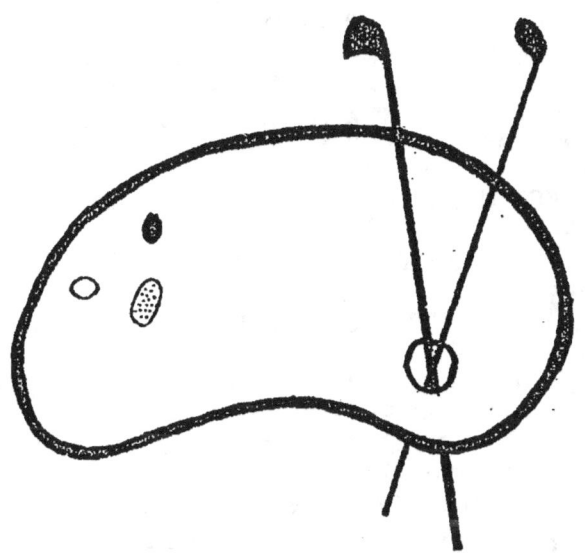

DEBUT D'UNE SERIE DE DOCUMENTS
EN COULEUR

MURRAY'S HANDBOOKS FOR TRAVELLERS.

WITH MAPS AND PLANS.

HANDBOOK OF TRAVEL-TALK.—ENGLISH, FRENCH, ITALIAN, AND GERMAN. 3s. 6d.

HANDBOOK FOR BELGIUM AND THE RHINE. 5s.

HANDBOOK OF NORTH GERMANY.—Including HOLLAND, BELGIUM, and the RHINE. 9s.

HANDBOOK OF SOUTH GERMANY.—THE TYROL, BAVARIA, AUSTRIA, SALZBURG, STYRIA, HUNGARY, and the DANUBE. 9s.

HANDBOOK OF SWITZERLAND,—the ALPS of SAVOY, and PIEDMONT. 7s. 6d.

HANDBOOK OF PAINTING.—THE GERMAN, DUTCH, FRENCH, AND SPANISH SCHOOLS. With Illustrations from the Old Masters. 2 vols. 24s.

HANDBOOK OF FRANCE.—NORMANDY, BRITTANY, the FRENCH ALPS, DAUPHINE, PROVENCE, and the PYRENEES. 9s.

HANDBOOK FOR NORTH ITALY.—SARDINIA, LOMBARDY, VENICE, PARMA, PIACENZA, MODENA, LUCCA, FLORENCE, and TUSCANY, as far as the VAL D'ARNO. 9s.

HANDBOOK FOR CENTRAL ITALY. Part I.—SOUTHERN TUSCANY and the PAPAL STATES, 7s.

HANDBOOK FOR CENTRAL ITALY. Part II.— ROME and its ENVIRONS. 7s.

HANDBOOK FOR SOUTHERN ITALY.—NAPLES, POMPEII, HERCULANEUM, VESUVIUS, &c. 15s.

HANDBOOK OF PAINTING. — THE ITALIAN SCHOOLS. — With Illustrations from the Old Masters. 2 vols. 24s.

HANDBOOK FOR GREECE.—THE IONIAN ISLANDS, ALBANIA, THESSALY, AND MACEDONIA. 15s.

HANDBOOK FOR TURKEY.—CONSTANTINOPLE, AND ASIA MINOR.

HANDBOOK OF EGYPT.—The NILE, ALEXANDRIA, CAIRO, THEBES, THE PYRAMIDS, MOUNT SINAI, &c. 15s.

HANDBOOK FOR MADEIRA AND PORTUGAL. 2 vols. 12s.

HANDBOOK OF SPAIN.—ANDALUSIA, RONDA, GRANADA, CATALONIA, GALLICIA, THE BASQUES, and ARRAGON. 2 vols.

HANDBOOK OF DENMARK,—NORWAY AND SWEDEN. 12s.

HANDBOOK OF RUSSIA,—FINLAND, AND ICELAND. 12s.

HANDBOOK OF LONDON.—PAST AND PRESENT. 16s.

HANDBOOK OF MODERN LONDON. 5s.

HANDBOOK OF DEVON AND CORNWALL. 6s.

HANDBOOK TO THE PUBLIC GALLERIES OF ART. 10s.

January, 1854.

Published Occasionally.

MURRAY'S RAILWAY READING.

Containing Works of SOUND INFORMATION and INNOCENT AMUSEMENT, printed in large Readable Type, *varying in size and price, and suited* for ALL CLASSES OF READERS.

Already Published.

BEAUTIES OF BYRON, POETRY AND PROSE.
THE ANCIENT EGYPTIANS. By SIR J. G. WILKINSON. 12s.
HISTORY OF THE GUILLOTINE. By MR. CROKER. 1s.
A MONTH IN NORWAY. By JOHN G. HOLLWAY. 2s.
THE DUKE OF WELLINGTON. By JULES MAUREL. 1s. 6d.
LIFE OF LORD BACON. By LORD CAMPBELL. 2s. 6d.
LOCKHART'S SPANISH BALLADS. 2s. 6d.
FALL OF JERUSALEM. By DEAN MILMAN. 1s.
LITERARY ESSAYS AND CHARACTERS. By HENRY HALLAM. 2s.
STORY OF JOAN OF ARC. By LORD MAHON. 1s.
LAYARD'S POPULAR ACCOUNT OF NINEVEH. 5s.
MUSIC AND DRESS. Two Essays. By A LADY. 1s.
GIFFARD'S DEEDS OF NAVAL DARING. 2s. 6d.
NIMROD ON THE TURF. 1s. 6d.
LIFE OF THEODORE HOOK. 1s.
THE EMIGRANT. By SIR F. B. HEAD. 2s. 6d.
THE FLOWER GARDEN. 1s.
LORD MAHON'S "HISTORY OF THE FORTY-FIVE." 3s.
CHARACTER OF WELLINGTON. By LORD ELLESMERE. 6d.
THE ART OF DINING. 1s. 6d.
THE HONEY BEE. 1s.
OLIPHANT'S NEPAUL AND THE NEPAULESE. 2s. 6d.
NIMROD ON THE ROAD. 1s.
LITERARY ESSAYS FROM "THE TIMES." 2 Vols. 8s.
NIMROD ON THE CHACE. 1s.
JAMES' FABLES OF ÆSOP. 2s. 6d.

January, 1854.

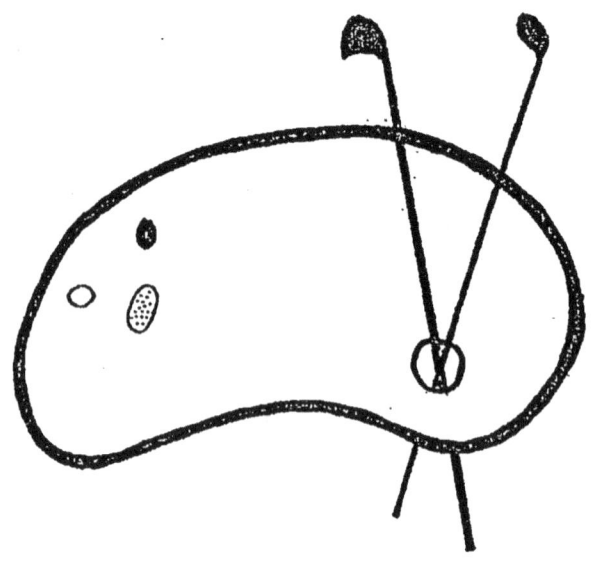

FIN D'UNE SERIE DE DOCUMENTS
EN COULEUR

L ^{25} 54

A HANDBOOK

FOR

TRAVELLERS IN FRANCE.

NOTICE TO THIS EDITION.

THE Editor of the 'Handbook for Travellers in France' requests that travellers who may, in the use of the Work, detect any faults or omissions which they can correct *from personal knowledge*, will have the kindness to mark them down on the spot and communicate to him a notice of the same, favouring him at the same time with their names—addressed to the care of Mr. Murray, Albemarle Street. They may be reminded that by such communications they are not merely furnishing the means of improving the Handbook, but are contributing to the benefit, information, and comfort of future travellers in general.

⁎ No attention can be paid to letters from innkeepers in praise of their own houses; and the postage of them is so onerous that they cannot be received.

CAUTION TO TRAVELLERS.—By a recent Act of Parliament the introduction into England of *foreign pirated Editions* of the works of British authors, in which the copyright subsists, *is totally prohibited*. Travellers will therefore bear in mind that even a single copy is contraband, and is liable to seizure at the English Custom-house.

CAUTION TO INNKEEPERS AND OTHERS.—The Editor of the Handbooks has learned from various quarters that a person or persons have of late been extorting money from innkeepers, tradespeople, artists, and others, on the Continent, under pretext of procuring recommendations and favourable notices of them and their establishments in the Handbooks for Travellers. The Editor, therefore, thinks proper to warn all whom it may concern, that *recommendations in the Handbooks are not to be obtained by purchase*, and that the persons alluded to are not only unauthorized by him, but are totally unknown to him. All those, therefore, who put confidence in such promises may rest assured that they will be defrauded of their money without attaining their object. English travellers are requested to explain this to innkeepers in remote situations, who are liable to become victims to such impositions. Notices to this effect have been inserted by the Editor in the principal English and foreign newspapers.—1847.

A HANDBOOK FOR TRAVELLERS

IN

FRANCE

BEING A GUIDE TO

NORMANDY, BRITTANY; THE RIVERS SEINE, LOIRE, RHÔNE, AND GARONNE; THE FRENCH ALPS, DAUPHINÉ, PROVENCE, AND THE PYRENEES;

THEIR RAILWAYS AND ROADS.

With Maps.

FIFTH EDITION, REVISED AND CORRECTED.

LONDON:
JOHN MURRAY, ALBEMARLE STREET.
PARIS: A. & W. GALIGNANI AND CO.; STASSIN AND XAVIER.
1854.

The Author reserves to himself the right of authorising a Translation of this Work.

THE ENGLISH EDITIONS OF MURRAY'S HANDBOOKS MAY BE OBTAINED OF THE FOLLOWING AGENTS:—

Germany, Holland, and Belgium.

AIX-LA-CHAPELLE	I. D. MAYER.—I. KOHNEN.	LEIPSIG	T. O. WEIGEL.
AMSTERDAM	KIRBERGER.—J. MULLER.	LIEGE	MAX KORNIKER.
ANTWERP	MAX. KORNICKER.	LUXEMBOURG	BÜCK.
BADEN-BADEN	D. R. MARX.	MANNHEIM	ARTARIA & FONTAINE.
BERLIN	A. DUNCKER.	MAYENCE	VON ZABERN.
BRUSSELS	S. MUQUARDT. — KEISSLING & CO.—A .DECQ.	MUNICH	LITERARISCH - ARTISTISCH ANSTALT.—I. PALM.
CARLSRUHE	CREUZBAUER & CO.—A. BIELEFELD.	NÜRNBERG	SCHRAG.
COBLENTZ	BAEDEKER.	PESTH	HARTLEBEN,—G. HECKENAST.
COLOGNE	L. KOHNEN.—A. BAEDEKER.	PRAGUE	CALVE.
DRESDEN	ARNOLD.	ROTTERDAM	A.BAEDEKER.—KRAMERS.
FRANKFURT	C. JÜGEL.	STUTTGART	P. NEFF.
GRATZ	DAMIAN & SORGE.	TRIESTE	MUNSTER.
THE HAGUE	VAN STOCKUM.	VIENNA	C. GEROLD.—BRAÜMULLER & SEIDEL.
HAMBURGH	PERTHES.		P. ROHRMAN.
HEIDELBERG	J. MOHR.		
KISSENGEN	S. JÜGEL.	WIESBADEN	C. JÜGEL.—C. W. KREIDEL.

Switzerland.

BASLE	SCHWEIGHA'USER.	LAUSANNE	HIGNOU & CO.—WEBER.
BERN	HUBER & CO.	LUCERNE	F. KAISER.
COIRE	GRUBENMANN.	SCHAFFHAUSEN	HURTER.
CONSTANCE	MERK.	SOLEURE	FENT.
ST. GALLEN	HUBER.	ZÜRICH	H. FUSSLI & CO.—H. F. LEUTHOLD.
GENEVA	KESSMANN.—MONROE.		

Italy.

BOLOGNA	M. RUSCONI.	PALERMO	CHARLES BEUF.
FLORENCE	MOLINI.—GOODBAN.	PARMA	J. ZANGHIERI.
GENOA	ANTOINE BEUF.	PISA	NISTRI.—JOS. VANNUCCHI.
LEGHORN	ROLANDI.	PERUGIA	VINCENZ. BARTELLI.
LUCCA	F. BARON.	ROME	GALLERINI—MONALDINI.—CUCCIONI.
MALTA	MUIR.		
MANTUA	NEGRETTI.	SIENA	ONORATO TORRI
MILAN	ARTARIA & SON,—MOLINARI.—SANGNER. P. & J. VALLARDI.	TRIESTE	HERMAN F. MÜNSTER.—FAVARGER.
		TURIN	GIANNINI & FIORE.—BOCCA.—MARIETTI.
MODENA	VINCENZI & ROSSI.		
NAPLES	DETKEN & CO		
NICE	SOCIETE' TYPOGRAPHIQUE—VISCONTI.	VENICE	HERMAN F. MÜNSTER.

France.

AMIENS	CARON.	MONTPELLIER	LEVALLE.
ANGERS	BARASSE'.	NANCY	GONET.
AVRANCHES	ANFRAY.	NANTES	GUÉRAUD.—FOREST AINE'.
BAYONNE	JAYMEBON.		
BORDEAUX	CHAUMAS.—LAWALLE.	ORLEANS	A. GATINEAU.—PESTY.
BOULOGNE	WATEL.—MERRIDEW.	PARIS	GALIGNANI,—STASSIN ET XAVIER.
BREST	HEBERT.		
CAEN	VILLENEUVE.	PAU	LAFON.—AUG. BASSY.
CALAIS	RIGAUX CAUX.	PERPIGNAN	JULIA FRERES.
DIEPPE	MARAIS.	REIMS	BRISSART BINET.
DINANT	COSTE.	ROCHEFORT	PENARD.
DOUAI	JACQUART.—LEMÂLE.	ROUEN	LEBRUMENT.
DUNKERQUE	LEYSCHOCHART,	ST. ETIENNE	DELARUE.
GRENOBLE	VELLOT ET COMP.	ST. MALO	HUE.
HAVRE	COCHARD.— MADAME BERTIN HUE.	ST. QUENTIN	DOLOY.
		STRASBOURG	C. F. SCHMIDT.
LILLE	VENACKERE.—BE'GHIN.	TOULON	MONGE ET VILLAMUS.
LYONS	GILBERTON & BRUN.—AYNE' FILS.	TOULOUSE	GALLON.—H. LEBON.
		TOURS	COUSTURIER.—BONTE.
MARSEILLES	MADAME CAMOIN.	TROYES	LALOY.
METZ	WARION.		

Spain.

MADRID	MONIER.	GIBRALTAR	ROWSWELL.

Russia.

ST. PETERSBURGH	ISSAKOFF.—N. ISSAKOFF.—BELLIZARD.	MOSCOW	W. GAUTIER
		ODESSA	VILLIETTY.

Constantinople.

WICK.

PREFACE.

The Handbook for France is the result of four or five journeys undertaken at different times between 1830 and 1841; and the Editor has covered the ground with a network of routes, described from personal observation, extending from Dunkirk to St. Jean de Luz; from Toulon and Hyères to Brest; from Grenoble and the Grande Chartreuse through Aubenas and Aurillac to the Porte de Venasque; and from Cherbourg and Mont St. Michel to Briançon and Embrun, and including the almost entire circuit of France. But in so vast a field many insterstices have been left to be filled up by the best printed information; and that so meagre in some respects, so abundant and scattered in others, that the collecting and arranging of the materials has been a work of very serious labour. The materials, indeed, for describing a large part of France are far more scanty than those which present themselves for Germany and Switzerland; and the writer may fairly say, that he has, in the following pages, laid down routes of which no account is to be found in French Guides. It would be unjust to omit to mention the admirable Guides of Vaysse de Villiers, from which he has derived essential information; but though they extend to nearly twenty volumes, they comprise only a small part of France, and only portions of their contents are calculated to interest English travellers. For their use this volume is compiled; and if any French readers think fit to take it up, they must not be surprised to find many details well known to them, and doubtless many errors, not a few of which will be equally discernible by the Editor's own countrymen. He trusts that in the statement of facts he has avoided invidious comparisons—that he has set down nought in such a light as to cause prejudice against the French, or to encourage or perpetuate estrangement between the two nations.

The chapters into which the book is divided are arranged according to the ancient Provinces, as being less minute, more historical, and better understood by English than the more intricate subdivisions of Departments. Though the latter are universally used by the French themselves, some centuries must elapse before *Champagne* and *Burgundy* cease to be remembered for their wines, *Périgord* for its pies, and *Provence* for its oil; nor will it be easy to obliterate the recollection of William of *Normandy*, Margaret of *Anjou*, and Henri of *Navarre*.

This volume contains no description of Paris, because to have included the capital would have extended this book to nearly double its present size, and because the "Paris Guide of Galignani's" is a very good one, and renders the preparation of another, for the present at least, unnecessary.

CONTENTS.

	PAGE
INTRODUCTORY INFORMATION	ix

SECTION I.

PICARDY.—FRENCH FLANDERS.—ILE DE FRANCE.—NORMANDY.

Introductory Information	1
Routes	3

SECTION II.

BRITTANY.

Introductory Information	103
Routes	109

SECTION III.

ORLÉANOIS.—TOURAINE.—RIVER LOIRE.—LA VENDÉE.—POITOU.—SAINTONGE.

Introductory Sketch of the Country	166
Routes	168

SECTION IV.

LIMOUSIN.—GASCONY.—GUIENNE.—THE PYRENEES.—NAVARRE.—BÉARN.—LANGUEDOC.—ROUSSILLON.

Preliminary Information	224
Routes	235

SECTION V.

CENTRAL FRANCE.—BERRI.—AUVERGNE.—VIVARAIS.—ARDÈCHE.—CANTAL.—BOURBONNAIS.—LYONNAIS.—THE CÉVENNES.

General View of the Country	335
Routes	339

Section VI.
PROVENCE AND LANGUEDOC.

	Page
Preliminary Information	421
Routes	424

Section VII.
DAUPHINÉ.

Introduction—Sketch of the Country	482
Routes	483

Section VIII.
BURGUNDY.—FRANCHE COMTÉ.

Routes	503

Section IX.
CHAMPAGNE.—LORRAINE.—ALSACE.—THE VOSGES MOUNTAINS.

Routes	515

Section X.
ILE DE FRANCE.—FLANDRES.—ARTOIS.

Routes	551
Index	563

HANDBOOK

FOR

TRAVELLERS IN FRANCE.

INTRODUCTORY INFORMATION.

CONTENTS.

a. MONEY—TABLE OF FRENCH FRANCS REDUCED TO £. *s. d.* x
b. TABLES OF WEIGHTS AND MEASURES . . . xii
    ,,   FRENCH FEET REDUCED TO ENGLISH FEET . xiii
    ,,   MÈTRES   —   Do. . . xiv
    ,,   KILOMÈTRES   ⎱   ⎰ENGLISH MILES⎱
    ,,   MYRIAMÈTRES ⎰— ⎱AND FURLONGS⎰ . xv
    ,,   LIEUES DE POSTE — Do. . . xv
    ,,   KILOGRAMMES   —   ENGLISH POUNDS . xv
    ,,   POUNDS   —   Do. . . xvi
    ,,   HECTARES   —   ENGLISH ACRES . xvi
    ,,   AUNES DE PARIS — ENGLISH YARDS . xvi
c. PASSPORTS AND POLICE. xvi
d. ROUTES ACROSS FRANCE—LONDON TO PARIS—STRASBURG
    —MARSEILLES, &c. xix
    MODES OF TRAVELLING—
        e. POSTING AND TRAVELLING CARRIAGE . . xx
        f. MALLES POSTES xxiv
        g. DILIGENCES xxv
        h. RAILROADS xxvii
        i. STEAM-BOATS xxviii
k. INNS—TABLES-D'HÔTE, ETC. xxix
l. CAFÉS xxxi
m. A TRAVELLER'S GENERAL VIEW OF FRANCE—POINTS OF
    INTEREST—SCENERY—ARCHITECTURE . . xxxii
n. LIST OF THE 86 DEPARTMENTS INTO WHICH FRANCE IS
    DIVIDED, AND OF THE 33 ANCIENT PROVINCES COM-
    POSING THEM xxxvi
o. THE ENGLISH ABROAD xxxvii
p. SKELETON TOUR THROUGH FRANCE . , . xxxix

a. MONEY TABLES.

a. MONEY.

In France, accounts are kept in *francs* and *centimes* (or hundred parts), the coinage being arranged on the decimal system. 1 franc contains 10 *décimes* (or double sous), and each décime 10 *centimes*.

FRENCH MONEY.

Silver Coins:—

		£	s.	d.	
Piece of 1 franc = 100 centimes = 20 sous	=	0	0	9½	to 10d. English.
,, ¼ ditto = 25 ditto	=	0	0	2¼ ⅛	
,, ½ ditto = 50 ditto	=	0	0	4¾	
,, 5 ditto = 500 ditto = 100 sous	=	0	4	0	
,, 2 ditto = 40 sous	=	0	1	7	to 1s. 8d.
,, 20 centimes = 4 sous.					

The ¼ franc pieces = 25 centimes have been called in and are now seldom met with.

Gold Coins:—

	£	s.	d.	
Louis d'or = 24 fr.	= 0	19	0	English.
Napoleon, or 20 franc piece	= 0	15	10½	
Half Napoleon, or 10 franc piece	= 0	9	6	
Double Napoleon, or 40 franc piece	= 1	11	9	

Copper Coins:

	£	s.	d.
Décime, or 2-sous piece	= 0	0	1
5 centimes = 1 sous	= 0	0	0½
1 centime	= 0	0	0 1/10

N.B. To find the value of centimes, remember that the *Tens* are all pennies, and the *Fives* halfpennies: thus 75c. = 7½d.—25c. = 2½d.—15c. = 1½d. within a fraction, but near enough for all practical purposes.

To reduce French francs to English money for common purposes, where minute exactness is not required, it is only necessary to divide the amount of francs by 25, or to substitute 4 for 100, thus:—

Francs.		£
100	=	4
1,000	=	40
10,000	=	400
100,000	=	4,000
1,000,000	=	40,000

The Bank of France issues *notes* for 1000, 500, 200, and 100 francs, but they are difficult to change out of Paris, not being received in the provinces without paying an agio.

FOREIGN COINS REDUCED TO THEIR VALUE IN FRENCH CURRENCY.

		fr.	c.	
English sovereign	=	25	50	to 25 fr. 20c. at par.
crown	=	6	2	
shilling	=	1	25	
Dutch Willem = 10 guilders	=	21	30	
guilder	=	2	15	
Prussian dollar	=	3	75	
Frederick d'or	=	21	0	
Bavarian florin = 20 pence English	=	2	15	
Kron thaler	=	5	81	
Austrian florin = 2 shillings English	=	2	57	

FRENCH FRANCS AND CENTIMES REDUCED TO THEIR VALUE IN ENGLISH POUNDS, SHILLINGS, AND PENCE.

	£	*s.*	*d.*		£	*s.*	*d.*
5 cents.	0	0	0¼ 8/10	10 francs	0	7	11
10	0	0	0¾ 8/10	11	0	8	8½
15	0	0	1¼ 7/10	12	0	9	6
20	0	0	1¾ 6/10	13	0	10	3¾
25	0	0	2¼ 5/10	14	0	11	1¼
30	0	0	2¾ 4/10	15	0	11	10¾
35	0	0	3¼ 3/10	16	0	12	8¼
40	0	0	3¾ 2/10	17	0	13	5¾
45	0	0	4¼ 1/10	18	0	14	3¼
50	0	0	4¾	19	0	15	0¾
55	0	0	5 - 9/10	20	0	15	10¼
60	0	0	5½ 8/10	30	1	3	9½
65	0	0	6 − 7/10	40	1	11	8¾
70	0	0	6½ 6/10	50	1	19	8
75	0	0	7 − 5/10	60	2	7	7
80	0	0	7½ 4/10	70	2	15	6¼
85	0	0	8 − 3/10	80	3	3	5½
90	0	0	8½ 2/10	90	3	11	4¾
95	0	0	9 − 1/10	100	3	19	4
1 franc	0	0	9½	200	7	18	8
2	0	1	7	300	11	18	0
3	0	2	4½	400	15	17	4
4	0	3	2	500	19	16	8
5	0	3	11½	750	29	15	0
6	0	4	9	1,000	39	13	4
7	0	5	6½	5,000	198	6	8
8	0	6	4	10,000	396	13	4
9	0	7	1½				

ENGLISH MONEY REDUCED TO ITS VALUE IN FRENCH FRANCS AND CENTIMES.

	Fr.	Cts.		Fr.	Cts.		Fr.	Cts.
1 penny	0	10½	12 shillings	15	12	15 £ sterl.	378	0
2	0	21	13	16	38	16	403	20
3	0	31½	14	17	64	17	428	40
4	0	42	15	18	90	18	453	60
5	0	52½	16	20	16	19	478	80
6	0	63	17	21	42	20	504	0
7	0	73½	18	22	68	30	756	0
8	0	84	19	23	94	40	1008	0
9	0	94½	1 £ sterl.	25	20	50	1260	0
10	1	5	2	50	40	60	1512	0
11	1	15	3	75	60	70	1764	0
1 shilling	1	26	4	100	80	80	2016	0
2	2	52	5	126	0	90	2268	0
3	3	78	6	151	20	100	2520	0
4	5	4	7	176	40	200	5040	0
5	6	30	8	201	60	300	7560	0
6	7	56	9	226	80	400	10,080	0
7	8	82	10	252	0	500	12,600	0
8	10	8	11	277	20	1000	25,200	0
9	11	34	12	302	40	5000	126,000	0
10	12	60	13	327	60	10,000	252,000	0
11	13	86	14	352	80			

b. WEIGHTS AND MEASURES.

A uniform decimal system of coins, weights, and measures was introduced into France in 1790, and since 1840 takes the place of all others.

In this new system all the measures of length, superficies, and solidity, the unit of weight, and the unit of money, are connected together, and are derived from one fundamental unit, deduced from the size of the earth, by means of geometrical and physical data, and each is capable of being verified at all times and in all places. This fundamental unit is called MÈTRE, and is equal to the ten-millionth part (0·0000001) of the distance from the pole to the equator.

The prefixes which express multiples are Greek:—

	MYRIA	KILO	HECTO	DECA,
represented by the capital letters	M	K	H	D,
expressing the numbers	10,000	1,000	100	10

The prefixes which express sub-multiples are Latin:—

	Deci	Centi	Milli	Deci-milli	Cent-milli
represented by	d	c	m	d-m	c-m,
expressing the fractions	0·1	0·01	0·001	0·0001	0·00001

By means of this system, with a small number of words, the division can be carried almost *ad infinitum*.

The measures of length are all either decimal multiples, or sub-multiples to the mètre, thus:—

Myria-	—	M.-m. =	10,000 Mètres.
Kilo-	—	K.-m. =	1,000 ,,
Hecto-	—	H.-m. =	100 ,,
Deca-	—	D.-m. =	10 ,,
		m. =	1 Mètre.
Deci-	—	d.-m. =	0·1 ,,
Centi-	—	c.-m. =	0·01 ,,
Milli-	—	m.-m. =	0·001 ,,

One great advantage of the decimal system of subdivision is, that, by the simple movement of a point, any one number of units is transformed into an equivalent number of superior and inferior units, thus:—$m489·365 = Dm48·9365 = Mm0·489365 = cm48936·5$.

LINEAR MEASURE.

French.			English.
The Mètre is	.	.	about 3 feet 3 inches.
,, Toise .	.	=2 mètres, or	,, 6 ,, 6 ,,
,, Pied (or foot) .	.	= ⅓ ,,	,, 1 ,, 1 ,,
,, Inch .	.	= 1/36 ,,	,, 0 ,, 1⅛ ,,
,, Aune .	.	= 1⅕ ,,	,, 3 ,, 11 ,,

Weights.

The Gramme	.	.	15·4340 grains
,, Decagramme	.	10	5·64 drams, avoird.
,, Hectogramme	.	100	3·527 ounces, avoird.
,, Kilogramme	.	1,000	2 lbs. 3 oz. 4½ drams, avoird.
,, Myriagramme	.	10,000	22·0485 lbs. avoird.

Capacity.

A Litre is	.	. 1000 grammes or 2·1135 wine pints.	15406·312 grains.

TABLES OF FRENCH MEASURES AND WEIGHTS.

TABLE A.—FRENCH FEET REDUCED TO ENGLISH FEET.*

French Feet.	English Feet and Decimal Parts.	French Feet.	English Feet and Decimal Parts.	French Feet.	English Feet and Decimal Parts.
1	1·066	40	42·631	79	84·195
2	2·132	41	43·696	80	85·261
3	3·197	42	44·762	81	86·327
4	4·263	43	45·828	82	87·393
5	5·329	44	46·894	83	88·459
6	6·395	45	47·959	84	89·524
7	7·460	46	49·025	85	90·590
8	8·526	47	50·091	86	91·656
9	9·592	48	51·157	87	92·722
10	10·658	49	52·222	88	93·787
11	11·723	50	53·288	89	94·853
12	12·789	51	54·354	90	95·919
13	13·855	52	55·420	91	96·985
14	14·921	53	56·486	92	98·050
15	15·986	54	57·551	93	99·116
16	17·052	55	58·617	94	100·182
17	18·118	56	59·683	95	101·248
18	19·184	57	60·749	96	102·313
19	20·250	58	61·814	97	103·379
20	21·315	59	62·880	98	104·445
21	22·381	60	63·946	99	105·511
22	23·447	61	65·012	100	106·577
23	24·513	62	66·077	150	159·865
24	25·578	63	67·143	200	213·153
25	26·644	64	68·209	250	266·441
26	27·710	65	69·275	300	319·730
27	28·776	66	70·341	350	373·018
28	29·841	67	71·406	400	426·306
29	30·907	68	72·472	450	479·594
30	31·973	69	73·538	500	532·883
31	33·039	70	74·604	550	586·171
32	34·104	71	75·669	600	639·460
33	35·170	72	76·735	650	692·747
34	36·236	73	77·801	700	746·036
35	37·302	74	78·867	750	799·324
36	38·368	75	79·932	800	852·612
37	39·433	76	80·998	850	905·901
38	40·499	77	82·064	900	959·189
39	41·565	78	83·130	1000	1065·765

1 French Foot = 1·06576543 English Foot.
1 English Foot = 0·93829277 French Foot.

* Tables A and B are abridged from Lieut. Becher's accurate work on Foreign Linear Measures.

b. TABLES OF FRENCH MEASURES AND WEIGHTS.

TABLE B.—FRENCH MÈTRES REDUCED TO ENGLISH FEET.

Mètres.	English Feet and Decimal Parts.	Mètres.	English Feet and Decimal Parts.	Mètres.	English Feet and Decimal Parts.
1	3·281	38	124·674	75	246·067
2	6·562	39	127·955	76	249·348
3	9·843	40	131·236	77	252·629
4	13·123	41	134·517	78	255·910
5	16·404	42	137·798	79	259·191
6	19·685	43	141·079	80	262·472
7	22·966	44	144·359	81	265·753
8	26·247	45	147·640	82	269·034
9	29·528	46	150·921	83	272·315
10	32·809	47	154·202	84	275·595
11	36·090	48	157·483	85	278·876
12	39·371	49	160·764	86	282·157
13	42·652	50	164·045	87	285·438
14	45·932	51	167·326	88	288·719
15	49·213	52	170·607	89	292·000
16	52·494	53	173·888	90	295·281
17	55·775	54	177·168	91	298·562
18	59·056	55	180·449	92	301·843
19	62·337	56	183·730	93	305·124
20	65·618	57	187·011	94	308·404
21	68·899	58	190·292	95	311·685
22	72·180	59	193·573	96	314·966
23	75·461	60	196·854	97	318·247
24	78·741	61	200·135	98	321·528
25	82·022	62	203·416	99	324·809
26	85·303	63	206·697	100	328·090
27	88·584	64	209·977	200	656·180
28	91·865	65	213·258	300	984·270
29	95·146	66	216·539	400	1312·360
30	98·427	67	219·820	500	1640·450
31	101·708	68	223·101	600	1968·539
32	104·989	69	226·382	700	2296·629
33	108·270	70	229·663	800	2624·719
34	111·550	71	232·944	900	2952·809
35	114·831	72	236·225	1000	3280·899
36	118·112	73	239·506		
37	121·393	74	242·786		

1 French mètre = 3·2808992 English feet.

TABLE C.—French Kilomètres and Myriamètres reduced into English Miles, etc.

KILOM.	Eng. Miles.	Fur-longs.	Yds.	Ft.	In.	KILOM.	Eng. Miles.	Fur-longs.	Yds.	Ft.	In.
1 =	0	4	213	1	11	8 =	4	7	169	0	4
2 =	1	1	207	0	10	9 =	5	4	162	2	3
3 =	1	6	200	2	9	1 myria. =	6	1	156	1	2
4 =	2	3	194	1	8	2 =	12	3	92	2	4
5 =	3	0	188	0	7	3 =	18	5	29	0	6
6 =	3	5	181	2	6	4 =	24	6	185	1	8
7 =	4	2	175	1	5	5 =	31	0	121	2	10

1 Kilomètre = 0·621 English mile.
1 Lieue de Poste = 2·422 English miles.

TABLE D.—French Lieues de Poste into English Miles and Yards.

L.	Mls.	Yds.	L.	Mls.	Yds.	L.	Mls.	Yds.	L.	Mls.	Yds.
1	2	743·061	11	26	1,133·671	30	72	1,171·832	400	968	1,544·428
2	4	1,486·122	12	29	116·732	40	96	1,562·443	500	1,211	170·535
3	7	469·183	13	31	859·794	50	121	193·053	600	1,453	556·642
4	9	1,212·244	14	33	1,602·855	60	145	583·664	700	1,695	942·749
5	12	195·305	15	36	585·916	70	169	974·275	800	1,937	1,328 856
6	14	938·366	16	38	1,328·977	80	193	1,364·886	900	2,179	1,714·963
7	16	1,681·427	17	41	312·038	90	217	1,755·496	1,000	2,422	341·070
8	19	664·488	18	43	1,055·099	100	242	386·107	2,000	4,844	682·140
9	21	1,407·549	19	46	38·160	200	484	772·214	3,000	7,266	1,023·210
10	24	390·610	20	48	731·221	300	726	1,158·321	5,000	12,110	1,705·350

TABLE E.—French Kilogrammes into English Pounds (Avoirdupois).

Kil.	E. Pds.	Kil.	E. Pds.	Kil.	E. Pds.	Kil.	E. Pds.	Kil.	E. Pds.
1	2·206	14	30·880	27	59·534	40	88·228	300	761·714
2	4·411	15	33·086	28	61·760	41	90·434	400	882·286
3	6·617	16	35·291	29	63·996	42	92·640	500	1,102·857
4	8·823	17	37·497	30	66·171	43	94·846	1,000	2,205·714
5	11·028	18	39·703	31	68·377	44	97·051	2,000	4,411·429
6	13·234	19	41·908	32	70·583	45	99·257	3,000	6,617·143
7	15·440	20	44·114	33	72·788	46	101·463	4,000	8,822·857
8	17·646	21	46·320	34	74·994	47	103·668	5,000	11,028·471
9	19·851	22	48·526	35	77·200	48	105·874	10,000	22,057·143
10	22·057	23	50·731	36	79·405	49	108·080	20,000	44,114·286
11	24·263	24	52·937	37	81·611	50	110·286	30,000	66,171·429
12	26·468	25	55·143	38	83·817	100	220·571	40,000	88,228·572
13	28·674	26	57·348	39	86·023	200	441·143	50,000	110,285·715

TABLE F.—FRENCH POUNDS INTO ENGLISH POUNDS (AVOIRDUPOIS).

Fr. Pds.	Eng. Pds.	Fr. Pds.	Eng. Pds.	Fr. Pds.	Eng. Pds.	Fr. Pds.	Eng. Pds.	Fr. Pds.	Eng. Pds.
1	1·080	14	15·116	27	29·152	40	43·188	300	323·913
2	2·159	15	16·196	28	30·232	41	44·268	400	431·884
3	3·239	16	17·275	29	31·312	42	45·348	500	539·855
4	4·319	17	18·355	30	32·391	43	46·427	1,000	1,079·710
5	5·398	18	19·435	31	33·471	44	47·507	2,000	2,159·420
6	6·478	19	20·514	32	34·551	45	48·587	3,000	3,239·130
7	7·558	20	21·594	33	35·630	46	49·666	4,000	4,318·840
8	8·638	21	22·674	34	36·710	47	50·746	5,000	5,398·550
9	9·717	22	23·754	35	37·790	48	51·826	10,000	10,797·100
10	10·797	23	24·833	36	38·869	49	52·906	20,000	21,594·200
11	11·877	24	25·913	37	39·949	50	53·985	30,000	32,391·300
12	12·956	25	26·993	38	41·029	100	107·971	40,000	43,188·400
13	14·036	26	28·072	39	42·109	200	215·942	50,000	53,985·500

TABLE G.—FRENCH HECTARES INTO ENGLISH ACRES.

Hect.	Acres.	Hect.	Acres.	Hect.	Acres.	Hect.	Acres.	Hect.	Acres.
1	2·471	8	19·769	15	37·067	40	98·846	200	494·229
2	4·942	9	22·240	16	39·538	50	123·557	300	741·343
3	7·413	10	24·711	17	42·009	60	148·268	400	988·457
4	9·884	11	27·182	18	44·480	70	172·980	500	1,235·571
5	12·356	12	29·654	19	46·952	80	197·691	1,000	2,471·143
6	14·827	13	32·125	20	49·423	90	222·403	2,000	4,942·286
7	17·298	14	34·596	30	74·134	100	247·114	5,000	12,355·751

TABLE H.—FRENCH "AUNES DE PARIS" INTO ENGLISH YARDS.

Aun.	Yds.	Aun.	Yds.	Aun.	Yds.	Aun.	Yds.	Aun.	Yds.
1	1·300	7	9·098	13	16·896	19	24·695	70	90·981
2	2·599	8	10·398	14	18·196	20	25·994	80	103·978
3	3·899	9	11·697	15	19·496	30	38·992	90	116·975
4	5·199	10	12·997	16	20·795	40	51·989	100	129·972
5	6·499	11	14·297	17	22·095	50	64·986	200	259·945
6	7·799	12	15·597	18	23·395	60	77·983	500	649·862

c. PASSPORTS AND POLICE.

A passport is indispensable to enable a stranger to travel in France.

British subjects about to travel on the Continent are recommended to procure a Foreign Office passport, and to have it countersigned, before leaving London, by the authorities of the various countries they intend to visit. (The visé of the French Consul costs 4s. 3d.) They will thus save much time and avoid inconvenience, the Foreign Secretary's passport being readily admitted all over the Continent.

An English passport may now be obtained at the Foreign Office, Downing Street, from the Secretary of State for Foreign Affairs, by British subjects properly recommended by a letter from a Banker, on payment of 7s. 6d., and it is the best certificate of nationality which an Englishman can carry abroad. Passports may be also obtained on payment of 4s. 6d., from British consuls in France, or from French consuls residing at British seaports, for 10s. Mr. Lee, bookseller, of West Strand, will procure passports and visés, and mount them in a case, at a fair price.

A French passport or visa may be procured in London, at the French Consul's Office,   , King William Street, London Bridge (price 5s.), open from 11 to 4 daily. The passport is at once made out, and, after a description of the person of the bearer has been inserted in it, and his own signature (which should be written legibly) has been attached to it, will be delivered to him. The description of his person, or *signalement*, should *not* be omitted in any passport for France : the want of it may lead, in remote parts of the country, to the bearer's detention or arrest ; and it is the more necessary to dwell on this point, because the officials of English ministers abroad, in making out passports for their countrymen, are apt to slur it over to save trouble. *Rentier*, or independent man, is a convenient designation for those who travel for recreation. An Englishman landing at any French port, and not intending to proceed inland, is not required to have a passport.

The following are the regulations issued by the Foreign Office with regard to passports :—

"1. Application for Foreign Office passports must be made in writing ; and addressed to Her Majesty's Secretary of State for Foreign Affairs, with the word 'passport' written upon the corner.

"2. The fee on the issue of a passport is 7s. 6d.

"3. Foreign Office passports are granted only to British subjects, including in that description foreigners who have been naturalized by Act of Parliament, or by certificates of naturalization granted before the 24th day of August, 1850 : in this latter case, the party is described in the passport as a 'naturalized British subject.'

"4. Passports are granted between the hours of twelve and four, on the day following that on which the application for the passport has been received at the Foreign Office.

"5. Passports are granted to persons who are either known to the Secretary of State, or recommended to him by some person who is known to him ; or upon the written application of any *banking firm* established in London or in any other part of the United Kingdom.

"6. Passports cannot be sent by the Foreign Office to persons already abroad. Such persons should apply to the nearest British mission or consulate.

"7. Foreign Office passports must be countersigned at the mission, or at some consulate in England, of the Government of the country which the bearer of the passport intends to visit.

"8. A Foreign Office passport granted for one journey may be used for any subsequent journey *if countersigned afresh* by the ministers or consuls of the countries which the bearer intends to visit."

In *cases of hasty* departure from England, when a traveller has not time to apply one day in advance, he may obtain a passport in any place in France where an English consul resides. A British consular passport is preferable to a foreign consul's.

To secure personally the necessary *visas* of French and foreign ministers to a passport, to enable the bearer to enter Austria or Italy, is not to be done under two days. The stranger who undertakes to do this for himself will find it a very disagreeable and tiresome business, the passport offices being open only at fixed hours, being situated in distant parts of the town, and being beset by crowds of applicants. In all the respectable Paris hotels (Meurice, Bristol, &c.), a commissionaire is appointed to attend to the passports, for which a fixed charge (4 to 5 francs) is made, and this saves the traveller a couple of days' running about from office to office. The signature of the Papal nuncio is essential for travellers going to Rome, and can be obtained only at Paris.

If the stranger is not going to Paris, but only to cross a part of France, on his way to another country, for instance, from Calais to Lille, on his way to Belgium, the passport which he brings with him is visé at the frontier and returned to him. If he wishes merely to make a short stay at the place where he has landed (Boulogne for instance), or in a contiguous department, and the period of his stay do not exceed one month, the local authorities deliver to him a limited passport, retaining the original in their hands.

Since the introduction of railways (1846) the passport system in France seems to have been relaxed in strictness, and a peaceably disposed traveller may sojourn months in the country and traverse it in many directions without its being even asked for. Still he is never safe without it. The Republic was more stern in requiring a passport than the Empire, and it should *always be carried about the person*. The Gens d'Armes are authorized to call for it not only in frontier and fortified towns, but in remote villages: they may stop you on the highway, or way-lay you as you descend from the diligence—may force themselves into the salle-à-manger, or enter your bed-room, to demand a sight of this precious document. It is needless to expatiate on this restraint, so inconsistent with the freedom which an Englishman enjoys at home; it is the custom of the country, and the stranger must conform, or has no business to set his foot in it. It must be allowed that the police perform their duty with civility, so as to render it as little vexatious as possible. They cannot enter a private house without a warrant.

Those who lose their passports, leave them behind, or do not take care to have them "en règle," are liable to be marched off to the juge de paix or préfet, often a distance of 10, 15, or 20 miles, on foot, unless they choose to pay for a carriage for their escort as well as themselves; and if no satisfactory explanation can be given, may at last be deposited in prison.

Before leaving France *or embarking at a French port* the passport must be stamped (visé) by the police authorities.

The duties of rural police are performed by

Gensdarmes, a fine body of men, chosen from the line, handsomely dressed, better mounted than any other French cavalry corps. Being settled in their native country, and not moved from place to place, they know every body and all the localities. Their salary amounts to 80*l.* a-year, out of which they have to provide their horse and uniform.

d. ROUTES TO PARIS AND ACROSS FRANCE.

d. ROUTES ACROSS FRANCE — LONDON TO PARIS — STRASBURG — MARSEILLES, &c.

LONDON TO PARIS BY RAIL AND STEAMER.

a. By Folkestone (Rail—express 2¼ hours), Boulogne (2 hours, steam), Paris (rail 7 hours).

By crossing from Dover or Folkestone to Boulogne, instead of Calais, some miles of land journey are saved.

At Folkestone the *Hotel* is comfortable, and by staying there during bad weather you may choose a calm day and an uncrowded steamer for crossing.

b. By Dover, Calais, Lille, 14 hours.

N.B. Owing to the smallness of the steamboats which cross the Channel between France and England they are constantly crowded to inconvenience, and in rough weather passengers are very liable to be wetted by the rain or spray. The passengers, especially ladies, should therefore take with them a small change of raiment in a hand bag, which must not be labelled at London Bridge.

As no luggage labelled and addressed "Paris" can on any account be opened at Boulogne or Calais, the traveller, without some separate provision, runs the risk of making the journey to Paris in wet clothes.

c. By Brighton, Shoreham, Dieppe, and Rouen, 16 hours.

Newhaven being a bar harbour, the steamer is compelled to start at a certain time of the tide, and if the train be late either the passenger, or at least his luggage, runs a risk of being left behind.

d. By Southampton and Havre, 18 to 22 hours.

Steamers in connexion with the S.W. Railway (trains from London, 7.30 p.m., daily) leave the Open Dock, Southampton, every night but Sunday.

LONDON to BÂLE, in SWITZERLAND, by Paris (12 hours), Strasburg (rail, 48 hours), Bâle (5 hours).

LONDON to GENEVA by PARIS, Tonnerre, Dijon (28 hours by railway and mail), (or from Châlons to Lons-le-Saulnier).

LONDON to MARSEILLES in 56* hours, by Paris (railway and steamer) 12 hours; Châlons-sur-Soane, 10 hours (railway express); Lyons, 5 hours; Avignon, 12 to 18 hours (steamers); Marseilles, 4 hours (rly).

The traveller bound for Marseilles should have his passport visé for that place direct on landing in France, which will enable him to retain his passport as far as Marseilles, and will save delay at Paris.

An English Government steamer plies twice a-month direct between Marseilles and Malta, where it meets the steamer coming direct from England. The fare is 9*l.*, including board, for a 1st class passenger; that of the 2nd class being 5*l*.. It leaves Marseilles on the 11th of every month, arriving at Malta early on the third day, or the 14th; and brings with it the London mail for India, which is made up on the 8th, unless it should happen to fall on a Sunday, when it is deferred till the following day. By this junction steamer letters can be dispatched from London three or four days later than by the packet that goes round by Gibraltar to Malta.

* 6 hours will be saved when the railways from Châlons to Lyons and Valence are opened.

e. POSTING.

The arrangements of the Mediterranean steamers are frequently changing; and it is therefore advisable to refer to the tariffs issued annually by the different companies.

You ought to reach Marseilles on the 10th or very early on the 11th of the month, in order to embark comfortably.

At Marseilles it is necessary to get the passport visé by the British consul and the local police; also a bill of health, and a permis d'embarquement.

French Government steamers ply from Marseilles to Alexandria, Constantinople, and Beyrout, touching at Malta, twice a month, 10th, and 25th. Other French Government steamers run from Marseilles to Malta, touching on the way at Leghorn, Civita Vecchia, and Naples, on the 9th, 19th, and 29th.

LONDON to BORDEAUX, by Orleans, Tours, Poitiers, and Libourne. The railway open all the way. Trains in about 25 hours.

LONDON to DUNKERQUE (screw steamer, 3 times a week) in 12 hours.

LONDON to BOULOGNE (steamer, 9 to 12 hours, 5 hours of open sea). This is an economical route, and not fatiguing for those who can stand the sea.

Owing to the prevalence of certain winds and currents, the shortest passages are from Dover to Calais (1 h. 40 m.), and from Boulogne to Folkestone (2 hours.)

e. POSTING. — PRIVATE CARRIAGE.

The French Post Book (Livre de Poste), published under the authority of the Government, is indispensable for persons travelling post, as it contains the exact distances from post to post, and the extra dues on entering and quitting towns (postes de faveur), *which are constantly changing*, likewise the legal distances from the chief *stations* of the chemins de fer to places in their vicinity. It may be had in all towns, and even at the post-houses.

By a law enforced throughout France since the 1st Jan., 1840, distances are no longer calculated by "postes,"* but by kilomètres and myriamètres. 1 kilomètre (*i.e.* 1000 mètres) = nearly 5 furlongs, or $\frac{5}{8}$ths of an English mile; 1 myriamètre = 10 kilom. = nearly $6\frac{1}{4}$ Eng. m. (or 6 m. 1 fur. 156 yds.). *See* table, p. xv.

The postmaster's authorised charge is, *for each horse*, 2 francs or 40 sous per myriamètre, or 20 centimes per kilom.

The *Postilion* is entitled by the law to demand only 1 franc per myriamètre or 10 centimes per kilom.; but it is customary to pay him 2 francs per myriam., or at the rate of a horse, unless he has misconducted himself, when he may be punished by limiting his pay to the tariff. He is bound by the law to drive the myriamètre within 46 and 58 minutes. The English, who generally want to go faster, are too often in the habit of giving him 50 sous per myriam., or 5 per kilom., which is at the rate of more than 4*d.* an English mile, *i.e.* more than a postboy in England gets. In fact, French postboys are not satisfied with 4 sous, but well contented with 5.

This extravagant remuneration is contrary to the express injunction of the French 'Livre de Poste,' which says, p. 42, "Les voyageurs conservent donc la faculté de restreindre le prix des guides à 1

---

* The old poste = 8 kilomètres.

franc, à titre de punition ; et ils seront invités par les maîtres de poste, et dans l'intérêt du service, à ne jamais dépasser la rétribution de 2 fr. par myriamètre."

The *cost of posting* with 3 persons in a calèche, through France, may be calculated at 8 francs par myriamètre, or 80 centimes par kilomètre. For 2 persons, with 2 horses and postboy, the rate is about 6 francs, or nearly 9*d*. per English mile.

The average speed of posting does not much exceed a myriamètre per hour, including stoppages.

In fixing the number of horses to be attached, the postmaster takes into account the nature, size, and weight of the carriage, and the quantity of luggage : a landau or berlin always requires 3 horses at least, generally 4 ; a chariot will require 3 ; while a britzka, holding the same number of persons, will need only 2.

To facilitate this, carriages are divided into 3 classes :—

1. Cabriolets and light calèches without a front seat, or having one narrower than the back seat, must have 2 horses.

2. Limonières, heavier carriages, chariots (coupeés) ; to these the postmaster may attach 3 horses, even when they contain only 2 persons.

3. The heaviest kind of carriages, berlines, landaus, barouches, whether closed or not, but having a front seat as wide as the back, 4 horses.

The posting regulations allot one horse to each person in a carriage ; but allow the traveller, at his option, and provided the postmaster agrees, either to take the full complement of horses, at the rate of 40 sous each, or to take 2 or 3 at 40 sous, and to pay for the rest at 30 sous without taking them. Thus a party of 4 persons in a light britzka may be drawn by 2 horses, paying 30 sous each for a third and fourth horse, which they are liable to take, or 3 francs extra for the 2 persons above the number of horses, thus compounding with the postmasters along the whole line of road. Where the carriage is so light as not to require as many horses as there are passengers, it is, of course, a saving of 10 sous a myriam. for each horse to dispense with them. Postmasters in France are too apt to withhold the third horse, even in cases where the weight of the carriage and the state of the roads require it to be put to. No one ought to submit to this when *first attempted* ; it will cause much loss of time on hilly roads.

The limitation of the number of horses on first setting out on a journey is of importance, because you are obliged to take on from every post station (except in the case of supplemental horses) the same number of horses that brought you to the relay.

One postilion may drive 4 horses, " aux grandes guides ;" where 3 horses are required, they may be harnessed one in front of the others, or " à l'arbalète." Formerly, in France, 3 horses required to be yoked abreast : and for this purpose shafts must be put to the carriage ; but this rule is not now enforced, and there is no difficulty in travelling with 3 horses and a pole, as in Belgium and Germany.

On certain hilly stages one or more extra horses (chevaux de supplément) are required to be attached to carriages ; and at the entry into and departure from certain large towns the postmaster is allowed to charge for a number of kilomètres exceeding the real distance of the stage, called "distances supplémentaires," de faveur, or formerly "postes royales." For example, 8 kilomètres beyond the real distance are charged on entering and quitting Paris. These privileges are defined by the 'Livre de Poste.' Those who merely pass through towns, changing horses but not stopping, are exempted from this extra charge.

The furnishing of post-horses does not, as in England, include *a post-chaise*, and those who mean to post in France must have a carriage of their own. It is true the French postmasters are obliged to keep a cabriolet or small calèche for hire, but it is usually a rickety vehicle holding only 2 persons, with no room for baggage beyond a sac de nuit, and is therefore seldom resorted to. The charge for it is the same as for a single horse, *i. e.* 40 sous per myriam.

Postilions are not allowed to pass another carriage on the road, unless the one in advance be drawn by fewer horses, or has been stopped by some accident. Travellers are supplied with horses in the order in which they and their couriers arrive; the malles postes and Government estafettes alone having a right of precedence.

A register is kept at every posthouse, in which the traveller may enter complaints against the postmaster or his servants in that or the neighbouring relays. These registers are inspected at stated times by proper authorities, and the charges are investigated.

Tariff *charge of post-horses* for conveying a carriage from the railway termini in Paris—for 2 horses and 1 postilion, 6 francs; 3 horses and 1 postilion, 8 francs 30 centimes; 4 horses and 2 postilions, 12 francs.

TABLE OF POSTING CHARGES IN FRANCE.

Kilomètres.	Three Horses, and Two "Petits Chevals" paid for but not used.		One Post-Boy.		Total.	
	fr.	c.	fr.	c.	fr.	c.
1	0	90	0	20	1	10
2	1	80	0	40	2	20
3	2	70	0	60	3	30
4	3	60	0	80	4	40
5	4	50	1	0	5	50
6	5	40	1	20	6	60
7	6	30	1	40	7	70
8	7	20	1	60	8	80
9	8	10	1	80	9	10
10	9	0	2	0	11	0
11	9	90	2	20	12	10
12	10	80	2	40	13	20
13	11	70	2	60	14	30
14	12	60	2	80	15	40
15	13	30	3	0	16	50
16	14	40	3	20	17	60
17	15	30	3	40	18	70
18	16	20	3	60	19	80
19	17	10	3	80	20	90
20	18	0	4	0	22	0

Carriages.

Duty on English Carriages.—English travellers, on entering France with a carriage not of French make, are called upon to deposit one-third of an *ad valorem* duty for it; a barouche or chariot is usually rated at 1000 frs. (sometimes you can get off for 600), and a landau or coach at 1500 frs. Travellers should be aware of this, in order that they may take with them ready money to meet this charge. A receipt, with an order upon the Bureau des Douanes, is given to the owner, entitling him to receive back $\frac{3}{4}$ths of this one-third, if the *same* carriage be taken out of France within 3 years. This order describes very particularly the carriage, and, on presenting it at the frontier, the money deposited is repaid, except $\frac{1}{4}$th (*i. e.* $\frac{1}{12}$th of the value of the carriage), which is all the duty paid.

Carriages landed in France, and *taken out of the country within six days*, are exempted from the duty of a third of their value, formerly levied on all carriages without exception.* This remission of duty, however, can only be obtained on condition that some respectable French householder will guarantee that the carriage shall quit France within the six days specified. The landlord of the inn at which the traveller puts up in Calais will effect this arrangement: but as he subjects himself to a penalty of a very large amount in case the above condition is not complied with, he requires the traveller to sign an undertaking to indemnify and hold him harmless in case of failure. An order to procure this remission of duty, issued by the French custom-house, and called "*acquit à caution,*" costs 5 francs, and must be delivered up on passing the French frontier.

Owing to the inferiority of the post-chaises in France (alluded to above), those who intend to travel post, and are not furnished with a carriage of their own, must buy or hire one.

A travelling carriage, strong and tolerably good-looking, may be hired at Calais, or Paris, or Boulogne, from one of the innkeepers, for 350 or 400 fr. (16*l.*) for two months, and 8 fr. a-day after the expiration of that time; the owner to pay for all necessary repairs. Thus the expense of crossing and recrossing the Channel, of shipping and unshipping, is spared.

Hired Carriages—Voitures à volonté.

It is difficult to fix a fair scale of prices to pay for the hire of a carriage and horses in different parts of France; the best guide is to calculate it at one-half or two-thirds of posting price for the same distance, exclusive of the carriage.

The carriage usually to be met with for hire is the cabriolet—a heavy, lumbering, and *jolting* vehicle: the charge for it is commonly 8 or 9 fr. a-day, exclusive of a pourboire of 2 or 3 fr. to the driver. It has neither the neatness nor the lightness of the gigs furnished at a country inn in England, but is necessarily clumsily built to stand the terrible cross-roads of France.

In out-of-the-way places often no other vehicle is to be found than a *patache*—a rustic cab, verging towards the covered cart, without its

---

* It is said that no duty is levied on carriages entering *by land.*

easy motion. He who rides in a patache must prepare to be jolted to pieces.

f. MALLES POSTES,

equivalent to the English mail-coaches, and kept up at the expense of Government, travel along the following great roads of France to carry the mail, and are allowed to take 2 or 3 passengers.

The various railways ramifying from Paris have superseded the 12 malles which used previously to start from the capital. The following malles postes keep up the communication between the railway termini and the stations most conveniently situated and the extreme limits of the territory of France; also between those provincial towns not as yet united by railways:—

1. Tonnere to Bâle.
2. Chartres to Brest, 36 to 37 hours.
3. St. Pierre de Vauvray to Cherbourg, 15¼ to 17 hours.
4. Châlons sur Marne to Metz, 10 hours.
5. Dijon to Geneva, 15 hours.
6. ——— to Besançon, 6 hours 194 kilom.
7. Lyons to Mulhausen, 24 hours.
8. Nevers to Avignon, by Moulins, Lyons, Vienne and Valence (1 place), 35 to 37 hours.
9. Nevers to Montpellier, by Clermont, St. Flour, Lodeve, 36½ to 42 hours.
10. Epernay to Sedan, by Rheims, 8½ hours.
11. Bar le Duc to Sarrebourg (until the railway is finished), 12 hours.
12. Châteauroux to Toulouse, by Limoges, Cahors, and Montauban, 30 to 33 hours.
13. Limoges to Pau, by Chalus, Périgueux, Agen, Auch, and Tarbes.
14. Toulouse to Bayonne, by Auch, Tarbes, and Pau.
15. ——— to Montpellier, by Narbonne, 16 hours.
16. ——— to Perpignan, by Limoux, 14 hours.
17. Bordeaux to Bayonne, 14½ hours.
18. ——— to Toulouse, 15½ hours.

The French mails are on the whole very comfortable, though the inside passengers have not very much room, and he that sits by the side of the conductor in the cabriolet is liable to be annoyed at every post-town by his companion's horn in his efforts to rouse the postmasters, and by his bustle in the delivery and receipt of the letter-bags.

The mails consist of a stoutly-built barouche which holds comfortably inside 2 or 3 passengers; painted of a light red colour, drawn by 4 horses with tolerable harness, with a seat in front for the postilion, and one behind for the conductor. Their rate of travelling exceeds that of the diligence on almost all the roads, equalling at least 9 or 10 Eng. m. an hour.

The price of places is nearly double that of the diligence, being 1 fr. 75 cent. per myriam. = to nearly 3*d.* a mile, the outside fare on an English mail.

As the malles postes take few passengers, it is generally necessary

g. DILIGENCES.

to secure a place some days beforehand. Places are taken at the post-offices in the towns whence or through which the malle poste passes. The passport must be shown if required before the name can be entered, and half the fare must be paid at once, the remainder before starting.

Baggage of passengers is restricted in weight to 25 kilogram. or 55 lbs.; all above that weight must be paid for. No portmanteau, or sac de nuit, of dimensions exceeding the following measurement, can be admitted into a malle poste:—

In length .	. 0^m, 70 décim.	= 26 pouces	= 27 English inches.
breadth .	. 0^m, 40	= 14	= 15
height .	. 0^m, 35	= 13	= 13

These regulations are strictly enforced, so that it is vain for those who travel with much baggage to think of availing themselves of the malle poste. There is room, however, for a writing-case or hat-box inside.

The fare includes all charges; nothing is to be given to the postilions; the conductor generally receives a small douceur, varying from 5 to 10 fr. according to the length of the journey, at the good will of the passenger.

Places cannot be *secured* except for three fourths of the entire distance which the mail travels; nor are passengers taken for short distances unless they are without baggage.

g. DILIGENCES.

The French stage coach or diligence is a huge, heavy, lofty, lumbering machine, something between an English stage and a broad-wheeled waggon. It is composed of three parts or bodies joined together: 1. the front division called *Coupé*, shaped like a chariot or post-chaise, holding 3 persons, quite distinct from the rest of the passengers, so that ladies may resort to it without inconvenience, and, by securing all 3 places to themselves, travel nearly as comfortably as in a private carriage. The fare is more expensive than in the other parts of the vehicle.

2. Next to it comes the *Intérieur*, or inside, holding 6 persons, and oppressively warm in summer.

3. Behind this is attached the *Rotonde*, "the receptacle of dust, dirt, and bad company," the least desirable part of the diligence, and the cheapest except

The *Banquette*, or Impériale, an outside seat on the roof of the coupé, tolerably well protected from rain and cold by a hood or head, and leather apron, but somewhat difficult of access until you are accustomed to climb up into it. It affords a comfortable and roomy seat by the side of the conductor, with the advantages of fresh air and the best view of the country from its great elevation, and greater freedom from the dust than those enjoy who sit below. It is true you may sometimes meet rough and low-bred companions, for the French do not like to travel outside; and few persons of the better class resort to it, except English,

France.

and they for the most part prefer it to all others. It is not suited to females, owing to the difficulty of clambering up to it. The diligence is more roomy and easy, and therefore less fatiguing than an English stage: but *the pace* is slow, rarely exceeding 6 or 7 m. an hour, and in bad weather, when roads are heavy, falling below that. Nevertheless, the diligences have undergone considerable improvement within the last 15 or 20 years; the horses are changed more rapidly; strips of hide have taken the place of rope harness; and, on one or two lines of road, the rate of travelling is accelerated to 8, or even 10 m. an hour.

The coach and its contents are placed in charge of the *Conducteur*, a sort of guard, who takes care of the passengers, the luggage, the way-bill, and the mécanique, that is, the break or leverage, by which the wheel is locked. He is paid by the administration, and expects nothing from the passengers, unless he obliges them by some extra service. He is generally an intelligent person, often an old soldier, and the traveller may pick up some information from him.

The large 1st class three-bodied diligences carry 15 passengers inside, and 4 out, including the conductor, and weigh when loaded 11,000 lbs., or about 5 tons. They are drawn by 5 or 6 horses, driven by a post-boy, from the box, instead of the saddle, as was formerly the case. Besides passengers, the diligence carries a great deal of heavy merchandise, such as in England would be sent by the waggon or canal-boat.

The *places* in the diligence are all numbered, and are given out to passengers in the order in which they book themselves, the corner seats first; and it comports very much with the traveller's comfort to secure one of them, especially in long journeys. Before starting, the passengers' names are called over, and to each is assigned his proper place. The average rate of the *fares* may be calculated at 45 or 50 centimes for 2 leagues, equivalent to a $1\frac{1}{2}d.$ a mile English, except for the coupé, which is somewhat higher. Never omit to ask for the receipt or bulletin for the fare paid, which constitutes your legal title to the place.

Two great companies, whose head-quarters are at Paris, the Messageries (Royales), Nationales and Messageries Générales (Laffitte, Caillard, et Comp[ie].), furnish diligences on the great roads of France, and correspond with provincial companies who "coach" the more distant and cross roads, so that there is no want of means of conveyance in any part of France between places of moderate consequence In many cases, however, the "turn-out" from provincial towns is of the worst kind, and the organisation is throughout inferior to the stage-coaching of England.

The two chief Messageries are equally good, and, generally speaking, superior to any of the minor companies; indeed, they manage to keep down their rivals, by a mutual understanding with each other.

N.B. On those routes upon which railways have been begun, the diligence pursues the line of the rail; the body of the vehicle being taken off from its wheels by a crane, and deposited, luggage, passengers and all, upon a truck attached to the train. On arriving at its destination it is taken off and placed upon a different set of wheels, and is instantly driven off.

g. DILIGENCES—h. RAILROADS.

N.B. During the *month of August* the diligences on all the great roads are thronged with schoolboys and collegians, with their parents and masters, in consequence of the breaking up of the establishments of education in Paris, all hurrying home at once into the provinces. It not unfrequently happens, that for a fortnight together every place in every coach is taken. The vacations at the public offices occur about the same time, and contribute largely to swell the crowd of travellers in August.

h. RAILROADS.

By a law passed in 1842, a system of railways was laid down for France, which, with slight modifications, is now being carried into effect. By this plan seven great arteries of railway communication were projected.

1. The Great Northern of France issues from Paris to Amiens, following the valleys of the Oise, Brêche, Arc, and Somme. From Amiens it is carried to Douay, where it forks, one branch running by Valenciennes to the Belgian frontier, the other by Lille to Calais and Dunkerque. Connected with this line are 2 great branches from Amiens to Boulogne and from Creil to St. Quentin.

2. A line from Paris to the W. coast of the Bay of Biscay has been completed as far as Chartres and Le Mans, but is in progress to Rennes.

3. A line from Paris by Orleans to Tours and Bordeaux, and thence to the Pyrenees at Bayonne, is in operation as far as Bordeaux. This line throws off an important branch from Tours to Angers and Nantes, which is open to traffic.

4. An artery (*Chemin du Centre*), branching from No. 3 line at Orleans, intended to proceed S. to the Pyrenees at Perpignan, is open as far as Châteauroux. Another branch of this line is in progress from Vierzon, by Moulins and Nevers, to Vichy, Clermont, and Roanne.

5. The Great Southern Railway, intended to connect Paris with Marseilles, is open by Tonnerre and Dijon as far as Châlons-sur-Saone and Lyons; the sections between Lyons and Valence, and Avignon and Marseilles, being also completed and under traffic: also a branch from Montereau to Troyes.

6. The eastern line, proceeding from Paris to the Rhine at Strasburg, is open. Branches extend from Metz to Forbach and Mayence —Metz to Thionville—Strasburg to Basle—La Fère to Rheims.

The Livret or *Guide* of *Paul Chaix*, published monthly, contains the time-tables, fares, &c., of all the French railways: it is the "Bradshaw" of France, and will be a useful companion to travellers in that country.

Railway passengers are compelled to deliver up their *luggage* blindly into the hands of the officials, by whom it is booked (*enregistré*), for which a fee of 2 sous must be paid, and a ticket is given, on delivery of which at the journey's end the baggage is restored to the holder. This gives rise to frequent inconvenience and serious mistakes and inevitable delay. The best way to obviate the nuisance is to take as little as possible, and to place it in one or more carpet bags, which will lie under *the seat* in the carriage.* 30 kilos (= more than 60 lbs. English) of luggage are allowed to every passenger free of charge.

RAILWAY STATIONS IN PARIS.

PARIS to	Boulogne, Calais. Amiens. Dunkirk.	Clos St. Lazare, 24, Place Roubaix, Faub. St. Denis.
———	Rouen, Havre, and Dieppe.	Rue d'Amsterdam.
———	Orleans, Tours, Nantes, and Bordeaux.	Boulevard de l'Hôpital, 7.
———	Lyons, Châlons, Marseilles.	Boulevard Mazas.
———	Strasburg, Metz, Bâle.	Rue et Place de Strasbourg.
———	Versailles, right bank, and St. Germain.	Rue St. Lazare, 124.
———	Versailles, left bank, and Chartres.	Boulevard Mont Parnasse, 44.

i. STEAM-BOATS.

The use of steam is very general on all the great rivers of France, but for purposes of travelling steamers are now nearly superseded by railways.

---

* Travellers arriving in Paris are exposed to a very annoying delay of seldom less than half an hour at the railway stations, arising out of the examination and slow delivery of their luggage.

They are obliged to wait until the whole of the luggage arriving by the train is laid out along tables, where it is examined by the Octroi and Custom-house authorities.

Families can avoid this annoying ordeal, by leaving it to be performed by their servants.

The examination of baggage, when it takes place, is rapid and superficial, except in cases of suspicion. A *porter must be found and paid* to carry it out of the station, as the foreign railway companies do nothing of the sort for their passengers.

The traveller who takes the omnibus must wait until the last person arriving by the train has left the station, *i. e.* as long as a chance remains of their picking up a new fare; and when the omnibus does start, it follows a circuitous course, dropping its passengers on the way at the different hotels. To avoid this the traveller should insist on his luggage being taken to a fiacre, of which there are always plenty in attendance at the gate of every railway station, which will convey him immediately to his hotel, and at a charge of a few sols more than he would have to pay to the omnibus.

Where the travelling party is numerous and the luggage abundant, the best and cheapest plan is to hire an omnibus to yourselves.

Travellers arriving in Paris should desire beforehand the owners of the hotels they intend stopping at to send a carriage with a *laquais de place* to meet them. The latter can remain with their servants to see their luggage examined, and to take it to the hotel. By doing this, a delay very annoying to ladies, especially when arriving in Paris, as is generally the case, by the night trains, may be avoided.

Inland Steam Navigation.

The Seine, from Havre to Rouen, from Paris to Montereau.
The Oise, to Compiègne.
The Loire, from Nantes to Angers;—Orleans, to Gien, Nevers, and Digoin.
The Allier, to Moulins.
The Aulne, Brest to Châteaulin.
The Charente, Rochefort to Saintes and Angoulême.
The Garonne, Bordeaux to Agen.
The Gironde, Bordeaux to the sea.
The Rhône, from Arles to Lyons and Seyssel.
The Saône, from Lyons to Châlons.
The Moselle, from Trèves to Thionville.

The rivers of France are more liable than those of Britain to rise and fall, and a sudden elevation caused by rains, or a want of water owing to drought, has equally the effect of arresting the navigation; the last by withdrawing the necessary depth of water, the first by filling the arches of the bridges so as to leave no room for the steamers to pass under them.

There are also a great number of coasting steamers; but the traveller should be cautious in trusting himself to them, unless the character of the captains and engineers be well ascertained to be of tried experience, as accidents not unfrequently happen, and even the French themselves do not place unlimited confidence in coasting steamers.

k. INNS, TABLES-D'HÔTE, ETC.

On the whole, the inns of France are very inferior to those of Germany and Switzerland, in the want of general comfort, and above all of cleanliness—their greatest drawback. There is an exception to this, however, in the bed and table linen. Even the filthy cabaret, whose kitchen and salon are scarcely endurable to look at, commonly affords napkins and table-cloths clean, though coarse and rough, and beds with unsullied sheets and white draperies, together with well-stuffed mattresses and pillows, which put German cribs and feather-beds to shame. Many of the most *important essentials*, on the other hand, are utterly disregarded, and evince a state of grossness and barbarism hardly to be expected in a civilised country; the provisions for personal ablution are very defective. Fail not to take a piece of soap with you, a thing never to be found in foreign bedrooms; indeed, the washing of floors, whether of timber or tile, seems unknown. In the better hotels, indeed, the floors are polished as tables are in England, with brushes attached to the feet instead of hands; but in other cases they are black with the accumulated filth of years, a little water being sprinkled on them from time to time to lay the dust and increase the dark crust of dirt.

French Inns may be divided into two classes:—*a*. Those which make some pretensions to study English tastes and habits (and a few of them have some claim to be considered comfortable), and, being frequented by Englishmen, are very exorbitant in their charges. Such are met with along the great roads to Paris, and thence to Geneva, Lyons, and Marseilles. *b.* Those in remote situations, not yet corrupted to exorbitance by the English and their couriers; where the traveller who can conform with the customs of the country is treated fairly, and charged no higher than a Frenchman. The expense of living in these country inns is moderate,—6 francs a-day board and lodging, and 10 sous to the servants.

In one respect the inns of France are more accommodating than those of Germany, that they will furnish at almost any hour of the day, at 10 minutes or ¼ hour's notice, a well-dressed *dinner* of 8 or 10 dishes, at a cost not greatly exceeding that of the table-d'hôte. When ordering dinner in private, the traveller should specify the price at which he chooses to be served, fixing the sum at 3, 5, or more francs, as he may please. In remote places and small inns, never order dinner at a higher price than 3 francs: the people have only the same food to present, even if they charged 10 francs. A capital dinner is usually furnished at 4 fr. a-head; but the traveller who goes post in his own carriage will probably be charged 6, unless he specifies the price beforehand. Travellers not dining at the table-d'hôte should bargain beforehand for their meals at so much per head (combien par tête), otherwise they will be charged for each dish *à la carte*, a recent innovation, and a method of fleecing the stranger which ought to be resisted. The usual charge for a table-d'hôte dinner is 3 fr. (including wine in a wine country, but not in the north,) and ought never to exceed that except in large towns and first-rate inns.

Bargaining for rooms before you enter an inn, though usual, sometimes leads the landlord to suppose that you are going to beat him down (marchander), and he may therefore name a higher price than he is willing to take, and thus you may cause the exorbitance which you intend to prevent. In French inns it is the universal custom to lock the door of your room when you go out of the house, and to leave the key with the porter; it is expected, and is indeed necessary for safety.

Tables-d'hôte, though very general throughout France, are not so much resorted to by the most respectable townspeople, or by ladies, as in Germany. The majority of the company frequently consist of "commis-voyageurs," Anglice, bagmen, who swarm in all the inns, and are consequently the most important personages. English ladies will be cautious of presenting themselves at a French table-d'hôte, except in first-rate hotels, where English guests form a considerable part of the company, and at the well-frequented watering-places. Even at Bagnères de Bigorre, Lady Chatterton relates, "We laughed a good deal at a scene we witnessed at the table-d'hôte yesterday, where a Frenchman, after helping himself to all the best pieces of the roast fowl, turned to the lady next him, and said, with a most insinuating smile, 'Madame ne mange pas de volaille.'"

There are no established *fees* for the *servants* at inns; ½ a franc a-day "pour le service," and something extra (5 or 6 sous) for Boots, "le décrotteur," is enough. At Meurice's Hotel, in Paris, the house charge for servants is only 1 franc a-day, and that sum is ample in any part of France.

Average Charges at French Provincial Hotels.

Bedroom, 1 fr. 50 c. to 2 fr. 5 c.
Salon, 3 fr. and upwards.
Breakfast, tea and coffee, with bread and butter, 1 fr. 50 c. ; with meat, 2 fr.
Dinner, table-d'hôte, 3 fr.—Apart 4 fr. to 5 fr. or upwards.
Bottle of vin ordinaire, 1 fr.—N.B. Included in the charge for dinner in wine-growing countries.
The better wines are sold in demi-bouteilles. When only a part of the bottle is consumed, the waiter puts it aside for the owner until another time.
Coffee, 1 fr. It is better to take it at a café, where it is always better, and costs only 8 or 10 sous.
Bougies (wax lights), 1 fr. Where this charge is made, that for the bedroom ought not to exceed 1 fr. 50 c.

l. CAFÉS.

We have no equivalent in England for the Cafés in France, and the number and splendour of some of these establishments, everywhere seemingly out of proportion to the population and to other shops not only in Paris, but in every provincial town, may well excite surprise. They are adapted to all classes of society, from the magnificent *salon*, resplendent with looking-glass, and glittering with gilding, the decorations of which have perhaps cost 4000*l*. or 5000*l*., down to the low and confined *estaminets*, resorted to by carters, porters, and common labourers, which abound in the back streets of every town, and in every village, however small and remote. The latter sort occupy the place of the beer-shops of England, furnish beer and brandy, as well as coffee, and, though not so injurious to health and morals as the gin-palaces of London, are even more destructive of time: indeed, the dissipation of precious hours by almost all classes in France produces as bad an effect on the habits of the people.

It is only to the superior class of cafés that an English traveller is likely to resort, and they furnish some agreeable resources to a stranger in a strange place. In the morning ladies as well as gentlemen may there obtain a breakfast of coffee or tea, better and cheaper than in an hotel, and far better than they can procure it in England ; in the afternoon, a demi-tasse of coffee well prepared, and a petit verre of liqueur ; and in the evening, in summer, excellent ices, sorbettes, orgeats, limonade, and other cool drinks ; and in winter a very tolerable potation called " punch," but differing from its English prototype. They are always supplied with the journals of Paris and the provinces, including, in the principal cities, " Galignani's Messenger," and have usually billiard-tables attached to them. Some of the best of these places in Paris and the large towns have a Salon des Dames free from tobacco-smoke.

In the evening they are most crowded, and even in the most respectable (except the first-rate Parisian cafés) the company is very mixed. Clerks, tradesmen, commis-voyageurs, soldiers—officers as well as privates—and men in blouzes, crowded about a multitude of little marble tables, wrangle over provincial or national politics, or over games of cards or dominoes, while others, perspiring in their shirt-sleeves, surround the billiard-table. The rattling of balls, the cries of waiters hurrying to and fro, the gingling of dominoes, and the tinkling bell of the mistress who presides at the bar, alone prevail over the harsh din of many voices, while the splendour of mirrored walls and velvet seats is eclipsed behind a cloud of unfragrant tobacco-smoke. Such is the picture of a French café!

A large cup of coffee (café au lait), with bread and butter, and an egg for breakfast, costs about 20 or 24 sous. A demi-tasse, or small cup, in the afternoon, 8 or 10 sous; a petit verre de cognac, 5 sous. The waiter usually receives 2 sous.

m. A TRAVELLER'S GENERAL VIEW OF FRANCE.

It has been the custom of the English, who traverse France on their way to Italy or Switzerland, to complain of the tiresome and monotonous features of the country, and to ridicule the epithet " *La Belle* France," which the French, who, it must be confessed, have in general no true feeling for the beauties of nature, are wont to apply to it. By a "beautiful" country, a Frenchman generally understands one richly fertile and fully cultivated; and in this point of view the epithet is justly applied to France. It is also most fortunate in its climate. Many of its vineyards, the most valuable spots in the country, occupy tracts of poor, barren, and waste land, which in our climate would be absolutely unprofitable. But in truth our countrymen are unjust in forming their opinion from the routes between Calais and Paris, and thence to Lyons, Strasburg, and Dijon, perhaps the least varied part of the kingdom, and at least no fair sample of its beauties. To this district, and to a large part of the province of Champagne, the descriptions of " wearisome expanse of tillage, unvaried by hill or dale, and extent of corn-land or pasture, without enclosures, supremely tiresome," are almost exclusively applicable. Throughout nearly one half of France, especially in Lower Normandy, Brittany, a great part of the country S. of the Loire, the vicinity of the Pyrenees, Limousin, Auvergne, and Dauphiné, enclosures and hedge-rows are almost as common as in England, and the variety of surface in some of these districts is far greater. Our own island, indeed, presents as it were a miniature of other lands—a concentration, within a small area, of scenery varying from flat fen and rolling down to mountains and precipices. In France, the features of nature are broad and expanded, and you must often traverse 50 or 100 miles to encounter those pleasing changes which, in Britain, succeed one another almost every 10 miles. If the English had confined themselves less to the beaten track in their way from the Channel to the Mediterranean, they would have verified the truth of this assertion.

More than 50 years ago, Arthur Young advised those "who know no more of France than just once passing through it to Italy, that, if they would see some of the finest parts of the kingdom, they should land at Havre, follow the Seine up to Paris, then take the great road to Moulins, and there quit it for Auvergne, and so to the Rhône at Valence or Viviers : such a variation from the common road, though it demand more time, would repay them by the sight of a much finer and more singular country than the road by Dijon." The traveller may at present farther vary his route by going from Paris by railway to Orleans, and thence by Bourges either to Clermont in Auvergne, or to Nevers and Moulins on the high road from Paris to Lyons.

The districts of France which chiefly recommend themselves by their beauty and variety of scenery are, in the north, Normandy, the banks of the Seine (the finest of the great rivers of France), the valleys round Vire, Mortain, and Avranches, the wild coast scenery of Brittany, and the course of the Rance, and of other streams near Quimper ; in the centre, the Loire below Tours, and parts of Limousin: Auvergne, the Cantal and Ardèche, the Rhône—by some preferred to the Rhine, on account of its more extended prospects ; in the east, the hills of the Jura, the mountains and valleys of Dauphiné, especially the vale of the Gresivaudan, the gorge of the Grande Chartreuse, and the savage magnificence of peak and glacier around Mont Pelvoux, a region which may be styled the Chamouny or Grindelwald of France. Among the Vosges and Ardennes are many soberly romantic scenes which have as yet attracted but little notice from travellers ; in the south, Provence, with its sunny sky, is too arid to deserve general praise, excepting that favoured terrace at the foot of the Alps along the shore of the Mediterranean, intervening between Toulon and Nice. The Pyrenees, however, without doubt, include the finest scenery in France, and, except in the want of lakes, are scarcely inferior to the Alps of Switzerland and Savoy.

This slight enumeration of the chief points of interest is filled up in ampler details in the introductions to the different sections into which this Hand-book is divided, with a view of enabling the traveller to lay down for himself the plan of a tour, embracing as many of these points as his time or inclination will permit.

"Bretagne, Maine, and Anjou, have the appearance of deserts. The fertile territories of Flanders, Artois, and Alsace are distinguished by their utility. Picardy is uninteresting. Champagne, in general, where I saw it, ugly, almost as much so as Poitou. Lorraine, Franche Comté and Bourgogne are *sombre* in the wooded districts, and want cheerfulness in the open ones. Berri and La Manche may be ranked in the same class."—*Arthur Young.*

On the other hand, these districts, which are not interesting in point of scenery, have a compensating recommendation in their architectural remains, and relics of antiquity. The heaths of Brittany are studded with extraordinary Celtic remains, and abound in most beautiful churches. Out of the midst of the monotonous plain of La Beauce rises the wondrous fabric of Chartres cathedral ; that of Bourges (colossal pile) overlooks the dull plain of Berri, as the spire of Strasburg surmounts the flat valley of the Rhine. Rheims, Troyes, Laon, &c., give an interest to the otherwise tiresome journey through Champagne; the sight of Amiens, Beauvais, and Abbeville, makes one forget the length of the way through Picardy and Artois; and the Roman remains of Nismes, Arles, St. Remy, Orange, and Antibes, equal to almost any in Italy, would alone compensate for a journey to Provence, even had it no other claims to interest.* France, however, is particularly rich in architectural remains, especially in Gothic architecture, of which it possesses some of the noblest specimens existing, viz., the cathedrals above enumerated; to which must be added those of Metz, and 3 churches at Rouen.

These glorious monuments of architectural skill and lavish devotion are far more stupendous in their proportions than the cathedrals of England, but have this peculiarity, that scarcely one of them is finished: thus, Beauvais has no nave, Amiens is incomplete in its towers, Abbeville has no choir, Bourges no spire. It has been said that a perfect cathedral might be made of the portal of Rheims, the nave of Amiens, the choir of Beauvais, and the tower of Chartres.

The rose or wheel windows are both more frequent and of larger dimensions than in English cathedrals, and contribute greatly to the beauty of those of France, where it is not uncommon to find three in one church. The quantity, variety, and richness of the *painted glass* which the ecclesiastical edifices still retain, in spite of Huguenot iconoclasts and revolutionary destructives, is quite marvellous: we have nothing to compare with it in England.

The churches in the N. of France are closed from 12 to 6, except the cathedrals, which re-open at 4. In the S. they remain open all day. The choir, its aisles and side chapels, are usually closed by an iron grating, and to obtain admittance one must apply to the *suisse*, or beadle, who struts about in cocked hat, sword, and laced livery.

The finest provincial cities are Lyons, Rouen, Bordeaux, Marseilles, and Nantes, all more or less distinguished for commerce, manufactures, and fine edifices. The minor provincial towns have a certain number of features in common which will not fail to draw the traveller's observation: such are the formal walk near the entrance or on the outskirts, often a mere platform, planted with rows of stunted trees, and the resort of nursery-maids, washerwomen, and recruits undergoing drill, except on Sundays or fête-days, when the dusty and gritty platform is crowded with a gay throng, to whom the sight of bright ribbons, shawls, and new bonnets, compensates for the want of other prospect. A walk into the country and across the fields is never thought of by the French artizan or shopkeeper, nor indeed are there any field paths, green shady lanes, or

---

* Mr. Petit's 'Architectural Studies in France, 1854,' should be perused and digested by every student of Gothic before he visits France. It is a book full of instruction and suggestion, and the illustrations are valuable memorials to refer to on returning from one's travels.

pretty villas, or neat cottages with gardens, on the outskirts of the towns, to invite him to sally forth. The *high roads* in France have been greatly improved since 1844; many are now macadamized: indeed, in spite of the desolating anarchy of 1848-50, the whole country shows unequivocal signs of great and increasing prosperity.

Every town of a certain size is surrounded with a wall or barrier for the purpose of levying the *octroi* or town duties on all articles for eating and drinking brought into it, and which go to the municipal caisse or corporation funds. All carts and carriages, public and private, are stopped at the gates in consequence, by douaniers, who search them, and the baggage contained in them, to ascertain that no "comestibles" are concealed in order to evade this tax. The space outside the gates usually swarms with low cabarets, guinguettes, &c., where the poor man may eat and drink at a cheaper rate than within the walls.

Arrived within the town, the traveller will commonly find narrow streets, with no pavement at the sides, but a huge gutter in the centre, neither clean nor sweet, lighted at night by lamps (réverbères), swinging from ropes attached to the houses on either side. After passing one or more barracks, the number of which and of soldiers is striking everywhere, the barrack being often a sequestrated convent or church, he will reach the Grande Place or square. On one side of it, or in some other conspicuous situation, appears a large white-washed building, graced probably with a portico in front, guarded by a sentinel, surmounted by a tri-color flag, and fenced round by a tall iron railing tipped with gilt spearheads. This is the préfecture or sous-préfecture.

There are many institutions and establishments in French towns deserving high commendation and general imitation in England: such are the Abattoirs, or slaughter-houses, always in the outskirts; the public Cemeteries, always removed beyond the walls; even the Public Walks to be found in every French town, though not suited altogether to English ideas of recreation, yet show an attention to the health and enjoyment of the people which is worthy of imitation north of the Channel.

In all the larger towns there is a museum of natural history, and generally of paintings, which, although for the most part of inferior merit, are commendable as institutions for public recreation.

Still more commendable are the public libraries and reading-rooms, arranged in convenient apartments, with salaried librarians, common in all French provincial towns. An amiable traveller observes. " I could not visit these libraries without wishing that similar institutions could be introduced into England, where the easy access to books in every part of the kingdom could not but prove at once agreeable and beneficial. The encouragement of such an object would be a wise application of the public money."—*Knight's Tour in Normandy.*

There are three authors whose works should be perused before entering France: Cæsar for its ancient history; Froissart for its feudal history; and Arthur Young, for the picture of France before the Revolution: his vivid local descriptions hold good to the present day.

n. LIST OF THE 86 DEPARTMENTS INTO WHICH FRANCE IS DIVIDED, AND OF THE 33 ANCIENT PROVINCES COMPOSING THEM.

Provinces.	Départemens.	Chefs-Lieux.
ILE DE FRANCE, WITH LA BRIE, &c.	Seine.	Paris.
	Seine-et-Oise.	Versailles.
	Seine-et-Marne.	Melun.
	Oise.	Beauvais.
	Aisne.	Laon.
PICARDIE.	Somme.	Amiens.
ARTOIS AND BOULONNAIS.	Pas-de-Calais.	Arras.
FLANDRE AND HAINAULT FRANÇAIS.	Nord.	Lille.
NORMANDIE.	Seine-Inférieure.	Rouen.
	Eure.	Evreux.
	Calvados.	Caen.
	Orne.	Alençon.
	Manche.	Saint-Lô.
BRETAGNE.	Ille-et-Vilaine.	Rennes.
	Côtes-du-Nord.	Saint-Brieux.
	Finisterre.	Quimper.
	Morbihan.	Vannes.
	Loire-Inférieure.	Nantes.
ORLÉANAIS.	Loiret.	Orléans.
	Loir-et-Cher.	Blois.
BEAUCE AND PAYS CHARTRAIN.	Eure-et-Loire.	Chartres.
MAINE.	Sarthe.	Le Mans.
	Mayenne.	Laval.
ANJOU.	Maine-et-Loire.	Angers.
TOURAINE.	Indre-et-Loire.	Tours.
POITOU.	Vendée.	Bourbon-Vendée.
	Deux-Sèvres.	Niort.
	Vienne	Poitiers.
BERRI.	Indre.	Châteauroux.
	Cher.	Bourges.
MARCHE.	Creuze.	Gueret.
LIMOUSIN.	Haute-Vienne.	Limoges.
	Corrèze.	Tulle.
ANGOUMOIS.	Charente.	Angoulême.
SAINTONGE AND AUNIS.	Charente-Inférieure.	La Rochelle.
PERIGORD.	Dordogne.	Périgueux.
GUYENNE.	Gironde.	Bordeaux.
	Lot-et-Garonne.	Agen.
	Lot.	Cahors.
	Tarn-et-Garonne.	Montauban.
	Aveyron.	Rhodez.
ARMAGNAC (PART OF GASCOGNE).	Gers.	Auch.
BIGORRE (PART OF GASCOGNE).	Hautes-Pyrénées.	Tarbes.
GASCOGNE.	Landes.	Mont-de-Marsan.
BÉARN AND FRENCH NAVARRE.	Basses-Pyrénées.	Pau.

n. PROVINCES.—o. THE ENGLISH ABROAD.

Provinces.	Départemens.	Chefs-Lieux.
COMTÉ DE FOIX.	Arriège.	Foix.
ROUSSILLON.	Pyrénées-Orientales.	Perpignan.
LANGUEDOC.	Haute-Garonne.	Toulouse.
	Tarn.	Alby.
	Aude.	Carcassonne.
	Hérault.	Montpellier.
	Gard.	Nismes.
VIVARAIS.	Ardèche.	Privas.
GÉVAUDAN.	Lozère.	Mende.
VELAY.	Haute-Loire.	Le Puy.
COMTAT VENAISSIN, ORANGE, &c.	Vaucluse.	Avignon.
PROVENCE.	Bouches-du-Rhône.	Marseille.
	Var.	Draguignan.
	Basses-Alpes.	Digne.
DAUPHINÉ.	Isère.	Grenoble.
	Drôme.	Valence.
	Hautes-Alpes.	Gap.
LYONNAIS & BEAUJOLAIS.	Rhône.	Lyon.
FOREZ.	Loire.	Montbrison.
AUVERGNE.	Puy-de-Dôme.	Clermont.
	Cantal.	Aurillac.
BOURBONNAIS	Allier.	Moulins.
NIVERNAIS.	Nièvre.	Nevers.
BRESSE, BUGEY, &c.	Ain.	Bourg.
BOURGOGNE (DUCHÉ).	Saône-et-Loire.	Mâcon.
	Côte d'Or.	Dijon.
	Yonne.	Auxerre.
COMTÉ DE BOURGOGNE, OR FRANCHE-COMTÉ.	Doubs.	Besançon.
	Jura.	Lons-le-Saulnier.
	Haute-Saône.	Vesoul.
CHAMPAGNE.	Aube.	Troyes.
	Marne.	Châlons-sur-Marne.
	Haute-Marne	Châumont.
	Ardennes.	Mézières.
LORRAINE.	Meurthe.	Nancy.
	Meuse.	Bar-le-Duc.
	Moselle.	Metz.
	Vosges.	Epinal.
ALSACE.	Bas-Rhin.	Strasburg.
	Haut-Rhin.	Colmar.
CORSICA.	Corse.	Ajaccio.

o. THE ENGLISH ABROAD.

It may not be amiss here briefly to consider the causes which render the English unpopular in many countries of the Continent. In the first place, it arises from the number of ill-conditioned persons (mauvais sujets) who, not being in a condition to face the world at home, scatter themselves over foreign lands, and bring no little discredit upon their country. But, in addition to these, there are many respectable and wealthy persons, who, through inattention, unguardedness, wanton expenditure in some cases, niggardly parsimony in others, but, above all, from an unwillingness to accommodate themselves to the feelings of the people they are among, contribute not a little to bring their own nation into disrepute. The Englishman abroad too often forgets that he is the representative of his country, and that his countrymen will be judged by his own conduct; that by affability, moderation, and being easily pleased, he will conciliate; whereas by caprice, extravagant squandering, or ill-timed niggardliness, he affects the reception of the next comer.

There are many points, however, in which our character is misunderstood by foreigners. The morose sullenness attributed by them to the Englishman is, in perhaps nine cases out of ten, nothing more than involuntary silence, arising from his ignorance of foreign languages, or at least from his want of sufficient fluency to make himself readily understood, which thus prevents his enjoying society. If an Englishman were fully aware how much it increases the pleasure and profit of travelling to have made some progress in foreign languages before he sets foot on the Continent, no one would think of quitting home until he had devoted at least some months to hard labour with grammars and dictionaries.

Englishmen and Protestants, admitted into Roman Catholic churches, at times are often inconsiderate in talking loud, laughing, and stamping with their feet while the service is going on: a moment's reflection should point out to them that they should regard the feelings of those around them who are engaged in their devotions. Above all, they should avoid as much as possible turning their backs upon the altar. In a church ladies and gentlemen should not walk arm in arm—as that is contrary to the usual practice of the people and to their idea of good manners: they should avoid talking together during service.

Our countrymen have a reputation for pugnacity in France: let them therefore be especially cautious not to make use of their fists, however great the provocation, otherwise they will rue it. No French magistrate or judge will listen to any plea of provocation; fine and imprisonment are the offender's inevitable portion. The general conduct of the French towards strangers, especially that of the peasantry, is courteous and kind, and in no country is the foreigner more sure of redress in the event of suffering from fraud or injustice, provided only he preserves his temper and applies to the proper authorities. In the case of an exorbitant bill, a stranger may resort to a respectable lawyer in the place; and without being compelled to stay and appear, as in England, by merely leaving his deposition properly attested, the fraudulent innkeeper may be compelled to disgorge.*

By the official returns it appears that there are at present in France 66,000 English residents. Supposing the average expenditure of each to be 5 francs a-day, the sum total will amount to about 4,820,000*l.*

---

* During the summer of 1852, an English clergyman, defrauded of part of his fare by a clerk in a diligence office, had the sum repaid to him by the offender, and an ample apology made to him, through the exertions of the Maire-adjoint of Vichy.—*G.B.*

per annum. In not fewer than 25 towns of France places of worship for the performance of the *English Church Service* have been established, and at most of these there are resident English ministers, many of them having the licence of the Bishop of London. With few exceptions the stipends are very small, and English travellers availing themselves of the privilege and benefit afforded by these places of worship should remember that they are in duty bound to contribute, according to their means, to the support of the establishments and their ministers.

p. SKELETON TOUR THROUGH FRANCE, TO EMBRACE THE PRINCIPAL OBJECTS OF CURIOSITY, AND TO OCCUPY FIVE OR SIX MONTHS.

HAVRE—By land up the N. bank of the Seine, halting to explore its beauties and curiosities.
Rouen (to Paris by railway).
Andelys.
Descend the valley of the Seine by railway to Havre.
Caen.
Bayeux (Cherbourg).
Vire.
Avranches and Mont St. Michel.
St. Malo.
Dinant (Brest and Quimper).
Vannes and Carnac.
Nantes—Clisson.
Ascent of the Loire to Angers. (Rl.)
Saumur.
Chinon.
Tours.
Loches — Chénonceaux.
Amboise.
Blois — Chambord.
Orleans.
Bourges.
Clermont — Puy de Dôme.
Mont Dore.
Cantal.
Le Puy.
St. Etienne.
Lyons.
Descent of Rhône — Valence.
Montelimart — Aubenas — Ardèche.
Viviers on the Rhône.
Orange.
Avignon — Pont du Gard.
Nismes.
Montpellier.
Narbonne.
Toulouse.
Descent of the Garonne.
Bordeaux.
Bayonne.
Pau.
Tour of the W. Pyrenees.
St. Gaudens.
Tour of the E. Pyrenees.
Perpignan.
Narbonne.
Montpellier.
Arles — Aix.
Marseilles.
Toulon.
Cannes.
Digne.
Sisteron.
Gap.
Embrun — Val Queiras.
Briançon.
Pass of Lauteret — Mont Pelvoux.
Bourg d'Oysans.
Grenoble — Vale of Gresivaudan.
Grande Chartreuse.
Bourg.
Châlons-sur-Saône.
Dijon.
Besançon.
Colmar.
Strasburg.
Nancy.
Troyes.
Châlons-sur-Marne.
Rheims.
Soissons.
Amiens.
Boulogne.

ABBREVIATIONS, &c., USED IN THE HANDBOOK.

The Points of the Compass are often marked simply by the letters N. S. E. W.

(*rt.*) right, (*l.*) left, — applied to the banks of a river. The right bank is that which lies on the right hand of a person whose back is turned towards the source, or the quarter from which the current descends.

kilom. for kilomètre.
m. for English mile.
Dépt. for Département.
Inhab. for Inhabitants.
Cent. for Century.
R. Rte. for Route.
p. for page.
Sta. Stat. for Railway Station.

The names of Inns precede the description of every place (often in a parenthesis), because the first information needed by a traveller is where to lodge. The best Inns, as far as they can be determined, are placed first.

Instead of designating a town by the vague words "large" or "small," the amount of the population, according to the latest census, is almost invariably stated, as presenting a more exact scale of the importance and size of the place.

Every Route has a number, corresponding with the figures attached to the Route on the General Map of France, which thus serves as an index to the Book, at the same time that it presents a *tolerably* exact view of the great high roads of France, and of the course of public conveyances.

The length of the Routes and the distances from place to place are measured in kilomètres.

LIST OF MAPS.

Course of the Seine and Railways	To face page 31.
———— Loire and Railways	. 177.
The Pyrenees	. 269.
Course of the Rhône and Railways	. 425.
General Map of France	. At the end.

HANDBOOK

FOR

TRAVELLERS IN FRANCE.

SECTION I.

PICARDY—FRENCH FLANDERS—ILE DE FRANCE—NORMANDY.

INTRODUCTORY INFORMATION.

Objects of Interest—Country of Normandy—Architectural Remains—Skeleton Tour.

ROUTES.

[The names of places are printed in *italics* only in those Routes where the *places* are described.]

ROUTE	PAGE
1 *Calais* to Paris, by *St. Omer*, *Hazebrouck*, *Lille*, *Douai*, *Arras*, &c., Amiens—RAILWAY.	3
2 Calais to Paris, by *Doullens*, Amiens, and Chantilly.	9
3 *Boulogne* to Paris, by *Abbeville*, Amiens, *Pontoise*, and *St. Denis*—RAILROAD	11
4 Calais to Paris, by Boulogne.—*Beauvais*	22
5 *Dieppe* to Paris, by *Gisors*.	26
6 Dieppe to Rouen (RAILROAD).	30
8 Paris to *Rouen* (RAILROAD).	30
9 Paris to Rouen.—*Lower Road*, by *St. Germain* and *Louviers*.	43
10 Paris to Rouen.—*Upper Road*, by Gisors or by *Magny*	47
11 The SEINE, A.—St. Germain to Rouen.—*Roche Guyon.*—*Château Gaillard*.	48
12 The SEINE, B.—Rouen to Havre	52
13 Rouen to Havre.—*Lower Road*, by *St. George Boscherville*, Jumièges, Caudebec, and *Lillebonne*.	55
14 Rouen to *Havre*—RAILROAD, by *Yvetot* and *Bolbec*	59
18 Havre to Dieppe and Abbeville, by *Fécamp* and *Eu*	64
21 Rouen to Alençon, by *Bernay*, *Broglie*, and *Séez*.	68
23 Rouen to Caen, by *Brionne* or by *Honfleur*	69
24 Havre to Caen	70
25 Paris to *Caen*, by *Evreux* and *Lisieux*.	71
26 Caen to *Cherbourg*, by *Bayeux*	78
27 Cherbourg to *St. Malo*, by *Coutances*, *Granville*, *Avranches*, *Mont St. Michel*, and *Dol*	87
29 Caen to Tours, by *Falaise*.—Alençon.	98
31 Caen to Rennes, by *Vire*, *Mortain*, and *Fougères*	99
32 Bayeux to St. Lo and *Avranches*	101
33 Fougères to Dinan	102

PICARDY and Ile de France, through which lie the routes to Paris from Calais and Boulogne, present no attractions of picturesqueness, but some interesting historical associations to Englishmen, and a few fine examples of Gothic architecture, the chief of which are the Cathedrals of Amiens, Beauvais, Abbeville.

Normandy, on the other hand, is full of interest in many respects:—it is remarkable for varied outline of swelling hills waving with corn; for beautiful valleys abounding in orchards, and in rich pasturages, on which large herds of cattle are reared, and traversed by winding rivers; for richness and careful cultivation; and above all, for remains of antiquity; venerable cities, the delight of the painter; noble cathedrals, abbeys, and churches, not confined merely to the larger towns, but scattered over the country, so that every little village, in some parts, possesses a fine specimen of Gothic architecture. Normandy is decidedly among the most attractive portions of France. Parts of the upper country are certainly flat, bare, monotonous table-land; but in its joyous sunny slopes and winding dales, in its hedgerows, orchards, thatched cottages with gardens, in the general character of the landscape of La Basse Normandie, especially in its verdure, frequent village spires, and white chalk cliffs, an Englishman recognises with pleasure the features of his own Fatherland, which no other part of the Continent affords. He may also take pleasure in remembering that this was the cradle whence came the wise and hardy bands of conquerors from whose possession of England that country dates her rising prosperity and greatness.

To those who are fond of Gothic architecture, especially to the architect and antiquary, Normandy will afford a rich treat. Rouen, a city possessing much of the old Teutonic character in its edifices, and containing not only a magnificent cathedral, but, if possible, a still finer church, that of St. Ouen, is certainly one of the most interesting places in France, and will alone furnish occupation for many days.

Caen is also interesting, though in a less degree; but in its vicinity are a great number of curious village churches. The ruined abbeys, Boscherville, Jumièges, &c., on the N. bank of the Seine, are remarkable examples of genuine Norman architecture; and the scenery of the river on whose banks and peninsulas they lie—the great water highway connecting Paris with its port of Havre—is so very pleasing, that it deserves to be seen both from land and water. The cathedrals of Bayeux (famed for its tapestry) and of Coutances also are noble edifices.

Normandy abounds in old *castles;* of which the most interesting, both in an historical and picturesque point of view, are Château Gaillard, the favourite stronghold of Richard Cœur de Lion; Falaise, the birth-place of William the Conqueror; and many others, the cradles of our English noblesse, whence they derive their titles; and above all, Mont St. Michel, which possesses a triple interest as an historical fortress, a remarkable ecclesiastical edifice, and a most grand and striking object.

The *Roman theatre* at Lillebonne deserves mention as an interesting example of an edifice of the kind, and almost the only one existing in Northern Europe.

The most picturesque parts of Normandy are the banks of the Seine from St. Germain to Havre, and especially from Rouen to Havre, though its innumerable islands, planted with rows of poplars and willows, are often monotonous; the vicinity of Vire and of Avranches charmingly posted on a hill top, whence the view extends to the Mont St. Michel, rising out of the sea, is peculiarly attractive.

The *Marine Arsenal, Dockyard,* and *Breakwater* of Cherbourg, at the extremity of the promontory called the Cotentin, which deserves to be explored for its geological peculiarities, must not be omitted among the curiosities of Normandy.

Skeleton Tour of 3 Weeks through Normandy.

Southampton to
1 Havre.
Tancarville.
3 Lillebonne.
Caudebec.
Jumièges.
4 St. George Boscherville.
7 Rouen.
Château Gaillard.
Descent of the Seine to Honfleur (or to Havre, and by another steamer to)
8 Caen.
10 Falaise and back.
11 Bayeux.
12 Valonges.
13 Cherbourg.
14 Coutances.
St. Lo.
15 Vire.
Mortain.
16 Avranches.
Mont St. Michel.
17 Dol.
18 Dinant.
19 St. Malo, and by steamer to
21 Jersey and Southampton.—Or from Dol to Dinant, Rennes, and Angers, on the Rly. from Nantes to Orleans, and so to Paris.

The best account of the architectural remains of Normandy will be found in Mr. *Gally Knight's* 'Tour in Normandy;' *Whewell's* 'Notes on German and French Churches;' *Turner's* 'Tour in Normandy,' one of the earliest descriptions of the country published in England or France; *Cotman* and *Pugin's* 'Illustrative Plates;' and *Caumont's* 'Histoire Sommaire de l'Architecture du Moyen Age.' *E. Frère's* 'Guide de Voyageur en Normandie, 1845,' which is, for the most part, a translation from this Handbook.

ROUTE 1.

CALAIS TO PARIS, BY ST. OMER, HAZEBROUCK, LILLE, DOUAI, ARRAS.—RAIL.

377 kilom. = 233¼ Eng. m.
4 trains daily—7 to 9 hrs.

This Rly., a branch of the Chemin de Fer du Nord, was completed 1848.

Terminus at Calais is on the Quay, close to the landing-place. It includes the Custom-house, Passport-office, and Refreshment-room (Buffet—hotel) all under its roof.

CALAIS. — *Inns:* H. Dessin. The bed-room in which the author of 'The Sentimental Journey' slept is still marked Sterne's Room; and that occupied by Sir Walter Scott is also ticketed with his respected name. H. de Paris, good, and more moderate than the more pretentious inns, is recommended. Quillac's Hotel. H. Meurice; no connection with the house of the same name at Paris. The preference generally given to Boulogne has diminished the custom of the hotel-keepers here; and this circumstance leads them to seek to indemnify themselves by an increase of prices. 10 fr. is the common charge for landing or shipping a 4-wheeled carriage; but M. Dessin has charged for landing a britzka and placing it on the railway truck 25 frs., with commission and other charges in addition, amounting to 44 frs. 14 c.—*a most extortionate charge,* which ought not to be submitted to.

For useful information on landing in France, see INTRODUCTION.

Calais has 12,508 Inhab.; it is a fortress of the second class, situated in a very barren and unpicturesque district, with sandhills raised by the wind and sea on the one side, and morasses on the other, contributing considerably to its military strength, but by no means to the beauty of its position. Within a few years it has been refortified, and the strength of its works greatly increased, especially to seaward. An English traveller of the time of James I. described it as "a beggarly, extorting town; monstrous dear and sluttish." In the opinion of many, this description holds good down to the present time.

The *harbour*, improved and lengthened by 282 yards since 1830, is not so deep as that of Boulogne. When the tide is low passengers must land in boats, and wait for their baggage until the steamer can enter.

Except to an Englishman setting his foot for the first time on the Continent, to whom everything is novel, Calais has little that is remarkable to show. After an hour or two it becomes tiresome, and a traveller will do well to quit it as soon as he has cleared his baggage from the custom-house, and procured the signature of the police to his passport, which, if he be pressed for time, will be done almost at any hour of the day or night, so as not to delay his departure. It is necessary to be aware of this, as the commissionnaires of the hotels will sometimes endeavour to detain a stranger, under pretence of not being able to get his passport signed. The owner of the passport must repair to the police-office himself to have it visé. Travellers not intending to go to Paris, but merely passing through the country on the way to Ostend, Brussels, or Marseilles, are not compelled to exchange their passport for a passe provisoire. (See *Passports: Introduction.*) Persons unprovided with a passport may procure one from the British Consul for 4s. 6d.

Calais has since 1830 become a manufacturing town; the bobbin-net (tulle) trade flourishes in rivalry of that of England; numerous *mills* have sprung up; steam-engines are multiplying; and the inner ramparts have been removed, to make way for factories. The gates remain open all night. Water is scarce here, and throughout Artois. 55 millions of eggs are exported hence to England annually.

The *Pier of Calais* is an agreeable promenade, nearly ¾ m. long. It is decorated with a pillar, raised to commemorate the return of Louis XVIII. to France, which originally bore this inscription:—

" Le 24 Avril, 1814, S. M. Louis XVIII. débarqua vis-à-vis de cette colonne, et fut enfin rendu à l'amour des Français; pour en perpétuer le souvenir, la ville de Calais a élevé ce monument." "As an additional means of perpetuating this remembrance, a brazen plate had been let into the pavement, upon the precise spot where his foot first touched the soil. It was the left; and an English traveller noticed it in his journal as a sinistrous omen, that, when Louis le Désiré, after his exile, stepped on France, he did not put the right foot foremost."—*Quarterly Review*. At the Revolution of July, 1830, both inscription and footmark were at once obliterated by the mob; and the pillar now stands a monument merely of the mutability of French opinions and dynasties.

The principal *gate* leading from the sea-side into the town is that introduced by Hogarth into his well-known picture. It was built by Cardinal Richelieu 1635.

No one needs to be reminded of the interesting incidents of the Siege of Calais by Edward III., which lasted 11 months, and of the heroic devotion of Eustace de St. Pierre and his 5 companions. Few, perhaps, are aware that the heroes of Calais not only went unrewarded by their own king and countrymen, but were compelled to beg their bread in misery through France. Calais remained in the hands of the English more than 200 years, from 1347 to 1558, when it was taken by the Duc de Guise. It was the last relic of the Gallic dominions of the Plantagenets, which, at one time, comprehended the half of France. Calais was dear to the English as the prize of the valour of their forefathers, rather than from any real value which it possessed.

The English traveller should look at the *Hôtel de Guise*, originally the guildhall of the mayor and aldermen of the "staple of wool," established here by Edward III. 1363. It has some vestiges of English Tudor architecture. Henry VIII. used to lodge in it.

In the Great Market Place stands the *Hôtel de Ville* (Town Hall). In it are situated the police-offices. In front of it are placed busts of St. Pierre; of the Duc de Guise, named le Balafré, who conquered the town from the English; and of the Cardinal de Richelieu, who built the citadel on the W. of the town: above it rises a belfry, containing the chimes. In the same square is a tower, which serves as a landmark by day and a lighthouse by night, to point out to sailors the entrance of the harbour.

The principal *Church* was built at the time when the English were masters of Calais. It is handsome, and surmounted by a stately tower and short steeple, which merit notice.

Lady Hamilton (Nelson's Emma) died here, a pauper, in great misery, Jan. 1815. Her body, enclosed in a deal box, was interred in the public cemetery, which was converted, in 1816, into a timber-yard, about 20 yards beyond the Porte de Calais, on the l. of the road to Boulogne. A pillar, set up by Mr. R. Barton, marks the spot.

The *walls* round the town, and the *pier* jutting out nearly ¾ m. from the shore, are admirable promenades, and command a distinct view of the white cliffs of England,—a tantalizing sight to the English exiles, fugitives from creditors, or *compelled* from other causes to leave their homes—a numerous class both here and at Boulogne. There are many of our countrymen besides, who reside merely for the purpose of economising; so that the place is half Anglicised, and our language is generally spoken. The number amounts at present to 4800 English residents in and around Calais. There is an *English Chapel*, Rue des Prêtres: service on Sundays, 11 A.M., 3 P.M.

There is a small *theatre* here.

Calais is one of those places where the fraternity of *Couriers* have a station. Travellers should be cautioned not to engage one, unless the landlord of an hotel, or some other respectable and responsible person, give him a character derived from *personal* knowledge; as many of these couriers remain at Calais only because some previous act of misconduct prevents them showing their faces on the opposite side of the Channel. The inn-yards are generally well stocked with carriages to be let or sold; they are mostly old and rickety vehicles, and the hire demanded for them nearly equals that for which an excellent carriage may be obtained in London.

Steamboats, 2 every day *to Dover*. The new English steamers usually make the voyage in 1½ to 2 hours. The French steamers are inferior. Fare, 10s. 6d. Carriages, 2l. 2s. Steamers go direct to London several times a-week, in 10½ or 12 hours.

Diligence daily to Boulogne and to Dunkerque.

Railways to Lille and Paris—to Lille and Brussels—to Mons and Namur—to Bruges, Ghent, and Antwerp. *Railways* are projected from Calais to Boulogne, and direct to Arras.

On leaving the Quai the line skirts the N.E. angle of the Citadel.

St. Pierre-les-Calais Stat. This is a sort of suburb of Calais, containing a population of 11,000.

The Rly. runs by the side of the river Aa: it crosses the Canal d'Ardres, near the Pont Sans Pareil.

Ardres Stat.

The plain between this place and Guisnes, a little to the W. of the road, is the *Field of the Cloth of Gold*, the scene of the meeting between Henry VIII. and Francis I., 1520, with their suites of 5696 persons and 4325 horses, called Le Champ du Drap d'Or, from the cloth of gold with which the tents and pavilions of the monarchs were covered.

Audruicq Stat.

Watten Stat.

St. Omer Stat. Inns: L'Ancienne Poste; Grande Ste. Catherine.

This is a third-rate fortress, whose means of defence lie less in its actual fortifications than in the marshes which surround it, and the facility afforded by the river Aa, on which it stands, of flooding the land round about, so as to leave only ¼ of its circuit unprotected by the waters. Although it contains a population of 19,344 souls, it is a very dull place. There are, however, two ecclesiastical edifices worthy of notice.

The *Cathedral*, at the upper end of the Rue St. Bertin, is a fine building, showing the transition from the round to the pointed style. The E. end is a good example of the polygonal termination of churches, with projecting chapels, so common on the Continent. The interior is good; — the small Lady Chapel has modern decorations.

At the opposite extremity of the same street stand the scanty remains of the famous *Abbey Church of St. Bertin*, at one time the noblest Gothic monument of French Flanders—in its present state a disgrace to the town, and a reproach to the government; for be it known that its destruction has been perpetrated since 1830! At the outbreak of the great Revolution the monastery was suppressed ; the Convention spared it ; and though under the Directory it was sold for the materials, unroofed, and stripped of its woodwork and metal, yet its walls remained comparatively uninjured until the magistrates barbarously pulled it down to afford employment to some labourers out of work! The fragment remaining consists of a stately tower built in the 15th century (1431-1461), displaying the ornaments of the florid Gothic in the mutilated panelling on its walls, and bits of tracery in its windows ; a small portion or the nave remains attached to it. The tower, threatening to fall, has been propped by an ugly, ill-contrived buttress of masonry ; there is some talk of converting it into a museum. The town is well seen from its top, but there is nothing else of interest in the view. Within the walls of the Abbey of St. Bertin the feeble Childeric III., the last king of the first race, ended his days ; here also Becket sought refuge when a fugitive from England.

A *Seminary* for the education of English and Irish Catholics exists here : it has succeeded the celebrated *Jesuits' College* founded by Father Parsons for the education of young Englishmen. Daniel O'Connell was brought up here for the priesthood ; and several of the conspirators engaged in the Gunpowder Plot were pupils of the same school. There are not more than 15 or 20 students at present. About 400 English reside here. *English Chapel*, Rue du Bon Pasteur, Sunday, 11 and 3.

Eblinghem Stat.

Hazebrouck Stat. is the point of junction of the lines from Calais and Dunkerque (by Cassel, Rte. 188).

This is a flourishing town of 7346 Inhab., whose Ch. is surmounted by a spire 240 ft. high, of open work, built 1493-1520.

Strazeele Stat.

Bailleul Stat. (*Inn*, Faucon), a town of 10,000 Inhab.

Steenwerck Stat.

Armentière Stat., a town of 7500 Inhab., mostly weavers.

Parenchies Stat.

The Rly. skirts the fortifications of Lille, and is joined by the Belgian section near the Porte de Fives.

LILLE STAT.

LILLE. (Flem. Ryssel.)—*Inns:* H. de l'Europe ; very dear ;—de Bellevue ; —de Commerce.

This city of 63,693 Inhab. is important both as a fortress of the first order for its strength, forming the central point of the defence of France on her N. frontier, and as a populous and industrious seat of manufacture, ranking seventh among the cities of France. It is chef-lieu of the Dépt. du Nord, and was formerly capital of French Flanders. The streams of the Haute and Basse Deule traverse the town, filling its moats and turning the wheels of its mills, and they are connected by a canal, by means of which the country for 1½ m. around the walls can be laid under water.

There are no fine public buildings proportioned to the size and wealth of the city, its monuments have been levelled by bomb-shells, and its objects of interest for the passing traveller, unless he be a military man, are few, as may be judged of by the following enumeration :—

Its *Citadel* is considered a masterpiece of the skill of Vauban, who was governor of it for many years. It is a regular pentagon, furnished with all the accessories which engineering skill can suggest, especially since the siege of 1792, and so strong, because commanded by no point, and capable of isolation by breaking the canal dykes, and filling its wide moats, that it is deemed impregnable. A great deal of misery, however, and enormous destruction of property, and injury to agriculture, would follow an inundation. The citadel is separated from the town by the *Esplanade*, a wide drilling ground, which serves also as a public walk, being planted with trees and traversed by the canal. Lille was captured from the Spaniards by Louis XIV. in 1667. At different periods, and under different masters, it has stood 7 distinct sieges; the one most memorable for an Englishman was that by the allied armies of Marlborough and Eugene in 1708, of 3 months' duration, during which the war was not merely waged above ground, but the most bloody combats were fought below the surface between the miners of the opposite armies, each endeavouring to sap and undermine the galleries of his opponent. Boufflers, the French commander, after a masterly defence, was compelled to capitulate, but upon the most honourable terms.

The *Hôtel de Ville* was anciently the palace of the Dukes of Burgundy. It was built by Jean-sans-Peur, 1430, and inhabited by the Emp. Charles V. It is a quaint rather than a handsome edifice, in the late Gothic style, but it has a prettily groined staircase in one of its tourelles, and a chapel built by Philippe le Bel and painted by *Arnold de Vuez*. One division of the building, appropriated to a *school of art*, contains a most interesting and valuable collection of 1200 *Drawings by old masters*, formed by the late M. Wicar, including 86 by *Raphael!* (sketches for the School of Athens, various Madonnas, La Perla, &c.), 197 by *Michael Angelo* (chiefly architectural—the Cupola of St. Peter's, Prometheus, Last Judgment), 10 *Fra Bartolomeo*, 15 *Francia*, 5 *L. da Vinci*, &c. &c., well worthy the inspection of all who take an interest in art.

The town also possesses a *Musée*, where, among a number of bad pictures, is one by *Rubens*, St. Catherine rescued from the Wheel of Martyrdom, painted for a ch. in the town. St. Cecilia and St. Francis are by *Arnold de Vuez* (a native artist of considerable merit, b. 1642); and there is a series of curious old portraits of the Dukes of Burgundy and Counts of Flanders.

The principal *Ch.* (St. Maurice) is in the Gothic style of the 16th cent., resting on slender piers, but is not very remarkable.

The huge *storehouses for corn* at the extremity of the Rue Royale, a street nearly a mile long, deserve notice. There are some very handsome shops in the *Rue Esquirmoise*. In the public walk adjoining the canal, a statue has been erected, by public subscription, to *General Negrier*, slain in the republican revolt of June 25th, 1848, at Paris, in putting down the anarchist insurgents.

The tall chimneys of numerous mills, even within the walls, announce the active industry which is working here, and show the unusual combination of a fortress and manufacturing town, while the country around, and indeed a large part of the Dépt. du Nord, is like a hive in population and activity, not unworthy of being compared with parts of Lancashire and the West Riding. The chief *manufacture* is that of *flax*, which is cultivated in the vicinity, and is spun into ordinary thread, and twisted to form the kind called *Lille thread*, by old-fashioned machines moved by the hand; besides which much linen is woven here. In the spinning of *cotton*, Lille is a formidable rival of the English. The making of tulles and cotton lace has fallen off. The extraction of *oils* from colza and the *seeds* of rape, poppies, linseed, &c., and the manufacture of *sugar from beetroot*, are very important, having given a great impulse to agriculture, as well as employing many hands and hundreds of windmills.

About 200 windmills are grouped around the walls of Lille in the vicinity of the road to Paris: they are used for grinding rape-seed and other oleaginous grains for oil. There are, however, not less than 600 windmills in this commune, which has taken the name of Moulins in consequence.

Brussels may be reached in 5 or 6 hrs. from Lille, by Rail—Rte. 186. The *terminus* at Lille is in the Faubourg de Fives. (See HANDBOOK N. GERMANY.)

Railways to Paris — to Tournay; Courtrai, Ghent: — (in 3 hrs.) Brussels and Ostende — to Dunkerque — to Calais.
Seclin Stat.
Carvin Stat.
Leforest Stat.
Douai Stat. — Here the Lille section of the Railway is joined by that from Valenciennes (Route 184).

Douai (*Inns*: H. de Flandres; — du Commerce) is a town of 17,501 Inhab., surrounded by old fortifications, seated on the Scarpe, defended by a detached fort, about 1½ m. distant, on the l. bank. It is the least *thriving* place in the Dépt. du Nord, and appears to be falling off in population; and though it covers more ground than Lille, does not contain half as many inhabitants. Like the Flemish towns, it has a picturesque *Beffroi*, in its market-place, rising above the Gothic *H. de Ville*, built at the end of the 15th cent., and many picturesque and other houses. It possesses a *library* of 30,000 vols., a collection of *pictures*, and contains one of the 3 *Imperial cannon foundries* in France.

From the 15th cent. the college or seminary of Douai, founded by an Englishman, Cardinal Allen, has educated *Roman Catholic* priests for England and Ireland. O'Connell studied here. There is a considerable trade in flax here.

The sculptor called John of Bologna is supposed to have been born here.

Every July a procession parades the streets of Douai, consisting of a giant of osier, called *Géant Gayant*, dressed in armour, 30 ft. high, attended by his wife and family, of proportionate size; the giant doll is moved by 8 men enclosed within it.

Diligence to Cambrai. A railway is projected by Cambrai to Rheims.
Vitry Stat.
Rœux Stat.
Arras Stat.

Arras. (*Inns*: Griffon; omnibus from Rly.; — Petit St. Paul; well recommended; — l'Univers. Arras is a large and fine city, formerly the capital of the Pays d'Artois, and now of the Dépt. du Pas de Calais; Pop. 23,485. It is a fortress of third class, seated on the Scarpe, and the passport regulations are strictly enforced. The entrance, between and amongst the lofty ramparts, shaded by loftier trees, is grand and imposing. In the interior it has quite the character of a Flemish town, especially in its *Grande Place*, surrounded by gable-faced houses, terminating in scallops and scroll-work supported on open arcades. On one side of it stands the *Hôtel de Ville*, a rather pleasing structure in the latest Gothic, resembling our Elizabethan, built 1510, surmounted by a *Beffroi*.

The first *Revolution* raged here with exceeding violence — a matter of little surprise when it is remembered that Arras was the birthplace of the monsters Max^n. Robespierre and his brother. They were the sons of an advocate, who abandoned them in their childhood and went to America, and they were educated at the College here, and maintained by the charity of some of the clergy of St. Waast. It is said that in one street all the inhabitants were guillotined, whence it was called the "Rue sans Têtes." One effect of this fury was the desecration of the greater portion of the religious edifices. The Cathedral fell like the rest, and only a fragment of it remains near the Place.

The *present Cathedral*, though in the form of a Latin cross, with flying buttresses, is a pure Italian edifice. Its interior, supported on classic columns, with side aisles and transepts, is plain but handsome. By a decree of the town council the external architecture of the old Gothic houses must not be altered.

Damiens, who attempted to assassinate Louis XV., was a native of Arras. The *cotton manufacture* is carried on to a considerable extent here.

Diligences to Cambrai. — The Railway descends the valley of the Scarpe.
Boileux Stat.
Achiet Stat.
Albert Stat.
Corbie Stat.
Amiens (*Stat.*) and the Railway thence to Paris are described in Rte. 3 (p. 16).

PICARDY.   Route 2.—*Calais to Paris—Chantilly.*   9

ROUTE 2.

CALAIS TO PARIS, BY DOULLENS, AMIENS, AND CHANTILLY.

281 kilom. = 174 Eng. m.

At present the quickest way from Calais to Paris is (Rte. 1) the Raily.

CALAIS is described in Rte. 1, p. 3.

The country about Calais, and for some distance inland, is low and wet, intersected by scummy ditches, and traversed by rows of pollard willows. It is drained by the canal de St. Omer, which falls into the sea at Calais: the tides are kept out by embankments. The villages are composed chiefly of mud cottages. The peasants, men as well as women, are frequently seen mounted on very high pattens to avoid the dirt. The road crosses the Pont Sans Pareil, thrown over the two canals from St. Omer to Calais, and from Ardres to Gravelines, at the point where they cut each other at right angles, 3 m. before reaching

16 Ardres, a small fortress.
8 La Recousse.
16 *St. Omer* (in Rte. 1).
18 Aire, another small fortress of the third class, contains a Gothic *Church*, *St. Paul's*, and a belfry built in the 18th century, rising above the public square. Mallebranche was born here. W. of Aire is Therouenne, and a little S. of it Guinegate.
13 Lillers.
11 Pernes.
13 St. Pol.

[15 m. N.W. of St. Pol, and 2 m. S. of the post station, Fruges, is *Azincour* (1415), a village of dirty farms and poor cottages, uninteresting but for its *battle-field*. Only the foundations remain of the castle mentioned by Shakspeare "that stands hard by." Azincour lies on the l. of the high road from St. Omer to Abbeville, which passes through the village of Ruisseauville, mentioned in all the accounts of the battle. The hottest of the fight raged between Azincour and the commune of Tramecour, where a wood still exists corresponding with that in which Henry posted his archers, who contributed so much to the victory, each armed with an iron-pointed stake, to fix in the ground before him and to serve the purpose of the modern bayonet.

Henry, like his great-grandfather Edward III., previous to Crécy, had marched, with a force of only 9000 men at the utmost, through a hostile country, from Harfleur on his way to Calais. On reaching the Somme below Abbeville he found the ford, by which Edward had crossed, staked, and was obliged to continue up the l. bank, finding every passage fortified and every bridge broken, until he arrived above Amiens, where he gained the rt. bank by a ford which had been left open. The French army, though more than six times the number of the English, retreated before him beyond St. Pol, and there drew up across the road to Calais to dispute his passage. There is thus a considerable similarity in the events attending the victories of Crécy and Azincour, and these two famous battle-fields are not more than 20 m. apart (see p. 15).]

13 Frevent.
15 Doullens, chef-lieu of an arrondissement in the Dépt. of the Somme, has a *Citadel* built by Vauban, now a state prison. *St. Martin's Church* is said to be remarkable for the lightness of the pillars which support it.
14 Talmas.
16 AMIENS, on the Railway (Rte. 3).
19 Flers.
13 Breteuil.—*Inn:* H. d'Ange et d'Angleterre, not good. The *Abbey of Ste. Marie* is an ancient Gothic building. Here is a station on the Railway, Rte. 3.

Diligence hence through Noiremont, 12 k., to Beauvais (p. 23), (16 k).
18 St. Just.

The park and château, formerly the property of the Duc de Fitzjames, are passed on the rt., shortly before reaching
16 Clermont-sur-Oise—Rte. 3.
10 Laigneville. The river is crossed at
Creil Stat. (Rte. 3).

A monotonously straight road, through an avenue of trees, partly skirting the forest, leads to
12 *Chantilly* (*Inns:* H. de la Pelouze, tolerably comfortable; H. d'Angleterre), a town of 2524 Inhab. The splendid *château*, built by the grandson of the Grand Condé, in the reign of

B 3

Louis XV., was levelled by the mob at the first Revolution. The Great Condé here spent his latter years, after retiring from military life, in the society of Racine, Boileau, Bossuet, and the other literary men of his age. The *Stables* remain—a splendid pile, capable of lodging 180 horses, but unfinished.

Condé took great pride in this beautiful retreat, and pleasure in embellishing it; and when Louis XIV., who had a claim on it, indicated a desire to obtain possession, he said, " Vous êtes le maître: mais j'ai une grâce à demander à V. M., c'est de me laisser à Chantilly comme votre concierge;" and the king had the moderation not to interfere. Condé's affairs were never in a more desperate condition than at the moment when he was honoured by a visit from his cousin and sovereign, 1671; nevertheless, nothing could exceed the magnificence of the entertainment, rendered memorable by the suicide of Vatel the cook, who ran himself through with his sword in despair because the fish did not arrive in time for dinner.*

Chantilly, one of the most beautiful spots in the vicinity of Paris, abounds in interest and in souvenirs of its most distinguished owner. A noble author,† who visited it in 1841, has touchingly described its vast natural forest, its limpid and purling streams, its green Arbele poplars, which have taken root in the ruins of the Grand Château, and now quite overshadow them, its green turf drives, and its hedges of hawthorn. *Le Petit Château*, built by the Montmorencys, is one of the most charming monuments of the style of the Renaissance in France. It is surrounded by water, and consequently the lower story is scarce habitable. The state rooms and gallery were adorned down to 1852 with the Battles of the Grand Condé, painted by Van der Meulen, now removed to Twickenham.

The *Chapel* contains a rich altarscreen in the style of the Renaissance, brought from Ecouen: here also is some fine painted glass, representing the story of Psyche. After the death of the Duc de Bourbon, the last of the line of Condé, Chantilly became the property of the Duc d'Aumale. *Le Petit Château* is allowed to be shown, and ought to be visited, but was sold December, 1853, in conformity with the confiscation decree of Louis Napoleon, with the park, &c., to the English bankers, Coutts and Co., for 11 million francs. An *Hospital*, built and endowed by the last Prince de Condé, remains a monument of his munificence to the town.

The *Jardin Anglais*, laid out before the Revolution, is very curious; the French garden is in bad taste—it has a noble *Terrace*.

The park and grounds are very beautiful, and are readily shown to strangers. The forest adjoining them has an extent of 6700 acres. *Races* are held here in May and October.

The body of the aged Admiral Coligny, the noblest victim of the massacre of St. Bartholomew, after having been hung up by the heels on the gallows of Montfaucon, was secretly brought hither by Montmorency, and buried in the *parish church* without the head, which was conveyed to Catherine de Medicis.

Chantilly is famed for its silk lace (*blonde*, so called from the light colour), made here to a less extent in the town itself than in the 20 or 30 neighbouring communes, the artificers being women and children. The manufacture was originally established 1710, by M. Moreau. There are now 7 large establishments; but they only give out the patterns and materials: the work is executed at the homes of the lacemakers. *Coaches* to the Creil Rly. Stat.

In the midst of the forest of Chantilly, on the dam at the margin of the Etangs de Comelle, is a pretty little Gothic building, flanked by 4 towers at the corners, called *Château de la Loge de Viarmes*, said to have been built by Queen Blanche of Castille, mother of St. Louis. Its carved ornaments of snakes, frogs, lizards, snails, intermixed with foliage composed of water-plants, are appropriate to the aquatic site. From the style of Gothic it appears to date from the 15th cent., and was probably erected by the Montmorencys for a hunting or fishing house. It was

---

* See Mad. de Sévigné's Letters.
† Lord Mahon :— Life of Condé.

restored carefully in 1826. Three avenues traverse the ponds; and here grand stag-hunts were held by the royal princes.

Not far from this is the ruined Cistercian Abbey of Royaumont, founded by St. Louis, 1230, who often retired hither from the world, tending the sick and eating with the monks. A wall and turret of the church, with bits of the refectory and cloister, alone remain, and are now converted into a cottonmill. The valley of the Oise in this vicinity is very rich and fine.

10 Luzarches has an interesting *Church* of the end of the 12th or beginning of the 13th cent.: its portal is ornamented with curious sculptures of martyred saints; and remains of an ancient castle of the French kings exist here on the top of the hill: they consist of a fragment of a square donjon and a chapel.

11 Ecouen. The chief building is the *Château* of the Montmorency family, built in the reign of Francis I., now the property of the Duc d'Aumale. It was converted by Napoleon into a seminary for the education of the daughters of members of the Legion of Honour, and placed under the direction of Madame Campan. It is now subordinate to the chief establishment of the order of St. Denis. The principal front was destroyed at the Revolution, the other 3 are well preserved. Within are traces of frescoes, of the 16th cent., which were whitewashed by Madame Campan. The elegant *chapel*, ornamented with carvings in wood and a richly-decorated chimney-piece, is a *chef-d'œuvre* of the style of the Renaissance.

Soon after leaving Ecouen a fine view of Paris presents itself. Champlatreux, the seat of M. Molé, is visible.

10 *St. Denis* (Stat. on the Railroad), in Rte. 3.

9 PARIS. See Galignani's Guide to Paris, and Rte. 4.

ROUTE 3.

BOULOGNE TO PARIS. — RAILWAY, BY ABBEVILLE, AMIENS, CLERMONT, AND PONTOISE.—CHEMIN DE FER DU NORD.

272 kilom. = 170 Eng. m.

5 *trains* daily; in 5½ to 8 hours.

BOULOGNE.—*Inns*: H. des Bains, situated close to the port, comfortable; a good cuisine and table d'hôte at 4 fr., good but dear. H. du Nord, also good. Barry's Marine Hotel, opposite the baths and steamers. H. d'Angleterre; moderate. H. de Londres; good, and great civility.

Boulogne-sur-Mer is a seaport in the Channel, or Pas de Calais, on the estuary of a small stream, the Liane, which forms a tide harbour, flanked on either side by wooden piers stretching out as far as low-water mark. It was the Roman GESSORIACUM. The old town occupies the summit of a hill, on which it was built for security in ancient times, and it is still encircled by its feudal ramparts, and entered by cavernous gateways. The new or Basse Ville, stretching down the slopes of the hills which border the harbour, and under the brown cliffs which partly line it, is the chief seat of commerce, and contains the best hotels, streets, and shops.

The number of inhabitants is 29,145, among whom are at least 7000 permanent English residents; indeed, Boulogne, having the advantage of being within 5 hours of London, has become, since the peace, one of the chief British colonies abroad; and, by a singular reciprocity, on the very spot whence Napoleon proposed the invasion of our shores, his intended victims have quietly taken possession and settled themselves down. The town is enriched by English money; warmed, lighted, and smoked by English coal; English signs and advertisements decorate every other shop-door, inn, tavern, and lodging-house; and almost every third person you meet is either a countryman or speaking our language; while the outskirts of the town are enlivened by villas and country-houses, somewhat in the style and taste of those on the opposite side of the Channel. There are at least 120 boarding-schools (pensionnats) for youth of both sexes, many of them under English managers.

Le Port. The margin of the harbour concentrates the chief bustle and business; here is the landing-place of the packets, and the *Douane*, whither passengers are first conveyed on their arrival to deliver their passports, and to be visited by the custom-house officers. *New Quays* have been built; a backwater with sluices for scouring the harbour mouth is planned. The tide rises from 18 to 27 ft. here.

The present entrance to the harbour was formed 1829, somewhat to the W. of the old, and allows the packets to enter 1½ hour earlier and later than in the old. It is flanked on either side by wooden piers, that which projects from the end of the quay forming a pleasant walk when the tide is in. The number of persons who disembark here annually amounts to 100,000 or 150,000, and hence the chief source of the prosperity of Boulogne.

On one side of the harbour, on the margin of a fine sandy beach, is the *Etablissement des Bains*, a showy building, fronted with colonnades, containing subscription, ball, and reading rooms. In front is drawn up in long array a number of genuine bathing-machines (voitures baignoires), to be found in very few places in France. Boulogne is much resorted to in summer as a watering-place, both by the Parisians and English, on account of sea-bathing, for which it is well adapted, having a fine sandy beach.

On the opposite (l.) side of the harbour is a semicircular basin, dug out of the sand by Napoleon, to contain the celebrated flotilla of flat-bottomed boats intended by him to transport an invading French army to the coasts of England, but happily not destined to reach our shores.

Almost all the 1300 vessels belonging to Boulogne are engaged in fishery, and the arrival and departure of the boats collects a crowd of fishermen and fisherwives in their singular and picturesque costume, such as the pencils of Prout and Stanfield are wont to portray. These people occupy a distinct quarter of the town on the N. side of the harbour, the streets of which are draped with nets hung out from the fronts of the houses to dry, and in dress and manners they are distinct from the rest of the inhabitants, speaking a peculiar patois, and rarely intermarrying with the other townsfolk. They are an industrious and very hard-working race, especially the women, and very religious: the perils and vicissitudes of their hard life reminding them more nearly than other classes of their dependence on Providence. The Boulogne fishing-boats are the largest and best worked in the Channel. A great number repair annually to the coast of Scotland for the herring fishery, and some go as far as Shetland and Iceland.

The Rue de l'Ecu, running parallel with the Liane, and the Grande Rue, ascending the hill towards the upper town, contain some of the best shops. About half-way up the Grande Rue is the *Museum* (in what was the Grande Séminaire). A sum has been voted for a new building expressly designed for it. It deservedly ranks amongst the best provincial collections in France, is highly creditable to the town, and owes a large part of its contents to private donations. The series of arms, dresses, implements, weapons, &c., of various nations, including the full dress of a Lapland lady given by Admiral Rosamel, is very extensive. Here is an imaginary model of the Tower of Caligula, which stood on the heights above the town: also engravings of the siege of Boulogne under Henry VIII.; a curfew of earthenware; some curious fragments of sculpture of the 15th and 16th cent. from churches, &c.; a Last Judgment, a bas-relief carved in wood very elaborately; an extensive series of medals,—among them that celebrated one, which took too much for granted, struck by Napoleon 1804, and bearing the inscription "Descente en Angleterre," "Frappé à Londres," of which 3 or 4 impressions alone are said to exist, the die having been destroyed. The quantity of Roman antiquities, of pottery, glass, bronzes, coins, utensils of various kinds, found in and about the town by excavations, is very remarkable, as well as their good preservation. In digging the foundations of the Abattoir on the road to Paris, a multitude of vases and other objects, with more than 1300 medals, relics of the Roman Bononia or Gessoriacum, came to light, and have been deposited here. A collection of siege pieces, or coins struck in haste in besieged towns, is curious, as well as a series of French Assignats, or paper money issued at the Revolution. The museum possesses a mummy pronounced by Champoillon one of the finest in Europe, for the number and brillancy of its paintings, &c.; it was brought from Biban el Molouk by Denon.

Persons interested in *natural history* will find collections in all departments, by no means contemptible in extent or preservation. The geology of the district is illustrated by a large series of specimens, including the ironstone of the Boulonnois, the marble of Marquise (lower oolite), and the coal. Of the *Picture Gallery* much cannot be said, but there are 1 or 2 tolerable modern paintings; a good sea-piece by *Delacroix*.

The Museum is opened to the public Thursday, Saturday, and Sunday, from 10 to 4; strangers may obtain admission on other days by giving a small fee to the concierge. Under the same roof is the *Public Library*, containing 22,000 volumes and 3000 MSS., many of them rare and richly illuminated, including the oldest copy extant of Bede's 'Homilies,' from St. Bertin.

The *Old Town* of Boulogne, on the summit of the hill, retains its three arched gateways, and the ancient ramparts which defended it in the 15th cent., but offered a vain resistance to the assaults and cannonading of the army of Henry VIII. The town was restored, however, to Henri II. of France by the English (1550), in the reign of Edward VI., by treaty, upon payment of 40,000 livres. In consideration of this a bronze bust of Henri (by David d'Angers) decorates the esplanade outside the gate des Dunes. The *Remparts* form an airy and agreeable walk, running uninterruptedly round the town, and commanding views in all directions, over the sea and port, and over the high ground to the E. occupied in turn by the camps of Caligula, Henry VIII., and Napoleon, and along the roads to Calais and Paris. In one corner of the walls is the old *Citadelle*, flanked by high round towers, and divided from the town by a fosse, but now much modernised externally, and converted into a barrack. In the midst of the old town, behind the Hôtel de Ville, rises the antique tower of the *Beffroi*.

The *Cathedral*, a large modern Grecian building, has been in progress since 1827, being built by subscription, on the site of a Gothic one pulled down at the Revolution. Beneath it extends a very curious and capacious *crypt*, supported on 2 rows of piers, 215 ft. long and 140 wide at the transepts, supposed to be the substructions of the ch. built in the 12th cent. by Ida of Lorraine, mother of Godfrey of Bouillon.

There are several *Nunneries* in the old town; that of the Ursulines is at No. 2, Rue de la Paille. The sisters, 40 or 50 in number, instruct a pension for young ladies. The Sœurs de Bon Secours (Rue St. Martin, No. 20) devote themselves to attend on the sick, and their services are much esteemed by the poor. The convent of the "Dames de la Visitation," about ¾ m. out of the town, near the St. Omer road, is the largest, and has a fine chapel, open on Sundays.

At Boulogne, in 1840, a landing and an ineffectual attempt at insurrection was made by Louis Napoleon.

Le Sage, *the author of Gil Blas*, who repaired to Boulogne in the latter years of his life to stay with his son, a canon of the cathedral, died 1747, in a house, No. 3, Rue du Château, as an inscription over the door points out. The existing building, however, is of much more recent date, and only occupies the site of the original house. Churchill the poet also died at Boulogne, whither he had come on a visit to John Wilkes, then a voluntary exile from England. Attempts made by the priests to obtain access to the dying man, in order to convert him to popery, were stoutly repelled by Wilkes.

There are 2 *English Chapels* here; one in the Rue du Temple, built by subscription of the English (1828), is capable of containing 1000 persons

—service at 11 and 3 on Sundays: the other in the Rue St. Martin in the Haute Ville.

The *Poste aux Lettres* is at No. 28, Rue des Vieillards; it is open from 8 A.M. to 8 P.M. The British Consul resides in the Rue des Vieillards.

In the *Cemetery* of the upper town is the grave of 82 female convicts from England, drowned in the wreck of the "Amphitrite," 1833, and others who perished in the Indiaman "Conqueror," 1843.

At *Capecure* a large flax-mill has been built, with 2 steam-engines, 6000 spindles, employing 1000 people.

Merridew, Rue de l'Écu, has an *English reading-room* and circulating library. Stubbs has another.

The *Office for Passports* is open from 9 to 2; but passports are countersigned at later hours in case of urgency. See Introduction, c.

On the very edge of the cliff, just above the sea-baths, a little to the E. of the port, are the scanty remains of solid brick walls known as *La Tour d'Ordre* (Turris Ardens, *i.e.* light-tower), supposed to be the foundations of a tower built by Caligula the Roman emperor, A.D. 40, when he marched to the shore of the Channel with an army of 100,000 men, boasting that he intended to invade the opposite coast of Britain, but contenting himself with gathering a few shells, which he called the spoils of the ocean. The tower is supposed to have been intended for a lighthouse, but the remains are very scanty, and from the falling of the cliff even these are likely soon to disappear.

On the same heights 18 centuries later another emperor—Napoleon—encamped an army of more than 180,000 men, designed to invade England, and placed under the command of Soult, Ney, Davoust, and Victor. Buonaparte himself, during his visits to the camp, occupied a temporary baraque, which was raised within a few yards of the Roman tower. Thence he could survey his flotilla of 2400 transports and flat-bottomed boats, and the shore on either side of the town, both under the cliff and upon the heights, bristling with batteries of cannon and mortars; while in the distance the vigilant fleets of England hovered incessantly. In one instance Nelson approached near enough to bombard the town and sink two of the floating batteries. "Boulogne," he writes, "was certainly not a pleasant place that morning; but it is not my wish to injure the poor inhabitants, and the town is spared as much as the service will admit." It is stated, however, that most of the bombs fell short, and that in excavating the new harbour many tons of them were dug out. He afterwards made an unsuccessful attempt with the boats of his squadron to cut out the flotilla in the teeth of the batteries, and burn it. Another attempt, in 1804, to burn the flotilla with fire-ships, made by Lord Keith, was attended with no better result.

The flotilla of Boulogne formed only part of the deeply laid scheme of Napoleon for the destruction of England. He designed to collect together the combined fleets of France, Spain, and Holland, which for years previously he had been constructing in the harbours of Antwerp, Brest, Cadiz, and the Mediterranean, and with a squadron of 70 ships of the line to sweep the Channel of the British. Under cover of this vast armament, he intended to have crossed over with the army of Boulogne, expecting to reach London in 5 days, where he designed to have proclaimed parliamentary reform, abolishing the monarchy and the House of Peers, and substituting a republic!! The troops of the Boulogne expedition were so nicely drilled, and every man so accurately informed of the boat which was to transport him, that at a preliminary review, in $10\frac{1}{2}$ minutes 25,000 were embarked; and relanded and drawn up on the shore again in 13 minutes more. The whole of these projects and combinations, however, were scattered to the winds; the fleet of England, under Sir Robert Calder, prevented the junction of those of the enemy, and Nelson finally annihilated them at Trafalgar.

A conspicuous memorial of this pro-

PICARDY.   *Route 3.—Boulogne to Paris—Railway.*   15

jected but unaccomplished invasion exists at the distance of nearly a mile from the town in the *Colonne Napoléon*, which surmounts the heights traversed by the road to Calais. It was begun by the grand army assembled for the invasion of England, as a monument to their leader and emperor. The first stone was laid by Marshal Soult, 1804; but its construction was discontinued after the departure of the troops, and the withdrawal of the subscriptions which they contributed out of their pay. Under Louis XVIII. it was resumed, with the ostensible design of commemorating the restoration of the Bourbons. In consequence, however, of the revolution of July it has resumed its original destination; and having been purged of carved fleurs-de-lis and royalist inscriptions, was dedicated, 1841, as a monument to Buonaparte, and surmounted by a bronze statue of him in his coronation robes by *Bosio*, and one of that sculptor's best works, while bronze bas-reliefs decorate the base. The pillar is of the Doric order, and 50 mètres = 164 ft. high, exclusive of the statue, 16 ft., and is constructed of marble from the quarries of Marquise. A winding stair leads up to the top, whence a view may be had of the white cliffs of England.

¾ m. farther, on the coast, a monument of marble commemorates the distribution of the Order of the Legion of Honour by Buonaparte to his troops, during one of his visits to the camp. Nearer at hand, attached to a small group of houses down in the hollow, 1½ m. from Boulogne, is the humble chapel of *Jésus Flagellé*; curious, because it exhibits an instance of the practice so common in the Romish Church of making votive offerings. It is resorted to by the fishermen of Boulogne and their families before they go out to sea; and they have lined its walls with votive pictures, even with lithographs, and hung its roof with models of their barks, each to commemorate some rescue from the perils of the great deep.

Railway to Paris (Rte. 3).

Steamers. To Dovor daily in 2 hours. The passage is very little longer than from Calais to Dovor, and 24 m. of tedious land journey are saved.—To Folkestone every tide in 2 hours.—To London: in summer almost daily, in winter 2 or 3 times a-week, in 10 or 12 hours.

Diligences. To Beauvais; to St. Omer; to Calais; to Samer; to Lille and Arras.

Landing and embarking at Boulogne (see INTRODUCTION). The porter's tariff for conveying luggage from the steamboat to the custom-house, and thence to the hotel, or to the owner's residence, is fixed according to weight.

Fr. Cents.
0 70 for 15 kilos (= 33 lbs.) or under.
1   0 for 15 to 100 kilos (= 220 lbs.).
1 50 for 100 kilos and upwards.

For excursions in the neighbourhood jackasses (baudets) are much in vogue.

Railway, Boulogne to Paris.

N.B.—Travellers by express trains are compelled to pay first-class fares from Amiens even for servants. This is not fair.

Between Boulogne and the mouth of the Somme (36 m.) the rly. is carried within a short distance of the sea. There is a tunnel of 200 yards, through the forest of Hardelot.

6 Pont de Brique Stat.

14 Neuchâtel Stat., a small village in a wooded hollow.

28 Etaples Stat. A town of 2500 Inhab. There is a viaduct over the Cauche, more than 900 ft. long.

39 *Montreuil* Stat. (Rte. 4, p. 22.)

55 Rue Stat., a poor and hitherto "out-of-the-way" town, with a curious old Ch.

65 Noyelle Stat. The railway runs near the N. bank of the Somme. [A branch line is projected from Noyelle to St. Valery; 5 kilo.

St. Valery, at the mouth of the Somme, 12 m. below Abbeville, was the port whence the fleet of William the Conqueror set sail to invade England. It is partially resorted to as a watering-place.]

At Blanchetaque Edward III. crossed the Somme with his army before the battle of *Crécy*, by a ford passable only at low water. The tide, rising immediately after, arrested the pursuit of the French forces, and compelled them to ascend the l. bank, while the English pursued their way up the rt.

The Somme is crossed by a bridge of 2 arches before reaching

79 *Abbeville Stat.*— *Inns*: H. de l'Europe; Tête de Bœuf. This is an industrious manufacturing town of 17,582 Inhab., which, from its situation on the Somme, here a wide river, is accessible for vessels of 150 tons. Those who will penetrate into its narrow and filthy streets will find some quaint specimens of ancient domestic architecture, timber houses, &c., but the chief object of interest, which really ought to be seen, is

The *Ch. of St. Wolfram*. The W. front, and 5 first arches of the nave, are a portion of a magnificent design, never carried out, commenced in the reign of Louis XII., under the Cardinal George d'Amboise. The façade is a splendid example of the flamboyant style, consisting of three gorgeous portals, surmounted by a pediment, and flanked by two towers; the whole covered with the richest flowing tracery, or panelling; the niches being filled with statues. The central door is curiously carved. The remainder of the church is a mean continuation of the first plan. *The prison* is a fragment of the old *Castle* of the Counts of Ponthieu.

Diligences to Eu and Dieppe (Rte. 18); to Rouen; to Beauvais; to St. Valery. Railway to Paris. From Abbeville to Amiens the line is carried up the valley of the Somme along its l. bank.

87 Pont-Rémy Stat. The village is on the rt. bank of the Somme. 6½ m. off lies Ailly le Haut Clocher, so called from the lofty steeple of its fine *Ch.*, in a style resembling Early English Gothic.

95 Longpré Stat.
102 Hangest Stat.
109 Picquigny Stat. The ruined *castle*, close to the Ch., with its terraces, mentioned in Mad. de Sévigné's 'Letters,' was built at the end of the 15th cent. This place gives its name to a Treaty, signed 1475, between Edward IV. and Louis XI., who met on the bridge; but so distrustful of each other, that a barrier of stout palisades and wooden bars, "such as the cages of lions are made of," says De Comines, was raised to divide them, leaving space between the bars only wide enough to allow them to shake hands.

Ailly Stat.

124 AMIENS STAT. — *Inns*: H. de France et d'Angleterre; H. de Paris; H. du Rhin, near the rly., good.

Amiens is an industrious manufacturing town of 46,129 Inhab., formerly capital of Picardy, now chef-lieu of the Dépt. de la Somme, and situated on that river, which passes through the town split into 11 branches, and renders essential service in turning the water-wheels of many of the numerous manufactories, whose tall chimneys are seen rising above the other buildings, and are clustered around the outskirts. The weaving of cotton velvets, chiefly for Spanish consumption, and the spinning of cotton and woollen yarn, are the principal branches of industry. Amiens is the cradle of the cotton manufacture of France, which dates no farther back than 1773.

The object which deservedly concentrates the attention of travellers at Amiens is the *Cathedral*, one of the noblest Gothic edifices in Europe. It was begun 1220, only two years later than Salisbury, though in a much more mature style than that edifice. It was designed and begun by the architect Robert de Luzarches, but continued and completed, 1269, by Thomas and Regnault de Cormont, except the W. front, not finished until the end of the 14th cent. Three vast and deeply recessed portals lead into it, the arches supported by a long array of statues in niches instead of pillars, while rows of statuettes supply the place of mouldings, so that the whole forms one mass of sculpture; an arrangement of constant occurrence in French Gothic, though rare in English. The sculpture of these porches merits attention; over the centre door the bas-relief represents the Last Judgment; the statues are those of the 12 Apostles. Over the rt.-hand porch are the Death and Assumption of the Virgin; over that on the l. is the legend of St. Firmin, the apostle of Picardy. Above the portals runs a colossal line of French kings, behind which appears a noble wheel-window; and the whole is flanked by two stately but unfinished towers.

"The interior is one of the most magnificent spectacles that architectural skill can ever have produced. The mind is filled and elevated by its enormous height (140 ft.), its lofty and many-coloured clerestory, its grand proportions, its noble simplicity. The proportion of height to breadth is almost double that to which we are accustomed in English cathedrals; the lofty, solid piers, which bear up this height, are far more massive in their plan than the light and graceful clusters of our English churches, each of them being a cylinder with 4 engaged columns. The polygonal E. apse is a feature which we seldom see, and nowhere so exhibited, and on such a scale; and the peculiar French arrangement which puts the walls at the outside edge of the buttresses, and thus forms interior chapels all round, in addition to the aisles, gives a vast multiplicity of perspective below, which fills out the idea produced by the gigantic height of the centre. Such terms will not be considered extravagant when it is recollected that the vault is half as high again as the roof of Westminster Abbey."—*Whewell.*

The entire length is 442 ft. The general character of the architecture is that of the early English, except the geometric tracery of the windows. The triforium is glazed, which gives great lightness to the interior. Just within the central porch are 2 fine brass effigies of bishops; that on the l. as you enter is Evrard de Fouilly, who laid the first stone of the church; that on the rt. Geoffroy d'Eu, " learned," as his epitaph tells us, " in medicine as well as theology." The splendid pulpit, the work of an artist of Amiens, Dupuis, is supported by statues of Faith, Hope, and Charity.

Placed at the crossing of the transept, the spectator may admire the 3 magnificent rose windows, all of elaborate tracery and varied patterns, filled with rich stained glass, each nearly 100 ft. in circumference, which form a great ornament to this church, and surpass everything of the sort which England can show. The font in the N. transept is an oblong trough of stone, probably of the 10th or 11th cent.

Round the wall which separates the choir from its aisles runs a low screen of stone, enclosing a series of curious sculptures, in high relief, representing on the S. side the legend of St. Firmin, and on the N. the acts and death of John the Baptist. They date from the end of the 15th cent.

The head of St. John the Baptist, brought from Constantinople at the time of the Crusades, has always been considered, and still remains, the most valuable relic possessed by this church. It is deposited in the side chapel dedicated to St. John. Several other heads of St. John existed before the Revolution in other churches of France, and one, indeed, in the neighbouring abbey of St. Acheul; but this, it was maintained, was the genuine one. Since the Revolution, the skull has been reduced to the frontal bone and upper jaw.

Attached to a monument of Canon Lucas, at the back of the high altar, and facing the Lady Chapel, is a weeping angel, which has received more praise than it seems to deserve on the score of art; it is known as " l'enfant pleureur." Blasset is the sculptor's name.

The *choir*, terminating in a semicircular E. end, the elegantly groined roof resting on compressed lancet-pointed arches, yields in beauty to no part of the church. It is also especially distinguished for the elaborately carved woodwork of its 116 stalls: in variety of invention and delicacy of execution there is nothing finer of the kind in Europe. The intricate details of the tabernacles and lace-like parapets, the bold drawing, and effective though coarse expression in the bas-reliefs, representing subjects from Holy Writ, the Life of the Virgin, &c., and the close imitation of nature in the twining tendrils and playful foliage of the vine and other plants, deserve minute attention. The carvers were Arnoult Boullin and Alex. Huet, menuisiers of Amiens: the work was finished in 1520. The diapering of fleurs-de-lis at the back of the seats was effaced by order of the government in 1830. To appreciate the vast proportions and examine the details of this cathedral, the visitor ought to ascend to the triforium gallery; thence he may mount the tower and enjoy the view over the vale of the Somme, remarking in his ascent the turret with the stone table, where Henri IV. posted himself to watch the retreat of the Spaniards in 1597. The roof is a wonderful piece of carpentry, 46 ft. high; a forest of oak and chestnut must be contained in it.

Within the cathedral of Amiens Edward III. did homage for Guienne to Philippe of Valois, 1329; and here, in 1385, Isabel of Bavaria was married to the idiot king Charles VI. The best description of Amiens Cathedral is that of M. Gilbert.

The other buildings in the town possess comparatively slight interest. The deserted *Ch. of St. Rémi*, now a stable, was a rich specimen of the latest florid Gothic, the beauty of which is destroyed by mutilations. Within it is a sculptured monument to the family Lannay. In the *Hôtel de Ville*, a building of 1600, the treaty of "the Peace of Amiens" was signed, 1802, by the plenipotentiaries, Joseph Buonaparte for France, Lord Cornwallis for England, Chevalier Azara for Spain, and M. Schimmelpenninck for Holland. The hall is hung with pictures of the modern French school, of slight merit. There is a *Museum*, containing some antiquities, paintings, &c.

A Boulevard surrounds the town, occupying the site of the ancient ramparts, and, being planted with trees, forms an agreeable promenade. A *Citadel*, however, remains, built on the rt. bank of the Somme by Henri IV., and strengthened by modern works. The Spaniards, in 1597, gained the city, which had claimed the privilege of exemption from a military garrison, through the stratagem of Hernando Tello de Porto Carrero, Spanish governor of Doullens, who, disguising himself and a band of companions as peasants, entered the town at early dawn, along with the market folk, driving a waggon laden with fruit, which he halted under the gateway. In passing the gate it was contrived that a sack of walnuts should burst; and while the unsuspecting guards were occupied on all fours scrambling for its scattered contents, the Spaniards fell on them and put them to the sword. In vain the portcullis was hastily lowered: the waggon had been drawn up so as to catch it as it fell, leaving a passage by which a party of armed Spaniards, in ambush outside, gained easy admittance.

Henri IV., not yet firmly fixed in his throne, felt the loss of Amiens as a severe blow, and hastened to recover it. He was aided in the siege and capture of the town, 1598, by a body of 4000 Englishmen, under Sir Arthur Savage, furnished by Queen Elizabeth.

Amiens was the *Samarobriva* of the Romans; and the *Ambiani*, the Gallic inhabitants of the district (whence the name Amiens), are mentioned by Cæsar. Here Merovée was proclaimed king by being raised on the shield of his victorious soldiers.

The following eminent persons were born in the town or its vicinity:— Peter the Hermit, preacher of the first crusade; Gabrielle d'Estrées, the cherished mistress of Henri IV.; Ducange, author of the 'Glossarium ad Scriptores mediæ et infimæ Latinitatis;' a *statue* of him (Du Fresne, Seigneur du Cange) has been set up in the square near the Stat.; Gresset the poet, author of 'Vertvert;' Delambre the astronomer.

The *Abbey of St. Acheul*, on the outskirts of the town, was converted into a Jesuits' college under the Restoration. The crypt under the church contains some ancient tombs and bas-reliefs.

Amiens is celebrated among gourmands for its *pâtés de canard*.

Railways from Amiens—to Paris, to Lille (Rte. 1), and to Abbeville.

Diligences daily to Beauvais (Rte. 4).

At Amiens our route enters upon the Great Trunk Railway from Paris to

Lille and Brussels, called *Chemin de Fer du Nord* (Rte. 1 and 184).
9 Boves Stat.
10 Ailly-sur-Noye Stat.
17 *Breteuil Stat.* — The town lies about 4 m. on the W.
Diligence to Beauvais, 17 m. (Rte. 4), and to Rouen.
15 St. Just Stat.
14 Clermont Stat.
Clermont-sur-Oise (*Inn:* Croissant, tolerable), a prettily situated town on the slopes of a hill, surmounted by the *Castle*, which is now a Penitentiary for women, and modernized. It was, however, an important fortress from the 10th to the 16th cent.; taken by the English 1359 and 1434, and by Henri IV. from the troops of the League 1595. The elder Condé, disgusted with the Court, retired hither, 1615, and fortified himself against attacks.
From the agreeable promenade *du Chatellier*, which surrounds its walls, jutting out over the valley, a beautiful view of its winding stream is obtained. Cassini, the astronomer and geographer, was a native of Clermont.
8 Liancourt Stat.
7 *Creil Junction Stat.*, a town of 1500 Inhab., on the l. bank of the Oise. Only the foundations of a tower remain of the old *Castle* in which Charles VI. was shut up during his madness. It stood on the island below the bridge, but was destroyed at the Revolution.
There is a large delft manufactory at Creil.
A branch railway diverges from Creil to St. Quentin, by Compiègne (Rte. 183), Noyon, and Chauny.
The railroad, hitherto carried along the high land of Picardy (chalk in part), here enters the valley of the Oise.
7 St. Leu Stat.
Diligence hence to Chantilly (Rte. 2, p. 9), and to Senlis.
8 Boran Stat.
6 Beaumont-sur-Oise Stat., a town of 2000 Inhab., surmounted by a ruined tower, part of its old castle.
From Beaumont the distance by rail is double the direct road to Paris.
7 Ile-Adam Stat.
6 Auvers Stat.

5 *Pontoise Stat.* (*Inns:* Grand Cerf; H. des Messageries), a town of 5400 Inhab., occupies a steep slope on the river Oise, here traversed by a *bridge*, whence its name. It is famous for calves and flour, and supplies Paris with these two articles. The Vionne, which here joins the Oise, turns 30 corn-mills.
The *Ch. of St. Maclose* is an interesting edifice presenting various styles; there is some painted glass in a chapel near the principal entrance. The *Palais de Justice* is a Gothic building.
Pontoise is a place of some historical notoriety. St. Louis, attacked by a violent illness, was here warned by a voice from heaven to assume the cross —1244. During the hard winter of 1437, when the ground was covered with snow, the English took the town by surprise, through the ingenious *ruse* of Talbot, who clothed his soldiers in white, under cover of which, in the obscurity of the night, they reached the foot of the walls unobserved by the garrison.
Coaches to Gisors and Chaumont.
8 Herblay Stat.
3 Franconville Stat. The rly. crosses the vale of Montmorency.
3 Ermont Stat.
3 Enghien Stat. *Enghien les Bains* (H. des Quatre Pavillons) is a very pretty village on the borders of the Etang de Montmorency, with a *Bathing Establishment* supplied with medicinal waters from a sulphureous spring. Not only on this account, but for the extreme beauty of its situation and environs, it is much frequented by the Parisians as a sort of French Richmond. The walks in the Parc de St. Gratian are pleasant.
Enghien is about 1¼ m. from *Montmorency*, whose beauties are much exaggerated by the Parisians. A road strikes off through Epinay-sur-Seine to *St. Leu*, celebrated for its château and park, which, before the first Revolution, belonged to the Duc d'Orléans, and was the favourite residence of Madame de Genlis. In the time of Napoleon it was given to Hortense, the Queen of Holland, and after the Re-

storation became the property of the Duc de Bourbon, who ended his days there miserably and mysteriously, being found hanging to the window-bolt (espagnolette) of his bed-room. Not a trace remains of the château of the last Condé, and even the grounds are all altered. It was purchased by the Bande Noire, sold for its materials, and streets built on the site, one appropriately called Rue des Vandeles. The Orleans family have erected on the spot an octagonal monument to the family of Condé.

The Comte de St. Leu, father of Louis Napoleon, is buried in the village church.

Montmorency is a dirty little town 14 m. distant from Paris. Its fine Gothic Ch., of the 15th cent., contains some good painted glass.

The house called L'Ermitage, about ½ m. off, has attained celebrity because Rousseau resided in it, 1756-58, and wrote there his 'Nouvelle Héloïse.' It was then the property of Madame d'Epinay, and really a peasant's cottage. It was afterwards occupied by Grétry the composer, who died here 1813. It still exists, but incorporated into a large and more modern mansion, in which are preserved Rousseau's bed, table, &c.

The line is carried past one of the detached forts which surround Paris, and skirts (rt.) the margin of the Seine shortly before reaching

5 *St. Denis Stat.*

The Abbey of *St. Denis* was one of the most important and wealthy religious foundations in France: its abbots were powerful potentates; Turpin was chancellor to Charlemagne, and Suger prime minister to St. Louis.

The *Abbey Church* has been the burial-place of the kings of France from the time of Dagobert (580), and is a building of great interest, in spite of the wanton dilapidations of revolutionary violence, which the restorations carried on under Napoleon, the Bourbons, and Louis-Philippe have not yet entirely repaired, and can never atone for. The W. front, flanked and surmounted by 2 towers, is in the Romanesque style, having been raised by Abbot Suger, 1134. It was in the porch of St. Denis that Henri IV. abjured the Protestant faith. Over the central portal, which is semicircular, is a bas-relief of the Last Judgment. A vestibule, crowded with piers to support the towers, leads into the nave, which was built 1281, and is of remarkable width, considering that the roof is of stone. The choir, dating from the earlier period of Abbot Suger, is, like that of Canterbury, narrower than the nave.

On the l., as you enter the nave, is the monument of Dagobert, a singular Gothic structure, raised to his memory by St. Louis. The bas-reliefs on it represent the pretended vision of a hermit, who reported that he had seen Dagobert in a boat pursued and scourged by devils, but defended by St. Denis, St. Martin, and St. Maurice. On the same side are the splendid monuments, in the style of the Renaissance, of Louis XII. and Anne of Brittany, whose recumbent effigies in marble are surrounded by 12 small statues, in niches, of the Apostles, admirable for design, attitude, and execution. The bas-reliefs round the base represent the battle of Agnadel and the entry of Louis into Milan. This monument is the work of Paulo Poncio. That beside it, of Henri II. and Catherine of Medicis his queen, is said to have been designed by Philip Delorme and executed by Germain Pilon. The royal effigies are repeated twice; below recumbent as dead, above kneeling: at the 4 corners are the Cardinal Virtues in bronze!

On the S. side of the nave is the cenotaph of Francis I. and Claude his queen, erected 1550, from designs of Primaticcio. The recumbent effigies are by the skilful hand of *Jean Goujon*, as well as the elegant arabesques which decorate the canopy. The frieze running round the base of the monument represents, in a series of marble bas-reliefs of good execution, the battles of Cerisol and of Marignano. The canopy is surmounted by duplicate statues of Francis and his queen, with their 3 children.

In the N. transept are placed monumental columns to Henri III., assassinated by Jacques Clement 1589, and to Francis II., husband of Mary Queen of Scots, its base surrounded by weeping angels. In the S. transept is a pillar in memory of Henri IV. The effigy of the Breton knight Du Guesclin, whose valour and renown procured him burial in the company of kings, but availed not to save his ashes from sacrilegious dispersion by the republicans, is remarkable for its diminutive size. The choir and its side chapels, elevated considerably above the nave, glow with modern decoration in painting and gilding, which rival heraldic blazonry in gaudy colours, laid on much too indiscriminately, and not in good taste. There is no lack of modern painted glass, a very small portion of the old having escaped the fury of the Revolution. Some fragments of that with which Abbot Suger decorated the building in 1140, still preserved in the apsidal chapels behind the choir, are regarded as the oldest in France. A red flag suspended behind the altar supplies the place of the once-venerated *Oriflamme*, the standard of the realm of France, but not used in battle since the time of Charles VII. It was originally the church flag of the Abbey of St. Denis, which was delivered by the abbot to the military guardian of the church whenever he went forth to fight its battles, and was supposed to secure victory to those who bore it. It supplanted St. Martin's cloak, which had previously served as the royal standard of France.

A flight of steps on either side of the choir leads down into the *crypt* beneath it. Here, along the aisle, are arranged chronologically the monuments of the kings of France from the time of Clovis. The statues called Clovis King of the Franks, and his Queen Clothilda, were brought from the portal of the church at Corbeil on the Seine at the Revolution. They are supposed to be works of the 11th or 12th cent., and are curious specimens of royal costume: the filleting of the queen's long hair is worth notice. Those of kings preceding the 13th cent. consist of rudely-sculptured effigies executed by order of St. Louis. His own bust and that of his queen, with statues of his two sons, painted and gilt, follow next in a separate chapel. The more modern statues of the sovereigns of the house of Valois and Bourbon are of white marble. The series is closed with those of Louis XVI., Marie Antoinette, the Duc de Berri, &c., executed for the Monument Expiatoire destined for the spot where the Duc de Berri was assassinated, but removed to the darkest corner of the crypt after the July revolution: in conception and execution they appear nearly the worst of the whole.

This long range of Royal tombs is now quite empty, in consequence of a decree of the Convention of 1793 ordering the destruction of the tombs of the ci-devant kings at St. Denis. In the course of 3 days 51 tombs were opened, rifled, and demolished; and the bodies of kings, queens, and princes, in every stage of decay, cast out in one indiscriminate heap into 2 trenches, hastily dug without the walls of the church, after being subjected to every species of brutal indignity. A soldier with his sabre cut the beard from the nearly perfect corpse of Henri IV. to wear it as a moustache on his own lip; and the valiant Turenne's body, so little injured by time that the likeness to his portrait was still recognised, was stuck into a glass case, and made a show to gratify idle curiosity. The broken monuments were conveyed, along with relics of saints and church-plate, to Paris, and owe their preservation and restoration to the praiseworthy zeal and care of M. le Noir, founder of the Musée des Petits Augustins. For 12 years after this sacrilege the Abbey Ch. of St. Denis, stripped of its lead to furnish bullets, remained roofless; having first been offered for sale for the value of the building-materials, and next used as a market-house. Napoleon, however, undertook its restoration, and caused the desecrated sepulchral vaults of the Bourbons to be fitted up as a mausoleum for his own family! His design, however, was frustrated by the Restoration. At present the central vaults below the high altar contain the confused mass of royal bones, withdrawn by order of Louis XVIII. from the ditch into which they had been cast, together with the burnt remains of Louis XVI. and Marie Antoinette, the coffins of Louis XVIII. and others of his family. In an obscure corner lies the last Condé, father of the Duc d'Enghien, who died at St. Leu.

The Rly. crosses the canal de St. Denis by a skew iron bridge, and the line of Fortifications of Paris, and passes (rt.) the hill of Montmartre.

PARIS.—*Terminus*, Clos St. Lazare, 24 Place Roubaix (see pp. 25–26, and *e*. Charge for posthorses).

ROUTE 4.

CALAIS TO PARIS, BY BOULOGNE, ABBEVILLE, BEAUVAIS, AND ST. DENIS.

272 kilom. = 168 Eng. m.

Diligences daily from Calais to Boulogne. *Railway* thence to Paris in 9 hours.

To the flat land immediately about Calais succeeds a hilly tract, unenclosed and uninteresting, which continues as far as Boulogne.

13 Haut Buisson.

The poor village Ouessant, or Witsand, on the sea-shore, about 4 m. N. of this, is supposed to be the *Portus Itius* of the Romans, the spot where Julius Cæsar embarked for the conquest of Great Britain. Roman remains are found in the neighbourhood. The harbour has long since been blocked up with sand; yet it was for centuries the landing-place for passengers from England.

9 Marquise, a town of 2000 Inhab., having in its neighbourhood mines of coal and iron of no great importance, and quarries of a coarse grey marble.

Ambleteuse, another poor village on the coast, deserves mention only as the spot where James II. disembarked, Jan. 5, 1689.

In the churchyard of Wimille, at the road side, 3 m. from Boulogne, the two unfortunate aëronauts, Pilâtre de Rosier and Romain, are buried; the balloon in which they had ascended from Boulogne (1785), intending to cross the Channel, caught fire at an elevation of 3600 ft., and they were miserably dashed to pieces. An obelisk has been erected to their memory.

The road, previous to descending from the open high ground, passes close to a fort thrown up by Napoleon in 1804; beyond which, about 200 yards on the rt., rises the Napoleon Column. (See p. 15.)

A rapid descent leads under the walls of the old town into the lower or new town of

13 BOULOGNE, in Rte. 3.

The high road to Paris is nearly deserted by travellers now that the Railway is open to Paris. It is destitute of interest, if we except the churches at Abbeville and Beauvais. These two towns are the best resting-places.

On quitting Boulogne the road commands, from an eminence which it ascends, a view into the valley of the Liane—thenceforth it is monotonous and dull. The *Railway* to Abbeville (Rte. 3) is carried a little to the W. of the post-road, nearer to the sea.

15 Samer (ruins of an abbey near this). *Inn*: Tête de Bœuf.

9 Cormont.

13 Montreuil-sur-Mer. *Inn*: H. de France. An ugly town and 2nd-rate fortress, on a hill rising out of the marshy valley of the Cache. It has a tall flamboyant church, with a fine W. doorway under the towers.

14 Nampont is situated within the Dépt. de la Somme, which anciently formed the province of Picardy.

9 Bernay.—La Poste, comfortable. The little seaport St. Valery is visible from the heights traversed by the road.

The wood seen on the l., at a little distance from the road, is a part of the forest of *Crecy*, the name of a village 12 m. from Abbeville; obscure in itself, but renowned for a victory gained in its precincts, Aug. 26th, 1346, by Edward III. and his 40,000 men over the French army of Philip of Valois 100,000 strong, commanded by the Count d'Alençon, which still, after the lapse of ages, remains one of the most brilliant in English annals. Here, upon that memorable day, to the winning of which the cannon, used, according to some, for the first time, contributed less than the clothyard shafts of the English yeomen, there fell, on the side of the French, the Kings of Bohemia and Majorca, the Duke of Lorraine, the Count d'Alençon (the king's brother), with 1200 knights, 1500 gentlemen, 5000 men at arms, and 30,000 infantry. Here it was that the Black Prince gained his spurs, and the feathers which the princes of Wales bear to this day.

7 Nouvion. An extensive manufactory of beet-root sugar is seen on the l., 2 m. before reaching Abbeville.

The most pleasing view on the whole road is that of Abbeville, and of the fertile vale of the Somme, in which it is situated, from the summit of the long and steep descent which leads down to it.

13 *Abbeville.* See Rte. 3. A Stat. on the Rly. to Paris.

[About 6 m. E. of Abbeville (bad road) is the *Abbey Ch. of St. Riquier*, a very splendid and interesting Gothic edifice, well preserved, having a beautiful flamboyant W. front, in the centre of which rises an elegant tower; while beneath it opens the main portal, having statues in its top and sides. "The details of the front are exquisite, well arranged, and well executed." The interior is also very fine; the nave flamboyant, the choir apparently earlier. On the walls of the treasury are curious and ancient frescoes; one in the style of the "Dance of Death." It is well worth a visit.]

The post-road crosses the Somme by two bridges on quitting Abbeville.

19 Airaines.

10 Camps.

13 Poix (Amiennois), which gives the title to the chief of the Noailles family. The road from Amiens to Rouen passes through this place.

14 Grandvilliers. H. d'Angleterre.

10 Marseille (Oise). During this stage the scenery is rather more interesting. Vineyards first appear a little to the N. of

19 *Beauvais. — Inns:* Hôtel du Cygne ;—d'Angleterre.

This is the chief town of the Dépt. de l'Oise: it has 13,082 Inhab. The central portion (la Cité) is very ancient, still in part enclosed by its old walls, which on the E. side have given place to airy boulevards planted with trees; many of the houses are of wood. The most conspicuous edifice, and the principal object of curiosity here, is the *Cathedral.* At a distance it appears a heavy and uncouth mass, overtopping the rest of the town with its prominent roof, which is supported by 3 rows of flying buttresses, surmounted by double ranges of pinnacles rising from broad buttress walls. It was commenced 1225, and the design of its founders and architects, excited to emulation by the splendour of Amiens, which had been begun 5 years earlier, seems to have been to surpass in vastness and magnificence all other Gothic edifices. They miscalculated, however, the resources both of their art and their treasury, and the result was repeated failure and final defeat; for the progress of the edifice was arrested when it was only half finished, and it remains a mere gigantic choir with transepts. As it is, however, this choir is the loftiest in the world, the elevation of the roof above the pavement being 153 ft.—13 ft. higher than that of Amiens ; but though more extraordinary, it is less pleasing than it. "The extension of its dimensions upward is carried to a degree which strikes the spectator as exaggeration. Amiens is a giant in repose; Beauvais a colossus on tiptoe."— *W.* To increase the wonder of the building, the architect designed to support it on half the number of piers employed at present; but in spite of the iron braces used to hold the piers in their places, the walls bulged out, and the roof fell twice. The only means, then, of maintaining it was by inserting intermediate piers in the wide spaces left between the original ones. The transepts, begun 1500, under the Bishop Villiers de l'Ile Adam (who, as well as his brother the Grand Master of St. John of Jerusalem, was a Beauvoisin), by the architects Jean Waast and Martin Cambiches, and finished 1555, are a fine example of the flamboyant style.

One compartment of the nave was actually begun when the architects (moved, it is said, by a vain ambition to rival the height of St. Peter's dome, and M. Angelo's masterpiece) abandoned it to raise a tower 455 ft. high, which lasted only 5 years, having tumbled down 1573. The choir, "though raised to a loftiness that strikes the beholder with awe and astonishment, displays the space between the tall and slender pillars so entirely filled with glass that the whole range of windows only appears like a single zone of light supported and separated by nothing but narrow mullions situated at wide intervals."—*Hope*.

In the interior the effect of the admirable painted glass, executed in the best period of the art, is very rich. That in the N. and S. rose windows is attributed to Nicholas Lepot, and that in some of the side chapels to Augrand Leprince, both celebrated as artists in this line in the 16th cent. In the choir are hung 8 of the *tapestries* for the manufacture of which Beauvais was celebrated, and which preceded by 3 years that of Gobelins. The monument in the N. aisle of the choir of Cardinal Forbin de Janson, surmounted by his kneeling effigy, is by Nicholas Coustou, and of good workmanship.

The entrances to the Cathedral are by the transepts: the portal at the extremity of the S. transept is loaded with flamboyant decorations, though, from the fury of iconoclasts, it has lost the statues which filled the niches. It is surmounted by a noble rose window, of very rich tracery. The façade of the N. transept has very much the character of English perpendicular Gothic; its portal, deeply recessed, with feathered mouldings to the arches, retains its original carved doors, which are surmounted by a bas-relief, in the tympanum, of a genealogical tree; the escutcheons suspended from the branches.

A ruinous building called the *Basse Œuvre*, on the W. of the cathedral, occupying part of the space which the nave, if carried out, would have covered, is curious as one of the most ancient buildings in France (8th or 9th cent.). The lower part of the outer walls displays masonry with bonds of tiles, and tiled arches in the manner of Roman edifices. The superstructure served as a church in the 10th cent.; in its interior square piers support plain round arches. It seems never to have had a stone roof.

St. Stephen's Church. The nave exhibits the transition from Romanesque to Gothic; it is very plain, with round pier arches, and round-headed clerestory windows. The W. front resembles a plain early English front of our own country. The painted glass is very excellent. The *Bishop's Palace*, rebuilt in the 15th cent., has externally the aspect of a castle surrounded by walls, and its entrance flanked by 2 large round towers.

Cæsar thus mentions the Bellovaci, the ancient inhabitants of the Beauvaisis: " Plurimum inter Belgas Bellovacos et virtute et auctoritate, et hominum numero valere."

The most remarkable event in the annals of Beauvais is its *Siege* by Charles the Bold in 1472, when, being destitute of garrison, it might have fallen by a *coup de main*, had not its citizens boldly closed their gates in the face of an army of 80,000 Burgundians, and maintained an obstinate resistance until succour arrived from Paris. The peculiar feature in this defence was the part which the wives and daughters of the townsfolk took in it, guarding the walls, and sharing in all the perils of the men. The chief heroine, Jeanne Hachette, appeared upon the breach at the moment of the fiercest assaults, seized a Burgundian standard which a soldier was endeavouring to plant on the walls, and, hurling the bearer to the bottom, bore it off in triumph into the town. Louis XI. rewarded the valour of the citizens by releasing them from taxes, and complimented the ladies by an ordonnance authorising them to take precedence of the men in the procession of St. Angadrème, instituted to commorate the raising of the siege. This procession is still kept up, on the Sunday nearest the 14th Oct.; the females lead the way, carrying the banner so valorously acquired by Jeanne Hachette, which is preserved in the *H. de Ville*. A statue of her, erected 1850, adorns the "Place."

At an earlier period (1357) Beauvais was the centre of the revolt of the serfs against their tyrannic lords, called *Jacquerie*, from Jacques Bonhomme (Goodman James), the familiar sobriquet of the peasantry. It extended over several provinces before it was put down by the armed force of the seigneurs banded together, and with fearful cruelty. Froissart thus describes an instance of wholesale vengeance performed upon the rebellious peasants by the Duke of Orleans, the Count of Foix, and the Captal de Buch: "They set fire to the town and burned it clean, and all the villagers of the town that they could close therein."

Diligence to Breteuil Stat. (Rte. 3.)
Railway—a branch to Creil Stat., passing by the valley of Thérain, 35 kilo., is in progress.

15 Noailles.
13 Puiseux.
10 Beaumont-sur-Oise (Hôtel du Paon), prettily situated on the l. bank of the Oise. Here vineyards first appear. Rly. Stat.

Before reaching Moisselles, a paved road, bordered with trees, strikes off to Viarmes, the Abbey of Royaumont, and Chantilly. (See p. 9.)

12 Moisselles. Rt. lie the forest of Montmorency, and that of Ecouen, with its immense château. (See p. 10.)

The road is carried through one of the *Forts* forming part of the outworks of the new Fortifications of Paris, before entering

13 *St. Denis*. (See Rte. 3.)

Travellers bound for the W. end of Paris turn to the rt. on quitting St. Denis, pass one of the new barracks for the garrison attached to the fortifications, and, leaving Montmartre on the l., traverse the Faubourg des Batignolles, up to the Barrière de Clichy.

France.

The post-road is drawn in a perfectly straight line from St. Denis to the Barrière St. Denis, keeping the heights of Montmartre on the rt. It crosses the canal which unites the Seine at St. Denis with the Canal de l'Ourcq, and cuts off a bend of the Seine. Further to the rt., and near the Seine, is the villa of the Prince de Craon, where Louis XVIII. signed the Charter in 1814.

9 PARIS. Galignani's Paris Guide appears so good as to relieve the Editor of this work from the necessity of entering into any description at present of the French Capital. The following information, however, may not be unacceptable to strangers.

Inns: —Hôtel Bristol, Place Vendôme, is the Mivart's or Clarendon of Paris; excellent, perfectly comfortable, capital cuisine. H. Wagram, Rue Rivoli, excellent. H. du Rhin, Place Vendôme. N.B. In first-rate hotels dinners served in private are now charged as in London, à la carte, each dish separately, which renders the charge per head very high. H. Brighton, Rue Rivoli, extremely clean, most civil landlord, charges moderate—a fine view over the Tuileries garden: the hotels in the Rue de Rivoli have the great advantage of sun in winter, and a covered walk under its arcades in wet weather; quiet and good. H. Mirabeau, Rue de la Paix; a good suite of 4 apartments 7 to 10 fr. and higher a-night. H. des Princes, Rue de Richelieu; expensive. Hôtel Meurice, Rue Rivoli; a comfortable and well-managed house, almost exclusively frequented by English and Americans: bed 3 fr. per day; breakfast, tea and coffee, with eggs, 2 fr.; dinner at table-d'hôte, without wine, 4½ fr.; lacquais-de-place 5 fr.; carriage 25 fr.; servants all round 1 fr. a-day, but less in proportion for family. H. Windsor, Rue de Rivoli; on the same plan as the H. Meurice, moderate in charges. H. Victoria, Rue Chauveau la Garde, near the Madeleine. H. de la Terrasse, Rue Rivoli, quiet; no table-d'hôte. Hôtel de Lisle and Albion, formerly Lawson's, in the Rue St. Honoré.

Boarding House. Madame Guilhom's Pension, 5, Rue des Champs Elysées; a very respectable establishment. The

c

best *Restaurants* are Café de Paris, on the Boulevard; Véron's, Véry's, and the Trois Frères Provençeaux, Palais Royal; Philippe, Rue Montorgeuil, is good and very moderate in prices.— *F.*

Galignani's Reading Room, 18, Rue Vivienne, in a court, is a great resource to the Englishman in Paris: here he will find all the best newspapers of all the world; here he will meet with his friends, a list of his countrymen visiting or residing in Paris being kept here, and may supply himself with books, or subscribe to the circulating library. *Galignani's Messenger* is a capital paper, condensing all the news of the English papers without reference to politics. It is a comfort to have it sent after the traveller from place to place as he moves about France, which MM. G. will undertake to do.

Messrs. Stassin and Xavier keep a very extensive assortment of English and foreign books, Rue de la Banque, près la Bourse.

Public and private carriages are stopped at the outer gate or barrier of Paris by the officers of the *Octroi*, whose duty it is to levy a tax upon all provisions, wines, &c. Railway baggage is also searched by them.

ROUTE 5.

DIEPPE TO PARIS, BY GISORS.

168 kilom. = 104 Eng. m.

Steamboats in summer from Brighton or Shoreham, Mon., Wed., Thurs., and Sat., and from Dieppe 4 days a week, making the passage in 8 hours. See " Hints on Landing in France." (§ *c. Introduction.*)

Dieppe.—*Inns:* H. Royal near the Quai—very good; H. Victoria, formerly Roi d'Angleterre; Grand Hotel des Bains (Morgan's), facing the sea, near the Baths; H. des Bains, next the Custom-house, on the Quai; de Londres; Taylor's Hotel.

The seaport town of Dieppe (17,000 Inhab.) is situated in a depression between two high ranges of the chalk cliffs which here line the coast, as white and nearly as tall as those of England. Through this gap the small river Arques flows into the sea, making an abrupt bend round the tongue of flat land upon which a part of the town is built, and forming a tolerable tide harbour fit for vessels of 500 tons, which is lined with quays, and cleared from mud by sluices. Dieppe is one of the chief fishing-ports in France, equipping annually 60 vessels of 9000 tons for the cod fishery, and many more for that of the herring. It is much frequented as a sea-bathing place in summer.

The streets of Dieppe are regular, and display few specimens of antiquity, in consequence of the bombardment of the town by the English, who, returning from an unsuccessful attack on Brest, 1694, revenged themselves by laying this town in ruins,—a reckless and inglorious exploit. The principal street runs parallel with the sea from the harbour to the castle, and contains some tolerable shops. The marketplace, especially on market-day, will display samples of the picturesque dresses and strange high caps of Normandy; perhaps one of those towering, helmet-like head-dresses, once the common head-gear of the women of the Pays de Caux (cauchoise), may present itself. The *Faubourg de Pollet*, however, on the W., inhabited almost exclusively by fishermen, is that in which the most character and peculiarity of costume is observable; and it includes a few old houses. This quarter can be reached now only by making the circuit of the harbour, the old bridge across it having been pulled down in order not to check the force of the waters discharged from the bassin de retenue behind.

In the town itself there is little to merit the stranger's attention.

The **Ch. of St. Jacques* stands in the square a little to the W. of the harbour. The body of the building is much hidden behind the flying buttresses, some of them consisting of open screen-work tracery with 8 mullions. The anti-Gothic slated cupola, however, above the cross, does not add to its beauty. The interior also is disfigured by yellow wash and wooden screens. The transepts are the oldest part, built in the 13th cent., as well as perhaps the arches of the choir: the nave is a little later, and the roof and many of the side chapels are not older than the 15th. The screens and curious carvings in the side aisles, especially that before the sacristy or trésor—a confusion of the Gothic and Italian styles—and that in the chapel of St. Yves, deserve notice as examples of French florid Gothic of the 15th and 16th cents. "The Lady Chapel is a late specimen of Gothic art. The bosses of the groined roof are of delicate filagree work, and the vaulting is ornamented with knots pendent from the ribs." Here is one of those strange representations of the Holy Sepulchre surrounded by figures of the 3 Maries and other holy personages, so common in Romish churches abroad, executed in a very inferior style.

The *Castle*, rising on the tall cliff at the W. end of the town, built in the 15th cent., is now a barrack, and modernised. It contains nothing remarkable. It is, however, a picturesque object, with its group of quaint cone-headed towers, its high bridge and drawbridge spanning a chasm which runs down to the sea; it commands a fine view, and it possesses historical associations of great interest. Within these walls Henri IV., retreating before the army of the League, found shelter among his "bons Dieppois," as he called them, who had been the first to acknowledge his right to the throne, before the battle of Arques. He made choice of Dieppe from the attachment of its inhabitants, the fidelity of its governor, and the advantage of an open communication by sea with England. While here he received from Queen Elizabeth a reinforcement of 1000 Scotch and 4500 English soldiers.

In 1650 the famous Duchesse de Longueville, so prominent among the leaders of the party of the Fronde, defying the royal authority, was compelled to take refuge in the castle; but being pursued even hither by the vengeance of Mazarin and Anne of Austria, she with difficulty at length escaped hence by night, and, making her way amidst storm and tempest, after innumerable escapes and adventures, embarked alone from the coast in an English vessel, dressed as a man, and at length succeeded in reaching Rotterdam.

Dieppe at present gives little token of its former celebrity and prosperity; yet 3 centuries ago it was the most flourishing seaport of France, and one of the first in Europe. The fleets of its adventurous merchants traversed every sea: one of them, indeed (Ango), riding in the Tagus with his merchant squadron, bearded the King of Portugal in his own capital; another captured the Canaries. Its skilful and hardy sailors distinguished themselves by their geographical discoveries and early settlements in the 15th and 16th cents. Claims are put forth for their having found out the passage round the Cape of Good Hope before the Portuguese. If it were so, they certainly kept the secret so close that they have lost the credit of it. They were among the first visitors of the New World, explored Florida, opening the fur trade in Canada, and establishing the earliest European colony in Senegal; whence, as well as from the East Indies, they drew the costliest gums, gems, precious stones, metals, and tissues, with which they for a long time exclusively supplied their luxurious countrymen. The importation of elephants' teeth from Africa is said to have given rise to the pretty *manufacture of carved ivory*, which still exists here, and is almost peculiar to Dieppe. The rivalry of the Port of Havre, and its superior advantages in internal communication up the Seine, were the ruin of Dieppe. The revocation of the Edict of Nantes, and the English bombardment, inflicted severe blows in addition; and although the extensive equipment of vessels for the fisheries of cod in Newfoundland, and of the herring, has long contributed largely to the support of the town, yet they are much fallen off at present.

Dieppe, however, is much frequented as a watering-place in summer. The *Etablissement des Bains* is situated on the beach, nearly under the castle. There are no proper bathing-machines; and the bottom is a mass of flint shingle, without sand. A series of little huts are erected at the sea-side, from which ladies issue in robes resembling those of nuns, and gentlemen in wide trousers, and thus bathe in public. Ladies are assisted by male dippers appointed for this service, if they require their aid. There are also *hot baths* near the beach.

English Ch. service, Sunday at 1 P.M., in the old Carmelite convent chapel.

Diligences to Havre and to Abbeville (Rte. 18).

Railway to Rouen and Paris (Rte. 6).

The *Environs of Dieppe* present several interesting excursions. About 2 m. to the E., on the cliffs above the sea, is a camp capable of holding many thousand men, once attributed to Cæsar, but now supposed to be Gallic, and called *la Cité des Limes*. It is triangular in form, defended on the landside by a rampart in places more than 50 ft. high. It is near the road to *Eu* (Rte. 18), 18¾ m. distant, where the *Château* of Louis - Philippe and the *Church* deserve a visit.

The most delightful walk, however, in the neighbourhood of Dieppe is to the ruins of the *Castle of Arques, which are far more interesting than the Cité des Limes. They are situated in the valley of the Béthune, at its junction with the Arques, less than 4 m. S.E. of Dieppe, and are celebrated for the momentous victory gained beneath the walls by Henri IV. and his devoted band of 4000 Protestants over the army of the League, 30,000 strong, under the Duc de Mayenne, which decided the fate of the Béarnais prince. The artillery from its walls contributed not a little to the result of that day. "Il en fut tirée," says Sully in his Memoirs, "une volée de quatre pièces, qui fit quatre belles rues dans leurs escadrons et bataillons." Three or four more discharges not only checked their advance, but drove them behind a bend of the valley to shelter themselves from the cannonade, and from this check they never recovered. The king, expecting the Leaguers to debouche down the valley to attack him, had disposed and intrenched his little band accordingly, when he suddenly found the advanced guard of the Duc de Mayenne in his rear, pushing forward to cut him off from his stronghold, Dieppe. Henri, with great quickness and dexterity, changed his front, threw up fresh ramparts to protect his flanks, and managed still to keep up his communication with Dieppe. Among the heroic traits of Henri on that anxious and hard-fought day, are his words to M. de Belin, an officer of the League, who scornfully inquired where Henri's forces were, to oppose so large an army: "Vous ne les voyez pas toutes, car vous ne comptez pas Dieu et le bon droit, qui m'assistent." A rude *obelisk*, raised on the brow of the hill, marks the spot where the deadliest struggle occurred.

The *Castle, a fine object at a distance, occupies a commanding position on a tongue of high land between two valleys, and covers a large area with its ruins; but its shattered condition, arising less from the hazards of war and the effects of time than the dilapidations of man, has robbed it of much of its picturesqueness. For a series of years, down to the end of the last cent., the government allowed it to be pulled to pieces as a mere quarry of building materials. It is difficult to fix the age of its shapeless walls, deprived of their casing of masonry; but it is probable that the oldest parts, viz. the *Donjon* and its enclosure, date from the time of our Henry II., who rebuilt the castle at the end of the 12th cent.; other portions are not older than the 16th cent. The English, under Talbot and Warwick, again obtained possession of it in 1419, and kept it for 30 years, down to the capitulation of Rouen, by which it was yielded to Charles VII.

The main entrance remains flanked by 2 massive towers of immense size; and portions of the piers of the drawbridge which led to it are still standing, but the 3 successive arches of the gateway are torn into nearly shapeless rents.

Within a pleasant walk from Dieppe, at the pretty but scattered *village of Varengeville*, stands *le Manoir d'Ango*, the château of the celebrated Dieppois merchant Ango,—the host and friend of Francis I. Though now converted into a farm-house, so little of its external form is defaced that the eye can readily trace all the richness of decoration which distinguished the style of the Renaissance when it was built.

" The walls are principally constructed of black hewn flint, which, alternating with a white stone, produce a very beautiful mosaic. They retain all the sharpness of their original construction; and the sculptures with which they are enriched are of the most classical and graceful form. A number of large medallions above the grand entrance, and along the façade of the principal corps de bâtiment, are remarkable: among them the portraits of Francis I. and Diane de Poitiers. In the interior are some finely sculptured fireplaces and the remains of a large fresco; but they are only to be discovered by groping amongst the greniers, into which the apartments once so splendid have been changed." —*Miss Costello.*

The following direct road from Dieppe to Paris by Gisors leaves Rouen altogether on one side, and is shorter by 8 or 10 miles, but few would omit visiting that highly interesting city. (Rtes. 6 and 9.) Besides, the raily. now renders the route by Rouen the quicker of the two. Diligences have in consequence ceased to run this way. The Gisors road strikes off to the l., 3 m. beyond Dieppe.

12 Bois Robert.
17 Pommeréval.

4 or 5 m. on the l. of our road lies Neufchâtel, famed for its excellent cylindrical cream-cheeses, called Bondes.

24 Forges les Eaux. A village and watering-place, possessing chalybeate springs once of some repute, but neglected at present. They are three in number—*La Reinette, La Royale,* and *Cardinale;* the two last named from Louis XIII. and Cardinal Richelieu, who visited Forges to drink the waters in 1632, the period of their highest celebrity, in consequence of Anne of Austria, after living childless for 18 years, here becoming enceinte with Louis XIV.;—an event which was attributed to a course of these waters.

21 Gournay, famed for its butter, is situated in the district anciently called Pays de Bray.

The *Church of St. Hildebert* was begun in the 11th cent., but not finished until the 13th, and its W. front, with pointed arches, is perhaps of the latter date. In the interior, very massive round piers support semicircular arches inclining to the horseshoe form. The sculptured ornaments of the capitals are very remarkable for variety of pattern. Herring-bone masonry occurs in the E. end. About 5 m. from Gournay is the *Abbey Church of St. Germes,* as grand and large as a cathedral, of the 13th cent.

12 Talmoutiers.

14 Gisors.—*Inn*: H. de l'Ecu. An ancient town of 3500 Inhab., prettily situated on the Epte. Its venerable ramparts are converted into agreeable promenades, whose plantations encircle the ruins of its commanding *Castle,* once the bulwark of Normandy on the side of France, and still retaining many interesting characteristics of a feudal fortress of the middle ages. The octagonal Donjon especially, and its enclosure, crowning the top of a high artificial conical mound, are of the most solid construction, and are works of the 12th cent., built by our Henry II. The walls of a dungeon under one of the towers have been curiously carved with a nail by some unfortunate prisoner. At an interview which took place here between Henry and Louis VII., the two monarchs agreed to assume the cross for the recovery of Jerusalem.

The *Ch. of SS. Gervais and Protais* presents a singular combination of styles, and an abundance of uncouth sculptures: it has a choir built in the 13th cent. by Blanche of Castille (it is said); the nave and remainder of the ch. are of a later period. The sculpture of the portal, richly carved, is of the latest style of French florid Gothic, and much overladen with ornament. The organ-loft, and an emaciated monumental effigy, both attributed to Jean Goujon, merit notice, and there is some fine painted glass in the windows. In the S. aisle is a singular twisted column, surrounded by spiral bands of tracery.

Gisors is on the high road from Paris to Rouen (Rte. 10).

19 Chars.
18 Pontoise (in Rte. 3).
10 Herblay. Here the road divides. the l.-hand branch leads to Paris by St. Denis (see Rte. 3); that on the rt. proceeds by Besons, where it crosses the Seine, and by

12 Courbevoie, to the Barrière de Neuilly, entering

9 Paris by the Arc de l'Etoile. See Galignani's Guide, and p. 26.

ROUTE 6.

DIEPPE TO ROUEN—RAILWAY.

61 kilom. = 37½ Eng. m.
This *Railway* was opened 1848.
6 trains daily: time 1½ to 2 hrs.
Terminus near the wet-dock (bassin-à-flot) at Dieppe.
A tunnel at Appeville, rather more than 1 m. long, carries the rly. into the valley of the Scie, up which, it runs for more than 18 m., crossing it 22 times. It is enlivened by several mills.

In the outskirts of Dieppe we cross the road to Havre. The high road to Rouen is passed on a level. l. Beyond Sanqueville are the ruins of the *Castle* of Charlesmesnil. The way is varied here and there at long intervals by villas or châteaux, without any claim to beauty. The numerous orchards are one of the characteristic features of Normandy, which is a cider, not wine-drinking, province.

17 Longueville Stat. stands on the domain of an abbey, the chief conventual building of which is now a cotton-mill. l. may be perceived the scanty ruins of the *Castle of Longueville*, celebrated during the wars of the Fronde, and for the courage and adventures of the Duchesse, sister of the Great Condé.

26 Auffay Stat. A considerable village, with several cotton-mills and tanneries, and a pretty church.

30 St. Victor Stat. William the Conqueror was the founder of the abbey, and his statue occupies a niche outside of the ch. The Scie rises about 100 yards to the l.

rt. About 2¼ m. is Tôtes. (Cygne, a small but clean country *Inn.*) The spinning and weaving of cotton furnish employment to the inhabitants. Mills and factories increase in number as we approach Rouen, the great centre of the cotton manufacture in France.

The summit level of the line is attained through the long and deep cutting of Frithemesnil, leading into the Valley de Clères. Here is an old castle in which is shown the bed of Henri IV.

Monville Stat.

The line of houses, factories, and chimneys, interspersed with villas, orchards, and gardens, almost uninterrupted, from Malaunay to Rouen, may remind an Englishman of the clothing district of the W. of England. In 1845 (Aug. 19) a terrific whirlwind swept down part of this valley, and in the course of 1½ minute demolished 3 factories, crumbling them like houses of cards, and all within them, people and machinery. 60 lives were lost, 100 were wounded, many were buried in the ruins.

The Dieppe Rly. falls into the line from Rouen to Havre near

Malaunay Stat. and the *Viaduct* of 8 arches. (Rte. 14.)

Before entering Rouen a pretty view is obtained of the blue hills which border the Seine; nor is the atmosphere thickened with so dense an envelope of smoke as hovers over the great manufacturing centres of England. A great part of the coal here used comes from England; the Dépt. du Nord furnishes also its supplies.

17 Rouen Stat. (in Rte. 8).

ROUTE 8.

PARIS TO ROUEN—RAILROAD.

137 kilom. = 84 Eng. m. *Trains* 6 times a day, in about 5 hrs.; Express in 2¾ hrs. *Terminus* in Paris, Rue d'Amsterdam. Fares, 16, 13, and 10 frs.

This railroad was commenced in 1841, and opened May 1843. Its engineer is Mr. Locke, who executed the London and Southampton Railway; many of the shareholders are English capitalists of Lancashire; and even most of the workmen were English. A considerable number of experienced "navigators," having been transported across the Channel, worked on it harmoniously with their French brethren, showing them the mode of operation. The rails are of French iron, which is much dearer than English; but the locomotives, though made in France (at Rouen), are executed by an English company, established there expressly to supply this railroad. The minute subdivision of property in France, and the great number of landholders with whom the company had to deal, occasioned some difficulty in obtaining the land over which the rly. passes, and caused the

PLANCHE (S) EN 2.
PRISES DE VUE

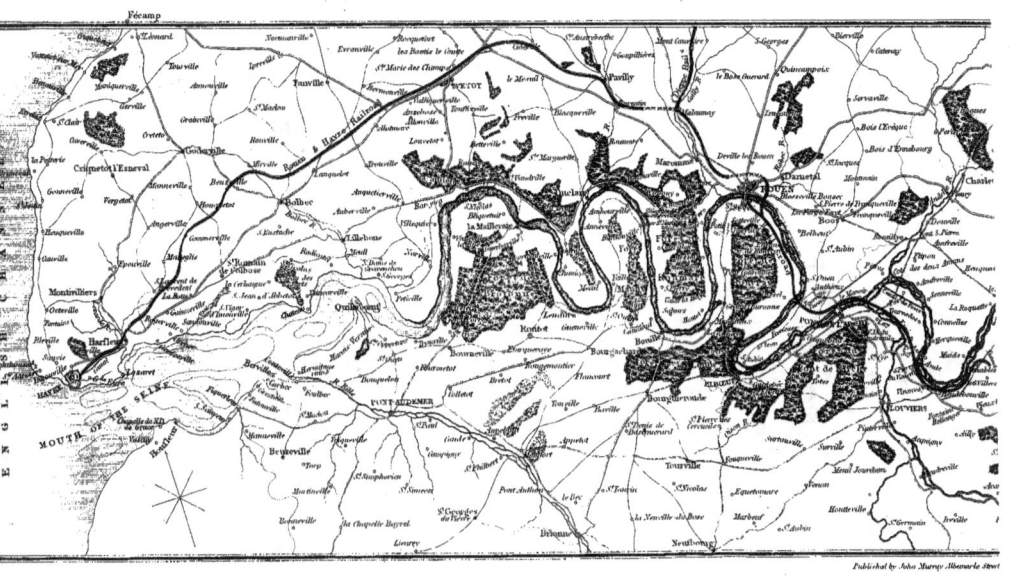

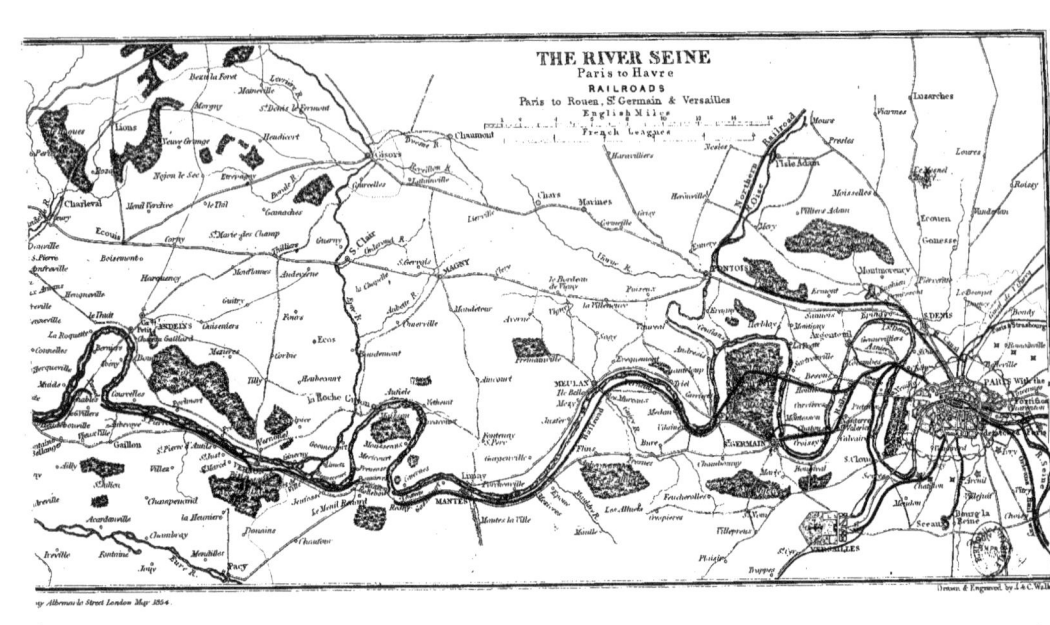

NORMANDY. *Route 8.—Paris to Rouen by Railway.* 31

number of contracts to be multiplied enormously; but the demands of the proprietors were by no means so exorbitant as in England.

The first part of the line is the same as that to St. Germain (Rte. 9). The rly., after passing on a bridge over the Rue de Stockholm, and through 2 tunnels under the Place d'Europe and other streets, quits Paris by Les Batignolles. The village of Clichy is passed on the rt. hand, and the Seine is crossed by a bridge of 5 arches before reaching the village.

4½ Asnières Stat., on the l. bank of the Seine, here crossed by another bridge, below that of the Chemin de Fer. The rly. bridge was ruthlessly burned by the Republican mob of 1848 and has since been rebuilt at great expense. The Versailles Railroad (rive droite) and the St. Germain Railroad here branch off to the l.

rt. Branch Railway to Argenteuil.

At Colombes, a small village, Henrietta Maria, widow of Charles I. and daughter of Henri IV., died in great poverty, 1669. The château which she inhabited no longer exists.

At Bezons the railway crosses the Seine by a bridge of 9 flat timber arches, each 100 ft. span, supported on stone piers. From this an embankment extends nearly a mile to a cutting at Houille which is also about a mile. Beyond this the embankment continues to the Seine, which is traversed for the second time by a bridge like the former, conducting to

17 Maisons Stat., at the end of the avenue leading to M. Lafitte's villa. (*Inns*: Hôtel Talma, so called because once the residence of the actor; good. Le Petit Havre.) The *Château* was the property of the late M. Jacques Lafitte, was built by François Mansard, 1658, for the Surintendant des Finances Réné de Longeuil, and is a handsome edifice of Italian architecture. Voltaire wrote ' Zaire' here; and he was here attacked with small-pox, which nearly carried him off. Before the Revolution it belonged to the Comte d'Artois, and was afterwards given by Napoleon to Marshal Lannes. The park has been cut into building lots, sold piecemeal, and studded over with villas, in the manner of the Regent's Park. Access is given to the new colony by the bridge of wood resting on stone piers. The distance hence to Paris is only 12 m. by land.

The rly. proceeds hence in a cutting across the forest of St. Germain, and follows the l. bank of the Seine by

9 Poissy Stat. (H. de Rouen), a small town on the l. bank of the Seine, the birthplace of St. Louis (1215), who was wont to sign himself by the modest style of Louis of Poissy. The font at which he was baptized is still shown in the *Parish Ch.*, a picturesque building, late Romanesque, with flamboyant additions, surmounted by 2 octagon towers and spires.

The *Conference of Poissy* was held 1561, with the hope of adjusting differences between the Popish and Calvinistic churches; Beza, with a train of doctors, appearing for the one party, and the papal legate, Cardinal Ippolito d'Este, for the other; and Charles IX. attended the first meeting with his mother, Catherine de Medicis. But the controversialists soon separated, without having approached to a reconciliation, each side believing it had the best of the argument.

A dirty and inconveniently narrow street leads to the long bridge of Poissy over the Seine, of 37 arches of different sizes, including the approaches, built, it is said, by St. Louis. The 3 central arches, now supplied by timber, were blown up in 1815 to prevent the passage of the allies; or, as some say, so long ago as in 1589, by Mayenne, the general of the League, to secure a safe retreat for his army from the pursuit of Maréchal de Biron, who had sacked Poissy because it refused to deliver its keys to the kings Henri III. and IV.

The greatest cattle-market in France is held here every Thursday for the supply of Paris with meat.

8 Triel Stat. In the ch. is an Adoration of the Shepherds, said to be an original, by *Poussin*, and some good painted glass. Here and at Vaux are extensive plaster quarries.

6 Meulan Stat. This town, on the rt. bank of the Seine, is partly built on

the slope of the hill, partly on an island in the middle of the river joined to the banks by an old stone bridge in two divisions.

8 Epone Stat. Here is a fine *Ch.*, 12th century.

The scenery of the valley is very pleasing, though the chalky white of the rocks is an eyesore. The banks of the river are enlivened with country houses.' The post-road runs at some distance from the river until it reaches Limay, the faubourg of Mantes, where it crosses from the rt. to the l. bank by the bridge. The rly. runs in a cutting to the W. of the town of

7 Mantes Stat. *Inn:* Grand Cerf—tolerable. This town is prettily situated on the margin of the Seine, whence it has gained the epithet La Jolie.

The chief building is the *Church of Notre Dame*, standing a little way above the bridge. It is a fine Gothic building; the body supported by flying buttresses, the roof covered with coloured tiles. The portals are pointed; the sculpture which adorns them is sadly mutilated. The interior, in the early pointed style, is very pleasing; its most remarkable feature being the height of the triforium gallery formed of triple arches, which, being carried quite round the E. end, and lighted by windows behind, gives a cheerful character to the ch. The tower at the W. end (a second or twin tower has been taken down) opens into the nave. It was built for Blanche of Castille and her son St. Louis by the architect Eudes de Montreuil.

The solitary *Tower of St. Maclou* is the sole remnant of another ch., built in 1344 with the toll dues exacted for leave to tow barges through the bridge on Sundays and holydays. It is deservedly preserved as a fine light Gothic structure.

It was among the glowing embers of the houses and monasteries of Mantes, which he had remorselessly caused to be burnt, that William the Conqueror received the injury in his corpulent person, caused by his horse starting, which proved mortal a few days after at Rouen. The castle of the French kings, where Henri IV. held the conferences with the Romish clergy which preceded his abjurance of the Protestant faith, was destroyed by the Regent Duke of Orleans.

Coach daily to St. Germain by the l. bank of the Seine.

rt. About half way between Mantes and Bonnières we pass *Rosny*, a dirty little village, contiguous to which, between it and the Seine, stands the *Château*, the birthplace of Sully, where he was frequently visited by his friend and master Henri IV., who slept here the night after his victory at Ivry. The king, having overtaken Sully on the road desperately wounded, carried on a litter, accompanied by his squires in a like plight, fell on his neck and affectionately embraced him. The château is a plain solid building of red brick, with stone quoins and a high tent roof, surrounded by a deep ditch; it was rebuilt by Sully at the beginning of the 17th cent. It is destitute of architectural beauty externally, and within has been modernised, although one room is still called Chambre de Sully. From 1818 down to the Revolution of 1830, Rosny was the favourite residence of the Duchesse de Berri, who erected here a chapel to contain the heart of her husband. The château has since changed hands repeatedly, and its present proprietor has pulled down the wings, which were modern, and added by the duchess. The grounds extend for some distance along the margin of the river, to which they owe their sole charm, the ground being perfectly flat, and traversed by long formal avenues.

In skirting the forest of Rosny, contiguous to the village, we are reminded of the sacrifice made by Sully, in felling in it at one time timber to the amount of 100,000 francs to pay his master's debts.

A great projecting buttress of chalk now intervenes, over which the high road is carried by a steep ascent and descent, and round which the Seine winds in a widely circuitous curve. The rly. pierces this by a *Tunnel* about 2480 yards long—driven through the chalk and a flinty conglomerate very hard to penetrate, commencing at Rolleboise, about 5 miles from Mantes, and

NORMANDY.   *Route 8.—Paris to Rouen—Pont de l'Arche.*   33

terminating on the W. at a short distance from

13 Bonnières Stat., the rly. having been previously carried over the highroad by a bridge. Bonnières is the stat. nearest to Evreux (Rte. 25), on the road to Caen and Cherbourg. Hence the railroad runs under the high ground close to the river as far as

10 Vernon Stat. *Inn:* Grand Cerf. This town (pop. 5300), which, like many others in Normandy, gives a name to a noble English family, is prettily situated, and its interior retains a venerable air of antiquity in its timber-framed houses; but its narrow streets, however picturesque, are by no means convenient on a great highway of traffic. There is preserved an ancient tower, tall and massive; and a Gothic *Ch.*, the choir of the 13th, the nave of the 16th cent., in which one monument only among many escaped the Revolution,—that of a lady of the family Maignard, — consisting of a kneeling effigy in marble (date 1610). At the foot of the bridge is a curious antique building, now a mill. Vernon possesses a *hospital* founded by St. Louis, an *artillery barrack*, and vast quarries of building-stone on the opposite side of the Seine.

The *Château de Bizy*, one of the finest seats in Normandy, the property of the Counts of Eu, and afterwards of the Duc de Penthièvre, was destroyed at the Revolution, and is now replaced by a plain country house belonging to the Orleans family. It is small and mean, but the grounds are beautiful and the walks through them agreeable. They are approached by a fine avenue on the outskirts of the town.

Coaches to Evreux, Dreux, and Chartres.

13 Gaillon Stat. A huge *penitentiary* occupies the place, and in part the remains, of the *Château* of the archbishops of Rouen. It was built 1515 for the Cardinal d'Amboise, out of the tribute levied on the Genoese, conceded to him by Louis XII., by the architects Jean Joconde and Androuet du Cerceau, and was adorned by the sculptor Jean-Juste de Tours. It was demolished at the Revolution, except the entrance portal flanked by 4 turrets, and covered with inscriptions and bas-reliefs, the clock tower, and the chapel tower. The gateway between the 1st and 2nd courts, a splendid example of the style of the Renaissance, was rescued by M. Lenoir and transported to Paris, where it has been reconstructed in front of the Ecole des Beaux Arts. Its architect was Pierre Fain, date 1509.

In the distance is seen the imposing ruin of *Château Gaillard*, the pet castle of Richard Cœur de Lion (Rte. 11), rising on a lofty rock washed by the Seine, but 5 or 6 miles N. of our road; so great is the circuit which the river here again makes.

Gaillon is the station nearest to Auteuil and the town of Andelys (omnibus runs thither), and hence an excursion may be made to the interesting castle of Château Gaillard (p. 50). Near le Grand Villers, two *Tunnels* are driven through the mass of a projecting promontory of chalk hill. The first or easternmost, of *Le Rule*, is a mile long, and the second, of *Venables*, 470 yards long.

13 St. Pierre de Vauvray Stat. The manufacturing town of Louviers is about 5 miles or 8 kilom. W. of this stat. (p. 46). *Malleposte* daily to Cherbourg, by Louviers, Lisieux, and Caen, 15¼ to 17 hrs. A *Rly.* is projected. Post-horses are kept here.

The Seine is traversed obliquely for the 3rd time by a bridge at Le Manoir just above the confluence of the Eure, and the rly. proceeds along the rt. bank of the Seine for a short distance to

12½ Pont de l'Arche Stat. at the extremity of the bridge leading to that town. Pont de l'Arche is a small town whose main street is a narrow and inconvenient lane leading to the bridge of 22 arches, by which the Seine is crossed by the post-road, a little below the junction of the Eure. The view from it is pretty; on the rt. is seen the Côte des Deux Amants (see Rte. 11). The tide ascends to this point.

The Gothic *Ch.* contains some curious painted windows: in one of them the inhabitants of the town, male and female, in the costume of the 16th cent., are seen towing barges through

c 3

the central arch of the bridge. *Coaches to Elbœuf* (Rte. 12).

The rly. next passes through the hill of Tourville by a short *Tunnel* of about 500 yards, and crosses the Seine, here divided into two arms, for the 4th time, by a bridge resting on the Ile des Bœufs, to

5 Tourville, Station for the populous and industrious town of *Elbœuf* (Rte. 12). Hence it proceeds onwards along the l. bank of the Seine through St. Etienne de Louvray and *Sotteville* (where the line to Havre diverges rt. and crosses the Seine) to its termination in the Faubourg St. Sever of the great city of

12 ROUEN: Terminus, Cours la Reine. *Postmaster's charge* 1 fr. 50 c. for each horse and each postilion in conveying a carriage from the rly. to any part of Rouen.

ROUEN.—*Inns*: H. d'Albion, on the Quai, clean and good;—H. d'Angleterre, good; excellent table d'hôte, dearer of late;—H. de Normandie, reasonable; —Hôtel Vatel, Rue des Carmes.

Rouen, anciently *Rotomagus*, the capital of ancient Normandy, and the chief town at present of the department of the Seine Inférieure, is agreeably seated on the Seine, and yields to no provincial city of France in its majestic and venerable aspect, in historic associations, and in magnificent buildings, the triumph of the ecclesiastical and civil architecture of the middle ages. It has this advantage also over most other ancient towns, that it is not a mere heap of dry bones, destitute of life and abandoned by commerce; its narrow streets of gable-faced, timber-fronted mansions, swarm like an ant-hill with busy crowds passing to and fro: it is a focus of trade, and the chief seat of the cotton manufacture in France. It may be called, indeed, the French Manchester. It contains 92,083 Inhab., and is surpassed in population by only 4 other cities in France.

The situation of Rouen on a river which affords ready access on the one hand to the sea at Havre (103 m. distant by the windings of the stream), and with the capital on the other, tends highly to promote its industry and commerce. The Seine, here more than 1000 ft. broad, forms a convenient port, accessible for vessels of 250 tons; and though the number of vessels is small, they add both to the picturesqueness and animation of the scene. Its banks are formed into fine broad *Quais*, and these are lined with handsome modern buildings, which have sprung up within the last 10 or 15 years, and serve as a screen to hide a rear rank of tottering timber houses, such as form the bulk of the city, and which previously extended down to the river-side. Modern improvements and additions, indeed, have of late greatly detracted from the venerable and picturesque appearance of Rouen; but the changes are skin-deep, confined to its exterior, and the stranger has only to plunge into its almost inextricable labyrinth of streets to find enough of antiquity to satiate the artist or the most ardent lover of bygone times; although, a law having been passed prohibiting the rebuilding of houses in wood, their number must diminish every year.

A *Boulevard*, occupying the place of the old fortifications which resisted Henry V. of England and Henri IV. of France, runs round the old town nearly in a semicircle, touching the Seine at its two extremities. This line includes within it all the most interesting public monuments and objects worth notice; outside of it spreads a supplement of populous fauxbourgs, occupied chiefly by the weavers and working classes, who also form the bulk of the population in the suburb St. Sever, on the l. bank of the Seine, having wider but not cleaner streets than the inner town, interspersed at intervals by tall smoking chimneys and lavishly glazed spinning-mills.

A walk through the town in the following order will carry the pedestrian to the things best worth observation; but if he wishes to see them thoroughly, he will find one or even two days not enough. The distances from one quarter of the town to another are considerable, to say nothing of the want of pavement, the dirt, and the bad smells which he will have to encounter. The Rue Grand Port, which runs up from the quai opposite the suspension-bridge, and which is at once the chief thoroughfare and includes the best shops, will bring you to the Cathedral; a little in the rear of it, to the E., is the ch. of St. Maclou, from the door of which the Rue Damiette, running due N., will bring you to St. Ouen, the noblest ch. in Rouen. A new street opened from the stone Bridge to the Place de l'Hôtel de Ville passes near St. Maclou and in front of St. Ouen. Close beside it, in the H. de Ville, is the gallery of pictures; but more worthy of attention is the Museum of Antiquities, Rue de Beauvoisin, near the Boulevard. Hence you must thread your way back to the river, visiting in turn the Palais de Justice, Tour de la Grosse Horloge, Place de la Pucelle (where Joan of Arc was burnt), and Hôtel de Bourgtheroude. As the churches are closed from 12 to 3, except on Saturday and Sunday, they should be visited in the early part of the day.

The **Cathedral of Notre Dame occupies with its W. front one side of the fruit and flower market. The vast proportions of this grand Gothic façade, its elaborate and profuse decorations, and its stone screens of open tracery, impress one, at first glance, with wonder and admiration; diminished, however, though not destroyed, by a closer examination, which shows a confusion of ornament and a certain corruption of taste. " It is viciously florid, and looks like a piece of rock-work, rough and encrusted with images and tabernacles, and ornamented from top to bottom." — G. Knight. The projecting central porch and the whole of the upper part were the work of Cardinal d'Amboise (1509-1530); the lateral ones are of an earlier period (13th cent.) and chaster style; and the sculpture adorning them deserves attention. Above the central door is carved the genealogy of Jesse. Over the l.-hand (N.W.) door is the Death of St. John Baptist,—in it may be seen Herodias's daughter dancing, or rather tumbling, before Herod: over this on the rt., much mutilated, the Virgin with Saints. Of the two stately flanking towers, that of St. Romain, on the N., rests on walls older than any other part of the building (12th cent.): it may be profitably ascended on account of the view. The rt.-hand, or S.W. tower, called *Tour de Beurre*, because built (between 1485 and 1507) with the money paid for indulgences to eat butter in Lent, is a far more beautiful structure, surmounted with an elegant circlet of stone filagree. It contained the famous bell, named George d'Amboise, melted at the Revolution; it is now gutted. Of the central spire the less that is said the better; it is a cage of cast-iron bars intended to replace a spire of wood burnt by lighting 1822; and judging from its shape and size, seen at a distance, might be taken for the parent of all the factory chimneys in and about the town. It reaches to a height of 436 ft. It is quite out of character with the rest of the building, and is intended to be gilt. A corkscrew or geometrical staircase of iron worms itself up the centre to a dizzy height.

The N. and S. fronts are in a style resembling the decorated of England, with geometric tracery. The very beautiful N. door, called *Portail des Libraires*, from the book-stalls which once occupied the court before it, was not finished until 1478. The opposite one leading to the S. transept, called *Portail de la Culende*, and nearly of the same age and style, is ornamented with bas-reliefs from the history of Joseph. The figure hanging, vulgarly supposed to represent a corn-merchant who suffered for using false measures, while his property was confiscated to build this entrance, is otherwise, and more accurately, explained to be Pharaoh's chief butler. The N. transept is flanked on either side by open towers of great beauty, and of such proportions as would fit them for the W. front of an English cathedral.

The *interior* measures 435 ft. in length, and the height of the nave is $89\frac{1}{2}$ ft. It is in the early pointed style. Above the main arches of the nave runs a second tier, smaller, but opening a so into the aisles; an arrangement not un common in Normandy, but rare in England. The three rose windows, in the nave and transepts, are very fine in size and decoration. In the end chapel, on the S. side of the nave, is the tomb and effigy of Rollo, first Duke of Normandy, and opposite to it that of his son William Long Epée: but the figures are not older probably than the 13th cent.

The *choir*, separated from the nave by a modern Grecian screen, was built between 1280 and 1300. The carving of the stalls, executed 1467, is extremely curious. The finest and oldest painted glass is to be found in the chapels of the choir aisles; it is of the 13th cent. Small lozenge-shaped tablets of marble, let into the pavement of the choir, mark the spots where the heart of Richard Cœur de Lion, and the bodies of his brother Henry (died 1183), of William son of Geoffroy Plantagenet their uncle, and of John Duke of Bedford, regent (prorex Normanniæ) under Henry VI. (1435), were interred. Their monuments, much injured by the outrage of the Huguenots in 1663, when all parts of the church suffered more or less, were removed, and lost until 1838, when the *effigy of Richard I.*, a rude statue 6½ ft. long, was dug up from under the pavement on the l. of the high altar. His "lion heart" was also found still perfect, but shrunk in size, enveloped in a sort of greenish taffeta enclosed in a case of lead, and is now deposited in the Museum. His body was interred at Fontevrault; but he bequeathed his heart to Rouen, on account of the great affection which he bore to the Normans. The effigy of limestone, much mutilated, represents him crowned, and in the royal robes, and is now placed in the *Lady Chapel* behind the high altar, which contains two other splendid and highly interesting monuments. On the rt. hand is that of Cardinal George d'Amboise, Archbishop of Rouen and minister of Louis XII., and his brother, a magnificent structure of black and white marble, in the style of the Renaissance, executed in 1525. The marble statues of the two cardinals, uncle and nephew, kneel below a covered canopy richly ornamented and gilt; behind is a bas-relief of St. George and the Dragon; above, in niches arranged two by two, are statues of the 12 Apostles; below are the Cardinal Virtues. The pilasters and intervening spaces are adorned with rich and fanciful arabesques. The bodies of the Cardinals d'Amboise were torn from the grave by the Revolutionists of 1793, the lead of the coffins melted, and the contents scattered.

On the l. side of the chapel is the monument of the Duc de Brézé, grand seneschal of Normandy; but more remarkable as husband of Diana of Poitiers, mistress of Henry II., by whom it was erected. The effigy of the distressed widow kneels at the head of an emaciated corpse representing her husband after death, stretched on a sarcophagus of black marble. She is in a mourning attitude corresponding with the words of the epitaph which she caused to be engraved on the tomb:—

"Indivulsa tibi quondam, et fidissima conjux,
Ut fuit in thalamo sic erit in tumulo."

A sentiment, however, which must be taken in an ironical sense; it is quite certain that she was not buried with him, but at her château of Anet, and it is probable that she was as true to her word in one respect as in the other. Above, in an arched recess, is the statue of the duke in full armour on horseback. This tomb is a splendid work of the age of Francis I.; and is attributed to Jean Goujon, or Jean Cousin.

A rich florid Gothic niche at the side, surmounted by a stone canopy of open work and intervening stems, was erected at an earlier period (1465) to Pierre de Brézé, grandfather of the preceding. Neither statue nor inscription remains.

The elaborately carved screen in front of the sacristy, executed in the latter part of the 15th cent., and its wrought-iron door, must not be passed without notice.

Passing the *Archevêché*, contiguous to the cathedral on its N. and E. side, we come to the

Church of St. Maclou, which ranks third among the churches of Rouen in beauty. Its grandest feature is its triple porch; it is a fine specimen of the florid architecture of the 15th cent., and the sculpture adorning it is of exquisite taste and beauty of execution. The traveller should pay attention to the wooden doors (including that on the N. side), beautifully carved with Scripture subjects, in bas-relief, by Jean Goujon, it is said, and to the elaborate winding stair of stone near the W. entrance, leading to the organ-loft. There is much painted glass in the windows. The *Cemetery* of St. Maclou is said to be very curious.

A newly opened street leads from the river to the * *Ch. of St. Ouen*, which surpasses the cathedral in size, purity of style, masterly execution, and splendid but judicious decoration, and is inferior only as regards historic monuments. It is beyond doubt one of the noblest and most perfect Gothic edifices in the world. Although it suffered considerably from the Huguenots (1562), who made 3 bonfires within the building to burn the stalls, pulpit, organ, and priests' robes; and from the republicans, who turned it into an armourer's shop, and raised a smith's forge in its interior, by the smoke of which the windows were blackened until they ceased to be transparent, it has escaped in a remarkable degree; and recent judicious restorations leave little to desire touching its state of repair.

The first stone of the existing edifice (for 4 other churches had preceded it) was laid 1318 by Abbot Jean Roussel; the choir, the chapels, and nearly all the transept were completed in 21 years, and the nave and tower finished by the end of the 15th cent. Thus, one plan being followed to the termination, the most perfect harmony of style prevailed throughout. The W. front, long unfinished, has recently been completed by the addition of 2 flanking steeples, surmounting 3 deep-set portals. It is a pity that the original design (still preserved in the library) has not been more strictly followed. The architect is M. Grégoire.

Above the cross rises the central tower, 260 ft. high, which, whether examined close at hand (as it ought to be) or seen at a distance rising above the town, is a model of grace and delicacy. It is an octagon composed of open arches and tracery, throwing out flying buttresses to the turrets in the angles, and terminates with a crown of fleurs-de-lis, which ancient royal symbol is also discovered in the pattern of the tracery of the windows, and in the painted glass.

The S. portal, called *des Marmouzets* from figures of the animals carved on it, deserves attentive examination, as a gem of Gothic work scarcely to be surpassed. It is surrounded by a fringe of open trefoil arches; while 2 groined pendants, 6 ft. long, drop from its vault. The bas-relief over the door represents the Death and Assumption of the Virgin: the whole has been restored.

The interior (443 ft. long, and 106½ ft. high), notwithstanding its size, is peculiarly light and graceful; the front pillars of its richly moulded piers run up uninterruptedly to the roof as ribs, the side ones bend under the arches. The clerestory being very large increases the effect of lightness; "the windows seem to have absorbed all the solid wall," and the roof is maintained in its place by the support of pillars and buttresses alone. All the glass is painted, and there are 3 noble rose windows filled with it. The stranger should look into the holy-water basin (bénitier) close to the W. door; he will find the beauties of the interior all mirrored on the surface of the water. The master mason under and by whom this noble ch. was reared is buried in St. Agnes' chapel, the 2nd on the l. in the N. choir aisle. His name was Alexander Berneval; and, according to tradition, he murdered his apprentice through envy, because the youth had surpassed, in the execution of the rose window in the N. transept, into the tracery of which the pentalpha is introduced, that which his master had constructed in the S. transept. Though the mason paid the penalty of his crime, the monks, out of gratitude for his skill, interred his body within the church which he had contributed so much to ornament.

The whole of the transept, choir, and lower part of the tower, are decorated in character, passing into the *flam-*

boyant in the upper story of the tower and in the nave.

The material used in the structure of St. Ouen is a limestone approaching to chalk, and containing flints, which have been often patiently cut through in the delicate carving and tracery. But the details of the building should be studied on the roof, upon the tower, and in the internal galleries. It will well repay the trouble of the ascent.

A very pretty *Garden*, whose great ornament, however, is the adjacent church, extends along the N. side of St. Ouen, behind the Hôtel de Ville; it was originally the convent garden. Within it, attached to the church, stands a very perfect *Norman tower*, with round-headed windows, in the style of the 11th cent.; it probably formed part of a previously existing church. It is called "La Chambre aux Clercs."

St. Ouen was archbishop of Rouen, and died 678.

The *Hôtel de Ville, a handsome building of Italian architecture, attached to the N. transept of the church, formed part of the monastery of St. Ouen, to which a modern front, with Corinthian colonnade, has been added, so as to give the building an official, civic air. Besides the public offices, it contains the *Public Library*, and *Le Musée des Tableaux*, a collection in which the good paintings bear a very small proportion to the bad. There is an ancient and curious picture, attributed to *Van Eyck*, of the Virgin and Child amidst Angels and Saints, "a delicious painting, and pronounced on good authority to be original"— (*E. o. S.*); the predella of an altar-piece, by *Perugino*, brought from Perugia; a copy of Raphael's Madonna di San Sisto; St. Francis in ecstasy, by *Ann. Caracci*; the Plague at Milan, by *Lemonnière of Rouen*; and an Ecce Homo, by *Mignard*.

The *Bibliothèque Publique* is a valuable collection of 33,000 vols., very accessible, being open every day from 11 to 4, and from 6 to 9, except Sunday and Thursday. Among the 1200 MSS., many richly ornamented with paintings, are the History of the Normans, by William of Jumièges, 11th cent.; a Benedictionary, which belonged to an archbishop of Canterbury; and a missal book of the 12th cent. The Gradual of Daniel d'Aubonne, 17th cent., containing about 200 vignettes and initials, is very beautiful.

**Le Musée des Antiquités*, in the suppressed convent de Ste. Marie, Rue Beauvoisin, from the number and rarity of the curiosities deposited in it, consisting for the most part of voluntary donations, is one of the most interesting sights in the town, and highly creditable to the administration of the department, by whom it was founded, 1833-4; no stranger should omit to visit it. The following enumeration will give an idea of the nature of the objects preserved here:— The door of the house in which Corneille was born; many Roman and Gallic tombstones, coffins, &c., dug up at Rouen and other places in the Dépt. de la Seine Inférieure; many fragments of Roman sculpture; specimens of pottery, glass, mosaics; inscriptions; together with a draped female statue of good work, but wanting the head, from the Roman theatre, Lillebonne.

It is chiefly, however, for works of art and antiquities of the Middle Ages, and the following period down to the 17th cent., that this museum is entitled to attention.

The windows, 15 in number, by which the gallery is lighted, are all filled with painted *glass* derived from suppressed convents, churches, &c., forming a chronological series from the 13th to the 17th cent.; very valuable and interesting, as showing the progress of the art. The most remarkable are those from the Church of St. Eloi, Rouen, 16th cent.; the miracle of St. Nicholas, from St. Godard (first half of 16th cent.), very fine. There is no collection of glass painting equal to this in France or England.

In glazed frames against the wall are hung *charters* and other ancient MSS., containing autographs of remarkable persons—among them, Wm. the Conqueror's mark, a cross (he could not write); and the signatures of our other Norman dukes and kings, among which those of Henry I. and Richard Cœur de Lion may be observed. Here also is now deposited the *heart* of the Lion-hearted King (see p. 36).

The shrine of St. Sever, which once contained the relics of that saint, formerly placed in the cathedral, is in the shape of a Gothic chapel, with silver statues of saints in niches round its sides. It is of oak, covered with copper plates gilt and silvered, and is an elegant piece of workmanship of the end of the 12th cent.: it has been restored. A crucifix, carved in stone, 16th cent.: at the foot of the cross the holy women; on the opposite side the Virgin and Child. Many other specimens of sculpture, of the 15th, 16th, and 17th cent., in stone and wood, from religious edifices: 5 bas-reliefs of the Last Judgment, in marble, from the Church of St. Denis-sur-Scie; in one, Christ is rescuing souls from the jaws (literally) of hell. Many capitals of Gothic columns richly sculptured.

An extensive collection of coins and medals; Roman, Gallo-Roman, French Norman, &c.

Casts from the bas-reliefs of the Hôtel de Bourgtheroude (p. 41), representing the interview of the Field of the Cloth of Gold between Henry VIII. and Francis I. A small collection of arms and armour; among them will be found the coat of mail of Enguerrand de Marigny, from the Church of Ecouis: also several early cannon and wall pieces, ancient furniture, cabinets.

A fragment of the famous bell George d'Amboise (see p. 35), which was melted into cannons and souspieces at the Revolution.

This *Museum* is open Sunday and fête-days from 11 to 4, and Tuesday and Thursday from 12 to 3; but it is always accessible to strangers.

In an adjoining building is a very respectable *Museum of Natural History.*

The amateur of stained glass should not omit to visit the churches of *St. Godard*, containing two windows 32 ft. high and 12 wide, and *St. Patrice*, where there are many more of still greater beauty, executed in the 16th cent. The architecture of these two churches is not remarkable; they are very late in the Gothic style.

The *Church of St. Vincent* has an exquisite Gothic porch, and very fine painted glass likewise.

Another church, *St. Gervais*, situated in the very remote faubourg Cauchois, near the Havre Railway terminus, is reputed the oldest structure in Rouen, and one of the earliest Christian monuments in France. The church itself is low, humble, and not remarkable; but below it is a *crypt* even more simple and unadorned, but exhibiting to the eye of the antiquary marks of construction as old probably as the 4th cent., in the courses of Roman tiles between the layers of rough masonry. It has an apsidal termination: in the side walls are holes for the *cancelli* or rails, to which the curtain was hung to separate the *chancel* from the rest of the church: the altar-slab is marked with 5 + +. The two low arched recesses in the walls are said to have been the graves of St. Mello and St. Avitien, the first archbishop of Rouen.

The circular E. end of the church itself, which rests upon this crypt, is in the earliest Norman style: and some of the pillars let into the wall, but too short to support the roof, have classic capitals. The Roman road to Lillebonne passed close to St. Gervais. William the Conqueror, tortured by the wound he had received at the cruel sack and burning of Mantes (p. 31), repaired to the retired monastery of St. Gervais to die. His death-bed exhibited a melancholy example of the vanity of earthly grandeur. Deserted by his own sons when the breath was scarce out of his body, forsaken by friends and courtiers, and plundered by his servants, his body remained stripped and deserted, until the pity and charity of an unknown knight in the neighbourhood provided the funds necessary for the funeral; and he himself escorted the body to its last resting-place at Caen. There are perhaps a dozen suppressed churches in Rouen, most of them converted into warehouses.

The *Palais de Justice* is a very interesting specimen of civic Gothic architecture, which may vie with some of the town-halls of the Low Countries. Reared at a time when the style had become fantastic in its forms and exuberant in its adornments, it yet displays so much originality of invention, beauty, and gorgeous magnificence, that it is hard to condemn it for a want of taste and purity.

It lines 3 sides of a square; the wing on the l. is the *Salle des Procureurs*, built 1493, as a sort of exchange for merchants, native and foreign, to meet in. It is a large and handsome hall, with an open roof, like a ship's hull reversed, 160 ft. long and 50 ft. high—a sort of Westminster Hall in miniature, and now serving the same purposes. The body of the building in the centre was raised 6 years later by Louis XII. for the *Cour d'Echiquier* of Normandy, the ancient supreme tribunal of the duchy, at least as old as the time of William the Conqueror, for which the name of parliament was substituted in 1515 by Francis I. This façade is decorated with all the ornament which the fertile resources of the architect afforded; the square-headed windows are set within the most delicate garlands of stone; the buttresses are studded with niches and crowned by pinnacles; and the lofty dormer windows, rising against the high-pitched roof, are surmounted by canopies of the most delicate open work, with pinnacles and statues, many of them executed by first-rate artists at Paris, and are connected by a pierced battlement of arches and tracery. For many years past this front has been undergoing a careful restoration; it is only a pity that it makes so slow a progress.

The chamber in which the parliament of Normandy met is now the *Salle d'Assises*. It has a fine roof of black oak, set off with gold; but the elegant pendants which hung from it have been removed, and the wainscoting, painted over with arabesques and old mottoes reminding judges of their duties, has been taken down or effaced by whitewash.

The large building behind the Palais, once the residence of the president of the parliament, is now the Cour Royale.

La *Rue de la Grosse Horloge*, not far from the Palais, one of the narrowest and most picturesque in Rouen, is so called from the antique clock gate-house, built 1527, by which it is spanned, adjoining the tower of the Beffroi, whence the curfew is still tolled every evening. In this street are several ancient houses. Nos. 115 and 129 deserve notice.

The *Place de la Pucelle*, known also by the vulgar name Marché aux Veaux, serves to record the fate of the heroic and unfortunate Jeanne d'Arc, the deliverer of her country, and the terror of the English, who was burned alive here as a sorceress 1431, on the spot marked by the contemptible modern statue placed upon a pump, which bears her name, but the outward aspect of Bellona! Her ashes were collected by the hangman, and cast into the Seine, by order of the Cardinal of Winchester. He and other prelates were spectators of her execution; and some of them, unmoved by her sufferings, even interrupted the priest who was confessing her, by their impatience, exclaiming, "Now, priest, do you mean to make us dine here?" After she was bound to the stake, and while the flames were rising around her, she begged her confessor to hold aloft the cross, that she might still behold the sacred emblem above the smoke; and she died expressing her conviction of the truth of her mission, and calling on the name of Jesus. The cruelty exercised upon this simple and gentle maiden (for in all her battles she never killed an enemy, and was always intent on preventing the effusion of blood) is a disgrace to the annals of England. In prison she was subjected to insult, insidious treachery, and even outrage; at her trial, in the chapel of the castle, she stood alone without counsel or adviser, browbeaten by her inhuman and bloodthirsty judges, yet baffling their cunning and sophistry by her plain straightforward answers.

But one of the saddest circumstances connected with the death of the forlorn maiden of Domrémy was, that her most active enemies and eventual betrayers were *her own countrymen*: the Bishop of Beauvais, her unjust judge, her accuser, and the false priest who was introduced into her cell on the pretence of friendship as a spy to betray her secrets, were all Frenchmen. Her own countrymen allowed her to be made prisoner at Compiègne without an attempt to defend or rescue her; it was they who sold her to the English; and Charles VII., her king, who owed his country and throne to her enthusiasm, appears neither to have cared for nor remembered the heroine of Orleans, from the hour when she fell into the hands of the English. He certainly neither attempted to ransom her, nor did he *protest* against her trial.*

It was not until 24 years from her death that a papal bull proclaimed her innocence; and a cross was raised by her own countrymen, once more become masters of Rouen, on the spot where she had been bound to the stake.

The great tower of the old castle in which she was imprisoned was demolished 1780. She was shut up in a cage of iron, and her feet were fettered, yet her spirit remained unbroken; and when some English nobles came to insult her, she answered, " Je sais bien que les Anglais me feront mourir, croyant après ma mort gagner le royaume de France; mais fussent-ils cent mille *Goddams* de plus qu'à présent, ils n'auront pas ce royaume."

On one side of the market-place, within a short distance of the statue, is an ancient mansion, which the common people call Maison de la Pucelle, but properly *l'Hôtel de Bourgtheroude*, constructed at the end of the 15th and beginning of the 16th cent., by William le Roux, seigneur of Bourgtheroude, nearly at the same period as the Palais de Justice. It is built round a courtyard, and its inner wall is ornamented with a series of bas-reliefs on tablets of marble, representing the interview of the Cloth of Gold, and the procession of the two kings Henry VIII. and Francis I., attended by their suite, among whom Cardinal Wolsey is conspicuous. Above these are other sculptures of allegorical figures, and the elegant hexagonal tower is decorated with pastoral subjects.

The *Convent of St. Amand*, recently pulled down, was a building of the same age: a few curious fragments alone remain in the Rue St. Amand.

There are several Gothic fountains in various parts of the city; the most curious are those of *La Croix de Pierre*, resembling in form Waltham Cross, but erected, 1500, by the Cardinal d'Amboise; it stands in the Carrefour St. Vivien. *La Fontaine de la Crosse* is a low Gothic structure of the 15th cent., elegantly adorned with tracery.

The house in which "Le grand Corneille" (Pierre) was born, the most illustrious of the natives of Rouen, exists in Rue de la Pie, No. 4; a statue of him has been erected by his fellow-citizens on the stone bridge. Fontenelle, his nephew, author of the 'Plurality of Worlds,' resided in the Rue des Bons Enfans, No. 132-134. The composer Boieldieu was also born here, and the town has raised a statue to him on the quay facing the Bourse.

The great *Lord Chancellor Clarendon* died here, in banishment, 1674.

The Crèches—an asylum for infant children while their parents are at work—may be seen here in full operation, and deserves a visit.

The edifice called *Les Halles*, situated between the cathedral and the stone bridge, appropriated to the purpose of a cloth-hall for the sale of the manufactures of Rouen, occupies the site of the ancient palace and Vieille Tour, in which King John Lackland is said to have imprisoned and finally murdered his nephew Prince Arthur.

The structure called *Monument de St. Romain*, opposite the cloth-hall (date 1542), was the spot where, by virtue of an ancient privilege conceded by King Dagobert, the chapter of the cathedral were entitled to claim, on Ascension-day, the release of a condemned criminal, how great soever his crime. This custom was intended to

* From a masterly and most interesting memoir of Jeanne d'Arc in the Quarterly Review, vol. 79.

commemorate the circumstance of a sentenced malefactor having been the only person willing to accompany St. Romain in his dangerous encounter with the dragon (gargouille) which infested the neighbourhood of Rouen. The monster, as it turned out, did not give much trouble; it was rendered powerless by the simple act of the saint making the sign of the cross over it, and, with his stole tied round its neck, allowed itself to be led quietly into the town. The privilege was maintained down to the time of the Revolution, though latterly under considerable modifications. In the front of the house at the corner of the Rue St. Romain and Rue la Croix de Fer, a curious bas-relief of the 16th cent., representing a school, is inserted.

Bridges.—The first bridge over the Seine here was built (1167) by Queen Matilda, daughter of Henry I.; it lasted till the middle of the 15th cent., when it was destroyed, and a bridge of boats substituted for it. In 1829 the upper bridge of stone was completed, and in 1836 the boats were finally replaced by *the existing suspension bridge*. An opening is left in the centre of this, between the supporting piers, under a lofty cast-iron arch rising 82 ft. above the river, to allow masted vessels to pass.

The *cotton manufactures* of Rouen are of such extent and importance as to render it the Manchester of France; they are greatly promoted by 3 small streams—the Robec, the Aubitte, and the Reuelle. A particular kind of striped and chequed stuff is called *Rouennerie* (toiles peintes, rayées, et à carreaux), because originally and more especially fabricated here. Spinning and weaving mills, dye-works, especially of Turkey red, printing and bleaching works, are most plentifully distributed, not only through town and suburbs, but over the adjacent country in a circuit of many miles, employing, on a moderate computation, 50,000 persons.

The *English Church service* was given up 1849. There are 800 English residents here.

At the *shop of Lebrument, bookseller,* Quai de Paris, the traveller may provide himself with many interesting works relating to the antiquities of Normandy, with views and maps.

The *Poste aux Lettres* is on the Quai du Havre, near the Custom-house; open from 8 A.M. to 8 P.M.

British Vice-Consul's address, Rue d'Orléans, 34.

The *Messageries Royales* in the Rue de Bec, 10. *Messag. Lafitte and Co.*, Rue Thouret, 15.

Railroads.—To *Paris*—Terminus in the Faubourg St. Sever. (Rte. 8.)—To Havre—Terminus in the Rue Verte, on the rt. bank of the Seine, but some distance from the river. (Rte. 14.)—To Dieppe.

Diligences to Caen daily, morning and evening; to Gournay and Beauvais daily; to Elbœuf and Lisieux; to Evreux and Orléans; to Pont Audemer and Honfleur; to Amiens, Angers, and Nantes.

Steamboats to Havre in 8 hrs.; to Elbœuf (Rte. 12).

Walks and Excursions.

The *Mont St. Catherine*, the escarped chalk hill on the E. of the city, rising above the Seine and the road to Paris, affords the best distant and panoramic view of Rouen, and will well repay the labour to those who are not afraid to face a steep ascent, 380 ft. high, which may be mastered in half an hour, starting from the extremity of the Cours Dauphin. The entire mass of the town is spread out below you, surmounted by engine chimneys mixed with spires, sending out its long lines of houses and factories up the hill sides and into the neighbouring industrious valleys, uniting it with distant villages; the noble spires of the cathedral and of St. Ouen rising out of the midst, the winding and sparkling river Seine, spanned by its 2 bridges and crowded with shipping, the Railway also crossing the river, and then pursuing its mole-like course, half above, half under ground, give a pleasing variety to the landscape. The marks of active industry are everywhere apparent, the bleach-fields strewn with white webs, the stream-courses marked by rows of factories and tall chimneys, the nooks in the hill sides choked with villages.

All along the top of the mount are traces of ditches and foundations of bastions, part of the strong *Fort* occupied by the Marquis Villars and the soldiers of the League during the siege of 1591, which were captured by Henri IV., and dismantled by him in compliance with the request of the citizens, with the memorable words, that "he desired no fortress but the hearts of his subjects." This post was taken by assault, chiefly through the bravery of Henri's English allies under the Earl of Essex, who challenged Villars to maintain, in single combat, on horse or foot, in armour or doublet, that his cause was the better and his mistress the fairer.

Not far from St. Catherine's is Blosseville *Bonsecours*, whose modern Gothic *Ch.*, with painted windows, was built 1846, to contain a figure of the Virgin, much resorted to by pilgrims. It has 3 portals in the W. front: it is stone vaulted, and it cost 40,000*l*.!

It is worth while to drive out to the château of *Canteleu*, on the road to Caudebec (Rte. 13), on account of its beautiful view, even if you go no farther.

A more distant excursion, which will occupy 1 day very agreeably, is to *Château Gaillard*, near Andelys (Rte. 11). The Paris Rly. passes within 3 m. of Andelys, and is the quickest way.

There are many interesting monuments of architecture in the vicinity of Rouen, among them the *Chapelle de St. Julien*, 3 or 4 m. S.W. of Rouen, on the l. bank of the Seine (Rte. 12); *St. George Boscherville*, 9 m. off, on the road to Havre (Rte. 13).

ROUTE 9.

PARIS TO ROUEN (LOWER ROAD), BY ST. GERMAIN AND LOUVIERS.

137 kilom. = 85 Eng. m.

Only one *Diligence*, in 10 or 12 hrs.; the rest are superseded by the rly. (Rte. 8).

This road to Rouen is far more generally interesting and more picturesque in scenery than the upper one, through Gisors, but is nearly 7 m. longer than it. It is carried down the valley of the Seine, quitting the bank of the river only to avoid its excessive windings. The high road from Paris to St. Germain commences at the "star," or radiation of routes which gives a name to the *Arc de Triomphe de l'Etoile*, the largest triumphal arch in the world, and the finest entrance into the French capital. Yet the eye scarcely appreciates its vastness: few would suspect that it is nearly as wide and lofty as the façade of Nôtre Dame, or that the aperture of the arch equalled that of its nave. The road skirts on the l. the Bois de Boulogne, famous for promenades, duels, and suicides — now shorn of its proportions to form a glacis for the new fortifications.

A cross road, called Chemin de la Révolte, leading from Neuilly to St. Denis, branches off on the rt.: near the entrance of it occurred the melancholy death of the Duc d'Orléans, who was killed in jumping out of his carriage, of which the horses had run away. An elegant Byzantine *Chapel* has been built on the site of the house in which he breathed his last: it is dedicated to St. Ferdinand, and is in the form of a Greek cross. It contains a monumental cenotaph, the effigy of the prince in his uniform reclining on a bed, by M. Triquety. On a pedestal to the rt. is an angel kneeling in prayer, one of the last works of his sister the Princess Marie. The painted windows were executed at Sèvres, from Ingre's designs.

The road next passes on the rt. the ruins of the *Château de Neuilly*, the most frequented residence of King Louis-Philippe, and beyond that village crosses the Seine by the celebrated bridge of 5 arches, each of 120 ft. span, the masterpiece of the architect Perronet, built 1772. Henri IV. and his queen were dragged into the water here in their cumbrous state coach, and narrowly escaped drowning: an accident which caused the ferry to be superseded by a bridge of wood. The park of Neuilly extends for some distance down the rt. bank of the Seine, and into the islands which here divide its stream. On the l. bank is seen the village and large barrack of

9 Courbevoie. A little beyond the posthouse, our road, a perfectly straight line hitherto, separating from the Route d'en haut (Rte. 10), bends to the l. and passes the Versailles Railroad (rive droite).

Mont Valérien, on the l., converted into the *citadel* of the fortifications of Paris, is not more than 1½ m. distant from the château of Neuilly. The Church on this height, founded on the débris of one destroyed by Napoleon, contains numerous relics : among them a fragment of the true Cross (!) and the Calvary attached to it has attracted pious pilgrims for several centuries. Madame de Genlis, the preceptress of Louis Philippe, was buried in the cemetery. The aqueduct of Marly and château of St. Germain are now seen in the distance.

At Ruel the Cardinal Richelieu had a magnificent residence. The large barrack on the l. of the road was occupied in the time of the elder Bourbons by the Swiss guard. In the little church of the village, built 1584, and decorated with a portico at the cost of Cardinal Richelieu, from the designs of Lemercier, is buried the Empress Josephine. A simple monument bearing her statue kneeling, by Cartallier, has been erected by her children, Prince Eugène (Duc of Leuchtenberg), and Hortense Beauharnois (ex-Queen of Holland), mother of Louis Napoleon, who has since been buried here herself. Josephine died, May 1814, at her favourite villa, hard by Ruel, *Malmaison*. Her pleasure-grounds have been cut up to be sold in lots; her conservatory and menageries, in which she took much delight, and the Swiss dairy and Merino farm, are swept away. The spot seems to have owed its charms chiefly to art; the soil is very sterile. Buonaparte spent 5 days here in June 1815, between his second abdication and his final departure for Rochefort, having been sent out of Paris by Fouché and the provisional government.

The road skirts the enclosing wall of Malmaison for some distance, and, soon after reaching the l. bank of the Seine, passes La Chaussée, where La Belle Gabrielle had a house, and *Marly la Machine*, so called from the cumbrous pile of wooden scaffolding and wheels constructed to raise the water of the Seine 300 ft. to supply Versailles, but now partly replaced by a steam engine. The *Aqueduct* of 36 arches, the loftiest 70 ft. high, by which the water is conveyed, is a conspicuous and fine object rising against the hill. The *Château de Marly*, built by Mansard for Louis XIV., was destroyed at the Revolution, having been purchased by speculators who pulled it down to sell the materials, and nothing now remains to mark that scene of a monarch's extravagance and magnificence. St. Simon, describing its construction, relates that whole forests of full-grown trees were brought from Compiègne, ¾ths of which died and were replaced by others; large tracts of wood were suddenly converted into sheets of water, and back again to shady groves; and all to adorn a small villa in a contracted valley without view, in which Louis might pass 3 or 4 nights in the course of the year.

The pavilion of *Luciennes*, on the brow of the hill above Marly, was the last residence of the notorious Madame du Barry, mistress of Louis XV.

Le Pecq is a suburb of St. Germain, stretching down the hill, on whose summit that town is built, to the margin of the Seine.

14 St. Germain-en-Laye (see below).

RAILROAD—*Paris to St. Germain*, 19 kilom. = 12 Eng. m. The distance is performed in less than 30 min. Trains (convois) go every hour: but see the printed bills. The Terminus (Embarcadère) in Paris is in Rue St. Lazare. This rly. received injuries from the Republican mob of Feb. 1848, to the extent of 1,700,000 frs.

The first part of this line as far as 4½ Asnières Stat. is the same as the Rouen Rly. (Rte. 8).

Colombes Stat. (Rte. 8).

The high road from Paris to Rouen is crossed within a short distance of

7 Nanterre Stat., a village celebrated as the birthplace of St. Geneviève, the patron saint of Paris, who preserved it by her prayers, according to the legend, from the invasion of Attila. The chapel of the saint, at which Anne of Austria came to pray for an heir, 1636, who was born 2 years after, no longer exists. Nanterre is famed for cakes.

Ruel Stat. (p. 44).

The Seine is crossed for the second time shortly before arriving at

3½ Chatou Stat., by 2 bridges resting on an island which here divides the river. The village of Chatou lies on the rt. hand of the rly. and rt. bank of the Seine. An atmospheric branch rly. has been constructed hence to St. Germain.

3⅔ Le Pecq Stat., opposite the village of Le Pecq, which is a suburb of St. Germain, and is connected with it by a bridge of stone, erected 1835, in the place of one of wood, by which, in 1815, the Prussian army under Blücher crossed the river on its march upon Paris.

The Rly. is carried (on the atmospheric principle) across the Seine and up the slope to the centre of the *Terrace de St. Germain*, ½ m. The steep ascent, from the bridge up to the town, is surmounted also by a broad road in zigzag, while a flight of stone steps affords access for the pedestrian to the *Terrace* which runs along the brow of the hill.

St. *Germain-en-Laye Stat.*—*Inns*: H. d'Angleterre — de Toulouse — de la Chasse Royale. There is a Restaurant on the slope of the hill, au Pavillon de Henri IV.; the best, but all dear. This deserted residence of kings is interesting from historical recollections, and pleasing from the grandeur of its site; but although it contains 12,000 Inhab., it has a melancholy air of abandonment in its grass-grown streets and straggling edifices. The huge gloomy pile of the *Royal Château* itself, the favourite residence of Marguerite de Valois, Henri II., Henri IV., Francis I., and the birthplace of Charles IX. and of Louis XIV., having been gutted at the Revolution, has nothing but its souvenirs to recommend it. It looks like a prison, and is actually converted into a military penitentiary, and surrounded by a wall for security. Those who will take the trouble to seek an order of admission from the commandant (which is not readily granted) may see the chapel, the eldest part and the least impaired, the hall of Francis I., the bed-chamber of Madame de la Vallière, and the trap-door by which the youthful Louis gained entrance into it after his mother had caused the door of the backstair to be walled up; also the Oratory of James II., and the chamber in which he died, 1701. This palace was assigned to him as a residence by his host Louis XIV., who was tired of the place himself, having taken an aversion to it because it commanded a view of his destined resting-place St. Denis. James resided here 12 years, holding the semblance of a court. Part of his body, " une portion de la chair et des parties nobles du corps," was buried in the *parish church*, recently rebuilt and faced with a Doric portico, where a monument was erected to his memory by George IV.

The only real attraction in St. Germain at present is its beautiful *Terrace*, stretching along the brow of the hill for 2400 metres = 1½ m., and commanding a delightful prospect over the valley of the Seine and its windings, with the aqueduct of Marly on the rt., Château of Maisons on the l., the rlys. and the Arc de Triomphe de l'Etoile, with the spires of St. Denis rising against the horizon, in front.

The *Forest of St. Germain*, one of the largest in France, having a circuit of 21 m., occupies a promontory formed by a sweeping bend of the river Seine. It is intersected by roads offering agreeable rides and walks in all directions. In the midst of it is the Pavillon de la Meute (Dog-kennel), begun by Francis I. Deer and roes are found in the remote parts.

The name of St. Germain-en-Laye comes from a chapel and monastery of St. Germanus, built in the reign of King Robert, in the midst of the forest then called *Silva Ledia*.

Many English reside here, on account of the cheapness of living and the pure air. The *Church service* is performed on Sundays in a private room.

There are 2 roads from St. Germain to Mantes; the one called Chemin de Quarante Sous, keeping on the S. side of the Seine, is the shorter by about 5 m., but more hilly; the other, the post-road, cuts across the S. extremity of the forest to Poissy. (See Rte. 8.)

The road descends the rt. bank of the river henceforth as far as Mantes, through

11 Triel (Rte. 8).

8 Meulan (Rte. 8).

The railroad is carried along the l. bank of the Seine, and passes in the rear of Mantes, where is a station.

15 Mantes.

About half-way between Mantes and Bonnières we pass Rosny.

The rly. is carried on a lofty terrace side by side with the high road as far as Rolleboise, where it penetrates in a tunnel through a hill which the road surmounts by a steep ascent. An abrupt curve of the river, here sweeping round by the château La Roche Guyon (Rte. 11), is thus avoided. The farther extremity of the tunnel opens out close to

13 Bonnières (Rte. 8).

About 1½ m. beyond this the road to Caen and Cherbourg by Evreux (Rte. 25) separates on the l. from that to Rouen, which skirts the margin of the Seine under a shady avenue of walnut and ash trees. A small rivulet flowing into it from the S., crossed by our road, was the boundary of the ancient province of Normandy, as it now is of the department of the Eure; and 2 m. farther on we reach

11 Vernon (Rte. 8).

There is another post-road from Vernon along the rt. bank of the Seine, by Andelys (22 kilom.), and Château Gaillard (Rte. 11), Pont St. Pierre (19 kilom.), Le Forge Féret (10 kilom.), to Rouen (11 kilom.), but it is longer by 3¾ m. than the following :

14 Gaillon.

The isthmus of the peninsula formed by this curve is traversed by the rly. in a tunnel (Rte. 8).

The post-road quits the borders of the Seine before reaching Gaillon, and does not rejoin it until Pont de l'Arche is reached.

At the village Heudebouville the road to Andelys and Château Gaillard (6 m. distant) strikes off to the rt. Here also the road to Rouen divides into 2 branches; the rt.-hand one, by Vaudreuil, though shorter, is more hilly, and takes the same time to travel, so that by Louviers is preferable. Tall chimneys and numerous huge red-brick buildings with many windows proclaim the manufacturing town of

14 *Louviers* (*Inns*: H. de Rouen, dear; du Mouton, good), advantageously situated on the numerous branches of the Eure; it is one of the 3 principal clothing towns of France, the other 2 being Elbœuf and Sédan. It contains 30 cloth manufactories, and 19 spinning-mills of woollen yarn, which employ from 7000 to 8000 persons in and around the town, though the number of Inhab. does not exceed 9927. The cloth of Louviers is remarkable for its fine quality; yet the town is not prosperous, being outstripped by its rival Elbouf. Its ancient features are fast being swept away. The *Ch. of Notre Dame*, shrouded behind the number of its flying buttresses, presents a mass of incongruities and sad mutilations, yet is well worth examination. Its S. portal, projecting forwards on fringed arches, with a pendant hanging from the centre, is decked out with an exuberance of florid ornament. It was built in 1496. The W. end has 3 portals, the centre supported by a Corinthian pillar. In the inside the nave and choir date from 1218, and exhibit the transition from the round to the pointed style; low and thick columnar piers support pointed arches, on which rests a glazed triforium of round-headed trefoil arches, with lancet windows under trefoil arches in the clerestory; the aisles are more modern. The bas-reliefs, carved in wood, of sacred subjects from the life of our Saviour, and the painted glass, merit notice, as well as the open gallery of filagree stone-work under the central tower, S. side.

The Gothic house with pointed windows, called *Maison des Templiers*, is probably as old as the 13th or beginning of the 14th cent.

Coaches—to St. Pierre de Vauvray station of the Rouen and Paris Rly.

A road branches off hence to Elbœuf (Rte. 11); *coaches* thither daily.

At Vaudreuil, 3 or 4 m. to the rt. of the road to Rouen, is a modern château, surrounded by the waters of the Eure, and a fine *church* (12th cent.), with a beautiful W. window.

A considerable tract of forest is passed between Louviers and Pont de l'Arche (Rte. 8).

To avoid a long bend of the river the road is carried over a high hill, whose top commands a charming view, but on the opposite descent regains the margin of the river before

17 Port St. Ouen, and thence runs beside it, skirting the foot of the chalk hills through a series of villages and hamlets to the extensive suburb of Eauplet, which extends up to the gate of Rouen. The entrance into the town on this side is by the Cours Dauphin, a raised causeway planted with an avenue of trees, having the Seine on the l. and the Champ de Mars on the rt. hand.

11 ROUEN (see. Rte. 8).

ROUTE 10.

PARIS TO ROUEN (THE UPPER ROAD), BY GISORS OR BY MAGNY.

By Magny, 119 kilom. = 73 Eng. m. *i.e.* 6¾ m. shorter than the lower rd. (Rte. 9), but much less interesting. By Gisors, 126 kilom. = 77¼ Eng. m.

9 Courbevoie,
14 Herblay,
9 Pontoise,   } in Rte. 5.
18 Chars,
18 Gisors,

From Paris to Pontoise by St. Denis (Rte. 2) is 3 kilom. = 1¾ Eng. m. longer, but there is a Rly. to Pontoise.

At Herblay the road by St. Denis joins that by Courbevoie. It is a tiresome road from Pontoise to

14 Bord'haut, a hamlet dependent on the village of de Vigny, whose fine old *Castle*, flanked by round towers, topped with extinguisher roofs, and surrounded by a moat, stands on the l. of the road. It was built by the Cardinal d'Amboise, minister of Louis XII., and is a picturesque and interesting specimen of domestic architecture in the beginning of the 16th cent.

13 Magny.—*Inn*: Grand Cerf. In the pretty *Church*, in the latest Gothic, passing into the Italian style, is a monument, consisting of 3 marble statues kneeling, to the memory of the family of Villerond (date 1617); another in bas-relief recording the virtues of M. Dubuisson, pastor of the parish, and a richly ornamented canopy, carved, and bearing statues, which covers the baptismal font.

We now enter the district anciently called *le Vexin*. The little river Epte divided the French from the Norman Vexin, and formed the boundary of Normandy. It is crossed at St. Clair-sur-Epte, whose ruined *Castle*, a mixture of late Norman and early pointed, is reputed the scene of the interview between Charles the Simple and the pirate Rollo; when the barbarian conqueror, called upon to do homage for the fertile province of Normandy, which he had in fact wrung from the weakness of the Frankish king, instead of kneeling to kiss the king's foot, seized the royal leg, and without bending carried it to his mouth, so as to upset the monarch from his seat, amidst the laughter of the rude warriors of the north.

The Epte is crossed on quitting St. Clair.

17 Thilliers-en-Vexin, in the midst of a monotonous plain of rich corn-land. Near the middle of this stage the road passes, at some distance on the rt., a village called Hacqueville, insignificant in itself, but deserving mention as the birthplace of the late *Mark Isambart Brunel*, the engineer of the Thames Tunnel, whom England is proud to own as her son by adoption, although France claims him by birth. He was educated in the college of Gisors, and when the vacations called him home his favourite resort was the shop of the village carpenter, whose tools and instruments had greater at-

tractions for the youthful engineer than Latin and Greek, and his allotted holiday task (devoirs). The writer of this has frequently heard him describe the wonder and delight with which he for the first time beheld (1784), on the quay of Rouen, the component parts of a huge steam-engine, just landed from England: "When I am a man," he said to himself, "I will repair to the country where such machinery is made."

15 Ecouis contains a fine Gothic *Church*, on the unusual plan of a Greek cross, founded by Enguerrand de Marigny, the unfortunate minister and high treasurer of Philippe le Bel, unjustly condemned to death without trial at the instigation of the succeeding king's uncle, Charles of Valois, and hung on the robbers' gibbet of Montfaucon. His monument, set up in this church at a time when his innocence and worth were acknowledged, was destroyed at the Revolution. That of his brother, Archbishop of Rouen, is still surmounted by his effigy in white marble. He went as ambassador to Edward III. in 1342, "and appeared at court in the guise of a warrior, not of a minister of peace." There are several other tombstones in the choir.

A rapid ascent and descent carries the road across the industrious and picturesque vale of the Andelle, in the midst of which is

9 Fleury-sur-Andelle. About 10 m. N.E. of this, and 2 from Lions la Forêt, are the ruins of the *Abbey of Mortemer*, begun 1154 by Henry II. of England. The church is pulled down; but some of the conventual buildings in the style of transition from round to pointed — including a fine *chapter-house* (date 1174) — remain. It was at Bourg-boudouin that Roland, the ex-minister and Girondist, committed suicide, 1793. As soon as he heard of his wife's death by the guillotine, he resolved not to survive her; but unwilling to endanger the generous friends who had sheltered him in their house at Rouen, he took leave of them, and, carrying a sword-stick in his hand, set out on the road to Paris. When he had got thus far, he sat down under a tree and stabbed himself, leaving about his person a note, written by his own hand, to this effect: "Whoever you may be who find me lying here, treat my remains with respect. They are those of one who devoted his whole life to be useful, and who died as he lived, virtuous and unsullied. May my fellow-citizens embrace more humane sentiments! When I heard of the death of my wife, I loathed a world stained with so many crimes." He perished an instance of the miserable fate which unerringly awaits those who, either from good or evil motives, are the first to plunge a country into revolution.

12 La Forge Féret.

From the brow of the steep hill leading down through deep cuttings into Rouen, a fine view is obtained of that city and the Seine. The upper and lower roads from Paris unite in the suburb Eauplet.

11 ROUEN (Rte. 8).

ROUTE 11.

THE SEINE, A.—ST. GERMAIN TO ROUEN.

The figures mark distances from place to place in French lieues = $2\frac{1}{2}$ Eng. m. From St. Germain to Rouen is 56 leagues, about 140 Eng. m.

The steam navigation has been abandoned in consequence of the completion of the Railway (Rte. 8).

The scenery of the Seine (*Sequana*, —from the Celtic *seach*, devious, and *an*, water) is very pleasing, almost meriting the epithet "beautiful;" its banks are abundantly studded with towns, villages, and châteaux, and are alternately wooded, or rise in round bare hills, sometimes presenting escarpments to the river, which, from the white colour of the chalk, are not altogether picturesque. There are not many *old* castles — Château Gaillard, however, is an imposing and interesting ruin, and perhaps, taken as a whole, the finest feature in the voyage. The number of islands in the river between Paris and Rouen is said to be 300. The circuitous windings of the river prolong the distance from Pecq to Rouen to 141 m., while by land it is only 71 m.

NORMANDY. *Route 11.—The Seine, A.—La Roche Guyon.* 49

Between St. Germain (or Pecq) and Poissy the river makes a bend of 21 m., enclosing as it were in a loop the forest of St. Germain (p. 45); by land the distance is 4½ m.

l. The river skirts the forest of St. Germain, passing Mesnil at the extremity of the terrace of St. Germain and the village. The Seine has been bridged to allow the rly. to pass at

l. Maisons (1). Rte. 8.

rt. Conflans (2½), a village having a suspension-bridge over the Seine, by which the road from Pontoise to Versailles crosses the river, is situated a little below the *confluence* of the Oise with the Seine, whence comes its name.

rt. Andresis is situated below the mouth of the Oise; it has a fine Gothic church.

l. Poissy (1¾); see Rte. 8. Poissy is not more than 5 m. by land from St. Germain, whereas by the windings of the river the voyage takes 1½ or 2 hrs. The most interesting objects on the river as far as Rosny and Rolleboise are described Rte. 8.

rt. Triel (2¼).

l. Verneuil.

rt. Meulan (2).

The island Ile Belle, opposite Meulan, is reputed the prettiest in the whole course of the river; but it is feared its shrubberies, and thickets, and plantations have been cut down.

l. Mantes (4¾), and rt. Limay, united by a bridge.

l. The Château of Rosny (½), a red brick building, with terraces on which Sully may have walked, clipped avenues, &c.

l. Rolleboise (½); between this place and Bonnières the curve made by the Seine measures 12 m., the direct distance is 3 m.

rt. La Roche Guyon (3½), one of the largest châteaux on the Seine, and one of the most striking objects, is a structure of different ages, part modern, part Gothic, situated at the base of a rock of chalk, which has been escarped artificially to make room for it. The kitchen, vaults, cellars, &c., are excavated in the rock, with merely fronts of brick. The oldest part is the tower on the eminence above, commanding the country far and near, and communicating with the château by steps cut in the hill side. On the summit of the hill is a large reservoir for water, excavated out of the rock. The château, long the property of the La Rochefoucaulds, now belongs to the family of Rohan. François de Bourbon, Comte d'Enghien, who gained the battle of Cérisoles, was killed here by a box thrown out of the castle window upon his head. The chamber and bed occupied by Henri IV. on his frequent visits to the castle are kept in their original condition. The attraction which drew him hither was the charms of the lady of the castle, the Marquise de Guercheville, whose high-minded reply to his assiduities deserves recording: "Je ne suis pas d'assez bonne maison pour être votre femme, mais je suis de trop bonne maison pour *être votre maitresse.*" The bourg adjoining the castle has a handsome Gothic church. "The houses of the poor people here, as on the Loire in Touraine, are burrowed into the chalk, and have a singular appearance; here are 2 streets of them, one above another."—*A. Young.* A *Suspension Bridge,* of 656 ft. opening between the piers, has been thrown across the Seine here.

l. Bonnières (1½).

rt. Limetz, a village at a little distance from the river, nearly marks the situation of the embouchure of the Epte, a small stream, which once formed the boundary or *limit* of Normandy. Charles the Simple, in 911, was fain to offer to the Norman Rollo all the territory extending from this streamlet to the sea, and with it his fair daughter Gisela, to arrest the exterminating inroads of the warriors of the North. The offer was accepted; and Neustria, receiving the name of its conquerors, became *Normandy.*

l. Vernon (2½), Rte. 8.

rt. The hills which border the river, with nearly precipitous cliffs, have a singularly wavy outline, their curved tops being saddled, as it were, with green turf, while between them dry valleys or coombes open out. They rise in the form of an amphitheatre, encircling an extensive plain. Nearly at the centre of the curve which the

France.   D

Seine here describes, on the summit of a commanding chalk cliff, rises

rt. *Château Gaillard* (6), the most picturesque ruin and interesting object, both from its situation and associations, in the lower course of the Seine. Immediately below its frowning antique towers and crumbling crags, a light and convenient wire suspension bridge has been thrown over the river.

The castle was begun and finished in one year by King Richard Cœur de Lion, in defiance of his rival Philippe Augustus, and in the face of the treaty of Louviers, by which he had bound himself not to fortify Andelys, the little town on the strand at the river side. He thus broke it in substance, while he kept to the letter. Exulting in his stronghold, as he first looked down from its commanding battlements on the defenceless town and exposed river below him, he named it, in the pride of his heart, his "Saucy Castle." Even now that it is reduced to a mouldering ruin, one cannot look up to its towering battlements, or gaze down from them upon the sunny landscape below —the glassy Seine flowing close at the foot of the castle rocks, then girdling the peninsula in front, and reflecting vine and corn clad slopes, trees, spires, and cottages in its surface—without sharing in this feeling of exultation of the fierce soldier king, in the possession of a stronghold which enabled him to defy his enemies, and overawe the country around, with the terror of his armed bands and unerring archers.

The eminence on which it stands projects forward, isolated from the neighbouring hills on all sides but one, where it is connected by a narrow tongue. This was cut through by a deep fosse skirting the outer line of wall. On all the other sides steep escarpments rendered the height inaccessible; towards the river, indeed, it presents a vertical precipice. Yet even along the edge of the cliff tall flanking towers were raised, some of which have long since toppled over, while others are tottering to their fall. But these were only the outworks; within them rose a citadel of singular form and strength,—a huge circular drum tower, having a wavy surface alternately projecting and receding, like a frustum of a fluted column. The circle is broken by the insertion of a round tower shaped externally like a dice-box on the side overhanging the Seine. This was the *Donjon*, and contained the royal apartments; its walls are 14 or 15 ft. thick. A second deep fosse surrounds this citadel, cut in the chalk rock, here interspersed with flints which were used in the building, and thus it served at once as quarry and defence. Extensive caverns, supported by piers of the rock left standing, branch off from one side of this fosse; they probably were used as stables. The original gateway into the citadel is no longer accessible, but entrance may be gained by clambering through a small sallyport in the corner. It is to be feared that only a small part of the existing ruins belonged to the castle of King Richard. At his death Philippe Augustus, waging war as the champion of Prince Arthur with John, laid siege to this castle. It was bravely defended by Roger de Lacy for 6 months, when he was finally starved into surrender. He had previously expelled from its walls the useless mouths, the old men, women, and children, to the number of 400 or 500; but the French king, wishing to distress the garrison, drove them back and refused them passage, so that the poor wretches, denied admittance into the castle, perished of famine in the ditches between the two armies. Château Gaillard continued to be the chief bulwark of Normandy down to 1606, when Henri IV. demolished it along with other castles as dangerous to the Royal authority. In 1314 two frail queens were immured within its walls, and one of them, Marguerite, wife of Louis X., was strangled here by order of her husband. David Bruce found an asylum here 1334, when an exile from Scotland, the castle having been ceded to him by Philippe of Valois. With a small garrison of 120 men it resisted for 16 months the forces of Henry V., and yielded at length because cut off from a supply of water by the wearing out of the ropes by which the buckets were let down into the well!

Against the face of the cliff above the Seine rises a curious pigeon-house tower, lined with cells for the pigeons, a common appendage to ancient fortresses, being a sort of natural larder. A chapel of recent date has been excavated in the rock near it.

The suspension bridge over the Seine beneath the castle opens a communication with Louviers (12 m.), rt. Below the castle rock crouches the town of Petit Andelys (no Inn); the large and conspicuous red building, surmounted by a dome at the lower end of it, is an *Hospital* founded by the Duc de Penthièvre.

Grand Andelys (*Inn*, Cerf, dear; the house is a curious and picturesque specimen of domestic Gothic architecture within and without; it was the residence of the Archbishop of Rouen, Pierre Harley, temp. Henri IV.). This town of 5000 Inhab. lies about 1 m. inland away from the Seine. The *Gothic ch.*, somewhat in decay, curiously Italianized on its N. side, contains some painted glass, and a rude representation of the neighbouring Château Gaillard carved in stone. It has many rich details, including a fine oriel. Turnebus, the Greek commentator, was a native of Andelys. The hamlet Villers, 3½ m. from this, was the birth-place (1594) of *Nicolas Poussin*, the painter; but the humble cottage of his parents is pulled down. A monument was set up to his memory (1851) in the market-place of Great Andelys. In the *Mairie* is a picture by him—Coriolanus among the Volsci, receiving his mother and wife.

La Fontaine de Ste. Clothilde alone recalls to mind the monastery founded here by the first Christian queen of France. It is swept away, but the water of the well is believed by the peasantry still to retain the virtues imparted to it by the royal saint, and to cure their children of stomachaches.

Andelys is about 4 m. distant from the railroad (Rte. 8). There is a direct post-road to Rouen by Pont St. Pierre; it is traversed daily by a diligence.

The Seine, leaving behind the white crags and towering ruins of Château Gaillard, makes a wide sweep along the base of a series of semicircular chalk cliffs. This curve of the river is 18 m. long, while the direct distance from (rt.) Thuit to the mouth of the Andelle is only 8 m. There is no place worth notice on the Seine between these two points. The railway emerges from a tunnel near (rt.) Venables, and skirts the river.

rt. (5¼). The pretty and industrious valley of the Andelle opens out into the Seine at the foot of a green hill, "the last of a long promontory," bearing the name of *Côte des Deux Amans*. It is the scene of the old romantic *Lai* of Mary of France—of the young lover who was to marry the mistress of his heart, a king's daughter, provided he could carry her to the top of the hill without stopping to rest. He fell dead under his precious burthen, exhausted with the exertion, just as he reached the summit; at which the king's daughter died of a broken heart, and was buried in the same grave with him. The hardhearted father, who had caused this catastrophe by imposing such cruel conditions, struck with remorse, founded on the spot where it occurred a convent whose existence is traced to an early period, but the building now standing on the top of the hill is not older than 1685.

At Romilly, 8 m. up the valley of the Andelle, are the most extensive copperworks in France, consisting of a foundry with rolling-mills. The banks of the Andelle are studded with fulling-mills. A bridge has been thrown across for the rly. a little above the influx of

l. The Eure, from which the Dept. is named, a considerable and useful river, on which stands Louviers, famed for its cloth manufacture (Rte. 9). The Eure falls into the Seine 2½ m. above

l. 3¼ Pont de l'Arche (Rte. 8). This town is only 12 m. from Rouen; whilst, in consequence of several serpentine bends, the distance by water is 33. The Seine abounds in islands in this part of its course, which increase the intricacies of the navigation.

l. A little below the bridge stand the remains of the Abbey of *Bon Port*, consisting of the refectory, and another monastic edifice, the ch. being quite destroyed. It was founded 1119 by Richard Cœur de Lion, in gratitude for his escape from drowning in the waters of the Seine, into which he had plunged in the heat of the chace while pursuing a stag. On reaching the bank, after a severe struggle with the current, he called the spot "bon port," and vowed to build a ch. The approach to the town of Elbœuf is marked by the number of tall chimneys, and the many floating arks moored in the midst of the river, used for washing wool.

1. *Elbœuf*, 3.

Elbœuf is exclusively a manufacturing town, and, if Rouen has any claim to be compared to Manchester, it may be called a French Leeds, as one of the principal seats of the manufacture of cloth; more than half of its 15,000 Inhab. and about 20,000 persons in the adjoining communes being weavers, or occupied in other departments of this branch of industry. Its situation on the l. bank of the Seine is advantageous to its prosperity. The wise enactments of the sage Colbert (1669) promoted greatly its already thriving commerce; but the revocation of the Edict of Nantes annulled their good effect, dispersing its industrious artisans, who settled in Leyden, Norwich, and Leicester. The manufactures of Elbœuf did not recover from this check until the events of 1815, relieving France from the competition of Belgium, gave them so decided an impulse that their produce is now threefold greater than it was then. The value of the cloth made here in one year is estimated at more than a million sterling.

The two Gothic *churches* of *St. Etienne* and *St. Jean* contain curious painted glass; in the latter is a window presented by the clothworkers' guild somewhere about 1466, in which various implements of the craft, such as shears and teasels, are introduced.

The working classes are generally industrious and economical, and are consequently far better off than those of Rouen.

Steamers 3 times a-day to Rouen.

1. The *Rocks of Orival*, a range of chalk cliffs beginning at Elbœuf, consisting of detached pinnacles and projecting shelves, formed by the hard flint layers enclosed in the rock, present a singular outline of fantastic forms. On a platform half way up their face a small chapel has found a niche; it is partly excavated in the rock, so are likewise many small dwellings around it. One of these needles of chalk, called Roche de Pignon, rises 200 ft. above the river. The Rouen Rly. crosses the river and an island in the midst of it at an oblique angle near Oissel.

rt. From Oissel ($2\frac{1}{2}$), marked by its spire, to Rouen the river is thickly set with islands bearing long rows of tall poplars. Beyond (rt.) Authieux the rt. bank rises in tall chalk cliffs, at the base of which, between them and the Seine, runs the road to Paris (Rte. 9), passing a series of villages and manufactories.

l. St. Etienne de Rouvray, $1\frac{1}{2}$. Wm. the Conqueror was hunting in the forest of Rouvray, which still exists behind this village, when the news was brought him of the death of Edward the Confessor, and of the usurpation of his throne by Harold, his brother-in-law.

rt. The high hill of St. Catherine (p. 42) and the spire of the Cathedral are conspicuous long before reaching

2 rt. ROUEN (Rte. 8).

ROUTE 12.

THE SEINE, B.—ROUEN TO HAVRE AND HONFLEUR.

34 leagues = $85\frac{1}{2}$ Eng. m. The distance to Havre by land is 53 m.

Steamers daily in summer, making the voyage in about 8 hours, *i. e.* a little longer time than the *diligence*.

The opening of the *Rly.* to *Havre* (Rte. 14) will probably put a stop to the steamers.

The scenery is so pleasing, that, notwithstanding the windings of the river, the voyage in fine weather is very agreeable.

The *places* where the steamers stop for passengers are marked by Italics.

The hour of starting varies so as to enable the vessels to meet the flood tide off Quillebœuf, and by the aid of it to pass the shifting sands there. The boats start from the Quai du Havre close to the Hôtel de Rouen. Fare 10 fr., carriages 30 fr.

For some distance below Rouen the river is intersected by numerous islands, long narrow strips of earth planted with willows and poplars: a scene of rich verdure, but somewhat monotonous. The hills near Rouen are dotted with white country houses of its citizens and manufacturers.

rt. The vale of Bapaume, beset with cotton factories, opens out.

l. Petit Quevilly (3 m. from Rouen). Here is an ancient little chapel of *St. Julien* in the Romanesque style, terminating in an apse having the windows and doors roundheaded, built soon after 1162 by our Henry II., who had a hunting-seat in the adjoining forest. Though now degraded into a barn, it is an edifice possessing an interest for the antiquary.

rt. Canteleu, a château of the time of Louis XIV.; its terraces and gardens were laid out by Le Nôtre, but have been modernised.

rt. Dieppedale, a long row of houses bordering the river.

l. Grand Quevilly once contained a Protestant ch. (temple) capable of holding 10,500 persons; but in 1685, through the machinations of the Jesuits, it was closed, and a few months after razed to the ground. This act of intolerance was committed shortly before the revocation of the Edict of Nantes entailed persecution and exile on the large and industrious Reformed community which then occupied this district.

l. *Moulineaux* (4), a prettily situated but poor village, on the high road to Honfleur (Rte. 23), has a ruinous but interesting ch. in the earliest pointed style; date the beginning of the 13th cent. On the hill above it are some heaps of stone, the very scanty traces of the walls of a *castle* destroyed by King John, which, according to the tradition, once belonged to *Robert the Devil*, a fabulous personage, a sort of Norman Blue Beard, who murdered his friends and mistresses, and in the end sold himself to the evil one. Some suppose him to have been Duke Robert, the father of William the Conqueror.

l. Near *La Bouille* and Caumont are extensive quarries of building-stone. Bare yellow cliffs line the river for some distance.

rt. St. George de Boscherville. This famous abbey stands at some distance from the Seine, near the Havre road (Rte. 13), and is only just visible from the river.

The Seine makes a bend 18 m. long between Rouen and this point; in a direct line they are not more than 10 m. apart.

rt. *Duclair* (5½), a pretty village traversed by the road to Havre (Rte. 13), squeezed in between the river and the rocks, one of which, an elevated crag, goes by the name of *la Chaire de Gargantua*. The rt. bank again sweeps round to the S., its elevated slopes covered with hanging woods.

rt. It is recorded that at the little hamlet of Mesnil, Agnes Sorel, mistress of Charles VII., breathed her last, in the arms of the king. An old building is still pointed out as her abode; it retains its chimneys of the 15th cent. It was called Mesnil la Belle; it is now a labourer's cottage. The l. bank below Mesnil has risen into round hills of considerable height, part bare, part wooded; houses few, and scenery solitary. To this succeeds on the rt. a plain, verdant and bosky, formed into a peninsula by the winding river, out of the midst of which rise the now spireless twin towers of Jumièges Abbey (p. 56).

l. The *Château de Mailleraye* (7½), situated at the water's edge, below the village of Guerbaville, where there is a large shipbuilder's yard, belongs to the Duc de Mortemart. It is an edifice of the 17th cent., in a park surrounded by green walls of straight clipped trees, and is a conspicuous object from the river, but not otherwise worth notice.

Below Mailleraye the river expands considerably, and its channel begins to be beset with the sand-banks which render its navigation so difficult, leaving only a narrow passage in the middle free.

rt. *Caudebec* (2¼), the most considerable and prettily situated town on the banks of the Lower Seine; its long terrace of houses, screened by an avenue of green trees, and surmounted by its elegant church spire, was a favourite subject of the landscape painter Vernet. It is described at p. 57.

rt. An humble structure at the foot of the steep wooded heights below Caudebec is the chapel of Notre Dame de Barre-y-va, much resorted to by sailors, who have covered its walls with ex-votos, paintings, models of ships, &c. The name probably comes from the circumstance of the much-dreaded Barre, or Bore, at the mouth of the Seine, ascending at times thus far.

rt. *Villiquier*, prettily placed, and forming an agreeable intermixture of trees and houses surmounted by a Gothic spire, is a fishing village and station of the pilots whose duty it is to carry vessels between this point and Mailleraye.

l. Vatteville la Rue.

The Seine, which has run nearly due S. from Caudebec, resumes its proper direction from E. to W. below Vieux Port, and preserves the same as far as its mouth. Its banks, retiring to a considerable distance from each other, allow it to expand into a wide but shallow estuary, frequently enlivened by large shipping, tug steamers (remorqueurs), &c.

l. *Quillebœuf*, an important town and small seaport which Henri IV. wanted to convert into a fortress, but which his widow Marie de Medicis dismantled, is built on a projecting promontory, at the extremity of which stands its massive church tower and lighthouse. It is the station of the pilots to the number of 110, with 28 apprentices (aspirants), whose duty it is to carry vessels through the intricate navigation of the mouth of the Seine, from Havre and Honfleur up to Villiquier.

This is the most difficult and dangerous portion of the whole river for vessels, on account of the sunk rocks and shifting sands, only to be passed during high tide. Shipwrecks occurred here almost every year before the introduction of steam towage, which, by enabling vessels to pass up, even when the wind is unfavourable, has diminished the delay and risk. So variable are the sand-banks off Quillebœuf that they have been known to change their position more than a league in the course of twelve months: this indeed occurred in 1840. The cause of this must be looked for in the sudden contraction of the river at this point to about ¾ m., while a little below it is 3 m. wide. The consequence is that the vast mass of water poured into the Seine by the rising tide forms capricious and powerful currents, and very commonly enters the river in the form of a lofty wave or wall of water, 3 to 6 ft. high, here called the *Barre*, and similar to the *Bore* at the mouth of the Severn. It stretches across from one bank to the other, marked by a line of white foam, sweeping all before it with a roar like thunder, heard forty minutes before it arrives. It seems to acquire the greatest force abreast of Quillebœuf, where it dashes over the quays, hurling vessels against them, and sometimes injuring the buildings, but it is perceived as high as Caudebec.

The still water produced at the point where the rising tide encounters the descending current allows the sand and mud, carried along by the river when in rapid motion, to fall to the bottom, and accumulate into shifting deposits of sand. Among these sand-banks the "Télémaque," a vessel said to have been laden with property belonging to émigrés, and with jewels of the Bourbon princes, was lost at the time of the Revolution. A recent attempt to raise the hull failed.

rt. Through the vista of the valley of the Bolbec, which opens out opposite Quillebœuf, a glimpse is obtained of the castle towers of *Lillebonne*, celebrated for its remains of a Roman theatre (p. 58).

rt. The opening of another small valley is marked on one side by a conspicuous conical white rock called Pierre Gante (? Géante), overhanging the Seine at a height of 200 ft., and on the other by the *Castle of Tancarville*, the venerable stronghold of the chamberlains of the Dukes of Normandy, planted on a pedestal of high cliff forming part of the headland called Nez de Tancarville. To the water-side it presents an open terrace, on which stands a modern mansion, with sash windows, and a tall watchtower, round on one side, and angular like a bastion on the other. Behind stretch two long lines of varied and stately towers connected by curtains forming a large triangular enclosure, once the castle courts, now grass-grown and encumbered with ruins. The country behind it is one dense forest, over which these ancient battlements peer majestically. The best-preserved portions are the gatehouse with caged windows, and grooves for double portcullis, and the contiguous tower dating from the latter half of the 15th cent. Here, within walls 9 ft. thick, may be seen the "cachots"— and the "chambre de question" which is frequently mentioned in the old archives. In the corner tower (l'Aigle), on the brow of the cliff overhanging the Seine, one or two old wallpieces, so constructed as to be loaded from the breech, are preserved. In this part only of the old castle do roofs and floors remain. All the rest is mere shattered walls, gutted towers, enclosures dark and overgrown with nettles and hemlock, which now luxuriate on the hearths of the Tancarville, Montmorencys, Harcourts, and La Tours d'Auvergne, its ancient owners. The chapel and the Salle des Chevaliers, with 3 fireplaces, are pointed out to strangers. The loftiness of some of the towers, and their singular form, deserve notice: the Tour de Lion is the segment of a circle; the Tour Coquisart, 60 ft. high, of 5 stories piled one over the other, and still surmounted by the stone-groined ribs of its roof, while all the rest is fallen, is in the shape of a triangle with curved sides. It communicates behind with the *Donjon*, which was detached from the body of the place and entered only by a drawbridge. It contains a well 300 ft. deep. The date of its construction is the early part of the 15th cent., and scarcely any portion of the castle seems older. The English under Henry V. burned down the preceding one 1437. The modern mansion is tumbling to pieces as fast as possible. From the noble owners whose names are mentioned above, Tancarville fell into the hands of Law of Lauriston, the South Sea schemer. It was plundered and demolished at the Revolution as the property of aristocrats and émigrés (the Montmorencys); but after having been for 20 years attached to a hospital at Havre, it has once more reverted to that family. The poor small hamlet of fishers' huts beneath the castle affords no tolerable accommodation for travellers. The distance from Lillebonne is 6 m., and from St. Romain on the road to Havre (Rte. 14) about 12 m.

Below this the banks of the Seine are too distant and destitute of objects of interest to need further notice, excepting the towns and ports of

rt. HARFLEUR, in Rte. 14.

l. *Honfleur*, described in Rte. 23.

Passengers can be put ashore here, where they can take the *diligence* to Caen. It is about 7 m. across to

rt. HAVRE, in Rte. 14.

ROUTE 13.

ROUEN TO HAVRE—LOWER ROAD, BY ST. GEORGE BOSCHERVILLE, JUMIÈGES, CAUDEBEC, AND LILLEBONNE.

86 kilom = 53¼ Eng. m.

Diligences have ceased to run.

Although the *Railroad* from Rouen to Havre (Rte. 14) is the quickest way, yet the following rte. is one of the most agreeable in Normandy, both for the pleasing view of the Seine which it commands, and for the succession of ancient ecclesiastical remains in the vicinity of which it passes. It is, however, hilly. A little way beyond the industrious cotton-spinning village of Bapaume, it surmounts the long and steep hill of Canteleu, fro whose top Rouen is seen to very great advantage, and the Seine winding away S. to double the ridge of which the hill of Canteleu forms a part. On the

l. is the *Château of Canteleu*, belonging to M. Elie Lefebure, which commands the view in perfection, and about 2 m. beyond it a road turning off to the l. leads to the *Abbey of St. George de Boscherville*, whose *Church* is one of the most ancient and unaltered monuments in Normandy. It was founded by Raoul de Tancarville, chamberlain of the Conqueror, previous to the Conquest, and consecrated in the founder's presence. From the precision with which its age is fixed, it has been termed "a landmark of Norman architecture;" as usual, it was destroyed at the Revolution, but the church was preserved for the use of the parish. It has the usual characteristics—vast proportions, simplicity, and austere grandeur. Its W. end has a round door ornamented with 5 mouldings, and 2 side towers, in whose upper story the pointed arch of a very early date appears. This may have been the part of the church last finished. The vaulting of the nave and transepts is also pointed, all the rest is Norman; the arches are carried round the ends of the transepts, forming 2 lofts or tribunes supported on a column, and there is an apse at the E. end of each, as in Winchester Cathedral, the older part of which is very like this church. The *Chapter-house* adjoining is of later date, 1157, and of mixed architecture, both round and pointed arches occurring in it. The capitals of its columns, sculptured with subjects in relief, such as the Passage of the Jordan and the Sacrifice of Isaac, merit notice.

Returning to the high road, you descend to the borders of the Seine, on which is situated the village and post-station.

20 Duclair (6 m. from St. George's), a row of houses between the river and the cliffs, one of which, from a supposed resemblance to a pulpit, is called *Chaire de Gargantua*.

The Seine once more takes a widely curving sweep, while the high road cuts across the neck of the peninsula. In the midst of this the twin towers of the *Abbey* of *Jumièges* are conspicuous. A cross road turns off to it near Yainville, whence it is about 2 m. distant.

It was the most important monastic institution on the banks of the Lower Seine for its extent, the number of its inmates, and its share in promoting learning during the dark ages, and it now towers venerable and majestic above the humble timber-framed and chalk-walled cottages of the village. It has been compared with some of the Romanesque churches of the Rhine in its plain but stately W. façade, surmounted by octagonal towers which have only recently lost their spires but between them the porch projects in an unusual manner. This and th entire nave as far as the cross, surmounted by a more massive central tower, one side of which only remains standing, is of unchanged early Norman (date 1067). The round arches are supported alternately on square piers and circular columns; their capitals, destitute of any sculpture, were ornamented with painted foliage, some traces of which still remain. The interior is in a state of ruin, entirely roofless, save a small fragment of vaulting in the aisles, and open to the rains of heaven; greensward supplies the place of pavement; the E. end, which was in the pointed style of the 13th cent., has been razed to its foundations. For the origin of this dilapidation the Revolution has to answer, but its consummation is of very recent date, this ancient and interesting fabric having been absolutely quarried and carted away to build barns with its masonry. The stone employed is a hard chalk enclosing flints, which are frequently exposed in the courses of the piers. The present owner fortunately has respect for the ruins, and watches over their preservation, having fitted up the old gatehouse for his residence. A number of curiously and rudely sculptured fragments, keystones, bas-reliefs, &c., have been discovered by him, and merit notice. Beneath a plain black marble slab, fractured into several pieces, and lying in a corner, was once deposited the heart of "Agnes Seurelle (Sorel), Dame de Breauté." She died near this, at Mesnil, and Charles VII., her royal lover, had apartments fitted up in the abbey in order to be near her. She was a benefactress to Jumièges, and the monks retained her heart, though her body was interred at Loches in Touraine. Breauté was the name of one of her domains; some have read the inscription erroneously " Dame de *Beauté*." Here also another mutilated monument has been brought to light. It consists of mutilated effigies of youths in royal garbs, with circlets on their heads, known by the name of "*les Enervés*" (*i. e.* the hamstrung), from a tradition that they represent the two sons of Clovis II., who, having rebelled and waged war against their father, suffered the cruel punishment of having the sinews of their arms and legs cut. They were then bound and set adrift in an open boat on the Seine, whose current wafted them down as far as Jumièges, where they were kindly received by the monks, and ended their days. On the S. side of the ch. are remains of the chapel of *St. Pierre*, a pointed work of the 14th cent.; and of a large vaulted apartment called " Salle des Gardes de Charles VII.," parallel with which runs a very extensive range of subterranean vaults, probably cellars, and the gatehouse.

The high road beyond Yainville and Le Trait is carried on a lofty terrace along the shoulders of the hills, commanding a most pleasing view of the windings of the Seine both upwards and down. Nearly in front the intervening slopes are covered with orchards and gardens, and on the opposite bank stands the *Château of Mailleraye*, a conspicuous and large edifice (Rte. 12). At the little village Caudebecquet, about 3 m. before reaching Caudebec, a road turning to the rt. leads in 1½ m. to another monastic ruin, of inferior interest to the other two, but of great antiquity, *St. Wandrille*, founded by the saint of that name in the 7th cent., and at first called Fontanelle. Here may be seen some elegant pointed arches, sole relics of a *church* sold and pulled down at the Revolution for building-materials. The conventual buildings, a palace in extent, are in the modern Italian architecture of the 16th or 17th cent., and have been converted partly into a manufactory of Jacquerie, partly into a bark warehouse and mill. The *Cloisters* behind them contain several arches, rich morceaux of flamboyant Gothic, and a Lavatory, with a few relics of sculpture, becoming fewer every day through wanton mutilation. Part of the Refectory is Norman, and lined with a circular arcade.

The good judgment of the monks is very conspicuous in the choice of the site for this convent, a nook shut out from the world in a side valley of the Seine, fertile, well watered, and wooded. St. Wandrille now stands a monument of the fall of ecclesiastic pomp and wealth. The hill side to the N. was terraced to form gardens and shady walks, now grown wild. On the top of the height above them is a little chapel of St. Saturnin, an early Norman structure (11th cent.), with 3 apses and windows like loopholes and walls of herring-bone masonry, many centuries older than any part of the convent below. St. Wandrille is about 4 m. from

16 Caudebec.—*Inns:* Poste; H. du Commerce, not very clean, but tolerable. This is one of the prettiest little antiquated towns on the Seine, with its quay and terrace along the waterside, shaded by trimmed elms, forming a screen before the row of houses which face the river. The old wooden buildings in the heart of it have been scarcely at all modernized, and are highly picturesque. In its outskirts the hills are dotted with neat villas and country seats. Its only remarkable edifice is its *Church*, a beautiful Gothic building in the florid style of the 15th cent., in the form of a parallelogram without transepts. It is surmounted by a tower having a short steeple of open stonework, the flamboyant tracery in it taking the form of fleurs-de-lis. Its flying buttresses and variously patterned parapets are very elegant. It was begun 1426, and stands at the side of the church. In the W. end, the gorgeous triple *portal*, with side porches bent back, all exuberantly ornamented with

D 3

carved foliage, statues, and niches, and the rose window above, merit notice. Also the N. porch.

Within, there is much fine painted glass of the 16th cent., and a wooden cover to the font, well carved in relief with subjects from the life of Christ. The spaces between the buttresses are occupied by small chapels; those at the E. end expand, and the central one, the Lady Chapel, behind the high altar, is distinguished by a finely groined roof, the ribs of which descend in the centre to form a *pendant of stone*, 14 ft. long, ending in a carved boss, or cul de lampe. In the next chapel of St. Sepulchre is a group of 8 figures, as large as life, representing the holy personages at the tomb of our Lord, under a florid Gothic canopy. The master mason of the church, William Le Tellier, is buried in the Lady Chapel: he was employed on it 30 years, down to his death, 1484, and in that time completed the upper part of the nave, the choir and chapels around it, including the Lady Chapel and its pendant.

The artist will find, in penetrating the dirty streets of the town, some picturesque bits among its timber-framed houses.

Caudebec was anciently a strong fortress; it was taken 1419 by the English, under Talbot and Warwick; and, during the wars of religion, Alexander Farnese, Duke of Parma, commander of a Spanish force sent in aid of the League, lost his arm in reconnoitring the ramparts, 1592. They have been long since swept away.

About 1½ m. up the valley, near the road which goes to Yvetot (Rte. 14), stands the *Church of St. Gertrude*, repaired 1841: it merits notice for its architecture, Gothic of the 16th cent., its stone tabernacle, and painted glass.

The Havre road beyond Caudebec quits the borders of the Seine, not to rejoin it until Harfleur is passed. It mounts a steep ascent and traverses a part of the table-land of the Pays de Caux. There is nothing of interest until you descend into the valley where lies the town of

16 *Lillebonne* (*Inn:* H. du Commerce), numbering 3500 Inhab., prettily situated on the stream of the Bolbec, and interesting on account of its Roman theatre—a relic of the ancient *Julia Bona* of the itineraries of Antonine and Ptolemy, capital of the *Caletes* (inhabitants of the Pays de Caux), of which the present town occupies the site, and retains (with a slight change) the name. The road, on entering the town, passes under the *old Castle* on the rt., and nearly over the space which must have anciently been the stage of the *Theatre*. On the l. hand is seen the semicircular portion allotted to the spectators, for the most part cut out of the hill, which, forming a gradual slope for the rows of seats to rest on, saved the cost of vast substructions—an advantage of which the Romans and Greeks usually availed themselves in their theatres. The remains consist chiefly of foundations, and have been laid open since 1812. The fragments of walls in the centre belonged probably to the orchestra, those on the slope of the side to the dressing-rooms. On the hill, among fragments of masonry, are several semicircular terraces, one above the other, with traces of the vomitories, or entrances: and round the whole runs a corridor or vaulted passage, gradually rising from the side to the centre, by which entrance was obtained to the highest seats. The walls and part of the vaults here remain tolerably perfect; they are supported by many spurs or buttresses. The walls are faced with ashlar masonry, or with small stones about the size of bricks neatly jointed, the centre filled in with rubble of flint strongly cemented with grouting, the whole banded together at irregular intervals by horizontal courses of red tiles. The stone employed is a porous but coherent calcareous tufa, or travertine, which is to this day deposited by the water of a neighbouring brook.

This is the best preserved, and indeed almost the only example of an ancient theatre in the N. of France, or of Europe. It measured across the chord of the arc 300 ft., and the dimensions of the circular corridor were

NORMANDY. *Route 14.—Rouen to Havre by Railroad.* 59

625 ft. The ground in and about the town can scarcely be turned up without disclosing ancient remains of one sort or another. In 1823 a fine bronze male statue (now in the British Museum) was discovered; and the Museum at Rouen has been greatly enriched from this mine of antiquities.

On the opposite side of the high road, looking down upon the theatre, is the *Castle*, a picturesque ruin, historically interesting as the residence of Wm. the Conqueror, who here called together his barons to unfold the momentous scheme of the invasion of England. The massive outer walls now serve to enclose a garden and modern house; close beside it is a tall round tower of beautifully even masonry, having walls 13 ft. thick, and some finely ribbed vaults; isolated by a deep fosse, crossed by a drawbridge. It is a construction of the 15th cent., built probably by the Harcourts, who owned the castle down to the Revolution. Not far off is a mutilated angular tower of the 13th or 14th cent., The great Norman hall, in which, according to the tradition, William met his barons in council, has been entirely swept away by the present proprietor, a cotton-spinner. The commanding elevation of these ruins gives them a magnificent view over the adjacent valley, with a peep, through a gap at its extremity, of the broad estuary of the Seine 3 m. below the town.

The *Parish Church* has a fine tower and spire, similar to that of Harfleur, but inferior, and a rich portal.

Owing to the abundant supply of water from the neighbouring hills, Lillebonne has become a manufacturing town, and cotton-mills have multiplied considerably about it, especially up the valley towards Bolbec: calicos and indiennes are principally made here.

The *Castle* of Tancarville (Rte. 12) is 6 m. distant from Lillebonne, by cross-roads, the latter part so narrow and steep as to be practicable only for a light carriage. A cabriolet may be hired for 12 fr. to go thither, and on to St. Romain on the Havre road (p. 55), waiting to allow the traveller to see the castle. The direct road from Lillebonne to Havre passes within 3 m. of the castle: the diligences go round by Bolbec. (Rte. 14.) Both roads meet at

18 La Botte.

In descending from the Plain de Caux towards

Harfleur, a fine view is obtained of that town, its noble spire, and the Seine beyond. The road hence to

17 HAVRE is described in Rte. 14.

ROUTE 14.

ROUEN TO HAVRE—RAILROAD.

95 kilom.=59 Eng. m.

4 or 5 trains daily, in 2½ and 3 hrs.

This line was opened 1847. Its engineer is Mr. Jos. Locke, and its construction is almost entirely due to English skill, enterprise, and capital.

It is carried, for the most part of the way, over the high and fertile tableland of the Pays de Caux.

It quits the line from Paris to Rouen (Rte. 8) at Sotteville, and, a little above the town of Rouen, crosses the Seine by a timber bridge of 8 arches, each 131 ft. span, its centre resting on an island; rebuilt since its destruction by fire by the mob of 1848. (N.B. Beautiful view of Rouen from the bridge.) This leads direct into the first *tunnel*, carried under part of St. Catherine's Hill (p. 42), 1133 yds. long. It describes a radius of about half a mile; the works were very difficult, owing to the rush of waters from springs in the chalk. The railway issues from it into the valley of Darnélat, filled with dye-works and cotton-mills, and crossed together with the 2 small streams which traverse it, the Robee and Aubette, by a rly. viaduct. The line speedily re-enters the chalk hills, and in 2 succeeding tunnels (one of them 1530 yds. long) sweeps round the town of Rouen, penetrating beneath the Boulevards St. Hilaire and Beauvoisine in a series of cuttings and tunnels, works of arduous execution and great engineering merit, made at great cost. It emerges at the

Rouen Stat., in the Rue Verte (built

by Tite, architect of the Royal Exchange), situated in a hole cut in the chalk, shut in by escarpment, excluding all view, and between 2 tunnels, and a long way from the heart of Rouen and the quays. On quitting the station you pass through the tunnel Cauchois, under the suburb of Bouvreuil and the cemetery of St. Gervais. A fifth tunnel succeeds, which ends near the village of Déville.

6 Maromme Stat.

Even after Rouen is a long way left behind, the country traversed by the road exhibits the vivifying effects of the cotton industry, in mills or factories, country-houses, villages, &c. The chief of these is Déville, situated in a pretty valley which bears its name.

3 Malaunay Stat.

Here is a *Viaduct* of 8 arches, and an embankment, over the Dieppe road. Near this the branch Railway to Dieppe (Rte. 6) diverges.

A 6th tunnel, nearly 1 m. and 3 fur. long, pierces the heights of Piccy-Poville, and the railroad crossing the high grounds is carried across the valley of

8 *Barentin*—Stat.

The curved *Viaduct of Barentin*, of 27 arches, each 60 ft. span, the central arch 108 ft. high, 765 yds. long, was constructed by Messrs. Mackenzie and Brassey. It gave way in the early part of 1846, covering the valley with rubbish. It was reconstructed in the short space of 6 months, at great cost, with the utmost care and solidity.

Barentin is a town of 2500 Inhab., in a small valley on the stream of the Austreberthe, which sets in movement many cotton-mills; the railway leaves it on the l. The railway has now emerged by gradual ascents out of the basin in which Rouen lies, to the table-land of the Pays de Caux, an elevation of about 400 feet.

2 Pavilly Stat.

11 Motteville Stat.

8 *Yvetot Stat*. (*Inn*, a cabaret) is an industrious little town of 9032 Inhab., with houses of timber, containing some manufactures of cotton, but destitute of objects of interest. The title of "Roi d'Yvetot" has given a wide celebrity to its name, and has greatly puzzled antiquaries and local historians, who have failed in proving the existence of any sovereign authority, or in discovering the origin of the title.

There is a tradition that one Gaulthier, Lord of Yvetot, having offended King Clothair, son of Clovis, and having been banished his presence, ventured to throw himself at the feet of the king while he was kneeling in prayer before the high altar at Soissons on Good Friday, thinking that the holiness of the place, and of the day of pardon for the sins of mankind, might obtain forgiveness for him also. Clothair, however, no sooner saw him than he drew his sword and slew him, but, repenting afterwards of his crime, and desiring to make atonement to Gaulthier, created his heirs kings of Yvetot. But this story has no good foundation. Béranger describes the king of Yvetot:—

" Il était un roi d'Yvetot,
Peu connu dans l'histoire,
Se levant tard, se couchant tôt,
Dormant fort bien sans gloire,
Et couronné par Jeanneton
D'un simple bonnet de coton."

Diligence to Caudebec. Rte. 13.

Here, in the very heart of the Pays de Caux, the traveller will now in vain look for the Cauchoise head-dress, once commonly worn by the women. It was a huge structure of cambric and lace, something between a cap and a helmet, and appears to have been the fashion even in England during the 15th and 16th centuries. The modern modes of Paris have driven it out of the field, even in remote Norman villages, and it is now rarely seen.

The *Pays de Caux*, through the centre of which the railroad runs, retains the name, slightly altered, of its ancient inhabitants in Cæsar's time, the Caletes (? Celts). It is a high table-land, only here and there intersected by river-courses, exceedingly fertile, though somewhat arid. Trees are rare on the high ground, except the usual avenues of fruit-trees on the road-side, and around villages and farm-houses, whose existence and position are invariably denoted by a sort of verdant rampart of stiff elms, planted in straight lines and double rows, on or near a high bank of earth; you may be sure that a farm or château is hid behind such an enclosure.

11 Alvimare Stat. *Coach* to Lillebonne.

8 Nointot Stat. [4 m. S. is Bolbec, a fresh-looking town of staring brick houses, which replace those of wood destroyed by a great fire in the last century: situated in one of the pleasant little valleys which intersect the Pays de Caux. It contains a vast number of cotton-mills, manufactories of calicos, printed stuffs, and handkerchiefs; printworks, bleaching-grounds, &c.; in short, it is one of the most industrious places in the Dépt. of the Seine Inférieure, 9630 Inhab. The abundant stream which runs through it, and is a main cause of this acitivity, turns no less than 113 usines before it joins the Seine below *Lillebonne.* That ancient town (see Rte. 13) is only 5 m. distant; its Roman Theatre merits notice.]

Bolbec lying in a depression of the table-land, high embankments and a viaduct were required to carry the railway across it.

At Mirville is a brick viaduct of 48 brick arches, the highest 106 ft. above the ground. Hence there is a steep incline (requiring an extra engine to surmount in coming from Havre) by which the railway descends nearly to a level with the Seine at

6 Beuzeville Stat. Coach to Fécamp.

8 St. Romain Stat.

HARFLEUR Stat. is situated on the Lézarde, a small stream now barely navigable for barges, and 2 m. distant from the Seine, yet Monstrelet calls it "le souverain port de la Normandie." The deposits brought down by the Lézarde have contracted its bed, and formed a fringe of land along the shore of the Seine, which has greatly increased the distance between the town and the estuary. Before the rise of Havre, Harfleur was the chief port of the mouth of the Seine, at which the wool of Spain and Portugal was imported and sent up to Montevilliers to be wrought, while by reason of its fortifications it was the key to the entrance of the Seine. In 1415 it resisted for 40 days the besieging army of Henry V., who, as soon as it had yielded, uncovered his feet and legs and walked barefoot to church to say his prayers, after which he collected the inhabitants to the number of 8000, and, turning them out of their houses with only the clothes on their backs, banished them and confiscated their property, substituting English colonists in their place. In 20 years, however, the town was surprised by a band of peasants, aided by a number of the former inhabitants, and the English were expelled. The tower, spire, and N. aisle of its *Church,* built in the 15th cent., it is said, by Henry V., and its fringed S. portal, are deservedly praised as masterpieces of Gothic. The E. end dates from the 13th centy. There is a fine timber-house (15th centy.) near the Ch.

The *Terrace* of the *Château of Orcher,* running along the heights above the town, commands a remarkably fine view of the river.

From Harfleur to Havre the railroad is carried along the side of a hill, sloping gently down to the Seine, whose embouchure is seen at intervals between the trees and houses. On the rt. a little above the road stands *Graville.* Its small church, prettily situated on a wooded bank, is Norman of the end of the 11th century. Its transepts are decorated externally with round intersecting arches, surmounted by figures of animals. The capitals of the pillars in the nave are sculptured with monsters. In the courtyard behind the Hôtel de Ville are caves in the rock, once the monks' cellars. The church was built in honour of St. Honoria. Her relics were removed for safety, at the Norman invasion, to Conflans, and confided to the custody of the monks, who, when the danger was overpast, refused to restore them. Notwithstanding this loss, the place where they *had been* retained its sanctity, so that more pilgrims and worshippers repaired hither than to the church at Conflans which actually held them! Remains of the masonry of a quay, with rings to attach vessels, are said to have been found under Graville. (?)

Passing numerous gardens and country houses, intermixed with inns, taverns, and guinguettes, composing the towns of Graville and Ingouville, so numerous as to form an uninterrupted street, we reach

7 *Havre Terminus*, close to the Cours Napoléon, and not far from Bassin Vauban. It covers 36 acres.

HAVRE.—*Inns: H. Frascati*, excellent, outside the walls, on the seashore, with a good table-d'hôte, reading-room, and neat and cheap warm-baths. *H. de l'Europe*, Rue de Paris, good. *Wheeler's*, on the Quai Notre Dame, near the steamers.

Havre, originally Havre de Grace, from a small chapel of Notre Dame de Grace which stood on its site, the port of the Seine and of Paris, one of the most thriving maritime towns of France, is situated on the N. side of the estuary of the Seine, and contains 28,000 Inhab. It is quite a modern town, owing its foundation to Francis I. (1516), and its prosperity to the judicious enactments of Louis XVI., though it has received its great impulse since the war, and has been rapidly gaining upon its elder rivals, Bordeaux and Nantes. It has no fine buildings nor historical monuments; its streets are laid down chiefly in straight lines, and at right angles with one another, and they are grouped round the basins, or docks, which communicate from one to the other by lock-gates, and are placed so as to form a triangle entered from the outer (avant) port. The quays bordering on the basins, lined with vessels, and choked up with cotton-bales, sugar-casks, &c., are the chief scenes of life. The strange cries and glittering plumage of parrots and macaws will remind the stranger of the connexion of the port with tropical countries. Its principal street (and it is a handsome one) is the Rue de Paris, extending through the Place du Spectacle from the Port d'Ingouville to the *round tower of François Premier*, at the entrance of the port, the only relic of the fortifications constructed by that monarch.

Improvements are to be made here, The old ramparts are to be removed, and Havre, Ingouville, and Graville, containing a population of near 70,000, are to be united into one, and to be surrounded by new and more extensive fortifications. The Citadel, built by Richelieu, in which Cardinal Mazarin shut up, in 1650, the leaders of the Fronde, the Princes of Condé, Conti, and Longueville, "the lion, the ape, and the fox, caught in one trap," to use the expression of Gaston of Orleans, has been dismantled. The release of these distinguished captives was at length effected (Feb. 1651) by one of those sudden popular risings so common in the history of the Fronde. Mazarin, prostrated from the height of power by this revolution, bethought himself how he might make friends of his former victims, and, disguised as a courier, posted off instantly from Paris, in order to be the first to tell the joyous news, and unlock the prison gates. Assuming an air of the most obsequious servility, he assured them he had no hand in their imprisonment, and stooped to kiss the boot of Condé, as the hero mounted his carriage, amidst salvos of artillery, on his way to Paris.

It is only by aid of a reservoir of water (*Retenue de la Floride*), regulated by sluices, that the mouth of the harbour, formed in the flat alluvium of the Seine, can be kept clear from the deposits of the river still in progress. The port is accessible for vessels during only four hours each tide; at low-water the port and avant-port are left dry. The three old docks are capable of containing 250 or 300 vessels, or more with inconvenience; the fourth dock, the Bassin de Vauban, the largest of all, situated outside the walls, and finished 1842, is a magnificent work, with a fine masting-machine and warehouses.

A 5th dock, destined for steamers, has been constructed at the extremity of the Retenue de la Floride.

The saying of Napoleon, that "Paris, Rouen, and Havre formed only one city, of which the Seine was the highway," explains the cause of the prosperity of Havre. It is the place of import of all the foreign articles needed for the supply of the French metropolis: like Liverpool with us, it is the chief *cotton port* of France, furnishing this commodity to the manufacturer of Rouen, Lille, St. Quentin, and even as far as Alsace, and from these cities it again receives the manufactured goods for exportation.

It is also the point of communication between the Continent of Europe and America; a great trade is carried on with the United States. The Declaration of Independence formed the groundwork of the present good fortunes of Havre. A line of American steamers runs twice a month to New York. Here also a great number of emigrants, many from Germany, annually embark for the New World.

The imports of Havre, though only one-half in quantity and weight of those of Marseilles (the chief seaport in France), are said nearly to equal them in value. The number of vessels belonging to the port is considerable. More than a million tons of shipping enter in and out yearly. Some of the principal mercantile houses here are English and American.

The shipbuilders of Havre enjoy a high reputation for the skill and science which they display in the construction of their vessels, which are capital sea-boats, yet their shipyards are nothing more than an open space on the sea-beach, outside the fortifications, fenced in with a wooden paling.

The annals of Havre are connected with the history of England at several points. Henry of Richmond embarked here, 1485, for Milford Haven and Bosworth Field, backed by 4000 men, furnished by Charles VIII. to aid his enterprise. The town was delivered over to the keeping of Queen Elizabeth by the Prince de Condé, leader of the Huguenots, 1562, and the command of it was intrusted to Ambrose Dudley, Earl of Warwick; but the English were ejected within a year, after a most obstinate siege, whose progress was pressed forward by Charles IX., and his mother, Catherine de Medicis, in person, sensible that the possession of Havre by the English would be a thorn in the side of France. Hatred of the English, indeed, had united all parties in France against them. The Protestant Condé served in the besieging army, which was commanded by the Constable Montmorency, previously the ally of the English. Warwick held out against vastly superior numbers, until his force was reduced by slaughter and the plague from nearly 6000 to 1500; he was himself shot in defending a breach, after which the place surrendered.

The fleet of William III., which had failed before Brest, made an ineffectual attempt in 1694 to bombard the town, as it had before done in the case of Dieppe with success. In 1796 Sir Sidney Smith, while cruising in the Channel, endeavoured to cut out a French ship of war from under the batteries, but became entangled in the currents and sandbanks of the Seine, and his vessel, having been perceived next morning lying high and dry, was captured by some gunboats, and he was sent a prisoner to the Temple in Paris.

Bernardin de St. Pierre, author of 'Paul and Virginia,' was born here in a house No. 47, Rue de la Corderie. Havre is also the birthplace of Mademoiselle Scudery, 1697, and of Casimir Delavigne.

There is an *English Chapel* in the Rue d'Orléans; service at 12 and 3¼ on Sundays. A handsome Grecian edifice, destined to contain a *Museum* and *Public Library*, has been raised on the site of the Old H. de Ville.

The *Cercle du Commerce* is a large commercial club-house, furnished with almost all the European newspapers and many American: strangers can be introduced to it by members.

The *Theatre* in the Place Louis XVI., or du Spectacle, at the extremity of the Bassin du Commerce, is one of the most striking buildings in the town.

Baths.—*Frascati*, on the sea-shore, not far from the pier, contains good hot and cold sea-water baths. In summer, bathing is carried on in the open sea. Cabinets are provided for dressing and undressing, and men and women bathe together, but covered up in bathing dresses. There are no bathing-machines; ladies are led out to a sufficient depth of water by the guide, who then seizes them by the shoulders, lays them on the surface of the water, and dips them by sousing their heads under water.

N.B. The draught of the tide is so strong as sometimes to overpower even skilful swimmers. The bathers lay hold of ropes attached to posts, to prevent their being swept away in stormy weather.

British travellers to Havre need not procure *Passports* in England, as they are permitted to land without them. They are to be obtained immediately on landing from Her Majesty's Consul [5 frs.], who has made arrangements for their delivery in time for the first train after the arrival of the steamers. These passports are countersigned at the *Bureau de Police*, Hôtel de Ville, at the corner of the Place François I., not far from the old round tower. The office is open at 8 o'clock a.m.

Passengers going to England require to have their passports viséd—the police office is open for that purpose an hour before the sailing of the steamer.

The *Custom-house*, corner of Quai Notre Dame and Grand Quai (entrance in Rue de la Gaffe), opens at 8—12, and 2 p.m.—5. After the baggage has been examined (see INTRODUCTION), the dues for the harbour on the landing, and for porterage, are fixed by and paid to an Englishwoman, who manages this department of the establishment.

Poste aux Lettres, Place Louis Seize.

Consuls reside here from Great Britain and from other maritime states of Europe, and from the U. S. and other Governments of America.

Railway to Paris (pp. 63, 60).

Diligences (offices, Rue de Paris, 49 and 101).—To Dieppe by Fécamp daily, in 9 hours (Rte. 18); to Caen (starting from Honfleur on the opposite side of the Seine) daily (Rte. 23).

Steamers to Rouen daily in 8 or 9 hours; to Caen daily in 4 hours (see Rte. 24); to Honfleur twice a day in $\frac{3}{4}$ of an hour (Rte. 23); to Cherbourg twice a week; to Morlaix in Brittany in 18 hours, every Saturday; to London 4 times a week; to Southampton *daily*, except Sunday (in summer), twice a week in winter; to Dunkirk, Rotterdam, and Hamburg twice a week; to Amsterdam; to St. Petersburg and Copenhagen twice a month. More than 40 steam-vessels, including tug-boats, belong to the Port du Havre.

The antiquarian and architect may visit the Norman Church of Graville, 2 m. on the Rouen road (p. 61).

Those who have an hour or two to spare at Havre cannot better employ it than in ascending the hill of *Ingouville*, a town of 12,000 Inhab., separated from Havre only by the gate, consisting chiefly of neat country-houses with gardens. The view from the top over the town of Havre—its forest of masts rising from amidst its buildings over the embouchure of the Seine, the distant hills of Calvados appearing on the horizon like an island, and over the heights of La Hève to the rt. (N.), crowned by its twin lighthouses—is very striking and pleasing.

The chalk cliffs under the lofty headland of Cap la Hève, on which the lighthouses are erected at a height of 300 ft., offer some fine rock scenery; but, except when the tide is low, the shingly beach is not favourable for walking. These rocks were the favourite haunt of the author of 'Paul and Virginia.'

ROUTE 18.

HAVRE TO DIEPPE AND ABBEVILLE, BY FÉCAMP AND EU.

171 kilom. = 106 Eng. m.

Diligence daily from the Beuzeville Stat. of the Paris Railway.

At Harfleur (p. 61) we turn out of the Rouen road, and ascend the pretty green valley of the Lézarde to Montivilliers, agreeably situated, with many trees about it, and containing some picturesque wooden houses. Its *Church* belonged to a once famous abbey of Benedictine nuns founded in the 7th cent. It is in the Romanesque style of the 11th cent., except the N. aisle, which is florid, and the Lady Chapel, early pointed. Notice should be taken of its elegant Norman tower, surmounted by a light spire, with a florid portal on one side of it, and a round doorway, ornamented with the embattled fret, on the other, and within, of the carved capitals of the columns, and a gallery of stone fret-work near the W. end.

16 Epouville. We now reach the high ground of the Pays de Caux (p. 60), but traverse a number of valleys or gullies intersecting it, running down to the sea, in every one of which a village or small town nestles; this renders the road a succession of ups and downs. When the harvest is cleared from the ground and sheep are feeding among the stubble, a long narrow cart, covered either with a coved wooden roof or thatched with straw—a sort of horizontal sentry-box on wheels—may be seen drawn up by the road-side or in the fields; it is the moveable bed of the shepherd, in which he shelters himself at night or in bad weather.

14 Goderville.

13 *Fécamp* (*Inns:* Poste, extortionate; H. du Commerce), a town of 10,000 Inhab., nearly fills the bottom and sides of a narrow valley opening out towards the sea between 2 high falaises or cliffs, on one of which stands a lighthouse. It has the advantage of being at once a seaport and a manufacturing town, owing to the abundant stream which, as it descends the valley, turns numerous cotton and other mills, besides which there are 3 steam saw-mills. The harbour is small and much sanded up, but is resorted to by colliers from Newcastle and Sunderland, and Baltic timber-ships, besides fishing vessels.

In the centre of the town stands the *Ch. of the Abbey of Notre Dame*, a large and fine edifice in the early pointed style, with some Norman features, built in the beginning of the 13th cent., except the 2 round arched apsidal chapels, behind the E. end, which are older, and the S. side of the choir, which is more modern and florid. The Lady Chapel, with its carved woodwork of the 16th cent., and the monuments in the side chapels of abbots Richard (1223), William (1297), and Robert (1326), consisting of altar tombs enriched with crocketed niches, bearing their effigies reclining under florid canopies, merit notice. Also some curious carvings of Scriptural subjects in the N. transept.

Fécamp was the retreat of Cuvier during the storm of the Revolution. He commenced his studies in natural history here on the sea-beach. On the top of the cliff behind the town, near the new lighthouse, 328 ft. above the sea-level, is the Gothic *Chapelle de N. Dame de Salut*, built by Henry I. of England, much resorted to as a place of pilgrimage by sailors and fishers. The fishwives sometimes mount up to it on their knees as a penance.

About 10 m. S.W. of Fécamp, on the coast, is the fishing village of *Etretat*, situated amidst rocks which have been excavated by the sea into arches, aiguilles, and other fantastic shapes. It is resorted to by French artists, and there is a tolerable and cheap little inn (Au Rendezvous des Artistes). The road thither is bad.

A hill, steeper than that which leads into Fécamp from the W., carries the road out of it on the side of Dieppe.

19 Cany, in its pretty green and wooded valley, is an agreeable contrast to the bare open land which precedes and follows. The *Château* belongs to the Duc de Luxembourg.

The road again approaches the sea at

12 St. Vallery en Caux, a fishing town of 5328 Inhab., with a port formed by locking the stream, which here descends to the sea.

14 Bourg Dun.

18 *Dieppe*, in Rte. 5.

A rudely jolting, one-horse patâche runs daily between Dieppe and Eu. A cabriolet costs 10 frs. to go and return. The road, as before, is carried over the high ground at some distance from the sea, and traverses in succession several valleys.

19 Tocqueville, a small hamlet. Beyond it a considerably larger village, Creil, with a massive church, is passed.

11 *Eu.*—*Inns:* Poste or Cygne; H. de l'Union, neither good nor cheap. Eu is a somewhat lifeless town of 3730 Inhab., on the Bresle, a small stream

which formed the boundary of Normandy, and which falls into the Channel 2 m. lower down at Treport. In the centre of the town is an irregular market-place, no two sides of which are parallel, overlooked by the E. end of the *Parish Church*, a heavy building and injured by modern reparations, externally propped up by huge flying buttresses. It is in the early pointed style; the triforium arches open into the aisles; the E. end is angular, but several of the side chapels are of late florid Gothic. Attention should be directed to the screen before that of St. Laurent, an Irish archbishop ; to the Entombment in another chapel composed of statues as large as life; and to the fantastic, spirally banded column in the S. transept. The church was restored by Louis Philippe, who gave several painted windows from the manufactory at Sèvres.

In the *crypt* (caveau) below the church are deposited a series of monumental effigies which were mutilated by the revolutionists 1793, and thrown into a vault filled with rubbish, but have been restored by the late king. The oldest is of St. Laurent, Archbishop of Dublin, who died at Eu (1181), whither he had repaired on a mission of peace, to reconcile Henry II. and the King of Ireland. The rest are of the counts of Eu, of the family of Artois; viz. Charles d'Artois, 1471—the head and hands are of marble ; of his father, Philip d'Artois, made prisoner at Nicopolis by the Turks, d. 1397 in Anatolia; Jean d'Artois, 1386, his surcoat studded with fleurs-de-lis of copper—he was taken prisoner at Cressy along with the French king; Isabella de Melun, his wife, in an elaborately carved dress, with dogs at her feet ; Jeanne de Saveuse, wife of Charles d'Artois, a pleasing countenance and curious costume; Hélène de Melun, his 2nd wife; Isabelle d'Artois, who died unmarried, 1397.

Eu is chiefly remarkable, however, on account of its *Château*, which belonged to King Louis-Philippe, who inherited it, with the Comté d'Eu, from his mother, daughter and heiress of the Duc de Penthièvre. His Majesty here received H. M. Queen Victoria in 1843.

The château is a low building of red brick surmounted by high tent-shaped roofs of slate, like the pavilions of the Tuileries, and is without architectural beauty. It was built 1578 by Henry of Lorraine, le Balafré Duc de Guise, on the site of a castle which had belonged in turn to the Lusignans, the Briennes, the Artois, the Clèves, and the Saint Pols, and which was burnt down by Louis XI. (1475), to punish the treachery of the Comte de St. Pol. It was much augmented by the late king, and splendidly fitted up, the walls being clothed with a collection of historical and family portraits, including those of the royal family and the various lines of the counts of Eu, to the number of 1100. Many of them are copies, others are mere furniture pictures; yet the collection is highly interesting, and the formation of it seems to have given rise to the grander gallery of Versailles, which this resembles on a miniature scale. There appears to be no other arrangement than that of making a certain number of pictures fit into certain spaces ; names, dates, nations, and families are intermixed, and the walls are covered with them from the top to the bottom of the house.

It is possible that the collection may shortly be dispersed. A few pictures are here noted down, as possessing some peculiar interest:—the Regent Duke of Orleans by *Mignard*. Napoleon, and his father, Charles Bonaparte ! There are several portraits of the frivolous and ambitious Anne Marie Louise de Montpensier, called sometimes la Grande Mademoiselle, who, after having aspired to the hands of her cousin Louis XIV., of the Grand Condé, of Charles II., and of the Emperor of Germany, was content at last to be married to Lauzun, a simple gentleman. She often resided in this château ; and one of these likenesses, at the age of 43, in which she is drawn holding her father's (Gaston Duc d'Orléans) portrait, is mentioned by her in her 'Mémoires.' Her bedroom is still preserved. Some of the drawings in the Cabinet de la Coquille, on the first floor, are by her. She became possessor of Eu by purchase from Mademoiselle de Guise, the last descendant of that family in a direct line, 1661. She bequeathed Dombes and Eu to the Duc du Maine, natural son of Louis XIV. by Mad. de Montespan, and father of the Duc de Penthièvre, in the vain hope of ransoming Lauzun her husband from the prison of Pignerol. She first commenced the historic gallery of portraits at Eu, and her collection forms the groundwork of that still existing. At the back of one of the portraits of herself there is written by her own hand, "Bergere alant a la faite du Vilage voisin." *Portraits continued*—of Louis XVI., Marie Antoinette his queen, the Dauphin their son, who died in the Temple, and all the other members of their family; those of Louis-Philippe and his family occupy the *Salon de Famille*—the most pleasing and interesting is the Princess Marie of Wirtemburg, the sculptor of the admirable statue of Jeanne d'Arc. There are 2 portraits of Louis-Philippe Egalité (d. 1793), one as a young man in civic dress, the other in uniform, by *Sir J. Reynolds.*

One of the most superb and interesting apartments is the *Galerie des Guises*, filled with portraits of that remarkable family, who once owned this château; among them, Claude de Lorraine, with the armour and sword with which he fought at Marignan; François de Lorraine, Duc de Guise, who was wounded in the face before Boulogne by an English lance, and who endured the pain of having the lance-head extracted from his cheek with a pair of pincers, while the surgeon rested his foot on the duke's head to obtain a purchase. He was the successful defender of Metz against Charles V., and the capturer of Calais from the English; he was killed by the poisoned bullet of Poltot, 1563. His son, Duc Henri le Balafré, was so called also from a wound in his cheek received from an arquebuse at the battle of Dormans. He began to build the château d'Eu 1578; he was the chief of the Ligue, the hero of the Journée des Barricades, and the murderer of Coligny on St. Bartholomew's night. He was assassinated by Henri III. at Blois (Rte. 53), 1588, together with his brother, the Card. de Lorraine.

Marie de Lorraine, daughter of Duke Claude, queen of James V. of Scotland, and mother of Mary Queen of Scots;—Queen Mary herself in her widow's weeds of white (royal mourning);—Catherine Duchesse de Montpensier, sister of Le Balafré, who revenged his death by instigating Jacques Clement to assassinate Henri III.;—the Duc de Mayenne, brother of Le Balafré, commander of the armies of the Ligue against Henri IV.;—Henri II. de Lorraine, Duc de Guise, conqueror and viceroy of Naples after Masaniello's rebellion.

"Le récit de cette salle a fait une longue digression sur les portraits qui y sont," are the words of Mademoiselle herself, in describing these very pictures in her own gallery; yet how momentous a tale does every countenance tell! Where shall we find such an accumulation of ambition, of crime, and of romance, as in that one family?

Of Louis XIV. there are several likenesses, also of his family, his mistresses, his generals, his court; and even more of Louis XV. In the billiard-room are Charles I. and II., Oliver Cromwell, Queen Elizabeth, Joan of Arc, and Agnes Sorel.

The superb *Salle des Rois* is so called because filled with portraits of kings and queens only: here are Marie de Medicis by *Van Dyk*, given by herself to Mademoiselle de Montpensier, and Henri IV. Here is a cast of the equestrian group of Jeanne d'Arc striking down for the first time an enemy, by the Princess Marie.

In the *Cabinet du Roi*, among portraits of H.M.'s own family, including his father, are Madame de Genlis, his preceptress; Pamela, afterwards Lady Fitzgerald; and Madame de Lamballe, who was murdered 1793.

The *Hall of Victoria* is decorated with pictures representing the visit of the Queen of England to Eu, painted by French artists.

The small *Chapelle*, a mixture of Gothic and Italian in its decorations, has some modern painted glass windows from Sèvres; one is a portrait of St. Amélie, after the picture by *Paul Delaroche*.

The *Parc* or grounds are less attractive than the palace; being a wilderness of trees, mostly woody elms, planted in rows with angular terraces; a gloomy canal, and muddy circular ponds beset with willows. No advantage has been taken of the slopes of the ground, — no taste shown in laying out the brotherhood of alleys and formal parterres. Only on the l. of the castle a few ancient beeches survive, beneath whose branches the Balafré Duc de Guise heard the suits of his vassals, and concerted plots against his sovereign. Here a small space was railed in by Louis-Philippe, who affixed this inscription:—" Ici les Guises tenaient conseil au XVIe siècle." At the extremity of the grounds is a terrace overlooking the gap through which the Bresle, quitting the bare and dull valley, enters the sea, and the little village Treport is perceived at its mouth. On this terrace is a brick *Pavillon*, fitted up by poor Mademoiselle, during the time she was banished to her estate at Eu by Louis XIV. for refusing to marry the paralytic and imbecile King of Portugal. Louis-Philippe restored it, and ornamented it with pictures of the events of her life.

The effigies of the Duc Henri de Guise (le Balafré), murdered at Blois, and of his wife Catherine de Clèves, are in the *Eglise du Collége*, originally of the Jesuits, who were established at Eu by le Balafré. The church, built out of the ruins of the old castle, as well as the monuments, were raised at her expense; they are rich in marble, but of no value as works of art. He is represented in armour, she in ruff and farthingale; there are duplicate effigies of both, attended by figures of Prudence, Strength, Faith, and Charity; Gillot was the sculptor. From the pulpit of this ch. Bourdaloue preached his first sermon.

On the Bresle, close to the palace, is a *mill* for making sea biscuits, sawing timber, &c., established by an Englishman.

Treport, the port of Eu, 3 m. distant, is a fishing village of 2265 Inhab., having an old *Church* seated on a height, approached by a flight of steps, remarkable for its elaborate W. *porch*, and for the roof of its nave distinguished by pendants of stone hanging from it, of the 14th century. Treport is supposed to be the *Ulterior Portus* of Julius Cæsar.

16 Valines.
18 *Abbeville* (Rte. 3).

ROUTE 21.

ROUEN TO ALENÇON, BY BERNAY, BROGLIE, AND SÉEZ.

143 kilom. = 89 Eng. m.
42 Brionne (Rte. 23).
15 Bernay (*Inn:* La Poste, Lion d'Or), a manufacturing town of 7244 Inhab. It once possessed an important abbey, founded by Judith, wife of Richard II. Duke of Normandy; the *Ch.* of which, now converted into warehouses, is one of the oldest Norman (Romanesque) buildings existing in Normandy, having been begun in the early part of the 11th century. It is large in its dimensions and perfectly simple in its style: plain square piers support equally plain circular arches. The columns attached to the piers are carved, and one is inscribed "Isambardus me fecit." The choir ends in an apse, and there is one in each transept. "The dome vaulting in circular courses over the aisles is exceedingly curious." In *St. Croix* are some painted windows, and the high altar was brought from Bec. *N. Dame de la Couture* is a Gothic ch. of the 15th cent. The houses in the *Grande Rue* retain curious porches and bits of Gothic.

10 Broglie, a town of 1052 Inhab. The *Church* is an ancient and singular building; along its W. front runs a row of interlacing circular arches; one side of the nave rests on very massive piers; the other is modernised, the piers pared down, and pointed arches substituted for round ones. The large and plain *Château* on a height surrounded by wood near this is the

family residence of the Duc de Broglie, ex-minister, and one of the most virtuous, enlightened, and eminent statesmen in France.

16 Monnai.
14 Gacé has a ruined *castle*.
12 Nonant.
12 Séez (*Inn*: La Corne), a poor little city with a population of only 5500, owing that title to the possession of a *Cathedral*, a fine edifice, the remarkable features of which are, the porch, 47 feet deep, under the W. front, flanked by 2 spires; the nave, 80 ft. high, of pure early pointed Gothic of the 13th cent.; the windows are double lancet and very elegant. The choir and transepts are in the decorated style of the end of the 14th cent.

A cathedral was built here in 1055, but no part of it exists in the present one, judging from the style. The town was burnt down in 1150 and 1353, and probably the cathedral also.

21 *Alençon* (Rte. 35).

ROUTE 23.

ROUEN TO CAEN, BY BRIONNE, OR BY HONFLEUR.

a. By Brionne 128 kilom.=79½ m.

The road after issuing out of Rouen crosses the Seine, and runs within a short distance of the l. bank, here bordered by chalk cliffs (Rte. 12), skirting on the l. the forest of Rouvray, to

12 Grande Couronne; thence by Moulineaux (Rte. 12) and near the castle of Robert le Diable to Bouille, where it quits the Seine, separating from the branch to Honfleur, which turns to the rt. (see below).

13 Bourgtheroude.

About 2 m. N. of the road, and the same from Brionne, are *the ruins of the Abbey of Bec Hellouin*, now of little importance or interest, but famous for having given two successive archbishops to the See of Canterbury, Lanfranc and Anselm. It has been demolished, except a tower of the 15th cent., and the vast conventual building erected in the 17th cent. is converted into a military stud-house.

17 Brionne.—*Inn:* La Poste, once the château of the seigneur of the place. Brionne is a small town on the Risle. The religious *council* which condemned the doctrines of Berengarius was held in the presence of William the Conqueror in the *Ch. of St. Denis.* There are some fragments of the walls of the *keep* of the castle in the middle of the Risle.

11 Marché Neuf.
14 L'Hôtellerie.
13 *Lisieux*, in Rte. 25.
17 Estrées.
13 Moult.
17 CAEN (Rte. 25).

Before reaching this the road falls into the great Route 25, from Paris to Cherbourg, and is fully described under that head.

b. By Honfleur 136 kilom.=84½ m.

To Caen by Pont Audemer and Honfleur, a *diligence* runs daily.

12 Grand Couronne.
13 Bourgachard.

At 5 min. past 1 on Sat. 19th Sept. 1829, the tower of the parish ch. sank down in a heap, crushing the nave and covering part of the churchyard. Had the accident occurred the following day, it being the hour of mass, the whole congregation must have been annihilated. There was a curious leaden font in this ch. A dreary district extends from this place as far as the pleasant valley of the Risle, one of the loveliest streams in Normandy, in which lies

23 Pont Audemer.—*Inn:* Pot d'Etain: the samlets (saumoneaux of the Risle) are excellent. This is a prettily situated town of 5400 Inhab., famed for its tanneries, of which it contains 40; besides which some cotton is woven here, its industry being greatly promoted by the Risle, which passes through it in small streams. It once had a castle, in besieging which, in the early part of the 14th cent., cannon were first used in France: it was razed by Du Guesclin. The *Churches* of Notre Dame des Prés, now a tanhouse, and of St. Germain, in the suburb, may furnish some points of interest to the antiquarian architect. The *Churches* of *St. Ouen* and of *St. Sepulchre* are said to be worth notice.

The *Terrace* of the château de Bonnebon presents a pleasant view. *English Ch.* service on Sundays, 45, Rue de Bernay. It is a pleasant walk to ascend the lovely banks of the Risle as far as the *Castle of Montfort*.

A direct road from Pont Audemer to Pont l'Evêque, avoiding the détour by Honfleur, is completed—by Beuzeville 14 kilom., to Pont l'Evêque 13 kilom.

At Fiquefleur we obtain a fine view over the embouchure of the Seine.

23 *Honfleur*. (*Inn:* Les Armes de France, a mere auberge.—Honfleur is famed for melons.) It is a seaport town of 10,000 Inhab. at the mouth of of the Seine, here 7 m. broad, on its S. bank, opposite to Havre, and communicating with that port daily by steamboats. The town is dull and utterly without interest to the traveller, and moreover very dirty, but its situation, backed by wooded heights, is very pleasing. Its commerce, once considerable, has been absorbed by Havre. Its harbour, protected by a stone pier not yet finished, is accessible only at high water, and is principally resorted to by fishing vessels, though some timber-ships unload here. 7000 dozens of eggs are exported weekly to England, besides butter and fruit. The chapel of *Notre Dame de Grace*, on the hill above the town to the W., much resorted to by sailors and filled with their ex-votos, is in a charming situation for the *view* over the Seine. It was formerly not uncommon for the crews of vessels which had escaped imminent danger at sea to make a pilgrimage hither in their shirts, barefooted and bareheaded.

The English Church Service was performed twice every Sunday (?) in 1844, in a building on the Route de Rouen.

The *Steamer* from Havre to Rouen calls off the port in going and returning. (Rte. 12.)

Steamers, twice a-day to Havre, 7 m. and back, start according to the tide: the passage takes up ¾ of an hour.

Diligences daily to Caen and Rouen.

After the long and stately avenue of trees leading out of Honfleur, the way to Caen possesses no great interest:

yet orchards and hedges give an English cast to the scenery. The head-dress of the women, a nightcap twisted like a Phrygian bonnet, is by no means elegant.

17 Pont l'Evêque, a town on the Touques. [Trouville, on the sea, at the mouth of the Touques (*Inns:* H. de la Plage;—de Paris;—de Bellevue), is a rapidly increasing bathing-place, much frequented from July to Sept. for sea-bathing: the sea is not so rough as at Havre, and the water is more salt. *Steamers* several times a-day to Havre.]

Here the road to Lisieux (Rte. 25) and Falaise branches S. ½ m. N. of our road, and 2¼ m. from P. l'E.; in the midst of the Pays d'Auze is Beaumont, a small bourg with an abbey, in which Laplace, the mathematician and author of the 'Mécanique Céleste,' was born.

18 Dozullé. We here cross the Dives, from whose mouth the Conqueror set sail for England.

12 Troarn.

14 CAEN, in Rte. 25.

ROUTE 24.

HAVRE TO CAEN.

Steamboats pass daily to and fro, starting as soon as the height of the tide allows them.

The voyage, which takes up about 4 hrs., 2½ of them on the open sea, is pleasant in fine weather. The steamer skirts the coast of the dépt. Calvados, in sight of the bathing-place Trouville (see above), and of the mouth of the Dives, where William the Conqueror tarried for a month to collect his fleet of 3000 ships and his army of 50,000 men. The mouth of the Orne is entered with difficulty on account of the sands and rocks, and we then thread its sinuous channel between low banks, but the landscape is enlivened by several ancient churches. A canal is in progress, by which some of the windings of the Orne will be avoided, and the distance from the sea to Caen, 10 m., abridged. If the vessel, owing to tempestuous weather, should miss the tide to cross the bar, it must wait outside, and lie off the mouth for 10 or 12 hrs. for the next tide; but this rarely happens.

"At length the city of Caen extends itself, terminated at each extremity by the venerable abbeys of William the Conqueror, and Mathilda his queen; the latter, surmounted by 3 towers, is nearest at hand, There are no traces of workshops and manufactories, or of their pollution; but the churches, with their towers and spires, rise above the houses in bold architectural masses, and the city assumes a character of quiet monastic opulence, comforting the eye and the mind."—*Palgrave*.

Abreast of the town the river is lined with sumptuous quays of solid masonry, alongside of which the vessel is moored.

CAEN. Rte. 25.

ROUTE 25.

PARIS TO CAEN AND CHERBOURG, BY EVREUX AND LISIEUX.

To Caen 223 kilom. = 138 Eng. m. Caen to Cherbourg 118 kilom. = 74 Eng. m.

This journey is best made by taking the Rouen Railway as far as St. Pierre de Vauvray Stat. (3 hrs.—see Rte. 8) —whence a *Malleposte* runs daily in 15¼ hrs. to Cherbourg, by Louviers and Lisieux, 251 kilom. = 125 m.

The Railway is to be continued to Cherbourg.

Diligences daily.

From Paris to St. Pierre de Vauvray is described in Rte. 8. A little beyond this we quit the route to Rouen, turning to the l. out of the valley of the Seine, up a wooded combe to an elevated and fertile but monotonous country.

15 Pacy-sur-Eure. 10 m. S. of this is Ivry, where Henri IV. gained a momentous victory over the Duc de Mayenne and the army of the League 1590.

At Cocherel, on the rt. bank of the Eure, 4 m. below (N. of) Pacy, Du Guesclin, in 1364, defeated the forces of the King of Navarre, Charles le Mauvais.

18 *Evreux* (*Inns:* H. du Grand Cerf, very good—de France, opposite the Cathedral), chef-lieu of the Dépt. de l'Eure, has 10,287 Inhab., and is prettily situated in a bowl-shaped valley shut in on N. and S. by hills, and watered by the Iton, an affluent of the Eure, divided into several branches. It has a considerable share in the cotton manufacture (ticking and stockings), here carried on by the hand-loom more than by the steam-engine. Its chief edifice is

La Cathédrale, presenting to the W. an incongruous front of Italian architecture, flanked by two towers, and surmounted in the centre of the cross by a loftier tower and florid spire, erected by the Cardinal de la Balue, favourite of Louis XI. The nave is in the Norman style, probably of our Henry I.'s time, since he burnt the town, with the permission of the bishop, on condition of rebuilding the churches. The upper part of the nave, and the rest of the ch., are pointed, and for the most part more modern than the reign of Philippe-Auguste, who again burnt the town to revenge himself on the treachery of Jean Sans Terre, in making it over to him during King Richard's captivity, but on Richard's unexpected return not only withholding it, but murdering the French garrison placed in the castle. The *choir*, supported on clustered columns with glazed triforium (1330-60), is very lofty and light. The Lady Chapel and the N. transept are still more recent (1465-75), and the *Portal* leading into it, in the flamboyant Gothic, elaborately ornamented, is deservedly admired, in spite of the injuries and loss of its statues inflicted by the Revolutionists. It dates from the beginning of the 17th centy. The beautiful rose window in the S. transept, and the wooden screens for the side chapels round the choir, showing the flamboyant Gothic style modified by the reviving Italian, also merit notice. The *Lady Chapel*, of elegant architecture (temp. Louis XI.), contains painted glass equally remarkable for its fine execution and perfect preservation. The woodwork enclosing the chapels round the choir, of mixed Gothic and Renaissance, merits notice.

The *Bishop's Palace*, built 1484, presents some curious details.

At the opposite end of the town is the *Ch. of St. Taurin*, attached to the séminaire; it is small, and resembles the cathedral in the various styles it displays, having shared like it the fortune of war and conflagration. The outer wall of the S. transept is ornamented with an arcade of semicircular arches, the pannels of which are prettily diapered with a pattern formed of red tiles let into the masonry. This is supposed to be a relic of the ch. built 1026 by Richard II. Duke of Normandy.

The *Chasse* or *Shrine of St. Taurin*, which once contained his relics, is preserved in the sacristy. It is a wooden box, shaped like a Gothic chapel, covered with plates of copper or silver gilt, enchased with a diapered pattern, and set round with bas-reliefs and small statuettes of bishops and saints; it is a work of the 13th cent. The architectural decorations are rich and in good taste: such shrines are now very rare. The precious stones which once ornamented it have been stolen or lost.

The streets of Evreux preserve many antique timber-framed houses, and on the Boulevards are traces of the walls which once defended it. It possesses a Beffroi called *Tour de l'Horloge*, built in the 15th cent.

Excavations made at Vieil Evreux (Mediolanum Aulercarum) have led to the discovery of a theatre, baths, &c., and of various relics now deposited in the Musée d'Antiquités.

The name of the premier English Viscount, Devereux Visct. Hereford, is derived from this town: the family traces its descent from Normandy.

Coaches go hence to Chartres and to St. Pierre and Vernon Stats. on the Paris and Rouen Railway (Rte. 50) daily.

The next post-station to Evreux is called

18 La Commanderie, from a castle and ch. of the Knights Templars, of which the ruins and some tombs of members of the order remain. It lies very high.

17 La Rivière Thibouville. A little to the N. is Harcourt, cradle of one of the noble houses of England, who trace their descent from a baron of the name who fell beside William the Norman at Hastings. There are scanty remains of a castle.

10 Marché Neuf.

14 L'Hôtellerie. The upland district traversed by the road forms part of the Pays de *Lieuvin*, celebrated for its fertility and excellent cultivation.

13 *Lisieux* (*Inns:* H. de France; H. d'Espagne), a thriving manufacturing town (11,473 Inhab.), prettily situated at the confluence of the Touques with the Orbec. About 3500 persons are employed in and around the town in weaving coarse woollens, flannels, horse-cloths, &c. Its main street exhibits specimens of ancient domestic architecture, timber-framed houses and pointed gables, well suited to the artist's pencil.

The **Church of St. Pierre* (formerly cathedral) faces an open square, with its W. front surmounted by a spire; one of its towers is rebuilding. It is in the early pointed style of the 13th cent., with lancet windows, holding a place between the Norman and the lancet Gothic of England. A preceding edifice, built 1143-82 (when the pointed style had scarcely begun to appear in this part of France) was burnt down 1226. Norman arches occur in the S. W. tower only; the outside of the S. transept is a fine example of the pointed style. The *Lady Chapel* was founded, in the 15th cent., by Pierre Cauchon, Bishop of Beauvais, and president of the unjust tribunal which condemned Joan of Arc, in expiation of "his false judgment of an innocent woman," as he expressly states in the deed of endowment.

Henry II. was married to Eleanor of Guienne, the divorced wife of Louis le Jeune, 1152, in this cathedral.

There is a very singular old wooden house in the Rue aux Fées.

Lisieux was the capital of the *Lexovii*, a Gallic tribe mentioned by Cæsar, and ruins of the ancient town (*Noviomagus*, l.) have been discovered at a short distance from the present one. Thomas à Becket retired hither 1169, during his exile from England. *Le Val Richer*, a small country house near Lisieux, is the summer-retreat of M. Guizot.

17 Estrées. The road from Lisieux to Caen is almost destitute of interest.

13 Moult.

17 CAEN. *Inns:* H. d'Angleterre; best and good; bed, 2 fr.; servants, 1 fr. 10 sous per diem;—H. de la Place Royale; not very clean, but moderate.

Caen, chief town of the Dépt. du Calvădós (so named from a long reef of rocks on its coast, on which a Spanish vessel, the Calvădós, was wrecked in the reign of Philippe II.), is situated on the Orne, 10 m. from its mouth, and has 43,079 Inhab. A smaller stream, the Odon, passes through the town and around the line of its old ramparts, to which it served as a fosse, before it joins the Orne, turning on its way several mills. Notwithstanding the antiquity of Caen, its wider streets, its large central square, in which stands the statue of Louis XIV., and its houses of white stone, give it a more cheerful air than Rouen, though less enlivened by passing crowds. The tall white Norman head-dress of the women, ornamented with lappets behind and sometimes with lace, is striking and quaint to a stranger's eye.

To the traveller Caen recommends itself by its numerous specimens of ancient architecture, to the permanent resident by the salubrity of its site and the cheapness of house-rent and provisions, which had caused our countrymen to settle themselves down here in a colony, until the troubles of 1848 put them to flight, and reduced their number from 4000 to less than 200.

Near the centre of the town, on one side of a small market-place full of bustle and quaint costumes in the early part of the day, rises the *Church of St. Pierre*, surmounted by one of the most graceful towers and spires, in the complete Gothic style, which Normandy can produce; the middle story, formed

France.

of tall lancet windows framed within reeded mouldings, is a model of strength and lightness. Its spire of stone, partly pierced à jour, was built 1308, and is 242 ft. high. The nave was constructed probably about the same time, the choir, more richly ornamented, rather later, while its roof and the chapels round the choir were added in 1521. The rich groining of the roof of the choir is surpassed in the chapels, where it assumes the form of pendent fringes, giving the roof a cellular character. The side walls of these chapels are pierced with arches and set with statues. Some of the capitals of the columns in the nave exhibit ludicrous carvings, such as Aristotle bridled and ridden by the mistress of Alexander, and Lancelot crossing the sea on his sword, from the old romances. The exterior of the E. end, well seen from the banks of the river, is as much Italian as Gothic, so entirely are forms and styles jumbled together.

Caen possesses two very remarkable monuments of the piety of William the Conqueror and his queen—or rather of their desire to appease the Pope for contracting a marriage within the prohibited degrees—in the churches of the Abbayes, Aux Hommes and Aux Dames: both founded 1066, and valuable in an architectural point of view, because their date is undoubted.

The *Church of St. Etienne*, or of the *Abbaye aux Hommes*, destined by the Conqueror as a resting-place for his own remains, was finished and dedicated by him in his lifetime, 1077, under Archbishop Lanfranc, who was the first abbot. The W. front is so perfectly and severely plain that it will probably disappoint expectations; it is surmounted by 2 stately towers and spires of later date (1200), which, with the choir, were rebuilt, or added to the original edifice, long after the time of William. The interior of the nave, however, exhibits the rigid severity and massy strength, with the grandeur of proportion, of the Norman Romanesque style. The ch. is 371 ft. long and 98 ft. high. The lower row of arches supports a gallery, having arches

E

of nearly equal span and ⅔ of the height of those below, an arrangement resembling the arcades of the Roman Coliseum. These upper arches originally opened into the aisles, the vaulting below them being of posterior date. The clerestory windows consist of a tall and short arch placed alternately on one side or the other to meet the curve of the vault. The choir, ending in an apse, and surrounded by apsidal chapels, is in the pointed Gothic style, answering to the early English of the 12th cent. (some say 1316-44). A plain grey marble slab in the pavement before the high altar marks the *grave of William the Conqueror*, the founder of the ch., but it has been long since empty: it was broken open, the costly monument erected over it by William Rufus destroyed, and the bones scattered, by the Huguenots, 1562, and lost without record, except one thigh-bone, which was re-interred. The Revolutionists of 1793 again violated the grave, and this also disappeared.

The funeral of the Conqueror, undertaken by the charity of a simple knight, as already detailed (p. 39), was singularly interrupted, even within the precincts of the ch., and before the service for the dead was concluded, by a cry from one of the bystanders, a man of low degree, who claimed the site of the grave, saying that it occupied the place of his father's house, that he had been illegally ejected from it in order to build the ch., and he demanded the restitution of his property. This claim, thus boldly made, in the presence of the dead monarch's son Henry, the chief mourner, being backed by the assent of the townspeople, who stood by, was not to be denied or rejected, and the bishop was obliged to pay down on the spot 60 sous for a place of sepulchre for the royal corpse. Even then it is related that, as the coffin was being lowered into the grave, it struck against some obstacle, fell, and was broken into pieces, so that the corpse, ejected from its tenement, diffused so horrid a stench through the ch., that the rites were hurried to a close, and the assembled priests and laity dispersed.

The exterior of this ch., surmounted by its 2 W. towers, its central octagonal tower, and 4 turrets on the E., has a peculiarly striking effect from a distance, and reminds one of the arrangements of some of those on the Rhine.

The adjoining conventual buildings (date 1726) have been converted, since 1800, into a *College* numbering not quite 300 students. On the W. side of the court adjoining is a handsome Gothic building (14th cent.), lately restored as a school, which occupies the site of the old Norman Palace, called Grand Palais. The ancient hall called *Salle des Gardes*, of the 13th or 14th century, still exists.

At the opposite end of the town, on the heights of St. Gilles, is the *Abbaye aux Dames*, and ch. of *la Ste. Trinité*, founded and consecrated 1066, though probably unfinished, by the Conqueror's queen, Mathilda, and destined by her for a nunnery of noble ladies. The conventual buildings attached to the ch. are quite modern (1726), and are converted into an *Hospital* (*Hôtel Dieu*), in which 40 sisters of the order of St. Augustine perform the duties of nurses of the sick: the choir of the ch. is railed off for their use. The ch., in the lighter and more ornate character of its architecture, displays so broad a contrast to the masculine plainness of St. Etienne, that it would scarcely be supposed that they had been both in progress at the same time. With the exception of the upper part of the W. towers, however, this edifice is a perfect and unaltered specimen of pure Norman Romanesque; the choir ending in an apsis, being of the same age and style as the nave. The piers are lighter, the engaged pillars project more, than in St. Etienne, the embattled fret here runs round the main arches, and instead of a lofty triforium the walls above them are threaded by a gallery supported by misproportioned pillars, exhibiting grotesque figures among the foliage of their capitals. The arches under the central tower are remarkably bold, and their archivolts are chased with the Norman lozenge. The one opening into the nave is obtusely pointed, but apparently of the same date. The choir, ending in a semicircle of double arches, one tier over the other, encloses in the centre the fragments of the black marble *grave-stone* of the foundress, broken in pieces by the Calvinists, who dispersed her remains, which, however, were collected some years after. Underneath is a *crypt* resting on 34 closely set pillars.

For the student of ancient architecture the following churches remain also to be visited. Not far from St. Etienne is *St. Nicholas*, another Norman ch., coeval with the two abbeys, having been built, except the tower and the pointed vaulting of the nave, between 1066 and 1083; it is now a hay-store, belonging to the Remonte de Cavalerie. It is unaltered, very plain in style, and ends in an apse.

St. Etienne le Vieux, though desecrated and in ruins, is a fine specimen of pointed Gothic: on the wall of the choir is a mutilated equestrian statue, said to be William I.

St. Jean has two unequal and unfinished towers, in the style of that of St. Pierre, but inferior to it in late pointed style.

St. Michel, in the suburb of Vaucelles, displays some curious architectural features; in the Norman tower the very long but narrow and round-headed windows deserve notice. The fringed portal is surmounted by a gable filled with elegant flamboyant tracery, in the style of the 15th or 16th cent.

There are many old houses, with curiously ornamented fronts of the 15th and 16th centies., in the Rue St. Pierre (Nos. 52, 18, 20, 54, 24, &c.), but they are fast disappearing.

The Hôtel de Valois, Place St. Pierre, now the *Bourse*, is of Italian architecture.

The *Castle*, surmounting the height to the W. of St. Pierre, built by William the Conqueror and his son Henry —held for a long period by the English, but finally taken from them by the brave Dunois, who compelled the Duke of Somerset with a garrison of 4000 men to surrender, 1459—has now the aspect of a modern fortress bastioned and counterscarped; but having been dismantled by a decree of the Convention, it is at present reduced to a barrack. The only Norman portions subsisting are the small *Chapel of St. George*, whose nave is probably of the 11th centy., though the earliest mention of it is in 1181; while the chancel, separated from it by a bold arch, is of the 15th centy.: another very interesting Norman hall has been ascertained to have been the original *Hall of the Exchequer of Normandy*, of the time of William the Conqueror. Both these buildings are now used as storehouses. From the ramparts there is a good view of the town.

In the *Hôtel de Ville*, which occupies with its Grecian portico one side of the Place Royale, is a *Collection of Paintings*. The only ones worth notice are a genuine *PERUGINO, Marriage of the Virgin, imitated by *Raphael in the famous Sposalizio* at Milan;— the Passage of the Rhine, by *Van der Meulen;* —Melchizedec offering bread and wine to Abraham, *Rubens;*—the Virgin with 3 Saints, by some old master, called *Albert Dürer*. Here is also the Library of 40,000 vols.

In the *Cabinet d' Histoire Naturelle* in the Palais de l'Université, Rue de la Chain, is a collection of the fossils of Normandy, including Ichthyosaurus, Plesiosaurus, and a very perfect crocodile from the neighbouring quarries of l'Allemagne. The collections made in the South Sea by Admiral Dumont d'Urville have been deposited here.

The *English Church Service* is performed on Sundays at 1, in the French Protestant *Temple*, Rue de la Geole.

The *Poste aux Lettres* is in the Rue de l'Hôtel de Ville.

Caen is well provided with *promenades*, formal avenues of trees;—the chief are called Grand Cours, and Cours Cafarelli, by the side of the Orne. The handsome *quais* bordering the Orne and the Odon near their junction form pleasant walks.

The women of the lower and middle classes in Caen, and throughout a large part of La Basse Normandie, are finely formed, fully grown, and handsomer than in most other parts of France.

The principal street, in which are the best shops, is the Rue St. Jean.

E 2

Froissart narrates the story of the capture of Caen in 1346, a short while before the battle of Crécy, by Edward III. and the Black Prince, who, being irritated by the resistance of the citizens, gave it up to plunder. It was then "large, strong, and full of drapery and all sorts of merchandise, rich citizens, noble dames, damsels, and fine churches." The English fleet returned home laden with its spoils.

Several of the leaders of the party of the Girondins, proscribed by the Jacobins of the revolutionary tribunal, and driven from Paris by the insurrection of May 31, 1793, retired to Caen to organise a revolt against the tyranny of the Mountain, but were entirely defeated and put down in a battle at Vernon. It was shortly after this event that Charlotte Corday (a native of St. Saturnin, near Séez), actuated by the spirit of resistance against the tyranny of the Terrorists, which prevailed strongly at Caen, set out hence to Paris to assassinate Marat. The Girondins used to meet in the Hotel, No. 44, Rue des Carmes.

Among the illustrious natives of Caen, the learned Huet Bishop of Avranches, born 1613, may be singled out; also the poets Clement Marot, Malherbe, Malfilâtre, and Ségrais; and the Oriental traveller and scholar Bochart.

Brummel, *the* Beau par excellence of the court of George IV. when regent, lived many years at Caen, and ended his days miserably here in a madhouse, *l'Hospice du Bon Sauveur*.

Malleposte daily to Paris (St. Pierre de Vauvray Stat.) and Cherbourg.

Diligences; to Lisieux and Evreux (pp. 71, 72), and to the Stat. St. Pierre de Vauvray on the Paris and Rouen Railway (Rte. 8), in 14 hrs.; daily to Cherbourg (Rte. 26); to Vire, Dol, and St. Malo (Rte. 27); to St. Lo, Coutances, and Granville (Rtes. 27 and 32); to Rennes and Nantes (Rte. 34); to Havre by Harfleur and Rouen (Rte. 23); to Tours by Falaise and Alençon.

Steamer to Havre.

The *making of lace* is said to occupy 20,000 women and children in and about Caen. The streets of the suburbs are lined with family parties seated round their cottage doors merrily twirling their bobbins. They make tulles, brodées, and blondes.

With this exception Caen has no claim to be a manufacturing town; though it was so in an eminent degree until the revocation of the Edict of Nantes banished all its most industrious artisans.

Environs. A cabriolet or other one-horse carriage may be hired for 8 or 10 francs the day.

The student of ancient architecture might spend many days profitably and agreeably in visiting the ecclesiastical and civil monuments which abound in the neighbourhood of Caen. The Dépt. du Calvădós is particularly rich in monuments of architecture; the distinguished archæologist of Caen, M. de Caumont, enumerates nearly 70 specimens of the Norman architecture of the 11th and 12th centuries existing in it.

a. On the outskirts of Caen, to the E., at the extremity of the Rue Basse St. Gilles, is a singular castellated mansion called *Les Gens d'Armes*, from 2 stone figures of armed men on the top. Though surrounded by battlemented walls and furnished with towers, it was not built as a place of defence, but as a maison de plaisance for one Gerard de Nollent, in the beginning of the 16th cent. Its walls are fantastically ornamented externally with medallion heads of emperors, &c.

b. There is a very beautiful and remarkable ruin near Caen, first described by *Prof. Whewell*, the *Abbaye d'Ardenne*, now a farm-yard. It has a fine gate-tower with a round-headed gate and pointed wicket, large stables, "a buttressed barn which puts to utter shame the largest of our edifices of this kind," and a beautiful *Ch.*, closely resembling in style the early English of our abbeys of Bolton and Newstead, now a barn or hay-magazine. Its W. front is especially noticeable; it has a rose within a pointed window, and a rich porch supported "on detached shafts."

c. Thann, Fontaine-Henri, La Délivrande, Luc.

A capital macadamised road, tra-

NORMANDY.   Route 25.—Caen—Thann—Luc.   77

versed by a diligence, leads N. of Caen, to Luc, a bathing-place on the sea, about 12 m. It passes several objects of architectural and antiquarian interest, to which ½ a day may be devoted with advantage, as follows. (N.B. This excursion may be made in a gig, costing 12 frs., in 5 or 6 hrs., including stoppages.)

From Caen a range of high table-land is ascended, on the summit of which is a *calvaire*, or crucifix. "The traveller will not fail to linger on the little hill just beyond the first crucifix. Here he enjoys a lovely prospect. The horizon is bounded by long lines of grey and purple hills: nearer are fields and pastures, whilst the river glitters and winds amidst their vivid tints; nearer still the city of Caen extends itself." It is worth while to walk thus far (2 m. from Caen), for the sake of the view.

7½ m. *Thann*. Here is a true Norman church, scarcely altered since the days of Henry I., when it was built, excepting the loss of its S. aisle. It is a good deal ornamented. The tower is capped with a hollow pyramid of stone, the oldest example of the nascent spire known. It is now deserted.

1¼ m. farther to the N. is the interesting *Château of Fontaine-Henri*, a seat of the family d'Harcourt, built in the first 30 years of the 16th cent., partly in the bastard Gothic, corresponding more with the late Elizabethan of England, partly in the Italian style, resembling the revived classic architecture of Audley End and Longleat. It is a mansion of no great size, but is distinguished by a preposterously lofty and steeply pitched roof, surmounting one wing, flanked by an equally lofty chimney. The most profuse decoration of sculpture is lavished on its singularly irregular façade. The ornaments of the windows, the panelling, balustrades, &c., are not inferior to those of the Palais de Justice at Rouen, which they much resemble. The *Church* of the village is Norman.

A second steep ascent, surmounted by another calvaire, commands a pleasing view over the sea, including 6 or 8 village spires, all having a strong family likeness to that of St. Pierre at Caen. A steep descent of about a mile brings you to the pilgrimage chapel of *La Délivrande*, to which the Norman sailors and peasants have resorted for the last 800 years. It is a small Norman edifice. The statue of the Virgin, which now commands the veneration of the faithful, was resuscitated in the reign of Henry I. from the ruins of a previous chapel destroyed by the Northmen, through the agency of a lamb constantly grubbing up the earth over the spot where it lay. Such is the tenor of the legend. The reputation of the image for performing miracles, especially in behalf of sailors, has been maintained from that time to the present, although it suffered much at the Revolution, when pilgrimages were forbidden. It was visited by Louis XI. in 1471.

It is a drive of 3 m. from this chapel along the low coast to *Luc*, another small watering-place, with an hotel (de la Belle Plage), said to be good.

12 m. from Caen, on the sea, is Corseulles, a small bathing-place and fishing port facing the terrible rocks of Calvădós. It is famed for its oysters. Paris receives from the "parcs aux huîtres" here $\frac{7}{10}$ of all that it consumes, amounting to 5½ million dozen annually. They are transported by light and fast carriages.

The *Church of Ifs*, about 3 m. S. of Caen, has a curious early-pointed steeple; but a still more remarkable tower and spire exist at Norrey, on the way to Bayeux (Rte. 26).

It is worth while to descend one of the *quarries of Caen stone*, so abundantly used in England during the middle ages, and of which the White Tower, old London Bridge, Henry VII.'s Chapel, Winchester and Canterbury cathedrals, besides many of our country churches, were built: they are situated within the circuit of 1½ m. to the W. and S. of Caen, near Maladrerie, on the road to Bayeux, and at Haute Allemagne. The rock is an oolite, equivalent to our Stonesfield slate, but without its slaty structure; it is extracted from subterraneous quarries through vertical shafts, in blocks 8 or 9 ft. long and 2 ft. thick. It is still employed in England; the new tower at the W. end of Canterbury Cathedral is built of this stone.

A visit to *Falaise Castle*, the birthplace of the Conqueror, will occupy a day; a *diligence* runs thither and back daily (see Rte. 29).

Another antiquarian and architectural excursion may be made on the way to Bayeux, to Frèsne-Camilly, Creuilly, and St. Gabriel (Rte. 26).

ROUTE 26.

CAEN TO CHERBOURG, BY BAYEUX.
121 kilom. = 74 Eng. m.
Malleposte daily in 8¼ hrs.
Diligences daily, meeting the Granville diligence at Carentan (Rte. 32.)
A Railway is to be made by 1855.

2 m. beyond Caen is la Maladrerie, so called from a lazar-house founded by our Henry II. for lepers of the town of Caen, now replaced by a huge penitentiary (Maison Centrale de Détention). Near this may be perceived the whims or wheels by which the Caen stone (see above) is raised out of the quarries. At St. Germain le Blancherbe the direct but not post road to St. Lo (Rte. 32) branches off to the l.

The first relay on the way to Bayeux, 12 Bretteville, is called l'Orgueilleuse, though of what it has to be proud is not evident, except its handsome steeple. This, however, is entirely eclipsed by the very fine open belfry and spire of *Norrey*, seen on the l. about 1 m. off the road.

This beautiful *Church*, which has been termed a miniature cathedral, is in the pure and simple Gothic style of our early English, and of the most elegant proportions, with an enriched choir, circular apse, and N. porch. "All the mouldings are deep, free, and repeated so as to give the greatest strength of line to all its parts." The tower owes its character of unequalled beauty to the 4 narrow and tall lancet arches which occupy the N. face of its belfry-story; the two central ones open so as to let daylight through.

In going from Caen to Bayeux a détour may be made to visit Frèsne Camilly, a church in the transition style, round arches prevailing in the body of the building, with indications of pointed arches in a panelled arcade on the exterior of the N. wall. At *Creuilly* the *Castle*, a construction of different ages, retains, among more modern additions, 2 round towers. It belonged to Robert of Gloucester, natural son of Henry I., and is now converted into a dwelling-house. The church is genuine Norman. A little farther is *St. Gabriel*, a ruined priory, founded by Robert of Gloucester, 1128: the choir of the church alone remains, and is a very remarkable example of florid Norman. This is a détour which will repay those of antiquarian taste.

There is another road from Bretteville to Creuilly, passing by Sacqueville en Bessin, whose *church* is curious, partly pointed, partly round.

On the direct road from Caen to Bayeux the country is not very interesting; orchards abound, or rather the corn-fields are planted with rows of apple-trees, under which the grain-crop ripens.

16 *Bayeux* (*Inns:* H. du Luxembourg; good;—Grand Hotel; small, but clean), a quiet and dull ecclesiastical city, with much the air of some cathedral towns in England, was anciently capital of the Bessin, and contains 10,303 Inhab. It is washed by a small stream, the Aure, which enters the sea at 5 m. distance. It consists of two main streets, including some ancient specimens of domestic architecture, running up a hill to a large open *Place*, lined with trees. Its only curiosities are its *Tapestry* and its

Cathedral, its chief ornament, though disfigured by a central cupola in a semi-Grecian style. The W. front is a fine elevation, in the pointed Gothic, surmounted by 2 steeples of the 12th cent., in the towers of which pointed arches alternate with round. The 3 *porches*, which, as well as that on the S. side, deserve attention for their bas-reliefs and ornamental foliage, are later in date and florid in style.

The interior is 315 ft. long and 81 high. The W. end of the *nave* consists of florid Norman arches and piers, whose natural heaviness is relieved by the beautifully-diapered patterns wrought upon the wall, probably built by Henry I., who destroyed the previously-existing church by fire, 1106. Above this runs a blank trefoiled arcade in the place of a triforium, surmounted by a clerestory of early-pointed windows very lofty and narrow.

The arches of the nave, nearest the cross and the *choir*, ending in a semicircle, exhibit a more advanced state of the pointed style, and are distinguished by the remarkable elegance of their graceful clustered pillars. They were built by Bishop Henry de Beaumont, an Englishman, 1205. The circular ornaments in the spandrils of the arches are very pleasing and of fanciful variety. The *stalls* are of oak, well carved.

The chapels in the side-aisles, and the exterior of the E. end, should not pass unnoticed. Under the choir is a *crypt*, probably the only part remaining of the original church, built, in 1077, by Odo, half-brother of the Conqueror, and fifty years bishop of Bayeux. It is supported on 12 pillars with rude capitals, and contains some episcopal tombs. In the *Trésor* is preserved the chasuble of St. Regnobert, in a casket of ivory, with enamelled ornaments, both apparently of Arab workmanship, said to be gifts of St. Louis.

The student of architecture may visit with profit the *Chapel of the Séminaire*, adjoining the *Hôtel Dieu*, a simple oblong plain groined hall, lighted by double lancet windows, and not unlike the E. end of the Temple Church in London: its date is 1206. Behind the altar is a singular recess, beautifully groined. The little Norman *Church of St. Loup*, in the outskirts of the town, on the way to St. Lo, also deserves notice.

The **Tapisserie de Bayeux* has been removed from the Hôtel de Ville—where it used to be unwound by the yard from a roller like a piece of haberdashery, and subjected to the fingers as well as eyes of the curious—to a new room in the *Public Library* (open 8 A.M. to 4 P.M.), where it is more carefully preserved, and quite as conveniently exhibited, under a glass-case. Many persons will look upon it merely as a long strip of coarse linen cloth, 20 inches wide and 214 ft. long, rudely worked with figures worthy of a girl's sampler. It is, however, a curious historical record of peculiar interest to an Englishman; and, although it presents such anomalies as horses coloured alternately blue and red, there is much spirit in the drawing. It is ascribed, with much probability, to the needle of Matilda, Queen of the Conqueror, and represents the Conquest of England, and the events which led to it. It was preserved in the cathedral until the Revolution, being hung round the nave on certain days. The earliest record of it is in an inventory of the effects of the church, taken 1476. Its series of rude worsted pictures represents such events as Edward the Confessor designating William as his heir; the treachery of Harold; the shipment and landing of the Norman army and battle of Hastings: in many of these scenes, Odo Bishop of Bayeux, the Conqueror's half-brother, is a prominent figure. The design has evidently been to represent Harold as a usurper, and William as the rightful heir to the crown, having other claims besides that of conquest. The Normans are drawn with shaven heads and chins, in armour of scales, helmets protected by nose-pieces in front, and shields shaped like boys' kites, sometimes bearing devices of crests (supposed to be of later invention) suspended by a belt round the neck. All the buildings have round arches. At the bottom runs a curious border of animals, including camels and elephants, said to represent fables from Æsop. (?)

The tapestry has been excellently engraved for the London Society of Antiquaries by the late Charles Stothard. When Napoleon was meditating the invasion of England, he caused this tapestry to be transported from town to town, and exhibited on the stage of the playhouses between the acts, to stimulate the spectators to a second conquest!

Wace, the author of the Roman de Rou, was a canon of the cathedral. According to it Harold actually did homage to William of Normandy, as heir of Edward the Confessor, for the throne of England. Many of the women about Bayeux still wear the Bourgogne or Bavolette, a rich and high head-dress, resembling that worn at the courts of the Dukes of Burgundy.

There are good *Baths* at the side of the river, and near them a pretty *Nursery Garden*.

Diligences daily to Caen (4), to Cherbourg and St. Lo, Granville and St. Malo.

In going from Bayeux to Cherbourg the *diligences* make a détour of 9 leagues by passing through St. Lo (Rte. 32); the *malleposte* takes the direct line, as follows, passing *La Tour en Bessin*, whose little *church* has a chancel in a style resembling the best English decorated; the nave is Norman, the tower and spire earlier than the chancel.

16 Formigny. Here the English were defeated (1450) in an engagement so decisive, that it occasioned them the loss of Normandy, which has never since been separated from the French crown. A monument on the rt. of the road marks the battle-field, and commemorates the victory. It must be borne in mind that Sir Thomas Kyriel, who commanded the English, an old soldier of Agincourt, who took little account of superior numbers on the side of the French, attacked, with a vastly inferior force, the army of the Comte de Clermont, and while thus engaged was assaulted in the rear by a second army, under the Constable de Richemont.

16 Isigny-on-the-Aure is accessible for vessels of considerable size, with the tide. Much butter is exported hence to England and elsewhere.

The river Vire, forming the boundary between the departments of Calvados and La Manche, is crossed about one-third of the distance.

11 Carentan (*Inn:* H. de la Place, good), a town of 3193 Inhab., in a low marshy situation, surrounded by fortifications no longer kept up, possessing an old *Castle*, which belonged to the Kings of France, and was besieged by Edward III., 1346, and a handsome *Church*, surmounted by a spire; it is Norman, with pointed additions, the E. end in the style of the 14th cent. There is some painted glass, but defective.

At Carentan we enter the peninsula of the *Cotentin*, so called from the "côtes"—coasts, which border it on 3 sides. It is a fertile and pleasing district, celebrated for its pastures, on which large herds are fed, everywhere enclosed within hedges, and abounding in old ruined castles and ancient churches. It is particularly interesting to Englishmen, as the cradle of some of the oldest and most noble English families. At every step the traveller will encounter obscure villages and hamlets, whose names are familiar to him as household words, as patronymics of great houses distinguished in French and English annals, most of whose founders left their country in the train of William the Norman. Such are Beaumont, Greville, Carteret, Bruce, Neville, Bohon, Perci, Pierpont; but these are only a few examples among many.

13 Saint Mère l'Eglise has a similar church to that of Carentan.

The ruins of the Abbey of Monteburg have been swept away to the foundation since 1817, having been sold in lots, and pulled down for the materials.

At Quinéville, 6 m. N.E. of this, on the coast, is an ancient monument of masonry, 27 ft. high, and 30 in circumference at the base, which is square, and surmounted by a hollow cylinder garnished round with 2 rows of pillars. It is called *la Grande Cheminée;* and though some writers have made it a Roman monument, it may be more safely pronounced a structure of the end of the 12th cent., and nothing more nor less than a chimney.

From the heights of Quinéville King James II. beheld the *sea-fight* of *La Hougue*, which destroyed all his hopes of regaining his throne. It is said that, in the heat of the battle, on seeing the French ships boarded and carried in succession, his English feelings so far prevailed, that he exultingly exclaimed to the French officers about him, " Look at my brave English sailors." (See p. 82.)

Through a pleasing country, to which the hedges and woodlands give a perfectly English character, not unlike parts of Sussex, to

17 Valognes (*Inns*: H. du Louvre, kept by M. Guetté, one of the best cooks in France; "the andouillettes and homards à la broche renowned " —*R. F.*; Grand Turc, tolerable), a pleasant town of 6940 Inhab., containing some large and handsome mansions, the residence of numerous genteel families. The castle of William the Conqueror is demolished; it was here that he was warned by his fool, in the middle of the night, of the conspiracy of the Seigneurs of the Bessin and Cotentin to surprise and assassinate him. He instantly mounted his horse, and escaped with difficulty to Falaise.

M. de Gerville, a distinguished antiquary and geologist, resides here.

Although Valognes possesses nothing in itself to detain the traveller, in its vicinity are several objects of high interest. *St. Sauveur le Vicomte* (10 m. S.) has a picturesque ruined castle and abbey (Rte. 27). At *Bricquebec* (9 m. S.W.) is a convent of Trappists. The geology of the Cotentin is very interesting; its tertiary beds, in which more than 300 species of fossil shells, identical with those of the Paris Basin, have been found, and its Baculite limestone, may be well studied in the quarries near Valognes.

At Alléaume, the Roman *Alauna*, a village contiguous to Valognes, are very scanty remains of a bath. A Roman theatre, described by Montfaucon, has been totally demolished.

An excursion may be made hence to *La Hougue* and *Barfleur* by Tamarville, (2¼ m.), where the Norman *Church* has an elegant octagonal tower (a rare form) composed of 3 stories of narrow round-headed arcades and windows.

St. Vaast la Hougue, 10 m. from Valognes, is a seaport town of 3500 Inhab., situated in a fine bay, with the fortified island and lazaret of Tatihou in front, provided with a pier 984 ft. long Previous to the rise of Cherbourg it was the chief port of the Cotentin. Vauban proposed to make it what Cherbourg is, the chief arsenal of France in the Channel, but the project was stopped, owing to the difficulty of quitting its port with a N. wind. The English frequently effected hostile landings here, to lay desolate the fair fields of France. King Stephen, in 1137, landed here, and the army which conquered at Crécy under Edward III. in 1346. Other armaments disembarked here in the reigns of Henry IV. and V.; and in 1574 a force of 5000 French and English Protestants, despatched by Queen Elizabeth under the Comte de Montgomery, to aid the cause of the Huguenots, made a descent upon Normandy at this point. La Hougue is chiefly known in English history, however, on account of the *sea-fight* of *Cap la Hougue* in 1692, when the united English and Dutch ships, under Admirals Russel and Rooke, annihilated the expedition prepared by Louis XIV. for a descent upon England, with the design of restoring James II. to the throne. The action commenced at some distance from the coast between Cape Barfleur and the Isle of Wight. The French admiral, Tourville, a man of great bravery, having orders from his master to engage at all odds, ventured to measure his strength with a fleet of 80 vessels, the largest which had entered the Channel since the Armada, while his own force did not exceed 44. It is supposed that he was ignorant of the junction of the Dutch, and that he counted on the desertion of Admiral Russel, who, it is well known, was in secret correspondence with James. However, nothing of this sort occurred; and, after a running fight, the French, in 3 divisions, retired to their own coast, pursued by the English. 3 of the largest ships, including the admiral's, le Soleil Royal, sought refuge in Cher-

E 3

bourg, where they were blown up by the English admiral Delaval. Tourville, hoisting his flag on board another vessel, conducted 12 into the bay of La Hougue, where he had time, before the arrival of Russel the day after, to prepare means for a stout defence, running them aground on the shallows with their broadside to the enemy. The French army, united with a body of Irish and English refugees, was drawn up on the heights above; while the artillery was embarked on floating batteries, à fleur d'eau, to assist in repelling any attack on the ships. James II., attended by Marshals Berwick and Bellefonde, who commanded his forces, was a spectator of the action which ensued. The only really brilliant part of the battle was the attack and capture of this armament by the boats of the English squadron under Sir George Rooke; these, and a few light frigates, only being able to approach near enough to take a part in the action on account of the shallows. In the teeth of a tremendous fire of musketry and artillery from shore and ships, the English sailors pulled up to the stranded vessels, boarded them all, one after the other, with loud huzzas, and pointed their guns against the French on the shore. All the 12 ships of war were burnt, together with a number of transports, 300 of which had been collected in this and the neighbouring ports to convey the army across to England.

A magnificent view of the coast may be obtained from the churchyard of *la Pernelle*.

About 7 m. N. of St. Vaast is *Barfleur*, an ancient and now nearly deserted town, built of granite.

Down to the end of the 12th centy. it was the most frequented port by which the communication between Normandy and England was maintained, in spite of the dangerous rocks around. Upon them perished the "Blanche Nef,"—the ship which conveyed William the only son of Henry I., with 140 young noblemen—through the fault of the intoxicated pilot and crew. The prince himself might have escaped had not an affectionate desire to save his natural sister, the Countess of Mortagne, caused him to turn back towards the foundering vessel. The boat which was bearing him to the shore was instantly filled by a crowd of despairing wretches, and all sank to the bottom together.

On the extreme point of the Cap de Gatteville, the W. horn of the great bay into which the Seine discharges itself, the E. headland being near Fécamp, about 1 m. N. of Barfleur, a magnificent *Lighthouse* was completed in 1835. It is 271 ft. high above the sea, and is constructed entirely of granite. The light is seen at a distance of 27 m. out at sea. There is a fine view from the top. Barfleur is 15 m. E. of Cherbourg: a good road leads thither. Near to it, about 2 m. E. of St. Pierre l'Eglise, lies the *Château de Tocqueville*, seat of the family " of *that* ilk," now belonging to the eminent writer on America, M. Alexis de T.; and on the other side of the village, the Château St. Pierre, a building of the 18th cent., seat of the Countess de Blangy.

At the distance of about 7 m. from Valognes the direct post-road from Valognes to Cherbourg passes, 2½ m. on the l., the small town of *Brix*, a memorable name, since it is the same as Bruis or Bruce in its primitive spelling. The noble family of that name was allied to the Dukes of Normandy, and from it sprang Robert Bruce the King of Scotland. The castle of the Seigneur de Brix, built in the 12th centy., is now reduced to a few ruined vaults and foundation walls. It was called *Château d'Adam*.

About 2 m. S.E. of Cherbourg, not far off the road, is the castle of *Tourlaville*, the magnificent seat of the family of Ravalez, now a farmhouse, belonging to the de Tocquevilles. Its position is beautiful and its architecture of high interest; part of it dates from the 15th centy., part was added in the reign of Henry II., and the Tour des 4 Vents (fine view from its top) has the character of Heidelberg Castle. "The bleeding heart and motto of the Ravalez family, 'Un seul me suffit,' are everywhere visible among the faded frescoes and gilding of its walls and ceilings"—*H.R.* There is nothing more to notice on the road, until from the top of the last hill a fine view of the sea is presented through the gap of the valley, with Cherbourg at its mouth. A winding descent through a picturesque gully, displaying here and there bare cliffs, terminates in a long avenue of trees, which forms the approach to Cherbourg. On the l. rises the eminence La Fauconnière, crowned by the telegraph; on the rt. the cliff of Roule exposes a precipitous escarpment, 350 ft. above the sea.

20 CHERBOURG.—*Inns:* H. de l'Europe, on the Quai Ouest du Bassin; H. de Londres, good restaurant—*R. F.*; H. de Commerce.

Cherbourg, one of the principal naval ports and dockyards of France, is situated at the N. extremity of the peninsula of the Cotentin in the Dépt. de la Manche, in the centre of a bay, the extremities of which are formed by Cap Levy on the E. and Point Omanville on the W. Its docks have been gained out of the rock, and its harbour won from the winds; for no pains nor cost have been spared to secure for France on this point, so advantageously projecting into the Channel, a naval arsenal and port, whence she may be ready to watch or annoy her rival on the opposite coast. The town lies in the hollow of the valley of the Divette, which opens out to the sea under the lofty falaise of the quartz hill of Roule, crowned by a fort. More than a dozen detached forts and redoubts have been erected on the hills behind the town, at distances varying from ½ m. to 1½ m. from the sea. Apart from its consideration as a naval station Cherbourg is insignificant; with dirty streets, reminding one of Portsmouth Point. Its commercial relations are very limited; but its extensive naval works employ about 10,000 out of its 25,000 Inhab., and upon them depends its prosperity. Among its few articles of export are eggs to the value of one million francs yearly sent to England. Cherbourg has a *Bassin de Commerce*, a commercial harbour, formed at the mouth of the Divette, never very full of shipping, but often visited by vessels of the English *Yacht Club*, who come over to lay in provisions and champagne. It is lined with quays, and the entrance to it is protected by stone piers, with a lighthouse at its extremity. The commercial port is quite distinct from

The *Dockyard* (Grand Port), situated on the N.W. of the town. Travellers desirous of seeing the dockyard must apply to the Major de la Marine, at the Vieux Port, on the E. of the commercial harbour, showing their passports, in order to procure a *ticket of admission.* He will appoint a gendarme to accompany them, to whom a couple of francs may be given for his trouble. The Grand Port occupies a nearly triangular space of ground, one side resting on the sea, and is surrounded by fortifications, surrounded by fossés cut in the rock, faced with granite masonry, and adding greatly to the strength of the place.

The *Port Militaire,* and *Arsenal de la Marine,* designed, as well as the Digue, by Marshal Vauban, whose plan, drawn by his own hand and signed, is preserved in the H. de Ville, were only partly begun by Louis XVI. They have been more than 50 years in progress; and the new works commenced since 1831 will take as many more, probably, to complete. The docks, floating basins (bassins à flot), &c., have been created by excavation by the aid of gunpowder out of the solid slate rock, which forms the foundation of the entire yard. From the stairs on the W. quai of the avant port, Charles X. and his family embarked in 1830. The 4 slips (Cales de Construction) are of very solid masonry; the lofty roofs rest on arches supported by piers of granite and slate; the arches are partly closed by wooden blinds. Adjoining them is a dry dock (*Forme de Radoub*), and beyond them are the Ateliers des Forges (smithy), des Machines (workshops filled with machinery for planing, turning, scooping, and cutting rods, beams, screws, &c., of iron); the Atelier de la Fonderie, roofed with zinc, furnished with 2 large and 6 smaller furnaces, and with iron cranes, &c. On the W. of the docks the *Magasins Généraux*, the *Parc et Caserne d'Artillerie*, and the *Caserne de Marine*, magnificent buildings, are nearly completed.

The Timber Shed (Hangar au Bois) is 958 ft. long, and supported on 130 stone pillars. The yard is supplied with water from the Divette by a long and expensive conduit.

Convicts are not employed at Cherbourg.

La Digue. The roads of Cherbourg, though protected on three sides by the land, are naturally open and exposed to the N. wind. To remedy this defect, the project of throwing a Breakwater across the bay's mouth, in the deep sea, has been favoured by every French government since that of Louis XVI. The old Bourbons, the Republic, the Empire, the Restoration, and Louis Philippe, have all desired to advance a scheme which should contribute to secure for France a safe and strong harbour on this part of her coast, exactly opposite Portsmouth, which would be an eye to watch and an arm to strike the English on the opposite side of the Channel. Hitherto the French have possessed no port for ships of war from Dunkirk (and that is fit only for frigates) to Brest. Now that the works have been carried on nearly 50 years, and more than 28,000,000 of francs, together with about 4,000,000 cubic mètres of stone, sunk in the operation, the Digue at length approaches to completion, since $\frac{2}{3}$ of it are now terminated, and its permanent duration seems probable, since for several years past no perceptible alteration has been produced by the action of the waves in the structure or profile of the base. For a long time the undertaking could be regarded only as a series of experiments and failures. The plan first adopted under Louis XVI. (1784) was that of forming truncated cones of timber, or huge broadbottomed tubs, floating them on empty casks to the proper place, sinking them, and filling them with stones, and heaping up others round about them. But a very brief exposure to a few storms overset some of the caissons, shattered the framework of others to pieces, and spread the stone and wood over the anchorage, so as to injure it. After a considerable interruption from the Revolution, another scheme was resorted to of forming a bank of small stones, and covering these with large solid blocks: this was continued down to the time of Napoleon, who, as was his custom, looked at the project in a military point of view, and at once directed the formation of a fort in the centre of the Digue. All exertions were thenceforth concentrated on this object; a mole was formed, a battery raised on it mounting 20 guns, a garrison of 90 men was established on it, and lodged in barracks erected for the purpose. In 1808, however, a storm of extraordinary violence burst upon the roads; the waves, carried to an unusual height, soon submerged all the buildings raised upon the Digue, and, by the impetuosity of their shocks, swept them all off, save the cabin of the commandant of the prison, and, forming a wide breach in the masonry, poured over and through it with tremendous violence. There were at the time upon the dyke 263 soldiers and workmen, of whom 194 were drowned, 69 were saved by finding shelter in hollows among the stones, and 38 got off in a boat which they managed to reach during a short lull, with great difficulty, since the vessels in the roads within the Digue were all driven from their moorings. By this disaster the operations of 16 years in sinking large blocks were nearly annihilated, and the whole mass of stone was reduced to the condition of a rubble bed, rendering it doubtful whether the plan of even protecting the roads at all was practicable. Nevertheless, Napoleon did not abandon it, nor did his successors lose sight of it. A survey made by order of the government in 1828 showed, however, that the foundations had shifted in the course of 40 years from the position in which they had been first placed to a considerable distance. Under the vigorous superintendence of Louis Philippe a new mode of proceeding was adopted in 1832. As the result of the schemes previously pursued had shown that the mere weight and volume of the stones thrown into the sea was insufficient to secure their fixity, a layer of beton, a species of concrete, composed of 1 part of small stones and pounded brick and 2 of lime, is now deposited on the loose stone heap, sloping on either side, and upon it a vertical wall of well-jointed and solid masonry, faced with granite, is raised. Even this, however, was destined to be the sport of the waves during a storm which occurred in 1836, the most terrible since that of 1808 : the coat of concrete was broken and turned over in places ; blocks of stone, weighing 3 tons, were raised 22 ft. high in the air, and carried over the wall to the inside of the Digue. At the end of 3 days 300 of them had found their way across, hurled with appalling violence and noise against the granite masonry, and acting upon it like battering rams, so that serious breaches and wide gaps were formed in the body of the breakwater. This is more or less the effect of every serious tempest.

More than 500 workmen are constantly employed upon the Digue, being lodged in barracks on the breakwater, and protected during their operations by a movable shed. The colossal structure now raises its head above the surface of the sea. At the present rate of progress it may be finished in 3 or 4 years.

The *Digue de Cherbourg* extends between the Ile Pelée and the Pointe de Querqueville, in length 4111 yards, or more than 2 m., leaving openings for the entrance and exit of vessels on the E. of 1257 yards, and at the W. of about 1½ m. The width at the base is 310 ft. The depth of the sea about the Digue varies from 36 to 45 ft. at low water. There are at each end lighthouses and forts, crossing their fire with those on shore, and guns may be mounted at intervals all along the Digue. The stone employed is partly from the quarries at the base of the Montagne de Roule, conveyed to the harbour along a tramway ; the slate comes from the excavations made in forming the docks, and the granite from Fermanville and Flamanville.

Persons desirous of seeing the Digue are required to have a permission from the authorities. Failing this, the best way is to hire a boat in the harbour and row off to it, the distance being about 2 m.

The following statement of comparative measurements in yards will show how much more serious an undertaking the Cherbourg Digue is than the Plymouth Breakwater :—

	Length.	Breadth.	Height.
Digue,	4111	103-310	22 } yards.
Break-water, }	1760	{ 120 at base, 16 at top,	14 }

The lapse of years however will alone decide whether the Digue will be completed successfully.

Commodore Sir Charles Napier, who visited Cherbourg during the Naval Review, Oct. 1850, thus described it :— "We have seen, almost within sight of our own shores, a splendid Breakwater of nearly 3 m. long rise from the bottom of the sea, 60 ft. deep, under which can lie at moorings 50 sail of the line with perfect safety, almost frowning on England. That breakwater, ere long, will be defended by 3 tremendous fortifications, independent of movable guns without number, to protect either entrance that may be attacked. On the Isle of Pelée opposite the breakwater, on the E. entrance, is Fort Imperial (or National), mounting 90 guns casemated, and guns pointing out of ports like a ship. Opposite this, on the main land, is Fort des Flamands, mounting many heavy guns; in its rear is the redoubt of Tourlaville.

"Opposite the breakwater, to the W., are the Forts of Querqueville, St. Anne, and Homet, and one intended to be built on a rock between the W. end of the breakwater and Querqueville. These forts will mount upwards of 150 guns. There are also strong batteries to the left of the basin, bearing on the roads. Within the breakwater, excavated out of rock and faced with stone, is the *avant port*, capable of containing 10 sail of the line alongside the quay, 30 ft. deep at low water springtides. In this port is a dock and 4 slips; in a line with this, and communicating with it, is an inner basin, in which 10 sail of the line can also lie alongside the quay. On two sides of this basin are magazines; and here also lies the sheer hulk. In the rear of Fort Homet there is another small basin, and two building-slips. This serves as a ditch to the fort, which is cut off from the mainland and island by a drawbridge; from the lower tier of guns another bridge conducts you over a ditch to a large barrack-yard, casemated; and two small stairs lead up to a second tier of guns.

"In the rear of the *avant port* and the inner basin inland, there is another basin in construction, which communicates with both. This basin when finished can accommodate 20 sail of the line alongside the quay. Here are 4 docks and 5 slips. To the l. of the great *avant port* there is another *avant port*, which leads to the steam basin, where there are 3 slips. The storehouses are large, well arranged, and close to the basins. There is also a port of refuge, leading to another steam basin, where, as in the other basins, the steamers can coal alongside the wharf.

"The splendid dockyard is surrounded by a high wall, and the wall is again surrounded by regular fortifications, with a wet ditch: and to protect the works, the heights in the rear, and, indeed, all round from Tourlaville, there is a double chain of strong redoubts. Independent of all these there is a commercial basin, with gates, in which merchant vessels lie afloat. Two piers project a considerable distance beyond the gates. Both the town and basin are outside the fortification."

These works would render Cherbourg, if not impregnable from the sea, at least very difficult to attack. On the land side it has hitherto been almost open, but the fortifications now in progress are intended to strengthen it there. The expenditure of money on the works here, including the Digue, considerably exceeds 400 millions of francs.

In 1758 the English, under General Bligh, effected a descent on the coast, to the number of 7000, in the face of 16,000 French troops, who offered no effective opposition. The English forces kept possession of Cherbourg for three days, in which time they destroyed all the naval and military works, docks, arsenals, &c., blowing them up with the powder which the French had left behind, burning the lock gates of the harbour and all the vessels of war and commerce. They levied a contribution of 44,000 livres on the town, but no injuries nor pillage of the inhabitants or their dwellings were permitted. To this the French themselves bear honourable testimony, acknowledging that the protection of British officers prevented any outrage. All the cannon were carried off, but the bells of the ch. were conceded to the entreaties of the curé, and allowed to remain.

Cherbourg has no antiquities to show, except the *Vieille Tour*, which formed part of the ancient fortifications, washed by the sea, and the *Ch.*, not far from it; both built about 1450, and neither possessing any interest.

The *Chapelle de Notre Dame du Vœu*, outside the town near the dockyard, owes its existence and its name to a vow made by the Empress Maude when caught in a fierce tempest, which threatened to overwhelm the vessel in which she was attempting to gain the port of Cherbourg, on her flight from the usurper Stephen, by whom she had been driven out of England. While still at her prayers, and in the agony of anticipated death among the waves, "Chante, Reine," exclaimed a sailor, "behold the land; your prayers are heard:" and from this circumstance, it is said, the spot where the queen landed, and near to which she built the chapel, now enclosed within the dockyard, was called *Chantereine*,—a name which it still retains. The *present Chapel* of the Vow is however modern, and stands on a different spot. Mathilda is not the only refugee sovereign whom Cherbourg has seen within its walls at various periods: besides Charles X., who here took a last farewell of his country, after abdicating the throne at Rambouillet, 1830, Don Pedro, ex-Emperor of Brazil, arrived here, 1831, when driven from his states, and James II. repaired hither after the battle of La Hougue.

The *Hôtel de Ville* contains a *Collection of* 164 *Pictures,* formed and bequeathed to the town by a native, Thomas Henry, himself an artist. " The best are (33) David, by *Herrera el Viejo ;* (34) Christ bearing the Cross, by *Alonso Cano* (called Murillo);—the majority are of the French school."— *R. F.* In the court-yard is a very curious chimney-piece, of the age of Louis XI., rescued from a demolished convent.

Consuls reside here from Great Britain and the maritime states of Europe and the United States of America.

There is a *Bathing Establishment* on the sands, to the E. of the old Arsenal and Jetée, but it is not well appointed.

" M. le Magnen et Fils, agents to the Royal Yacht Club of England, are very obliging, and their wines, especially their clarets, are excellent." —*R. F.*

The *Poste aux Lettres* is on the Quai du Port.

Malleposte daily to the Paris and Rouen Rly.

Diligences daily to Caen; to St. Lo, Coutances, and St. Malo. Inferior coaches daily to Valognes ; to Barfleur; to St. Vaast; to Bricquebec.

Steamers to Havre twice a week; to Weymouth once or twice in the summer.

Excursions may be made to the Phare de Gatteville ; Barfleur, and La Hougue; to the interesting Châteaux of Martinvaast (p. 87), belonging to the Comte Dumoncel; of Flamanville, a splendid mansion; of Tourlaville; of Blangy (p. 82).

Querqueville 5 m. W. of Cherbourg, is a hamlet whose name is variously derived from the oak, *quercus,* which once surrounded it, or, with more probability, from its small *Church* (kerk) of *St. Germain* standing by the side of the parish ch. This is one of the oldest monuments of Christianity in Normandy. It is in the form of a cross; its chancel and transepts, lighted by loophole windows, all end in apses, and all this part is of herring-bone masonry; the nave and tower were added at a subsequent period. The ornaments of the towers, stripes of stone projecting from the wall, surmounted by the round arch, resemble those of Barton on the Humber, Barnack, and others in England.

The fort of Querqueville is one of the defences of the roads of Cherbourg, and its lighthouse points out the entrance to them.

13 m. farther to the W., beyond Beaumont, the Cap la Hague (often confounded on the maps with La Hougue) stretches out towards Alderney (called by the French Aurigny), from which island it is only 9 m. distant. Both the cape and the island, as well as the Cape Flamanville, are of granite, the fundamental rock of the Côtentin, supporting the grauwacke and clay slates, which for the most part appear on the surface of that district. Opposite Cap la Hague, on a rock called le Gros du Raz, about a mile out at sea, stands a lighthouse.

The Trappist Convent at Bricquebec, and the Castle and Abbey of St. Sauveur le Vicomte, are described in Rte. 27.

ROUTE 27.

CHERBOURG TO ST. MALO, BY ST. SAUVEUR, COUTANCES, GRANVILLE, AVRANCHES, MONT ST. MICHEL, AND DOL.

205 kilom. = 127 Eng. m.

Diligences daily from Cherbourg by Carentan and Coutances to St. Malo.

Persons travelling in their own carriage may vary the road back to

20 Valognes, the first post-station (p. 81), by going round by Octeville (1 m.), where is a Norman church with an octagonal tower and curious carvings (a Last Supper, &c., in bas-relief) older than the reign of Henry II.; and Martinvaast (2½ m.), where is a still older ch. in the same style, and unaltered, with slender half-pillars, supporting Ionic capitals, outside its semi-

circular E. end, and a cornice of grotesque heads under its eaves: its lofty stone vaulted roof is supported on horse-shoe arches. It stands in a sequestered spot, with a fine old yew beside it. There is a fine *Castle*, still inhabited, hard by. Bricquebec (8 m. from Valognes), a village, including an ancient *Castle*, whose lofty donjon keep, 100 ft. high, in shape a decagon, seated on a high mound, remains tolerably perfect (date 14th cent.), as well as the walls of the outer enclosure. Other portions are as late as the 16th, and some as early as the 11th cent. It belonged in turn to the families of Bertram, Paisnel (Paganel) and Estouteville. It was taken from the last by Henry V. after the battle of Agincourt, and bestowed on his favourite William de la Pole, Earl of Suffolk, who parted with it to ransom himself from the hands of the French.

In the adjoining forest, on the hill des *Grosses Roches*, are three Druidical monuments of the kind called "Galeries Couvertes." A little more than a m. N. E. of Bricquebec is the *Trappist Convent*, founded 1823 by M. Onfray, on a spot of ground just cleared from the forest. Its inmates, 32 in number, of whom 12 are priests, are bound by strict vows to silence, communicating by established signs on indispensable matters, living on coarse dry bread, a few vegetables, a salad with a spoonful of oil, a little milk, and a bit of cheese, and one plateful of a meagre potage, which on fast-days is reduced to 6 oz. of bread in the morning and 2 or 3 at night, with a fixed allowance of herbs and roots. They are prohibited from wearing linen even when ill, and sleep with their clothes on, upon a straw mattress piquée, 2 inches thick. They are allowed one sort of meat when sick, but fish is forbidden. They rise daily at 2 A. M.; and on fête-days at 12 or 1, and spend their time in prayer, reading, and work.

There is a cross-road from Bricquebec to St. Sauveur. On quitting Valognes our route separates from Rte. 26, and turning to the l. passes by Columby (a church with pointed lancet windows) to

15 St. Sauveur le Vicomte, where there is a picturesque and imposing *Castle* of the Tessons and Harcourts, but given by Edward III. after the treaty of Bretigny to John Chandos, one of the most famous captains of the wars of Edward III. and the Black Prince. He built the square and lofty keep-tower, one of the gateways, and other portions. In the 17th century it became a hospital, and continued such down to the Revolution. Although falling to ruin at present, it is the best preserved feudal fortress on the Côtentin.

Here are also ruins of an *Abbey*, which in 1831 were being pulled down for the sake of the materials. The church was beautiful, the groundwork Norman (1067-1160), with additions, in the pointed style, of the 13th century.

Between St. Sauveur and Bériers the post-road passes near the *Abbey of Blanchelande*, founded by Richard de la Haye, a favourite of Henry II. (1115-85) who had been captured by corsairs, and passed many years in slavery. It is beautifully situated, and consists of the abbot's house, still perfect and inhabited by a farmer, and part of the *Church*, in which late insertions have been added to an original Norman structure.

10 La Haye du Puits. The castle, dating from the 11th cent., the only thing of interest in this obscure little town, has been pulled down within the last 15 years to mend the roads! The last remains, a fine old machicolated tower, have probably by this time disappeared.

At Lessay is another abbey and church in the Norman style, begun in the 11th cent., but not consecrated till 1178. "It is of one character, plain, but grand throughout; and possesses a noble central tower. The W. portal is more ornamented than the other parts, and exhibits the dog-tooth moulding, which does not appear in England till nearly the end of the 12th century."—*Knight*.

18 Périers.

16 *Coutances*. (*Inns:* H. de France, dear; H. d'Angleterre, tolerable.)

Coutances, at present a somewhat lifeless town of 8957 Inhab., is built upon a nearly conical hill, the summit of which is occupied by the *Cathedral*, proudly predominating over other buildings, with its 3 towers. The high road, carried in a broad winding terrace along the flank of the hill, round the outskirts of the town, forms an agreeable walk, while on the opposite or E. side are more formal and gloomy promenades closely planted with avenues of trees.

The *Cathedral is one of the finest churches of Normandy, in the early pointed style, free from exuberant ornament, but captivating the eye by the elegance of proportion and arrangement. "The whole is of a piece, complete in conception and execution. The lofty towers terminating in spires, both finished and alike, flank its W. front." "Its interior is very lofty, more than 100 ft. from the floor to the keystone of the vault. Cluster piers divide the nave from the aisles: coupled pillars surround the choir (which ends in a hexagon). Most of the windows are of later date than the body of the building."—*Knight.* "The peculiarities of this cathedral are, the side porches close behind the towers; the open screens of mullioned tracery, corresponding with the windows, which divide the side chapels; and the excessive height of the choir, which has no triforium, only a balustrade just before the clerestory windows. The central tower is wonderfully fine in the exterior; it is apparently an expansion of the plain Norman lantern as at Caen. Some of the painted glass is in the oldest style: diapered patterns in a black outline, on a grey ground."— *Palgrave.*

A magnificent cathedral was built at Coutances in the 11th cent. with contributions partly furnished by Tancred de Hauteville and his 6 sons, the conquerors of Sicily and Apulia, who were natives of the diocese of Coutances; "it was consecrated 1056 in the presence of William Duke of Normandy, 9 years before he conquered England."

Some of the antiquaries of Normandy have maintained that the existing edifice is the one completed at that time, and have claimed in consequence for their country the invention of the pointed style in the 11th centy.; but as no buildings either in W. France or in England were constructed in that style until 130 years after, and as, on the contrary, all the buildings erected during that period are in the round style—for instance, the church of Lessay, only 9 m. off, consecrated 1178—there is no reason to concede their claim. The evidence upon which they found it is, that the *Livre Noir*, (a mere account of the advowsons of the diocese, compiled 1250) makes no mention of the rebuilding of the church after the 11th cent. There exists, however, proof, from inscriptions on the walls of the side chapels, that several of them were dedicated, and therefore probably built, in the latter half of the 13th cent. (1274), and it is also known that the church was nearly ruined in 1356 by the army of Geoffrey d'Harcourt, so that it must have needed serious repairs, though the record of them is lost, executed probably about the end of the 14th cent. (*See Knight's Normandy.*)

From the top of the fine lantern tower a view may be obtained of the sea, with the distant island of Jersey on the W., and of the rock of Granville.

The *Ch. of St. Pierre* is in the florid Gothic style of the 15th cent.

The steep and narrow valley which bounds the town on the W. and is traversed by the terraced road leading to Granville, before mentioned, is crossed by the remains of an *ancient Aqueduct*, consisting of 5 perfect arches, and 15 piers supported by buttresses, called *Les Piliers*, which is also the name given to the village or suburb in which it is situated, $\frac{1}{4}$ m. out of Coutances. In most guide-books and descriptions of the town it is called a *Roman* aqueduct, but its pointed arches, its buttresses with offsets, and coarse irregular masonry, prove clearly that it is not so, but a work of the middle ages, probably monkish. It is supposed to have been erected in the 13th cent.

by one of the noble family De Paisnel (Paganel.)

Coaches to St. Lo (Rte. 32) daily; to Granville 3 times a day.

Those who love old Gothic ruins, either for their picturesqueness or architecture, will be repaid by an excursion hence to the *Abbey of Hambye*, about 13 m. to the S.E. It may be taken on the way to Granville, making a détour of 6 or 7 m. A good road leads through a pleasing but hilly country by Mesnil l'Aubert and St. Denis le Guest, leaving *Hambye l'Eglise* ¼ m. to the rt., to Bourg d'Hambye, a scattered village, with a small but clean cabaret, furnishing only homely fare, —coffee, milk, cheese, and cider. The old *Castle* of Hambye, whose keep, 100 ft. high, stood on an eminence over the Bourg, is swept away to mend the roads. Happily a better spirit is now abroad in France, and the government holds out an example to England of zeal for the preservation of the many noble or curious edifices dispersed over the country.

It is a pleasant walk of 1½ m. from the Bourg to the *Abbey*, but the road thither, through narrow lanes, is practicable only for light cars.

The little *Abbey of Hambye* nestles in a retired valley, sheltered under picturesque cliffs by the side of a trout-stream (the Sienne) the beau idéal of a monastic site. The roof and W. end are gone, the ivy begins to creep up the mouldering walls, and destruction is advancing apace, yet there is much beauty in the narrow arches which enclosed the choir, resting on columnar piers, in the style of the 15th centy. Behind them are side chapels much older, having round and pointed arches in combination, which marks the period of transition. The tower in the centre of the cross rests on square piers which become octagonal below by chamfering. The convent buildings are now occupied by a farmer. The *Chapterhouse*, a double pointed vault elegantly groined, resting on angular pillars and entered by a fine doorway deep sunk in its early English mouldings, is now turned into a woodhouse: it should be seen. This abbey was founded by William de Pagnel 1145, but renovated, or probably rebuilt, in the 15th cent. by Joanne de Pagnel, the last of her family, who was buried in the church with her husband Louis d'Estouteville, the defender of Mont St. Michel against the English (p. 93). Their tombs were destroyed at the Revolution.

About 5 m. from Hambye is *Perci*, cradle of the Earls of Northumberland. The high road to Granville may be regained at Bréhal.

The direct road from Coutances to Granville has no interest.

19 Bréhal. Trees diminish in size and number on approaching the sea, glimpses of which and the island of Chaussey are seen at intervals. The entrance to Granville is by a steep descent, excavated partly through a deep hollow way; on the rt. a natural wall of rock separates the road from the sea-shore, and through a gap cut in it access is afforded to the baths and sea-beach. In front rises a high hill, its slope cut away evenly and levelled, until it is as steep and smooth as the roof of a house, in order to form a glacis for the fort on its top. A bend in the road presently discloses to view the lower town and harbour.

10 *Granville*. — *Inns:* Trois Couronnes; H. du Nord, abominably dirty. Neither good. This is a small but tolerably prosperous seaport (7600 Inhab.), chiefly resorted to by fishing vessels, but driving some commerce along the coast and with Jersey (33 m. distant) and Guernsey.

Its situation is singular, built in steps or terraces under a rocky promontory projecting into the sea, surmounted by the fort, whose presence restricts many of the buildings from rising above one story in height. Under the shelter of this eminence lies the little port, screened by it from the N. winds. A new town is gradually spreading itself along the low margin of this harbour, and up the banks of a stream so small that it is generally swallowed up in soapsuds, and contributes, with the filthy abominations of the town itself, especially at low water, when the harbour is drained to the lees of mud, to produce a state of atmosphere barely tolerable. The sombre hue of the buildings, whose walls are dark granite and their roofs black slate, renders Granville on a near examination as unattractive to the sight as to the smell, and moreover it contains no objects of interest.

The stranger desirous to rescue himself from *ennui* must repair to the noble *Pier*, begun 1828 and still unfinished, enclosing an older one in its much wider circuit. It is very strongly built, so that guns can be mounted on it. The tide rises and falls here at times from 40 to 44 feet.

Steamers go hence to Jersey (in 3 hours) and to St. Malo once a week.

The *Church* at the W. end of the town is a low gloomy building, chiefly in the late flamboyant style, though it has some round arches. It is of grey granite, even the capitals of its columns being worked in that hard stone.

In order to ascend the hill above the old town it is advisable not to thread the labyrinth of filthy alleys, steep slopes, and stone steps which compose it, but to issue out by the road to Coutances, and then scale the steep slope no farther than the walls of the fort, a point which commands a good sea view. Close under the cliffs lie the *baths* (Salon des Bains) and *reading-room*, which can be approached only through the breach in the rock before alluded to, leading also down to the sands, a fine smooth and broad expanse, quite shut out from the town. There are no machines; instead of them bathers are enclosed in cases of canvas carried in the fashion of sedan-chairs, and they must walk into the water thick-clad: the ladies led by the women: the men are banished to the distance of ½ m. to the N.—*British Consul* here.

Though Granville is not a particularly strong place, it resisted effectually the attack of the peasant army of *Vendéans*, 30,000 strong, on their ill-fated march, N. from the Loire, in 1793, led on by the gallant Larochejacquelin. The inducements of the royalists to make this attempt were the hope of opening a communication by the sea with England, whose government had promised to send them succour; and to secure a fortified place where they could deposit in safety the women and children, the sick and the priests, who embarrassed the operations of the army. The Vendéans, being destitute of artillery to breach the ramparts, were unable to resort to a regular siege. The attempt to storm the place, though conducted with the most dashing courage, was foiled. More than once these brave soldiers gained the ramparts, sometimes supplying the want of scaling ladders by sticking their bayonets into the chinks of the masonry, but as often they were swept off by grape and musketry from the walls and gunboats in the harbour, until at length they were forced to retire with a loss of 1800 killed. Their army never advanced farther N.; this was the culminating point of their success, and from henceforth they were compelled to retreat. During this attack the suburbs of the town were set on fire by the republican commander of the fortress and burnt down.

It is a very pretty ride from Granville to Avranches; the view obtained from the height, after crossing the wooded dell of Sartilly, of the peaked rock of Mont St. Michel, is especially striking.

[About 4 m. N.E. of Sartilly is the ruined abbey of *Luzerne*. The granite church, in the transition style, is tolerably perfect: it was completed 1178, except the nave, which is later. The conventual buildings, turned into a cotton-mill at the Revolution, are fast going to decay. The situation in a wooded valley is very beautiful. The road from Sartilly is wretchedly bad.

26 *Avranches*.—(*Inns*: H. de Londres; very good, *clean*, and moderate: table-d'hôte 1¼ or 2 fr., breakfast 1½ fr.; garden behind. This house would prove a cheap and pleasant residence for a few weeks. H. de France; H. de Bretagne; both tolerable. H. d'Angleterre.) Avranches (Abrancæ), a town of 7269 Inhab., is now chiefly remarkable for its very beautiful situation on the sides and summit of a high hill, the last of a widely extending

ridge, rendered accessible for the high road by broad terraces carried up its steep slope in zigzags. *The view which you obtain in ascending, and especially that from the little mound on the l. of the road before you enter the town, in front of the Sous-Préfecture, is one of the most beautiful in the N. of France. The landscape abounds in wood, with partial clearances of well-cultivated corn-land, through the midst of which winds the river, flashing in glittering pools until expanding into a broad estuary it meets the sea, which borders the horizon. But the prominent feature of the view is the peaked rock of Mont St. Michel, and the twin islet of Tombeleine rising grandly from the hem of the waters.

Under this mound is a *Public Walk* planted with trees, formerly the garden of the Archevêché, in the midst of which a statue of General Valhubert, a native of Avranches, who fell at Austerlitz, is set up.

The cathedral of Avranches, one of the noblest in Normandy, and the chief ornament of the town, was destroyed by the mob at the Revolution: its site remains an open platform, commanding an extensive view, and now named *Place Huet*, from the celebrated Bishop of Avranches. All traces of the church are swept away, save one or two flagstones and a broken column, said to be the stone upon which Henry II. kneeled, a humble penitent, before the Papal Legates, to make atonement for the murder of Becket, " which had affected him more than the death of his own father or mother." After swearing on the Gospels that he had neither ordered nor desired it, he here received the Papal absolution, 1172. The stone stands at what formed part of the door of the N. transept, and is surrounded by a chain.

There are some portions remaining of the old *ramparts* of the town.

Another point of view, preferable perhaps, in some respects, even to that above described, is obtained from the *Jardin des Plantes*.

There is an extensive *Public Library* here, containing 10,000 volumes and some old MSS., among which was discovered a copy of Abelard's treatise called 'Sic et Non,' published 1836 by M. Cousin. A *Museum of Antiquities and a Picture Gallery* have been added.

The beauty of the situation, the salubrity of the air, and the cheapness of living, have rendered Avranches a favourite residence of the English, who form a considerable colony here. The *English Ch. Service* is performed in a room once a barrack, in the Boulevard de l'Ouest, where it joins the Rue Sanguière.

The *Post Office* is in Rue St. Gervais.

There is a way practicable for a light carriage, with a guide, from Avranches to Mont St. Michel, across the sands when the tide is out; but as there are two watercourses to wade through or cross in a boat, it is preferable to go round by Pont Orson. As is the case on Lancaster sands, the rise of the tide here is so excessively rapid at times, that a fleet horse, it is said, could not outrun it.

In going to Pont Orson and Dol you quit Avranches by another series of zigzags overlooking the bay of Cancale with Mont St. Michel in the midst, rising above a beautiful foreground of trees, and at Pont au Baud, at the bottom of the hill, you cross the little river Selune.

At Louis, 3 m. short of Pont Orson, a cross-road turns off on the rt. to the Mont St. Michel by Ardevon.

22 Pont Orson. *Inn:* Croix Verte; tolerable; it will furnish a horse and car for 5 or 6 fr. to go to Mont St. Michel, and this is the best point to start from.

The *Castle*, now entirely swept away, was intrusted by Charles the Wise, 1361, to Du Guesclin, to hold as a frontier post against the English. During his absence on a foraging expedition, however, it was very nearly lost, through an understanding between an English prisoner, Felton, and the waiting-maids of Du Guesclin's lady. The attempt was discovered, as the enemy were scaling the walls, by his sister, a stout Amazon, who overthrew the ladders into the ditch, and the treacherous waiting-maids were sewed up in sacks and drowned in the river.

The interesting granite *Church*, partly Norman, with a transition W. end and pointed choir, contains, in the N. aisle, a singular series of carvings in stone, representing the Passion—but so mutilated as to lose much of their value; also a very old stone altar-table, with sculpture mutilated, in the N. aisle.

A good macadamised road, leading from Pont Orson to *Mont St. Michel, 5 m., renders this by far the best approach to the Mount. It passes near Beauvoir and Ardevon, where are the remains of conventual farm-buildings, anciently belonging to the monks of the mount. The road terminates on the margin of "la Grève," *i.e.* the sands, extending for many square leagues all round the mount, and left bare for 4 or 5 hours by the sea, which interrupts the passage to it between 1 and 2 hours near high water. "At neap-tides (aux eaux mortes) the rock is not surrounded by water at all at any part of the day. At spring-tides (aux eaux vives) it is surrounded twice each day, and then the sea sometimes breaks into the soldiers' mess-room."—*G.B.A.*

The distance across the Grève to the mount is about a mile; the driest track is firm and perfectly safe for horses or carriages, but on either side are quicksands, which render it dangerous to diverge. There always remain behind a few pools which would reach above the ankles of a pedestrian. There is something mysterious and almost awful in the aspect of this solitary cone of granite, rising alone out of the wide, level expanse of sand. One might imagine it the peak of some colossal mountain just piercing through the crust of the earth, but deprived, at the moment of its appearance, of the geological force necessary to rear it aloft. Slight as is its elevation, its isolated position in the midst of the sea, and its heaven-pointed top, render it the prominent object of every view from the surrounding coast, and from a long distance give it the appearance of being much nearer at hand than it really is. On approaching it, it is found to be girt round at its base by a circlet of feudal walls and towers, washed by the sea; above these rise the quaint irregular houses of the little town, plastered as it were against the rock, and piled one over another. Above them project the bare beds of rock, serving as a pedestal from which the lofty walls, high turrets, and prolonged buttresses of the conventual buildings are reared aloft, surmounted in their turn by the pinnacles and tower of the church (now bearing a telegraph), which crowns the whole, and forms the apex of the pyramid.

Not inferior in interest to its outward aspect are the historical associations connected with this shrine of the Archangel Michael—the successor of Bel and the Dragon—the saint of high places. Holy hermits succeeded to Pagan priests in the possession of this natural temple, which Norman dukes and kings further honoured by building a church, and converted into a fortress almost impregnable in ancient times. Henry I. here effectually resisted his two elder brothers. Here Henry II., in 1166, kept his court and received the homage of the turbulent Bretons, whom he had subdued with a strong arm. This was the only fortress which held out for the French king when all Normandy was overrun by the armies of the conqueror of Azincour; successfully withstanding 2 sieges, in 1417 and 1423, under the brave Louis d'Estouteville. The shrine of St. Michel was for ages visited yearly by thousands of devotees from far and near, and the records of the convent preserve the names of more than a dozen royal pilgrims who have repaired hither to prostrate themselves as penitents before it, and to load it with their bounty. The Revolution dispersed the monks, interrupted the pilgrimage, and changed the destination of the building to a Prison, in which 300 aged priests were immured until death should release them. Its prisons and oubliettes, however, are of far greater antiquity. Who has not heard of the iron cage of St. Michel, which, though originally of metal bars, was afterwards changed to one of thick beams of wood placed 3 inches apart? Its last occupant was an unfortunate Dutch journalist, who was seized most unjustifiably, beyond the territory of France, for having abused the unscrupulous tyrant Louis XIV., who treated the Dutchman as he did the Italian prisoner of the iron mask. St. Michael's Mount in Cornwall, which bears so remarkable a resemblance to this, though on a smaller scale, was one of the foreign dependencies of the abbey.

The entrance to Mont St. Michel is by 3 gates, one within the other, the second flanked by 2 of the cannon with which the English forces of Henry V. ineffectually bombarded the mount in 1424, firing from them stone balls 1 ft. in diameter. Near this the arms of the knights of St. Michel, with a lion for supporter, are seen carved in the wall: the third gate is provided with a portcullis, and within it is the little inn (not very inviting; crabs, shrimps, and other fish may be got here). The town (so to call it) consists of one narrow, steep, and very foul-smelling lane. The best way of ascending is by the ramparts, turning to the rt. after passing the gate, up a succession of grass-grown flights of stairs "hanging to the side of the rock," provided with machicoulis at the side to annoy an enemy below. The uppermost gateway, leading into the castle convent, stands midway across a flight of steps, and is flanked by 2 bartizans or turrets; it "is very scenic and baronial," built probably 1257; but the chamber of knights and princes now re-echoes to the clank of chains and the rattle of the shuttle and beam. The present destination of the building is a prison for ordinary criminals and political offenders. For this reason only parts of it are accessible for the minute examination of strangers; and others are concealed by screen-partitions. The formality of delivering the passport, and requesting admission of the governor, having been gone through at this gate, the stranger is conducted by dark mysterious vaults and passages, up and down gloomy stairs. The convent-building, called "the Marvel," consists of 3 stories, the lower one a series of vaulted crypts, once used for stables; above this 2 noble halls, probably erected by Philip Augustus, who was a great benefactor; and above all the cloister and dormitory. The *Cloisters, the most beautiful part of the building, and a gem of Gothic architecture, unique of its kind, were built between 1220 and 1228. Towards the court they are supported by a double row of pointed arches resting on thin granite pillars, leaving an exquisitely groined narrow vault between the rows. The pillar of one arch alternates with the point of the next, so as to allow a most graceful carved volute or sprig, issuing from the capital of every alternate pillar, to be seen. The spandrils of the arches are filled up with a vegetative creation of foliage, sprigs, flowers, garlands, such as is scarcely to be equalled anywhere for fanciful variety, and sharpness and excellence of execution; the whole is surmounted by a cornice of flowers, and is in good preservation. It highly merits to be drawn in detail. The arches and carvings are of soft limestone brought from a distance; all the rest of the buildings are of granite, and the rock of St. Michel itself is of that stone.

The *Chambre des Chevaliers*, below the cloisters, is a noble hall or nave, of 4 finely-vaulted aisles, supported on 3 rows of pillars, and measures 98 ft. by 68. The chapters of the knights of the order of St. Michel, founded 1496 by the bigot Louis XI., who twice repaired hither as a pilgrim, were held in it. This is now filled with the looms at which the prisoners are compelled to work, and is not shown to strangers. La Salle de Montgomery, or monks' Refectory, is also a fine Gothic apartment.

The *Church* of the convent consists of 2 parts, of different ages and styles. The Romanesque nave, in the massive style of the 12th cent. (about 1140), with slightly ornamented capitals and a wooden roof, is now used as a chapel for the convicts. The pointed Gothic choir is of the 15th cent. (1452-1521):—the mouldings of the arches are carried down into the reeding of the piers without any interruption of capitals. The arches are closed up with walls, into which curious Scriptural bas-reliefs, such as Adam and Eve driven from Paradise, Noah's ark, &c., St. Michael killing the dragon, very grotesquely treated, are let in. The piers supporting the central towers having given way, owing to the injury they received from a fire, the last of the 8 or 10 conflagrations, several of them caused by lightning, which at different times have consumed the abbey, the arches of the transept are staved up by a complicated framework of timber to prevent the roof falling.

Beneath the choir of the church a circle of drum-like pillars, set very close together, with one in the centre, supports the superincumbent weight, and forms a curious crypt.

The view from the top of the church, elevated 400 ft. above the sands, from amidst its florid buttresses and pinnacles, now much mutilated, is curious. The Rochers du Cancale, on the coast of Brittany, the town of Avranches, and the neighbouring rock of Tombeleine, are the most conspicuous objects; all around is, as the tide ebbs or flows, either a waste of sand, interspersed with pools and channels of rivers, or a wild expanse of tossing waves.

"The sea has receded from this coast of late years, so that it barely reaches the Mount except at spring-tides, and it then rises with such rapidity as to be extremely dangerous, especially as it renders the sand *quick* for some distance in advance of it."—*J.H.P.* Formerly, owing to the short stay the sea made round the walls at every tide, the castle was hardly accessible by a boat, and from this circumstance, and its amphibious position, changing twice a-day from land to water, its strength as a fortress arose.

The river Couësnon, crossed by a bridge on quitting Pont Orson for Dol, forms the boundary between Normandy and Brittany. A fertile and very picturesque country succeeds, well wooded; in fact, one entire orchard, the cornfields being invariably planted with rows of fruit-trees. A last view is obtained of Mt. St. Michel from a lofty hill over which the road is carried.

The caps worn by the women hereabouts consist of a piece of white linen, bent like a roof, laid on the top of the head, the front, or gable, turned up in a sort of scroll, exactly corresponding with that seen on monumental effigies in English churches, of ladies of the 15th and 16th cent.

19 *Dol.*—*Inns:* La Grande Maison, not very good; homely, but not dear; Hôtel de Notre Dame.

Dol is a remarkable town, as bearing thoroughly the aspect of ancient days: the black hue of the granite of which its houses are built, contrasting sometimes with splashes of whitewash dashed over them, the heavy projecting gables, the arcades of various heights and patterns running under the houses, the quaintly carved granite pillars on which they rest, all give a peculiar character to the place, and offer some good bits for the artist's pencil, while he may fill a sketch-book with costumes in its market-place. It has 3990 Inhab. and a considerable corn-market held in a desecrated church (des Carmes) distinguished by fine flamboyant W. window and a Norman nave.

The chief building is the *Cathedral* (before the Revolution an episcopal see), build of sombre grey granite, uniformly in the early pointed style, except the porches; that on the S. leading into the nave being florid, and having carvings in white stone like those in the cloister of Mont St. Michel. The arches of the nave have deep mouldings, and rest on circular piers, composed of a group of 4 columns, the inner one towards the nave being detached half-way up to the roof, where it becomes engaged like the rest. The choir, more ornamented than the nave, but in the same style, has a square E. end, like the English churches, but behind the high altar is an open arch of two divisions separated by a slender pillar admitting a view into a small Lady Chapel behind. The space above this arch is occupied by a large E. window filled with old and good painted glass. These are the most striking points in this fine edifice, which is worthy of attention for its similarity to the Gothic of England; indeed many of the churches of Brittany are said to be the work of English architects.

There is an antique building called *le Palais* or *Maison des Plaids*, apparently Romanesque.

The old *walls of Dol remain tolerably perfect, wanting the gates; many of their flanking towers and bastions are surmounted with deep machicoulis, and the whole is surrounded by a fosse. A high *Terrace* walk has been formed on the outside of this, and planted with trees. On the side of the town next the cathedral a view is obtained from this walk of the solitary eminence of Mont Dol, a granite rock something like Mont St. Michel, only rising out of the dry land. (See below.)

These antiquated fortifications of the 15th and 16th cent. were defended by the Vendéans after their retreat from Granville against the Republican army, which was beat off after a bloody combat of 15 hours' duration, and compelled to retreat.

The tract of land between Dol and the sea, a distance of 3 m., is chiefly marsh gained from the waters by embankments; very fertile, but teeming with miasma, which, however, has diminished of late from improved drainage. A tremendous irruption of the sea, reclaiming its own, in the beginning of the 17th cent., overwhelmed this district.

About a mile outside of Dol, and ¼ m. to the l. of the Rennes road, is one of those Druidical stones, so common in Brittany, called Menhirs (see p. 105). It is known as *la Pierre du Champ Dolent*, a name which probably marks it as a funereal monument, perhaps on some field of blood or battle. It is a rude, skittle-shaped obelisk of granite, a single block, 30 ft. high above ground, and 8 or 10, it is said, below, rising in the midst of a cornfield, and surmounted by a wooden cross.

On the way to St. Malo you pass on the rt. the *Mont Dol*, a granite rock surmounted by a telegraph, rising out of the flat land, and most probably once an island in the bay of Mont St. Michel, for the sea no doubt once extended thus far. Where the road reaches the present margin of the bay the shore is lined by a long scattered village, composed of nearly as many windmills as cottages. Not a boat can approach them, owing to the shallowness of the water, although the tide comes up to their doors twice a day. On the W. shore of the bay, however, is the small port of *Cancale*—4880 Inhab.—visible on the rt., backed by high cliffs, famed for the oyster-beds on the *Rochers de Cancale* below them, whence Paris and a large part of France are supplied.

In 1758 an army of 14,000 English, under the Duke of Marlborough, landed here, but after fruitlessly summoning St. Malo, which was found too strong to be taken by assault, they re-embarked, having burned a few small vessels; and, as H. Walpole said, "The French learned that they were not to be conquered by every Duke of Marlborough."

28 *St. Malo.*—*Inns:* H. de France, kept by M. Gogué, once cook to Lord Melville; good, and not dear, but horribly and inexcusably dirty, considering that the mistress is English; rooms at 1, 2, and 3 frs. per bed; table-d'hôte at 5, 3 frs.; déjeûner à la fourchette, 2 frs. 50 c. No W.C.'s! The house is the one in which Châteaubriand was born;—H. de la Paix, equally good. This fortified seaport town (pop. 10,100) may be styled a little French Cadiz from its position on a rocky island (l'Ile d'Aron) communicating with the mainland by a long causeway called *Le Sillon:* the mouth of the river Rance, which forms the port, being separated from the open sea by the island and this causeway. The town fills the island completely, so that its picturesque walls and flanking towers, surmounted by a deep cornice of machicoulis, rise at once from the water's edge, washed by the waves; and the houses and buildings squeezed closely together, having no room for lateral extension, rise to the height of 5 or 6 stories above its narrow and filthy lanes.

The tides rise here higher than at

any other point in the Channel, viz. to an elevation of 45 to 50 ft. above low-water mark, and the harbour, which is protected by a stout pier, is drained perfectly dry at ebb, so that carriages and foot passengers cross it to go to the populous suburb *St. Servan* (9984 Inhab.), in places covered an hour or two before with 4 fathoms of water. But a solid wall of granite, designed to be carried across from St. Servan, with lock-gates in the centre wide enough to admit steamers and frigates, so as to retain the tide, and form a floating dock (bassin à flot) of very large dimensions, has been begun. This if finished would open a second approach from the Rennes road to St. Malo, across a bridge to be thrown over the lock-gates. These works, unfortunately, are making very little progress (1851). After an expenditure of more than 6 millions of francs symptoms of failure have shown themselves in the pier and quays, and it seems likely that this vast undertaking will be abandoned.

The harbour is lined with a broad *quay* running just under the town walls, and here the steamers moor when the tide permits them to enter. The *Town walls* afford an almost uninterrupted walk around the island, and the circuit may be made in ¾ of an hour. The view out to sea is varied by the little archipelago of islands;— white, angular, bare rocks which raise their bristling heads around the roads: the larger ones crowned with forts and batteries. That called La Conchée is occupied by a strong citadel built by Vauban; and Cisambre, 6 m. off, is also strongly fortified. The smaller isles and the sunken rocks attached to them render the access to the port difficult.

The public buildings are of no interest: on the side of the town nearest the Sillon, and separated from it by a bridge, is the *old Castle*, which, together with a large part of the fortifications, may have been constructed in the 16th cent. by Anne of Brittany, who placed over one of the towers this inscription — " Qui qu'en grogne, ainsi sera, c'est mon plaisir." The *Cathedral* very capacious and much modernised, has a choir something like that of Dol, and a new gaudy Gothic altar from Paris, with several marble statues worth notice.

The sabbath is more strictly observed by the Malouins, and indeed in Brittany generally, than in most other parts of France.

English service is performed in a small old chapel, in the suburb of St. Servan, on Sunday.

The statue opposite the Hôtel de Ville is that of *Duguy Trouin*, a native of St. Malo (born 1673), and a naval hero of whom the French are very proud, "parcequ'il a chassé les Anglais sur toutes les mers."

The illustrious Châteaubriand first drew breath in the Rue des Juifs, No. 15, in the house which is now the H. de France, in the room marked No. 5, from the window of which the sea and his tomb are visible. The Abbé de la Mennais, author of Paroles d'un Croyant, and Mahé de la Bourdonnais, governor of the French East Indies, who took Madras from the English, 1746, were also Malouins.

On the sea-shore, by the side of the Sillon, just beyond the castle, on the rt. of the road from Dol, are *Sea-baths* and a *Subscription Reading-room*. There is a large expanse of sand extending at low water as far as a little rocky island in front, well adapted for bathing, but unprovided with machines.

St. Malo was bombarded by an English fleet in 1692, and by another under Admiral Berkeley, 1695—both times with slight result. In June, 1758, an army under the 2nd Duke of Marlborough, having landed in the Bay of Cancale, burned 80 vessels lying in the harbour of St. Malo.

St. Malo flourished during the last war, when it was styled the "Ville de Corsaires," fitting out privateers to prey on the commercial ships of England; many large fortunes were then made.

The best view to be obtained of St. Malo is from the half-ruined *Fort de la Cité*, situated on the promontory a little to the W. of St. Servan, reached by the first turning on the rt. after you

France.

F

enter that suburb from St. Malo. Hence from a considerable elevation you look down upon the town, upon the singular inlets of the sea branching out into the land which form the harbour, and on the archipelago of little islands grouped around its entrance. Among them the islet of Grand Bay, situated to the S.W. of the town, chosen by Châteaubriand for his last resting-place, and bestowed upon him by the municipality of his native town, is conspicuous. His fellow-citizens erected a tomb on it to contain his remains. Immediately beneath the spectator on his l. rises the triangular tower of the *Solidor*, a feudal fort 60 ft. high, with flanking towers at its angles, approached by a drawbridge. It is now a prison.

At *St. Servan* the Union Boarding-house is recommended; charges 5 fr. a day, or 100 fr. a month, exclusive of wine.

Diligences daily to Rennes (Rte. 41) and Paris (Rte. 35), to Brest (Rte. 36), to Dinan (Rte. 41), to Dol and Caen (Rtes. 27 and 31).

Steamers. It is a pleasant excursion up the river Rance from St. Malo to Dinant. A small steamer ascends and returns with the ebb, when the state of the tide permits. (Rte. 41.)

Steamers twice a week to and from Jersey, where they correspond with the boats to Southampton.

ROUTE 29.

CAEN TO TOURS, BY FALAISE, ALENÇON, AND LE MANS.

232 kilom. = 143½ Eng. m.

A daily communication is kept up by diligences, but with interruptions, and the traveller is compelled to wait 3 or 4 hours at a time for the coach which is to carry him on. A separate conveyance runs from Caen to Falaise and back daily.

About 7 m. from Caen, and 2 or 3 to the rt. of the road, lies Fontenay le' Marmion, cradle of the family of Marmion.

20 Langannerie. The country for the first 2 stages is bare, open, and monotonous, until the castle of Falaise is perceived on the rt. rising out of a picturesque valley.

6 m. short of Falaise, and nearly 2 to the l. of the road, lie the *rocks of St. Quentin,* sometimes called *Brèche du Diable,* a rocky gorge bounded by precipices, pinnacles, &c. It has been compared with Cheddar Cliffs, only on a much smaller scale.

15 *Falaise.* Inns: H. du Grand Cerf; H. de France, good. This ancient and not very prospering town of 9580 Inhab. occupies the summit of a lofty platform, bordering on a rocky precipice, or *Falaise*, whence its name. One very populous suburb has extended into the narrow ravine below this precipice; and another, situated at the distance of 1 m. to the E., called Guibray, now rivals the town itself in size and population, and is distinguished for its Fairs established by William the Conqueror, held in August, celebrated for the horses then brought to market. Falaise is a dull lifeless town at present, having only one object of interest to the passing traveller —the *Castle*, one of the few real Norman fortresses remaining in France, the ancient seat of the Dukes of Normandy, and the birthplace of William the Conqueror. It is a grand and picturesque ruin, occupying a commanding position at the extremity of the town, where the platform is cut into a narrow promontory by gullies which isolate it on 3 sides, rendering it a place of great strength, until the invention of gunpowder. To this it was indebted for the 9 sieges which it had to endure. The approach to it is behind the modern Hôtel de Ville. A college or *grammar school* has been planted within the exterior court. A grassy terrace walk along the ramparts, shaded with trees, leads to the Norman *Donjon Keep,* an oblong square, whose walls, supported by high and massy buttresses, rise abruptly from the edge of the precipitous rocks de Norrou. It is now a mere shale, partly filled with rubbish; its walls show traces of herringbone masonry, and retain several round-headed windows, of 2 lights supported on short pillars, and

having capitals carved with Runic knots. In one corner a cell is shown in which, according to the tradition, the Conqueror was born. From those windows and ruined walls you look down into the Val d'Ante, so called from the small stream which runs through it, crowded with mills and tanneries. It was while gazing upon this scene, according to the tradition, that Duke Robert, the father of the Conqueror (like David of old), first espied Arlotte, the tanner's fair daughter, and became at once so smitten with her charms, that he made her his mistress, and continued faithful to her until death.

The keep is surpassed in elevation by *Talbot's tower*, a cylinder of beautifully smooth and perfect masonry, rising beside it to a height of more than 100 ft., crowned with a rim of broken machicoulis. Its walls, 15 ft. thick, enclose a winding stair leading to the top, and a well opening into each of the 5 vaulted stories. The chapel is converted into a powder magazine. This tower is supposed to have been built by "Valiant Talbot," who was lord warden of the "Marche Normande," after the capture of Falaise by Henry V., between 1418 and 1450. Henry assaulted the castle from the top of the still loftier cliff Mont Mirat, on the opposite side of the ravine, where traces of his intrenchments still remain: the siege lasted more than 4 months. On the other side of the castle is a relic of another siege, viz. the breach in the wall by which Henri IV. carried the fortress by assault, after 7 days of cannonade, in 1589.

A bronze equestrian *statue of Wm. the Conqueror* was set up by his fellow townsmen in 1851, in Trinity-square, at the foot of the Castle. He is represented in the attitude of leading on his followers to invade England!

The churches are not remarkable. A considerable portion of the old town *walls* remain, running round the edge of the ravines, through which the stranger may ramble agreeably, either upwards into the suburb of Val d'Ante, the birthplace of the Conqueror's mother, below the castle keep, or, issuing out of the picturesque "Porte des Cordeliers," the only gate remaining perfect, he may follow the direction of the Ante downwards through shady lanes, and re-enter the town by the dismantled Porte St. Laurent.

The *Saturday market* exhibits a larger collection and greater variety of quaint old Norman female headdresses than any other in Normandy perhaps.

There are several cotton-mills in the vicinity, and the weaving of nightcaps occupies a considerable number of hands.

22 Argentan.—*Inn:* Trois Maures (?). A town of 6147 Inhab., on the Orne, surrounded by ramparts.

23 Séez (in Rte. 21).
21 Alençon (in Rte. 35).
14 La Hutte.
9 Beaumont-sur-Sarthe.
15 La Bazoge.
11 *Le Mans* (in Rte. 46). Railway to Tours in 1856.
21 Ecommoy.—*Inn:* Poste.
20 Château du Loir.—*Inn:* Poste. The *Castle*, after which this village is named, is gone; it was built 1080 by Robert *Eveille-chien*, Duc d'Anjou. The cliffs near this are hollowed into caves, serving partly for houses to more than 100 poor families, partly as cellars for the richer.
20 La Roue in Touraine.
20 Tours (in Rte. 53).

ROUTE 31.

CAEN TO RENNES, BY VIRE, MORTAIN, AND FOUGÈRES.

171 kilom. = 106 Eng. m.
2 Diligences daily.
The road conducts through some of the most pleasing scenery in Normandy; at first it ascends the valley of the Odon, in which lies
13 Mondrainville. We now enter the *Bocage* of Normandy, a pretty *wooded* district, situated about the source of the Orne, Odon, and Vire.
12 Villars Bocage; here is an hospice, founded 1366 by Jeanne Bacon, of Mollay.
15 Ménil au Zouf.
12 *Vire* (*Inns:* H. St. Pierre, clean and moderate, fine view; Cheval

Blanc, not good), a picturesque antique town (pop. 8000), the capital of the Bocage, situated on a lofty eminence, bordered by ravines. A Norman *Castle* occupies the extreme point of the promontory, naturally inaccessible on 3 sides, owing to the precipices which surround it; and on the 4th originally separated from the town by a deep ditch. It is now reduced to the fragment of the tall *keep*, a construction of the 11th cent., having been dismantled 1630, by order of Richelieu, but its ruins are preserved, and surrounded by a sort of dusty pleasure-ground or plantation belonging to a private individual. It commands a view of the country around, streaked with long lines of "tenters" upon which cloth is hung, and especially of the 2 valleys beneath it, called, *par excellence*, *Les Vaux de Vire*, whence comes the word Vaudeville, originally applied to the merry and humorous drinking songs composed among these valleys by one Oliver Basselin. He was a native of Vire, and owner of a fulling-*mill*, which still remains at no great distance from the town. He flourished in the 15th centy., and is reported to have been present at the battle of Formigny. His chansons, chiefly in praise of good wine and his native province, soon became so popular over France, that their name was transferred to those truly national dramas peculiar to the French stage, in which the plot or story is carried through chiefly by songs.

In the narrow and steep streets of Vire may be found many specimens of ancient domestic architecture, well adapted for the artist's sketch-book. The *Ch. of Notre Dame* is a fine building; but the chief boast of Vire are the *walks* in and about it. Terraced paths are carried up the hill side amidst thickets and plantations, commanding at intervals very pleasing views.

The valleys in the neighbourhood, generally shut in by craggy heights and copse-covered slopes, abound in mills of paper and *cloth*, in which the clothing for the French army is made. This gives employment to half the inhabitants of Vire. On the 10th of August the "Fête des Drapiers" is celebrated here, and more than 10,000 persons assemble under the apple-trees, which are illuminated at night for the occasion.

Vire has a gastronomic celebrity for chitterlings (andouilles) and for pastry.

Diligences, several daily, to Avranches through a beautiful country, "rich swelling hills, green meadows, and vast seas of waving wood. The first view of Avranches, about 8 m. before you get there, with the rich foreground, the spire of the town crowning the height, and the sea beyond, with Mt. St. Michel rising out of it, is truly striking."—*W. J.*

[10 m. S.E. of Vire is *Tinchebray*, where Robert of Normandy succumbed in battle to his younger brother Henry, 1106. This victory secured a throne to the one prince, and a prison for life to the other.]

13 Sourdeval.

10 Mortain. (*Inn*: La Poste, opposite the Ch.; not bad, but not clean.) Mortain, a decayed and lifeless town, occupies a position nearly resembling that of Vire, and at least equally romantic. "The valleys are narrower, the steeps more rocky and better wooded; the river at the bottom is more considerable, and a wide extent of distant Campagna is seen through the jaws of the ravine. The whole scene put me in mind of Italy and of Tivoli, and the cascades which we heard from above and visited afterwards helped to keep up the resemblance."—*G. Knight*.

"You *descend* to the side of the old *Castle*, but when you arrive there you find it a most suitable spot for an eagle's nest. A jutting cliff, only connected to the height by a narrow ledge of rock, afforded just space enough for a feudal fortress. The strength of this fortress made it once a place of importance. Here dwelt the brothers and the sons of kings of England." The whole of this venerable structure has been levelled with the dust, and in its place now rises the staring modern *Sous-Préfecture*.

The *Collegiate Ch.* has been groundlessly pronounced to be a work of the year 1082, when a church is known to have been founded here. But the only fragment remaining of that epoch is a circular doorway leading into the nave on the S. side, ornamented with zigzags and saw-tooth ornaments; the rest is of the pure and unmixed early pointed style of the 13th cent., and the clumsy junction of the new wall around the old circular portal is very apparent. The arches of the nave rest on thick short pillars; those of the choir are narrower.

About a mile out of the town, seated in a secluded valley, is the *Abbaye Blanche*, founded 1105. The *Church*, restored with care 1850, is in the Transition style, round-headed windows alternating with pointed. An early pointed cloister also remains tolerably perfect. The abbey is now a Séminaire for the education of priests.

The *Cascades* of Mortain are the finest, and indeed almost the only ones, in Normandy.

About 8 m. from Mortain are the ruins of the *Abbey of Savigny*, b. 1173, in the Transition style, but partaking more of the round than pointed character.

15 St. Hilaire du Harcouet is the entrepôt for the agricultural and manufacturing produce of a large part of Brittany:—its markets are greatly frequented. The frontier of Brittany is crossed about 4 m. to the N. of

11 Louvigné. At the door of the present posthouse M. de Lescure, the Vendéan chief, died of his wounds, and was buried at the road-side—site unknown.

16 *Fougères.*—*Inn:* H. St. Jacques. This town (4635 Inhab.), once a frontier fortress, the key of Brittany on the side of Normandy, "is full of picturesque interest. The old town, built on a steep acclivity, shows traces of the Middle Ages; the ancient arcades still obtrude in places upon the streets. It is still surrounded by antique ramparts. There is a *Church* of some architectural interest, and a charming *promenade*, on a high eminence commanding romantic prospects."—*G*.

Attached to the town walls, at the lower end, is the huge and picturesque ruined *Castle*, of which the Donjon, built by Olivier de Clisson, and la Tour de Melusine, so named by the former owners, the Lusignans, from the *Fair M.*, from whom they claimed descent, are the oldest parts of the castle; the rest of the 14th and 16th cent.; and the outer towers and curtains are still later. Its approaches and defences are very curious. In 1794 Fougères was seized by the Vendéans.

20 St. Aubin du Cormier. Near this La Trémouille gained a decisive victory, in 1488, over Francis II. Duke of Brittany, the Duke of Orleans, afterwards Louis XII., and others, who had leagued against the Crown.

10 Liffré.

18 RENNES (in Rte. 35).

ROUTE 32.

BAYEUX TO ST. LO AND AVRANCHES.

90 kilom. = 55¾ Eng. m.
Diligences daily.

13 Vaubadon.

The road traverses a portion of the extensive forest of Cerisy. The *Abbey of Cerisy*, one of the most considerable in Normandy in olden time, lies on the rt. of the road. The church still exists, an early Norman building of the same plain character as St. Stephen's at Caen (p. 73). It was founded 1030, by Robert Duke of Normandy, and completed by his son William the Conqueror.

21 St. Lo (*Inns:* Cheval Blanc; Soleil Levant; far from good, and very dirty), named from St. Lo, or Laudus, who lived in the 6th centy., and came from this part of Normandy, is picturesquely situated, and its *Cathedral*, standing prominently on the brow of the hill, has an imposing appearance, with its double towers and spires, but as a building it is not of much interest. The W. end is florid, of the 15th centy.; it has three fine porches, but the upper part is defective and irregular; and, as well as the choir, exhibits marks of slovenliness in its builder. The nave is better, in the pointed style of the 12th centy. Outside the Church, in the S.W. angle, is a fine stone pulpit, with a pyramidal canopy

over it. Charlemagne founded here, in the 9th centy., the once celebrated Abbey of *St. Croix*; but this building was swept away at the invasion of the Northmen, and the present *Eglise de St. Croix*, a very curious edifice in the early Norman style, does not appear older than the 11th centy. The nave arches rest on pillars, and the S. side is plainer, and apparently older than the N. Over the round-headed doorway at the W. end is a bas-relief representing St. Lo restoring sight to a blind woman. The adjoining conventual buildings are of late dates; they are now converted into a *Stud* (haras) for improving the breed of horses.

St. Lo is chef-lieu of the Dépt. de la Manche, and numbers 8941 Inhab.; it has a manufacture of fine cloth, but possesses no great attraction to the stranger. There is a small terraced platform to the W. of the cathedral, called *Petite Place*, which commands a view of the vale of the Vire. The modern *H. de Ville* is built with considerable taste in the style of the Renaissance.

Diligences twice a day to Coutances (Rte. 27), passing within a short distance of *Hauteville*, the humble village which sent forth the bold Baron Tancred and his six sons to conquer Sicily and Apulia. On the way from St. Lo to Vire (Rte. 31) lies the town of Torigni. The building now used as an Hôtel de Ville is one wing of the *Château* of the family of Matignon, Counts of Torigni, one of whom, by marriage with Louisa Grimaldi, became Prince of Monaco. In 1793 the building was turned into a prison, and the park, terraces, and gardens sold piecemeal.

The *Ch. of St. Laurent* is early Norman, and that of *Notre Dame* retains traces of the same style.

The road from St. Lo to Avranches lies through

19 Villebaudon. The little humble village *Perci* was the cradle of the ancestors of the house of Northumberland.

15 Villedieu les Poêles derives the adjunct to its name from the number of coppersmiths, who drive a thriving trade in pots, pans, and other articles, which the French call dinanderies and quincailleries. These artificers were originally settled here by the Knights Templars, who employed them in making decorations for churches. Here are many furnaces for melting the copper, and mills for rolling it into sheets.

22 Avranches (Rte. 27).

ROUTE 33.
FOUGÈRES TO DINAN.

80 kilom.

A fine view of Mount St. Michel before reaching

Autrain, on the road between Avranchances and Rennes.

Bazouges la Perouse. In the *Church* is a fine painted window of the life of Christ, preserved from destruction 1591 (as appears by the parish register) by a ransom of 180 livres, paid to an English leader of marauders. On the way to Combourg, at the roadside, stands a Menhir, *La Pierre Longue*.

Combourg, a poor small town, famed for its sausages and horse-fair. The *Castle* has belonged to the Chateaubriands for 150 years, and before them to the Durases. Chateaubriand, the author and minister of Louis XVIII., spent part of his boyhood here, and his chamber and study remain unaltered. It is a square building with towers in the 4 corners, enclosing a small court: it is in perfect preservation, with its wall-galleries and loopholes. The present entrance, by a long flight of steps, is modern.

4 m. from Dinan, in the midst of a thick wood (rt.), are the ruins of the *Castle* of the ancient family of the *Coetgvens*, the last of whom was the Duchesse de Duras. Beneath are large subterranean dungeons.

Lanvanay. The viaduct is crossed to reach

DINAN. (Route 41.)

SECTION II.

BRITTANY.

INTRODUCTORY INFORMATION.

1. *Character of the Country.* 2. *People.* 3. *Language.* 4. *Celtic Remains classified.* 5. *Superstition.* 6. *Churches, Carvings, Flamboyant Gothic, Bone-houses, Kersanton Stone.* 7. *Connection with England.* 8. *Chouannerie.* 9. *Books to consult.* 10. *Tour of Brittany.* 11. *Accommodation for Travellers.*

ROUTE	PAGE	ROUTE	PAGE
34 Paris to *Rennes*, by Versailles, Rambouillet, Chartres, Le Mans (Railway), and *Laval* . . .	109	42 Morlaix to Nantes, by *Huelgoat, Carhaix, Pontivy*, and *Josselin*	141
35 Paris to Rennes, by Versailles, Dreux, Verneuil, Alençon, and Laval (RAILROADS to *Versailles*)	120	44 Brest to Nantes, by *Quimper, Lorient, Auray, the Druidical remains of Carnac, Vannes,* and *Roche Bernard*	144
36 Rennes to *Brest* by *St. Brieuc* and Morlaix	124	45 Rennes to Vannes, by *Ploermel.*—Excursion to Carnac .	153
38 St. Brieuc to Brest, by *Paimpol, Lannion*, Morlaix, *St. Pol de Léon*	132	46 *Le Mans* to *Nantes*, by *Angers*	153
41 St. Malo to Nantes by *Dinan,* Rennes, and *Châteaubriand* .	137	47 Dreux to Argentan, by l'Aigle	165

1. There can scarcely be a more abrupt contrast to the smiling land of Normandy than that presented by the neighbouring province of sombre, poverty-stricken Brittany. Here we find an atmosphere of mist and moisture ; and a soil based on hard granite, best fitted for heath, furze, and broom, the very broom (*genêt*) which supplied our first Plantagenet with his crest and name. In many points the country bears a strong resemblance to Scotland; the same wide, barren moors, the same deep and picturesque wooded dells and storm-beaten coasts. Here, however, are no grand lofty mountain chains like the Grampians: the highest ridges of the Menez-Arrés hills, the back-bone of the peninsula of Brittany, rarely surpass 1200 ft. above the sea-level.

2. In civilization it is behind almost every other part of France: its *inhabitants* are of Celtic origin, speaking a language of their own, allied to, and, indeed, essentially the same as, the Welsh and Cornish, so that Breton sailors landing on our coasts can make themselves understood by the Welsh there. It is exclusively spoken to the W. of a line drawn from the point of Finisterre through Chatelaudran and Pontivy; the "Vrai Bretagne Brettonnante," as Froissart calls it, to distinguish it from "La Bretagne Douce," where French is spoken. One of the principal objects of interest and study for the stranger in Brittany is its inhabitants, who have been kept distinct from the rest of France by position as well as difference of language.

The peasantry are almost as wild as their country, excessively quaint in their costume, wearing broad-brimmed hats and flowing hair, and in some districts trunk hose (bragous bras = breeks) of the 16th cent.; in others wrapped up in goat-skins, like Robinson Crusoe, a costume which they retain as it was handed down from their ancestors. They are usually mean and small in their persons; coarse-featured in face; squalidly filthy in their habitations; rude and unskilful in their agriculture. They are almost unchanged in their manners, customs, and habits: modern innovation has not entirely rubbed off the rust of long-continued habit; old legends and superstitions still retain their hold on the popular mind. They present a curious picture of a primitive state of society; and if a century behind their neighbours in what is called improvements, they are at least not corrupted by revolutions and commotions. In no part of France are the people, both of upper and lower orders, more observant of their religious duties, of festivals, fasts, &c.; nowhere are the churches so thronged.

"There is much picturesque beauty in Brittany, though of a character not so imposing at first sight as that of countries moulded on a grander scale. Scenery of great and winning loveliness is to be found on the banks of the Trieux, the Lannion, the Châteaulin, and the Rance, and in many other secluded and scarcely accessible valleys, where the 'broomie knowe,' the wooded dell, and the rocky cliff alternately border the brawling mountain torrent, as it flashes along its stony bed, or is pent up in the still pool of an old water-mill, which looks as if it had stood untouched (as it has perhaps) from the time of the 'good Duchess Anne.' The quaint and antique aspect of the buildings adds much to the picturesque character of the country. Some, as in Dinan, Morlaix, Quimper, &c., are framed of timber, with projecting stories resting on grotesquely carved brackets; but generally the houses both in the towns and villages are of grey granite, with massive round or ogee arched imposts to the doors and windows, often enriched with Gothic mouldings; and presenting, from the peculiar colour and grain of the stone, an appearance of antiquity even in buildings recently erected. The churches again are features of great interest and beauty scattered profusely over the country, and many a ruined castle or tower, or dilapidated 'manoir' with its old avenue, huge granite portals, round turrets, and 'extinguisher' roofs, recalls the days of the Breton chivalry. Add to these characteristic features, that the country is usually very intricate and thickly wooded, the enclosures being small and surrounded by high earthen banks, upon which, from six to ten feet above the level of the road or field, grows a close phalanx of timber-trees, oak, elm, or ash, gnarled and pollarded into grotesque forms, and intercepting all view, so as to give rise to constant excitement, as the scene changes almost at every step that the traveller advances."—*G. P. S.*

"The Bretons are impetuous and violent in their temper, and give way to furious bursts of passion when angry. Their way of living is homely and frugal to a degree, even when in circumstances to afford better fare. Of drink they unquestionably are fond, but it is not a regular habit with them to indulge in strong potations—water is usually drunk at meals, and cider in small quantities on Sundays and feasts. Wine is hardly ever tasted in the province, but brandy is cheap and good, as in other parts of France. They live much upon buckwheat, made into cakes, and mix rye with their wheat into a coarse meal, which forms a dark-coloured bread; these, with savoury esculents, and at times salt-fish and meat, constitute the staple of their subsistence. With a climate unfavourable to production, or rather to the maturity of their produce (for the sun is even more coy in Brittany than in the British Isles), and a soil generally of a cold wet character, the Bretons labour under far greater difficulties than their Norman neighbours as to tillage. Yet if they would be guided by wise advice, much progress might be imparted to their well-doing. Even now some improvements have obtained, especially since 1834, and capital is finding its way to the land, although most commonly in the shape of a loan to the occupant, who pledges his land for the amount. When a Breton saves a little money, he buys more land, if he can; he never seeks to apply more money to the land he has already under culture. The most perceptible feature of difference, perhaps, between Normandy and Brittany, is that, in the former, large and commodious farm-buildings are observed around the farmer's dwelling, whilst in Brittany it is rare to see a barn, or granary, or any roomy out-house—in short, the Bretons pursue the wasteful habit of threshing out their corn in August, and housing it in the grain; paying enormously for such labour (to an ambulant class called "les batteurs"), and losing the otherwise valuable season of warmth and daylight for cleaning and working the soil against seed-time. But having no barns, they must do this. Stacking is unknown, and besides, there is no sheltered floor for threshing on in winter; the threshing grounds, as in Italy (here termed "aires"), are in the open space adjoining the cultivator's dwelling, and are composed of bare earth, swept clean. It is a pretty incident in rural life when you behold all the family at this work, in fine weather, singing as the flail twirls to enliven their toil; but the inconceivable drawback which it forms to profitable farming obtrudes itself upon the mind of the traveller and impairs his pleasure at this primitive pastoral picture."

"The indescribable forms of many of the caps worn by the Bretonnes are worth remarking. Both Norman and Breton caps are pleasing auxiliaries to the scenery, which they enliven by their snowy whiteness. Old point lace is not unfrequently discerned on peasant heads, and these curious and costly 'coiffures' sometimes adorn the brows of more than one generation in turn. When caught in the rain the women instantly cover their fine caps over with a coloured handkerchief. It is the Bretons who chiefly man the navy of France: their qualities are eminently suited to the seafaring life, and the perseverance and patient courage they display stand out in contrast with the natives of other provinces of France, and denote a totally different origin."—*G*.

4. Of *Ancient Monuments* of different ages there is no lack in Brittany, and, above all, of Celtic Remains; those extraordinary masses of rude unhewn stones whose objects, age, and uses have never been satisfactorily accounted for, but which are supposed to have been in some way connected with the religion of the Druids, and their number would prove this country to have been the chief seat of that mysterious worship. In Great Britain we possess a few, and, above all, we have in Stonehenge a more stupendous monument than any elsewhere; but in Brittany the number is enormous; almost every wild heath possesses one or more. They are most numerous, however, on the storm-beaten promontories and islands of the W. coast; especially in the Morbihan, which includes the wondrous stony array of *Carnac* and the monstrous granitic obelisks of *Lokmariaker*, larger than any single blocks at Stonehenge, but now fractured.

These rude Remains are of several different kinds, distinguished by the following names:—

a. *Menhir* (literally long stone: Ir-min-Sul; long stone of the sun) is a monolith in the form of a rude obelisk set upright on one end, whose height much exceeds its breadth. There is a menhir near Dol which rises 30 ft. above the ground, but the largest specimen of this class known is at Plouarzel, near Brest; it exceeds 42 ft. in height. Those at Lokmariaker, now laid prostrate and broken by violence, were more than 60 ft. high, and were thick in proportion.

b. *Peulven* (pillar of stone), an upright stone of inferior height to the menhir; the single stones at Carnac are generally of this class.

c. *Dolmen* (from "taal," table, and "maen," or men, stone), in England commonly called Cromlech, is an arrangement of rude blocks, by which one or more upright stones are made to support a horizontal block or slab. Sometimes they nearly resemble a table; the upright stones serving merely as props or legs, and are called in French pierres levées, or pierres couvertes; at others the supporting stones are wide slabs, so arranged as to fit close to one another, and so lofty as to allow a man to walk upright beneath the horizontal roof-stone which they support. Kits Coity House in Kent is an instance of this kind, and there are others in Cornwall, but they are far inferior in size to those of Brittany, which are often 60 or 80 ft. long. The French sometimes call them "allées couvertes."

d. *Kistvaen* is similar to the Dolmen, inasmuch as it consists of two rows of upright stones supporting flat blocks; but the stones are smaller, and the whole structure lower and longer; it appears to correspond with the "Hunnengräber" of North Germany. The most remarkable example is on the island *Gavre Innis* near Lokmariaker.

e. *Galgal* is a tumulus, barrow, or cairn; the largest known is the *Butte de Tumiac* on the shore of the Sea of Morbihan.

The Celtic remains are not confined to Brittany, though most numerous there; they occur almost invariably on some flat open plain at a distance from the hills, in situations corresponding with Salisbury Plain and Dartmoor in England. Brittany appears, like our Mona, to have been the sacred land of the Gauls, the centre of their worship, to which probably the various nations and tribes repaired on pilgrimage at stated times to pay their devotions.

Of the particular destination or object of these rude elevations in general, or of the individual uses of the different classes enumerated above, no satisfactory explanation has been offered. The accumulated ranges, the long avenues of stones of Carnac and Erdevan, amounting to thousands in number, may have stood in the place of temples where rites of initiation and purification similar to the Grecian mysteries may have been performed. The upright solitary menhir may have been a symbol of some individual deity, as the sun; the dolmen may have served as an altar or shrine, and the galgal and kistvaen were probably monumental. Equally unexplained are the mechanical means by which a rude people contrived to transport, and to elevate one above another, such huge masses.

5. Their mysterious influence is not yet, by any means, effaced from the mind of the lower orders in Brittany. The first teachers of Christianity in this region found this attachment to superstition so strong, that, after in vain attempting to eradicate it by overthrowing and destroying these rude stones, they altered their plan to that of engrafting, to a certain extent, their own faith upon the old idolatrous worship of stones and fountains, converting the dolmen into a chapel, and making the menhir serve as a pedestal to a crucifix, which it commonly does even to the present day.

The influence of paganism lingered long in these remote wilds, attached as it was to visible objects: indeed, the inhabitants of Ouessant are said to have been idolaters until within 150 years.

Hence has arisen a strange jumble of Paganism and Romanism; thus pilgrimages are made to fountains by those who desire to be relieved from some malady, by pouring its holy water over the affected part: and visits are paid in the depth of night to some solitary menhir by the barren woman, who hopes to become fruitful by rubbing her bosom against the hard stone. Some of these inanimate objects also are supposed to possess virtue to cure the diseases of cattle. Heathen divinities were replaced by saints, of which the number in Brittany exceeds that of any other part of Romanist Europe; most of them are peculiar to the country, their names being unknown elsewhere, and their canonization conferred rather by the popular voice than with the authority of the Pope. Almost every church has its own strange legend, and on its saint's day a pilgrimage or *Pardon* is celebrated, when indulgence for past sins is obtained, and the penitent pilgrims are no sooner shrived than they begin to run up a fresh score at the riotous festivities which follow these assemblies. These pardons, or village festivals, which are nearly equivalent to the German kirchweih, the Flemish kermes, and the English *wake*, deserve the attention of strangers, from the illustrations they afford of Breton life, manners, and costume.

6. In *Ecclesiastical Monuments* Brittany is not so well furnished as Normandy,

but the architecture is of a different style, chiefly the florid or flamboyant Gothic, and of a much later period: indeed, even in architecture, Brittany seems to have been behind the rest of the world, and the fashions of building only reached it when superseded in other parts. The following excellent remarks apply generally to all parts of France, yet will not be out of place here. "The most obvious characteristics of the *Flamboyant style* are the flat 3-centred arches of doorways, the entire independence of different pilasters upon the same pier as regards the vertical height of their base mouldings, the scrupulous interpenetration of different mouldings, and the absence of capitals if the arch mouldings are continued on the pier, or their dying gradually into the pier by penetration if they are not continued on it."—*G. B. A.* There are some peculiarities in "the Breton style," which render it well worthy the attention of architects. In elaborateness and profuseness of ornament, in the minuteness and delicacy of carving, especially of the foliage (for the figures are inferior), there are some churches in Brittany which yield to few in any part of Europe. As instances may be mentioned those of *Folgoat* near Brest, *St. Pol de Léon*, which is remarkable for its exquisite spire, *Théogonec* near Morlaix, *St. Herbot* near Poulahouan, and the cathedral of *Nantes*.

The Department of Finisterre is the quarter in which churches more especially abound, and it is quite as profusely supplied as Lincolnshire, and many of the village churches are of unusual size and richness. "In the churches near Brest, instead of building a tower with 4 walls, containing windows or panel work, the practice seems to have been to raise stages or floors, one upon another on open arches, so as to make a kind of square pagoda, not contracting in dimensions, through which in certain directions the light is seen and the arch piers look comparatively small. This peculiarity deserves attention from architects."—*G. B. A.*

Several of the churches, even in remote situations, as at St. Herbot, are decorated internally with *carvings in wood* and stone; roodlofts still exist at Folgoat, St. Fiarre le Fahouet (of oak painted and sculptured), Lambader, &c., though scarcely found elsewhere on the continent: painted glass is also by no means uncommon. These very gorgeous churches of Brittany were erected principally from the end of the 14th to the beginning of the 16th cent.

Formerly the churchyards and even roadsides were adorned with *Crucifixes* of most elaborate execution, and comprising a multitude of figures; "most of them suffered by the Revolution, but many exquisite examples remain almost as perfect as those of Plougastel near Brest, St. Théogonec, &c., and hardly a single point of intersection of two roads can be passed which is not marked by a more or less mutilated cross, oftentimes restored by the piety of the present generation."—*G. P. S.*

The *Bone-house* or *Reliquaire* will be constantly found in the Breton churchyards, and illustrates a curious custom. To allow "the rude forefathers of the hamlet" to repose quietly in the grave is opposed to the ideas of piety and affection in these rude people: after a certain number of years the survivors are required to show their remembrance and respect for their parents and relations by removing the skulls and bones from the coffin and placing them in the Ossuary,—where the former are arranged on shelves, open to the view of all, each with the name or initials in black paint written across the fleshless brow. There is a curious Reliquaire in St. Herbot.

One cause of the profuse decoration of these churches, and of their excellent preservation, may be referred to the materials employed—a greenstone, peculiar to Brittany, called *Kersanton* (St. Anthony's house), remarkable for the facility with which it is worked, and its tenacity in withstanding the weather. Its composition is not exactly understood, but it is supposed by mineralogists to consist of mica and amphibole, in particles minutely disseminated. It is found only in two localities, on the W. of the harbour of Brest, near the escarped rocks of Quelern, between the river of Faou and that of Landerneau. It is regarded as volcanic, both from its composition and because the rocks adjacent to it show marks of dislocation, caused apparently by its intrusion. The weather has scarce any destructive effect on it, even after the lapse of ages; and its peculiarly bright green colour gives to a portal carved out of it the appearance of being cast in bronze.

Of churches in the Romanesque or Norman style the examples are few; among them are the church of Dinan and the *chapel of Lanleff*, which, after all the disputes of learned antiquaries respecting its origin and great age, is probably merely an equivalent to the round churches of England.

The cathedral of Dol nearly corresponds in style to the Early English; and the tradition of the country attributes it and some of the later churches to English architects. This is not surprising, considering the long and early connection between Great Britain and Little Britain to the S. of the Channel— *Armorica*, as it was styled, which the careful researches of historians and philologists have proved to have been colonised by natives of Britain after the 6th century, partly during the Roman dominion, partly after the invasion of the Saxons. From Brittany, if we believe the native traditions, we derive our most popular romances, our nursery and fairy tales. Arthur here held his court with the Knights of the Round Table; and the cradle of Merlin was on the Ile de Sein, a low sand-bank in that stormy sea La Baie de Trépassés.

7. Many of the names of places closely resemble those of Wales and Cornwall. Brittany also has its *Cournouaille*, equally celebrated with our own for wrestling matches, still held annually, at which the true Cornish hug is said to be given; and for wreckers, whose infamous trade is promoted by the ever-raging sea and iron-bound coast. The Droit de Bris, right of "jetsam and flotsam," is, however, nearly abolished in France as in England: and the time is past when a race or whirlpool was as productive to a landlord as a mine or fishery.

English armies have fought and bled on this soil of Brittany; and the chivalric heroes of our history, Edward III., Chandos, Sir Walter Manny, were opposed to no unworthy antagonists in the Du Guesclins and Clissons. In the castle of Elven, Henry of Richmond passed 15 years of his youth, though a prisoner, yet protected from the vengeance of the Yorkists.

A perusal of Froissart will be a good preparation for a visit to Brittany.

8. Brittany, old-fashioned in all things, is still the stronghold of that old-fashioned virtue, loyalty to its sovereign; and, besides sharing in the horrors and glory of the war in support of the legitimate monarch, which had its rise in La Vendée, was the seat of a hard-fought contest of its own, called *La Chouannerie*, from the cry, "chou, chou," in imitation of the night-owl, the signal for onset among the Breton peasantry, originally employed as a sign by smugglers in their nocturnal expeditions. Memorials or recollections of these struggles will be encountered by the traveller at every step.

9. Those who desire full information respecting the antiquities, customs, legends, and poetry of the Bretons should read *Souvestre's* excellent work, 'Les Derniers Bretons,' and *Freminville's* ' Finisterre and Morbihan.' For its churches and Druidic remains consult *Merimée*, 'Sur les Monumens de l'Ouest de la France;' for its history, *Daru*:—*Miss Costello's* 'Bocages and Vines,' *Mr. Trollope's* 'Brittany,' are interesting English works; and *Mrs. Stothard's* 'Tour in Brittany,' and *Villemarqué's* ' Chansons Populaires de la Bretagne,' will repay the perusal.

10. *Skeleton Tour of Brittany.*

Brittany is accessible to travellers from England, by steamers either direct from Southampton to St. Malo, a very good starting-point, or from Southampton to Havre, and thence by land through Normandy, or by steamer to Morlaix.

BRITTANY. *Route 34.—Paris to Rennes by Versailles.*

The traveller coming from Paris may commence his tour at Rennes, but the capital of la Bretagne does not possess any of the characteristic features of the province.

Dol.
St. Malo.
Dinan.
St. Brieuc.
{ Lanleff.
{ Paimpol.
{ Treguier.
Morlaix.
St. Pol de Léon.
Folgoat.
Brest—dockyard.
Pointe St. Matthieu.
Châteaulin (by water).

Carhaix.
} Folgoat.
} St. Herbot.
(Châteaulin.
Quimper.
Quimperlé.
Auray.
Carnac and Lokmariaker.
[Peninsula of Rhuys.]
Vannes.
Roche Bernard.
Nantes.

11. *Accommodation for travellers*, even in the large towns, is inferior to that of the rest of France; while in spots at all remote from the high road the filth is most disgusting, the fare miserable.

The following excellent description of the chief inn of the chief town of the province is from the private diary of a tourist:—

"The Hôtel de France, if it be not good, is at all events highly amusing as a curiosity. It is something akin to what the 'Swan with Two Necks' in Lad Lane, or the 'Four Swans' in Bishopsgate Street, probably were 40 years since. You get a good dinner for 2 francs at the table-d'hôte, exclusive of a fair table wine; and, by dint of importunity at the kitchen, some coffee and bread and butter for breakfast. You also get your bed made in time to get into it again at night; but you never see a servant except one who flits round at the table-d'hôte. The yard is crowded with diligences and baggage, and strewn with straw and ordures, and the proprietors are incognoscible beings. Everything seems to move on by unseen agency; yet you really want for nothing material if you will but give up getting the *bell* answered. This inn is in fact a sample of the 'Tom Jones' inn of the 18th cent., and the landlady at Rennes (whom we succeeded in finding out before we left) was a French counterpart of the English one of that day: slaving daily at her stews and stoves, like any necessitous hireling, in a dress indicating the most rigorous economy. But the virtue of prudence and the desire of accumulation occupy the foreground in the mind of a French 'bourgeoise.' The landlord we learned had a delightful country house out of Rennes, whence he daily visited his gainful but ill-appointed 'auberge.' No trade so profitable as an aubergiste, it would seem, in a frequented town of France."—*G*.

ROUTE 34.

PARIS TO RENNES, BY VERSAILLES, RAMBOUILLET, CHARTRES, LE MANS (GREAT WESTERN RAILWAY OF FRANCE TO LE MANS), AND LAVAL.

kilom. = 230 Eng. m. Trains daily to Chartres. Terminus, Boulevard Mt. Parnasse.

From Paris to Versailles there are 2 railroads, one on the l., the other on the rt. bank of the Seine. The l. bank railway is continued from Versailles to Chartres and Le Mans.

a. *Chemin de Fer, Rive Gauche,* 16¾ kilom. = 11¼ Eng. m. Terminus, Boulevard Mont Parnasse, 44. Trains go every ½ hr. Those starting at the hour are stopping trains, those at the ½ hour quick or direct. Time employed 20 to 25 minutes, with stopping train 35 minutes.

Before issuing beyond the line of the

new fortifications you see on the rt. Grenelle and Vaugirard, now forming a town of about 6000 Inhab., most of the houses being cabarets, the resort of the working classes on Sundays and fête-days; and on the l. Montrouge, where are numerous quarries of building stone.

Beyond the Lines the railway passes between the detached forts of Vanvres and Issy, a village whose name is fancifully derived from a temple of Isis! In the *Séminaire*, which still exists as a sort of country-seat dependent on that of St. Sulpice, Fénélon was interrogated by a conclave of bishops, styled the Conference of Issy, on certain points of doctrine, and here the Cardinal Fleury died, 1745.

rt. Vanvres. The *Château*, formerly the property of the Condés, built here by Mansard for the Duc de Bourbon, now belongs to the Collége Louis le Grand.

5 Clamart Stat. The village, half hid among the trees, on the l., was the retreat of La Fontaine, of the Abbé Delille, who wrote here his poem 'L'Imagination,' and of Condorcet.

Emerging from a deep cutting we traverse on a lofty *viaduct* (Pont du Val) of 2 rows of arches, one above the other, 108 ft. high and 145 ft. long, the bosky dell of Val Fleury, commanding a pretty view of the château of Meudon on the l., while the Seine is perceived on the rt.

2 Meudon Stat. A little on the l. lies the bourg of 3000 Inhab. Rabelais was curé of Meudon, 1550.

The *Château*, now belonging to the nation, approached by a fine avenue of 4 rows of lime-trees, was built by the Grand Dauphin, son of Louis XIV., who died in it, from designs of Mansard, 1699, by the side of an older château now destroyed, the work of Philibert Delorme, which the widow of the minister Louvois sold to Louis XIV. During the Revolution the Comité du Salut Public converted it into a factory for inventing and perfecting warlike engines, and surrounded it with a permanent camp to keep out spies. The existing château was fitted up for Marie Louise by Napoleon, 1812. The best things about it are its situation, its gardens laid out by Le Nôtre, but lately re-arranged on a more modern plan, and its *terrace*. The view from the terrace is very fine. There is a breeding-stud for race-horses here belonging to the Duc. de Nemours.

The Forêt de Meudon is a favourite holiday resort of the Parisians. Near this the fatal accident occurred on this railway, May 1842, when, by the fracture of the axle of a locomotive, several of the foremost carriages of a long train were crushed, thrown upon the engine-furnace, and set on fire, and more than 100 persons were burnt alive, together with the railway-carriages in which they were locked up, in the space of about $\frac{1}{4}$ hour. An expiatory chapel, dedicated to Notre Dame des Flammes, has been erected on the spot where this catastrophe occurred. Another cutting succeeds, and the railway passes under the Meudon avenue.

1 Bellevue Stat. was named from a villa built in a few months to please Madame de Pompadour, but pulled to pieces during the Revolution.

rt. *Sèvres Stat.*, contiguous to Bellevue, is described farther on (p. 120). The high road, and the chemin de fer, rive droite, now run parallel and within a musket-shot of our line.

A deep cutting through part of the crown forests leads to

4 Chaville Stat., so called from a village on the l.

1 Viroflay Stat. l. Railway to Chartres diverges.

4 *Versailles Station* (in the Avenue de la Mairie).

---

b. *Chemin de Fer, Rive Droite.* Terminus in Paris, Rue St. Lazare, 120, the same as the St. Germain and Rouen railways, and the 3 railways use the same line of rails as far as Clichy. Trains every $\frac{1}{2}$ hour (stopping), and every hour direct, from $7\frac{1}{2}$ A.M. to 10 P.M., $22\frac{3}{4}$ kilom = 14 Eng. m.; time in going 30 to 35 minutes.

After crossing the Seine by the Pont d'Asnières Stat. beyond Clichy, this railway turns to the l. out of the St. Germain line (See Rte. 8) to

Courbevoie Stat., whose large barrack, built by Louis XV., is seen on the l., and beyond it the Arc de l'Etoile. The avenue leading from it, after passing the Seine by the Pont de Neuilly, branches out into two roads leading to Rouen, the upper and the lower, both of which are crossed by the railway before reaching

Puteaux Stat. A fine view is obtained of Paris and the Seine from this part of the line, while skirting on the rt. the flanks of Mont Valérien, now converted into one of the citadels of Paris.

Suresnes Stat.

St. Cloud Stat.

The Imperial Château, built or altered by Mansard for the Duc d'Orléans, brother of Louis XIV., has been the scene of great events. Here the fatal Ordonnances of July 1830 were signed, which lost Charles X. the throne; here Napoleon, like Cromwell before him, laid the foundation of his power on the memorable 19 Brumaire (Nov. 11, 1799), by expelling with his armed grenadiers the Council of Five Hundred from the *Orangerie*, in which they held their sittings;—two of the most momentous of the Revolutions of France. It was a favourite residence of Marie Antoinette and of Bonaparte, and is now occupied by the President.

The interior is handsomely furnished, and contains some paintings chiefly of the modern French school, Gobelin tapestry, Sèvres vases, &c. The finest apartment is the Salon de Mars; the most interesting for its associations, the *Orangerie* already mentioned. Even more remarkable than the Château is the *Parc de St. Cloud*, laid out by Le Nôtre, always open to the public, and well worthy of a visit on account of the beautiful view which it commands over the winding Seine and the country around Paris, for its artificial cascades, and its waterworks, which play the 1st and 3rd Sunday of every month. The *Grand Jet d'Eau* rises from the centre of a circular basin, at the extremity of a long avenue, to a height of 137 feet, and discharges 5000 gallons per minute. The copy of the beautiful circular temple at Athens, called the *Lanterne de Démosthène*, should not be passed unobserved.

In this part a fair is held on the 7th September, and lasts 3 weeks, one of the most celebrated and frequented of all the fêtes near Paris.

The name of St. Cloud is a contraction of St. Clodoald, grandson of Clovis, who escaped alive when his brothers were murdered by their uncle Clothaire, by hiding himself in a wood here, and living as a hermit. Here, in the Maison de Gondi, Henri III. was assassinated by Jacques Clement, 1589, while his army, united with that of Henri of Navarre, was encamped on these heights preparing to attack Paris. The father of Louis-Philippe was born here.

The railway is carried under a part of the park of St. Cloud in a *Tunnel* more than 1650 ft. long.

Sèvres Stat. Both railways have stations here, but at some distance from the village, as well as at

Viroflay Stat. 1. The railway to Chartres diverges about 1 m. beyond Viroflay.

rt. The small village of Montreuil, famed for peaches, is the birthplace of General Hoche, who commenced life as an under groom in the royal stables, and rose to be commander of the army of the Moselle.

Versailles Station, Rue Duplessis, Boulevard de la Reine.

[Near Magny—Les Hameux are the scanty remains of the once celebrated abbey of *Port Royal des Champs*, destroyed by royal decree 1709, at the instigation of the Jesuits, as the headquarters of Jansenism, after the nuns, its tenants, had been subjected to the most cruel persecutions in order to compel them to subscribe to the bull of Alexander VII. against the doctrines of Jansen. In 1644 a number of learned men and profound divines, professing the same doctrines, settled in a farmhouse near the convent, called La Grange, repairing hither for study; and here composed those works which, as "they were published anonymously, are known by the name of their place of residence. Arnauld, Nicole, are among the Messieurs de Port-Royal,—an appellation so glorious in the 17th cent."—*Hallam*. Boileau and Pascal were their friends, and Racine, who wrote their history, their pupil.

"He whose journey lies from Versailles to Chevreuse will soon find himself at the brow of a steep cleft or hollow, intersecting the monotonous plain across which he has been passing. The brook which winds through the verdant meadows beneath him stagnates into a lage pool, reflecting the solitary Gothic arch, the water-mill, and the dovecot, which rise from its banks, with the farmhouse, the decayed towers, the forest-trees, and innumerable shrubs and creepers which clothe the slopes of the valley. France has many a lovelier prospect, though this is not without its beauty, and many a field of more heart-stirring interest, though this, too, has been ennobled by heroic daring; but through the length and breadth of that land of chivalry and of song, the traveller will in vain seek a spot so sacred to genius, to piety, and to virtue. That arch is all which remains of the once crowded monastery of Port-Royal. In those woods Racine first learned the language — the universal language — of poetry. Under the roof of that humble farmhouse, Pascal, Arnauld, Nicole, De Sace, and Tillemont meditated those works which, as long as civilization and Christianity survive, will retain their hold on the gratitude and reverence of mankind. There were given innumerable proofs of the graceful good humour of Henri IV. To this seclusion retired the heroine of the Fronde, Ann Geneviève, Duchess of Longueville, to seek the peace the world could not give. Madame de Sévigné discovered here a place 'tout propre à inspirer le désir de faire son salut.' From Versailles there came hither to worship God many a courtier and many a beauty, heartbroken or jaded with the very vanity of vanities—the idolatry of their fellow-mortals. Survey French society in the 17th cent. from what aspect you will, it matters not, at Port-Royal will be found the most illustrious examples of whatever imparted to that motley assemblage any real dignity or permanent regard. Even to the mere antiquarian it was not without a lively interest."— *Stephen.*

The magnificent *Château de Dampierre,* in the vale of Chevreuse, has lately been restored by its owner, the Duc de Luynes, one of the richest nobles in France. It has been adorned with paintings by *Ingres,* and with sculptures by *Simart.* The park has an area of 2000 acres. The valley is one of the prettiest and least visited spots in the vicinity of Paris. The Château is curious.

32 La Verrière Stat.

39 Lartoire Stat.

48 *Rambouillet Stat.*, a dull town of 3000 Inhab., remarkable only for its *Château,* long the residence of the kings of France, down to the time of Charles X., who, after the July revolution, here signed, in conjunction with the Duc d'Angoulême, his abdication of the French throne, Aug. 2, 1830, under pressure of the news that the mob of Paris, armed, was on its march hither, seeming to threaten results not unlike those which befel Louis XVI. at Versailles, Oct. 1789. It is a gloomy and ugly pile of red brick, with 5 flanking towers of stone, destitute of interest beyond what it may derive from its history. A chamber is shown in the great round tower where Francis I. died, 1547, aged 52. The dreary park and extensive forest adjoining, the favourite sporting ground of Charles X., are now hired to private clubs of sportsmen. The château was converted by Louis Napoleon into a Seminary for officers' daughters, 1852.

Beyond this the road becomes more hilly and varied. The rly. descends the valley of the Guesle, following its sinuosities, as far as

61 Epernon Stat., no tolerable *Inn.*

The name of this town of 1600 Inhab. was changed from Autrist to Epernon by Henry III., who created it and the district around a duchy for his favourite Nogaret. It retains portions of its old walls and towers, and is prettily situated on the banks of the Guesle, under a commanding rock of limestone.

Maintenon Stat. is situated between

the ruined aqueduct of Louis XIV. (see below) and the imposing modern rly. viaduct of 32 arches, 65 ft. high, raised on light piers. The *Château* attached to this little town was given by Louis XIV., with the estate and title of Marquise de Maintenon, to Françoise d'Aubigné, widow of Scarron, at the time when the king made her his wife. Their marriage is said to have been celebrated in the chapel of the castle by the Père la Chaise in the presence of Harlay and Louvois, 1685, she being 50 years old and Louis 47. The *Castle* stands on the margin of the Eure, and now belongs to the Duc de Noailles; parts of it are said to appertain to the original structure raised by Cocquereau, treasurer of finance to Louis XI. and Charles VIII. The bedroom of Mad. de Maintenon, and her portrait in robes trimmed with ermine and fleurs-de-lis, are shown.

The valley of the Eure is here crossed by the imposing ruins of the *Aqueduct*, constructed 1684, at the mandate of Louis XIV., to convey the waters of the Eure from Pont Gouin to Versailles, but afterwards abandoned for the machine at Marly.

" As Louis had committed the blunder of building in a place without water, he proposed to remedy his mistake by conveying the river eight leagues, by a new channel, to adorn his park. To accomplish this it was necessary to join two mountains at Maintenon, and form an aqueduct: 40,000 troops were employed in this great work, and a camp formed expressly for the purpose. From the unhealthiness of the work or of the air, a great mortality ensued; the dead were carried away in the nighttime, that their companions might not be discouraged; but the loss of many thousand lives to please the wanton caprice of a despot excited no sympathy and created no surprise. The war of 1688, however, interrupted the labour, and it was never afterwards resumed."—*Lord John Russell*. It was partly pulled down, after a lapse of 65 years, to build the villa of Crécy for Mad. de Pompadour. The remains consist of 47 arches, 42 ft. wide and 83 high. The total length of the canal, of which this was to form a part, would have exceeded 33 m. if completed.

On leaving Maintenon behind we enter the fertile plain called *La Beauce*, comprising some of the finest cornland in France. In the early summer it is an uninterrupted ocean of waving corn as far as the eye can reach—without hedges, little varied by trees or houses. "In crossing this monotonous plain I was much struck with the number of churches. I counted at one time about 13, yet the villages are neither numerous nor large."—*P. H.*

78 Jouy Stat.

Rather more than 1 m. from Chartres the river Eure is crossed. The twin steeples of Chartres are conspicuous a long way off.

88 CHARTRES *Station*.— *Inns:* Post, or Grand Monarque, best; Hôtel Duc de Chartres; H. de France, indifferent.

Chartres, a city of 14,439 Inhab., once capital of the fertile Beauce, and now of the Dépt. d'Eure et Loire, is situated on a slope, at the bottom of which runs the Eure, washing the only remaining portion of the old fortifications and two of the city gates. The *Porte Guillaume*, one of these, is picturesque; the rest have been pulled down, the ramparts levelled into walks, and the town thrown open. Chartres is remarkable in a *commercial* point of view for one of the largest corn-markets in France, held every Saturday, where the produce of the Beauce is disposed of; and in point of *architecture*, for its

** *Cathedral*, one of the most magnificent in Europe, conspicuous far and near, with its two tall but unequal spires surmounting the hill on which the city stands. Its most striking and interesting features, after its vast dimensions and elegant proportions, are its two rich and singular lateral portals, its painted glass, scarcely equalled in France, and its three rose windows.

There is much perplexity in the dates assigned to different parts of the building, but, with the evidence of style, we may pronounce the *Crypt*, running under the whole extent of the choir aisles, to be the only part remaining which was built by Bishop Fulbert, 1029. He was aided in his pious foundation by gifts from the kings of England, France, and Denmark, and a great body of people came over from Rouen to work at it, encamping in tents around while it was in progress. The ch., as it exists, was not dedicated until 1260, and the greater portion of it may safely be referred to the 13th centy.; but the W. front was completed in 1145, except the elegant crocketed N. spire raised in 1514, partly at the charge of Louis XII., by Jean Texier, an architect of the Beauce: it is 304 ft. high, and the upper part of beautifully light and delicately executed work. It is well worth ascending for the view, not only of the surrounding country, but of the Cathedral itself. In the W. front, which is simple in its style, we have to remark the triple portal of pointed arches; that in the centre, called *Porte Royale*, supported and flanked by statues of royal saints. These are attenuated figures with formal plaited drapery, characteristic of the Byzantine sculpture of the 12th centy. Above the door is the image of Christ in an oval, with the symbols of the 4 Evangelists, as designated in the vision of Ezekiel, around him. Below these are the 14 Prophets in a row, and in the arches above the 24 Elders of the Apocalypse, playing on musical instruments of the middle ages. The sculpture of the right-hand portal relates to the life of the Virgin, and in that of the l. is seen Christ, again surrounded by angels, with the signs of the zodiac, and the agricultural labours of the twelve months.

Far finer are the two entrances on the N. and S. sides, consisting of triple projecting Gothic porticoes (something like the W. end of Peterborough), resting on piers, or bundles of pillars, with side openings between them. The stately statues which line the sides and vaults are of a superior style of art, and of a later date (14th cent.) than those of the W. front.

The interior is of such consistent vastness in all its parts, that its dimensions do not perhaps strike the spectator, at first sight, to their fullest extent, but its length is 422 ft., and the height to the apex of its roof 112 ft. The style throughout nave and choir is the vigorous early Gothic. In the centre of the nave a maze or labyrinth, of intricate circles, is marked out on the pavement in coloured stone: to follow it through its windings (1320 ft. long), saying prayers at certain stations, was probably at one time a penitential exercise. The ch. possesses a perfect treasure of *Painted Glass*, more than 130 windows being completely filled, and few being quite destitute of this splendid ornament. They date, for the most part, from the 13th centy. Some of the glass is ½ inch thick. The 3 rose windows at the end of the nave and transepts are remarkable for their size, 30 or 40 ft. diameter, and their complicated tracery, but it is somewhat clumsy. The windows, both in nave and choir, illustrate subjects from the Bible, or legends of saints; in the lower compartments are frequently seen representations of various trades—shoemakers, basket-makers, &c.—showing that their guilds or corporations were the donors.

Attached to the E. end is a chapel dedicated to St. Piat, in the form of an oblong; it was founded in 1349, and is flanked by two round towers externally.

The choir has double aisles and a semicircular E. end; in the inside 8 marble bas-reliefs, of Scriptural subjects, mediocre in design and execution, are inserted, and behind the high altar is a huge marble piece of sculpture, in the taste of the time of Louis XIII., not consistent with the character of the building. The outside of the screen, which separates the choir from its aisles, is ornamented with a series of very remarkable Gothic sculptures, each representing an event in the life of Christ or the Virgin Mary, in 45 compartments surrounded with the most elaborate tracery and tabernacle work; they were begun 1514, and continued down to the middle of the 17th century, and are interesting as some of the final efforts of Gothic art. The execution has been compared to "point lace in stone, and some of the sculptured threads are not thicker than the blade of a penknife."

In the choir of Chartres cathedral Henri IV. was crowned, 1594; Rheims, the ancient scene of the royal coronation, being at the time in the hands of the Leaguers. The ceremony was performed by the bishop of the diocese, and, as the "Sainte Ampoulle" was not to be got at, a vial of holy oil, said to have been given by an angel to St. Martin of Tours, to cure a bruise, was brought in procession from the Abbey of Marmoutiers, and with this the king was anointed. This cathedral narrowly escaped destruction by fire in 1836 : fortunately the roof and interior of the towers were alone consumed.

"The origin and splendour of this cathedral are owing to the circumstance that it was the earliest and chief church in France dedicated to the Virgin, and thus the object of vast pilgrimages. The sacred image, supposed to date from the time when this place was the centre of the Druidic worship, as described by Cæsar, stood in the crypt. It was burned and the crypt sacked in 1793. The church still contains the relic of the *Sacra Camisia*, given by Charles le Chauve; and there is a black image of the 12th centy. in the N. aisle, which attracts much devotion. It is worth while to ascend the tower—not for the panorama, which is only over a vast plain, but in order to have a near view of the painted glass inside the cathedral. A full account of every window will be found in the elaborate History of the Cathedral by the Abbé Baltran, price 4½ francs."— *A. P. S.*

After exploring this noble and surpassing edifice, the traveller will probably have little desire to look at inferior churches, yet *the only* other curiosities here are

The *Church of St. Pierre* (St. Père), contiguous to a huge caserne, once a convent, and not far from the river; —although very inferior to the cathedral, it presents a remakable lantern-like E. end, filled with rich painted glass. The lantern character is increased by the triforium, running all round the choir, being open and glazed.

The choir, though pointed, must be very early in the style, the piers having a Romanesque character, the nave slightly different, and apparently later, yet retains the transition appearance in its columns. Its triforium is a row of trefoil-headed arches, supported on pilasters.

St. André, also near the river, and now a magasin de fourrage, filled with straw and hay, is yet interesting to the student of architecture as an early, plain, and severe example of the pointed style. In the W. façade a circular-headed doorway is surmounted by a triplet of lancet windows, and these by a bold rose window. The piers supporting the nave arches are cylindrical, marking the transition from Romanesque to Gothic. The choir, which was carried across the Eure, is destroyed. A curious crypt extends from the south aisle down to the river, and below its level. St. André is supposed to have been founded 1108.

An *Obelisk* has been set up in the Marché aux Herbes, to record the fact that *Marceau* was a native of Chartres, —"Soldat à 16 ans, Général à 23 ; il mourut à 27." The original inscription mentioned his exploits in destroying the rebel Vendéans at Le Mans and Laval. The revolutionary hero Pétion was born here.

The *Corn Market* is exceedingly well regulated ; business is transacted for ready money, and is usually over in ¾ hour. The measuring and selling of the grain, and receiving payment for it, are managed by a corporation of women, of long standing, remarkable for their integrity, and implicitly trusted by the owners.

There are a public *Library* of 30,000 volumes and a *Museum* in the town.

Malleposte to Brest.

Diligences daily to Orleans and Rouen by Evreux (Rte. 50). To Tours by Vendôme (Rte. 54). To Nantes.

Railway to Paris by Versailles:—to Le Mans :—in progress to Rennes.

The little village *Bretigny*, 6 m. from Chartres, gives its name to the treaty of peace, signed 1360, between France and England, by which

Edward III. renounced his claim to the throne of France, and released the French king, John, taken prisoner at Poitiers, upon payment of a vast ransom, and delivery of numerous hostages. A violent storm which fell upon Edward and his army near Chartres, and "reminded him of the day of judgment," caused him to make a vow (looking towards the towers of the cathedral) that he would give peace to France, and led to this important treaty.

The journey from Chartres is continued through the monotonous but fertile and well-cultivated corn-plain of La Beauce.

La Loupe Stat.

[Courville. 3 m. S. of this is the Château de *Villebon*, where the illustrious Sully died. It is a square building of brick, with towers at the angles, and not many years ago retained its ancient furniture, even to the bed on which the great minister expired. The Eure rises about 15 m. to the N. of Courville.] At Montlandon the fertile Beauce terminates, and the country becomes hilly.

Nogent-le-Rotrou Stat., a town of 7070 Inhab., contains a ruined *Castle*, the residence of Sully, and his *Monument* in the chapel of the *Hôtel Dieu* founded by him. It bears the marble statues of himself and his wife by Boudin, 1642, and a long inscription at the back.; it escaped the fury of the Revolution, but the grave itself was violated, and the bones disinterred and scattered. The word Nogent is an abbreviation of the Latin Novigentium ; Rotrou was the name of a count of Perche, in which district it is situated. The river produces crawfish in great abundance. (*Inn*: St. Jacques.) The railroad follows the direction of the Huisne river from Nogent nearly to Le Mans.

Ferté-Bernard Stat. is a prettily situated town in the Dépt. de la Sarthe, Within it the *Parish Church* is an interesting Gothic building, having a richly sculptured external gallery, with the words "Salve Regina" cut in stone, and 3 chapels, from the vaulted roofs of which hang stone pendants.

Near Connerré is a large Dolmen or Druidic monument of rude stone slabs, like Kits Coity House in Kent. (§ 4.)

St. Mars-la-Bruyère indicates by its name the desolate sandy heaths in the midst of which it is situated.

Le Mans Stat. (*Inn*: Le Dauphin), once capital of the province of Le Haut Maine, now chef-lieu of the Dépt. de la Sarthe, is situated on the l. bank of the river Sarthe, a little above the junction of the Huisne, and has 20,000 Inhab.

The principal edifice is the *Cathedral* of St. Julien, which is well deserving of attention. It is in two styles ; the *nave*, Romanesque, though with pointed arches, dates probably from the 12 cent., but its side aisles and walls, and the plain W. front, are not later than the 11th, perhaps much earlier. Indeed, the external masonry of the side walls, resembling Roman construction, is probably part of the original church, founded in the 8th or 9th cent. Above the W. door are portions of reticulated masonry, and an ancient bust of a king or bishop ; on each side are figures supposed to represent the 2 signs of the zodiac, Capricorn and Sagittarius.

On the S. side is a very richly-carved Romanesque *doorway*—a round arch preceded by a pointed porch, flanked by statues of kings and saints, resembling the W. door at Chartres, and with angels in the vault. It is much mutilated, unfortunately.

The *Choir* is a beautiful production of the 13th centy., the period of perfection in pointed Gothic architecture. It is surrounded by 11 chapels, and its windows are filled with beautiful painted glass, little inferior to that of Chartres, except in preservation. In the transept is a fine rose window, together with much stained glass of the 14th or 15th cent., a date rather more modern than that of the choir.

This church contains the monuments of Berengaria of Sicily, queen of Richard Cœur de Lion, brought from the abbey of Epau, and much defaced ; of Charles of Anjou ; and of Langey du Bellay, distinguished as a soldier and as a writer in the reigns of Francis I. and Henri II. The last is attributed to Germain Pilon ; its arabesques and bas-reliefs in marble are well worthy attention.

An undressed block of silicious sandstone, standing on one end, has been incorporated into the wall of the church on the outside ; it is supposed to be a Druidic stone.

The Church of *Notre Dame du Pré* is probably of the 11th cent.

Notre Dame de la Coûture (de culturâ Dei) has a very old choir, supposed to have been begun 990 ; both arches and vaulting are round and of rude construction ; it has a very elegant portal, adorned with sculpture of considerable merit (Last Judgment). The conventual buildings to which it was originally attached are now the *Préfecture*, but contain besides the *Library* and a *Museum*, partly devoted to natural history, partly to paintings of a very inferior order, but possessing one curiosity at least, viz. a portrait of Geoffroi Plantagenet, enamelled on copper, a very early specimen of that class of art : it was anciently placed in the cathedral where he was buried. There are also many objects of Roman antiquity found in Le Mans and the neighbourhood, at Alonnes pottery, &c.

St. Pierre is supposed to be the oldest church here, that is to say, the lower part of its walls.

The *Séminaire*, originally the Abbaye de St. Vincent, has a noble façade and a fine staircase. There is a handsome theatre.

Many specimens of ancient domestic architecture remained here until lately, but are fast disappearing, and the town is becoming modern and commonplace. There used to be some old houses in the *Grande Rue*. Nos. 7, 10, and 12 deserve attention ; the last is known as the house of Queen Berengaria, but appears not to be older than the 15th century. It contains a chimney-piece adorned with bas-reliefs. The house of Scarron (husband of Madame de Maintenon) is pointed out near the cathedral. The vestiges of the Roman rule at Le Mans are not considerable : the chief are the remains of 3 subterranean aqueducts, by which the city was supplied with water from a distance. A portion of them may be seen in a cellar of the Rue Gourdaine. Fragments of the Roman town walls still exist ; but all traces of an amphitheatre, discovered in the last century, have been swept away.

Le Mans was the birthplace of Henry (II.) Fitz-Empress, the first of the Plantagenet kings of England: a name derived from the plant or sprig of broom (genêt), the abundant production of his native province Anjou and Maine, which his father, Geoffroi, used to wear in his cap.

A great trade is carried on here in clover-seed, which is sent over in large quantities to England. The chief article of manufacture is *wax candles*. Le Mans is also famed for poultry ; its poulards and chapons supply the markets of Paris.

Le Mans witnessed the ruin and final dispersion of the Vendéan army in 1793. Worn out by the disastrous fatigues of a six months' campaign, they were here assaulted by the Republican forces under Marceau's command. Very obstinate was the resistance made by the Royalists in the streets and great square of the town before they were finally expelled, with their leader, Larochejacquelin, who was wounded in the action. Then ensued the most fearful carnage, not only of the Vendéan soldiery, but of their miserable wives and children, who accompanied them. By the joint exercise of cannonades of grape and platoons of musketry, discharged upon the defenceless crowd, under the order of the commissioners of the Convention, upwards of 10,000 persons were slaughtered on that occasion.

Conveyances daily to Caen by Alençon and to Tours (Rte. 29).

Branch Railway from Le Mans to Mezedon, by Alençon and Argentan. It has 5 bridges over the Sarthe, and will be opened 1856 or 1857.

The Railway to Rennes (230 m. from Paris) is in progress through Laval and Vitré.

From Le Mans to Laval the post-relays are

14 Coulans.
19 La Lune Brulon.

18 La Métairie de Beauvais.
10 Soulgé-le-Bruant.
16 LAVAL. (*Inns*: Tête Noire;— Cour Royale), a curious ancient town, chef-lieu of the Dépt. de la Mayenne, on the river Mayenne, has 16,500 Inhab. The oldest part consists of black timber houses, each story projecting beyond that below it, until the gable overhangs the street; but a new quarter has risen on the W., where the streets are wide and regular. On the rt. bank of the river, close to the old bridge, the *Castle* of the seigneurs of La Trémouille rises from a basement of rock, on which its lofty wall is raised, flanked at one end by a machicolated round tower. It was built in the 12th centy., and its *Chapel* on round arches is perhaps of that date, but there are many later additions, and the jambs of some of the windows facing the inner court retain some rich ornaments in the style of the Renaissance (15th or 16th centy.). It is now a *prison*.

The *Cathedral* presents a singularity of ground plan, taking the form of a right angle, occasioned by the sloping ground on which it stands. It is a curious Gothic edifice. The nave and choir (except the aisles and side chapels, additions of the 15th and 16th centuries, in the flamboyant style) are not older than the 12th centy. The E. end is square; the porch is a wretched addition of recent times. Under the ch. are very extensive substructions and crypts, thrown up in consequence of the slope of the ground to form a platform or pedestal for the building.

St. Vénerand, a ch. of the 15th or 16th centy., has a little painted glass.

The *church* in the village of Avenières, adjoining the town, built 1040, deserves the notice of the architect. Its choir, in the early pointed style, is surrounded by 5 apsidal chapels, and 2 others open into the transepts. Above the cross rises an elegant stone spire of decorated Gothic. The church contains a miracle-working image of the Virgin.

The architect and antiquary ought not to leave unseen the little ruined *Ch.* of *Grenoux*, 2 m. from Laval. It is destitute of all ornament. The structure of its masonry, small square stones with intervening bonds of tiles, marks the style of a period not later than the 9th cent. Within it is a monument of a knight and his lady.

Laval is essentially a manufacturing town, occupied in the production of linens and cottons (toiles, coutils, siamoises), and of linen thread, large quantities of which are spun here. A market for the sale of these productions is held every week in the *Halle aux Toiles*.

Laval was the centre from which arose the Royalist insurrection of 1792, called *Chouannerie*, either from 4 brothers named Chouan, its first leaders, of the village St. Ouen des Toits, or from the cry of the owl, imitated by the salt-smugglers of this district as a signal to their confederates, and afterwards adopted during the struggle, by the peasant guerrillas, to announce the enemy's approach.

One of the most glorious victories of the Vendéans was gained in Oct. 1793, a little to the S. of the town. Defeated in several previous combats, and driven across the Loire, with a large Republican army in pursuit of them, their enemies believed the war extinguished. Barrère announced this intelligence to the Convention in Paris: "La Vendée is no more, the brigands are exterminated, a profound solitude reigns in the Bocage, covered with cinders and watered with tears:"—but at the very time that these words were being uttered, Larochejacquelin had carried Laval at the point of the bayonet; then, turning round on his pursuers, he exhorted his brave bands to efface the memory of their former defeats, and to fight for the preservation of their wives and children who accompanied them, now far from their homes. Lescure insisted on being carried through the ranks on his death-litter, mortally wounded as he was, to encourage the Royalists by his presence, and to share their peril and toil. The Vendéans, obeying the appeal, on this occasion rushed upon the enemy in close column, routed them entirely, and pursued them beyond Château Gonthier, with a loss to the

Republicans of 12,000 men, among whom were the redoubted garrison of Mayenne, who were mostly cut to pieces, and of 19 cannon. The conflict began at les Croix de Bataille, 2 m. S. of Laval. So precipitate and complete was the rout, that the remains of the Republican army, reduced to 12,000 men, were not collected and reorganised until 12 days had elapsed, and not before they had left the town of Angers in their rear.

21 La Gravelle. There are large coal-works at St. Pierre la Cour, near this.

16 Vitré (*Inn:* La Poste) is in appearance a town of the middle ages, Gothic and irregular, retaining the greater portion of its feudal fortifications, high and thick *walls* flanked by towers, surmounted by machicolations, and surrounded by a deep ditch. They appear not later in date than the 15th cent. On one side of them, but detached from them by a ditch, stands a venerable and picturesque *Castle* of the Seigneurs de la Tremouille, now converted into a prison and falling to decay. In the court is an elegantly ornamented structure, half Gothic, half Italian, supposed to have been a pulpit. At the time of its construction the lords of the castle were adherents of the reformed faith, and the inscription, which may still be read around the console, "post tenebras spero lucem," probably alludes to the persecutions they suffered.

The *Ch. of Notre Dame* is in a style indicating the decline of Gothic art; attached to it, on the outside, is a stone pulpit, and within one of the chapels hangs a frame containing 32 small enamels, probably from Limoges.

The peasants of this part of Brittany wear a dress of goatskins with the hair turned outwards, which gives them a somewhat savage aspect, and reminds one of Robinson Crusoe.

About 3 m. S. of Vitré is the *Château des Rochers*, long time the residence of Madame de Sévigné; her bedroom and the cabinet where she wrote many of her charming letters are pointed out, and there is a fine portrait of her by *Mignard*, but the furniture, &c., of the interior has been altered.

[Near Essé, 7 lieues S.W. of Vitré, is a very fine Druidical monument called "la Roche aux Fées," consisting of 43 large rough blocks of stone—34 upright, supporting 8 others which form a roof.]

The Vilaine river, after which the department is named, rises near Vitré; our road runs parallel with its course as far as Rennes, crossing it by a stone bridge at

15 Châteaubourg.

2 m. beyond this the road passes close to a large slate-quarry excavated to a depth of more than 100 ft.

9 Noyal. The country possesses little interest.

12 RENNES.—*Inns:* H. de France, rebuilt 1851; table-d'hôte 4 frs.;— H. de la Corne de Cerf, well situated and moderate charges;—H. Jullien (formerly H. de l'Europe). This town, once capital of Brittany, now chef-lieu of the Dépt. Ille et Vilaine, is situated at the confluence of these two streams, and contains 37,900 Inhab. Here are few antiquities; the town has an entirely modern aspect, arising from a dreadful fire which in 1720 reduced nearly the whole to ashes. It lasted 7 days, and consumed 850 houses, besides nearly all the public buildings; the ancient and solidly built clock tower crumbled to pieces on the third day, calcined by the flames. The public buildings, of a date subsequent to this catastrophe, display for the most part the bad taste of the 18th centy.

The streets are uniform; and, "notwithstanding the sober and gloomy hue of which the houses are chiefly built, Rennes is rather a handsome city," but dull. Considerable improvements have taken place, many narrow streets have been removed, and a new bridge has been thrown over the Vilaine.

The stately *Palais de Justice*, in the handsome Place du Palais, was the parliament house of the States of Brittany, and is the most remarkable building here. It contains one fine large Salle, des Pas Perdus, and several apartments rich in gilded ceilings and stucco ornaments, Cupids bearing festoons, &c., with roofs and panels painted by Jouvenet. Its date is 1670.

The interior of the *modern Cathedral*

"is a very spacious, lofty, and imposing *Hall* of Grecian architecture; the principal aisle having a richly decorated vaulted roof, supported by massive and well-proportioned fluted Corinthian columns. On the whole the effect is striking, but not all ecclesiastical." *M. A. S.*—*St. Melaine* retains a Romanesque porch supported on engaged pillars with curiously carved capitals, probably of the 12th century. The telegraph on the top of the cathedral is one of the chain communicating between Paris and Brest.

There is a very handsome modern *Theatre*, situated in another respectable square, with covered arcades around it, lined with shops.

In the modern *Hôtel de Ville* facing the theatre is a collection of pictures removed from the damp Musée in which they were before deposited: the greater part are of little worth. As a curiosity may be cited a Judgment of Solomon painted by *King René of Anjou*, but much injured, faded and dingy in hue. There is a Lion Hunt, said to be by *Rubens* (?)

Here is also the Public Library, containing 30,000 volumes, and many rare MSS., among them a charter of Don Henry of Trastamare, granting lands in Spain to Du Guesclin.

The chief attraction of Rennes, however, is its *Public Walks*, especially that called *le Mont Thabor*, planted with fine trees and commanding a pleasing view over the town, and valley of the Vilaine. A miserable statue of Du Guesclin has been set up in it. The other walks are *le Mail*, extending down to the junction of the Ille and Vilaine, *le Mont de Madame*, and *le Champ de Mars*.

One of the old town gates, *la Porte Mordelaise*, is preserved opposite the new cathedral; the entrance is by a pointed arch, and the masonry includes a stone bearing a Roman inscription, dedicated by the town of Rennes (*Redonis*) to the Emperor Gordian; it is no longer legible. Through this gate the ancient Dukes of Brittany made their solemn entry into Rennes on their accession, but before passing it they swore to preserve the Catholic faith and the ch. of Brittany, to govern wisely, and to execute justice; they were then conducted into the ch., where, after 2 days spent in prayer, they were crowned with the golden circlet, and girt with the ducal sword.

The manufactures of Rennes are sail-cloth, which it supplies to the French navy, and some table linen. The butter (*beurre salé*) is excellent, especially that of Prévalaye, large quantities of which are sent to other parts of France.

Rennes has a communication by *Canal* with St. Malo and the Channel on the one hand, and with Nantes and Brest on the other.

Diligences daily to Le Mans Rly. Stat. for Paris, and to Brest (Rte. 36); to Dinan and St. Malo (Rte. 41); to Caen (Rte. 31); to Nantes (Rte 41).

ROUTE 35.

PARIS TO RENNES, BY VERNEUIL, DREUX, ALENÇON, AND LAVAL.

355 kilom. = 220 Eng. m. *Rail* to Auteuil.

c. *The High Road*, now deserted for the railway (Rte. 34), quits Paris by the Barrière de Passy. The village of Passy was the residence of Benjamin Franklin, 1788. He occupied the house No. 40, Rue Basse, previously Hôtel de Valentinois. The Abbé Raynal died here, 1796, and Bellini, the composer, 1834. Béranger has long lived in a very modest house here. The road runs along the rt. bank of the Seine through *Auteuil*, 2 m. farther on, which was also the residence of many eminent men. The wise and good Chancellor d'Aguesseau lived and died here; an obelisk in the churchyard marks his grave. Boileau's house is still pointed out, Rue de Boileau 18, and Molière composed here a great part of his works. Condorcet and Madame Helvetius had also houses here. The park and château de St. Cloud are conspicuous on the hill to the rt. The river Seine is crossed by the Pont de Sèvres, a short way before entering le Bourg de

12 *Sèvres* (Pop. 4000), situated on the l. bank of the river, 6 m. distant

from Paris, between 2 hills, the hill of Meudon on the l. and that of St. Cloud on the rt., along whose slopes the 2 railways to Versailles are carried. Sèvres, like Faenza and Delft, gives its name to the china made in it, and for which it is principally known. The *manufactory* is in the large building on the l. of the road, erected 1755, when the works were transferred from Vincennes, and purchased by Louis XV. It is now the property of the nation, and employs 150 persons. Admission to see it is given by the directeur, M. Brongniart, a distinguished mineralogist and geologist, to whose scientific researches the manufacture owes much of its present perfection. Besides the show-rooms filled with objects for sale, there is a very complete and curious *Porcelain Museum* here, consisting of clay, earthenware, and china of all countries and periods, from the oldest Greek and Etruscan vases down to the most recent productions of the nations of Europe and Asia, China, Japan, and the East Indies, and of many of the rude tribes of America. Here is a series of all the objects made in the establishment since its commencement, marking the change of fashion and forms: also the various materials, earths, calces, colouring matters used in the manufacture. The Kaolin, or white clay, comes from St. Yreix near Limoges. The paintings are very remarkable from the talents of the artists employed, (among whom Madame Jacotot and M. Constantin rank highest,) and the skill displayed in the burning of the colours gives an equal pre-eminence to Sèvres ware. Several pictures by ancient and modern masters have been copied in the size of the originals; some were painted on the china tablet in Italy and sent over to Sèvres to be burnt, and again sent abroad to be retouched. The Sèvres manufacture is celebrated for its white unglazed ware, *biscuit de Sèvres*, the white glazed ware, the elegance of the shape, and the beauty of the painting.

The *manufacture of painted glass*, erroneously supposed to be lost, has been revived and brought to considerable perfection within a few years; also the imitation of precious stones.

The park of St. Cloud (p. 111) reaches as far as Sèvres; there are 2 entrances to it from the town.

The road continues between the 2 railways as far as Versailles, and enters that town by the Grande Avenue de Paris.

7 VERSAILLES. — *Inns:* H. du Réservoir and H. de France. (See Galignani's 'Paris Guide.')

Railroad to Chartres. (Rte. 34.)

The road to Rennes and Brest, in quitting Versailles, passes between the park wall and a large sheet of water called Pièce des Suisses.

A little way on the rt. lies *St. Cyr*, converted by Napoleon into an Ecole Militaire, 1806, for 300 pupils—a destination which it still preserves; but it was originally founded by Louis XIV., at the suggestion of Madame de Maintenon, as a school for 250 young ladies of noble birth, and Mansard furnished the designs for it, 1686. Racine's tragedies of Esther and Athalie, written for the pupils of the establishment, were here first brought out, in the presence of the King and Madame de Maintenon. She retired hither after Louis's death, and dying here, 1719, was buried in the church. At the village of Trappes the road, leaving on the l. the route to Nantes (Rte. 46), passes through a dull country to

19 Pontchartrain.

11 La Queue.

13 Houdan. — *Inns:* l'Ecu; le Cygne. There is a handsome Gothic *Church* and an old *Tower*, part of the ancient fortifications, in this town of 2000 Inhab.

7 Maroles.

The river Eure is crossed at Cherisy.

12 *Dreux* — (*Inn:* H. du Paradis) (Durocassis), a town of 6400 Inhab., on the Blaise, a tributary of the Eure. It was on the plain between the two rivers that the battle, known as la Journée de Dreux, one of the bloodiest in the French religious wars, was fought between the Roman Catholics, under the Duc de Guise, who was victorious, and the Huguenots, under the Prince

G

de Condé, who was made prisoner, 1563. The Duc de Guise shared his couch the night after with his mortal enemy, and slept soundly by his side.

The hill which rises above the town is crowned by the ruins of the *Castle* of the Comtes de Dreux, which was captured with the town from the Duc de Guise by Henri IV.: the remains of the very old *Donjon* or keep tower of brick, of a handsome Norman gateway, and of a Gothic chapel, built 1142, still exist. The space enclosed by the walls is planted and converted into a garden, in the midst of which rises a modern *Chapel*, in the form of a Greek temple surmounted by a cupola, erected by the late Louis Philippe, when Duc d'Orléans, to replace one destroyed at the Revolution, which was the burial-place of his maternal ancestors. Beneath it are interred the Duchesse de Penthièvre, the remains of the Princesse de Lamballe, who was massacred at the Revolution, the Princesse Marie of Würtemberg, the accomplished daughter of the King, and the Duke of Orleans. Louis Philippe expended vast sums in adorning the edifice with the best productions of modern French Art. The entrances to the Chapel are Gothic: the dome is painted in fresco with the 12 Apostles. Some of the painted glass is very fine, and the sculpture on some of the tombs is exquisite, the finest of all being an Angel, in a bending attitude, the chef d'œuvre of the late King's daughter—finer even than her well-known Jeanne d'Arc. The *Chapel of the Virgin* is enriched with carving, with pendants from the roof, and with painted windows of modern glass, representing religious subjects. The King built a long low range of apartments for the residence of himself and his family when he visited the spot—and they are left just in the state in which he quitted them. The sum laid out here by Louis Philippe exceeded 4,000,000 francs. Around the hill are carried agreeable walks. Its top is surmounted by a telegraph-tower, and the view from it is very extensive.

The *Gothic Parish Church*, its lower portions in the style of the 13th cent., the upper part and tower in that of the 16th, contains the graves of Rotrou, a dramatist of the 13th cent., and of Philidor the chess-player, both natives of Dreux.

The *Hôtel de Ville*, part Gothic, part the revival style of the 16th cent., now turned into a museum, contains a curious chimney-piece, and a bell, cast in the reign of Charles IX., bearing a representation, in relief, of the procession of the Flambards.

There are numerous manufactures of coarse cloths, serges, &c., in the arrondissement of Dreux.

Diligences to Paris by Versailles:—to Chartres and Rouen daily.

[11 m. N.E. of Dreux are the scanty remains of the Château d'Anet, built by the architect Philibert Delorme for Diana of Poitiers out of the funds furnished by the liberality of her royal lover Henri II., 1552, on the site of a castle which belonged to her husband Louis de Brézé, to which she retired to pass her widowhood. When she first became acquainted with the king she was 31, and he a youth of 13, yet she maintained her influence over him to the day of her death, in spite of the Queen, Catherine de Medicis, and he wore her colours—the widow's weeds, black and white—to the last, and her symbol, the crescent of Diana, is conspicuous in all his palaces. She was buried in the *Chapel*, which still remains, surmounted by a cupola, but her monument was removed to Paris, 1793, when her body was torn from the grave and lost. The château was almost entirely pulled down at the Revolution; part of the façade was transported to Paris, where it has been re-erected at the Ecole des Beaux Arts. The ruins are pleasantly situated on the banks of the Eure. That stream traverses, a little lower down, the *Plain of Ivry*, the scene of one of the most decisive victories gained by Henry IV. over the armies of the Ligue, 1590, composed of French and Spaniards under Mayenne. Henri's words to his soldiers before the battle were—" Je veux vaincre ou mourir avec vous. Gardez bien vos rangs, ne perdez point de vue mon panache blanc, vous le trouverez toujours au chemin de l'honneur." The monumental obelisk erected on the spot to commemorate the battle was thrown down 1793, but restored by Napoleon.] The *Ch. of St. Remé* near Dreux is a fine example of the flamboyant style.

On the Avre, a tributary of the Eure, are several manufactories: the paper-mills of the very eminent stationer and publisher Didot, 2 or 3 cotton-mills belonging to Mr. Waddington, and the woollen yarn mill of Mr. Vulliamy—the 2 last Englishmen, who employ a great number of persons. The mechanical power is water only.

14 Nonancourt.

The site of the house in the market-place, near the church, in which Henri IV. slept the night before the battle of Ivry, is pointed out.

11 Tillières-sur-Ayre.

10 Verneuil.—*Inns:* Poste; Cheval Blanc. This interesting old town, of 4000 Inhab., contains several remarkable specimens of Gothic architecture—the finest being the *Tour de la Madeleine*, a magnificent work in the most gorgeous late Gothic style, surmounted by a stunted spire. Verneuil was once a place of strength:—under its *walls*, which partly remain, a fine specimen of fortification of the 12th cent., was fought a bloody battle, August 17, 1424, between the French and English, which, after two days of hard and uncertain contest, terminated in favour of the Regent Duke of Bedford, and was the last great victory obtained by him. The bravest leaders and most efficient troops who fought on the side of the French were the Scotch. Their commanders, the Earl of Douglas, who had been created Duke of Touraine, his son, the Earl of Buchan, and many other knights were slain. The English army was inferior in numbers to the enemy, yet it left 1600 dead on the field, while on the side of the French there fell 4000, including Scotch and Italian allies. As usual, the English archers contributed mainly to the victory. Attached to the portion of the fortifications not yet removed, is a tall tower, 60 ft. high, on the margin of the Avre, called *la Tour Grise*.

The road by Argentan and Falaise branches off here (Rte. 29).

16 St. Maurice.

22 Mortagne.—*Inn:* H. de France. An old town (5158 Inhab.) which claimed to be capital of la Perche. It is situated in a commanding position on a hill, surmounted by the high road in a series of zigzags, in order to reach the principal square. It was a place of strength, often besieged, and suffered much from the horrors of war. During the contests of the League it was taken and pillaged by the two parties 22 times in $3\frac{1}{2}$ years. Parts of its ramparts remain. Its only supply of water is obtained by means of a steam-engine pump, from springs at the bottom of the hill. The *Church* is remarkable for the pendants in the roof of its nave.

The *canvas used for pictures* is made at Mortagne, besides other coarse cloths, and some porcelain.

[7 m. N. of Mortagne, at Soligny, is the convent of *La Trappe*, founded in the 12th cent., but owing its celebrity to the severe rule of the order enforced, 1666, by the Abbé la Rancé, who, so far from leading a dissipated life in his youth, as is commonly reported, is proved, by documents and letters published by M. Gonod, to have always lived "strictly and ascetically. The well-known story of his conversion is a pure fable."—*G*. The convent was suppressed 1790, by a decree of the Assemblée Nationale, and its church destroyed with the tomb of La Rancé, but the monks were restored in 1814 by the exertions of M. Lestrange. They are interdicted from all intellectual labour, and only allowed to work in the fields.]

16 Mesle-sur-Sarthe. The Sarthe, a tributary of the Loire, is crossed here.

10 Ménil Broust.

13 *Alençon (Inns:* none good; Poste;—Grand Cerf;—H. d'Angleterre), chief town of the Dépt. de l'Orne, has a population of 14,500, and is a thriving place, situated on the Sarthe, near the junction of the Briante, in an open plain. Its manufactures consist chiefly of cotton and woollen, hempen and linen cloths, called "*Toiles d' Alençon*."

G 2

The making of point lace, "Point d'Alençon," established here by Colbert, for which the town was long celebrated, has now nearly disappeared. Cider and perry (poiré), the common drink of the country, are sold to a considerable extent, in casks called *pipes*.

The public buildings are not very remarkable. The *Cathedral* consists of a Gothic nave, built in the 16th cent., having some painted glass, injured by a storm, 1821, and a pulpit approached by a staircase cut in the pier, attached to a plain modern choir. The crypt beneath the church contains the remains of the Ducs d'Alençon—lately opened.

Three battlemented towers of the old *Castle*, built by Wm. de Bellesme 1026, are converted into a prison, and the *Préfecture* is a brick building, which once belonged to the Duchesse de Guise.

One of the most atrocious of the Revolutionary leaders, Hébert the anarchist, editor of the infamous journal Père Duchesne, was a native of Alençon. He was led trembling and weeping to the scaffold, to which he had condemned so many thousand innocent persons, in 1793, exhibiting in his last moments the most abject cowardice.

The name Diamants d'Alençon is given to the crystals of smoky quartz (rock crystal), found in the neighbouring granite quarries; where the beryl also occurs. Alençon is built of granite, which becomes the predominant rock of the country further W. The cultivation of wheat becomes rarer, buckwheat takes its place; broom and rushes abound.

Diligences to Tours and Caen. (Rte. 29.)

11 St. Denis. The river Mayenne rises near this, and is crossed about half way to

13 Prez en Pail, in the Dépt. de la Mayenne; the portion of it traversed by the road is a dreary country, unenclosed and covered with heath.

18 Le Ribay.

The high road to Brest merely skirts a suburb of Mayenne, leaving the town itself on the rt.

18 Mayenne.—*Inns*: Belle Etoile; —Tête Noire. A town of 10,000 Inhab., situated ⅔ on the rt. bank and ⅓ on the l. of the Mayenne. Its manufactures of calicoes, linen cloth, and tickens employ 8000 persons in and around the town. The *Castle*, now in ruins, is a picturesque object, on the rt. bank of the river, near the bridge. It belonged to the seigneurs of Mayenne, and was taken after a 3 months' siege, by the English, under the Earl of Salisbury, 1424. Many of the streets are very narrow, and so steep that it requires 8 or 10 oxen to draw a cart up them.

The road descends the valley of the Mayenne, having the river on the rt. but out of sight, to

13 Martigné.

17 Laval. }
Rennes. } (See Rte. 34.)

ROUTE 36.

RENNES TO BREST.

240 kilom.=149 Eng. m. *Malleposte* daily in 18 hours. *Diligences* daily.

10 Pacé.
13 Dedée.
14 La Barette.
16 Broons is remarkable only as the birthplace of Bertrand Du Guesclin, the great captain of France in the 15th century. He was 10th child of Robert Du Guesclin, and remarkably ill-favoured to look upon. He first saw the light in the castle of La Motte Broons, of which no vestiges remain, but the place where it stood is marked by an avenue of trees, and a *Monument*, erected at the cost of the department, by the side of the road to Brest, about 1 m. out of the town.

12 Langouèdre.

15 Lamballe (4400 Inhab.) was the chief place of the Comté of Penthièvre; the castle of the counts was reduced and dismantled by Cardinal Richelieu, 1626, to punish a rebellious seigneur. The *Ch. of Notre Dame*, on the top of the hill whose slope is occupied by the town, was originally the castle chapel, and is a fine Gothic building. Thick cylindrical piers, surmounted by capitals in bands, support the lancet

arches of the nave, whilst the choir rests on clustered pillars, the arches being surmounted by a double triforium gallery. It has a wooden roof. In a side aisle is some good carved woodwork, with decorated and flamboyant tracery, perhaps the remains of a roodloft. Part of the church was built 1545.

The road to St. Malo (Rte. 41) diverges from this.

Glimpses of the sea are obtained on the rt. before reaching

20 *St. Brieuc.*—*Inns:* Croix Blanche, clean and good: dinner, wine, bed, and tea for breakfast, 4 fr. 50 c.;— H. Tassin, middling and moderate.

There is nothing worth notice in this town of 14,053 Inhab.; it is situated on the Gouet, and has a port called Légué, 2 m. lower down the stream, provided with a long quai, accessible for vessels of 400 or 500 tons to unload at. On the top of a hilly promontory, commanding the bouchure of the river, stands the ruined *Tour de Cesson,* built 1395, to defend its entrance, but blown up 1598, after the war of the League, by order of Henri IV. Such, however, was the thickness of the wall, and the coherence of the mortar, that one half of the cylinder remains standing, braving the tempests, while the other lies shattered into a few large masses at its base, as it fell. There is a pretty walk from St. Brieuc to Légué, through a narrow ravine, traversed by a small tributary of the Gouet.

St. Brieuc was taken by the Chouans in the Vendéan war, 1799.

An interesting antiquarian and architectural excursion to Lanleff, Paimpol, &c., may be made from this (Rte. 38).

17 Châtelaudren, a small town on the Leff.

14 Guingamp (Hôtel des Voyageurs) is a very picturesque town, situated in the vale of the Trieux, which abounds in pleasing scenery (7200 Inhab.). It formed part of the vast possessions of the Ducs de Penthièvre, and descended from them to Louis-Philippe. The site of their castle, razed to the earth, is occupied by a grove of trees, and serves as a promenade; but fragments of the town walls remain. Its *Church,* surmounting the other buildings, part Gothic, part in the style of the revival, has some peculiarities, viz. grotesque heads projecting from the shafts of its piers.

The *Fontaine de Plomb,* in the middle of the Place, is rather an elegant work of Italian artists in the 15th cent., it is supposed.

The *Chapel of Notre Dame de Grace,* 3 m. out of the town, is well deserving a visit, although its rich decorations in sculptured tracery and figures have been much mutilated. "Its elegant spire, finely proportioned pillars, and light arches, are still worthy of admiration; and much of the grotesque carving which formed the cornices of the nave and aisles may still be seen." —*Trollope.* It was erected in the 14th cent. by Charles of Blois.

19 Belle-Ile-en-Terre.

The Dépt. of Finisterre, in la Basse Bretagne, the ancient Armorica, is entered before reaching

19 Ponthou.

15 *Morlaix* (*Inns:* H. de Provence; good and moderate;—H. de Paris) is a flourishing little port and town of 10,500 Inhab., picturesquely seated in a valley wide enough only for the tidal river or creek which runs up it, lined with 2 quays and 2 rows of houses, "behind which the hills rise steep and woody on one side, on the other gardens and rocks and wood; the effect romantic and beautiful."— *A. Young.* The rock rises so close behind the houses as to give rise to a proverb, "From the garret to the garden, as they say at Morlaix." It is only 6½ m. from the sea, and is reached by vessels of considerable tonnage. To the stranger its chief attraction is the unaltered air of antiquity which it retains in its older quarters, such as the Rues des Nobles and du Pavé, and the thoroughly Breton character of its street architecture and houses overhanging the footway, each story, fronted with an apron of slates, more nearly approaching its neighbour on the opposite side of the way, until the inmates of the garrets may shake hands. The grotesquely carved corner

posts, ornamented with figures of kings, priests, saints, monsters, and bagpipers, the Gothic doorways, the sculptured cornices, would enrich an artist's sketch-book, and furnish employment for many days. The costume of the people also is thoroughly in keeping with the buildings; their pent-house brimmed hats, their loose trunk hose, their shaggy locks hanging like manes down their backs, are all thoroughly characteristic of la Bretagne Bretonnante (§ 2).

Sad havoc, however, has been made in this antique town by modern improvements; and the opening formed for the new Rue Nation-Royale, by which the road to Brest issues out on the W., has swept away a crowd of crazy but picturesque constructions, whose loss would have made poor Prout sigh.

Two small streams, descending from separate ravines, but uniting above the town, are arched over to furnish space for the market-place and modern Hôtel de Ville; below which, expanding naturally, and partly by their bed being artificially excavated, they form a port, lined with quays and lofty picturesque houses, resting on covered galleries or arcades called *Lances*. One of the houses on this quai is particularly remarkable for its carved staircase. Beside these quays several merchant vessels may usually be seen lying, together with a variety of small craft.

The churches are not remarkable: *St. Mathieu* is Gothic; in *St. Melaine* is some good carved screen-work.

Many of the houses in the Rue du Pavé and Rue des Nobles (especially the staircase of one high up on the right hand) deserve notice; they are richly ornamented in the flamboyant style.

The *Gothic fountain* of the Carmelites, and the *Chapel* of the Convent of St. François, may be visited by those who have time. The *Manufacture Nationale de Tabac*, a large building on the W. quay, is said to produce the worst tobacco in Europe.

In 1522 the fleet of Henry VIII., who was at that time incensed with Francis I. for seizing the ships and goods of English merchants in French ports, on its return from escorting the Empr. Charles V. to Spain, under the command of Henry Earl of Surrey, entered the river, in number 50 vessels, and, effecting a descent in the neighbouring bay of Dourdu, surprised Morlaix. The English set fire to it in 4 different places, pillaged it, massacred the inhabitants, and burnt to the ground great part of it, "together with some right fair castles, goodly houses, and proper piles."—*State Papers*. They retired to their vessels loaded with booty; but 600 of the hindmost were intercepted by the infuriated inhabitants, and cut off with great slaughter near a spring, still called *Fontaine des Anglais*, or, as the Bretons, like their Welsh kinsmen, style them, the Saxons.

Near the said fountain begins a very pleasant promenade, planted with trees, called *Cours Beaumont*, which extends nearly 1½ m. down the l. bank of the river. The views from it of the river and the wooded valley are very pleasing.

The site of the old castle, planted with trees, also commands a fine view of the town.

Morlaix is the native place of General Moreau.

Diligences daily to Brest; to St. Malo; to Rennes; to Lorient.

A well-appointed *Steamer* runs from Morlaix to Havre, 70 leagues, in 20 hrs., once a week, fare 30 fr.

The churches of Kreisker, at St. Pol de Léon, and of Folgoat, may be visited by making a détour on the way to Brest (Rte. 38). Another interesting excursion is to the mining district of Huelgoat and Poulahouen (Rte. 42).

Rather more than half way (9 m.) between Morlaix and the next relay the village of Théogonec is passed, remarkable for its fine *Church*, in the style of the Renaissance; a vast edifice, richly decorated with sculptures in the dark Kersanton stone. Its delicately carved pulpit, its reliquary, and its Calvary, deserve notice.

21 Landivisiau has a *Church* also, with a very fine S. portal filled with statues of the 12 Apostles; and at the

W. end a most elegant tower and spire, well worth studying.

[The *Church of Lanbader*, 5 m. N. of this, on the road to St. Pol, surmounted by an elegant tower and spire, was originally attached to a commandery of Templars, ruins of which exist near the tower. Within is a beautifully pierced and carved *roodloft* and screen of wood, composed of exquisite flamboyant tracery; also a staircase in the same style. The chains of some knight, liberated from slavery among the followers of Mahoun, still hang in the choir.]

3 m. short of Landerneau, on a hill above the village *La Roche Maurice*, stand the ruins of its castle, reduced to 3 shattered towers, but very picturesque in its outline and position.

In the churchyard is an *Ossuary*, filled with skulls and dry bones, ornamented in front with a sculptured frieze, representing the *Dance of Death*, executed 1639. The *Church* is Gothic, and built 1559, and contains some good painted glass. The carved portal in Kersanton stone, and the sculptured roodloft of wood within, are worth notice.

16 Landerneau (*Inn:* Hôtel de l'Univers), a pretty town, seated in the hollow of a valley on the Elorn, whose mouth forms one branch of the roadstead of Brest. There are some picturesque Gothic bits among its old houses. 4963 Inhab.

The roads to Brest from Morlaix, from Carhaix (Rte. 42), and from Quimper (Rte. 44), all converge at this point.

A little beyond Landerneau, on the l. of the road, between it and the river Elorn, a ruined gateway, draped with ivy, is the sole subsisting relic of the *Castle of the Joyeuse Garde*, now known as Château le Forêt, the cradle of chivalry, the seat of Arthur, Lancelot du Lac, and the Knights of the Round Table. Of course there is no pretension that the existing remains are of their time. No satisfactory explanation is given of the origin of the name Joyeuse Garde, but it is supposed to be a perversion of a Breton term.

20 BREST.—*Inns:* H. du Grand Monarque, good and moderate;—H. de Provence. N.B. The gates of Brest are closed at 10 P.M. in summer, and 9 in winter; no entrance after. Foreigners must give up passports at the gates.

Brest, the chief naval seaport of France, an arsenal of war, and fortress of first class, is very advantageously situated near the W. extremity of the Dépt. Finisterre (the Land's End of France), on that portion of her territory which projects most to the W. between the Channel and the Gulf of Gascony. It stands on the N. side of one of the finest harbours in the world, nearly land-locked, accessible only through a narrow and well-fortified throat, *Le Goulet*, and extending far inland in 2 branches, one running up to Landerneau, the other towards Châteaulin. The town is built on the summit and sides of a kind of projecting ridge, and some of its streets are too steep to be passable except on foot. A narrow but deep creek, which is in fact formed by the mouth of the small stream the Penfeld, running up from the harbour behind this ridge, serves as the basin to the dockyard, and divides the town on its l. bank from the suburb *La Recouvrance* on its rt. The communication between the town and suburb is kept up by numerous ferry-boats. Close above the mouth of this creek, which is not more than a musket-shot across, and is defended by several tiers of batteries on either hand, rise the feudal round towers and colossal curtains, not less than 100 ft. high, of the picturesque *old Castle*, which belonged to the Ducs de Bretagne. It was besieged in vain by Du Guesclin and Clisson, was long held by the English, having for governor, 1373, the brave warrior Robert Knolles. It was yielded up by Richard II. 1395, in consideration of 12,000 crowns, and was finally modernised by Vauban, 1688, who formed casemates in the interior of its massive towers, and platforms with embrasures for cannon on their tops. From its walls there is a good view of the port and dockyard, but the Fort de l'Ecole, on the opposite side of the water, commands one still finer, including the roadstead also. There are numerous dungeons beneath the castle, and extensive vaults.

The inner port of Brest, or creek above mentioned, is so narrow, that if the town had any commerce it would not be large enough to hold the merchant vessels; but there is no deficiency of depth (25 ft. at low water), and 30 or 40 ships of war might lie within it in single file. Above the castle the shores of both sides of this creek are enclosed by a high wall, separating the dockyard within it from the town. The mouth of the creek is closed by a boom. The population of Brest is said to exceed 32,000, though, to avoid the additional contributions on large towns, it is put down in the census at 29,860. There is accommodation in the numerous barracks for a garrison of nearly 10,000 men.

Although Brest is enclosed within ramparts, there are several fine open spaces within its walls; such are the square called *Champ de Bataille*, innocent of any other combat than a sham fight, and the *Cours d'Ajot* (so named from an officer of engineers who laid it out), a promenade agreeable on account of the fine trees which shade it, and the beautiful view of the roads, appearing like a vast lake, which its terrace commands, but infested all the morning by parties of recruits undergoing drill.

More rain, it is said, falls in Brest than in any other town of France, and the whole department of Finisterre is peculiarly exposed to storms, winds, mists, and fogs.

In 1548 Mary Queen of Scots, then a child 5 years old, landed at Brest, and a few days after was affianced to the Dauphin Francis at St. Germain.

The *Dockyard*, or *Port Militaire*.— The authorities connected with the dockyard (major de la marine, &c.) will not admit foreigners to see it without an order from the Ministre de la Marine at Paris. The Bagnes and Hôpital de la Marine, the most interesting objects here, can be seen on presenting the passport. The dockyard of Brest is situated on the 2 sides of a narrow but deep creek or arm of the sea, running up in a winding direction between high and steep rocks, which intrude so near upon the water that it is only by paring them down that space is formed for the buildings, and for the quays and yards required in front of them. The first view, looking down from above into this narrow ravine, lined with long and massive ranges of buildings rising tier over tier in the form of an amphitheatre, is exceedingly striking. On one side is the *Voilerie* (sail-house), *Magasin Général* (slop-shop), and *Corderie* (ropery), of 3 stories, surmounted by the *Bagne*, and above it rises the *New Hospital*. On the opposite side are various atéliers, forgeries, *Atélier d'Artillerie de Marine* (burnt in 1833). The *Foundry* (for casting cannon), and the *Quartier des Marins*, or sailors' barracks, where they are lodged when in port in the same manner as soldiers— an admirable establishment, which might be advantageously copied by the English Admiralty—fill up the opposite side. The level space at the water's edge is occupied by slips (cales de construction), only 2 of which are covered, about 8 being uncovered, dry docks (formes), at times converted to the purpose of building ships. It is surprising that the first dockyard of France should possess so few covered slips. There are, besides, timber-yards, boat-sheds, water-cisterns supplied by a steam-engine where vessels fill their tanks, sheds for containing the new tanks, and government cellars, while a very large space near the sea entrance of the dockyard is covered with dismounted cannon. Here also is placed a trophy from Algiers, a brass gun 20 ft. long, which forms an excellent column reared on its breech. The precautions against fire and theft are very rigid; a vigilant guardian watches in every apartment, a door-keeper at every door; cisterns are placed at short distances, with tubs full of water every 8 or 10 yards.

The ground occupied by most of these buildings has been gained, as before observed, by excavations out of the hill-side. Greatly as the space on either side of the water has been widened by artificial means, the cliffs even now approach too near the slips and timber-sheds, preventing a free circulation of air, causing dampness, and consequently dry rot. Near the timber-sheds is the *Musée Maritime*, filled with models, ships' heads, &c., but containing nothing very remarkable.

On both sides of the port, roads are carried up the steep sides of the confining heights in zigzag terraces, so that they may easily be surmounted by heavy carriages.

The *Victualling Office* (Direction des Subsistances et Parc aux Vivres) is near the mouth of the port, on the rt. bank, and includes the bakehouse, containing 24 ovens, the slaughterhouse, kitchens, &c. In 1802-3, when the combined Spanish and French fleets lay in the roads, 50,000 rations were supplied hence daily.

The Bagnes (from bagnio, Ital., bath; the Christian slaves in Turkey and Barbary were employed in heating the baths of the sultans, pachas, deys, &c.) contain about 3000 convicts (forçats), condemned to forced labour for a certain term of years or for life. Their dress is a jacket of dirty red serge, fitting no better than a sack, yellow trowsers, and a green, red, or yellow cap: the green cap denotes one condemned for life; the yellow sleeve one twice sentenced. The worst offenders are heavily loaded with shackles fastened to a ring riveted fast round the leg. The chain and shackle together weigh more than 7 lbs., and usually cause a wound on the leg at first. It is not, however, the hideous dress nor the clanking chains which render the forçats repulsive; it is the countenance marked with bad passions and villany, which indicate the degradation of human nature. The worst offenders are coupled two together to the same chain. They work in gangs, each gang accompanied by a plante or garde chourme, a fierce-looking moustache, with a tranchant sabre, accompanied by a soldier with a loaded musket. The *Prison of the Bagnes* has a long façade, with more of architectural ornament and style in its pediment than usually marks a prison destined for doubly and trebly dyed criminals. It contains 4 salles, lofty, wide, and airy, filled with large wooden platforms, having sloping tops like desks; these are the bedsteads of the forçats, who recline on them upon a small mattress provided with a coarse quilt of sackcloth, the chain of each being passed over a bar of iron running along the foot of the bed, but allowing tether enough to move a distance of 5 or 6 ft. Only the better class of convicts are allowed a thin mattress.

As soon as their allotted task for the day is done out of doors, they are allowed to repair hither; some have writing-desks, others employ themselves in handicrafts, many in making toys out of cocoa-nuts, horsehair, &c., by which they may earn a little money. At gunfire the names are called over, and in an hour profound silence is required; the night, passed on a hard board, is a time of suffering, especially in winter, from the cold.

Their daily allowance of food includes a pint of wine, a measure of biscuit, or ½ a loaf of brown bread.

The 4 salles are closed by strong iron gates at night, but stand open during the day; there are, however, plenty of guards at hand, and immediately behind the Bagnes rises the *Caserne de la Marine Militaire*, which could pour in some hundred men in a few minutes in case of revolt. The forçat, degraded as he is, is not allowed to be struck by his guards or keepers; his punishment, if he does wrong, is either solitary confinement in the black hole, a series of cells in the court behind the building, or deprivation of his wine, &c., coupling to another prisoner, or flogging with the rope's end. As a further preventive of tumult or rebellion, the walls of each salle are pierced with embrasures through which 2 cannon show their mouths; they are loaded with grape, and would enfilade the chamber, and sweep it from end to end.

Outside the dockyard, a little higher up the hill than the prison, rises the

Hôpital de la Marine, an edifice of great extent, though of unpretending architecture, of which Brest may well be proud. It was begun 1824. It contains 26 salles, each with 53 beds; and is attended by between 30 and 40 Religieuses, Sœurs Fidèles de la Sagesse as they call themselves, who are also lodged within the building. So far from being revolting, as is the case in many hospitals, it is a pleasing sight to enter one of the salles; its cleanliness puts to shame the confined frowsy wards of Greenwich Hospital. Here are wide, airy apartments, the roofs without speck, the floors, though of tile, sedulously polished and provided with pieces of carpeting, each window hung with white curtains, each bed of metal, also with white curtains and furniture. The salle des officiers is superior to the common rooms, even elegant. The kitchens, laboratories, linen-closet, &c., are in the same style. Even the convicts, when sick, are received and nursed in this establishment.

A *British Consul* resides here.

At Hébert's library and reading-room, Rue d'Aiguillon, the papers may be seen, and many interesting works on Brittany, especially those of MM. Souvestre and Freminville, obtained.

Malleposte daily to Chartres in 36 hours: *diligences* daily to Rennes; to St. Malo; to Lorient, Auray, and Nantes. A *railroad* to Paris by Chartres is in progress.

Steamer every other day traverses the roads.

The *Roadstead of Brest* lies between the great promontory of Finisterre on the N. and the smaller peninsula of Quélern on the S., which approach so near as to leave a passage only 1749 yards broad between them, called the Goulet. The Mingan rocks, rising in the midst of this channel, contract the entrance still more, and compel vessels to pass close under the guns of batteries which line it on either side, and command it by a cross fire. The road consists of numerous bays, into which several rivers empty themselves, the principal being the Elorn from Landerneau, and the Châteaulin, which is navigated by a steamboat. In some places the harbour is 3 m. broad, and the area of its surface is estimated at 15 square leagues. All the fleets of France might lie snugly within it, and a hostile ship dare not venture within its entrance without the risk of being battered to pieces. Not only are the jaws of the harbour bristling with fortifications "à fleur d'eau," but the works are carried inwards so as to command the anchorage, and the batteries spread outside to the rt. and l. of the entrance, while every eminence is crowned with other forts commanding those below. The number of cannon and large mortars which could be brought to bear on an enemy from the batteries of the Goulet, and of the coast ouside of it, is not less than 400, while 60 pieces sweep the anchorage from the forts within the Goulet. On the N. of the Goulet, in the midst of the bay of Bertheaume, are 2 island forts, united together by a rope bridge, and by one of wood with the shore. The extreme fort on this side is the batterie de St. Mathieu, under the ruined abbey (p. 131), and close to the new lighthouse. On the S. of the Goulet lies the Bay de Camaret, one of whose numerous and formidable batteries goes by the name of *Mort Anglaise,* commemorating the miserable defeat of the expedition which landed here 1694 from a British fleet commanded by Admiral Berkeley. On approaching the shore, the English found it bristling with armaments: batteries were thrown up on all sides, gunners at their posts, troops of horse and foot drawn up behind the guns, and, as soon as the English began to disembark, 3 masked batteries opened on the ships a destructive fire. 900 men under the command of General Tollemache, who persisted in landing in the face even of such formidable preparations, reached the shore, and were almost immediately cut to pieces, the ebbing of the tide having left their boats dry, and cut off their retreat. And thus the expedition failed miserably. What wonder? The news of the intended descent had been betrayed to Louis XIV. and James II. more than a month before by the

Duke of Marlborough, the hero of Blenheim! These are the words in which he communicated the intelligence to his old master James:—"The capture of Brest would be a great advantage to England, but no advantage can prevent or ever shall prevent me from informing you of all that I believe to be for your service; therefore you may make your own use of this intelligence."—*Macpherson's State Papers*. In the interval between the receipt of this letter and the sailing of the armament, the skill and activity of Vauban had put the intended landing-place in such a state of defence, by throwing up batteries, disposing cannon, and collecting troops, as to render success hopeless, defeat inevitable.

The *Pointe des Espagnols* owes its name to a body of Spaniards, about 600 strong, who occupied it for several weeks, 1594, and threw up an earthen redoubt, which was captured by assault. The peninsula of Quélern is defended by lines, drawn across the isthmus which connects it with the mainland, nearly a mile long, consisting of bastions faced with masonry, constructed by Vauban, mounting 60 pieces of cannon. From a point near these lines, just above the Bay of Camaret, *the finest view* is obtained of the roads of Brest and their defences, with the point of St. Mathieu and the archipelago of Ouessant on the N., and on the S. the Bay of Dournenez and the Pointe du Raz.

The defences above enumerated do not include those of Brest itself, amounting altogether to 400 pieces of cannon, nor of the intrenched camp behind it, numbering 60 more cannon and mortars.

Excursions.—The country about Brest is far from picturesque, but it contains many objects of interest.

The *Menhir of Plouarzel* (§ 4), about 10 m. N. W. of Brest and 3 beyond the village of St. Renan, is the loftiest of those singular Celtic monuments now remaining in Finisterre. It measures 35 ft. in height, and stands on an eminence in the midst of a wild heath. Whatever its original destination, it is still looked on with awe by the peasantry, and singular superstitions are associated with it. Often in the dead of night the barren woman repairs hither, hoping to procure the boon of fruitfulness by rubbing her naked breast against the hard granite.

Near the mouth of the pretty river Aber Ildut, which flows past St. Renan, are the quarries of granite which furnished the pedestal for the obelisk of Luxor, erected in the Place Louis XV., at Paris.

3 m. N. of St. Renan, at Lanriouaré, is the graveyard of the 7777 saints, a walled enclosure, never trod by the peasants except with bare feet and head uncovered; it is paved with slabs, and marked by a cross.

The ruined *Abbey of St. Matthew*, situated on the extreme W. cape of Finisterre, N. of the Rade de Brest, is about 15 m. W. from Brest and 10 from St. Renan. The roads from both places converge at the little town of Le Conquet, where La Grâce de Dieu is a decent cabaret. Conquet suffered from an English fleet sent forth by Queen Mary, 1558, to ravage the French coast, and to surprise Brest, "because it was known not to be well garrisoned, and was thought the best mark to be shot at for the time." But the English commander contented himself with a far more inglorious enterprise. Landing at Conquet, "he put it to the saccage, with a great abbey, and many pretty towns and villages, where our men found good booties and great store of pillage."—*Holinshed*. Thence it is a walk of 3, m. along the tops of the cliffs, battered below by the waves, to the storm-fretted ruins of *St. Matthew's Abbey*, which stand on the bleak exposed promontory above the sea—the most W. spot of France, and, with the exception of Cape Finisterre in Spain, of the European continent. It occupies a position similar to St. Mary's Abbey, Whitby, so as to be the first and the last object seen by the mariner quitting or entering the Bay of Brest. Whatever wind may blow, it is rare but it rages a hurricane around these mouldering arches and piers, which yet have braved for 5 centuries the pelting storm and whistling wind. The architecture is pointed in the greater part of the building, with some Romanesque portions and round arches. It is of solid granite, simple in style, and without ornament. Close beside the ruins a *Lighthouse* has been erected. There is much savage grandeur in the scene around, viewed from this point, increased by the sullen roar of the mighty Atlantic chafing in the eaves and fissures of the rocks below. In clear weather the eye ranges over the dangerous strait called *Passage du Four*, beset with rocks, between the mainland and the granitic islands Molène, Beniguet, and *Ouessant*. The last is supposed by some to be the Ultima Thule of the ancients: its inhabitants remained idolaters down to the 17th century. The indecisive naval action of Ushant (as we call it) was fought off this island, 1778, between the French Fleet under D'Orvilliers, and the English under Keppel and Palliser. On the S. the roads of Brest and the peninsula of Quélern lie open, and on the horizon appears the Pointe du Raz.

On the E. side of the roadstead, and on the shore of the estuary of the Landerneau river, opposite to Brest, lies *Plougastel*, remarkable for a *Calvary* attached to its cimetière, one of the most remarkable of the Gothic monuments of Finisterre. The 3 customary crosses, carved in Kersanton stone (§ 6) are surrounded by an army of stone saints on foot, raised on a platform with bas-reliefs running round it. A multitude of sculptures, rudely but forcibly executed, representing scenes of the Life and Passion of Christ. Some of the subjects, such as the entry of our Saviour into Jerusalem to the music of the bigniou (bagpipe), the Temptation, and Hell, are treated in a homely manner, approaching the grotesque, marking the hand of a rustic artist. "Notwithstanding its Gothic character, it appears by an inscription upon it to have been executed in 1602 : but we must remember that the middle ages lasted longer in Brittany than elsewhere."—*Souvestre*.

The costume of the women of Plougastel is remarkable for its elegance.

Ferry-boats ply between Brest and the point of Plougastel.

The fine Gothic *Ch. of Folgoat* (Rte. 38) would form an agreeable day's excursion for any one who interests himself in architecture. He might take the patache which runs daily from Brest to Lesneven and back.

ROUTE 38.

ST. BRIEUC TO BREST.—COAST ROAD BY PAIMPOL, LANNION, MORLAIX, ST. POL DE LEON, and FOLGOAT.

The distances are marked in lieues communes of 3 Eng. m., measured from place to place.

This rte. properly consists of two excursions from the high road from Rennes to Brest: it carries the traveller to a succession of interesting churches and ecclesiastical remains well worth visiting, though much of it lies over cross roads; no posting.

St. Brieuc (Rte. 36). A wretched patache runs between this place and Paimpol, passing near the little port of Binic, through Plouha.

Thus far there is nothing remarkable, unless the traveller diverge about 1 m. to the l. of the road beyond Binic, to visit the beautiful Gothic chapel of *Lantec*, which has been compared with the Ste. Chapelle at Paris, but is far inferior to it.

From Plouha the antiquarian traveller should diverge to the l., to visit a ruined building, known as the

7½ *Temple de Lanleff*, about 8 m. from Plouha. A carriage cannot easily get within a mile of it, owing to the badness of the roads. It has been the subject of much controversy, some writers calling it a Pagan Temple: but in truth it is nothing more than an early Christian church, probably of the 10th or 11th cent., in the form of a rotunda, like the English churches of the Temple, St. Sepulchre, Cambridge, Little Maplestead, &c. But the building which it perhaps most nearly resembles is the round church at Nymegen, in Holland, attributed to

Charlemagne, but now in ruins. It consists of 2 concentric walls, the inner one a cylinder, 30 ft. high, resting on 12 circular arches, supported on square piers, with engaged columns on each side, of granite, having rudely carved capitals of monsters, human faces, rams' heads. Outside of this runs a lower concentric wall, destroyed for a considerable part of its circuit, but which once extended quite round the inner wall, and thus formed the aisles of the church. It is pierced with narrow loopholed windows, which widen inwards, the early form common in churches built before glass came into use. The edges of the vaulted roof which covered this aisle may still be traced, and a small portion of the aisle is included in the modern church; but whether the vaulting of it be as old as the walls on which it rests cannot be distinctly affirmed. This ruin now forms a vestibule to a little village church. As a ruin, it is too rude in its architecture to be pleasing, but in the midst of it rises a noble *yew-tree*, tall and straight, surmounting the old wall with its dark canopy of foliage. The tradition of the country is, that it was built by the Templars, the "Moines Rouges" as they are called. It is just possible that Gothic architecture in Brittany was not more advanced in the 12th cent. than this building indicates.

Lanleff is about 24 m. from St. Brieuc and 7½ from

2½ Paimpol (*Inn*: H. du Commerce, formerly Pelican), a town of 2112 Inhab.

On the sea-shore, 2 m. to the E. of Paimpol, are the ruins of the *Abbey* of *Beauport* (in 1841 the keys were kept at Paimpol, and should be obtained before setting out). It is beautifully situated on the shore of a retired bay. The remains consist of a *Church*, now roofless and deprived of the choir, in the pointed style, built 1202, with a W. front showing an early English character, together with several conventual buildings at the E. end. An elegant small chapterhouse, its vaulted roof supported on a row of circular pillars, is so perfect that it is now used as a school. On the N. side are an extensive vaulted cellar, and an apartment of a superior character, also vaulted, which was the grand refectory. These serve the purpose of farm-buildings at present, being divided between 2 tenants.

From Paimpol to Treguier is about 9 m., passing through Lezardrieux, where the river Trieux, descending from Guingamp, is crossed by a fine wire suspension-bridge resting on lofty piers.

The castle of *La Roche Jagu*, near this, is an interesting specimen of domestic architecture, now in ruins, finely situated on the Trieux above Lezardrieux. It is a semi-castellated mansion, entered by a low doorway closed by an oaken door and a heavy iron gate of cross-bars. Although dismantled, it is inhabited by a peasant. There is a fine view from its roof.

Another still larger and loftier suspension-bridge thrown over the Jaudy leads into

3 Treguier (*Inn*: Hôtel de France, tolerable), a town of 3178 Inhab., occupying the summit and slope of a hill.

The *Church* in the market-place, formerly the cathedral, has a fine S. porch, the vaulted roof panelled, and the divisions filled with quatrefoils, and a doorway ornamented with statues in niches, of good workmanship. The piers of the nave are irregular in form, and its arches vary in width. The N. transept is Romanesque, with circular arches and well-wrought capitals to its pillars. Contiguous to it is a tower in the same style, and probably of the 11th cent., though named Tour de Hastings, after the Danish pirate of a much earlier period. This tower is best seen from the cloisters, where some mutilated effigies of ecclesiastics and knights are deposited.

In a farmhouse a little way out of the town, called Kermartin, is preserved the *bed of St. Yves*, a favourite Breton saint. It is a cupboard bedstead, the front of dark wood finely carved.

4 Lannion (*Inn*: H. de France), on the Guier, possesses a market-place

filled with odd old houses, several of a very peculiar style of architecture, and nothing else worthy of remark but narrow and dirty streets. A *diligence* runs daily to Morlaix. There is a post-road hence to Guingamp, 32 kilom., and another by Plesten, 18 kilom., to Morlaix, 19 kilom.

The district extending N. from Lannion to the sea, between the rivers Guier and Jaudy, is the very cradle of romance. King Arthur held his court at Kerdluel, graced by the presence of the Paladins, Lancelot, Tristan, and Caradoc; and a short distance off the coast is an islet called Agalon or Avalon, which the Bretons maintain to be King Arthur's burial-place, thus depriving Glastonbury of that honour.

About 6 m. S. of Lannion, on the E. bank of the Guier, between it and the road to Guingamp, is the *Castle Tonquedec*, one of the largest and best preserved in Brittany. It was built in the 13th cent., and dismantled by order of Richelieu, after having served during the wars of the Ligue as a royal fortress. It consisted of 3 courts defended by moats, drawbridges, and portcullises. In the inner court is the *keep*, a tall round tower, " accessible only by an opening in its 2nd story, approached by 2 drawbridges, supported midway upon an isolated square pier." The staircase was formed in the thickness of the wall. " In many respects these ruins are well worth coming some distance to visit. To the antiquary they are precious as a specimen of the finest military architecture of the 13th cent. For the sketcher they combine the requisites to form a lovely landscape."—*Trollope.*

The direct road from Lannion to Morlaix (about 23 m.) passes St. Michel-sur-Grève, a spot where the sea encroaches on the shore, and a little farther we enter the department Finisterre. On the sands near this, according to the legend, King Arthur fought the dragon.

The *crypt* under the church of Lanmeur is of great antiquity, and encloses the holy fountain which caused its foundation, and is still held in repute by the common people. The piers which support the crypt have serpents carved on them.

About 5 m. N. of Lanmeur, close upon the coast, lies the village of *St. Jean du Doigt*, whose church, containing the precious finger of St. John, from which it is named, is a favourite place of pilgrimage with the peasantry, who repair hither to the number of 12,000 on the eve of St. John. The church has a wooden roof elegantly carved and painted, and surmounted by a spire of lead; it also possesses a ciborium bearing enamelled medallions on the 12 Apostles, a beautiful crucifix of the 16th cent., a chalice and a patina presented by Anne of Brittany, who was a patroness of St. John's finger. She built the hospice by the side of the church to receive pilgrims.

Souvestre mentions a singular little chapel called the Oratoire, between this and Plougasnon, in which the young girls who are about to marry in the course of the year hang up their hair as an offering to the Virgin; this ancient Gaulish custom, however, is diminishing every year.

7½ *Morlaix* (Rte. 36).

There is nothing very interesting beyond Morlaix until the towers and spires appear of

5 St. Pol de Léon.—*Inn*: Hôtel du Commerce, tolerable.

This ancient and almost deserted ecclesiastical city reminds one of St. Andrew's in Scotland, and St. David's in Wales, in its remote position near the sea-shore, in its decayed state, and in its ancient edifices. It possesses 6700 Inhab. and 2 very fine churches.

The *Cathedral*, dedicated to St. Pol, is flanked at the W. end with 2 fine towers, whose central stories, pierced with long and elegant lancet windows (like St. Pierre at Caen), are surmounted by spires, also pierced through to the sky. They open to the choir beneath, so as to form a sort of vestibule as at Peterborough. The nave is in the early pointed style, probably of the 13th cent.; the transepts display Romanesque features; in the S. transept is a fine circular window, its tracery cut in granite. The trough-shaped bénitier near the W. end was probably a tomb, and from its rude sculpture is certainly very old. The *choir*, longer, more ornamented, and of later date than the nave, is surrounded by double aisles, and ends in a Lady Chapel ; it contains some good carved wood-work of the 16th cent. The S. porch, a rich florid work with foliage delicately cut in Kersanton stone, merits examination.

The boast of St. Pol is the spire of the *Church of Creizker* (the word means centre of the town), 393 ft. high; a structure of open work of great lightness and grace, though constructed entirely of granite. The richly ornamented square tower is surmounted by a very boldly-projecting cornice, above which rises the spire, its masonry cut to imitate overlapping tiles. The whole rests on 4 pillars, not particularly thick, but the arches of the aisles act as buttresses to support it. This spire was built at the latter end of the 14th cent. by John IV., Duke of Brittany; according to tradition the architect was English. The N. portal, florid and fringed, is very rich and in good taste, though much injured; the rest of the church is not remarkable. These are the curiosities of this dull town, and after exploring them one is happy to leave behind its grass-grown streets, and the melancholy which they inspire.

3 m. to the N. lies the little port of Roscoff. Half-way, near Chapel Pol, are some Celtic remains, several dolmens, and a menhir (§ 4).

Roscoff is filled with sailors and smugglers, and contains a vegetable prodigy, *a fig-tree*, in the garden of the Capucin convent, whose branches, supported by scaffolding, would shelter beneath them 200 persons. The church, though of the time of Louis XIV., has a Gothic character, while its details are Italian; below it are 7 very curious bas-reliefs in alabaster.

Opposite Roscoff lies the little island of Batz, separated from the mainland by a strait which may be crossed in 10 min. In the cemetery there is a monument of granite to the memory of a lady who succoured the proscribed and fugitive priests during the Revolution.

The young Pretender landed here after his hazardous escape from Scotland, subsequent to the battle of Culloden.

The road from St. Pol to Brest lies through

7 Lesneven.—*Inn*: Grande Maison; tolerable. Some Roman remains, urns, &c., found a few miles S.-E. of this dull little town on the way to Landivisiau, have been supposed to mark the site of the long-lost Breton town *Occismor*.

Pursuing the road to Brest, 1 m. beyond Lesneven, on a dreary, bleak, unsheltered spot, we reach the village of *Folgoat*, marked in the distance by its tall spire, little inferior to the Creizker, of unusual splendour for a village, attached to the *Church of Notre Dame*, one of the most remarkable Gothic buildings of Brittany. It owes its origin to the following circumstance: —This spot was once haunted by an idiot-boy, who was in the habit of begging alms of those who passed, using at the same time this one unvaried exclamation, "Oh! Lady Virgin Mary!" so that the place became known as "ar fol coat," the fool of the wood. The fool died, and in a short time there sprang up from his grave, even out of his mouth, according to the legend, a beautiful lily, whose leaves bore inscribed upon them the name of Mary. This miracle was noised abroad, and, coming to the ears of John de Montfort, then warring with Charles de Blois for the dukedom of Brittany, he vowed to build a church on the spot if he triumphed over his rival. In consequence, after the victory of Auray, he laid the first stone on the spot where the lily had sprouted forth, but the church was not finished until 1423, by his son John V., who, in an inscription legible on the l. of the W. portal, claims to be its founder.

It is built of the very dark greenstone called Kersanton (§ 6), which gives the edifice on the whole a gloomy appearance, but it is well adapted for delicate sculpture, and by the sharpness with which it has retained the delicate touches of the artist's chisel, shows how great judgment he exercised in selecting it. Almost every part of the church, inside and out, deserves minute inspection; the fertile invention, laborious pains, and dexterous skill of the sculptor are visible in almost every part, though the edifice has been sadly injured through neglect. This is more especially conspicuous externally in the W. portal, the canopy of which fell down 1824; but round the portal runs so delicate a wreath of thistles and vine-leaves, perfect in their prickly flowers and stems, and even in the very fibres of the leaves and the curves of the stalks and tendrils, as cannot be seen without wonder. Birds also (chardonneret) and serpents are interspersed among the leaves. Above the door is a bas-relief of the Nativity, the Adoration of the Magi on one side (St. Joseph with wooden shoes has all the character of a Breton peasant), and of the Shepherds on the other. Below, the centre pier is formed into an elegant niche enclosing the bénitier under a graceful canopy, and supporting it on a bracket. Among the foliage here and in other parts may be seen the ermine, the armorial device of the dukes of Brittany, bearing their motto, "Melius mori quam fœdari." The thistle (chardon) and the goldfinch (chardonneret) also recur repeatedly in the ornaments of various parts of the church.

A far more beautiful porch is attached to the S. transept. Here 12 very exquisite niches line the vault leading to the door, in the mouldings around which similar leaves and wreaths are reproduced with far greater truth and delicacy. The stone from its peculiar colour has all the effect of bronze. This portal is believed to have been built by Anne of Brittany, as the arms of France united to those of Brittany are visible on it.

The sloping, open parapets which decorate the gables of the transept, the tracery of the E. windows, especially the central one surmounted by a rose, and the elegant arched niche at the E. end below it, on the outside of the church, constructed to receive the waters of the miraculous *fount,* which burst forth from beneath the high altar itself, are not to be passed unnoticed. The water of this spring is held in great repute by pilgrims, who, regardless of bystanders, strip themselves to apply it to all parts of their persons.

Within the church on the rt. as you enter is the *Fool's Chapel,* covered with frescoes nearly destroyed by the damp. Every capital, cornice, and border merits attention for the minute carving; but the chief object of interest is the *jubé* or *roodloft* between the choir and nave: it consists of 3 round arches most elegantly fringed, surmounted by canopies resting on panelled pillars, and supporting a gallery, of rich open work, pierced with quatrefoils. The foliage composing the crockets is an elaborate yet natural imitation of the most complicated leaves, and the two angels who occupy the place of finials are well designed.

The E. window, seen from within, surmounted by its rose, is admirable for its tracery: the high altar below it is a single slab of stone, 14 ft. long, supported on a front of niche-work filled with statuettes. The side screens and side altars are all more or less worthy of observation. There are numerous statues of saints curious for their costume. But the chief peculiarity of this church is the manner in which the sculptor who decorated it has rendered into stone the productions of the vegetable creation.

The roof of the church does not agree with the rest in splendour, and is evidently not completed conformably with the original plan.

The *Gothic College* on the N. side of the church was built by Anne of Brittany; she, as well as Francis I., were lodged in it when they came on a pilgrimage to Folgoat.

The country between St. Pol and Brest is very dreary; much heath, furze, and broom;—the cottages are poor dingy peat-covered hovels, among which a few starveling black sheep seek a scanty mouthful: few trees appear higher than brushwood. There are many beggars, some of them rivalling in their rags the mendicants of Ireland.

We fall into the great high road

from Paris about a mile before entering 6¼ *Brest,* in Rte. 36.

ROUTE 41.

ST. MALO TO NANTES BY DINAN AND RENNES. — ASCENT OF THE RIVER RANCE TO DINAN.

To Rennes direct 71 kilom. = 44¼ Eng. m.; thence to Nantes 107 kilom. = 66¼ Eng. m.

The détour by Dinan is 13 kilom. or 8 Eng. m. longer than the direct road. St. Malo is described in Rte. 27.

A *Steamer* ascends the Rance 3 or 4 times a week, when the high tide permits (N.B. not at neap tides). There is some beauty in the scenery, but no comfort in the voyage except when the tide is up. It takes 3 hrs. There is a lock (barrage éclusé) to be passed midway, at Châtelier, which is not pleasant: by means of this a depth of more than 6 ft. is alway maintained in the Rance at Dinan.

Owing to the variation of the tides on this coast, amounting to 40 ft., the current of the Rance is desperately rapid, and the river fills and empties with remarkable celerity.

The places passed in succession upon either bank are—

rt. St. Servan and the Castle of Solidor, p. 98.

l. St. Suliac, the prettiest village on the Rance.

l. Port St. Hubert, a little watering-place in a charming situation.

l. Plouer.
rt. Pleadihen.
Châtelier.
l. Tadens.

The river is confined between lofty precipices nearly all the way to Dinan, and may vary in breadth from ¼ to ½ m. Sometimes expanding into wide reaches, it resembles a Scotch lake.

The high road from St. Malo to Dinan runs on the E. side of the Rance, but only now and then in sight of it, and is devoid of interest until it comes in view of Dinan.

The postmaster charges 4 kilom. extra on quitting St. Malo at high water, on account of the circuit round the port which his horses are obliged to make, instead of crossing direct to St. Servan, as is done when the tide is out.

35 Châteauneuf, a strong fort covering the high road to Rennes; here are remains of an old castle.

We here quit the direct road to Rennes by St. Pierre de Plesguin 13 kilom.; Hédé 20 kilom. (p. 140); *Rennes* 23 kilom. = 34¾ Eng. m.

Some of the prettiest scenery of the Rance may be seen by those who, travelling *by land,* choose to quit the high road and their vehicle about 8 m. short of Dinan, walk over to the river at l'Ecluse, and ascend its rt. bank.

Pursuing the post-road, the picturesque towers and spires of Dinan are seen crowning the summit of a rocky steep. *A granite viaduct*—a work worthy of the Romans—carries the carriage-road across the valley of the Rance nearly on a level with the town, so as to avoid the tedious and toilsome descent and ascent formerly incurred by travellers approaching from St. Malo or Paris. The arches, are 10 in number; the principal piers, rising from the bed of the Rance, are 130 ft. high; the whole of solid masonry. The work was begun by Louis Philippe, but lingered until 1852 for want of funds.

18 *Dinan.—Inns*: H. de Bretagne, outside the gate, on the road to Brest, homely, clean, and cheap, best; H. du Commerce; Poste; both in the Place Du Guesclin.

The country in which Dinan is placed is perhaps the most beautiful in Brittany. The situation of the town (8044 Inhab.) is very romantic, on the crown and slopes of a hill of granite, overlooking the deep and narrow valley of the Rance, flowing 250 ft. below it. The sides of the hill are excessively steep; but, notwithstanding, houses and streets have been built along the face of it to the water's edge. The Rue de Jersuel, which stretches down to the old bridge, is so precipitous as to be impracticable except on foot, and it is even difficult for a pedestrian to descend its slippery pavement; yet this originally formed the only approach to the town on the side of St. Malo, through a pointed and ribbed Gothic gateway.

The modern road from St. Malo, after making a wide sweep and many turns under the old walls, in order to master the hill, enters the town by the Porte St. Louis close to the old and picturesque *Castle*, built about 1300, and often inhabited by Anne of Brittany, but now a prison. It was besieged by the Duke of Lancaster, 1389, and successfully defended by Du Guesclin against the English. It stands on the edge of the ravine on the outskirts of the town, and isolated from it by a deep fosse. The present entrance has been forced through a wall into the chapel, a finely vaulted chamber. A recess on one side, beside the altar, in which the lord or lady of the castle might hear mass without being seen, is called the oratoire of Anne of Brittany. The deep cornice of machicolations which crown the Donjon tower give it a very picturesque appearance, and there is a pleasing view from its top.

The *Place Du Guesclin* receives its name from that Breton hero, whose statue (in decayed plaster!) is placed in the midst of it ; and from the circumstance of its having been the lists in which he fought and vanquished an English knight, "Thomas of Cantorbie," whom he challenged to single combat for seizing treacherously, in time of truce between the two nations, his brother Oliver, 1359.

The *Cathedral of St. Sauveur* is an interesting edifice to the antiquary, in the Romanesque style, such as is more commonly met with in the S. of Europe than in the N. The crumbling nature of the granite of which it is composed gives it the appearance of greater antiquity than it really possesses. The lower part of the W. front and the S. side are probably of the 12th or even 11th centy.: the rest is modernised. The central portal, a round arch deeply recessed within mouldings and pillars (the two outer ones detached), is flanked on each side by blank arches, containing statues of the four Evangelists standing on lions, &c., under curious Romanesque canopies. From the wall above, the winged lion and ox, attributes of of St. Mark and St. Luke, project in high relief. The buttresses against the S. wall are in the form of round attached pillars, or square pilasters surmounted by capitals. Nothing within the church merits notice except a black tasteless slab in the N. transept, bearing engraved on it and gilt a double-headed eagle, whose outspread wings are crossed by a bar, below which a quaint inscription, in gold letters, informs us that the heart of Bertrand Du Guesclin (spelt g u e a q u ī) reposes beneath it, while his body lies among those of kings at St. Denis. Now, at least, neither statement is any longer true. The slab was found among the ruins of the church of the Jacobins, now razed to the ground; and all traces of the heart, and of the tomb of the Lady Tiphaine, the wife of Du Guesclin, by whose side the heart was deposited, are gone : the body shared the fate of the royal ashes at the desecration of St. Denis in the Revolution. The old town wall and watch-towers still remain; the streets in the older quarters abound in picturesque bits of architecture ; and no spot in Brittany is better fitted to exercise the artist's pencil.

The admirer of ancient domestic architecture should explore the narrow streets, with overhanging houses, the basements planted on pillars, each story projecting on corbels, which form the nucleus of the town. Arcades resting on carved granite pillars or wooden posts are very prevalent. Besides the steep Rue de Jersuel already mentioned, the Carrefour d'Horloge, so called from its lofty granite clock-tower, the Rue de la Vieille Poissonnerie (where is a house bearing the date 1366), and the Rue de la Croix (where the house of Du Guesclin and his lady Tiphaine is shown near the Hôtel de Ville), are the most remarkable in this respect. *The Canal d'Ille et Rance* begins at Dinan.

The English settled in Dinan are reduced from 400 to 100 since 1848: they have a *Chapel* here, in the Ancient Tribunal, Rue de la Lainerie, in which the English Church Service is performed on Sunday at 11½.

Medical men, M.M. Guillard and Piedvache.

Mademoiselle Roussin keeps a tolerable circulating *library*.

Mrs. Barr's Boarding-house, Rue de St. Malo, is recommended. Families can be received for one or more days. It is kept by the widow of a captain of the 33rd.

The *Steamer* from St. Malo ascends the Rance as far as the bridge of Dinan. (See p. 137).

Diligences daily to Rennes and Le Mans, to Brest, to St. Malo, to Dol, and to St. Brieuc in 5 hrs.

On the outside of the town, under the old walls, now overgrown with ivy, while the ditches are converted into gardens, run agreeable *Terraces*, commanding beautiful views over the vale of the Rance. The Mont Dol and Mont St. Michel are visible, it is said, from some points. There are manufactories of fine linen and of sailcloth in and about the town.

Excursions almost without end, each varying from the other, may be made on horse and foot in this delightful neighbourhood.

a. At the distance of less than a mile from the Porte St. Louis, prettily situated in the bottom of a dell, through which a streamlet falls into the Rance, lies the village of *Lehon*, where are the ruins of a once celebrated abbey and a castle. The *abbey* is entered by a fine circular archway within deep mouldings : the church, now roofless, is in the early pointed style : it is called La Chapelle des Beaumanoir, from being the burial-place of the family of that name, whose tombs were broken open at the Revolution, and the remains dispersed, while their monumental effigies, originally placed in the niches on either side of the church, have been removed to the Mairie. There are 4 figures of warriors armed, and an ecclesiastic, all in high relief; the drapery well executed, the hands folded in prayer. One of them is said to have been the leader of the Bretons in the famous "Combat des Trente." (See Rte. 42.)

The steep wooded height above the village is crowned by the *Castle*, now reduced to a square enclosure of walls levelled down to the surface of the potato-field which they enclose, having round towers in the angles and centre of each face. It was taken by Henry II. of England, 1168. From this castle-crowned height a beautiful view opens out of the village and abbey at its feet, of the course of the Rance and the romantic valley through which it flows. The navigation above this is continued by means of a canal which unites the Rance with the Vilaine.

The walk may be very pleasantly extended from this along the slopes of the hills, by paths across the fields behind the Hospice des Aliénés, towards the Village of St. Esprit, where there is a curious *Gothic crucifix* of granite, with figures of the first and second persons of the Trinity, now much mutilated. The charm of this walk, however, is the fine view it presents of the antique towers and spires of Dinan, on the opposite side of the valley to the rt., and the insight it affords into the curious system of labyrinthine lanes by which a great part of Brittany is traversed. The country is well wooded, abounding especially in oaks, and each field is surrounded by hedges. The lanes by which it is intersected in all directions, owing to the soft and crumbling nature of the soil, differ little from ditches worn down 8 or 10 ft. below the surface of the fields, and vary in character between a pool or slough of mud and a mound of hard bare rock. A stranger is almost sure to lose his way among them, so intricate and numerous are their crossings. The country, seamed and grooved by these hollow ways, is like a rabbit warren, and this thoroughly explains how the Chouans and Vendéans were able, among such fastnesses, to put to defiance so long the armies of the Republican Government.

b. On the opposite side of Dinan, about

1 m. distant, at the bottom of a really romantic little valley, is the spa or *Eaux Minérales*, a source of saline sulphureous water, good for liver complaints, much resorted to in summer. Alleys have been planted and a sort of pump-room built, which contribute little to the beauty of the spot, though they cannot spoil it. A walk along the paths, cut through the trees along the steep sides of the dell, is highly to be recommended.

c. The *Château de la Garaye* is a ruined mansion of the time of Francis I., exhibiting in its falling walls and towers some picturesque bits of architecture, in the style of la Renaissance, intermixed with Gothic ornaments. The last owner, M. de la Garaye, quitting the gay world, converted this house into an hospital, while, with his wife, he devoted all his time and fortune to the care of the sick. To fit themselves for this duty they both studied medicine and surgery, and the lady became an excellent oculist. The hospital was destroyed at the Revolution, which the benevolent founders fortunately did not live to see, having died 1755-7; but the monument over the graves even of these benefactors of the district, in the churchyard of Faden, did not escape destruction from the ruthless hands of the Republican spoilers.

d. e. The *Castles of Montafilant* and *Guildo* on the sea-coast near Plombalay.

f. About 10 m. N. W. of Dinan is the *Château of La Hunandaye*, an interesting old castle surrounded by rampart and ditch, and tolerably perfect, in the form of a pentagon. It is supposed to have been built in the 13th century, by Olivier de Tournemine. It is to be reached only by a cross road, intricate to find without a guide, passing through Corseul, where Roman remains have been discovered.

About 10 m. beyond the castle, on the coast, is St. Cast, where an ill-contrived expedition of the English was ignominiously defeated in attempting an inroad on Brittany in 1758, with a loss of 822 men, including 42 officers, killed and taken prisoners.

From Dinan to Rennes it is worth while to take the route by *Hédé*, for the sake of the *Ruined Castle*, occupying a very picturesque site and commanding a beautiful view. In the chapel of Montmuran, near Hédé, Du Guesclin was armed a knight.

On the road from Dinan to Rennes the small town of Evrau is passed; it is situated on the *Canal* which joins the Rance to the Ille. The castle of the Beaumanoir here is now modernised. The country beyond is very tame; fields and hedgerows, and few villages. Country-houses, where they occur, lie at a distance from the road, without lodges or dressed grounds.

29 La Chapelle Chaussée.
24 *Rennes*, in Rte. 34.

There are 2 roads from Rennes to Nantes:
—a. By Derval 107 kilom. = $66\frac{1}{4}$ Eng. m.
  16 Bout de Lande.
  11 Roudun.
A high hill is crossed before reaching
  17 La Breheraye.
   9 Derval.
  12 Nozay.
  14 Bout de Bois.
  14 Gesvres.
  14 NANTES, in Rte. 46.
—b. By Châteaubriant 119 kilom. = 73 Eng. m.
  18 Corps Nuds.
  17 Thourie.
  18 Châteaubriant (*Inn:* H. des Voyageurs, small, but clean), a town of 3673 Inhab., at the intersection of several roads. Its ancient walls remain nearly intact. The *Castle* was dismantled by Henri IV. and Louis XIII., but part of it, including a spiral stair leading to the chamber in which, according to tradition, Françoise de Foix was bled to death by her husband Jean de Laval (1525 or 37), are incorporated in the public offices. The *Ch. of St. Jean de Béré* is an interesting Romanesque structure.
  18 La Meilleraye.

About 1 m. on the l. of the road lies a *Monastery of the Order of La Trappe*. It was sold as national property 1793, and was repurchased 1816 by a Romanist Society of Trappists, who had been settled at Lulworth in Dorsetshire, but their number has been greatly diminished (to 25) since 1830, in consequence of their having mixed themselves up with the Chouan insurrection of that period.

19 Nort is a small town on the l. bank of the Erdre, which becomes navigable here for steamers. One plies daily between Nantes and Nort, to and fro. Below this the Erdre swells out into the form of a lake; on its rt. bank are Chapelle-sur-Erdre, and the castle of la Gâcherie, residence of the Princess Marguerite de Navarre, sister of Francis I., and authoress of the romances known by the title Heptameron.

A little farther is the castle of Blue Bleard (Gilles de Retz), whose story is told in Rte. 58.

18 Carquefou.

11 NANTES, in Rte. 46.

ROUTE 42.

MORLAIX TO NANTES, BY THE MINES OF HUELGOAT AND POULAHOUAN, CARHAIX, PONTIVY, JOSSELIN, AND PLOERMEL.

This is a cross-country road, *not* a post-road, but traversed by a Diligence. It is described because it includes several places of interest.

There is a good view of the picturesque town of Morlaix (Rte. 36) from the heights crossed on quitting it. The road gradually approaches and surmounts the chain of the Menez Arrés hills, through a desolate country chiefly moorland. The summit level is reached at Croix Court, which is also the boundary of the arrondissements of Morlaix and Châteaulin. About 1½ m. beyond Le Mendi, a hamlet 12 m. from Morlaix, a road turns off on the rt. to

Huelgoat (4 m. farther). Here is only a poor *Inn* (Lion d'Or), which, however, can furnish a clean bed and something to eat. Huelgoat is a town of 1200 Inhab., in a remote and thinly-peopled district celebrated for its *Mines* of lead containing silver mixed with it. They are situated about 1¼ m. from the town, in the midst of a picturesque valley, through which runs a rushing stream, concealed from view at one particular spot by an *éboulement* of colossal fragments of rocks.

The path to the mines is carried through thick woods by the side of a narrow canal or aqueduct, conveying water to move the machinery and the hydraulic pump by which the mine is kept dry. This machine is a masterpiece of mechanical skill, constructed by M. Juncker, an engineer of Alsace, and related to Cuvier. It well deserves the minute attention of all who take an interest in mining or machinery, and has been thought worthy of an eulogistic report, read to the Academy of Science by M. Arago. It has the force of 280 horses, and raises 3 cubic mètres 53 centièmes per minute, a height of 754 ft., effected by a column of water equal to 21 cubic inches falling from a height of 196 ft. It has been at work for many years night and day; its movements are free from the least irregularity or the slightest noise. It is entirely under ground, at a considerable depth below the surface. The process of separating the silver from the ores by amalgamation with mercury is also very curious. M. Juncker, who for many years directed these works, introduced considerable ameliorations on the Saxon method, by means of which large masses of very poor ores have been worked, which were formerly rejected; by this means the prosperity of the Huelgoat mines has increased much of late years. Permission to enter the mines is readily given by the director. The best time for visiting them is at six o'clock, when the gangs of miners are shifted, and the nightworking set relieve those who have toiled through the day. The descent is made by a bucket and rope. The vein of lead has been traced for more than ½ a mile in a clay slate of the upper Silurian formation. The lead ore (galena) is sent to Poulahouan to be smelted.

In the *Church* of Huelgoat is a curious reading-desk (lutrin) resting on a pedestal resembling the classic tripod, but of wood, each of the 3 sides ornamented with a figure in bas-relief of a classic character. On one is a man with long hair and a mace over his shoulder, with no other clothing than a short cloak; on another a young man in classic garb, bearing a torch in one hand and a dart in the other; on the third a female bearing a cup and vase, in the guise of a Bacchante. It has been well described by M. Freminville; but nothing is known of its origin or the meaning of its carvings.

The *Ménage de la Vierge* is a species of cave formed by fallen masses of granite rock, through which a small stream of black water and of unknown origin flows, in places out of sight. It is possible with a sure foot and steady head to descend into the gulf. Near this is a *Rocking Stone*.

The *Cascades of St. Herbot* are worth the walk to them, less on account of the waterfalls themselves than for the scenery of the little valley in which they lie, varied with dense woods and bare jutting rocks. The village *Church*, surmounted by a fine square tower on a height above, contains the tomb and effigy of the anchorite St. Herbot, some carved screen-work in the choir, and a *roodloft* of elaborate and beautiful workmanship in the style of the Renaissance. There are 2 painted windows of rich colour with the date 1556. It has a fine W. portal in the decorated style, but bearing the date 1516, an ogee arch ornamented with frizzled foliage, and a still more beautiful S. porch, but the statues are poor. Herbot is a veterinary saint, who cures the diseases of animals, provided a lock of the beast's hair be laid on his altar.

At *Branilis* in the parish of Locquefret, about 6 m. from Huelgoat, at a distance from any village, surrounded by 3 or 4 hovels, is a fine large *Church* in the best style of Gothic art, surmounted by a spire, and internally adorned with carving in stone and wood, and with painted glass, now all going to decay.

Poulahouan, on the direct road from Morlaix to Carhaix, contains other lead-mines, but inferio in extent and productiveness to those of Huelgoat. Here, however, are the *smelting-houses* in which the ore from both mines is reduced. The galleries of the mine have been driven horizontally $\frac{3}{4}$ of a mile and vertically more than 600 ft. in the grauwacke.

There is a direct road (15 m.) from Huelgoat to

Carhaix (La Tour d'Auvergne is a good little *Inn:* game very cheap; partridges 3d. a brace), a primitive town (2000 Inhab.) among the hills, in the midst of that most unsophisticated district of ancient Brittany, Cornouailles. It abounds in old houses, with projecting cornices and carved timber-work, and is inhabited by people as old-fashioned as their dwellings.

Here is shown the house in which La Tour d'Auvergne (Théophile-Malo Corret) was born, in 1743; who, stern republican as well as brave warrior, steadily refused rank, but died the "premier grenadier de France," in the battle-field on the banks of the Danube. A statue of him by the sculptor *Marochetti* is erected in the Place. In the *Château de la Haye* are preserved his heart, an early portrait, his sword, and his boots. The canal from Nantes to Brest will send a branch to Carhaix.

A little way out of the town on the road to Callac is an ancient structure, said to be a Roman aqueduct. There is also a Roman road which can be traced for more than a mile on the way to St. Gildas. Richard Cœur de Lion was defeated at Carhaix, 1197, by his rebellious vassals, the nobles of Brittany. Six high roads—to Brest, Morlaix, St. Brieuc, Vannes, Châteaulin, and Quimper—unite here.

A direct road leads from Carhaix to Lorient, by Le Faouet, and over the high range of the Montagne Noire. Not far from Le Faouet is a very handsome Gothic chapel.

The road to Pontivy and Vannes quits the Dépt. of Finisterre soon after leaving Carhaix, passes Rostrénen (Dépt. Côtes du Nord), beyond which it crosses the Brest and Nantes Canal, and reaches

Pontivy (*Inn:* H. des Voyageurs), an ancient town with old walls and gates, to which a new quarter was tacked on by Napoleon, who changed the name of the place to Napoleonville. At the restoration of the Bourbons, however, his name and his public works were dropped; and many of the buildings remain half finished. The river Blavet, now rendered navigable to the sea at Lorient, and the canal from Brest to Nantes, afford openings for some commerce. The *Castle* of the Dukes of Brittany is of ancient foundation, but the actual edifice was rebuilt 1485. It is very picturesque, but rapidly falling to ruin. The fine church tower and spire of St. Nicodème is 2½ lieues from Pontivy.

About 6 m. N. of the road to Josselin is *Rohan*, cradle of the noble family of that name, now a poor and insignificant village, but prettily situated. Of the *Castle*, now neglected by the princes its owners, scarcely a morsel of wall remains above the surface; the last fragments having been pulled down to build cottages with the stones.

Posting is established on the road between Pontivy and

34 Josselin. — *Inns:* Poste; Croix d'Or. The *Castle of Josselin,* an ancient feudal fortress, founded on a rock above the river Oest, was the residence of the famous Constable de Clisson, who added a donjon, now destroyed, to the building, and died here, 1407, in a chamber facing the river, still pointed out. The oldest parts are the round towers, on the outside, built of slate. The most remarkable portion of the building is the inner front, in the irregular but picturesque style of Gothic in its latest form, equivalent to our Elizabethan, and dating probably from the 16th centy. It is surmounted by pointed gables, and no two divisions correspond; the windows, surmounted by Gothic canopies, are interspersed with parapets of interlacing tracery, in the midst of which the words "à plus," the motto of the Rohans, to whom the castle still belongs, cut in letters of stone, are constantly recurring. From the initials A. V. with a coronet, it is supposed to have been built by Alain VIII. Vicomte de Josselin.

The *Tomb of Olivier de Clisson,* in the Ch. of Notre Dame, was violated at the Revolution, and the effigies of himself, and his wife Marguerite de Rohan, through whom he inherited the castle, were broken to pieces. The mutilated fragments were to be seen lately in the sacristy. A modern mausoleum has been erected, in execrable taste.

In the midst of a wild open heath, half way between Josselin and Ploermel, a modern obelisk marks the spot where the *Combat des Trente* took place. Here, if we may believe Breton poets and writers of modern date (for ancient authority is wanting for the event, and many have doubted whether it ever occurred), close to an oak, which has long since disappeared, called "chêne de mie voi," a battle is said to have been fought 1351, between 30 Bretons on the side of Charles de Blois, and 30 partisans of Jean de Montfort, consisting of 20 English, 4 Flemings, and 6 Bretons, there not being enough English on the spot to form the full complement of combatants. The challenge was given by Du Beaumanoir, the Breton leader of the garrison of Josselin, to his opponents, who composed part of the garrison of Ploermel, in consequence of an alleged infraction of a treaty by the latter. The English were led on by a knight whom the French call Brembro (? Pembroke), and after a very stout resistance were vanquished, chiefly owing to the death of their leader. The combat of the 30 is not mentioned in the oldest copies of Froissart, the contemporary chronicle of the wars of Brittany, and is doubted by Daru in his History; notwithstanding which the monumental obelisk erected since the Restoration, in the place of one destroyed at the Revolution, headed "Vive le Roi! Les Bourbons toujours!" gives a list of the names of the 30 Bretons engaged in it.

12 Ploermel, in Rte. 45.

15 Malestroit.—There is no posting from this place to

Redon, a town of 4500 Inhab., on the Vilaine, a tidal river up to this point, and navigable for vessels of considerable size, while the navigation is continued by locks above this to Rennes.

The *Church*, originally belonging to the Abbey, is a fine Gothic building with a semicircular E. end. The conventual buildings are turned into a college.

The *Château de Beaumont*, in the vicinity of the town, retains 3 towers of considerable antiquity attached to its modern constructions. There are extensive slate-quarries near this.

19 Rozay.
24 Bout de Bois. We here enter Rte. 41 a, p. 140.
14 Gesvres.
14 NANTES. (Route 46.)

ROUTE 44.

BREST TO NANTES, BY QUIMPER, AURAY, VANNES, AND LA ROCHE BERNARD.—EXCURSIONS TO LORIENT AND TO CARNAC AND LOKMARIAKER.

307 kilom. = 191 Eng. m.

Diligence (mail) daily, in 36 hours, including 3 or 4 hours stoppages. It is a finely constructed road, though hilly from Brest to Le Faou.

The high road from Brest to Châteaulin makes a great circuit in order to avoid the creeks jutting out of the Bay of Brest: it follows the Paris road to

20 Landerneau (Rte. 36), then turns abruptly S. to

19 Faou, seated on a river which becomes all slime at low water. The costume of the people in this part of Brittany is such as was worn in England in the time of Charles I. and II.—slouched hats, trunk hose (bragou bras, *i. e.* brogues or breeks), very wide, and with many folds, the hair hanging down the men's backs, reminding one of the pictures in Isaac Walton. The black charcoal-burners thus attired have a very singular appearance. The women here wear a sort of cravat round their necks. The Pardon (§ 5), celebrated four times a year at Rumengol near Faou, is attended with very curious ceremonies.

From the high ground beyond Faou a pretty view is obtained on the rt.; the road, which is very hilly, next dips into a wooded and picturesque dell, at the bottom of which is a royal manufactory of gunpowder, called Pont de Puis. Another hill surmounted, and we reach the banks of the Châteaulin river at *Port de Launay*.

[A *steamer*, at one time, ran from Brest to Port Launay, 2 m. short of Châteaulin, traversing the Rade de Brest through its entire length, and enabling the stranger fully to enjoy the beauties of that fine salt-water lake. For a general description of it, and of the vast range of batteries which defend it, see Rte. 36.

rt. The Pointe des Espagnols, the extreme projection of the peninsula of Quélern, and l. the Pointe de l'Armorique, both strongly defended by forts. During the wars of the Ligue, a Spanish force sent over to aid the Duc de Mercœur in his resistance to Henri IV. took possession of the point, and, intrenching themselves on it, completely commanded the entry of the roads. Their fort was at length captured by assault by Maréchal d'Aumont, assisted by 1800 English, commanded by Col. Norris, sent over by Queen Elizabeth, after an obstinate defence, and all within it were put to the sword — the French say, chiefly through the savageness of the English. The English formed the forlorn hope in scaling the breach; and here the veteran mariner Frobisher, the tamer of the Spanish Armada, got his death-wound.

The peninsula of Quélern, consumed on both sides by the ever-restless waves, exhibits a fringe of notched and jagged rocks, which, as they become undermined by the ocean, are constantly giving way. Immense fissures are formed every year in the ground above, and are followed by numerous landslips. These bare and exposed promontories, covered with heath and cut up and corroded by the waves, were the chosen site of the worship of the Druids, and abound in those curious Celtic remains called Druidic stones. (§ 4.)

1. The Bay of Daoulas, or "Double Murder," is so called from the slaughter of two saints by a pagan chief, which gave rise to an *Abbey* whose ruins still remain. They are chiefly of the 15th centy., with earlier portions in the round style. Near this are the quarries of the Kersanton stone, so much used for the churches of Brittany. (§ 5.)

rt. The steamer next entered the inlet of Châteaulin, bending round the projecting promontory Landevennec, on which are ruins of a church attached to a once celebrated Abbey, the Breton Chartreuse, which was destroyed at the Revolution, and its valuable charters and MSS. sent to Brest to be made into cartridges by the artillery.

The banks of the inlet, now contracting into a river, are picturesque, but the course of the stream is very winding.

At Port de Launay the voyage for steamers ends; the river Aulne being crossed by a weir and lock a short way above this, to render it navigable for barges as far as Châteauneuf, where the canal to Nantes commences.]

There are many slate-quarries on the banks of the river near to

19 Châteaulin. — *Inn:* none tolerable. A small, but not remarkable town, in a pretty, park-like valley, having a bridge over the Aulne, and an old castle in ruins on a rock behind it. At *Pleyben*, 7 m. E. of this, is a fine Gothic *Church*, with a lofty tower and well-preserved sculptured portal, bearing inside of it statues of the 12 Apostles; the windows are adorned with painted glass. In the churchyard is a very curious *Calvaire* resting on 4 arches, on the sides and the top of which our Saviour's passion is represented in bas-reliefs and statues, more than 120 in number, not ill drawn, the drapery especially. The costume is

France.

that of the 16th centy., yet the date affixed to the monument is 1650.

Quimper may be reached from Châteaulin in about 2½ hours. The road here quits the valley of the Aulne by a steep ascent 3 m. long; from the very top of which, an open moorland tract, you still look down upon Châteaulin and its valley. This ridge is called the Black Mountain. It was near this part of the road that a party of intrusive clergy and bishops, appointed by the Revolutionist government, proceeding to a confirmation at Brest, were stopped, dragged out of the coach by a party of Chouans, and murdered on the highway.

28 Quimper (Corentin), — *Inn:* H. de l'Epeé, the only good one.

Quimper is capital of the Dépt. Finisterre, though it has only 9860 Inhab., while Brest has 30,000. It bears the stamp of antiquity as much as any town in Brittany, and is still partly surrounded by the walls and watch-towers erected for its defence by Pierre de Dreux, who, though a bishop, was also a great captain in his time. The *Cathedral* rears its stately W. front, with a deep sculptured portal, rich in foliage, but much fractured, between two massive towers, on one side of the market-place. It is a large and fine edifice, begun 1424, and has this peculiarity, that its nave is not on a line with the choir, which inclines considerably to the N.E., although the irregularity is not so perceptible as to be a defect. The interior is of a stately height; in the S. aisle is a curious grated niche. The pulpit is carved and gilt. The sculpture of the porch is like that of Folgoat in the beautiful treatment of the foliage. The towers though massive are not heavy, being set off by the slit windows 30 ft. high which pierce them, and by the light open parapet with which they terminate.

The ruined *Ch. of the Cordeliers*, begun 1224, with its elegant though mutilated cloister, and a large window looking over the Rue St. François, and the chapel of *Locmaria*, on the outskirts of the town to the S., apparently older than any in Quimper, and

H

a work of the middle of the 12th centy., will be appreciated by the antiquary.

The best and most modern houses line a quay on the rt. bank of the Odel, which flows through Quimper in the form of a canal. On its l. bank stands the Préfecture, fronting a sort of Champ de Mars, behind which a tall and steep hill rises, covered with a hanging wood, cut into terraces and zigzag paths, forming an agreeable public walk, leading to the top, whence there is a fine view of the river, which expands greatly below the town.

Quimper is said to be an agreeable residence; its situation is very pretty, and some trout-fishing might be had in the neighbouring streams: the climate is bad, however.

For those who have time and inclination, there remain to be visited near Quimper the picturesque manoir of *Coat Bily*, a little to the rt. of the road to Châteaulin (date 1517); the elegant and well-preserved chapel of *La Mère de Dieu*, 16th cent.; the *Moustoir*, an ancient fortified mansion on the way to Concarneau.

A new high road has been made from this to the *Pointe*, or *Bec du Raz*, a storm-beaten promontory, surmounted by a lighthouse, which, though nearly 270 ft. above the sea, is constantly covered by the spray during tempests. The spot has little grandeur, but a savage wildness; the sea around is always tempest-tossed, and the shore of the Baie des Trépassés, so called from the number of dead bodies washed upon it, is perpetually covered with wrecks. The flat, bare, rocky peninsula of Penmarch abounds in Celtic remains. Near Soc'h is a Druidic parallelogram of upright stones, and the finest dolmen in Finisterre, consisting of 16 vertical slabs supporting two horizontal or tabular stones. (§ 4.)

The road out of Quimper to Quimperlé has been carried round the flanks of the hills, instead of over their tops.

21 Rosporden stands on the borders of a large pond.

25 Quimperlé (no good *Inn*) is seated amidst hills, on a brawling river, the Elle, and is a pretty town. 5300 Inhab.

The large mass of building on one side of the Place, now serving as *Mairie*, &c., was originally a convent of Benedictines, attached to which, behind, is the *Ch. of Ste. Croix*, a building calculated to interest the antiquary and architect, from its age (10th or 11th cent. ?), and its form, a rotunda surmounted by a dome with 4 projecting apses, one of which has been modernised. The arrangement of the central piers, concave inwardly, convex outwardly, the pilasters attached to them, the narrow, loopholed, roundheaded windows high up in the wall, all mark its antiquity. 3 flights of steps lead up to the altar, beneath which is a curious and still more ancient crypt, entered from the outside. It contains the grave of St. Gurlot: the Bretons thrust their arms through a hole in his tombstone, in order to be cured of rheumatism. Above the main entrance to the church is a bas-relief of good execution, of the age of Francis I., representing the 4 Evangelists and the Theological Virtues.

There is another church (*St. Michel*) on the top of the hill, its groundwork Romanesque, with additions of the 12th and 15th cents.

Travellers bound for *Lorient* (where the H. de France is a good *Inn*) take a route to the rt. of our line on quitting Quimperlé. There is nothing remarkable in that dull modern town of straight streets and 19,095 Inhab., save its *Dockyard*, which is not readily shown to an Englishman, and which he need not care to see, as it is much inferior to those of his own country. The town is strongly fortified, and stands in the angle between two creeks, one of which, the estuary of the Scorff, forms the port militaire, the other the port marchand. They unite below the town, where they are met by the estuary of the Blavet from the E., and expand into the Roads; but as the dockyard occupies nearly the entire margin, and is surrounded on all sides by a high wall, all view of the water is excluded from the town, and contributes nothing to remove the monotonous dulness of its dirty streets, whose meagre houses look as though they were built merely to be knocked down. An excellent bird's-eye view of the dockyard may be obtained from the top of the tower of the parish church.

At the entrance of the *Dockyard* is the house of the *Préfet Maritime*. The adjacent buildings are part of those erected by the "Compagnie des Indes Orientales," whose establishment here, 1666, converted into a town a previously obscure village. The company was dissolved 1770. Law of Lauriston, the South Sea schemer, occupied the house which is now the *Préfecture*. Near to it stands a narrow look-out tower 180 ft. high, overtopping all other buildings, affording a view of the whole roadstead and of the coast far and wide; near this is a small astronomical observatory. Lorient is exclusively a building dock; there are no bagnes nor convicts here. There are 15 or 16 building-slips (cales) here and on the opposite side of the creek, but only one has a permanent roof, fit for first-rates; the rest are mostly for frigates and steam-vessels. A new *Fonderie* near to the shed for masting vessels, 2 large mast-houses, and very extensive workshops, provided with a steam-engine, have been finished.

The roads open out at the lower extremity of the creek which forms the port: they are partly dry at low water. Some way down is the Ile St. Michel, covered with the yellow buildings of the Lazaret, and beyond it, on a projecting point, the fortress of *Port Louis*, commanding the entrance of the harbour, mounting 500 cannon (?)

A *steamer* goes from Lorient to Nantes, and *vice versâ*, every week, touching at Belle Isle, a barren rock, which was captured by the English, under General Hodson and Admiral Keppel, in 1761.

The estuary of the Scorff is crossed by a wooden bridge in going to Auray from Lorient.]

———

A coach runs between Quimperlé and Nantes daily in about 24 hrs., through Lorient and Hennebon. The direct road to Hennebon passes out of the Dépt. Finisterre into the Morbihan about 6 m. from Quimperlé.

The river Blavet is crossed by an iron suspension bridge to reach

24 Hennebon (H. du Commerce; tolerable), an antique town, 4477 Inhab., prettily situated on its l. bank, once the chief port of Morbihan. Its name must be familiar to all who have read Froissart, through the noble defence which it made in the succession war of Brittany 1342, during two sieges sustained by Jeanne de Montfort against the armies of Philippe de Valois and Charles of Blois. The capture and imprisonment in Paris of Jean de Montfort would have ruined his cause in Brittany but for his heroic countess, who, possessing the courage of a man and the heart of a lion, threw herself into Hennebon, strengthened its works, filled it with provisions, and animated the courage of the garrison and inhabitants to resist to the last extremity. To marshal troops, to lead them to the onset, to fight hand to hand armed cap-à-pied with sword and casque, to manage a war-horse with the skill of the most adept cavalier, to preside in council, or dictate treaties; such were the accomplishments of this noble dame. Several times did she boldly sally forth at the head of her troops to assail the enemy, and on one occasion set fire to his camp; and when the besiegers turned round to defend it in such numbers as to cut off her retreat into the town, she forced her way through them and effected her escape to Auray, whence, after beating up the country around for 5 days, she returned in triumph to Hennebon with a force augmented from 300 to 600 men, and entered the gates in safety. At length the last extremity arrived; provisions were nearly exhausted, her counsellors advised surrender, and articles of capitulation were drawn up. She was forced unwillingly to consent to yield, provided at the end of 3 days succour did not arrive from England. On the eve of the 2nd day, as she was gazing from her watch-tower, she perceived the

H 2

English fleet, which had been detained by contrary winds, entering the mouth of the Blavet full sail, bringing the brave knight Sir Walter de Manny, with a strong force of English knights and archers, and plenty of provisions. All thoughts of surrender were now abandoned; and, after one or two successful sorties, the siege was raised. Two years after this, Edward III. in person landed here with an army of 12,000, which laid siege to Vannes. In 1375, however, the town was taken by Du Guesclin, and the English garrison all put to the sword, except the commanders Wisk and Prior, who were reserved for ransom. The only relics now remaining in the town from that period of bloodshed are a portion of the town-wall on the side of the river, and an ancient *gate* which led to the castle; it is a pointed gateway between 2 very massive round towers, and is now a prison. The *Church* is said to have been built by the English; it is unfinished, and only remarkable for a lofty and elegant portal, recessed and fringed, not unlike that at Harfleur, surmounted by a crocketed steeple. There are some picturesque old houses here.

[Near Baud (a poor town, destitute of a tolerable inn), 15 m. N. of Hennebon, is the statue called *Venus of Quinipily,* from a castle of that name now razed to the ground, on whose site it is placed. It is of granite, coarsely worked and badly designed; the arms are crossed in front over a piece of drapery like a stole, descending halfway down the thighs; in other respects it is naked. Nothing is known concerning its origin, and the conjectures are very vague. One writer supposes, from its Egyptian character, that it was a Gallic Isis, and it is called Venus only in the inscriptions on the pedestal set up 1689. This much is certain, that down to the 17th centy. it was worshipped with foul rites, and is even now looked on with superstitious veneration by the peasantry.]

A dreary and monotonous country of moor and heathland is crossed on quitting Hennebon to reach

13 Landevan.

15 Auray (*Inn*: Pavillon d'en Bas; tolerable), a town of 3734 Inhab., on the Auray; in nowise remarkable, but from its position it is the best starting-point for a visit to the Celtic antiquities of *Carnac* and *Locmariaker.* Jolting gigs may be hired here for 10 fr. to go and return.

The Castle of Auray, no part of which is now standing, is said to have been founded by King Arthur. A battle fought under its walls, 1364, settled the succession to the dukedom of Brittany in favour of young De Montfort, son-in-law to King Edward III., who owed the victory to his English allies, led on by the brave John Chandos. In the opposite ranks fought Du Guesclin, who was made prisoner by Chandos, and Olivier de Clisson, who lost an eye in the battle. Charles de Blois was slain in the thickest of the fight, and there fell on his side not less than 5000 men, while the English lost a very small number.

St. Anne d'Auray is a celebrated pilgrimage *church* 6 m. from the town, frequented usually by 6000 devotees from all parts of Brittany in the month of July, but not otherwise remarkable. It is a modern and not handsome building.

In another direction, about a mile from Auray, is the nunnery of the *Chartreuse,* occupied by the Sœurs de la Sagesse, who instruct a school for the deaf and dumb. Attached to their church is the *Expiatory Monument,* erected by the Bourbons to the memory of the 950 unfortunate Emigrés and Royalists who composed the ill-advised expedition to Quiberon, 1795, and who either fell there, or were shot by the Republicans on the banks of the Auray, at the spot marked by a Grecian temple not far distant from the Chartreuse. Another monument, which has been placed in the church to record their unhappy fate, is not a work of merit, either in general design or in the execution of the bas-relief intended to adorn it. It bears the names of those who fell.

The village of Breech was the birthplace of George Cadoudal, a leader of the Chouans. Morbihan was the centre of their insurrection.

The *Excursion to Carnac and Locmariaker* may be made in one day by pursuing the following plan, and provided the traveller can walk 8 m., the only mode of passing between these two places being on foot. If the wind be favourable he may hire a boat for 10 francs and descend the Auray to Locmariaker, a pleasant voyage of a little more than an hour; if he visit Gâvr Innis (*N.B.* in this case take candles and matches), 1 or $1\frac{1}{2}$ hr. more is required: from Locmariaker on foot to Carnac will take 2 hrs. He must, however, beforehand, hire a gig at Auray, and send it on to Carnac to wait for him. He may return to Auray in the gig in $2\frac{1}{2}$ hrs.

In sailing down the estuary of the Auray he will pass

rt. The Château de Plessis Kaer, a Gothic castle, with additions of the time of Francis I., and the ruins of another, called Rosnareu. Near this the boatmen assert that ruins of the piles of a bridge, which they attribute to Cæsar, may be discovered at low water in the bed of the river.

rt. A perfect Château, called Kerentrec. The river now widens out, and a little farther on we enter

The *Morbihan* (Little Sea), an inland sea or archipelago from which the department is named, so thickly beset with islands that the common belief assigns them a number equal to the days of the year. The shores on all sides have a most jagged outline, fringed with capes, creeks, and inlets; they are of granite, barely covered with the scantiest vegetable soil, supporting a growth of barren heath; very often the surface is mere bare rock. 2 narrow peninsulas or arms, projecting from the E. and W., separate this gulf from the sea, allowing only a narrow passage between them. This archipelago is very difficult to navigate—a perfect labyrinth of islands, separated by intricate passages which only the experienced navigator can thread. The land rises but little above the sea; it is sterile in the extreme; the peasantry are miserably poor, and barely win a scanty crop from a soil whose proper productions seem heath and furze. Yet this melancholy and mysterious but uninviting district seems to have been the head-quarters of the religion of the Druids—the number of barrows, cairns, dolmens, menhirs, &c., is extraordinary (§ 4).

The island of *Gâvr Innis*, or Gaffr' né, nearly opposite Locmariaker, may be visited on the way thither, diverging a mile or 2 to the E. It is "an island of granite about $\frac{1}{4}$ m. long, of granite covered with turf, in which rises a tumulus 30 ft. high and 300 in circumference. It is traversed by a subterranean passage or cromlech, consisting of 13 and 14 vertical props at the sides and 10 cap-stones. Some of them are covered with engraved lines forming patterns somewhat resembling the tattooing of a New Zealander.— *Lukis.* The only way to get to these islands is to take a boat from Locmariaker. The Auray boatmen either cannot or will not go over.

Locmariaker is a poor village, possessing accommodation only of the commonest kind for a traveller. It stands on a heathy promontory projecting between the ocean and the Gulf of Morbihan, but is deserted by the tide at low water, so that one must land at a sort of pier a little to the N. of the village, near the *Mont Hellu*, a mound of stones or galgal, about $\frac{3}{4}$ m. N. W. of the village. There is another similar mound to the S. E. called *butte de* Cæsar. The most interesting of the Celtic monuments lie to the N. of the village, between it and the Mont Hellu. Contiguous to the last house is a menhir 20 ft. long, overthrown like every other in this district; a little to the l. on an eminence is a dolmen, the top stone of which is 12 to 15 ft. square, and in parts 3 ft. thick. Still farther to the N. lies prostrate and broken into 4 fragments the *largest Menhir* known; it measures nearly 60 ft. in length, and 5 or 6 ft. in height as it lies. It is difficult to imagine by what force so huge a mass can have been snapped short across, with such clean fractures. Some have attributed its fall to lightning. Near to it is another dolmen called *Dol ar Marchant*, the Merchant's Table, which seems larger than any other in the neighbourhood; it consists of 2 table-stones, one of them 16 ft. by 12, supported on 3 vertical ones; it is possible to creep under it, and remark the singular figures cut on its under surface. Between it and the Mont Hellu, a vast heap of cinders is said to have been found (?)

There are many other similar monuments near Locmariaker, but these are the principal ones.

Locmariaker (i. e. place of the Virgin Mary) is supposed to occupy the site of the ancient *Dariorigum*, the capital of the Venetes: its position agrees with Cæsar's description of their "oppida in extremis linguis, promontoriisque posita," and some substructures of houses laid bare near the village are attributed to the Romans.

[The *peninsula* of *Rhuys*, which, with that of Locmariaker, form, as it were, the natural piers separating the Sea of Morbihan from the Atlantic, contains the following objects of curiosity. 1. Le *Grand Mont*, called also *la Butte de Tumiac*, situated about 4 m. from Sarzeau, an obscure little town, but memorable as the birthplace of the author of Gil Blas. It is the largest tumulus existing in France, 100 ft. high and 300 in circumference, and is planted near the extremity of the promontory. 2. The ruined *ch.* of the *Abbey of St. Gildas de Rhuys*, remarkable because it was the retreat of Abelard in 1125, who narrowly escaped poisoning at the hands of the refractory and ill-conditioned monks, whose dissolute manners he wished to repress. The remains consist of a modern nave, and a very ancient choir in the Romanesque style, terminating at the E. end in 3 semicircular chapels. The walls of the transept are partly of herring-bone masonry. The date of the oldest part of the building is probably 1038. The tomb of the saint is pointed out; an ancient font deserves notice. St. Gildas is about 21 m. from Vannes. On the way to St. Gildas from Vannes, 3, the *Castle of Succinio* may be visited.

It is a fine and perfect feudal fortress, built 1260 by John the Red, Duke of Brittany. It has nearly the form of a pentagon flanked by 6 round towers. It was the birthplace of the Constable de Richemont, who defeated the English at Formigny.]

Between Carnac and Locmariaker a deep frith of the sea penetrates far inland, and is crossed half way by a ferry; the way is very intricate, from the number of paths, so as scarcely to be found without a guide, and the road is very bad. The distance, 8 m., is practicable only on foot.

The Ferry of Cherispere over this inlet is prettily situated, and commands a view of the little port of La Trinité in the bay of Crach.

A little to the W. of the ferry, near some salt-works, at the bottom of a shallow dell, is a rude monument to mark the grave of a royalist, shot on the spot, 1801.

The approach to Carnac is marked by the prominent Cairn, or *Tombelle de St. Michel*, so called from the chapel surmounting it. It is a cone of loose stones artificially heaped together, standing at the E. extremity of the great army of rocks of Carnac, of which it commands a view, as well as of the sea and promontory of Quiberon.

Carnac. Inn: H. des Voyageurs, an humble auberge.

The great *Celtic Monument of Carnac*, the most extensive in France, is situated about $\frac{3}{4}$ m. from this remote village, and is traversed by the road from Auray. In the midst of a wide heath, as dreary and blasted in aspect as that "near Forres," extends this brotherhood of grey stones,—rude blocks set on end, angular, showing no marks of polish, and hirsute with the long moss which has covered the hard surface of the granite, and marks the length of time they must have stood in their present position. At first sight it is difficult to distinguish any order, so many are overthrown, and the gaps left in the lines by depredations are so numerous and wide; indeed, every house and every wall in the vicinity seems to have been built out of this ready quarry. The great mass of the stones extends between 2 windmills. They are arranged in 11 lines, forming 10 avenues, with a curved row of 18 stones at one end, touching at its extremities the two outside rows.

The ranks are best preserved, and the stones are highest, near the farm called *Menec*. There are, it is said, not less than 12,000 stones, blocks of the granite which forms the basis of the country, and which is barely covered with soil, and in many places projects naked above it. None exceed 18 ft. in height, and a very large proportion are cubical masses not more than 3 ft. high. They give one the idea of a regiment of soldiers, and the tradition of the country respecting their origin is, that St. Cornely (Cornelius), hard pressed by an army of Pagans, fled to the sea-shore, but, finding no boat to further his escape, uttered a prayer, which converted his pursuers into stones. Of the numerous theories invented by learned antiquaries to account for the origin and object of these stones, several are not less absurd nor more probable than the legend just mentioned; none are satisfactory. The opinions perhaps least unworthy of consideration would suppose either that it was a burial-place on the site of some great battle-field, and that each stone marked a grave,

or that it was a great temple dedicated to serpent worship. It was probably connected with some of those rites of initiation which formed part of the Druidical religion, and were derived from the same source as the Greek Mysteries.

At *Erdevan*, about 8 m. W. of Carnac, and again at *St. Barbe*, between Carnac and Erdevan, there are similar assemblages of stones, but not so numerous. Some have maintained that these three systems of rude pillars were once united, but there is no evidence of this. The piles of stones invariably follow the same direction from E. to W. One can scarcely see Carnac without comparing it with Stonehenge; and it must be admitted that, in spite of the vast multitude of stones, the few and gigantic masses of Salisbury Plain are far more impressive than the long array of the petrified army on the heath of Morbihan. At Carnac there are no cross-stones raised on the top of the upright slabs, as at Stonehenge.

The *Peninsula of Quiberon* stretches 10 m. S. into the sea, a little to the W. of the village of Carnac. Its name is associated with melancholy recollections of the ill-contrived and ill-executed expedition, consisting of 6000 French emigrants in the pay of England, who were landed there from a British fleet 1795, and, after a futile attempt to break through the Republican armies opposed to them, were for the most part driven into the sea by General Hoche. The surprise, by Hoche, of Fort Penthièvre, which guards the neck of the peninsula, and of which the émigrés had made themselves masters on first landing, decided the fate of the expedition. Sombreuil, their brave leader, when expelled from it, drew up his little band on the farthest extremity of the sand, where they made the most determined resistance, so as to call down the admiration of their antagonists and fellow countrymen. Humbert, the republican general, advanced with a flag of truce, and promised that their lives should be spared if they laid down their arms. A storm prevented the

British fleet rendering them any assistance; one corvette alone for a time checked the Republicans by its destructive fire, and a few of the fugitives were brought off in the boats of the squadron; but many, including women and children, perished in the waves. 950 unfortunate men, most of them persons of rank or station, who capitulated on promise of amnesty, with their commander, Sombreuil, were, in spite of that, conveyed to Auray as prisoners of war, and shot there (see p. 148). The descent on Quiberon was an example of the danger of disgrace and failure which England runs by "waging a little war."

The road from Auray to Carnac is not good; the latter part is very bad.

Diligence, Auray to Nantes, in 12 hrs. There is nothing to note between Auray and

18 *Vannes.—Inn*: Hôtel du Commerce, tolerable. This town, capital of the Dépt. of Morbihan (population 12,000), is built at the extremity of a narrow inlet, branching out from the Gulf of Morbihan, and about 15 m. from the open sea. It possesses in an eminent degree the character of antiquity which distinguishes most Breton towns, in its narrow streets, overhanging houses, massive town walls and gates, but has no curiosities to detain the stranger. The portal of carved Kersanton stone, the towers of the *Cathedral*, and a tower in the centre of the town erroneously called *Tour du Connétable*, because Olivier de Clisson was said to have been confined in it 1387, are the only buildings worth mentioning. 3 or 4 old convents, suppressed at the Revolution, now serve for barracks and similar purposes.

The castle into which the Constable de Clisson was entrapped, under pretence of asking his opinion of the new fortifications, by John (IV.) de Montfort, who then locked the door upon him, and loaded him with chains, was the *Château de l'Hermine*, which was razed to the ground in the 16th centy. Clisson owed his life to the forbearance of the governor, Bazvalan, who (like King John's Hubert) pretended compliance with De Montfort's order to murder his prisoner, but, when his master's anger cooled, informed him of his captive's safety. Clisson was not released, however, without paying a heavy ransom.

A sailing-boat with a favourable wind will cross the Sea of Morbihan to Locmariaker, on the way to Carnac (p. 149), in about $2\frac{1}{2}$ hours; but as no conveyances are to be obtained at either of these places, most persons will prefer the land journey viâ Auray.

Excursion through the *Promontory of Rhuys*.

The pedestrian may walk by the Castle of Succinio (p. 150) to Sarzeau (where is an humble *Inn*), St. Gildas Abbey, and back to Sarzeau for the night; next day by Butte de Tumiac to Port Navalo, whence cross in a boat to Gâvr Innis and Locmariaker (see p. 149).

Diligences daily to Rennes (Rte. 45); to Brest; to Nantes.

Through a country abounding in heath and broom, we pass through

9 Theix, and

15 Muzillac, to

16 Roche Bernard, on the l. bank of the Vilaine, which is here crossed by a remarkably fine *Suspension Bridge* of iron wire, supported on 2 piers of granite masonry, each approached by 3 lofty arches of granite. The opening between the two points of suspension measures 626 ft., the elevation of the roadway above high-water mark 108 ft. In its general appearance it resembles the Menai bridge; it was constructed under the superintendence of M. Leblanc, the engineer des Ponts et Chaussées. It was completed 1839, and subjected to the trial of its strength which the French law requires, by placing 2 rows of 115 carts and carriages heavily laden on the carriageway, and of 117 barrows filled with stones on the footpath, which it stood without the least sympton of weakness.

The road leading to and from the bridge is well engineered, and leaves the town of Roche Bernard on one side. *Inn*: Hôtel Silvestre, tolerable, on the new road, ¾ m. S. of the bridge. Those who remember the tedious and dangerous ferry which this bridge replaces, and all the trouble and inconveniences of embarking and disembarking, will rejoice in the improvement.

There is nothing of interest beyond this; the country is very dreary, with few hills; the road in the Dépt. of the Loire Inférieure is only beginning to be macadamized.

19 Pont Château.

15 Le Moere. At Savenay, on the rt. of our road, in December, 1793, the last relics of that daring army of Vendéan peasants, which had crossed the Loire 6 weeks before 80,000 strong, now reduced to 8000 or 10,000, made a last stand against the Republicans, but their obstinate bravery was of little avail against overpowering numbers. They fought long after their ammunition was exhausted, even women taking part in the combat, but were at length cut to pieces or made prisoners, 3000 only escaping back into La Vendée.

11 Le Temple. Glimpses of the estuary of the Loire, running parallel with our road, are seen on the rt. Near Santron, through which the road passes, is the Château de Buron, one of the residences of Madame de Sévigné. The approach to Nantes is marked by the number of neat country houses.

23 NANTES (in Rte. 46).

ROUTE 45.

RENNES TO VANNES BY PLOERMEL, AND TO CARNAC.

92 kilom. = 57 Eng. m.
A *diligence* daily.
15 Mordelles.
20 Plélan.
24 Ploërmel (*Inn:* H. du Commerce), a town of 5207 Inhab.

In the *Parish Ch.*, a low and heavy structure of the 12th centy., are the monumental effigies in armour of Dukes John II. (1305) and III. (1341) of Brittany. They were brought from the church of the Carmelites, founded by John II., who had fought in Syria against the Infidels, and had visited Mount Carmel; the sculpture is good, and they are tolerably perfect: the church was destroyed at the Revolution. These statues are interesting examples of the costume and armour of the time. There is some painted glass in the church.

About 7 m. W. of Ploërmel is the Castle of Josselin (Rte. 42).

10 Roc St. André.

16 Pont Guillemet.

Beyond this, about 1 m. to the rt. of the road, is the ruined *Castle of Elven*, one of the best preserved fortresses of the middle ages in Brittany, built on the model, it is said, of some castle in Syria. It stands on a flat, surmounted by a lofty octagonal keep-tower. Elven is interesting to an Englishman, because young Henry of Richmond (afterwards Henry VII.) was shut up in it for many years, along with his uncle the Earl of Pembroke, by Francis II., Duke of Brittany. The two English fugitives, escaping from their own country after the battle of Tewkesbury, were driven by a storm on the coast of Brittany, and Henry remained a prisoner nearly 15 years, until 1484. when, escaping into France, he accepted the invitation of friends in England to supplant the tyrant Richard III.

18 *Vannes*. (Rte. 44: where the excursion to the *Druidical Monuments of Carnac* is also described.)

ROUTE 46.

LE MANS TO NANTES, BY ANGERS.

kilom.= Eng. m.
Diligence daily.
Le Mans is described in Rte. 34.

The road, on quitting Le Mans, crosses the Huisne just before it falls into the Sarthe, and then runs along the l. bank of that river as far as

16 Guécelard. On the outskirts of Le Mans, not far from the bridge over

the Huisne, the buffoon Scarron threw himself into the river, to conceal himself from the pursuit and taunts of the mob, whose derision he had excited by parading the streets during the Carnival tarred and feathered, by way of masquerading. The result of this frolic, so little becoming his position as canon of the cathedral, was, that he caught a rheumatism in his limbs which rendered him a cripple for life.

Maize begins to grow to the S. of Le Mans, but nowhere to the N. of that place.

7 Fouletourte.

The road descends into the pretty valley of the Loir (*N.B.*, not to be confounded with the Loire), a little before it reaches

19 La Flèche (*Inn:* La Poste), a town of 6500 Inhab., prettily situated in a country where vineyards begin to be cultivated with advantage. The large edifice, now the Ecole Militaire, was built by Henri IV. as a Jesuits' College, 1603, but turned into its present destination by Napoleon. The heart of Henri is still preserved in the church. The *Church of St. Thomas* is a heavy Romanesque edifice.

[20 m. N. W. of La Flèche is Sablé (*Inn:* Croix Verte, comfortable and moderate), "a beautiful little town on the Sarthe, with a château built by M. de Torcy, foreign minister in the reign of Louis XIV. (1696-1715), and nephew of Colbert, still in the Torcy family. Near Sablé are immense marble quarries. Anthracite *coal* is worked at La Ragotène."—*L.* About 2 m. beyond Sablé, ½ an hour's walk by the river side, is the *Abbey of Solesmes*, purchased since 1830 and re-occupied by a society of Benedictine monks, who devote themselves to study in this picturesque retreat. The church is remarkable for 4 groups of statues, called *Les Saintes de Solesmes*, enclosed in niches, each surrounded by a rich framework of architecture and sculpture, in a style of Gothic approaching to the Renaissance. The groups of statuary represent, 1. The Entombment of our Saviour; the head of Christ and the figure of the Magdalen are particularly well executed. Above the recess rises an ogee arch decorated with the richest foliage of thistles and mallows. It bears the date 1496. 2. Christ disputing with the Doctors; the figures, in the dress of the 15th centy., are somewhat coarse, reminding one of a Dutch painting. 3. On the l. of the choir, the Communion of the Virgin. 4. Death of the Virgin, in the N. transept. These sculptures have been variously attributed to Italian artists, and to the Frenchman Germain Pilon, but without authority. An altar in the S. transept has been lately fitted up with fragments of other statuary found among the ruins of the abbey. The stalls in the choir, carved with the genealogy of Christ, are worth notice.]

The road to Angers follows the valley of the Loir downwards, running at the foot of gentle hills covered with vineyards.

13 Duretal is a town of 1500 Inhab., overlooked by two picturesque embattled towers, part of a *Castle* built by Foulques Nera, Comte d'Anjou.

14 Suette.

The Loir now bends away from the road to the W., and 6 m. below this falls into the Sarthe.

On approaching Angers the road passes near some of the vast quarries of slate, which forms a principal production of the district.

19. ANGERS.—*Inns:* no good inn. Cheval Blanc, in the heart of the town, best;—H. le Roy;— H. de Londres, dirty and ill-conditioned.

Angers, chef-lieu of the Dépt. Maine et Loire, is situated on the Maine, called Mayenne in the upper part of its course, a little below the junction of the Sarthe with it, and about 5 m. above the influx of the Maine into the Loire. It has 33,000 Inhab. Modern improvements, the formation of a broad quay along the l. bank of the river, the substitution of tall, regular white stone houses, like those of the Rue Rivoli, for the old gable-faced cottage-built structures, have greatly innovated upon the thoroughly antique character which Angers previously bore. A broad formal boulevard, planted with young trees, replaces the old fortifications,—

"The flinty ribs of this contemptuous town;"
... "those sleeping stones,
That as a waist did girdle it about,
By this time from their fixed beds of lime
Have been dishabited." *King John.*

The "strong barred gates" are all down, and only one tower remains near the upper bridge of those "saucy walls." Black Angers, as it was called from the sombre hue of its buildings of slate, is now like an old coat with a modern trimming: but plunge into the midst of its labyrinth of buildings, scale its steep and narrow streets, many of them inaccessible to wheel carriages, and you will find traces enough of the Angers of olden time, the capital of Anjou, and residence of its dukes. In few towns of France will the antiquary, artist, or architect find a greater number of interesting antique churches and houses than here.

Most of the old houses are timber-framed, their fronts gable-faced, the roofs, and often fronts, covered with scales of slate, which abounds in the neighbourhood and forms the common building-stone, and many of the door and corner posts, the joists and cornices, bear rich Gothic carvings. The most venerable relic of antiquity is the *old Castle,* at the water-side, close to the suspension bridge. Its walls were originally washed by the waters of the Maine, until its moat was partly filled to give place to the new quay. If its size and preservation be jointly considered, it is perhaps the finest feudal castle in France. 17 colossal towers surround it; they are 70 to 80 ft. high, close set along the walls, shaped like dice-boxes, thick below, narrow waisted, and having bands of white stone let into the black rough slate of which they are built, so as to give them the appearance of being hooped. A broad and deep ditch isolates the castle from the rest of the town; it is entered by a massive gateway under a perfect portcullis, and within its portal is the furnace where lead and pitch were melted for the benefit of invaders. This castle was begun by Philippe-Auguste, and completed by Louis IX. It serves at present for a prison, barrack, and dépôt of powder. The part which served as a palace of the Dukes of Anjou, overlooking the river, is now in ruins, but shows the architecture of the Renaissance. It stood between the high tower called *Du Moulin,* because it once supported a windmill, and that called *Du Diable,* because close to it was the fearful Oubliette, down which criminals were cast alive. From this tower there is a capital view of the town, its spires and other buildings, of the river and its bridges; while a slight glimpse of the Loire also, deep set in its distant valley, may be gained. There is a neat chapel, now filled with fire-arms, showing, in the delicate tracery of its windows, a good example of Gothic. Beside it is a small building flanked with turrets, in which, it is said, King René of Provence and Anjou was born. The view from the terrace outside the castle-gate is less extensive, but nearly as good, as that from within the walls, and on the whole the castle is more imposing from without than interesting within.

On one side of the open space surrounding the castle stands a handsome modern building, originally *L'Académie d'Equitation.* Mr. Pitt (afterwards Lord Chatham) and the Duke of Wellington received part of their education at the military college here, now removed to Saumur, which occupied this edifice, still called *L'Académie.* The Duke was here one year. It has been converted since the Revolution into a caserne de cavalerie and dépôt de remonte. No trace or tradition is preserved of either of these great men, of whose education it may be said "fas est et ab hoste doceri."

The Cathedral of St. Maurice is everywhere conspicuous from its elevated position and its delicate tapering twin spires, whose effect is somewhat marred by thrusting between them an ugly pavilion, an addition of the Renaissance (1540). The W. portal, a work of the 12th centy., is remarkable for the richness and good preservation of the sculptures surrounding its elegant early-pointed arch; they retain indeed even their colouring. On either side are 4 saints, male and female; above, the curved niches are filled with smaller statues, angels, &c., while the tympanum is occupied by the Saviour, surrounded by the attributes of the 12 Apostles. The workmanship is good, the faces expressive, the draperies elaborate, but the whole displays the stiff style of Byzantine art of the period. Higher up, in a row of niches, are 8 statues of Dukes of Anjou, later in date (15th centy.) and inferior in execution. On the l. hand as you enter, passing from below the carved organloft, is an antique bénitier of oblong form, in verde antique, supported on lions, a Byzantine work of the Lower Empire; it was brought from the East, and presented to the church by King René. The church consists of a very long nave without aisles (12th cent.), each division of the side wall being a wide pointed arch resting on the ground without pillars, and an upper arch rising from engaged groups of pillars having Romanesque capitals, enclosing a pair of narrow circular-headed windows. The greater part of these windows, as well as those of the nave and choir, are filled with painted glass of the richest colour and very old (13th centy.), forming one of the chief ornaments of the church. This and other churches in the Angevine style are destitute of triforium or clerestory. The choir and transepts are short, the E. end is multangular. In the choir (end of 12th cent.), on the l. as you look towards the apse, is a splendid Flamboyant doorway. Both transepts (1225) terminate with fine wheel windows, the other windows are pointed, and below these along the wall runs a rich pointed arcade. The nave is about 80 ft. high, and nearly 54 ft. wide, stone vaulted. Local historians lay great stress on its roof being supported without flying buttresses, but their place is supplied by huge clumsy square piers at least 8 ft. by 10 square, and retaining the same thickness up to the roof, raised outside between each pair of windows and at the angles of the transepts, and thus the wonder is removed. Margaret of Anjou was buried in St. Maurice, but her tomb was destroyed at the Revolution.

Not far from the cathedral is the *Musée*, placed in a building erected by an intendant of the province, afterwards converted into the Séminaire, and added to in the time of Louis XIV. Its cloister and winding staircase are curious examples of the latest Gothic style.

It contains a large collection of mediocre paintings, mostly of the modern French school. Among them is placed a *Vase* of antique Egyptian porphyry, obtained by King René from the East, which for a long time passed for one of the water-pots used at the marriage feast of Cana. It bears 2 bearded masks carved on it, and is broken, which is not surprising considering its thinness. Here is a fine bust of Napoleon by *Canova*, in marble, condemned to be broken at the Restoration, but saved by being hid in a garret. One room is filled with casts from the works of the living French sculptor *David*, given by him to his native town. His statues of Guttemberg, inventor of printing, for Strasburg, of General Foy in a Roman dress, of Armand Carrel in loose pantaloons plaited round the waist, of the Greek girl at the tomb of Marco Botzaris; his busts of Göthe, Hahnemann the homœopathist, and Jeremy Bentham, appear best worth notice. He has also executed a series of medallion heads of celebrated persons of the 19th century.

The Museum of *Natural History*, situated in the upper story of the building, is reached by a corkscrew stair remarkable for its lightness and its singular groined roof. The collection is exceedingly well arranged and named. The geology of the department is illustrated in a series of specimens by themselves. Among a few antiquities is the crosier of Robert d'Arbrissal, founder of Fontevrault, found in that Abbey; it bears a semipagan representation of St. Michael and the dragon, of gold (?) partly enamelled. The shoes of Joanne de Laval, 2nd wife of King René, high-heeled and ornamented with open work; also an aërolite, which fell in one of the fauxbourgs of Angers 1822, deserve attention. The *Library* possesses some curious old MSS.

Not far from the Musée is the ruined church of *Toussaints*, attached to a convent now converted into a *Dépôt des Subsistances Militaires*. It is an elegant pointed building, and almost identical in style with the early English. It is a cross church without aisles, with lancet windows, richly cut capitals, and corbels, from which springs the roof destroyed at the Revolution. The E. window is a wheel, apparently of later date.

The massive and stately tower of *St. Aubin*, in the early pointed style, unfinished and surmounted with a conical roof of slate, is now converted into a shot-tower. Not far from it is the *Préfecture*, on the site of the ancient convent of St. Aubin; along the corridor on the l. hand, now released from a coating of plaster, runs a colonnade of florid Norman architecture, of very early date, and of curious and elaborate workmanship. The small round arches rest alternately on piers faced with pilasters, and on detached pillars arranged in 2 rows, each 5 deep. All the pillars, cornices, and mouldings of the arches are elaborately and sharply carved, very perfect, and no two alike. The mouldings running round the arches consist of bearded heads, monsters, animals, fish, &c. In the midst is a circular portal, the lower part of which is sunk rather below the surface of the ground, supported on cut columns of varied patterns, and surmounted by a series of Runic bands, cords, and foliage, each confined to one stone, and radiating from a common centre. Next to this is a double arch ornamented with fresco paintings instead of sculpture, the subjects being Herod on his Throne, the Massacre of the Innocents, the Temple of Jerusalem, and the Nativity and Adoration of the Magi, who are seen on horseback approaching Bethlehem. The style of drawing bears a near resemblance to the tapestry of Bayeux; the colours are very perfect. These arches formed part of the Refectory of the convent.

The *Eglise de St. Martin*, now converted into a magazine of fagots, and piled up to the roof with them, so as to be scarcely visible, will yet interest the antiquary from its age and structure, though the nave, the oldest part, is nearly all destroyed, and the rest is probably not older than the 12th and 13th centuries. The stone dome covering the central tower rests upon thick round pillars set in the 4 inner angles of the walls which support the tower. Its windows are round-headed and long. The choir (date end of 12th or beginning of 13th cent.) ends in a polygonal apse.

At the extremity of the town to the N. is the *Church of St. Serge*, remarkable for a choir built 1050 by the monk Vulgrin, who became abbot, supported on 6 columns of peculiar lightness and height, from whose freely cut capitals rises an elegant pointed roof; behind it is a square Lady Chapel. The style indicates the transition from Romanesque to early pointed. The windows are without tracery, for the most part round-headed, enclosed within pointed arches. The transepts seem of a much older date than the choir; the nave is in the late Gothic of the 15th centy. St. Serge is entered by a vestibule or atrium.

Here is a finely-carved spiral staircase of wood; every panel contains a different sculpture and composition.

In the same quarter of the town is the *Jardin des Plantes*, an agreeable walk in hot weather under shady trees, near to the *Séminaire*, a vast edifice.

Among the more interesting specimens of ancient domestic architecture, with which the streets of Angers abound, may be mentioned a corner house, in the Place behind the cathedral, adorned with curious carvings in wood; that called *Hôtel des Marchands* in the Rue Baudrière; and another in the Rue du Figuier, known as the *Hôtel des Ducs d'Anjou*, for what reason is not evident, since René, the last Duke of Anjou, died 1480, and this building cannot be older than the 16th centy., and is in the style of Francis I.'s time, with more of Italian than of Gothic in the composition of its architecture.

The square turrets, or projecting oriels, at its angles are singular. In the Rue St. Sang is a house called *Abraham*, and another called *Adam* in the little Place St. Maurice, end of Rue St. Aubin, deserving notice.

The *wire Suspension Bridge* close to the castle over the Maine fell in 1849, during the march of a regiment of infantry across it; the greater part were precipitated into the river and nearly 250 men were drowned.

In the suburb of *la Doutre* (beyond, or on the further (or rt.) bank of the Maine) are several buildings deserving notice for their antiquity. The *Eglise de la Trinité* is a Romanesque building probably of the 11th and 12th centuries. It consists of a long nave without aisles, having in the side walls a series of apsidal recesses under pointed arches. The choir, very shallow, and formed of a central and 2 side apses, is separated from the nave by a wall pierced with a pointed arch, which contracts the view of the high altar, but serves as a support to the *Tower*, which is square below, octagonal above, and very elegant.

Close to this church, indeed touching it, is a second equally ancient and in a nearly similar style, *l'Eglise de Ronceray*, once attached to a famous nunnery founded in the 10th century by Fulk Count of Anjou, who placed under the rule of its abbess the whole suburb. It is now included in the extensive range of buildings forming the *Ecole des Arts et Métiers*. The church serves as a chapel for the students; it is plain excepting some rich Romanesque arches and pillars.

On the same side of the river, a little higher up, is the *Hospice St. Jean*, founded by Henry II. King of England and Duke of Anjou, 1153. The great hall, said to be of that date, is a fine apartment, lofty and airy, its groined and pointed roof supported on 2 rows of light pillars. Here the beds of the patients are ranged in rows, the males separated from the females by a low partition. The office of nurses is performed by nuns; the whole is kept very orderly, the linen-closet particularly neat. The cloisters between the great hall and the church are partly in the Romanesque style; double pillars support the arches; a round portal with deep mouldings leads into the *Chapel*.

A decayed Barn near the hospital is still older than it. It is Norman, with 3 aisles, like old Westminster Hall, and deserves to be drawn.—*F. P.*

At the opposite extremity of the Suburb Doutre, below the suspension bridge, near the Nantes road, is the vast *Nunnery du Bon Pasteur*, surrounded by high walls. The sisters keep a school for females.

Very extensive *Boulevards*, planted with trees and lined with some very handsome houses, the Mairie, &c., occupy the site of the old walls, and communicate with a wide open space for the exercise of troops, called *Champ de Mars*, traversed by the road to Saumur. Some of the houses about it bore until lately the marks of bullets fired in the attack of Angers by the Vendéan army, 90,000 strong, 1793.

The forces of King John laid waste Brittany in 1199, and to that period we must refer the scene in Shakspeare "Before the walls of Angiers," where the citizens are summoned by both the rival kings—"Ye men of Angiers, open wide your gates."

Angers occupies a fortunate position near the mouth of 3 navigable rivers, in a country producing lime, coal, and slate.

Angers is famed for its *nursery* gardens; there are not less than 30.

The neighbourhood abounds in *Slate Quarries*, which employ between 2000 and 3000 men, and supply a large part of France. They furnish 80 millions of slates yearly, which are exported to the value of 1½ million of francs per annum.

The most considerable, *Le Grand Carreau*, is about 4 m. off, a little to the l. of the road to Saumur. It is nearly 400 ft. (105 mètres) deep, and occupies an area of 4000 mètres. Besides the yawning open excavation, a considerable cavern, approached by a horizontal gallery on one side of the quarry, has been driven under ground. It is a grand sight, like an underground cathedral, and well worth a visit. It is approached by vertical ladders, and frail extracting machinery overhangs the precipice. At times serious slips, or *éboulements*, produce very dangerous avalanches of rock.

10 m. from Angers, beyond the Loire at Pont de Cé, is the interesting *Château de Brissac*.

2 *Steamers* daily to Nantes. (See Rte. 58.)

Diligences daily to Le Mans (Rte. 46); to Alençon, Rennes, Brest, L'Orient, Vannes, Laval, Choles.

Railways to Paris by Tours; to Nantes; to Saumur.

The post-road to Nantes quits Angers by the Suburb Doutre, and, leaving the Mayenne on the l. hand, reaches the Loire at

17 St. George-sur-Loire.
  8 Champtocé.
13 Varades. ⎫
13 Ancenis. ⎬ *Railway* described in Rte. 58.
  9 Oudon. ⎪
15 La Seilleraye. ⎭

14 NANTES STATION.—*Inns:* H. de France, in the Place Graslin, close to the theatre, clean and good; H. des Colonies and du Commerce, 2 hotels united into one, and very good, comfortable, and cheap; H. des Voyageurs, Rue Molière, good ; H. de L'Europe, reasonable ; H. de Paris, Rue Boileau, good.

Nantes, the ancient residence of the Dukes of Brittany, when that province was independent—which disputed with Rennes the title of capital of the duchy, now chef-lieu of the Dépt. de la Loire Inférieure—is situated on the l. bank of the Loire, at the influx into it from the N. of the Erdre; the junction of the two rivers being in the middle of the town. The Sèvre (Nantaise) from the S. flows into the Loire a little below Nantes. There are at least 16 bridges in the town over these various streams. It is distant about 40 m. from the ocean, and is a flourishing seaport, the fourth in rank and population in France, numbering 77,992 Inhab. Though less prosperous since the loss of St. Domingo to France, and of late outstripped by Havre as a port, it has remained nearly stationary in population and commercial prosperity for the last 50 years: it is still the seat of much respectable opulence and active industry. As a town it is one of the handsomest and most pleasing in France. Its fine *Quais*, extending about 2 m. along the Loire, and on both sides of the Erdre, and the wide open space left by these two rivers, enlivened with small craft, remind the traveller somewhat of the busy aquatic towns of Holland—Amsterdam and Rotterdam, and give a very cheerful character to Nantes, which is, besides, far less dirty than most French towns. In the new quarters it has streets lined with houses not unworthy of Paris. The Place Royale and Rue d'Orléans contain the chief shops, while the old quarters, belonging to the capital of the ancient duchy, abound in picturesque houses, gable-faced and overhanging the narrow streets. Those who admire and would seek out picturesque bits of street architecture, now fast disappearing even from the old town under modern improvements, must penetrate the Rues de la Poissonnerie, where the house "aux Enfans Nantais," so called from the carved figures of the martyrs St. Donatien and St. Rogatien, at the corner of the Place du Change, deserves particular notice: it dates from the 15th centy. There are other old houses in the Rues du Calvaire and de la Juiverie. In the Rue de la Boucherie is a house said to have been inhabited by Anne of Brittany.

The most prominent and remarkable edifice is the *Cathedral of St. Pierre*, externally an unsightly pile, from the unfinished towers not rising much higher than the roof. The three lofty portals of its W. front, however, are striking for size and the great number of small bas-reliefs and other sculptures adorning them. It was begun 1434, and finished about the end of the centy. The *nave*, of the same age, "a remarkably fine structure of admirable proportions and great effect, in pure Flamboyant style," is very imposing on account of the great elevation of its roof, 120 ft. above the pavement, and the elegance of its arches; but its windows are destitute of tracery. The *modern* wood-carving in some of the side chapels, and the stone-work of the organ-loft decorated with pendants, a delicate work of the 16th centy., deserve notice. Attached to this noble nave is a plain Romanesque choir, inferior in height and plain in style, probably of the 11th centy.: it was already enclosed in new walls, corresponding with the nave, preparatory to pulling down the old structure, when the works were stopped for want of funds near the latter end of the 15th centy. The solitary transept on the S. side, which had been alone completed, is now partitioned off, and serves to contain the splendid *Monument* (removed from the suppressed Carmelite convent) of Francis II., last Duc de Bretagne, and his wife, Marguerite de Foix, raised to their memory by his daughter, Anne of Brittany. It is a splendid work of art in the style of the Renaissance, executed by a Bas Breton artist, Michel Colomb, a native of St. Pol de Léon, who preceded Jean Goujon. It was fortunately secreted at the Revolution, and thus preserved from destruction. It is a large altar tomb of marble, black, white, and red, raised to a height of 5 ft. Upon it repose the recumbent figures of Francis and his wife; three angels support their heads, and their feet rest on a lion and greyhound. In the four corners stand statues as large as life in white marble: of Justice, with sword and scales, said to be a portrait of the Duchess Anne; of Power, strangling a dragon (heresy), which she draws out of a tower; she is attired with helmet and breastplate, and has a scarf wound round her arm: Wisdom or Prudence, double-faced, bears a mirror and a compass; and Temperance holds a lantern in one hand and a bit in the other, as attributes. These statues are well designed, and executed with great delicacy, which is particularly conspicuous in the draperies. Along the sides of the tomb small statues of the 12 Apostles are ranged in niches, and below them are figures of mourners in coloured marble. The patron saints of the Duke and Duchess, St. Francis d'Assisi and St. Margaret, stand at their feet, St. Louis and Charlemagne at their head. The remains of the illustrious dead, for whom this splendid tomb was raised, having been torn up and scattered in 1793, the body of the Constable de Richemont, one of the generals who contributed to drive the English out of France in the reign of Charles VII., was deposited within it in 1815. The N. transept and the choir of this ch. are in progress of completion, to correspond with the nave, and it is proposed to pull down the old choir.

Beyond the cathedral a broad and much-frequented promenade, occupying the site of the old fortifications, and forming a sort of boulevard, extends from the Loire to the Erdre, under the names *Cours St. Pierre* and *Cours St. André*. The former is approached by a broad and stately flight of steps from the Loire, and is ornamented with statues of the Duchess Anne and the three Breton heroes,— the constables Du Guesclin, Clisson, and De Richemont. Between the two walks stands a *Column* raised to the memory of Louis XVI., and surmounted by his statue; but since 1830 made to commemorate a combat between some young men of the town with the troops of the line, in which 10 of the former were killed, during the July Revolution. The brass plate which records this states that "Des ouvriers Anglais ont fait graver cette inscription." 'Tis a pity English workmen cannot mind their own business, without meddling with the politics of a foreign country.

The *New Church of St. Nicholas*, from designs of M. Lassus, well deserves attention: it is a grand Gothic edifice still in progress, but the choir is completed.

The *Castle*, a massive and venerable edifice of the 14th centy., partly modernized in the 16th by the Duc de Mercœur during the wars of the League, flanked with bastions, still bearing on them the cross of Lorraine, stands at the extremity of the Cours St. Pierre, on the margin of the Loire, surrounded on the land side by a deep fosse. Its massive round towers are built of slate and granite: a portcullis still defends its entrance, and the interior contains several constructions of the 16th centy., in the latest Gothic, the windows surmounted with canopies. In one is a curious spiral staircase. Most of the Kings of France, from Charles VIII. downwards, resided for a time within its walls. The powder magazine is said to have been the *Chapel* in which Anne of Brittany was married to Louis XII. (?), thus becoming for the second time Queen of France. She certainly was born here, and made the castle her residence. In this castle Henri IV. signed the *Edit de Nantes* for the protection of the Protestants in 1598, revoked, to the injury and stain of France, by Louis XIV.

In 1654 it was the prison of the Cardinal de Retz, who escaped by letting himself down by a rope from the bastion de Mercœur into a boat moored in the Loire, which at that time, and until the present quai was formed, washed the castle walls. The attention of the sentinel meanwhile was taken off by a bottle of wine given him to drink, and his eye was deceived by the cardinal's red cloak and hat slipped off and hung over the battlements. De Retz, reaching the shore by means of the boat, instantly mounted a horse provided for him by his friends, which, however, quickly threw him and dislocated his shoulder. In spite of this accident and the pain it caused, he rode to a place of safety, the Château de Beaupreau, whence he effected his escape through Spain to Rome. Madame de Sévigné describes her visit to the castle in 1648, shortly after, and the Duchess de Berri was shut up in it previous to her removal to Blaye. That adventurous Princess, after having long encouraged disaffection and fermentation in Brittany and La Vendée, was finally detected, after a concealment of 5 months within the city, which had eluded the vigilance of the Police, Nov. 1832, in the *house No. 3, Rue Haute du Château*, facing the castle, which belonged to two ladies, named Du Guigny, zealous partisans of the Bourbon cause. Her presence in this house had been betrayed to the government by a Jew, named Deutz, previously a confidant of the duchess and her friends, and a party of soldiers and police were despatched thither instantly. They searched the whole building from top to bottom, but found her not. Confiding, however, in their information, a party of gendarmes was left behind to keep watch. Some of them, posted in a garret, remained a whole day beside a fire which they had lighted, when on a sudden they were startled by voices and the sound of kicks, proceeding from an iron door which formed the back of the chimney, and, to the surprise of the soldiers, out scrambled four persons—the duchess, a lady, and MM. de Menars and Guibourg, who had passed 16 hours in a secret hole or hiding-place, entered by a door 20 inches wide, and too low for a man to stand upright in. Not only this oppressive confinement, but even the heat of the fire, was endured patiently, and without the slightest noise, until they were nearly suffocated, and the duchess's dress, entirely scorched by the iron door being heated red hot, was on the point of catching fire.

Nantes possesses a *Museum of Paintings*, rather above the average of provincial collections, though a large portion are copies; situated in the upper part of the Cloth Hall, Rue de l'Arche-Sèche. The greater part were collected by one M. Cacault, of this town. Among the curiosities may be specified a head of a Crusader painted by *Canova*; an old church painting of a Holy Family, on two shutters; a head of Christ, brought from the cathedral; portrait of Queen Elizabeth (? artist unknown); portraits of the children of Henri II., by *Janet*; a Bull, by *Brascassat*, a modern artist, good. Here is a copy of Napoleon's bust by *Canova*.

Travellers who have leisure to devote any time to a *Library* will find that of Nantes, above the Halle aux Grains, Quai Brancas, an especially rich collection of 30,000 volumes. A MS. copy of the Cité de Dieu of St. Augustin, of the year 1375, is remarkable for its beautiful miniatures.

The *Archives*, deposited in the Préfecture, contain a mass of curious documents relating to the history of Brittany; many ancient charters of Abbeys, &c., and the trial of that most infamous of criminals, Gilles de Retz, Maréchal de France, who was burnt on the Chaussée de la Madeleine (Rte. 58). It is in Latin, and will not bear translation.

In the *Musée d'Histoire Naturelle*, Rue du Port Communeau, may be seen a collection illustrating the geology of the department, formed by the late M. Dubuisson; besides several fragments of antiquity found in the neighbourhood, and a mummy, presented by the Egyptian traveller Caillaud, who is a native of Nantes.

A handsome new *Palais de Justice* was finished 1852.

An Arcade called *Passage Pommeraye* leads by a flight of iron steps from the Rue Crébillon to the Rue de la Fosse.

The *Quais*, lined on the one side by handsome houses, and on the other fringed with shipping, present a lively scene, and form an agreeable walk about 2 m. long (at least in the lower part, where they are gravelled). An Englishman, in traversing them, may remember with some interest that it was at this port that the young Pretender embarked on the expedition of 1745, in a fast-sailing brig, the Doutelle, provided by one Walsh, a French subject settled at Nantes, who accompanied him. He was disguised as a student of the Scotch college at Paris, and for better concealment had allowed his beard to grow. On the quais are situated the Halle aux Grains and the *Bourse*, which is not remarkable for excellence of architecture. The Quai de la Fosse is lined by a fine row of trees, reminding one a little of the Boompjes of Rotterdam. Near its lower end, where the shipbuilders' yards commence, in which the steamers for the Loire are constructed, is a building, insignificant in itself, but remarkable for its associations, and they are melancholy, called *Salorges*. built as an entrepôt for colonial merchandise, and still serving as a warehouse. Who has not heard of the *Noyades* and republican marriages; the invention of Carrier, the most detestable, perhaps, of the monsters of the revolution, when sated with single murders by the guillotine, and thirsting for more blood, and the excitement of executions on a large scale? It was in front of the Salorges that they took place, and that building served as a temporary place of confinement for the miserable victims, who were dragged hence and put on board barges (gabarres) furnished with a sliding valve (soupape) or trap-door in their bottom. These boats, when towed into the middle of the river, and deserted by the crews, were sunk with their load of 20 or 30 human beings, by pulling from the shore a cord attached to the valve. To prevent the possibility of escape for the strong swimmer, or poor wretch who might be cast ashore alive by the current, armed men of the bloody band called Compagnie de Marat, composed of the most abandoned wretches whom the lowest dens in Nantes could pour forth, were stationed on the banks to fire on those who rose to the surface, while others, armed with swords, cut off the hands and fingers of such as struggled to reach the boats. As many as 600 human beings perished on one day; the total number of persons thus destroyed has never been correctly ascertained, but 25 of these Noyades or executions by water are known to have taken place, and the number who perished has been variously estimated at 6000 or 9000! At first the wholesale butchery was perpetrated at night, but, emboldened by impunity, and supported by a portion of the citizens, almost exclusively of the class of little tradesmen, the tyrants did not hesitate to immolate their victims in broad day. The most atrocious feature in these massacres is the number of women and of young children who were thus consigned to eternity, without the possibility of having committed any offence, by the exulting savages who then ruled the people's destinies. When a remonstrance was made against the murder of the children, "Ce sont des louveteaux, il faut les détruire,— Ce sont des vipères, il faut les étouffer," were Carrier's answers. The experiment of the Noyades was first tried on 24 priests condemned to transportation (déportation). " Le decret de déportation a été exécuté verticalement," was Carrier's boast. The Mariages Républicains, as another refinement of cruelty was called in mockery, consisted in binding together a man and woman, back to back, stripped naked, keeping them exposed for an hour, and then hurling them into the current of "la baignoire nationale," as the bloodhounds termed the Loire. That river, as it were indignant at crimes scarcely paralleled in the history of the world, threw back upon its banks, at each returning tide, the corpses with which it was choked, until the air became pestilential, and its very water and fish poisonous. When Carrier was at length called to account for his crimes, which, however, had been connived at, if not approved, by the Convention a short while before, and asked for proofs of the accusations against him, he was answered, "Vous me demandez des preuves? faites donc refluer la Loire." But these are only a part of the revolutionary atrocities committed at Nantes: to the victims of the Noyades must be added those who perished by the guillotine, by disease, famine, and terror in the prisons, and, above all, by the fusillades, which took place day after day on the Plaine de Sainte Mauve, where, at one time, 500 children, the eldest not more than 14, were mowed down by musketry, and where deep ditches, dug for the purpose, were filled with corpses heaped confusedly one over the other. The population of Nantes, which amounted in 1790 to 81,000, was reduced to 75,000 in 1800, and the number who were slaughtered in 1793 belonging to the town and surrounding country is estimated at 30,000. It is painful to describe these horrors, but they form an integral part of the history of Nantes, and that which is here detailed is only a sample; they might be greatly expanded.

The Vendéan war has also left some sad souvenirs at Nantes. In the attack of the town by the Vendéan forces on the 29th June, 1793, their leader, the gentle Cathelineau (the cárter), was mortally wounded in penetrating into the *Place Viarme,* now the cattle-market, and his fall was the cause of their retreat. Not far from this spot another of their generals, Charette, was shot, at the corner of the Rue de la Miséricorde, April, 1796.

Fouché, the police minister, Duc d'Otrante, Marshal of France, regicide, and minister of Louis XVIII. in 1814, was born at Nantes.

The *New Quarter* of the town, the West End of Nantes, was commenced 1784, by M. Graslin, ancien fermier-général, after whom the Place containing the theatre is called. He seems to have exhausted the Biographie Universelle for names to the adjoining streets; among them appear the Rue Jean-Jacques, Rue Racine, Rue Franklin, Rue Crébillon, &c. The houses are built of white stone from the neighbourhood of Saumur.

The commerce of Nantes, though no longer what it was, is still of great value; in 1836 it was carried on by 458 vessels, but more than $\frac{1}{2}$ of them were of less than 100 tons. Owing to the want of water in the Loire abreast of the town, vessels of more than 200 tons burthen are obliged to unload at Paimbœuf (p. 164), 24 m. lower down, near its mouth.

A *Canal* is in progress to connect Nantes with Brest by the Erdre; it will be about 230 m. long when finished.

The importations consist of sugar, coffee, cotton, and other colonial produce. Much corn and flour is exported to England since 1849.

Nantes is gradually changing from a commercial to a manufacturing town. The most considerable manufacture is that of cotton-yarn; in 1837 there were 16 mills in the vicinity of the town.

There is a singular manufacture here of preserved dinners ready cooked (Conserves Alimentaires), prepared by the firm Colin et Comp^{ie}, Rue de Salorges, No. 9, which sends forth, hermetically sealed, all kinds of provisions, so as to be capable of perfect preservation in all climates, and for any length of time. 150,000 boxes of young peas and 800,000 boxes of sardines (pilchards) are embalmed in one season, and 8 oxen can be cooked at once in a single boiler. Roasting is carried on by heated air, and boiling by steam, in a kitchen roofed with glass. The proprietor of the establishment employs in the autumn 800 persons in curing and packing sardines alone, and monopolizes all the green peas which come to market in early spring to supply his wants.

The suburb of Nantes on the S. side of the Loire is spread over a series of islands, formed by the branches of that river and the Sèvre, connected together by no less than 6 bridges in one line, over all of which the roads to Bordeaux and Clisson pass.

Consuls from Great Britain and the United States reside here.

The French *Protestant Ch.* is in the Rue des Carmélites, in the chapel of the former convent. (*N.B.* About to be rebuilt.)

The *Poste aux Lettres* is in the Passage Pommeraye.

Prosper Sebire, bookseller, Rue Crébillon, No. 17, has a number of views, maps, guides, &c., relating to Nantes: a capital plan of Nantes, price 1 fr.

Fiacres stand for hire in the principal squares.

Omnibuses (said to be a Nantais invention, transferred from this to Paris) run along the Ligne des Ponts from the Place du Commerce to the Pont de Permil, and along the quays from the Bourse to the Chantiers de Construction.

Diligences daily to Le Mans; to Brest, 2 hrs.—Rennes, 3—Bordeaux, 4—Poitiers—to Bourbon Vendée, 2.

Railways to Angers and Tours.

Steamers daily ascend the Loire to Angers in 7 or 8 hrs., starting from the Quai du Port Maillard. *Steamers* down the Loire to Paimbœuf daily; and to St. Nazaire when the high tides permit; to Bordeaux 3 times a month; to Lorient and Quimper once a week.

Steamer on the Erdre to Nort starts from the Quai Céneray, behind the Préfecture (Rte. 41)—a pleasant excursion of one day there and back.

Environs of Nantes.—The immediate vicinity of the town displays great marks of opulence and prosperity, in its numerous and neat white villas, many of them quite in the English style, and in the great number of factory chimneys, many of them new.

About 5 m. S.W. of Nantes extends the *Lake de Grand Lieu*.

The excursion most commonly recommended to a stranger is that to *Clisson*, the Richmond of Nantes, 18 m. S. of the town, on the borders of La Vendée, described in Rte. 60. It is a pretty spot, though its beauties have been considerably exaggerated by local enthusiasts. You may go thither by the omnibus in the morning, visit the castle and all its curiosities, and return by the same conveyance at 7 P.M. But as this may leave the traveller a prey to ennui for several hours after exhausting the sights of Clisson, it is even possible to hire a cabriolet, and see Tiffauges, returning to Clisson in time for the omnibus.

The Loire below Nantes

Is navigated by steam-vessels, but with caution, on account of the numerous sand-banks.

1. A little below Nantes the Sèvre Nantaise enters the Loire.

On the island of *Indret*, 7 m. below Nantes, the French government have an establishment for the construction of steam-engines. More than 800 workmen are employed here. The steam-engines turned out here are very bad, far inferior to those made by private establishments. Indret is well situated at the mouth of the Loire, so as to have a speedy communication, safe from cruisers in time of war, with the great dockyards of Brest, Lorient, and Rochefort.

The estuary of the Loire is 3 m. broad abreast of

1. Paimbœuf (30 m. below Nantes). This place may be regarded as the outport of Nantes, since large vessels above 200 tons burthen stop here and discharge their cargoes into lighters (gabarres). The loss of St. Domingo, and the long-continued wars under Napoleon, reduced the population of this

town from 9000 to 4000, which it does not exceed at present.

2 *Steamers* ply daily to Nantes in 4 hrs. *Coaches* go hence to the watering-place of *Pornic*, 12 m. S. of Paimbœuf, situated on the shore of the bay of Bourgneuf, opposite the island of Noirmoutiers, the last retreat of the Vendéan bands. Comfortable accommodation is to be had in the Etablissement des Bains. The town was burnt in the Vendéan war. An old castle overlooks its little fishing-port.

ROUTE 47.

DREUX TO ARGENTAN, BY L'AIGLE.

Verneuil. (See p. 123.)
14 Chaudé.
8 L'Aigle—the scene of the frolic between the Conqueror's sons, when William and Henry threw the water over Robert. Here are 2 rather curious *Churches.*
16 St. Lanburge.

The road passes by a great government stud (Haras) and through a forest.
16 Nonan.
22 Argentan (in Rte. 29).

SECTION III.

ORLEANOIS. — TOURAINE. — RIVER LOIRE. — LA VENDEE.—
POITOU. — SAINTONGE.

ROUTE	PAGE
48 Paris to Orleans	168
49 Paris to *Orleans* (RAILWAY)	169
50 Rouen to Orleans by Chartres	175
51 Paris to *Sceaux*—RAILWAY	175
52 THE LOIRE (A).—*Gien* to Orleans	176
53 THE LOIRE (B).—Orleans to Tours, by *Blois* and *Amboise.*—RAILWAY. [Châteaux of *Chambord* and *Chénonceaux*]	177
54 Chartres to Tours, by *Vendôme*	191
56 Tours to *Loches* and Châteauroux	191
57 Tours to Saumur, by *Chinon* and Fontevrault	193
58 THE LOIRE (C).—Tours to Nantes, by *Saumur* and Angers (RAILWAY)	195
60 Nantes to Poitiers, by *Clisson*	204
61 Saumur to Saintes and Bordeaux	207
62 Nantes to Bordeaux, by *Bourbon Vendée*, *Rochelle*, *Rochefort*, and *Saintes*	208
64 Tours to Bordeaux, by *Poitiers* and *Angoulême*—RAILWAY	213
65 Poitiers to Châteauroux, by *St. Savin*, *Montmorillon*	222
66 Poitiers to Rochefort by *Niort*	223

INTRODUCTORY SKETCH OF THE COUNTRY.

ARRIVED on the borders of the Loire, which divides France nearly in the centre, the traveller already finds himself amidst sunny landscapes, under the influence of the more genial climate of the south. The provinces bordering on that great river—Touraine, Orléanois, Anjou, Poitou—have been styled "the garden of France;" and the golden vineyards, the blooming orchards, the yellow cornfields (especially those of La Beauce, the granary of France), and the acacia hedges bear testimony to the facile bounty of Nature. But little pains have been taken to improve her gifts; an ornamental garden or pleasure-ground is rarely seen: the earth seems to bring forth abundantly with less than the average amount of painstaking: "c'est le pays de rire et de ne rien faire." The Loire, which forms its chief feature, is decidedly inferior in beauty to the Seine. In Touraine its banks are flat and monotonous, and it is only after passing Tours that it becomes really picturesque. Near Saumur it is a romantic stream; and from thence, with slight interruptions, nearly all the way to Nantes, the "considerable boldness of its banks, the richness of the culture, the wooded islands, and the animation derived from the swelling canvass of active commerce, conspire to render it eminently beautiful: but for the rest of its immense course it exhibits a stream of sand, and rolls shingles through the valley instead of water."—*A. Young.* "Quel torrent révolutionnaire que cette Loire!" was the expression of Barrère the democrat: and the unbridled impetuosity of its course, its sudden inundations and changes of bed, justify the epithet, and are as detrimental to the utility as to the beauty of this main artery of France. The inundation of the Loire in October (18th and 19th), 1846, was the most extensive and disastrous of that river on record. It burst through the Levée or dyke in several places above and below Orleans, spreading over the plain round Orleans to an extent of 39 kilomètres; while in the streets of Orleans the water rose 5 mètres. 100 barges, with bargemen, were sent from Paris to assist the inhabitants of the city and neighbourhood, isolated by the flood. In winter the Loire rages, and swells, and has too much water, just as in summer it has too little. Its broad shoals greatly disfigure the landscape; its shallows and sandbanks render the passage of steamers intricate. Navigation is limited to very small vessels, and is frequently arrested in the dry months. The cave dwellings excavated in the cliffs of soft chalk (craie tufeau) along the river banks, and the long Levée or dyke raised to protect the right bank between Blois and Angers, a distance of 96 m., from inundations, will be remarked as peculiar features in the borders of the Loire. The descent of the Loire from Orleans to Nantes is productive of much interest, partly derived from its venerable cities, gloomy castles, and the great events in French history which have passed upon its banks.

These provinces of France, especially Touraine, were the chosen residence of her kings (les Valois) down to Louis XIV., and they afford a hundred sites preferable to the sands and morasses of Versailles. The vast and castellated Chambord, bristling with turrets and pinnacles, studded with Diana's crescent, where the Emp. Charles V. was entertained by his good-natured enemy Francis I.; the gloomy Blois, haunt of bigotry and scene of the deep-plotted assassination of the Guises; Amboise, the favourite abode of the warrior Charles VIII., and also witness to conspiracy and wholesale massacre; Chénonceaux, the retreat of Diana of Poitiers; Plessis, the den of the timorous bigot Louis XI.; Chinon, where passed the careless revelry of the indolent Charles VII., and the opening scene of the wondrous career of "the shepherd girl of Domrémy;" Fontevrault, the last resting-place of the lion-hearted Richard; Loches, with its dungeon of sighs and tears, a provincial Bastille, contrasting with more agreeable recollections of the beauteous and gentle Agnes Sorel; Dampierre, where Margaret of Anjou's life and sorrow ceased; and Nantes, which saw Henri IV. put his hand to the edict of toleration, and in later times witnessed the heroism and frailty of a daughter of Bourbon, his descendant :—all these are national monuments—integral portions, as it were, of French history. It is a region of interesting associations and recollections: here Joan of Arc first unfurled her victorious banner; here the chief events of the contests of religion in the 16th century occurred; this soil is watered with the blood of Guise and Condé; the fields of La Vendée are fattened with the unburied bones of the thousands who fell in the cause of loyalty, and in opposition to revolution and irreligion.

All the places above-named or alluded to well deserve to be visited by the traveller. Orleans, though retaining few traces or relics of the Maid; Blois and Amboise; Tours, a fine city, though seated on a flat, amidst dust and glare; Saumur, once the stronghold of Protestantism; Loches, for its architectural remains and historical souvenirs, and pleasing situation in the charming valley of the Indre; black Angers, cradle of our early Plantagenet monarchs—all abound in specimens of ancient architecture, all possess more or less claims to attention. Chénonceaux is a charming specimen of the old French château, with turrets and extinguisher towers; without, all crinkum crankum—and within, lined with tapestry and armour; preserved unimpaired, and well kept up. Aizy-le-Rideau is nearly as perfect and beautiful, but with less interesting associations.

S. of Nantes, between the Loire, the sea, and the Sèvre Niortaise, lies La Vendée, celebrated in the history of the wars of the Revolution for its adhesion to royalty and opposition to innovation. The framework or foundation of that country is composed of the elevated plateau of the Gatine, whose crest is in no wise distinguishable, and which presents a series of hills, furrowed by narrow glens or valleys, through which run a few muddy streams. "It is an inextricable complication of heaths, brooks, heights, hollows, and little plains having no connection with one another, and apparently no general water-shed. It is covered with trees, yet has no forests; every field, every dwelling is surrounded by quick hedges, abounding with close-set trees, and surrounded by ditches, forming complete natural redoubts. The lines of communication from place to place are hollow ways, cut so deep below the surface of the ground that a man's head in walking along them will not appear above it, and their vertical sides are surmounted by hedges. They are narrow, shady, and muddy or rutty, according to the season, and intersect one another so as to form a multitude of crossways, looking all like one another. There are few high roads, no large towns; the villages are scattered and thinly inhabited, estates very much subdivided, houses concealed by trees and bushes, and a peasantry of primitive and rude manners; these are the combination of circumstances which have made this district a complete labyrinth, perfectly adapted as the theatre of the civil war which so long and so fearfully desolated it. It is divided into three parts: the *Marais*, comprising the sands, salt marshes, and ponds bordering the sea-shore, intersected by dykes and canals, abounding in pastures, destitute of drinking-water; the *Bocage*, covered with thickets and heaths, rough and bristling, much cut up and well cultivated; and the *Plaine*, very rich and highly cultivated, abounding with corn and vines."

The traveller disposed to visit the theatre of the Vendéan war may do so from Nantes by way of Clisson; but the character of the country and its inhabitants is fast changing under the system pursued by Napoleon and Louis-Philippe; and intersected, as it has been by them, with a network of high roads, it has lost much of its primitive character.

The *Rly. to Orleans and Tours* brings this interesting country in a manner to the gates of Paris, and opens the readiest line of communication between Paris, Lyons, Tours, Bordeaux, and the South of France.

ROUTE 48.

PARIS TO ORLEANS.

119 kilom. = 74 Eng. m.

The high road is now superseded by the Railroad. Mallepostes and diligences are transferred to it. See Rte. 49.

The high road to Orleans quits Paris by the Barrière d'Enfer; it passes through Bourg-la-Reine, where Condorcet, proscribed by the Convention, arrested and placed in jail, put an end to himself by poison concealed in a ring, 1794. It leaves about 1 m. to the rt. the town of *Sceaux*. (Rte. 51.)

12 Berny. Chatenay, about a mile to the rt. of Berny, was the birthplace of Voltaire, 1694. He was born in a house which belonged to the Comtesse de Bóignes.

8 Longjumeau, a small town on the Yvette.

Beyond this the road skirts the hill of Montlhéry (Rte. 49).

12 Arpajon. The Marolles Stat. of the Rly. is about 1 m. to the l. of this town (Rte. 49).

12 Etrécy, a walled town.

Morigny, on the l. of the road, beyond the river Juine, has a fine Ch.

8 *Etampes*, a Stat. on the Rly. (Rte. 49.)

Beyond this the road enters the monotonous plain of La Beauce, famed for growing corn.

9 Montdésir.

At Méreville, on the l., about midway in this stage, is the Château of Comte de Laborde.

10 Angerville.

14 Toury.

14 Artenay. Here the road from Chartres falls in. (Rte. 50.)

6 Chevilly.

We here enter the *Forest of Orleans*; Cercolles is a small hamlet in the heart of it, inhabited by woodcutters. The suburb Bannier, more than 1½ m. long, precedes the town of

14 ORLEANS (in Rte. 49).

ROUTE 49.

RAILWAY.—PARIS TO ORLEANS, AND BRANCH TO CORBEIL.

121 kilom. = 75 Eng. m.
Trains go to Corbeil (30 kilom. = 19 Eng. m.) in 1 hour, or 55 min., 8 times a day on week-days; every hour on Sundays and fête-days.

The Trains to Corbeil stop at intermediate stations, which are distinguished by the letter C.

Trains to Orleans 7 times a day, in 3 and 4 hours. *Fares:* 12 fr. 60 c., 9 f. 50 c., and 3rd class uncovered 6 fr. 35 c.; a place in the coupé 15 fr. Carriages 62 to 82 fr.

The railway was completed to Orleans in 1843.

Terminus in the Boulevard de l'Hôpital, close to the Jardin des Plantes. The line, at first skirting the walls of the Hospital of the Salpetrière, is carried through a pretty country, at the foot of the slopes which border the l. bank of the Seine. It approaches the river closely at each curve which the Seine makes, and commands pleasant views of it. There are many pretty villas and country-houses on the river banks, and villages are numerous.

It skirts the walls of Ivry, and of Vitry, famed for its nursery-gardens, on the rt.

10 Choisy Stat. is close to a viaduct of 8 arches, which also support the towing-path along the Seine; 4 of the arches are left open to allow a passage between the Seine and the town. Choisy is a very thriving manufacturing town, whose population has increased within a few years to more than 3000. It was called Choisy-le-Roi, because Louis XV. made it one of his residences; the *Château* which he built for himself and Madame de Pompadour is demolished, except a fragment, now turned into a china manufactory. There are also manufactories of morocco leather (the largest in France), of glass, and of beetroot sugar, and a chemical work. Close to the station the Seine is crossed by a bridge of 5 arches, built 1802. The château and village of Orly are seen on the height to the rt. The rly. skirts the parc of Villeneuve-le-Roi. A new bridge over the Seine gives access to it. We approach the vine-clad slopes bounding the valley of the Seine.

6 Ablon (C. Stat.). Ablon is composed almost entirely of neat villas. One of the 3 Protestant churches which the reformers of Paris were allowed by the Edict of Nantes to possess stood here.

2 Athis Mont (C. Stat.).

9 Juvisy Stat., situated at the foot of a hill on the rt., is remarkable for its antiquity. Its bridge over the Orge anciently formed the boundary between the kingdoms of Paris and of Orleans. Isabella of Bavaria was arrested here as she was carrying off the Dauphin.

[At Juvisy the *Branch Rly. to Corbeil* separates from the main line to Orleans, turning off to the l., but continuing along the margin of the Seine, and running near the high road to Lyons (Rte. 105). It passes through Châtillon, a little port on the Seine. At Viry is the fine garden of the Duchesse de Raguse.

3 Ris (C. Stat.), close to Laborde.

Here is a suspension bridge buil' over the Seine by the late M. Aguado, the Spanish banker.

The rly. cuts through a part of the park of Petit Bourg, broken up and parcelled out by its owner, the late M. Aguado. The *Château*, when it belonged to the Duc d'Antin, was often the residence of Madame de Montespan, who was visited here by Louis XIV.

4 Evry (C. Stat.).

3 Corbeil (C. Stat.) is a considerable manufacturing town of 3900 Inhab., on the Seine, here crossed by a bridge, at the influx of the Essonne. Here are very extensive *Flour Mills* and a corn warehouse (Magasin), belonging to Government, for the supply of Paris. The *Ch. of St. Spire* (Exupère), rebuilt 1437, after a fire, contains the tomb of Jaques de Bourgoin, founder of the college of Corbeil, 1661, and the casket or reliquaire containing relics of St. Leu and St. Rembert. The little church

France.   I

of *St. Jean en l'Ile* was built by the Templars in the 13th centy.

Omnibus from Corbeil to Fontainebleau (Rte. 105). A continued street connects Corbeil with the village of Essonne.

At Juvisy (19 kilom. from Paris) the *Orleans Line*, curving a little to the S.W., enters the valley of a small stream, the Orge, the railway crossing previously the high road to Antibes. It traverses the gardens of

3 Savigny Stat., a village with a castle, fortified 1486 by Étienne de Vesi, chamberlain to Charles VIII. The handsome *Château* occupying its place is now the property of the Princess Dowager of Eckmühl. A great hemp market is held here. A viaduct of 3 arches over the Yvette leads to

2 (rt.) Epinay Stat., which is $2\frac{1}{2}$ m. distant from Longjumeau on the post-road (Rte. 48). The quarries near this furnish paving-stones for the streets of Paris. Another viaduct of 5 arches carries you from Epinay Stat. You next skirt on the l. the forêt de St. Geneviève: on the rt., beyond the Orge, you see the château of Vaucluse; Villiers, and its villas of Paris citizens; and Longpont, whose church of the 14th centy. is the sole relic of its ancient abbey. A portion of the parc of the handsome château d'Ormay is traversed before reaching

4 St. Michel-sur-Orge Stat. *Montlhéry* is about $1\frac{1}{2}$ m. on the rt. Its ancient castle, of which a tower remains, built (1012) by Thibaut-File-Etoupe, forester of King Robert, was the terror of the kings of France in feudal times, and has been made famous by Boileau in the poem of the Lutrin :—

" Ses murs dont le sommet se dérobe à la vue,
Sur le cime d'un roc s'allongeant dans la nue,
Et présentant de loin leur objet ennuyeux,
Du passant qui les fuit semblent suivre les yeux."

A bloody but indecisive battle was fought between Montlhéry and Longpont, 1465, between Louis XI. and the troops of the so-called "Ligue du Bien Public," commanded by the Comte de Charolais, afterwards Charles the Bold, of Burgundy. The spot still goes by the name of Cimetière des Bourguinons.

The line passes through the midst of the collection of hamlets called

3 Brétigny Stat., beyond which the rly. attains a summit level, and descends into the valley of the Juine shortly before.

5 Marolles Stat. The village and château lie a little on the l.; Arpajon (2400 Inhab.) is about 1 m. off on the rt. Beyond Cheptainville we pass through the park appertaining to the château of *Mesnil Voisin*, the property of the Duc de Choiseul Praslin, a building of brick and stone on the borders of the Juine.

4 Lardy Stat. Farther on to the l. is another château, Chamarande. The rly. skirts the walls of

5 Etrécy Stat. It here approaches the post-road, which passes through Etrécy, a walled town, and the two run parallel for some distance.

7 *Etampes* Stat. Here refreshments may be had. Close to the Stat. rises a ruined tower called *Guinette*, the only remains of the royal castle and palace, built in the 11th centy. by King Robert, and dismantled by Henri IV. It is formed externally of 4 segments of circles.

Inn: H. du Bois de Vincennes.

This interesting ancient town, of 8000 Inhab., carries on a considerable trade in flour, the produce of its 40 water-mills, and in wool. The main street is about 4 m. long from octroi to octroi. The *Ch.* of *Notre Dame* is distinguished by its very elegant spire, with tall pinnacles, of the period of transition from the Romanesque to Early French style. *St. Jules* is another fine transition Ch. The tower, square, but curiously raised on an octagon base, has 4 gables with crockets, of the end of the 12th centy. *St. Martin* has a detached W. tower built at the time of the Renaissance in imitation of St. Jules: it leans considerably, from its foundations having given way. The royal castle, resembling in its ground-plan that of Clifford's Tower, York, was given as an *apanage* to various remarkable personages, among others to the mistresses of the three French kings, Francis I. (Anne de Pisseleu), Henri II. (Diana of Poitiers), and Henri IV. (Gabrielle d'Estrées). The town consists of one long street, and retains several picturesque old houses of the age of the Renaissance: one of them is attributed to Diana of Poitiers. The H. de Ville is an antique building with turrets.

Omnibus twice a day to Pithiviers.

A high embankment, a bridge over the Louette, and a steep incline carry the Rly. from Etampes.

4 Monnerville Stat. The Rly. crosses the stream of the Chalonette on a viaduct, and ascending the valley of l'Hémery reaches the upland plain of La Beauce and a second summit level. It crosses the post-road on a bridge shortly before reaching

5 Angerville Stat. Coaches run hence once a day to Chartres. 14 m. from this is Pithiviers, famed for *pâtés d'alouettes*, for *almond cakes*, and for its trade in saffron. From this point the post and railroad run side by side, within a short distance of each other, so that the description of the one will serve for both.

13 Toury Stat.

14 Artenay Stat. Here the road from Chartres falls in (Rte. 50). A little to the W. of the road, near Rouvray, an English detachment of about 2000 men, under Sir John Fastolf, escorting a convoy of provisions to the army besieging Orleans, defeated a force 4000 strong, consisting of French and Scotch, commanded by Dunois and the Count of Clermont, who endeavoured to intercept them. The French left 500 dead on the field, among them Sir John Stewart, constable of Scotland. This engagement, fought February 10, 1409, was called " The Battle of Herrings," from the salt fish for Lent, which formed the bulk of the provisions intended for the English.

A few months later, June 18, and nearly on the same ground, at Patay, the English forces under the same commander, retreating dispirited from Orleans, were put to flight at the first onset by the French, led on by Jeanne d'Arc. Fastolf ran away, and the brave Talbot, who never turned back on an enemy, being left to fight almost alone, was made prisoner together with Lord Scales.

6 Chevilly Stat. Fossil remains of gigantic quadrupeds (Deinotherium) have been discovered near Chevilly.

14 ORLEANS TERMINUS a little to the E. of the Porte Bannier.

ORLEANS.—*Inns:* H. d'Orléans, close to the railway, good; H. du Loiret, very clean and comfortable; H. de la Boule d'Or, good.

Orleans (the Roman *Genabum*, named afterwards Aurelianum, from M. Aurelius, who rebuilt it in the 3rd centy.) occupies an extensive level area on the l. bank of the Loire; it contains 45,000 Inhab., and is chef-lieu of the Dépt. of the Loiret. In a town so important for its situation, nearly in the centre of France, midway on the course of the sunny but shallow Loire, of consequence in a military point of view as commanding the passage over that river from the N. to the S. provinces of the kingdom, and conspicuous in history from a very early period—the traveller will probably expect more of interest than he will find. Orleans is not conspicuous for trade or manufactures, and is deficient in tangible historical memorials, chiefly owing to the cacoethes of pulling down for the sake of what is called improvement, which has prevailed to a most destructive extent during the last 50 years in the town council. The town gates and walls have been destroyed, several of the latter since 1830, and above all, nearly every memorial of the heroine of Orleans, Joan of Arc, has been swept away.

A tolerably handsome street leads from the bridge over the Loire to the irregular *Place du Martroy*, which occupies nearly the centre of the town, and is prolonged from it under another name (*Rue de Banier*) to the Barrière de Paris and the rly.

A wide and handsome new street (Rue Jeanne d'Arc) has been driven through a dense mass of old houses from the Rue Royale to the W. front of the *Cathedral* (St. Croix), the chief building of the town, which this opening now for the first time allows to be seen to advantage. The remarkable

I 2

circumstance connected with this church is, that it was built as it now stands, in the 17th centy., at a period when Gothic architecture was not only on the decline, but had fallen into disuse. Notwithstanding this, it is a beautiful edifice, in a pure style, and reflects credit on its architects, and on Henri IV., who furnished the funds, to atone for the destruction by the Calvinists of the former church, to ingratiate himself (vain hope!) with the Jesuits, and to liberate himself from the pope's excommunication. He laid the first stone 1601, and the building, unfinished at his death, was continued under Louis XIII., XIV., and XV. The design of the W. front was made, 1764, by the architect Gabriel, and modified by his successor, M. Paris. It consists of 3 somewhat plain pointed portals, surmounted by 3 rose windows flanked by 2 towers of equal height (280 ft.) and of great elegance: the circular top is capped by a circlet of cut stone; below this runs a light arcade with fringed arches; in each tower are 3 circular windows. Over the W. portal are some incongruous coats of arms, supported by cherubs, including the shield of the old Bourbons, now lilyless. The S. porch is a Grecian abomination; indeed the exterior is in many respects faulty. The *nave* is flanked by double aisles. The magnificent effect of the interior depends in a great degree on the large size of the clerestory windows (double that of the side aisle windows).

A portion of the former cathedral, blown up 1567 by the Huguenots, who had previously turned it into a stable for their cavalry, in spite of the remonstrances of the Prince de Condé, still remains in the N. choir aisle: the choir ends in an apse. There is nothing else to notice in the interior. The other churches are either modern or so mutilated as scarcely to deserve notice. *St. Aignan* is the finest; its much injured portal and nave are in the florid style. Under it is a Romanesque crypt; its towers are surmounted by a pyramid. The houses Nos. 2 and 4 in the Place adjoining this church, formerly the Convent of St. Aignan, were built and inhabited by Louis XI. They are of plain red brick, with high pitched slate roofs, having dormer windows, and resemble closely the remaining fragment of the château de Plessis les Tours (Rte. 53). *St. Pierre-le-Puellier* (Petrus Puellarum) has a Norman N. porch and an ancient apse.

Next to the cathedral, the stranger will find the most to interest him in the *Musée*, in the ancient *Hôtel de Ville*, a picturesque edifice of the time of Charles VIII. and Louis XII., situated Rue des Hôtelleries, not far from the Rue Jeanne d'Arc. Here is placed a cast of the *statue* of the heroine by Louis Philippe's daughter. Besides a considerable number of ordinary pictures it contains a curious collection of local antiquities, carvings in ivory, wood, and stone, which once ornamented the houses and churches of Orleans, chiefly of the 15th and 16th centy. Amidst old furniture, cabinets, chimney-pieces, bas-reliefs and statues, is an elaborately carved chest, bearing the history of Solomon and David in relief; another, which came from St. Aignan, is ornamented with a representation of the coronation of Louis XI. A Massacre of the Innocents in stone, an enamelled triptic, and some elaborate iron-work, locks, &c., with Gothic patterns, *chefs-d'œuvre* of the hammer and anvil, also deserve notice.

Not far from the Musée, in the Rue des Albanais, and Rue Neuve No. 22, is the *house of Diane de Poitiers*, so called because she is supposed to have been laid up in it with a broken leg; but it appears to have belonged to the Bishop of Orleans, and was built 1552. The inner front facing the court is a good specimen of Italian architecture, such as we see in the works of Inigo Jones.

Owing to the excessive filth and bad pavement of the older streets of Orleans, the stranger will do well not to trust himself to thread their labyrinths, but should rather keep to the great thoroughfares and the quays, and should only dive into the side streets to visit some particular object and return. The *Rue du Tabourg* contains some interesting specimens of domestic architecture, as the house of Jeanne d'Arc (No. 35), described below, and that of Agnes

Sorel (No. 15), which is well worthy of examination, on account of its carved wood and stone work, its doors, the reliefs round the galleries facing the court, their roofs, and the staircases. The style of architecture and ornament, and the coats of arms, fleurs-de-lis, &c., render it probable that it was erected by Charles VII. for his mistress previous to 1470.

No. 28, Rue de la Recouvrance, called *Maison de François Premier*, is supposed to have been built for the Duchesse d'Etampes 1540, and in its general arrangement and sculptures (including the Salamander of Francis) is a good specimen of the *Renaissance*.

At one extremity of the Place du Martroy is a *bronze statue* of Jeanne d'Arc, erected 1804, affected in attitude, incorrect in costume, and entirely in bad taste: around the pedestal are bas-reliefs, representing her exploits and death. An ancient statue, erected on the bridge soon after her death, was broken to pieces by the Revolutionists of 1792, to melt into cannon! We have reserved to the last the enumeration of the few remaining memorials, souvenirs, and relics of the heroic *Maid of Orleans*. A careful inquiry has discovered only the following:—

In the Salle du Conseil of the *Hôtel de la Mairie* is a portrait of her, painted 1581, from an older picture, it is said; it represents her in a theatrical attitude, and in a female costume of the time of Francis I., and apparently deserves little confidence as a likeness. A view of the town, hung up here, shows its ancient configuration about the time of the siege. King Louis-Philippe has presented to the town a bronze cast of the statue by his gifted daughter, by far the worthiest representation of the inspired Maid.

The Maid entered the city on Friday, April 29th, 1429, in the teeth of the English army, which was vastly superior to the French force. She had convoyed a supply of provisions from Blois to the famished townsmen, who, as she rode in triumph through their streets on her charger, in full armour, bearing her sacred banner, looked on her as their guardian angel sent from heaven. She was lodged in the *house* of Jacques Bouchier, treasurer of the Duc d'Orléans, which she had selected, with that sense of modesty which always actuated her, because she would there be under the protection of a matron of good repute, his wife. It stood close to the Porte Renard (long since removed), and only in part exists in the house No. 35, *Rue du Tabourg*. The chamber which she occupied is removed, and a sort of *pavilion* of Italian architecture, erected in the latter part of the 16th centy., occupies its place.

The scene of the chief exploits of the Maid was the *old bridge*, which stood considerably higher up the river than the present one (b. 1761), and rested in the centre on an island. It was defended at its extremity, on the S. bank of the Loire, by a fort, or Tête du Pont, called *Les Tourelles*, which had fallen into the hands of the English before Jeanne's arrival, and, together with another tower in the centre of the bridge, formed a strong post, whence the English greatly annoyed the besieged by a battery of cannon planted on it. It was while reconnoitring the town from this battery that the English commander, the Earl of Salisbury, was mortally wounded by a shot from the walls, which drove a splinter into his head.

The Maid in her enthusiasm decided that this post should be first attacked; and though her design was opposed by the most skilful of the French commanders, they were obliged to yield, because she carried the people and soldiery with her. As the bridge had been broken between the Tourelles and the town, when that fort fell into the hands of the besiegers, a chosen band of troops with the Maiden at their head was pushed across the Loire in boats, and began the attack upon the Tête du Pont on the l. bank, which formed part of the Bastille des Tourelles. It was defended by a picked body of 500 English soldiers, under Sir Wm. Gladsdale, who for many hours kept their assailants at bay by their unerring flights of arrows and fire of cannon. At length the Maid, seeing her countrymen falter, snatched up a ladder, and planting it against the walls began to mount to the escalade, but an arrow pierced her corslet, and she fell as one dead into the ditch. She was with difficulty rescued by her own people from being made prisoner, and was borne to the rear. Here, however, after a few woman's tears called forth by the anguish of the wound, she received, as she said, the consolation of "her voices," and, encouraged by St. Michael, St. Catherine, and St. Margaret, &c., hurried back once more to the contest. Great was the dismay of the English when they beheld her, whom a few minutes before they had supposed mortally wounded, again leading the assault, and waving on high her magic banner. To the feeling of supernatural agency being exerted against them, was now added the failure of arrows and ammunition, and the hopelessness of aid from their army on the opposite bank. The spirits of the French proportionately increased, and they now began to assault the Tourelles from the side of the town, throwing beams over the broken arch to render it accessible. 300 men had fallen on the side of the English, but the surrender of the fort was at length decided by the death of their leader, whom a cannon-shot hurled into the river as he was crossing the drawbridge. That same evening the courageous Jeanne, whom but the day before the English had tauntingly desired to "go home and mind her cows," entered Orleans in triumph by the bridge which had remained many months closed; as she had herself foretold before she began the attack. Next day the English broke up the siege, burning the remaining bastilles which they had erected around the town to hem it in, and retreating from before the walls. Thus in seven days from her arrival in the town had the Maid accomplished its deliverance.

Opposite to the spot where the old bridge terminated, on the l. bank of the river, stands a small cross called *Croix de la Pucelle;* and the *cellars,* underneath the neighbouring cabaret called Le Bœuf, are part of the celebrated Tête du Pont included in the English bastille called *Les Tourelles.* They are now below the surface of the ground, but receive partial light from the old loopholes, which seem designed for the firing of cannon, and are furnished with rings above, from which it is probable that the guns were suspended by chains, as carriages were not then in use. The fort has two branches, and there is a vaulted passage from it, which the people say led to the river. In its present state the fort is nothing more than a damp, dirty, low cellar, possessing this interest alone, that it is perhaps the sole remaining contemporary relic of the siege.

The life of the Maid of Orleans has been admirably told in the Quarterly Review, No. 138, by one who has used the discrimination of the practised historian in sifting the true from the false, and has unravelled, for the first time, the mystery of her story, without depriving it of any of the charms of romance.

During the Wars of Religion, at another siege of Orleans, 1563, the Duc de Guise, the conqueror of Calais and defender of Metz, who commanded the Catholic army which invested the town, was assassinated before its walls by a fanatical young Huguenot, Poltrot de Méré. He was shot near the village Olivet (Rte. 70), and died a few days after in the Château de Caubrai. Orleans was then justly regarded as the stronghold of the Protestant party, and continued so until the revocation of the Edict of Nantes banished those who followed the Reformed faith. Previous to that event its population amounted to 54,000.

Francis II., husband of Mary Queen of Scots, ended his insignificant life at Orleans, whither he had repaired to assist at the meeting of the Estates, in the building now the Mairie. In his last illness, at the instigation of his mother, Cath. de Medicis, he sent a deputation of pilgrims to Notre Dame de Cléry, promising to purge the kingdom of heretics if he ever recovered. The vow was accomplished not by him, but by Charles IX., at the instigation of the same wicked mother, in the St. Bartholomew's night.

Cæsar mentions Orleans in the following passage: "Carnutes Genabum concurrunt, civesque Romanos, qui negotiandi causâ ibi consisterant, interficiunt."

Promenades are formed round the town upon the line of the former ramparts.

Post-Office in the Rue d'Illiers.

Alphonse Gatineau, bookseller, has a shop well provided with guides, views, maps, and plans.

Railways to Paris, 7 trains daily; to Vierzon and Moulins; to Tours and Bordeaux (Rte. 53) and Nantes.

Diligences:—to Gien, to Montargis and Briare, to Roanne.

Steamboats on the Loire, (?) in summer, to Gien, Nevers, up the river (Rte. 52).

Environs. The objects of interest in the vicinity of Orleans are—

Notre Dame de Cléry, the burial-place of Louis XI. (Rte. 53.)

The *Château de la Source*, the residence of Lord Bolingbroke (Rte. 70), is about 5 m. off; a cab costs 4 or 5 fr. The way thither leads across the bridge over the Loire to the village of Olivet, whither omnibuses run every hour from Orleans, where the road turns to the l. The château is named from the little river Loiret, which here rises at once out of the ground in full flood, from a natural basin, but injured by art, close under the walls of the château, in the midst of the parc. After a course of only 10 m. it falls into the Loire, giving, however, its name to the department. With this exception, the grounds, laid out in the formal French style, have little interest; nor has the château itself any other than what it derives from having been the residence of Bolingbroke, who rented it from the proprietor during the latter years of his life when exiled from England. He was visited here by Voltaire. He wrote here his Reflections on Exile. There is a second and more copious source, produced, at the beginning of the last century, by the artificial means resorted to to confine the waters of the old source, which, in consequence, broke a new passage for themselves.

Not far from La Source, near the road, is another handsome *Château—de la Fontaine*.

ROUTE 50.

ROUEN TO ORLEANS BY CHARTRES.

201 kilom. = 124 Eng. m.
11 Port St. Ouen, } (Rte. 9).
17 Louviers,
23 *Evreux* (Rte. 25).
13 Thomer. Our route traverses the fertile but monotonous district of *La Beauce* (Belsia), one of the granaries of France, on a table-land extending nearly from the Seine to the Loire; of which Chartres is considered the capital.
15 Nonancourt.
14 Dreux (Rte. 35).
16 Péage.
16 *Chartres* (Rte. 46). Diligence to Angerville Stat. (Rte. 49). It takes about 10 hrs. to travel hence to Orleans. At the village of Berchères are stone-quarries from which Chartres cathedral was built. The road traverses the fertile corn-lands of La Beauce.
26 Allonne.
19 Allaines.
15 Artenay, on the Paris Railroad (Rte. 49), and in the Dépt. du Loiret.
6 Chevilly.
14 ORLEANS (Rte. 49).

ROUTE 51.

PARIS TO SCEAUX—RAILWAY.

Terminus in Paris, Barrière d'Enfer.

The peculiarity of the line is, that, for the sake of economizing outlay, it is constructed upon steep slopes and curves of narrow radius, which are traversed in safety by railway trains called *trains articulés*, owing to the carriages being made to turn on their wheels like road carriages, the invention of M. Arnoux.

Arcueil Stat.
Cachan Stat.
Bourg-la-Reine Stat. (see Rte. 48) is situated in the valley, at the foot of the ascent on whose summit is situated the town of Sceaux. The intervening space is traversed by means of curves

carried along the face of the slope in zigzags (lacets) of small radius.

The town of *Sceaux* was once famed for its splendid *Château*, built by the Minister Colbert (1760), afterwards enlarged by the Duc de Maine, whose duchess assembled around her here a literary circle the most eminent in France. It was destroyed, except some of the offices and the menagerie, at the Revolution, and its park, laid out by *Le Nôtre*, ploughed up. A part of it has been made a public garden, and part belongs to the Duc de Trevise (Mortier). The Terrace is a favourite walk of the Parisians. Sceaux is now celebrated for its large cattle-market, and has a considerable glass-manufactory. Florian, the novelist, who resided in the château and died here, is buried in its Cimetière.

ROUTE 52.
THE LOIRE (A)—GIEN TO ORLEANS.

62 kilom. = 38½ Eng. m.
2 Diligences daily.
Steamers 3 times a week. (?)

The scenery of this part of the course of the Loire is not particularly interesting. When the height of water permitted, steamers used to ascend as high as Nevers, and sometimes even to mount the Allier by Moulins to Digoin (Rte. 105). From Gien to Nevers the course of the Loire is described in Rte. 105.

Gien is a town of 5530 Inhab., on the rt. bank of the Loire, here crossed by a bridge, on the road from Orleans to Lyons. Its old church, *St. Etienne*, has been injured by repairs. Near it is a portion of the ancient *Castle*, now turned into the préfecture. It was at Gien that the Maid of Orleans crossed the Loire on her way from her native village, to announce her divine mission to "Charles the Dauphin" at Chinon.

l. A mound of earth, called Motte du Leon, is supposed to be a Celtic tumulus.

About 12 m. below Gien lies

l. Sully, a town of 2145 Inhab., possessing a wire suspension bridge, and an old *Castle*, resting its front upon the Loire, and separated from the town by a deep ditch. It is remarkable as the residence of the minister of Henri IV., Maximilian de Béthune, first Duc de Sully, who purchased it from its former possessors, the family de la Trémouille; and in the alterations which he made in the building everywhere effaced their arms to substitute his own, along with cannons, grenades, bullets, and similar ornaments. He passed here the latter years of his life, after his disgrace under Louis XIII., maintaining considerable state with his regiment of lancers, and occupying himself with the preparation of his work 'Sur les Economies Royales,' which he printed at a press established in one of the towers. It remained in the possession of his descendants down to 1807, when the last Duc de Sully died. One of them fitted up a little theatre in the château, and was visited by the literary men of his times, among them by Voltaire, who here commenced his *Henriade*. The building is now going to decay, and is no longer inhabited: in one corner a few bits of tapestry, old portraits, &c., have been brought together; also a statue of Sully.

rt. The *Ch. of St. Bénoit*, one of the oldest and finest in the Dépt., was originally attached to a monastery, destroyed 1792. Its tower was lowered in consequence of a revolt of the monks against the royal authority under Francis I. It has a curious N. portal, some carved stalls, and one or two curiosities in the sacristy.

rt. Châteauneuf. Here are remains of a fine château.

The river is crossed by another suspension-bridge at

l. Jargeau, a town of 2358 Inhab., 12 m. from Orleans. It still retains a portion of its old walls, within which a few hundred English soldiers, with their commander, the Earl of Suffolk, shut themselves up, after the raising of the siege of Orleans, to resist the attacks of the French led on by Dunois and the Maid. She was struck down into the ditch by a stone while mounting a ladder to scale a breach made in the walls by the besiegers' cannon; but, recovering herself, instantly rose, and encouraged her followers by her voice

PLANCHE (S) EN 2.
PRISES DE VUE

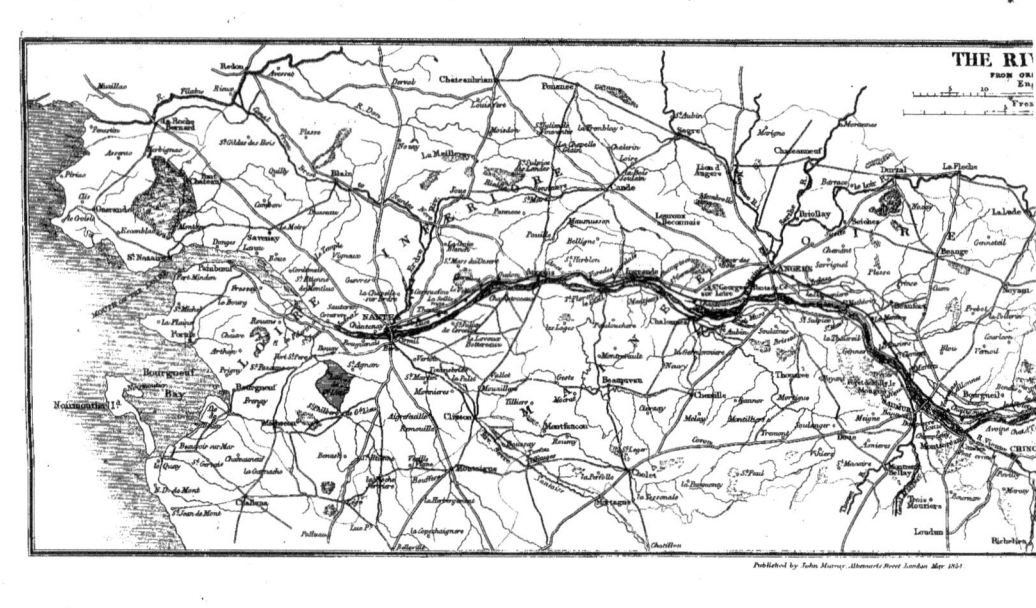

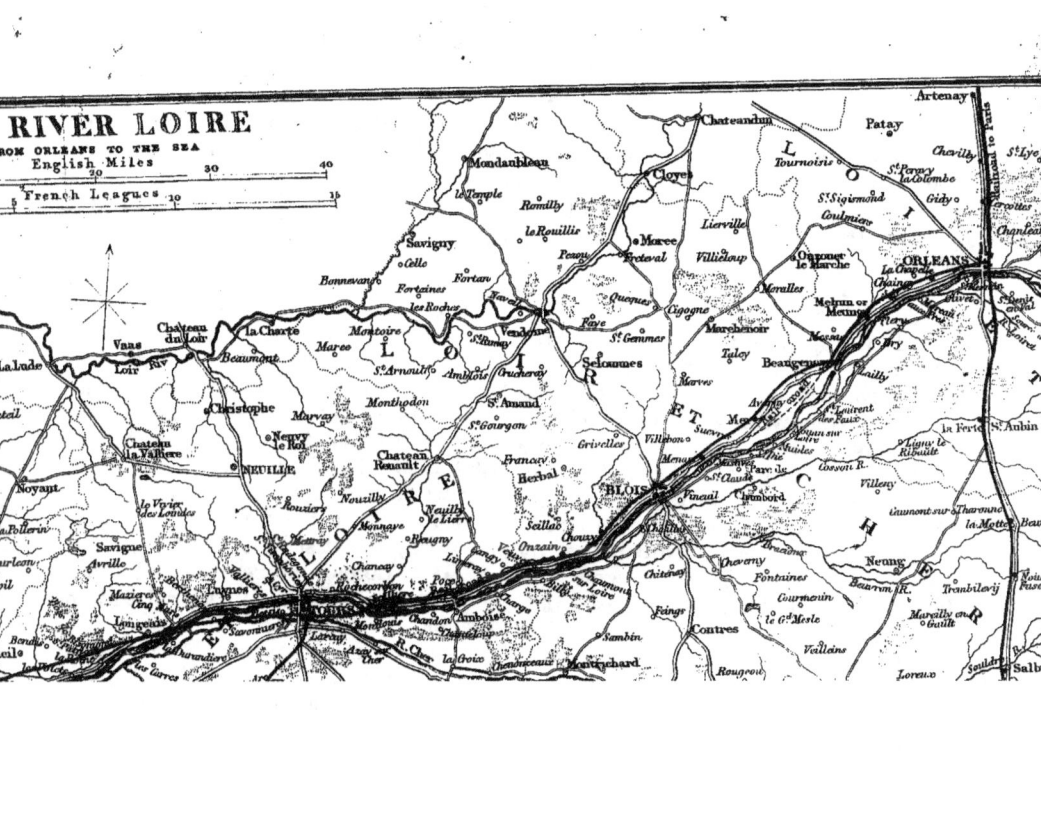

and waving banner. The town was taken, and almost all the garrison put to the sword, in spite of the endeavours of the Maid to prevent the shedding of blood. Suffolk was made prisoner.

The *Ch. of St. Etienne and St. Vrain*, though injured by the Huguenots 1562, is still a fine building.

rt. A little below Checy, at Combleaux, is the opening of the Canal d'Orléans, which unites the Loire with the Seine.

rt. ORLEANS, Rte. 49.

ROUTE 53.

THE LOIRE (B).—ORLEANS TO TOURS —RAILWAY BY BLOIS AND AMBOISE. — EXCURSIONS TO CHAMBORD AND CHENONCEAUX.

Railroad along the rt. bank of the Loire, 115 kilom. = 73 Eng. m.

4 or 5 trains run daily in $3\frac{1}{4}$ hrs.

Steamers have been superseded by the railway, and no longer run.

The course of the Loire from Orleans to Tours lies for the most part through a wide valley, slightly varied by hills of very moderate height: its scenery, therefore, consisting chiefly of slopes covered over with vineyards, of low banks and islands, fringed with willows and poplars, is somewhat monotonous, though of a sunny character, and relieved now and then by a frowning old town such as Blois or Amboise, or by a formal château. Lower down a yellow streak of cliffs hollowed out into caves and subterranean dwellings frequently forms the bank. The river itself winds very much: its shallow waters occupy a bed too large for them to fill in summer, and it is obstructed by shifting sandbanks.

The first thing worth noticing after quitting Orleans is,

1. The outlet into the Loire of the Loiret, a stream not 30 feet broad, which yet gives the name to a department. On the peninsula between the rivers once stood the abbey St. Mesmin, whose fertile territory was the gift of Clovis to the monks. A part of the church and traces of the gardens remain. The road to Cléry crosses the Loiret by a bridge at St. Mesmin.

7 La Chapelle Stat.

7 St. Ay Stat.

1. Opposite to St. Ay,* whose vineyards produce the best wine in the Orléanois, the spire of *Notre Dame de Cléry* may be perceived about 3 m. from the Loire, on its l. bank. This little town, 9 m. from Orleans, contains a very fine *Church*, remarkable for the veneration in which its image of the Virgin was held by Louis XI., who was buried within its walls. Its name must be familiar to every reader of 'Quentin Durward.' Louis, passing this way in his frequent journeys into Touraine, always performed his devotions to our Lady of Cléry, whose leaden figure he carried in his cap. The existing church was almost entirely built by him, in the place of an older one ruined by the English under Salisbury, 1428. He selected it as his burial-place in preference to St. Denis, because he believed he had recovered from a severe illness by the intercession of the Virgin. A grave was made for him in his lifetime, in which he used to lay himself at full length to ascertain whether it fitted him: but this, as well as the statue in bronze which adorned the tomb, was destroyed by the Huguenots 1563. The existing monument is said to resemble the preceding one, except that the statue is in marble: it was executed by Michel Bourdin, an artist of Orleans, for Louis XIII. Louis is represented bareheaded, on his knees in an attitude of prayer, upon a black altar-tomb with four angels in the corners. The image of the Virgin is said to be the identical one before which Louis spent so many hours in prayer: it is black. Independently of its fine architectural proportions, the church possesses several objects of interest,—as the sculpture of the Sacristy, much mutilated, the carved wood-work of its stalls, the fine painted glass of the E. window, 16th cent., and the Chapel of the family of the Counts of Dunois, in which Tanneguy du Châtel was buried, 1477. A wretched road leads from this to Meung on the Loire.

The Loire is crossed by a wire suspension-bridge at

* *Post-road.*—13 St. Ay.

6. **Meung**, or **Mehun** Stat., a town whose name occurs in the annals of the English campaigns. It has a Romanesque *church*, and a red ruined *Castle* close beside it, partly concealed by trees, and backed by a hill.

l. In the churchyard of Lailly, Condillac was buried without a line to mark the spot. An irregular bridge of some 30 arches, the oldest parts of which date from the 15th or 16th cent., is thrown over the Loire at

7 *Beaugency** Stat. (*Inn:* l'Ecu de Brétagne, good), an antique town of 4849 Inhab., prettily situated between two hills. Conspicuous above its old houses rises the square *Donjon tower*, of great antiquity (10th or 11th centy.) and solid construction, 115 feet high, adjoining the *Castle* built by le beau Dunois. The *H. de Ville*, designed by the architect Viart of Orleans 1526, has an elegant front ornamented with the arms of the Card. de Longueville and of the Comte de Dunois. The *clocher de St. Firmin* is the only remains of the ch. of that saint, and is now attached to the Hôtel Dieu. Beaugency gives its name to one of the best wines of the Orléanois.

Some miles off, beyond the Loire, is Eugene Sue's Sybarite château, the effeminate and selfish splendour of which was thought so inconsistent with his Republican professions.

The high road runs at the back of the town, skirting without entering it, and for the next 3 stages separates itself from the Loire, to avoid its windings, and passes the little town of

12 **Mer** Stat. and **Suèvres**,† and the village of

11 **Menars le Château**‡ Stat., so called from the well-built but ill-kept château, which belonged to Madame de Pompadour, and under Louis XVIII. to the Duc de Bellune. It is now the property of the Prince de Chimay, who has established a college here.

l. St. Dié, nearly opposite Suèvres, is about 1¾ m. distant from the Palace of Chambord. (See p. 180.)

9 *Blois*§ Stat.—*Inns:* H. d'Angleterre, best; close to the bridge, comfortable, cheerful, and reasonable; civil landlord. H. de Blois, in the centre of the town.

This ancient and picturesque town, chef-lieu of the Dépt. Loire et Cher, containing 14,000 Inhab., is built upon a steep slope, crowned by its historic and gloomy castle at one end of the ridge, and by the cathedral at the other.

The quarter which reaches down to the river consists of modern houses, forming a handsome quay lined with rows of trees, and along it, between the town and the river, the high road passes. A bridge of 11 arches, surmounted by an obelisk in the centre, unites Blois with its suburb Vienne on the l. bank.

Numerous streets of stairs running up the hill, and winding narrow lanes lined with picturesque old houses, form the bulk of the town, and must be threaded to reach the very interesting

*Castle, for ages the residence of kings and princes, and the scene of momentous events, crimes, and murders. It has been degraded to a barrack, and was allowed to go to ruin until 1845, since which the government, with laudable zeal, has restored it to its pristine splendour, with excellent taste, under the direction of M. Duban, who restored the Ste. Chapelle at Paris. It is said that 480,000 fr. have been spent at Blois. The interior is well worth visiting, and affords an excellent idea of the decorations of houses in the 16th and 17th cent. The E. front, of red brick, facing the square, is of the time of Louis XII., who rebuilt this edifice, in which he was born.

The fine Gothic portal, surmounted by a niche or oriel, is not in the centre of the façade: it leads into a court, the E. side of which is lined with a cloister, resting on pillars carved with a netlike panelling. On the rt. hand (N. side) is the pile raised by Francis I., corresponding in style (Renaissance) with part of Chambord. That on the W. was commenced under Gaston Duc d'Orléans from the designs of Mansard, but never finished; that on the l. (S.) is the most ancient and least like a

---

* *Post-road.*—13 k. Beaugency.
† 13 Mer.   ‡ 10 Menars.
§ 8 Blois.

palace, the work of the early Dukes of Orleans. An elegant winding staircase of stone, on whose rich roof the Salamanders of Francis I. have been lately replaced, leads into the suite of rooms in which the tragedy of the Guises was consummated. Tradition, as it seems, gloating over this deed of blood and deception, has preserved the memory of the minutest particulars connected with it; and, though the interior was stripped of almost all its decorations at the Revolution, and the walls whitewashed like those of a prison, points out the chamber and oratoire of Catherine de Medicis, the contriver of the plot,—the *cabinet of Henri III.*, where he distributed with his own hand the daggers to his 45 gentlemen in waiting, who were to rid him of his rival, the hero of the barricades,—the *Vieux Cabinet*, at the entrance of which the victim, sent for by the king, was set upon by his assassins as he was turning aside the tapestry hung over the door, and fell pierced with more than 40 wounds,—the outer chamber where the body lay for 2 hours with a cloak and a cross of straw thrown over it, until the royal murderer, issuing from his den to look at the corse of the once mighty Henri le Balafré, spurned it in the face with his foot, saying, "Je ne le croyais pas aussi grand," and then ordered it to be burnt, and the ashes thrown into the river. During the progress of the murder, prayers were being offered up for its success in the adjoining chapel, distinguished by the pendants which still ornament its roof. This happened on the 23rd December, 1588:—on the following day the Cardinal de Lorraine, brother of the Balafré, was murdered in cold blood in another part of the castle. The ground floor at the N. E. angle of the building is occupied by the *Salle des Etats de Blois*, to attend the meeting of which the Guises had been enticed hither from Paris, their stronghold. It was while seated at the council board in this hall, eating prunes de Brignolles, that the duke was summoned by the royal page to attend the king. This hall is supposed to be as old as the 13th centy.: a row of pointed arches supports its double, barn-like roof of wood. The king's throne was placed against the wall on one side.

One other memorial of that age of crime and superstition remains to be noticed,—it is a sort of *pavillon* raised upon an old tower, detached from the S. side of the castle, projecting over the Ch. of St. Nicholas towards the river: this was the *Observatory of Catherine de Medicis*, to which she used to retire, with her astrologer, to consult the stars. It bears the inscription "Uraniæ Sacrum." A stone slab, like a tombstone, in front of the pavillon, served as a support for the astrolabe. The beautiful porcelain floorings in the rooms of Catherine de Medicis deserve notice.

A good general view of the gloomy château is gained by turning to the l., as you issue out of the great gate, through a vaulted passage into the Place du Collége, above which it rears aloft its sombre mass from a basement of grass-grown buttresses. Here we may remark the window from which Queen Marie de Medicis let herself down to escape when banished to Blois by the King her son, on the murder of Maréchal d'Ancre.

In the *Eglise St. Vincent*, now belonging to a sisterhood, facing this Place, is the tomb of Gaston d'Orléans, who passed here, in a sort of exile, the last 8 years of his insignificant life.

The *Ch. of St. Nicholas* is a very fine Gothic edifice, chiefly belonging to the 12th centy., surmounted by a central tower (pyramidal roof) and 2 W. towers (one rebuilt). The choir ends in an apse of 7 arches resting on single shafts, and there are 3 apsidal chapels behind. The manner in which the capitals are executed, the regularity of the arches, and the elegance of the circular Gothic dome which surmounts the central tower, deserve notice. This ch. has been restored.

The terraced *Gardens* attached to the former Evêché form a very agreeable walk, commanding a fine view of the town and river, extending to the distant towers of Chambord and Chaumont. The *Cathedral*, or Ch. of the Jesuits, said to have been built by Mansard, has been repaired. Not far from it a Maison des Fous, a handsome

180 Route 53.—*The Loire (B.)—Blois—Chambord.* Sect. III.

edifice, has been built. A vaulted sewer, partly cut in the solid rock, by some attributed to the Romans and called an *aqueduct*, runs under a considerable part of the town. It is known to the common people as the Pont de César.

A new square has been erected, having on one side the Préfecture, on another the Palais de Justice, and on a third the Halle au Blé.

In the old streets of Blois may still be found some interesting specimens of domestic architecture of the 16th centy. The H. d'Alluye retains an elegant portico in its inner court, and some rooms on the ground floor, but little altered. Miss Costello mentions a curiously-carved house in the Rue Pierre de Blois, leading to the Evêché; and there is an elaborately-sculptured staircase of wood representing St. George and the Dragon, with a central balustrade corded to the top, and compartments filled with various compositions.

Among the illustrious *natives* of Blois may be named the learned divine and chronicler, Peter of Blois, who died in England A.D. 1200; Louis XII.; and Denys Papin, for whom the French have claimed the invention of the steam-engine.

In 1814 the Empress Marie Louise, with the King of Rome, and the remnant of the Imperial court, government, and army, were despatched hither by Napoleon, who made his wife regent; and the last Imperial decrees were dated from hence.

Diligence to Vierzon Stat., on the way to Bourges, by Romorantin and the Sologne.

[The interesting *excursion to the Château de Chambord* may be conveniently made from Blois, whence it is about 12 m. distant, a 2 hrs.' drive. *Omnibus* daily to and fro; a carriage with 1 horse 8 fr., with 2 horses 15 fr. The road thither runs up the l. bank of the Loire in sight of the Château of Menars on the opposite bank, on an embankment or Levée, nearly as far as St. Dié, a village with a small *Inn* (au Grand Chambord), 1½ m. distant from the château. A cross road, in very bad condition, leads thence to

*Chambord, the Versailles of Touraine, until Louis XIV. deserted that beautiful province to fix the royal residence in a swamp close to the metropolis. It has no beauty of site to recommend it, being placed in the midst of a sandy flat, surrounded by a park 21 m. in circumference, where the roe and deer cross the traveller's path. The château itself, though somewhat fantastic, is on the whole a grand edifice, surmounted by a vast group of turrets, minarets, and cones, which rise conspicuous at a distance from a solid basement, the chief features of which are 6 round towers of prodigious size, 60 ft. in diameter, which seem the types of all those which characterise French châteaux. Its architecture marks the transition between the fortified castle and the Italian palace, and is a fine specimen of the age and taste of Francis I., who built it, after his return from captivity in Spain, on the site of a favourite hunting lodge of the Counts of Blois, engaging Primaticcio to furnish designs for it. He laid the foundation of it 1526, and employed 1800 men constantly on its construction until his death. It was afterwards continued, though with less zeal, by Henri II. and Charles IX.; and even Louis XV. added the low screen at the back, which, though from Mansard's designs, is ugly, and of course inappropriate to the style of the original. It is at present the property of the Duc de Bordeaux, having been purchased for him and presented to him by public subscription. He has been confirmed in his possession, though the Bourbons have forfeited other estates in France, by the decision of the French law courts. Its 440 chambers, though uninhabited, are undergoing judicious repairs in capital style and in good taste, the rental of the estate, amounting to about 3000*l.* a year, being entirely spent by its present possessor on its restoration. The sum already expended amounts to about 40,000*l.*

Enclosed within the building a *central* tower rises above all the rest, called *Donjon*, or Tour de la Fleur de Lis, from the lily of France, in stone, 6 ft. high, which surmounted it. After having escaped the hammer which defaced all its minor brethren so profusely scattered over the building, at the first Revolution, this monster lily was destined to fall at the second.

This tower is filled with a very beautiful double spiral staircase, an architectural curiosity, so contrived that 2 parties may pass up or down at the same time without meeting, scarcely even seeing each other. It opens on each floor upon 4 corridors, branching from it like the arms of a cross, vaulted. The compartments of their roof were once filled with the Salamander and F. of Francis I. One of these corridors was converted under Louis XIV. into a theatre, for the first performance of Molière's Bourgeois Gentilhomme, in which Molière and his troop performed before the King, for the first time, 1670. The device of Henri II. and Diana of Poitiers, the H. and D. entwined with the crescent, are distributed over the parts which he built, but left unfinished.

It is worth while to mount to the terrace and top of the tower to examine the details of the building, its solid masonry inlaid with morsels of black slate cut into the shape of lozenges, crescents, &c. Its rich niches, its classic chimneys converted into ornaments instead of being eye-sores, its balustrades and flying buttresses, are all curious specimens of the style of the Renaissance, resembling somewhat the Elizabethan architecture of Burleigh. The roof is like the hull of a ship, and must contain a forest of timber. From the top of the tower you look down upon the wide forest and wilderness of a park with its avenues.

Since the commencement of the liberal repairs and restorations now in progress, it is once more a pleasure to traverse the labyrinth of rooms, though showing no traces of the frescoes with which they were decorated by Jean Cousin. The well-read traveller, in imagination, can repeople their halls and corridors with the brilliancy and beauty of the courts of Francis I. and Henri II., recalling the time when Charles V. was entertained here on his passage through France, 1539, by his generous rival, or that when poor Ma-demoiselle de Montpensier here lost her heart to the fickle Lauzun.

Among the occupants of Chambord since it was deserted by its royal owners, was Marshal Saxe,—that veteran of a hundred fights, to whom it was given by Louis XV. He brought with him 6 cannon taken from the enemy, and a regiment of lancers, whom he reviewed daily from the terrace, although with one foot already in the grave. He died here 1750. It afterwards became the asylum of Stanislas King of Poland, and his queen Maria Leczinska. It was plundered and dismantled by the mob of 1792, and sold as national property. Napoleon bestowed it in 1809 upon Marshal Berthier, from whose widow it was purchased by a body of Loyalists, and presented to the Duc de Bordeaux, as already mentioned.]

[Another excursion may be made from Blois to Valençay by Selles, an old town on the Cher. The *Château of Valençay*, built by Philibert Delorme in the reign of Francis I., is interesting architecturally as a specimen of the style of the Renaissance, and historically as the prison-house allotted by Napoleon to Ferdinand VII. of Spain from 1808 to 1814, and still more as the residence of M. de Talleyrand during the latter part of his life. The larger rooms contain portraits of monarchs (Napoleon and Louis-Philippe presented by themselves) and of statesmen, his contemporaries. His study and bedchamber remained in 1843 exactly as he left them: his shoes, one furnished with steel spring and bandages for a club foot, his walking sticks, his desk, writing materials, together with his robes, stars, and orders, in a glass case, may still be seen.

Talleyrand's last resting-place is in a vault beneath the chapel of a small nunnery, in a narrow street off the Place at Valençay. It is entered through an iron trap-door in the floor, and in one corner a dark stone sarcophagus contains all that remains of the wily minister of so many sovereigns. By the marriage of a niece of the Duchesse de Dino, it now belongs to the family Montmorency.

Returning to Selles, the traveller

may proceed down the valley of the Cher to Chénonceaux, and thence to Amboise or Loches, passing through St. Aignan, where there is a magnificent *Château* of various ages, formerly belonging to the Ducs de St. A. It is inhabited and kept up with beautiful gardens and terraces, fine trees, and profusion of flowers; the gardens open to the townspeople.]

Bidding adieu to Blois, its frowning castle, whose W. front looking down the Loire is imposing and more cheerful than the rest, with the astrological tower of Catherine de Medicis in front of it, and the pepper-box dome of the cathedral in the distance, we resume our journey between vine hills and willow beds.

rt. Hereabouts begins the colossal dyke called *La Levée*, commenced in very ancient times under the Carlovingian monarchs, and augmented and improved by different kings of France, to restrain the furious Loire within its bed, and check its destructive inundations. It runs along the rt. bank as far as the mouth of the Mayenne, below Angers, a distance of about 100 m. It is faced with masonry kept in constant repair, and the high road is carried along its top. It is a considerable work, though vastly inferior to the dykes of Holland, and was burst through by the inundation of 1846. There are other very extensive dykes on the l. bank in different portions of the river's course.

This high embankment conceals from the view of those who travel by water the wide and fertile plain beyond it; only now and then the tops of houses are seen rising above it.

9 Chousy Stat.*
6 Ouzain Stat. The first object to be noticed below Blois is,

1. The *Château de Chaumont*, a conspicuous building picturesquely situated on a height, with machicolated towers, forming 3 sides of a square. It was the residence of Cath. de Medicis, whose chamber is shown, and who here spent her time in plotting and in reading the stars until the death of her husband, Henri II., when she obliged his mistress, Diana of Poitiers, to exchange her bijou château of Chénonceaux (p. 184) for this, which, however, Diana does not appear to have inhabited. It was the birthplace of the Cardinal George d'Amboise, 1460, the wise and popular minister of France under Louis XII. The arms, still visible, cut in the masonry, are a blazing hill,—chaudmont.

Limeray Stat.
rt.* Veuves: a little beyond this the Loire enters the province of Touraine, and the Dépt. Indre et Loire.

The high road does not pass through Amboise, but through a suburb on the opposite bank of the river.

1. *Amboise Stat.†—Inns:* Lion d'Or; cheap and homely. At the Cygne, on the rt. bank of the river, close to the Poste aux Chevaux, the landlord keeps a good horse and cab, and charges to Chénonceaux 8 fr., or thither and to Loches 15 fr.

Amboise, an old and languid town of 4600 Inhab., stands on the l. bank of the Loire, here divided by an island, upon which the 2 bridges which cross the river rest.

The principal and most conspicuous object is the *Castle*, long the residence of the Kings of France, and late the property of the King of the French, Louis Philippe. Its buildings, flanked by round towers roofed with cones, reduced to a very small portion of their original extent, occupy the platform of a lofty rock, escarped in front and rear. Louis Philippe, who inherited the castle as the descendant of the Duc de Penthièvre, caused the old houses to be swept away from the base of the rock, so as to form an opening from the bridge to a *tunnel* which he bored through the rock and under the castle. It is vaulted with masonry. Two enormous towers, 90 ft. high and 42 in diameter, spring from the ground at the base of the rock, and rise to the level of the other towers. They contain 2 winding, inclined planes of so gradual a slope that horses and even carriages can ascend them to the summit of the rock. The one in front has been closed to form a saloon, but that behind, on the l. as you emerge from the tunnel, still gives

---

* *Post-road.*—10 Chousy.   * *Post-road.*—11 Veuves.   † 12 Amboise.

access to the castle, and is remarkable for its elegant florid Gothic doorway and groined roof. This and most of the other existing buildings date from the time of Charles VIII., who was much attached to Amboise, having been born here, 1470; he also died here, 1498.

During the latter part of Louis Philippe's reign (1847), the castle was converted into a prison, in which the brave Arab chief Abd-el-Kader and his family were immured. He was released by Louis Napoleon, 1853.

In the interior of the château there is nothing worth seeing. The improving hand of the late possessor had pierced holes as big as the embrasures of a battery in its old and massive walls, to admit broad day into vaults once perhaps cachots or oubliettes, but now, by the aid of whitewash, ventilation, and stoves, converted into comfortable kitchens, larders, pantries, and cellars; while the upper rooms, papered, polished, and filled with cast-off furniture from the Palais Royal, preserve no traces of antiquity. Yet in them perhaps was decided the bloody doom of those 1200 miserable and misled Huguenot prisoners concerned in the well-known "*Conjuration d'Amboise*," which had for its object to extricate the young and simple king Francis II. from the clutches and influence of the Guises, 1560. The secret of the plot was betrayed to the Duc de Guise by one of the conspirators, and its leader, La Renaudie, seized and hung on a gibbet in the centre of the bridge. The remainder of the conspirators were dispersed and everywhere seized; the castle walls were decorated with the hanging bodies of the criminals, and the courts and streets of the town streamed with blood, until the wearied headsman, resigning his axe, consigned the remainder to other executioners, who drowned them in the Loire. Such was the extent of the carnage that the court was driven from Amboise by the stench of the dead bodies. This butchery formed the prelude to the still more horrible tragedy of St. Bartholomew. In 1470 the exiled Queen Margaret of Anjou and her son, through the intervention of the cunning Louis XI., were reconciled in this castle to her quondam foe, by whom her own husband had been dethroned, the Earl of Warwick, the kingmaker. Hatred to Edward IV. became the bond of union, and they agreed in vowing vengeance on him.

The *gardens* are well kept up, and the view from their terraces is as good as that from the château itself, which is not worth entering, as it contains no paintings or architectural decorations, and is simply furnished as a country gentleman's house. Within the garden, however, stands the *little Chapel*, one of the most exquisite morsels of profusely florid Gothic in France, restored by Louis Philippe in a manner creditable to French taste. It is in the form of a cross, was built for Anne of Brittany, and is dedicated to St. Hubert, whose miraculous meeting with the stag, having a cross growing between its horns, is curiously carved over the rich doorway. This and the interior are panelled throughout, or decorated with foliage of the most delicate sculpture. The leaves, showing all their fibres, crisped and curled round the edges like kail, are cut behind in a style more common in ivory than stone. Interspersed among the foliage are singular and grotesque figures; along the wall runs a sort of frieze of stone-work; the roof is elaborately groined, and the pendants hanging from it carved with grotesques, the whole reminding one of the richness of Henry VII.'s chapel, without its arrangement. Underneath is a crypt in which was originally placed the *Holy Sepulchre*, now removed to the chapel of *St. Florentin* in the town below. It consists of a group of figures as large as life, well executed in baked clay and coloured, representing the entombment of our Lord. The figures are said to be portraits of the family of an intendant of the palace named Babou, the three Marys being likenesses of his daughters, who were in turn mistresses of Francis I., as the story goes!! Marie de Beauvilliers and Gabrielle d'Estrées, mistresses of Henri IV., were daughters of 2 of these ladies.

The *Ch. of St. Denis*, restored, is interesting to the architect and antiquary.

In the cliff a little above the castle, and entered from the garden behind a private house, are very singular caverns called *Les Greniers de César*. They consist of a lofty, narrow excavation running in a direct line into the rock, evidently once divided into three stories, as the broken edges of the chalk vaulting which formed the roofs and floors still remain; and by their removal the three are thrown into one. The walls are covered with cement. At the extremity is a round, vaulted chamber lined with masonry; at one side runs a staircase cut in the rock, descending towards the river and ascending to a level with the roof of the high excavation, where it leads to three other similar vaulted chambers, constructed, it is supposed, to hold corn. There is a tradition that Cæsar, after conquering the Gallic confederation, reached the Loire at this spot, and formed a camp, traces of which still exist on the cliff above, together with these caves below it, to serve as storehouses.

It seems likely that these caves had a much later origin, though their destination was probably for granaries or cellars.

Amboise is said to derive its name from its position between the two streams, " ab ambabus aquis," the Loire and the Amasse, which here falls into the Loire.

[A very pleasant excursion may be made from Amboise to *Chénonceaux*, 10 m. S. The road lies through the forest of Amboise (till 1852 a domain of the Orleans family), passing on the rt. the pagoda of the park of *Chanteloup*, whose magnificent château, the retreat of the Duc de Choiseul, discarded minister of Louis XV., when banished from the court to his estate by way of punishment, has disappeared. After the Revolution it belonged to le Comte Chaptal, the distinguished chemist and minister of Buonaparte, who established here a refinery of sugar from beetroot, which he first brought to perfection. The château was pulled down and sold about 1830 by the "bande noir."]

At Bléré (*Inn:* H. de la Promenade) we reach the valley of the Cher; and a road turning to the l. up the rt. bank of the river, covered hereabouts with black vines (gros noir), leads to the village of Chénonceaux (possessing a poor auberge), which is connected by an avenue with the

Château de Chénonceaux.

In front of the building extends a stately terrace lined with stone balustrades set with orange-trees, approached by a flight of steps; and adjoining is a pleasure garden.

Château Chénonceaux has nearly as many *souvenirs* about it as Amboise, but not of so disagreeable a kind. It was built in the more joyous days of Francis I. Its picturesque round towers, bartizans, and bridged moat, though still preserving the shape of a castle, were not meant for defence; and its front is covered over with graceful and delicate Italian ornaments, such as are seen at Longleat, at Audley End, and in works of Inigo Jones. It stands on the river Cher: literally *on*, for it is built partly upon a bridge, and the river passes under it. At a distance it is most picturesque, with its green court, its single advanced round tower, occupied by the *Concierge*, and pretty formal gardens around. Its interior is almost unaltered since the day it was built, besides, what is so rare in France, being well and carefully kept up, retaining all its old furniture, old cabinets, old china, enamels, and glass. Its vaulted hall is hung with armour, its walls are covered with stamped cloth, its doors are screened by tapestry curtains which draw aside, and the rich ceilings are of blue ground studded with stars. You are shown the very glass out of which Francis I. drank; Mary Queen of Scots' mirror, &c. But its chief interest depends on the persons who have lived in it. It was given by Henri II. to his mistress, Diana de Poitiers, who enlarged it by extending the bridge, previously constructed over only part of the river, quite to the other side, and raising upon it a handsome, but less quaint and interesting building, of two stories. Hither her royal lover used to repair after

Sect. III.   *Route 53.—The Loire (B)—Chénonceaux.*   185

hunting in the neighbouring forest of Loches. Her initial D is plentifully introduced combined with his H, thus ⟨HD⟩. She was, however, dispossessed of her fair mansion, on the death of Henri, by the wicked and unscrupulous Catherine de Medicis, whose bedroom, with the original furniture, is still shown. It was afterwards for some time occupied by Louise de Lorraine, widow of Henri III.: her chamber is still hung with black. Nor does the list of distinguished inmates cease here, for near the end of the last century all the wits of the time used to assemble here, drawn together by the owner of the mansion, Madame Dupin, a beautiful, amiable, and accomplished lady, who died so recently as 1799, at the age of 93. In her time, Voltaire, the exiled Bolingbroke, Rousseau, and many others, were her constant visitors; and in the little, dusty, faded theatre, which occupies the end of Diana's gallery, Rousseau's opera, 'Le Devin du Village,' was performed for the first time. The collection of historical portraits, including all the persons who have lived here, is very curious; among them a whole-length portrait of Diana, said to be by Primaticcio, in the costume of her namesake, the goddess, with a dog in a leash, a bow at her back, and wearing a taffeta petticoat, embroidered with golden fleurs-de-lis. · Here are also portraits of Henri IV., of Sully, of Rabelais, and a cast of the sweet face of Agnes Sorel from her monument at Loches. The most remarkable thing about Chénonceaux, perhaps, is that it escaped the ravages of the Revolution, owing solely to the respect which the character of Madame Dupin, its mistress, commanded. Strangers are obligingly admitted by the present proprietor, le Comte de Villeneuve, to see the interior.

Loches (Rte. 56) is about 18 m. S. of Chénonceaux; the road runs partly through the forest of Loches. It is a dreary ride.

rt. The road to Tours, below Amboise, is carried along the Levée, at no great distance from the Loire.

Noisay Stat.

Vernau Stat.

13 Vouvray Stat. Here the Rly. is carried across the Loire to its l. bank on *a bridge*.

l. Mont Louis Stat. This village, composed partly of caves cut in the rocks, was the place of meeting of an ecclesiastical assembly, convened to witness the reconciliation of Henry II. with Thomas Becket only 3 months before his assassination.

rt. Frillière.* Near this the banks of the river rise into considerable heights; and on the top of a projecting promontory stands, conspicuous from afar, rt., the feudal beacon-tower, called *Lanterne de la Roche Corbon*, not unlike a great factory-chimney of modern times. It anciently communicated by telegraphic signals with the Castle of Amboise. It is about 50 ft. high, and stands on the very verge of the cliff, above the small village of Roche Corbon, remarkable because most of its habitations are cut out of the limestone (craie tuffeau). They are sometimes faced with walls, at others with partitions of the living rock, and are prettily festooned with vines. One mass of rock which must have slipped from above, and now lies in a nook, is turned into 2 cottages of 2 stories. These habitations seem comfortable, and are mostly provided with little gardens in front. Some large excavations which belonged to the castle of Roche Corbon, with fragments of masonry, remain. It is worth while to climb up to the top of the rock, beside the Lanterne, to look down upon the Loire from thence—a pleasing prospect. It is possible to scramble through the vineyards along the top of the cliff nearly to St. Radegonde, and so to reach Tours ($4\frac{1}{2}$ m.), but there is no path.

rt. A row of villas with formal gardens, interspersed with villages, line the bank nearly all the way to Tours, whose cathedral towers form a fine object in the distance.

rt. The round tower, rising at the water-side, close to the road, together with a gate-house and a few crumbling foundations of pillars and walls, are

* *Post-road.*—12 La Frillière.

the sole remains of the once magnificent *Abbey of Marmoutiers* (Majus Monasterium), one of the richest in France, founded by St. Martin, in which the sainte ampoulle, or vessel of holy oil, given by an angel to St. Martin to rub a bruise which he had received, was preserved, an object of veneration with pilgrims. It was sent to Chartres to anoint Henri IV. at his coronation.

1. Just above the city of Tours is the mouth of the *canal* or cut which joins the Loire to the Cher, whose course is nearly parallel with the Loire, and only 13½ m. S. of it.

10 l. TOURS *Terminus* on the S. side of the town. It is also terminus of the lines to Bordeaux (Rte. 64) and Nantes (Rte. 58).

TOURS.*—*Inns*: H. de l'Univers, a large and handsome building, one of the best in France, fitted up with every English convenience, clean and moderate; H. de Bordeaux; both these are near to the railway terminus; Faisan, good; H. de Londres, comfortable; La Boule d'Or, in the Rue Nationale.

Tours, chief town of the Dépt. Indre et Loire, and once capital of Touraine, is situated in the midst of the fertile but flat valley of the Loire, on its l. bank, and between it and the Cher, and has 28,000 Inhab. The highway from Paris to Bordeaux and Bayonne here crosses the river by its *bridge* of 15 arches, 1423 ft. long, and traverses the whole extent of the town through its main street, the *Rue Impériale* or *Nationale*, a fine avenue running in a direct line from the bridge, near which a statue of Descartes is erected, and containing the principal cafés, shops, and offices of the diligences. At its entrance from the bridge stands on the rt. the *H. de Ville*, and on the l. the *Musée*, while in front run quays and planted platforms, serving as promenades. The town is no longer remarkable for the many objects of curiosity which it possessed before the sweeping convulsion of the Revolution; and the charms of its situation, in an unvaried plain, have been greatly overrated by the French.

* *Post-road.*— 12 Tours.

The Loire, though a fine river at certain seasons, contributes less to its beauty than might be expected, owing to a great part of its channel being left bare in summer, so that only three or four of the arches of the bridge bestride the shrunken stream, while the rest traverse wide, ugly beds of bare gravel. Owing to the flatness of the surface and the dust there are few interesting walks or rides in its immediate vicinity. However, our description of the town shall assume the form of a walk which may occupy a long morning or a short day.

Starting from the main street, the Rue Nationale, a turning on the l. (Rue de la Scellerie) leads you past the *Poste aux Lettres* to the Archevêché, approached by a handsome Italian portal, at the side of which rises the stately *Cathedral* of *St. Gatien*. The W. front, consisting of 3 lofty portals enriched with florid ornaments, niches, and foliage, surmounted by a window having a 4-pointed head, astonishes by its vastness: it dates from about 1510. The 2 towers which flank it are 205 ft. high; their domed tops, carved as with scales, are somewhat later than the rest, and of a debased Italian style, not conformable with the lower part.

The interior, 256 ft. long and 85 ft. high, is in a mature and noble style of Gothic resembling early English, with varied capitals to the columns. The choir was begun 1170, and the nave carried on to completion in the reign of St. Louis; but the W. end is still later, of the 15th century. In the beautiful old painted glass surrounding the choir, and shedding a venerable gloom about the altar, may be seen the arms of St. Louis, of his mother, Blanche of Castile, and those of the town, a group of towers. The fine rose-window in the N. transept is injured in effect by a thick stone prop carried through the middle to support the roof. At the angle of the S. transept and aisle is the marble monument of the 2 only children of Charles VIII. and Anne de Bretagne, in consequence of whose early deaths the succession passed to the branch of Valois Orléans.

Figures of the 2 princes, watched by angels, recline on a sarcophagus of white marble decorated with the arms of France, with dolphins, bas-reliefs, and ornaments in the style of the *Renaissance*: it is the work of 2 Touraingeaux artists named Juste, contemporaries of Jean Goujon.

It is worth while to ascend the towers on account of the view, which includes Amboise, Plessis les Tours, and the course of the Loire and Cher. The woodwork of the roof, a masterpiece of carpentry, covering the stone roof, and the elegant, light, spiral staircase (*Renaissance*), resting on a crown of open groins or ribs, in the N. tower, should be seen at the same time.

Passing from the cathedral towards the quay, a circular and machicolated tower is seen on the rt., enclosed within the Cavalry Barracks: it is the only remaining part of the *Castle* built by Henry II. of England in the 12th centy. From this tower Charles de Lorraine, the son of the Duc de Guise le Balafré, imprisoned by Henri III. after his father's murder at Blois, escaped by letting himself down by a rope. Turning to the l. and following the line of the quay, you reach the iron *wire Bridge* (Pont Suspendu) erected by M. Seguin 1847, and lower down the stone *Bridge* (b. 1762) already mentioned: several of its arches have given way at different times, owing to the river undermining its foundations.

The *Musée* contains a collection of nearly 200 bad pictures, chiefly copies, and some casts; it is open to the public only on Sundays, 12–4. A Last Judgment, brought from the chapel of the castle of Plessis, may be mentioned as curious.

A little way up the Rue Nationale, on the l. in going from the bridge, is the *Ch. of St. Julien*, until 1847 desecrated and turned into a remise and coach-house for diligences, but happily rescued by a subscription raised among a few private persons amounting to 80,000 frs. It is a fine pointed edifice, date 1224, except the lower part of the W. tower, which is founded upon circular arches, with Romanesque capitals belonging to an older church. The building is undergoing repairs in order that it may be rendered fit for divine service. There are 3 or 4 desecrated churches here.

The first street on the rt. is the Rue de Commerce; and No. 30, said to have been the Chancellerie de Louis XI. (now Hôtel Gouin), is the handsomest old mansion in the town, and a perfectly preserved specimen of the style of the *Renaissance* (16th centy.) adapted to domestic architecture: its front is richly decorated with coats of arms, scroll-work, &c.; its dormer windows are terminated by crocketed gables; a turret projects in front, below which is the entrance, and round the bottom runs a light trefoil balustrade.

Continuing our walk along the Rue de Commerce we come to the Rue des Trois Pucelles, where the house No. 18 passes for that of *Tristan l'Hermite*, the ill-omened executioner of Louis XI. (see 'Quentin Durward'), though there is no authority for the designation. It is a brick mansion, apparently of the 15th centy.: its front terminates in a gable, and is flanked by a stair turret, 70 ft. high, curiously vaulted with brick, overtopping the neighbouring houses and commanding a view of Plessis. Its door and windows are enriched with florid canopies, that over the door supported on twisted columns; but the remarkable feature, to which alone the house owes its name, is that the string courses dividing the 3 stories are formed by ropes in relief, ending in fantastic knots so as to resemble the noose of a halter. The same ornament occurs on the tomb of Anne of Brittany, and on her chantry at Loches, and was adopted by her as an heraldic badge of her widowhood. This house may have belonged to her or to some of her retainers. On the wall may be read the motto, "Assez aurons, et peu vivrons," and "Priez pour —." The court-yard walls are similarly decorated, and on the ground floor is an elegant vaulted recess for a lavatory. In the same street, on the opposite side, is a house of evidently much greater antiquity (14th centy.), having a vaulted ground floor, and an arcade of pointed arches running along its first floor.

In going hence to the Vieux Marché, a corner house, now a shop, is remarkable for the carvings on the front, representing the Holy Family.

In the centre of the market-place itself is a white *marble fountain*, La Fontaine de Baune, of considerable elegance, in the *Renaissance* style, executed by the brothers Juste. Among its ornaments are the porcupine, the crest of Louis XII., and the ermine of Anne of Brittany.

Two Towers, rising on either side of the Rue St. Martin, are conspicuous objects in all views of the town: one, containing the clock, having a domed top, is called the Tour de St. Martin, or d'Horloge; the other, La Tour de Charlemagne, was so named, it is said, because his wife Luitgarde was buried below it. They deserve notice and mention as the only remaining relics of the vast *Cathedral of St. Martin of Tours*. The palladium of this celebrated building was the shrine of St. Martin, the first metropolitan of Tours (A.D. 340), which became to the barbarians of the dark ages what Delphi was to the Greeks—the oracle which kings and chiefs came to consult in the beginning of the 7th centy. The concourse of pilgrims to this shrine occasioned the old Roman town *Cæsarodunum* of the *Turones* to swell to ten times its original extent. The great ecclesiastical establishment, of which this church was the centre, spread civilization and religion through the country, and its archbishop became the patriarch of France and one of the most influential persons in the state. At the head of the chapter even the kings of France were proud to enrol themselves.

Its treasures in precious metals, jewels, &c., amounted to 575 marcs of gold and 2200 marcs of silver in 1562, when it was pillaged by the Huguenots, who broke the images, melted the lamps, and burnt the relics deposited here. After flourishing for 12 centuries, the church, an enormous edifice, was utterly destroyed at the Revolution, excepting two towers out of the five which adorned it. On viewing the space which now intervenes between them, some idea may be formed of its extent. One of these stood at the W. end, the other at the N.W.; both seem from their style to date from the 12th centy. Attached to that of St. Martin may be seen Romanesque pillars and capitals of an earlier edifice. Louis XI., through gratitude for supposed benefits derived from the Saint's intercession, surrounded St. Martin's shrine with a railing of solid silver which weighed nearly 6776 marcs. His needy follower, Francis I., had it taken down and converted into good crown-pieces, which were called "testons au gros bonnet."

Bishop Gregory of Tours, a native of the city, was buried within the walls of this church.

A florid Gothic portal, forming the front of a house in the street running from the market to the Rue St. Martin, was one of the residences of the chapter.

The *Halle au Blé* is another secularised church, dedicated to St. Clement, gutted to a mere shell. It is a building of the 16th centy.; its florid N. porch, though mutilated, still retains portions of foliage cut with much delicacy. There is nothing to be seen within.

The new *Palais de Justice* is a splendid building. There are extensive *Barracks* at the river-side near to the suspension bridge.

Plessis les Tours, the castellated den of the tyrant and bigot Louis XI., with which all the world is acquainted through the admirable descriptions of 'Quentin Durward,' is situated in the commune of La Riche, adjoining a humble hamlet of scattered cottages, on a perfectly flat plain, about a mile distant from the Halle au Blé, on the W. of Tours, passing the Barrière des Oiseaux, and beyond the Hospice Générale. Visitors to Plessis must not expect anything in the shape of a feudal castle, for it was built at a time when the fortress was giving place to the fortified mansion. When complete, it must have been somewhat like the older parts of Hampton Court and St.

James's Palaces, which were built not many years after Plessis, with this difference, that the niggardliness of Louis, and his apprehension of danger, caused it to be built in so plain a style, and with so many defensive precautions, walls of enclosure, drawbridges, battlements, and wet and dry ditches, that its external appearance must have corresponded with that of a gaol much more than of a palace. The small fragment now remaining, so far from having about it the least trace or character of a castle, looks like a mean ordinary dwelling: indeed it formed part of the inner constructions, but was surrounded by three ramparts and fosses. It is of plain red brick, with quoins of stone and sash windows, surmounted by a high pitched roof, and almost all traces of the scanty ornaments have been destroyed. Beside it is a stair turret, recently raised 16 or 20 ft., with a wooden addition at the side, to convert it into a *shot-tower!* Originally a cloister ran along the front. The interior is modern, except the stair, and contains nothing worth notice. All traces are gone of the pitfalls, fosses, &c., which originally surrounded the castle; but on the l., as you approach the house, are seen the foundations of walls of masonry; and a door, below ground, leads into a range of vaulted chambers barely lighted by small windows, which may once have served for prisons, as they now do for cellars. It is evident that the palace was well supplied with dungeons. At the end of the small terrace walk in the garden is another vault, called the *prison of Cardinal de la Balue*, who was shut up for betraying his master's secrets to Charles of Burgundy: it has been repaired, but the lower steps of a stair, the lower part of the fireplace, the grated bars and shutters are old. At the back of a cottage, nearly facing the garden gates, is a small vaulted chapel, now filled with casks, said to be the *Oratory* of Louis XI., where he passed hours in abject prayer to the Virgin and Saints for cure of his complicated maladies. The present doorway has been broken through the wall where the altar stood;

the two small windows are nearly stopped up. Louis ended his miserable life here, 1483. Plessis was converted into a Dépôt de Mendicité about 1778; it was sold and pulled down at the Revolution. Plessis lies on the tongue of land between the Loire and Cher, about 1 m. from the Cher, and 9 m. above their junction.

Between Plessis and the Hospice is an old house, called *La Rabaterie*, having a square turret at the back which passes for the residence of Olivier le Daim, the barber and minister of Louis.

There remains little else to describe at Tours. Under the mutilated church of *Notre Dame la Riche* (originally called La Pauvre) is a cave, vaulted, and having pillars in the corners, where it is said St. Gatien, the predecessor of St. Martin, first preached Christianity to the Gauls, A.D. 251, but it is now shut up.

At the *Préfecture* is placed the *Public Library* of 40,000 volumes, including some curious MSS.; for example, a copy of the Gospels in gold letters on vellum, which belonged to the church of St. Martin, upon which the King of France took the oaths as premier chanoine of that church; Les Heures of Charles V. of France and of Anne de Bretagne; and numerous Missals, besides early printed books. The library is open Tuesday, Wednesday, Thursday, and Friday, 12-4.

The most respectable *Café* is that *de la Ville de Paris*, Rue Nationale.

The *Poste aux Lettres* is in the Rue de la Scellerie, and the *Theatre* in the same.

The number of English established in and around Tours is considerable, but has diminished since 1848: they have a subscription *club*.

The *English Church* service is performed every Sunday at $11\frac{1}{2}$ and $4\frac{1}{2}$ in the chapel, Rue de la Préfecture.

Railways:—To Angers and Nantes; to Poitiers, Angoulême, and Bordeaux; to Paris, by Orleans; in progress to Le Mans.

Diligences daily, to Loches, Bourges, and Chinon; to Le Mans, Vendôme; to Chartres and Laval.

Steamers (?) to Nantes (in 11 hrs.) Tours was long famed for its manufacture of silk, established 1480 by Louis XI., who brought over and settled here Italian weavers. This branch of industry, however, was ruined by the revocation of the Edict of Nantes, by which the population was reduced from 80,000 to less than one half. This tyrannical act transferred 3000 families, with their wealth and industry, from France to Holland, and the manufacture dwindled away at Tours to take root at Lyons. Tours has now no manufacture of great importance, but receives some life from being a place of much passage, planted on one of the great high roads of France. The *pruneaux de Tours*, once so celebrated, are now far less esteemed in commerce than the dried plums of Gascony and Provence.

Tours is a city of some importance in history. The *Turones*, its ancient inhabitants, joined the league of the 64 Gallic towns under Vercingetorix against Julius Cæsar, and are mentioned by Lucan, "Instabiles Turones circumsita castra coerunt." The Lande de Miré, about 9 m. to the S.W. on the road to Azay-le-Rideau, is supposed to be the place where the Saracens under Abderahmen were defeated by Charles Martel, and Europe saved from the Mahomedan yoke, A.D. 732.

One of the chief mints of France was established in the middle ages at Tours, whence come the *livres Tournois*, silver pieces (libra or as of the Romans), the equivalent of francs at present, which were coined here.

The *Porte Hugon*, which stood at the end of a street running down to the Loire, is said to have given the name of Huguenots to the Protestant party in France, who, being very numerous in the town, but checked and watched by their enemies, used to meet beyond the walls, issuing out stealthily through this gate at nightfall. A more probable derivation of Huguenot is from the Swiss Eidgenossen, *i.e.* Confederate. Another memorial of the days of persecution of the Protestants is retained in the name *Rue Renard*, persons suspected of heresy being pursued in the streets by the Romanists about 1562, hunted down with the cry "au Reynard," and often massacred.

Touraine was bestowed as an *apanage* on Mary Queen of Scots and her short-lived husband Francis, and she is said to have drawn revenue from it, as Duchess of Touraine, even while in captivity in England, but it was afterwards given in her lifetime to the Duc d'Alençon, brother of Henri III.

It is a pleasant walk of about 4 m. along the road to Orleans up the rt. bank of the Loire to the singular village *La Roche Corbon*, excavated out of the rock (p. 185). It would be better to ride thither, and thus avoid the long dusty road.

The *Colony of Mettray*, about $4\frac{1}{2}$ m. from Tours, established by two philanthropic French gentlemen, the Vicomte Bretignères de Courteilles and le conseiller Demetz, deserves very high praise, and will be visited by all who take an interest in the improvement of their fellow-creatures. The objects which its founders and directors have in view are, the education, reward, and restoration to society of juvenile offenders who while in the public prisons have distinguished themselves by good conduct and by signs of penitence. This is sought to be effected by teaching them the mode of gaining an honest livelihood, chiefly by agricultural labour. The ground on which the establishment stands was given by the Vicomte; it is conducted by him and his friend in person, and is supported by voluntary donations and annual subscriptions.

More distant and highly interesting excursions may be made to Amboise (p. 182), Chénonceaux, 24 m. off (p. 184; 4 hrs.' drive), Loches (p. 191), and to that curious and unexplained monument of antiquity La Pile de St. Mars (p. 196).

M. Souillé furnishes good *horses* and carriages.

ROUTE 54.
CHARTRES TO TOURS, BY VENDÔME.

139 kilom. = 88 Eng. m.
Diligences daily.
15 La Bourdinière.
16 Bonneval.
An ancient Benedictine convent here is converted into a cotton-mill.

14 Châteaudun, a town of 6500 Inhab., standing on the banks of the Loire. Its most conspicuous building is the ancient *Castle* of the Counts of Dunois, surmounted by a prodigious tower, 90 ft. high, built by Thibaut le Tricheur in the 10th centy. The ancient name of the town, whence comes the modern, was Castellodunum.

During the next stage the road descends by the side of the Loire, passing the Gothic castle of Montigny on a height beyond the river.
12 Cloyes.
17 Pezou.

11 Vendôme.—*Inns:* H. Gaillarde, good; Lion d'Or, not bad. A town of 9470 Inhab., on the Loire, at the foot of vine-clad slopes. Above it rise the picturesque ruins of the *Castle* of the Ducs de Vendôme, demolished at the Revolution, when the graves of Jeanne d'Albret, mother of Henri IV., and of several Bourbon princes, were rifled, and their tombs destroyed. Near the Lion d'Or is a fine flamboyant *Ch.*, containing good painted glass, with elaborate and beautiful wood carvings in the stalls of the choir. It has an early Gothic tower and spire. Nearly opposite to it are very curious remains of a *Norman* Domestic edifice of unusually early date. Several smaller churches will repay the notice of a lover of church architecture. There is a *College* here.

We now cross the Loire for the 4th time, and quit its valley to traverse a monotonous plain to
14 Neuve St. Amand.
12 Château Regnault, a town of 2500 Inhab.
15 Monnaye (Indre et Loire).
15 Tours, in Rte. 53.

ROUTE 56.
TOURS TO LOCHES AND CHÂTEAUROUX.

108 kilom. = 67 Eng. m.
Diligences, daily, to Loches, in about $4\frac{1}{2}$ hrs.

You continue along the road to Bordeaux (Rte. 64) for about 2 m. after crossing the Cher; then turn to the l. Several small villages are passed whose houses are caves cut in the soft rock, the fronts built up with masonry, the roofs covered with vines, from the midst of which peer the chimneys. After passing the prettily situated village of

19 Cormery (interesting *Church*, and a detached spire of a ruined abbey) we reach the borders of the Indre, which flows through one of the richest and most fertile valleys of Touraine; in the midst of which stands

21 *Loches. Inns:* H. de la Tour; cheap, and obliging landlord: H. Grand Monarque. This is one of the most picturesque towns of Touraine, far more striking than Chinon or Amboise; its buildings are huddled together round the base of a lofty rock, from whose commanding top the romantic ruins of its historic and ill-omened *Castle* still frown over the landscape, forming the grand and striking feature in every view. In and around the town the number of religious houses, which clustered around the castle, is remarkable. Many of the buildings remain. The town still retains several of its old *gates*, grooved for the portcullis, and garnished with holes for stockade beams, and in its streets are some old houses. Pop. 4753.

On the opposite bank of the Indre lies the suburb of Beaulieu, connected with the town by a row of bridges. The river winding through the vale overspreads its bottom with a carpet of the richest verdure, fringed with willows and poplars, and turns the machinery of one or two mills.

The *Castle of Loches*, though long a royal palace, in which James V. of Scotland was married to Magdalen of France, and where Francis I. held his splendid court and received the Emperor Charles V. on his way from Spain to Ghent, is better known and has a more terrible reputation as a prison of state, especially during the reign of Louis XI., when "the sound of the name of Loches was yet more dreaded than Plessis itself, as a place destined to the workings of those secret acts of cruelty with which even Louis shamed to pollute the interior of his own residence at Plessis. There were in this place of terror dungeons under dungeons, some of them unknown even to the keepers themselves; living graves, to which men were consigned with little hope of further employment during the rest of their life than to breathe impure air, and feed on bread and water. At this formidable castle were also those dreadful places of confinement called cages, in which the wretched prisoner could neither stand upright nor stretch himself at length; an invention, it is said, of Cardinal Balue."—*Scott.* Louis appointed Olivier le Daim, the barber, who was also his prime minister, governor of the castle and gaoler. It is composed of a pile of buildings of various ages, partly in ruins. The most conspicuous of all is the tall white Donjon tower, rising at the extremity of the platform of rock to a height of 120 ft., and overhanging the verge of the precipice. Its walls of even and perfect masonry, supported by buttresses in the form of circular pillars, pierced by scanty round-headed windows above, and by mere slits below, mark it as a work of the Norman style, probably of the 12th centy., though some attribute its construction to Foulques Nerra, Comte d'Anjou, in the 11th. In its size, form, and arrangement of the entrance stair, within a projecting lower tower, it is not unlike the White Tower of London, and the castles of Newcastle or Rochester. Its walls, 8 ft. thick, are now empty, gutted of the four stories into which they were divided. It stands within the enclosure of the town gaol, a part of the castle having been converted into that ignoble purpose. Beside it rises a picturesque group of less ancient towers, in one of which, circular in form, are the terrible *Cachots* of Louis XI., extending downwards in four stories below one another. Two of them contained the iron cages invented by Cardinal Balue, who himself expiated his treasonable betrayal of his master's secrets to the Duke of Burgundy by a confinement of 8 years in one of them. In another, Ludovico Sforza, *il Moro,* Duke of Milan, the prisoner of Louis XII., was confined from 1500 until 1510, when death released him. Here Philip de Comines, the historian, was also shut up in 1486; the Duc d'Alençon, 1456; Charles de Melun, who was beheaded, 1468; and many more victims of tyranny. These dungeons are vaulted, and dimly lighted by small windows, whose deep recesses, in walls 10 or 12 ft. thick, are crossed by double iron gratings. The cages existed down to 1789.

At the other end of the castle platform, on the l. as you ascend from the town through the arched gateway, is a more modern pile of building, now serving as the *Sous-Préfecture.* At one end of the terrace behind it, within a small tower, is placed the monument of *Agnes Sorel,* mistress of Charles VII., who was born, 1400, in the neighbouring château of Fromonteau. Upon a base of black marble reclines the effigy of La Belle des Belles, well sculptured in white limestone, her hands uplifted in prayer, with two angels bending over her head and shielding her with their wings, and two lambs reclining at her feet. She is gracefully attired in long robes, and a simple circlet surrounds her brow; her countenance exhibits a refined character of beauty, modesty, sweetness, and gentleness, not unworthy of the Madonna of Raphael, and befitting one whose influence over a king was never exercised but for good. It has been proved, however, by an acute historian, that she could in no wise have contributed to stimulate Charles to the assumption of hi dominions and the expulsion of the English, not having been seen by him until 1431, after the death of Jeanne d'Arc. When Charles died, the ungrateful monks of Loches, whom the bounty of Agnes had cherished and her bequests had enriched, were desirous of ejecting her remains and tomb from their church, on the score of some scruples as to the purity of her life; but even Louis XI., much as he hated Agnes, reproved such ingratitude, telling them

Sect. III.   Route 57.—Tours to Saumur.   193

that if they abandoned her body they must also resign her legacies: so the bones remained in their place until the Revolution, when the grave was violated, and the monument was preserved from destruction only by the interference of the préfet.

Between the Sous-Préfecture and the Norman keep stands the *Ch. of St. Ours, a very interesting monument of ecclesiastical architecture, meriting in a high degree the attention of every student of Gothic architecture.* In its outline it presents 4 conical roofs, 2 of them raised on towers, and 2 intermediate, covering the nave with cupolas of stone. To the W. of the belfry-tower is a low square porch, protecting a large and very perfect Romanesque W. doorway, rich in mouldings and sculptured figures. Beyond the other steeple is the E. apse: the transepts are short. A pointed arch divides the nave into 2 square compartments, each covered with an octagonal cupola of stone. According to records, the building was completed, as it stands, 1180, but the E. apse and crypt are older, probably of the 11th cent. Observe the sculpture throughout—the capitals, the corbels in tiers supporting the domed roofs of the nave, the cylindrical font. The crypt, beneath the choir, was the place of devotion of Louis XI.

In the suburb Beaulieu, 1 m. E. of Loches, is a beautiful Church, with a fine Romanesque tower. The view of Loches hence is very good.

The rest of the road lies up the pretty vale of the Indre to

21 Châtillon-sur-Indre, a town of 2700 Inhab., in the Dépt. l'Indre, and the ancient province of Berry.

23 Buzançais, a town of 3800 Inhab., on the rt. bank of the river, whose branches are here crossed by several bridges.

23 Châteauroux, in Rte. 65.

ROUTE 57.

TOURS TO SAUMUR, BY CHINON AND FONTEVRAULT.

76 kilom. = 47 Eng. m.

* This church is perfectly delineated in Petit's 'Architectural Studies in France.' France.

Diligences daily.

This route issues out of Tours lined by avenues of poplars, and crosses at the distance of 1½ m. the river Cher, a little to the E. of Plessis les Tours (p. 188). The Cher runs for about 15 m. below this nearly parallel with the Loire, before uniting itself to that river. Along its N. bank runs a considerable levée or dyke constructed by Madame de Vermandois, abbess of Beaumont les Tours, to protect the land between it and the Loire from inundations. After crossing the flat land, passing numerous white hamlets and villas, the road ascends and traverses an extensive table-land before entering the valley of the Indre, on whose banks stands

24 Azay-le-Rideau, a small town prettily situated, 15 m. from Tours. On the l. of the road, nearly concealed by trees and surrounded by branches of the Indre, is the Château, one of the best preserved specimens in France of the semi-castellated manor-house, in the style of the Renaissance. It was built by Gilles Berthelot in the reign of Francis I., and over the chief portal, enriched with sculpture and combinations of three classic orders, may be discerned the emblem of that king, the Salamander, with the motto "Nutrio et extinguo," and the initials of Diana of Poitiers. The carving has been thought worthy of Jean Goujon; the entire façade and the staircase are very elegant, the wall partly panelled, and the compartments filled with diversified patterns. The interior has been preserved nearly unaltered, and contains old furniture and a collection of portraits. A bed, supported in the 4 corners by carved figures, is of very elaborate Gothic workmanship. A neatly kept garden surrounds the house. The present owner is M. de Biancourt.

A considerable tract of forest is traversed on the direct road from Azay, before it descends by the hollow way behind the castle of

22 Chinon. — Inns: H. de France, best, but miserable. — Chêne Vert, dirty. A deserted and dull town (6700 Inhab.), which yet deserves a visit, owing to its pleasing position on the rt. bank of the Vienne, and on

K

account of the numerous and interesting historical associations attached to its utterly ruined *Castle*, the French Windsor of our Plantagenet kings, as it has been termed, where Henry II. breathed his last, uttering curses on his own sons, whose disobedience had hastened his death. It was the favourite residence, also, of the French monarchs, from Philippe-Augustus to Henri IV., and the scene of Joan of Arc's first public appearance. The remains are of vast extent, but too much demolished, and too white in colour, to be very picturesque. They occupy the summit of a lofty platform of rock, rising nearly 300 ft. above the town and river. A natural escarpment surrounds it on 3 sides; where the cliff was not naturally vertical, it has been cut away, and huge walls of smooth masonry have been built up from below to a level with the top of the cliff, so as to render it hopeless, before the days of gunpowder, to scale or batter such a fortress. Between the river and the rock crouch the buildings of the town. Behind the castle, in a deep hollow, runs the road to Tours, originally commanded by the castle embrasures; and a deep gully or fosse is cut through the rock on the 4th side, to isolate the promontory from the ridge of which it forms the termination.

Several of the tall flanking towers remain tolerably perfect; the rest is all crumbling wall. The 3 divisions into which the castle was separated by deep dry ditches may still be discovered. In the central division, above the entrance to which rises the tall Donjon, the only part now inhabited, are shown the royal apartments; and among them the very one in which Joan the Maid, the simple shepherdess of Domrémy,* recognised Charles the Dauphin, though disguised in plain attire, and, singling him out from among the crowd of courtiers, led him apart to the recess of the window, where she unfolded to him "secrets known only to himself and to God." The scene of that interview, and of the splendours of the court of the careless and luxurious Charles, whom even the loss of a kingdom could

* See Lord Mahon's Life of Jeanne d'Arc.

not recall from indolence and pleasure, is now a broken ruin open to the sky, with one or two transoms remaining in the windows, and a few traces of paint upon the walls. Close beside it is a very deep square tower, adjoining one of the ditches, and without openings, said to have been the Oubliettes down which prisoners were cast.

Crossing a bridge into the 3rd court, we find around it the towers of *la Glacière*, in which Jacques de Molay, Grand Master of the Templars, is said to have been confined; the *Tour du Moulin*, so called because it was surmounted by a windmill, standing at the farthest extremity, and of very solid structure; and the *Tour d'Argentau*, from which, as the story goes, a secret passage led beyond the wall to the Maison Robardeau, the retreat of Agnes Sorel, Charles's mistress. Among all these fragments, the only trace of the original Norman castle is to be found in the round tower du Moulin; the rest seems not older than the 15th centy.

The view from the walls is very pleasing, extending for a long distance up and down the fertile valley,—" a glowing and glorious prospect; a green expanse of groves and vineyards all blending into one,"—with the winding Vienne sparkling and flashing among the green meadows, or foliage of poplars, walnut-trees, and vines, nearly as far as its junction with the Loire, which, however, is not visible. Fontevrault, the last resting-place of Henry II. and his undutiful son the Lion-hearted Richard, is concealed from view by intervening heights.

There is nothing worth notice in the town of Chinon itself. No tradition is preserved of the hostelry in which the Pucelle was lodged on her arrival from her native village, and where she was kept two days before she could obtain admission to the king, until his councillors had ascertained whether she was a sorceress. Nor can the ch. be pointed out in which she spent the greater part of each day in prayer while she resided here. It was at Chinon that she first received from the king her suit of knight's armour, and an escort of a squire, a confessor, and 2 pages. Here she first girt on the mysterious sword found in the ch. of St. Catherine of Fierbois, and here unfurled her white banner sprinkled with fleurs-de-lis, made expressly for her under the direction of her mysterious "voices."

The rocks behind the town, underneath the castle, have been quarried for ages to supply building materials, and these *subterraneous excavations*, called *Les Caves Peintes*, have attained a great extent. There is nothing worth seeing in them, nor is it a task of pleasure to explore them.

Chinon is the country of Rabelais, who was born 1483, in the farm-house called *la Devinière*, in the commune of Seuilly, a little way on the l. of the road to Saumur, on the opposite side of the Vienne. He commenced his education in the school of the neighbouring abbey, whose monks he afterwards ridiculed in his writings.

At Champigny, about 9 m. S. of Chinon, is a chapel containing very remarkable painted glass, representing the life of St. Louis.

It is a very delightful drive from Chinon to Saumur, through a country teeming with fertility, amongst orchards, and walnut groves, and acacia hedges, while beneath the fruit-trees springs up a crop of corn, without exhausting the soil. The valley of the Vienne terminates at Candes, remarkable for its fine ch. (p. 196), where that river falls into the Loire; and our road, emerging upon its l. bank, is carried along it, through most pleasing scenery, to

30 Saumur, described, with the rest of the road, in p. 198.

At Montsoreau, close to Candes, our road passes within 3 m. of the *Abbey of Fontevrault*. The excursion thither is described in p. 197.

ROUTE 58.

THE LOIRE (C): TOURS TO NANTES, BY SAUMUR AND ANGERS—RAILWAY.

Rly.—196 kilom. = 122¼ Eng. m. 3 Trains daily, in 6¼ (fast) to 8 hours.

From Tours this rly. follows the l. bank of the Loire as far as Cinq Mars

The prettiest part of the course of the Loire lies below Tours, in the neighbourhood of Saumur, and thence to Nantes. For some distance below Tours, however, its banks continue low, and its bed, everywhere too large for its stream, is left bare and unsightly in summer. In winter the river sometimes rises 20 ft. above its ordinary level; and from these irregularities it is unfit for the permanent establishment of water-mills or manufactories on its banks. It is confined on both sides by levées as far down as Angers.

The *high road* continues, as before (p. 182), along the Levée, or river dyke, often on a level with the tops of the houses and cottages, which, together with the fertile fields, orchards, gardens, and vineyards, it protects from the inundations of the Loire, commanding, both on the river and land side, an extensive view.

rt. St. Symphorien, nearly opposite Tours, forms a sort of suburb to that city; and not far from it is the pretty hamlet of St. Cyr, where a cottage, called La Grenadière, is at present the retreat of the veteran poet Béranger.

14 Savonnières Stat.

rt. Luynes* is a small town at the opening of a valley into the Loire, backed by a limestone cliff, pierced with numerous cave dwellings, on the top of which stands the old *Castle*, commanding the country around. It was the residence of the seigneurs of Luynes, and among them of the first duke, the favourite of Louis XIII. and Constable of France, who gave his own name to the castle and town, previously called de Maillé, 1619. Not far off are the ruins of an *aqueduct*, said to be Roman, of which nearly 50 square pillars and 8 arches remain. Luynes is the birthplace of Paul Louis Courrier, the celebrated political writer; he was found shot dead near his own residence, Veretz, on the banks of the Cher, not far from this, 1825.

The Rly. crosses the Loire on a bridge of 19 arches at

* *Post-road.*—10 Luynes.

rt. 21 Cinq Mars Stat., or more correctly St. Mars, since the name is supposed to be a contraction of St. Medard. Near this village, whose ruined castle gave a title to another favourite of Louis XIII., who fell by the executioner's axe, under the relentless rule of Cardinal Richelieu, is the curious ancient monument called *La Pile de Cinq Mars*, a square tower of brick, 92 ft. high and 13 ft. wide on each face, surmounted originally by 5 pinnacles 10 ft. high, one of which was thrown down by a storm 1751. The origin, use, and age of the pile are equally unknown. Some attribute it to the Romans, others to the Celts. It is destitute of door, window, or other opening, and is perfectly solid. On the S. face the bricks are arranged in a pattern so as to form 12 compartments. It was *probably* a funereal monument.

The traveller continues to pass entire villages, cut in the yellow chalk rock, or *tuffeau*, whenever it rises into cliffs favourable for human habitations.

l. The Cher, after running parallel with the Loire for about 15 m., enters it a little above Cinq Mars, but sends off a branch which continues to run parallel with it until it joins the Indre, 9 m. lower down.

rt. 26 Langeais* Stat., another little town, has also a *Castle*, in tolerable preservation, which is remarkable because the marriage of Charles VIII. with Anne of Brittany was celebrated within its walls—an event which united that important province to France. It is well preserved and furnished in antique style. The gate-house serves as a gaol. This castle was built, in the 13th centy., by Pierre de Brosses, minister of Philippe le Hardi, after having been barber to his predecessor, St. Louis. He ended his career on the gibbet of Montfaucon, being hung for high treason in poisoning his master's son, and accusing the queen of the crime.

rt. St. Patrice Stat. Near this is the Château of Rochecotte, where the Chouan leader of that name was born; it belongs to the Duchesse de Dino, now Princesse de Talleyrand, who was often visited here by her uncle, M. de Talleyrand.

rt. Trois Volets.*

l. Nearly opposite this, backed by a wooded hill, is the Château d'Ussé, belonging to one of the family of Larochejacquelin, but partly built by Vauban, its original owner.

rt. Chouzé,† on the confines of Touraine. Near this, if anywhere, the valley of the Loire exhibits its garden-like character, an exuberant vegetation, with trees of large growth, capable of furnishing some shade to the road,— among them the graceful feathery acacia, which also forms the hedges,— vines, Indian corn, and mulberry-trees, prevail.

La Chapelle-sur-Loire Stat.

47 Port Boulet Stat. Omnibus to Chinon, about 10 m. up the valley of the Vienne (Rte. 57).

At Port Boulet the Loire is crossed by a wire suspension-bridge of 5 spans, leading to

l. Candes, opposite to which place we pass out of Touraine into Anjou.

l. The river Vienne here pours itself into the Loire; and immediately below it stands the pretty white town of Candes, where St. Martin of Tours breathed his last. It has an interesting ch., of which the apsidal choir seems to be of the 12th centy., and the nave of the 13th (1215). Its S. porch is remarkable, though much mutilated; 14 statues in trefoil-headed niches adorn the façade, with smaller niches below them filled with heads. The porch itself is a vestibule supported by a light central column, in the manner of the chapter-houses of English cathedrals. The W. end is flanked on either side by a machicolated buttress, and includes a circular window, now stopped up. The tomb of St. Martin is shown in this ch. The possession of his remains was warmly contested between the Poitevins and Touraingeaux.

A small brook alone separates Candes from Montsoreau, whose *castle*, now parcelled out among poor people, was the seat of that cruel Comte de Montsoreau who became the executioner of the Protestants of Anjou by carrying out the

* 14 Langeais.   * Trois Volets.   † 12 Chouzé.

infamous St. Bartholomew decrees of Charles IX.

[3 m. up the little retired and wooded valley behind Montsoreau lies the *Abbey of Fontevrault*, one of the richest in France in ancient times, where 150 nuns and 70 monks submitted to the rule of an abbess, who was always a lady of high degree. This singular establishment, which thus combined members of both sexes, was founded by a Breton monk, Robert d'Arbrissel, 1099; who by his powerful preaching converted and led after him a multitude of followers of both sexes and all ages, amounting to 3000, whom he at length settled here, in a sequestered forest, on the borders of Touraine and Anjou. In spite of the scope for scandal, the convent maintained its existence for 9 centuries, down to the Revolution. It has an interest to Englishmen, from having been the burial-place of several of our Plantagenet kings. A tolerably good road leads to the poor village of Fontevrault, where the inn (Croix Blanche) does not look promising.

The *Abbey* is now converted into a prison (Maison Centrale de Détention); one of the largest in France, covering 30 or 40 acres with its courts and ranges of building, occupied by 500 women, 1200 men, and 300 boys; the entrance is in the little *place* close to the inn. The prison is not shown without an order from the préfet; and this is necessary now even to admit strangers into the ch. to see the tombs, which they can do without coming in contact with the prisoners. Above the abbey building rises a singular *octagon*, which was in fact the *Kitchen* of the monastery,* called *Tour d'Evrault*; it dates from the 12th cent.

The *church*, approached by a covered way, from which you look through loopholes into the prison-yards, is an interesting building of Romanesque architecture, ending in an E. apse, with apsidal chapels. It is supposed to have been begun by Foulques, 5th Comte d'Anjou, 1125. Its nave is now partitioned off, and, by the introduction

* It is described in Turner's Domestic Architecture.

of 2 floors, is converted into dormitories for the prisoners. The *Royal monuments* are transferred to the S. transept, enclosed by bolts and bars and grilles, in a dark corner, mutilated and broken by the Vandals of the Revolution, who rifled the graves of their contents, and scattered the royal dust. The effigies, in spite of the injuries they received, are interesting from the evident marks they exhibit of being portraits; they retain still a little of the colouring with which they were ornamented. They are recumbent statues of Henry II. and Richard Cœur de Lion, represented in their royal robes without armour; the drapery of complicated execution. Richard is remarkable for his lofty stature (6½ ft.) and broad forehead; he wears moustache and a beard; his hair is cut short. The two female effigies are in better preservation; they represent Eleanor of Guienne, queen of Henry II., and Isabelle d'Angoulême, widow of King John; the last a statue of considerable beauty. It is much to be desired that these neglected effigies of our kings should be transferred from their dark prison-house to Westminster Abbey, where they would form an interesting link in the series of British historical sculpture. There can be no longer any harm in separating them from graves rifled and empty, and from an abbey now become a prison. The French government owes us some return for our ready compliance with its wishes to possess the bones of Napoleon.

The body of Henry II. was brought hither from the neighbouring royal residence of Chinon, and laid in the sanctuary previously to interment. When Richard, his undutiful son, approached, the dead body is said to have shuddered convulsively, and to have sweated drops of blood while he remained in its presence; "the very corpse, as it were, abhorring and accusing him of his unnatural conduct." At a short distance from the abbey is a curious cemetery chapel, or *Lanterne des Morts*.]

1. Souzé, a little below Montsoreau, contains a castellated mansion, behind which are vast excavations in the rock,

which is pierced through and through like a rabbit warren to furnish dwellings for people of the poorer sort.

1. Still lower down is Dampierre, where Margaret of Anjou ended a life of ambition and sorrow, in misery and poverty, in a house granted to her by Louis XI., who had ransomed her at the price of 50,000 crowns from the hands of Edward IV., after 5 years of imprisonment, dating from the battle of Tewkesbury.

55 Varennes Stat.

1. The approach to Saumur is marked by the number of windmills on the heights, below which stands the domed church of Notre Dame des Ardilliers. Beneath its cupola runs an inscription celebrating the suppression of heresy throughout his dominions, and the expulsion of its followers, by Louis XIV.; a subject rather of shame than of boast, on a spot which suffered in turn the massacre of St. Bartholomew, the atrocities of the Dragonnades, and finally ruin from the revocation of the Edict of Nantes.

The convent attached to this ch. is now the *Hospice de la Providence*, attended by charitable sisters: a portion of the patients, including the insane, are lodged in cells and vast dormitories cut in the cliff behind.

rt. La Croix Verte,* a suburb of Saumur, at the extremity of the bridge opposite to the town, contains the post-house.

1. 64 *Saumur Stat.*—*Inns:* Hôtel Budan best; beautifully situated, fitted up with English comforts;—one of the best in France. A very pleasant light effervescing wine grown in the vicinity may be had here. Belvédère, on the quay. H. de Londres. H. de France.

This cheerful white town is one of the most picturesque on the Loire. Seen from the river or the bridge, its quaint Hôtel de Ville, near the waterside, surmounted by a tent-like roof and pinnacled turrets, its church spires and towers, overhung by the castle behind, have a very pleasing effect. The town itself, however, is torpid,

* *Post-road.*— 16 Croix Verte. 4 kilom. extra are paid by those who take the horses into or from Saumur, crossing the bridge.

though its population amounts to 15,000 souls, and it does not possess many curiosities.

On the handsome quay which lines the river stand a modern edifice which combines theatre and market-house, and the above-mentioned antique *Hôtel de Ville*, a square building of black and white stone, with a peaked roof as high as its walls, a cornice of trefoiled machicolations running under it, and turrets or bartizans in its corners. It was anciently included in the fortifications, and joined the town walls, and, therefore, has few openings in the lower part. The front towards the court-yard has not the same castellated character, but is enriched with florid Gothic ornaments, very elegant, and recently restored. The date of the building is probably the 15th centy., about the time of Louis XI. The upper story is converted into a *Museum*. The best part of its limited collection are the *antiquities* found in the department; such as Roman vases, statues, spear-heads, axes, &c., of bronze; a complete set of Roman carpenter's tools, Roman weights, glass, cinerary urns (30 of them dug up in one spot), pottery, &c. But its chief curiosity is a Roman trumpet of bronze, 5 ft. long. Among the Celtic remains are several stone axes, dug up under one of the Dolmens in the neighbourhood, and a Druid knife of flint, from that of Bois Berard.

St. Pierre, the principal Ch., in the centre of the town, is disfigured by a modern Italian façade, and its massy tower is surmounted by a recent spire. Its interior, originally built without aisles, in the Angevine fashion, has had side chapels added. It is in the pointed style.

More curious for its age and architecture is the Ch. *Notre Dame de Nantilly*, on the outskirts of the town. The oldest parts, the N. side, the nave, and E. apse, in the Romanesque style, have been supposed to date from the 5th or 6th, but cannot be older than the 11th centy. The S. aisle is an addition of the 15th centy., nearly as wide as the nave itself, and the pillars between are nothing more than the old buttresses. The roof of the nave is slightly pointed, with platebands running across from pier to pier. In the S. aisle is the oratory of Louis XI. Against one of the piers is a basrelief of John the Baptist preaching in the wilderness, renewed 1830. The Ch. is hung with curious antique tapestries, probably of the 16th centy., productions of the looms of Flanders, if we may judge by the style of art. In one, representing the siege of Jerusalem, one soldier appears to be discharging an instrument like a matchlock, (?) but all the others are armed with bows and arrows. In this Ch. are buried Gilles Archbishop of Tyre, keeper of the seals of St. Louis, whose crozier is preserved here, and the nurse of King René of Anjou.

The *Castle*, standing conspicuously on the top of the ridge which rises like a wall above the town (Sous-lemur is a fanciful derivation of its name), is only worth entering for the view, from its terraced bastions, over the Loire and the rich flat land on either side of it, not forgetting the pretty gardens at the base of the walls. The tall *Donjon*, circular below and octagonal above, and flanked by four turrets, is a magazine for powder and fire-arms, and is shut to strangers.

The wise Protestant leader, Duplessis Mornay, was appointed governor by Henri IV., and under his prudent and fostering care Saumur was a stronghold of the Protestants, and a flourishing town of 25,000 inhabitants. The revocation of the Edict of Nantes annihilated its prosperity, by expelling the industrious Huguenots, and reduced its population to *one-fourth*.

One of the greatest exploits of the Vendéan army was the capture of Saumur, June 10, 1793, by storming the heights, on which the Republican army, 15,000 strong, had formed an intrenched camp, defended by 100 pieces of artillery. Henri de Larochejacquelin forced the intrenchments of the town from the side of the meadows of Varen, exciting his followers to the capture of a redoute by throwing his hat, conspicuous for its white plume, into the midst of the enemy, crying "Qui va me le chercher?"—an appeal not lost upon his followers, especially when enforced by his own example in taking the lead. Foremost of his band, with only 60 of his men to back him, he burst his way into the town, clearing the streets before him as far as the bridge. Here, seizing two cannon, he turned them against the enemy, drove them quite across the river, and on the road towards Tours, thus separating them from the garrison of the castle, which surrendered the day following. The Vendéans obtained this victory with a loss of only 60 killed and 100 wounded, and with a gain of 60 pieces of cannon, 10,000 muskets, and 11,000 prisoners, who were released after having one side of their head shaved, and promising not to serve against La Vendée—humane conditions, contrasting strongly with the atrocious system of massacring their prisoners, already adopted by the Republicans at the command of the Convention.

Detached from the town, to the S.W., on the rt. hand as you issue out of the main street, is the *Ecole de Cavalerie*, for the instruction, in all branches of information suited to their profession, of between 3000 and 4000 sous-officiers, who are drafted hence into different regiments to instruct their corps. There are large *riding-schools*, covered and open, in which the various exercises of the manège are performed with much precision. This establishment was transferred from Angers hither at the latter end of the last century.

Some remains of the old fortifications may be seen in the Rue du Petit Mail; they consist of two feudal towers and a prison-house. In the quartier *des Ponts*, the suburb which fills the island on which the bridge rests, is a house built by King René of Anjou, and called *Maison de la Reine Cicile* (de Sicile). Its once highly ornamented front, in the latest Gothic, not unlike that of the H. de Ville in style, has been so deplorably defaced that it retains little interest, but it may still be worthy to employ the artist's pencil.

Within about 1½ m. of Saumur, on the S., stands one of the largest, most perfect, and best preserved Druidical monuments in France, the *Dolmen of Bagneux* (§ 4). It is a chamber composed of huge blocks of unhewn stone set upright to form the walls, with others laid across them for a roof, in the manner of a house of cards. This rude cot measures more than 50 ft. in length, yet consists of only 14 stones, 4 on each of the sides and on the roof, one at the W. end, which is closed, another at the E., now thrown down, serving as a threshold over which you step to the present doorway, formed by bricking up the mouth. The largest stone measures 24 ft. by 21 ft., and 2¾ ft. thick. The stones are set so close, that originally a man could not force his body between them. The blocks composing it are of the sandstone found in this district, but not near at hand, nor near the surface. Among the adjoining vineyards stands an upright stone, also of Celtic origin. Not ½ hour's drive from Saumur, on rt. of road to Poée in going to the larger Dolmen, you pass another *pierre-couverte*, formed of only 6 stones, in the manner of Kits Coity House in Kent.

The road to these Druidic stones, on issuing out of Saumur, crosses the small river Thoue by a handsome new bridge of 3 segmental arches, called Pont Fouchard, thence by cross roads proceeds to the village of Bagneux, beyond which they are situated.

Anne Lefèbre, who became Madame Dacier, the learned translator of Homer, was born at Saumur.

Diligences daily to Le Mans; Chinon, Cholet; Poitiers and Bordeaux; to Niort and Saintes; Rochefort.

l. The Ecole de Cavalerie is seen as you quit Saumur. The whiteness of the houses about Saumur is remarkable, and arises from the pure colour of the stone, which, being readily cut, is formed into smooth, nicely jointed masonry, and gives even to humble cottages the aspect of villas. They add much to the pleasing character of the country, peering from amidst the luxuriant foliage. Acacia hedges, vines, and walnut-trees, with orchards and rich crops of corn, cover this really beautiful district, upon which all the bounties of nature seem to have been lavished.

l. The village of Tuffeau receives its name from its quarries of tufa, worked into vast subterranean catacombs, which have furnished building materials for the surrounding district.

l. Trèves is conspicuous owing to its pretty Gothic tower, 100 ft. high. It was built by Foulques d'Anjou, 1016, and given by Charles VII. to his Chancellor, Robert-le-Maçon, for saving his life at the capture of Paris by the Burgundians: it is carefully kept up by its present owner. Not far off is the *Ch. of Cunault*, attributed to King Dagobert, and, though not' of his time, at least of great antiquity: 11th to 13th century.

rt. 80 Les Rosiers Stat. l. Nearly opposite, the very ancient *Ch.* of Gennes rises on the top of a hill: it is dedicated to St. Eusèbe, and is said to have been used by the early Christians. The ruined nave is built of small stones, alternating with bands of tiles in the fashion of Roman masonry. The N. door is arched with bricks intermingled with stones, and in the wall above is a row of small semicircular arches. Gennes lies in a remarkably pretty situation, on a streamlet called Avort.

La Menitré Stat.

l. The vast conventual buildings of *St. Maur*, with 16 windows on a row in front, deserve to be looked upon with respect as the retreat of those learned and laborious Benedictines who, in the 17th centy., under the patronage of Richelieu, 1621, compiled those ponderous folios—stores of learning and erudition,—' L'Art de vérifier les Dates,' 'Gallia Christiana,'—the Collection of French Historians—the Monumental Antiquities, &c. "Works of general and permanent advantage to the world at large; showing that the revenues of the Benedictines were not always spent in self-indulgence, and that the members of that order did not uniformly slumber in sloth and indolence."—*Sir W. Scott*. Among the

Sect. III. R. 58.—Angers to Nantes, Railway—The Loire (C). 201

most eminent names which distinguished this society of learned monks are those of Felibien, Montfaucon, Vaissette, Lobineau, and Mabillon.

A wire bridge of 5 spans has been constructed at

rt. 89 St. Mathurin* Stat., nearly opposite St. Maur. At Daguénière, a little lower, the Levées de la Loire terminate, after running by the riverside from Blois hither, a distance of nearly 100 m.

Near this the railroad to Angers† and Nantes turns away from the Loire, to rejoin it about 20 m. lower down.

96 La Bohalle Stat.
102 Trélazé Stat.
105 La Paperie Stat.

Below this the Loire is split into a number of channels by considerable islands, which are connected together by a series of 4 bridges of more than 100 antiquated arches of wood and stone, equally inconvenient for boats which pass under, and for vehicles which go over them, measuring altogether about 4600 ft.

rt. Ponts de Cè. A town of 3520 Inhab., on the rt. bank of the Loire, which is here nearly 2 m. distant from the l. bank. It is about 4 m. from Angers (Rte. 46). Some antiquaries have attributed its origin to Ce-sar, who, according to them, also bequeathed to it the first syllable of his name—a theory which is considerably thwarted by the fact that the name was anciently written Ponts de Scez. The bridges form an important passage over the Loire. A bloody engagement was fought here in the Vendéan war, 1793.

109 ANGERS STAT. (in Rte. 46.)

[1. About 7 m. S.E. of Ponts de Cè is the *Château de Brissac*, seat of the noble and ancient family of that name, consisting of a handsome Italian palazzo, between two older castellated round towers, of such solid construction that it was found impossible to remove them when the centre was built, and they were in consequence

* *Post-road* from Saumur.
15 Les Rosiers.
11 St. Mathurin.
† 21 Angers, on the Mayenne, is described in Rte. 46.

amalgamated with it. It is conspicuous for the red colour of the stone. The general effect of its façade, though of a mixed character, is stately and good, but the details of carving have been destroyed by mutilations. The château was ransacked, stripped, and dismantled during the Vendéan war, and returned to the Duc de Brissac at the Restoration a mere shell. It is still uninhabited, but contains only a few articles of antique furniture.]

115 Bouchemaine Stat.

rt. The Loire is joined by the Maine (called Mayenne above Angers) about 6 m. below Ponts de Cè. On the point of land between them stands the village of

La Pointe Stat., where are numerous white villas and walled gardens of the citizens of Angers.

The Rly. crosses the Maine near La Pointe.

Below the junction of the Maine the Loire is sensibly augmented in expanse and depth, and its banks attain a more considerable elevation than above, rising into hills, often in abrupt precipices from the water's edge.

rt. One of these heights, called Coulée de Serrant, is clothed with vines, the growth of which is much esteemed. The Château de Serrant, the stately mansion of Count Walsh, is one of the finest on the Loire, and is situated 3 m. from the river, between it and the high road to Nantes. Its gardens, park, and orangery are said to be fine and well kept up. In the chapel is a marble monument by Coysevoix to the Marquis de Vaubrun, killed at the passage of the Rhine. The family is of Irish origin, having emigrated with James II. A portrait of the Pretender, still in their possession, was a gift from him to their ancestor, who fitted out the vessel which conveyed Charles Edward from Nantes to Scotland in 1745.

The pretty wooded Ile de Béhuard contains a *chapel* of Our Lady, founded on a rock, whose uneven surface forms its floor, and projects upwards in a point 4 or 5 ft. high. It was for ages a place of pilgrimage, and was visited with superstitious veneration by Louis

XI., whose faded portrait, a contemporary work in fresco, remains on the wall. Both he and his son lavished on it considerable gifts. By accident it was forgotten at the Revolution, and remains undespoiled, retaining many ex-votos, some church plate, &c. Its walls, still displaying the fleurs-de-lis and other coats of arms with which they were painted, are hung with the chains of Christian captives rescued from Algiers.

rt. The *Ch.* of the small town of Savenières (Pop. 2500), opposite the Ile Béhuard, has parts of extreme antiquity. The front and part of the S. wall of the nave, of singularly constructed masonry, consisting of black slate alternating with bands or layers of red tiles, arranged in fern-leaf pattern, intermixed with white tufa stones, are probably as old as the 6th or 7th centy. The doorway is more modern. The choir and E. apse, added in the 11th or 12th cent., display on their external walls and around the windows rich Byzantine ornaments and mouldings.

l. The triple rock of Rochefort was anciently crowned by a fortress of which nothing now remains but a few fragments of wall. It was destroyed by Henri IV. 1598.

120 Les Forges Stat.
123 La Poissonnière Stat.
129 Chalonnes Stat.

Between (l.) this picturesque town, surmounted by the square tower of its castle, and (rt.) St. George (at some distance from the Loire, on the high road), the river traverses a small *coalfield*, which has been worked to a considerable extent of late, though it produces only an inferior quality of coal. This bed, extensively developed throughout the Dépts. Maine and Loire, occurs at the bottom of the true coal formation, and is fit only for burning lime; but that lime, being employed as manure, has converted much barren ground into corn-land, and converted this part of France, since 1849, into a granary for supplying Great Britain with wheat. The quantity of flour exported from Nantes is enormous.

At Chalonnes another suspension-bridge has been thrown over the Loire.

l. The eminence crowned with a modern-looking ruin, through whose numerous windows and roofless walls the sky appears, is Mont Jan; whose name, according to etymologists, has something to do with Janus—though they cannot exactly agree what the connection is. The ruins are those of a convent of Cordeliers: it had been converted into a sort of state prison, of which the monks were the gaolers, when it was burnt during the Vendéan war.

rt. 137 Champtocé Stat.,* a little village opposite Mont Jan, and situated on the post-road, which here again joins the Loire, is surmounted by the imposing ruins of a feudal castle, celebrated from the crimes of its owner in the reign of Charles VII., the infamous Gilles de Retz, Sieur de Laval, a monster in human shape, the bugbear of the surrounding country, called Barbe Bleu, and the original of our well-known *Blue Beard;* who, although clothed by us in a turban, in reality comes from the banks of the Loire. His history affords a remarkable instance of the superstitions of the 15th centy., and of the impunity for his atrocities which a feudal seigneur enjoyed in that dark age. Having run through an enormous fortune by extravagance, and impaired by excesses his constitution in early youth, the Sieur de Retz sought to renovate both by magic. He kept in his pay an Italian alchemist and magician, who induced him to believe that a charm could be produced from the blood of infants, which would restore him to health and fortune by using it as a bath. For this end children and young persons were spirited away and murdered in the deep dungeons of his castles or in the solitude of his forests, to the number, it is said, of more than 100; he himself, in most cases, plunging the poignard in their breasts. At length the whole country rose up against the tyrant; and his suzerain, Duke Jean V. of Brittany, having heard the charges against him, caused him to be seized and tried: he was

* *Post-road* from Angers.
17 St. George-sur-Loire.
 8 Champtocé.

Sect. III. Route 58.—The Loire (C)—St. Florent. 203

found guilty, condemned, and burnt at the stake in Nantes in 1440, after making full confession of his misdeeds. The peasant still regards with horror the ill-omened walls and vaults in which the monster raised the devil, and sold himself to Satan, according to the popular belief.

rt. 142 Ingrande Stat., a long line of houses raised upon a terraced wall stretching along the strand, is placed exactly on the boundary of ancient Brittany and Anjou, and between the modern Départements of Loire Inférieure and Maine et Loire. The name was originally "Ingressus Andium," the entrance of the country of the Andes, *i.e.* the Angevine.

rt. At Montrelais are extensive coalmines, some of the pits extending under the river. The coal is not good enough for the steamers, which burn English coals.

l. The heights of St. Florent are marked by two piles of building; the vast but not picturesque ruins of the Abbey of Montglonne, whose foundation is traced to Charlemagne, burnt down and destroyed by the Republicans in the Vendéan war; and a little below it, the church of St. Florent, surmounted by a modern-looking tower, by the side of which rises a *Pillar* to the memory of the brave Vendéan general, Bonchamps, but now surmounted, as if in insult and mockery, by the symbol of revolution, which he died in combating, the drapeau tricolor. Wounded mortally in the fatal fray of Chollet, he was brought hither by the routed Vendéans to die. He closed his career with an act of mercy in rescuing the lives of 4000 Republican prisoners, who had been taken and shut up in the church, and against whom the irritated Vendéans were already pointing their cannon, worked up to madness by defeat, by the mortal wound of their general, and by terror for their wives and families. The commands and entreaties of the dying hero, and nearly the last words he uttered—" Grâce aux prisonniers "—had the effect of saving them from military execution, when nothing else could have rescued them. Bonchamps expired in a miserable hovel, in the village of Meilleraye, on the opposite side of the Loire, but is interred within the ch. of St. Florent, and a monument of marble by David is erected to his memory. St. Florent was the scene of the most memorable event in the war of La Vendée, which all who have read Madame Larochejacquelin's touching Memoirs will remember—the passage of the Loire by the Vendéan army after their rout at Chollet, 1793. They reached the narrow strip of level ground at the base of the semicircle of heights on the l. bank, in number nearly 100,000, half of them unarmed, old men, women, and children; the enemy pressing on in the rear, the country behind smoking with the conflagration of their homes by the Republicans, who, to use their own words, "left behind nothing but ashes and piles of dead." The tumult of such a multitude crowding down to the 25 small barks which alone could be mustered to ferry them over, the cries of children seeking parents or relations, the groans of the wounded, the alarm caused by the enemy, formed a scene of pain, confusion, and despair, which Madame de Larochejacquelin compares with the awful spectacle that the world must behold at the Day of Judgment. The whole multitude, however, were transported across in safety before the arrival of the enemy, whose advanced posts reached the river the day after.

The broad expanse of the river is divided by an island, between St. Florent and

rt. 151 Varades Stat.,* the spot where the fugitives, when landed, waited the junction of their companions. It is a town of 4000 Inhab.

Passing many monotonous clumps and rows of willows, we reach the *suspension-bridge* of wire, supported by wire shrouds or stays, erected 1839, of five arches, more than 1300 ft. long, which leads from La Vendée to the little town of

rt. 163 Ancenis Stat.† (*Inn:* H. de France; small, but clean and comfortable—*H. M.*), a town of nearly 4000

* *Post-road*—13 Varades. † 13 Ancenis.

Inhab., having remains of an old castle of the Ducs de Béthune at the waterside, above the bridge, now reduced to a few strong walls and towers. The large barracks are formed out of a ci-devant convent of Ursuline nuns.

Here a broken remnant of the Vendéan host, which had crossed at Varades, endeavoured to recross a few weeks after, shattered by the recent defeat of Le Mans. Larochejacquelin, on this occasion, volunteered to cross the river in the only boat which could be found on the l. bank, to bring over some hay-barges attached to the opposite shore; but while so engaged he was attacked by the enemy and driven into the woods. A gunboat of the enemy sunk the barges destined to transport his followers, and thus cut off all communication between them and their general.

l. On the top of a hill covered with brushwood stand the ruins of the castle of Champtoceaux, in which Jean de Montfort was kept a prisoner by Marguerite de Clisson; and at the foot of the hill a bridge or pier of 2 arches projects into the river, designed by the owner of the fort above to facilitate the levying of toll on the vessels which passed, in feudal times.

rt. The tall black octagonal tower of Oudon,* 5 stories high, surmounted by machicolations, overlooks the flat land and a series of islands which here intersect the river. It was built probably in the 13th centy.

rt. After passing a group of pseudo-castellated modern constructions, worthy of a tea-garden, and called after their founder, a citizen of Nantes, Les Folies Siffait, we approach the

rt. 176 *Castle of Clermont*, Stat., on the top of an abrupt and lofty escarpment, yet not destitute of foliage, forming one of the most picturesque scenes on the Loire, but unendowed with any historical interest.

rt. La Seilleraie,† at a little distance from the river, was several times visited by Madame de Sévigné, who dates some of her letters hence, and its gardens were laid out by Le Nôtre. The apartment and portrait of the Sévigné are

* 9 Oudon. † La Seilleraie.

preserved, and the mansion contains other portraits by Mignard, Le Brun, &c.

rt. The precipitous heights gradually give place to gentle undulations, which, below the rocks of (184) Mauves Stat., subside into a flat monotonous plain, out of the midst of which, in the distance, the towers of the cathedral of Nantes are seen to rise. Islands and sandbanks greatly multiply in this part of the river, interspersed with dykes of stone heaps to regulate the river, and a few insignificant villages occur at intervals.

196 NANTES STATION.* (Rte. 46.)

ROUTE 60.

NANTES TO POITIERS, BY CLISSON.

178 kilom. = 110¼ Eng. m.

Diligence daily in about 19 hrs., and several from Nantes to Clisson.

Our road, before it gets clear of the suburb of Nantes (St. Jacques), is carried over the different branches of the Loire on a series of 7 bridges, united by causeways, about 2 m. long, lined with houses. Beyond the last bridge the road to Bordeaux (Rte. 62) branches off to the rt. About 2 m. S. of Nantes we find the country, though nearly level in surface, covered with vineyards.

13 Tournebride.

The little village *Le Pallet* is celebrated as the birthplace of Abelard; the crumbling brier-grown foundations of a square tower behind the church on the l. of the road are called the remains of the house of his father Béranger.

The stream of the Sèvre Nantaise runs nearly parallel with our road, a little on the rt., as far as Clisson.

A small bridge carrying the road over a valley is stated in an inscription to have been built "l'An 2 du Règne de Napoléon le Grand."

15 *Clisson.—Inns:* Poste, beyond the bridge, fine view; H. de France.

This small town (21 m. from Nantes) is celebrated for its very romantic situation in the deep, narrow, bosky valley of the Sèvre, on one side of which towers the stately old *castle*. The scene has a somewhat Italian character.

* 14 Nantes.

As the town was destroyed in the Vendéan war, its houses are mostly modern, and contribute little to the beauty of it. A handsome new *Bridge* of 12 arches, 54 ft. high in the centre, rising on very lofty double piers, now spans the valley, carrying the road to Poitiers across, without descending the very steep slope which leads to and from the river. The perspective of the interior of the bridge from below, through its arched piers, forms a vista like that of a cathedral.

The *Castle of Clisson*, the cradle of that illustrious family from which sprang the famous Olivier de Clisson, the fierce and successful antagonist of the English in the wars of the 14th centy., who was thought worthy to succeed Du Guesclin as constable of France, stands on the l. bank of the Sèvre. It is based on the rock, or, where that was wanting to furnish a foundation, huge sustaining walls have been raised from the bottom of the valley, on a line with the escarpment of the rock, to support its towers and bastions. Where not protected by an escarpment, it is surrounded by a fosse. On the l. of the grass-grown courtyard, after entering by the gateway of the Tour des Pélerins, so called from the crusader Clisson, who built it after his return from Palestine, is a vast pile separated by ditches from the rest, entered by several gates in succession, containing the great hall, the tall donjon, of which one side only remains, and the kitchen, with its wide fireplace. From some of the windows a fine view is obtained over the two valleys of the Maine and Sèvre. All this part of the building is in a state of complete ruin, occasioned by the civil war of La Vendée. Before that broke out the castle belonged to the family of Rohan-Soubise, and had fallen into neglect, but its destruction was completed by the Republican army in 1793. When the town was set on fire and destroyed by them, a number of its unfortunate inhabitants, chiefly old men, women, and children, sought refuge within the castle walls, and remained in its gloomy vaults and dungeons, whither they had conveyed some of their cattle also, for a little time unnoticed. But no sooner was their retreat discovered by the army of Kleber, than they were dragged forth from their hiding-place, and hurled *alive* down a deep well in the second court of the castle, now stopped up, and marked by a cypress planted near it. For many hours the feeble and half-stifled cries of these unfortunate creatures were heard issuing from its depths, before they utterly perished. The number thus destroyed is variously stated at 100 and 405; the latter, it is to be feared, is nearest the truth. The story of the well of Clisson is one of the blackest spots on that page of atrocities.

The pretty grounds of *La Garenne*, once highly extolled, perhaps too highly, as "a show-place," but now no longer kept up, are indebted for the considerable beauty which they possess to the full stream of the Sèvre, which flows past them, to the fantastic rocks piled one above another rising near its margin, and to the fine trees dipping their branches in its waters, alternating with rich flat meadow land, which here gives variety to the valley, and to the glimpses of the old castle seen at certain points. Winding walks are carried through the park, decorated at intervals with monuments and statues, a temple of Vesta, a grotto called after Heloïse, and a Roman milestone of the age of Antonine found on the road to Poitiers. The Garenne owes its artificial embellishment to the brothers Cacault, who deposited their collection of paintings here, and to M. Lemot, a sculptor; successively its owners, who built the house on the height now deserted.

The *Villa Valentin* is a would-be Italian cascina on a height above the Maine.

On leaving Clisson you pass on the top of the hill the little *Chapelle de toute Joie*, so called by a lord of Clisson who received on this spot the joyful news of the birth of a son, and built it in consequence.

The road from Clisson to Poitiers has been made about 15 years, and is part of a network of lines of communication formed to facilitate not only commercial intercourse, but the passage of large bodies of troops; they will contribute more than anything else to alter the primitive state of society in this part of France. Clisson is on the very verge of La Vendée (p. 168), which begins on the l. bank of the Sèvre; but our road, running parallel with the river, skirts, but does not enter it.

14 Torfou, a village almost exclusively composed of new houses, the old having been destroyed in the civil war. One of the greatest victories of the Vendéan peasantry was gained near this over a Republican army superior in numbers by 10,000 men, including the terrible garrison of Mayence,—veterans and reputed the best soldiers in France, and commanded by Kleber. A pillar set up on the post-road, about a mile beyond Torfou, at the junction of four highways, marks the scene of the battle, which occurred Sept. 19, 1793. Its four sides bear the names of Charette, D'Elbée, Lescure, and Bonchamps, the four Vendéan leaders who took part in it. The day would have been lost for the cause of the Royalists, soon after the action began, had not Lescure rallied around him 1700 peasants of the village of Echanbrognes, who stood the brunt of the assault for two hours, until the division of Bonchamps came up.

About 3 m. from Torfou in a direct line, and more than 4 by the post-road, passing the column (where turn to rt.), is the *Castle of Tiffauges*, an extensive ruin on a high table-land between the l. bank of the Sèvre and a small rivulet (la Crume) falling into it. The donjon stood on the rocky height overlooking and commanding the gap through which the high road to Les Herbiers is carried. The inner courts, now separated merely by a few foundations of wall, are converted into productive corn-fields; but behind two cottages, built in the midst of them, runs a pile of building skirting the brow of the cliff, originally occupied by the seigneur, and more perfect than any other part. The most picturesque bit is a round tower projecting over the rivulet, containing a fine vaulted apartment and a spiral stair, probably of the 16th centy. Round the top runs a covered gallery, resting on the corbels of the machicolations. These chambers now serve as store-rooms for hay, corn, and other farm produce, and the inner wall is prettily draped with vines. By a little postern you may descend into the valley of the Crume. This castle is said to have been one of the residences of the wicked Gilles de Retz, the Bluebeard of the Loire (p. 202); it was dismantled by Card. Richelieu.

The part of the valley on which the village Tiffauges stands is rocky and somewhat bare of grass. A cotton-mill has been built under the castle. There is no good inn.

Those who take the direct line between Torfou and Tiffauges will have an opportunity of learning what sort of a country La Vendée was before Napoleon and Louis-Philippe intersected it in all directions by broad, open, macadamized high roads. At the distance of a few hundred yards from either village you find yourself in a labyrinth of lanes branching in all directions, worn down by cart-wheels or winter torrents considerably below the surface, lined on either side with trees or hedges, which close above your head and form a covered way like a subterranean passage. So numerous are these deep paths, and so intricate their crossings, that even the inhabitant is apt to be misled by them, while the frequent stagnant pools and sloughs of mud, alternating with deep ruts or projecting bosses of bare granite rock, render the passage through them harassing and fatiguing. At the same time, the country is so thickly wooded by thickets and hedgerow trees, which surround every small field, that it is difficult to see your way far before you. It can easily be understood what a complete stronghold such a district would become when defended by a brave peasantry, fighting close to their own homes, and thoroughly acquainted with all its intricacies. 20 years ago, it must be remembered, only two high roads, properly so called, existed in La Vendée—that from Nantes to Bordeaux, and from Tours to Poitiers; and these were 70 m. apart. The peasantry were all accustomed to the use of the gun; many were old poachers and capital marksmen. The tactics which they adopted was a species of skirmishing, never attacking the enemy but to advantage, themselves choosing time and place, when and where they found him entangled in the toils. At the word of command from their chief, these rude bands assembled at the place of rendezvous, scattered themselves on the enemy's approach, lining every hedge and copse, from which a murderous fire opened on all sides, the Vendéan marksmen picking out their men, while they themselves were invisible or unassailable.

15 Mortagne (Vendée) on the Sèvre was burnt down, like Torfou, in the Vendéan war, and has been since rebuilt. It was long the headquarters of the Royalist army. At *Chollet*, 8 m. N.E. of this, a manufacturing town of 8897 Inhab., entirely rebuilt since its destruction in the civil war, two actions were fought in 1793; in the first of which the Vendéans lost one of their bravest leaders, M. Lescure, who was shot through the head, and in the second suffered a more fatal defeat, which, in fact, decided the war, and drove them across the Loire (see p. 203). Before this battle began, on the 13th of October, 1793, the whole Vendéan army heard mass by torchlight, performed by the curé of this parish. On the first attack, the peasants, who here, for the first time, marched in close column, succeeded in driving back the enemy, and a party, headed by Larochejacquelin and Stofflet, even captured a park of artillery; but a charge of the Republican cavalry, and an attack from the garrison of Mayence, the so-called "invincibles," turned the scale; the Vendéans were utterly routed, and their best general, the brave and generous Bonchamps, was carried off the field mortally wounded.

At a short distance from Nouaillé, on the road from Chollet to Saumur, a third leader of the Vendéans, Henri Larochejacquelin, fell, March 4, 1793. For a long time after the wreck of the Royalist cause, he had carried on a successful partisan warfare, issuing out from the fastnesses of the Forest of Vezins at the head of a few determined followers, and spreading dismay among the Republican outposts. He was shot by a grenadier, while in the act of offering him quarter. At his death, the Convention could, for the first time, with safety and truth, proclaim that La Vendée had ceased to exist. An apple-tree is pointed out as marking the spot where he fell.

18 Châtillon-sur-Sèvre, destroyed also, except three houses, in the civil war, is now rebuilt. It was called Mauléon down to 1737.

22 Bressuire (*Inn*: H. de France), a new town built on the ashes of one ruined by the same disastrous war. Here are grand remains of a *Castle* built by the English.

31 Parthenay (*Inn*: H. des Trois Piliers), a poor town of 4024 Inhab., though carried by storm by the Republican forces under Westermann, escaped annihilation, and retains some fragments of antiquity, in the ruins of its *castle*, the *gate of St. Jacques*, and the *Ch. of St. John*, said to be a structure of the 9th centy. The town stands on the rt. bank of the Thoue, a tributary of the Loire, in a hilly district.

25 Ayron.
25 POITIERS. (Rte. 64.)

ROUTE 61.

SAUMUR TO SAINTES AND BORDEAUX, THROUGH PARTHENAY, NIORT, AND ST. JEAN D'ANGELY.

Montreuil. Here is rather a fine church and conventual establishment.

Thouars. Road rather hilly, but good. Thouars is beautifully situated on a hill, with the river Thoue running round it at a very considerable depth, so as to give it the appearance of an island. Here is a very fine old château, which originally belonged to the ancient family of Tremouille. It was sold at the Revolution, and was to have been broken up, but the town authorities purchased it, and it is now the Mairie. Here is also an old and curious Romanesque church. The front

has been handsomely decorated with images of saints, but they are all mutilated or badly preserved. To
Parthenay (Rte. 60), a poor town, the country hilly.
St. Maixent. Here is a very fine church of the early Gothic, and a curious old chapel under the principal altar, where are deposited the remains of St. Maixent and St. Leger; the former founded the church, &c. To it is attached a fine originally Benedictine monastery, which is now a seminary for priests. There is a very fine staircase in the convent. There are in the church some very beautiful wood carvings.

Niort. *Inns*: H. du Raisin de Burgogne, good and clean; the best;—H. de France, fair (Rte. 66). The country in the immediate neighbourhood of Niort is very picturesque and very rich, growing vines which produce a very fine vin ordinaire.

St. Jean d'Angely (*Inn*: H. de France, very good and reasonable). There is nothing remarkable here; the prison has an ugly Italian façade. It was the commencement of an immense cathedral, but want of funds prevented its completion.

Saintes,
Blaye, } See Rte. 62.
Bordeaux,

ROUTE 62.

NANTES TO BORDEAUX, BY BOURBON VENDÉE, LA ROCHELLE, ROCHEFORT, AND SAINTES.

345 kilom.=214 Eng. m.
Diligences daily. It is an uninteresting drive.

Steamers thrice a week between Nantes and Bordeaux. *N. B.* Some trustworthy person should be consulted as to the efficiency and safety of the boats before embarking.

On quitting Nantes by the six bridges at the extremity of the Faubourg St. Jacques, our route turns to the rt. out of that to Clisson (p. 204), and crosses, on a handsome new bridge, the Sèvre Nantaise, just above its junction with the Loire.

21 Aigrefeuille.
A little beyond this the road enters the department of la Vendée, and thenceforth traverses the centre of the district which was the theatre of the terrible civil war of 1792-93.

13 Montaigu, prettily situated on a height above a small stream called the Maine, in the midst of the Bocage of la Vendée, has fallen from the condition of a town to a village since the war, when two-thirds of its houses were burned, and a large part of its inhabitants massacred. The terrace of the *château*, not now inhabited, commands a good view.

After crossing the Maine, a wild, open, heathy country succeeds, producing furze, broom, and a little barley or buckwheat, as far as

24 Belleville.

13 *Bourbon Vendée* (*Inns*: H. des Voyageurs; H. de l'Europe—both slovenly and comfortless), a new town of right-angled streets and ugly fresh-looking houses, founded by Napoleon in the very centre of the rebellious province la Vendée, and destined by him to be called Napoléon-Vendée, is now the chef-lieu of the Dépt. La Roche-sur-Yonne, an ancient appanage of the Bourbons, occupied nearly the same site, and now, united with it, forms a suburb. It has not quite 5060 Inhab. Destitute of commerce or manufactures, in a situation deficient in any advantages required to render a town flourishing, in the midst of a district of barren open heath, it stands about the dullest town in France, and a melancholy example of the folly of establishing a town by word of command. "It is exactly what one might expect it would be from the hasty and arbitrary manner of its creation. A huge oblong 'Place' forms the centre and principal part of it. From the sides and corners of this 8 or 10 streets branch off at right angles. The buildings which compose this square are almost all public edifices, each looking more mesquin and meagre than the other, and all having the appearance of being stretched out at the least possible expense to the greatest possible extent of front, for the purpose of

Sect. III. *Route 62.—Nantes to Bordeaux—La Rochelle.*

making them go as far as possible towards the composition of the proposed town. A *theatre,* on the steps of whose portico the grass was growing, forms part of one side. A huge *Hôtel de Ville,* which seems deserted and shut up, stands opposite to a great barn of a church. A *préfecture,* a court-house, a mairie, and enormous barracks, surrounding a court in which a dozen regiments might manœuvre at once, occupy the most of the remaining space. The barracks have been constructed so much in haste and with so little solidity that they are already beginning to fall to ruins—new ruins, the most unsightly spectacle. They are deserted, and apparently abandoned to their fate."—*Trollope, W., France.*

Conveyances go from this to Nantes, Bordeaux, Saumur, and Les Sables.

About 4 m. to the W. (2 of them not fit for carriages, but only for the pedestrian) are the ruins of the *Abbey of Fontanelles;* a Gothic chapel remains in excellent preservation.

Les Sables, 20 m. W. of Bourbon Vendée, on the sea, is a town of some interest, curiously placed on a narrow sand-ledge, at the margin of a bay forming a large and beautiful crescent. The sands are smooth and extensive. A fleet of 70 fishing-vessels may be seen at times entering the roads in one hour, sweeping from the wide sea into a deep narrow channel between two piers, and so entering the large harbour at the back of the town. There are two peculiarities in the female costume here,—a small bell-shaped laced cap, and an enormous blue hood of cloth-shreds or wool, giving to their upper figures the shape of a huge beehive.—*Inn:* H. de France, fair, and civil people.

The same dreary, unenclosed, and heath-clad land extends to

22 Mareuil, beyond which a fine corn country commences.

Between Les Sables and Luçon (25 m.) is the Castle of Talmont, a lofty picturesque feudal ruin.

10 Luçon, a dull and dirty small town, in a situation which is unhealthy on account of its vicinity to the marshes, connected with the sea by a canal, and having a population of about 3000. Luçon was the episcopal see of Cardinal Richelieu, having been a sort of family living, into which he, though bred up for a soldier, was inducted at the age of 22. Its Gothic *cathedral,* surmounted by a tall spire of open-work, is the principal building.

10 Moreilles. Our route now lies across a district which may be called the Fens of France, a series of marshy flats, traversed by numerous rivers, the chief of which are the Vendée and Sèvre Niortaise ; it is intersected also in all directions by canals, and, notwithstanding the drainage effected by them, is unhealthy from malaria. A solitary conical mound rising out of the flat on the l. of the road is crowned by the village of Chaillé. The limits of la Vendée and the stream of the Sèvre Niortaise are crossed shortly before reaching

17 Marans, a town of 4000 Inhab., 9 m. from the sea, which exports corn from la Vendée and flour from Niort.

Before half the next stage is traversed the road crosses the canal from la Rochelle to Niort. Near this the marshes of la Vendée terminate, and the marly lands of the Aunis begin. At

15 Grolaud the canal is crossed.

A picturesque group of towers and spires, visible from a considerable distance, announces the approach to

9 *La Rochelle.—Inns:* Poste, very good ; H. de France. This third-rate fortress, and commercial town of secondary importance, is situated on the sea, on the shore of a bay in front of which rise the Iles de Ré and d'Oléron. It was capital of the district of Aunis, and is now chef-lieu of the Dépt. de la Charente. Before its memorable siege of 1628, it had a population of 27,000 ; at present it contains no more than 14,857.

Its little *port* is entirely enclosed by the buildings of the town, and consists of an outer tidal basin, and an inner wet dock, protected by a pier, and flanked at its entrance on either side by the round towers of la Chaîne and St. Nicholas, built 1418 out of the remains of the castle. A quay, planted with trees, runs round the harbour, and forms an agreeable promenade.

Its chief commerce consists in the exportation of the brandy made in the adjoining province of l'Aunis, the finest in France, of wine, corn, and flour.

At low water, the remains of the famous *dyke*, thrown out into the sea by order of Richelieu during the siege of 1628-29, and which contributed mainly to the surrender of the town, by interrupting all supplies and succour from England, are distinctly visible. This long pile of stones, stretching for a distance of 1640 yds. from the point of Coreille to that of Fort Louis, was built by the engineer Metezeau.

In the *Hôtel de Ville*, a handsome building in the style of the Renaissance, of the time of Francis I., is shown the chamber in which the heroic Guiton accepted the office of mayor on the very eve of the siege, "on condition," said he, "that I be allowed to plunge into the heart of any one who speaks of surrender the dagger which I hold in my hand, which I insist shall be placed on the table of the council-chamber where we meet, to be used against myself first, should I be weak enough to propose a capitulation." Influenced by so obstinate a spirit of resistance, the citizens held out for 14 long months against the vast force brought against them, commanded by Cardinal Richelieu in person, and supported by the presence of Louis XIII. At length, when famine, which followed the vigilant blockade established on the land side, by throwing up lines 3 miles long, and by the dyke before-mentioned drawn across the harbour, had reduced the numbers of the besieged from 27,000 to 5000, la Rochelle, the bulwark of the Protestant cause in France, which had remained in the hands of the Huguenots since the first unsuccessful siege of 1573, was yielded up to the king, and its fortifications levelled, except the two towers at the mouth of the harbour. The ill success of the two expeditions fitted out by Charles I., whose favourite, Buckingham, contributed to the failure of the first by his incompetence, and who was assassinated by Felton while about to assume the command of the second, prepared the way for its fall. The town never regained its previous prosperity, though Protestants are still numerous here. By its capture, Richelieu destroyed the political influence of the Calvinists in France. The chair of Guiton, and the council-table of marble, are still preserved in the H. de Ville. His house, at the Rue Guiton, is also pointed out—a building in the style of the Renaissance, flanked with tourelles. Six or eight of the old town gates remain, and the Tour de la Lanterne, a conspicuous structure, surmounted by a spire, dates from 1445.

The Gothic *Porte de l'Horloge*, whose architecture announces it to be a work of the 16th centy., is another relic of the time of the *siege*, and there are some old houses still standing which must also have existed at that memorable event, when streets and houses were rendered infected by the dead bodies too numerous for the living to bury. Such was the extreme misery to which the inhabitants were reduced, that one of them declared that for a whole week he had kept his child alive solely by blood drawn from his own body. One of the articles of capitulation was, that the invincible Guiton should continue in the office of mayor, retaining all his dignities: he is lost sight of, however, after the siege.

The town was again fortified by Vauban in the reign of Louis XIV. The tower of the church of *St. Sauveur*, the loftiest in the place, now used as a shot-tower, commands from its top a view embracing the Iles de Ré, whose town, St. Martin, resisted all the efforts of the English under Buckingham to capture it, 1628; and of *Oléron*, a long, low bank of land, separated from Ré by a strait called Pertuis d'Antioche. Still nearer, not 2 m. off the shore, is the Ile d'Aix, opposite the mouth of the Charente: the fort and batteries upon it, defending the entrance of the roads, were captured by the English 1757, but have been greatly strengthened since that time. An attempt was also made, 1809, by the English, to destroy the French fleet here by fireships, and was partly successful, as, out of 14 vessels, 4 ran ashore and were burnt, and 2 were captured.

For some years past a singular plague of white ants (Termes lucifugis), originally imported from India, has infested the buildings of La Rochelle, especially the Prefecture and the Arsenal.

There is an *Etablissement des Bains* here, situated on a fine Promenade or Mall, a grove of trees stretching along the shore; nice gardens are attached. Much salt is made near the town, by evaporating the sea-water.

A *steamer* plies daily between La Rochelle and l'Ile de Ré.

Rochelle is the birthplace of Réaumur, inventor of the thermometric scale named after him, and of Billaud Varennes, member of the National Convention.

Coaches to Paris by Poitiers daily; —5 times a day to Rochefort.

An uninteresting tract of flat marshy land intervenes between Rochelle and Rochefort. Near the village of Passage stood an ancient town, Châtelaillon, which preceded La Rochelle, and has long since disappeared, owing to encroachments of the sea.

14 Trois Canons.

17 Rochefort (*Inns*: H. des Etrangers; H. Grand Bacha), a fortress of 4th rank, but standing third in importance among the naval arsenals of France, is built on the rt. bank of the Charente, about 10 m. from its junction with the sea, and contains 15,911 Inhab. The river is deep enough to float vessels of the largest size abreast of the town, having 20 ft. water at ebb, and 40 ft. at the highest tides, and five forts at its mouth protect the dockyard from hostile approach. Its position is well chosen, owing to its vicinity to the roadstead formed at the embouchure of the Charente, by the protection of the islands of Ré, Oléron, and Aix. In order further to defend the roadstead, a fort is being constructed at their mouth, on a sandbank called the Boyard, between the Ile d'Aix and Ile d'Oléron; and a million of francs was voted for the purpose 1840. Rochefort is quite a modern town, founded in 1644 for the establishment of a dockyard by Louis XIV., or rather by his wise minister Colbert, who saw the necessity for a second port and arsenal on the ocean besides Brest. Its streets are built at right angles, and the only buildings of consequence are those connected with the *Port Militaire* or *Dockyard*. Admission is given by the Major de la Marine, on application of the British consul, and on exhibition of the passport. Among the vessels on the stocks are several large war-steamers; the model-room contains some curiosities. To describe the sailmakers' shops, the cable-twisting loft, the workshops whose machinery is set in motion by a steam-engine, would be nearly to repeat what has been said of Brest and Cherbourg. The only novelty to an Englishman, acquainted with the British dockyards, will be the *Bagne*, or convict prison, capable of containing 2200 forçats, but occupied by only half that number.

The largest and most remarkable edifice here is the *Hôpital de la Marine*, outside the town, consisting of nine separate masses of building, containing 1200 beds. It is excellently arranged, and well kept up, cleanly in the extreme. There is a tolerable anatomical museum attached to it.

The town was originally very unhealthy, owing to its low situation among the marshes; but these have been drained, and fevers are become rare.

In the Grande Place is a *fountain* adorned with figures representing Old Ocean shaking hands with the Charente!

In 1809 Lord Cochrane penetrated into the *Basque Roads*, between the Ile de Ré and the Ile d'Oléron, with a small squadron, and burnt 5 vessels of the French fleet destined for the W. Indies, he himself steering the leading fire-ship, charged with 1500 barrels of powder and 400 shells, through the concentrated fire of 1000 guns!

On the 3rd July, 1815, Napoleon arrived at Rochefort, seeking to escape to America, and lodged at the Préfecture; but finding that the Bellerophon, an English line-of-battle ship, was at anchor in the Rade des Basques, and that there were no possible means of evading it, he went on board on the 15th, and sailed for England, after in vain attempting to obtain a pledge from Captain Maitland for safe-conduct.

A *Steamer* runs 4 or 5 times a-week from Royan, a small port on the N. bank of the Gironde, 29 m. from Rochefort to Bordeaux: the voyage takes 7 hours. Coaches convey passengers between Rochefort and Royan, fare 4 fr. 25 c., and total to Bordeaux 8 fr. In going to Royan (a small watering-place opposite the lighthouse of the Tour de Cordouan [Rte. 69]), the Charente is crossed by a ferry. The road traverses an uninteresting flat, only redeemed by drainage from the state of a pestilential marsh, called Les Marennes.

A *Steamer* ascends the Charente to Saintes (35 m.) every morning, returning in the afternoon: the passage takes 4 hours.

The voyage up the Charente is agreeable, though somewhat monotonous, from the windings of the river and the unvaried nature of the green flat pasture-lands on its banks. Near to Saintes it passes the ruined *Castle of Taillebourg*, on an isolated rock, near which St. Louis defeated the English in 1242.

Those who travel by land from Rochefort to Bordeaux cross the Charente by a magnificent new suspension bridge, in the place of the old ferry, close under the town of Tonnay-Charente, which Louis XIV. had fixed upon for the site of his dockyard, a design which was defeated by the enormous demands of its owners for the purchase of the ground. The Gothic *Castle*, having a park and gardens attached to it, is the ancient seat of the family of Mortemart. A great quantity of brandy is exported from hence, almost all the vineyards on the banks of the Charente being cultivated for the manufacture of eau-de-vie (see p. 213): 6000 casks, a large part of the produce of Cognac, is annually shipped here for England.

11 St. Hypolite.
13 St. Porchaire.
On the l. bank of the Charente stands

14 *Saintes* (*Inns:* H. du Bâteau à Vapeur ; best and very good), formerly capital of the province Saintonge: it betrays in its name the antiquity of its origin, as chief city of the *Santones*, and has many traces to prove its importance under Roman rule.

The principal and best preserved ancient monument is the *Roman Arch of Triumph*, upon the bridge over the Charente, serving for a principal entrance into the town, constructed of a coarse limestone, originally very plain, and now, after the lapse of ages, much injured by the weather, which has rounded the angles of the stone, and converted the joints of the masonry into gaps. It is a heavy pile of masonry, pierced by two arches, and destitute of all architectural beauty, 38 ft. high. Five inscriptions upon it, now half effaced, record that it was raised (in the reign of Nero) to the memory of Germanicus, of Tiberius his uncle, and of Drusus his father, by Caius Julius Rufus, priest of Roma and Augustus. It was saved from destruction in 1665 by Blondel the architect, who at that time rebuilt the bridge; and it was repaired in 1844, when the arch was pulled down, but the separate stones were marked for re-erection. It is said to have been built originally on dry land, and that the river has since altered its bed, and isolated the arch; but this seems doubtful.

There are also considerable remains of a *Roman Amphitheatre*, near the church of St. Eutrope, in the faubourg. Though nearly equal in size to the grand circus of Nismes, it is very inferior in an architectural point of view, being built of small stones squared, and destitute of ornament, and it is now reduced to a few fractured vaults and arches. The oval of the arena measures 70 ft. in its greatest length, and 57 ft. in width. The

Sect. III.	*Route 64.— Tours to Libourne.*	213

dens destined for the wild beasts still remain, and there are fragments of an aqueduct, contrived, it is supposed, to convert the arena into a naumachia for aquatic spectacles. (?) Many antique fragments, capitals, inscriptions, sarcophagi, &c., are preserved in the garden of the sous préfecture. Such are the few traces of the former magnificence of the ancient *Mediolanum Santonum*, one of the most important cities of Aquitaine.

The *Ch. of St. Eutrope* is a structure of the 11th centy. : its huge crypt is the most curious part of it; some of the capitals of columns have quaint carvings. The spire was built in the 15th centy.

The detached tower of the *Cathedral*, a fine Flamboyant structure, conspicuous from the pinnacles which surmount it, occupies the site of the church built by Charlemagne in fulfilment of the vow of his father Pepin, after defeating on this spot Gaiffre Duc of Aquitaine. The portal is ancient.

The public *Library* contains Fénélon's Bible, with notes in his own hand.

The population of Saintes amounts to 11,000. The Charente is here a tidal river, but navigable only for barges. Much eau-de-vie is sent down to the sea for exportation.

[About 18 m. to the E. higher up the river, on the road to Angoulême, is the town of *Cognac* (*Inn:* H. d'Orléans, poor outside, very comfortable, but dear), which gives its name to the best brandy in France, produced from vineyards in its vicinity, and along the banks of the river near Jarnac and Angoulême (Rte. 64), in the department of La Charente. The quantity produced annually does not exceed 6000 butts (tierçons), but the number sold under the name "les fines Champagnes," by which the best quality is distinguished, exceeds 15,000 butts. Cognac contains numerous distilleries, and is the staple place for the brandy produced in the surrounding districts. The vines cultivated for its manufacture are allowed to grow to greater luxuriance than those used for winemaking, and run along the ground, whence they acquire strength, while the earthy flavour which is inseparable from wine produced from creeping vines is dissipated in the process of distillation.

Francis I. was born at Cognac, while his mother Louise de Savoie, Duchesse d'Angoulême, was residing in the castle; but, according to tradition, he first saw the light under an elm-tree, where his mother was unexpectedly brought to bed. A stone now marks the spot.]

A Diligence runs from Saintes to Mortagne on the Garonne, to meet the steamer to Bordeaux.

The road from Saintes to Bordeaux is carried through

12 La Jard.

9 Pons, a town of 4000 Inhab., picturesquely seated on the l. bank of the Seugne. Its castle, distinguished by a keep-tower, 100 ft. high, built in the 11th century, is now a prison. Théodore Agrippa d'Aubigné, grandfather of Madame de Maintenon, and a favourite of Henri IV., was a native of Pons.

11 St. Genis.

12 Mirambeau.

17 Etauliers, Dépt. de la Gironde.

The road reaches the banks of the Gironde at

13 Blaye, described in Rte. 69.

Steamers ply daily between Blaye and Bordeaux.

15 Graviers. There is a direct road from Etauliers to Graviers, avoiding the détour by Blaye round two sides of a triangle; but not long since this road was impracticable for carriages for want of repair.

14 Cubsac is on the high road from Paris to Bordeaux. (Rte. 64.)

10 Carbon Blanc. } (Rte. 64.)
11 BORDEAUX.

ROUTE 64.

TOURS TO LIBOURNE AND BORDEAUX, BY POITIERS AND ANGOULÊME RAILWAY.

345 kilom. = 210 Eng. m.   *Railway.*
Tours to Poitiers—101 kilom. = 60 Eng. m. — was opened July 1851.

Poitiers to Angoulême—112 kilom.—opened 1853. Angoulême to Bordeaux —183 kilom. = 83 Eng. m. — was finished 1852.

This railway in the first part of its course crosses 4 or 5 rivers, tributaries of the Loire, in succession, on viaducts, and the ridges separating their respective valleys in deep cuttings. Soon after quitting Tours it passes the Cher, and the rich green pastures bordering on it, on an embankment and a bridge of 6 arches, 590 ft. long; next it is carried over the valley of the Indre on a long viaduct of 59 arches, 30 ft. span, 65 ft. high, 2624 ft. long.

13 Monts Stat. 2 m. rt. is Montbazon, a small town, with a *castle-keep* on a rock.

22 Villeperdue Stat. A mile or two on the l. is the Chapel of *St. Catherine de Fierbois*, whither Joan of Arc sent from Chinon to fetch the sacred sword, "marked with 5 crosses, lying in a vault," which she afterwards bore in all her battles. She had previously passed through the village, however, on her journey from Lorraine to Chinon, and had doubtless then remarked the weapon; but the vulgar belief attributed its discovery to divine inspiration. Near this is a handsome modern Gothic *château*, built, 1850, by the Marquis de Lussac.

33 Ste. Maure Stat: here a road to Chinon branches off. (See p. 193.) Here are ruins of a *Castle* which belonged to the family of Craon. The plain around Ste. Maure is thought to be the site of the battle between Charles Martel and the Saracens under Abderahmen.

The river Creuse is crossed at

45 Port-de-Piles Stat., about ½ m. above its junction with the Vienne. [Higher up, on the rt. bank of the Creuse, and 3 m. to the l. of our road, is the village of La Haye, the birthplace of the philosopher Descartes. The house in which he was born (1596) is preserved.]

[About 7 m. S. of La Haye, also on the Creuse, is the *Château de Guerche*, built by Charles VII. for Agnes Sorel, his mistress, where she resided when the king was at Loches, and where he used to visit her on his way to and from the chace in the neighbouring forest. It is a massy pile, rising 100 ft. above the waterside, flanked by 4 towers at the angles. It retains in its interior some traces of fresco painting, and the punning initials of his mistress's name, an A over L (*A-Sur-Elle*). In the chapel is placed a statue of Agnes.]

49 Les Ormes Stat., on the Vienne. —The château belongs to the family d'Argenson, and has fine gardens.

The railroad runs parallel with the Vienne, through

Dangé, and

53 Ingrande Stat.

68 *Châtellerault Stat.* (*Inns:* H. de l'Espérance, good; Tête Noire, fair dining-place), a smoky town of mean houses, on the rt. bank of the Vienne, is one of the chief seats of the *Manufacture of Cutlery* in France, which gives employment to about 600 families, out of its 12,433 Inhab., who work for large houses. There is also a royal manufactory of swords and bayonets (armes blanches), established 1820.

The Duchy of Châtellerault was bestowed by Henri II. upon James Hamilton, 2nd Earl of Arran, Regent of Scotland, 1548, to induce him to consent to the projected match between his ward, the infant Queen Mary, and the Dauphin Francis. The duchy was forfeited to the crown, and has never been restored.

The Vienne is navigable for a short distance higher up. A portion of a gateway flanked by turrets, erected by the Duc de Sully, stands at the extremity of the bridge over it.

76 Barres de Nintré Stat.

82 La Tricherie Stat.

89 Clain Stat. For the last 3 stages the railroad has continued to ascend the valley of the Clain. That stream traverses a rocky and wooded ravine, of much picturesque beauty: a bridge and viaduct are crossed before arriving at

10 POITIERS STATION, nearly a mile from the town by the road, but much less by the pathway. — *Inns:* H. de France; bed 2 fr., dinner 3 fr., tea 1 fr., coffee 15 sous;—H. de l'Europe, good; —Trois Piliers.

Poitiers, the capital of ancient Poitou, an early possession of the kings of England, who were its dukes down to the time of Charles V. (1371), stands on a rounded eminence of considerable height, the summit of which is occupied by the Préfecture and Palais de Justice. From this its streets sweep down in steep slopes, or curve, in winding mazes, to the small river Clain, which encompasses nearly ¾ of its circuit, while the smaller river Boivre encircles another part, so that they formed, in ancient times, a sort of natural fosse round its ramparts, now almost entirely swept away by town-council improvements. The number of inhabitants is about 28,000, but it has neither commerce nor manufacture of any great importance, as might indeed be surmised from its dull and empty streets, excepting the market-place, which is a scene of much bustle and densely crowded.

It has an *Ecole de Droit*, numbering between 200 and 300 students, but of greater celebrity in former times than at present. Lord Bacon in his youth studied here. The town still contains more than a dozen *nunneries*, chiefly serving as boarding-schools for the education of young females.

The curiosities of Poitiers are chiefly of an antiquarian nature. It possesses a remarkably large number of churches, all more or less interesting to the lover of architecture and antiquity,—and, as some of them date from a very early period, and others were commenced later, and continued down to comparatively modern times, they form a very instructive series by which to study the progress and change of style in building.

Notre Dame de Poitiers, in the market-place, nearly opposite the Ecole de Droit, presents a remarkable example of the florid Romanesque style in its W. façade, which is nearly covered with sculpture from top to bottom. It rests on a triple arcade; the central arch forming the entrance being circular, the two side arches pointed, but all decorated with mouldings and capitals of the same character of richness and singularity. The rest of the façade, on each side of a tall window, is occupied by arcades filled with statues and bas-reliefs; and the usual pointed oval frame (vescica piscis) within the gable contains 2 statues. The whole is flanked by 2 round turrets. The probable date of this façade is the middle of the 12th centy.

The interior is of a more severe style, but sadly defaced by modern painting: it has an apsidal E. end, with circular arches and hooped vaulting, except the side chapels, one of which, in the S. aisle, an addition in the florid style of the 15th centy., contains a rich recess to include a somewhat grotesque group of sculpture meant to represent the Entombment.

The Salle des Pas Perdus, attached to the *Palais de Justice*, which originally formed part of the palace of the Comtes de Poitou, is a vast hall, with an open wooden roof; its walls are decorated with arcades, circular on one side and pointed on the other, yet both perhaps nearly of the same date, the 12th centy. The front, recently thrown open, is said to have been built by Comte Jean de Berry.

The *Cathedral*, dedicated to St. Peter, is said to have been founded by Henry II. of England. The 2 towers, similar in style, but unequal in size,—the semicircular N. doorway, in which the capitals of the pillars are human figures, stiff, but good in style,—and a large part of the body of the building, whose round and pointed arches are intermixed, as in the Salle de Justice,—may possibly be of Henry's time.

The building is divided into 3 aisles, the central one being much the widest. The piers, composed of 4 engaged shafts, surmounted by sharply-cut capitals, are very elegant. There are several painted windows, and a fine rose at the W. end, hid, internally, by the organ. Very solid buttresses support the walls and roof.

A little way behind the E. end of the cathedral stands the *Ch. of St. Radegonde*; the lower part of whose elegant Byzantine tower, though masked by a florid porch, is probably of the 11th centy., as well as the white marble *bénitier*, shaped like a horse-trough, within it. Above it is a curious niche, containing the statue of a saint. The Romanesque choir is raised upon a very old *crypt*, perhaps older than any part of the upper structure, partly cut out of the rock. In this is deposited the black marble Coffin of St. Radegonde, resorted to, in the month of August, by thousands of pilgrims, chiefly of the lower orders, who throng the low vault to kiss the worn marble Sarcophagus (on which some curious ornaments of an early age may be discerned), and to bring their sick children to be cured. The saint's empty coffin, it appears, still retains the virtue of healing possessed by her body, before it was burnt by the ruthless Huguenots in 1562. In the S. wall of the nave is a small chapel, fenced with iron bars, called "*Le Pas de Dieu*," because it contains the stone impressed by the footmark of our Saviour, who here appeared to St. Radegonde, according to the legend! It is covered over by an iron case to protect it. Part of the internal decorations of this ch. are, like the porch, of the 15th centy., and some of the sculpture is by no means appropriate to a church.

The building called the *Temple de St. Jean*, now converted into a *Musée*, and previously a church, is, next to the Roman Circus, the oldest edifice in Poitiers, and one of the oldest Christian monuments in France; on which account, as well as from the style of its architecture, it deserves particular attention from those who take an interest in antiquities.

It is an oblong building, measuring about 40 ft. by 25, its greatest length being from E. to W., and its walls on these sides terminating in obtuse gables. The masonry is very neat; and on 3 of the walls, inside as well as out, a sort of arcade is introduced, consisting of a circular arch, flanked and surmounted by small triangles resembling pediments. This debased style of building, arising from want of skill in the architects, and of funds in the founders, followed the Roman, at the fall of the Empire, and preceded the Romanesque, and it is probable, therefore, that the Temple de St. Jean dates from the 6th or 7th centy. It appears to have been a *Baptistery*, judging from the well in the centre of its floor, about 8 ft. deep, having a pipe running obliquely into it. The style of construction is decidedly post-Roman.

To convert it into a ch., a semicircular apse was thrown out from the E. wall, and a sort of porch was raised before the W. The style of building in these alterations denotes a date probably not later than the 10th centy.; and the curious frescoes, still visible on the inner walls, are perhaps nearly as old. The bull's-eye windows by which it is lighted were originally round-headed windows, the lower part of which has been bricked up. This edifice was condemned, a few years ago, by the municipal authorities, to be pulled down, because it stood in the way of the road to Limoges. Luckily there were found in Poitiers some admirers of ancient art to save it from destruction.

The *antiquities* deposited within consist chiefly of broken fragments of Roman sculpture and architecture; a mile-stone of the age of Alexander Severus, and some inscriptions; also a curious Byzantine bas-relief representing St. Hilarius.

The following churches deserve the notice of the antiquary and architect, in addition to those already mentioned. *St. Hilaire*, finished 1049, has lost a portion of its nave. The apsidal choir rests on 7 lofty columnar piers. The Ch. of *Moutiersneuf* is also Romanesque, but has been much restored since the Revolution. *St. Porchaire* has a curious portal with bas-reliefs.

In the *Public Library* are some fine illuminated MSS.

The Romans have left traces of their settlement here, on the site of Gaulic *Limonum*, a city of the *Pictavi*, in the remains of an *Amphitheatre*, which is best approached through the Inn called Hôtel d'Evreux. At the back of the stable-yard is a tolerably perfect wedge-shaped vault, now filled with hay; and leading to it, a part of the vaulted corridor which ran round the building on the ground-floor. The oval interior of the Circus is now converted into the inn garden, and some houses have been built upon the sloping constructions around it which formerly supported the rows of benches. There is no doubt that other vaults and corridors remain under them. The hardness and regularity of the masonry, in the portions of the wall exposed to view, are such as characterise all Roman constructions.

The town of Poitiers is surrounded by narrow valleys or ravines on all sides but the S.W., where a neck of land connects it with the high ridge whose extremity it occupies. In ancient times the town was defended on this side by strong walls and a deep ditch dug across the isthmus. The space immediately within these walls is now converted into a *Promenade*, called de Blossac, from an intendant of the province in the last centy. It would be a very agreeable walk were it only kept clean, for the terraces, resting on the foundations of the old walls, command a pleasing view into the deep valley of the Clain below.

The *Bains du Belvédère*, not far from this walk, are comfortable, and the charge moderate.

From the heights on the rt. bank of the Clain there is a very good view of the picturesque town of Poitiers, but no path runs along them. The writer of this took an agreeable but scrambling walk, issuing out of Poitiers by the Paris gate, crossing the bridge over the Clain, then ascending through vineyards behind the Faubourg, and keeping along the edge of the cliff as far as the road to Limoges, where he recrossed the Clain by another bridge, at the back of St. Radegonde.

About 1½ m. out of the town, a little to the l. of the road to Limoges, on a height, is a *Dolmen*, or Druidic monument, called *Pierre Levée*. It is a block of calcareous sandstone, about 13 ft. long and 3 thick, resting at one end upon upright stones, but at the other deprived of its support. Rabelais attributes its erection to Pantagruel, "pour le divertissement des escholiers de l'Université," who resorted hither to carouse.

At about an equal distance from the town, in another direction, a little to the l. of the road to Angoulême, are remains of a *Roman Aqueduct*, which supplied water to the town and circus. 4 or 5 of its arches are still tolerably perfect, but they are neither imposing nor very ornamental.

Poitiers is historically very celebrated. The invading tide of the Saracenic hordes penetrated in the 8th centy. thus far into W. Europe, at a moment when the fate of Christianity seemed trembling in the scale. At that epoch, having already conquered Spain, they poured through the defiles of the Pyrenees, overspread Aquitaine, advanced up to the walls of Poitiers under their famed chief Abdelrahmen, and burned the Ch. of St. Hilaire to the ground. They were even threatening to pass the Loire, when they were met, somewhere between Poitiers and Tours, by Charles Martel, in 732. This contest between the E. and the W., between the Gospel and the Koran, ended in the defeat of the Saracens, 300,000 of whom, it is said, but on the doubtful authority of a single chronicler, were left dead on the field; and the remnant retired, never more to trouble Christendom in the W. The site of the battle-field has never been exactly ascertained, and no discovery of bones has been made, which would surely mark the scene of so enormous a slaughter. At an earlier period (507) the plains of Poitiers had been the scene of the defeat of Alaric King of the Visigoths, by Clovis.

Poitiers is distinguished in English history by the signal victory gained under its walls, in 1356, by the army of the Black Prince, consisting of English and Gascons, who early in that year had invaded the S. of France, and spread desolation through Languedoc, Limousin, and Auvergne, as far as the gates of Bourges in Berry. The prince's whole force did not exceed 12,000 or 14,000 men, and the expedition had no other design than that of a foray to "harry" the fair fields of France.

L

France. On his way back to Bordeaux, however, suddenly and unexpectedly, on 9th September, he encountered the army of John King of France, amounting to 60,000 men, of whose vicinity, and even of their march to meet him, he had been entirely ignorant.

"God help us!" said the prince, "we must now consider how we can best fight them." The Pope's Legate, Cardinal Talleyrand, assuming the office of peacemaker, in vain endeavoured to prevent the impending strife and bloodshed; even Edward himself offered to acquiesce in any reasonable terms, consistent with his honour, to be permitted to go free. He offered to give up all the towns and castles he had taken, together with the prisoners, and not to bear arms against the French king for the space of 7 years. The French, however, confident in numbers, would listen to no conditions but the surrender of the Black Prince and 100 of his principal knights. The result is well known. The English owed the success of the day, under Providence, to their well-chosen position, to the deadly and skilfully aimed arrows of their yeomen, which availed more than the lances of their knights, and to the stout hearts of their leaders, the Black Prince and Lord Chandos, and of all the English under them.

On that day France beheld the flower of her chivalry laid low, while her king, John, was led into captivity. The noble dead were buried by the townsfolk in the churches of the Cordeliers and Jacobins within the town. The field of battle is fixed by Froissart near the village Maupertuis, about 5 m. N. W. of the town, near the road to La Rochelle.

Diligences.—Daily to Limoges; to Rochefort (Rte. 62); to Nantes (Rte. 60); Niort, Les Sables, Châteauroux, Civray.

Railway to Angoulême was completed 1853.

The country possesses little interest. On quitting Poitiers, it leaves l. the Faubourg de la Tranchée, and traverses a short tunnel.

104 St. Benoit Stat.
108 Legugé Stat. The course of the Clain is followed to

120 Vivonne Stat., passing another tunnel.
133 Couhé-Verac Stat.
150 *Civray Stat.* The old town lies 2 m. l. It has a Romanesque *Ch.* whose façade is curiously ornamented with sculptures, including signs of the zodiac, somewhat like Notre Dame at Poitiers, but dating probably from the early part of the 12th centy. At Charroux, 8 m. farther off, are remains of an *Abbey*, now reduced to a tower about 80 ft. high, rising from 2 circular arcades, one above the other, supported by piers formed of bundles of shafts. This was originally the central tower of a very curious ch., consisting of a circular choir, preceded by a rectangular nave: but all the rest is destroyed. The abbey was founded by Charlemagne, but these ruins are not older than the 11th or 12th centy.

A few m. N. E. of Civray is Geuçay (H. du Lion d'Or), where there is a very fine and picturesque *Castle* of the 12th or 13th centy., the walls in good preservation. And near it is the *Ch. of St. Maurice*, a Romanesque structure, central tower, apsidal chapels, and the other usual features of a fine ch. of the 12th centy.

The Railway now enters the valley of the Charente, and passes the ironwork of Taizé Aizé.

166 Ruffec Stat.—*Inns :* H. des Ambassadeurs; the pâtés de perdrix aux truffes unrivalled.—*Ld. B.* Poste, very good.

6 Les Nègres. At
11 Mansle the river Charente is crossed.
14 Churet.
172 Courcome ⎫
176 Moussac ⎬ Stats.
182 Luxé ⎭

The Charante is crossed at Foulpouque on a bridge of 5 arches. The Castles of la Terne and la Titerne are passed.

The cultivation of the vine now becomes general. The wines produced about Angoulême and along the borders of the Charente are of inferior quality, but fit for converting into brandy.

200 Vars Stat. Between Pontouvre and Bourgets we cross the Touvres.

[A few miles up this picturesque stream is the Imperial cannon-foundry of Ruelle; charcoal is exclusively employed as the fuel for the smelting furnaces, and is abundantly supplied by the neighbouring forests.

Farther on, in the same direction, is La Rochefoucauld, whose castle was the ancient residence of the family of that name, its most noted scion being François, author of the celebrated 'Maximes.' It escaped destruction at the Revolution, and still belongs to the same family, though no longer inhabited by them. It is a huge pile, flanked by round, cone-roofed towers at the angles, forming 3 sides of a square, and, with the exception of the antique donjon, was erected, 1527, by Antoine Fontan, in the style of the Renaissance. A range of arcades serves as a passage along the inner façade, and a curious and richly ornamented spiral stone staircase leads to the upper stories. Below the castle are very extensive *Caves*, not now entered, which served as a refuge to the Huguenots in the wars of Religion. There are similar natural caverns all along the valley of the Tardonère, the largest of which, les Grottes de Rancogne, are about 3 m. above La Rochefoucauld. They are traversed by a streamlet, and contain some stalactites.]

A tunnel conveys the railway train entirely through the hill on which stands the town, in order to reach

213 *Angoulême Stat.*   a

11 *Angoulême.—Inns:* L   Poste, good; the landlord's pâtés of foies de canards, famous; the cuisine excellent; —H. des Etrangers, diligence-house; —Croix d'Or, at the foot of the hill, good but dear.

Angoulême, the ancient capital of the Angoumois, now of the Dépt. de la Charente, occupies a situation, not unlike that of Poitiers, on the top of a high hill, terraced round with remains of the ancient ramparts above, while below it is nearly encircled by the course of the Charente, and by another small stream falling into it. The town is distinguished by far more life, industry, and trade, than Poitiers, and possesses, with its suburbs, a population of 20,000. Though planted on the top of an isolated hill, more than 200 ft. above the Charente, it is most abundantly supplied with fountains of fresh water, pumped up by machinery recently established. Its houses, being of a very white stone, easily cut, have a cheerful appearance: it has many new streets and a few old buildings. Its most pleasing features, however, are the series of *Terrace-walks* running round it, in the place of the old ramparts, and commanding a charming view of the industrious valley deep below, of the winding Charente fringed with verdure, of the suburbs, and the *paper-mills* on the river banks, which furnish the staple article of manufacture here. By far the finest portion of these terraces is the *Promenade Beaulieu;* and a series of walks and shrubberies extend down the slopes below it towards the bottom of the valley. In the midst of them stands a column dedicated, by precipitate loyalty, to the Duchesse d'Angoulême in 1815, re-dedicated, since 1830, "à la Liberté."

In the irregular *Place,* serving for the market, in the centre of the town, stands the old *Castle,* distinguished by its 3 picturesque feudal towers and tall donjon, now converted into a prison, and surmounted by the telegraph. It contains a number of vaulted apartments, but possesses nothing of interest, save the recollection that it was the residence of the ancient Counts of Angoulême; that Marguerite de Valois, Queen of Navarre, was born in it,—the most accomplished princess of her day, "La Marguerite des Marguerites," as her brother François I. called her; and that its walls gave shelter to Marie de Medicis. She retired hither, after her husband's assassination, under the protection of the Duc d'Epernon, governor of the Angoumois, who has been suspected of being the accomplice of Ravaillac; while the queen-mother herself is not free from suspicion—"The death of Henry did not sufficiently surprise her."

The *Cathedral* is rather a curious than a beautiful edifice, in the Romanesque style, rebuilt from its foundations in 1120. It suffered at the Revolution; and till very lately bore over

L 2

its frontispiece the ill-effaced inscription, "Temple de la Raison," set over it at that period. It is surmounted by a fine tall tower, of 6 rows of semicircular arcades, rising on the N. side. The W. front is in the style of the churches of Italy; almost the whole space being divided by circular arcades, resting on elegant columns, enclosing statues much mutilated, surmounted in the pediment by a statue of the Saviour (once supposed to be Jupiter), surrounded by the attributes of the 4 Evangelists. The *nave* has no side aisles, and its roof is formed of 3 vaulted cupolas, a style of construction not known to the N. of the Loire. At the cross rises an octagonal tower. The choir ends in an apse. Numerous additions and repairs were made to the interior, after the barbarous devastations committed by the Huguenots in 1562 and 1568.

Among modern buildings, the *Palais de Justice* is by no means contemptible. In the attic has been placed the public *Library*, containing 14,000 vols., and a small collection of Natural History.

Outside the town, to the N., in the escarped rock below the ramparts, is the *Grotte de St. Cybard*, a holy hermit, whose real name was Eparchus, who occupied it as his cell, and died here in the 6th century. By the sanctity of his life he caused the foundation of arch. and monastery, which extended from the cave to the Charente, and was once much frequented by devout pilgrims, but both are now swept away. In the grotto, which Charlemagne himself approached on bended knees in order to perform his devotions, mass was said daily down to the time of the Revolution. This oldest Christian monument in Angoulême is respected by its present owner, but no longer serves as a church.

Ausonius makes mention of this town under the name *Ioulisma*, fancifully derived from "In collis summâ," and gradually softened down, as some conjecture, into the modern Angoulême.

Angoulême and the surrounding province were governed, from the 8th cent. down to 1303, when they were united to France, by a long line of independent counts, 19 in number; first of the race of Taillefer, and, after 1180, of the house of Lusignan. It also belonged to the English, and was some time the residence of the Black Prince after the battle of Poitiers, 1360. One of the town gates, not pulled down until 1808, was named *Porte de Chandos*, from the brave English knight who built it, while Constable of Aquitaine for Edward III. A house in the Rue de Genève is pointed out as that inhabited by Calvin, who sought refuge here 1533, and taught Greek to maintain himself. The *Place de Murier* receives its name from a mulberry-tree which stood in the midst of it while it was the convent garden of the Jacobins. During the outrages committed by the Calvinist soldiery 1562, when they captured and sacked the town, the monk Michel Grillet was hung to its boughs, in the presence of the Admiral Coligny, whose death he is said to have foretold with his dying words, saying, "You shall be thrown out of the window, like Jezebel, and shall be ignominiously dragged through the streets."

Among the remarkable persons natives of this place are Ravaillac, the assassin of Henri IV.; Poltrot, who shot the Duc de Guise le Balafré, before the walls of Orleans; and Montalembert, the inventor of a system of fortification.

The *Naval School*, established here at the suggestion of the Duc d'Angoulême 1816, was suppressed 1830, and transferred to Brest, and the building in the Faubourg l'Houmeau still remains closed.

The manufactures of Angoulême consist of paper, made in numerous (36 ?) mills in the neighbouring valleys, and brandy.

Capital *pâtés de perdrix aux truffes* are made here.

The Charente is navigable up to the quay below the town. A *Steamer* runs to Saintes (Rte. 62) 3 times a week.

[18¾ m. W. of Angoulême, on the way to Cognac (Rte. 62), is *Jarnac*, where a handful of Protestants, commanded by the Prince de Condé, engaged the royal army commanded by the Duc d'Anjou, doubling their force in num-

Sect. III.   Route 64.—Tours to Bordeaux—Cubsac.

ber, and were defeated. Condé fell, after giving the signal for a third charge, which he led, with one arm in a sling, and his leg shattered. Young Henri, Prince of Béarn, his nephew, was a spectator of the bloody affray, but was not permitted to take part in it.]

Many cuttings and embankments occur before we reach

220 La Couronne Stat., near to which the ruins of the *Abbey* of *la Couronne* are seen on the l., in the midst of a green valley abounding in paper-mills. After escaping destruction at the Revolution, it has been demolished for the sake of the material since 1808, and is now reduced to a mere fragment, including the W. front with a fine doorway, and part of a rose-window over it.

The Railway leaves the old post-road on the rt. It crosses on a lofty viaduct of 12 arches the valley of the Coutabière. The ruins of Castle Larochaudry on the top of a rock are seen before reaching

225 Moulhiers Stat.

233 Charmaul Stat. [Some miles on the rt. lies Barbezieu (*Inn:* Boule d'Or), a town of 2500 Inhab.] The tunnel of Livernan, the longest on the line, measures 1310 mètres.

247 Montmoreau Stat. Here is a fine Romanesque Ch. lately restored, and fragments of a Castle.

263 *Chalais* Stat. This town with its château (Renaissance) belongs to the family Talleyrand.

277 La Roche Chalais Stat. The town is a mile off.

294 *Coutras Stat.* Memorable for the battle between the Protestants under Henri of Navarre and the Roman Catholics, fought on the plain near the confluence of the Dronne and l'Isle, 1587.

303 St. Denis Stat. Department of the Gironde.

312 *Libourne Stat.* (*Inns:* H. de France ; des Princes), a town of 11,552 Inhab., situated on the rt. bank of the Dordogne, here a tidal river, capable of receiving vessels of 300 tons burthen, and crossed by a bridge of brick, like that of Bordeaux, at the confluence of the l'Isle, which is traversed by an iron bridge. It is neat and regularly built, and is one of the " Bastides" or free towns founded by Edward I.* It is said to occupy the site of the " Condatis portus" mentioned by Ausonius.

The Rly. quits Libourne by a bridge of 9 arches over the Dordogne, planted by the side of that which carries the road to Bordeaux.

The viaduct of Arvers over the marshes consists of 100 small arches, and is $3\frac{1}{4}$ m. long. The Rly., following the Dordogne, makes a wide sweep before it arrives at

318 Vayres Stat.

322 St. Sulpice Stat., in a country of vineyards. A few miles from this, lower down the river, is

[Cubsac, on the rt. bank of the Dordogne, here a broad estuary, formerly crossed in ferry-boats, in which passengers and carriages were embarked. The transit occupied from $\frac{1}{4}$ to $\frac{1}{2}$ an hr., and was sometimes attended with danger, and always formed a serious interruption to the communication between Bordeaux and the French metropolis. For this disagreeable ferry an iron-wire *Suspension-bridge*, the longest in France, and indeed in Europe, is substituted. It was begun 1835, and finished 1839, at a cost of 3,000,000 fr., by the engineer Fortuné de Vergèz. It is divided into 5 curves supported on 6 pair of piers, consisting of hollow open columnar shafts or towers of cast iron. The roadway of the bridge is raised 93 ft. above the water, so as to allow vessels of large size to pass under it ; and the approaches to it, from either bank, are by a series of lofty stilted arches, 29 in number, on either bank, which have a striking effect. The bridge itself has much the appearance of the Brighton chain-pier, and is of slight construction, being warranted to stand no more than 40 years, it is understood. Besides the suspending wire cables, others are attached to the summits of the piers, in the manner of stays or braces, to steady them. The length of the central, or suspension-bridge, is 1640 ft., and the 29 arches, on either side, measure 656 ft., making a total length

* See p. 228.

of 2952 ft., or more than ½ a mile : it is 20 ft. wide.

The Dordogne joins the Garonne 10 m. below this bridge, and their united waters form the estuary called the Gironde, after which the department is named.

The tongue of land which separates the Dordogne from the Garonne, across which our road lies, is a fertile district, chiefly laid out in vineyards and cornfields, and scattered over with country seats. It is called the "Entre Deux Mers."]

341 *Lormont* Stat., on the Garonne. Near this are 4 tunnels.

The approach to Bordeaux is very striking; the Railroad is carried along the rt. bank of the broad Garonne, until the city of Bordeaux appears lining its opposite concave bank.

345 *Bordeaux Terminus* is close to the magnificent *bridge*, one of the finest in Europe, consisting of 17 arches of stone, the walls and spandrels being brick, with stone quoins, 1534 ft. ong, traversing the Garonne, from the little suburb la Bastide to the city of Bordeaux. Until 1821 the Garonne was passed by a ferry; and the want of a bridge has confined the city exclusively to the l. bank of the river. A bridge of wood was begun in the time of Napoleon, but was abandoned soon after for one of stone, which was completed, 1821, by a company of shareholders, who are repaid by the tolls during 99 years for their outlay, which amounted to 260,000*l*. (6¼ millions of francs). The architect was M. Deschamps.

A vaulted passage runs under the roadway, between it and the arches, for the whole length of the bridge : this gives a great height of wall between the crown of the arches and the parapet.

As the French are fond of comparing this bridge with that of Waterloo, the dimensions of both are here given in English feet.

	Length.	Width.	No. of Arches.	Width of Arch.
Bordeaux	1534	47	17	85*
Waterloo	1326	40	9	118

* Only the 7 central arches have this width, the rest are smaller.

The view of Bordeaux from the bridge is very striking. Opposite the bridge stands the Porte de Bourgogne, erected to commemorate the birth of the Duc de B., grandson of Louis XIV.

Passengers are conveyed in omnibuses from the station, over the bridge, to

BORDEAUX, in Rte. 73.

ROUTE 65.

POITIERS TO CHÂTEAUROUX, BY ST. SAVIN ;—EXCURSION TO MONTMORILLON.

119 kilom. = 73½ Eng. m.

This cross-road, not much travelled, leads to some interesting antiquities.

23 Chauvigny, a town of 1000 Inhab., occupies a commanding height on the rt. bank of the Vienne. It was, in feudal times, a strong fortress, and still possesses the ruins of 3 distinct *Castles* built on the same plan, a square flanked by turrets. The *Donjon*, on the top of the hill, shows on one side a breach in its wall, made by a battery of cannon in the 16th century, during the wars of Religion, and now filled up with bricks arranged herring-bone fashion. One of the castles, the most modern, probably of the 13th or 14th century, with pointed windows, now serves as a prison. There are many old houses in the upper town dating from the 15th and 16th centuries.

The *Church*, also in the upper town, is a very interesting Romanesque building, decorated with all the ornaments of Byzantine art externally, and also within; the capitals of its columns being carved with mermaids, monsters, &c., as well as with Scriptural subjects.

19 St. Savin has a *Church* decorated in its porch, nave, and crypt, under the choir, with fresco paintings, representing Scriptural subjects from the Creation, the figures as large as life, and tolerably well preserved. Those in the crypt describe the legend of St. Savin and St. Cyprien, and are of smaller proportions. They are probably the work of Greek or Italian artists in the 11th, or at earliest of the 10th century, and are certainly very valuable as monuments of early art. It has been

remarked, as a proof of the antiquity or the Eastern origin of these frescoes, that the horsemen are represented riding without stirrups. The whole ch. was originally covered with paintings; those in the choir have been effaced by whitewash. The ch. itself is a very ancient specimen of Romanesque architecture; it is entered by steps leading down into it, and the W. end seems to have been separated from the rest, so as to form a Narthex, like the Galilee of some English churches. The choir and shallow transepts end in apses.

[At *Montmorillon*, 12 m. S. of St. Savin, "in the courtyard of what was the baronial castle, and is now a college, there is an ancient and very curious chapel. Originally it must have been the domestic chapel of the lords of the adjacent castle, doubtless erected by them, and for their private use. It consists of a subterraneous crypt, which probably was the family vault, and an octagonal chapel above it, with a conical roof. Part of this building is in the round style, and part in the pointed. That part which is in the round style may belong to the 11th cent. The pointed part cannot be older than the 13th. But the most remarkable feature in this building, and that to which it owes its celebrity, is a group of rudely sculptured figures which occupy a recess above the doorway. Various explanations of this singular group have been offered by the learned, but none of them are satisfactory, and the problem is more difficult to solve, as some of the figures are taken from ordinary life, and some are allegorical."—*H. G. K.* The most singular and inexplicable, perhaps, are two female figures, the one corpulent, having toads or scarabs hanging from her breasts; the other meagre, entwined by serpents, and suckling them. This *Church* has been repaired by the Government. Under an arch on the rt. is the tomb of Etienne de la Hire. "A few miles W. of Montmorillon is *Lussac les Châteaux* (*Inn:* Trois Pigeons), where there are a small Romanesque church, and the ruins of 2 *castles*, and of a bridge which connected them, the towers of which remain in the water, but the arches, probably of wood, have been destroyed. The scenery is very picturesque; there is a cavern in the rock."—*J. H. P.*

18 Le Blanc. The abbey of Fronquambant is again taken possession of by the Trappists. The fine ruined *Ch.* of the 12th and 13th centuries is being restored by them.

18 Scoury.
11 St. Gaulthier.
15 Lothiers.
15 Châteauroux. (R. 70.)

ROUTE 66.

POITIERS TO ROCHEFORT BY NIORT.

132 kilom. = 80 Eng. m. A Railway is in progress, by Rochelle.

Poitiers (in Rte. 64) to
6 Croutelle, on the road to Bordeaux.
17 Lusignan on the Vonne (*Inns:* H. Ste. Catherine;—Lion d'Or) gave its name to the noble family which rescued Jerusalem from the Infidels and for some time occupied its throne. The castle was surprised and razed by the Catholics 1574, and a public walk occupies its site. The *Church*, a dilapidated building, has a curious portal, ornamented with the signs of the zodiac.
14 Villedieu du Perron.
15 St. Maixent (*Inn:* L'Ecu de France —extortionate), an old walled town, 5500 Inhab., on a height above the Sèvre.
10 La Crèche.
13 *Niort* (*Inns:* H. du Raisin de Bourgogne; H. de France—good), a modern town, chef-lieu of the Dept. of the Deux Sèvres, on the Sèvre Niortaise, 22,000 Inhab.

The *old Castle*, surmounted by 2 keep-towers, each flanked by 8 turrets, remarkable as the birthplace, or at least the cradle, of Madame de Maintenon, whose profligate father, Constant d'Aubigné, was confined in it, is now the *Maison d'Arrêt*.

10 Frontenay.
13 Mauzé.
12 Surgères.
10 Muron.
16 Rochefort, in Rte. 62.

SECTION IV.

LIMOUSIN—GASCONY—GUIENNE—THE PYRENEES—NAVARRE—
BÉARN—LANGUEDOC—ROUSSILLON.

PRELIMINARY INFORMATION.

§ 1. *Scenery of Limousin and of the Pyrenees.* § 2. *Objects of interest in the Pyrenees.* § 3. *Comparison with the Alps; Forests, Gaves, Lakes, Ports or Passes, Valleys, Cirques or Oules.* § 5. *A Dash into Spain.* § 6. *Inhabitants.* § 7. *Cagots, Sporting.* § 9. *History, the English in the Pyrenees, Froissart, the Black Prince, Wellington.* § 10. *Characteristics of the chief Watering-places, the Baths.* § 11. *Works on the Pyrenees.* § 12. *Directions for Travellers, Approaches and nearest Routes, Starting-points.* § 13. *Skeleton Tours.* § 14. *Passports, Accommodations, Inns, Conveyances, Guides, Horses, Chaises à Porteurs.*

ROUTE	PAGE
70 Orleans to *Toulouse*, by *Vierzon, Châteauroux, Limoges,* and *Montauban* (RAILWAY) . . .	235
71 Limoges to Bordeaux, by *Perigueux* and Libourne . . .	249
73 The GARONNE.—Toulouse to Bordeaux, by *Moissac, Agen, Marmande*	252
74 The Gironde from Bordeaux to La Tour de Cordouan.—Wine District of *Médoc.*—*Château Margaux, Lafitte,* and *Latour*	261
76 Bordeaux to *Bayonne, St. Jean de Luz,* and the Spanish Frontier	266
77 Bordeaux to Bayonne, across *Les Grandes Landes*	274
78 Bayonne to Pau, by *Orthez* .	276
79 Bordeaux to Auch, by Castel Jaloux and *Nerac*	277
80 Bordeaux to *Pau*	278
82 Pau to the Spanish Frontier, by *Oloron* and *the Val d' Aspe*.	282
83 Pau to *Eaux-Bonnes* and *Eaux-Chaudes.—Pic du Midi d' Ossau,* and *Spanish Baths of Panticosa*	283
84 The *Col de Torte.*—Eaux-Bonnes to Cauterets or Luz .	289
85 Pau to *Lourdes, Cauterets, Luz, St. Sauveur, Barèges,* and *Bagnères de Bigorre.* — The Mountain Road, with Excursions to the *Lac de Gaube,* Gavarnie, Brèche de Roland, Mont Perdu, Pic du Midi, &c.	290
86 Bagnères de Bigorre to Bagnères de Luchon.—*Mountain Road,* by the *Hourquette d' Aspin, Arreau,* Col de Peyresourde, and *Val de l' Arboust.* — Excursion to the *Lac de Seculéjo*	305
87 Pau to *Bagnères de Bigorre* and *Bagnères de Luchon,* by *Tarbes.*—Post Road.—Excursions to the *Val de Lys, Port de Venasque,* and *Val d' Aran* .	308
90 Toulouse to Pau, by *Auch* and Tarbes	321
91 Toulouse to Bagnères de Luchon and Bagnères de Bigorre, by *St. Gaudens* . .	322
93 Toulouse to Narbonne, by *Carcassonne.—Canal du Midi* .	323
94 Narbonne to *Perpignan,* Port *Vendres,* and the Spanish Frontier	326
95 St. Gaudens to Foix and Carcassonne, by *St. Girons* . .	328
97 *The E. Pyrenees.*—Toulouse to *Foix* and *Puycerda.*—The Valley of the *Ariége.*—*Vicdessos.*—*Andorre*	329
98 *The E. Pyrenees.*—Perpignan to *Mont Louis* and Puycerda, by the *Valleys* of the *Tet* and *Tech.*—Ascent of the *Canigou*	332

§ 1. *The scenery of Limousin,* through which province the following Routes conduct the traveller to the Pyrenees, is thus described in the excellent work of Arthur Young:—

"In regard to the general beauty of a country, I prefer Limousin to every other province in France. It does not depend on any particular feature, but is the result of many. Hill, dale, wood, enclosures, streams, lakes, and scattered farms are mingled into a thousand delicious landscapes, which set off everywhere this province."

The length of the portion of the chain of the Pyrenees running between the Mediterranean and the Bay of Biscay, and forming the boundary line between France and Spain, is estimated at about 270 m. The highest parts of the chain are near the centre, and it descends considerably towards the Mediterranean and the Gulf of Gascony. The highest summits do not occur on the central ridge or main chain, but on the buttresses running out from it to the S., and therefore belong to Spain. Only one summit within the French frontier, the Vignemale, attains an elevation of 11,000 ft., while 3 in the Spanish portion of the chain exceed that measure. The average length of the valleys running up from the plain to the crest of the mountains is about 36 m.

§ 2. Without doubt some of the finest scenery in France is to be found among the Pyrenees, which, though inferior in height, and on the whole in *grandeur* of scenery, number of snowy peaks, and area of crystal glaciers, to the Alps, yet possess beauties peculiar to themselves, of which the Alps cannot boast. The sunny atmosphere, which they owe to their more southern latitude, gives a warmth or glow to the landscape which will in vain be sought farther to the N.; and this genial climate, while it banishes perpetual snow to a height of about 9000 ft. (*i. e.* 1300 ft. above the Alpine snow-line), also spreads a richness of sylvan decorations over these mountains unparalleled in Swiss scenery. Heights which in a more northern region would either be condemned to nakedness, or to a scanty growth of lichens, are here clothed in verdure to the very top; and precipitous rocks, elsewhere rejecting all vegetation, are tufted in every cranny and fissure with brushwood, especially with box, which thrives and spreads wonderfully.

But the pride and boast and chief charm of the Pyrenees are their vast forests, the seas of undulating foliage which clothe their sides and tops, not merely of dark monotonous fir, but oak and beech: examples of these are presented in the upper part of the Val d'Ossau, near Gabas, in parts of the Val d'Argelez and Val d'Aure.

The meadows which carpet the lower slopes and bottom of the valleys equal if they do not surpass those of Switzerland in intense verdure produced by irrigation and sunshine, and approximate to the even surface of an English lawn; and while the plains of Languedoc and Provence are parched into a yellow desert, here the hues of spring are prolonged into summer and autumn, and the traveller is constantly refreshed by vernal gales.

§ 3. The brawling rivers (*Gaves* is the local name, derived from the same Celtic root as our *Avon*) are remarkable, beyond those of almost any other country, for their excessive purity, and for tints resembling beryl and chrysoprase. The waterfalls are second rate, quite inferior to those of Switzerland; those above Cauterets are pretty, and perhaps the finest. That of Gavarnie, the loftiest in Europe but one (in Norway), though 1300 ft. high, is a mere thread of water. Lakes are almost entirely wanting, and here the inferiority of the Pyrenean mountains to those of Switzerland is most decided. The Lacs de Gaube, of Seculeijo (or Lac d'Oo), and the Lac Bleu, though very interesting from the adjuncts of scenery, precipices, and streamlets dashing into them, are mere mountain tarns, yet they are the finest and almost the only sheets of water.

The chain of the Pyrenees has in a considerable degree the character of a vast wall drawn from sea to sea, inasmuch as it preserves an almost unvarying ridge, notched by frequent passes or cols, rarely more than 1000 ft. lower than the summit of the crest which surmounts them. The consequence is, that the passes leading across the chain are generally higher than among the Alps, far higher in proportion to the comparative elevation of the Pyrenees, and that they are much less accessible for high roads; indeed only two are practicable for carriages—the Pass of the Bidassoa, at the W. extremity, close to the Bay of Biscay, and that of the Col de Pertus, at the E., along the shore of the Mediterranean. There are however at least 50 passes known to, and used by, the shepherds and mountaineers, and most of them practicable on horseback. They are here called "*Ports,*" a very expressive name, for in many instances they are literally doors cut in the crest of the mountains leading from France into Spain. The most striking of these, and well worth the traveller's attention, are the "Brèche de Roland," and the Port de Venasque, the passage of which reveals the grandest, and almost the only, view of the Maladetta, the monarch of the Pyrenees.

The valleys of the Pyrenees run nearly at rt. angles with the great dorsal ridge, descending from the central spine into the plain in a series of basins and gorges: the most considerable are the valleys of the Garonne and Ariège.

The most beautiful on the French side of the chain are the Val d'Argelez (which no one should omit seeing), Val d'Ossau, and valleys of the Garonne, Adour, and Lys, Val d'Aure, and Val d'Aran.

The most grand gorges are those leading from Pierrefitte to Cauterets and Luz, and that of Mahourat leading to Pont d'Espagne, and the approach to Eaux-Chaudes.

§ 4. Several Pyrenean valleys have a termination quite peculiar to themselves —in a *Cirque* or *Oule* (a local word, meaning pot, Latin *olla*), a vast circle or semicircle, excavated in the mass of the mountain, walled round by precipices of great height, surrounding two-thirds or three-fourths of the basin, and leaving no opening but that by which the waters escape. The finest of these Cirques is that of Gavarnie, at the commencement of the Val de Lavedan: its walls are loftiest and most perfect; that of Troumouse at the head of the Val d'Héas is larger, but not so deep: another occurs at the bottom of the Val Estaubé. The nearest approach to this peculiar formation of the vale head in the Alps is at Leuk; but the precipices of the Gemmi, which wall it round, want the semicircular arrangement, as well as the waterfalls, the towers, and cylinders of rock, which give the grand character to the scenery of Gavarnie.

The valleys of the Pyrenees are separated from one another by lateral ridges descending like ribs or buttresses from the great chain, over which the communication is maintained by numerous minor cols, called *Portillons,* or in some parts *Hourquettes.* Such are the interesting passes of the Tourmalet and of the Hourquettes d'Arreau and d'Aspin.

Most visitors to the Pyrenees make a point of ascending one of the high peaks in the vicinity of the baths, either for the sake of the view, or to say they have been on such or such a peak: hence, "Avez-vous fait quelques ascensions?" is a common inquiry. The mountain which may be ascended with least trouble, and which repays well by its prospect, is the *Pic de Bergons,* above Luz. The *Pic du Midi de Bigorre,* conveniently reached from either Barèges or Bagnères de Bigorre, is loftier and more difficult. Less easy still are the Pic du Midi d'Ossau, the *Canigou* in the E. Pyrenees, and the Brèche de Roland; while the still more lofty Vignemale is no easy task to surmount, and the Mont Perdu is both difficult and dangerous—an exploit for a practised mountaineer; and the Maladetta wears snow on its crest never trodden by human foot until 1842.

§ 5. *A dash into Spain,* of three or four days' duration, will add much to the variety and interest of a journey among the Pyrenees. The points whence it may be made with most advantage are either from Bayonne to St. Sebastian, from Eaux-Bonnes or Cauterets to the Baths of Panticosa, from Gavarnie to Busaruelo and Fanlo, or from Luchon to Venasque and the Val d'Aran. The scenery on the Spanish side of the Pyrenees is far grander and wilder than on the French. Those who attempt to explore it must be prepared to "rough it;" they will encounter a wild people, rude villages, accommodations of the very worst kind, yet very expensive, paths scarcely passable, and cookery nauseous to those unused to it, owing to oil and garlic. The sudden transition from France to Spain, the total difference of people, language, manners, habitations, food, combined with the grander features of the mountain scenery, yield the chief zest to such a journey. An invitation to one of the *Spanish Bullfights*, which are held every year in all the large towns of the N. of Spain, may tempt some to penetrate farther into the country. (See for details the HANDBOOK FOR TRAVELLERS IN SPAIN.)

§ 6. The inhabitants of the Pyrenees, composed of various races, interesting for their antiquity, customs, costumes, &c., are worthy of the attention of the traveller. At the W. extremity of the chain, S. of Bayonne, you have the *Basques*, the aborigines of W. Europe, who have seen Carthaginians, Celts, Romans, Goths, Saracens, pass before them, and still remain in possession of their mountain home, part in France, part in Spain, speaking a language which has nothing in common with any other of Europe. (See Rte. 76.).

The peasantry of Béarn, who occupy the beautiful Val d'Ossau and its tributaries, the land of Henri IV., in the midst of which he spent the years of childhood, are a fine race, retaining much of their primitive simplicity of manners, along with their ancient costumes; the men wearing the berret or cap, like the Lowland bonnet of the Scotch, and a red sash round the waist ; the women covering their heads with the red hood or capulet. In the E. Pyrenees the people of Foix and Roussillon have a considerable resemblance, in character, dress, and language, to the Catalans of Spain.

§ 7. The proscribed and outcast race called *Cagots* exist more in tradition than in reality at present among the Pyrenees. In these mountains there may be families who have intermarried with them, or are descended from them, but the ban of caste no longer hangs over them. They are said to have been weak in body and mind, low in stature, sallow in countenance, and to have lived only in the remotest valleys, shunning their fellow-men. There are various theories to account for their origin and name, none of them satisfactory—for example, that they are the descendants of the Goths, dispossessed of Aquitaine by Clovis—"chiens de Goths," whence Cagots, by a somewhat forced derivation. 2nd. That they sprang from the Saracens who stayed behind in France after their defeat by Charles Martel. 3rd. That they were lepers, banished from human haunts for fear of infection ; or, what seems probable, fugitives tainted with heresy and driven apart from the community by the prejudices and aversion of the Romish priesthood. They are now nearly lost through intermixture with the mass of the population.*

§ 8. *The Sportsman* may still find some occupation among the Pyrenees in the pursuit of the bear, the ibex or bouquetin, and the chamois or izard, though these animals are growing rare. The bouquetin, especially, is almost extinct ; if anywhere, he may be found on the Maladetta. The izard is not uncommon, and the best localities for enjoying this chace are Eaux-Bonnes, where are some capital guides (see Rte. 83), the snow-fields of the Vignemale, the Mont Perdu, and the Maladetta, or in the Spanish Val de Broto.

The izard is hunted either by stalking, in the manner in which the red deer is stalked, though with much more difficulty and danger, amidst precipices, glaciers, and snow-fields, until, after a tedious pursuit, the huntsman may have the chance of a steady shot, or by driving the animals by guides and mountain

* The best account of the Cagots is contained in the 'Histoire des Races maudites de la France et de l'Espagne, par N. Fr. Michel,' Paris, 1847; an excellent work, and reliable authority.

shepherds towards the spot where the chasseur is posted. Success in this case entirely depends on the perfect knowledge possessed by the guides of the habits and haunts of the izard.

The rivers are so much netted as greatly to interfere with the sport of angling; a scientific fisherman, however, would doubtless find full scope for the exercise of his rod among its innumerable Gaves and mountain streams.

§ 9. *History and Antiquities.*—The passage of the Pyrenees by Hannibal, and afterwards by Cæsar, with large armies, are the earliest events of importance connected with these mountains. The pass by which they crossed was that of Pertus, at the E. end of the chain. Charlemagne's advance into Spain, in 778, was through that of *Roncesvaux*, where he received the memorable check so celebrated in history and romance, chiefly at the hands of the hardy mountaineers, the Basques, who fell upon his rear guard while entangled in the defiles, and killed many of his "paladins and peers," amongst them the renowned Roland, who has left his name upon the highest mountain ridge of the chain in the so-called Brèche, cleft through the rock, according to the tradition, by a swashing blow of his celebrated sword Durandal. The valleys and passes of the Pyrenees, like those of all other border countries, abound in *castles* and watch-towers, relics of feudal times, when war and rapine was the business of a great portion of the inhabitants, especially of all who claimed to be noble or gentle. Those who would know something of the history of these ruined hill forts, and of the mode of life of those who occupied them in the 14th century, of the marauding expeditions which went out from them on border forays, to harry the cattle or fair fields of some neighbouring chief, of ambuscades to rob the burgess of the neighbouring towns of his merchandise, or capture some wealthy ecclesiastic or seigneur of eminence, and clap him into the deep dungeon until a ransom was paid, must refer to the delightful pages of *Sir John Froissart's Chronicles*, the oldest and best handbook for the Pyrenees, which he traversed and threaded in various directions, picking up anecdotes for his history.

In his time many of these strongholds were held by English garrisons for the Black Prince, the province of Gascony, with Bigorre, having been ceded to the English as part of the ransom of the French king, John, captured at Azincour. The tradition of the country, indeed, attributes the building of some of the castles to the Black Prince. He led an English [*] army into Navarre, to

[*] The name of BASTIDES (applied to the citizens' boxes in the neighbourhood of Marseilles) was the name of the FREE TOWNS founded in the 13th and 14th centuries, which are very numerous in many parts of France. They are often called the ENGLISH TOWNS, and many of them were undoubtedly founded by the kings of England, especially that wise and politic monarch Edward I.; but many were also founded by the French kings and by the counts of Toulouse, and it is doubtful which had the priority. They are all readily distinguished by the regularity of their plan, the streets being in straight parallel lines, with narrow lanes at the back serving for mews, and usually a narrow passage between each house, so that each plot of ground was complete in itself, and each house independent of its neighbours. The cross streets are at right angles with the others. There is usually a central market-place with a covered way or piazza round it, the covered way being often high enough and wide enough for two carts to pass; and it is usually vaulted over, the vaults often retaining their original character where all the superstructure is modern. The church generally stands in one corner of the market-place. These towns were always fortified; and in many cases the old walls with their turrets and gateways remain perfect. From this circumstance, and from their regular military plan, they are commonly considered as military towns only, built during the wars between the French and English. But this is only a part of the truth; they often were so, but they also played an important part in the history of civilization. They were pre-eminently FREE TOWNS; all their inhabitants were *freemen*, and they were endowed with liberal privileges against the oppressions of the nobles or lords of the neighbouring castles; especially they had the important privilege of FREE TRADE. They often served as places of refuge for the serfs, when driven to desperation by the exactions of their masters. It was in defence of their privileges, much more than for the sake of either party, that they were always ready to fight and defend their city from the attacks of the barons. They may often be recognized at once on the map by the names of Ville-Franche or Ville-Neuve, of which there are some scores in all parts of France. Others had more specific names, as Libourne, Saint Foy, Montpazier, &c. &c. Perhaps one of the most

reinstate Pedro the Cruel on the throne of Spain, through the pass of Ronceval, the scene of the "dolorous rout" of Charlemagne.

Four centuries and a half later the Pyrenees once more became connected with English history, and in a more glorious cause.

"Many of these romantic heights are endeared to an Englishman by the recollection of gallant deeds of British valour performed at the close of the Peninsular war."—*S.* To visit the scenes of the masterly passage of the Bidassoa, and of the Adour below Bayonne, the spot where the fatal sortie took place under the walls of that fortress, the heights of Orthez, and those where the hard-contested but decisive and final battle of Toulouse was fought, cannot but add to the interest of the journey. It will augment the satisfaction of an Englishman, on visiting the theatre of the war, to know that the British commander, so far from displaying the insolence of a conqueror on entering the French territory, took measures to repress rigidly all acts of plunder on the part of his troops, by careful discipline. No inconsiderable difficulty was at first experienced in restraining the Spaniards, smarting under the oppression and wrongs inflicted on their own fatherland by the soldiery of the country which they then entered in triumph, and expecting to avenge upon its inhabitants the injuries they themselves had suffered. The firmness of the British commander, however, succeeded in alleviating, as far as possible, the horrors of war to the French; and the two following extracts, one from a general order of the Duke issued after the passage of the Bidassoa, the other from a letter written by him to a Spanish officer, will show how great care he took to effect this.

General Order.—" The Commander of the Forces is particularly desirous that the inhabitants should be well treated, and private property must be respected, as it has been hitherto.

" The officers and soldiers of the army must recollect that their nations are at war with France, solely because the ruler of the French nation will not allow them to be at peace, and is desirous of forcing them to submit to his yoke; and they must not forget that the worst of the evils suffered by the enemy in his profligate invasion of Spain and Portugal have been occasioned by the irregularities of the soldiers, and their cruelties authorized and encouraged by their chiefs towards the unfortunate and peaceful inhabitants of the country.

" To revenge this conduct on the peaceable inhabitants of France would be unmanly and unworthy of the nations to whom the Commander of the Forces now addresses himself; and, at all events, would be the occasion of similar and worse evils to the army at large than those which the enemy's army have suffered in the Peninsula; and would, eventually, prove highly injurious to the public interests." * * *

To General ——, a Spanish Officer.—" I did not lose thousands of men to bring the army under my command into the French territory, in order that

important was Libourne, founded by Edward I., at the highest point to which the River Gironde was navigable for the wine-vessels. In consequence of this favourable situation it grew rapidly in wealth and population, and in the fourteenth century it bid fair to rival Bordeaux, the jealousy of whose citizens led them to petition for the curtailment of the privileges of the inhabitants of Libourne, in which they ultimately succeeded; but it long continued a place of importance, both in a military and a commercial point of view. A similar history would apply to many of the others, and the success of these new towns often caused the decay of the more ancient ones in the same neighbourhood, which had clustered round the walls of some castle or abbey for protection. Such was the case with St. Emilion, near Libourne, which now has a most desolate appearance; scarcely a house seems to have been built since the fifteenth century, and it is quite a storehouse for the antiquary. It may be observed that the English bastides are generally more regular and perfect in plan than the French ones, which some attribute to their being the earliest, and the French ones bad copies of them—others to their being the latest, and built when the system was brought to greater perfection. The original charters of nearly all the English bastides are still preserved among the national archives in the Tower of London.—*J. H. P.*

the soldiers might plunder and ill-treat the French peasantry, in positive disobedience to my orders; and I beg that you and your officers will understand, that I prefer to have a small army that will obey my orders, and preserve discipline, to a large one that is disobedient and undisciplined; and that, if the measures which I am obliged to adopt to enforce obedience and good order occasion the loss of men and the reduction of my force, it is totally indifferent to me; and the fault rests with those who, by the neglect of their duty, suffer their soldiers to commit disorders which must be prejudicial to their country."
— *Wellington Dispatches.*

§ 10. *Hot Springs—Character of the Watering-Places—Baths in the Pyrenees.*—The bounty with which Nature has poured forth, throughout the whole range of the Pyrenean mountains, mineral sources of healing quality, of various kinds, adapted to the various ills to which flesh is heir, is truly surprising, and an interesting natural phenomenon. It has been calculated that in the whole chain there are not less than 200 springs, many of them of a high temperature.

It has been observed, that they usually issue forth to light near the junction of the primitive rocks, as granite, gneiss, or slate, with some other formation, chiefly limestone.

The value of these natural medicines was not unknown to the Romans, traces of whose constructions have been discovered near more than one of the hot sources.

Here follows a list and a brief character of a few of the principal watering-places, beginning from the W., with a notice of the nature of the mineral waters attached.

Eaux-Bonnes.—A fashionable resort, consisting of a row of eighteen or twenty fine tall houses, chiefly modern, and Parisian in their style, and rather expensive, in a wild mountain nook. The water is sulphureous. It is recommended for those afflicted with complaints in the lungs.

Eaux-Chaudes.—Water sulphureous, nearly like Eaux-Bonnes, from which it is only 3 m. distant; good but limited accommodation, romantic scenery around.

Cauterets.—Sulphureous water. A neat little mountain town, in an upland valley surrounded by colossal peaks. Plenty of accommodation, and good; also a place of fashionable resort. In autumn frequented by many Spaniards. Climate bracing, if not cold, from the elevation of its site. Excursions numerous. Its waters and site are considered efficacious in bronchial complaints and rheumatism.

St. Sauveur.—Feebly sulphureous. An attractive watering-place of a few dozen lodging-houses. Charming walks; fine scenery.

Barèges.—A complete hospital, thronged with miserable invalids; inferior accommodation; a poor village in a dreary gorge, which nothing but the hope of recovering health would render endurable beyond an hour or two; yet the efficacy of its waters is astonishing, and in a medical sense it deserves its celebrity, more extended over Europe than that of any other Pyrenean bath. It is often quite full in the season, and lodgings dear. A sharp atmosphere, owing to its great elevation.

Bagnères de Bigorre.—Saline springs; weak; one ferruginous spring. A considerable town, something more than a mere watering-place, seated just within the roots of the Pyrenees on the verge of the plain, and not much raised above it; warm climate. Various amusements; pleasant excursions. The tepid baths are efficacious only for slight complaints; the waters are not powerful remedies.

Bagnères de Luchon.—Seated in the bottom of a basin surrounded by mountains; resorted to for pleasure as well as cure. Its waters are sulphureous and hot—efficacious in rheumatic complaints or cutaneous affections. There are charming excursions in its vicinity.

At every French watering-place is a medical inspector appointed by the government, and invalids intending to take a course of the waters had better put themselves in communication with him. He will assist them respecting lodgings, and assign to them a fixed hour for bathing, which they will retain during the whole time of their stay—a measure often indispensable during the season, owing to the number of bathers, in order to obtain access to the bath at all.

The *Bath Houses* (*Etablissements Thermals*) of the Pyrenees are very far behind those of Germany in orderly and medical arrangement; the waters, in many cases, losing some of their properties in their passage from the source to the baths. But their chief inferiority is in want of cleanliness. The cabinets des bains are dark hot cells; the baths themselves, though of marble, mere troughs, calculated to inspire disgust in those who either do not need, or are not thoroughly convinced of their sanative power.

Works relating to the Pyrenees.—The best of all the descriptions of the Pyrenees are the works of Ramond (the Saussure of these mountains), 'Observations dans les Pyrénées,' and 'Voyages au Mont Perdu.' To these may be added, *Vayse de Villiers*, 2 vols. of Itinéraire; and Charpentier's Geological Essai, &c., now superseded by the more recent geological papers by Elie de Beaumont and Dufresnoy, in the Transactions of the French Geological Society. In English, we have Mrs. Ellis's very pleasant little volume, Lady Chatterton's charming work, more recent and more comprehensive, and the Hon. Erskine Murray's 'Summer in the Pyrenees,' which relates especially to the little-visited valleys in the E. part of the chain.

The very amusing 'Letters from the Pyrenees, 1843,' of Mr. Paris, a hardy and intrepid pedestrian, have shown the way into some of the most remote valleys rarely visited and never yet described by any English writers.

§ 12. DIRECTIONS FOR TRAVELLERS IN THE PYRENEES.—APPROACHES AND MOST DIRECT ROUTES.

1. The extension of railways through France since 1845 has greatly facilitated access to the Pyrenees. The best and quickest route is by Paris; Orleans; Tours; Poitiers, by railway in about 42 hours, to Bordeaux, which may be reduced to 36 hours when the Rly. is finished from Poitiers to Bordeaux. Thence to Pau, a land journey of about 125 m., 2 or 3 days' posting, 18 hours' diligence; or up the Garonne to Langon, and thence by land to Pau.

2. From Paris to Orleans, Vierzon (railway), Limoges, Toulouse, Bagnères, is a long and uninteresting land journey.

3. Paris to Châlons-sur-Saône, by rail; thence to Lyons and Avignon, by steamer; to Beaucaire, Nismes, and Montpellier, by railway; by land or canal to Toulouse; a land journey thence of nearly 90 m. to Bagnères.

The best starting points for making the tour of the Pyrenees are Pau for those coming from the W., and Toulouse for travellers approaching from the E. Those who do not intend to make a permanent stay at any of the watering-places should dismiss their heavy baggage before they plunge into the mountains, sending it on by *roulage*, from the one extreme point of their intended tour to the other, from Pau to Toulouse, or *vice versâ*.

The Brunnen of the Pyrenees, ensconced each in its own beautiful valley, form good halting-places for the passing traveller who visits these mountains merely from curiosity to explore their beauties, and he may thus terminate almost every day's journey in a comfortable hotel, or at least in tolerable quarters. Almost every valley is accessible by a good *carriage road*, but it stops at a certain distance, without surmounting the mountain ridge, or penetrating into Spain, except the two extreme passes at the E. and W. ends of the chain. As there are few carriage roads over even the lateral ridges from one valley into another, those who travel only in carriages must retrace their steps down the valleys. Pedestrians and equestrians (and the only way to see the Pyrenees to advantage is on foot or horseback) may pass, in most instances, by foot or bridle paths, out of one valley into another across the minor ridges which separate them, and thus enjoy some of the finest scenery without going twice over the same ground. The great chain can only be crossed in the same way, by bridle or foot paths, over some of the many Ports or Cols, more than 50 of which are enumerated between the Bay of Biscay and the Mediterranean.

§ 13. SKELETON TOUR OF THREE OR FOUR WEEKS, TO INCLUDE THE MOST INTERESTING OBJECTS IN THE W. PYRENEES.

PAU. Starting-point to—
Eaux Bonnes et Chaudes.
* Pic du Midi d'Ossau.
* Col de Torte.
* Val d'Azun.
Argelez.
Cauterets.
* Pont d'Espagne, Lac de Gaube [or from * Eaux-Chaudes to Panticosa in Spain, by Pont d'Espagne to Cauterets].
Gorge of Pierrefitte.
Luz, or St. Sauveur.
Gavarnie.
* Brèche de Roland, back to Luz [or to Busaruelo and Fanlo in Spain, and back].
* Val d'Héas.
* Vignemale.

Barèges.
* Tourmalet.
* Pic du Midi de Bigorre.
Bagnères de Bigorre.
* Lac Bleu.
Hourquette d'Aspin.
* Arreau.
* Tramesaigues and the Val d'Aure.
* Port de Peyresourdes.
* Lac de Seculéjo.
Bagnères de Luchon.
Val de Lys.
* Port de Venasque, Venasque, Viella.
* St. Beat, in Val d'Aran.
* Toulouse.
N.B. This mark * denotes places which cannot be reached in carriages, but only on horseback or foot.

CARRIAGE TOUR BY POST-ROADS.

Pau, Eaux Bonnes et Chaudes.
Louvie, Lestelle, Lourdes, Argelez, Cauterets.
Pierrefitte, Luz, Barèges.
Lourdes, Bagnères de Bigorre, Valley of Grip, Arreau (? no posting).
Lannemezan, Cierp, Bagnères de Luchon.

Cierp, St. Beat.
St. Gaudens.
Toulouse.

N.B. Ladies may be *carried* up to most of the points of interest in a chaise à porteur.

COMPLETE ITINERARY OF THE FRENCH PYRENEES FROM BORDEAUX TO PERPIGNAN.*

Days.	Night Quarters.	Objects of Interest.
1	Mont de Marsan.	
2, 3	Bayonne.	Citadel (Sortie). Embankments to turn the course of the Adour.—St. Pierre d'Arruby.—Biarritz.
4, 5	St. Sebastian and back, by Diligence.	Interesting ride, through scene of the war in Spain. —Irun and Hernani, curious Spanish towns.— See Citadel of St. S. and walk to Passages.

* Compiled from the notes of J. J., a most experienced traveller in the Pyrenees, obligingly communicated to the Editor.

Days.	Night Quarters.	Objects of Interest.
6	St. Jean Pied de Port.	(*Inn*: Soleil) on the slope of a hill, crowned by the citadel.
7 8	Roncesvalles, 15 m. from St. Jean.	Arrange about passport and procure a guide and horse at St. Jean. It will take a day to go, and the same to return.—A poor village.—The Abbey is tenantless; but there is an Inn.—A stone cross on the plain marks the spot where Roland fell.
9	Oloron.	By Mauléon (Hôtel Vefour good), a Basque town, and Tardetz.
10	Val d'Aspe.	Bedous, best sleeping-place, but bad.—Take provisions—at least white bread.
11	Eaux-Chaudes: Val d'Ossau.	Cross from Escot by the Col de Marie Blanche, and Plan de Benou (the bed of a former lake), to Bielle in Val d'Ossau.
12 13	Eaux-Bonnes.	Ascent of Pic du Midi d'Ossau.
14	Pau.	By Diligence. Or, if you do not wish to visit Pau, cross Col de Torte and descend Val d'Azun to Argelez.
15	Cauterets.	By Lourdes (Argelez, ascend Val d'Azun, as far as Pouy le Hun).—St. Savin.
16	Cauterets.	Ascend Monné; 10 hrs. up and down.
17	Panticosa.	Visit, on the way, the Pont d'Espagne and Lac de Gaube.
18	Eaux-Bonnes.	By the Case de Broussettes.
19	Argelez.	By Col de Torte and the beautiful Val d'Azun, 12 hours' walk.
20	Luz.	Pic de Bergons.—St. Sauveur.
21	Luz.	Gavarnie and Brèche de Roland. If Val d'Héas also, you must sleep at Gavarnie and scale the Brèche next day.
22	Grip or Bagnères de Bigorre.	By Barèges, which may be seen en passant. Turn off at foot of Tourmalet, and ride up by the Lac d'Oncet to the top of the Pic du Midi. Sleep at Grip, if unable to reach Bagnères. Start early.
23 24	Bagnères de Bigorre.	See marble-works.—Baths.—Walks.—Visit Lac Bleu.—Pic de Monné.
25	Arreau.	Ascend Penne de l'Hyeris. Cross Hourquette d'Arreau.
26 27	Aragnouet or Hospice de Coubise; miserable quarters.	Ascend Val d'Aure by Vielle, beyond which it splits into several branches. That called Val d'Aragnouet and Gorge de Couplan contains *magnificent* mountain scenery, forests, cascades.—Return to Arreau.
28	Bagnères de Luchon.	By Val de Louron, Port de Peyresordes, and Lac d'Oo. If time admits, ascend by Scala to upper Lake.
29	Bagnères de Luchon.	Val de Lys.—Go or return by Sopra Bagnères.
30	Luchon or Venasque.	Port de Venasque—Trou du Taureau—returning by Port de Picade, to Luchon. *N. B.* This excursion may be extended to Venasque, and round the Maladetta to Vitallez and Viella.
31	Val d'Aran: Lez.	By Port de Portillon to Œil de Garonne.—Castel Leon.—Bososte.—Sleep at Baths of Lez.

Days.	Night Quarters.	Objects of Interest.
32	Cierp or Luchon.	Below Lez the finest part of Val d'Aran.—St. Beat.
33	St. Bertrand de Comminges; Inn in Haute Ville.	See the church and remains of Lugdunum Convenarum below the town.—Ride up Val de Barouse to Mauléon. The mountains are pierced with caverns.
34	St. Gaudens.	Visit la Basse Grotte de Gargas, 5 m. from St. Bertrand, near Tyberan.—Cross the Neste to St. Gaudens.
34	St. Girons; poor Inn.	By Diligence to St. Martory, where hire a horse to St. Girons, on the Sallat, a bad cross road, but practicable for vehicles.
35	Foix.	By Remont and La Bastide de Seron.
36	Tarascon.	Visit Iron Mines of Vic de Sos.
37, 38	Ax or Mt. Louis.	Cross to Puycerda and Bourg Madame by Port de Morens. Arrange with the Douane to take a horse across the frontier. Sleep at Bourg Madame or at Cabannes under the walls of Mt. Louis.
39	Prades.	Ride by Olette down Vale of Tet.
40	Prades.	Ascend Canigou: must start early. Next day to Perpignan and Narbonne.

§ 14. PASSPORTS—CONVEYANCES—ACCOMMODATION FOR TRAVELLERS.

Passports.—Those who mean to enter Spain should obtain a Spanish Consul's visé at Bordeaux or Bayonne, to prevent their being mistaken for refugees or smugglers;—they should also provide themselves with the SPANISH HANDBOOK.

Mallepostes from Toulouse to Bayonne and from Limoges to Pau. *Diligences* run regularly from Bordeaux and Bayonne to Pau and Tarbes, from Toulouse to Bagnères and Tarbes, which is the point of concentration for conveyances from all directions; and in summer a constant communication is kept up between all the watering-places. The diligences, however, are ill appointed and very slow, and the routes they follow exceedingly circuitous. They are of use to the pedestrian in conveying his luggage from place to place.

Inns are far inferior to those in the German watering-places: the best are at Pau, Eaux-Bonnes, Cauterets, Luz, and Bagnères de Bigorre (by far the best), but they have all the fault of filth. Those at Barèges are inferior.

The *charges* vary much, especially for rooms, according to the season, rising exorbitantly when the places are full. Provisions are cheap.—Bed, 1 f. 50 c. to 2 f.; dinner (table-d'hôte), 3 f.; breakfast à la fourchette, 2 f.; tea or coffee, 1 f. 50 c. On ordinary occasions the traveller's expenses ought not to exceed 8 f. per diem; and if he stop a week or longer in an hotel, he may easily bargain for 6 f. The chance-traveller is often asked 3, 4, or 5 f. for the worst bedroom for a single night during the season.

	Fr.	cent.
Expenses at Bagnères de Bigorre. Board and lodging at an hotel for a month or 6 weeks, per diem	5— 6	0
Calèche and 2 horses	16—18	0
A horse, exclusive of feed	3— 4	0
,, ,, for a month	60—80	0
A room in the town	1 f. 50 c. to 2 f.	
Bath at a fixed hour	1	0
Warm linen	0	10
Chairmen (porteurs)	0	40

Izard venison, game, ortolans, truffles, mountain-trout, green figs, and strawberries, are among the delicacies which await the traveller in the Pyrenees.

"The remote valleys—Val d'Aran, Val d'Aure, and all those on the Spanish side—are miserably off for inns; travellers should always take provisions thither, or at least white bread, as the rye-bread, which can alone be procured, is apt to disagree with strangers."—*J. J.*

Riding horses, or rather ponies, very unprepossessing to look at for the most part, yet hardy and capable of work, and well used to the mountains, are kept at all the watering-places. The charges for them are moderate, viz. 5 f. a day, including the feed, or 3 f. paying the forage, which it is not advisable to do. It is the custom of the French visitors at the baths to unite in large parties, and invade some quiet valley, or interesting point of view, in troops of cavalry 50 or 60 strong, and to establish there a pic-nic. Very little regard is paid by these riotous assemblages to the beauties of nature. Awakening the echoes with the loud cracks of the whip with which they urge on their jaded hacks, they scour along the rough roads, up hill and down dale, attired in the most fantastic costume—men and women wearing the red sashes of the peasantry, and broad-brimmed felt hats; while even the ladies assume neat white pantaloons, sometimes set off with boots and spurs.

Guides.—There are very excellent and trustworthy professional guides, well acquainted with the mountains, and many of them capital mountaineers and skilful sportsmen; though not, perhaps, so good as the guides of Switzerland or Savoy. The best are met with at Eaux-Bonnes, Cauterets, Luz, Bagnères de Bigorre and Luchon. A guide receives 5 f. a day, feeding and lodging himself. A horse must be provided for him, unless the traveller is willing to be retarded by his following on foot.

For return-money, 4 f. a day each for horse and man, until the guide can reach his home from the place where he is dismissed, is the fair allowance; but 5 f. are generally asked.

Chaises à Porteur.—There is scarcely an excursion off the high-road, however distant, or a mountain-top, or other spot, however difficult of access, which ladies may not reach by the aid of a chair on poles. Each lady will require from 4 to 6 chairmen; the cost is 15 f. a day, and 3 or 4 f. pour boire. This conveyance has been pronounced by a lady traveller "at once the gentlest, safest, and most agreeable mode of conveyance imaginable. The chairmen will go anywhere and everywhere; and instead of being rocked and jolted in a dislocating machine, those who cannot walk, and fear to ride, are carried about like petted children, without the risk of fatigue or the probability of danger."—*Mrs. Boddington.*

ROUTE 70.*

ORLEANS TO TOULOUSE BY CHÂTEAUROUX, RAILWAY [CHEMIN DE FER DU CENTRE], LIMOGES, AND MONTAUBAN.

570 kilom. = 353 Eng. m.

Railway — Orleans to Châteauroux, 143 kilom., in progress to Limoges. A *Malleposte*—Châteauroux by Limoges to Toulouse in 33 hrs. Diligences daily. A bridge carries the line across the Loire. It nearly follows the line of the post-road.

* The Editor has not travelled this route beyond Vierzon, and will be glad of corrections or additional information from those who have.

The *tunnel* of l'Allouet is 1236 mètres long, and is lighted by 18 openings.

An avenue of trees leads from the bridge of Orleans to the suburb St. Marceaux, abounding in country houses; and a little farther on is the industrious village of Olivet (3250 Inhab.). Here the river Loiret is crossed by a bridge, about 2 m. below its source, and 5 or 6 above its termination in the Loire. The *Château of La Source*, the residence of the banished Lord Bolingbroke, near this, is described in Rte. 48. Below the bridge, between it and the Château de Ponty, on the l. bank, it is pretended that the assassination of the Duc de Guise by Poltrot took place: he was conveyed to Caubray, where he breathed his last.

The Railroad, as far as Vierzon, traverses the district of *la triste Sologne*, noted for its barrenness; a large part of it being waste land, heath, and common; a dead flat of hungry sandy gravel, the surface slightly varied, and the scenery monotonous. The name Sologne (*Segalonia*) has been derived from "segale," seigle, barley, the crop chiefly produced on its unprofitable soil. (?)

23 La Ferté St. Aubin Stat. At the entrance of this village, on the l., stands the Château of Lowendahl, named after a Danish general who served in the armies of France along with his friend Marshal Saxe, and was made Maréchal de France for his share in the capture of Bergen-op-Zoom. It now belongs to the Prince d'Essling, son of Marshal Masséna. It is a low building, surrounded by water. The name *Ferté*, an old form of fortifié, denotes the existence, in ancient times, of a castle, embattled and fortified by royal permission, granted to the seigneur.

39 Lamotte Stat., Dépt. Loire et Cher.

46 Nouan le Fuzelier Stat.

58 Salbris Stat.

70 Theillay Stat.

80 *Vierzon Junction Stat.*—The railway to Bourges, Nevers, Moulins, and Vichy (Rte. 103), here branches l. from the line to Châteauroux. (*Inns*: Croix Blanche; H. des Messageries.) Vierzon, a town of the Dépt. Cher, and of the ancient province of Berry, enlivened by the Canal de Berry, which passes through it, running side by side with the river Cher. By means of it the iron of Berry, manufactured in furnaces not far distant from the town, is exported; and coal is brought hither to smelt it. Pop. 4700. At Vierzon the tiresome Sologne has terminated; the valley of the Cher is rather cheerful, and on its borders are some vineyards. The Evre and the Cher are crossed on quitting Vierzon.

96 Chery Stat.

100 Reuilly Stat.

109 St. Lizaigne Stat.

117 Issoudun Stat.

128 Neuvy Pailloux Stat.

144 *Châteauroux Stat.* — *Inns*: La Poste (Ste. Catherine); H. de France. This town, chef-lieu of the Dépt. Indre (Pop. 13,847), is of little interest to the traveller, but of considerable industrial importance, owing to its extensive cloth manufactures, the sale of which is estimated at 4 millions of francs yearly. The wools of Berry are almost exclusively used in their fabrication. Some trade is also carried on in iron, there being more than 40 iron furnaces in the department. The *Castle*, on an eminence above the Indre, close beside the modern Préfecture, is a gloomy building, flanked by turrets, probably of the 16th centy. It was the prison, for 23 years, of the unfortunate Clémence de Maillé, Princesse de Condé and niece of Richelieu, who here ended a life of suffering, 1694. The Grand Condé, her husband, repaid her devotion to him, and ill-requited affection, by procuring from Louis XIV. an order for her imprisonment; and his last dying request to the king was, that she should never be set free. Her grave in the ch. of St. Martin was violated 1793. The town owes its name to an older *château*, built in the 10th century by one Raoul de Déols. One of the old *town gates*, a venerable structure, still remains.

General Bertrand, who accompanied Napoleon to St. Helena, was a native of Châteauroux.

At Bourg Dieu, or Déols, situated within 1½ m. of Châteauroux, are the ruins of an ancient monastery, and a ch. containing, in a crypt under the altar, a curiously carved marble sarcophagus.

Railway to Limoges (135 kilom.) in progress, 1854. It crosses the valley of the Garetempe on a viaduct more than a mile (2 kilom.) long.

Malleposte to Toulouse by Limoges in 33 hours. *Diligences* to Tours by Loches. (Rte. 56.)

15 Lothiers, a dreary country of heath, to

14 Argenton, a town of 4000 Inhab.,

on the Creuse: it had once a large castle flanked by 10 high towers, dismantled by Louis XIV., and farther reduced to ruin in recent times.
15 Le Fay.
25 La Souterraine.
16 Morterolles.
17 Ville au Brun.
17 Morterol.
12 Chanteloube.
15 Maison Rouge.
14 LIMOGES (*Inns:* Boule d'Or, dirty; H. Richelieu, not much better; H. de Perigord), the capital of the ancient province of Limousin, at present chef-lieu of the Dépt. Haute Vienne, is a commercial and manufacturing town, situated on the rt. bank of the Vienne. Pop. 27,611.

It is very picturesque in its ancient street architecture, but has few curiosities to show to the passing stranger. The Revolution swept away the greater number of its churches, many of which were curious from their antiquity. Of those which remain the most interesting are

The *Cathedral* of *St. Etienne*, begun in the 13th centy., and slowly continued down to the 16th, when the work came to a stand; and the building has since remained a mere fragment, consisting of the *Choir*, the N. transept, and two compartments of the nave, now blocked up by a common partition wall, while at the spot to which it ought to have extended rises an isolated belfry, now in a very insecure condition, separated by a wide gap from the rest of the edifice. Under this tower is a Romanesque porch belonging to an older cathedral. The ch. is built of granite, and terminates in an apse. The interior is not remarkable in itself, but contains a *Jubé*, or roodloft, removed without reason, 1789, from its proper place between the choir and nave, to one side of the nave. It is a curious jumble of flamboyant Gothic ornaments and tracery, with sculpture in the style of the Renaissance (date 1543). It has been seriously mutilated, and its niches robbed of their statues, but contains curious bas-reliefs, among which are represented the Labours of Hercules.

Its construction is attributed to Bishop Langeac, whose *Tomb* is remarkable for the richness and elegance of its decorations, far superior to those of the Jubé. It was prepared for him before his death, 1541, and includes some admirable bas-reliefs, well worth examination in spite of their mutilations; among them one, representing "Death on the White Horse," is much praised. Two other monuments, that of Bishop Regnault de la Porte, of the 14th cent., and of Bernard Brun his nephew, deserve notice.

St. Michel-aux-Lions is the most conspicuous object in the town, owing to its tall and graceful tower and spire, planted on the highest ground, surmounting the other buildings. This ch., erected 1364, is named from the rudely sculptured figures of lions which ornament its porch; the lightness and height of the 8 lofty pillars supporting the roof are alone remarkable in the interior.

An old *Cross* of granite, in front of the ch. of St. Aurelian, deserves mention for the elaborate workmanship bestowed on it, which has recently been concealed under a coat of oil paint.

The *Episcopal Palace* is a handsome building of granite, with a fine *Garden* attached to it.

Although Limoges was an important place in Roman times, under the names *Lemovices* and *Augustoritum*, there are no remains of Roman buildings. The only trace of the amphitheatre, to which Molière alludes in *M. de Pourceaugnac*, Act I., Scene 6, is the name *Les Arènes* given to a burial-ground. Its site is nearly covered by the *Place d'Orsay*, on one side of which runs a terrace, whence there is a view over the valley of the Vienne. A Latin name, "*Aqua lenis*," is said to be retained in the *Fontaine Aigoulène*, and its water is supplied through a Roman conduit.

The ancient fortifications of Limoges have been thrown down, planted, and converted into boulevards and public walks; nothing therefore remains as a relic of that terrible siege (1370) and capture by assault of the place by the Black Prince, who, irritated at its revolting from him, through the treachery of its bishop, swore by the soul of his father that he would have it back again. Too ill to ride on horseback, he directed the operations from a litter, and, having forced a breach by blowing up a tower, entered through it, and, denying quarter to its wretched inhabitants, allowed 3000 men, women, and children, to be massacred—a blot on the fair fame of his heroic career, the verge of which he had already reached,-for the hand of death was upon him, and he breathed his last six years after.

Limoges is distinguished by having been the birthplace of the upright chancellor d'Aguesseau, born 1688. Vergniaud, the Republican orator, the leader of the Girondins, beheaded by Robespierre 1793, Marshal Jourdan, the conqueror at Fleurus, Marshal Bugeaud, and Dupuytren the surgeon, were also natives. Limoges likewise produced in the 15th and 16th centuries a series of artists, among whom the names of Laudin, Noel, Leonard, Courtois, Rexmore, are conspicuous, eminent for the beautiful paintings in *enamel* which they produced, still so highly esteemed all over Europe. Nayllier, the last master in this *genre* of art, died 1765, and the art died with him. It appears to have originated as early as the 12th centy., and was brought hither by Greeks from Byzantium, but was at its acmé in the time of Francis I. The private cabinets of M. Germeau and M. Maurice Ardent, of Limoges, contain some very remarkable specimens of enamels.

The *Manufacture* at present most prevalent here is that of *porcelain*, due to the discovery in this neighbourhood (at St. Yrieix) of the *kaolin*, or pure white porcelain earth, consisting of the decomposed felspar, arising from gneiss, which alone furnishes a fit material for the manufacture. The substance appears to owe its origin not to a mere disintegration of the gneiss, but to an electro-chemical decomposition, and combination with neighbouring rocks, especially such as are ferruginous. Sèvres is supplied hence with the kaolin, and nearly 2000 persons are employed in and about Limoges in making china. There are also some cotton and woollen mills.

The Limousin horses are a celebrated breed, in much request for the French cavalry; they are reared in the prairies bordering on the Vienne.

Mallepostes to Toulouse;—to Perigueux, Auch, and Pau.

Diligences to Toulouse, Bordeaux, Poitiers, Angoulême, Clermont, Moulins, Blois, Valençay.

The road from Limoges to Bordeaux, by Perigueux, is described in Rte. 71.

[At the town St. Junien, 18 m. from Limoges on the way to Angoulême, is a very curious *ch.* of the 11th centy., containing at the back of the high altar a curious sarcophagus of white marble, adorned with reliefs in the Byzantine style of art. It contains the relics of the saint, much visited by devout pilgrims. In the lower part of the town near the bridge is a chapel of the 15th centy., of *Notre Dame;* and 1 m. out of the town, on the borders of the Vienne, are the ruins of *St. Amand.* M. Mérimée observed in its transept a basin hollowed out of the rock, supplied by a spring of running water, into which little pieces of bread had been cast by the peasants, as offerings to St. Amand, who is believed still to work miracles, though his shrine has been destroyed for ages.]

At Boisseuil, 7 m. from Limoges, we leave about 1 m. to the rt. the ruined *Castle of Chalusset,* a curious example of the art of fortification in the middle ages, situated on an isolated rock at the junction of two streams. It must have been very strong both by its natural position and its outworks. It has been referred to the 12th centy.

20 Pierre Buffière. Arthur Young praises much the beauty and variety of the country to Brives, hill and valley, a quick succession of landscapes.

21 Beausoleil.

18 Uzerche, a picturesque little town on a conical hill, converted into a peninsula by the bend which the Vezère makes round it. It has a curious Romanesque *ch.* on the crest of the hill, surrounded at the E. end by 5 apsidal

chapels, partly destroyed. Under it is a *crypt*, containing the tomb of St. Coronat, in a niche, closed in front by a wooden railing. Insane persons are shut up within it for a night, in the belief that they will thereby recover their reason!

The road to Tulle here turns off to the l.

[*Tulle* (*Inn:* H. de Lyon), a town of 8000 Inhab., singularly placed in the fork of a deep narrow valley of the Corrèze, a fresh bubbling stream, which runs through it, bordered for a considerable distance with houses, many of them ancient and picturesque. The *Cathedral* had a slice cut from it, in Revolutionary times, to make way for a public walk. The nave only remains, of granite, in a severe and early style of Gothic.

The town has an important manufactory of fire-arms.

Diligence to Clermont by Ussel, and to Mont Dore les Bains.

About 10 m. W. of Uzerche is the *Château de Pompadour*, anciently the residence of a noble family, several of whom were governors of the province of Limousin, whose name was never sullied, until, after the extinction of their line (1722), it was bestowed upon the mistress of Louis XV., the daughter of the bankrupt butcher Poisson.

25 Donzenac. Picturesque varied country; groves and forests of chestnut.

10 Brives (*Inn:* H. de Bordeaux, clean, comfortable, and a good cook, who makes capital pâtés) enjoys a fine situation in the valley of the Corrèze; but its favourable appearance at a distance is not realised in its interior, which contains nothing remarkable but an ancient *Gothic house* attributed to the English: it is said to have been the residence of the governor. Brives is the birthplace of the Cardinal Dubois, son of an apothecary, who became tutor and afterwards minister to the Regent Duke of Orleans; and of Marshal Brune, one of the generals of the Republic, assassinated at Avignon 1815.

The culture of the vine and of maize flourishes near this.

The road has now reached a hilly country: it passes within a short distance of the castle *de Noailles*, cradle of the noble family who derive their ducal title from it, now in ruins; a modern château has been built not far off. The old feudal *Castle of Turenne*, situated about 2 m. to the E. of the road, on the Tourmente, a tributary of the Dordogne, gave a name to another great family, illustrious by deeds as well as by descent: the Ducs de Bouillon obtained the domain and viscounty of Turenne by alliance. Within its walls the wife of the Great Condé, a fugitive with her son from the pursuit of Mazarin, was received amidst a crowd of enthusiastic partisans of the Fronde, in 1650, and sumptuously entertained for 8 days; during which, taking counsel with the Ducs de Bouillon and de La Rochefoucauld, she planned the memorable rising in the South which was called the civil war of Guienne. She here summoned her vassals and retainers to mount the fawn-coloured scarf, and to rally round her for the rescue of her husband from prison. At the order of the Duc de Bouillon the tocsin was sounded in the 400 villages of his vicomté of Turenne, and the peasants at once flew to arms and flocked round his standard.

20 Cressensac (Dépt. Lot).

Truffles flourish in the uncultivated ground around this village.

16 Souillac, a miserable little town in the deep valley of the Dordogne, on its rt. bank.

After crossing the river, a steep hill, nearly 3 m. long, requires to be surmounted, in effecting which the postmaster is authorised to attach a pair of oxen to all four-wheeled carriages. 2 m. on the l. is the village and château of La Mothe Fénélon, not the birthplace, as some have stated, of the author of Télémaque, but a property belonging to his family. A hilly country, arid, barren, and uninteresting, all the way to Cahors.

16 Peyrac.

18 Pont de Rodes.

17 Pelacoy. Near this is Murat, and a little beyond it La Bastide, the birthplace of Joachim Murat, general of cavalry, and King of Naples. He was the son of an aubergiste who was

steward in the family of the Talleyrands.

A long but gradual descent of nearly 5 m. leads down into the valley of the Lot.

The very distant outline of the Pyrenees, 150 m. off, may be distinguished in clear weather near

16 *Cahors*. (*Inns*: H. des Ambassadeurs, not very clean, but excellent cook; Trois Rois; de l'Europe, good.) Cahors, the *chef-lieu* of the Dépt. le Lot (Pop. 12,050), is situated on the top and round the base of an escarped rock, on a wide sweeping bend of the river Lot. It is a very ancient town of narrow streets, full of antique edifices, to which a new quarter has been added. The name comes from its ancient appellation, *Divona Cadurcorum*, and there still exist the scanty remains of a Roman amphitheatre, and of a conduit, which conveyed water to it from the village St. Martin de Vern, through La Roque, where are vestiges of the arches of an aqueduct.

The *Cathedral*, a truly fine edifice, consists of a large nave, surmounted by two hemispherical cupolas, in the Byzantine style; a portal and the choir are Gothic. The Bishop's Palace is now the Préfecture. The bishop originally bore the title of count, and enjoyed the privilege of wearing a sword and gauntlets, which he deposited on the altar when he said mass. When he took possession of his diocese, he was received at the gate of the town by his vassal, le Vicomte de Sessac, bareheaded, without cloak, with one leg bare, and the foot in a slipper, and was conducted by the count in that guise to his palace, and waited on by him there at table. This curious tenure had fallen out of use before the Revolution.

The surprise and capture of Cahors in 1580 was one of the most brilliant exploits of Henri IV. (when King of Navarre). He reached the town by a forced march of 30 m. under a burning sun, and, posting his men in ambuscade among the walnut-trees, awaited the nightfall; when, silently approaching the gate, he blew it up with a petard, and entered himself the seventh, followed by 700 men, and leaving 700 outside to check the arrival of reinforcements to the garrison. The bursting of the gate had alarmed the town, which was strongly guarded, and a shower of stones and tiles from every housetop assailed the Navarrese troops and their general. The combat was carried on throughout the night, and yet, when dawn appeared, the assailants had gained but a very small footing. Henri was strongly advised to retire, especially when intelligence was brought of the arrival of succour to the town; but the king, setting his back against a shop, persisted in fighting on, exclaiming, "Ma retraite hors de cette ville sera celle de mon âme hors de mon corps." The reinforcements were driven back, but Henri still had to struggle step by step, to lay siege to every street, and almost to every house. It was not until the fifth night that Cahors submitted. Henri's soldiers, irritated by the resistance made by the garrison, put a great many to the sword.

On the open promenade de Fossé, in front of the college, is placed a statue of Fénélon, who was a student here. One of the *bridges* over the Lot, built in the 14th and 15th cents., is curious, being surmounted by 3 gate-towers, to defend the approach to the town. Cahors is the native place of Pope Jean XXII., whose name was Jacques d'Euze; his *Castle* is pointed out near the entrance to the town, on the side of Paris; also of Clement Marot, the poet, author of sonnets, ballads, &c. (1495), and page to Marguerite, sister of Francis I.

The country around produces a good deal of *wine*, which is not much known, but is not bad, and *truffles* in abundance.

21 La Magdeleine.

17 Caussade stands on the fertile plain watered by the Loire; it is a town of 5000 Inhab., famed for turkeys stuffed with truffles.

In the next stage the river Aveyron is crossed, and we enter the wide and fertile plain of Languedoc, which extends to the foot of the Pyrenees with little interruption.

23 *Montauban* (*Inns*: H. de France;

de l'Europe ; clean, and comfortable), chef-lieu of the Dépt. Tarn et Garonne, is a good-looking little town, with clean and wide streets, on the rt. bank of the Tarn, here lined by a fine quay, and crossed by a brick bridge of the 13th cent., but modernized, at the end of which stands the *Préfecture*, a square building with 4 turrets at its angles. There is not much to be seen in the town. The *Cathedral* is a large modern building of Italian architecture, with a frontispiece at the W. end.

"The *Promenade* of Les Terrasses on the borders of the Trescon, and on the highest part of the ramparts, commands that noble plain, one of the richest in Europe, which extends on one side to the sea, and in front to the Pyrenees, whose towering masses, heaped one upon another in a stupendous manner, and covered with snow, offer a variety of lights and shades from their indented forms and the immensity of their projections. This prospect has a sort of oceanic vastness, in which the eye loses itself ; an almost boundless scene of cultivation ; an animated but confused mass of infinitely varied parts, melting gradually into the distant obscure, from which arises the amazing frame of the Pyrenees, rearing their silvered heads far above the clouds."—*A. Young.*

Montauban is a flourishing manufacturing town, producing various kinds of woollen cloths, hair stuffs (cadis, molletons), which are exported to the colonies. It has 24,660 Inhab., nearly one-half of them being Protestants, and there is a *Protestant College* here for the instruction of pastors.

In the 16th and 17th cents. Montauban was a stronghold of Protestantism, its inhabitants having early embraced the Reformed doctrines, and being prepared to defend them. It endured in consequence a very memorable siege in 1621, from the royal army led on by the favourite Luynes, who brought hither his master Louis XIII. ; but, instead of witnessing its fall, after nearly 3 months of fruitless assault, Louis and his minister were forced to withdraw, such was the obstinate bravery of the inhabitants and the skill of their governors. Under the reign of Louis XIV., and the influence of Madame de Maintenon, the Protestants of Montauban were singled out to suffer the direst persecutions, inflicted by the so-called *Dragonnades*, or quartering of regiments of soldiers on them, who exercised every species of licence, inquisitorial tyranny, and cruelty, with the design of forcing them to become Roman Catholics.

At the farther extremity of the bridge over the Tarn we pass under an arch of brick into the extensive suburb of Ville Bourdon, founded by the Protestants expelled from Toulouse in 1562.

We enter the grand route from Bordeaux to Toulouse (Rte. 73) a little short of

22 Grisolles. The Garonne runs parallel with our road, at a little distance on the rt., through a plain of unequalled fertility. The British army, under the Duke of Wellington, passed the river, before the battle of Toulouse, by 2 pontoon bridges above the small town of Grenade on the l. bank nearly opposite Castelnau, 15 m. below Toulouse. The road crosses the river Lers a little farther on. The capture of the bridge over it at Croix Daurade, by a gallant charge of the 18th hussars, on the day before the battle, secured a communication between the columns of the allied army, part of which marched up the rt. and part up the l. bank of the Lers, to attack the strong position of Marshal Soult.

12 St. Jory.

The approach to Toulouse lies over a bridge, flanked by 2 columns, thrown across the *Canal du Midi*, which, half encircling the town on the N. and E., joins the Garonne about a mile to the rt. of this bridge in the Faubourg d'Arnaud Bernard.

The *Obelisk* on the height to the l. marks the centre of Marshal Soult's position at the battle of Toulouse, which, though strongly fortified by redoubts and cannon, was carried by the Allies (see p. 248).

17 TOULOUSE.—(*Inns*: H. de France, H. de l'Europe, kept by Bibent, Place

Lafayette; good situation; comfortable; good cuisine. H. Souville; very good. H. du Midi. H. Casset.)

In the midst of the great plain of Gascony and Languedoc, beginning at the very foot of the Pyrenees, and stretching from them nearly 100 m. N., stands Toulouse, the ancient capital of Languedoc, and now of the Dépt. of Haute Garonne. It is built on both banks of the Garonne, just above the point where the Canal du Midi, connecting the Atlantic with the Mediterranean, falls into it, after winding round the N. and E. sides of the town. The river is crossed by a brick bridge connecting the city with the suburb St. Cyprien on the l. bank of the river.

It is far from being a handsome city; its streets are irregular and dirty, its houses and even churches of brick; and neither public nor private buildings are distinguished by special architectural beauty: but it ranks as the seventh city in France, from the number of its inhabitants (77,400), and the extensive trade and commerce of a provincial capital which it enjoys. It is interesting from its historical souvenirs, as the capital of the kingdom of the Visigoths from 413 to 507, when it was destroyed by Clovis on the battle-field of Vouillé near Poitiers; as the place where the art of the Troubadours was encouraged at the gay court of its counts; as the scene of the papal crusade against the Albigenses, headed by an English leader, and as the seat of the ancient Parliament of Toulouse. But the Revolution has, as usual, done its worst to extirpate all tangible relics of bygone days.

The *Place du Capitole* (once Place Royale), a handsome square of regular modern buildings (one of which is an exceedingly sumptuous *café*), is the centre of bustle and traffic; the chief market-place, and the point of departure of the main thoroughfares. It is named from *le Capitole*, or Hôtel de Ville, so called either from the tradition that in the time of the Romans the Capitol of the Tolosates may have stood here, or from the meetings of the civic chapter (capitolium), whose members were also called capitouls, on this spot. The building presents externally a modern front, finished 1769, with eight columns of red Pyrenean marble in the centre, and includes, besides the municipal buildings and the archives, the *Theatre* in the l. wing. The principal apartment, running along nearly the whole length of the first floor, is the *Salle des Illustres*, or hall of the worthies of Toulouse, so called from 38 terra-cotta busts of men of note, born in and near Toulouse, or connected with it, each with a pompous Latin inscription below it, filling as many gilt niches in the walls. In real truth, a great many —as Riquet, engineer of the Canal du Midi, Pope Benedict XII., &c., have no connection of birth with the town; and many more, though really citizens, have no claim to renown beyond its walls. Among those of most general celebrity may be mentioned Raymond St. Gilles, Count of Toulouse, one of the leaders of the first crusade; Cujas, the lawyer ("*cujus merum nomen plus laudis amplectitur quam quælibet oratio potest*"), who was rejected by the university here when a candidate for the professorship of law; and P. Fermat, the mathematician, inventor of the integral calculus, b. 1608.

In this hall are held every year the meetings of the *Société des Jeux Floraux*, deriving its origin from the ancient troubadours, but founded, it is said, by one Clémence Isaure, a Toulousan lady, who revived the science of the "gai Scavoir" in the 14th centy. (1333). Her very existence, however, is not a little doubtful, as there is no mention of her in the archives of the town, though her statue is preserved in the Capitole. In spite of these doubts, the society has adopted her as its patroness and founder, and every year at the beginning (3rd) of May, after making a pilgrimage to the church of the Daurade in which her tomb once was, it distributes, to various competitors, prizes consisting of golden and silver flowers, the violette, amaranthe, eglantine, souci, and lis, for the best original compositions in verse, and essays in prose, for which the directors give the subject. The society maintains about equal importance, and the prize compositions have nearly the same literary value, as those of the bardic meetings held in Wales. Although the existence of Clémence is uncertain, there is no doubt of the antiquity of the society, and it claims for itself to be the oldest literary institution in Europe, dating from 1333. Indeed, it appears that in that year a number of Troubadours, or Mainteneurs du Gai Scavoir, citizens of Toulouse, met in a field near the town to distribute prizes to the composers of the best verses.

In the same room with the statue of Clémence Isaure is preserved *the axe* with which Henri Duc de Montmorency, the victim of the implacable Cardinal Richelieu, and one of the last of the great vassals of the crown of France, was decapitated. It is a sort of huge carving-knife, and was made in the town. The execution took place 1632, in the first court of the Capitole, at the feet of the statue of Henri IV., in whose reign that part of the building was erected. In the 2nd court on the rt., two barred windows mark the dungeon in which the duke was confined, and belong to the oldest portion of the building. Here also is the old *Salle de Consistoire*, with ornamented roof and chimney (? if still existing). The council chamber of the senators of the town, or capitouls, equivalent to the échevins elsewhere, no longer exists.

The antiquity of the municipal privileges of Toulouse, and of the meetings of the magistrates, who were elected by the people themselves, and who were recognised by Raymond V. as far back as 1152, deserves notice. These rights, of 5 centuries' duration, were infringed, in spite of the remonstrances of the citizens, by Louis XIV., who caused the capitouls to be appointed at Paris by royal ordonnance.

The *Place du Capitole* is a good starting-place from which to visit the chief curiosities of the town.

**L'Eglise St. Sernin*, the largest, oldest, and most perfect ecclesiastical edifice here, is a plain building of brick and stone in the Romanesque style, finished and consecrated 1090, by Pope Urban II. It is conspicuous for its lofty octagonal *Tower*, formed by 5 tiers of arches, each story less in size than that below it. The upper part is of the 14th cent., the lower corresponds in style with the church below. Of its 2 S. *porches*, one is distinguished by a curious early Byzantine bas-relief over the door, and by the capitals of its columns representing the murder of the Innocents, expulsion of Adam, &c.; the other, a double portal leading into the S. transept, bears carved capitals of the 7 deadly sins. By the side of it, within a modernised chapel, open to the air, are several tombs of early counts of Toulouse. The interior is remarkable for its very long *Nave* (not unlike that of St. Albans, but flanked by double aisles). The E. end is semicircular and its arches round; close-set columns support the vault above the high altar-painted with the colossal figure of Christ and the symbols of the 4 evangelists. From the aisle behind it project 5 apsidal chapels, decorated with curious carvings of saints and legends in wood. Here also is a model of the church as it stood before the Revolution, showing that it formed an isolated fortress, apart from the town, walled in by towers and battlements. Some curious Byzantine bas-reliefs in white marble, said to have belonged to the old church of St. Sernin, built by Charlemagne in the 8th centy. (?), are let into the wall of the aisle behind the choir; they represent our Saviour, angels, and saints. The *Crypt* under the choir, modernised in the 15th centy., was the place of deposit of relics in great number and esteemed of immense value. Before the Revolution this church indeed boasted of possessing the bodies of no less than 7 of the apostles; that of St. James was, it is true, a duplicate, another of his bodies being preserved at Compostella! This motto was blazoned over the entry — "*Non est in toto sanctior orbe locus.*"

The wooden stalls of the choir are

well carved in the style of the 16th centy.

The *Church of St. Taur*, situated in the street leading from the Capitole to St. Sernin, derives its name from the wild bull to whose horns the body of the martyr St. Saturnin was bound by his heathen persecutors. The struggles of the furious animal having detached it from the cords on this spot, a church was in consequence erected. That at present existing has nothing remarkable but its flattened fronton belfry, surmounted by angular arches.

The *Church of the Cordeliers*, a brick building of great loftiness, erected in the 14th centy., is now turned into a magasin de fourrage, and filled with hay; that of the *Jacobins*, surmounted by a conspicuous brick tower, rising in arches having straight-angled heads, is of vast size, and of brick, like the other churches. It has become a barrack, and is divided by floors, the lower story serving as a stable for artillery horses.

Issuing out of the Place du Capitole by the Rue de la Pomme, we come to the *Cathedral*, or *Eglise St. Etienne*, remarkable for the irregularity and want of concord in all its parts. The large and beautiful rose window is out of the line of the centre of the main portal immediately below it; the centre of the nave is parallel with the side aisle of the choir, and its two walls do not correspond. The nave was built by Raymond VI., Comte de Toulouse, in the 13th centy., at a time when he was favouring the heretical Albigeois, and was excommunicated in consequence by the Pope. Raymond was besieged within the walls of Toulouse by Simon de Montfort, Earl of Leicester, appointed by Innocent III. head of the crusade against the heretics. He met his death in one of the suburbs of the town, from a stone discharged by a mangonel, whilst he was endeavouring to repel a sally of the citizens, in the 9th month of the fruitless siege, on St. John Baptist's day, 1218. Count Raymond's construction is the oldest part of the church, and was doubtless intended to be removed by those who raised the very elegant Flamboyant *Choir*. It was begun 1272, but not roofed until 1502, by the Cardinal d'Orléans, son of the brave bastard Dunois, who built also the clocher and the singular isolated column called *Pilier d'Orléans*, which fronts you as you enter the nave. There is some good painted glass in the choir. The tower is singular from its form, having two broad sides and two narrow.

In the Rue des Arts is the *Musée, deposited in the desecrated church of the Augustins, and comprising a large collection of bad paintings, copies, &c., filling two rooms, one of them being the old church itself, which has been re-roofed and re-floored. The best pictures are a *Perugino*, St. John Evangelist and St. Austin; a *Vander Meulen*, Siege of Cambray; and a curious painting of the eight capitouls forming the town council of Toulouse in 1645. A good collection of *casts* from the antique is placed in the chapterhouse, an elegantly vaulted and groined apartment of the 14th centy., supported on light pillars. The *Collection of Antiquities* in this museum is the most interesting sight in Toulouse; it is placed under the admirable direction of M. du Mège, who may be considered its founder. The locale which it partly occupies is the elegant Gothic *Cloister* of the old church, the traceried arches of which are supported on pillars of marble in pairs, producing an effect not unlike the Campo Santo at Pisa.

In addition to a small series of Egyptian sculptures, there are numerous inscriptions, Roman and Gallic, votive altars, &c., with fragments of statues and of marbles, from various places in Languedoc and the Pyrenees, showing that the quarries of the Pyrenees were worked by the Romans. The most remarkable part of the collection, however, is the three following series, forming an almost uninterrupted chain in the history of art, from the Gallo-Roman period to the Renaissance or cinque-cento through the Gothic period.

1st. A very large collection of antiquities dug up near the small town of Martres, on the l. bank of the Garonne, a little below St. Gaudens, and proved by M. du Mège to be the ancient Calagorris. In consequence of the excavations undertaken at his suggestion, it has become a Gallic Pompeii. The discoveries consist of a series of about 40 busts and medallions of Roman emperors, and of members of their families, from Augustus and Claudius down to Gallienus, forming a tolerably complete portrait gallery; of a number of small statues of gods and goddesses, of good execution, especially in the drapery, including Isis, Venus, Diana, Jupiter, Serapis, Esculapius, Harpocrates; a series of bas-reliefs, much mutilated, representing the Labours of Hercules; a mosaic of the head of a river god; a number of Corinthian capitals, friezes, and other architectural ornaments. Among the bronzes are a pair of *wheels* and the *pole of a Roman chariot*, very rare and interesting objects, dug up at Fa, near the Bains de Rennes. Two bas-reliefs, with inscriptions relating to the two Emperors Tetricus, have given rise to much discussion among antiquaries. They were found at Nérac.

2nd. A collection of works of art of the middle ages, consisting of bas-reliefs, statues, monuments, portals, and a long series of curiously carved capitals of columns obtained from ecclesiastic edifices and Christian monuments destroyed or desecrated at or since the Revolution, beginning with early Christian tombs, sarcophagi, and coffins, covered with sculpture rude and debased in point of art, but showing Roman influence, bearing Christian symbols combined with heathen subjects, the cross, X, P, the vine-branch, &c. One of these, brought from the outer wall of the church of La Daurade, where it went by the name of *Tombeau de la Reine Pedauque* (pes aucæ, queen goose-leg), bears six bas-reliefs of the multiplication of loaves and fishes, the raising of Lazarus, and other Scriptural events, which were adopted as types symbolical of the goodness of God, and of the resurrection, by the early Christians. Another sarcophagus from St. Orens, at Auch, displays, with similar symbolical allusion, the sacrifice of Isaac, and Lazarus deplored by Martha, with Adam and Eve. Others of these tombs come from the very ancient cemetery of St. Saturnin in Toulouse. Several bas-reliefs which ornamented a portal of that church are preserved here; one represents 2 females seated, their legs crossed; one holds a ram, the other a lion: the names of these two signs of the zodiac being written at the side, and below one of them, "Hoc factum est in tempore Julii Cæsaris." They are supposed to have formed part of a Zodiac, or Julian Calendar, attached to that church. It is not improbable that they were executed in the time of Charlemagne. From St. Sernin also comes a carving of a hawk, with a human head, treading under foot a monster, inscribed "Crocodilus:" the allegory seems derived from Egypt. A *pedestal in white* marble, bearing 4 figures in relief, 2 of them saints with palms (St. Justus and Rusticus), the Virgin, and a crowned king, supposed to be Charlemagne, holding a lotus-headed (?) sceptre, and wearing a cross on his breast, was brought from the Cathedral of Narbonne, of which he was the founder. The curious *Portal of the old Church of La Daurade*, pulled down in 1812 when the monastery attached to it was converted into a tobacco manufactory, has been re-erected here, as nearly as possible in its original condition. Its circular arch is supported by statues, instead of pillars: attached to it are 4 figures in bas-relief,—David playing on the Harp, and the Virgin and our Saviour, with a king and queen, founders or benefactors of the church.

In like manner, the *Portal of the Cathedral Chápterhouse* at Toulouse, decorated with figures of the Apostles in bas-relief, has been removed hither.

Here are numerous statues, partly coloured and gilt, of Christ, the Virgin, Apostles, and Saints. A series of more than 60 capitals of columns, almost all differing in form and decoration, the greater part ornamented with subjects minutely carved from the Bible or Legends of Saints. The casts of sculptures from the church of St. Victor at Marseille, and from that of Moissac, merit attention, as well as many monumental effigies of noble knights and high-born dames, and holy ecclesiastics, mitred abbots, bishops, and several archbishops of Toulouse, here deposited.

The museum also boasts of possessing the *ivory horn* of the renowned *Roland*, richly carved—formerly preserved in the treasury of the church of S. Sernin.

A third division of the museum contains *Monuments of the Renaissance*, including casts from a portion of the carved wood screen-work in the Cathedral of Auch, and church of St. Bertrand de Comminges. A Pietà, in white marble, from the Eglise des Carmes at Carcassonne, several fragments of statues, bas-reliefs, &c., by *Bachelier*, a sculptor of Toulouse, and pupil of Michael Angelo, 1485-1567. A relief, in white marble, of boys dancing, by *Pierre Paul Puget*, is very clever.

The plastered and stuccoed church of *La Daurade* derives its name from the *gilt* mosaics of a former church, of which no traces are now left: the monastery attached to it, on the quay, a little below the bridge, is now the Manufacture Royale de Tabac.

There are numerous specimens in the streets of the grand but exaggerated architecture of the Renaissance; one, perhaps the best, is attributed to Primaticcio's design, and is situated near the bridge over the Garonne.

If the stranger will continue past the bridge, up the street, on the rt. bank of the Garonne, called Rue du Couteliers, he may view the *Hôtel St. Jean*, of Italian architecture, that called *Hôtel Daguin*, or more commonly *Maison de Pierre*, a gaudy specimen of the style of the Renaissance, and nearly opposite an ornamental portal, in much better taste, designed by *Bachelier*, already mentioned.

Still farther on is the *cannon foundry*, occupying the ancient nunnery of Sainte Claire; and a little beyond it *Le Couvent de l'Inquisition*, an obscure edifice retaining 'its old ill-omened name, but now belonging to a religious brotherhood engaged in education. It is memorable for crimes which stain the annals of Toulouse. Here alone, in France, was that accursed tribunal allowed to take root. Here, as in Spain, it brought with it its usual train of tyrannous atrocities, torturing, imprisoning, roasting at the stake the living, tearing up the dead from their graves, or refusing Christian burial to persons deceased. It was first established here, in the time of Count Raymond VII. (1221), by the ecclesiastical council assembled to exterminate the heresy of the Albigenses, which, at the beginning of the 13th centy., had overspread the entire S. of France, under the connivance or encouragement of Raymond VI., of Toulouse, one of the wealthiest and most powerful princes of his time. St. Dominic himself, the founder of the Inquisition, visited Toulouse to water the thriving offset from his own terrible foundation: the cell which he occupied was shown until 1772.

The *Place de Salin* was the scene upon which the French Autos da Fé were enacted.

The house No. 50, Rue des Filatiers, was in 1762 occupied by a respectable Protestant family, named Calas. The father, Jean Calas, carried on the trade of a draper, and prospered, in good repute with his neighbours, and in contentment at home. The only exception to his domestic happiness was the conversion, by a priest named Durand, of his third son, Jean Louis, to the Roman Catholic faith. The youth had, in consequence, been sent from home, receiving a small allowance from his father.

On the night of the 13th-14th October, 1761, cries were heard issuing from the house of Calas, and the chief of police, with an escort of soldiers, on entering it, found near the door the dead body of the eldest son of Calas, Marc Antoine by name.

A procès verbal was prepared, declaring that he died, hung by himself; which there can be no doubt is the truth, for he was of a melancholy temperament; but a malicious cry was raised in the crowd by a voice unknown, that he had been strangled by his father, to prevent his abjuring Calvinism as his brother had done, and the report spread, and was partly believed by the fanatic Toulousans. The elder Calas was in consequence accused of the murder of his own son, before the Parliament of Toulouse; and that ancient and venerable assembly, without listening to one-tenth of the evidence which had been prepared, and without any proof of his guilt, sullied its reputation for justice by condemning him, at the age of 63, to be tortured and broken on the wheel, and his remains burnt and scattered to the wind.

The act of condemnation, in virtue of which this atrocious judicial murder was committed, runs as follows:—
"La Cour le condamne à être livré aux mains de l'exécuteur de la haute justice, qui, tête, pieds nus, et en chemise, la hart au col, le montera sur le chariot à ce destiné, et le conduira devant la porte principale de l'Eglise de Toulouse; où, étant à genoux, tenant entre ses mains une torche de cire jaune allumée, du poids de deux livres, il fera amende honorable, et demandera pardon à Dieu, au Roi, et à la justice, de ses crimes et méfaits; ce fait, le remontera sur le chariot, et le conduira à la Place St. George de cette ville, où, sur un échaufaud, qui y sera à cet effet dressé, il lui rompra et brisera les bras, jambes, cuisses, et reins; ensuite l'exposera sur une roue qui sera dressée tout auprès du dit échafaud, la face tournée vers le ciel, pour y vivre en peine et repentance de ses dits méfaits, servir d'exemple, et donner de la terreur aux méchants, tout autant qu'il plaise à Dieu de lui donner la vie; et son corps sera jeté dans un bucher préparé à cet effet sur la dite Place, pour y être consumé par les flammes, et ensuite (ses cendres) jetées au vent. Préalablement le dit Calas sera appliqué à la question ordinaire et extraordinaire, sera le dit Calas père étranglé, après avoir resté deux heures sur la roue. Jugé le 9 Mai, 1762.—Cassan, Clairac, rapporteurs." He bore the torture inflicted on him in the Hôtel de Ville with the greatest firmness, answering all questions with the utmost clearness, and giving no advantage to his interrogators, but persisting in maintaining his innocence. On the scaffold, after suffering with the most patient resignation the agonies of his punishment for 2 whole hours, during which he was subjected to the mental rackings of a Romish priest, being still fully alive, the signal was given to the executioner to inflict the "*coup de grâce.*"

"De faux témoins ont égarés mes juges," exclaimed he, before breathing his last breath; "je meurs innocent: Jésus Christ, qui était l'innocence même, voulut mourir par une supplice plus cruel encore." The very Dominicans who attended Calas exclaimed as he expired, "Il est mort un juste!" With his murder an end was put to the martyrdoms and cruel persecutions of the Protestants which had disgraced the South of France for almost a century, and chiefly owing to the praiseworthy exertions of Voltaire in defending Jean Calas and exposing his persecutors. His sentence was reversed and his innocence proclaimed by the Conseil Royal at Paris.

The *Palais de Justice*, totally modernised externally, and for the most part a new building, was the seat of the Parliament of Toulouse, where its sittings were held. The fine ceilings ornamenting its interior have been retained in two apartments: one, carved with reliefs in compartments, representing the Labours of Hercules, is by no means contemptible; the other is richly gilt.

At a short distance below the bridge the navigation of the Garonne is interrupted by a weir thrown across it to supply water to the large corn-mill of the town, called *le Basacle*, rebuilt 1814.

Between this mill and the church of La Daurade is the mouth of the *Canal* de Brienne, constructed by the archbishop whose name it bears, to remedy the interruption in the navigation caused by the mill-weir. It runs nearly parallel with the Garonne for about ¾ mile below the Basacle, and then falls into the *Canal du Midi*. A fine avenue of trees leads to this junction. Here the 2 canals are crossed by small bridges, between which, on a level with the water, is stuck a large piece of sculpture, in high relief, of white marble, representing some unmeaning allegory, without allusion to the founder of the great work, Riquet, and contemptible in execution.

A few hundred yards below this, the *Canal du Midi*, after sweeping round the E. and N. sides of the city of Toulouse, enters the Garonne through a basin provided with double locks, and guarded against ice by a sort of pier. The Garonne is at this point 144 mètres, or 473 feet, above the level of the Atlantic.

The navigation of the Garonne, though carried on by barges, is very difficult, owing to rocks and stems of trees in its bed, from Toulouse to the junction of the Tarn. A lateral canal has been projected from Toulouse to Castels in Dépt. de la Gironde. For a description of the *Canal du Midi* see Rte. 93.

At the battle of Toulouse the inner bank of the canal, towards the town, was lined with French troops, and every bridge over it strongly defended by têtes de pont and intrenchments. In an attack made by the British Light Division upon the bridge nearest the embouchure of the canal, designed by Wellington merely as a feint, but converted by Picton, in disobedience to orders, into a hopeless assault, the British were repulsed with a loss of 400 men.

A *monument* has been erected, in the grounds of the Château Gragnague, on the N. side of the canal, to a British officer of great merit, Colonel Forbes, of the 45th regiment. Several other English monumental tablets are also placed in the Protestant Church of Toulouse.

The best point of view for surveying the *field of the Battle of Toulouse* (April 10, 1814), as well as for viewing the town, is the *Obelisk* of brick, erected by the city, "Aux Braves morts pour la Patrie," occupying the site of one of Marshal Soult's redoubts, taken by the English, on the height of Calvinet. It is reached by traversing the fine oval *place*, and the broad *Avenue Lafayette* (originally d'Angoulême), crossing the canal at the flying bridge, or Pont Matabiau, and ascending at the back of the Ecole Vétérinaire. The view owes its chief interest to the distant chain of the Pyrenees, occupying the horizon, whose peaks may be discerned, in fine weather, from the Canigou on the E. to the Pic du Midi de Bigorre on the W., with the Maladetta, Crabioules, and Mt. Perdu in the centre. The city itself is not striking; the country around is very flat and monotonous, and the Garonne runs in too deep a bed to form a feature in the landscape.

The most important part of Marshal Soult's position, at the time of the battle, was along the heights called Mont Rave, composed of two platforms, Calvinet (on which stands the obelisk) and Sypierre, both of which had been fortified, several weeks beforehand, with 5 redoubts, and intrenchments between them, mounted with a great many guns. The position was supported by the canal, and by the ramparts by which the town was then surrounded in the rear of the canal; and in front the position was covered by the Ers. That stream was at the time unfordable, and all the bridges over it were blown up, or strongly guarded, except that of Croix Daurade, taken by the British Hussars the day before the battle. General Beresford's division, which achieved the victory, had to make a flank movement, marching for 2 m. up the rt. bank of the Ers, under the fire from the heights, over ground naturally very difficult, marshy, and intersected by watercourses, but rendered almost impassable by artificial inundations. After passing Calvinet, the British troops formed, and, charging up the height, took first the redoubt on Sypierre, and afterwards those on Calvinet. Here, however, a terrible struggle took place : the British, "clinging to the brow of the hill," in spite of the masses opposed to them, stood fast on the ground they had gained; and though the French made desperate efforts from the canal, they never retook Calvinet. A previous attack on Calvinet, made in the early part of the day by the Spaniards, had been very different in its result ; so quickly, indeed, did they retire, that the Duke of Wellington said of them, "he never before saw 10,000 men running a race;" 1500 of them were slaughtered on the slope of this hill, chiefly in a hollow road upon its flank, raked by a battery from the Pont de Matabiau on the canal, which "sent its bullets from flank to flank, hissing through the quivering mass of flesh and bones," to use the words of Colonel Napier.

At 5 o'clock P. M. Soult withdrew his whole army behind the canal. The next day he remained inactive, and on the night of the 11th was "forced to abandon" Toulouse, leaving behind 1600 wounded and 3 generals, to fall prisoners into the hands of the allies. They lost in this battle 4659 men and 4 generals; the French nearly 3000, and 5 generals killed or wounded; a useless waste of human life, since Napoleon had abdicated on the 4th April, some days previously, though that event was unknown to either of the commanders. There can be no doubt that the charge brought against Marshal Soult of fighting this battle though aware of what had happened at Paris is unfounded, and the Duke of Wellington himself has nobly vindicated him from it. The forces of the allies amounted to 52,000 men; but of these only 24,000, and 52 guns, were actually engaged in the battle; the French had 38,000 men, with from 80 to 90 guns. This is the estimate drawn out with the utmost fairness by Colonel Napier.

The country immediately about Toulouse is generally flat and uninteresting, and, being besides arid, and burnt up in summer, the want of shade and verdure, and the excessive dust, offer no inducements to explore. Its fertility, however, is very conspicuous.

Toulouse is joined by a *bridge* of brick, pierced with round holes between the spandrels of the arches, and terminating in an archway, with the suburb of St. Cyprien, which was invested by General Hill and one division of the British army at the time of the battle.

The principal *Cafés* are in the Place du Capitole. The market held here is very abundantly supplied : fruit, vegetables, poultry, and wine are very cheap; butter and milk dear; ortolans, truffles, figs, pâtés de *foies de canards*, are the delicacies which await the gourmand here.

Mallepostes daily to Châteauroux by Montauban and Limoges; to Narbonne and Montpellier; to Bordeaux by Agen ; to Bayonne by Auch and Pau.

Diligences—daily, to Paris (Châteauroux Stat.) ; to Bordeaux ; to Tarbes, Pau, and Bayonne; to Auch and Bagnères de Bigorre; to St. Gaudens and Bagnères de Luchon; to Carcassonne in 9 hours ; to Foix, Ussat, and Ax; to Villefranche (Aveyron) ; to Narbonne and Montpellier; to Perpignan by Limoux; to Alby.

ROUTE 71.

LIMOGES TO BORDEAUX, BY PERIGUEUX AND LIBOURNE.

215 kilom. = 133½ Eng. m.
Malleposte as far as Perigueux.
Diligences daily.
Through a hilly country we reach the first relay at

12 Aixe, on the Vienne, a small town skirted by the road.

23 Chalus. The post-house and inn is situated at some distance from this little town, which is only remarkable for its *Castle of Chabrol*, rising above it in picturesque ruins. Beneath its walls Richard Cœur de Lion received his death-wound from the arrow of a youth named Bertrand de Guerdon. The tamer of the infidel, and hero of the Crusades, thus ended

a chivalrous life of nearly constant warfare, before the petty fortress of a vassal, the Viscount of Limoges, which he had besieged in consequence of a quarrel about the division of a treasure found in the viscount's domain, of which Richard claimed the whole, or a larger share than had been conceded to him. The castle was soon taken, and the garrison of only 38 men were hung by the king's order, except the bold archer who had sped the shaft so fatal to him. The youth avowed, when brought before the dying monarch, that revenge for the death of his father and two brothers, slain by Richard, had prompted him to free the country of its oppressor. His life, though magnanimously spared by Richard, was taken after his death; and he is said to have been flayed alive by order of Richard's minister. The most conspicuous part of the castle yet remaining is a circular *donjon*, entered by a doorway high up in the wall, and no longer accessible without a ladder. The tower is entirely gutted. Around it are grouped some shattered fragments of buildings, including a portion of a chapel. A little conical stone, rising out of the meadows in the front of the castle, in the valley below it, is pointed out as the spot where Richard had placed himself to reconnoitre the fort, when the arrow struck him in the l. shoulder. The stone is called *Maumont*.

The bridge of Firbeix, 3 m. from Chalus, crosses the boundary line of the ancient provinces of Limousin and Perigord.

13 La Coquille.
15 Thiviers.
13 Palissou.
19 *Perigueux* (*Inns:* H. de France; good;—H. de Perigord, famed for its *Pies*, turkeys stuffed with truffles, &c.; —du Chêne Vert), the chef-lieu of the Dépt. Dordogne, contains 12,157 Inhab., and is situated on the rt. bank of the river L'Isle, which was canalised in 1837. The town, composed of streets narrow, tortuous, and dirty within, is fringed by green alleys externally.

Its *Cathedral of St. Front* is a very remarkable ch., the type of the ecclesiastical architecture of the neighbouring provinces of France, and undoubtedly Byzantine both in its character and origin. It consists of 5 domed compartments, the choir, nave, transepts, and crossing, each being covered by a separate stone cupola or dome. It is very worthy of note that St. Front is an exact copy, in plan and dimensions, of St. Mark's at Venice, with which it is nearly contemporary in age. At the W. end is a vestibule of earlier date, surmounted by a tower 197 ft. high, in stages, while at the E. end is an apsidal chapel of the 14th or 15th centy. The arches supporting the domes are pointed, and this is said to be the earliest instance of the use of the pointed arch in France. The domes are now hidden on the outside by walls of masonry. In a chapel is a bas-relief in wood, representing the Assumption of the Virgin, of elaborate execution.

The *Préfecture* is a handsome modern building.

The first ancient name of this city was Vesuna, retained in the *Tour de Vésune*, a circular tower of Roman construction, 100 ft. high, its walls 6 ft. thick, hooped with brick bands at intervals, without doors or windows. It is supposed to have been a tomb, and is situated in a suburb called La Cité, which contains other ancient remains of a *Roman amphitheatre* (very picturesque) and *arch*. At a later period the name Vesuna was changed to *Petrocorii*, mentioned by Cæsar, whence Perigueux. The *Château de la Barrière* is a most curious building, raised on Roman foundations, which themselves show evidence of hasty construction. Other portions date from the 10th to the 17th centy. Part is inhabited by the Comte de Beaufort, being his paternal inheritance recovered after the Revolution.

The streets of Perigueux contain some curiously ornamented houses of the 16th century: one at the corner of Rue l'Aiguillerie bearing the date 1518; 2 others in Rue Taillefer, Nos. 31 and 37; and a 4th at the end of the Rue de la Sagesse, ornamented with arabesques and carvings, merit notice.

There are some buildings and vaults which are as old as the 12th and 13th centuries.

The celebrated *pâtés de Perigueux*, well known to all gourmands, are made of partridges combined with truffles, and form an article of considerable export.

The road descends the valley of the L'Isle nearly all the way to Libourne, crossing the stream opposite Castel Fadaise.

Passing under the castle of Montancey, we reach

18 Massoulie.
17 Mussidan.
17 Montpont.
18 St. Médard (Dépt. Gironde). A few m. to the rt. lies Coutras, where Henri IV., while still only King of Navarre, gained a bloody victory over the forces of the League under the Duc de Joyeuse, who lost his life on the field, along with many other great lords, 1587. Coutras is visible from a hill overlooking the valley of the L'Isle, surmounted before reaching

20 *Libourne* (Rte. 64), a rly. stat.

Railroad, Libourne to Angoulême and Tours;—to Bordeaux.

Diligence to Perigueux.

[An interesting excursion may be made from Libourne up the valley of the Dordogne to *St. Emilion*, a town of 3100 Inhab. (3 m. distant), celebrated for its wines, and one of the most remarkable in France for the antiquity of its buildings. It is, as it were, a town of the middle ages preserved to our times ; with its crenellated ramparts, watch-towers, and 6 gates still perfect. There is not a house in it less than 3 centuries old. It is seated in a sort of ravine or quarry, and many of the dwellings are caves hewn in the rocks. It has a ruined *Castle, le Château du Roi*, built by Louis VIII., surmounted by a square keep-tower, in a style resembling the Norman, most singular ; in fact unique. A very singular rock-hewn church of great age. It consists of a nave (barrel-vaulted) with aisles, and piers formed of square masses of the sandstone left standing. Over it, on the top of the rock, a lofty Gothic steeple has been erected, and a ·rich portal of the 14th cent. is applied to the face of the rock. A round Gothic church, called the *Rotonde;* the *Parish* or Collegiate *Church*, a fine building, reduced to the nave and W. portal, of the 12th centy. On the S. side is a curious *Cloister*, and not far off rises a graceful tower, octagonal above, square below, commanding from its top a very fine view; the ruins of several other churches and convents; and a handsome building, the *Palais du Cardinal* de Cantarac. The Girondins Guadet, Pétion, and Barbaroux sought refuge for a time in the cave dwellings here, but were captured and slain here, 1794.]

[About 12 m. S.E. of this is Castillon, under whose walls was fought, in 1453, the battle in which valiant Lord Talbot, Earl of Shrewsbury,

"The Frenchman's only scourge,
Their kingdom's terror, and black Nemesis,"

hemmed in by a French force greatly superior to his own, was slain, at the age of nearly 80 years, gallantly fighting, along with his son, the Lord Lisle, whom his father in vain counselled to depart out of the field, seeing that all was lost,—a real incident, which has furnished Shakespeare with a fine scene. The result of Talbot's defeat and death was the capture of Bordeaux from the English, and their final expulsion from Guienne. Near Montraval, on the rt. bank of the Dordogne, a tomb was formerly pointed out under the name of Talbot's ; but it is known that his body was transported by his friends to England. 3 m. from Castillon, on the l. of the road, but accessible only by rough cross-roads, is the *Château of St. Michel de Montaigne*, the birthplace of Montaigne, the philosopher essayist, Shakespeare's favourite author. It is a considerable building, never fortified, and remains nearly as described by him in his Essai des Trois Commerces. The room which was his library is preserved in the gate tower, over the entrance, and its roof is inscribed with Greek and Latin sentences ; among them some from Ecclesiastes also—

"Homo sum : humani à me nihil alienum puto." There is a pleasing view from the terrace. The ch. is near the house.]

The great line of railway from Paris to Bordeaux passes through Libourne (see Rte. 64). The old road to Bordeaux, after crossing the bridge over the Dordogne, passes through

16 Beychac.

15 BORDEAUX itself will be found in Rte. 73.

ROUTE 73.

TOULOUSE TO BORDEAUX BY MOISSAC, AGEN, MARMANDE ;—DESCENT OF THE GARONNE.

256 kilom. = 158½ Eng. m. *Malleposte* daily in 16 hours, and *diligences*.

Steamers ply on the Garonne from Agen or Marmande to Bordeaux : a good restaurant on board. The Garonne is a winding stream, much more picturesque than the Loire.

The first 2 stages from Toulouse by

17 St. Jory, and

12 Grisolles, are the same as Rte. 70; but we turn to the l. out of the road to Paris by Montauban, before reaching

16 La Vitarelle.

The Garonne runs nearly parallel with the road, but so far off (1½ to 2 m.) as scarcely to be seen.

After skirting the little town of St. Porquier, and crossing the road from Montauban to Auch, we reach

13 Castel Sarrazin, a town of 7000 Inhab., carrying on some trade in the corn grown on the fertile plain around. Opinions differ as to the origin of the name ; some deriving it from the Saracens, who may have built the *castle*, of which scanty remains exist, to secure themselves in this part of France ; others, from Castel-sur-Azin, the name of the small stream running through it.

The river Tarn, flowing down from Montauban to join the Garonne, is crossed before entering

7 Moissac (*Inn :* Grand Soleil), a town of 10,165 Inhab., on the rt. bank of the Tarn.

Its *Ch. of St. Pierre and St. Paul,* once attached to a celebrated abbey founded by Clovis, or more probably by St. Amand of Maestricht in the 7th centy., has a very remarkable *portal*, which was added in the early part of the 12th centy. to the still older church. It is a deeply recessed porch, preceding a pointed arch, the mouldings and tympanum of which, over the door, are enriched with the most fantastic sculptures, designed with the utmost boldness and fancy. Figures of apostles, saints, angels, bas-reliefs, fanciful patterns and mouldings, have been dashed off with wonderful freedom. The central pier, supporting the doorway, and the side walls, under the porch, are similarly adorned. In the interior are some very early mosaics.

The *cloisters*, a range of pointed arches, resting on twin pillars with singular capitals, were constructed in 1110, as is recorded on one of the pillars.

An ancient fountain in the town merits notice.

A hilly stage intervenes between Moissac and

10 Malause, a prettily situated town, whose ancient castle has been destroyed since the first Revolution. The flat land ceases here, and the country around is very pleasing : the Garonne, which the road now approaches more closely, is a charming feature in the landscape.

The little town of Valence is passed, and a few miles further the road runs along a sort of terrace or quay by the side of the Garonne, through

12 La Magistère.

10 Croquelardit.

About half way between Toulouse and Bordeaux lies

rt. 10 *Agen.*—*Inns :* H. du Petit St. Jean, comfortable ; good cuisine, famed for its Terrines de Nérac and pâtés aux truffes ; pretty garden ;— H. de France, good and cheap.

Agen, chef-lieu of the Dépt. Lot et Garonne, is a very old town, chiefly of narrow streets, with 15,000 Inhab., agreeably situated on the rt. bank of the Garonne, between it and the gently sloping height, covered with trees, vineyards, and country-houses, called Côte de l'Ermitage. The Garonne is here crossed by a bridge of stone, and also by a *Suspension-bridge*, between which and the town runs a beautiful avenue of trees, forming an agreeable promenade called *Les Graviers*. The old Ch. of *St. Caprais* is a fine Romanesque building, very broad, with numerous apses, and has been well restored. There are a few scanty remains of the cathedral of St. Etienne, destroyed at the Revolution, and its site is now become a beast-market.

The *Prefecture* was originally the episcopal palace, and is a handsome edifice.

The *Canal* is carried over the Garonne here, on a 3rd *Bridge* or ponderous stone *Aqueduct* of 23 arches, of good architecture.

The town was known to the Romans under the name Aginum. The early Christians suffered severe persecution here from the Roman prætor ; and St. Vincent, the 2nd bishop, and many followers, underwent martyrdom, being torn to pieces on the spot now occupied by the Fontaine St. Vincent. Agen suffered much from the fortunes of war, especially in the 14th century, when, by sieges and assaults, it passed repeatedly from the hands of the French to the English, and *vice versâ*. During the wars of the League it was taken by the Maréchal de Matignon, with the aid of an engineer, who blew in one of the gates with a petard, 1591. Marguerite de Valois, who was in the town at the time, had great difficulty in securing a horse, with a pillion, for herself to escape, and post-horses for a portion of her maids of honour, many of whom were compelled to decamp "on foot without masks, others without riding-habits."

Those who have time should walk to the top of the rocky height of *L'Ermi-tage*, on the way to Villeneuve, for the sake of the view over the beautiful valley of the Garonne and the distant Pyrenees. In a pretty gorge or recess in the slope of the hill is the curious house of the erudite Julius Scaliger, whither he retired, in the reign of Francis I., after migrating from his native city, Verona. He died here 1558, and here his no less learned son, Joseph Julius Scaliger, was born. Agen is also the birthplace of Bernard Palissy, inventor of a beautiful species of earthenware, the Wedgewood of the 16th century, and not less scientific for his age; also of Lacépède, the naturalist. Here was born, and still dwells and sings, a rustic poet named Jasmin, a perruquier by trade, the last representative of the Troubadours. His songs are very popular throughout the S. of France, in the country of the Langue d'Oc.

A great number of plum orchards clothe the neighbouring slopes and fields, and produce the celebrated *prunes d'Agen*, which form an article of considerable export.

Steamers navigate the Garonne as far up as Agen, when the river is of proper height: the descent hence to Bordeaux requires 8 hours, the ascent 11 or 12. You reach Agen from Bordeaux about 6 or 7 p.m. The vessels are clean but small, so that they do not take carriages, which must be sent by land by voiturier.

Mallepostes to Auch and Pau ; to Limoges and Orleans ; to Bordeaux and Toulouse. The traveller bound to the Pyrenees may turn off here to Pau, by Lectoure.

10 Pont St. Hilaire.

11 Port St. Marie. Here is a suspension-bridge over the Garonne.

Near the village of St. Côme, on the rt. of the road, the remains of a tower, called *Tour de St. Côme*, constructed of small square stones, and supposed to be of Roman origin, are worthy of notice. It stands at a short distance from

10 Aiguillon, a town of nearly 2000 Inhab., on the l. bank of the Lot, about a mile above its influx into the Garonne. Its principal building is the large *château*

on an eminence, left unfinished by the Duc d'Aiguillon, minister of Louis XV. by favour of Mad. du Barry. But it is said to include portions of older construction. The duchy was created by Henri IV. 1599, to bestow it upon the Duc de Mayenne. The old castle, so stoutly defended by the English in 1346, when besieged for 5 months by Jean Duc de Normandie, son of Philippe de Valois, with an army of 60,000 men, no longer exists. Although the prince directed against it 20 assaults in 7 days, and though he had sworn not to move until it was taken, he was compelled to retire from before its walls without having succeeded, being called off by intelligence of his father's defeat at Crecy.

The Lot is crossed here by a bridge of 8 arches, built by Napoleon.

11 Tonneins (*Inn*: H. d'Angleterre), a cheerful-looking town, chiefly of modern buildings, remarkable for the beauty of its situation, on the rt. bank of the Garonne, containing 6500 Inhab., half of whom are Protestants. There are extensive manufactures of rope here, and a royal manufactory of *tobacco*, large quantities of which are cultivated around Tonneins, and throughout the departments of Lot and Lot et Garonne, under the inspection of the excise.

There is a suspension-bridge over the Garonne here.

17 *Marmande* (*Inns*: H. de France; —H. de la Providence;—Tête Noire; good, clean, and reasonable—*M. L.*), a town of venerable aspect, many of its houses being timber-framed, but possessing no objects of interest to the traveller. Pop. 8257.

Below Marmande the navigation of the river is more sure, and steamers ply more regularly, than above. One or two vessels run daily to Bordeaux, corresponding with the diligences to Toulouse.

The road avoids the windings made by the river below Marmande, being carried in nearly a straight line to

11 La Mothe Landeron, which lies within the Dépt. of the Gironde.

l. The lofty old ruined tower of Meilhau remains long in sight of those who travel by water, owing to its position at the extremity of an acute angle or elbow made by the river.

A fine suspension-bridge of a single curve, 558 ft. wide in the opening, spans the river at

9 La Réole (Cerf Volant: a mere public-house, but clean beds and good food)—a town of 4000 Inhab., retaining the ruins of an ancient castle, which Froissart says was built by the Saracens. The vast Benedictine convent, rebuilt in the 17th century and suppressed at the Revolution, has been converted into a nunnery. The Gothic church attached to it has been allowed to go to decay.

9 Candrot.

The ancient town of St. Macaire, retaining its feudal walls and possessing a fine Romanesque church, is passed shortly before reaching the suspension-bridge, 656 ft. long, which carries the road over the Garonne into

9 Langon (*Inn*: H. de France; homely but clean), a miserable town of 3745 Inhab., partly surrounded by old walls, on the l. bank of the Garonne, which could be crossed only by a ferry-boat down to 1831, though Langon lies on the great line of traffic between Bordeaux and Toulouse.

The high roads from Bayonne and Pau to Bordeaux (Rtes. 76 and 80) unite with that from Toulouse at Langon. The tide runs up as far as Langon.

The post-road hence to Bordeaux is described in Rte. 76.

The banks of the river are here clothed with vineyards, whose produce, chiefly white wines, enjoys some reputation and fetches a considerable price, being known by the name of Vins de Grave. Sauterne and Barsac are both grown in the commune of

l. Preignac, not far from Langon. Bertrand de Gout, who became pope under the name of Clement V., was born in the very picturesque *castle* of Villandraut, about 8 m. S. of Preignac.

l. Barsac, whence comes the white wine named after it, is a town of 2896 Inhab.

rt. Cardillac was the seat of the Duc d'Epernon, governor of the province of

Guienne in the 17th century; the first duke, who was the favourite of Henri III., but died in the prison of Loches, built the *Château* (1598), which is now converted into a female *Penitentiary*. His splendid monument, attributed to Girardon, erected by his son in the parish church, was destroyed at the Revolution, except one statue now in the Louvre. There is a great manufacture of wine-casks here.

12 (l.) Cérons, an old castle.

1. Podensac, 15 m. from Bordeaux.

rt. At Langoiron, at the foot of the slope, are ruins of a *castle* built apparently in the 14th century: near this l'Ami des Enfans, Berquin, was born.

l. Portets is the place where the inhabitants of the Landes embark their rosin and timber, the produce of that sandy district, which stretches S. from the Garonne near this to the Adour.

12 (l.) Castres.

13 (l.) Bouscaut, at some distance from the river. Among the numerous villages which crowd the banks of the Garonne none appear to deserve particular mention. On approaching Bordeaux the wooded and vineclad (rt.) heights of Floirac form a pleasing feature in the view. The bridge is described in Rte. 64.

11 (l.) BORDEAUX. — *Inns*: H. de France et Rouen, very good;—H. de la Paix; beds, 2 frs.; sitting-room, 3 frs.; —H. de Paris, frequented by English, good;—H. de Richelieu, good situation; no table-d'hôte;—H. des Américains, commercial, good table-d'hôte.

Bordeaux, the second seaport-town of France, chef-lieu of the Dépt. Gironde, containing 124,000 Inhab., is placed on the l. bank of the Garonne, on a spot where its voluminous stream, deep enough for vessels of 1200 tons burthen, makes a very regular curve, which, being lined with handsome buildings of varied architecture, chiefly Italian, forms a noble crescent, lined with quays not less than 3 m. long, surmounted by several Gothic towers and antique spires in the background. No city in Europe can display a more splendid quay than this. The river abreast of the town, 2000 ft. wide, and 18 to 30 ft. deep, is filled with shipping up to the magnificent *Bridge*, the handsomest in France. (See Rte. 64.) This noble exterior, equally striking to the stranger whether he approaches by water or by land from the side of Paris, is borne out by the aspect of a large part of its interior, which has a courtly rather than a commercial air. The Rues du Chapeau Rouge and de l'Intendance, running E. and W. through the heart of the town, nearly separate the old town, of narrow and insignificant though very populous streets, from the N. or more modern quarter, consisting of wide openings, broad streets, extensive places, and avenues, and gardens running into one another, which render Bordeaux a sprawling city, difficult to get over on foot, but omnibuses and neat fiacres are fortunately very abundant.

The Place and Allées de Tournay are so named from an ancient intendant of the province, who in 1750 led the way in improving the city.

Some of the finest streets and rows of houses, and the open *Place Louis-Philippe* terminating at the river side with 2 lofty rostral columns, occupy the site of a citadel called Château Trompette, built by Vauban for Louis XIV. to overawe the Bordelais, dismantled under Louis XVI., and removed since the Restoration. The construction of this new quarter has united with the town of Bordeaux the vast Quartier des Chartrons (so called from a convent of Chartreux), stretching down by the river side, and once a distinct faubourg.

One of the most conspicuous, and at the same time handsomest buildings, is the *Theatre*, of good Italian architecture, faced with a Corinthian portico of 12 arches and isolated on all sides; it is situated in a very central part of the town. It was erected 1780, under the direction of the Duc de Richelieu, by the architect Louis.

The *Cathedral* of St. André is distinguished by its 2 elegant spires, 150 ft. high, at the end of the N. transept, said to have been erected by the English, who held possession of Bordeaux for nearly 300 years, and flanking a pointed portal, enriched with statues and bas-reliefs, above which is a fine rose-window surmounted by a gable. The nave, partly in the round Romanesque style, partly, towards the W. end, repaired in a bungling manner in the 15th centy., after the destruction of a part of the church by an earthquake, is destitute of aisles, and remarkable only for its breadth—56 ft., which, being out of all proportion with its height, deprives it of the chief merit and characteristic of Gothic architecture—elevation. The choir is more elevated, and in a more truly Gothic style, with a triforium gallery and lofty clerestory windows; it is probably of the same age as the spires, and is also said to be by English architects. Our Richard II. was christened, and the marriage of Louis XIII. with the Infanta of Spain, Anne of Austria, was solemnized in this church, 1615.

Opposite the W. end of the cathedral are the Palais and Hôtel de Ville.

Near the E. end of the cathedral, but quite detached from it, is the *Tour de Peyberland*, a noble structure 200 ft. high, square below, and supported by buttresses, but gradually diminishing from its base until it terminates in a circular top. It was originally surmounted by a spire, which rose to a height of 300 ft. It is named from Pierre Berland, who rose from being the son of a poor labourer in Médoc to be bishop of Bordeaux; he caused it to be erected in 1430. During the Reign of Terror it was condemned to destruction; but the spire alone suffered, the rest resisting all attacks, owing to its solidity. Its handsome windows, however, were stopped, and it was converted into a shot-tower, but it has been repaired and reconsecrated as a belfry once more.

L'Eglise Ste. Croix, situated quite at the S. extremity of the town, near the quay, considerably above the bridge, is supposed to be the oldest church here, though a much earlier age has been assigned to it by some than it can claim, as its oldest parts cannot date farther back than the 10th or 11th centy. Its W. front, quite without uniformity, owing to its partial destruction and subsequent repairs, is a specimen of richly decorated Romanesque architecture, and from its age and quaint ornaments deserves some notice. Its semicircular portal and 2 lateral closed arcades are surrounded by mouldings elaborately carved, some with singular and unexplained naked groups of figures, intermixed with cable mouldings. In the tympanum above the door are 3 rows of bas-reliefs, in a style curiously resembling the Egyptian. The rest of the façade, and the wall of the tower rising on the one side, are occupied by arcades; groups of twisted or grooved pillars flank the portal, and 3 tiers of 4 small pillars, placed side by side one above the other, serve instead of buttresses to the tower.

The interior is of later date and inferior interest; its clustered roof rests on clumsy drum-like piers, partly plain, partly surrounded by shafts, some of them surmounted by curious stiffly-carved capitals. It contains a handsome canopied tomb of an abbot, in decorated Gothic. In a chapel on the l. as you enter, the panelled walls of which are decorated with tolerable paintings from the life of the Virgin by an old Italian artist, Vasetti, is an oblong baptismal font, bearing on 2 sides well-executed bas-reliefs of the Last Supper, with decorated ornaments.

In descending the quay from Ste. Croix, you pass, a little above the bridge, near the church of

St. Michael, situated nearly on a line with the bridge, and distinguished by its lofty detached tower, deprived of much of its effect by being hemmed in with mean houses. Its N. front is a superb Gothic elevation in the florid style (15th centy.). It has an elegant rose window framed within a richly decorated arch, whose mouldings are curved back below it. Under it is a florid *porch*. Over the door are placed a pair of bas-reliefs representing the Sacrifice of Isaac and the Paschal Lamb, dating from the 16th centy.; they are separated by a charming group of wonderful expression, representing Judas's kiss. Within the church, at the back of this portal, over the door, is another group, an "Ecce Homo," of the same period, and a century earlier than the bas-reliefs on each side of it, which represent St. Michael destroying the Dragon, and Adam and Eve. The nave and choir are nearly uniform, and of noble pointed Gothic; the choir (about the 13th centy.) has a triforium and clerestory running behind the high altar, so that the E. end is like any compartment at the side, except that the space below, behind the altar, is filled with a shallow apse.

There are a few good painted windows, and in the N. side of the nave a chapel furnished with an altar in the richest and most overladen Renaissance style. Within its niches are 3 graceful statues —the Virgin and Child, St. Catherine, and St. Barbara.

Near the W. end stands the elegant detached *belfry*, 178 ft. high, which now bears the telegraph, but was originally surmounted by a steeple, and rose to a height of 300 ft. It is of octagonal form, supported by elegant buttresses, and was built between 1472 and 1480. In the vault beneath it are shown from 40 to 50 human bodies, interred in the vault below before the Revolution, and preserved by its dry and antiseptic qualities, until they are now like leather, or salt fish,—a disgusting sight.

St. Seurin (St. Severin), situated beyond the Place Dauphine, in the Allées d'Amour, is remarkable for a finely carved triple S. porch, consisting of a trefoil-headed door, enriched with statues of good workmanship, well-executed draperies, and dating from 1267. They represent the 12 Apostles and 2 more sacred personages.

The W. front is modern, but is a tolerable attempt to follow the Romanesque style. The W. porch consists of 3 detached low vaults, one within the other, supported on pillars with curiously carved capitals.

Within this church, on the rt.-hand or S. wall, is a curious bas-relief within a pointed arch above a doorway, now walled up, representing a pope saying mass (supposed to be Clement V., Archbishop of Bordeaux), assisted by a cardinal. On the opposite wall is another bas-relief of 7 figures in niches. The Gothic woodwork of the choir is curious, but sadly bedaubed with paint. Under the seats are numerous grotesque groups. The high altar is decorated with 14 curiously carved bas-reliefs of marble, framed, representing the legend of St. Severin, Bishop of Bordeaux in the 5th centy. On the one side of the chancel stands the *Bishop's Throne*, a curiously carved seat, under a canopy, all of marble, richly sculptured. This church was the cathedral before St. André. Under the choir is an early crypt with 3 aisles and semicircular arches. At the W. end rises a tower surrounded by a double row of circular arcades.

In the *Chapelle of the College*, a bold Gothic structure, is the *monument of Montaigne*, the essayist, a native of Montaigne St. Michel in Périgord, who was mayor of Bordeaux in 1553. He is represented in full armour, according to the custom of the period, laid on his back, with his hands joined in prayer. The statue is a well-executed work of the 16th centy. At No. 17, in the Rue des Minimes, stood his modest mansion, in which he lived and died, 1592, now pulled down.

These are the most remarkable ecclesiastical edifices of Bordeaux, but it retains still a monument of the Roman city *Burdigala*, in the fragment of an amphitheatre, now called *Palais Gallien*, not quite accurately, because, though possibly built in the reign of the Emp. Gallienus, it was not a palace, but a circus, capable of containing 1500 persons. It is supposed to have been built by Tetricus, one of the so-called 30 tyrants, who assumed the purple here. It was condemned to destruction 1792, and has been since gradually pulled down to build houses, so that it is now reduced to mere fragments, interesting to the antiquary alone, of an oval wall formed of small stones with layers of tiles between them, interrupted by the broken archways which lead into it. The interior is occupied by houses and workshops, and 2 streets cross in the centre of it: so that you may stand in the midst of its area and scarcely recognise these ancient remains.

Bordeaux has preserved 2 of its feudal town gates: one, now called *Tour de l' Horloge*, built 1246 by Henry III. of England, surmounted by 3 pointed turrets, formed part of the old Hôtel de Ville; the other, Porte de Caillou, at the end of the Rue du Palais, was built 1492, to commemorate the victory of Charles VIII. at Fornova. The old Bourse, in the Place d'Aquitaine, now an office of roulage, but built as a palace for Charles IX., and the old *Evêché* in a narrow street near it, are picturesque examples of the architecture of the 16th centy.

Bordeaux, like almost every other chef-lieu de Département in France, has a *Gallery of Paintings*. They are placed in the numerous saloons of the Hôtel de Ville; but, except for their number, they are in no wise remarkable, and the less said of their merits the more true the description. There are, however, some tolerable works of the French school.

The *Musée*, situated in Rue St. Dominique, a street leading out of the Chaussée de Tourny, contains a collection of antique fragments, inscriptions, altars, &c., chiefly Roman, found in the vicinity of Bordeaux; 2 sarcophagi, with bas-reliefs, of inferior merit and late date; also fragments of the marble bas-reliefs, representing the battle of Fontenoy, and the capture of Port Mahon from the English by the Duc de Richelieu, which ornamented the pedestal of the statue of Louis XV. in the Place Royale, destroyed at the Revolution. Here are some relics of Napoleon, including his tooth-brush! and the star of the Legion of Honour which he wore. In the *Musée d' Histoire Naturelle* are tolerable collections of shells, of the fossils of the neighbourhood of Bordeaux, marked by blue tickets, and of the marbles of the Pyrenees. A specimen of a sea-eagle was shot at La Teste. These museums are open daily to strangers.

In the same locality, Rue St. Dominique, is the *library* of more than 100,000 volumes, partly the bequest of a member of the old Parliament of Bordeaux, partly the remains of conventual libraries forfeited at the Revolution. A copy of Montaigne's Essays with marginal notes in his own hand, and the first French translation of Livy illuminated, are among its curiosities.

The *Bourse*, the centre of the commerce and trade of the city, is situated on the quay at the extremity of the Rue Chapeau Rouge, between it and the Place Royale. The merchants meet here daily, under a glass dome which covers the inner court of the building, 98 ft. long by 65 broad.

The commercial importance of Bordeaux is due to its situation on a fine navigable river, where the rise and fall of tides amounts to 20 ft., in which vessels of more than 1000 tons may ride at anchor, at a distance of about 70 m. from the sea. It is connected by the same river, through the Canal du Midi, with the Mediterranean. The commerce of Bordeaux is carried on chiefly with South America and Mexico, the United States, French colonies, and Great Britain. Its principal articles of trade and exports consist in wines, known in France as vins de Bordeaux, and in England as *claret*, a name of doubtful origin. From 50,000 to 60,000 tuns of wine are exported annually. Nearly half of the best quality and highest price is sent to Great Britain; very little is consumed in France. The Quartier des Chartrons is the focus of this trade; here the principal wine-merchants have their counting-houses and cellars.

The *Cellars of MM. Barton and Guestier*, leading bankers and wine-merchants, 35, Cours des Chartrons, are among " the lions " of Bordeaux. They are 2 stories in height, and commonly contain from 8000 to 9000 casks (barriques) of wine, never less than 4000 or 5000. The duty paid by this house in one year alone to the British government has amounted to 300,000*l*.

For an account of the wines of Bordeaux see Route 74.

Among the *delicacies* furnished by the Bordeaux markets to the table are *Royans*, a species of sardines (pilchards), caught in autumn; *Ceps*, a sort of mushroom cooked in oil; *Muriers*, small birds something like beccaficas; and *Ortolans*, caught in August, near Agen and the Pyrenees.

The Café de Paris is a tolerable Restaurant.

Consuls reside here from the chief powers of Europe and America; Great Britain is most respectably represented by Mr. Scott, No. 7, Place du Champ de Mars.

The *English Ch. service* is performed on Sundays at the English Protestant Ch., 8, Cours des Chartrons, at 11 a.m. and 3 p.m.

The *Poste aux Lettres* is at No. 5, Rue Porte Dijeaux: a letter reaches London in 48 hours from this.

Public baths on a very extensive scale, in two fine buildings on each side of the Place Louis-Philippe.

Newspapers of all countries, English, French, German, Spanish, &c., may be found in great abundance at the *Cercle*, 7, Place de la Comédie, opposite the theatre.

The only *resident English physician* is Dr. Coppinger, Place Dauphine, 43.

Paul Chaumas Gayet, the bookseller, 34, Rue fossé du Chapeau Rouge, keeps a number of topographical works, maps, &c., besides the newest French publications.

Besides the *Grand Théâtre*, mentioned already, open commonly three times a week, there is a smaller *Théâtre Français* or *des Variétés*, near the extremity of the Rue de l'Intendance, adjoining the Place Dauphine.

Omnibuses run along the quay from one end to the other, and in a direction across the town, from the river to its outskirts.

Fiacres stand for hire in the principal *places*: they are better but rather more expensive than those of Paris, charging 2 f. for the course, or, by time, 2 fr. for the first hour, and 1 f. 80 c. for every hour after.

Conveyances. — *Mallepostes* daily to Bayonne in 17 hours; to Nantes in 22 hours; to Toulouse in 16 hours.

Diligences daily to Toulouse, several; to Bayonne in 17 hours; to Pau, Bagnères, Cauterets, and the Pyrenæan baths; to Nantes, by Niort, Rochefort, and La Rochelle.

Railway to Paris, viâ Libourne, Angoulême, and Tours; to La Teste; to Bayonne in progress.

Steamers to Nantes twice a week.

Steamers on the Garonne.—*Down the river,* to Blaye and Pauillac daily, starting from the quay abreast of the rostral columns; to Royan. Coaches thence to Rochefort 29 m. several times a week in 7 hours.

Up the river, daily to Langon, Marmande, and Agen (Rte. 73), on the way to Pau or Toulouse (one of the least fatiguing approaches to the Pyrenees), starting from the quay just above the bridge; but it takes 12 or 14 hours to reach Agen.

Environs of Bordeaux.

A *railroad* connects Bordeaux with La Teste, an inconsiderable place 31 m. distant—a journey of about 2 hours, near the sea, on the borders of a great salt lake in the flat district of the *Landes*, whose sole productions are salt and pitch from the large fir forests.

This railroad has been made through a line of country where no previous traffic existed, to a spot possessing no commercial or manufacturing importance. It has consequently been a source of annual loss to its owners hitherto; but having been chosen as the starting-point of the Grand Trunk Railway from Bordeaux to Bayonne (1855), whose traffic will run along it nearly ¾ of its length, its projectors may perhaps be reimbursed eventually (see Rte. 77).

An excursion to La Teste (*Inn:* La Providence?) will give the traveller some notion of the nature of the sandy district called Les Landes, and will probably afford him an opportunity of seeing some of its inhabitants mounted on stilts. Here are several bathing establishments, and an Agricultural Association for redeeming the barren Landes.

The *banks of the Garonne* below Bordeaux, and the *wine district of Médoc*, which produces the claret, are described in Rte. 74.

The Garonne above Bordeaux, in Rte. 73, p. 252.

The excursions to the Château de la Brède, the birthplace of Montesquieu, 2 hours' drive (Rte. 76), or to Blanquefort, the castle of the Black Prince, p. 261.

Passages in the History of Bordeaux.

The earliest mention of Bordeaux is in the geography of Strabo, who calls it Βουρδιγαλα, under which it was known to the Romans, and described in some pretty verses by Ausonius the poet, who was born here in the 4th centy. :—

" Impia jamdudum condemno silentia quod te,
O patria, insignem Baccho, fluviisque, virisque,
Non inter primas memorem. * * *
Burdigala est natale solum, clementia cœli
Mitis ubi, et riguæ largu indulgentia terræ;
Ver longum, brumæque breves, juga frondea subsunt,
Fervent æquoreos imitata fluenta meatus."
AUSON. *Claræ Urbes.*

Hadrian created it the capital of 2nd Aquitania.

Bordeaux belonged for nearly 300 years to the kings of England, who obtained it along with the duchy of Aquitaine by the marriage of Eleanor of Guienne, sole heiress of the last native duke, with Henry II., in 1152, and her inheritance became the fruitful cause of strife between England and France.

The Black Prince, having been invested by his father with the government of Guienne, resided many years at Bordeaux. Hence he set forth on that adventurous foray into the centre of France which led to the battle of Poitiers. Here he held a brilliant court, to which Don Pedro the Cruel repaired, when driven out of Spain, with his two fair daughters, who were here married to the English Princes John of Gaunt and the Earl of Cambridge.

Here the Black Prince's son, Richard II., was born, and surnamed from his birthplace Richard of Bordeaux.

The Bordelais retained their affection for the English long after the downfall of our sway in the rest of France, in the reign of Henry VI.; revolting from the rule of Charles VII. to receive within their walls the valiant Talbot (1453), but his speedy defeat and death forced them again to submit to the French monarch.

Bordeaux was the seat of one of the provincial Parliaments of France, or high court of justice, composed of laymen and ecclesiastics, who registered the royal decrees and transmitted them to the lower courts.

One of the most momentous events of the civil war of the Fronde was the siege of Bordeaux, undertaken by the royal army, with Mazarin, young Louis XIV., and his mother, at its head, while the city held for the Princess de Condé, the Dukes of la Rochefoucauld and Bouillon, at the head of their vassals, assisted by the townspeople and backed by the Parliament of Bordeaux. The heroic wife of the Great Condé, having escaped the clutches of the Cardinal, who already held her husband in prison, and wished to transfer her and her son to like durance, traversed the country from Chantilly, and after a series of adventures and escapes threw herself into this city, where the interest of the Condés was strong. Her beauty, eloquence, and forlorn position enlisted in her favour the enthusiasm of the magistrates and townspeople, and upon her persuasion they agreed to admit her allies and resist the force of Mazarin. She captivated all hearts, and became as it were queen of Bordeaux, then the second city of the empire; and Condé, while shut up in Vincennes and employed in watering his pot of violets, learned with surprise that his feeble princess was acting the part of a general, conducting the defence of a town, and exposing her life on the walls. The defence was conducted with such obstinacy, that, at the end of several weeks, Mazarin, having made little progress, was happy to offer fair terms to the Frondeurs. The citizens of Bordeaux were right glad to be released from the blockade just at the approach of the vintage, for their warlike enthusiasm had begun to cool at the prospect of being shut out from their vineyards.

A great impulse was given to the French Revolution by the inhabitants of Bordeaux. At the beginning of the reign of Louis XVI. the Parliament of Bordeaux, having refused to acknowledge the edict of the king, was banished to Libourne, and in consequence contributed largely to the clamour for the assembling together of the States-general. Many of the persons of greatest eloquence and talent sent as members to the Legislative Assembly, including Vergniaud, Gaudet, Gensonné, Ducos, &c., were returned by the department of the Gironde, whence the party which they composed was called the *Girondins*; but having themselves brought on all the evils of the Revolution, they were swallowed up by the monster they had created, and guillotined for the most part by the stronger party of the Montagne, which succeeded them in the Convention. Bordeaux had a Reign of Terror of its own; the guillotine was erected in the square near the centre of the town, called Place Dauphine (in honour of the Dauphin, afterwards Louis XIII.), but then named Place de Justice, and some of its best citizens were sacrificed. No less than 500 persons suffered death here, whom either envy of their merits, or cupidity for their wealth, caused to be condemned under the false charge of conspiracy against the sovereignty of the people.

The names of some of the streets afford a curious commentary on the history of the town, and a proof among many of the mutability of the French nation. The *Place Louis-Philippe* was Place Louis XVI. down to 1830, and a statue of that king had been prepared, and its pedestal actually erected, when the July Revolution broke out. The *Cours de Douze Mars* was the name given to the row of houses now called *Trente Juillet*, because on the former day, in 1814, the Duc d'Angoulême made his triumphant entry into Bordeaux, at the invitation of the Mayor Lynch (whose name has also been erased from a street which bore it), and amidst the acclamations of a part of the inhabitants.

On the 8th March in that year 2 divisions of the British army, under Marshal Beresford, marched upon Bordeaux; where the presence of the dauntless Duchesse d'Angoulême, who had thrown herself into the town to revive the dormant spirit of loyalty towards her family, and the intrigues of the Duc d'Angoulême, contrary to the advice and wishes of the Duke of Wellington, caused the premature proclamation of the Bourbons by the royalist mayor. The Duke had expressly declared that "he could not interfere to produce any declaration in favour of the Bourbons, nor to support their measures by military force."

ROUTE 74.

THE GARONNE AND GIRONDE FROM BORDEAUX TO LA TOUR DE CORDOUAN; THE WINE DISTRICT OF MÉDOC.

100 kilom. = 62 Eng. m.

Steamers daily to Blaye and Pauillac—4 or 5 times a week to Royan; fare, 15 and 8 frs.

Diligences daily along the S. W. side of the river to Château Margaux and Lesparre, through the midst of Médoc, and along the rt. bank to Blaye. The road on the W. side of the Garonne passes Bouscat and Bruges, so named by Flemish settlers established here by Henri IV. to drain the marshes, and *Blanquefort*, whose picturesque *castle*, a favourite residence of the Black Prince, still preserves part of its outer circuit walls, round towers, and fosse, and some of its apartments entire. The leopards of England are only half effaced from the walls. It is a picturesque object. Thence the road runs to Margaux.

Bordeaux Wines.

The long tongue of land stretching N. from Bordeaux, between the sea on the one hand and the Garonne and Gironde on the other, is called *Médoc* (quasi medio aquæ), because nearly surrounded by water. It is the N. termination of the extensive district of sand hills and sand plains, called Les Landes, extending from Bayonne north, which changes to a bank of gravel on approaching the l. bank of the Garonne, and forms a narrow strip of land nowhere more than 1 or 2 m. broad, raised from 50 to 80 ft. above the river, which is planted with vines, and contains some of the most precious vineyards in the world. The transition is abrupt from this gravel bank near the river to the mere Landes or sandy waste running to the W. and S. of it, producing nothing but firs, furze, and heath. The soil of Médoc is a light gravel, and indeed, on the spots where some of the best wine is produced, it appears a mere heap of white quartz pebbles rolled, and about the size of an egg, mixed with sand. The best wine is not produced where the vine-bush is most luxuriant, but on the thinner soils, where it is actually stunted—in ground fit for nothing else; in fact, where even weeds disdain often to grow. Yet this stony soil is congenial to the vine, retaining the sun's heat about its roots after sunset, so that, in the language of the country, it works (travaille) in maturing its precious juices as much by night as by day. The accumulation of sand and pebbles, of which this soil is composed, is apparently the spoils of the Pyrenean rocks, brought down by the torrents tributary to the Garonne and other great rivers, and deposited in former ages on the borders of the sea. At the depth of 2 or 3 feet from the surface occurs a bed of indurated conglomerate, called *alios*, which requires to be broken up before the vine will grow, as it would stop the progress of the roots, being impenetrable to their fibres. The vine is trained exclusively in the fashion of espaliers, fastened to horizontal laths, attached to upright posts at a height not exceeding 1½ or 2 feet from the ground, running in an uninterrupted line from one end of the vineyard to the other. Manure is scarcely used in the culture, only a little fresh mould is laid over the roots from time to time; but the plough is driven between the vines four times every season, alternately laying open and covering its roots: this is performed by oxen, who, with steady and unvarying pace, thread the ranks without treading on the plants. Manure destroys the fine quality of the wine, and moisture or standing water is most injurious to the plant. The vine begins to produce at 5 years of age, and continues productive sometimes when 200 years old, provided its roots have found a congenial soil to insinuate (pivoter) their fibres, which they sometimes do to a distance of 40 or 50 ft., when the soil is dry and deep enough to protect them from the sun. The wines are classed into growths (*crus*), according to their excellence, and only a very small part of the strip of land before mentioned is capable of producing the "premiers crus;" indeed so capricious is the vine, that within a few yards of the finest vineyards it degenerates at once. The following list will show the classification of Bordeaux wines, or clarets as we call them in England (though whence the name, or what its meaning, are unknown in Médoc), together with the average quantity of each produced in one season. The tun, or *tonneau*, contains 4 hogsheads, called *barriques*.

First Growths.
Château Margaux	140—160
Château Lafitte	120
Château Latour	100
Haut Brion	60— 80

Tuns.

The last is properly a vin de Grave, grown on the Garonne above Bordeaux, yet is classed with Médoc wines; it is less in repute now than formerly.

Second Growths.
Mouton (Lafitte)	120—146
Léoville, the best of the wines of St. Julien	145—186
Rauzan (Margaux)	75— 95

Tuns.

La Rose Gruau, Pichon Longueville, Durfort, Degorse, Lascombe, Cos-Destournelle, in all about 800 tuns.

It is needless to enumerate those of 3rd, 4th, and 5th rate growths, many of which are produced in the vicinity of the first-rate vineyards, at the villages or in the communes of Margaux,

Lafitte, Latour, without partaking in their excellences. The goodness of a season will sometimes give an excellence to second-class wines, while in bad years those of first-class sink to mediocrity, and are not fit for exporting to England (such is the importance of maintaining the character of these wines there), but go to Holland, or are retained in France. This is so well understood, that some years ago the proprietor of the vineyard of La Rose used to hoist, on a flagstaff above his house, the English flag in good years, the Dutch in middling, and the French in bad years. England consumes more than one-half of the premiers crus, and very little of inferior sorts; Russia takes a good deal, Paris little of the best; Holland is the great mart for wines of second quality; and the third-rate sorts, or vins ordinaires, are chiefly used in France. An erroneous notion prevails in England that clarets are prepared for the English market by a certain mixture of brandy. This is not the case; brandy would destroy the wine. A mixture does take place to adapt the wines to the English palate; but they are doctored with strong-bodied (corsés) Rhône wines, and chiefly with Hermitage, the principal consumption of which is for this purpose. The practice of mixing is very general. The characteristic of the good wines of Bordeaux is their aroma or bouquet; spirit they have none, and will distil away into nothing, yet the aroma will be retained and penetrate even through the Rhône wine, when it is judiciously added. The average price of a hogshead (barrique) of genuine wine of first growth, in the cellar of the first houses at Bordeaux, is 50*l*., which, with carriage, duty, bottling, &c., amounts to 80*l*., rather more than 70*s*. a dozen. A first-growth wine of a fine vintage is scarcely to be had at a less price; indeed, the whole produce of Château Margaux has been sold on the spot for 1000 francs the hogshead, in the case of a very first-rate vintage. Very great skill is shown, and much experience required, in the making of the wine, in the compounding of various growths and qualities, and in the preservation of it: a promising vintage often disappoints expectations, while a bad one sometimes turns out excellent; indeed, all that can be said of the premiers crus is, that they are the wines which most often succeed. The total produce of Médoc, in average years, is from 150,000 to 170,000 hogsheads, of which about 6000 go to England.

Travellers desiring to visit the principal vineyards of Médoc may take the steamer to Pauillac (which may be reached in 4 hrs., or 6 against tide), which is not far from Lafitte and Latour, or the coaches which run daily will convey them to Margaux. The high road thither, and thence to Pauillac, traverses the centre of the narrow strip of land forming the wine district. For some distance out of Bordeaux it passes a series of country houses.

The Garonne below Bordeaux is a fine broad tidal river, but very much charged with mud, having few features of interest, its banks being chiefly low, while an intervening fringe of marsh and meadow land, grown over with willows, separates the river from the vineyards, little of which can be seen from the deck of the steamer.

Nothing can be finer than the view of the long crescent quay of Bordeaux, and the broad river crowded with shipping, many of them 3-masted vessels, as the steamer casts off from the quay, opposite the rostral columns, and skirts the long Faubourg des Chartrons.

rt. Lormont is a picturesque eminence, covered with wood and vineyards, interspersed with some neat country-houses on its top and below its steep side. In a recess under the hill stands the village, with a domed church, surmounted by a château.

rt. Below Montferrand, a small village hid by poplars, is a large *Château*, the residence of the late M. de Peyronnet, one of the ministers of Charles X. who signed the ordonnances.

rt. The tongue of land between the Garonne and Dordogne, called Entre Deux Mers, which produces a vast quantity of wines of inferior quality, draws to a termination at the low point called Bec d'Ambés. The union of the two rivers forms the broad estuary of the *Gironde*, whence the department is named. The monsters of the revolutionary Mountain, after overwhelming in 1793 their antagonists the Girondins (so called because the leaders came from this part of the country), swamped even the name of the department, which for several months bore that of "Ambés." A long line of low hills, faced towards the water with cliffs, lines the l. bank of the Gironde and Dordogne. Looking up the Dordogne, you perceive, on an eminence, Bourg, a small town of 3855 Inhab., where Louis XIV., when a child, resided with his mother, Anne of Austria, for nearly a year (1649-50), during the continuance of the siege of Bordeaux. Mazarin, in order to superintend the operations and watch the leaders of the Fronde within the city, had repaired in person to the S., dragging with him the King, the Regent, and the Court. The ladies in waiting complained bitterly of the want of a theatre to enliven the ennui of their residence, and the cardinal got angry with the mayor because the whole place could not furnish a sedan-chair to carry him through the steep and dirty streets. The extensive vineyards around Bourg produced the wines (claret) esteemed the best in the district 200 years ago, before the cultivation of the vine in Médoc had commenced, which does not date farther back than 250 years.

rt. The steamer stops to set down or take up passengers at the Pain de Sucre, a landing-place at the mouth of the Dordogne, close under the Bec d'Ambés, and about 1½ m. below Bourg. Two large islands are here formed in the middle of the Gironde.

l. Nearly abreast of the Pain de Sucre a glimpse may be obtained of the mansion of *Château Margaux*, situated some distance inland : it is an Italian villa, the handsomest in Médoc, and belongs to the heirs of the Spanish banker, the Marquis d'Aguado, though rarely inhabited, owing to the malaria which prevails around it. It stands in the midst of the vineyards producing the celebrated wine of Château Margaux, the most esteemed growth of Médoc. The grape which yields it is small and poor to the taste, with a flavour slightly resembling that of black currants. The Château is about ½ m. from the village of Margaux, which abounds in neat whitewashed villas, seated in little gardens, amidst acacia hedges and trellised vines. It is about 20 m. distant from Bordeaux. At Delas is a tolerable *Inn*.

rt. The yellow cliffs along the riverside are pierced to form cellars, in which is deposited the wine grown above them : and for a considerable extent near Gauriac they are excavated in quarries of building-stone. At the base of the cliffs are several small villages.

rt. *Blaye*. The dead walls and gloomy-looking modern bastions of the citadel of Blaye are seen projecting over the river at a height considerably above it. In the midst of them stands a fragment of the old feudal fortress, whose towers may be seen surmounting the turfed ramparts. This citadel was chosen as the prison of the Duchesse de Berri, who was confined here in a double sense after her capture in La Vendée (see Nantes), having been brought to bed of a daughter in 1833. After a detention of 7 months she was sent back to Naples. The body of Roland the Brave was, according to tradition, transported hither from Roncesvaux by Charlemagne, and interred in the *Church of St. Romain*, with his sword *Durandal* at his head, and his famous horn of ivory (Oliphant), with which he had awakened the echoes of Fuentarabia, at his feet. The body was afterwards transported to St. Sernin, at Bordeaux.

Opposite Blaye several islands have been formed in the middle of the river by the deposits brought down by the Dordogne and Garonne, and are constantly increasing. On one of them is planted the little fort *du Pâté*, so called from its round shape. It crosses its fire with that of the fortress of Blaye on the rt. bank, and of Fort

Médoc on the l., and thus commands the passage of the Gironde.

To the N. of Margaux the vines decline in quality; and it is not until after an interval of several miles of inferior vineyards that we reach others, producing wine of reputation, in the vicinity of

l. Beycheville, lying within the commune of *St. Julien*, a name of note on account of the wine grown in it. The *Château de Beycheville*, situated on the height in the midst of valuable vineyards, is the seat of M. Guestier, Pair de France, ancien Député, and one of the first wine-merchants of Bordeaux.

Here begin some of the most renowned vineyards of Médoc, which lie crowded together in almost uninterrupted succession, within a narrow space, stretching about 6 m. N. of Beycheville.

About 1½ m. off is *Château Léoville*, which produces one of the best second growths, nearly equalling the first growths. The estate is divided between Mr. Barton and M. de Las Cases. In the same commune is the vineyard of *La Rose*, a prime second growth; and in the adjoining one of St. Lambert is the vineyard of *Château Latour*, yielding a well-known wine, premier cru. The estate, which does not exceed 330 acres, was sold a few years ago for 60,000*l*. The second growths, Pichon-Longueville and Mouton, come from the same quarter.

l. Pauillac (*Inn:* H. de France), a small seaport, behind which, at the distance of about 1½ m., is the vineyard of *Château Lafitte*, producing one of the three best wines of Bordeaux; it is the property of Sir Claude Scott, and does not yield more than 400 hogsheads yearly. The region of good wines extends N. as far as Lesparre, but the wines are far inferior to those of the commune of Pauillac.

The aspect of the vine district of Médoc is that of an undulating country, slightly raised above the Garonne, affording here and there peeps of the river between the gentle hills and shallow gullies which intersect it. It abounds in marshes and stagnant pools, *France*.

which render it unhealthy, so that the châteaux which occur in it are inhabited only for a small part of the year by their proprietors. Yet the district is populous, a group of cottages being attached to almost every vineyard, and inhabited by the peasants who cultivate it. The vineyards are open fields; even those of greatest value being for the most part unprovided with walls, or even hedges, in order to avoid the loss of any space of ground which must be left round the margin to allow the plough to turn. When the grapes begin to ripen, a temporary fence is formed round the vines, of twisted boughs interwoven with furze, to keep out the dogs, which are most destructive consumers of grapes. Further to deter both bipeds and quadrupeds from committing depredations, guards armed with guns are posted on the watch, day and night, while streaks of paint, and bits of white paper stuck upon poles, announce that the vineyard is strewn with poisoned sausages, and that the grapes themselves are smeared with some deleterious mixture. The vines are planted in quincunx order on ridges (about 3 ft. apart): they are trained to espaliers, and not allowed to rise more than 2 ft. above the ground. In the best vineyards they barely cover the soil, but allow the singular mass of pebbles, of which it almost exclusively consists, to appear between the rows. The growth of the vine is confined within a narrow line of demarcation, and the transition is most abrupt from the most precious land to an uncultivated sandy desert. The distance of a few feet makes all the difference. The vintage takes place in the month of September, and it is then that Médoc presents a scene of bustle, activity, and rejoicing. The proprietors then repair hither with their friends and families to superintend the proceedings and make merry: vignerons pour in from the l. bank of the Gironde, to assist in the gathering. Busy crowds of men, women, and children sweep the vineyard from end to end, clearing all before them like bands of locusts, while the air resounds with

N

their songs and laughter. The utmost care is employed by the pickers to remove from the bunches all defective, dried, mouldy, or unripe grapes. Every road is thronged with carts filled with high-heaped tubs, which the labouring oxen are dragging slowly to the *Cuvier de pressoir* (pressing-trough). This is placed usually in a lofty outhouse, resembling a barn, whence issue sounds of still louder merriment, and a scene presents itself sufficiently singular to the stranger. Upon a square wooden trough (pressoir) stand 3 or 4 men with bare legs all stained with purple juice, dancing and treading down the grapes as fast as they are thrown in, to the tunes of a violin. The labour of constantly stamping down the fruit is desperately fatiguing, and without music would get on very slowly; a fiddler, therefore, forms part of every wine-grower's establishment; and as long as the instrument pours forth its merry strains, the treaders continue their dance in the gore of the grape, and the work proceeds diligently. The next process is to strip (égrapper) the broken grapes and skins from the stalks, with an instrument called dérapoir, and to pour the juice and skins into vats to ferment. The skin rises to the top, and the wine is drawn off into hogsheads as soon as fermentation is carried to the proper extent, in judging of which the utmost experience is required, as on it depends much of the quality of the vintage.

At Trompe-Loup is the Lazareth, where vessels from the Levant perform quarantine.

1. The cultivation of the vine ceases to the N. of Castillon, and the extreme point of Médoc, towards the mouth of the Gironde, consists of rich pasture-land, famed for its breed of cattle, and some corn-fields. It lies on a level with the surface of the sea, and was redeemed from the condition of marsh by a colony of Flemings, invited over to France by Henri IV., who surrounded it with sea-dikes like their own country.

rt. Mortagne. A diligence runs hence to Saintes in communication with the steamer.

rt. *Royan* (Inns: H. de Bordeaux, best: d'Orléans) is a neat small seaport town in the Dépt. of the Charente, about 25 m. from Rochefort, whither a *Diligence* runs. (Rte. 62.) It is a station of pilots, and is resorted to for sea-bathing. Steamer to Bordeaux in summer, in about 8 hrs.

On an isolated rock outside the mouth of the Gironde, which is beset with dangerous sandbanks, rises the lighthouse called *La Tour de Cordouan*, whose beacon guides mariners entering or quitting the river. It is a circular structure of three stories, the central one being domed like a church, from the midst of which rises a sort of pepper-box turret. It was designed in the reign of Henri II. by *Louis de Foix*, one of the architects of the Escurial, 1611, who is said to have died here, and to have been buried within it. It replaced a lighthouse founded by the English 1362-71, while the Black Prince was governor of Guienne. (See Rymer.)

ROUTE 76.

BORDEAUX TO BAYONNE, ST. JEAN DE LUZ, AND THE SPANISH FRONTIER.

227 kilom. = 141 Eng. m.

Malleposte daily in 14 hours, diligences daily in 19 hours, to *Bayonne*.

A *Railway* is in progress: commencing by the line to La Teste (Rte. 73, p. 259), it traverses the Landes to Dax, to which place it may be opened in 1854-55.

For a mile or two out of Bordeaux a succession of neat villas lines the road, and the ground is mostly laid out in vineyards. Here, however, the vines grow upright, and are not trained along the ground as in the more famous district of Médoc (p. 261). Their produce is a wine as black as ink, full of spirit, from which brandy is distilled. Before the end of the stage the country becomes open and heathy; it is, in fact, the border of that extensive region of flat sand called the *Landes*, to avoid which the high road to Spain makes a considerable circuit. (See Route 77.)

11 Bouscaut. Between 2 and 3 m. to the rt. of La Prade, a hamlet which is passed about the middle of this stage, lies the *Château de la Brède*, the birthplace and family seat of Montesquieu. It is a low many-sided castle, probably of the 15th centy., surmounted by a circular donjon entirely surrounded by the waters of the Guèmort, which forms a broad fosse around it, and served anciently to defend it from foes, since it can only be entered by three bridges (once drawbridges). it is far from imposing, either without or within; but retains its primitive condition nearly unaltered, together with some old portraits of the family Secondat, and, above all, the *chamber* of Montesquieu, with his simple bed, arm-chair, &c., nearly as he left it. The wainscoting on one side of the fireplace is rubbed by the motion of his foot resting against it, a habit attributed to him when seated in his easy chair, lost in thought, meditating on his works. It was here that he composed his work 'Sur la Grandeur et la Décadence des Romains,' while it is reported that the dark feudal cachot beneath the castle, which is entered by a stair from his room, was his resort while he was preparing his reflections 'On the Liberty of the Subject.'

12 Castres.—*Inn:* H. la Providence, good, but small. The road ascends the valley of the Garonne, but at the distance of 3 or 4 m. from the river, whose banks are described in Rte. 73.

12 Cerans. *Barsac*, passed in this stage, produces one of the best *white wines* grown on the Garonne; and 4 or 5 m. S. of Preignac lies the château of *Sauterne*, which gives its name to the best of all the white wines of this district.

12 Langon, on the l. bank of the Garonne, is described in Rte. 73. (*Inns:* Cheval Blanc; H. de France). Here the road to Toulouse (Rte.73) branches off, and our road quits the Garonne and turns nearly due S. penetrating through a portion of the Petites Landes. Few houses and no villages occur before

15 Bazas, an ancient town of 4300 Inhab., which existed in the time of the Romans, and is mentioned under the name Vesates by Ausonius, whose father was born here. It has a Gothic Church, once a cathedral, without transepts. The sculpture on the 3 portals of its façade is much defaced. Bazas retains on its outskirts fragments of the old town walls.

"About 6 m. W. of Bazas is Uzeste, a small village, with a *church* of the 13th cent., chiefly built by Pope Clement V., who died there in 1314. His tomb of black marble is preserved. His *Castle*, about 2 m. distant, is a fine ruin. See Villandraut, p. 254."—*P.* (*Inn:* Lion d'Or; small, but clean beds.)

17 Captieux lies in the midst of sand wastes and pine forests; the country presents all the characters of the Landes, and the road enters the Dept. so called shortly before reaching

15 Les Traverses.

15 Roquefort (*Inn:* H. de France; civil, and good fare), an insignificant town of 1600 Inhab., named from the rocks of tufa which border the bank of the Douze, a tributary of the Adour. This place must not be confounded with Roquefort, famed for cheese, in the Dept. Aveyron, near Rodez.

[About 20 m. W. of this, in the midst of the sandy Landes, is an obscure and wretched hamlet, called *Labrit* or *Albret*. It was the cradle of the Sires d'Albret, one of the oldest families of France, from whom sprang the illustrious Henri IV., the son of Jeanne d'Albret.]

Here the road from Bordeaux to Pau branches off to the l. (Rte. 80.)

12 Caloy. The chain of the Pyrenees, 30 leagues distant, may already be discovered in clear weather.

10 Mont de Marsan. (*Inn:* H. des Ambassadeurs; capital sleeping-place, civil people, good cuisine, and moderate charges. Ortolans may be had in August.) This is the chef-lieu of the Dept. des Landes (4463 Inhab.), and enjoys some commerce by virtue of its position at the junction of two streams, the Douze and Medou, which, becoming navigable here, take the name of Medouze. It is united with the Garonne by the Canal des Landes, nearly 60 m. long, designed to open a communication between Bayonne and Bordeaux when the sea is closed in time of war.

Roads branch off hence to Pau (Rte. 80), and to Orthez.

The road hence is somewhat less dull: it lies through extensive forests of spindly pines, whose sides are rasped or grooved to extract the *resin* which exudes from the wound, and is collected in a hollow at their foot.

13 Campagne. Beyond

14 Tartas, where the Medouze is crossed by a new bridge, are some fine oak woods.

11 Pontons. As before, the same alternation of pine woods and bare sand, not a pebble to be seen. Pyrenees well seen beyond Pontons.

Pouy, a village on the l. of the road shortly before reaching Dax, was the birthplace of the philanthropic founder of the order of Sœurs de la Charité, and of foundling hospitals, St. Vincent de Paul. When a boy he tended his father's flock in the sandy heaths near the Lazarist convent of Buglose. The road passes through the village of

12 St. Paul de Dax, about a mile distant from the town of Dax (*Inns :* H. St. Etienne ; de St. Esprit), which lies on the l. bank of the Adour, and is reached by a bridge of wood. Its name probably comes from its *hot springs* (de aquis), which are one of the curiosities of Guienne, and doubtless induced that bath-loving people the Romans to found here their settlement Aquæ Augustæ Tarbellicæ. They rise nearly in the centre of the town, and are received in a large square basin enclosed with porticoes, whence rise such clouds of steam as in a frosty morning to envelop all the town. The temperature at the source is 212° Fahrenheit, a scalding heat. The water is nearly tasteless, and, though only partially used medicinally, is much employed by the washerwomen. There are several other sources in and about the town. Near the bridge are portions of the old fortifications ; and Roman masonry may, it is said, be discovered in their substructions. Pop. 5509.

The tertiary strata near Dax abound in fossil shells.

The postmaster is entitled to charge 2 kilom. extra on carriages which cross the Adour into Dax from St. Paul.

The road beyond Dax traverses numerous forests of cork-trees, which, being stripped of their flaky bark to stop the claret bottles of the merchants of Bordeaux, have a singular effect, from the dark brown colour of their naked trunks. A new skin speedily repairs the loss of the old.

15 St. Geours.

The Pyrenean range now forms a grand feature in the landscape. They are not unlike some views of the Grampians, in which sharp peaks here and there surmount intervening round-backed hills : the most conspicuous and picturesque peaks seen from this are the Arrhune in France, and the Quatre Couronnes in Spain. Near

13 Cantons, a large pond or étang is passed, and a peep is obtained over the Bay of Biscay on the rt.

The direct road from Bordeaux across the Grandes Landes (Rte. 77) falls into ours at St. Vincent, and the Landes cease altogether at Oudres.

The descent upon Bayonne presents that town under a striking aspect, seated on the Adour, surrounded by fortifications. A short way before you reach the Octroi, a lane on the rt. leads down to the *Cimetière Anglais*, a simple enclosure between 4 walls, planted with poplars ; it contains the remains of many brave British soldiers, and several officers of the Coldstream Guards, who fell in the sortie from Bayonne, April 14, 1814. Bayonne is entered by the Faubourg of St. Esprit, in which is situated the *Citadel*, the strongest of the military works. The town itself is reached by a new stone bridge over the Adour, and, after crossing the angular strip of land between the rivers, by a stone and iron bridge over the Nive.

19 BAYONNE.—*Inns :* H. St. Etienne ; H. du Commerce ; H. de l'Europe.

Bayonne, a strong fortress of the first class, commanding the Passes of the W. Pyrenees, and one of the two carriage-roads leading from Spain into France, has an agreeable situation at the junction of the Nive with the Adour, and is divided into three parts

PLANCHE (S) EN **2.**
PRISES DE VUE

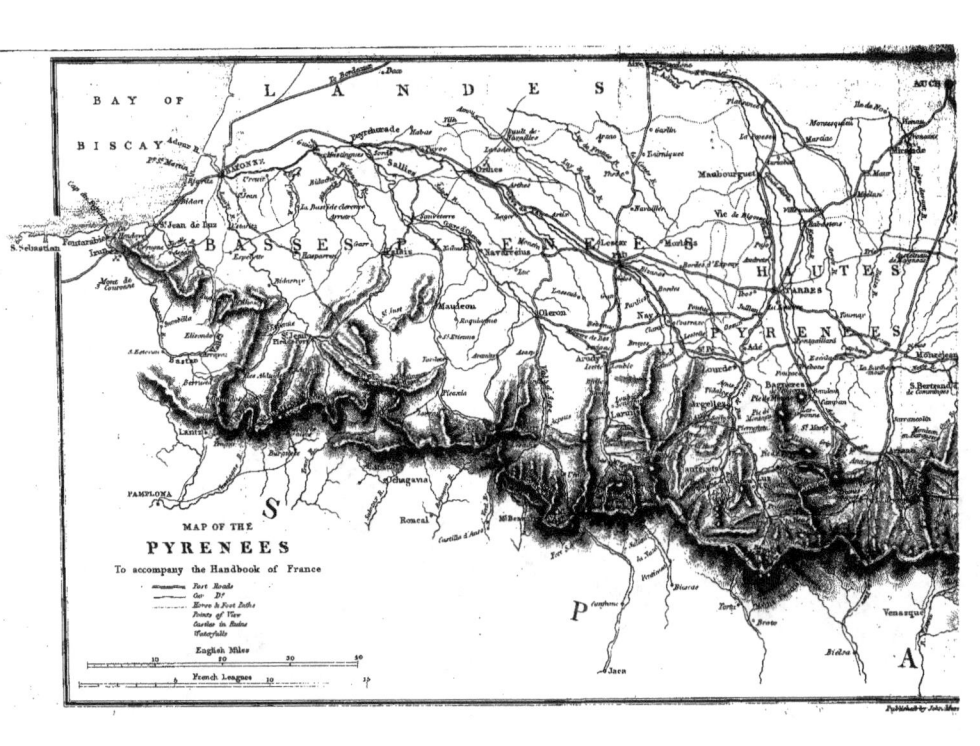

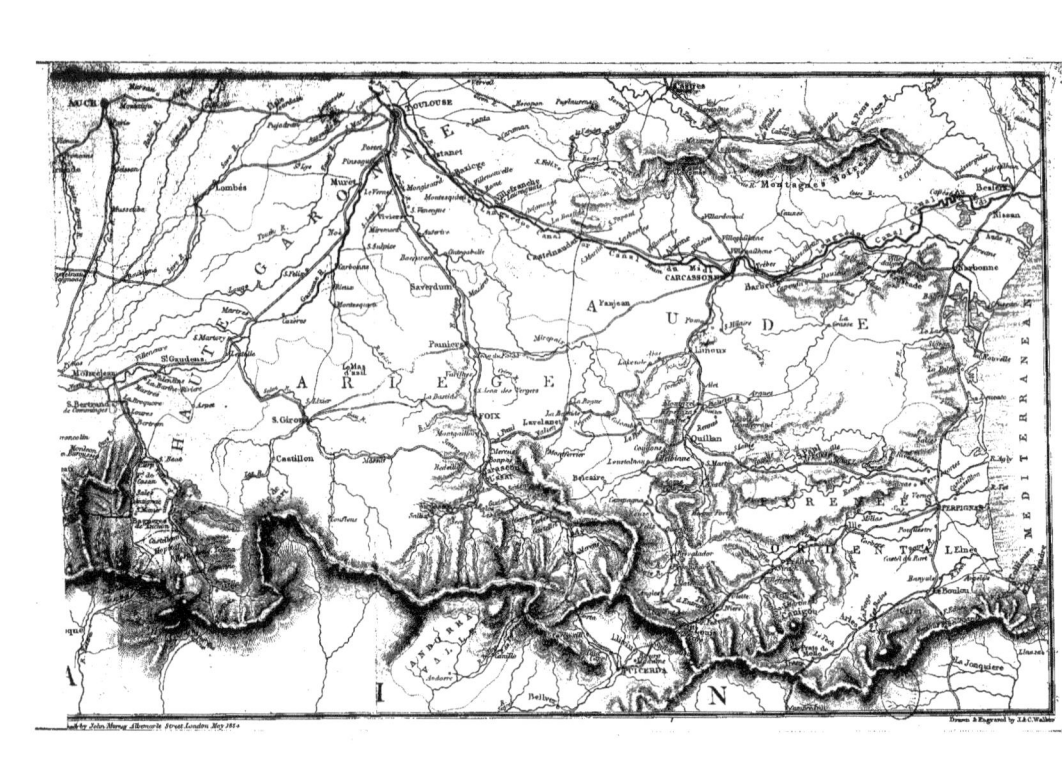

by these fine broad rivers, which are lined with quays, and always include a small quantity of shipping. The suburb St. Esprit, on the rt. bank of the Adour, lies within the Dépt. des Landes, and alone includes 5897 Inhab. (more than the chief town of the dépt.), among whom are 2000 Jews, descendants of those expelled at different times from Spain. On an eminence rising above this suburb, just at the lower end of it and commanding with its formidable batteries the town, both the rivers, and the plain to the N., rises the *Citadel*, the most formidable of the works laid out by Vauban, and greatly strengthened, especially since 1814, when it formed the key to an intrenched camp of Marshal Soult, and was invested by a detachment of the army of the Duke of Wellington, but not taken, the peace having put a stop to the siege after some bloody encounters. The last of these, a dreadful and useless expenditure of human life, took place after peace was declared, and the British forces put off their guard in consequence. They were thus entirely taken by surprise by a sally of the garrison, made early on the morning of April 14th; which, though repulsed, was attended with the loss of 830 men to the British, and by the capture of their commander, Sir John Hope, whose horse was shot under him, and himself wounded. The French attack was supported by the fire of their gunboats on the river, which opened indiscriminately on friend and foe. 910 of the French were killed. Admission to the citadel is obtained by a ticket from the commandant; but, except to a military man, it possesses nothing of interest. Steep approaches, resembling inclined planes, lead up to it, deep fosses surround it, nearly vertical walls, 40 feet high, and numerous bastions flank and enfilade every access to it; visitors are not allowed to mount the ramparts.

Bayonne Proper occupies the triangular space between the two rivers, and stretches for a considerable distance up the bank of the Nive, which is crossed by 3 bridges. Its total population, excluding St. Esprit, is 16,299 souls. Many of the streets have a half Spanish character from the piazzas running under the houses. The handsomest quarter of the town is that adjoining the theatre, newly built, consisting of fine tall houses.

The only building of consequence is *the Cathedral*, ugly externally, but within a fine lofty church in the pointed Gothic of the 13th centy., with choir and transepts very short. The arms of England are still visible on its roof. The cloisters behind, in the florid style, nearly the largest in France, deserve notice. From the top of its tower there is a good *view* of the distant Pyrenees, of the town, rivers, and citadel, and of the spot a little below it, at the extremity of the long avenue of trees, where a part of the British army under Sir John Hope crossed by a bridge of boats furnished from the fleet of Admiral Penrose, and transported with much difficulty over the bar, Feb. 23-27, 1814, in order to invest the citadel.

As very malignant calumnies have been spread by some French writers respecting the conduct of the Duke of Wellington's army in France, it may not be amiss to refute them by the unexceptionable testimony of one of their own writers, and an eye-witness, the late M. Vayse de Villiers, author of the *Itinéraire de la France*, the best guide-book for that country. He traversed the theatre of the war only a few months after the occupation by the Duke of Wellington, and states that, so far from laying waste the country to a distance of a league around Bayonne, as a French writer had asserted, "Il avait établi une telle discipline qu'il était accueilli partout comme libérateur."—*Route de Paris en Espagne*, p. 91.

The Duke's own immortal Dispatches show with what severe discipline he prevented the troops, Spanish and English, under his command, imitating the cruel injuries which the French army had inflicted on Spain and other countries invaded by them.

The construction of the bridge over

the Adour below Bayonne, and the passage of the Allies across it, display the genius of Wellington in conceiving, combining, and executing a measure deemed impossible by his opponents; and is styled by Colonel Napier "a stupendous undertaking, which will always rank among the prodigies of war." The impediments consisted in the breadth of the river, the rapidity of its current, the height to which the tide rises (14 feet), the difficulty of procuring and transporting the materials of the bridge : since, if sent by land, through bad and difficult roads, they must have alarmed the enemy; if by water, the bar, passable only at high water, and surf at the river's mouth, rendered the entrance of boats next to impossible. The latter measure, however, had been decided on by the Duke; and to effect this purpose a little flotilla of chassemarées had been prepared in the Spanish harbour of Passages. But the long prevalence of storms and contrary winds had rendered its approach impracticable; and the gallant Sir John Hope, to whom the execution of this measure had been intrusted by the Duke of Wellington, at last on the 23rd of February, 1814, began to push his troops across upon a raft attached to a hawser; and thus, in the teeth of a strong fortress and garrison of nearly 15,000 men, 600 men of the Guards gained the opposite bank; the French gunboats which guarded the river being silenced by rockets, three of them burnt, and a sloop of war driven up the river under the guns of Bayonne, while the same effective weapons kept the garrison at bay. Next morning, in spite of the tempestuous weather and the raging surf on the bar, which was so furious as to leave no strip of black water to point out the passage;—without pilots, with no landmarks on the shore, the little fleet made for the mouth of the Adour. Each vessel had an engineer on board, and a supply of timber, cables, &c., and, aided by men of war's boats from the fleet, they boldly dashed into the midst of the breakers, blindly seeking the entrance. Several of the foremost, mastered by the wind and the waves, ran aground or were dashed ashore, and their crews perished. This did not deter the others, however; one more fortunate boat discovered the only safe channel, and the rest, following in its wake, gained smooth water within the bar—a glorious and gallant exploit. The 26 chassemarées thus introduced were moored head and stern by ropes stretched over the dykes which line the river at a spot where it is 800 ft. broad, at a distance of about 3 m. below Bayonne. Platforms of loose planks were laid between the boats, and the ropes were left slack, so as to allow the bridge to rise and fall with the tide; yet this seemingly frail structure was strong enough to bear the heaviest artillery, and it was finished by the 26th. This deep-laid scheme entirely foiled Marshal Soult, whose attention had been drawn off by the British general to an attack among the Gaves, the tributaries of the Adour high up the country, at the very moment when the passage of that river was effected close to the sea.

Bayonne is a town of commerce as well as of war, though its port is of comparatively small use, on account of the shifting bar at the *mouth of the Adour*, which can only be passed at high water, and not without danger at some seasons, though the employment of tug-steamers now diminishes the risk. In the 14th or 15th centy. the Adour changed its bed, owing to its mouth becoming obstructed by shifting sands or dunes blown up by the winds, and running N. parallel with the coast within this sand-wall, until it found an outlet either at Cape Breton or at Vieux Boucaut. This lasted down to 1579, when the engineer, Louis de Foix, restored it to its old channel, called Boucaut Neuf. In 1684, however, it broke a fresh channel for itself to the l., in the direction of the Chambre d'Amour, but was brought back again shortly after to the bed by which it still finds a passage to the ocean through a waste of sand-hills.

The commerce of Bayonne consists chiefly in Spanish wool, which is largely imported, and in an extensive smuggling trade carried on with that country.

Excellent *chocolate* and *eau de vie* are made here; but the *Bayonne hams*, so called because largely exported hence, are reared and cured among the Pyrenees, near Orthez and Pau. Some ships are built here.

From what has been said, it will be perceived that Bayonne has few sights to amuse the passing stranger. The well-supplied *markets*, abounding in fruit and vegetables, sold at the cheapest rates, are worth a visit; and these, or the promenades, will afford an opportunity of seeing the Bayonnaise ladies, who are remarkably pretty, as well as the Basquaise peasants, who are also distinguished by pretty faces and good figures, and contrast with the inhabitants of the Landes to the N. of Bayonne.

Those who desire a pleasant shady walk and fresh air should repair to the *Allées Marines*, an avenue of trees more than a m. long, on the l. bank of the Adour, below the town and opposite the citadel, reaching down almost to the bend of the river, near which the Duke threw his army across.

A little way outside the town is the dilapidated *Château de Marrac*, destroyed by fire in 1825 and gutted. It belonged to Napoleon, who here received the degraded sovereigns of Spain, Charles IV. and his queen, and her minion Godoy likewise. The Emperor also brought hither to meet them Ferdinand Prince of Asturias, whom, by false pretences, he had entrapped from Madrid in 1808: and in this château, under threat of death or imprisonment, they resigned to him their hereditary rights to the crown of Spain.

Bayonne was the capital of the ancient district, enclosed within the Adour and Bidassoa, called Pays de Labourd (from *Lapurdum*), by which it was known down to the 10th centy. The name Bayonne is merely the Basque Baia una, a port. Hence comes the word *Bayonnette*, said to have been invented in this neighbourhood (see p. 274), and first made here. The gloomy old *Castle* opposite the Sous-Préfecture, now a barrack, was probably the residence of Catherine de Medicis when she dragged hither her weak son, Charles IX., to that secret conference with the Duke of Alva, in 1563, at which, it is now known, the massacre of the St. Bartholomew's night was suggested and decided on. Yet Bayonne has the rare credit of refusing to execute the bloody orders of Charles IX. to slay all the Protestants in the town, owing to the firmness of the governor, Dapremont, Vicomte d'Orthez, who told the king that the town of Bayonne included only good citizens and brave soldiers, but not a single executioner.

The chief place of resort for the inhabitants of Bayonne out of the town is the little watering-place of *Biaritz*, described farther on (p. 272.)

Cambo, in the vale of Nive, is also a pretty watering-place, with mineral baths. *Inn:* H. des Etrangers.

A short but interesting *excursion into Spain* may be made by taking the diligence to St. Sebastian (*Inn:* Parador Real), which starts every morning. You pass through a portion of the country which was the theatre of the Carlist war, visit the citadel of St. Sebastian and the singular land-locked harbour of Passages, eat an olla, and smoke a cigarillo, and may return to Bayonne the following afternoon. See HANDBOOK FOR SPAIN.

The *British Consul*, residing at Bayonne (Captain Graham), will sign his countrymen's passports for the journey.

In the coach-offices and inns at Bayonne will be found hung up advertisements of approaching *Bull Fights*, to be held at Vittoria, Tolosa, Saragossa, and other places in the N. of Spain, in the vicinity of the French frontier.

Conveyances:—*Mallepostes* daily to Bordeaux in 14 hours; to Toulouse in 21 hours.

Railway to Bordeaux in progress.

Diligences daily to Bordeaux (2 or 3); to Toulouse; to Pau, by Orthez.

Conveyances into Spain; to Madrid—*Malleposte* travels by night, and is three nights on the journey.

Diligences, belonging to different companies—to Madrid.

Diligences every other day to Tolosa and St. Sebastian in 10 hours.

The Southern Road quits Bayonne by the Porte d'Espagne, through which Napoleon poured so many gallant armies in succession into the Peninsula. The road is hilly the whole way to the frontier, and from time to time affords glimpses of the season the rt. After passing a number of country-houses, amongst which, at a little distance on the l., stands the Château de Marrac (p. 271), a fingerpost at the end of 2 m. points the sandy way to *Biaritz* (*Inns:* H. de Monhau; rooms small, but clean and comfortable;—H. des Ambassadeurs;—H. Dumont); a little secluded watering-place, lying 3 m. on the rt. and about 5 m. from Bayonne. It consists of a group of whitewashed lodging-houses, cafés, inns, traiteurs, cottages, &c., generally of an humble character, scattered over rolling eminences and hollows bare of trees, on the sea-shore, here fenced with cliffs 40 or 50 feet high, excavated by the waves into numberless quiet coves and curious caverns. In these the sea at times roars and chafes, perforating the rock with holes, and undermining huge masses, which are detached from time to time; and some of them, left like islands at some distance from the shore, still project above the waves. From the tops of these cliffs, especially that which bears the ruins of an old fort or lighthouse, you look over the wide expanse of the Bay of Biscay, bounded on the rt. by the French coast, on which rises the new *Phare*, showing the way into the mouth of the Adour; and on the l. by the shore of Spain beyond St. Sebastian, with peaks of distant Sierras rising behind it. The limpid purity of the sea and the smoothness of the sand render bathing in the sheltered bays most agreeable. French ladies and gentlemen " en costume des bains " consume hours in aquatic promenades. The ladies may be seen floating about like mermaids, being supported on bladders, corks, or gourds, attired in woollen trousers covering the feet, and overshadowed by broad-brimmed hats.

The geologist will be interested to recognise in the rocks of Biaritz the fossils of the lower chalk and greensand, though the rock here assumes an external character very different from that we are accustomed to in England. Beyond its sea-bathing, its rocks, and its view, Biaritz must be the dullest place upon earth, except to those who have other resources of friends, &c., on the spot. Omnibuses and coucous are constantly plying between the baths and the Porte d'Espagne of Bayonne. The ancient mode of conveyance hither, which is peculiar to the spot, but is now becoming obsolete, was to ride " *en cacolet*." In this mode of conveyance, the rider, seated on one side of a hack, in a wooden frame fitting to a horse's back, as a pair of spectacles does to a human nose, occupies the place of a pannier on one side of an ass's back, while his conductor, usually a stout and buxom lass, fills the opposite division, and by her weight the balance is preserved. Some little skill is required in mounting, for, unless both parties jump into their seats at the same moment, he who reaches it prematurely runs the risk of destroying the equipoise and of being capsized into the dust, and the same in dismounting. It is chiefly peasants and market-women, now-a-days, who ride en cacolet; though, under the ancien régime of the Bourbons, the frolicsome Duchesse de Berri, when on a visit to this part of France, was wont to resort to this primitive conveyance.

There are 3 lines of custom-houses on the road from Bayonne to the Spanish frontier. The 3rd, or innermost, is not more than 5 m. from Bayonne. A large fresh-water pond within a funnel-shaped basin is passed shortly before reaching.

11 Bidart. We now enter the *Pays Basques*, inhabited by that peculiar race who speak a language having no relation with any other in Europe. They occupy in France only a small part of the S.W. corner of the Dépt. des Basses Pyrénées, but are much more widely disseminated in Spain, where they form the mass of the population of 5 provinces. The French and

Spanish Basques are distinguished by their speech, and also by their costume, consisting of the red beret, a cap resembling that of the lowland shepherd in Scotland, a red sash round the waist, and sandals made of hemp, called Espartillas, on the feet, and a stout stick in the hand. They are supposed to be the descendants of the "Cantabrum indoctum ferre juga nostra," who sided with Hannibal in opposing the Romans, who contributed mainly to the defeat of Charlemagne and Roland in the pass of Roncesvaux, and whose boast is that they were never conquered. In France they are confined to portions of the arrondissements of Bayonne and Mauléon, which formed part of the ancient kingdom of Navarre.

9 St. Jean de Luz.—*Inns:* H. de France, very good; Poste; St. Etienne. A frontier town of France, at the mouth of the Nivelle, where it falls into a small creek or bay, over which a new bridge has been thrown. The inroads of the sea for some time past have washed away parts of the town, breaking through the dykes thrown up to protect it, and the shifting sands at the mouth of the Nivelle have almost entirely blocked up its port. The town is distinguished by its narrow street and whitewashed houses, some of considerable antiquity. Here is the 2nd Douane. The suburb on the l. bank of the river is called Sibourre. The marriage of Louis XIV. with Maria Theresa, Infanta of Spain, was celebrated here 1660.

In Nov. 1813, the British army, under the Duke of Wellington, crossed the Nivelle close to this town, after attacking and carrying the very strong intrenched position occupied by the French army upon the heights on the l. bank of the river.

In the midst of barren, heathy, high ground stands

5 Urugne, last post-station in France. The forms of the mountains are picturesque, especially of that called *Montagne d'Arrhune*, rising above Urugne, which is visible even on the other side of Bayonne. Before reaching this point the traveller finds, contrary probably to what he could have expected from books, that the mountain chain of the Pyrenees by no means terminate in France, but stretches W. in lofty ridges and bare peaks tossed about in wild confusion, traversing Spain to its farther corner, and ending in Cape Ortegal in the Asturias.

Beyond Urugne, the antique Château of Urtubi is passed. Louis XI. came hither, 1462, to meet the King of Aragon, John II.

The French frontier *custom-house* is placed at *Behobia*, a small village (*Inn:* H. de la Bidassoa, kept by Fayes, good) on the rt. bank of the Bidassoa, which here separates France from Spain. The baggage of travellers entering France is strictly searched; and after it has undergone the process, they will do well to have it plombed, to save themselves from a repetition of the same twice between this and Bayonne. 10 sous is the charge for plombing each package.

The wild and lofty mountains around and behind Behobia, called Montagne Verte and Mendele, now so solitary, were strongly fortified by Marshal Soult in 1813, to defend the *Passage of the Bidassoa*, which the Duke of Wellington effected nevertheless, in the face and in spite of them. In the course of several months preceding, intrenchment behind intrenchment had been thrown up by the French; every weak point had been strengthened, and the whole line of slopes and precipices, from the sea to the Arrhune mountain, bristled with ramparts and batteries, defending the fords of the river; the bridge of Behobia being then broken down.

From the middle of the existing wooden bridge, which unites France to Spain, the stranger looking up the stream will perceive the green knoll or mamelon of St. Marcial; on this a strong battery was planted by the Allies, which covered the passage, by the ford higher up, of one division, consisting of Spaniards, under Gen. Freire, who won from the French the heights of Mendele. The most formidable part of the French position was the Montagne d'Arrhune, not only from its elevation, steepness, and tremendous precipices, but from the redoubts, intrenchments, abattis, &c., thrown up on it, wherever there appeared the least facility of approach, and from the strong body of troops who held every commanding point, sweeping the slopes and ravines with their cannon and musketry. The Duke of Wellington employed nearly 20,000 men in the attack of this mountain, which was gained, as it were, inch by inch, the enemy being driven from one work after another up to the very summit, where they occupied a rocky height called the Hermitage. This was nearly impregnable, and they defended it for some time merely by rolling down stones upon their assailants. The bones of many a brave man are probably even now whitening among the dells and clefts of that rugged mountain: many who were wounded were left to perish where they fell, from the difficulty of discovering them among these vast solitudes.

A lower ridge, or projecting buttress, of the Montagne d'Arrhune, is called *La Bayonnette*, from that weapon of war, invented extemporaneously, it is said, on this spot, by a Basque regiment, who, having run short of ammunition, assaulted the Spaniards opposed to them by sticking the long knives which the Basques commonly carry into the barrels of their muskets, and thus charging the enemy. This must have occurred some time in the 16th or early in the 17th century. The ridge of the Bayonnette was stormed and carried by the Allies 1813, before they gained the Arrhune.

Behind St. Marcial opens out the Valley of the Bastan, the cradle of the Bidassoa. Close below the bridge of Behobia is a little island, reduced by the washing of the current to a narrow strip of earth, tufted with grass and willows. This is the historically celebrated *Ile des Faisans*, on which the conferences were held between the French Minister Mazarin and the Spanish Don Louis de Haro, which led to the famous treaty of the Pyrenees, 1659, and the marriage of Louis XIV. with the daughter of Philip IV. Each party advanced from its own territory, by a temporary bridge, to this little bit of neutral ground, which then reached nearly up to the bridge. The piles which supported the Cardinal's pavilion were visible not many years ago. The death of Velasquez, the painter, was caused by his exertions in superintending these constructions; duties more fitting to an upholsterer than an artist.

The Bidassoa forms the line of demarcation between the two kingdoms only for about 12 m.: it enters the sea about 5 m. below Behobia, between Andaye on the French side, and the ancient walled town of Fuentarabía (accent on the i) on the Spanish, after passing near the town of

9 Irun, first Spanish post-station. (See HANDBOOK FOR SPAIN.)

Between Irun and Fuentarabia are the 3 fords discovered by the Duke of Wellington, on the information of Spanish fishermen, by which he carried one division of his army across, and, gaining the first permanent footing in the French territory, turned the rt. of the French position, and the strongly defended heights near Andaye (once famed for distilling brandy). These fords were practicable only at certain states of the tide, and for 3 or 4 hours, being covered by the sea, to a depth of 14 ft., at high water. Soult was therefore perfectly unprepared for an attempt to cross at this point, and his troops were deceived by the tents of the British camp being left standing as though still occupied. At the close of a fierce thunder-storm, early on the morning of Oct. 17, the allied army formed into 7 columns behind banks and ridges, issued forth at a given signal, and winding slowly, like snakes, across the broad sands, effected the passage.

ROUTE 77.

BORDEAUX TO BAYONNE, THROUGH LES GRANDES LANDES.

About 116 Eng. m. The Railroad now in progress from Bordeaux to Bayonne adopts at first the line to *La Teste*, p. 259 ; but before reaching that place diverges S., and closely adheres to the direction of the following route, diverging, however, to Dax (Rte. 76).

This was once the high road into

Spain; but since the construction of the route through the Petites Landes (Rte. 76), and the removal of post-horses from this line, it has been almost entirely abandoned, although it is 25 m. shorter than the other. In fact, it traverses a country scarcely practicable for carriages, owing to the want of proper materials for the roads; a small portion only, near Bordeaux and Muret, being paved. The accommodation for travellers is, of course, very scanty. Many of the old post-stations enumerated below, with the distances from one to another, are mere single houses or stables, established solely as relays, and perhaps now abandoned.

3 Gradignan. Beyond this village fields give place to heaths and pine-woods, interspersed with a few patches of barley and a little maize; for these crops will grow wherever manure and industry can be employed upon the soil. The surface of the ground is of a dull grey or ash-coloured sand. A few flocks of lean, tattered, ill-conditioned sheep wander over this waste, tended by shepherds renowned for walking on stilts (échasses). By the aid of these they are not only enabled to stalk over the prickly bushes, and avoid the inconvenience of filling their shoes with sand, but they gain an elevation not afforded by the even surface of the ground, from which they can overlook their flock, and prevent their sheep straying. They carry a long pole, which, when stuck into the ground, forms a support, and against it they can rest and knit stockings all the day through. A stranger, unprepared for the sight, would have some difficulty in explaining the nature of the extraordinary tripod thus formed; and the sheep-skins worn by the peasant would not diminish the mystery. The peasants of the Landes are all accustomed to the use of stilts, and with a very slight exertion, and not a very quick movement, will clear the country at a pace which would keep a horse at a hard trot, by the aid of these wooden legs. "The inhabitants are rather diminutive in size, and not a very long-lived race. They endure severe privations—among them, the want of water. Even the lower animals must here change their nature to accommodate themselves to the soil. I saw large flocks of ducks which, I was assured, had never seen a pond!"—*F.*

There is at least one thing which appears peculiarly at home among the Landes, which seems to rejoice in this dry sand, and to flourish in the most robust vigour—the *pine* (Pinus maritima). Nearly $\frac{1}{4}$ of the Dépt. des Landes is covered with dark forests of this tree, and the distribution of it is greatly increasing, since, from the value of the timber and of the rosin which it produces, and the facility with which it is grown, large districts have been planted by order of the government. The Landes, it must be remembered, are not confined to the dept. so called, for we have hitherto been traversing that of the Gironde, and it is only between Bélin and the next station,

3 Muret, that the boundary line of the Dépt. des Landes is passed. Here the small river Leyre is crossed, which falls into the sea at La Teste. Like all the streams of the district, its waters are brackish; and one of the chief evils to which the inhabitants are subject is the want of good water.

2 Bellevue.
2 Puch.
3 Barps.
2 Hospitalet.
2 Bélin, a small town.
3 Lipostey.
4 Bonhère. Here used to be the best inn on the line.
3 Belloe, a single cottage.
4 La Harie.
3 Esperon.
4 Castels.

The *Pignadas*, or pine-forests of the Landes, furnish a large quantity of rosin, which is obtained by grooving the trunk, or scarifying the bark, 3 or 4 ft. above the root, and allowing the pitch to flow into a hollow below.

4 Majèse. An inn here formerly.
3 Les Monts.
2 St. Vincent. Here our road falls into the post-road from Bordeaux to
9 BAYONNE (Rte. 76, p. 268).

The wild district of the Landes stretches uninterruptedly from the Garonne at Bordeaux to the Adour at

Bayonne, and from the sea to Mont St. Marsan and Dax.

The inhabitants of the Landes occupy a low position, physically and morally, in the scale of civilisation.

ROUTE 78.

BAYONNE TO PAU, BY ORTHEZ.

105 kilom.= 65½ Eng. m.

Malleposte to Pau and Toulouse daily. *Diligences* daily by Orthez and by Oloron.

The road turns to the rt., out of that to Bordeaux (Rte. 76), on the top of the hill above St. Esprit, the suburb of Bayonne. It runs in a direction nearly parallel with the Pyrenees, through a country abounding in heath, having the Adour at some distance on the rt., until, a few miles beyond

17 Biaudos, that river is crossed: the descent upon it is fine. The Gave de Pau falls into the Adour a little below the bridge; henceforth we ascend the rt. bank of that stream all the way to Pau. Hereabouts the Gave divides the district called Chalosse from the Pays Basque (see p. 272).

20 Peyrehorade (*Inn:* H. de Voyageurs; second rate), a prettily situated town, on the Gave de Pau, just below its junction with the Gave d'Oloron, under a height crowned by a ruined *Castle* mentioned by Froissart. About a mile out of the town a turning on the rt. carries the new road to Pau by Oloron (unfinished 1841) across the Gave de Pau, by a new wire suspension bridge. It passes through Sorde, a walled town, Sallies, so called from its strong brine spring, which furnishes the salt used in curing Bayonne hams, and Sauveterre.

The road from Peyrehorade to Orthez crosses, shortly before entering

16 Puyoo, a rivulet which anciently formed the boundary-line between the kingdoms of France and Navarre.

The fertility of the plain, the abundant watercourses, the luxuriant festoons of the vines, and the magnificent views of the Pyrenean range, give great interest to this portion of the route. At Berenz, Sir Stapylton Cotton's division of cavalry, and Picton's 3rd brigade, crossed the Gave before the *Battle of Orthez.* That victory was achieved, Feb. 27, 1814, by driving the French from a very strong position on the heights above Orthez, extending from the town to the high road to Dax and the village of Boés. The retreat of the enemy ended in a flight, and they were pursued by the British, the same night, as far as Sault de Navailles. A wound received by the Duke of Wellington in the critical moment of pursuit contributed to save the French from greater loss. They attribute their defeat to a superiority of force on the side of the Allies, but the impartial estimate of Col. Napier sets down the numbers of Soult's army at 40,000 (including 4000 or 5000 raw conscripts), and that of the Duke at 37,000. The British cavalry outnumbered that of the enemy by 1000. The French lost nearly 4000 men killed, wounded, and prisoners; the Allies, 2300.

12 Orthez (*Inns:* H. Jennes;—H. Bergerot) is a somewhat dull town of 7000 Inhab., though situated at the junction of 6 roads,—to Spain, by St. Jean Pied de Port, to Dax, to Bordeaux, to Oloron, to Pau, and to Bayonne. It has an old Gothic *bridge*, which resisted the attempts of the French to mine it and blow it up, consisting of 4 arches, surmounted in the centre by a tower from which, according to tradition, the Calvinist soldiers of the army of the Comte de Montgomery, after taking the town by assault, 1569, and putting to the sword most of its defenders, precipitated into the river the Roman Catholic priests who were found with arms in their hands, and who refused to abjure their religion. Jeanne d'Albret, Queen of Navarre, mother of Henri IV., established here a Protestant College. The little Inn La Belle Hôtesse was Froissart's "La Lune."

Orthez was once a place of greater importance, as residence of the Princes of Béarn down to the end of the 15th centy., when they removed to Pau. The *Castle de Moncada*, built by Gaston de Foix, IV., 1240, after the pattern of a Spanish castle of that name, is reduced to a few ruined walls, overtopped by one stately tower, left to attest its former splendour, on a height above the town. It is mentioned by Froissart, who paid a visit to Gaston Phœbus Comte de Foix, 1388, and was received into the household, in order to obtain, from the Count's own mouth, information for his history respecting the wars in Gascony and Spain. He describes the death of Gaston de Foix, at the neighbouring village of Riou, on his return from hunting the bear, and the celebration of his funeral in the Church of the Cordeliers at Orthez, where he was buried in front of the grand altar. The Castle of Orthez was the scene of unparalleled crimes during the life of the brutal Gaston Phœbus, who filled its dungeons with the victims of his unbridled passion; among them his own kinsman, the Viscomte de Châteaubon, Pierre Arnaut, the faithful governor of Lourdes, who, because he refused to betray his trust, and surrender the fortress, was stabbed by Gaston's own hand, and thrust into a dungeon to perish; and, finally, his own son and only child, whom he killed with his knife, in the dark cell into which he had caused him to be thrust. The *churches* of *La Trinité* (1107) and of *St. Pierre* deserve notice.

The very picturesque peak called Pic du Midi d'Ossau is visible near this.

20 Artix. About 4 m. before entering Pau, the road passes, at a short distance on the l., the curious old and decayed town *Lescar*, supposed by some to be the ancient *Beneharnum*, whence the district of which it was originally the capital was called Béarn. The town was sacked and ruined during the wars of Religion, 1569, by the troops of the Comte de Montgomery. On a detached eminence, rising above the town, stand the Castle and the *Ch.* of *Notre Dame*, a decayed edifice, 10th centy., partly in the Romanesque style, containing carved oak stalls in the choir, and a curious mosaic pavement under the flooring. The early princes of Béarn, including Henri d'Albret, grandfather of Henri IV., and his wife, the Marguerite des Marguerites, were buried in it; but their tombs were destroyed either by the Huguenots or the Revolutionists. There is a fine view of the mountains from the cathedral terrace.

The *Jesuits' College*, founded here by Henri IV. after his conversion, has been turned into a manufactory.

Still nearer to Pau, on the l. of the road, is Bilhère, where Henri was nursed by a peasant, whose humble dwelling is still preserved and pointed out with some pride to strangers. The eminence rising on the opposite bank of the Gave, its slopes covered with verdure and vineyards, is the *Côte de Jurançon*, which produces the best of all the Pyrenean wines.

The road, before entering Pau, skirts the woody ridge which forms its beautiful Parc; and which, intervening between the river and the road, conceals the view of the mountains.

20 PAU (Rte. 80).

ROUTE 79.

BORDEAUX TO AUCH, BY CASTEL JALOUX AND NERAC.

186 kilom. = 115 Eng. m.
The road is the same as Rte. 76 as far as
61 Bazas.
14 Grignols.
15 Castel Jaloux, a town of nearly 2000 Inhab., owing its name and origin to a *Castle* built by the Seigneurs d'Albret, on the l. bank of the Avance, now in ruins.

At Barbaste corks are made. Henri IV. had a flour-mill here, whence he was sometimes called "le Meunier de Barbaste:" it still exists.

17 Pompiey. The road passes a little to the S. of the castle of Xaintrailles, the birthplace of Pothon de Xaintrailles, a knight celebrated in the wars against the English in the reign of Charles VII., who took the valiant Talbot prisoner at the battle of Patay.

13 *Nérac* (*Inn:* Tertres; famous for its *pâtés*, or *terrines* de perdrix), a town of 7090 Inhab., pleasingly situated on the Baïse, once capital of the duchy d'Albret. It was an ancient possession of the family d'Albret, who built and resided in the venerable *Castle*, which remained nearly entire down to the Revolution, but is now demolished, excepting one wing, and its fosses turned into gardens. Yet even this fragment is interesting, because within its walls Marguerite

d'Angoulême, Queen of Navarre, held her court, assembling around her the men most distinguished by learning and literary genius of the time; among others, Calvin, Beza, Clement Marot, here found an asylum from persecution down to 1534. At a later period, the "Bon Roi Henri," whose mother resided in the castle to within four months of his birth, passed here a portion of his youth. His chamber is pointed out at the W. end of the building. Here, in 1579, Catherine de Medicis held a conference. The tomb of Pothon de Xaintrailles was destroyed along with the ch. of Cordeliers, at the instigation of the Calvinists.

The promenade called *La Garenne* was once the park of the kings of Navarre, planted by Marguerite de Valois. A bronze statue of Henri IV. has been erected to his memory by a private individual, inscribed "Alumno, mox Patri Nostro Ho. IV."

The *Fontaine de St. Jean* is overshadowed by 2 elms, planted by Henri IV. and Marguerite de Valois.

Corks are manufactured here for the wine-merchants of Bordeaux.

We enter the Dépt. de Gers before reaching

22 Condom (*Inns*: Cheval Blanc; Lion d'Or), a town of 7144 Inhab., and of considerable trade. It has a handsome Gothic Ch.

19 Castéra Verduzan.

Near this village are mineral springs, one sulphureous, the other chalybeate, which are received into a *Bath-house*.

24 Auch, in Rte. 90.

ROUTE 80.

BORDEAUX TO PAU.

195 kilom. = 120 Eng. m.
Diligences daily in 20 hours.

Roquefort is a tolerable sleeping-place; so is Mont de Marsan (p. 267), but it is 12 m. out of the way.

The Bayonne road (Rte. 76) is followed as far as

108 Roquefort (*Inn*: H. de France), and by the diligence as far as Mont de Marsan (22 kilom.).

The mountains of the Pyrenean chain are visible even to the N. of this, rising ridge over ridge abruptly from the low plain of Gascony, so as to give the greatest effect to their elevation, with a grandeur worthy of the barrier wall between two great kingdoms.

No villages of consequence, and few habitations, occur on the sandy tract between Roquefort and

16 Villeneuve de Marsan, on the Medou. *Inn:* H. de France, good.

The district of sandy and heath-clad common, stretching from the sea-coast E. through the Landes (Rte. 77), gives place to cultivated and enclosed ground near

22 Aire (Poste, a mere auberge), a poor, old town, of 4028 Inhab., on the l. bank of the Adour, near which a detachment of the French army, retreating from Orthez, were defeated, a few days after that battle, by Lord Hill, who also gained possession of the French magazines here, and at St. Sever, lower down the Adour.

A steep ascent leads out of the valley of the Adour, and a table-land separates it from

17 Garlin.

12 Auriac.

From the top of each eminence, as you surmount it, a splendid view of the Pyrenees expands before the eye.

21 PAU.—(*Inns:* H. de France, at the corner of the Place Royale; very good and excellent cuisine; table-d'hôte, 3 fr.;—H. de l'Europe, Rue de la Préfecture, improved;—La Poste, Place de Henri IV., good; beds, 3 fr. to 1 fr. 50 c.; café au lait and eggs, 1 fr. 25 c.; table-d'hôte, 3 fr.;—H. de Daurade, ditto.) Good *lodgings* may be had at the Bains de la Place Royale. Try here the white wine of Jurançon, which, when good, deserves commendation, but it is very strong.

Pau, ancient capital of the little kingdom of French Navarre and Béarn, now chef-lieu of the Dépt. des Basses Pyrénées, stands on a lofty ridge, forming the rt. bank of the river, or Gave de Pau, and has 15,171 Inhab. Its situation is perhaps scarcely surpassed by that of any town in France, if we consider the magnificent view over the chain of the W. Pyrenees, which expands in front of it. The

English have shown their good taste in having chosen it for their residence, especially in winter. *The View*, reminding one somewhat of that from the platform at Berne, though far inferior to it, is well seen either from the Castle and its terrace, or from the extremity of the oblong, formal, gravelly promenade near the centre of the town, called the Place Royale, or from the *Parc*. This Parc is a fine natural terrace, running along the rt. bank of the Gave, thickly covered, on its top and sides, with noble trees, affording a grateful shade in the heat of the day, and provided with seats wherever, through gaps in the foliage, the different parts of the view appear to advantage. This spot formed part of the domain anciently attached to the old castle, and a communication between the castle and the Parc, through a formal square planted with rows of trees, called *Plante*, has been established by a handsome bridge of two arches, thrown over the high road.

The range of the Pyrenees, as seen from Pau, presents a strikingly beautiful and varied outline of peaks, cones, and ridges, often cut like a saw, rising against the S. horizon. Among the mass of summits, and precipices, and bold forms, are two pre-eminent from their elevation and shape—the Pic du Midi de Pau to the W., a peak with sides nearly vertical and cloven crest, rising at the extremity of the beautiful Val d'Ossau; and to the E., the Pic du Midi de Bigorre. These members of the great central range are disclosed to view through the gaps of a subordinate chain of round-backed and wooded hills forming the middle distance; while in the foreground appear the venerable Castle of Pau, the torrent, or Gave, its banks beautifully fringed with trees, the picturesque bridge, and the ruins of another bridge destroyed by its inundations. Within the scope of this view appear Jurançon, a village famed for its wines, and Bilhère, where Henri IV. was nursed. It is a glorious prospect, to be dwelt upon and seen over and over again.

Pau owes its chief renown to its having been the birthplace of the "Bon Roi" Henri IV., who drew his first breath (Dec. 13, 1553) in its ancient, time-honoured, historic *Castle, the most conspicuous and interesting building in the town. It stands statelily upon the ridge above mentioned, overlooking the river and bridge, at the point of a sort of promontory formed by a small rivulet which cuts its way through the town, and behind the castle walls at the bottom of a deep ravine, to throw itself into the Gave, just below it. The five towers of the Castle, and the outer wall which unites them, and serves to support the upper stories, are the oldest part, and supposed to date from the time of Gaston Phœbus Comte de Foix, who founded the castle about 1363. The tallest tower, or *Donjon*, named after Gaston, rising at the E. end to a height of 115 ft., is of brick, furnished with loopholes. The windows have been stopped up in modern times. A copy of the contract for erecting it (dated 1375) still exists, and in it the Count himself engages to furnish the bricks from the Tuileries de Pau. In the gutted and half-ruined *Tour de la Monnoye*, rising on the side of the castle next the river, from the bottom of the eminence on which it stands, to a level with the terrace, Margaret de Valois, it is said, gave an asylum to Cavin and other persecuted Reformers, and took great delight in listening to their discourse, although she never actually abandoned the Roman Catholic faith. This tradition, however, requires confirmation. The tower was used as a gaol until the Restoration (1814). The little oblong court-yard of the castle is destitute of architectural beauty; but the *Tour de Montauzet*, on one side of it, contained, according to popular belief, the oubliettes. It is about 80 ft. high, and its walls, to a height of 40 ft., were originally destitute of any opening, the gate at the bottom having been broken through in 1793, when the castle was sacked and despoiled by the Revolutionists. It stands within, and detached from, the outer wall of the castle, from which a small drawbridge, thrown over the gap, gave access to it through a little door. Within the thickness of its walls 7 or 8 confined dungeons exist, lighted by very small apertures, barred. The upper story only is provided with a window, looking into the court, and with a fireplace. Its wall, on the side of the court, is spotted with the marks of the shot fired by the Biscayans when they assaulted the castle during the troubles or civil wars in Béarn (1569), in the absence of Jeanne de Navarre.

Opposite the tower of Montauzet is the grand staircase, the vaulting of which, divided into squares, contains rich carvings, among which may be observed the letters H. M., the initials of Henri II. of Navarre and Margaret, the grand-parents of Henri IV., by whom it was built. The entire restoration of the interior was undertaken by Louis-Philippe, with very good taste and splendour. The King revived, as far as possible, the ancient decorations, injured by the Revolutionists, who first stripped and ruined this ancient palace, and then degraded it to a barrack, and he replaced those which they destroyed by others as far as possible in accordance with the age and style of the edifice. The walls of the chief apartments have been covered with tapestry, and the rooms filled with ancient furniture of the period, collected at vast expense.

In an apartment on the first floor is preserved a very interesting relic—the *cradle in which Henri IV. was rocked, consisting of a large tortoise-shell, inverted and suspended by cords, like the scale of a balance. It is at present surmounted by a trophy of flags, embroidered by the Duchesse d'Angoulême, the staves of which serve to support it. When the castle was sacked in 1793 by the Republicans, bent on destroying all traces of royalty, they would certainly not have spared this; but, luckily, another tortoise-shell was substituted in its place, which was broken and burnt with every insult. The parties who preserved the original shell were M. d'Espalunge d'Arros, commandant of the castle, who devised the pious fraud; M. Beauregard, the possessor of a collection of natural history, who exchanged a tortoise-shell of the same size for the cradle, which he afterwards concealed for many years in the roof of his house; and M. Lamaignère, concierge of the castle, who, at great risk, conveyed away the true cradle, and substituted the false in its place. A contemporary statue of Henri IV., preserved here, represents him leaning on his truncheon, after the battle of Ivry; it has little merit as a work of art. In front of the state apartments projects a balcony, commanding a view of the chain of the Pyrenees unsurpassed for its beauty. In the second story of the castle, in the room adjoining the Tour de Mazères in the S.W. corner, Henri IV. was born. Here his venerable grandfather, Henri d'Albret, taking in his arms the new-born infant, after his lips had been rubbed with garlic, according to the custom of Béarn, poured down his throat some drops of Jurançon wine, the best which the country affords, to give him a strong constitution! On the day of Henri's death, in 1610, there is a tradition that the castle was struck by lightning, which broke in pieces the royal escutcheon! Jeanne d'Albret was also born in the castle, 1528. It was alternately the prison of Reformers and Romanists during the religious wars and troubles of Béarn; and was the refuge of Theodore Beza and other Protestant teachers whom Jeanne de Navarre protected from persecution.

Among the costly and curious articles of old-fashioned furniture collected by Louis-Philippe to decorate the castle, and restore it to its ancient splendour, may be mentioned the bed, in the chambre-à-coucher du Roi, said to be that of Henri IV.; it is curiously carved with medallion heads of the kings of France: in an adjoining room is the bed of Jeanne d'Albret, and a state chair, richly carved, bearing her arms, presented by Marshal Soult. The chapel has been newly fitted up, and has a painted window of Sèvres glass. The apartment leading to it contains some magnificent presents made by the late King of Sweden to the town of Pau, his birthplace.

They consist of vases of porphyry of large size, superb tables of various kinds of porphyry, conglomerate, &c., and a chimney-piece of serpentine, all the produce of Sweden, and of great value and beauty.

Bernadotte, King of Sweden, son of a poor saddler in Pau, was born in a house Rue de Tran, No. 6. He quitted his native town, 1780, as a drummer boy in the Régiment Royal de la Marine. Some of his relations still remain in very humble situations in the neighbourhood.

It is a somewhat remarkable coincidence, that of the two most eminent men and sovereigns who first drew breath at Pau, the one abandoned the Protestant faith, the other the Roman Catholic, in order to secure a throne.

The low ugly Ch. of *St. Martin* is only remarkable because in it Jeanne d'Albret, the most sagacious and accomplished princess of her age, after our Elizabeth, first received the communion according to the form of the Reformed church, on Easter-day, 1560. Viret, the Reformer, preached from its pulpit.

A *Statue of Henri IV.* has been set up in the Place Royale; the bas-reliefs on the pedestal represent events of his life.

The *College*, at the E. end of the town, was originally a convent of Barnabites, founded by Henri IV., after he had abandoned the faith of his mother, in order to conciliate the Roman Catholics.

In the *Mairie* there is a collection of marbles of the Pyrenees, and a picture, by *Deveria*, of the birth of Henri IV.

The *Poste aux Lettres* adjoins the *Préfecture*, where is deposited a very curious collection of old records, deeds, &c., relating to the ancient state and history of Béarn, including the Fors (fueros, privilèges) of Béarn; autographs of its most illustrious Béarnois sovereigns, and a list of the contributions collected in Béarn towards the ransom of Francis I. from captivity.

There are *Hot Baths* (for 75 c.) at the extremity of the Place Royale adjoining the Basse Plante.

There is a *Musée* devoted chiefly to the natural history of the Pyrenees, above the new *Halle*, where the markets are held.

The town of Pau in itself is not very handsome or remarkable. Its chief street is the Rue de la Préfecture, which on market-days presents a bustling scene; here are the chief shops, such as they are.

Many English, as before observed, make Pau their residence, chiefly for the winter months, when its mild and dry climate, and the stillness of atmosphere peculiar to it, are a great recommendation—See Sir James Clark's excellent work on Climate.

Pau has been greatly resorted to of late by the wealthy Parisians also; good houses are consequently difficult to procure, and though provisions are cheap, house-rent is enormously high; a moderately good suite of apartments costs more than a similar set at Paris. A number of new houses have been built.

A *Protestant Church* has been built in the Rue des Cordeliers, mainly by the handsome contributions of the Duchess of Gordon. It is unfortunate that it should be so very ugly a building. The English Church service is performed in it every Sunday by a resident clergyman at 11 a.m.

Mr. P. Hodgson resides here as H.B.M.'s vice-consul and as English banker.

A *Circulating Library* of English and French books is kept by Lafon. Bassy's shop, Rue du Collége, is the best for prints, views, &c.

A *pack of hounds* is kept by an American gentleman, who hunts twice a week in the season.

Conveyances.—Malleposte to Toulouse and Bayonne. Diligences *daily:* to Bordeaux in 20 hrs.; to Bayonne, 9 hrs.; to Barèges, Luz, and Cauterets, 12 hrs.; to Bagnères de Bigorre, 36 m.; to Toulouse, by Tarbes, Trie, and Lombez, in 20 hrs.; to Oloron in 3 hrs.; to Eaux-Bonnes in 6 hrs.

*Commerce.—*From the swine, reared near this and at Orthez, are derived the so-called *Jambons de Bayonne;* they are said to owe their excellent flavour to the abundance of acorns in the woods where the swine are herded, and to the salt of Sallies with which they are cured. There is a considerable manufacture of chequered handkerchiefs here.

Baggage may be transmitted from this to Toulouse, or *vice versâ*, by the house of Turettes et Comp., commissionnaires, or at a somewhat higher cost by the diligence.

Pau, situated at the termination of the plain, and at the roots of the *Pyrenees*, is excellent head-quarters for travellers' intending to explore those mountains and the valleys which penetrate into their recesses. Of these, no one surpasses in beauty of scenery the *Val d'Ossau*, which opens out to the S. immediately in front of Pau, and terminates in the magnificent Pic du Midi d'Ossau.

The excursions to Eaux-Chaudes and Eaux-Bonnes, about 26 m. distant, situated at the head of the valley of Ossau, near the base of the Pic, are described in Rte. 83; that to the Val d'Aspe in Rte. 82.

The *Ch. of Ste. Foi*, at Morlaas, 6 m. N.E., in the Romanesque style of the 11th centy., is interesting, but much dilapidated. It has a splendid W. portal with much carving (12th cent.), and a rich chapel containing an altarpiece of the 16th cent. Morlaas was capital of Béarn down to the 13th cent.; it is now a village of hovels.

Lescar, the antiquated town, 4 m., and Bilhère, 1 m., where Henri IV. was nursed, are mentioned in Rte. 78.

Cauterets is about 45 m., and Bagnères de Bigorre 36 m., from Pau (Rte. 85).

ROUTE 82.

PAU TO CAMPFRANC IN SPAIN, BY OLORON AND THE VAL D'ASPE.

113 kilom. = 70 Eng. m.

A post-road as far as Urdos.

Diligences daily to Oloron in 3 hrs. The road has been greatly improved on the side of France, with the design of making it a highway to Madrid.

The road as far as Gan is the same as Rte. 83; beyond that place it crosses the hills to

17 Maison la Coste Belair.

16 Oloron. — (*Inns:* H. des Voyageurs, chez Lustalot, best ;—H. Condesse ;—Poste. This is a large and prosperous manufacturing town of 6500 Inhab., on the Gave d'Oloron, a river formed by the junction at this spot of the Gaves d'Ossau and d'Aspe. The oldest part of the town occupies the summit of the hill, and includes the *Ch. of Ste. Croix*. A lofty stone bridge thrown across the stream unites Oloron with the suburb St. Marie, containing 3400 Inhab. Its *Ch. of St. Marie* shows the transition from Romanesque to Gothic: it has a fine Roman portal, and its sacristy contains some costly priests' vestments. At the side of the Gave is the new Séminaire.

The objects manufactured here are the chequered handkerchiefs so much in vogue as a head-dress among the peasantry of Aragon and Gascony, and also the berrets worn by the Béarnais. There is some trade in Spanish wool.

Diligences go in summer to Eaux Chaudes and Bonnes (Rte. 83), and to Urdos.

The *Val d'Aspe*, at the mouth of which Oloron stands, contains scenery of great beauty, though it wants the boldness of many other valleys in the Pyrenees. A gradual ascent along a good road leads up it, following the course of the stream. At Asaspe the traveller has entered the Basque country, and is already in the heart of the mountains. The Gave is crossed at Escot, near which a Latin inscription, cut in the rock by the wayside, commemorates the first making of this road by the Romans, under one Valerius, and twice more before reaching

24 Bédous, last post-town in France, 1200 Inhab.; it has a tolerable but dirty Inn. Here the vale swells out into a basin shape. In the neighbouring village of Osse there is an isolated Protestant community of 30 families, who have preserved their faith in the midst of Roman Catholics for ages.

An Obelisk of marble has been reared near the village of Accous (Aspa Luca) to the memory of Desporins, the poet of the Pyrenees—their Burns, who was born here.

Grand defiles succeed to this basin; and in the midst the Pont d'Esquil, a bold antique arch, forms a fine object. Above Accous the new road has been blasted out of the rock. After passing the villages of Aigun and Etsaut we reach a grand rocky defile at the ruined fort Portalet, which once entirely barred the passage up and down the valley: it was destroyed by the Spaniards. Near this Buonaparte caused a road to be formed at vast expense, partly by excavating a shelf out of the face of the vertical precipice, partly by building up terraces of masonry for the conveyance of timber for shipbuilding from the neighbouring forests.

17 *Urdos*, a poor village of 300 Inhab., at which the carriage-road ends. Above it has been constructed a very remarkable *Fortress*, entirely hewn in the natural rock, within the shoulder of a hill, rising in a succession of stages to a height of 500 ft. The appearance of this mountain, from without, gives little indication of the long galleries and batteries excavated in its interior. A small masonry façade, battlemented and flanked with bartezan turrets at the base of the hill, and some loopholes and embrasures for cannon pierced in the face of the cliff, explain, to those who are prepared for it, the nature of this outpost of France, which is the work of 10 years of excavating, and is capable of holding a garrison of 3000 men.

11 Paillette (no post-horses) is the last place in France. The journey into Spain as far as Jaca is a distance of 30 m., and must be performed on mules. On the way, 10 m. short of Jaca, lies

23 Campfranc, a village about equal in population to Urdos.

ROUTE 83.

PAU TO EAUX-BONNES AND EAUX-CHAUDES.—EXCURSION TO THE PIC DU MIDI D'OSSAU, AND THE SPANISH BATHS OF PANTICOSA.

42 kilom.= 26 Eng. m. to Les Eaux. Several *diligences* go daily from June to middle of Sept. in 6 hrs., returning in about 4 hrs.; very slow.

A voiture may be hired at Pau for the journey at the rate of 20 fr. a day: 2 days are charged to Eaux-Bonnes. The road is very good, but up hill most of the way. For those who travel only in carriages it leads into a cul-de-sac; and to prosecute their journey to other parts of the Pyrenees they must return nearly to Pau.

After crossing the bridge over the Gave du Pau, the village of Jurançon, distinguished by its groves of fine oaks, is passed on the rt.; it is famed for its wine, perhaps the best grown in the Pyrenees. The vineyards producing it extend along the slopes from this to Gan. One of the houses near the road was occupied for many years by the late Lord Elgin, when released from the dungeons of Lourdes by Napoleon, as prisoner on his parole. The well-wooded, verdant, shady valley, up which the road runs, is watered by the Néez, or Neiss, a clear stream rushing over the limestone rocks, whose slaty foliations, crossing the direction of its current, resemble a flight of steps. In this country the vines are either trained over trellises upon cross bars of wood, or are allowed to climb up the trees, whence their long tendrils sweep down over the hedges: the box-tree flourishes, and would attain great size were it not constantly cropped. At the village of Gan, on the l., also locally famous for its wines, is seen an old *castellated house*, in which Pierre Marca, the historian of Béarn and Archbishop of Paris, was born 1594. The front towards the court is said to possess some architectural interest. Interesting remains of a *Roman Villa*, with elaborate mosaics, were found here in 1850 by an English gentleman. Here the road to Oloron (Rte. 82) turns to the rt. Above Rébénac rises its château on a hillock; and a little beyond, on the l., the copious source of the Neiss bursts out of the rock. A long and toilsome ascent leads up to the village of Sévignac, situated on the top of the ridge separating the Neiss and other streams flowing into the Gave de Pau from the tributaries of the Gave d'Oloron, flowing out of the Val d'Ossau, which we now enter. It here expands into the form of a basin, round which the Gave takes a wide turn, passing by the village of Arudy. In descending the wooded slope from Sévignac, several glimpses are afforded of the Pic du Midi d'Ossau, a grand object; but near the bottom of the hill, and as far as the Pont de Louvie, his cleft crest and precipitous cone appear in full majesty, filling up the vista at the extremity of the Val d'Ossau. This is a magnificent view on a clear day, and in advancing up the valley it is soon lost. Rocks and precipices of limestone now line the road, which is partly cut out of them. On their smooth surface, or in their narrow chinks, the box delights to fix itself. They furnish the slabs of black and grey marble with which the door-posts and lintels of even the humblest cottage are here adorned. The Gave d'Ossau is crossed at the end of the village of

27 Louvie Juzon; and here also the road from Oloron (Rte. 82) to Les Eaux falls in, at the H. des Pyrénées (indifferent accommodation), at the end of the bridge.

The great transverse *Val d'Ossau*, which we are now about to ascend, and in which the Eaux are situated, is one of the most interesting among the Pyrenees, for its picturesque beauties, and for the people who inhabit it. They still retain much of their ancient customs and costumes. The women are distinguished by the scarlet *capulet*, a sort of monk's hood, serving at once for bonnet and shawl, descending as far as the shoulders. Whether sitting or walking, and even when carrying burthens on the head, the spindle and distaff are never out of their hands. They are inferior in stature and features to the men, which may perhaps be owing to the hard and unfeminine labours which devolve upon them; it is common to see them holding the plough, and carrying sacks of manure on their heads, or spreading it over the land. The men, however, are not idle; they are absent on the high mountain pastures tending their flocks and herds, or following the hardy trade of woodcutters and charcoal-burners a great part of the year.

The men are chiefly distinguished by the wide cloth cap or *berret*, properly and most commonly of brown colour, which, overhanging the brow and assuming very picturesque folds, sits very becomingly on a head of hair allowed to grow thick and of even length all round the neck, but cut short in front. They wear short jackets and knee-breeches, also brown, the colour of the undyed wool of the sheep, and round the waist a brilliant red sash of silk or woollen is tied. To defend them from rain or cold they carry the white or brown *capa*, which resembles a sack, unseamed, on one side, pulled over the head. An artist would find many good subjects among them, very picturesque countenances, such as are seen in pictures of Van Eyck and Albert Dürer.

The mountains around the valley abound in *Izards* (chamois), which are sometimes met with in troops of 40 or 50. The chasse aux izards is a common amusement of visitors at the baths, under the guidance of experienced huntsmen, of whom there is no lack. The haunts most frequented by the izard, in this district, are the Pics d'Arcizet, de Gazie, and de Sesque. *Bears*, though less common, are sometimes killed.

Flocks of sheep form the chief wealth of this valley; but as they are led up to the mountains in April, and do not return till the end of summer, they are seldom seen, except by those who traverse the high mountains. They are guarded by a remarkable breed of dogs of large size, very courageous, whose duty is less to drive the flock, as the shepherd's dog of England and Scotland, than to protect it from the wolf and bear.

The rustic fêtes, dances, &c., still kept up in some parts of the Val d'Ossau, especially at Laruns (Aug. 15), are well worth seeing, as they collect some of the finest specimens of the men of the valley, and of its primitive costumes. They have a peculiar musical instrument called *tambourin*, a lyre or zithern of 6 strings, struck with a stick by one hand, while the other holds the rustic mountain flageolet; it thus corresponds in simplicity and mode of playing to the old English tabour and pipe.

The part of the valley which we first enter is shut in by lofty mountains of bold forms and steep sides, separated by a plain of considerable breadth, through which winds the torrent, and it is scattered over with numerous villages. It is cultivated in patches to a considerable height, and covered below with large fields of maize, or with meadows deriving their bright verdure from well-managed irrigation, and producing, by means of it, three crops of hay in a year.

Within a mile of Louvie you pass, on the opposite bank of the Gave, the ruins of *Castel Jaloux*, or *Geloz*, occupying the top of one of two little hillocks; the other, also anciently enclosed within its ramparts, is now crowned by a small chapel. This stronghold was the key of the Val d'Ossau, and residence of its viscounts in early times, while the valley formed a separate state, independent of Béarn.

In the *Ch.* of the village of Bielle, the finest in the valley in the pointed style, are 4 columns of marble, which, it is said, were so much admired by Henri IV., that he begged them of the inhabitants, but was met with this ingenious reply in the negative : " Nos cœurs et nos biens sont à vous, disposez en à votre volonté; quant aux colonnes, elles appartiennent à Dieu, entendez-vous en avec lui." The pillars themselves seem too poor to have excited the admiration of the king, but it was probably in the days of his boyhood, when wandering among his native mountains, that they struck his fancy.

A little before reaching the village of Laruns, one of the most considerable in the valley, a snow-white gash or scar, high up on the mountain side to the l., marks the situation of the *white marble quarry* of Louvie Soubiron, producing a stone well adapted for the sculptor's purpose. It has been employed at Paris for the statues in the Place de la Concorde, and for the bas-reliefs on the outside of the Madeleine. It is harder than that of Carrara, but is sometimes traversed by grey veins.

The situation of Laruns, encircled by high peaks and ridges, which impend on all sides above it, is very striking: among them the distant Pic de Gers raises his conspicuous head. The *Church* appears originally to have had no windows much larger than loopholes, though wide ones have been broken through in modern times: its font or bénitier, of the white marble mentioned above, is carved outside in the fashion of a basket, and within bears the inappropriate figures of mermaids.

On issuing out of Laruns you might suppose that you had arrived at the termination of the valley, so completely is it blocked up by the mass of the mountain *Hourat;* but after crossing the furious and injurious winter torrent, the Larienzé, and reaching the mountain foot, two roads are found to diverge; that on the l. to Eaux-Bonnes (p. 288), that on the rt. to Eaux-Chaudes, both places being equally distant (4 kilom. = 2½ Eng. m.) from this spot.

The shoulder of the mountain, which, as it were, laps over, and conceals from the view of those below the upper part of the Val d'Ossau, has been cut down, and scooped out, by the aid of the auger and of gunpowder. The *new road*, completed 1847, a very wonderful and laborious work, is carried to Eaux-Chaudes directly through this gorge into the valley, and thus avoids the steep and awkward ascent and descent of the Hourat. After passing this gloomy portal of the valley, a sudden change of scene takes place. Before you opens out a lofty ravine of mountains, almost precipitous, rising from 1000 to 1500 ft. above your head, and approaching so close to one another at their base as to leave no room for culture or meadow, only space for the torrent below, here called Gave de Gabas, which chafes and tumbles from rock to rock, boring the limestone, by its whirlpools, into cauldrons and pits. The deep fissure, at the bottom of which it takes its course, is well seen near the bridge, which transfers the road from its l. to its rt. bank. From this point the river forces its way out into the lower Val d'Ossau, through the remarkable gorge just described, which long bade defiance to the passage of any road.

The approach to the Eaux-Chaudes is grand; the height and steepness of the mountains, now robed from top to bottom in box-bushes, now starting out in lofty precipices of bare limestone, scarred by the course of torrents, which at times descend in long falls like white ribbons, and the variety imparted to the road by the projecting shoulders round which it winds, give interest to this part of the journey. At length the last projection is doubled, and a view opens of the group of houses called

17 *Eaux-Chaudes.* — *Inns:* H. de France, best, and very good;—H. des Pyrénées is entered by the upper story; the rest of the building lies below the level of the road, and is traversed by long dark corridors; while in a vault below are the *Baths*. Dinner at 5; table-d'hôte 3 fr.; breakfast, or tea, 1 fr. 50 cents.; beds 2 fr. There are 6 or 7 other lodging-houses, which form the bulk of the place. It lies wedged in, as it were, in the midst of the long trough of the valley, between lofty precipices, towering overhead, and often draped with clouds. The houses are founded upon granite, which here first makes its appearance, jutting up in a round boss behind the village. In its rise it has considerably elevated the limestone above it, as may be perceived by the remarkable curve in the strata, visible on the face of the precipices on the l. bank, opposite the baths. The hot springs burst forth out of the granite, close to the junction of the limestone. This phenomenon of the outbreak of hot sources near the points of contact of granitic or trappean rocks is of frequent occurrence among the Alps and Pyrenees.

In spite of the name, Eaux-Chaudes, the temperature of the waters is not so high as at many other Pyrenean springs, the hottest not exceeding 95° Fahr.; and one of them is cold. The principal sources are Lou Rey (le Roi), named from Henri IV., a frequent visitor, 93°, and L'Esquirette, 95°, the most sought after, and most highly mineralised. The waters are sulphureous, and are supplied from 6 springs, 3 of which, used for bathing, are conveyed into the bath-houses; the others, used for drinking, partly burst out from the rock into rude little basins, whither invalids resort to fill their glasses. A handsome *Etablissement des Bains*, including pump-room, promenade, and baths, chambers for the resident physician, and some sets of rooms for guests, has been constructed at the expense of the Government, which gave 80,000 fr., and of the town of Laruns, which gave 30,000 fr., on the platform of rock below the hotel. Into it the waters of 3 of the springs are conducted. This new building is furnished with 5 baths, besides douches, and contains *billiard-room*, *café*, and *reading-room*. The Eaux-Chaudes baths are resorted to, both by the real invalid in search of health, and the passing traveller attracted by the beauties of nature.

There is, however, at least one very interesting excursion to be made from this, viz. to *Gabas* and the *Pic du Midi d'Ossau*. Horses may be hired at 3 fr. to 4 fr. for the day; guides 4 fr. The valley of Ossau is a frequented passage between France and Spain, along which 15,000 mules pass annually. Its scenery, above Eaux-Chaudes, is far grander and more varied in its mountain outlines and vegetation than below; and the whole range of the Pyrenees presents few more interesting rides than that to Gabas (6 m.). The fine near view obtained, in proceeding thither, of the Pic du Midi, which is out of sight at Eaux-Chaudes, would alone well repay the trouble. About ½ m. beyond Eaux-Chaudes the Gave is crossed by a bridge of wood, called Pont d'Enfer, above which, on the rt., a small cascade, named from the neighbouring but elevated hamlet of Goust, descends the mountain. In this portion of the valley the limestone has entirely given place to granite, which forms the substance of the mountains, and the vegetation which covers them is of a beauty and variety unrivalled. It is at this point that we pass into the zone of fir-trees, whose dark files, covering the mountain tops, descend half-way, mixing like mourners in the crowd of trees of lighter foliage—birch, beech, hazel, alder, and oaks, which rise from amidst an undergrowth of box, mixed with a wonderful profusion of wild flowers. At times the road mounts to a great height above the torrent; and there is a fearful pleasure in looking down, over the tree-tops, upon its waters, writhing, struggling, and serpentining in the dark depths below. The firs in the forests around were formerly sent to Bayonne, to supply timber for the French navy, being hurled down the steep mountain sides, and floated down into the Gave d'Oloron.

Gabas is a poor hamlet, the last in France, having a small cabaret, which will furnish a very tolerable dinner to a sharp appetite, and where Malaga wine may be had good. At the extremity of the hamlet is the French *Douane*. Hence a fine view of the forked summit of the Pic du Midi is obtained. It is well worth while to take a walk (2 hrs. to and fro) beyond the Douane, crossing the bridge, and following the path to the rt. of the road and l. of the Gave. The pines here are magnificent. From Gabas also the *ascent of the Pic du Midi* is made, following the rt.-hand branch of the valley above Gabas. It takes 3 hrs., passing the Cabanes de Magne-Baigne, to reach the Crête de Pombie, at the base of the peak itself, which is of granite, very steep, and takes 1¾ to 2 hrs. to surmount.

Should the traveller be disposed to take a peep at Spain, he may go from *Les Eaux-Chaudes to Panticosa*, an Arragonese watering-place, a long day's journey of about 14 *hours*, including a rest of 2 hrs. Start by 6 A.M. at the latest. The *charge* for a guide is 5 fr., and 5 fr. for each horse per diem (nourriture comprise): the guide finding himself in food and bed. Each lady ought to have a guide to attend to her horse on the Spanish side of the road.—*G. M. S.*

The route is quite easy, neither very steep in any part nor difficult to find, as there is a broadly-marked horse-track the whole way. The col is rather swampy in spring, after the melting of the snow.

The carriage-road up the valley terminates at

2 hrs. Gabas. A steep mule-path turning to the rt. leads to the *Plateau of Bioux Artiques*, which commands so grand a view of the Pic du Midi that Lady Chatterton says it is worth while to come all the way from England to enjoy it alone. It is only 1¼ hr. from Gabas. The mule-path turning to the l. from that place, on the E. side of the mountain, leads into Spain, past the solitary house called

2 hrs. Case de Brousette, the last in France, which will furnish good homely fare. It has been built as a sort of refuge, half-way between Gabas and Salients.

1 hr. The passage or col called Le Port d'Anéou is an hour's walk above this; a mule-path of gradual descent leads from it, by the side of the stream of the Gallego.

2 hrs. Salients, the first Spanish village, is reached by a steep descent, a little beyond the Custom-house. While the horses are resting here you may take a cup of excellent chocolate at the Posada, and visit the little Ch. and its trésor. The village of Panticosa is 2½ hours' ride hence; and 2½ hrs. more of difficult ascent, by a winding path, through a narrow and savage gorge, called El Escular, are required to reach *The Baths*. They consist of 4 or 5 large buildings, in a wild, romantic situation, at a height of more than 8300 ft. above the sea level, in a confined hollow basin or valley, half of which is occupied by a lake surrounded by wild mountains of granite. The inn here is provided with a capital cuisine Française, and there is a daily table-d'hôte during the season. Accommodation, *i. e.* a clean room, may be had at the house of Don José Juan Torla. 3 or even 4 frs. a night are asked for a bed sometimes, in June, July, and August; but living is more moderate; for chocolate at 9 A.M. and 4 P.M., dinner at 1, and supper at 9, only 4

frs. 15 sous. The season lasts only for 3 months.

The Spanish Valle de Broto is one of the few remaining haunts of the ibex or bouquetin. The return to Eaux-Chaudes may be varied by going round the W. side of the Pic du Midi d'Ossau, traversing the Plateau of Bioux Artiques to Gabas.

From Panticosa village you may reach Gavarnie, or Broto, or Torla, in one long day, by climbing the Pass of Bendeneta. A guide is necessary, however. The scenery is very grand. See HANDBOOK FOR TRAVELLERS IN SPAIN.

From Panticosa to Cauterets is a journey of 8 hrs. on foot, and a little more with mules, over the Col de Marcadaou, one of the most desolate passes in the range, traversed by a very rough mule-track, but at times, when the snow is deep, it is impassable for mules. For the greater part of the way there is no marked track. From Panticosa the ascent, for 2 hrs. of hard climbing, is up the face of a rock covered with débris. Another hour over swampy ground, bearing patches of melting snow, brings you to the foot of the col. The ascent from this to the frontier is as steep as a staircase, for about 1½ hr. The descent on the French side, passing some grand pines, equally steep, ½ hr. Another hr. brings you to a hut at the foot of the col. Hence to the Pont d'Espagne another hr., and from the Pont to Cauterets ½ hr., though 2 hrs. are required to ascend. (Rte. 85, p. 295.)

One of the first sights which travellers are invited to see at Eaux-Chaudes is the *Grotte*, situated in the rock on the l. side of the valley, 2 hours' walk above the baths. 'Tis scarce worth the trouble.

The road to Eaux-Bonnes, branching off to the l. at the bifurcation beyond Laruns, crosses the Gave de Gabas by a bridge, whence there is a good view of the dark and narrow gorge through which that stream issues out of the upper valley (see p. 285). A steep ascent, carried up in a terrace along the mountain side, succeeds, and does not terminate till the road reaches Eaux-Bonnes. On the l., low down, lies the castle of Espalunge; and higher up, on the shoulder of a mountain, the village d'Aas looks down upon our road. The stream flowing at the bottom of the valley is a tributary of the Gave d'Ossau, called the Valentin. At the very entrance of Eaux-Bonnes a narrow, rocky gully, with a torrent at its bottom, is crossed by a wooden bridge. This stream is the contribution sent forth by the confined nook in which Eaux-Bonnes stands, partitioned off, as it were, from the vale of the Valentin by a ridge of rock of no great height, and concealed from view until you are about to enter it. Beyond the bridge above alluded to is the fashionable and much-frequented watering-place

17 *Les Eaux-Bonnes*, consisting of a street of 20 or 30 hotels and lodging-houses, of large dimensions and many stories, which would not disgrace a German watering-place. On one side of the street is an open space, laid out as a shrubbery, and planted with trees, named Jardin Anglais. The village is cradled in the lap of the mountains, niched in a complete cul-de-sac, with precipices rising all around close to the houses, so that the rock has been blasted in order to make room for some of them. Above these cliffs, to the S.E., towers the majestic *Pic de Gers*, the grand feature in all the views of this neighbourhood; while nearly due E. rises the serrated ridge of the Col de Torte.

Inns: H. de France et de l'Europe, chez Taverne Aîné (good, and civil landlord);—H. de Petit Paris, chez Cazères;—La Poste;—Quatre Nations; —H. des Etrangers. The *charges* are high, but vary according to the season and the throng of visitors. In the height of the season, in spite of the number of lodgings, rooms are frequently not to be had, unless ordered beforehand. The apartments are not well furnished. Meals are supplied, even in the hotels, by traiteurs, at the rate of 4 fr. per diem, including breakfast and dinner at table-d'hôte; or 5 fr. if sent into the visitor's private apartments; children 2 fr. 50 cents., and servants 3 fr. The season opens in June and lasts till October, being at its height in July and August. Taverne Aîné keeps a *circulating Library*.

There are 4 or 5 *springs* here of warm sulphurous water, stronger than those of Eaux-Chaudes, but of lower temperature, the hottest not exceeding 91° Fahrenheit. The principal ones rise at the foot of the craig called Butte du Trésor, and are conducted into the *Bath-house* at the extremity of the village. The water of one source is subjected to artificial heating to fit it for baths. The cold spring alone is used for drinking. Caution is necessary in using the waters: bad consequences have arisen from a stranger taking even a glassful to taste. It is usual to begin with a table spoonful and a half. Dr. Daüralde, the resident physician, has a high reputation for his treatment of consumption and spine complaints. The waters are considered good for complaints of the lungs and chest, and very efficacious in the early stages of consumption. Their reputation is of long standing, for the Béarnais soldiers of Henri d'Albret, wounded in the battle of Pavia, repaired hither for the cure of their injuries, and first gave the water the name of Eau d'Arquebusade.

The *walks* around Eaux-Bonnes cannot be too much praised: they have chiefly been made by M. Eynard of Geneva; except the *Promenade Horizontal* (so called to distinguish it from the others, chiefly steep ascents), this being admirably conducted on a level, and therefore suited for invalids. It commands noble views of the Valleys d'Aas and d'Ossau: it is already completed for 3 m., and it is to be carried on to les Eaux-Chaudes.

The well-wooded cliffs around have been rendered accessible for invalids by zigzag paths and terraces. The summer-house on the top of the Butte du Trésor commands a view of Laruns and the Val d'Ossau. Other paths lead down to the pretty but trifling waterfalls of the *France*.

Valentin. The finest fall is that named *Du Gros Hêtre*, from a beech-tree, now cut down, about 3 m. distant. Another very delightful walk of 1½ hr., at first under the shade of the beech-trees, leads to the Promenade Jacqueminot, so called from a general who caused it to be cut.

Salanave is a *guide* to be recommended, and has good horses.

Persons residing at Eaux-Bonnes should not omit to explore the Val de Gabas above Eaux-Chaudes, with its luxuriant forests and its noble Pic du Midi, the grandest mountain in this district (see p. 286). It is a drive of an hour, or a walk of 2, to Eaux-Chaudes by the road.

The mountain-path over the *Col de Torte* from Eaux-Bonnes to Argelez forms Rte. 84.

ROUTE 84.

THE COL DE TORTE.—EAUX-BONNES TO CAUTERETS OR LUZ.

It takes 11 or 12 hrs. walking to Argelez. Send round the baggage. There is not a single auberge, even of the worst kind, as far as Arruns. Beware of the shepherds' dogs, which are very savage.

On leaving Eaux-Bonnes, by the road near the source, you traverse part of the mountain called Le Trésor. Keep the upper path, and, leaving the first bridge and cascade on your l., you come to a second bridge; pass it, keeping the torrent on your rt. The road is as yet well marked by horses, &c., and sufficiently steep to make a person unaccustomed to mountain-paths feel not particularly comfortable. In 2 hrs. thence, on horseback, you can make the Col de Torte; and, although the path is not always very distinct, you may know the Col by a remarkable rock which elevates itself on the l., and is like the root of an eye tooth. The descent on both sides is remarkably steep, and would induce most persons to descend from their horses. Leaving the valley of Assun and the river Assun on your l., keep under the Pic de Gabisos till you come to some châlets. The next Col is then right before you—a green and heathy mount.

o

The descent from Col de Torte and ascent of this Col takes 1¾ hr. on foot. This part of the way is very complicated, and especially in the valley between the two Cols is not well marked. In descending this Col, the path is soon found; and the view, from Arruns, of the Hermitage and mountains which fill up the end of the valley, *i. e.* d'Arrui and La Rivelle, is one of the finest in the Pyrenees. The descent from the Col to Arruns occupies a good hour of walking. From hence there is good road to Argelez, about 1¼ hr., or Pierrefitte, at least ¾ more. Argelez- (See Route 85.)

It would be making a toil of a pleasure to attempt to reach Cauterets in 1 day from Eaux-Bonnes, at least on foot; especially as the road from Argelez to Cauterets is so magnificent, so pleasing, and so varied, that it alone deserves a day.

ROUTE 85.

THE PYRENEES. — PAU TO LOURDES, CAUTERETS, LUZ, ST. SAUVEUR.—GAVARNIE, BARÈGES, AND BAGNÈRES DE BIGORRE, MOUNTAIN-ROAD.—EXCURSIONS TO THE LAC DE GAUBE.—BRÈCHE DE ROLAND AND MONT PERDU.—THE PIC DU MIDI, &c. &c.

A daily communication of diligences is kept up in summer between all the principal watering-places of the Pyrenees.

Distances from Pau — to Cauterets, 68 kilom. = 42 Eng. m.; to Luz and St. Sauveur, 71 kilom. = 43¾ Eng. m.; to Barèges, 76 kilom. = 46¾ Eng. m.; to B. de Bigorre.

This route includes some of the most interesting objects and places in the Pyrenees; and the drive from Lourdes to Luz and Cauterets in particular is a continued succession of the most beautiful scenery.

The road ascends the rt. bank of the Gave du Pau, through a plain of considerable width, nearly covered with maize and flax, and passes between festooned vines slinging their tendrils between the apple and cherry trees. One village rapidly succeeds another, but they contribute little to the cheerfulness of the drive, as the houses turn their backs on the traveller, whose gaze is met by dead walls. He has, however, something more interesting to occupy his attention in the varying forms of the mountains which he is gradually approaching. But there is one exception in the village of *Coarrase*, where the Gave is crossed by a bridge ; for its old tower, crowning a mound on the rt. bank, is part of the castle in which the Bon Henri IV. was confided from his early years to the care of Susanne de Bourbon, Baronne de Missans, and by the wisdom of his mother brought up in the rough fashion of the peasants of his native country, dressed like them, fed like them, sharing in their sports, and traversing the rugged rocks with bare feet; thus acquiring the vigour of body and strength of mind which enabled him to surmount in after-life so many hardships, dangers, and difficulties. Beside the ruin a modern château has been built.

The feet of the mountains are fairly gained at

24 Lestelle.—*Inns:* H. de France ; an excellent country inn : Poste. The Gave, running in a contracted rocky bed, is here spanned by a bold arch most picturesquely draped with ivy. Just outside of this village, at a spot where the road is hemmed in between a fine wooded hill, spotted with chapels or stations, and the river, stands the *Pilgrimage Ch. of Bétharram*, an ugly modern building, containing a statue of the Virgin reported to have miraculous powers, which attracts a multitude of devotees from a distance in the month of September. Here also is a *Séminaire* for the education of priests.

Traversing a narrow defile again on the rt. bank of the Gave, which is hemmed in between barren brackencovered hills, we pass into the Dépt. des Hautes Pyrénées, and from ancient Béarn into Bigorre, shortly before entering the little manufacturing town of St. Pé. It is chiefly inhabited by nailers, who obtain iron from the forges of Asson, and by comb-makers, who supply the Spanish ladies with combs of box-wood for their hair. It has a curious Romanesque church with apsidal terminations, and sculpture over the door. Much roofing slate is exported hence.

16 Lourdes (*Inns:* Poste, bad;—H. Lafitte, better) consists of a picturesque but somewhat gloomy-looking hill fort, seated on a rock, around which the town of narrow dirty streets and shabby houses group themselves. This *Castle* was once the key of the valley of Lavedan, or of the Gave de Pau, commanding the 4 roads which unite here from Tarbes, Bagnères, Argelez, and Pau. It is reached by flights of stairs, and entered by a small drawbridge, and a door 4 feet high and only wide enough for one person to squeeze through; but, not being strong according to modern rules of art, is rather of use as a barrack than a fortress. It was long a state prison, and in 1804 Lord Elgin was incarcerated within it by Napoleon, who caused him to be seized in his passage through France from Constantinople. Far different was its importance in ancient times; it was held for the English monarchs, and the Black Prince, as part of the country of Bigorre, which was yielded up to the English by the French king John as part of his ransom, in conformity with the treaty of Brétigny. Froissart gives a very long account of its varied fortunes, which render this feudal fortress interesting for all who are acquainted with its history. He tells us that when the Black Prince came over to take possession of Aquitaine, which his father had given him to hold in fief, he and his princess, while on a visit to the Comte d'Armagnac at Tarbes, rode over to Lourdes, which he had a great desire to see. He was much pleased, "as well with the strength of the place as with its situation on the frontiers of several countries, for those of Lourdes can overrun the country of Arragon to a great extent, and as far as Barcelona in Catalonia." The Prince intrusted the command of it to a knight of Béarn, one of his household, in whom he had great confidence, Sir Peter Arnaut, to guard it well. When the war broke out with France, he held it fast, and, assisted by many bold adventurers, made repeated incursions through Bigorre and all Languedoc, sometimes to a distance of 30 leagues. "In their march out they touched nothing, but on their return all things were seized, and sometimes they brought with them so many prisoners and such quantities of cattle that they knew not how to dispose of or lodge them. They laid under contributions the whole country except the territory of the Comte of Foix, where they dared touch nothing without paying for it. Tarbes was kept in great fear, and was obliged to enter into a composition with them." In 1369, not very long after the visit of the Black Prince, Lourdes was actually attacked by the French army commanded by the Duc d'Anjou, and at the end of 16 days the town, defended only by a palisade, and much injured by the machines which the duke brought to bear against it, was won; but the enemy made no impression on the citadel above, which bade defiance for six weeks longer to all efforts to take it. The governor remained true to his oath sworn to the Prince of Wales to guard his stronghold, and resisted the offer of a large sum from the Duc d'Anjou to deliver it up. Another attempt was made to induce this faithful châtelain to betray his trust, by Gaston Phœbus, who invited him to his castle of Orthez. Before setting out, however, Pierre Arnaut confided his stronghold to his brother Jean, who took the same oaths of fidelity. Gaston, irritated at the stedfast honesty of Arnaut in refusing his proposal to yield up the castle, in a brutal fit of rage stabbed him in 5 places with his poignard, and thrust him into a dungeon, where he perished. The atrocious crime availed him not; for Jean, the brother of his victim, proved as trusty a governor and skilful a captain as the murdered Pierre.

There is nothing to be seen here, but the artist-traveller may probably get a sketch of the castle and its picturesque donjon. The sides of the valley are very bare and uninviting near this.

The direct post-road from Pau to Bagnères branches off from Lourdes, whence it is distant 21 kilom. (Rte. 87.)

When Lourdes is left behind we are in the heart of the mountains, but the valley continues for some time stern, rocky, bare; showing marks in its gashed sides and rock-strewn bottom of the fury of the torrents.

Here and there a feudal hill fort rises upon its rocky perch, a relic of the days when nearly every valley of the Pyrenees was the scene of almost constant border warfare.

This unpromising vestibule, however, leads into what has not unjustly been called the Paradise of Argelez, where the valley of Lavedan (for so this part of the watercourse of the Gave de Pau above Lourdes is called) expands into a wide basin renowned for its picturesque beauty, fertility, and cultivation, and ranking among the finest in the Pyrenees. This altered scene opens out to view after passing the widely conspicuous dismantled tower of Vidalos, which, rising in the midst of the valley upon a monticule, conceals the village behind it.

Rich maize crops or verdant pastures occupy the bottom, interspersed with orchards alternately powdered with blossom or laden with fruit, walnut, fig-trees, and vines; but the tilled land extends far up the slopes, and the grand mountains around are clothed with forests of noble growth, the whole scattered over with houses and villages, which add to the whole the charm of much cheerfulness. In the midst of this lies the pretty village or small town of *Argelez*. (*Inn:* H. de France, clean and reasonable.) Argelez stands 1575 ft. above the sea-level, but, from its sheltered situation, enjoys a climate where winter tarries so short a while that its presence is scarcely perceived; where the snowflake melts as soon as it falls, and spring begins when the valley above and below is buried in snow. In summer, however, it is intensely hot. It is precisely in the midst of these beauties of nature that man appears most miserable: the maladies of goître and cretinism are very prevalent about Argelez.

[The *Val d'Azun*, opening out on the W. opposite Argelez, and extending up into the central chain between the mountains called Pic du Midi d'Azun and Pic de Gabisos, includes some very fine scenery, and is well worth exploring. A path leads up by Anzizans, a beautiful spot, to Arrens, the highest village (8 m.); but beyond it stands the pilgrimage chapel of N. D. de Pouey la Hun, a picturesque building on a pedestal of rock overlooking the valley. From Arrens a mountain-path runs to Eaux-Bonnes (Rte. 84), crossing two ridges, the second being the Col de Torte.]

Beyond Argelez the scanty remains of the ancient abbey of St. Savin, long ago sequestrated, are passed high up on the hill to our right. The view from the convent-garden is beautiful, and the church, said to be as old as Charlemagne, is *very* curious. The valley of Argelez terminates at

19 Pierrefitte.—No good *Inn*. This village, whose population seems to live by begging, much to the traveller's annoyance, is the centre from which the road to Cauterets and to Barèges separate: it is seated at the foot of a lofty and conspicuous mountain, which seems to block up the passage, and which, in fact, gives rise to 2 minor valleys. The road to Luz, Barèges, and St. Sauveur runs up that on the l., and the way to Cauterets is on the rt. of this mountain. The highest point of the ridge dividing the valley of Cauterets from that of Luz is named the Pic du Midi de Viscos: it is 7030 ft. above the sea-level. The whole way to Cauterets lies through a narrow gorge, where the cheerful beauty of the lower valley gives place to savage grandeur. A good carriage-road, which took 4 years to complete, is carried through it, rising immediately behind Pierrefitte, before it penetrates into the defile, in well-contrived zigzags, either elevated on terraces of masonry or cut out of the hard rock: it is a fine work of engineering, not inferior, as far as it extends, to some

of the celebrated roads through and over the Alps. The ascent by the old road was both difficult and dangerous; 4 horses and 3 pair of oxen being attached to a carriage to drag it up. A portion of the old way remains, and serves as a short cut for the pedestrian, whence he may survey to advantage the mouth of the narrow gorge, in the depths of which the torrent struggles along. It is a rent burst through vertical strata of slate, yet, except where its sides are absolutely perpendicular, they are either carpeted with bright patches of green meadow or covered with trees and brushwood, among which the hazel thrives. At a short distance from the mouth of the gorge, the view, looking back upon the vale of Argelez, is peculiarly beautiful, from the contrast of rugged, gloomy wildness in the foreground, with the sunny richness beyond of groves, pastures, and corn-fields. Near the middle of the pass, which, *longo intervallo*, may recall to the Swiss traveller some features of the Via Mala, the road surmounts in a series of graceful curves a bed of limestone or marble, called *Butte du Limaçon*, which stretches across the valley like a dam. Over this the Gave tumbles in a long rapid, which frets its waters into foam as white as snow. To this succeeds a slight opening in the valley, and a tall pointed mountain appears at its extremity, clad in fir: at its foot lies Cauterets; though intervening hills conceal it from view until you are close upon it.

11 *Cauterets.*—Inns: Lion d'Or, comfortable; H. du Parc; H. de France.

There are tables d'hôte twice a day at the chief inns, and families may be supplied with meals in their rooms by a traiteur. Cauterets, though in a spot so remote and elevated (3254 ft. above the sea), with savage mountains encircling it in an amphitheatre, and overhanging its roofs with their peaks and pine forests, has a perfectly townish air, with an octroi at its entrance, paved streets of inns and lodging-houses, and in the centre an irregular market-place. It is one of the chief Brunnen of the Pyrenees, containing nearly 1000 permanent Inhab., — abounding in agents, guides, horse-jobbers, and itinerant marchands, who beset the traveller the moment he sets foot within it. The number of houses is about 200; most of them have the door-posts, window-sills, and thresholds of grey marble, and over every other door is emblazoned "Chevaux ou voitures à louer." Invalids repairing to Cauterets to take the waters must address themselves to the inspector (Dr. Buron), who will inscribe their names in a book, and allot to them an hour for taking the bath, to remain fixed during the whole of their stay, with a chaise à porteur to convey them if required.

The chief building is the modern pump-room or *Etablissement des Bains* built near the foot of the hill, to receive the waters of the source called *les Espagnols*, one of the most powerful and hottest in the Pyrenees. It is so named from its having at an early period, according to tradition, cured the ailments of a king of Arragon, or from being much frequented by Spaniards, who cross the mountains in great numbers to repair hither. The new building is supplied with water in pipes carried down the slope of the hill de Perraute, from the source, situated at a considerable elevation, where the old bath-house stands. The bathing apparatus and accessories are constructed on the most approved plan dictated by the experience of modern science. The older bath-houses in the same direction are little better than wretched sheds, approached by paths so steep and stony as to require much exertion on the part of the robust to surmount; yet up them the invalid was formerly compelled either to toil on foot or be carried in a chaise à porteur.

The *Mineral Springs* here are sulphurous and hot, varying only in the quantity of the same ingredients, and in warmth from 102° to 122° Fahr. There are about 16 distinct sources, six of which rise on the hill of Perraute, above the town to the E., and the remainder are situated higher up the valley, on the banks of the Gave, from 1 to 1½ m. distant. They are said to present, in their strength, warmth, and qualities an epitome of almost all the sulphurous sources scattered over the Pyrenees; some of them being even more powerful than those of Barèges, others as mild as St. Sauveur. The chief of the springs on the banks of the Gave, and the one most resorted to, is the *Raillère*, whose waters are received in a building of some pretensions, faced with a portico, on a raised terrace, at the foot of a granitic mountain, destitute of trees or verdure, but covered over with fallen blocks of stone, which descend its slopes in dreary ruin. From 6 to 8 in the morning all the world of Cauterets repairs to this desolate spot, and during the dense season bathers assemble here at a much earlier hour, even at 4 in the morning. The road is thronged with sour-faced invalids; open sedan-chairs upon poles, covered with a canvas hood, of which 50 or 60 are kept in the town, hurry to and fro, occupied by muffled females; peasant women in red capulets mingle with Paris dandies in white berrets and red Béarnais sashes (la mode des Bains): black ecclesiastics in broad-brimmed hats, Capuchin monks in brown sackcloth and hoods, and Spaniards of swarthy olive-coloured visage and stately gait, their heads swathed in mottled handkerchiefs, their persons muffled up in the embozo of their cloaks, which are often no better than horsecloths, offering a singular combination of dignity and poverty, — such are the component parts of the motley and picturesque crowd which repairs daily to La Raillère. There are 23 Cabinets des Bains at La Raillère, with 2 douches and a fountain for drinking.

Above the Raillère is a group of other springs and a cluster of little bath-houses, built one above another against the hill-sides: the principal are the *Bain du Pré*, beneath a stream of fallen rocks, grown over with lichens, Petit St. Sauveur, Mahourat, B. des Œufs, and des Yeux. The *Source de Montmorency* is a sort of grotto, whose waters, too hot for the hand to bear, deposit a white, greasy slime; and the *Bain du Bois*, the highest in this direction, contains 4 cabinet baths, with a douche in each, and beds for the invalid who may desire to encourage the perspiration produced by the bath, and 2 piscines or large baths: the charge for one is 20 sous.

July and August are the *season* when Cauterets is most visited: lodgings are then very dear; poorly furnished apartments sometimes costing as much as 4 or 5 fr. each per diem.

There is a subscription reading-room or club here, called *Cercle*.

Several formal avenues and alleys on the outskirts of the town, by the side of the road to Pierrefitte, and the Parc on the margin of the Gave, satisfy the wants of French visitors as promenades, but must appear wearisome to English: indeed, except in the society of friends, or with the inducement of illness to make one tarry, the attractions at Cauterets are few.

The Grange de la Reine, an humble farm, so called from Queen Hortense having once been belated in crossing the mountains, and having passed the night there, is a good point of view for the basin of Cauterets, about 600 ft. above it. The mountain called *Peak of Monné* commands a far more extensive and very striking view, but is a serious mountain to climb; 10 hrs. up and down.

The sportsman may be thankful to know, that the rivers abound in trout, and that the chace of the izard and the bear may be pursued on the neighbouring mountains between the Vignemale and the Pic du Midi d'Ossau, with some prospect of success at the latter end of spring. These wild animals are, however, becoming rare even in these their last retreats. Jean Destapins is a capital guide and chasseur.

Chaises à porteur cost 15 fr. a day, and 3 fr. pourboire to the porteurs, who are very agile and sure-footed; ladies are often carried by them as far as the Lac de Gaube. Good *ponies* may be hired here.

Nobody thinks of quitting Cauterets without making the customary excursion (one of the most interesting in the Pyrenees) to the *Pont d'Espagne* and *Lac de Gaube*. There is a bridle-road all the way, well marked but steep at its farther extremity, and the excursion may be performed by men without a guide, though those who wish to save time will take a guide and mount him on a horse. It requires about 2 hrs'. good walking to reach the Pont d'Espagne, and 45 min. more thence to the Lac de Gaube: the return may be effected in less time.

Passing the source de la Raillère, and other springs and baths already mentioned, and winding between the mountains Perraute and Peyrénère, whose sides are strewn with rocks fallen from above, the road ascends by the margin of the Gave, through a wild narrow valley, the lower parts of the mountains bounding it wooded at first with trees and bushes, and afterwards with pine forests, while the upper parts rise in bare precipices, serrated peaks, and pointed aiguilles of granite.

The torrent leaps down from the upper to the lower slopes of the valley in several fine *falls*, the best of which is the cascade *de Cerizette*, where travellers usually dismount and scramble down into a rude scene of rocks, wood, and water. Further up, the road winds through a wild spot called "Le Grand Chaos," consisting of immense blocks of limestone fallen from above.

About 6 m. from Cauterets is the *Pont d'Espagne* (5150 feet above the sea), in itself a simple structure of pine trunks thrown across the torrent, here confined in a narrow chasm between rocks, just below the juncture of the Gave descending from the Lac de Gaube with that from the Marcadaou. The streams unite by leaping together into the chasm under the bridge, in picturesque *Falls*, but of no great magnitude. They are best seen about 20 or 30 yards on the path leading into Spain. These are but accessories to the sublime scene around, which, from the predominance of black fir forests, surrounded by granite cliffs shooting upwards in spires and pinnacles, our friend and fellow-traveller (*T.*) assures us, reminded him somewhat of Norway.

[The valley above the Pont d'Espagne, called Val de Jarret, continues of great grandeur, and is traversed by a path on the l. bank of the stream by the Marcadaou pass to the baths of Panticosa in Spain. (See Rte. 83.) The road is good as far as "some saw-mills, ¾ hr. above the Pont. The road then becomes stony and steep, ill fitted for horses, and you go faster on foot. From the saw-mills to the summit is about 1 hour's walk. From the top (4 hrs. from Cauterets) you descend in ½ hr. to some small lakes, by a rather difficult path. Thence to Panticosa, 3 hrs., a fatiguing descent, but not dangerous, down a staircase, as it were, of granite. The journey occupies 8 hrs. good from Cauterets. It is well worth while to ascend the Marcadaou Pass, even if you do not cross into Spain, as far as the frontier, as the view towards Spain is magnificent—far finer than that from the Brèche de Roland. It comprises 4 chains of snow-clad mountains.]

To reach the *Lac de Gaube* you must turn to the l. close to the Pont d'Espagne. Immediately above it you turn aside over another small wooden bridge, called Pont de Joseph, and, alighting at a small hut or cabaret, you gaze down from a green knoll upon a magnificent fall, "La Cascade," the whole body of water discharged from the Lac de Gaube, tumbling from a considerable height. Returning over the bridges, you take the l. hand very steep path, which strikes up the mountain side through the pine wood, and at first by the side of a torrent, and over many patches of boggy ground. It is here that a guide is useful. After about ¾ hour's walk (2 m.) over trunks and roots and shattered stones, you reach this lonely basin of green water. It is not more than 2½ m. in circumference, yet is the largest lake among the Pyrenees, and lies at an elevation of 1788 mètres = 5866 ft. above the sea-level, and is 300 or 400 (?) ft. deep. The steep precipices on either side are bare, except where seamed with lines of straggling black firs, alternating with streams of fallen rocks; but the entire centre of the picture is filled with the noble mass of the *Vignemale*, one of the highest mountains in France, white with eternal snow, crowned by crags and by glaciers which feed the lake through a small fall. The only habitation is the fisherman's hut, which now serves as a restaurant (furnishing lake trout for the hungry traveller's breakfast at a high rate), planted upon a ridge of granite, stretching across the valley, and damming up the waters of the lake. On a projecting rock a little *monument of white marble*, railed in, is the record of the melancholy fate of a young Englishman, named Pattison, and his wife, who, within one month of their marriage, were drowned in the lake. They had trusted themselves to the frail skiff of the fisherman to row across the lake; and it is supposed to have been accidentally overset, for no human eye beheld the accident. Their bodies were conveyed to Witham in Essex. A detestable, lying romance, grafted on their sad story, destitute of all truth, is sold on the spot—let no one buy it.

The *ascent of the Vignemale* is sometimes made from the lake, which is either crossed in the boat, or skirted by the path on the l. The clue to the ascent is the Gave, which forms the waterfall at the extremity. Following its bank, you ascend in succession, in the course of 1½ hour's walk, 5 different stages or steps of the mountain, each of which the torrent clears by a leap. The mass of the mountain is alpine limestone, which here overlies the granite prevailing from La Raillère to the Lac de Gaube. The Gave has its origin in the foot of a glacier stretching nearly up to the top of the mountain. Its crest is topped by 3 peaks detached from one another; the lowest of the 3, called Petit Pic, is alone accessible. The highest is 11,001 ft. above the sealevel, surpassing every other in the French Pyrenees. The view is said to extend into Spain and over a large part of the French chain. This excursion cannot be performed without the aid of approved and experienced guides.

[There is a difficult mountain path among broken rocks and the débris of glaciers, from the Lac de Gaube over the shoulder of the Vignemale, keeping that mountain on the rt., through the *Col or Port d'Ossoué* and down the *Val d'Ossoué* to Gavarnie. It requires 8 or 10 hrs., and should not be undertaken without good guides, being one of the most difficult expeditions in the Pyrenees.]

The course usually taken by persons proceeding to Bagnères, Barèges, and Gavarnie, from Cauterets, is to retrace their steps down the valley as far as Pierrefitte (see p. 292), and thence ascend the gorge leading up to Luz, which is so interesting in its scenery that no one should omit to explore it.

It is a truly magnificent defile, differing from that to Cauterets, being rather less gloomy, but scarcely superior. It abounds in rich foliage throughout. Near the 3rd bridge over the Gave a new road has been made with much engineering skill, running 200 or 300 ft. lower down than the old, which mounts a very steep ascent, only to descend immediately after. It is alternately a shelf cut with vast labour out of the rock, or a terrace built up with masonry; with an abyss under foot, and towering masses over head. The chasm through which the Gave flows is very striking: it is a rent so narrow that its sides seem to overlap each other, and never to have been completely parted. The green torrent chafing along, and worming its way through the depths between the rocks, is a beautiful object. Where the new road, in one even gradual ascent, meets the old, the gorge opens into a basin-shaped vale, remarkable for its rich carpet of verdure, cultivated in patches, having little villages planted a considerable way up its sides, until fields give place to forests. The mountains by the separation leave space for a small plain nearly in the form of a triangle, entered by a narrow defile at each of its angles. On the S.W. opens that of Gavarnie, at the mouth of which lies St. Sauveur, on the S.E. that of the Bastan leading to Barèges, guarded at its mouth by the Castle of St. Marie. From both of these issue Gaves which, meeting in the midst of the plain, escape by its third or N. angle through the defile leading to Pierrefitte, and traversed by the carriage-road. [rt. A road branches off direct to St. Sauveur.] At the upper end of the plain between the defiles of Gavarnie and Barèges, at the foot of a lofty mountain called Pic de Bergons, lies the little village of Luz. An avenue of formal poplars traverses the verdant flat meadows, gushing with rills of water, to which they owe their emerald tints and rich crops of grass, and leads into

Luz (*Inn*: H. des Pyrénées or Poste, Mad. Cazeaux). Luz or St. Sauveur are the best head-quarters for an expedition to Gavarnie and Barèges. Grandet's lodging-house is also recommended.

Luz is a cleanly village, situated on a crystal Gave of rapid flow: to the refreshing stream of one of its tributary brooks, under the inn windows, horses and pigs repair to bathe all day long. The pigs in particular seem to have acquired unwonted habits of cleanliness in this country, and to enjoy excessively the ablutions of their sides administered by the swineherd, who bastes them with a wooden ladle.

The *Church of Luz*, enclosed within a castle furnished with battlements and loop-holed walls, is a great curiosity, bearing as it does the mixed character of the order of the Templars,—half monks, half soldiers,—by whom it was founded. They were planted here to guard the frontier in troublous times, forming an outpost of Christians against the Saracens at first, and Spaniards afterwards. The church, entered by a machicolated gate under a projecting turret, is a Romanesque building probably of the 11th centy. The carved doorway, and the arcade of straight-sided arches, running round the E. end on the outside, deserve notice; also a *small doorway* now walled up on the S. side, through which alone, according to a tradition which wants confirmation, the proscribed race of *Cagots* were allowed to enter the church, where they occupied a chapel apart from the rest of the congregation. Crêpe de Barèges is made at Luz.

The knoll behind Luz crowned with the ruins of a hermitage commands a very pleasing view, looking down into a valley on either hand, and is easily accessible. A path may be found to descend on the opposite side to St. Sauveur, crossing the road to Gavarnie, and the small wooden bridge over the Gave.

It is not more than $\frac{1}{2}$ a m. by the level road from Luz to the *Baths of St. Sauveur*, a narrow street of white *Inns* (H. de la Paix: H. de France, best, clean, and good cuisine; charges 6 fr. a-day, bed and board) and lodging-houses planted on a narrow terrace or ledge, on the top of a rocky cliff, about 200 ft. above the Gave on its l. bank, and just within the jaws of the romantic and beautifully wooded defile leading to Gavarnie. Its most conspicuous edifice is a mean modern church in the form of a *Rotunda*, badly built. Near it rises a *pillar*, which, by the erasure in 1830 of its inscription, has ceased to commemorate the event to which it owes its existence, viz. the presence of the Duchesse d'Angoulême at these baths. It stands in the so-called *Jardin Anglais*.

In the middle of the village are the *Baths* (Etablissement Thermal), one of the handsomest in the Pyrenees, containing 14 or 16 baignoires, supplied from springs of sulphurous water, resembling those of Cauterets, but less warm, and less rich in gas. They are considered efficacious in female complaints, for nervous affections, &c. Thus the greater number of invalids here are ladies, while at Barèges the male sex abounds. Being weaker than those of Barèges, a course of them is recommended as a good preparation for the stronger waters of Barèges.

The name St. Sauveur is said to be derived from an inscription set over the healing source by a bishop of Tarbes, at what period is unknown:—"Vos haurietis aquas de fontibus Salvatoris."

The carriage-road up the valley stops at St. Sauveur: a wooden bridge opposite the baths leads over to the other side, where a bridle-road is carried.

At St. Sauveur, as well as at Luz, horses and guides may be had at the usual charges. Jacques St. Laur, of Luz, who may be heard of at Madame Cazaux's, is an excellent guide. Bernard and Martin are also recommended. Another guide, Pierre Sanio, made the ascent of the Maladetta in 1842.

The summit of the *Pic de Bergons*, the hill behind Luz and opposite St.

Sauveur, 6117 ft. above the sea, is one of the best points of view among the Pyrenees, and one of the most accessible; since even ladies may *ride* up without difficulty, or be carried in a chaise à porteur. About 2 hrs. are required to reach the summit, and 1½ to descend. From the top may be seen the Cirque of Gavarnie, the Brèche de Roland, and Tours de Marboré, and the more distant and loftier Mont Perdu to the S.; to the W. the Vignemale; to the E. the sterile valley of Barèges, and the Pic du Midi; to the N. the Vale of Lavedan and the plains beyond it.

There is a path, not easy to find without a guide, over the mountains from St. Sauveur to Cauterets: the journey takes 5 hrs. on foot; but the high road (already described) is much grander in scenery, and as smooth as a bowling-green all the way, though it makes a wide détour.

Cirque de Gavarnie—Brèche de Roland— Mont Perdu.

The valley of the Gave de Gavarnie, at whose mouth stands St. Sauveur, contains some of the most striking scenery in the Pyrenees, and terminates in the most remarkable of those *Oules* or *Cirques* peculiar to the Pyrenees, and already described, § 4. The distance from Luz or St. Sauveur to the Cirque de Gavarnie is about 15 m. A good but narrow horse-road runs thither, and the time employed, riding as fast as stones, gutters, and steep and frequent ascents and descents will permit, is rather less than 3 hrs.; but ladies riding at a gentler pace will take 4 or 5. It takes 4 hrs. to walk; no guide is needed to Gavarnie, only thence up to the Brèche one is indispensable. On reaching the foot of the bridge leading to St. Sauveur, you turn short to the l., without crossing, and ascend by the road along the rt. bank of the Gave, passing the baths on the opposite side. The grand scenery of the defile begins at once:—umbrageous woods alternating with precipitous rocks—mountain peaks of picturesque form rear their heads aloft; below gapes a confined chasm. The road is a narrow shelf, cut in the face of a rocky precipice, down which the eye gazes 300 or 400 ft., sheer into the green and frothy river, within the half-opened fissure below. One difficult pass around an angular shoulder of the mountain is called *Pas de l'Echelle*, because, before the present road was cut, it could only be traversed by a hazardous stair, descending on one side and ascending on the other. Here the peasants of Bigorre defeated a force of Miquelites (Spanish troops), who invaded the frontier for the last time in the wars of Louis XIV., 1708. There are ruins, down in the hollow, of an old fort called *Escalette*, the vestiges of which are nearly gone. Many small falls are passed and torrents crossed by high and narrow bridges, suspended over deep gulfs: many of the water-courses are bestridden by mills, not much larger than boxes; a row of such, close together, seen on the hill-side, near the romantic double *bridge of Sia*, look like beads on a white string.

Twice the valley expands, into the basins of Pragnères and Gèdre, and it is more often throttled (étranglé) by narrow defiles. On approaching the village of Gèdre, from the hill above it, you have a fine view, for a short space, of the snowy mountains called Tours de Marboré, and of the Brèche de Roland, a gap in the wall of rock which crests the mountain, looking like a notch made in a jaw by the loss of a single tooth. It was cut through, according to the legend, by Roland, the brave Paladin, with his trusty blade Durandal, to open a passage in pursuit of the Moors. To the rt. of it the false Brèche, a similar gap, is seen. They both lie immediately above the Cirque of Gavarnie, and are soon lost to view behind intervening mountains, as the valley curves, and they are invisible from the Cirque itself. At Gèdre there is a small *Inn* (N.B. fleas), and a sight scarcely worth notice, but to which travellers are invited, called *Grotte de Gèdre*. It is an imperfect arch, formed by the torrent scooping out the rock, partly grown over with creeping shrubs. There is a pleasant excursion from Gèdre across the shoulder of the Vignemale to the Lac de Gaube, 4 hrs'. walk.

[The opening on the l., behind Gèdre, through which the torrent issues, is the mouth of the *Val d'Héas*, one of the largest and deepest valleys which penetrate the granitic region of the Pyrenees, containing fine wild scenery, and terminating in the Cirque de Troumouse, situated a little to the E. of that of Gavarnie. In coming from Luz the valley is entered by a road turning to the l., on the height which precedes the village of Gèdre. It keeps up on the slope for some distance, then ascends along the rt. bank of the Gave, under the shade of fine trees, ashes and sycamores. The torrent descending on the l. from the Cambiel is next crossed on a bridge; a sombre gorge succeeds, leading to the village of Héas, remarkable for its *chaos* of granite blocks, about 4 m. from Gèdre, which have fallen from the mountain above, across the valley, and resemble that of Peyrada, described farther on. This enormous land-slip took place in 1650, blocked up the torrent, and formed a lake behind it, which lasted until 1788, when its waters, sweeping away the dam, broke out, inundating the valley below, and thus the lake was tapped and emptied.

Here is the *Chapelle de la Vierge d'Héas*, 4910 ft. above the sea-level, resorted to yearly between the 15th of August and the 18th of September, by hosts of pilgrims from afar, who come to worship and kiss her miraculous image, which is dressed in gold-embroidered stuffs, and hooded with the red capulet of the country. Before the rude chapel was built by the shepherds of the valley, to shelter it, the image sought refuge upon an enormous block of granite, the largest and most elevated of the group of fallen fragments, called *Le Caillou de l'Arayé*, which is much reverenced in consequence. It is a wild and naked spot, with little cultivation. Beyond it the gorge d'Aguila opens out to the E. About 6 m. farther on the valley ends in the *Cirque de Troumouse*, a semi-circular wall of precipitous mountains, enclosing a verdant plain. It is larger than Gavarnie, but not so imposing, yet deserves to be seen. You may walk hence over the Coumélie mountain to Gavarnie. No provisions to be had at Héas."

The road to Gavarnie from the prettily situated village of Gèdre skirts the flanks of the mountain Coumélie, between hedges of box, and reaches in a little space the *Chaos* or *Peyrada*, an éboulement or slip of masses of gneiss fallen from above, so extensive that it looks as though a mountain had tumbled to pieces. It is a grand and savage scene. The path winds, in zigzags, through a perfect labyrinth of blocks, many of them as big as a house, and far larger than the Cumberland Bowder stone, piled one above another in extreme confusion, forming mysterious cavities and sheds between them. These fragments sweep down to the Gave, and partly conceal it; their fall must have occurred long ago, from the lichens which cover their surface, and was probably produced by the action of the atmosphere, especially of frost, so powerful an agent in fracturing and disintegrating the slaty structure of the gneiss. Beyond the Chaos the road passes under the base of the Pimené, a picturesque mountain, rising on the l. to a height of 9384 ft.

In passing the Pont de Barregui the peaks and glaciers of the *Vignemale* are disclosed to view for a short time, at the extremity of the Val d'Ossoué (p. 296), up which runs the mountain path to Cauterets by the Lac de Gaube.

Gavarnie is a poor small village, 4623 ft. above the sea-level, with a small *Inn*, furnishing fresh trout and cutlets.

The modernized and uninteresting *Ch*. contains the skulls of 12 Templars (?) beheaded in the reign of Philip le Bel; such is the tradition, and the Order certainly had a commandery in this desolate spot. One of the heads is said to be that of a female.

Behind Gavarnie rise the black walls of the *Cirque*, surmounted by eternal snow shutting in the valley. It appears close to the village, and the stranger will scarcely believe that he has 3 weary m. to trudge or ride, which will take nearly an hour, before he can reach its farther extremity. Three shallow, basin-shaped valleys, partly strewn with stones, partly carpeted with grass, seemingly at one time lake basins, are passed, before you surmount the small projecting wall of rock which masks the entry to the Cirque, and once, doubtless, dammed up the waters of the Gave. Here, shut out from the world, and, as it were, arrived at its end, you gaze up to the vast semicircle of rocks around, the tall rampire of a kingdom, at the base of which France terminates. The precipices forming its sides, varying in height from 1000 to 1400 ft., are divided into 3 or 4 steps or stages, upon each of which a glacier, covered with white snow, is heaped: not a scrap of vegetation relieves their bare sides. Down the vertical faces of the rocks stream 12 or 15 thin cascades, like white threads; but there is one on the l. hand, where the precipice is least interrupted, which falls in one white cord, only twice broken by ledges, nearly 1266 ft. high: it is reputed the highest fall in Europe, and is the head water of the Gave de Pau; but so small is it in volume that it dissipates into spray before reaching the bottom. These streamlets are the drainage of the glaciers above, and all, joining the Gave, escape from the Cirque by the only opening, that by which the traveller enters. The floor of the Cirque is an uninterrupted and irregular heap of rubbish and blocks of rock, the ruins of the neighbouring mountains, which have fallen from above, very toilsome to walk over; and in the midst are one or two patches of dirty snow, nearly consolidated into ice, under which the Gave flows in a hollow vault. It takes nearly ¼ an hr. from the entrance to reach the foot of the high waterfall, where the geologist may find specimens of the fossils contained in the rocks of the Cirque, which have been ascertained by M. Dufresnoy to be identical with those of the chalk. An English traveller would certainly not recognize, otherwise, that formation, in the dark cliffs around, so unlike in colour and texture to the white chalk of England.

The mountains rising above the Cirque, but not visible from within its enclosure, are to the E. the *Cylindre*, 10,050 ft., so called from its shape, whose base is embedded in the great glacier, whence springs the high fall; the Tours de Marboré, 9964 ft., forming part of the Mont Perdu; and on the W. the Brèche de Roland, and farther on the Fausse Brèche.

The ascent of the *Brèche de Roland* is made from the Cirque of Gavarnie: it is fatiguing and difficult, but not dangerous, provided the head be steady. Some provisions, and a wine or brandy flask, should be taken. It occupies 4 hrs., and 2 to descend; slow walkers take 3½ to 4 hrs. to ascend, 3 to descend. The ascent commences from the corner of the Cirque on the rt. hand, opposite to the high fall. A stranger would scarcely find the spot; no path leads to it, and there is no apparent break or interruption in the perpendicular wall of the Cirque. The strata of the limestone are here vertical, and a buttress of it slightly projecting from the mass furnishes the means of scaling the precipice along the abrupt and shattered edges of the slaty rock, here divided like the leaves of a book, set on end, but shivery on the surface. The broken angles and splinters serve as steps, in which one may insert the toes and fingers, but it is as abrupt as the ascent of a ladder. The path winds round some smooth projecting shoulders of rock, and round the edges of 1 or 2 cliffs, which alternate, higher up, with steep slopes, covered less with grass than with fallen stones. These steep grassy banks form a pasturage, called Las Serrades, for the flocks of some Spanish shepherds, who rent them from the commune of Gavarnie. There is no intermission to the steepness of the ascent, no flat interval between the slopes; it takes more than 1 hr. of "treadmill work" to rise above the high cascade. It is a glorious sight to look *down* from this upon the precipices and waterfalls, and the great glacier which feeds them, at which, shortly before, you gazed *up* with aching neck. Hence the Tours de Marboré are well seen; and at this height, about noon, the roar of avalanches succeeds to the monotonous dash of waterfalls, which before alone interrupted the solitude. The Cirque is soon after lost sight of: above your head rises an expanse of snow and glacier covering a steep slope, inclined like the roof of a house, surmounted by the wall of rock, in the midst of which is *Roland's Breach*, and another similar embrasure on the rt. of it, called Fausse Brèche. As the glacier is too abrupt to ascend, you leave it on the l. hand, and begin to climb a less steeply inclined snow-clad slope, which at some seasons is denuded down to the slaty rubbish below the snow. It is a work of some fatigue to surmount this, and crampons and a pole are generally furnished by the guide. When two-thirds of the acclivity are surmounted the guide turns to the l. across the glacier, whose surface is so highly inclined that it is not possible to scale it from below. Even to cross it when the snowy surface is hard or slippery requires great caution. The mountaineer sets his foot down firmly with a stamp, to secure a firm hold, and drives in his pole well at every step he takes: a false move would send you at once to the bottom. A few paces beyond the glacier brings you to the *Brèche*. That insignificant notch in the mountain brow seen from Gèdre has now expanded into a colossal portal 300 ft. wide, 350 ft. high, and 50 ft. thick—9337 ft. above the sea-level. The ridge or crest in which it is formed is literally, not metaphorically, a wall of rock, varying in height from 300 to 600 ft., which here divides France from Spain, escarped on both sides, and not more than 50 or 80 ft. thick. Through this singular opening—as it were a window in the mountain, nearly square in its angles, and not much wider above than below—Spain is seen; a most uninviting prospect of rugged and bare mountains and valleys, filled with stones and snow in the foreground, while the distance is formed by the hazy plain of Arragon rising high up against the horizon. On the French side there is more of interest in the striking forms of the Vignemale, the Pic du Midi de Bigorre, the Bergons, and a hundred other peaks.

The Brèche is said by Raymond to be visible from Saragossa and Huesca; and a practised eye, knowing where to search for these cities, might, with the aid of a telescope, in a clear state of the atmosphere, be enabled to discern them from hence.

The threshold of the Brèche is angular, like the roof of a house, and the frontier line runs directly along it, so that one may sit astride of it, with one leg in France and the other in Spain.

All along the front of the Brèche, on the French side, the glacier is scooped out into a deep fosse or cavity, by the action of the sun's rays pouring from the south, through the opening, as Raymond has well explained, so that it cannot be approached directly, but only by skirting the edge of the cavity. The ascent was accomplished by the Duchesse de Berri in 1828, but it is not fit for ladies in general.

The Brèche de Roland is used by the inhabitants of several villages on the Spanish side as a pass into France, and especially by smugglers. Through it lies the way to ascend the *Mont Perdu*, whose top may be reached in 6 hrs. from the Brèche, descending at first some hundred ft., and skirting the crumbling slopes of the Marboré on the l. Travellers usually pass the night in a poor hut near its base on the high table-land called Millaris, scattered over with slaty débris, and traversed by rents and deep fissures. Mont Perdu is composed of 4 stages or terraces, faced by abrupt escarpments, each receding farther back than the one below. The 2 lower steps are easily ascended by means of a talus of marly débris fallen from above. The 3rd and 4th are very difficult to scale, especially the 4th, which can only be reached through a sort of chimney, serving as an outlet for the melting snow. The summit of the Mont Perdu is 11,168 ft. above the sea-level, second in height to the Maladetta alone among the Pyrenees; and it was first surmounted in 1802 by Raymond after two dangerous and fruitless attempts. It is not to be tried without the aid of a skilful guide. One may ascend from the hut of the Millaris and return from the summit to Gèdre on the same day.

Very *interesting* excursions may be made from Gavarnie into Spain to Busaruelo (3½ hours), and one hour beyond towards Torla, through the grandest scenery, returning the same day; and, 2ndly, over the Brèche de Roland to Fanlo, Nerin, and the rivulet Bellos. See HANDBOOK FOR SPAIN.

Barèges and Pass of the Tourmalet to Bagnères de Bigorre.

From Luz to Barèges is a continuous ascent of about 4¼ m. A much improved and well-constructed road now shortens what was once a very tedious drive; the old road being constantly washed away by the torrent.

The accommodation at Barèges is so very inferior that the traveller bound for Bagnères by the Tourmalet had better lengthen his day's journey by starting from Luz than put up at Barèges.

On quitting Luz you pass on the l. the ruined castle of *Ste. Marie*, one of the last possessions retained by the English in the S. of France, since it held out for the Black Prince nearly as long as Lourdes. It stands on a mount, at the point where the valley of Barèges, or of the Bastan, opens into the plain of Luz. This is one of the least attractive valleys of the Pyrenees; the mountains around it are not picturesque in their forms, and the fissile and easily disintegrated shale composing them, crumbling down and filling up the bottom and sides of the valley, has been cut through by the Bastan and other furious torrents which seam the mountain's sides. From time to time vast masses of débris are washed down, and éboulements ensue, which stop up the watercourses until a débâcle occurs, and spreads desolation below it. Such catastrophes are of frequent occurrence; and the main torrent, the Bastan, is a very scourge. The great elevation of the valley above the sea contributes to its cheerless and forbidding character; and it is in such a situation, at a height 4180 ft. above the sea-level, confined by gloomy mountains which almost seem to overhang it, that

7 *Barèges* stands, a watering-place better known by name, perhaps, in distant countries, than any other among the Pyrenees, and in deserved repute with those who are really ill and in earnest to get well, on account of the cures effected by its waters, but void of all other attractions, destitute even of a tolerable inn (H. de France; best, but very uncomfortable: cuisine dirty and bad;—H. de la Paix; worse still). There is nothing to see here, so that our advice to travellers for amusement is, pass through, and tarry not. Being the loftiest of the Pyrenean baths, its atmosphere is chilly and variable even in the height of summer. It contains about 70 houses, chiefly lodgings, with two miserable cafés, arranged in a long dull street, running by the side of the Gave. The buildings next the stream, which are *meant to last*, are based on huge buttresses of masonry, without which precaution they would long ago have been swept away by the inundations of the torrent. A wide gap, however, is left in the midst, upon which only a few temporary booths and huts of wood are raised, for the winter avalanches sweep down from the mountains Ayré on the S. and Midaü on the N., through the wide gaping gashes in their sides, which open out opposite the vacant space, and bury this part of the town under the snow for several months of the year. In consequence Barèges is inhabited only during summer and autumn, and is abandoned for the rest of the year, except by a few persons, who take care of the houses, to the wolves and bears, which often come down and prowl about the streets. An Englishman, who came hither in the midst of winter, found the entire

population reduced to 30 men and women, collected around the great public bath for the sake of the heat of the water, all busily employed knitting. At the beginning of summer the owners return and dig out their houses from the snow, which covers them up to the first floor. The triste air of the place is greatly increased by the number of cripples, sick, and invalids you encounter at every step. This may be called the Hospital Brunnen of the Pyrenees, being visited yearly by 1000 or 1200 genuine invalids, to whom the prospect of regaining health is a sufficient attraction. The French government have established here a military *hospital*, capable of receiving 300 men and 100 officers (perhaps more) for 50 days. The cures effected by the waters are wonderful: their efficacy is very great in gunshot and other wounds, in curing sores, in relieving rheumatism, stiffness of the joints, and scrofulous complaints. They cause old wounds, or ill-cured ulcers, to open afresh at first, then relieve them by discharges, drawing to the surface extraneous bodies long imbedded in the flesh, and promoting the exfoliation of carious portions of bone, and finally close the wound in a healthy manner.

The *mineral water* is very strong, its principal ingredient being sulphuret of sodium, with portions of carbonate, muriate, and sulphate of soda, azote, sulphuretted hydrogen, and animal matter. It is derived from 6 to 7 different springs, the most potent being that called *Le Tambour*, but the supply is scarcely adequate to the demand. They are conducted into a miserably-arranged, dirty, and ill-smelling bath-house, where they fill 16 baths, for the use of which 1 fr. is charged, and into 3 piscines or public baths capable of holding from 12 to 20 persons each. One of these is appropriated to the soldiers, another to the civil service, the 3rd to the poor. Admission to them is settled by order of precedence, and they are in use all day and all night. Indeed so precious is the fluid, that the water from the bath-house is said to be turned into the piscines. The piscines are horrid vaulted dens below ground, their roof serving as a promenade, filled with vapour; and the water has a greenish-yellow tint. The waters have a strong smell of rotten eggs, and a nauseous oily taste; after standing they are covered on the surface with a film of glairy unctuous substance, which they also deposit on the sides and bottom of the bath, called Barégine by French chemists. These valuable medicinal springs rise (as usual in the Pyrenees) near a junction of the slate rock with the granite, and force their way to the surface through a mass of débris composed of the neighbouring rocks. They were first brought into notice by a visit which Madame de Maintenon paid to them 1676, by advice of the royal physician Fagon, for the sake of the young Duc du Maine, natural son of Louis XIV., and her pupil. The "gouvernante" dates several of her letters from hence; and after a protracted residence she had the satisfaction of bringing back the little cripple so much better that he could enter the room to meet the king walking. She reached this place by crossing the Tourmalet, the road by Lourdes not being then made, and lodged in the Maison Maraquette. Barèges was once nearly swept away by the bursting of the Lac d'Oncet.

A scanty and stunted wood of firs and alders is planted on the hill above Barèges on the S. It serves as a partial protection from avalanches, and below is converted into a *promenade* by walks cut along the slopes.

The fine tissue called *crêpe de Barèges* is not made here, but at Bagnères de Bigorre and at Luz.

Diligences go daily in the season to Lourdes, where they correspond with those to Pau, Toulouse, and Bagnères. The direct road to Bagnères, and by far the most interesting, is over the *Tourmalet*, but it is not practicable for carriages. Horses and guides may be obtained at Barèges.

Besides the excursions described under the head of Luz, which may be made from Barèges nearly as well as from that place, is the ascent of the *Pic du Midi de Bigorre*, which lies but a short way off the road to Bagnères by the Tourmalet, and will now be described.

The distance from Barèges to Bagnères de Bigorre across the Tourmalet is about 18 m. Including a halt to rest the horses, it takes up from 7 to 8 hours. A good bridle road, which might be made passable for chars, leads up the Bastan valley on the l. bank of the torrent. The valley looks very dreary from the barrenness of the mountain tops, and the deep gashes cut in their crumbling sides by the avalanches which rush down them in spring. Yet the course of the falling snow is so regular, that on the very margin of these gashes cottages are built, each protected by a tuft of trees, and along their slopes a few cultivated patches of corn stretch upwards. Two torrents descend from the rt., out of the vales of Lienz and Escabous, at whose head lie nearly a dozen small tarns, or lakes. After passing these, the Bastan is crossed, and the main ascent begins.

[About 1¾ hr's. walk from Barèges you pass on the l. a path striking N. up a small valley towards the *Pic du Midi de Bigorre*. That majestic mountain, which, though 9553 ft. above the sea level, is free from snow in summer, rises on the l. of the pass of the Tourmalet, and is accessible, even on horseback, in 4½ hrs. from Barèges. The path is steep, and in many places dangerous, there being scarcely room for a horse to step. It is possible to ride to within 100 yards of the summit. The way lies by the margin of the Lac d'Oncet, a picturesque tarn at the foot of the peak, nearly closed in by precipices, about 2000 ft. below the summit. The view from the top is magnificent. It wants the numerous lakes of the Righi, but in other respects is superior. The Pic stands at the outer verge of the Pyrenean range: it descends with only one break to the plain, and affords a view towards Bordeaux and Toulouse, bounded only by the limit of vision. It comprises on the N. the plains watered by the Adour and Garonne; on the S. the great chain, including the step-like mass of the Mont Perdu, the Cylindre, Tours de Marboré, Brèche de Roland, and Vignemale, covered with glaciers; while among a multitude of peaks to the E. rises the Maladetta, the loftiest of the Pyrenees, forming a conspicuous point in this immense semicircle of mountains. There is another way down through the Hourquette de Cinq Ours and the ravine leading from the Lac d'Oncet to Trames Aigues in the valley of Grip. See below.]

The *Tourmalet* is a low curved ridge, such as would be called a col in the Alps—an isthmus uniting the Pic du Midi with the main chain of the Pyrenees, over which lies the passage from the valley of the Gave de Pau into that of the Adour. The old and shorter road is carried up to the col in a series of sharp zigzags, over heaps of shivered shale: the pedestrian will save time by taking it. The new path is longer, and runs more on a level, round the shoulders of the hills. Those bound for the Pic du Midi take this path. On the rt. rise three bristling mountains of fine form, the Caubère, the Campana, and the Pic d'Espade. The summit of the Pass is 7141 ft. above the sea-level: the view from it is not very striking; but as you look back the Monné and mountains above Cauterets are visible beyond it. The vale of Grip opens out far more pleasingly than that of Barèges, carpeted with beautiful pastures; it is the cradle of the infant Adour, which rises near the base of the Pic d'Espade. After a mile or two of gradual descent, the valley makes an abrupt dip, down which the path is carried, by a series of very steep zigzags called Escalette, to a hamlet occupied by shepherds, called Trames Aigues (3½ hours from Barèges), at the mouth of a gorge through which the pyramidal mass of the Pic du Midi appears in full majesty. This is the finest object on the pass: its bare precipice, when lighted up by the sun, exhibits the most singularly contorted strata, imitating the lines on an agate. It remains in sight only for a short distance; but from no point does this mountain appear to greater advantage. The summit of the Pic is reached from Bagnères by ascending this valley.

Near Artigues, a hamlet on the rt. beyond the river, is a cascade formed by one of the tributaries of the Adour, and a little lower down is another, the *Garret*, in the course of the Adour itself, beneath a black fir forest, which covers the shoulder of the mountain like a bear skin, above the village of *Grip*. Grip is a prettily situated group of scattered cottages, including a very tolerable country Inn, famed for its trout (H. des Voyageurs, chez Cazères): it is the one nearest Bagnères—4 hours' walk or ride from Barèges, and 3 from Bagnères de Bigorre. Grip is much frequented by visitors from both baths, on account of its waterfalls and its pleasing position, precisely in the part of the valley where trees flourish, corn begins to grow, and pastures become most verdant. The Pic du Midi may be reached in 5 h. from this, descending in 3 h. A mule path all the way; but up to the Lac d'Oncet, where it joins the path from Barèges, it is steep and rough.

From Grip to Bagnères de Bigorre there is a good carriage road, which, at Ste. Marie, falls into the *valley of Campan*, and the route to Luchon by Arreau (Rte. 86). The aspect of the Val de Campan from this point, and in descending to Bigorre, is less attractive than in ascending, owing to the arid, bare, and stained escarpments of the limestone cliffs (Jura limestone) on the rt. bank of the Adour; but there are some fine views on the l., looking up the tributary valleys towards the Pic du Midi.

Ste. Marie, 7½ m. from Bagnères, lies near the point of junction of two valleys, up one of which runs the road to Grip and the Tourmalet, and up the other, that to Luchon by Arreau. The village of Campan, lower down, which gives its name to the valley, is not remarkable, but every traveller is pestered as he passes to visit the grotto, which is not worth seeing.

16 The Pics du Midi and de Montaigu are well seen below this through the fine opening of the vale of Lesponne to the l.: near its entrance stands the mansion of St. Paul.

At Baudéan, a small village a little lower down, Baron Larrey, the army surgeon and favourite of Buonaparte, who accompanied him on his various campaigns, was born 1766, in a humble house marked by a marble tablet. The valley of Campan is fertile, well cultivated, and populous, with a considerable show of picturesque beauty. The precipitous mountain rising on the rt. is the *Penne de l'Hyeris*, often ascended on account of its view. The Pont de Gerde, over the Adour, leads to it.

2 m. short of Bagnères, close to the road, is Médous, a sequestrated and abandoned Capuchin convent, reduced to uninteresting ruins. A copious source of clear water rising here serves to turn a marble mill. On the outskirts of Bagnères, the road passes close under the promenade called Allées Maintenon.

BAGNERES DE BIGORRE (Route 87).

ROUTE 86.

THE PYRENEES—BAGNÈRES DE BIGORRE TO BAGNÈRES DE LUCHON—MOUNTAIN ROAD, BY THE HOURQUETTE D'ASPIN, ARREAU, COL DE PEYRESOURDE, AND VAL DE L'ARBOUST—EXCURSION TO THE LAC DE SECULÉJO, OR LAC D'OO.

This is now a good carriage-road, and the journey may be made in one day, say 14 hours, allowing 2 hours for rest. The charge for a carriage and pair of horses, including the use of leaders for the steep ascent of the pass, is 70 fr. The journey may be divided by sleeping at Arreau. The total distance may be about 40 m., exclusive of the excursion to Seculéjo, which is about 12 m. more, to and fro, off the direct road. The route abounds in picturesque beauties; it ascends the Val Campan (described in Rte. 85) as far as the village of

7½ m. Ste. Marie (4 hours' walk from Arreau).

We here leave, on the rt., the road to Grip and the Tourmalet, and, crossing the Adour, ascend gradually along the bank of its E. tributary, up the Val de Séoube, and, passing through a scattered and picturesque village, reach (in 2 hours' walking),

Paillole, a group of cottages, with a small Inn (Ferme St. Jean) where an omelette and trout may be had, in the midst of green pastures, encircled by noble forests, which seem to have suffered little diminution from the woodman's axe. In the mountain on the E. side of the valley, composed of transition limestone, are the *quarries of Espiadet*, yielding the marble called of Campan, a great deal of which was employed in the decoration of the royal villa of Trianon. After being long abandoned, they are now again worked by M. Geruzet of Bagnères. At Campan itself, where the rocks are of the Jura limestone, no marble is obtained.

The ascent to the Col, or *Hourquette d'Aspin*, is carried up from the farm cottages of Paillole, at first in zigzags, entirely through forests of fir, composed of fine trees of ancient growth, covering the hill sides far and wide. Through gaps among the trees, the bare Pic d'Arbizon (?) is seen, from time to time, on the rt., at the head of the valley. The trees thin out before reaching the top of the pass, whose open curved slopes are covered with turf. The Hourquette d'Aspin (1½ hour from Paillole) commands *one of the finest views in the Pyrenees*. Look back, and the Pic du Midi de Bigorre and the Pic d'Arbizon rise majestically above the pine forests; forward, and the billowy forms of many mountains, and the junction of many valleys, peaks, ridges, and hollows, one behind another, are presented to view, and the horizon is closed by the snowy top of the Maladetta, or at least of the Monts Maudits. The slope of the hills, on the side of Arreau, is so steep that the descent upon that town, which appears lying in a hole, as it were, no more than a rifle shot off, is only effected by most complicated tourniquets, or winding terraces, the vagaries of which are most extraordinary and tantalising: 4 or 5 times, when you think you are close to Arreau, the road turns away to penetrate nearly to the head of the valley, on the rt. or l., and it takes a good hour from the top of the pass to reach the town, which is about 5½ hrs.' ride or walk from Bagnères.

Arreau (*Inn :* H. de France, clean and tolerable) is a small and triste town, nowise remarkable except for its situation, nearly in the midst of the picturesque Val d'Aure, which runs up into the Pyrenees, between the Val de Campan and the Val de Luchon, at the junction of the Nestes (or torrents) de Louron and d'Aure, which turn several saw-mills: the number of inhabitants is about 1600. Here is a curious castellated *Church* of the Templars.

Lower down the valley, near Sarrincolin, are the marble quarries of Beyride and Camous.

[The upper part of the Val d'Aure unfolds scenery whose extreme beauty and magnificence will well recompense the pedestrian disposed to explore it, and prepared for the wretched accommodation which is to be found. Indeed it is advisable to take provisions of some kind, or at least white bread. A path along the l. bank of the Neste leads through the villages of Cadéac (½ hr.), Ancisan, Guichen, all ancient settlements of the Templars, to Vielle (Aure), 5 m., a village with a wretched inn (H. d'Espagne). Over this part of the valley the Pics d'Arbizon and d'Azet rise in great grandeur. Continue along the l. bank from Vielle, 1½ hr., to Tramesaigues (not to be confounded with the place of the same name mentioned further on), a village having sulphureous springs, a very picturesque ruined castle on a height, and a curious *Ch.* of the Templars, with a wooden clock tower, and a singularly ornamented door. It is one of the most romantic spots in the Pyrenees. From the l. bank you have the best view of the Templar ch. and castle opposite. Cross here by a bridge and return to Vielle by the rt. bank (1 hr.). The only place where you have a chance of getting anything to eat at Tramesaigues is chez le Douanier. The upper part of the valley is well worth exploring by any one who can rough it. Before reaching the village the valley divides, and 2 paths strike off into Spain, one due S. by the Port de Plan, the other inclining to S.W. by the Port de Bielsa, passing Aragnouet, whence a path mounts over the Port de Cambiel to Gèdre, at the mouth of the Val d'Héas. (Rte. 85.) The *Port de Cambiel* is a depression between the mountains of Cambiel and the Pic Long, nearly 8000 ft. high, whence the Vignemale and M. Perdu are well seen.]

There is a mule-path from Arreau to B. de Luchon, by the *Port de Pierrefitte* (7 hours' walk), which is loftier and finer in point of scenery than the Col de Peyresourde, but a bad road; a guide is required at least up to the Col, as it is difficult to find.

An excellent carriage-road, but very circuitous from its windings and zigzags, has been made from Arreau over the *Port de Peyresourde* to Luchon. It runs up the Valley of the Neste de Louron, which, at first narrow, widens out, and becomes populous higher up, and is studded with a great number of old feudal castles, now in ruins, but which once defended the passage into Spain, perched on conical rocks. That of Bordères, on the l. bank, was the stronghold of the Counts of Armagnac, owners of the valley, the last of whom, John V., in the reign of Louis XI., 1475, on account of his infamous union with his sister, was excommunicated by the pope, and deprived of his princely domains by Louis. Below this, looking back, there is a good view of the windings of the road to the Col d'Aspin and of the town of Arreau, which looks well only at a distance. At Avejan, above Bordères, the road crosses to the rt. bank, and, gradually ascending by narrow lanes flanked by trees and hedges, through the villages Estravielle and several others, reaches Loudervielle, distinguished by its square feudal watch-tower projecting over the valley, and confronted, on the opposite side, by a rival fort, based upon a rocky pedestal now quarried for slates. Above this, the vale of the Louron divides into 2 branches, terminating in the Ports de la Pez and de Clarbide, leading into Spain, but difficult, if not dangerous, and little used; and between them rises the grand Pic de Génos. Near the Port de la Pez are remains of a tunnel 200 ft. long, commenced by some speculators, who designed to bore through the mountain in order to reach the Spanish pine forests, and make use of their timber. The scheme was abandoned. The ruined gallery is situated high above all habitations, and to visit it would take up a day.

We pursue our course up the valley no farther, but at Loudervielle (2¾ hrs'. ride from Arreau) turn to the l. up a very steep stony ascent leading to the *Col de Peyresourde*, 4452 ft. above the sea, which separates the Val de Louron from that of L'Arboust, covered with coarse pasturage dotted over with a few fir-trees. The view from the summit over the chain of the Pyrenees, including the Maladetta, is very grand. Cultivation is carried up very high in the opposite valley; but the woods (arbusta), from which, doubtless, it derives its name, are greatly diminished. Before descending, a narrow path, difficult for horses, strikes off on the rt. direct to the Lac d'Oo, or de Seculéjo. The carriage-road to Bagnères makes a considerable détour, descending the valley nearly as far as an ancient, half-ruined, solitary ch., planted on a singular mound, by the side of which rises the brand or split fir tree set in readiness to be lighted on "The Eve of St. John" (1¾ hr. from Loudervielle).

[In order to reach the beautiful Lac d'Oo you turn to the rt. at this ch., and by a very narrow and stony bridle path, through the fields and along the slopes of a hill which drops down upon the village d'Oo and its picturesque castle, you enter the Val d'Asto, as this branch of the Val de l'Arboust, at whose upper end lies the Lac de Seculéjo, is called. It is very narrow and deep, closed in by impending mountains, and at its head by glaciers. The horse-path up it crosses the clear stream of the Oo or Go, just outside of the village, and following the rt. bank of the stream, threads stony lanes between pastures of vivid green under the shade of ash-trees. Next, it emerges upon open meadows, beyond which it begins to mount in earnest, by a long series of zigzags, a high step stretching across the valley, which from below or above appears a precipice, yet is made accessible for horses, but is very toilsome to surmount. We now enter the fir-woods; the mountains, sternly grand, rise beetling over the path, which is at one spot a mere shelf cut in the face of the rock. At length the valley is traversed from side to side by a natural dam of slate rocks, whose strata are vertical. Behind this the little oval basin, called *Lac d'Oo*, or *de Seculéjo*,* lies snugly cradled, shut in all round, save on the side of the dam, by precipices of great height, which, though vertical, are tinged green by partial vegetation. In front, a very fine cascade forms the centre of the picture, and is reflected in a white streak upon the dark mirror of the lake below. The waters of the lake escape in a fall over a gap in the slate-dam already mentioned, upon which also stands a hut where horses may be put up, and common refreshments obtained. The lake abounds with trout. Here a small toll is paid for keeping up the path, which higher up ceases to be practicable for horses.

The waterfall of the Lac d'Oo is fed from a still higher reservoir, the *Lac d'Espingo*, drawing its supplies from the contiguous glaciers. It may be reached either by a narrow path along the l. or E. margin of the Lac d'Oo, or by crossing it in a boat kept to convey people to the foot of the fall, and then by clambering up at the side of it through a rent in the slate rock, whose broken laminations serve as steps (scala); next, passing above the cascade, it reaches the upper lake *D'Espingo*, 1¼ hour's walk from Lac d'Oo. The savage wildness and awful stillness of this scene render it very impressive. There is a third lake close beside it, called Saounsat, in which fish cannot live, though trout are found in its neighbour, lying at the foot of the Mount Espingo, amidst scenery far more savage than that of the lake d'Oo. The rest of the way is pathless, and for some distance over beds of snow, and not to be explored without the aid of experienced guides. The course usually taken is to leave on the l. the 3rd lake and also a 4th, and making a detour push upwards through a natural breach in the rocks, by which the precipice may be surmounted—a fatiguing scramble. Some rounded summits of rock and snowy banks are next crossed, until the summit is reached, the rocky edge of a basin filled with snow, in whose depths lies another lake which remains ice-bound nearly throughout the year, fed by an extensive glacier. A walk of 1¼ m. across this snowy basin leads to the col called *Port d'Oo*, 9850 ft. above the sea-level, the loftiest col or pass in the Pyrenees, and exceeded by very few among the Alps, leading to the Spanish town of Venasque (R. 87). There is here no gap or opening in the rocky wall, only a narrow ridge, 20 ft. wide, commanding a scene of wildness not to be described. On the l. of this pass lies the vast glacier of the Port d'Oo, the second in extent, next to that of the Maladetta, among the Pyrenees. It is 5 hrs. walk from the Port d'Oo to the Spanish town of Venasque, and about 10 hrs. from Luchon. (Rte. 87.)

It takes about 1½ hr. to ascend from the village d'Oo to the Lac d'Oo, and 3 hrs. to descend from the lake to Luchon.]

In going from Luchon to the Lac d'Oo you turn to the l. out of the Val de l'Arboust at the village of Cazeau; beggars and goîtres abound here. The carriage-road leaves Cazeau on one side, but passes through the villages of Garen, &c. Lower down is St. Aventin, a large village named from a chapel of that saint.

After crossing the minor stream of the L'Oueil, the fine avenue called Allée des Soupirs leads into

BAGNERES DE LUCHON (R. 87).

ROUTE 87.

THE PYRENEES.—PAU TO BAGNERES DE BIGORRE, AND TO BAGNERES DE LUCHON, BY TARBES.—POST ROAD.—EXCURSIONS TO THE VAL DE LYS, PORT DE VENASQUE, AND VAL D'ARAN.

To B. de Bigorre, 60 kilom. = 37 Eng. m.; thence to Luchon, 78 kilom. = 48 Eng. m.

Diligences daily, but very slow.

---

* The situation of the Lac d'Oo is very like that of the Upper Gosau lake in Salzburg.

Route 87.—*Pau to Bagnères de Bigorre.*

The following is the direct post-road between the two Bagnères: it runs through the plain to the N. of the Pyrenees, affording only distant views of them. To enjoy fully their beauties, the traveller must pursue Rtes. 85 and 86.

A high table-land, in part uncultivated, is traversed both before and after reaching

16 Bordes d'Expouy.

The village passed on the rt., shortly before entering Tarbes, distinguished by its lofty ch., is Ibos.

23 Tarbes.—*Inns:* H. du Grand Soleil, good and moderate;—H. de la Paix (try coquille aux champignons);—H. de l'Europe. Sir John Froissart put up at the Star, and commended his hostel. Tarbes, cheflieu of the Dépt. des Hautes Pyrénées, is pleasantly situated on the clear Adour, in the midst of a fertile plain, in full view of the Pyrenees. It has 12,663 Inhab. and some manufactures, but contains few objects of interest. Several public walks contribute to the public health and recreation, the principal and most striking of which is the *Place Maubourguet*, where are the principal inns and cafés. There is also a pleasant walk by the side of the river. The buildings are not remarkable. On the Place Marcadieu the markets and extensive yearly fairs are held. The market-people, in their various costumes, are worth seeing. There is a fine bridge over the Adour, and a portion of its water is distributed in canals through the town. The French government has a *stud* (Haras) here for improving the breed of horses. The officials are very civil. The chief building is a modern *Cathedral*, said to occupy the site of the Castle of the Counts of Bigorre, of which Tarbes (the city of the Tarbelli was the capital. The English monarchs retained possession of Bigorre, which, with Guienne, formed the dowry of Queen Eleanor, for 300 years, down to the reign of Charles VII. The Black Prince kept his court at Tarbes; Froissart describes his visit to the Count d'Armagnac.

The distant *view* of the Pyrenees is scarcely equal to that from Pau, but the Pic du Midi de Bigorre here forms the prominent object, and the mountains about Luchon are also visible. Tarbes was the birthplace (1755) of the infamous Bertrand *Barrère* de Vieusac, member of the National Convention, the meanest and most dastardly as well as the most cruel of the monsters of the Revolution. (See *Edin. Rev.* 1844.)

A smart action was fought at Tarbes, in the interval between the battle of Orthez and that of Toulouse, in which the British army drove the French from their position, and compelled them to retreat. One French brigade was attacked by the 3 rifle battalions: —" The fight was short, yet wonderfully fierce and violent; for the French, probably thinking their opponents to be Portuguese, on account of their green dress, charged with great hardiness, and being encountered by men not accustomed to yield, they fought muzzle to muzzle, and it was difficult to judge at first who would win. At last the French gave way." But out of the 120 men who fell on the side of the British, there were 12 officers and 80 men of the Rifles.—*Napier*.

The road from Tarbes to Cauterets and Barèges, by Lourdes (19 kilom.), is described in Rte. 85. Tarbes is the key to the communication with all parts of the Pyrenees.

Mallepostes go daily to Pau and Bayonne; to Auch and Toulouse; to Auch, Agen, and Limoges.

Diligences go to Lourdes and Barèges; also to Bagnères; to Toulouse and Bordeaux; to Bayonne, Auch, Agen; to Bagnères de Luchon, by Lannemezan, a long stage of 20 Eng. m.

From Tarbes our road ascends the l. bank of the Adour; gradually advancing within the embrace of the mountains, which rise in height in proportion as we advance. The country is richly cultivated, copiously irrigated, and thickly peopled; no less than 8 villages being passed on this stage. A little off the road lies the Château d'Odos, where Marguerite Queen of Navarre, sister of Francis I., died, 1549. Near Montgaillard, the road from Lourdes, Barèges, and Cauterets, to Bagnères, falls in on the rt. At

Trebons, the Val d'Ossouet opens out on the rt., and runs up towards the Pic de Montaigu.

A little below Pouzac occurs a church, walled round like that of the Templars at Luz. About 2 m. below Bagnères, on the rt. bank of the Adour, near the farther extremity of a wooden bridge over that river, the geologist will discover a knob of hornblende or trap rock (ophite), which appears to have affected the rocks about it, since a little lower down, the granite is found decomposed, intermixed with a limestone which has assumed a large granular structure.

The knoll passed on the rt., a little behind the village of Pouzac, before reaching the town, is the *Camp de César*, so called from an intrenchment upon it.

21 BAGNÈRES DE BIGORRE.—(*Inns:* H. de France, most respectable landlord (M. Uzac) and one of the best and cheapest hotels in the Pyrenees; comfortable apartments, and excellent table-d'hôte; Galignani is regularly taken in; persons making some stay may board and lodge for 6 fr. per diem;—Frascati, a large establishment, including mineral baths and springs, a concert room, billiard and coffee rooms;—H. de Paris, good;—H. du Grand Soleil; du Bon Pasteur, good; de la Paix.)

Bagnères is the most town-like of the Pyrenean watering-places in extent, amusements, shops, &c., having a permanent population of 8000, often augmented by 6000 or 8000 strangers intent upon pleasure as well as health, during the season, which lasts from the end of June to the end of September. It is a cheerful town of whitewashed houses, set off with blue marble window-sills and door-jambs, delightfully situated, just where the plain of Tarbes begins to contract into the vale of Campan, and the slopes which bound it to change from hills into mountains, whose noble peaks and masses rising to the S. form the background of all the beautiful views in and about the town, while undulating slopes, trees, fields of maize, vines, and villas fill up the foreground. It stands at a height of only 1852 ft. above the sea-level; and its fault is the fervid heat, dust, and glare during part of the summer, unfanned by the mountain breezes. The Adour, on whose l. bank it is built, is here greatly reduced in breadth and volume by the numerous artificial cuts and canals, which borrow its waters for the purpose of irrigation, and to turn marble, paper, and other mills. A large part of these streams also is made to circulate through the streets; and thus they contribute to clean them, while they freshen the air. Every street and lane has its own clear gutter, at which the housewives wash their linen and domestic vessels before their own doors; while to the deeper canals, horses, asses, and pigs repair twice a day, and after wading knee deep, are ladled over with water thrown from their backs by a wooden scoop.

Montaigne preferred Bagnères above all the Eaux-Thermales which he had visited, "comme celles où il y avait plus d'aménité de lieu, commodité de logis, de vivre, et de bonne compagnie;" and on almost all these heads it still continues to deserve praise. The climate is warmer and less variable than that of the mountain baths; the cost of living and price of provisions are moderate, lodgings being very numerous, since almost every householder in the town lets either part or the whole of his domicile.

To the passing traveller its chief attractions are the picturesque beauties of the valleys and mountains around, which afford endless resources: in the town itself are scarcely any curiosities or sights.

The tall, octagonal, Gothic *tower*, rising near the H. de France, belonged to a church of Jacobins, suppressed at the Revolution. The church of St. John, which belonged to the Templars, but is now converted into a playhouse, retains a fine pointed doorway, enriched with mouldings. One or two feudal towers remain of the ancient *fortifications*, relics of the days when Froissart describes Bagnères as "une bonne, grosse ville, fermée," whose peaceful citizens suffered sorely from a neighbouring den of thieves, or castle, or, to borrow Froissart's words,

"Ceux d'icelle ville avoyent trop fort temps, car ils estoyent guerroyés et harriés de ceux de Malvoisin qui sied sur une montagne." (See p. 313.) Bagnères was given up to the English by the Treaty of Bretigny; and, as a border fortress on a line of passage into Spain, it was taken by Henry of Trastamare by storm, after the death of his brother, Don Pedro the Cruel. One of the towers, called de Malfourat, still stands opposite the Thermes.

Bagnères de Bigorre owes its reputation as a watering-place to its warm *saline springs*, varying in temperature from 87° to 123° Fahrenheit. They are good for disorders of the digestive organs, and resemble those of Baden-Baden, but contain a smaller quantity of saline substances. They were known to the Romans, as inscriptions found in and near the town prove; indeed the name Bagnères is not improbably traced to the Latin "Balnearia." The sources rise, to the number of about 40, within the space of 3 or 4 hectares, out of a shaly, calcareous rock, supposed to be the equivalent of the Jura limestone.

The *Public Bathing Establishment*, or *Thermes*, situated at the extremity of the town, under Mount Olivet, is the largest building in it, and the handsomest and most cleanly in the Pyrenees, though the arrangements for conducting the mineral waters to it are said to be defective, and to deprive them of a part of their medicinal properties. The six springs, La Reine (named from Jeanne de Navarre, mother of Henri IV., who used it 1567), Le Dauphin, Roi de Lannes, St. Roch, Foulon, and Des Yeux, are conducted into the building and distributed among its 29 baths and 4 douches. The water is previously received and cooled down in open tanks; and it is in this situation that the substance called by French chemists Barégine, but whose nature, whether animal or vegetable, conferva or oscillatoria, has not yet been ascertained, collects on the surface.

There are about 20 other private establishments in and around the town; indeed it is only necessary to bore into the ground to a certain depth to obtain with certainty a warm saline spring. The most fashionable and frequented bath, and the water apparently most efficacious, is that of *Le Salut*, rather less than a mile out of the town, in a great recess in the flank of the Monné hill. The bath-house is a solitary building, approached by a long avenue of poplars, winding through the pretty green valley, crowded at all hours, but chiefly in the morning, by bathers on horseback or foot, or in sedan chairs. It contains only 10 baths, so that, during the season, they are in request at all hours. The water of the Salut is saline, with a sulphureous smell; and it has the property of blackening silver. It has scarcely any perceptible taste, only a sort of milky feel in the mouth.

Bagnères also possesses a chalybeate spring, *Fontaine Ferrugineuse* (or d'Angoulême), almost the only one in the Pyrenees, situated on the E. flank of the Mount Olivet, in the direction of the village of Pouzac (p. 310). Granite is stated to have been found by digging, within a few feet of the spring, which doubtless originates in that rock.

The vale of Campan above Bagnères abounds in the beautiful marbles for which the Pyrenees are famed: they are much used in Paris, and the working of them gives employment to many persons here. The *Marbrerie* of *M. Géruzet* is on a very extensive scale, and the modes of cutting, turning in the lathe, and polishing large blocks, by machinery moved by the river, are well worth seeing. Tables, chimney-pieces, buffets, pillars, slabs, as well as vases and other articles, are made here; and no less than 20 varieties of marble are employed. The prices are not extravagant: a list of the different varieties is printed with the cost. The most beautiful are the green and flesh-coloured marbles of Campan, the blood-red or Griotte, filled with fossilized shells of the nautilus, whose spirals are disclosed in cutting. The quarries whence they are derived occur in the transition limestone formation. M. Géruzet is also banker and agent of Coutts.

The knitting of the *fine wool* of the Pyrenees, derived from Spain, gives employment to the greater part of the females, young and old, in and about the town, who may be seen sitting at their cottage-doors, in the roads and streets, hard at work. The articles made here are counterpanes, mittens, aprons, caps, work-bags, besides shawls and scarfs of woollen gauze, rivalling in thinness fine lace. The so-called *crêpe de Barèges* is not made at that place, but in Bagnères and Luz. The principal dépôt for this kind of articles seems to be chez Mademoiselle Laffourque.

The *English service* is performed on Sunday at 11½, in a room in the bathing establishment. There is a permanent Protestant French service throughout the year. The Rev. Mr. Frossard is established as Pastor here and Protestant Missionary. He is collecting funds to build a church.

There is a *Theatre* here in a desecrated church.

Concerts and balls, during the season, are given at Frascati's, a superb establishment, which was formerly a gambling-house. There is good fly-fishing in the Adour between B. and Tarbes.

Diligences—4 or 5 daily to Tarbes; thence to Pau, Auch, Bordeaux, Limoges; daily to Toulouse, to Bagnères de Luchon, to Cauterets, Luz, Barèges (nearly 40 m. distant by the post and coach road, 20 by the Tourmalet). (See Rte. 85.)

Guides and *ponies* for excursions in the mountains are very numerous. The landlords of the H. de France or other inns will recommend the most trustworthy.

Chaises à porteurs, or sedan-chairs, are much used by invalids to go to the bath. To be carried to the Bain de Salut and back costs 1 fr.

The *Promenades* most frequented in and near the town (besides the *Avenues de Salut* already mentioned) are the *Coustous* (? Côteau), a long platform in the midst of the town, lined with houses and cafés; shaded with trees, under which a sort of fair is kept up throughout the season, in temporary booths occupied by itinerant marchands. It is crowded in the cool of the evening.

The *Allées de Maintenon*, a row of trees planted along a bank above the road leading to Campan, are named from the lady who became the wife of Louis XIV., but who visited these baths in the capacity of gouvernante to his deformed child, the Duc du Maine, for the benefit of the waters, in 1675, 1677, and 1681.

The *pleasantest walk* in the morning is along the slopes of the *Mont Olivet*, the wooded hill rising behind the Thermes. Numerous shady paths are cut through the trees, whence you may survey the vale of the Adour. One path skirting the flanks of the hill leads to the chalybeate spring.

In the rear of Mont Olivet and of the Bains de Salut rises the loftier cone-topped mountain *Bédat*, which takes more than half an hour to ascend, but is accessible on horseback.

By crossing the two bridges over the two main arms of the Adour, by which the road to Toulouse quits the town, and turning to the rt., after passing the second, up a steep road in zigzags, the *Palombière* is reached; a row of trees on the top of the hill, between which the fowlers stretch their nets in September and October, to catch the migratory flocks of wild pigeons, aided by boys hoisted aloft in a sort of cradle at the top of a pair of poles 130 to 150 ft. high above the ground—a position which seems terrific, owing to the bending of the poles beneath their weight. On the approach of the birds the boy throws down a piece of wood somewhat in the shape of a pigeon, which making a whizzing noise causes the birds to stoop in their flight, so as to come within the reach of the net, which the fowler allows to fall on them by loosening the cords. There is scarcely a better point than this to look up the valley of Campan and survey the magnificent mountains at its head, bounding it on the S.W.; the Pic du Midi and the Pic de Montaigu, with the Penne (*Pen* or *Ben*, Celtic, head) de l'Hyéris rising on the l. In the midst, the white buildings of Bagnères are spread out, backed by the dark masses of the Mont Olivet, the Bédat, &c. The Adour makes little figure in the view, so much are its streams frittered away; but below the town to the N. its wide, cultivated plain expands to view for miles and miles, until it unites with that of the Garonne.

More distant excursions, of great beauty and interest, are to the Valley of Grip and its cascades; to Trames Aigues, on account of the fine view thence of the Pic du Midi, described at p. 304; the ascent of that Pic also, p. 305.

The most beautiful scenery of the Vale of Campan is to be found within the branch of it called *Val Lesponne*, opening out near the Château de St. Paul, between Baudéan and Campan, and running up between the Pic du Midi on the S. and the Pic de Montaigu on the N. Its lower portion has chiefly the pastoral character of rich verdure, alternating with cultivated fields. Beyond the village Lesponne it contracts in width, its aspect alters and becomes wilder; bare rocks and rugged crags succeed to dark forests of beech and pine: the forms of the mountains are very striking. About 2 m. above Lesponne a gorge, opening on the rt., displays the entire mass of the Montaigu, a noble spectacle; and the streamlet traversing it descends the steep rocks in a pretty fall. Half an hour's walk farther, and the valley divides: the branch on the rt. leads, in 3 h., over the pass called Hourquette de Baran by Villelongue, to Pierrefitte in the Val d'Argelez; that on the l., disclosing the noble form of the Pic du Midi, leads up to the *Lac Bleu*, in which the stream of the Val Lesponne takes its rise. The ascent to it is very steep and fatiguing, though achieved by ladies: it is cut through the mica slate rock, covered at first by a wood, beyond which are extensive pasturages. The lake itself "is an oval basin, or tarn, about 2 m. long, at the top of a mountain, surrounded by bare craggy peaks of the most curious formation, within whose declivities the snow always remains. It is a solitary spot, with no house, or tree, or living thing to be seen in its vicinity, a stillness almost death-like reigning around. It might be dreary, but for the rich warm colouring of the rocks, the depth and stillness of the water, and its intense blue, whence it takes its name."—*Ellis.* It takes 6 or 7 hours, on foot, to reach Lac Bleu from B. de Bigorre. Higher up is another smaller tarn, difficult to approach, distinguished as the *Lac Vert*, another of the head-waters of the Adour.

The shortest and most romantic way to Bagnères de Luchon from B. de Bigorre is the road by Arreau over the Hourquette d'Aspin, at the head of the Val de Campan, and through the Val de Louron, described in Rte. 86. The circuitous post-road doubles the mountains, and skirts their roots between the valley of the Adour and that of the Garonne, as follows. It quits Bagnères by crossing the Adour, and for the two first stages is identical with that to Toulouse. A steep hill precedes

12 Escaladieu, where the post-house occupies part of the buildings of the ancient *Abbey*, now in ruins, charmingly placed on the borders of the Arros. It now belongs to a gentleman of Bordeaux, who has fitted up a portion of the building as a dwelling. The chapel remains, with some fragments of Gothic sculpture. A little beyond it the ruins of the *Castle Maurezin* (i. e. Mauvais Voisin, a name given by the inhabitants of the neighbouring towns, who suffered from the depredations of the bands of marauders sheltered in this stronghold) crown a detached hill. It witnessed many exploits during the occupation of this country by the English. It was besieged 1374, by the Duc d'Anjou, with an army of 8000 men; and the strength of the castle was so great that it would have held out for a very long time, but, the well which supplied it being without the walls, the besiegers cut off the communication, and as the weather was hot and the cisterns dry, not a drop of rain having fallen for six weeks, the garrison were obliged to come to terms. The Duc d'Anjou allowed them to depart, saying, "Get about your business, each of you to your own countries, without entering any fort that holds out against us; for if you do so, and I get hold of you, I

France.   P

will deliver you up to Jocelin (his headsman), who will shave you without a razor." He also allowed them to carry off as much of their booty as they could convey in trunks on sumpter horses.—*See* Froissart.

Capbern, a little farther on the road, is a small village, on one side of which, ½ m. off, in a retired nook, are the Sulphureous Springs of *Capbern*, having a bathing establishment, 3 hotels, and several lodging-houses attached to it. It is a place of increasing resort, owing to the virtue of its waters.

14 Lannemezan (*Inn* not good). On quitting this small bourg, a road branches off, S., into the Val d'Aure, to Arreau (Rte. 86). There is a short cut for the pedestrian, or equestrian, to St. Bernard by La Barthe, where is a good little country inn, opposite the ancient square tower, at the E. end of the village.

16 Montrejeau (*Inn* not good), a town of 3034 Inhab., in front of the opening of the Vale of the Garonne, whose vista is terminated by the grand peaks and ridges attached to the Monts Maudits, ranking among the highest of the Pyrenees; at whose foot, on the S., rises the Ebro, and on the N. the Garonne. It is a truly magnificent view. The stream of the Neste d'Aure falls into the Garonne a little above this. Here the road to Toulouse (Rte. 91) turns off to the l.; and that to Luchon, crossing the Garonne, begins to ascend its valley. On its rt. bank lies the ancient and curious walled town of

St. Bertrand de Comminges (Lugdunum Convenarum), situated at the opening of the Val de Barousse, upon and around a solitary rock, rising picturesquely out of the plain. Its summit is crowned by a Gothic *church*, the finest among the Pyrenees, in the Pointed style, whose choir and organ are ornamented with wood carvings, of very remarkable excellence, executed apparently in the 16th or 17th century. The painted glass, and a monument of a bishop (date 1351) in white marble, deserve notice. Upon the walls are a series of rude and ancient (? fresco) paintings of the Miracles of St. Bertrand; and some relics of the saint are preserved in the sacristy. Here is hung up the skin of a crocodile, which is said to have infested the neighbourhood and to have been destroyed by the saint! In a fragment of the cloisters, which have only recently been pulled down, are some curious old tombs. This church was once a *cathedral*, and the town itself, now deserted (847 Inhab.), was the capital of a comté, and a bishop's see. Many of the houses belonged to the canons and chapter. The inn is in the upper town.

The *Grotto* of Gargas, 5 m. S. of Montrejeau, in the wooded hill extending between the Garonne and Neste, is the finest in the Pyrenees for extent and the beauty of its stalactites: the entrance is a hole so small that it is necessary to crawl through on one's hands and knees.

The high road, leaving St. Bertrand on one side, again crosses the Garonne, by the Pont de Labroquère, and pursues its l. bank, through scenery of great interest, in which well-cultivated fields, enclosed by festoons of vines, hanging from tree to tree, form the foreground, and grand mountains the distance, by

18 Estĕnos—to Cierp, where we quit the Garonne, and enter the Vale of the Pique, which becomes its affluent at Cierp, a picturesque village both on account of its antique cottages, and from its position, under cliffs which nearly overhang it, at a point where the vistas of 2 valleys, meeting, disclose noble views. There are quarries of a beautiful marble near this.

A road runs from Cierp up the Valley of the Garonne (Vallée d'Aran), one of the most beautiful in the Pyrenees, to St. Béat, the last town of France, situated in a narrow gorge between high mountains. (See p. 321.) St. Béat is not more than 5 m. from the Spanish frontier.

The Valley of the Pique, which is very picturesquely varied with wood, rock, human habitations, and cultivated fields, presents a succession of savage contractions, and smiling basin-shaped expansions, covered with verdure, the river alternately winding over the plain and dashing through the gorge; its upper end terminated by the grand snowy peaks contiguous to the Port de Venasque. The road, which now makes several awkward ascents and steep descents, is about to be carried on a regular terrace. When the iron furnaces of Guron are passed, we traverse, near Pont de Casaux, the defile, before the geological rupture of which, the basin of Luchon must, doubtless, have been a vast lake. Some have considered this "rupture" a work of art, and have attributed it to the Romans.

21 *Bagnères de Luchon.—Inns:* H. Bonnemaison; Gypsy Villa, an English family house; H. de Londres, a café and reading-room attached; H. du Commerce. The accommodation and cuisine at the inns are inferior to that afforded at Bagnères de Bigorre. Strangers about to stop some days here had better hire lodgings, of which there are enough to accommodate from 1500 to 2000 persons.

The situation of Bagnères de Luchon is somewhat like that of Bigorre, except that the mountains are loftier, and entirely surround the flat, fertile plain on the edge of which it stands, forming a sort of oval basin in the very heart of the Pyrenees. On the W., close to the town, the Val de l'Arboust (Rte. 86) opens out; on the S., high among the clouds, rise bare, serrated ridges, destitute of vegetation, but contrasting grandly with the luxuriantly cropped plain near at hand.

Luchon is a town of 2000 Inhab., of narrow streets and mean houses, less neat and civilised than B. de Bigorre, with the exception of the Allée de Pique, leading to the river, and the *Allée des Bains*, a triple avenue of limes, lined with buildings, including the chief inns and best lodging-houses. Another avenue stretches up the hill to the entrance of the Val de l'Arboust; and a third, of poplars, crosses the valley from the church towards the river Pique. These Allées enable the pedestrian to move to a considerable distance under shade, protected from the sun, and enjoying the view of the mountains which close the upper end of the valley. This range of peaks and precipices, among which the Pic de la Pique is conspicuous, screens from view the Maladetta, the Monarch of the Pyrenees. In the middle distance rises the tower of Castle Vieilh, which stops the mouth of the gorge to the S.

At the end of the Great Allée are the *Baths*. A splendid *new Thermal Establishment* is being built on the plan of those at some of the German Spas, to which the architects were purposely sent to obtain the best plan. It will cost more than 600,000 fr. Many of the *Bath-rooms* already finished combine every comfort. The price of the bath depends on the hour at which you take it. During the morning and middle of the day it is 20 to 22 sous. At 4 A.M. and 5 P.M. it diminishes to 12 or 14 sous. The Baths stand at the foot of a precipitous wooded hill of slate, called Super Bagnères: the waters issue forth at the junction of the slate with the granite; they are sulphureous (except two, one saline, the other ferruginous?), and vary in temperature from 77° to 152° Fahr. The waters are good for rheumatic complaints, paralysis, and cutaneous disorders, but are injurious in nervous diseases, and to persons of sanguine temperament. They are taken internally as well as in baths.

By driving horizontal galleries into the rock of the mountain behind, near the old sources, an experiment which was 2 years in progress, hotter water, and a more copious supply, have been obtained, but some of the old springs are dried up in consequence.

The Romans were well acquainted with the hot springs of Luchon; many altars and inscriptions, now in the museum of Toulouse, have been dug up here, some of them dedicated *Deo Lixoni*, from whom the place would appear to be named.

Protestant service is performed in a *chapel* built by an Irish gentleman, Mr. Corneille, at his own expense.

Zigzag paths run up the hill behind the baths, through the wood, and along the face of the hill; and have been extended to the English gardens lately laid out.

The chief *season* of these baths is June and July to the middle of September.

About 200 *horses* and ponies are kept here for hire, at the usual charges, and are in constant request in fine weather. *Guides* are proportionably numerous; among them Laffont, called Prince, is hardy, experienced, and trustworthy, and has very good horses; he knows every step of the country around, and every mountain peak. Baptiste Aen is trusty and experienced. Bertrand Estrujo is a capital *guide*, especially for ladies. He speaks Spanish and knows the region of the High Pyrenees. His horses are also good. At Luchon the quality of the horse is often of more importance than that of the guide, except on very severe mountain excursions.

Diligences—daily, 3 to Toulouse; 1 to Auch; 1 or 2 to Bagnères de Bigorre.

The inhabitants of the valley of Luchon and its tributaries appear an inferior race to those of the valleys in the W.; not so well off, nor so well clothed. In their dress the berret gives place to an ugly night-cap, and the capulet, if retained, is black, instead of red. Beggars are very numerous, and goîtres not uncommon; yet the lower parts of the valleys are fertile, producing two crops of corn in the year; the first of wheat or maize, the second, late in September, when the fields are literally white, for the harvest of buck-wheat. Many goats are kept, which find sufficient food in the luxuriant herbage of the rocks; and the tinkling bells of the scampering flock, as they enter the town at sunset, produce a merry sound.

The *Cascade of Montauban*, on the E. side of the valley, is a very romantic spot, and, though the fall is inconsiderable, forms an agreeable walk. It is approached through a garden made by the curé of the village, who devotes to his parish the douceurs left by visitors.

A farther scramble up the course of the stream will repay the *hardy* pedestrian by bringing him to another Fall; and still further on, after about 1 hour's good walking, he will come to an *Oule* or vast circular excavation in the rock. Fine views into the valley beneath. The summit of the high hill called *Super Bagnères*, rising close above the houses of the town, and made accessible for some distance by paths, commands a nobly magnificent panorama of the flat land on the N., and of the mountains E., W., and S., including the *Maladetta*, whose glaciers appear through a gap in the chain.

The *Excursions* to be made from B. de Luchon are superior to those from B. de Bigorre, and are indeed the finest in the Pyrenees. *a.* That to the beautiful *Lac de Seculéjo* or *Lac d'Oo* will be found in Rte. 86, p. 307; 4 h. are required to go thither, and 3 to return.

b. Ascent of the *Pic de Monné* well repays the visitor for the fatigue of a ride of about $9\frac{1}{2}$ hours, including 2 hours' rest. A guide is necessary. You follow the road to Arreau by Col de Peyresourde (Rte. 86) nearly as far as St. Aventin, before which you turn rt. into a bridle-road leading into the valley of Oueil, which you traverse through its whole length, through the villages of Benqué Debas and Benqué Dessus and Maregne, to Bourg.—Here the horses rest, and the summit of the Pic may be reached from Bourg in $1\frac{1}{2}$ hour, riding all the way except about $\frac{1}{4}$ m. below the top, where the mountain-path disappears. The panorama of mountains seen from this spot is magnificent, including the chief summits of the range. The return may be made through the Val de l'Arboust, which lengthens the journey by 1 hour.

c. The *Val de Lys*, so called, not from its lilies, but from an old or provincial form of the word *eau*, water, from the number of streams and waterfalls, is a ride of 2 h. or a walk of 3, the distance being 7 or 8 m. The road to it ascends the valley from the baths, having the Pique at some distance on the l. It passes, also on the l., the pictureque border tower of *Castel Vieilh*, perched on a projecting crag, before the mouth of the Gorge de St. Mamet, watered by the Bourbe, leading, by the pass of the Portillon, into the Spanish Val d'Aran. This tower was designed to defend the entrance into the Val de Luchon by the ports of Portillon and of Venasque. Soon after passing it the road crosses the Pique to its rt. bank, and ½ a m. farther, leaving on the l. the road to Venasque, it recrosses the Pique, to enter the fine wooded gorge out of which the Lys issues to unite with it. After a mile and a half's pleasant ride through the wood, under the shade of beech and hazels, the gorge expands into a green basin-shaped valley, of a truly pastoral character; the pastures covered with herds occupying its bottom being overlooked by very lofty mountains, girt with fir woods, especially at its upper end. It is there shut in by the snowy peaks and glaciers of the Crabioules, rising above the fir-clad precipices, which look like a festooned curtain of black drapery drawn across the valley head. The centre of this curtain of foliage is streaked by the white lines of the foaming cascades which form the lions of this valley. The principal one leaps down into the valley, about 200 yards above the little *cabin*, half châlet, half pot-house, where visitors put up their horses, and may obtain some common refreshments. The slate rock is cleft by a very narrow fissure or groove, called *Trou d'Enfer*, down which the fall, really a picturesque one, dashes. The other fall, on the l., called Cascade de Cœur, is less striking in character and less accessible; it is fed by the glaciers of the Tuque de Maupas. The glacier of Crabioules, which feeds the other, is very difficult of access, owing to its steep inclination and its crevices. It joins, on the W., the glacier of the Portillon d'Oo and the Port d'Oo. The pedestrian should go to the Val de Lys or return from it by the hill of Super Bagnères, the height behind Luchon, whence he will enjoy a magnificent view.

ḍ. None of the excursions from Luchon, nor indeed in the whole range of the Pyrenees, surpass that to the Port de Venasque. It is somewhat difficult, yet is achieved by ladies in chaises à porteur. The expense for taking up one lady is 60 frs. It is practicable on horseback, and no one should omit it who has strength and love of fine scenery. It may be accomplished in 9 hrs., allowing 1½ hr. halt at the Port. A guide is necessary. The road is the same as that just described as far as the 2nd bridge over the Pique above Castel Vieilh. Leaving the opening of the Val de Lys on the rt., without crossing this bridge, you continue up the valley of the Pique, through park-like scenery, under the grateful shade of beech forests interspersed with firs and yews, between whose branches appear the rugged crags of the Pic de la Pique on the opposite side of the torrent. The ascent is gradual up to the Hospice de Bagnères (1¼ hr. ride), the last habitation in France, where the horses are commonly allowed half-an-hour's rest to prepare them for the fatigue in store for them. It is a large, massive, dirty stone house, like a Refuge on a Swiss mountain pass, belonging to the Commune of Luchon, intrusted to an inn-keeper who resides here till the 20th December, and on his departure leaves behind a store of bread and wine, wood and straw, for the entertainment of wayfarers, who cross the pass even in the depth of winter. No one avails himself of this provision without leaving behind money in payment for it. The house is on a par with a common cabaret, affording only the commonest necessaries, and appears a miserable hovel to those who need neither food nor shelter. It stands in a grassy hollow at the foot of high hills, some way below the head of the valley where the Pique takes its rise at the foot of the mountain called La Picade, over whose shoulder lies the pass of the Port de Picade. The path to it scales the hill behind the house, and it is a good 2 hrs. ascent, chiefly over grass, to reach the Port.

Opposite the house, at rt. angles to the vale of the Pique, a colossal semicircular recess, or natural cirque cut out of the mountains, which surround it with bare precipices, opens out; it is a scene of dreary solitude, disturbed only by the hoarse raven or the howling blast. It is approached by a little wooden bridge crossing the Pique in front of the hospice, under the singular Pic de Picade, rising on the l. hand.

"We were all puzzled, as our horses' heads were turned towards the glen and we commenced the ascent, to tell how men on foot, much more laden beasts, were to pass up and over this wall in any part of its circumference. Up, however, we went, toiling for 2 hrs. incessantly along a slightly traced path, always winding in zigzags, over large stones or rough beds of débris fallen from the mountains, alternating with smooth solid rock. Our little jaded horses did the work wonderfully well, taking to the steep staircase road most willingly, and clambering among the cliffs like kids, never making a false step. As we mounted higher, however, 'the rushing mighty wind,' which sweeps down the gully with a hideous howl and a force perfectly tremendous, rendered it difficult to keep one's seat. There is a proverb, that, in ascending the Port de Venasque, 'a father will not look back at his son, nor a son wait for his father.' About 3-4ths of the way up is a small ledge or recess in the face of the mountain, in which lie 4 small, deep-sunken tarns or ponds, frozen over a great part of the year. The steepness of the mountain and the shortness of the zigzags constantly increase till, near the top, the angle of the slope is so highly inclined that the path turns abruptly at every 6 or 8 ft.; and as the ground is covered with loose splintery shale, the horses have no secure footing. The rocks in front hide all view until the moment when you enter the *Port*, a wedge-shaped fissure cut into the crest of the mountain;—a mere gate, not more than 6 ft. wide. On passing this doorway, you step from France at once into Spain. To tarry in the singular portal or port-hole was impossible on account of the wind, which threatened to blow us back again more quickly than we had entered; so we descended a few steps, driving our horses before us, and seated ourselves on the smooth slate rock, which here dips downward as abruptly as the roof of a house. But what a scene opened before us—not a glimpse of which had been perceived before! We beheld an enormous mountain, the highest of the Pyrenees, called the *Maladetta*, or *Accursed*—I suppose from the utterly barren and dreary air of it and everything about it. Its huge round top and ridges are covered with everlasting snow, except where one or two bristling black peaks break through it; its lower part is shrouded with scanty fir-trees: a great gulf or deep ravine separates it from the bare slope on which we stood; not a sign of human habitation or cultivation; all around a desert, as though a corner of the world forgotten and left unfinished."—*MS. Journal.**

This road has lately been improved, so that not only ladies, but even the fat and infirm, may easily surmount it in a chaise à porteurs, or even on horseback.

The pass called *Port de Venasque* (reached in 2 hrs. from the Hospice of Bagnères) is cut through the mountain wall called Penna Blanca, at an elevation of 7917 ft. above the sea-level, but at a considerable depth below the crest of that mountain. The frontier line, near its top, is marked by an iron

* In Blackwood's Magazine, No. CLXV., will be found a most vivid and true description of the Port de Venasque. The final ascent is thus related by its observant author:—
"Our position became at every step more interesting and extraordinary; for to all powers of observation this cul-de-sac was so perfect, and all means of exit so inscrutable, that not one of the party, after the most mature inspection, could form a conjecture as to the continuation even of the very pathway, much less of the pass itself, which appeared to elude our grasp as we drew near, and yet must, if it really existed, be now close at hand. At length, in rounding a sharp corner, the pass started into view, about 50 ft. above our head. . . . The poor animals, as if conscious that the severest portion of their task was drawing to a close, exerted themselves with redoubled efforts to accomplish the remaining—I may say—steps in the ladder. . . .
"Another march brought me to the breach, when I drew up, and in motionless and speechless admiration sat with my eyes riveted on the stupendous scene so singularly, so suddenly revealed . . . The Maladetta was immediately in front, without a single intervening object, standing in all its dreary nakedness, like the ghost of some mountain belonging to a departed world."—*S.*

cross. In the depths of the hollow below the Port, within the Spanish territory, the Essera takes its rise, and a low ridge stretching across at its head unites the Maladetta with the main chain and the mountains of the Port de Venasque. To the E. of this ridge, on the l., lies the mysterious *Trou du Taureau*, an oval basin or gulf without visible outlet, excavated in the limestone rock to a depth of 80 ft., which, swallowing up the waters descending from the N.E. slope of the Maladetta, is believed to convey them *under* the intervening mountains into the French Valley of Artigues Tellina, where, rising again to light, they form the
Source of the Garonne. This phenomenon merits the personal investigation of travellers.

The *Maladetta*, erroneously included in some maps in the central chain, and even placed within the French frontier, is an outlier or buttress, lying to the S. of the dorsal spine of the Pyrenees, and entirely shut out by it from France, as it were by a screen of peaks and ridges. Though the highest of the Pyrenees, 11,426 ft. above the sea-level, it loses much of the effect of elevation when seen from the Port de Venasque, on account of the great height of the Val d'Essera, out of which it rises. The highest of its summits, the Pic de Nethou, had never been reached until 1842, when it was surmounted by a Russian officer named Tchitchacheff, with one French companion and 3 guides. The glacier upon its N. flank is the largest in the Pyrenees, and is dangerous to cross on account of the crevasses. In 1824 a guide, named Barran, perished miserably in one of them, owing to the covering of snow giving way beneath him, before the eyes of two French gentlemen, pupils of the École des Mines, who heard his agonising cries as he gradually sank down, without being able to render any assistance. The crags and snows of the Maladetta are the favourite haunt of the izard; and many a bold chasseur dares all the perils of the mountain in pursuit of them.

The *Spanish town of Venasque* is about as far from the Port to the S.W. as Luchon is to the N., *i. e.* a walk of 4 hrs.; but the way is very rough and difficult, following at first the windings of the Essera, wading the torrents which fall into it, and threading the mass of rocks and rubbish fallen from the gigantic wall of Penna Blanca on the rt.: no danger, however. The scenery far more magnificent than on the French side, the Val d'Essera being esteemed by some travellers as fine as any scene in the Pyrenees. Some way down is the Spanish Hospice, "a vile posada," serving as a guard and custom-house, occupied by carabineers, and supplying the place of a hospice swept away by an avalanche in 1838, which resembled that on the French side of the pass. From this to Venasque, about 10 m., the path runs by the side of the Essera, and is very difficult. The scenery of the gorge is grand but savage, its striking feature being the number of its waterfalls, and rapidity of the torrents descending into it. A bath has been built on the opposite slope of the valley.

The path from the Port d'Oo (see p. 308) descends the Val d'Astos. The sides of the mountains are stripped of wood near
Venasque, which is suddenly disclosed to view by a bend in the valley. It is a wretched dirty and foul place. Its most conspicuous feature is the gloomy *Castle* by which it is surmounted, originally a stronghold of the middle ages, converted by modern works into a fortress, which was besieged and taken by the French in 1809, and possesses no great strength. It is surrounded on three sides by deep ravines.

In the principal street, Calle Mayor, are several picturesque old houses ornamented with sculptured figures, coats of arms, &c., and some of these retain the towers which originally served for defence. The *Church*, at the end of the town farthest from the castle, is a curious Romanesque building, fitted up in the Spanish style, with carving, gilding, &c. Another church was destroyed by the French, who did much mischief here. "The

Inns are ventas of the most miserable class, unfit to shelter an English dog. Strangers are received, as a great favour and at a high price, in 2 houses belonging to rich, proud Arragonese. It is necessary to make a bargain before you discharge an article of baggage, and ½ an hour is spent in haggling. They demand 10 frs. for a miserable supper, bed, and small cup of chocolate in the morning. You *may* get off with 7 frs." — *G. M. S.* There is nothing tolerable but the beds, which are clean, and the chocolate.

You may return from Venasque to the Spanish Hospice and over the Pommereau into the gorge of Artigues Tellina, visiting on the way the Œil de Garonne, sleep at Viella, and reach Luchon by St. Béat the 3rd night.

The excursion may be prolonged round the base of the Maladetta, from Venasque, through wild and magnificent scenery, by the Port de Castanéze, 3 hrs.; village of C., 4 hrs.; Vitalles, 2 hrs.; Hospice de Viella, 4 hrs., situated amidst stupendous scenery; Port de Viella, 2 hrs., 8322 ft. above the sea, and very grand; town of Viella, 2½ hrs., in the Val d'Aran.

Venasque to Luchon—
a. by the *Port de Picade*.
b. by the *Port de Pommereau*.

The ridge of the Penna Blanca, through which the Port de Venasque opens, is traversed, about 1½ m. to the E. of it, by another pass, called Port de Picade, reached by turning to the l. across the meadows at the base of the mountains, whence the Port de Venasque looks as though it had been formed by chipping a bit out of the Sierra, and then scaling a steep ascent encumbered with rubbish, and not marked by any path. On the top you pass out of Arragon into a corner of Catalonia, and look down upon a chaos of wild peaks and ridges. Here you have the choice of two passes, the shortest the Picade; on the l. is a very narrow path carried along the shattered edges of the slaty stone, barely traced among shivers and splinters of rock upon the very ridge or crest of the Sierra, along the brink of the precipice. It is a grand wild spot, and is named Picade from the gigantic obelisk of rock which rears itself aloft. It leads back to the Hospice de Bagnères by a path marked with tolerable distinctness on the grassy slopes, and, though steep, much easier than that up to the Port de Venasque. Thus the traveller has passed from France into Spain through one door or gap in the great separation-wall between them, and returned through another.

b. The pass on the rt. hand, after reaching the crest of the Port de Picade, is called *Port de Pommereau*, and leads into the vale of the Garonne, the upper part of which is called the *Val d'Aran*, and, though lying on the French side of the Pyrenees, belongs to Spain. The descent runs through the grand gorge of Artigues Tellina, covered, as you proceed down it, with dense intact forests of primæval growth, in the midst of which, in a deep hollow at the foot of precipices, 10 minutes distant from the path, one of the chief *sources of the Garonne* issues forth from a series of cavities encumbered with broken rocks called Œil de Djoueou, and by the Spaniards Ojos de Garonna, "the Garonne's eye." It is said that the copious stream which here bursts forth to-day is the torrent whose cradle is the snows of the Maladetta, and which, after being lost in the Trou de Taureau (p. 319), pursues its way under ground, through the caverns of the limestone mountains, as far as this spot, where it rises a ready-made river. This is one of the most important sources of the Garonne. A little farther down lies the Hospice of Artigues Tellina. The part of the lovely valley below this is covered with pastures. Much timber is cut in the forests, and floated down the Garonne to Bordeaux. Near the junction of the valley of Artigues Tellina with that of the main stream of the Garonne of Viella, the river is crossed by a bridge near the ruined *Castel Leon*, destroyed by the French in the war of the Succession. The *Val d'Aran* contains 32 towns and villages, 69 churches, and 20,000 Inhab.; it runs up towards the great chain, 14 m. above Castel Leon; 5 m. up it lies Viella, the chief place of the valley, containing 900 Inhab., 8 m. below the Port de Viella. Below Castel Leon, at Las Bordas, the path to Luchon by the Portillon and the Val Burbe stretches off to the W. Good sleeping quarters may be found in a farm-house at Viella, $2\frac{1}{2}$ hrs. Lower down is Bosost, the second place in the valley, a miserable village, but in a charming situation. On the outskirts of the village of Les are *Baths* supplied by sulphureous springs, and a boarding-house or *Inn*, belonging to the proprietor, affords the best accommodation in the valley. Below this a fine view is obtained of the Maladetta. Here the Val d'Aran puts on its greatest beauty and grandeur, which cause it to rank high among the Pyrenean valleys. The river is jammed in between the rocks near a bridge over a tributary stream, called Pont du Roi, which marks the frontier of France; it is the custom-house post, &c. The Val d'Aran belonged to France down to 1192, when it was transferred as the dowry of Beatrix de Comminges to her husband, a prince of Aragon. It was ravaged by the Carlists in the late war. Fos is the first place within the French territory. The valley contracts lower down to a grand defile, in the midst of which lies St. Béat (3 hrs. below Bosost), a very picturesque and interesting old town, consisting of a narrow street overhung by beetling cliffs; a ruined castle stands on a rock in the midst of the defile. The scenery around is most lovely. The *Inn* (Fortan's) is not good, but it is one of the best in the valley. There is an excellent carriage-road from this to Cierp and Luchon.

There are quarries of marble here.

At Cierp, 6 m. below St. Béat, the Garonne is joined by the Pique coming from Luchon, and our road falls into the high road from Bigorre and Toulouse (p. 314), leading thither.

⁎* More detailed and accurate information respecting the Val d'Aran, the scenery S. of the Maladetta, and Venasque, would be acceptable to the Editor.

ROUTE 90.

TOULOUSE TO PAU, BY AUCH AND TARBES.

188 kilom. = 116 Eng. m.
Malleposte, daily in 15 hrs.
Diligence, daily.
Toulouse is in Rte. 70.

At the radiation of roads outside the Faubourg St. Cyprien, called Patte d'Oie, the branch on the rt. is that which leads to Auch; it crosses, at the distance of 2 m., the stream of the Touch.

18 Leguevin.

15 L'Île Jourdain (H. de France), a town of 2000 Inhab., on the rt. bank of the Save.

18 Gimont.

9 Aubiet. The road runs through a highly cultivated and very productive country, in a direction nearly due W., not inclining in the least to S., all the way from Toulouse to

17 Auch (*Inns:* H. de France; best, and very good), the chef-lieu of the Dépt. du Gers, a town of 9935 Inhab., and see of an archbishop, situated on the top and slopes of an eminence washed by the Gers at its base, and crowned by the *Cathedral*, begun in the reign of Charles VIII., and completed, by the tasteless addition of its inappropriate Grecian portico, in that of Louis XIV. The church is 347 ft. long, and 74 ft. high. The *painted glass* is of rare richness of colour, but is coarse in design; it was executed (1513) by Arnaud de Moles. The *carved woodwork* of the choir is equally remarkable, and is scarcely surpassed in France. At the back of the stalls are well-executed figures of Virtues, &c., in bas-relief, enclosed in niches and canopies of elaborate workmanship (date 1525-7). The choir is separated from the nave by a gallery (jubé), or rood-loft.

Long flights of stairs lead from the lower town to the upper: many old houses are preserved here. The *Place Royale*, in the higher and better quarter of the town, is a handsome square; adjoining it is the *Cours d'Etigny*, so named from a magistrate by whom it

P 3

was laid out, commanding a glorious view of the chain of the Pyrenees.

Auch was anciently capital of the *Ausci* (whence Auch), afterwards of the Comté d'Armagnac, and seat of the primate of Aquitaine.

A *malleposte* runs hence daily by Agen to Limoges (Rte. 73, 70).

15 Vicnau, Dépt. Gers.

9 Mirande. *Inns:* H. Dupuy; very comfortable; there is a large establishment of baths attached to it—*L. Y. Soleil*; good.

13 Miélan. Soon after crossing the Arras we descend a slope, commanding the view of the Pyrenees, among which the Pic du Midi de Bigorre, rising directly in front, is grandly conspicuous, into the plain of the Adour, which stretches hence to the foot of those mountains, and enter

16 Rabastens, an old town mentioned by Froissart. A perfectly straight road connects this place with

19 *Tarbes*, in Rte. 87.

23 Bordes d'Expouy.

16 PAU (Route 80). There is a second and more direct road from Toulouse to Tarbes, which, though unprovided with post-horses, is taken by the *diligence* daily in 22 hrs., passing through Lombez, Boulogne, and Trie.

ROUTE 91.

TOULOUSE TO BAGNÈRES DE LUCHON AND BAGNÈRES DE BIGORRE, BY ST. GAUDENS.

To B. de Bigorre, 144 kilom. = 90 Eng. m.; to B. de Luchon, 135 kilom. = 84 Eng. m.

Diligences daily.

The first part of the road, across the great plain of Languedoc, and along the l. bank of the Garonne, though seldom in sight of the river, is very monotonous. The Pyrenees are yet too distant to form an important feature, but the richness of the soil and abundance of the crops are very remarkable. The Duke of Wellington attempted the passage of the Garonne at Portet, a village on the l. of the high road, 6 m. above Toulouse, but the width of the river proved too great for the pontoons provided, and the army consequently crossed lower down, below Toulouse. The confluence of the Ariège with the Garonne takes place opposite Portet.

20 Muret.

The army of the Comte de Toulouse, aided by Pedro II., king of Arragon, amounting to 40,000 men, was defeated under the walls of Muret by Simon de Montfort, who made a sortie with 14,000 men, and cut the besiegers to pieces, leaving Pedro dead on the field.

13 Noè, on the l. bank of the Garonne. At Carbonne, above this, some way to the l. of the road, Lord Hill crossed the Garonne with 18,000 men; but, finding the roads impassable, speedily returned to march along the l. bank, against St. Cyprien, the faubourg of Toulouse.

27 Martres. In a field near this, interesting Roman antiquities have been discovered, consisting of an immense number of busts, statues, reliefs, inscriptions, &c., now deposited in the museum of Toulouse, marking this as the site of the ancient town *Calagorris Convenarum*.

There is a bridge over the Garonne at St. Martory. A new road has been made to skirt the town, and avoid the narrow streets of

28 St. Gaudens (*Inn:* H. de France; good), an old and gloomy town of 5000 Inhab., at a little distance from the Garonne: it has a *church* of considerable antiquity, in the Romanesque style, with 3 apses at the E. end, and small round-headed windows. The road to Bagnères de Bigorre diverges on the rt. at St. Gaudens, up the l. bank of the Garonne to Montrejeau, where it falls into Rte. 87.

From St. Gaudens, by St. Girons, to Foix and Carcassonne, is Rte. 95.

The Garonne is crossed by the road to Luchon, a short way out of the town; and from the slope leading down to it there is a fine view of its windings and of the distant Pyrenees.

At the distance of 6 or 8 m. farther the road passes abruptly from the plain into the midst of the mountains, by ascending an eminence, the extreme root or spur of the Pyrenees, to avoid a wide curve of the Garonne, but descends upon the river at the foot of the opposite slope. An uncommon view is here presented of the interesting town of St. Bertrand (Rte. 87), which our road leaves on the rt. "You break at once upon a vale, sunk deep enough beneath the point of view to command every hedge and tree, with St. Bertrand clustered round its large cathedral on a rising ground. If it had been built purposely to add a feature to a singular prospect, it could not have been better placed. The mountains rise proudly around, and give their rough frame to this exquisite little picture."—*A. Young.* The Garonne is crossed at the Pont Labrequere to

27 Estenos, described, with the rest of the road, to

21 Bagnères de Luchon, in Rte. 87.

ROUTE 93.

TOULOUSE TO NARBONNE, BY CARCASSONNE.—CANAL DU MIDI.

156 kilom. = 97 Eng. m.

Malleposte daily in 16 hrs. to Montpellier.

Diligences daily. With post-horses in 6 hrs. to Carcassonne.

Bateaux de Poste daily, along the Canal du Midi from Toulouse to Agde: a very tedious conveyance (35 hrs.), to which, for the most part, the lower classes only resort: the boats very uncomfortable, no restaurant, the delays from locks excessive: boats are changed at Beziers.

The road, on quitting Toulouse, passes on the l. the hill of Pech David —a good point of view to see the Pyrenees from; and skirting, at a short distance on the l., the *Canal du Midi*, continues to run nearly parallel with it for several stages. This great and useful public work, sometimes called Canal des Deux Mers, because it unites the Mediterranean with the Atlantic, was executed under Louis XIV., by the enterprising Paul Riquet, though the design is clearly sketched out in the Mémoires de Sully. It was commenced 1666 (100 years save 6 before Brindley, in England, began the Bridgewater Canal), and finished 1681, the year before Riquet's death. It measures, from the basin where it joins the Garonne at Toulouse, to the Etang du Thau, near Agde, where it falls into the Mediterranean, 244 kilom. = 151 Eng. m.; it is 20 mèt. (65 ft. 7 in.) wide at the surface, and 10 mèt. (32 ft.) at the bottom. It cost more than 16 million livres = 33 million fr.

It has 64 locks, and many other considerable works, reservoirs, &c., which will be enumerated as we approach them. These, though wonderful for the time when they were constructed, have been surpassed by many in England, and even in France. The articles transported along the canal consist chiefly of corn, oil, soap, wine, brandy, &c.; it is navigated by barges of 100 tons, but the traffic is not very extensive, judging from the number of voyages yearly to and fro, which is only 960. It is closed for a month or 6 weeks once in 3 years for the "chômaee" (stand-still), in order to be cleaned.

Our road lies across a rich corn country, but monotonously flat, which before the end of summer becomes parched, dusty, and arid.

12 Castanet. The canal, and the river Lers, running parallel with it, are crossed at

12 Bazière.

11 Villefranche, a town of 2400 Inhab., consisting of a long street traversed by the road.

Beyond Avignonet we pass from the Dépt. Haute Garonne into that of l'Aude, and a little farther skirt on the rt. the *Bassin de Naurouze*, an artificial reservoir formed for the supply of the canal, which here attains its summit level (point de partage). The water is derived from a still higher and larger reservoir, le Bassin de St. Féréol, measuring 5249 ft. by 2558 ft., situated on the flanks of the Montagne Noire, whence it is conducted hither in an artificial channel to be discharged into the two seas. The descent of 208¼ ft. between this and Toulouse is effected by 18 locks, and that of 719 ft., down to the level of the Mediterranean at Agde, by 46 locks. Riquet intended to have founded a town upon the basin of Naurouze—a design not yet accomplished; but an *obelisk*, by way of *mo-*

nument, was erected to him by his descendants, on this spot, 1825. A little island has been formed in the basin opposite the mouth of the Canal by the deposits brought down by it. After crossing this main feeder of the canal, there is nothing to notice until reaching

22 *Castelnaudary* (*Inns:* La Flèche; Notre Dame), a town of nearly 10,000 Inhab., on an eminence, skirted at its base by the Canal du Midi, which here expands into a *bassin*, much larger than that at Naurouze, the only thing remarkable here. There are stone quarries and lime-kilns near.

The name has been traced to "Castrum Novum Arianorum," the name given by the Visigoths to the town, which they refounded. It suffered severely in the crusade against the Albigenses, having been taken both by Simon de Montfort and the Comte de Toulouse: and in 1237 the inquisitors enacted an auto-da-fè here; in which, in their desire to root out heresy, they not only burnt many persons alive, but many dead bodies, dragged ignominiously from the grave for this purpose. The most memorable event in the annals of Castelnaudary is the *battle* fought here on the banks of the Fresquel, 1632, between the forces of Louis XIII. and of Gaston Duc d'Orléans, at which the unfortunate Duc de Montmorency was wounded and made prisoner, and soon after conveyed hence to Toulouse to be beheaded.

12 Villepinte. The rounded outline of the Black Mountain bounds the view on the N.

8 Alzonne, a town of 2000 Inhab.

16 CARCASSONNE.—*Inns:* H. Bonnet, very good, baths hot and cold; St. Jean Baptiste, tolerable, on the Boulevard. This chef-lieu of the Dépt. de l'Aude, a city of 18,483 Inhab., is traversed by the river Aude, and by the Canal du Midi, which, at first carried at a distance from its walls at the request of the inhabitants, has, in recent times, received at vast expense another direction, in order to bring it up to the town, where it now forms a large *bassin*.

Carcassonne itself is composed of two parts, the modern town on the plain and the old town on an eminence above it, forming a picturesque background with its venerable towers and commanding battlements. The lower and newer town, cheerful, flourishing, and industrious, consists chiefly of modern-built houses, in streets ranging at right angles with one another, surrounded by boulevards, occupying the site of its ramparts, including squares planted with trees and furnished with marble fountains, and running with freshening rivulets. It contains several large woollen factories, and not less than 7000 persons of the town and its vicinity are employed in the *manufacture of cloth*, chiefly exported to the Levant, Barbary, and S. America, where it is esteemed for its brilliant dyes. From this and other sources of commercial prosperity it has increased, in the course of 4 or 5 centuries, from a suburb to be the town itself, while the original city on the height has dwindled down into an insignificant faubourg. Beyond this, however, it has no claim to detain the passing traveller. Its modern cathedral, and ch. of St. Vincent, whose tall tower stands on the line of the meridian of Paris, are not remarkable.

The *avenue of trees* planted along the margin of the canal, and embellished with a column of the red marble of the country to the memory of Riquet, its founder, leads to the aqueduct bridge by which the canal has been carried over the stream of the Fresnel in recent times.

The *old town*, on the height beyond the Aude, deserves the notice of all who have artists' taste for paintable bits or take an interest in antiquities, as retaining unchanged, to a greater extent perhaps than any other in France, the aspect of a fortress of the middle ages. A traveller with such tastes must not be deterred from entering by odious smells, steep, narrow, and desolate streets, with the grass growing in many of them, and the houses falling to ruin, for it has been abandoned entirely to persons of the poorer class and to artisans, composing a population of paupers pent up within its narrow enclosure. It is enclosed by double *ramparts and towers:* a portion of the inner line is attributed to the

Visigoths with much probability; and the rest, including the castle, with its curious postern, seems to be of the 11th or 12th centy., while the outer circuit has been referred to the latter end of the 13th centy. The former are therefore the same defences which withstood for a time the assault of the army of Crusaders under the fierce Simon de Montfort and the Abbot of Citeaux, who, reeking with the blood spilt at Beziers, laid siege to Carcassonne, where a vast number of fugitives, together with the Viscomte de Beziers, had taken refuge. At the intercession of the King of Arragon, his uncle, the papal legate promised to spare his life and those of 12 others with him; but the brave young warrior rejected these terms, declaring that he would sooner be flayed alive than betray one of those who had endangered themselves for his sake. Finding, however, that, owing to the number of men, women, and children who had poured in from the surrounding country, it was impossible to hold out, he managed to let them escape by a secret passage, and surrendered under a promise of safe-conduct for himself. He was nevertheless seized treacherously, and soon after died in prison, while of those who remained in the town 50 were hung and 400 burnt alive. In 1356 this fortress effectually resisted the Black Prince, who burnt the suburb below, and ravaged with fire and sword the whole of Languedoc. A curious sally-port, or *barbacane*, projects from the walls on the side nearest the modern town; and one of the towers has been split into two, but the one half, though fallen down, has not broken to pieces —such is the thickness and solidity of the masonry. The legend respecting it is, that Charlemagne, after in vain besieging for several years the town, which held out, though defended only by one Saracen woman named *Carcas*, was about to raise the siege in despair, when this tower gave way of its own accord, and opened a breach by which his army entered. The figure of this Saracen Amazon is still to be seen rudely carved over the Porte Narbonnaise, on the E. side of the town.

The *Ch. of St. Nazaire*, formerly cathedral, in the middle of the old town, consists of a Romanesque *nave*, part of the ch. dedicated by Pope Urban II. in 1096, supported by massive piers round and square, and of a Gothic *choir* and transepts added at the beginning of the 13th centy. In this part of the ch. are two fine circular windows, and some painted glass of great brilliancy of colour, though inferior in drawing. On one side of the high-altar a slab of red marble is said to mark the grave of Simon de Montfort, Earl of Leicester, that cruel and ambitious warrior, who, steeled in the holy wars, in the school of the Templars and Assassins, turned at the bidding of the Pope the sword whetted against the infidels upon the heretical Christians, the unfortunate Albigenses. The marble monument of a bishop, date 1264, is placed in a side-chapel. In one of the side-chapels of the nave is a curious *bas-relief*, representing an assault of a besieged town, probably of the 13th centy. This ch. has been restored.

Near the centre of the town is a very wide and deep well, into which, according to tradition, the Visigoth kings threw their treasures.

Carcassonne was the birth-place of the Revolutionist *Fabre*, who called himself *d'Eglantine* because he had gained the prize of the golden sweetbrier in the floral games at Toulouse: he began his career as an actor, and ended it on the guillotine in 1793.

Diligences daily to Narbonne, and the Rly. Stats. of Montpellier, Nismes, and Marseilles; to Perpignan by Limoux; to Toulouse.

At Caunes, 12 m. N.E. of Carcassonne, are the quarries of marble commonly used in churches and other public buildings in the S. of France. They are associated with slates of the transition series, and furnish 4 sorts: 1, flesh-coloured, much employed by Louis XIV. and XV.; 2, marbre cervelas; 3, grey marble containing encrinites; 4, Griotte, including nautili. One variety is called "œil de perdrix."

On quitting Carcassonne, the road crosses and runs for some distance by the side of the Aude. The canal makes a bend to the N., its new channel being cut through deep excavations. The cultivation of the olive begins near this, though the tree can scarcely be said to flourish hereabouts.

14 Barbeira.

Near this, a little to the N. of the canal, is the drained lake of Marseillette, converted from a useless pool or morass into 2900 hectares of excellent arable land by the enterprise and capital of Madame Lawless, an Irish lady domiciled in France. The drainage was completed 1850, by the construction of a tunnel near a mile long, and the ground is now portioned out into 24 farms.

13 Moux.
15 Villedaigne.

The country between this and Narbonne contracts into a narrow gorge between white naked rocks.

13 *Narbonne*, in Rte. 126.

ROUTE 94.

NARBONNE TO PERPIGNAN, PORT VENDRES, AND THE SPANISH FRONTIER.

To Perpignan is 62 kilom.= 40 Eng. m. *Diligences* twice a day.

The road is very uninteresting, skirting on the rt. the low chains of the Corbières, consisting of bare rocks without trees or herbage; only a few bristly plants, and tufts of the heath which produces the Narbonne honey; and on the l., the salt lagoons, or shallow lakes, called Etangs de Bages, de Sigean, de la Palme, and de Leucate, which here line the shore of the Mediterranean, bordered with mud and sand. The district is unhealthy, owing to the miasma from this marshy tract. At intervals, when the road surmounts a slight eminence, a glimpse may be obtained of the open sea beyond the étangs.

21 Sigean, situated on the margin of the lagoon of the same name, was the scene of a victory gained by Charles Martel over the Saracens, 737.

The few trees near the road are all bent in one direction, to the S.E., by the violent winds from the N.W., which prevail here for 8 months out of the 12.

16 Fitou stands on the edge of the large étang, called de Leucate, from a half-deserted town on the tongue of land between it and the sea: a place of strength and importance during the period when Roussillon belonged to Spain, and Leucate stood on the frontier of France. The extremity of the chain of the Pyrenees, stretching into the sea, may be discerned near this.

10 Salces. The fort on the rt., before entering this village, was built by the Emperor Charles V.; it is now a powder-magazine.

The little town of Rivesaltes, famed for its wine, lies about $1\frac{1}{2}$ m. on the rt., upon a small stream often dried up, the Agly, which is crossed by the road half way between Salces and Perpignan.

The two branches of the torrent-river Tet are crossed in order to reach Perpignan; between them stands the suburb Notre Dame; and on the rt. bank the lofty and singular castle of *Castellet*, a double tower of brick, surmounted by machicolations erected by Charles V., now a military prison.

15 PERPIGNAN.—*Inns:* H. des Ambassadeurs;—du Commerce;—de l'Europe;—Petit Paris, good;—du Midi.

Perpignan, chef-lieu of the Dépt. des Pyrénées Orientales, also a first-class fortress of great strength, defending the passage by the E. Pyrenees from Spain into France, is placed on the rt. bank of the Tet, about 6 m. above its termination in the sea, in the midst of the level plain of Roussillon, and contains 19,122 Inhab., exclusive of its garrison. As Roussillon, of which province it was the capital, was not permanently united to France until the Treaty of the Pyrenees, in 1659, it is not surprising that both the town, in its narrow dirty streets covered with awnings, its semi-Moresque buildings, its houses furnished with wooden balconies and courts (patios), and its inhabitants, especially the lower orders, should resemble those of Catalonia, on the S. side of the Pyrenees, in their physiognomy, language, dress, dances. Those to whom Spain is unknown will be struck with this novel character; but beyond this there is not much to interest the stranger here. Almost all the public buildings date from the Spanish period, and are of brick or rolled pebbles. The *Cathedral*, begun 1324, and continued by Louis XI., during the time he held Roussillon in pawn from the king of Arragon, consists of a very broad and lofty nave. The altar-screen, of beautiful carved work, partly wood, partly stone, in the style of the Renaissance, deserves notice; and the massy frame-work, gilding, tapestries, &c., which decorate this part of the ch., are thoroughly Spanish in style. The font, of marble, in the form of a tub, is very old; some attribute it to the time of the Visigoth kings. Adjoining this ch. are remains of a still older ch., now in ruins, called *St. Jean le Vieux*. Of the ch. and *convent* of the Dominicans, now a military store, a portion, in the Romanesque style, belongs to the edifice which St. Dominic, the Inquisitor, inhabited when he entered Roussillon. The building called *La Loge* (from the Spanish Lonja, exchange or bazaar) is a curious example of the mixed Moresque and Gothic styles of the end of the 15th centy. Its façade, exhibiting flamboyant ornaments, foliage and tracery, though much mutilated and injured by alterations, and the covered galleries round the court behind, merit notice. The ancient University contains the public library of 20,000 vols., and the commencement of a museum.

The *Citadel*, separated from the town by a wide glacis, and surrounded by a double line of works, is considered very strong, and commands the town. The inner ramparts were raised by Charles V., the outer by Vauban; and in the midst rises a tall square castle, or *Donjon*, built by the kings of Majorca, and the remains of a *ch.*, whose façade is remarkable, and is said to resemble that on Mount Sinai. The portal is a pointed arch, faced with slabs of marble, red and white alternately, resting on columns whose capitals represent fighting dragons. On one of the ramparts, an arm carved in stone (dextrochère), projecting from the parapet, was formerly pointed out as marking the spot where the Emperor Charles V., going the rounds at night, found a sentinel fast asleep at his post, and, pushing him into the fosse, himself took the musket, and did duty until relieved by the guard. This has been recently destroyed. From the citadel a view may be obtained over the plain of Roussillon, extending 15 m. on all sides, save that towards the sea not more than 6 m., and surrounded by a semicircle of mountains, the most elevated being the Pyrenees on the S., though they are still distant. The only mountain which makes a conspicuous figure is the *Canigou*, the highest of this portion of the chain.

Perpignan is more remarkable as a fortress than a place of commerce, but some trade is carried on in *wines* of Roussillon, also in Cork, from the mountains.

For information regarding passports on entering France from Spain, see INTRODUCTION, *d*.

Diligences twice a day to Narbonne; daily to Toulouse, by Limoux; and to Barcelona in 2 days.

M. Arago, the mathematician and astronomer (d. 1853) was born at Estagel, a poor village near Perpignan.

About 17½ m. S.E. of Perpignan is the seaport of Port Vendres; the road to it passes

12 *St. Elne*, the ancient *Illiberis*, mentioned by Pliny as "ingentis quondam urbis tenue vestigium," and by Livy as the place where Hannibal first encamped, after crossing the Pyrenees on his march to Rome, " Pyræneum transgreditur, et ad oppidum Illiberis castra locat." It was rebuilt by Constantine, who gave it the name of his mother Elena. It has a very ancient *Ch. of St. Eulalie*, once the cathedral, and episcopal see of Roussillon before Perpignan. It dates from 1019, and is in the Romanesque style, but with a pointed roof; it is quite plain internally, but the *cloister* adjoining is very richly ornamented with carvings, bas-reliefs, &c., and is worth notice. It is entered from the ch. by a pointed doorway resembling that in the citadel of Perpignan. Many inscriptions and bas-reliefs are let into the outer walls of the ch.; one of them is called the Tomb of Constans, who was assassinated at Elne by order of Maxentius. Elne is now reduced to a poor village. On

quitting it the river Tech is crossed, and Argelez is passed. Beyond this the E. extremity of the Pyrenean chain, dropping down into the sea, forms, by its projecting buttresses and roots, a number of headlands and retreating coves or bays. On the shore of one of these lies

14 Collioure (Cauroliberis), defended by numerous forts, the whole commanded by the citadel of St. Elne, between this and Port Vendres. At the entrance of the harbour rises a little rocky island bearing a Church of Pilgrimage, dedicated to the Virgin. The town contains about 2000 Inhab., and is surrounded by vineyards: the rocks, bare as they are, suffice to maintain the vine, and even the aloe, and produce some of the best wines in the department.

About 2 m. beyond Collioure is

3 *Port Vendres* (*Inn*: H. du Commerce), a town of 1305 Inhab., and a harbour of some consequence, as it is the only port of refuge between Marseilles and the Spanish frontier, and is accessible for frigates. It is defended by 4 forts and 4 batteries, but is entirely commanded by the heights behind. It has gained of late in prosperity, from its increased communication with Africa, most of the troops destined for Algiers being embarked here. 3 or 4 *steamers*, plying between Marseilles, Barcelona, Gibraltar, and Cadiz, touch here (?) every week. The marble *obelisk*, 100 ft. high, in the square was raised to Louis XVI., who caused the harbour to be cleared, excavated, and made useful, 1780. The ancient name of this place was *Portus Veneris*, from a temple of Venus, built here by the Romans. There is a mule-path hence into Spain, by the village and Col of Banyuls to Lanza, the first place in Catalonia.

The interesting road up the valley of the Tech, from Boulou, is described in Rte. 98.

———

The high road into Spain from Perpignan continues to cross the monotonous plain of Roussillon, but, as it gradually approaches the Pyrenees, commands a fine view of the Canigou on the rt.

22 Boulou lies at the foot of the mountains on the Tech, whose valley is described in Rte. 98. The stream is crossed as you quit Boulou, and about a mile farther the ascent begins, the road making considerable curves, up to the pass or *Col de Perthus*, which may be reached in 1½ hr. Half way, upon the l. of the road, is the ruined castle of L'Ecluse. At the summit on the rt. of the col, on a height above the little village of Perthus, stands the fort of Bellegarde, constructed by Louis XIV., in 1679, to command the passage into Spain. It is a regular pentagon with 5 bastions, in one of which, facing Spain, General Dugommier, killed in the battle of the Montagne Noire, on the road to Figueiras, 1794, is buried.

This pass was crossed by the conquering army of Pompey, who erected upon it a trophy of his successes, inscribed with the names of 876 places which he had subdued. Cæsar followed not long after, and raised an altar by the side of the monument of Pompey, over whose lieutenants he had, in turn, been victorious. No traces of either now remain.

Junquiera, the first Spanish town, 15 m. from Boulou, and the road to Barcelona, are described in the HANDBOOK FOR SPAIN.

ROUTE 95.

ST. GAUDENS TO CARCASSONNE BY ST. GIRONS AND FOIX.

189 kilom. = 117 Eng. m.; road good, and very pretty, but hilly. St. Gaudens is in Rte. 91.

At St. Martory the road quits that to Toulouse, and crosses the Garonne by a picturesque stone bridge. Cross a stone bridge of 5 arches before entering Mane, a poor village. The fine old *Evêché of St. Elize*, perched on a steep rock, now a lunatic asylum, is passed about 1 m. before reaching

47 St. Girons (*Inns*: H. de Biros;— H. de France, not good), a "dull and crumbling" town of 3895 Inhab., close to the junction of the Salut with the Gau. The walk along the river is delightful. Good road, but against the

collar, to La Bastide. A new, well-made road, avoiding hills, to
44 Foix, in Rte. 97. Road hilly, but good, to
27 Lavelanet (H. chez Elanet).— Good road, chiefly descent, to
21 Chalabre (*Inn*: H. d'Espagne, not good). Very mountainous, but good road to
25 *Limoux* (*Inn*: H. Lion d'Or, good; H. du Parc), a small town of 7188 Inhab., pleasantly situated in a valley on the River Aude. The rich soil of the neighbouring vineyards produces the famous wines of Limoux and Blanquette. *Diligences* to Toulouse, and twice a day to Carcassonne, and once a day to Foix.
25 CARCASSONNE. H. Bonnet, good. (Rte. 93).

ROUTE 97.*

THE EASTERN PYRENEES. — TOULOUSE TO FOIX AND PUYCERDA.—THE VALLEY OF THE ARIÉGE.— VICDESSOS.— ANDORRE.

81 kilom. = 50 Eng. m. to Foix, 18 lieues thence to Puycerda = 50 Eng. m.

A post-road as far as Foix. *Diligences* run daily to Foix, Ussat, and Ax.

At Portet the road turns to the l., away from that to Bagnères de Luchon (Rte. 91), and crosses the Garonne by a brick bridge, nearly opposite the influx of the Ariége, and afterwards runs along the l. bank of that river.

26 Viviers.

A little above Beccarest is Cintegabelle, where Lord Hill passed the Ariége in 1814.

22 Saverdun, a town of 3000 Inhab., was the birth-place of Pope Benedict XII.; he was the son of a baker or miller. At Mazères, a little to the E. of our road, Gaston de Foix, Duc de Nemours, the hero of the battle of Ravenna, was born 1489. Crossing the Ariége, by a bridge at Saverdun, the road ascends its rt. bank to

15 Pamiers (*Inns*: Croix d'Or;

* Routes 97 and 98, not being described from personal knowledge, may perhaps be somewhat inaccurate, and the Editor would feel much obliged to any traveller who has travelled on these lines for notes to correct them.

Grand Soleil), a cheerful and pretty town. Pop. 7459. A *Cathedral*, surmounted by an octagonal Gothic tower of brick, spared by Mansard when he rebuilt the nave in the style of the 17th centy. A beautiful *promenade*, on an eminence beyond the Cathedral, looks out upon the distant Pyrenees. About 12 m. W. of this the philosopher Bayle, author of the Dictionary, was born, 1647, in the obscure village of Carla le Comte.

The road still runs along the rt. bank of the river; the valley contracts in width and increases in beauty at Varilhes.

19 Foix (*Inns*: Rocher de Foix;— H. la Coste, indifferent and dear), the ancient capital of the Comté de Foix, is now the chef-lieu of the Dépt. l'Ariége, which is nearly coequal with the Comté de Foix. It is one of the smallest chef-lieux in France, as its population does not exceed 4110. It has a very picturesque site, at the junction of a stream called the Larget with the Ariége. It fills up the mouth of the valley, here narrow and bounded by precipitous hills, and lines either bank of the rapid river, whilst an isolated rock, rising from amidst the houses, sustains the ancient *castle* of the Counts of Foix, who resisted with such invincible courage the attacks of the kings of France and Arragon, and whose line terminated with the chivalrous Gaston. It is known by the name of *Les Tours*, an appropriate one, as its lofty towers, built of a coarse whitish marble, and preserved unstained by the dryness of the climate, stand prominent. Part, also, of the ancient ramparts have resisted time's decay; and the antique character of many of the houses, together with " the magic of a name," have thrown a colouring over it that makes it, although now unimportant and remote, a spot interesting to the tourist.

The *Castle*, now converted into a gaol, and much injured by modern erections, is approached by a very narrow, steep path, bending, with very abrupt turns, along the edge of the precipice. Of its 3 fine towers, all of different ages and all anterior to the 15th centy., the tallest, or donjon, 136 ft. high, is also the oldest, having been built 1362 by Gaston Phœbus, Count of Foix: it commands a fine view from its top. Simon de Montfort in vain besieged this stronghold, in 1210, during the wars of the Albigenses; and at a later period, 1272, Philippe le Hardi, unable to take it by other means, began to undermine the rocky pedestal, with the intention of toppling it over, together with the fortress on the top of it ! Such, at least, is the popular tale; and though there seems little possibility that such a threat could have been accomplished in days when gunpowder was unknown, it had the effect of inducing the garrison to surrender.

Excepting the castle, there is little in the town to attract notice,—but the country around is lovely.

The *Préfecture* was originally part of the abbey of St. Volusien, suppressed at the Revolution. The church of St. Volusien, rebuilt by Roger II., Comte de Foix, is a heavy Gothic building.

A considerable trade in iron, the staple of the Dépt. l'Ariége, derived from the mines of La Rancié, in the Vicdessos, is carried on here. The metal is embarked on the Ariége at Autrerive, below St. Foix, for exportation.

Diligence to Toulouse.

The valley above this is bare of trees, but productive in corn and wine; the vine itself being frequently planted on the heaps of boulder-stones cleared away from the fields, where they are otherwise so numerous as to hinder cultivation. Tarascon, a smaller town than Foix (1555 Inhab.), having also its ancient castle on a rock above it, stands at the point of convergence of several valleys,—that of Vicdessos, in which the iron-mines of La Rancié are situated, traversed by a carriage-road as far as Sens, that of Saurat (near the entrance of which is the fine cave of Bédeillac), up which runs a carriage-road to St. Girons, by the Col de Portet and town of Massat (1000 Inhab.), and that of the Ariége.

[The valley of Vicdessos is rendered one of the most industrious in the Pyrenees by its iron mines and works. It is further embellished by the neat houses and gardens of the iron-masters and miners, and by several picturesque old castles, among which that of Méglos is very conspicuous. The *mines of Rancié*, situated 460 ft. above the village of Sem, reached by a difficult path in zigzags which takes an hour to surmount, have been worked for many ages, but without a proper system; and it is supposed that the supply of ore will be exhausted in 20 years. The ore is chiefly the hydrate and carbonate of iron, and is very rich, often yielding 60 per cent.; but as it requires to be brought down from the mine on mule-back, and to be transported often 40 or 50 miles to the furnace, and as the fuel (charcoal) must be sought for in many situations from a like distance, the metal produced is very dear, in spite of the cheapness of labour. Yet nearly 60 furnaces are supplied from hence in the Dépt. of Ariége alone. The iron ore is found deposited in caverns, veins, and hollows within the strata of a limestone rock, belonging apparently to the lower Jura limestone (lias) formation, and within a short distance of the fundamental granite. The ore has been worked horizontally to a depth of 300 mètres, and vertically to a height of 600 mètres. Owing to the unskilfulness, want of concert, and heedlessness of the miners, the ore has been extracted without any regard to economy or safety of life; the roofs and walls of the galleries and chambers excavated, having no proper support, are constantly giving way in consequence, and serious loss of life has frequently attended these éboulements. Many of the galleries leading into the mines have been blocked up by the ruins. At the village of Vicdessos, which is surrounded by furnaces (forges), there is a clean inn. There is a path up the Val de Sallix, over the mountain-pass called Port d'Aulus, into the Val d'Ercé, and by Aulus and Oust to St. Girons.]

A little more than a mile above Tarascon lie the *Bains d' Ussat*, a group of lodging and bath-houses, &c., including 2 large and comfortable *Hôtels*

(Des Voyageurs, close to the road, and L'Etablissement, on the opposite side of the river), which the traveller may conveniently make his head-quarters when exploring the neighbouring valleys. They stand, shaded by trees, within a few yards of the river, at a point where the valley is closed by mountain-walls of limestone, barely allowing a few box-bushes to take root in their crevices, but traversed by numerous caverns, in some of which fossil bones have been found. The *Grotto* cave on the l. bank of the river, above the H. des Voyageurs, is of considerable extent, requiring an hour to reach its extremity, and is worth a visit. The *waters* are warm, acidulous, and, when administered in baths, are said to have a calming effect over the nervous system, and are much used by females. The baths are hollows excavated in the ground, lined with marble, filled naturally by the water rising from beneath.

The high road runs up the l. bank of the Ariége, but there is a path along the rt. from Ussat to Tarascon. Above Tarascon the vale of the Ariége makes an abrupt bend to the E., round the N. base of the Mont St. Barthélemy, one of the loftiest of this portion of the chain of the Pyrenees, whose top, surmounted by snows and glaciers, appears, from time to time, domineering over the upper valley on the l. The Pont de Gudane carries the road over the stream of the Aston, descending from the lofty and snowy range separating France from Andorre. Numerous old ruined castles, built originally to command the valley or defend the frequented passage through it into Catalonia, occur at intervals, rising on peaked eminences above the valley; but the largest and most lordly and picturesque of all is that of *Lordat*, near Cabannes; its origin is attributed to the Moors or Goths. Iron-works in equal number alternate with these feudal remains; thus the romantic associations of former times combine with the active industry of the present to add an interest to a valley which derives so many attractions besides from the beauties of nature. Its ancient inhabitants were called *Tectosages*, from the *sagum*, or cloak, which they wore, which has descended to the present generation, who, by a curious coincidence, still designate it by the same name, in their patois, "*un sayo.*"

Ax, 13 m. above Ussat.—*Inns:* H. d'Espagne; H. de France; both extremely dirty. Ax is a town of 2000 Inhab., prettily situated amidst granitic mountains, at the junction of 3 valleys, out of which issue 3 mountain torrents, whose streams combine, in or near the town, to form the river Ariége.

In the name Ax it is easy to discover the Latin *Aquæ*, derived from the hot *sulphureous springs* which burst out on all sides; indeed there appears to be a natural kettle of boiling water under the town. More than 30 hot sources issue forth in different parts of it, varying in temperature from 113° to 168° of Fahr.; and in order to obtain cold one must resort to the river; and even it, in some parts, is rendered tepid by hot springs rising in its very bed: the snow rests but a few instants on a soil so thoroughly heated from below. Besides the application of the waters to baths, of which there are 2 or 3 establishments, and for drinking, it is turned to various domestic and economic purposes by the inhabitants, who wash not only their linen, but a vast quantity of wool in its tepid streams. The town itself is a miserable collection of dirty lanes, the only considerable buildings being the hotels and hospitals, one of which has been constructed by government for military patients. Near the hospital is an ancient bath, established in 1200, and still called *Bassin des Ladres*, or Lepers' Basin.

The carriage-road up the valley ceases shortly before reaching Merens —a poor village; beyond it the mountains close in and form a long, gloomy defile; it afterwards expands into an open, stony, and uninteresting tract. A very rough and steep path leads to Hospitalet (12 m. from Ax), a journey of 3½ h. on horseback. This is a poor hamlet, but has a small inn. 1½ hour's ride above this is the pass or col over the mountain, called *Port de Puymaurins*, upon which a custom-house is planted. [Close to this pass, on the W., begins the territory of *Andorre*, a small neutral state between France and Spain, which has been allowed by its powerful neighbours, partly through its insignificance and poverty, to maintain an independent existence, under a republican form of government, for six centuries since the days of Charlemagne, resembling in this respect the republic of San Marino in Italy. It is shut in by high mountains on all sides but the S., where the river Embalire issues out towards the Spanish town of Urgel. Its population amounts to about 15,000, and its capital, Andorre, numbers about 2000. It is governed by a council of 24, a syndic, and 2 viguiers, or magistrates, appointed, one by the sovereign of France, who, as protector of Andorre, receives 960 fr. of tribute yearly, the other by the bishop of Urgel. It consists of 3 valleys, hemmed in by grand mountains of great elevation: its productions are limited nearly to wood and iron; and from the sale of these (and from smuggling) the inhabitants are enabled to purchase corn and other necessaries, which their barren and lofty country refuses to yield. For the traveller there is no accommodation; and he that ventures thither, if he be not prepared to sleep in the open air, with some risk of starving, should carry letters with him from persons of authority at Ax to some of the wealthy proprietors. The only English traveller who has given an account of Andorre, derived from a personal acquaintance with the country, is the Hon. Erskine Murray.]

After passing the crest of the great chain by the Port de Puymaurins, the path descends the S. slope, through a very wild valley, strewn with rocks, passing the hamlets of Porté and Porta, near which a path strikes off to the rt. up a minor valley into Andorre. Between Porta and Courbassil is the old ruined castle, after which the vale is named, called *Tour du Carol*, built, according to popular tradition, by the Moors; but upon the conquest of this country and their expulsion from it by Charlemagne, the towers were christened Carol, after him. They occupy a very picturesque position on the top of an immense isolated mass of granite, rising in the midst of this narrow and rugged valley. Beyond Courbassil is the village called Tour de Carol, situated within a mile of the Spanish frontier, which is marked neither by stream nor mountain, but is a mere imaginary line at this point. About 2 m. within it lies the Spanish town of Puycerda, 13 m. from Hospitalet. See HANDBOOK FOR SPAIN.

The road hence to Perpignan, by Mont Louis and the Valley of the Tech, is described in Rte. 98.

ROUTE 98.*

EASTERN PYRENEES.— PERPIGNAN TO MONT LOUIS AND PUYCERDA, BY THE VALLEYS OF THE TET AND TECH.— ASCENT OF THE CANIGOU.

About 47 Eng. m.

A post-road as far as Olette, but not always provided with horses.

The vale of the Tet, up whose rt. bank our road ascends, is flattened down and absorbed in the great plain of Roussillon, near Perpignan, and it is not until after leaving behind, at some distance,

24 Ille, a walled town of 3000 Inhab., that the road enters fairly among the mountains. From Vinça, another town, the ascent is gradual to

18 Prades. This town of 3013 Inhab. possesses a tolerable *Inn*, but is in no wise remarkable, except for its pretty situation on the rt. bank of the Tet, in a valley abounding in corn, wine, and fruits, vineyards terraced up the hill-sides, maize and hemp fields. "The banks on the rt. and l. are spotted with villages, and clustered with old châteaux." Prades lies at the N. base of the Canigou, whose summit may be reached by 8 or 9 hours' walk up the vale of Lentilla.

There is, however, another and more interesting way of approaching the Canigou, pursuing the high road into Spain (Rte. 94) as far as Boulou (22

* See note to Route 97.

kilom.), where it turns to the S.W. up the *Valley of the Tech*. At Ceret, 6 m. up, the river is spanned by an ancient bridge of a single bold arch, 144 ft. in the opening, whose construction is attributed to the Visigoth kings, but which in reality is not older than 1352. It is very narrow, and the arch thins out towards the keystone. Ceret, a town of 3000 Inhab., is about a mile farther; and 7 m. above it is the small fort of Arles-les-Bains, constructed by Louis XIV., on the top of an eminence, from whose base issue hot sulphureous springs of a temperature of 157° Fahr. They were known to the Romans, and the vaulted chamber in which one of them is still received is of their building, but is remarkable only for its solidity. Between this and the town of Arles are some iron-forges, where the ore derived from mines situated high up on the N. flank of the Canigou, and brought hither on mules' backs, is smelted. The Tech is again crossed before entering the town; it has 2000 Inhab. The *Ch.* is ancient; the front and portal enriched with curious carving, in white marble, dated from 1045. On the l. of the façade, under a sort of shed, is a very ancient sarcophagus resting on 4 feet, filled with miracle-working water, which is never exhausted, and is sold at 20 sous the vial-full. It owes its virtues to the coffin having enclosed the relics of two saints, which were brought from Rome to free the neighbourhood of Arles from dragons, lions, &c., which then infested it! Adjoining the Ch. is a cloister, a range of pointed arches on slender pillars, of the 13th centy., without a roof.

About 10 m. distant among the mountains, and approached by steep paths, from which fine views are obtained of the Canigou, is the Romanesque Ch. of Coustouges, which may interest the antiquary, as it is supposed to date from the 9th centy.

8 m. above Arles, in the Valley of the Tech, lies Pratz de Mollo, a frontier town of 4000 Inhab., surrounded by old-fashioned fortifications, but commanded on the height above by the efficient Fort Legarde, constructed from the plans of Vauban. A mule-path runs hence over the mountains to the Spanish town Compredon.

The *ascent of the Canigou*, which projects forward from the great chain of the Pyrenees, and rises, almost isolated, above the plain of Roussillon, to a height of 9141 ft., was made by Mr. E. Murray from Arles. He followed the mule-paths leading to the iron-mines, as far as the old tower of Batères, standing on a ridge whence you look down upon both valleys of the Tech and Tet ; and after 3 or 4 hours' scrambling from this ridge, "up steps, along precipices, and over snow wreaths," attained the summit; whence the eye surveys the plain of Roussillon, and the coast of the Mediterranean, with Perpignan on its margin ; the valleys bordering on the Tet ; the mountain range of Catalonia on the S.; and on the W. the chain separating Roussillon from the Vale of Ariége. "The ascent or descent to Valmania is so difficult and dangerous as to deter many an aspirant from attempting to surmount it; but no one, with a tolerable pair of legs, good lungs, and not unaccustomed to mountain climbing, ought to be discouraged: should he succeed, he will find himself amply repaid for his toil and fatigue." Valmania is a hamlet, composed of a few miners' houses, and a very humble cabaret, which will afford night shelter, and fresh eggs, with vin du pays, in a wild situation under an old ruined castle. The iron-mines occur near the junction of a limestone (of the age of the chalk) with the granite. It is a five hours' walk hence to Prades, descending the vale of the Lentilla, through picturesque scenery, and joining the high road near Vinca.

Above Prades the plain of the Tet contracts into a valley; and, after passing the old *castle* of Ria, the cradle of a noble line, whence came the Counts of Arragon and Barcelona, narrows to a gorge at Villefranche, a town fortified by Vauban, but not strong, because commanded by the neighbouring heights, which squeeze it in as it were, and leave barely space for its two narrow streets, and the river below.

8½ m. from Prades, in the vale of Corneilla, which penetrates S. from this into the flanks of the Canigou, lies *Vernet*, a watering-place, supplied by hot sulphurous springs bursting out of a slaty quartzose rock, which here composes the Pyrenæan chain. They are useful in cases of rheumatism, paralysis, wounds, and ulcers. The place was visited by Ibrahim Pasha in 1846. Above Vernet rises the ruined abbey St. Martin de Canigou.

The high road crosses the Tet, by a bridge, on quitting Villefranche, and terminates soon after, giving place to a mere mule-path.

16 Olette. 2 m. farther the cultivation of the vine ceases; the valley becomes sterile and wild; the road, ascending more rapidly, traverses a narrow defile, guarded and closed, in ancient times, by walls, towers, and gateways, whose ruins still remain. To this succeeds an open expanse, a table-land of green meadow, a pastoral scene, surrounded by fir-clad heights; and in the midst, at a distance of 10 m. above Olette, stands

Mont Louis (a tolerable *Inn*), a frontier fortress (442 Inhab.), built 1684 by Vauban to guard the passage from Spain.

The town consists of 8 short streets, in straight lines, crossing one another at right angles, surmounted by the *Citadel*, whose casemates afford shelter for 800 men. A road runs N. from this to Carcassonne (Rte. 93), and a path over the mountains by Langles into the vale of the Ariége.

About 2 m. from Mont Louis, and at a height of 1150 ft. above it, 5114 ft. above the sea-level, is the pass over the mountains, called *Col de la Perche*. The path from it descends into the basin-shaped valley of the Cerdagne Française, traversed by numerous streams, the chief of which is the Seyre, or Segre, a tributary of the Ebro. The territory of France has here been pushed, for some distance, down the S. slope of the backbone of the Pyrenees, in the same manner that the Spaniards occupy the head of the vale of the Garonne, on the N. of the chain (Rte. 87). 5 m. below the col is Saillagousa, a town of 400 Inhab.; 2 m. farther is Llivia; and 3 m. more carry the traveller across the frontier to the first Spanish town, Puycerda (10 m. from Mont Louis). See HANDBOOK FOR TRAVELLERS IN SPAIN.

The road from Puycerda to Toulouse is described in Rte. 97.

SECTION V.

CENTRAL FRANCE—BERRI—AUVERGNE—VIVARAIS—ARDECHE—CANTAL—BOURBONNAIS—LYONNAIS—THE CEVENNES.

ROUTE	PAGE
103 Orleans to Clermont by Vierzon, *Bourges* (Nevers), Moulins, and Vichy (*Railway*)	339
104 Paris to Dijon, by Melun, *Fontainebleau, Sens, Joigny, Tonnerre* [*Auxerre*].—Paris and Lyons Railway A	344
105 Paris to Lyons, by Fontainebleau, *Montargis, Nevers*, Moulins [*Baths of Vichy*]	356
106 Dijon to *Châlons-sur-Saône*, by Paris and Lyons Railway B	363
107 Nevers to Châlons-sur-Saône, by Château-Chinon and Autun	366
108 Châlons-sur-Saône to Lyons, by *Mâcon*.—*Descent of the Saône*	367
109 Moulins to *Clermont* and *Le Puy*.— *Volcanoes of Auvergne*	379
110 Clermont to *Mont Dore les Bains*	392
111 Mont Dore les Bains to Le Puy, by Issoire	396
112 Clermont to Lyons, by *Thiers*	397
114 Clermont to Toulouse, by the *Cantal* and *Aurillac*	398
116 Clermont to Toulouse, by *St. Flour*, the *Baths of Chaudes Aigues, Rodez*, and *Alby*	401
117 Montauban to Beziers, by *Castres*	406
118 Lyons to Le Puy, Aubenas, *Mende*, and Nismes.—*Railway to St. Etienne*.—The *Cevennes*	406
119 Roanne to Valence on the Rhône, by *St. Etienne* and *Annonay*.—*Railway* from Roanne to St. Etienne	411
120 Le Puy to Alais	414
121 Valence to Nismes, by *Privas, Aubenas*, the *Volcanoes of the Ardèche*, and *Alais*.—*Railway* from *Alais* to *Nismes*.—The *Cevennes*	415

CENTRAL FRANCE.

GENERAL VIEW OF THE COUNTRY.

AMONG the crowds of English travellers who annually roll along the high road and railway from Paris to Lyons on their way to Italy, complaining of the dull monotony of France, how few have taken the trouble to ascertain what beauties and curiosities were presented by the districts which they almost skirted with their carriage-wheels—Auvergne, the Vivarais, the Ardèche, and Dauphiné! Auvergne, little known even to the French themselves, except among men of science, in whose works it is minutely described, is best approached by quitting the high road to Lyons at Moulins, and ascending the valley of the Allier to Clermont. The road thither, and for some distance beyond, traverses a country contrasting remarkably with that left behind at Moulins in varied surface, fertility, and abundance of foliage. It is thickly inhabited, and sprinkled over with towns and villages, not hidden, but planted on the road side or on the top of conspicuous eminences, where they alternate with ruined castles. The chief source of interest, however, in Auvergne consists in its *extinct volcanoes*, which of themselves deserve to attract visitors from all quarters of the globe. Even the distant outline of these commanding mountain groups marks them as something uncommon, while on a nearer approach their structure and composition furnish undeniable proof of their extraordinary origin. Many of them swell into domes, showing that

" The earth hath bubbles as the water has;"

others are formed into craters as regular and perfect as those of Etna and Vesuvius, assuming the shape of a funnel or inverted cone. In many instances the lava streams may be traced from the very lips of the crater out of which they originally flowed for miles over the country, capping the hill tops and filling up the valleys.

Castles of the feudal ages, dismantled by the levelling politician Richelieu, or by the unbridled fury of the Revolutionists, abound in Central France and contribute to adorn the landscape. In the volcanic country they are usually perched on a platform of basalt crowning some conical peak, which is the relic of a great bed of the same rock which once overspread the country. These ready-made pedestals, from their isolated position and precipitous sides, afforded security for property in troublous times, and impunity for violence and rapine.

The best head-quarters for exploring Auvergne are Clermont, at the foot of the Puy (or Pic) de Dôme, whence numerous excursions may be made over the Phlegræan fields of France, and *Mont Dore les Bains*, a very interesting spot, situated within another volcanic chain, the Monts Dores. Farther S. lie the volcanic groups of the *Cantal*, between Murat and Aurillac, whose scenery is striking and very peculiar; of *Velay*, in the midst of which stands the town of Le Puy, one of the most singular and picturesque in France; and of the *Ardèche* or *Vivarais*. Both the Cantal and Le Puy are accessible by good roads from Clermont, but there is a want of communication between them, and a carriage can only proceed from one to the other by a long détour, while the Ardèche is accessible by good roads only from the Rhône. The pedestrian and geologist will find his way readily across the country.

Aubenas, in the Ardèche, has a good inn; Vals, too, which is even more centrical, affords very fair accommodation, where travellers may put up while exploring its basaltic causeways, its domes of ashes, and craters of scoriæ, on which the chesnut luxuriates. The pedestrian and equestrian can pass from Le Puy, by Langogne, direct to Thueyts and Montpezat. (Rte. 121.)

The best mode of travelling through Auvergne is *on horseback:* the horses of the country are hardy, safe, and strong.

Bordering upon the Ardèche to the S. extends the wild mountain chain of the *Cevennes*, which may be termed a *moral* extinct volcano, the last stronghold of persecuted Protestantism in France, "Le Désert," as its own inhabitants called it, while, further in allusion to the children of Israel, they styled themselves "Les Enfans de Dieu." The Cevennes fill a large part of the departments of La Lozère and Gard; and, by tracing up to their sources on the map the rivers Tarn, Gardon, Vidourle, and Herault, the reader will ascertain the theatre of that dire struggle, in the course of which 30,000 Cevenols perished in battle or on the scaffold, and a much larger number of royal troops fell, between November 1702 and December 1704. The boundaries of the Hautes Cevennes are precisely marked by the lozenge-shaped outline formed by the head waters, or forks, of the Tarn, and the two Gardons, that of Andouze and that of Alais. The Basses Cevennes lie S. of this, between the Gardon d'Andouze and the Vidourle. These mountains are a natural citadel, an inextricable labyrinth of gorges and defiles well fitted for desultory warfare, where a handful of bold defenders could hold out against a host; with mountain peaks and ridges for camps; passes and gorges for ambuscades; forests to rally in, in the event of defeat; and for escape and refuge, mountain paths, trodden only by the wild goat, and caves haunted by the fox; but which the Cevenols converted into arsenals and storehouses. The best disciplined troops availed nothing in storming these bulwarks of nature; and army after army, sent forth by the bigot Louis XIV., at the instigation of the Jesuits, was annihilated by rude peasants, and their leaders were recalled with disgrace. But the miseries of war, the assassinations, burnings, pillagings, slaughter of females and infants, were not confined to these mountains: they spread far and wide down into the plain, to the ocean on the S., to the Rhône on the E., and N. beyond the Ardèche: the incursions of the peasants in their forays, pouring down from the hills, repeatedly spread consternation up to the very walls of Nismes, Uzès, Alais, and Montpellier; and their leaders in disguise boldly penetrated into the interior of these towns when in search of provisions or intelligence. And who were these chiefs? Simple peasants, shepherds, labourers, carders of wool, and weavers, who exercised the double office of military leaders and prophets; a singular compound of psalm-singing and throat-cutting, combining the strongest religious fanaticism with much worldly vanity, love of fine dresses, and of plunder; and above all, the most dauntless courage. One or two had served as soldiers in the ranks, during the war of the Alps; but this could not have given them that skill in generalship which enabled them repeatedly to bring their wild hordes to face troops four, six, or eight times more numerous, not only in the mountains, in advantageous positions, but also in the plain, with so much skill as to call forth the admiration even of Marshal Villars. The story of the poor peasants of the Cevennes differs but little from that of the Covenanters in Scotland, except that the oppression which the Cevenols endured was more cruel. It affords a remarkable proof how fruitless are the efforts of bigoted persecution and tyrannic cruelty, even when backed by unlimited power, in procuring passive submission. When, in an evil hour for France, Louis XIV., listening to the advice of Louvois and Bossuet, backed by the Jesuits, revoked the Edict of Nantes, made it a crime to pray except according to his own religion, banished the Reformed pastors to distant lands, pulled down the churches, and let loose the Dragonnades to torture the people into conformity, a strange fermentation was produced in the public mind, heated by the perusal and misapplication of particular parts of the Bible. Prophets and prophetesses began to spring up among the Protestant community. That wild enthusiasm, bordering on insanity, which roused up the Maid of Orleans to resist the oppression of the English, here seems to have developed itself among a whole community. The disease of prophesying seems first to have broken out in Dauphiné, but soon spread, like an epidemic, across the Rhône, and a large proportion of the cases were mere boys and girls, and all untaught peasants. The ignorant peasantry, believing the ecstasies of these preachers to be inspired by the Holy Ghost, flocked from far and near to listen, and, deprived of the sober guidance of their own exiled pastors, imbibed the fervour of fanaticism. The spirit of resistance began to show itself, drawn forth by the recital of their wrongs, the denunciation of their tyrants, and the assurance of support from heaven: conventicles were held, in spite of the terrors of prison, torture, and the soldiery, in the open air among rocks and caverns. The desire of vengeance on the instrument of their suffering, a bigoted priest who had acted the part which Archbishop Sharp is supposed to have done in Scotland, and who was assassinated by a fanatic French Balfour of Burley, was the signal for denial of mercy on the part of the ministers of Louis, and of open rebellion on the side of the Cevenols. Hereupon commenced the insurrection of the *Camisards*, as the persecuted outcasts of the Cevennes were called by their enemies, it is supposed from the white shirt (in Languedocian, *Camisa*) which they wore over their clothes to distinguish themselves. The whole of the Protestant communities were organized, chiefly by the leaders Roland and Cavalier; troops were levied from the different parishes, and each furnished its quota to the ranks and the commissariat or a contribution of money; and losses in the ranks were filled up by fresh levies. The

Cevenol force never exceeded 3000 in arms at one time, and was divided into three brigades under different chiefs, each of whom had his own post and district (generally near his own home) among the hills. Such troops and commanders, intoxicated by the wild harangues of prophets and prophetesses who accompanied the expeditions on horseback, and made their hearers believe that their bodies should be as stone against sword and musket, and who led them into action with some inspiriting psalm, produced acts of most dauntless daring and prowess, and a total disregard of the numbers brought against them. The seizures, tortures, executions, by breaking on the wheel and burning alive (the common modes of punishing a Camisard), led to reprisals on their part—to murders of priests, sacking and burning of popish churches. Yet, horrible as were the acts of vengeance and violence committed by the Cevenols, they were equalled, if not surpassed, by the crimes, plunder, and murder of women and children, perpetrated by the ruffian soldiery in the pay of Louis, especially by the guerrilla bands called Florentins. The royal troops carried fire and sword into every village; and the unscrupulous generals and governors of Louis acting in Languedoc resorted to the atrocious measure of devastating the whole of the Upper Cevennes; destroying by fire and axe 400 hamlets and villages, and driving away the inhabitants. The Camisards did not attempt to defend their homesteads, but retorted by carrying fire and sword over the fertile plain, and spreading terror into the cities of Nismes and Montpellier. The rebellion was at length arrested, less by any successes gained against the Protestants in the field, by the number of troops employed against them, and the skill and generalship of the four marshals of France despatched in turn to take the command, than by the cautious policy of one of them, Marshal Villars, in cajoling and bribing the Cevenol leaders.

Though the struggle of the Cevenols ended in failure—though the tolerance of their faith, according to the Edict of Nantes, the chief object for which they contended, was denied them—though the insurrection was followed, not by alleviation of their wrongs, but by persecution continued for half a century,—yet these misguided sufferers, who bled upon their native mountains, who were broken alive on the wheel, burnt alive on the pile, tormented in dungeons, or pined away their lives in gaol, gave a terrible lesson to tyranny and religious bigotry, and shook the "Grand Monarque" on his throne. Even at the present time their country has not recovered from the desolation inflicted by the destruction of its houses and temples. Many parishes, destitute of places of worship, meet for prayer in the open air, and the traveller in passing through them may be arrested by the distant sounds of psalmody, or in passing an abrupt turn in his road may come upon a congregation of peasants attentively listening to the pastor, who holds forth from the top of the rock, or from beneath the shade of a venerable tree. Many families trace their descent from the chiefs of the insurrection. The people are poor, and the greater part of their country, especially the Upper Cevennes, is not easily accessible for want of roads. There is but little traffic along the two highways from Mende to Nismes (Rte. 118), and from Aubenas to Alais (Rte. 121), which skirt or traverse it. Manufactures, however, are gradually creeping up its remote valleys from the S.; and the railway completed between Nismes and Alais, and the neighbouring coal-field, cannot fail to give an impulse to traffic and commerce. The traveller will find little picturesque beauty, owing to the bare aridity of the hills, the want of foliage and of verdure.

Its history and ancient associations form its chief interest. An Englishman may be willing to be reminded, as he traverses this district of former strife, that many of the Irish officers and soldiers who fought at the battle of the Boyne on the side of James II., and afterwards accompanied him to France, were employed here against the Protestants; that the Cevenol leaders were encouraged by the ministers of William III. and Queen Anne, and received

CENTRAL FRANCE. *Route 103.—Bourges.* 339

promises of assistance, but promises only; that on two occasions British fleets, under Sir Cloudesley Shovel, approached the coast of Languedoc to support the insurrection with troops and arms, but failed in effecting that purpose; that the band of Cevenol insurgents expelled from France by the intrigues and negotiations of Villars was formed into a regiment under their chief Cavalier, and fought in the English army commanded by Peterborough in Spain, at Almanza, where they were almost cut to pieces by their own countrymen; and that Cavalier, their leader, died a pensioner in Chelsea Hospital.

A full account of the war of the Cevennes, and the events which led to it, will be found in Peyrat, *Histoire des Pasteurs du Désert,* Paris, 1842.

For the geology of Auvergne, Velay, and the Vivarais, there is no work so good as G. P. Scrope's *Central France,* with illustrations from the author's sketches. Consult also Lyell's Geology, and the French works of M. Elie de Beaumont; those of MM. Lecocq and Bouillé, and of M. Bertrand de Doux. Miss Costello's *Summer in Auvergne* may also be referred to. Merimée's *Notes d'un Voyage en Auvergne* contains the most complete account of the monuments of that district.

ROUTE 103.

ORLEANS TO CLERMONT, BY VIERZON, BOURGES [NEVERS], MOULINS, AND VICHY. RAILWAY.

111 kilom. = 69 Eng. m. to Bourges. 71 kilom. thence to Clermont.

Railroad. 4 trains daily.

This road is the same as Rte. 70 as far as

80 Vierzon Junction Stat. About a mile out of the town, on the banks of the Canal, is the village Les Forges, consisting of extensive furnaces, where the iron of Berry is wrought in large quantity.

90 Foecy Stat.

96 Mehun Stat., near to the river Yèvre. A fragment, consisting of 2 machicolated towers, alone remains of the *castle* in which Charles VII. spent much of the early part of his reign in indolence, and at last ended his days; allowing himself to die of starvation, through the fear of being poisoned by his son, afterwards Louis XI., 1461. The demolition of the building has been chiefly effected since 1812, down to which time the chamber of the king, and that of his mistress, Agnes Sorel, were still pointed out.

103 Marmagne Stat.

112 BOURGES Stat.—*Inns:* none good.

Bourges, anciently capital of Berry, and now of the Dépt. of the Cher, is situated nearly in the centre of France, upon a considerable eminence, rising abruptly out of an uninteresting and flat country, *watered* by the river Auron, and has 22,465 Inhab. It possesses little trade and no extensive manufacture; though some cloth is woven and some iron ore is smelted in it. Its streets may be divided into 2 classes: those of very ancient houses with gables facing outwards, many of them having frame fronts of timber, generally occupied by shops; and streets of dead walls and portes cochères, denoting the habitations of families of independent fortune, and in easy circumstances, in which class Bourges abounds. The opening of the railway seems to have thrown some little life into these dead walls. The number of silversmiths is remarkable in a provincial town. The highest platform of the hill on which the town is built is occupied by the *Cathedral of St. Etienne,* a colossal and magnificent edifice, one of the finest in France, conspicuous, with its 2 solid towers, far and near. Its W. façade presents a row of no less than 5 deeply-recessed portals, all ornamented, in a style of peculiar richness and originality, with sculpture; that in the centre, higher than the rest, is decorated, above the carved wood doors, with a bas-relief of admirable execution, representing the Last Judgment. In the centre, Christ seated amidst Archangels, and the Virgin and St. John on either side, on their knees: below, on his rt., the Good led to the Gate of Paradise by St. Peter; on the

Q 2

1. the Wicked seized by Demons and hurled into a fiery Cauldron, which divers Imps are exciting with the Bellows: 6 rows of niches, filled with figures of the Angelic Choir, Saints, Patriarchs, &c., line this deep porch on either side. The varied expression of the countenances, the elevated character of many, the easy flow of the drapery, and the good execution of the whole, bespeak the work of an eminent sculptor, but his name, as well as that of the architect of the building, is unknown. The portals have been lately restored, with great care and skill, in a species of clay. The injuries are attributed to the Protestants; but if they be the result of a popular commotion, and not of the mere progress of time, they are wonderfully slight. The other portals have smaller reliefs, from Scriptural and legendary stories, and fewer niches, but equally deserve examination. Those on the rt. of the spectator represent the stoning of St. Stephen, and the Acts of St. Ursin; on the l. the Death of the Virgin, and St. Ursin and St. Just preaching the Gospel in Berry. The foliage between the mouldings can scarcely be surpassed for delicacy.

The oldest part of the ch. is the lateral doorways on the N. and S. sides; they are circular arches, adorned with florid Norman ornaments and statues, in a stiff style dating probably from the 12th centy. The N. door is covered by a projecting porch of later date. The N. and most perfect *tower* was founded 1508, and finished 1538. Its builder was Guil. Pellevoisin : it is 199 ft. high; it is called the butter tower, because built with the money raised from indulgences to eat butter in Lent. The S. tower is inferior in elegance.

The interior consists of one long and vast parallelogram, without transept, but, to make amends, provided with double aisles on each side, those next the centre being 65 ft. high, and furnished, like it, with triforium and clerestory, worthy of a cathedral nave, extending all round the choir. Beyond the outer aisle are 18 chapels. The vaulted stone roof of the central aisle, 117 ft. high, is supported by 60 piers, with capitals in the Early English style, presenting the most varied and striking perspective.

The chapel, built by the jeweller Jacques Cœur, and his son John, 88*th* Archbishop of Bourges, 1446, now converted into a *Sacristy*, is remarkable for its glass, and for the very delicate sculpture of the portal. One of the chief boasts of this cathedral is the quantity, excellence, and good preservation of the *painted glass* of the windows of the choir and chapels. They include specimens of the art from the 13th down to the 17th centy. The chapels containing the finest examples of the later state of the art are those of Jacques Cœur, St. Loup, St. Denis: those in the chapels of Tullier and Coppin are the work of Lécuyer, an artist of Bourges (d. 1556). One of the most modern specimens is a beautiful Ascension of the Virgin, given, 1619, by the Maréchal de Montigny, whose portrait, with that of his wife, is seen in the corner below.

In the *crypt*, an early Pointed structure, running below the choir, in a semicircle, is deposited the monument of Jean le Magnifique, Duc de Berri, son, brother, and uncle of kings, and nephew of Charles V. of France, erected by his own nephew, Charles VII. His effigy, in marble, of good execution, was brought hither from the Sainte Chapelle, which he built, now destroyed. Here are also the effigies in marble of the Maréchal Montigny and his lady, and the statue of the Virgin, of good design. Louis XI., son of Charles VII., b. at Bourges 1423, was baptized in the cathedral by Huri d'Avanjour, 89th archbishop.

Adjoining the cathedral, on the S., is the *Archevêché*, a handsome edifice, in the Italian style, with gardens attached, traversed by fine avenues of limes. Here Don Carlos of Spain was lodged as a sort of state prisoner. A little way from it the *Caserne d'Artillerie*, an immense building, formerly the Grand Séminaire, surrounded by numerous detached buildings, stables to accommodate the men and horses, of whom 800, with all their train and equipments, are commonly stationed here.

The city of Bourges is still surrounded by *Remparts*, converted, for the greater part of their extent, into a public promenade, and planted with trees. It was formerly defended by 60 watch-towers, all of which have been demolished except 6 or 8. Two of these, behind the archevêché and cavalry barrack, opposite the promenade called the Cours Seraucourt, deserve notice, as being undoubtedly Roman. One is formed of huge blocks of stone, now much worn at the edges, a style of durable masonry (opus incertum) employed by the Romans in their great works; the other is of smaller stones, with layers of large tiles in bands; the substructure of the wall, as far as the garden of the préfecture, is of the same kind. These Roman relics are of some interest. Joseph Scaliger and d'Anville are satisfied that Bourges is the ancient *Avaricum* (named from the river Avara, now Evre), chief town of the Bituriges (Berry), mentioned by Cæsar in his Commentaries (viii. 13), "Oppidum quod erat maximum munitissimumque, in finibus Biturigum, et totius Galliæ urbs prope pulcherrima." On account of its importance and beauty it was the only city of the Celtic Gauls which they spared to burn to the ground, when, like the Russians in Moscow, they resorted to that expedient as a last resource to check the conquering armies of Julius Cæsar.

At the entrance of the Garden of the Préfecture, close to the Promenade de Seraucourt, is a Romanesque portal of the 11th centy., removed from the *Ch. of St. Ursin*, now destroyed. It is a circular arch, enclosing curious sculptures in relief, representing the 12 Months of the Year; a Boar Hunt, &c.; Scenes from Æsop's Fables, as the Stork and the Fox; a Fox drawn by Geese; of very good execution.

Next to the cathedral, the most interesting building is the *Hôtel de Ville*, originally the private mansion of Jacques Cœur, a citizen of the town, a great capitalist and successful merchant and jeweller, and finance minister to Charles VII., who, after lending his master 200,000 gold crowns, was torn from his palace, cast into prison, and condemned to death and confiscation of his property—a sentence commuted by the king into perpetual banishment. The cause of his accusation and condemnation remains a mystery. The building, begun 1443, is in the late or florid Gothic style, of great magnificence, yet not overladen: the walls alone cost 130,000 livres. There is no uniformity of parts; no one wall or window corresponds with another—all is varied, yet all is harmonious. The entrance is flanked by a most elegant tourelle, and is surmounted by a projecting balcony, or open oriel of elegant tracery. Two figures, sculptured in stone, on each side, are said to be the servants of Jacques Cœur, on the lookout to warn him of danger from the officers of justice, but are more probably a mere freak of the architect. This elegant palace is distinguished, like many other French domestic edifices of the 15th centy., by its circular coneroofed towers, containing spiral staircases. Its windows, surmounted by flat arches, are ornamented below with open tablets of quatrefoils, among which is introduced the punning device of Jacques Cœur, the heart, and the scallop-shell of the pilgrim to St. James's Shrine. On a little Gothic balustrade between the outer gateway and its flanking turret the motto of Jacques Cœur, "A vaillants Cœurs rien impossible," is most elaborately carved in tall Gothic characters of stone. Over the doorways in the court are singular bas-reliefs: observe that on the l. of the great entrance, and that over the kitchen. The *chapel* above the gateway deserves to be seen, but especially the upper part, divided from the lower by a modern floor, its groined roof being elegantly painted in fresco, probably by Italian artists, with angels in flowing robes of white upon a blue ground, representing the multitude of the angelic host, bearing scrolls, inscribed, "Gloria in excelsis Deo, et in terrâ pax," &c.: the figures are well foreshortened, and in good preservation. In the lower part of the chapel are 2 elegant niches, nearly blocked up. The rest of the interior has been sadly mutilated and altered, to fit it for conversion into lawcourts, stripped of panelling, cornices, and chimney-pieces, so that the chapel alone is now worth entering. This palace was appropriated as a residence to the youthful Condé, destined to become *Le Grand Condé*, while pursuing his studies at the Jesuits' College here.

The *Caserne de Gendarmerie*, in a street behind the Hôtel de Ville, not far off from it, was the house of Cujas, professor in the *University*, which existed here from 1465 to the Revolution. It is of brick, of very solid construction, built towards the end of the 16th centy., and displays about its doors, windows, and turrets, some fragments of elegant decoration. It will be remembered that Bourges had great fame as a school of law.

The Convent of the *Sœurs Bleues*, in the Rue des Vieilles Prisons, originally the mansion of the family Lallemand, and built probably about 1512, has an irregular front, flanked by tourelles, gracefully decorated with arabesque patterns, bas-reliefs, &c., in the style of the Renaissance, which will please an architect. It contains a little family oratory, about 10 ft. by 15, surmounted by a roof of 3 stone slabs, divided into 30 compartments, each filled with some device, as a Globe on Fire, a Hand gathering a Chesnut, or other pattern, rebus, relief, or ornament, alternating with the letters R E, often repeated, most elaborately carved, but of which the meaning is difficult to explain. These buildings and others of the same age in other parts of France in the same debased style of Gothic, have a curious resemblance to the contemporary architecture of Scotland, as shown in many castellated mansions still existing.

Bourges was the residence and refuge of Charles VII., at a time when three-fourths of his kingdom of France belonged to the English, when he was little more, in fact, than "king of Bourges."

Bourges has a *museum*, a receptacle of antiquities, of various ages, and other curiosities, without order or arrangement. A series of 6 weeping figures (pleureuses), in alabaster, from some monument; a model of the Saint Chapelle, mentioned above, now destroyed; an ebony cabinet, ornamented in the style of the Renaissance, from Agnes Sorel's castle, Bon-sire-aimé, and some portraits, including those of Louis XVI. and Marie Antoinette, merit notice.

Bourges is the birthplace of Louis XI., and of *Bourdaloue*, one of the first pulpit orators of the French Church.

The *Railway* is continued from Bourges by
123 Moulins Stat.
129 Savigny Stat.
138 Avor Stat.
148 *Nérondes* Stat.
161 La Guerche Stat.
170 *Le Guétin Junction* Stat. [Here a branch Rly. diverges l. 11 kilom. to NEVERS Stat.] (Rte. 105.)
St. Pierre Stat.
MOULINS Stat. (in Rte. 103.)
Varennes Stat. (82 kilom. from Guétin).
St. Germain des Fossés Stat. Here the line diverges, and a branch proceeds l. to Roanne.
The Allier is crossed at St. Germain by a long viaduct.
Vichy Stat. (Rte. 105, p. 360).
CLERMONT Stat. (Rte. 109).

Bourges to *Montluçon* and *Neris les Bains*. Diligences daily. Country flat and of little interest. By
18 Levet.
13 Jariole.
A little on one side of the road is the ruined *Abbey of Noirlac*, so named from a dark pool near it. It is now converted into a China manufactory, including *The Ch.*, a large and still perfect structure, and a good example of the transition Gothic of the latter part of the 13th centy., 1289. The kitchen and refectory, supported on pillars, still remain, as well as the cloister.

16 St. Amand Montrond, a neat town of 6636 Inhab., on the Marmande, about a mile from the rt. bank of the Cher. Only a few shapeless ruins remain of its *Castle*, once an important stronghold, belonging to the princes de Condé, in which the sickly infant who grew to be le Grand Condé was nursed and reared. His heroic wife, the Princess Clémence de Maillé, after her escape from Chantilly, 1650, threw herself and her son into this castle, whence, after

gathering around her the dependants and retainers of the house of Condé, she set forth to cross some of the wildest provinces of France in order to join the Dukes of Bouillon and La Rochefoucald, and put herself at the head of the army of the Fronde, which kept possession of Bordeaux against Mazarin. Montrond was the birth-place of Gaston de Foix; it was fortified by the Duc de Sully, who wrote here his "Adieux à la Cour:" after enduring a siege of a whole year's duration, 1652, from the royal forces, it was compelled to surrender to the Comte de Palluau, who levelled the fortifications. The last tower which remained standing has been pulled down, in order that the proprietor may make gardens and terraces on the site.

About 21 m. S.W. of St. Amand is the *Château de Meillant*, built 1511, for Charles, Seigneur de Chaumont, somewhat in the style of the house of Jacques Cœur at Bourges, with similar external ornaments, balustrades, and projecting towers to contain the snail-shell stairs, but vastly inferior to it. The blazing hill, sculptured in various parts, is intended as a sculptured pun on the owner's name, *Chauds Monts.* The decorations of the interior are not supposed to be later than the 18th centy. On the towers are sculptured figures of sentinels threatening all who approach, like those on the battlements of Alnwick.

The road from St. Amand is very agreeable, running by the side of the Cher. At Drevant, on its rt. bank, traversed by the road, extensive substructions of a theatre, and other Roman buildings, have been laid bare.

A branch of the Canal du Cher runs parallel with the Cher and the high road from St. Amand to Montluçon, and the coal mines of Commentry, where it terminates.

18 Meaulne.

16 Reugny (Dépt. Allier).

15 Montluçon (*Inns:* H. de France, and de l'Ecu), a very ancient town of the province of the Bourbonnais, having 8810 Inhab., picturesquely situated on the slope of a hill, whose base is washed by the Cher, and its summit crowned by a *Castle*. During the middle ages it was a strong fortress; and, from its position near the frontier of the French king's domains, had often to sustain the attacks of the English. A part of its old walls, and their flanking watch-towers, still remains, constructed with great solidity. The donjon, and a few towers on the summit of the hill, are all that remains of the *castle* of the Ducs de Bourbon, which commanded the town, as its ruins still command an extensive view.

A hilly and uninteresting road to

8 *Néris* (*Inns:* Grand Hôtel;—H. Leopold), a watering-place of considerable resort within a few years, but well known to the Romans, who must have had a magnificent establishment here, judging from the architectural fragments—columns, friezes, foundations of walls—discovered from time to time. Yet it is only since 1821 that the French have begun a *bath-house*, which is not yet finished, and which, with several boarding-houses attached to a poor village of 800 Inhab., compose the place. The *mineral waters* are warm, alkaline, but nearly tasteless, so that the inhabitants employ them for culinary purposes and for drinking; they are furnished from 4 sources, one of which, La Source Nouvelle, burst forth, 1757, at the time of the earthquake at Lisbon. They are exclusively used for baths, being introduced into the houses. They resemble the spring of Schlangenbad, have the same unctuous feel to the touch, the same smoothing effect on the skin, and sedative influence on the nerves. It is usual to go to bed after taking the bath, in order to promote perspiration. There are also douche and mud-baths, and 3 piscines or public baths.

The very pretty promenade, or *Jardin des Bains*, occupies the site of an *amphitheatre*, built by the Romans for the recreation of visitors to these remote baths of *Aquæ Neri*, as Néris was anciently called. Concentric terraces mark the stages on which the seats were placed; and traces remain of one of the passages which divided them into cunei, or wedges. There are considerable fragments of walls.

The *Church* is a very ancient Romanesque edifice, in the form of a basilica, ending in 3 apses. The arches in the nave are pointed, those in the choir round. From the rude sculpture of the capitals, its date has been referred to the 11th centy.

The country around is pleasing, and the situation very healthy.

The road to Clermont is carried through a wild hilly district, passing out of the coal formation into a country of primitive rocks shortly before reaching

18 Montaigu, a little town appropriately named from its site on a pointed hill, crowned by a castle, situated in the Dépt. Puy de Dôme.

At Menat are quarries, whence tripoli or polishing slate is obtained: it is produced by the spontaneous combustion of iron pyrites among beds of bituminous clay. It contains impressions of vegetables, fish, and insects. Near this the road ascends a long and steep hill, commanding a very extensive view over the volcanic ranges of Auvergne, and near at hand looks down upon the Castle of Blot, seated amidst rugged rocks. The river Sioule is crossed before reaching

27 St. Pardoux. The very peculiar forms of the volcanic mountains of the Puy de Dôme cannot fail to arrest attention.

We now enter the fertile plain of the Limagne d'Auvergne.

23 Riom }
15 *Clermont* } described in Rte. 109.

ROUTE 104.

PARIS TO DIJON, BY MELUN, FONTAINEBLEAU, MONTEREAU, SENS, JOIGNY [AUXERRE], AND TONNERRE.—PARIS AND LYONS RAILROAD A.

Terminus Boulevard Mazas, on the rt. bank of the Seine, not far from the Pont d'Austerlitz. 4 trains daily to Châlons—fast in 10 hrs., slow in 12½ hrs. ¼ an hr. halt for refreshment at Tonnerre. The first part of this railway, from Paris to Tonnerre, was opened 1849. It is carried up the valleys of the Seine, Yonne, Armançon, Brenne, and Oze.

The river Marne is crossed by a bridge of two divisions, respectively of 2 and 3 arches, at *Charenton*, a village of 1900 Inhab., containing a *Lunatic Asylum*, a large building. Two of the detached forts for the defence of Paris here guard the passage of the Seine, one on each bank.

At Alfort is a large veterinary college.
rt. flows the Seine.
Villeneuve St. George Stat.
l. is the Forest of Senars.
Viaduct of 9 arches over the valley of the Yéres river.
Brunoy Stat.
2nd viaduct of 28 arches 72 ft. high.
Combes la Ville Stat.
l. m. is Brie Comte Robert.
Lieusaint Stat.
Cesson Stat.
A handsome bridge of 3 arches of cast iron traverses the Seine at le Mée.

44 Melun Stat. (*Inn:* H. de France), a town of 7528 Inhab., chef-lieu of the Dépt. Seine et Marne. It is mentioned in Cæsar's Commentaries under the name Melodunum. In 1520 it was besieged and taken by the armies of Henry V. and the Duke of Burgundy, but the English were ejected 1530.

Diligence to Provins by Nanjis.
51 Bois le Roi Stat.

There is a very fine *viaduct* of 30 arches, 66 ft. high by 33 wide, at Avon. In the old church of the village, Monaldeschi, favourite of Christina Queen of Sweden, murdered by her orders (p. 346), is buried. A small square stone in the pavement, near the bénitier, marks the grave.

59 FONTAINEBLEAU STATION is about 1 m. E. of the town—omnibus thither.

10 *Fontainebleau*. — *Inns:* H. de France, facing the *Palace;* good. Ville de Lyon, very clean, comfortable, and moderate; Aigle Noir.

This town, seated in the midst of the Forest of Fontainebleau, has swelled, under the influence of the presence and smiles of royalty, to a population of 10,000, from a poor hamlet in the time of Louis VII., who first built a castle here (1162). It owes its consequence entirely to its

**Château Royal, a palace of much historical interest, but not very imposing as an edifice, externally, in spite of its extent; the masses of building composing it, though they enclose 6 courts, being limited to low ranges of 2 or 3 stories, chiefly of brick. The oldest and the greatest part of the existing edifice dates from the reign of Francis I., excepting the chapel.

Time, neglect, and violence had greatly dimmed the splendour of this venerable seat of kings, when Louis-Philippe undertook to revive it; and his judicious and splendid restorations, following closely the style and character of the different periods at which it was originally constructed, have added greatly to the magnificence and interest of the palace.

The entrance is by the "Cour du Cheval Blanc," so called from a plaster cast of the equestrian statue of Marcus Aurelius at Rome, which Catherine of Medici set up in it, but it no longer exists. In the midst of this court, near the foot of the horseshoe stair, Napoleon took leave of the remnant of the Old Guard, who had followed him to the last, midst his reverses, previously to his departure for Elba, 1814, an event commemorated by the well-known picture of "Les Adieux de Fontainebleau."

The apartments first entered are those fitted up for the late Duc d'Orléans, on the occasion of his marriage; they had been originally occupied by Catherine de' Medici and Anne of Austria, whence they got the name Appartements des *Reines Mères*. Here Pope Pius VII. was lodged, rejecting all the magnificence and comforts prepared for him by his imperial jailer, who desired that his forced residence of 3 years should have the appearance of a visit rather than an imprisonment. Napoleon attempted in a private interview to wring from the old man his consent to the Concordat, by which he renounced temporal power. The ceiling of the *salon*, recently restored, is very gorgeous.

In the *Chapelle de la Trinité*, whose paintings are inferior and faded, the marriages of Louis XV. with Maria Leckzinska (1725) and of the late Duc d'Orléans (1837) were celebrated. The *Galerie de François I.* is one of the most striking in the palace; perfectly characteristic of the style of art of the period of the Renaissance; and it supplies specimens of some of the productions of the Italians attracted, at the king's bidding, to France, where they founded a school of art. Its roof is of walnut wood, its walls are richly panelled and covered with stucco, scroll-work, carvings, trophies, devices, among which the Salamander of Francis is often repeated alternating with terms, or Caryatid figures, medallions, bas-reliefs. These serve partly as frames to 14 pictures, in fresco, the work of *Rossi* (Maître Roux), a Florentine, and his scholars. One of Danaë, however, is attributed to *Primaticcio*, who is supposed also to have designed the ornaments. The paintings, now too much faded or injured to be appreciated, are chiefly mythological subjects, chosen for their allegorical reference to the life of Francis. In the first he is represented opening the Temple of Art and Taste to a crowd of blind persons; next comes a Triumph, in honour of the victory of Marignan, led by a caparisoned elephant; then the Rape of Europa; the Burning of Troy; Æneas carrying off Anchises, &c. In the centre is a bust of Francis. The paintings of the age of Francis I. were of so licentious a character, that Anne of Austria thought right to cause a great part of them to be effaced in 1653, when she became Regent, and this will account for the slight remains now existing. The *Cabinet de Travail* contains the little round mahogany table at which Napoleon, in 1814, signed his abdication, a fac-simile of which, blotted and scrawled, is suspended on the walls. His bed-room remains nearly as he left it. The *Salle du Trône* is of the age of Louis XIII. and XIV., but the throne was set up by Buonaparte. The *Boudoir de la Reine* was fitted up for the unfortunate Marie-Antoinette by Louis XVI., and the metal window bolts (espagnolettes) are said to have been wrought by his own hand, and are masterly specimens of his skill in smith's work. The *Galerie de Diane* is a long corridor, built 1600, but decorated with paintings relating to that goddess, by modern artists. Below it runs the *Galerie des Cerfs*, which was in 1657 the scene of the atrocious murder of an Italian, the Marquis Monaldeschi, by 3 assassins hired for the purpose by Christina of Sweden, at that time residing in the château as the guest of Louis XIII. The reason assigned by her for the crime was some alleged betrayal of her secrets by Monaldeschi, who was her high chamberlain, and had enjoyed her full confidence. She subjected him to a sort of mock trial, in which she acted as judge and jury. She sent for a priest to confess him before she gave orders for his murder, which was executed in the confessor's presence. Monaldeschi seems not to have been free from suspicions of his mistress, for he wore under his dress a coat of mail, which turned the first thrusts of the sword of the assassin. The French court was content to give a hint of displeasure at this atrocity, but the queen remained here until 1659. This gallery is now subdivided into small apartments, and is not shown.

The suite of rooms called *Salons de Réception* comprises one called *de François I.*, containing Gobelins tapestries, of recent date, as brilliant as oil paintings, and a chimney-piece ornamented with Sèvres china. A second is named after *Louis XIII.*, because he was born in it; and the *Salle de St. Louis* is ornamented with a high relief of Henri IV. on horseback, over the fire-place. The *Salle des Gardes* is admirably and most richly restored: the paintings on the walls are in the style of those of the Loggie of Raphael. The chimney-piece rests on 2 figures of Strength and Peace, and in the centre is a bust of Henri IV.

The *Salle du Bal*, or *Galerie de Henri II.*, is the most splendid of the recent restorations, and one of the finest things in the palace. The paintings have been renovated with as much care as possible, yet, it is to be feared, retain little of the master pencils of *Primaticcio*, and his pupil, *Niccolo del Abbate*, by whom they were executed. The ceiling is most gorgeous and elaborate with ornaments; the walls are of consistent richness. Everywhere appears the crescent of Diana of Poictiers, and her initial D. linked with that of her royal lover, H. The chimney-piece, glittering with fleurs-de-lis, and resplendent with marbles, was the work of the sculptor *Rondelet*.

The *Chapelle de St. Saturnin*, on the ground floor, is said to be of the time of Louis VII., and the oldest part of the palace; but the repairs of Francis I., who found it in ruins, have disguised and altered it so that little of its primitive structure can be traced. It was originally dedicated by Thomas à Becket. In its windows is some good modern painted glass, from the designs of the late talented Princess Marie d'Orléans.

The *Porte Dorée*, a splendid portal, decorated with revived frescoes, originally by Rossi, leads from the Cour Ovale to the *Allée de Maintenon*, "named by the proudest and vainest king in Europe after his plebeian wife." The Oval Court is also called Cour du Donjon, from an elevated pavillon on an archway in the style of the Renaissance, and includes the oldest part of the Palais. The other entrance to it is called Port Dauphine, because built at the birth of Louis XIII., 1601.

The *gardens* at the back of the palace are not, on the whole, very remarkable to one accustomed to those of England. That called *Jardin Anglais* is bordered by a triangular pond, in the midst of which rises a pavillon surrounded by water. The "Fontaine de Belle Eau," which gave the name to the place, rose, it is said, within the garden; but the source has been lost in forming the artificial ponds.

Philippe le Bel was born and died at Fontainebleau; the emperor Charles V. was lodged in the Salle des Poëles, and entertained here by Francis I., 1539; Henrietta Maria sought refuge here when the cause of Charles I. became hopeless, 1644; here the Maréchal de Biron, betrayed by his agent Mafin, was arrested for conspiracy against Henri IV., 1602, and conveyed to the Bastille; the Grand Condé died here 1686, and Louis XIV. here signed

CENTRAL FRANCE.   *Route* 104.—*Fontainebleau.*   347

(1685) the Revocation of the Edict of Nantes.

The *Sandstone quarries* around Fontainebleau not only furnish paving stones for the chausséed high roads around the town, but are transported in quantities down the Seine to Paris. The rock sometimes presents very pretty groups of crystals, covered over with fine sand, well known to every mineralogist.

The band of the Cavalry Regt. stationed here plays every Thursday and Sunday afternoon in the Gardens of the Château.

Café Reillier, Place au Charbon, is the best. *Post Office*, Rue St. Merry, No. 49. *Baths*, No. 33 same street.

English Church Service in the Temple Protestant, Rue du Cimetière, No. 1 bis, not far from the Post Office, every Sunday at 3-30 ; French Service at 12-30.

Local souvenirs made of the wood of the juniper (Genévrier) are made and sold here.

Carriage hire with 2 horses, 12 fr. per diem; saddle-horse, 6 fr.; donkey, 2 fr.: may be engaged at any of the hotels.

It is scarcely possible to praise too highly the woodland scenery of *La Forêt de Fontainebleau*, the constant resort of French artists in summer, which would require weeks to explore thoroughly. An excellent *Guide* has been published by M. Denecourt, a veteran officer of Napoleon, who has devoted himself to "la Forêt." His *map* is *essential* in tracing the various picturesque routes which he has indicated, by the paths which he has cut through the wildest parts. His routes are made clear to the wanderer by arrows painted on the rocks or trees.

The forest of Fontainebleau extends over an area of about 23,700 hectares. This attractive hunting-ground induced the monarchs of France, ardent lovers of the chase, to build a palace within it, and make it their favourite resort. At the Revolution of 1830, however, all the deer were exterminated. Only a small portion of the forest is occupied with full-grown trees; but here and there it has preserved noble groves of oaks and beech, of majestic size and luxuriant foliage,

which may have sheltered the jovial François I., the Bon Roi Henri IV., Louis XIV., and Napoleon. A large space is covered with broom, heath, and underwood, and with extensive plantations of black fir, from the midst of which picturesque masses of bare sandstone rock (grés de Fontainebleau) break through, and give great variety and picturesqueness to the forest scenery. The points best worth visiting are—to the rt. of the road from Paris, the *Gorges d'Apremont* and *de Franchard*, above which are remains of a hermitage, as old as the days of Philippe-Auguste, destroyed by Louis XIV.; and to the l. of the road *La Vallée de la Solle*, Le Gorge aux Loups, and Nid de l'Aigle.

"La Croix du Grand Veneur," an obelisk on the grand route, at a place where 4 roads meet, receives its name from a spectral Black Huntsman, supposed to haunt the forest, who appeared here to Henri IV., according to the story, shortly before his assassination. The forest is so intersected with roads radiating in all directions, that it is difficult to find one's way without a map or a guide.

Railway continues

64 Thomery Stat.

On the borders of the Seine are grown the fine Chasselas *grapes* called *Fontainebleau grapes*. 5000 or 6000 baskets of them, packed in heather, are sent down the Seine every week in autumn, to supply the markets of Paris. The vines are trained along the houses and walls of the village, sheltered by narrow roofs from the rain. Even the streets are vineyards, and every foot of wall is covered with vines.

Viaduct at St. Mammès of 30 arches, 62 ft. high, 32 ft. wide.

68 Moret St. Mammès Stat. Moret is a picturesque old walled town on the verge of the Forest of Fontainebleau, with ancient *Ch.* and *Castle*.

79 *Montereau Stat.*

Montereau (*Inn:* Grand Monarque, the only one, but exorbitant charges) is a town of 4153 Inhab., occupying a pleasing situation, and one very advantageous for commerce, at the junction of the two navigable rivers the

Seine and Yonne, whence it has gained the adjunct to its name Montereau-faut-Yonne—where the Yonne *fails*, or is lost in the Seine. The most considerable part lies on the l. bank of the Yonne. Both rivers are crossed by bridges, and the one over the Seine (or rather an older bridge in the same situation) was the scene of the murder of Jean-Sans-Peur, Duke of Burgundy, in the presence and by the orders of the Dauphin (afterwards Charles VII.), during a conference between them, and in spite of the precautions which had been resorted to of erecting double barricades to divide the persons of the 2 princes. The blow was struck by Tanneguy du Chastel. The conference was designed to bring about a reconciliation, in order that the two parties might combine to resist the invasion of France by Henry V.

l. Here the branch Railway to Troyes (Rte. 143) diverges.

"The traveller who approaches Montereau from the side of Paris involuntarily halts on the summit of the heights of Surville, which overhang the town on the N., to gaze on the lovely scene which lies spread out, like a map, beneath his feet: he would do well to remember that there, beside the little cross adjacent to the château, stood Napoleon during the last and not the least of his many victories, on Feb. 18th, 1814. On the evening of the 17th the French troops assembled in imposing masses on these heights (which they had gained only after a severe conflict), and which commanded the bridge and town beneath. The artillery of the Guard was placed on either side of the road near the cross, and the Emperor took his station, in person, amidst the guns, to direct their fire, for the enemy still held the town. Such was his eagerness to annihilate the dense masses of the enemy crowding over the bridge, that he himself, resuming his old occupation of a gunner, with his own hand, as at Toulon, levelled and pointed a cannon upon them."—*Alison*. The allies were so hotly pursued by the French cuirassiers, that they were driven over the Seine, and out of Montereau, having barely time to blow up the bridge over the Yonne, which checked the pursuit in the direction of Sens.

The Railroad ascends the pleasant and fertile valley of the Yonne.

89 Villeneuve-la-Guiard Stat.—*Inn:* H. de la Souche, tolerable. Landlord a wheelwright.

112 Pont-sur-Yonne Stat., pleasantly situated on green banks fringed with tall poplars and silvery willows. The country is full of vineyards; and a larger proportion than ordinary of the châteaux of the old noblesse seem to be in existence near the churches of the villages, or peeping over the trees.

113 SENS Stat.—*Inn:* H. de l'Ecu; very good. This ancient capital of the Sennones is now but a small city, containing 10,335 Inhab., partly surrounded by its original ramparts. It is remarkably clean, with little *becks* of water running through the streets, supplied from a stream called the Vanne, which falls into the Yonne hard by. The *Cathedral*, dedicated to St. Stephen, is one of the finest of its style, early Gothic, or Transition Norman, resembling Canterbury, whose builder was William of Sens; it has undergone a thorough repair. The tracery in front of the transepts is the perfection of flamboyant detail. The painted glass deserves peculiar attention. It was executed by Jean Cousin, a native of Soucy, a village near Sens, who attained great excellence in this as well as in other branches of art. The colouring is extremely harmonious. The tomb of the Chancellor Duprat has partly escaped the general destruction; the bas-reliefs around it are very curious. (Temp. Francis I.) There is also a monument to the dauphin, son of Louis XV., and his wife, by Coustou. In the *Treasury*, among other curious relics, are shown the vests and mitre of Thomas Becket, his alb, girdle, stole, maniple, and chasuble, to all appearance genuine; they have been repaired. He fled to Sens 1164, when he escaped out of England from the wrath of Henry II.

The altar of *St. Thomas* is said to be the same at which Becket performed his devotions, and is very ancient. He resided, while in this city, in the *Abbey* of St. Columbe, now occupied by the Sœurs de l'Enfance de Jésus. The Cathedral has 2 of the largest Bells in France; one weighs 16½ tons. 3 of the old town gates, the Portes Notre Dame, St. Antoine, and St. Remy, still remain: they are probably as old as the 14th cent.

The walls of Sens, which, on the south side, extend in a straight unbroken line, exhibit in the lower portions magnificent remains of Roman, some say Gaulish, masonry.

[At Vallery, 12 m. to the W. of Sens, the Grand Condé is buried in the Ch., which contains a costly monument of marble. The Château was designed by Philibert Delorme.]

An open chalky country follows Sens till you reach

127 Villeneuve-le-Roi (or sur-Yonne) Stat., a remarkably pretty and peculiar town, with much scope for the use of the pencil and sketch-book. The principal street is terminated by a gate at each end, of feudal times, yet apparently more for ornament than defence. The church, in the style of the Renaissance, is richly ornamented.

135 St. Jullien-du-Sault Stat.

146 Joigny Stat.—Inn: Duc de Bourgogne; dear. This town (Pop. 6056) is also pleasantly situated on the Yonne. It derives its ancient name (Joviniacum) from Jovinian (see Rheims). A fine quay, closed at either end by an iron gate, runs along the side of the Yonne, from one end of the town to the other. The old town, scarcely accessible, owing to its steep and numerous streets, contains 3 Gothic churches —St. Jean, which stood within the castle ; St. André, attached to the priory ; and St. Thibault.

[Coaches several times a day from Joigny Stat. to Auxerre—Vermanton, Vezelay, Clamuz — La Charité and Nevers.

12 Bassou.

17 Auxerre.—Inn: Léopard, on the quai, next the Poste; civil people. This city of 12,673 Inhab., very prettily situated on the l. bank of the Yonne, and chef-lieu of that Dépt., is seen to great advantage from a distance. The grand mass of the cathedral, and two or three other large churches, and a ruined spire, all rise finely above the houses.

The *Cathedral has a splendid though unfinished façade, in the Flamboyant Gothic style, which prevails throughout the edifice, except in the choir, in the early Gothic (1215-30). " The transepts are covered externally with the boldest flowing tracery, occasionally standing free from the wall. The doors and rose windows are magnificent."—Petit. The nave was finished about 1350. Within, it is beautifully proportioned ; and the painted glass, principally in mosaic patterns, is splendid. Here is the tomb of Jacques Amyot, whilome bishop of this see, and celebrated for his racy translation of Plutarch, so excellent in its style as almost to form an era in the history of the French language. The chapter of Auxerre was at one time one of the richest in France, but they freed themselves from most of their superfluous possessions by indulging in the luxury of litigation.

St. Germain, now attached to the Hôtel Dieu, on the height, is in a plainer style than the cathedral ; it has lost part of its nave, but possesses a lofty choir, and transepts. Underneath are curious crypts, one below another; in the lower are some tombs of early counts of Auxerre. It has an ancient tower, which belonged to the W. front, but is now detached.

St. Pierre is a large and handsome specimen of Italianised Gothic, begun at the end of the 16th centy., and finished 1672. St. Eusèbe is a Romanesque church in its nave, and detached tower, with a choir in the florid style, begun 1530.

There is a curious old clock tower over a gate-house, " with an ugly skeleton spire of iron bars," in the Place du Marché.

" The Boulevards, in the place of the ancient walls which surround the town on 3 sides, present a variety of prospects; the moats are filled with plantations of acacia, gardens, and vines; the fine old towers are covered with festoons of ivy."—Miss Costello.

A considerable quantity of wines

(chiefly ordinaires), the growth of La Basse Bourgogne, are sent down the Yonne hence to Paris. *Châblis*, about 12 m. E. of this, on the road to Tonnerre, gives its name to a wine of superior quality, prized for drinking at breakfast or with oysters.

10 Champs. A good road, avoiding the hills and St. Bris, leads from Auxerre to Semur, keeping along the banks of the Yonne, through the pretty villages of Champs, Vincelles, and Cravaut-Vermanton.

15 Vermanton. *Inn:* Etoile.

19 Lucy-le-Bois (no *Inn*) stands in a sheltered and rather pretty valley. The rocks around, and the stone heaps at the road-side derived from them, abound in fossils of the lias and gryphite limestone.

About 6 m. from Vermanton, and 9 from Lucy-le-Bois, to the S., are the *Grottes d'Arcy*, a series of natural caverns in the limestone, many of vast extent, abounding in stalactites, and in bats, separated from one another by natural divisions, through which it is often necessary to crawl on hands and knees. The entrance to them is by a door inserted in an opening in the rock of a wooded dell, on the borders of the Cure. A guide, with candles, can be obtained at the village ; the best time to visit them is during dry weather. The largest cavern is about 25 ft. high, 30 wide, and 400 long.

9 Avallon (*Inn:* Poste), a pleasantly situated town, nearly surrounded by a ravine. Around it runs a broad terrace walk, under lime-trees, about 500 ft. above the bed of the Cousin. The *Ch.* is ancient, and has a curious Romanesque portal. Parts of its interior are singular.

[8 m. off the road, to the E., is *Vezelay*, a decayed town, capital of the district of *Le Morvan*, situated on a hill 2000 ft. high, commanding a noble view, surrounded by embattled walls, and entered still by feudal gateways. It contains a very remarkable *Abbey Ch.*, dedicated to the Madeleine, finely seated on the summit of a hill. The ruinous W. front lost one of its towers by the attack of the Huguenots in 1569; the lower part of it is Romanesque, the upper a late Pointed Restoration, poor in effect. Another tower rises from the angle between the nave and S. transept. The W. doors lead into a sort of porch, destined, like the Galilees in some English cathedrals, for catechumens : 3 other doorways open out of this vestibule into the nave; that in the centre is very rich in sculpture, and supported by an ornamental shaft, on which rests a transom covered with a procession of figures, in relief. The tympanum of the arch above it is filled with a large bas-relief : the figure of the Saviour forms the centre, attended by groups of saints reading or writing. One of the archivolts above is carved with a zodiac, the signs of which are intermingled with monsters forming 29 medallions. The interior of the nave is very impressive from "its great length, its gloom, and the simplicity of design which pervades its Norman features." It has no triforium, and is surmounted by a cradle roof. These walls doubtless echoed to the voice of Becket in 1168, when he repaired to Vezelay on Ascension-day, when the church was crowded, and, mounting the pulpit, cursed by bell, book, and candle, all those who maintained in England "the Customs of their Elders." This proceeding so enraged Henry II. that he threatened to confiscate all the Benedictine abbeys in England, if the Order continued to shelter Becket in France. A flight of steps leads up into the choir, which, with the transepts, is a fine specimen of early complete Pointed Gothic. It is surrounded by 8 round pillars, each of a single stone, and it is lighted by lancet windows. The axis of the choir differs from that of the nave, inclining a little to the l.

Attached to the S. transept is the *Chapter-house*, a low vaulted chamber, its roof resting on 2 clumsy central piers in the Romanesque style. Here, it is said, the monks assembled, with tears in their eyes, before their expulsion in 1154, through the rebellion of their vassals, the townsfolk, aided by the forces of the Comte de Nevers. The oldest part of the existing church is the nave, from the porch E., and the crypt; and they probably date from 1050, the previous church having been destroyed, "prope ad nihilum redactum," in the middle of the 10th centy., and its restoration begun 1008. The W. front is probably of the 12th centy., and the choir of the early part of the 13th. Scarcely any remains exist of the domestic buildings of the abbey, which were so vast that kings, with their suite, could be lodged in them without discomfort to their monkish inmates. The entire length of the building is 404 ft.; the height of the choir 70 ft.

Vezelay is now a poor wretched town; its church is dropping to pieces, the roof and walls being cracked and crumbling, yet it possesses interesting historical associations. Here, on March 31, 1145, St. Bernard assembled a solemn Council of the Church, and preached in the presence of Louis VII., to a multitude assembled in the open field (the church being too small to hold them), the necessity of a new Crusade, with such impressive eloquence, that the universal cry for the Cross burst from the crowd around; and the supply of crosses not being sufficient, the Abbot of Clairvaux tore his own red robe to pieces to distribute among his willing hearers. The king, on his knees, first received the sacred symbol from him; the nobles followed his example; and the year following he set out from hence, with his army, for the Holy Land. In 1190 Richard Cœur de Lion and Philippe-Auguste repaired hither to assume the pilgrim's cross at the head of their armies.

Theodore Beza, the Reformer and Calvinist theologian, was born at Vezelay, of noble parents, 1519. On the way to Vezelay you pass the church of *St. Père*, whose tower is "an almost unique specimen of transition, or very early complete Gothic. The detached shafts, and canopies at its angles, and its several stages of open windows, give it an air of lightness and elegance such as I have never seen surpassed in later buildings."—*Petit*. The château de Bazoche belonged to Marshal Vauban, who was born in the village St. Leger de Foucheret, in Le Morvan. His room and bed and sword are still preserved in it—also 4 cannon used at the siege of Philipburg. His body is buried in the chapel, his heart is removed to the Invalides.]

To the S.W. of Avallon stretches the extensive tract of woodland called La Forêt de Morvan, which supplies Paris with fuel, the wood being cut every 10 or 15 years, by portions at a time, and transported down the Yonne and Seine in rafts of faggots.]

From Joigny *the Railroad* is carried to
155 La Roche Stat.
A bridge of 6 stone arches crosses the Yonne.

St. Florentin Stat.—A pretty town at the junction of the Armance and Armançon. Its *Church*, founded 1376, is said to possess fine painted glass, and a curious double staircase. The walk of the Prieuré commands a view. [About 14 m. S. of St. Florentin Stat. lies the *Abbey of Pontigny*, remarkable as having been the residence of many English prelates, and the retreat of Thomas Becket during his exile, 1164-6. While here he carried the practice of the austerities of the Cistercian order to the very extreme, and while in prayer before one of the altars of the church had a divine vision, accompanied by the words, "Thomas, Thomas, my church shall be glorified by thy blood:" such, at least, is the Romish legend. The Abbey was devastated by the Huguenots, who unroofed and burnt the church and Abbey, and broke open the tombs, 1567; and the destruction of the conventual buildings and confiscation of the revenues were effected at the Revolution. The *Church*, however, still remains, and, though dilapidated, is a grand edifice, in a severe style of early or transition Gothic, uniform throughout, erected 1150 by the munificence of a Count of Champagne, the finest church in Burgundy after Sens and Auxerre. It is 354 ft. long and 68 ft. high, and is lighted by narrow lancet windows. Behind the high altar is the

Shrine of the English Saint, Edmund Archbishop of Canterbury, an ark or chest of wood, carved and gilt, with a top in the form of a roof, and statues of saints around it, supported by 4 stone statues of angels as large as life.

Attached to the S. transept is a chapel, now in ruins, dedicated to St. Thomas the Martyr, who was driven from Pontigny by the threat of Henry II. to banish the Cistercians from England, if they sheltered him in France. It retains some traces of frescoes, executed 1520. Among the English refugees who found shelter here was Stephen Langton, Archbishop of Canterbury, when banished from England by King John, together with his suffragans. The church of Pontigny is to be repaired.]

The railroad from St. Florentin follows the valley of the Armançon, and the line of the Canal de Bourgogne upwards, through

184 Flogny Stat., where is a wire bridge, to

197 *Tonnerre Stat.*—(*Inns:* Lion d'Or; Poste.) This is an old and dull town, of 4310 Inhab., on a steep slope, on the summit of which stands the *Ch. of St. Pierre,* commanding a fine view of the town from its rocky platform, and containing the interesting monument, in marble, of Marguerite de Bourgogne, Queen of Sicily, who founded the noble *Hospital* in this town, endowing it with large revenues, which it still enjoys. Her effigy, finely sculptured in the costume of the time, reclines upon the tomb. Here is also buried, under an imposing monument, Michel le Tellier, Marquis de Louvois, Minister of War to Louis XIV. It is the work of Girardon. *St. Pierre* and *Notre Dame* possess some architectural interest as Gothic churches.

The gnomon traced on the walls of the hospital, in 1786, is interesting as a scientific memorial.

205 *Tanlay Stat.*—Here is one of the finest châteaux in Burgundy, and tolerably well kept up by its owner. It is a good specimen of the style of the Renaissance, the oldest part having been begun, 1559, by Coligny d'Andelot, brother of the Admiral Coligny, the leader of the Protestants, and the chief victim of the St. Bartholomew's night. A chamber in the *Tour de la Ligue* is pointed out as the place where he and the other leaders of the party, the Prince de Condé, &c., were in the habit of meeting; and it is still covered with faded frescoes, representing, under the disguise of the gods of Olympus, the leading characters of the time; Catherine de Medicis as Juno (but with a double face?), and her son, Charles IX., as Pluto; Condé as Mars. The larger and more splendid portion of the château, including numerous additions to the original plan, was built between 1643 and 1648 by Particelli d'Emery, Surintendant de Finance under Mazarin, from designs of Le Muet, except the Petit Château at the entrance of the great building, which is a beautiful specimen of the Renaissance of the 16th centy. At the extremity of the grand *Canal,* flanked by avenues, beneath which Coligny and Condé may have walked, is the Château d'Eau, from which artificial streams burst forth.

219 Ancy le Franc Stat.

The *Château* was begun in 1555, from designs, it is said, of Primaticcio, and decorated with frescoes still existing. In 1688 it became the property and residence of Louvois, minister of the Grand Monarque, who owned besides the Comté of Tonnerre, and other vast neighbouring possessions brought to him by his wife, Anne de Souvré, the richest heiress in France. The Marquis de Louvois established iron-forges here. The château is well kept up, and surrounded by park and woods.

225 Nuits-sous-Ravière Stat.—Coaches to Bourbonne les Bains; Châtillon, Bar-sur-Aube.

233 Aisy-sur-Armançon Stat.—Soon after quitting this place you enter the department of the Côte d'Or, so famous for its vineyards.

243 Montbard Stat.—(*Inn:* Point du Jour.) This unimportant and dirty town was the residence of the naturalist Buffon, who was born 1707, and lived in the *Château,* which still exists. The *gardens* attached to it are arranged in terraces along the slope of the hill, and

decorated with orange-trees. In an isolated antique tower, rising in a corner of them, now going to decay, and stripped of its furniture, Buffon formed his study, and composed most of his works. Nothing but bare walls now remains. The gardens, now open to the public, were laid waste and destroyed by the Revolutionists, but one relic of their ancient condition was preserved in a small pillar of marble raised by the son of Buffon in front of the lofty tower which contained his father's study, and bearing this inscription,

"Excelsæ turris humilis columna,
Parenti suo filius Buffon, 1785."

"The *Château*, now occupied by the widow of Buffon's son, who was one of the first victims of the guillotine at the Revolution, contains portraits of Buffon and his assistant Daubenton. Two of the rooms are lined with coloured prints from the Natural History of its great owner. *His tomb*, in the parish church, was destroyed at the Revolution, the lead of his coffin melted, and his bones scattered."—*Costello*.

[*Fontenay* is a sequestered abbey, a few miles from Montbard, whose founder was one Evrard Bishop of Norwich. It was devoted to monks of the Cistercian order. Its ruined buildings are now converted into a paper manufactory, belonging to the respected family of Montgolfier. The chapter-house and cloisters are still fine specimens of Gothic architecture. The church, converted into every-day purposes, is less striking; but it contains several mutilated ecclesiastical monuments.]

Coaches from Montbard to Autun, Semur, Saulieu, Chatillon, Langres.

Les Laumes Stat.
279 *Verrey* Stat.
288 Blaisy-Bas Stat.

The *Tunnel of Blaisy* is about 2½ m. long, and cost more than 10 million francs.

298 Malain Stat.
310 Plombières Stat.

The Rly. cuts through the bastions of the town, in order to reach

315 DIJON STAT. (*Inns*: H. du Parc, comfortable but dear; H. de la Cloche, near the Rly. and Cathedral, fairly good), the ancient capital of the Duchy of Burgundy, now the chef-lieu of the Dépt. de la Côte d'Or, contains 29,000 Inhab. The first view of this once important and opulent city is peculiarly agreeable and striking. The Jura faintly bounds the horizon. Dijon lies outspread on the plain below. The great fortress-like masses of the churches, and the Palace of the Dukes of Burgundy, standing out boldly from the buildings of the town, mark themselves forcibly on the landscape, quite as advantageously as the greater richness of battlemented turrets and of crocheted spires.

The artist may pass several days here agreeably and profitably.

St. Benigne, originally a conventual Ch., became the Cathedral after the Revolution, when it was much injured. It is a fine building of the 13th and 14th cent., with a bold W. front. Its *spire* enjoys local celebrity, but is an obelisk of wood (1742), on open legs, and its spiral leading lines add to its appearance of insecurity. Here have been recently discovered the remains of Duke Philip le Hardi and some fine brick slabs with effigies of Burgundian nobles. In the nave is the slab tomb of Udislaus King of Poland, 1388. The organ is large and fine.

St. Jean (1466), now *Marché du Midi*, behind the Cathedral, is a fine cross Ch., with a painted roof of wide span and good flamboyant windows. The choir was destroyed 1810. Bossuet was baptized here, and was born in the adjacent house, 10, Place St. Jean.

Notre Dame is a singularly fine Ch. in the purest Gothic, somewhat like Ely, and remarkable for the boldness of its construction. The E. end, a beautiful specimen of early pointed, was finished 1229. The front exhibits a beautiful play of light and shade. At one corner of this façade, where it was intended a tower should rise, still stands the clock brought (1382) from Courtrai, by *Philip le Hardi*, an epithet which his general conduct deserved, though, in this achievement, *the Cruel* would have suited him better, for he plundered and burnt the town, and massacred the inhabitants. Jacques

Marques, a Flemish mathematician, was the maker of this clock, which, in the opinion of Froissart, was the most curious existing, whether in Christendom or in the heathen lands, and hence selected by the duke as his trophy. The bells are struck by two hammermen, and who are called *Jacquemars* by the badaud of Dijon—a corruption of their maker's name.

St. Michael's Ch. was consecrated 1529. Its front is a splendid example of the *Renaissance*. The portal is composed of three circular arches, with a very fine frieze above. The ornaments of this front are generally Italian in their details, yet so put together that the whole becomes a perfect Gothic cathedral.

There are a great many desecrated churches here, degraded into stables, coach-houses, warehouses, &c., though in tolerable repair, and worthy the attention of the architect; such are *St. Etienne*, a covered market; *St. Philibert*, cavalry stables.

Next to the *Theatre*, distinguished by its noble octostyle Corinthian portico, stands the ancient *Palace* of the dukes of Burgundy, which, after the union of the duchy to the crown of France, became the *Palais des Etats*, and is now the *H. de Ville*. It has been so completely modernised in its principal front, that the great interest possessed by the building would hardly be anticipated. Parts of its interior, however, are old, such as the Hall and the low vaulted chambers beneath, and it is still surmounted by a large and massy feudal tower. A curious well, in another part, marks the site of the *Sainte Chapelle*, in which chapters of the order of the Golden Fleece were held, 1433. Thus the building retains many of the features of the residence of the premier dukes of Christendom.

"The style prevailing in this and the other buildings of the 15th centy. in Dijon, and which may be properly called the Burgundian style, has many of the features which we afterwards find in our Tudor architecture, and the aspect of the building softens down from the castle to the palace or mansion. Besides the Civic Offices, and the *Oratoire*, or Protestant Chapel, this building contains a *Museum*. The ancient hall and adjoining chambers have been very judiciously chosen as the place of deposit for the very rich and important monuments of the middle ages which are there preserved. The following articles may be particularly noticed. The crozier of St. Robert, the first abbot of the Cistercian order (ob. 1098). The wooden cup of St. Bernard, undoubted relic of this truly great and pious man, whose memory cannot be, however, relieved from the atrocities occasioned by the Crusades. The ornaments were probably added after his canonization. Toilet furniture of the Duchesses of Burgundy; caskets and boxes of ivory, beautifully carved. A purse supposed to have belonged to Isabella of Portugal, third wife of Philip the Good, of leather richly embroidered, and apparently of oriental workmanship. The chief ornaments of the collection are the magnificent *Tombs* of Philippe le Hardi, the founder of the second race of the Dukes of Burgundy (1342—1404), and of Jean-sans-Peur, his son and successor (1371—1419). These tombs, the sculptures on which are perhaps the finest specimens existing of mediæval art on this side of the Alps, have suffered strange vicissitudes. Both were erected in the Chartreuse of Dijon, founded and endowed by Philip, and selected by him. Upon the suppression of the Chartreuse they were removed to St. Benigne, where they rested but a short time, as in 1793 the Council of the Commune decreed their destruction. The bases remained at St. Benigne, but the figures were dispersed: some were placed in the Museum, others in private cabinets, and some abandoned in a lumber-room. In 1818 the department determined upon their restoration. This labour, though costly, was comparatively easy, for, although pulled to pieces, these pieces were as little defaced as possible. We see them in a state very little different from the original splendour. The tomb of Philippe le Hardi represents him in a recumbent posture, in his full ducal robes. He is crowned with the ducal coronet, a plain circle without flowers, and his hand grasps the ducal sceptre. By the side is a space for the statue of his consort, but it never was filled. The sides of the tomb are ornamented with arcades filled with elaborately sculptured statuettes, in alabaster, of friars, represented as mourners, but with skilful variety of feeling. The draperies are admirable. Claus Slater, the Dutchman, was the artist.

The tomb of *Jean-sans-Peur*, slain on the Bridge of Montereau, 1419, matches entirely with that of his father both in material and in design. His ducal robe is *semé* with the device which he adopted, the *rabot*, or carpenter's plane, assumed by him in opposition to the ragged staff of his political adversary, the Duke of Orleans. By his side is his consort, Margaret of Bavaria. Her robe is white, *semé* with the well-known little flower which bears her name.

The chimney-piece of the Great Hall is said to have been built in 1504, after a fire which destroyed the roof in 1502; but it was probably only restored. It is perhaps 50 ft. in height by 20 in breadth, and it is a magnificent specimen of Gothic art. Here is preserved a model of the beautiful Sainte Chapelle, the chief Gothic ornament of Dijon: desecrated at the Revolution; pulled down and sold, 1807.

The *paintings* in the Museum are numerous, but much of the usual kind found in provincial collections: some of the portraits are interesting, especially those of the Duchess of Burgundy.

The *Palais de Justice* has a fine Renaissance front, restored, and a large Hall.

Some curious relics of domestic architecture and early art are to be met with in the town. In a street near St. Michael's is a very elegant stone seat or sofa. "In a house entered through a shop, not far from Notre Dame, is a Gothic staircase, on the top of which stands the figure of a man with a basket on his shoulder, whence spring, in the form of a plant or tree, the vaulting ribs of the roof; these are foliated in a very bold manner. The whole is of good execution, though evidently late in the style.

The *Public Walks* are, indeed, a leading feature in Dijon, surrounding the walls as with a belt of foliage, and there is perhaps no other provincial town in France so well provided. They run partly in the form of *Boulevards* outside of, and parallel to, the old ramparts, which themselves form elevated terraces. The *Parc*, about a mile out of the town, reached by the Cours du Parc, was laid out, 1610, by Le Nôtre for the Great Condé, its owner, when governor of the province, who gave free admission to the public.

Dijon has the renown of being the native place of Bossuet, the divine, born in the house No. 12, Place St. Jean; of Crebillon; of Guyton Morveau, the chemist; and of Maret Duc de Bassano. St. Bernard was born in the village *Fontaines*, about a mile beyond the walls, and his father's castle is still in existence beside the curious church.

The *trade* in the *wines of Burgundy* is concentrated in Dijon; the district which produces the most celebrated wines lies to the S. of the town, and is traversed by the Railroad to Châlons-sur-Saône, passing Clos de Vougeot, Nuits, and Beaune. (Rte. 152.)

10 min. walk from the town, by the Rly. Stat., stands the *Asyle des Aliénés*, formerly the Chartreuse, founded by Philip le Hardi, 1383, as a burial-place for the ducal house, many of whom were buried here, including Charles the Bold, until the Emperor Charles V. removed his body in 1550 to Bruges. The existing remains are scanty:—the entrance gate, part of a tower, the kneeling effigies of Duke Philip and his Duchess prefixed to the portal of the modern chapel, and the well or cistern known as *Les Puits de Möise* (1399) executed by Claus Slater (the sculptor of the ducal monuments). It consists of figures of Moses, David, Jeremiah, Zachariah, Daniel, and Isaiah, hexagonally placed under rich canopies, and upon elaborate pedestals. The figures are well preserved.

Conveyances.—*Mallepostes* to Besançon, to Geneva, daily.

N.B.—The quickest way to Geneva is from Châlons-sur-Saône by Lons-le-Saulnier.

Diligences to Nancy; to Vesoul; to Dôle and Geneva; to Besançon; to Belfort; to Pontarlier; to Gray.
Railroads to Châlons-sur-Saône (Rte. 106); to Paris by Tonnerre.

ROUTE 105.

PARIS TO LYONS.—ROUTE DU BOURBONNAIS, BY FONTAINEBLEAU, MONTARGIS, NEVERS, AND MOULINS.—THE BATHS OF VICHY.

473 kilom. = 293 Eng. m.

From Paris to Lyons the Raily. (Rtes. 104-106) is usually followed.

From Paris to Nevers the Raily. by Orleans (Rte. 103). *Diligences* no longer run between Paris and Nevers.

The road, soon after quitting Paris by the Faubourg St. Marceau and the Barrière d'Italie, passes at a short distance on the rt. of *Bicêtre*, an hospital for old men, a lunatic asylum, and a penitentiary. Its name is said to be a corruption of Winchester, because it is thought to occupy the site of a country-house built, 1290, by John Bp. of Winchester; another derivation is from its owner in the 15th centy. (1410), John Duc de Berry, in Latin, "Dux Bituricensis." The oldest of the existing buildings are chiefly those constructed by Cardinal Richelieu, as an asylum for wounded soldiers, which was afterwards transferred to the Invalides.

Nearly 4500 criminals are confined here, including convicts awaiting their transmission to the hulks.

The road, which is paved, runs through an avenue of trees along the table-land which sinks down into the valley of the Seine.

8 Villejuif. At the entrance of this town, on the l., stands an obelisk, marking the N. base of a triangle, established for the construction of Cassini's Map of France: a similar obelisk, at Fromenteau, marks the other extremity of the base.

11 Fromenteau.

Napoleon, hastening to the relief of Paris, March 30th, 1814, here met the head of the column of dejected troops who informed him of the surrender of the capital to the allies; in consequence he was forced to return to Fontainebleau, where he soon after signed his abdication. Near Juvisy our road crosses the railroad to Orleans (Rte. 49), and runs for some distance parallel with the branch to Corbeil.

12 Essonne, a small town, in a hollow, on the Essonne, which falls into the Seine, 1½ m. below, at Corbeil (Rte. 49), where the branch-rly. terminates.

There are several *châteaux* near this part of the road, Villeroy on the rt., Coudray on the l.; but they contribute in no respect to adorn the road, as the parks, and lodges, and seats of England. On the l. the Seine, winding through its fertile valley, is a pleasing feature.

11 Ponthierry.

8 Chailly.

About 5 m. short of Fontainebleau, we enter its noble *Forest*, p. 347.

10 *Fontainebleau* (Rte. 104).

On quitting Fontainebleau our road passes an *obelisk* or Pyramid, planted in the midst of a star (étoile) formed by the divergence of 11 roads; among them those to Orleans, to Montereau, and to Nemours, the last of which we follow.

For 4 or 5 m. the road continues through the Forest; then issues out into a plain of sand, amidst which the traveller's carriage flounders; in summer enveloped in tormenting dust, in winter sinking up to the axles in mud. The pavement ceases near

13 *Nemours*, a town of 3830 Inhab., deriving its name from the woods (nemora) which once surrounded it. The *old Castle*, the residence of the Ducs de Nemours, of the line of Savoy, still exists, flanked by 4 towers, and includes several institutions.

The *Parish Ch.*, originally attached to the Priory of St. John, is a fine building. St. Pierre is the oldest in the town.

Mirabeau was born (1749) at Bignon, 15 m. from Nemours, on the road to Sens.

We continue by the side of the small river Loing all the way to Montargis, through

13 La Croisière.

7 Fontenay.

14 Montargis (*Inn:* Poste;—H. de Lyon; not good), a town of 7757 Inhab.,

on the borders of an extensive forest, at the junction of the *Canal de Briare* with that of Orleans, by the side of which there are public walks. The castle, which for a long time formed part of the domain of the crown, and, serving as a royal nursery, was called "le Berceau des Enfans de France," is entirely destroyed. It was of vast extent; but was sold in 1809, to a démolisseur, for 60,000 fr. Over one of the fireplaces in its great hall (for it had no less than 6) was a fresco painting, representing the combat between "*the Dog of Montargis*" and the murderer of its master, Macaire, which is said to have taken place, in the presence of Charles VI., in the lists of the Ile Nôtre Dame at Paris. The sagacity of the dog not only indicated the spot where his master was buried in the forest of Bondy, but also singled out the murderer; and the king, according to the spirit of the laws of the time, directed that the cause should be tried by a duel between the dog, as accuser, and the accused. After several attacks, the dog seized his adversary, who was armed with a club, by the throat, and compelled him to confess his crime. In 1652 the Grand Condé, then a rebel against the royal authority, arriving before Montargis with a small force, summoned it to surrender. The magistrate hesitated, but Condé, taking out his watch, declared he would sack the town and slay the inhabitants if it were not given up in an hour. This produced the desired effect, and gave rise to the saying, "que M. le Prince avait pris Montargis avec sa montre."

The country in which Montargis lies belongs to the district anciently called Gâtinois; it has little interest. The road is carried in a straight line, through a dull district, to

17 Nogent-sur-Vernisson.

A road strikes off from this to Gien on the Loire (Rte. 52).

[About 5 m. to the E. lies Châtillon-sur-Loing, in whose ancient *castle* the Admiral Coligny was born, 1516. After his murder on the Bartholomew's night his body was cut down from the gallows of Montfaucon, upon which it had been shamefully hung by his Romanist assassins, and conveyed by his cousin Montmorency to his wife, who concealed it for many months before she could venture to commit it to the tomb at Chantilly. Châtillon belonged to the family of Condé.]

12 La Bussière has a handsome château of the 15th centy. From the summit of a hill, on approaching Briare, the valley of the Loire bursts into view: the pleasing effect of the broad winding river, and its vine-clad banks, is much enhanced by the previous barrenness and monotonous road.

16 Briare (*Inn:* Poste), a town of 2730 Inhab., on the rt. bank of the Loire, has given its name to the *Canal*, begun by Sully, and completed 1642, remarkable as the first attempt to open a communication between 2 river basins by means of supplies of water stored up on the summit level (point de partage). It runs from the Loing at Montargis to the Seine at St. Mamet, thus opening a communication between Paris and the S. and centre of France. From Briare there is a post-road along the rt. bank of the Loire by Gien (Rte. 52) to Orleans, where the traveller may take the railroad to Paris.

17 Neuvy. *Inns:* Poste, small, but the bed-rooms comfortable.— *W. M. H. de Nièvre*, clean. Here is the quiet, unpretending country seat of the late Marshal Macdonald, in an English-looking park. Across an undulating country, commanding, from time to time, peeps of the Loire, the road proceeds through

14 Cosne (*Inn:* Grand Cerf—*H.N.*), where there are iron-forges; and a little way above which the town of Sancerre is seen on the opposite bank of the river.

15 Pouilly.

13 La Charité (*Inn:* Poste, pretty good—*C. B.*), an ancient town of 5000 Inhab., still partly surrounded by ramparts, flanked by watch-towers, of the 14th centy. It is said to have derived its name from the benevolence shown to travellers by the Monks of St. Benedict; and its arms are 3 open purses, on a field azure. Its *Ch.* (*Notre Dame*) must originally have been a very fine Romanesque building; but the nave

is, in part, destroyed, and the aisles and other portions modernised. The *choir*, however, surrounded by pointed arches, on light piers with elegant capitals, and the front, are probably as old as the latter part of the 12th centy. The church, which had 5 doors (4 Romanesque and with bas-reliefs still remaining), 5 aisles, and 5 apses round the choir, was in great part destroyed by fire, 1204, and was restored by Philippe-Auguste. A ruined tower is the only remaining relic of the monastery, whose priors were so wealthy and powerful, that in the 16th centy. the Pope found it necessary to interfere and regulate the number of knights who should form their escort when they went abroad.

The road to Bourges here crosses the Loire on a stone bridge (Rte. 103): there is also a suspension bridge. A *diligence* goes daily to Bourges.

At La Marche are ruins of a Romanesque *Ch.*, which, from the rudeness of its architecture and carved capitals, is probably as old as the 10th centy. Under its E. end is a crypt.

13 Pouges. There are mineral springs about a mile from this.

From the top of a hill surmounted in the course of this stage, a fine view is presented of the valley of the Loire and of that of the Allier, which joins it a little below Nevers; the latter river, however, is not visible.

At Fourchamboult there are extensive iron furnaces and forges, perhaps the largest in France, where the iron conservatories in the Jardin des Plantes, the arches of the Pont du Carrousel, the frame-work for the roof of Chartres cathedral, and the piers for the bridge of Cubsac, were cast. They employ between 2000 and 3000 workmen.

12 *Nevers* (*Inn:* H. de France), an unprepossessing, dirty, but ancient city of 17,085 Inhab., chef-lieu of the Dépt. de la Nièvre, formerly capital of the Nivernois, is situated on the rt. bank of the Loire, at the confluence of the Nièvre. It is mentioned by Cæsar in his Commentaries, "Noviodunum oppidum Æduorum, ad ripas Ligeris opportuno loco positum." He deposited here his money-chest.

The oldest ecclesiastical edifice here is the Romanesque *Ch. of St. Etienne*, very plain, both within and without. The date is proved by the charter to be 1063. It is entered by descending several steps. The transepts are separated from the body of the church, opening below in a wide arch surmounted by smaller arcades. *St. Sauveur*, near the Loire, another Romanesque church, is turned into a warehouse; *St. Genest*, an example of the Transition into the Pointed style, is also desecrated into a brewery.

The *Cathedral* of St. Cyr, on the hill top, somewhat heavy externally, consists of a nave and choir, built in the 13th, 14th, and 15th centuries, with an apse at both ends; that at the W. is Romanesque, and probably of the 10th centy.; beneath it is a large crypt. The nave and choir have not the same axes, the choir inclining perceptibly to the S. (rt.) The tower is flanked at the angles by colossal figures, in bad taste. The decoration of the interior is praiseworthy; the capitals of the columns sculptured with rich foliage, of admirable workmanship. All the statues were mutilated at the Revolution. There are some painted glass and old tapestries in the choir; and in the S. transept a rich flamboyant *doorway*, leading to a fanciful spiral staircase, is a remarkable example of what Mr. Willis calls "interpenetration," or the running of several series of mouldings into one another: these complicated interlacings pervade not only the canopy of the arch, but even the pinnacles.

The *Hôtel de Ville*, also on the height facing an irregular Place, formerly palace of the Dukes of Nevers, built by the princes of the line of Clèves, is an edifice in the flamboyant style, retaining several of its picturesque turrets and gables.

The old *walls* and *towers* of the 15th centy. still remain. One of the *town gates*, a relic of the fortifications erected by Pierre de Courtenay, Seigneur de Nevers, at the end of the 12th centy., rebuilt 1393, still exists in the *Porte du Croux*, black with age and dirt. Another entry into the town is by a *triumphal arch*, erected to commemorate the battle of Fontenay, 1746.

CENTRAL FRANCE. *Route* 105.—*Moulins.* 359

Behind the H. de Ville is a public *garden*, formerly the park of the palace.

Nevers is a thriving, busy manufacturing town, now connected with Orleans and Paris by Rly.; its potteries are 8 centuries old, and employ 700 persons: in its iron-works chains and cables for suspension bridges are made; the iron used is that of Berry. There is a *royal cannon-foundry*, for the navy, where 125 pieces are cast annually. Not far from Nevers, the lateral canal of the Loire is carried over the Allier in an aqueduct called *Pont Canal de Guétin*, a work of magnitude, completed 1845.

Mallepostes to Avignon and Lyons—to Montpellier, by Clermont, St. Flour, and Lodeve.

Railway. A branch line connects Nevers with Guétin Stat. on the Rly. from Vierzon to Moulins and Clermont (Rte. 103)—from Vierzon to Orleans and Paris.

The road crosses the Loire by a heavy bridge of 20 arches on quitting Nevers, and, leaving that river on the l., proceeds to ascend the valley of the Allier, its tributary. The scenery between Nevers and Moulins is on the whole very pleasing, the country much enclosed with hedge-rows, and generally fertile. The river Allier is seldom seen, concealed as it is by trees, in the flat valley through which it passes.

12 Magny.

11 St. Pierre le Moutier. Near this is a large pond. Hence a road strikes off to Bourges and Orleans.

8 St. Imbert.

10 Villeneuve-sur-Allier (Dépt. Allier).

12 *Moulins* (*Inns:* H. de France, very good, but dear; Lion d'Or, and des Princes, exceedingly good), a cheerful town, without the activity of much trade or commerce, pleasantly situated on the rt. bank of the Allier. It is chef-lieu of the Dépt. d'Allier, and contains a population of 15,398.

It is a comparatively modern town, and has no fine buildings. The *castle* is reduced to a square tower, of the 15th centy., called *La Mal Coiffée*, and some buildings erected by Cath. de Medicis.

The *Cathedral of Notre Dame* consists merely of a lofty choir in the Florid style of the 15th centy.: its vaulted roof is elaborately groined. It contains an old painting of the Virgin and Child, the two shutters of which, now detached from it, and hung against piers, bear portraits of Pierre II., Duc de Bourbon, and his wife, Anne of France, attended by their patron saints, attributed to *Ghirlandajo*.

In the *Chapel of the College* is the monument of Henri Duc de Montmorency, who suffered, under the heavy hand of Richelieu, for having conspired against him and his master, Louis XIII., and was executed at Toulouse, 1632. His widow, Marie Orsini, conveyed his remains to this chapel, then attached to the Convent of the Visitation, of which she became superior, spending in it the rest of her days. The monument, attributed to an Italian sculptor, *Agheri*, consists of the reclining statue of the duke, in Roman armour, resting on his helmet, with his duchess beside him in an attitude of grief and resignation; the expression of profound sorrow in her countenance is perfect, and the draperies are very beautifully executed. On either side is an allegorical figure—Valour, a sort of Hercules, and Liberality, a coarse female. The fact of this monument being in honour of a man beheaded for conspiring against a king preserved it from demolition at the Revolution.

Marshal Villars, the opponent of Marlborough, and Marshal Berwick, natural son of James II. by Arabella Churchill (Marlborough's sister), who won the battle of Almanza from the English in Spain, were both born here.

Here Lord Clarendon wrote the greater part of his 'History of the Great Rebellion,' in exile.

Some cutlery, of an inferior kind, is made at Moulins; the manufacture has much fallen off.

At Moulins the very interesting road through the Limagne, Clermont, and the Volcanic district of Auvergne, strikes off up the valley of the Allier (Rte. 109). *Diligences* run daily, and a *Malleposte* to Clermont and Montpellier. It is possible to go this way to Lyons by Montbrison, and to Marseille by Le Puy and St.

Etienne, though, in both cases, it is a détour.

Diligences go hence also to Vichy (see below). Railway in progress to Vichy and Clermont (Rte. 103).

No one will quit Moulins without thinking of Sterne and his Maria, the scene of her melancholy story being laid here.

[*a*. The watering-place of *Bourbon l'Archambault*, a town of 3017 Inhab., frequented on account of its mineral waters, is about 19 m. W. of Moulins. The waters are saline, and are supplied by a hot spring, and a cold spring called *Source de Jonas*. There is a bath-house in the middle of the town. There are very considerable and picturesque remains of the ancient *castle* of the early Sires de Bourbon, and a fragment of the apse of the *Ste. Chapelle*. Diligences run daily from Moulins to the Baths in summer, and the road thither passes through *Souvigny*, a poor village 5 m. from Moulins, containing an *Abbey Church*, which is one of the most remarkable Gothic monuments in the province for size. The central nave, the apses at the E. end, and the crypt below the choir, date from the 11th centy.; the more recent portions from 1446, when the church was rebuilt. The *nave* is flanked by double aisles, the outer ones nearly as broad as the centre. In the N. aisle is a curious fragment of an octagonal pillar covered with sculptures—signs of the zodiac, mythical beasts, &c.—in the Byzantine style. The *Chapelle Vieille*, on the S. side, is separated from the choir and transept by a stone screen, beautifully carved with flamboyant tracery. It encloses the monument of Louis Duc de Bourbon, and Anne his wife, bearing their recumbent figures, of white marble, sadly mutilated by the Revolutionists. A recess, or niche, in the wall opposite, displays, amidst rich flamboyant tracery, the word "Espérance," the motto of the Order of the Thistle, founded by the Duke. This chapel, the greater part of the choir, the vaults, and windows of the nave, 4 divisions of the outer S. aisle of the nave, and the remains of the cloisters on the S. side of the chapel, are supposed by M. Merimée to have been built 1441. On the N. side of the choir is *La Chapelle Neuve*, similarly decorated, and even more injured by the Vandals of '93, containing the tombs of Duc Charles, and his wife, Agnes de Bourgogne. The date of this chapel is somewhere about the end of the 15th or beginning of the 16th centy.

b. All persons who take an interest in Gothic architecture should visit Souvigny from Moulins: in spite of its mutilations, it is a very interesting church. The Auberge de la Poste was the ancient Priors' palace. At *St. Menoux*, not far from Souvigny, is another ancient *church*, once attached to a Benedictine abbey, but much decayed. The *choir* is the most interesting portion, and a good example of the florid Romanesque.]

15 Bessay.

15 Varennes.—Poste; a comfortable little Inn.—*C. B.*

11 St. Gerard-le-Puy.

[From this a road turns off to the fashionable watering-place of *Vichy*, 61 kilom. from Moulins = 39¼ Eng. m., through a rich but unpicturesque country, the only objects of interest being the Puy de Dôme and Mont Dore; visible the whole way.

Vichy (*Inns*: every one lives in boarding-houses; of these there are 6 or 8.—H. Guillermen, best, good table-d'hôte; H. de Corneil, civil people; H. de Paris is most frequented by Parisians; H. Velay. In none is the accommodation first-rate. The guests live together, taking their meals in public, consisting of a breakfast à la fourchette at 10, and dinner at 5. Nobody is allowed to be served in his own room, unless illness prevent his appearance in public. The *charges* for board and lodging vary from 8 fr. to 12 fr. per diem.

Vichy is situated in a poplar-planted flat, in which the broad brawling Allier occupies a great river-bed, crossed by a bridge ¼ m. long; little eminences with old bourgs and round towers here and there, of which Old Vichy is one, rising on the rt. bank of the river. There is besides a new external quarter, or suburb, of handsome lodging and boarding houses, connected with old Vichy, on a height above, by a fine *promenade*, shaded by avenues of plane-trees. This is the watering-place; now one of the most frequented in France; and here rise the *mineral springs*, of acidulous alkaline water, which has been compared with hot soda-water, their principal ingredients being carbonate of soda and carbonic acid gas, and their peculiarity the small quantity of iron, in proportion to these ingredients, which accompanies them. They operate with advantage on the digestive and urinary organs, and are efficacious in long-standing stomach disorders, obstruction and enlargement of the spleen.

There are 7 springs, varying in temperature from 86° to 111° Fahr., but differing only slightly in the proportion of the same ingredients; 3 of them are received in the *bath-house* (*Bâtiment Thermal*), a very handsome building, faced on the ground floor by a long colonnade, containing, in the upper story, a cabinet de lecture and ball-room; and in the lateral ranges 72 baths, tolerably well appointed, and 4 douches. The principal source, or the one most used for drinking and exportation in bottles, is that called *Grand Grille*. The water, received into stone basins, has the appearance of boiling, from the quantity of gas which bubbles up through it. The season begins here in the early part of May, and ends by the middle of September.

The routine of a day is as follows:— As early as 6 the crowd assembles to drink the waters, which takes up an hour or two: the band plays during the season from 8 to 10 A.M.: 10 is the hour of breakfast: to this succeeds, after an interval, the Bath, for those who are recommended to bathe. Tickets (cachets) are obtained by applying to the manager (Directeur), who sits at his desk at the end of one of the galleries, and who arranges the hour at which each person can bathe. Bath-tickets cost 5 frs., and without a ticket no one is allowed to bathe. Owing to want of method and arrangement, patients have often to wait 2 or 3 hours after the time appointed. The table-d'hôte dinner takes place at 5; and in the evening the company assemble in the drawing-room (salon) of the hotel, where cards or music afford resources for passing the evening. Precedence is determined by the order of arrival, those who have been longest resident occupying the upper seats at table, &c. There are occasional balls at the rooms, but, as the physicians are masters of the ceremonies, they begin at 8½, and usually end before 11: raking is not allowed. *A season-ticket* (carte d'abonnement personnel), which costs 20 frs., admits a visitor to all the balls and concerts of the season. They are conducted by *Strauss*, who resides on the spot, which is a guarantee for the music. Frequent collections (quêtes) are made at the instigation of the curé, for the good of some charity or parish school, and the poor-box is commonly carried round by a lady and gentleman. On quitting Vichy it is customary to give 5 frs. or more to the manager for charitable purposes.

N. of the great Round Tower, the only one remaining out of 7 which defended the walls, stands the mansion which Madame de Sévigné occupied, and from which she wrote some of her Letters: see vol. v.

The Rocher des Celestins, at the foot of which the springs rise, so called from a convent in ruins on its top, presents a curious geological phenomenon, being composed of vertical strata of a tufacious rock, almost pure arragonite, no doubt deposited from mineral springs, projecting in shattered slabs above the surface, and abutting at a short distance against horizontal strata of the same tufa.

The situation of Vichy is agreeable, but not striking, in an open and highly cultivated country, the celebrated Limagne d'Auvergne (Rte. 109); in fact, Vichy's main attractions are its waters.

Some pleasant *Excursions*, however, may be made in the neighbourhood, and many troops of *donkeys* are kept for the use of the guests.

The valley of the *Sichon* affords pleasant walks or rides, and its stream some trout.

More distant expeditions may be made to the *Château of Effiat*, a building of the 17th centy., now delapidated, but still inhabited, and retaining its formal garden flanked by fosses. It was erected by Marshal Effiat, who was ambassador to England to negotiate the marriage of Henrietta Maria with Charles I., and father of Cinq Mars, beheaded by Richelieu at Lyon.

At the village of *Cresset*, an old feudal fortress, with crumbling ramparts, 2½ m. from Vichy, a fair is held at the latter end of June, to which the peasants resort to be hired as servants. On this occasion the monotonous but somewhat laughable dance of the country, "La Bourrée," is kept up with great perseverance by the *younger* peasants.

The quickest way from Paris to Vichy is to take the Orleans, Vierzon, and Moulins Railway as far as completed, which will soon be to Vichy.

The *castle of Randan*, a modern mansion with pretty grounds, on the site of that in which Bayard tarried so long, paying court to its noble *Châtellaine*, was bequeathed by Madame Adelaide, sister of Louis Philippe, to the Duc de Montpensier.

Until the Rly. is finished, *diligences* go daily to Moulins, on the way to Paris; to Roanne, on the way to Lyons; to Clermont (Rte. 109), &c.

———

The road to Lyons has now quitted the valley of the Allier, and enters on a hilly country. The mountains of Auvergne appearing to the S.W., and those of Forez more to the E., form features in the landscape.

10 La Palisse.—*Inn:*
Between this and la Pacaudière the road traverses a hilly tract.

The road crosses a deep ravine by a very lofty bridge, called Pont de la Vallée, shortly before entering

8 Droiturier.

7 St. Martin d'Estréaux is seated on a height, in the midst of a barren and hilly country.

7 La Pacaudière. Here we are once more in the valley of the Loire, though that river is not reached until, after passing

12 St. Germain l'Espinasse, we arrive at

12 *Roanne* (*Inns:* none good; H. du Centre; Poste, best; two call themselves H. du Midi), a town of 12,000 Inhab., deriving importance from its situation on the l. bank of the Loire, at the point up to which it is navigable against the stream as well as downwards. It has a great transit trade: the manufactures of Lyons, the iron and coal of St. Etienne, the productions of the S. provinces of France, and the imports from the Levant, conveyed hither from the Rhône by railway or canal, are transported hence, down the Loire, to Nantes, or through it, and the Canal de Briare, to the Seine and Paris. There are also considerable manufactures of cotton in the town and its neighbourhood. There is an old *Ch. St. Etienne*, rebuilt 1549, near the château, and a *bridge* over the Loire which cost 3 million francs.

The *Railroad* from Roanne to St. Etienne and Lyons is described in Rte. 119; it is very inferior, as a line of conveyance, to those in the vicinity of Paris. Carriages are not taken by it. The Loire is crossed by a fine stone bridge on leaving Roanne, and the road proceeds across the plain for some distance parallel with the railroad. About half way to

17 St. Symphorien-en-Lay, the ascent of the Montagne de Tarare begins. The ascent has been made comparatively easy by a truly alpine road, carried up in a series of zigzag terraces, sweeping round the shoulders of the hills, and crossing the gorges on handsome bridges of masonry, protected, at the sides, by stone studs like milestones.

15 Pain Bouchain. Near this is the summit of the pass, about 3000 ft. above the sea. You reach the foot of the descent at

12 Tarare (*Inn:* H. de l'Europe, beds clean; fare middling—*W. M.*; le Soleil), a wonderfully thriving manufacturing town of 7762 Inhab., seated in a narrow valley. The weaving of *muslins*, remarkable for their fineness, is the staple branch of manufacture, and it is calculated that between 3 and 4 millions of pieces are produced annually. It is said that as many as 52,000 persons are employed

in the town and surrounding country on this branch of industry. The weavers ply their trade in damp cellars, which are neither floored nor warmed by fire, in order to keep up the moisture necessary for weaving fine webs, and to prevent the breaking of the thread.

The road continues along the narrow valley of the Tardine from Tarare to

11 Arnas, where the country opens out.

19 Salvagny.

A few m. to the l. of the road is the copper-mine of Chessy, which produced the beautiful blue ore of copper so well known to the mineralogist, but it is now abandoned.

As you approach Lyons the scene becomes extremely fine, and immediately above the city you look down upon it, extending along the banks of the two great rivers, surrounded by an amphitheatre of hills. Handsome country seats, gardens, and vineyards are dotted over the landscape, bespeaking the wealth and prosperity (in a mercantile sense) of the district. As the town is entered by the quay of the Saône, it assumes a most picturesque character, the grey rough rocks forcing themselves, as it were, into the city, protruding between the lofty houses—a singular mixture of nature and art.

14 Lyons, described in Rte. 108.

ROUTE 106.

DIJON TO CHÂLONS-SUR-SAÔNE BY BEAUNE, AND THE WINE DISTRICT OF THE CÔTE D'OR, CHAMBERTIN, CLOS-VOUGEOT, NUITS, ETC. — PARIS AND LYONS RAILWAY (B).

69 kilom. = 43 Eng. m. 6 Trains daily in 2 hours.

Dijon is in Rte. 104.

This Railroad carries the traveller along the skirts of the vineyards, producing the *Burgundy wines*, which rank amongst the best and most famous in France. The country, wherever it presents an advantageous slope, is entirely laid out in vines, and what it loses in picturesqueness it gains in richness. It is besides very populous; there are said to be 40 or 50 villages between Dijon and Beaune, a distance of 26 m.

"About 1 m. S.W. of Dijon begin the hills which form the celebrated *Côte d'Or*, which, judging by the eye, average from about 800 to 1000 ft. in height, continuing to range at the distance of about a m. from the road. It is a wall of hills, covered with vineyards, which ascend in terraces their sunny sides, and then spread along the table-land on the summit. The colour of the soil, as seen through the well-trimmed tufty vines, is of yellowish red; and it may be asked whether the name of the range arises from this prevailing colour of the ground, or from the richness of the product. Here the best Burgundy is grown, and here, as in almost all other vine countries, we find the singular and perplexing phenomenon (but perhaps nowhere so forcibly apparent as here), that whilst one tract of small extent produces the finest quality, another hard by, enjoying the same aspect, and as far as we can judge, either by our unaided senses or by chemical tests, the same soil, can never be made to bring forth a wine of equal flavour. In richness of flavour and in perfume, and all the more delicate qualities of the juice of the grape, they unquestionably rank as the finest in the world; and it was not without reason that the Dukes of Burgundy were designated as the 'princes des bons vins.' The soils on which these valuable wines are grown consist, in general, of a light black or red loam, mixed with the *débris* of the calcareous rocks upon which they repose. The principal vineyards of the *Côte d'Or* are all situated between Dijon and Chagny, and describe an *arc* of a large circle exposed to the S.E. and protected from the N.W. by the range of hills that stretches behind them. The vines are planted in trenches, at the distance of about 2 ft. apart, and are trained on poles to the height of 30 to 40 inches. In the best vineyards they are extremely old, and when old vines are replaced by others, a larger crop, but of an inferior quality, is obtained. The choice red growths of the *Côte d'Or*, are the Clos-Vougeot, Nuits, Beaune, Volnay, Pomard, Chambertin, Richebourg, Romance, and St. George. They are all distinguished by their beautiful colour and exquisite flavour and aroma, combining, in a greater degree than any other wines, the qualities of lightness and delicacy with richness and fulness of body. Many other crops are intermixed with the vineyards,—potatoes, clover, and maize, —whilst cherry, almond, and walnut trees are dotted over the fields. One need not wonder that the Kings of France should have coveted this rich Burgundian territory. This is about the highest latitude N. where maize can be grown to any advantage."—*F. P.*

Gevray Stat. Here is the vineyard of *Chambertin*, about 15 or 20 acres in extent, but divided among numerous proprietors.

Vougeot Stat. The enclosure (*Clos*) *de Vougeot* produces the prince of Burgundy wines. It originally belonged to the monks of the neighbouring Abbey of Citeaux, who carried its culture to the highest perfection, never selling it, but making presents of what they did not consume themselves. At the Revolution it was bought by MM. Tourlon at Revol, and still later was resold to M. Ouvrard (?) and Aguado, the loan contractor. Its recent proprietors have enlarged it by taking in some of the neighbouring land; but the present extent of the vineyard is only 112½ English acres (48 hectares): the average annual produce is about 200 hogsheads. The soil near the top of the hill consists of small fragments of whitish limestone, mixed with shells, of which the hill is composed: in the lowest part of the vineyard it merges into a nearly pure clay. The vines nearest the top, in the dry soil, produce the best wine; on reaching the clay it falls off, and becomes the mere vin du pays.

"The vintage is in general soon over, the proprietor employing often from 400 to 450 vintagers at the same time. For the red wine, the grapes as they are brought in are thrown into large cases or troughs, and there trodden by a number of men, with large wooden shoes, till the grapes are nearly all broken. They are then taken up in baskets, with interstices wide enough to allow the grapes to pass through, when a portion of the stalks, generally about two-thirds, are taken out. If the whole of the stalks were taken out, the quality of the wine, as has been repeatedly proved, would be inferior. The whole is then put into the vat into which the *must*, as it ran from the treading, had been previously carried. A space of about 12 inches is left unfilled at the top, and a sliding lid is then put over, which floats upon the surface. As soon as the fermentation becomes violent, the swelling of the mass lifts the lid to the height of six inches above the mouth of the vat. As, however, the skins and the stalks had previously risen to the surface, none of the liquor escapes. A very small space, formed by the looseness of the lid, is considered sufficient to allow the gas to escape, until the rising of the lid allows a greater space; and it is perhaps owing to the confinement of the gas that the lid is raised to such a height. If the weather had been very warm when the grapes were gathered, and still continues warm while the fermentation is going forward, the wine is soon made. The fermentation is sometimes over in 30 h., at other times it continues 10, 12, and even 15 days, The best wine is always produced from the most rapid fermentation. When the fermentation slackens, the liquor begins to subside, and, when it is entirely over, sinks within the top of the vat, but not so low as when the vat was first filled, for the *marc*, or, in other words, the stalks and skins, are completely separated from the liquor, and float upon the top.

"As soon as it is known by the subsiding of the head, and by the taste and examination of the wine, that the fermentation has ceased, the wine is drawn off into large casks, which contain about 700 gallons each. Every 3 or 4 months it is pumped by means of the syphon and bellows into another vat of the same dimensions, when a man enters by the small opening left in the end of the vats, and washes out, with a brush and cold water, any lees which may have been deposited. The Burgundy of the Clos-Vougeot receives no other preparation, and it is treated in this manner as often as may be judged requisite, till it is disposed of. They commence selling it when 3 and 4 years old, but the wine of very favourable seasons is retained by the proprietor till it is 10 or 12 years old, when it is bottled and sold at the rate of 6 fr. a bottle. The price of the wine of ordinary vintages, from 3 to 4 years old, is from 500 to 600 fr. the hogshead, but seasons occasionally occur when the wine is not better than the *Vin Ordinaire* of the country."—*Busby*.

Nuits Stat., a town of 2700 Inhab., in the midst of the celebrated vineyards Romanée, Richebourg, La Tache, &c. The *vins de Nuits* were brought into fashion 1680, by Louis XIV., for whom they were exclusively prescribed by the chief physician, Fagon, as a means of restoring his strength.

[6 or 7 m. E. of Nuits is the celebrated *Abbey of Citeaux*, founded 1090 by Robert de Molesme, in which St. Bernard assumed the cowl 1113, which sent forth to assume the keys of St. Peter no less than 4 popes, and which numbered 3600 tributary convents of the Cistercian order, of which it was the head. Great part of the abbatial buildings still exist, and are used as a Penitentiary; near them is a large Agricultural College.]

15 *Beaune Stat.* (*Inns*: Poste;—H. d'Angleterre) contains 10,800 Inhab., and owes its prosperity to its being the chief seat of the *wine trade in Burgundy*, about 80 mercantile houses being engaged in it; the annual exportation amounts to 30,000 or 40,000 butts.

The *Hospital* (Hôtel Dieu), founded by Nic. Rollin, chancellor of Philip Duke of Burgundy, 1443, presents in its court some good bits of Gothic, and there is a fine Gothic hall. Here is a remarkable early painting, a Last Judgment, by *Albert van Ouwater*. The Bouzeoise, a limpid stream full of green weeds floating with its current, traverses the town.

Beaune is the birthplace of the senator Monge, the savant and favourite of Napoleon.

Coaches daily to Autun (Rte. 108).

[At *Cussy la Colonne*, 12 m. S.W. of Beaune, is a Roman pillar or monument, bearing bas-reliefs; but it is accessible with difficulty by cross roads. At *Nolay*, near it, Carnot, the republican general and engineer, was born.]

The country immediately about Beaune has much amenity, and in its neighbourhood are produced the wines of Volnay and Pomard, the former being characterised by its light and grateful aroma and delicate tint, the latter having more body and colour: they are sometimes mixed with the red wines to give them fire. Savigny, Beaune, Meursault, and several other vineyards in the neighbourhood, all produce excellent wines, and, generally speaking, all the growths of that district are remarkable for the purity of their flavour.

Meursault Stat. A vineyard.

Chagny Stat. This town is full of interesting subjects for the sketch-book, particularly of domestic architecture; one house in the principal street, with a row of trefoil windows, is particularly striking. The tower of the *Ch.* is also curious; it is a perfect specimen of the transition into the Pointed from the Norman style.

16 *Châlons-sur-Saône Stat.*—(*Inns*: Trois Faisans;—H. du Parc; H. de l'Europe.) The Saône, which runs through this town of 15,719 Inhab., and which, from this point, becomes an important river, navigable for steam-boats, gives it much water-side activity. The *Canal du Centre*, which joins the Saône to the Loire, commences here, and affords an outlet for a considerable traffic and transit of goods to the Mediterranean and Atlantic from the central departments of France. Châlons is the Cabillonum of Cæsar, whose Commentaries should be one of the handbooks of every traveller through the districts of Gaul. A fine granite column, standing, or rather raised, on one of the Places, is unquestionably a relic of the Roman age.

The town is dull, but clean, for France; and there is little worth seeing. But the quai, facing the river, is lined by good houses, and is the most lively portion. The *Cathedral* (St. Vincent), lately restored, in tolerably good taste, with the addition of 2 new towers, is in the early Gothic, when the peculiarities of that style were beginning to mix themselves with the older Romanesque. The *Hospital of St. Laurent*, on the island in the Saône, has some good painted glass, which, it has been suggested, should be removed to the cathedral. At present it is necessary to traverse the sick ward in order to see it. The date of this vaulted dormitory, and of the hospital itself, is 1528.

Steamers down the Saône to Lyons in Rte. 108.

Diligences daily to Lyons; to Autun; to Geneva.

Abélard died (1142) at the Abbey of St. Marcel, about 2 m. from Châlons, now destroyed except the Ch.; he was buried there, but afterwards removed to the Paraclet.

Railway to Paris in 10 hours.

ROUTE 107.

NEVERS TO CHALONS-SUR-SAÔNE, BY CHÂTEAU-CHINON AND AUTUN.

154 kilom. = 101½ Eng. m.

Diligences daily from Nevers Stat.

Railway from Orleans and Vierzon is described in Rte. 105.

19 Maison Rouge (Nièvre).

22 Châtillon-en-Bazois. Hilly road, extensive views.

10 Moulin Mauguin.

15 Château-Chinon, an ancient town (Pop. 3000), built on a considerable height, with traces of old fortifications, not far from the sources of the Yonne. Under its walls Louis XI. beat the army of the Duc de Bourgogne, 1475, and put the inhabitants to the sword.

17 Pommoy.

20 *Autun.* (*Inns:* La Poste; Chablis good here;—La Cloche.) In September a fair is held which lasts the whole month: the inns are then intolerable, and the town one scene of bustle and confusion. The first view of this interesting city is very pleasing. It is supposed to have been the ancient *Bibracte*, capital of the Ædui, mentioned by Cæsar as "oppidum maximæ auctoritatis apud eos," but its name was changed, in the time of Augustus, into *Augustodunum*, modernised into Autun. Tacitus describes its importance as a fortress and great city, and states that the most illustrious of the youth of Gaul were educated here. "Autun, now a town of 11,094 Inhab., stands at the foot of a range of well-wooded hills. The Roman ruins, hoary-grey, situated low down near the river, distinguish themselves by their fine and peculiar forms. Amongst the masses of buildings, crowned by the cathedral and its lofty spire, is the *Temple of Janus*, as it is called, though without any sufficient authority, a square building, of which 3 sides are standing, near the river. It is denuded of ornaments, but imposing, from its proportions and its solidity. It probably dates from the time of the Lower Empire. *The Two Roman Gates* are beautiful and very perfect. They are both nearly on the same plan; double arches below, and ranges of smaller arches above, ornamented with pilasters. The *Porte d'Arroux* is Corinthian, the *Porte Saint André* Ionic. They are evidently of the Lower Empire, and the *purist* will find fault with the details; but if you will put away criticism, and enjoy the objects, the effect is most satisfactory. Nothing can be more charming than the appearance of the delicately-cut arches, coming off against the blue sky."—*F. P.* The *Roman walls of Augustodunum*, within which the present city has shrunk, are very massive and curious, and large fragments still very perfect exist.

Just without Autun, upon the Dijon road, is a singular pyramidal mass of masonry, called the *Pierre de Couars*. It is about 50 ft. in height, and was probably originally much more lofty. The facing is entirely destroyed. It is quite solid, and is probably sepulchral: antiquaries suppose it to be the tomb of Divictiacus (?).

Autun had a noble *amphitheatre*. The ruins are now encircled by other buildings, but the general site of the Roman city is a perfect mine of antiquities. Many were collected by the late M. Jovet. Here also is a fragment of the tomb of the wicked Brunehault, who was buried at the abbey of St. Martin, a curious structure, now razed to the ground.

The *Cathedral of St. Lazare*, lately repaired, exhibits an interesting variety in its style of architecture. The lofty spire, covered with foliaged crockets, is a masterpiece of Gothic; so also is the rood-loft, composed of delicate and elaborate filagree-work. But a large proportion of the building is in the Romanesque style, and displays the closest imitation of Roman art; indeed, it is copied from the neighbouring Porte d'Arroux. The elegant flamboyant decorations of the chapels in the nave, and especially of the door of the sacristy, a charming bas-relief of Christ and the Magdalene, in the chapel which serves as baptistery, the painted glass in the Chapelle St. Nazare, representing the genealogy of the Virgin, and the Martyrdom of St. Symphorien, by *Ingres*, deserve also particular attention.

In all parts of the city you may see the disjointed and lamentable fragments of the ancient edifices by which Autun was once adorned. There is a good collection of the *geology* of the district in the Petit Séminaire, of which the Abbé Landriot is superior.

St. Symphorien suffered martyrdom here for refusing to join a procession in honour of Cybele.

Autun, it will be remembered, was the see of *Bishop* Talleyrand.

Coach daily from Autun to Beaune Stat. (Rte. 106.)

Not far from Autun are the two valuable coal-basins of Epinac (to the N.) and of Creuzot, which are worked by pits, in some cases more than 650 ft. deep, and employ, together with the iron-works (usine), about 4000 workmen. Mineral oil for lighting the mines is obtained by a distillation from the bituminous schists accompanying the coal. The Romans used these very schists to line the walls of their houses at Autun.

At Creuzot are extensive iron-furnaces, but the iron-ore requires to be brought from a distance. From Epinac (where are considerable glass-works for making wine-bottles) the coal is transported on a tramway to the Canal de Bourgogne, and thence, by water, to Paris and Alsace. The Canal du Centre traverses the coal-field of Creuzot (see p. 365). There is a new very hilly road, direct from Autun to Mâcon (104 kilom.), by Marmagne (21 kilom.), Mont Cenis, and Cluny.

"Soon after quitting Autun you enter the forest of Morvan (p. 351). The road ascends, but with frequent dips. It is richly wooded, and some of the little glens are lovely. The sides of the road are clad with alder and beech, with here and there a fine oak-tree lifting up his head above his compeers. The rocks show between and amongst the verdure, and you see and hear the rushing of the little rills, dashing by or in the road."

17 St. Emiland. "Beyond St. Emiland you begin to find yourself in another climate. Vines reappear in great luxuriance, and, unlike other parts of France, they are often trained in festoons and arcades; a mode equally disadvantageous to the produce, and advantageous to the beauty of the scenery."—*F. P.*

14 St. Léger.
8 Bourgneuf.
12 *Châlons-sur-Saône.* (Rte. 106.)

ROUTE 108.

DESCENT OF THE SAÔNE.—CHÂLONS TO LYONS, BY MÂCON.

Railroad from Châlons to Lyons to be opened in 1854, except tunnel leading into Lyons.

Steamboats every day. The distance by the river is about 100 m. The voyage is far preferable to the land journey, and is performed in 5 or 6 h. descending. Meals are served on board. A steamer (le Parisien) ascends in little more than 7 h.; leaving Lyons at 5 A.M., it reaches Châlons by 12¼, in good time for the Express Train to Paris. The captain of the steamer will take charge of the carriage, embarking and landing it, and the luggage, and will forward them to and from the hotel. Some of the steamboats are not large enough to convey carriages. The *expense with* a carriage ought not to exceed that of posting, including the passenger's fare, but the charges vary. The steamers are liable to be arrested by too much water in the river, in which case there is not room for the vessel to pass under the bridges, as well as by too little, and to be delayed by fogs.

The post-road is good and picturesque. *Malleposte* daily, and *Diligences* run daily to and fro, but take 16 hrs., double the time of the steamer.

The *post-road* runs along the rt. side of the Saône, sometimes close to it, at others out of sight of it, but so little removed from it that the course by water or land may, without inconvenience, be described together.*

rt. immediately below Châlons is the mouth of the *Canal du Centre*, and a basin or dock for barges entering or quitting it.

The banks of the Saône are at first tame, but improve as you approach Lyons.

rt. †Tournus (*Inns:* Sauvage; H. de l'Europe; both tolerable), a town of 5311 Inhab., possessing a wooden bridge of 5 arches over the Saône. Its *Church*, formerly attached to a venerable abbey, now destroyed, is a very plain edifice, in the Romanesque style, but interesting to the student for its architecture and antiquity. It is surmounted by a central tower, flanked with Corinthian pilasters at the angles, and has 2 other towers at the W. end. Its nave, preceded by a narthex or vestibule supported on 2 rows of short thick pillars without capitals, is probably of the 10th centy. The nave is roofed with a series of cradle-vaults, placed transversely, separated by cross arches, so as to divide it into compartments.

In the Place de l'Hôtel de Ville is a granite column, reputed an antique.

The charming painter *Greuze* was a native of Tournus: the house where he was born is marked by an inscription: he died at Paris, 1805.

1. Fleurville, a bridge over the Saône.

* *Post Road.*—18 Sennecy.
From some of the eminences surmounted by the road, towards the E., you see the chain of the Jura, and, in favourable weather, the white snow of Mont Blanc, which may at first easily be mistaken for a cloud, distant as the crow flies about 100 miles.
† 10 Tournus.

1. St. Albin* has a curious, early pointed Gothic church; the windows lancet. The costume of the villagers is picturesque.

Near the river vineyards cover the slopes, which are a prolongation of the distant range of the hills of Charolois.

rt. *Mâcon.*†—(*Inns:* Le Sauvage; a view of the river; tolerable;—H. de l'Europe, on the Quay, good.) Mâcon was heretofore the capital of the country of the Mâconnois, and ruled by its own sovereigns from the time of Louis le Débonnaire until it passed to the house of Burgundy. The country was often settled as an appanage upon the younger branches of the family. The present population of the town, which is not flourishing, is 12,653: it is cheflieu of the Dépt. Saône et Loire. The conjoint devastations of the Huguenots, who exercised the greatest cruelties and atrocities here, and of the Revolutionists, have nearly denuded Mâcon of all its ancient religious structures; hence the necessity of erecting a new church, which, until recently, was an unheard-of event in France. The towers of the *Cathedral* are standing, but mutilated, together with a very small portion of the body of the building, now turned into a blacksmith's forge. The river is crossed by a *Bridge* of 13 arches. From it, but still better from a little *Esplanade* planted with poplar trees beyond it, a view of Mont Blanc may be obtained. In the neighbourhood of Mâcon are many very fine prospects of the ranges of the hills of the Bourbonnois and Charolois, the latter being a continuation of the Côte d'Or.

Mâcon is thus mentioned by Cæsar: "Tullium Ciceronem Matiscone, rei frumentariæ causa, collocat." It is the birthplace of the living poet and French politician M. Alphonse de Lamartine. His Château, St. Point, not far off, is sold.

Mâcon is the centre of a great trade in the *wine* grown in its arrondissement, though at some distance from the town itself, and from our road; at the foot of the hills on the W. The best sorts are the growths of Thorins and Moulin

* *Post Road.*—16 St. Albin.
† 14 Mâcon.

CENT. FRANCE. *Route* 108.—*Châlons to Lyons—The Saône.* 369

à Vent, which are red, and the Pouilly, a white wine. Romanêche, situated in the midst of this wine district, 12 m. from Mâcon, possesses an important mine of manganese, which gives activity to many manufactures.

[22 kilom. = 15 m. N.W. of Mâcon is *Cluny*, a large place (*Inn:* H. de Bourgogne), once famous for its ancient and wealthy *abbey*, of the order of St. Benedict, which, before the Revolution, had 600 religious houses dependent upon it, and enjoyed a revenue of 300,000 fr. a year. It was so utterly destroyed in 1789, that of its noble Gothic church, which had 5 aisles and double transepts, only the 2 towers remain, with some fragment of wall, and the *chapelle de Bourbon*, 15th centy. The town, which has a population of 4152, and carries on some manufactures, is built on the site and with the materials of the abbatial buildings. The *cloisters* form a sort of public square, and a fragment of the Abbot's Palace is converted into a private dwelling. Here is a government stud (*Haras*).]

The country on the l. bank of the Saône formed part of the ancient divisions of La Bresse and Dombes; its inhabitants are a primitive race, by no means enlightened.

The banks of the Saône acquire some elevation and picturesqueness below Mâcon; the Jura mountains being all along a feature in the view to the E.; the nearer hills studded with white châteaux and villages. The *Château de Corielles*, flanked by 4 round towers, stands at some distance off the road to the W.

rt. At St. Romain, a suspension-bridge.

l. Toissey, an ancient town of the principality de Dombes, partly hid by poplars and willows.

rt. Belleville.* A bridge.

About 13 m. to the W. is Beaujeu, capital of the province of Beaujolais, in the midst of a district famed for its wines.

l. Montmerle, a village situated below a considerable island, has a suspension-bridge: other bridges are thrown across at Fléchère, Beauregard, and at Frans, opposite to

rt. Villefranche.* "A small town; has rather a cheerful aspect. The *church* has been a beautiful specimen of the florid Gothic, though small."

There is a bridge at St. Bernard.

rt. Anse is the port of Villefranche.

l. *Trévoux* is an ancient town of 2239 Inhab., on the slope of a concave hill, surmounted by the ruins of its old *castle*. It possesses now no interest beyond that connected with the recollection of its having once been capital of the principality of Dombes, and the place where the Jesuits compiled and printed the very learned works called the 'Journal de Trévoux,' 1701, and 'Dictionnaire de Trévoux,' 1704, a sort of Encyclopædia. Their house remains, marked by the shield of arms of the Order of St. Ignatius.

Dombes was acknowledged as an independent state by the French kings (except Francis I.) from Philippe-Auguste down to Louis XIV., owing them only allegiance and aids of men in case of war. It had a parliament of its own, which met at Trévoux, and the right of striking money, down to 1762. It is supposed to have been the Roman Triviæ, near which Septimius Severus beat the army of his rival Albinus, and thus secured the empire for himself.

Through pretty scenery, between banks thickly scattered with habitations, the Saône, considerably contracted in width, passes under the richly-wooded heights called Mont d'Or, rising 1000 ft. above the river, on the rt., by Belle Ile,

l. Neuville, with its suspension-bridge, and

rt. Couson, opposite to

l. *La Roche Taillée*, so called from the cutting which Agrippa caused to be made through it, to allow the passage of one of the great Roman highways.

Lower down is *L'Ile Barbe*, the favourite retreat of Charlemagne, linked to either bank by a suspension-bridge. (See p. 378.)

* 14 Villefranche. Here the road turns away from the river, avoiding its windings, and following a nearly straight line by
18 Limonest.—Hills, and long descent into
11 LYONS. (Route 105.)

* *Post Road.*—13 Pontaneveaux.
11 La Croissée.

R 3

The valley of *Rochecorbon*, with its wood and fountain of *Roset*, was a favourite haunt of Rousseau.

1. La Tour de la Belle Allemande (described p. 375), and
rt. Pierre Scise. (See p. 374.)

The entrance to Lyons has been compared to the "approach to Bristol under the slopes of Durdham and King's Down, and the rocks of Clifton Hot Wells; but the river Saône is larger, and the cliffs not so high."

LYONS (French, Lyon).—*Inns:* H. d'Univers, Rue de Bourbon;—H. de l'Europe, good;—H. de Provence, et des Ambassadeurs, opposite the Post Office, in the Place Bellecour;—H. de Rome, Place St. Jean, quiet, no tabled'hôte;—H. du Nord, a well-kept house, cuisine good, chiefly for bachelors, not far from the H. de Ville;—H. du Parc.

There are few more stately cities, in external aspect, in striking situation, seated as it is on two great rivers, the Rhône and Saône, or in the lively air of bustle and commerce diffused through its interior, than Lyons, the second city of France, the chief seat of manufactures, the focus where the commerce of the North and South converges. It is a fortress of 1st class, and chef-lieu du Dépt. du Rhône. Its pop. amounts to 155,169, or 200,000 including its suburbs.

The appearance of grandeur, however, is limited to its quais, bridges, and noble rivers, to the steep and commanding heights of Fourvières on the rt. of the Saône, and to the two Places Bellecour and des Terreaux; it is deficient in fine streets and long open thoroughfares. The interior is one stack of lofty houses, penetrated by lanes so excessively narrow and nasty as not to be traversed without disgust.

It is worth the stranger's while to remember, as a clue to find his way through this labyrinth, that the streets whose names are written on black plates run parallel with the course of the two rivers, those on yellow plates at rt. angles to them.

Lyons stands on both banks of the Saône and Rhône, but the largest part occupies the tongue of land between these two rivers, extending from the heights covered by the populous suburb of La Croix Rousse, the residence of the silk-weavers and the hot-bed of insurrection, down nearly to the confluence of the rivers, towards which the quarter of Perrache has pushed forward buildings. On the l. bank of the Rhône are the suburbs of Les Brotteaux, the scene of revolutionary executions, and of Guillotière, where a new town is rapidly rising; on the rt. bank of the Saône, the suburbs of Vaise, through which you enter Lyons from Paris, of Fourvières, mounting up the face of a slope so abrupt as scarcely to be accessible for wheel carriages, of St. Irénée behind it, and of St. George, lower down, near the water-side. These dry topographical details will be best understood when the traveller has scaled the Height of *Fourvières*, which *he should do the first thing after his arrival*, on account of the view it commands. To reach it you pass between the Palais de Justice and the cathedral, ascending the steep and narrow streets above the cathedral, which are very foul and stinking.

You pass behind the huge straggling hospital of *Antiquailles*, occupying the site of the Roman palace in which Claudius and Caligula were born, now assigned to the reception of 600 patients, the most miserable wretches of this populous city, afflicted with madness and all sorts of incurable and disgusting diseases, to the care of whom 27 Frères Hospitaliers and 67 Sœurs devote their lives. Up narrow lanes, and steep stone stairs, partly in front of shops in which rosaries, medals, pictures, candles, and wax models of different parts of the body for suspension in the church, are displayed before the eyes of devout pilgrims, you reach The *Ch. of Notre Dame de Fourvières*, whose lofty dome is crowned by a colossal gilt copper figure of the Virgin: it is only remarkable for the quantity of ex-votos, paintings, &c., to the number of 4000, with which its walls are covered, offered to the altar of the miracle-working figure of our Lady of Fourvières, whose intercession is stated, by an inscription over the entrance, to have preserved Lyons from the cholera. Close beside the

Ch. a speculator has built a *tower*, by way of observatory, 630 ft. above the Saône, and from it, even better than from the terrace beside it, a most magnificent view may be obtained. The city of Lyons appears unrolled as a map beneath your feet, including the two noble rivers visible to their junction, the Saône crossed by 8 or 10 bridges, the Rhône by 7. Beyond it stretch fields, plains, and hills, dotted over with country houses, and the distance is closed (in clear weather) by the snowy peak of *Mt. Blanc*, nearly 100 m. off, this being one of the farthest points from which it is seen. More to the S. the Alps of Dauphiné, the mountains of the Grande Chartreuse, and the Mont Pilas appear. The Ch. of Notre Dame is seated on the very summit of the hill, and is said to occupy the site, and retain the name, of the Roman *Forum Vetus*, built by Trajan. Numerous but inconsiderable Roman remains have been brought to light on the hill, the principal being an amphitheatre within the *Jardin des Plantes*, and a fragment of an aqueduct.

In the faubourg St. Irénée, behind Fourvières, is the *Ch. of St. Irénée*, an uninteresting modern building, but erected on the grave of that saint and martyr, and upon subterranean vaults, in which, it is said, the early Christians met for prayer, and were afterwards massacred, by order of Septimius Severus, A.D. 202. In the midst of this crypt, an ancient Romanesque building, resting on plain columns, is a sort of well, down which the bodies of the Christians were thrown, until it overflowed with the blood of the 19,000 martyrs, for such is the number reported to have fallen, according to the legend, and a recess is filled with their bones.

The upper Ch. was destroyed, and the crypt much injured, by the Calvinists, 1562.

The *Cathedral of St. Jean Baptiste*, on the rt. bank of the Saône, has 4 towers, two of which flank the W. front, and two, more massive, but shorter, from the transepts. The W. front is the most recent part, not having been completed until the reign of Louis XI.: its bas-reliefs and statues are curious, but they have suffered from the Calvinistic iconoclasts of the 16th centy.; these injuries have usually, but unjustly, been attributed to the infamous Baron des Adrets, since he was not in Lyons at the time when they were perpetrated. "The greater portion of the cathedral is of the age of St. Louis; but, though Gothic, the attentive observer will remark some curious imitations of Roman ornaments, particularly in an incrusted band or frieze of red and white marble, composed of masques and foliage, copied from the antique, with considerable exactness, running round the principal apse. The painted glass windows are remarkably fine. The centre tower, which opens into the cross, contains a rose window, which produces a peculiarly good effect. In a side aisle, on the floor, stands the once celebrated clock, made or built by Nicholas Lippeus of Basle, in 1508. It is very much like that at Strasburg, exhibiting various processions of little figures, the courses of the sun and moon, and the like; but it is quite out of repair; and to be called in action it requires the administration of half a franc to the sacristan."—*F. P.* "The clerestory presents an interesting series of windows, giving, in order, the gradations from plain lancets and circles, without foliation, or even a containing arch, to the perfect mullioned window, with flowing tracery" (*Petit*), a good lesson for the student. *The Bourbon chapel*, built by the Cardinal Bourbon and his brother Pierre, son-in-law of Louis XI., is remarkable for its ornaments, principally flowers and foliage of the most delicate sculpture. Amongst them the thistle or *chardon* is repeatedly introduced; a pun or rebus, allusive to the *cher-don* which the king had made to Pierre in the gift of his daughter.

"The see of Lyons, the religious metropolis of the Gauls, ascends to the era of the primitive church, its founders having been St. Pothinus, an Asiatic Greek, in the 2nd centy., and St. Irenæus, disciples of the apostles, both of whom suffered martyrdom here. Before the Revolution the cathedral enjoyed many high privileges. The canons had the title of Counts of Lyons: and in the service many ancient usages are retained; amongst others, yellow or native wax alone was used for the tapers, and no instrumental music was allowed. Adjoining the cathedral is a building, part of the ancient *Archiepiscopal Palace*, which seems to be of the 9th centy. According to popular opinion, Becket lodged here; but as it is not known that he visited Lyons, though Anselm did, the two archbishops may have been easily confounded; several anthems and hymns yet sung in the cathedral are said to have been composed and set to music by Becket."—*F. P.*

On the quai, a little above the cathedral, opposite the Pont Seguin, destroyed by the flood of 1840, is the new *Palais de Justice*, a handsome building, faced with a colonnade of 24 pillars. Baltard is the architect.

On the opposite side of the Saône, about ½ m. lower down, at the end of a street running up from the Pont d'Ainay, is the *Church of the Abbey of Ainay*, a very remarkable monument, both of Pagan and Christian antiquity. "The centre of the cross is supported by 4 ancient granite columns, supposed to have belonged to the altar erected at the confluence of the Rhône and Saône (which originally met close to the Ch.), in honour of Augustus, who resided for 3 years at Lyons, by the 60 nations of Gaul. In the representation of that altar existing on medals there are only 2 pillars, 1 on either side of the altar, each supporting a statue of Victory; but these lofty columns, each of a single shaft, having been cut in two, now form the 4 supporters, of somewhat low proportions, to the central lantern." The measurements of the diameter of the sections in each pair show how they were joined. Their capitals, an imitation of the Corinthian, are mediæval. The original capitals were Ionic. The Ch., as a building, was in existence before 937 (its foundation as a monastery was much earlier), and these are possibly of that æra. The outer tower is probably Carlovingian; but the building has recently been restored, in some parts awkwardly, so as to prepare much perplexity for the antiquarians who are yet unborn. Beneath the sacristy are the *dungeons* in which Pothinus and Blandina were immured previously to their martyrdom.

"The sufferings of these witnesses for the truth rest upon a document of great authenticity, the Epistle of the Churches of Vienne and Lyons to the Brethren in Asia and Phrygia. Pothinus, chosen bishop of Lyons, and then 90 years of age, was sent back into this dungeon, where he expired after two days' confinement. For Blandina, who was a converted slave, greater tortures were reserved. After being scourged and exposed to the fire in an iron chair, she was delivered over to the beasts in the amphitheatre. These events took place during the persecution under Marcus Antoninus, the implacable enemy of Christianity, A.D. 177.

"These dungeons are gloomy cells, without light or air, below the bed of the adjoining river. The apertures by which they are entered are so low that you must creep into them upon hands and knees. They adjoin a crypt which, until the Revolution, was used as a chapel: traces of Roman work are here distinctly seen. It has been restored to use.

"The middle-age name of Ainay is *Athenacum*, and most of the historians of Lyons are unanimous in supposing that it is built upon the site of the *Athenæum* founded by Caligula, and the buildings of which joined to or included the Augustan altar. It was a school of debate and composition, in which pleaders competed for the prize. Great honours were bestowed upon the successful competitors; but those who failed were liable, according to the statutes of the imperial founder, to the most severe and humiliating punishments—to be chastised with a ferula, or thrown into the river, and to obliterate their own compositions by licking them out with the tongue: hence even the most gifted would approach the altar with trepidation and fear" (*F. P.*), and hence the line of Juvenal—

"Palleat, ut nudis pressit qui calcibus anguem,
Aut Lugdunensem rhetor dicturus ad aram."

Some other remarkable churches, &c., have been spared:—*St. Nizier*, a splendid example of the flamboyant Gothic. The bosses of the arched roof are curiously pointed. The portal, in the style of the Renaissance, is a work of the architect Philibert Delorme, in the 16th centy. Several hundred of the insurgents in the insurrection of 1834 were pursued within the walls of this church by the soldiery, and killed there.

St. Pierre has a curious Carlovingian portal, in perfect preservation, though barbarously coated with oil-paint.

The square called *Place des Terreaux*, one side of which is occupied by the Hôtel de Ville, and another by the Museum or Palais des Beaux Arts, was the scene of the execution of Cinq Mars and De Thou: "they perished on the scaffold, the one like a Roman, the other like a saint;" thus atoning for their share in a conspiracy against the unrelenting Cardinal Richelieu. Here also, in 1794, the guillotine was erected, and actively kept at work until the square became so flooded with human blood, that the Terrorist chiefs, fearing to rouse the sensibility of the people, resolved on a wholesale massacre, by musketry and grape, in the Brotteaux, on the other side of the Rhône.

The *Hotel de Ville* (1447-55), with its lofty roofs and bold projections, is not unworthy of the ancient consulate, who, before the Revolution, were a most influential and useful magistracy, though much reduced in authority by Henri IV. In this building sat the Revolutionary Tribunal which, under Challier before the siege of Lyons, and after it under Couthon, Collot d'Herbois, and Fouché, despatched so many thousand victims to perish by the guillotine and the fusillade. Collot d'Herbois, the chief of these tyrants, had been an actor, and in that capacity had been hissed off the stage of Lyons. He vowed vengeance against the town in consequence of this affront; and amply did the savage glut his desire for it.

The *Palais des Beaux Arts*, or Museum, in the ancient convent of St. Pierre, contains some very remarkable specimens of Roman antiquity. A *Taurobole*, or square altar, 5 ft. high. "The *Bronze Tables* containing the speech made by Claudius, when Censor, in the Roman senate (A.D. 48), on moving that the communities of *Gallia Comata* should be admitted to the privileges of the citizenship of Rome—an act of the highest national importance. They are beautifully cut, and the letters are as sharp and as legible as if they had just issued from the engraver's hands. In these engravings we have probably the very words or composition of Claudius himself. They were discovered in the year 1528, on the heights of St. Sebastian. Claudius was born at Lyons on the very day when the altar of Augustus was consecrated.

"In contemplating a relic of this description in the city to which it belongs, we become sensible how much of its interest would be diminished by depositing it in any situation out of its proper locality. A very fine mosaic pavement, representing the *games of the Circus*, in which the Spina, and the gates whence the chariots started for the race, are fully given, was found at Ainay, 1800. Several other pavements were found in or near the city, including one of Orpheus and the Beasts, brilliant in colour, with many sepulchral and other inscriptions."—*F. P.*

The legs of a bronze horse, extracted from the bed of the Saône, are remarkable.

In the *Picture Gallery* are several paintings of celebrated masters.—*Pietro Perugino*: The Ascension, the heavenly choir in the sky, the Apostles and Virgin below; one of the best works of the master, a magnificent painting; given to the city by Pope Pius VII. *Rubens*: St. Francis, St. Dominic, and the Virgin interceding for the world, against which the Saviour is about to launch his thunder; finely coloured, but coarse, profane, and offensive in the composition. The Adoration of the Magi. *Spagnoletto*: St. Francis after Death, as placed in the tomb by Gregory IV.; the ghastly glare of the eye and rigidity of the frame are truly, but somewhat painfully, represented. *Palma Vecchio*: Portrait of his daughter Violante (called a Titian), the same face by Palma existed at Dresden. *Caracci*: The Baptism in the Jordan. A Portrait of a Canon of Bologna. *Guercino* The Circumcision, very fine. *Teniers*: St. Peter delivered from the Prison, or rather soldiers gaming in the guardhouse; for what is called the subject is rendered merely an accessory. *Perugino*: St. Gregory and St. James. *A. Dürer* (?): The Empr. Maximilian and the Empress. A Portrait of Jacquart, inventor of the silk-loom named after him, by *Bonnefonds*. Portrait of *Mignard*, by himself. Portrait of William III. of England, *Van Heem*. Here are preserved *Poussin's* original drawings for the 7 Sacraments; also a small collection of majolica, porcelain, and Limoges ware.

A School of Design established at Lyons has been attended with remarkable success in improving the manufactures. A portrait of Jacquart, in imitation of an engraving, but produced by the loom invented by him, is both a monument to his memory and a proof of the skill attained by his townsmen.

In one of the apartments are placed the busts of some of the illustrious natives of Lyons, as Philibert Delorme, architect; Bernard Jussieu, the botanist; Jacquart, inventor of the silk-loom; Suchet, marshal of France; Poivre, governor of L'Ile de France, who introduced pepper.

The *Museum of Natural History* is very creditable to the town, by its extent; and most useful and instructive to the student, by its *excellent systematic arrangement*, according to orders, families, genera. It is tolerably well filled in all the departments of natural history; but where specimens of a genus are wanting, the place is supplied by a drawing.

Among the *minerals* are a very complete and valuable series of *marbles*, antique and modern, of Italy, France, &c. ; a suit of the blue and green copper-ores from the mine of Chessy, on the Saône, now abandoned. The mineralogical and geological topography of France is illustrated in a collection of rocks and fossils from the different departments.

"The *Bibliothèque Publique* is the best provincial collection in France. The consulate of the city took great pride in this institution, which was originally annexed to the college. It contains many manuscripts, and about 80,000 printed volumes. Amongst them are many valuable and all but unique articles of the early printers— the delight and despair of the bibliomaniac. During the siege of Lyons in 1793, the library suffered greatly from the bombardments and the cannonade to which the city was exposed. The roof of the library was beat down, large heaps of the books were covered by the rubbish, and it might have been wished that they could have continued so during the reign of the Convention. Some were carried to Paris ; others stolen. The foregoing were at least preserved for literature. But the library was turned into a barrack; the National Guard lighted their fires and boiled their coffee with the volumes, which they employed in preference to any other combustible; and a Juge de Paix in a different canton caused a cartload to be brought to him every décade for the same purpose; for, said he, they are all books of devotion, and we do not exactly seek truth in the age of reason."—*F. P.*

In the suburb of Vaise, on the rt. bank of the Saône, on the line of the old fortifications, and just above the road leading to Paris and Châlons, rise the scanty remains of the escarped rock of *Pierre Seise*, or Encise, so called from its having been cut through by Agrippa, in order to open a military road. It is now used as a quarry, and the proprietors are carting off the picturesque and beautiful by wholesale. Upon this rock stood a castle, formerly the dwelling of the Archbishops, and of which the central tower was remarkable for its symmetry. It was demolished during the Revolution, perhaps in consequence of the odium which it acquired by having been anciently employed as a state prison, and also because it was offensive to the inhabitants from its domineering over the town. In this castle Ludovico

Sforza, called Il Moro, was confined by Louis XII. ; he was afterwards removed to the castle of Loches, where, being occasionally confined in an iron cage, he sank under the misery he sustained. So closely was he incarcerated, that the exact time of his death is unknown: some writers place it in 1508, others in 1510. (See Rte. 56.)

Here also Card. Richelieu shut up M. de Cinq Mars, for conspiring against his authority and corresponding with Spain; and De Thou, the son of the historian, for not betraying the conspiracy.

Farther on, upon the opposite (l.) bank of the Saône, is an antique castle, surmounted by a lofty tower, called *Tour de la Belle Allemande*, from a tradition of a German damsel being immured in it while her beloved was shut up in Pierre Scise. He, as the story goes, having escaped, by leaping into the Saône, was swimming across the river to join her, when he was perceived by the castle guard, and shot at the foot of the tower.

"The charitable institutions of Lyons are numerous. The principal one is the *Hôtel Dieu*, on the quay facing the Rhône, between the Pont de l'Hôtel Dieu and Pont Guillotière: it is the most ancient, perhaps, now subsisting in France, having been founded by Childebert, and Ultrogotha his queen. The present edifice was built by Soufflot, architect of the Pantheon, but the front is recent. The plan of the building is that of a cross, and it is arranged upon the Panopticon principle. An octagon altar is placed under the central dome. From this the wards radiate, and the crucifix and the officiating priest can be seen from every bed in the hospital. The chambers are very lofty and spacious. Amongst other attendants are 150 sisters of charity."—*F. P.*

The building was destroyed during the siege of 1793, when filled with wounded, by shells and red-hot shot: a black flag, hoisted upon the building to avert the deadly shower, seemed only to attract towards it a larger share of the fire; and after the flames had been in vain extinguished 42 times, it was finally consumed. From an inscription discovered not long since in a courtyard of the Hôtel Dieu (once a Protestant burial-ground), it would seem that Mrs. Temple, daughter of Young, author of the 'Night Thoughts,' who died at Montpellier, 1736, was actually buried here. By the archives in the H. de Ville, it appears that 729 livres were paid for permission to inter her.

On the quay of the Rhône, below the Pont Guillotière, is the still larger *Hospice de la Charité*.

The *Place Bellecour*, one of the largest squares in Europe, perhaps too large, since it covers 15 acres, and only one side has any pretension to architectural merit, has been rebuilt since 1793-94. The bronze statue of Louis XIV. in the centre was restored by Charles X. On the capture of Lyons by the republicans, the total annihilation of the town, and of all its chief buildings, public and private, which had escaped the 11,000 red-hot shot and the 27,000 shells hurled against it during a bombardment of several weeks, was decreed by the National Convention, in order to humble the pride of the Lyonnais. The demolition of the houses of the Place Bellecour was directed by Couthon, who, borne on a litter, on account of illness, gave the signal by striking with a little hammer on the door of each condemned house, repeating the words "Je te condamne à être démolie au nom de la loi." A mob of discharged workmen and others of the lowest classes then hastened to carry into effect these commands. Lyons, the chief manufacturing town of France, was reduced to a heap of ruins, and the expense of merely pulling down amounted to 700,000*l.*—a sum larger than that which built the Hôtel des Invalides at Paris. Thus was fulfilled the decree of the Montagne, that "Lyons should no longer exist," that "even its name should be effaced," and that of "Commune Affranchie" substituted. This decree enacted also that a column should be erected on its ruins to bear these words:—

"Lyon fit la guerre à la Liberté;
"Lyon n'est plus."

The *Siege of Lyons*, which preceded this wanton razing of the town, was undertaken by the National Convention, to punish and bring back to their side the people of Lyons, who, irritated by the vexations, and horror-stricken by the tyranny, of the club of Terrorists and the municipality, had risen up in arms against them, and made prisoner, tried, and executed their president, the infamous Challier, a Savoyard, and once an abbé. In consequence 60,000 troops were collected from all quarters against this devoted town. Its defence was intrusted to about 30,000 of her citizens, who cheerfully manned the walls, resolving that their oppressors should not capture the place without marching over piles of ruins and heaps of dead. After an heroic resistance of 63 days, during which acts of the utmost bravery and scenes of the direst misery were exhibited, after all the surrounding heights had been gained by the enemy, and 30,000 persons had perished within the walls, famine began to arrest the power of all further resistance, and the town was yielded, Oct. 9, 1793.

The *Suburb of Perrache*, between the Saône and Rhône, receives its name from the architect who conceived and executed the plan of removing the confluence of these rivers, which, before 1770, were united a little below the church of Ainay, to its actual situation. He effected this by strong embankments; and the greater portion of the land thus gained is either built over, or is prepared for building. Here is the Terminus of the railroad to St. Etienne. (Rte. 118.)

In the Place Louis Napoleon is a statue of the Emperor, by Nieuerkerk.

Until the commencement of the present century the Rhône merely skirted the city, and Lyons may be said to have been confined to its rt. bank; or, as Gray in his letters humorously describes the confluence, "the Saône goes through the middle of the city in state, while he (the Rhône) passes *incog.* outside the walls, but waits for her a little below."

Since that time the l. bank of the Rhône has been covered over with houses, forming the suburbs of Brotteaux and Guillotière. Several streets of fine and lofty houses are now building here, and a new bridge in construction over the Rhône will connect them directly with the business quarter of the city. At the back of these new constructions an embankment has been formed, and a military canal dug, protected by forts, so as to serve the double purpose of securing the neighbourhood from the inundations of the Rhône and the attack of an enemy. In the *Brotteaux*, at the extremity of the street called Avenue des Martyrs, a *monumental Chapel*, in the form of a pyramid, perpetuates the memory of the miserable victims of one of the worst atrocities of the Revolution. After the siege and capture of Lyons, as narrated above, the guillotine proved too slow an instrument of slaughter of the accused or suspected victims, condemned, with or without cause, to suffer by the mandate of the revolutionary tribunal. The bloodthirsty and infamous tyrant Collot d'Herbois therefore conducted the prisoners, by 60 at a time, under the escort of soldiers, to a field beside the granary of La Part Dieu. Here, with their hands bound behind their backs, they were fastened by ropes to a cable attached to a row of willows; and at the end of the line two cannons, loaded with grape-shot, were so placed as to enfilade the whole. At the first discharge few fell dead; a second and third, directed against the poor wretches, mutilated, wounded, and deprived of their limbs a great number, but left the greater part still alive, rending the air with their agonizing shrieks, so that the soldiers were obliged to finish the work with their swords or the butt end of their muskets. So laborious was the task, and so imperfectly performed, that some were found breathing 12 hrs. after, when their bodies were covered with quicklime, and thrown into a hole for burial. These heart-sickening massacres were repeated, by the aid of grape-shot or musketry fired by platoons of soldiers, until the number of victims amounted to 2100. Collot d'Herbois and Fouché looked on while these deeds were done; and the former, when informed, on one occasion, that a band of prisoners about to be led forth to death exceeded by two the number condemned for execution, replied,

"Qu'importe ! s'ils passent aujourd'hui, ils ne passeront pas demain."

The miscreant Collot d'Herbois, exulting in his atrocities, forwarded from time to time to Paris reports of his proceedings to the Convention, from which these are extracts. He says of himself and colleague, "The sword of the law is falling on the conspirators at the rate of 30 at a time; that they have already despatched 200, and they were occupied, in the most unceasing manner, in the discharge of their functions." 3 days after he writes, "I send you a second list; the number now amounts to 300. A more grand act of justice is preparing; 400 or 500, with whom the prisons are filled, are one of these days to expiate their crimes: the stroke of powder shall purge them from the earth by a single discharge." In a vault beneath the chapel are shown about 200 skulls and skeletons, the relics of the miserable sufferers by this tyranny.

At the extremity of the suburb of La Guillotière is an ancient castle called *Château de la Motte*, in which Henri IV. was married to Marie de Medicis.

The *Bridges*. There are 7 over the Rhône:—the *Pont Morand*, of wood, opposite the Place des Terreaux, leading to Les Brotteaux, named after its architect, who perished by the hand of the revolutionary assassins; *Pont Lafayette* (formerly de Charles X.), of wood, on stone piers; *Pont de l'Hôtel Dieu*, a suspension bridge; *Pont de la Guillotière*, between the Hôtel Dieu and la Charité, leading to the Place Bellecour, is of stone, 539 yards long: it is the oldest of all the bridges, its foundation being referred to Pope Innocent IV., 1190, though no part of the present structure is of that age. The high road to Savoy passes over it. A very curious silver buckler, bearing a representation of the Continence of Scipio, in relief, was found at the base of one of its piers.

The bridges over the Saône, between L'Ile Barbe and La Mulatière, are 10 in number. The principal are *Pont de Tilsit*, a beautiful stone bridge, leading from the Place Bellecour to the Archevêché; the *Pont Seguin*, a suspension bridge (destroyed 1840), named after its engineer, opposite the Palais de Justice; and higher up, the *Pont du Change*, an old stone bridge.

The Quartiers des Capucins, between the Place des Terreaux and Croix-Rousse, and of St. Clair, are chiefly inhabited by rich capitalists and manufacturers. The former stretches up the foot of the hill of Croix-Rousse, separated from the faubourg of that name by a line of antiquated ramparts and bastions.

The *fortifications of Lyons* consist of 18 detached forts arranged in a circle of $12\frac{1}{2}$ m. around the town, crowning the heights of St. Croix and Fourvières, on the rt. bank of the Saône, and of Croix-Rousse, above the suburb of that name; and the circuit is completed round the fauxbourgs Brotteaux and Guillotière. They owe their origin to the fearful insurrections of the workmen and others, which took place as a consequence of the July Revolution in 1831 and 1834; and they are at least as much designed to repress intestine revolt as to withstand invasion from without. A garrison of 6000 men would suffice to defend them. The chief work, the *Fort Montessay*, is so constructed that its guns entirely command, and could level with the dust, the *faubourg of La Croix-Rousse*, the St. Antoine of Lyons, a moral volcano teeming with turbulence and sedition; while a fortified barrack on the Place des Bernardines separates it, at will, from the rest of the city. From this faubourg issued, in 1831 and 1834, the armed insurgents who for several days held possession of the town, having expelled the military, until an army could be assembled large enough to put them down, which was only effected with a loss of more than 1000 lives. In these revolts (for they were far too serious to fall under the name of riots), this ill-starred and ill-conditioned city experienced a renewal of many of the horrors, the bloodshed, and misery of the first Revolution. Many workmen were obliged to quit the town for their share in these disturbances, and settled in Switzerland. Even under a Republican government Lyons required a permanent army of 30,000 to enforce order —to do the work of police!

The Croix-Rousse is principally inhabited by silk-weavers, who live in densely crowded narrow streets, where 12 to 20 families are piled one above another in the lofty houses.

Silk is the staple manufacture of Lyons; in the extent of it she surpasses every other town of Europe. The manufacture of silk was first established in Lyons in the year 1450. In variety of design, in taste, in elegance of pattern, and in certain colours, the manufactures have a superiority over the English. "They can work 25 per cent. cheaper ; but the hand-loom weavers of Lyons are nearly as ill off as those of Spitalfields."—*Laing.* There are no huge factories here: the master, instead of having a certain number of workmen constantly employed in his own premises, merely buys the raw material, and gives it out to be manufactured by the weavers, dyers, &c., at their own houses, by themselves and their families. The patterns are produced by draughtsmen (generally a partner of the master manufacturer), and the laying or preparing of the pattern (mise en carte) is the province of another artiste. There are about 31,000 silk-looms in and about Lyons. The silk-weavers are, bodily and physically, an inferior race ; half the young men of an age for military service are exempted, owing to weakness or deformity. Of late manufactories of cotton, hardware, &c., have been established in Lyons; it is also the centre of money transactions with Switzerland and Italy.

The *Conseil des Prudhommes* is a commercial tribunal, composed half of masters, half of workmen, designed to settle disputes, respecting wages and such matters, between the two classes, and between masters and apprentices, in a spirit of conciliation. It is of immense service, and exists in other manufacturing towns, and might, perhaps, be imitated with advantage in England. Every workman is provided with a "livret de bonne conduite," in which particulars of his ability, industry, and conduct are entered from time to time, so that it serves as a passport for him when in want of work, provided it shows a good and steady character.

The *Condition des Soies* is an establishment in which the quality and goodness of raw silks brought hither for sale is tried, by exposing them to heat, at a temperature of $72\frac{1}{2}°$ to $77°$ Fahr. The weight of the silk is then ascertained, and marked by a sworn estimator, and fraud is thus prevented.

There are several *Theatres*, the chief one behind the H. de Ville, another in the Place des Célestins, which abounds with *cafés*.

The *Post Office* is in the Place Bellecour.

Omnibuses traverse the town from end to end; and *cabriolets* and fiacres stand in the Places des Terreaux and Bellecour, and on the Quai de Retz. N.B.—Before 8 A.M. a carriage costs 6 fr. for however short a distance.

Malleposte daily to Châlons in 6 h. thence to Paris by Rail in 10 h.; to Strasbourg in 36 h.

Diligences daily; 4 to Châlons-sur-Saône; to Turin by Chambéry in 38 h. ; to Aix-les-Bains ; to Avignon ; to Strasbourg, by Lons-le-Saulnier, Besançon, Belfort, Colmar; to Clermont, by Montbrison, to Grenoble; to Geneva in 13 h.; to Moulins and Nevers Stat. on the Rly. to Orleans.

Railways to Châlons; to Valence and Avignon in progress.

Railroad to St. Etienne. Office, Place Bellecour, whence omnibuses go to the terminus in the Quartier Perrache. Trains 3 times a day. (See Rte. 118.)

Steamers on the Rhône start for Vienne, Valence, Avignon, and Arles, every morning at 4 or 5 A.M., from the Quai on the Rhône (see Rte. 125) —to Valence at 1 p.m. stopping there for the night and resuming the voyage next morning.

Steamers on the Saône for Châlons, starting from the Quai (Rte. 106) every morning, from 4 to 6 A.M.

The *Environs of Lyons* are correctly described by Gray the poet: "The hills around are bedropped and bespeckled with country houses, gardens, and plantations of rich merchants and bourgeois." These villas are much more numerous than in the vicinity of Paris.

"*L'Ile Barbe,* an island in the Saône,

above Lyons, nearly surrounded by escarped rocks, and connected with the banks of the river by a wire bridge, was the frequent residence of Charlemagne; and at the upper extremity is a watch-tower, on which, according to tradition, the emperor sat and contemplated his Paladins, heading his army, as it marched along the banks of the river. This castle seems not older than the 15th centy.; and a chapel on the island dates, probably, from the 12th. Many curious antique fragments are dispersed in the island."—*F. P.*

A few Historical Notices of Lyons.—The ancient city of Lyons, the Roman *Lugdunum*, founded, according to Dion Cassius, by Munatius Plancus (B.C. 40), occupied the heights of Fourvières. Here Augustus and Severus resided. The central fountain in the *Jardins de Plantes* stands in the arena of a Roman Amphitheatre. Here still exist traces of the vast *Aqueduct*, constructed, it is said, by the soldiers of Marc Antony, when his legions were quartered here, to supply the town with water from the distant mountains of La Forez. It may be still traced for miles, crossing the valleys on arches, of which the most considerable remains are at Bionnat (6 arches), Chapponost, Chardonniers and Oullins.

Remains of Agrippa's 4 great roads, which met at Lyons, radiating thence to the Pyrenees, through the Cevennes, to the Rhine, to the Ocean through Picardy, and to Marseilles, may also be traced.

The settlement of the early Christians, and the persecutions they endured in the 2nd and 3rd centuries, have been alluded to in p. 372.

Lyons was possessed and governed by its archbishops, who held it by a grant from the Emperor of Germany, during the 12th and part of the 13th centy., and was not restored to the French crown until the reign of Philippe le Bel.

The silk manufacture was established here in the middle of the 15th centy. by Italian refugees, and was nearly ruined by the revocation of the Edict of Nantes, which dispersed most of its best workmen to Spitalfields, Amsterdam, Crefeld, &c.

The events which occurred at Lyons during the first Revolution have been detailed at p. 375.

In 1815 Lyons threw open its gates to Napoleon on his return from Elba; the troops intended to defend it having at once deserted the standard of the Bourbons, to gather round the tricolor, in spite of the exertions of the Comte d'Artois and Marshal Macdonald to keep them to their duty.

ROUTE 109.

MOULINS TO CLERMONT AND LE PUY.
VOLCANOES OF AUVERGNE.

To Clermont 95 kilom. = 59 Eng. m. *Malleposte* in 6 hrs. daily to Clermont, and in 36 to Montpellier.

A *Railway*, a continuation of the line from Orleans and Vierzon to Moulins, is in progress (1854) to Clermont, by St. Germain des Fossés, where it sends off a branch to Roanne.

Clermont to Le Puy, 122 kilom. = 75 Eng. m. *Diligences* daily.

Moulins is described in Rte. 105. This road contrasts agreeably with the monotonous dulness of that from Paris to Lyons, and is interesting from the natural beauties and rich cultivation of the country which it traverses; but, more than all, for the phenomena of the extinct volcanic mountains of Auvergne, through the midst of which it passes. It proceeds nearly due S. from Moulins, up the valley-plain of the Allier, the chief tributary of the Loire, first crossing by a bridge to its l. bank. The upper part of this valley above Aigueperse was anciently called *La Limagne*, and is believed to have been once a lake basin, in which were deposited the fresh-water marls, sands, &c., which now contribute so much to its fertility.

12 Châtel Neuve, or de Neuvre. The mountains of Forez, which divide the waters of the Allier from those of the Loire, are seen on the E.

12 St. Pourçain (*Inn*: Poste), a town of 4000 Inhab., on the Sioule. An Ecce Homo, carved in the stone, in the church here, is praised.

The road, leaving the Allier on the l. at St. Pourçain, ascends the vale of the Sioule. It is a flat and uninteresting stage to

16 Mayet d'Ecole.

8 Gannat. There is a road hence to the Baths of Vichy (Rte. 105). Our route is shaded by luxuriant walnut avenues.

The hill rising on the l. of the road, about 1 m. N.E. of Aigueperse, is called *La Butte de Montpensier*, and is composed of yellow marly limestones. There is a fine *view* from its top. Between it and the road is a *hole* which exhales carbonic acid nearly pure, so that small animals which come to drink from the pool of water which often collects at the bottom are apt to be suffocated. The common people, attributing this to the water, called it *La Fontaine empoisonnée*.

9 Aigueperse (*Inn*: Poste; comfortable) is the first town in the Dépt. Puy de Dôme, and is celebrated as the native place of the Chancellor d'Aguesseau, born at the Château de la Roche: his statue may be seen in the *Hôtel de Ville*. Its name is derived from "acqua sparsa," from the streams around it. The *choir* of the principal church, attached to an ugly modern nave, deserves notice as a pure specimen of the Gothic of the 13th centy.; its lofty roof is sustained by long graceful columns. Here is a painting of the Nativity, attributed to *Ghirlandajo*, in a stiff style (the figures said to be portraits of princes and lords of the Bourbonnais), and a St. Sebastian (?), locked up. There is also a *Sainte Chapelle* here, founded, 1475, by Louis, Dauphin d'Auvergne, inferior to one at Riom.

The Abbé Delille, author of 'Les Jardins,' was born here 1738.

"O champs de la Limagne, ô fortuné séjour,
J'ai revu les beaux lieux qui m'ont donné le jour."

The hill of Chaptuzat, on the rt. of the road, is quarried for building-stone; the rock is an oolite. Above it, and on many other eminences throughout the Limagne, beds of a tertiary limestone occur, entirely formed of the cases of insects resembling the caddis-worm, or May-fly, incrusted by carbonate of lime, and formed into a hard travertine, called "calcaire à friganes," or indusial limestone. The cases, or tubes, are coated over with shells of Paludina, often to the number of 100 around one tube, and 10 or 12 tubes are packed within the space of a cubic inch. These insects must have inhabited the lake which once covered the valley of the Limagne.

Near Riom the country becomes interesting, and exhibits the characteristic features of the scenery of Auvergne,—a rich vegetation and beautiful verdure, produced by the abundant irrigation; a varied outline of country, with towns, castles, and villages perched on the tops of eminences commanding the Limagne.

16 Riom (*Inns*: Colonne; H. du Palais; Ecu de France) is a town of 12,500 Inhab., the second in the Dépt. Puy de Dôme, in a cheerful situation, but built of dark lava from the quarries of Volvic, and paved with volcanic stones. It is encircled by boulevards planted with trees, in one part widening out into a platform called *Pré-Madame*, where a monument of granite has been raised to the memory of General Désaix. It is a perfect treasury of domestic architecture, chiefly of the Renaissance period.

The *Sainte Chapelle*, attached to the Palais de Justice, is, like that of Paris, a light and lofty lantern of stone, built 1382, the piers which support the roof forming the separations between the windows. It has, however, suffered material injury from being divided horizontally, by a floor, into 2 stories: the lower one is converted into a law court (Cour Royale), and is stripped of its painted glass in order to throw a light upon the proceedings; the upper one, turned into a record office, is filled with old musty deeds, so that its really beautiful stained windows can scarcely be seen.

St. Amable is a curious church, which will interest the architect and antiquary. The date of the nave, the oldest part, seems uncertain. The lower arches are pointed, and rest on piers, having engaged pillars on 3 sides, but plain on the inner face; above them runs a gallery of circular arches roofed with a demi-vault, which serves the purpose of a range of flying buttresses to support the roof of the central aisle. The little sculpture employed is very rude. The choir is in the Gothic style of the 13th centy. the arches alternately pinched up and expanding. The W. front and cupola above the cross are tasteless additions of the 17th centy.

About a mile from Riom, on the W., is the village of Mosac or Mosat, whose *church* has been attributed to Pepin ; but the only part which can be referred to the 8th or 9th centuries is the W. porch, now walled up. The nave, in the Romanesque style, seems to belong to the early part of the 12th centy., and is remarkable for the beautifully executed capitals of its columns: the only windows are in the aisle. The choir and rest of the church are of the 15th centy., and uninteresting. In the sacristy is preserved a silver-gilt *shrine*, in the shape of a sarcophagus, ornamented with enamels in the Romanesque style, made in the middle of the 10th centy. It contained the relics of Saints Calmidius and Numadia.

At *Volvic*, a few miles farther to the W. of Riom, are the vast *quarries* of lava which have furnished the stones for building that town and Clermont. The lava current in which they are excavated has issued out of the extinct crater called Puy de la Nugère. They are partly subterranean, partly open to the sky; they have been worked since the 13th centy., and give employment to the whole neighbouring population. The stone is porous, resembling trachyte, and contains specular iron in its cells; it is easily worked, and the bed furnishes blocks 20 ft. by 6 ft. in size. When first extracted, it is of a grey or slate colour, but darkens by exposure to the air ; it is used for rude works of sculpture. The *church* of Volvic is ancient.

Volvic is built at the foot of the volcanic cone called Puy de la Bannière, on the lava current which has flowed from it, and appears to have crossed and covered that from Puy de la Nugère.

On an eminence near Volvic stands the very romantic ruined *Castle* of *Tournoëlle*, in ancient times one of the strongest in Auvergne, so that it resisted long and stoutly a besieging army under Guy Dampierre and Renauld de Forez, Archbishop of Lyons, in 1213, and again 1590, when it was defended against the forces of the League by Charles d'Apchon. The remains are accessible by a steep path, and part of them are tolerably perfect: the oubliettes, or dungeon, entered only by a small hole from above, still exist under the round tower.

There is a footpath or horse-road direct from Volvic to Clermont.

About a mile before entering Clermont, the suburb of Montferrand, a cluster of narrow streets conspicuously seated on a limestone eminence, crowned by an old *church* dedicated to Notre Dame de Prospérité, is passed. It was anciently an independent town and fortress, and was called Montferrand le Fort. It was surprised and pillaged by the English, under Perrot the Béarnais, 1388. Froissart, in his Chronicles, recounts at length the story of its capture.

An avenue of trees, nearly a mile long, leads into

15 CLERMONT, or Clermont-Ferrand. —*Inns*: H. de l'Ecu ; very good. H. de l'Europe. H. de la Paix (Boyer's); good, and tolerably clean.

Clermont, once capital of Lower Auvergne, now of the Dépt. du Puy de Dôme, is a cheerful town, which, in consequence of recent improvements, has lost the gloomy character which once distinguished it, its houses, built of dull grey lava, being now whitewashed. Its principal interest is derived from its situation on a hill, composed chiefly of volcanic tuff, in the fertile Limagne, in the midst of a mountainous country, at the foot of that extraordinary range of extinct volcanoes which rear their conic or crater-shaped forms around, surmounted by the mountain of the *Puy* (*i. e.* Pic) *de Dôme*, whence the department is named, which, though apparently overhanging Clermont, is nearly 5 m. distant. The population amounts to 32,427, including the suburbs.

On the outskirts of the town, nearly all round its circuit, except on the N.W., runs a line of boulevards, or "places," the chief of which are the

Place de Jaude, a wide oblong dusty space on which fairs are held, surrounded by houses; the *Place de Taureau*, on which a monument has been raised to Gen. Désaix, a native of Clermont; and the *Place Delille*, by which the Paris road enters the town, named after the poet, who was also an Auvergnat.

Clermont is destitute of fine public buildings: the principal edifice is the *Cathedral*, externally an irregular pile of dark lugubrious hue, from the black lava of Volvic, of which it is built. It suffered serious injury from the frenzy of the Revolution, being stripped of its ornaments and monuments, and condemned by the mob to be levelled with the ground, but was saved by the exertions of a citizen and magistrate, M. Verdier Latour, under the pretext that it would be useful to hold popular meetings in. It is, notwithstanding, an interesting example of the mature pointed Gothic, begun 1248, and carried on till 1265, by the architect Jean Deschamps (J. de Campis), but never completed. The interior, therefore, is all of a piece, presenting one harmonious whole, remarkable for its lightness and loftiness, the vaulted roof (of tufa) being more than 100 ft. above the pavement. There are fine rose windows in the transepts. The painted glass is very beautiful; that in the choir is of the age of St. Louis (13th cent.), and displays his arms quartered with those of Spain: the glass in the large window of the nave is of the 15th and 16th cents., and inferior; it has, besides, suffered from a hailstorm in 1835.

In one of the side chapels of the choir is an ancient *sarcophagus* of white marble, adorned with sculptures well executed.

The *N. portal* suffered least at the Revolution, is very richly adorned with sculptures, and deserves notice.

From the top of the tower the stranger may survey to advantage the town, and the volcanic mountains, the valley of the Limagne, and the plateau of Gergovia, the scene of Cæsar's discomfiture. (See p. 387.)

The most ancient and interesting church, in an architectural point of view, is *Notre Dame du Port*, a Romanesque edifice of the 10th or 11th centy., judging from the evidence of style, but said to date from 870, and perhaps portions of the very curious *crypt* may be of that age. It is encrusted externally with rude mosaics. The tower above the W. door is modern (1823), but in tolerable taste: the S. doorway is surmounted by curious bas-reliefs, much mutilated, and partly hidden behind woodwork; yet Christ between two six-winged cherubims, and the Adoration of the Magi, and the Baptism of Christ, may be distinguished below. The interior possesses some modern painted glass by a native artist, M. Thévenot; and in the crypt is a black image of the Virgin, said to have been found at the bottom of the well, which is supposed to work miracles, and is resorted to by pilgrims on the 15th May.

In the N.E. corner of the town, not far from the last-named church, is the Place Delille, in the midst of which has been placed a fountain of elegant design in the style of the *Renaissance*, with some mixture of Gothic, executed 1515, for the Bishop Jacques d'Amboise. In the same quarter, on the l. of the road to Montferrand, is the *Cimetière de la Ville*, in whose chapel a curious antique sarcophagus, richly sculptured, has been converted into an altar.

In the Faubourg St. Alyre, to the N.W. of Clermont, and at the foot of the eminence on which it is built, rises a remarkable calcareous spring, called *Fontaine pétrifiante*, issuing out of a volcanic peperino resting upon granite. It resembles that of Matlock, except that its deposits are more copious and quickly formed, from the larger quantity of calcareous matter suspended by the carbonic acid with which it is impregnated. It has deposited in the course of ages a mass of travertine or limestone, 240 ft. long, 16 ft. high, and 12 ft. wide at its termination. It has formed over the rivulet a sort of natural bridge, *Pont de Pierre*, which is in fact nothing more than a huge stalactite, while a second bridge is in progress, and gradually increasing. So abundant is the quantity of lime held in solution in the water, that the pipes and troughs through which it passes would be chocked up with stone, were they not cleared out every 2 or 3 months. By breaking the fall of a jet of the water, and allowing its spray to descend upon any article subjected to it, such as bunches of grapes, baskets, nests, eggs, hedgehogs, &c., they become encrusted with the calcareous sediment, or petrified, as it is vulgarly called; and in this way even very fine casts are obtained from medals, &c.

The fountain and bridge are situated in a garden, within which is a bathing-house supplied from its waters.

The *Musée*, or Etablissement Scientifique, a building situated on the S. side of the town within the ill-kept but beautifully-situated botanic garden, contains—1. A collection of *Natural History*, particularly rich in the mineral products of Auvergne, which may be studied with advantage by the geological traveller previous to travelling through the country, as the specimens are arranged topographically. 2. The *Public Library* of 15,000 vols., including some curious ancient MSS., and a folio bible of the 12th centy., illuminated with vignettes.

Here is a statue of Blaize Pascal (b. 1623), and a bust of Delille, both Auvergnats.

In a corner of the Jardin Botanique, a number of antiquities, inscriptions, fragments of columns, &c., and a head in relief of the Gallic Mercury (?), dug up in the vicinity, have been deposited here, but are very little cared for, being exposed to the weather in the open air.

The terraced walks called Place du Taureau and Place de la Pôterne command fine views of the surrounding mountains.

Clermont has been the seat of several ecclesiastical *Councils*: the most remarkable was that held in 1095, which may be said to have lighted the spark of the crusades in Europe, the train having been laid by Peter the Hermit. It was convoked by Pope Urban II., who presided in person over the vast assembly at the head of his cardinals, of 13 archbishops, and 205 bishops. The place of meeting is supposed to have been an open space to the rear of the church of Notre Dame du Port. Here, from a throne raised in the midst, around which were grouped the tents of tens of thousands of enthusiastic hearers, the pope pronounced that eloquent discourse which melted all to tears, and was followed by the universal shout of "*Diex le volt*" (Dieu le veut); when the cloaks of red cloth worn by the noble bystanders were torn into shreds, to form the badge of the cross, then first adopted and laid on the breast of all who took the vow.

Clermont is supposed to be the ancient *Augustonemetum*.

Conveyances.—*Mallepostes* to Moulins Stat.:—to Montpellier, by St. Flour, in 60 hrs.

Railroad in progress to Moulins Stat.

Diligences daily to Moulins Stat. for Paris; to Lyons; to Le Puy and St. Etienne; to Montpellier, to Aurillac, to Alby and Toulouse, to Tulle, Limoges, and Bordeaux; to Bourges.

Small carriages and saddle-horses may be hired at a moderate rate, by aid of which numerous interesting excursions may be made in the

Environs, the beauties of which can be reached only by passing over a dreary intervening space of dusty road between high walls. It is not therefore advisable to make these excursions on foot.

The ascent of the *Puy de Dôme*, the highest mountain in the neighbourhood, 4846 ft. above the sea-level, is very interesting on account of the insight it affords into the geological phenomena of the district. It may be performed in the following manner:— You may hire a char-à-banc at Clermont for 8 or 10 fr. to go and return. No carriage can advance farther than to the foot of the cone, the rest of the ascent must be performed on foot; it is practicable on horseback if the beast be sure of foot: the distance is about 6 m. A steep, but well-engineered road, commencing at the barrier, passing at first over black basalt, and afterwards over the more modern lava, scoriæ, and calcined stones, which have issued from the Puy de Pariou, leads, in about 1½ hr., to the hamlet and cabaret of la Barraque, where the road divides, the l.-hand branch leading to the Puy de Dôme and Mont Dore, the rt.-hand to the Puy de Pariou and Pont Gibaud, and passing on the l. the ruined Castle of Montrodeix. A guide may be hired at la Barraque, and the carriage may proceed nearly to the base of the Dôme, beyond which is a very steep ascent, partly over coarse grass, mixed with bilberry bushes, partly over the bare crumbling rock of which the mountain is composed; a variety of trachyte, called Domite by the French geologists, because peculiar to this locality. It is so porous, that it retains no water on its surface, and the mountain in consequence does not possess a single spring. The summit is most easily accessible from the S., where a sort of zigzag path has been carried up its side. The Puy (pic) de Dôme rises to a height of 1600 ft. above the table-land around; it is the largest in mass and the most central of the group of volcanoes of Clermont. Viewed from the W. only has it the form of a dome, but its name is said to come from *dumus*, the thicket which once covered its sides. From the top the eye surveys the singular range of igneous mountains, craters, domes, lava currents (called *cheires* in the dialect of the country), and heaps of scoriæ, the produce of volcanoes, which, though extinct within the period of all human tradition, were once as active as Ætna or Vesuvius, and converted the surrounding district into the Phlegræan Fields of France. In many instances the vast lava currents, flowing across the country for miles, may be traced up to the funnel-shaped craters which poured them forth. The fertile Limagne lies expanded to view, traversed by the winding Allier. On the S.W. rises the rival group of volcanoes of the Monts Dore; the remainder of the panorama is somewhat uninteresting over a monotonous country. The range of hills of the Monts Dôme rises from a granitic platform, and stretches "18 m. in length by 2 in breadth. They are usually truncated at the summit, where the crater is often preserved entire, the lava having issued from the base of the hill; but frequently the crater is broken down on one side, where the lava has flowed out. Had these cones of loose sand and ashes been in existence previous to the Deluge, they must have been swept away, or greatly altered, by the power of a current of water. Had these volcanoes, again, been in activity in the time of Cæsar, he would scarcely have failed to observe them when encamped on the neighbouring plateau of Gergovia (p. 387), or to have mentioned them in his Commentaries."—*Lyell's Geology.* See *Scrope* and *Daubeny* on *Volcanoes.*

The experiments instituted by the philosopher B. Pascal, to determine the weight or pressure of the atmosphere, were made on the Puy de Dôme, within view of his native town.

A chapel, dedicated to St. Barnabe, formerly stood on the summit; and the blocks of basalt, brought from a distance to build it, still strew the mountain side.

In descending from the summit, every one should visit the crater called the *Hen's Nest, Nid de la Poule,* at the base of the Petit Puy de Dôme, a regular bowl-shaped hollow, 294 ft. deep, and nearly the same in diameter.

Still farther to the N., the *Puy de Pariou* deserves to be ascended, because it is one of the most beautifully regular and perfect volcanic cones and craters existing in Auvergne. The sides of this bowl-shaped hollow are composed of scoriæ and pozzolana, thrown up so regularly from below, that they taper upwards into a narrow ridge so little degraded by time or by the weather, that in many places it is barely wide enough for one person to walk along it. The crater is 300 ft. deep, and 3000 in circumference, measured along the brim of the bowl. It has the figure of an inverted cone. "It is clothed to the bottom with grass; and it is a somewhat singular spectacle to see a herd of cattle quietly grazing above the orifice whence such furious explosions once broke forth. Their foot-tracks, round the shelving side of the basin, in steps rising one above the other, like the seats of an amphitheatre, make the excessive regularity of its circular basin more remarkable."—*Scrope*.

The lava from this crater flowed down in one undivided stream, bristling and rugged on its surface, like that of a river blocked up by floating masses of ice. After descending as far as la Barraque it encountered a small knoll of granite. The lava has accumulated against this impediment into a long and elevated ridge, "which still bears the appearance of a huge wave about to break over the seemingly insignificant obstacle; but an easier issue offered itself in two lateral valleys." The rt.-hand branch "entered the valley of Villar, a steep and sinuous gorge, which it threaded, exactly in the manner of a watery torrent, turning all the projecting rocks, dashing in cascades through the narrowest parts, and widening its current where the space permitted, till, on reaching the Limagne, it stopped at a spot called Fontmore, where its termination constitutes a rock, 50 ft. high, still quarried for building-stone. From the base of this rock gushes a plentiful spring, the waters of which still find their way from Villar, beneath the lava, which usurped their ancient channel."—*Scrope*.

The left-hand branch "plunged down a steep bank into the valley of Gresinier, replacing the rivulet which flowed there with a black and shagged torrent of lava; entered the limits of the Limagne at the village of Durtol; and, following the course of the stream, did not stop till it reached the site of the village of Nohanent. Here, as at Fontmore, an abundant spring busts forth from the extremity of the lava current. The springs of the valley of Durtol find a passage beneath the lava concealed among the scoriæ, which always form the lowest part of a bed of lava, and flow on in these subterranean channels till they burst forth at the limits of the lava, in the same manner that the Arveiron and other Swiss rivers issue from beneath, under the termination of a glacier. Above Nohanent, consequently, is seen the anomaly of a valley without any visible stream; and the inhabitants of Durtol are condemned in seasons of drought to the strange necessity of seeking at Nohanent, a distance of 2 m., the water which flows below their own houses. A similar phenomenon is common throughout Auvergne, wherever a current of recent lava has occupied the bed of a mountain rivulet not sufficiently copious or violent to undermine the lava above, or open a new side channel through its former bank."—*P. Scrope*.

"A little to the N.W. of the Puy de Pariou is the *Puy de Cliersou*, whose 'figure is most precisely that of a bell,' and which is curious from the numerous perforations made in it for the purpose of obtaining trachyte for sarcophagi."—*T. J. T.*

Instead of returning from the Puy de Dôme by la Barraque and the high road, you may strike down into the Val de Fontanat to *Royat*, a poor and filthily dirty village, 2 m. from Clermont, which has twice been nearly swept away by inundations of the torrent which flows past it. It is built on one of the branches of the lava-current which has issued from the Puy de Gravenoire. The torrent, flowing through the valley, has cut through the bed of basaltic lava to a depth of 65 feet, exposing, at the bottom, a sort of grotto, out of which gush numerous copious springs, some of which, conducted in an aqueduct to Clermont, supply the town with fresh water. There are many other sources higher up the valley, issuing out at intervals from the rocky sides. The *Roman Baths*, rediscovered by the curé, are said to be as efficacious as those of Mont Dore, but lack notoriety. When the workmen first cleared them out, the waters rushed in so fast as nearly to drown and parboil them. The scenery of the vale of Royat is overpraised by the French; but a fine view is gained of the Puy de Dôme from some part of it, and the lava-current, one stratum of which is filled with burnt corn as thick as plums in a pudding, is highly curious. The *church* is remarkable for its antiquity (anterior to the 11th centy.); it has a crypt supported by low columns, and a spring rises in the midst of it. In front of the church is a curious cross.

The *Puy de Gravenoire* is composed of scoriæ and pozzolana; the latter is used in the country to make mortar, and is commonly called "gravier noir," whence the name of this hill.

The conical basaltic summit of the *Puy de Girou*, 3 or 4 m. to the S. of Clermont, is an excellent point for obtaining an extensive view over a considerable portion of Auvergne.

At *Pontgibaud*, 13 m. from Clermont, on the road to Limoges, may be seen a feudal castle of the 14th centy., which once belonged to the family Lafayette, and was visited by Montaigne; and the smelting-houses, where the argentiferous lead from mines in this neighbourhood is refined and separated. The village and castle stand on a lava-current, which has issued from the base of the very perfect and regularly-conical crater called *Puy de Come*. The course of this current deserves observation: descending the granite slope, it has covered the ground on which Pontgibaud now stands; then, pouring in a broad sheet down a steep granite hill into the valley of the Sioule, it has usurped the ancient bed of that river for more than a mile, and, crossing the more ancient stream of Louchadière, near Pichadoire, terminates there. The river has, in consequence, worked out for itself a fresh bed between the lava and the granite of its W. bank, and in one place has laid bare a singular basaltic colonnade, formed of jointed pillars, partly vertical, partly twisted. "In the ravine between the smelting-house and the castle is a small isolated knob of granite which separates the two great lava currents of Louchadière and Come. The former continues a short way down the rt. bank of the river, and then crosses it."—*T. J. T.*

At some little distance to the N.W. of Pontgibaud are the ruins of the *Chartreuse de Porte Sainte Marie*, while in an opposite direction, a little to the S., near the margin of the lava current from the Puy de Come, is the *Fon-taine d'Oule*, a grotto whence issues a streamlet which is partly frozen in the hottest weather of summer, but in winter preserves a temperature considerably higher than that of the outer air. "Several of the more interesting Puys are easily accessible from the road between Clermont and Pontgibaud; and of these two may be particularly specified, viz. the *Puy du Grand Sarcouy*, 3799 ft. above the sea-level, composed of domite, of a striking, flattened hemispherical form, and having on its S.E. side a large artificial excavation, about 70 ft. long, 30 wide, and 35 high, from which the trachyte was quarried in ancient times for sarcophagi; and the conical *Puy de Chopine*, 3910 ft. above the sea, of a singularly complicated and confused geological structure, and composed chiefly of domite, granite, and basalt: the view from it is very fine."—*T. J. T.*

The *Puy de Louchadière* may be visited from Pontgibaud by the crossroad leading to Volvic.

The excursion to the volcanoes and *baths of Mont Dore* is described in Rte. 110.

The *Puy de la Poix*, about 3 m. from Clermont on the Lyons road, is mentioned in Rte. 112.

The Limagne, or valley of the Allier, is far more interesting above Clermont, on the way to Le Puy, than below it. Here it is truly a luxuriant garden, teeming with the most varied productions.

Soon after quitting Clermont, by the road to Issoire, we skirt a lava current from the mountain Gravenoire, called Plateau de Beaumont, a very characteristic specimen of a lava stream, which, although partly covered with vines, exhibits, even to the unscientific eye, in a manner not to be mistaken, compact and porous lava, ashes (scoriæ), and volcanic dust (pozzolana). Beyond rises the singular peak of *Montrognon*, a basaltic dyke bursting through fresh-water strata, crowned by an old *castle*, built by the 1st Dauphin of Auvergne (not by Cæsar), and demolished, like so many other feudal fortresses, by the Card. Richelieu. The basaltic prisms on which it is founded are the most regular which occur in this district. Our road next passes, within a short distance on the rt., the *Hill of Gergovia* (4½ m. from Clermont), memorable as the site of the chief city of the *Arverni* (whence Auvergne), so nobly defended by the Gauls and their chief Vercingetorix against Cæsar, who was more seriously worsted here than in any other of his numerous campaigns, having run great risk of being made prisoner, and having left his sword in the enemy's hands. The hill of Gergovia is as interesting for its geology as for its history : it is a table-land, composed of a base of fresh-water marls, capped by a sheet of basalt, surrounded by steep escarpments, absolutely inaccessible on the N. and W., while on the S. and E. it presents a slope in the form of steps, occasioned by the horizontal strata of rock composing it. At the base of the eminence flows a small stream, the Auzun, whence the Gaulish garrison are supposed to have drawn water, there being no springs upon the plateau itself ; and one of Cæsar's first objects was to cut them off from this supply. The hill called La Roche Blanche, surmounted by a tower of the middle ages, though called Tour de César, is conjectured to be the Gaulish post seized by two Roman Legions in order to effect that object. Cæsar's camp is supposed to have been formed on a detached and lower eminence, called Le Crest. The only traces of human habitation on the top of the table-land of Gergovia are some scanty foundations of walls, some Roman coins, and Gaulish axes of flint, found from time to time, and a rampart or agger of loose stones, which may be traced near the margin of the plateau. In the ravine above the village of Merdogne a section of the strata composing the hill is exhibited, consisting of beds of white and greenish marls, nearly 300 ft. thick, intersected by a basaltic dyke, which has greatly altered the marl in contact with it. In the flanks of this hill also are found extensive deposits of the limestone formed of the cases of insects mentioned before.

The road to Le Puy, unlike the monotonous chaussées of most other parts of France, winds and undulates between and over varied heights, sometimes crossing a lava current or basaltic dyke, and is generally shaded from the sun by luxuriant walnut-trees. Scarcely an eminence but possesses some interest, either from its volcanic origin, or from its picturesquely-placed castle in ruins, or village, which, in this district, is almost invariably perched on the hill-top, The country is very populous as well as fertile, and intersected by numerous roads.

"The *Puy de Marman*, a little to the N. of Vayre, is celebrated among mineralogists for the beautiful crystallized specimens of mezotype contained in the volcanic tuff and basalt of which it is composed. In the same neighbourhood interesting fragments of charred wood, whose bark has been converted into mezotype, are met with in the tufa of the Puy de la Pignette, situated a little to the N. of Mouton." —*T. J. T.*

After passing the populous village Vayre, we reach, by a steep descent, the post-station

24 Coudes, situated on the bank of the Allier. The *castle* of Montpeyroux, on an adjoining eminence, now reduced to a round tower, and some fragments of walls, belonged to Philip Augustus. "Near Coudes a variety of sandstone, termed *Arkose*, is quarried for millstones. Between Coudes and Montpeyroux veins of fibrous arragonite occur in travertine, and farther down the river Allier at Corent there are gypsum quarries which afford fine specimens of fibrous gypsum."—*T. J. T.* From Coudes through a lovely country, which keeps the attention constantly alive.

In the ravine des Etouaires, near the village of Perrier, an interesting geological section is presented. Here fossil remains of extinct quadrupeds, mastodon, tapir, rhinoceros, elephant, &c., have been found in alluvial beds, covered by volcanic breccias, and alternating with them. Near Vayre and at Perrier the rock has been excavated to form cave-dwellings ; above Perrier rises the tower of Maurifolet.

A view of the Monts Dores rising on the W. may be obtained near

s 2

11 Issoire (*Inn:* Chez Roussard, Poste), an ancient town of 5990 Inhab., situated on the Couze, a short way above its exit into the Allier. The ch. of *St. Paul* will interest the architect and antiquary, as a characteristic specimen of Auvergnat architecture, as it prevailed in the 10th and 11th centuries. It is in the Romanesque style, ending in 5 apses at the E., surmounted at the cross by a tower, the upper part of which, and also the W. front, are modern. The exterior of the wall at the E. end is singularly decorated with rude mosaics, and with 12 medallions, representing the signs of the zodiac, let into the wall under the cornice. Under the window of the N. transept are 2 bas-reliefs, representing the Angel appearing to Abraham, and the Sacrifice of Isaac. In the interior the arches are semicircular, the side aisles and transepts being covered with a stone roof, forming the quarter of a circle, and thus serving as a buttress to support the tower and central walls of the nave. There is an extensive crypt under the choir.

The chancellor Duprat was born here. The chief manufacture is that of copper kettles.

After passing through St. Germain Lembron, and leaving a little on the l. the coal-mines and steam-engines of St. Florine beyond the Allier, we quit the volcanic country, and the Dépt. du Puy de Dôme, to enter that of la Haute Loire, shortly before reaching

20 Lempde (*Inn:* Poste), situated on the rt. bank of the Alagnon. Here the road to St. Flour, Montpellier, and Aurillac (Rte. 114) branches off. It is the line of a malleposte.

15 Brioude. — *Inn:* H. de la Poste. The very fine Romanesque *ch. of St. Julien* is curious for its semicircular E. end, with chequered patterns in a coarse mosaic of particoloured stones on the outer walls, and round its 5 projecting apsidal chapels, of elegant design. The interior is lofty; the arches of the choir are pointed, and the capitals of the columns adorned with foliage: the arches of the nave are round, and the capitals of the columns supporting them are partly very grotesque, partly display a nearly pure classic character. At the W. end, which is almost bare externally, is a sort of inner vestibule or narthex, supporting, on low arches, 3 chambers, one of which, the chapel of St. Michel, is decorated with curious antique *frescoes* of the 13th centy. The canons of the church of St. Julien the Martyr anciently bore the title of counts.

[The very curious Ch. of *La Chaise Dieu* is distant 18 m. from Brioude, nearly due E. The monastery of the Casa Dei, now ruined, and attached to a dilapidated little village (Cheval Blanc is the inn), is situated at a considerable elevation, on a high mountain. It was founded in the 11th century by St. Robert, a canon of Brioude, and became the most opulent convent in Auvergne. Of this original structure nothing exists, except, perhaps, an external gateway. The monastic buildings were destroyed at the Revolution. The *Ch.* alone remains, and is a noble edifice in the pointed Gothic style, begun 1343, chiefly at the expense of Pope Clement VI., a native of Chaise Dieu, who laid the first stone, and is buried under a mutilated *monument*, surmounted by his effigy, wearing the triple crown. The *carved woodwork* of the 156 stalls in the choir is much admired, and deservedly. On the N. wall, which encloses the choir, are traces, now nearly defaced, and obliterated by moisture, of a Dance of Death, painted in fresco, probably in the 15th centy. Here are preserved some of the most curious ancient *tapestries* remaining in France, executed probably at the beginning of the 16th centy., woven partly with gold thread. The tomb of another pope, Gregory XI., and of an abbot, in the S. choir aisle, deserve notice. Two sides of the *cloisters* remain tolerably perfect, and are of a good style. Contiguous to the ch. rises a tall square *donjon tower*, the only remains of the ancient fortifications which surrounded the monastery. It is surmounted by a bold cornice.]

2 m. beyond Brioude, on the road to Le Puy, at the wretched village of

La Vieille Brioude, the Allier, here running in a deep and rocky bed, is crossed by a *Bridge* of a *single arch of stone*, which was long celebrated as being the widest in span of any known, measuring 181 English ft. and 90½ ft. in height, but now surpassed by the stone arches of Turin and of Chester (200 ft. span). It is a very noble arch, and constructed of Volvic lava. It replaces a more ancient bridge (b. 1451), of equal dimensions, which fell down in 1822. Immediately beyond the bridge, the road begins to ascend, and continues over a hilly and uninteresting country, almost constantly mounting higher, for many leagues. A little beyond the poor village of

21 St. George d'Aurat, the château de Chavagnac is passed, at the distance of 1½ m. on the l. of the road: it is remarkable as being the birthplace of Gen. Lafayette.

By a long, though gradual ascent, which the diligence takes 3 hours to surmount "au pas," the Montagne de Fix, separating the valley of the Allier from that of the Loire, is passed. Measured at the village of Fix, this road is 3197 ft. above the sea-level, and one of the highest carriage-roads in France.

18 Limandre.

We are now again upon volcanic rocks, belonging to the basin of Le Puy. The small river Borne, which runs into the Loire below Le Puy, is crossed, and the road is carried down its valley, passing, at a distance of 4 m. from Le Puy, under the black rock of basaltic breccia, escarped and inaccessible on all sides but the N., which bears the ruined *castle of Polignac*, seat and cradle of that ancient family, the branche aînée of the name, whence sprang the Cardinal, a diplomatic servant of Louis XIV., and the well-known minister of Charles X. It was pulled to pieces during the fury of the Revolution, and all the lands sold; but the mouldering and picturesque ruins, which still bristle on the top of the rock, were repurchased by the family. They consist of rude but strongly built walls, often double and treble, with flanking towers at intervals, surmounted by a square donjon tower. Part of the pile of buildings which served as dwellings may be as old as the 12th centy. There is little to be seen except an enormous *mask*, rudely carved in granite, of a bearded human face, with a wide orifice for the mouth. According to the tradition, a Temple of Apollo occupied the summit of the rock before the castle, and from this mouthpiece (somewhat after the fashion of the Bocca della Verità at Rome) oracles were delivered: hence some have gone so far as to derive Polignac from "Apollinis Arx." (?) Sunk in the platform of the castle is a well, called *Puit de l'Oracle*, from a tradition that the oracles were delivered from it through the mask, which is said to have covered the well. At a depth of 20 ft. this well communicates with a vaulted chamber, supported on circular arches, resting on square piers, designed doubtless as a cistern, into which rain-water was conducted by pipes, now stopped up. About 25 paces from the well is the *abyme*, a hole about 40 ft. deep and 15 wide, cut in the rock, probably designed as a storehouse. The *ch*. of Polignac, at the foot of the castle rock, is an ancient Romanesque edifice.

Upon a sudden turn of the road, here bordered by basaltic columns, a very striking view is presented of Le Puy and its volcanic rocks; the "spiry pinnacle" of St. Michel's, resembling more an artificial obelisk than a natural eminence, and Corneille, starting up from amidst the masses of buildings, while on the rt. appears Espailly (p. 392).

19 LE PUY. — *Inns:* H. des Ambassadeurs;—Palais Royal; good;—H. du Commerce. Le Puy, anciently capital of the Velay, and now of the Dépt. de la Haute Loire, with 14,924 Inhab., is, at a distance, one of the most striking, uncommon, and picturesque towns in France. Excepting the broad modern Boulevard, through which the high roads from Clermont and St. Etienne pass, which stands on level ground, the buildings and narrow streets of the old town are carried up a steep slope, surmounted by a tower-

ing, table-topped mass, called *Rocher de Corneille*, whose summit, vertically escarped and mouldering in the form of turrets, is surmounted by the ruins of an old *castle*, the stronghold and place of retreat from danger of the former bishops. This rock is a volcanic breccia, resting on a calcareous base.

Far more remarkable, though less lofty, is the *Rocher de St. Michel*, an isolated rock of basaltic tufa, which, from its needle shape, gives the name *de l'Aiguille* to the suburb in which it stands. It rises from the margin of the stream of the Borne to a height of 265 ft., with a thickness of 500 ft. at its base, and 45 or 50 on its top. It is a fragment of the vast bed of volcanic rock once covering the country around. The rocks of Corneille and Polignac are also relics of it; and, because harder than the rest, all three have resisted the erosive processes of rivers and the atmosphere, which have scooped out into valleys the intervening portions, and washed away the débris. Faujas de St. Fond absurdly supposes the Aiguille of St. Michel to have been projected by a volcanic eruption from below, and consolidated in its actual form. The sides of this truncated cone, or sugar-loaf, are nearly vertical, and its top is surmounted by a small *chapel*, which just fills the platform, dedicated to Michael, the saint who loves such airy sites. This building, rendered accessible by a winding stair partly cut in the rock, is in the Romanesque style, and was constructed at the cost of a dean of the cathedral in the 10th centy. Its Moresque portal, a circular arch under a trefoiled arch, is ornamented with curious sculptured mermen, bas-reliefs, and chequered stone-work, composed of black scoriæ, white sandstone, and red tile, in the style of marqueterie. The interior presents a low irregular choir, supported by short pillars with carved capitals.

From the top of the rock a good view is obtained of the vine-clad hills covering the slopes of the valley, dotted over with white country-houses, boxes, and pavilions, built in the midst of the vines, also of the white escarp-ments of the tertiary strata, laid bare here and there.

Near the foot of this rock stands an octagonal building which has long passed for a heathen *temple of Diana*, though destitute of any pretensions to such a title, being, in fact, a Christian edifice in the Romanesque style, and perhaps originally a *baptistery*: some say a chapel of St. Claire. A small apse projects from its eastern side, and it is entered by doors on the N. and W. It has an octagonal roof, with a hole in the centre, resting on columns placed in the angles. It may have been built by the Templars, who had property in this suburb.

A road slopes upwards from St. Michel, under the Rock of Corneille, past the Hospital, and the little turning box, in which enfans trouvés are deposited after ringing a bell to announce their arrival, through the "Rue de la Raison," to

The *Cathedral*, which rears its singularly streaked W. front high over the other buildings. The regular approach to it is up the steep streets leading from the market-place to the long flight of steps under the huge cavernous vaulted portal, which is prolonged in a sort of corridor beneath the church. As the slope of the hill denied to the architect level ground sufficient to extend his church to the W., he was forced to raise an artificial platform for it upon these vast substructions. The doorway is flanked by 2 pillars of Egyptian porphyry. It is a heavy ungainly building, in the Romanesque style; its interior not improved by the repairs and stucco applied at the expense of Louis XVIII. The oldest parts of the church are the choir, including 4 compartments of arches on either side, and the transepts; each compartment is cross-vaulted; the probable date is the 10th or 11th centy. This church is chiefly remarkable for a miracle-working image of *Notre Dame du Puy*, which for many centuries has attracted thousands of devout pilgrims, who still repair hither, though in less number than formerly. Among its visitors in former times are numbered several popes, and the following kings :—Louis VII., Philippe

Auguste, Philippe le Hardi, Charles VI. and VII., Louis XI., Charles VIII., and François I. : its visitors at present do not exceed 4000 annually, and are chiefly of the lower order of peasants. One cause for this falling off may be that the existing image deposited over the high-altar, a black group of the Virgin and Child with shining faces, is a modern work, executed by a sculptor in the town, whose name is well known, from recollection of the original, which was destroyed at the Revolution. The original Notre Dame du Puy, believed to have been made by the Christians of Mount Lebanon, or, according to some accounts, by the prophet Jeremiah himself, and brought to Europe at the time of the Crusades, was of cedar-wood, singularly swathed round with bands of papyrus glued to it, and partly inscribed. Upon this the features of the face, of negro tint, the flesh of hands and feet, and the draperies, were painted in distemper, in a rude style, probably by some artist who copied from Egyptian models.

A marble tablet on one side of the church records the names of 20 priests of the diocese slaughtered in the Revolution, 1793-4 and 8.

The *monument* raised to the Constable Du Guesclin, whose body reposed some time at Le Puy, after his death at Châteauneuf de Randon, and whose entrails were buried here, has recently been restored in a chapel on the N. side of the Gothic *Church of St. Laurent*, in the lower part of the town. His effigy represents him in armour, except the helmet, lying on his back, his hands raised in prayer. The head is modern, but copied from a cast of the original, destroyed by the Baron des Adrets and his followers, and is considered to have some claim to be looked on as a portrait.

The collections in the *Musée*, not far from the cathedral, are of considerable interest as local curiosities in art and nature. Besides some mediocre paintings (among them Henrietta Maria, queen of Charles I., a copy from *Vandyke*; a faint but curious portrait of Henri II., in the style of *Janet*; and a good landscape by *Huysman*), are some Roman antiquities, a bas-relief of a Stag and Boar Hunt, found on digging the foundations of the Evêché ; also 3 Genii or Cupids fishing (one with 2 dolphins of very fair execution), from Margeaix ; a cippus hollowed out into a sarcophagus, bearing figures of arms, cut in relief, among them a crossbow (?) ; cast of a bronze hand, with a Greek inscription, recording a treaty of peace ; a cast from the so-called Mask of Apollo, at Polignac (see p. 389); one or two groups of Gothic sculpture, nuns, female saints, &c. ; carvings in ivory, in Byzantine and Gothic styles ; a portion of the inscribed *papyrus* in which the image of N. D. de Puy was swathed, preserved at the time the image was burnt, at the Revolution ; some old furniture ; an abbot's seat, carved in the style of the Renaissance ; and an arm-chair of Gothic work, bearing the arms of Polignac. Those who take interest in the *geology* and *mineralogy* of the district will find the collections here not only the best part of the whole museum, but one of the best arranged and best named cabinets which any provincial museum in France possesses, under the inspection of M. Bertrand de Doué, the able expositor of the geology of Velay. The formations of La Puy en Velay, the Vivarais, and the Ardèche may be studied in distinct series of specimens, topographically arranged, side by side with a series of the volcanic rocks of Vesuvius, for the sake of comparison.

Here are preserved the bones of rhinoceros, hyæna, deer, &c., found by Dr. Hibbert, a Scotch geologist, at St. Privat d'Allier, in a matrix of scoriæ, between two layers of basaltic lava ; a discovery of great interest, as proving the recent date at which the volcanoes of the Velay were in activity ; also fossil bones of Palæotherium, of Anthracotherium Velaunum, so named by Cuvier from Le Puy, the locality where it was found ; of hippopotamus, found in the terrain du transport near Polignac ; and fossil fruits from the coal-measures at Longeac.

The manufacture of *cotton lace* gives employment to the females of the lower classes in and about the town ; and some specimens are shown at the museum of great beauty.

About 1 m. W. of the town is the village of *Espailly*, surmounted by another castle-crowned *rock* of volcanic breccia. Charles VII. was residing here during the occupation of France by the English (1422), when news was brought of the death of his father, and his scanty train of followers proclaimed him King of France in the ancient fashion, by raising him aloft on a shield, at the same moment that the infant Henry VI. of England was proclaimed, with all pomp, at Paris, the successor to the French throne. There are good displays of basaltic columns here, called *Les Orgues d'Espailly*; and on the opposite side of the river, in the eminence of Denise, several coarse varieties of precious stones, sapphires, zircons, and garnets, are found in the basalt, and in the sands of the neighbouring streamlet of Riou Pezzouliou. Fossil remains of Anthracotherium and other extinct animals have been found in the marly limestone near Espailly.

The *Castle of Polignac* is a walk of about an hour, not far from the road to Clermont.

The *Roche Rouge*, an isolated mass of basalt, rising abruptly out of the granite rock to a height of 60 ft., about 3 m. to the E. of Le Puy, will interest the geologist. Its name is probably derived from the colour of the lichens which grow on it. It is nothing more than the expanded portion (renflement) of a basaltic dyke, which, from superior hardness, has resisted the action of the weather, while the softer granite around has been disintegrated. The dyke is continued on either side in a vein often not more than a foot wide.

Diligences twice a-day to St. Etienne; daily to Clermont, and to Langogne.

The views of the town from the surrounding heights from the roads to Espailly, Polignac, St. Etienne, are very striking. Mr. Scrope prefers the extensive *panorama* from the more distant *Mont d'Ours*, and observes, with some geological enthusiasm,—" There are, perhaps, few spots on the globe which offer a more extraordinary prospect than this. To the eye of a geologist it is superlatively interesting, exhibiting in one view a vast theatre of volcanic formation, containing igneous products of various natures belonging to different epochs, and exhibited under a great diversity of aspect."

" The traveller bound from Le Puy to the Volcanic District of the Vivarais and Ardèche may take the diligence to Pradelles, and thence strike across the country, by bad cross-roads, to Aubenas, by Thueyts (Rte. 118, 121), or, more directly, by a mule-road to Montpezat; in the course of which he may visit the *Mt. Mezène*, the highest volcanic mountain in Central France, presenting some wild and singular views. He may also pass the curious mountain called *Gerbier des Joncs*, at the foot of which rises the Loire. There is scarcely any accommodation on this route, which can hardly be performed in a day; and the people are rude and forbidding."—*P. F.*

ROUTE 110.

CLERMONT TO MONT DORE LES BAINS.

I. Grande Route, 53¼ kilom.= 33 Eng. m.

Diligences creep, in 9 or 10 hours, miserably slow.

II. Petite Route, hilly and not good for carriages, 42 kilom. = 27 Eng. m.

It is a hilly journey by either of these routes, beginning to ascend from the Barrier of Clermont to La Barraque (see p. 384), then leaving the Cone of the Puy de Dôme on the rt. and the ruined castle of Montrodeix on the l.; its walls formed of basaltic prisms.

The road reaches the summit level of the chain of the Monts Dôme, at a spot called Moréneau, between the Puys de Leschamps, covered with wood, and de Montchié, a volcano, furnished with 4 craters, which has been cut away at the base to give passage to the road; and trunks of trees charred have been disclosed by the section of the trachytic rock. Descending the opposite slope, it crosses the stream of the Sioule, here in its infancy. Before reaching Pont des Eaux, the turreted Castle of Cordés is for some distance conspicuous. At

St. Bonnet a basaltic clinkstone is quarried, to serve as roofing slate, as bridges, fences, &c.: the thin slabs ring like a bell when struck.

29 Rochefort.

The ruined *castle*, on the summit of a basaltic rock, once belonged to the Dauphins of Auvergne.

The road continues to ascend through a hilly and bleak country, often blocked up by snow in winter. About 3 m. beyond the village of Laqueuille the road to Mont Dore branches off to the l., out of that to Aurillac by Muriac, and, crossing another ridge, descends upon the village Murat le Queire, in the valley of the Dordogne, and proceeds up the rt. bank of that stream to

24 *Mont Dore les Bains* (see below).

No. II. *La Petite Route* is the same as No. I. until reaching the village Laschamp, 3 m. beyond La Barraque; or, on foot, more directly and agreeably by Thadde. As there are few villages, the route may most conveniently be traced by the Puys which are passed, viz. Gravenoire and Charade on the rt.: La Bache and Lassolas, also on the rt., are extremely well preserved, and are completely thrown open on the S.W. side, towards which they have diverted their lava streams. There is here quite a circle of craters, among which Mont Jughat and Mont Chat are conspicuous.

21 Randanne (a roadside Inn, with one bedroom: respectable travellers may procure a bed in the Château). In the vicinity, at the foot of the Puy de Montchal, lived the patriotic philosopher le Comte de Montlosier, who settled himself down here, after his return from exile in 1816, in the midst of an unproductive wilderness, the home of his fathers having been destroyed in the Revolution, and, by the enlightened agricultural improvements which he introduced, redeemed a large tract from unproductive barrenness, and "bid the desert smile." He is buried in a small Gothic *chapel*, erected on a pretty spot within his estate; the priests having refused interment to his remains within consecrated ground, on account of his writings against the Jesuits.

A road just practicable for a char leads in about 3 m. on the l. to the sheet of water called *Lac d'Aidat*, formed by the volcanic current from the Puy de la Vache, damming up the course of 2 rivulets. On its borders Sidonius Apollinaris lived, and an inscription on the wall of the curious early *church* marks the place of his interment. "To the rt. is the *Puy de la Rodde*, a fine crater opening to the S., and commanding an extensive view of the Puys, the streams of lava, and the mountains of Mont Dore. Abundance of fine crystals of Augite are found in it."—*T. J. T.*

After attaining the table-land of Baladaud, which commands an extensive view, but is itself bleak and uninteresting, it is an uninterrupted and steep descent into the vale of the Dordogne. It is clothed with wood, and interesting. At Quereilh the traveller turns abruptly to the l., and enters the valley enclosing

21 *Mont Dore les Bains*. Inns: H. de Paris, chez Chaboury le Jeune, best, first-rate;—H. Bellon, good;—H. de Lyon (chez Baraduc); *charge*, living en pension, 4 to 7 f. a day. There is a daily table-d'hôte at most of them. The rivers and lakes furnish trout, and the mountains roe venison. The people here, little accustomed to English, are disposed to make exorbitant charges, experimentally, trying to hit the mark of the standard which English are made to pay elsewhere. This small watering-place is a village at a height of 3411 ft. above the sea-level, in an upland valley, the cradle of the river *Dor*-dogne, surrounded by an amphitheatre of volcanic hills, their sides clothed with verdant meadows or black pine forests, but torn and gashed at intervals by ravines and gullies, down which numerous streams dash in small cascades from the bare table-land above. The village lies at the distance of about 2 m. from the Pic du Sancy, the highest summit in central France, 6217 ft. above the sea-level, and the culminating point of the Mont Dore, that vast volcanic excrescence which has broken through the fundamental granite rock, and, stretching from this point to a distance

of 8 or 10 m., measures 18 leagues in circumference. It is seamed and fissured by deep valleys radiating in all directions from the common centre, the chief of them on the N. side being the valley of the Dordogne, or of Mont Dore. The crater from which this eruption burst forth is not distinctly marked, owing to the dilapidations in its sides caused by volcanic convulsions, by the wearing down of torrents, and even by the effects of the weather; but there can be no doubt that we see the traces and remains of the lava walls which surrounded it in "the elevated peaks which still bristle over the circus-like gorge occupying the very heart of the mountain. This was probably the site of its central crater, but now, branching off into deep and short recesses, it forms the upper basin of the principal valley, and the recipient into which 2 mountain rills, the Dor and the Dogne unite, at the source of the noble river which henceforward bears their joint names."—*Scrope*, 98.

The mineral springs, on account of which Mont Dore is resorted to from June to the beginning of September, are 8 in number, 2 being cold, the rest of a temperature of 106 to 113 Fahrenheit; they issue out of the trachytic rock, at the foot of the eminence called Plateau de l'Angle. They are alkaline, and are efficacious in complaints of the lungs, when unattended with inflammation, in disorders of the stomach, and in rheumatism. They are conducted into a very handsome *bathing establishment*, built, like the rest of the houses, of a trachytic lava, resembling that of Volvic, but obtained from a neighbouring quarry. The most copious source, *La Madeleine*, is also used for drinking, and large quantities are exported in bottles. It, as well as that called Le Bain de César, is enclosed in *Roman masonry,* proving that bath-loving people to have made use of these warm springs. Numerous architectual fragments, columns, &c., very curious, in a rich semi-barbarous style, have been discovered here, supposed to have belonged to a temple whose foundations exist, and go by the name of *Le Panthéon*.

The angler may catch some trout in the Dordogne below the Baths.

A *char-à-banc* holding 4 to 6 people costs 15 frs. a day. Capital, sure-footed mountain *horses* may be hired at the rate of 3 frs. a day; also guides, and chaises-à-porteurs with bearers for ladies, for the numerous interesting excursions in the vicinity of these baths. In front of the bath-house is a pretty green promenade, encircled by the windings of the Dordogne, over which a suspension bridge has been thrown, conducting to a path which leads to the base of the *Capucin*, the isolated, cowl-shaped rock, conspicuous from all parts of the valley, named from a detached pinnacle, jutting forward on one side, said to resemble a monk in a hood.

The *Champ de la Foire* is a cattle-market formed by levelling a group of basaltic columns. The tops of the prisms make a natural pavement.

The direction of the valley of the Dor from its head, at the base of the Pic de Sancy, to a short distance below the baths, is nearly due N. and S. In its E. side, not more than ½ an hour's walk above the baths, a singular breach or fissure is perceptible, worn away by the descent of a stream called *La Grande Cascade*, which has cut through the rock, and exhibits, in the face of the precipice, an instructive geological section of a series of beds of trachyte, tufa, and basalt. Vast blocks have been detached and hurled below, so that the stream, after its leap of nearly 80 ft., is almost hidden from view.

The Valley of Mont Dore is a region of woods and waterfalls; the latter, though not of any great elevation or grandeur, add an interest to the many pretty scenes around; by far the finest is the *Cascade de Quereilh*, shooting perpendicularly downwards; a miniature Staul-bach.

On the W. side of the valley, opposite to the Grand Cascade, is the gorge called *Vallée d'Enfer*, excavated out of a volcanic rock, consisting of scoriæ and other fragments, bearing the marks of fire, over which rise the naked summits of the Pic d'Aiguiller. The breccia is in many places penetrated by vertical dykes of dark porphyritic trachyte; and such a dyke forms the separation, called Les Fernes, between the gorges of Enfer and La Cour. Similar dykes are seen traversing the precipices of the Pic d'Aiguiller exposed to the view at the end of the Val d'Enfer.

The ascent of the *Pic de Sancy* may be made in 2 hours from the baths, on foot or horseback, or in a chair; proceeding to the head of the valley, past the gorges d'Enfer and de la Cour, and turning to the l., near the ravine of La Craie, where a steep ascent begins, through a fir wood, in the depths of which lies the Cascade du Serpent, passing the marsh in which the Dore rises. The Pic (6171 ft. above the sealevel) is reached by passing the high Col between it and the Puy Ferrand. The distant objects seen from it are the volcanic group of the Cantal to the S., and the Monts Dôme to the N., while near at hand yawns a labyrinth of valleys and gorges, with peaks bristling around on all sides; and numerous small lakes glitter in the depths, among them the crater Lakes de Pavin and that de Chambon.

Another very interesting excursion is to the *castle of Murol*, situated to the E. of the baths, crossing the mountains by the Puy de Diane and the pretty little Lac Chambon. There is a road thither directly over the Mont Dore by la Croix Morand, but, as it requires to be repaired every spring after the melting of the snow, inquiry should be made whether it is passable. Murol, the village, is built at the base of the red scoriaceous volcanic hill called Puy de Tartaret, upon a lava current which has issued from it, at a period long after the formation of the volcanic rocks of the Mont Dore. Murol is nearly surrounded by a dense forest, one of the finest in Auvergne. Homely and rustic accommodation at the public-house kept by Morin.

The *castle*, one of the largest relics of feudal times in France, and a very picturesque object, crowns the summit of a detached eminence topped with basalt, affording a platform just large enough to hold the fortress, whose walls rise up, as it were, in continuation of the vertical precipices beneath them. It consists of a double enclosure, an outer wall flanked with bastions, dating from the 16th centy. and an inner circular wall, surmounted by machicolations of the 15th. In the midst rises a round tower, or *donjon*, commanding the country far and near, and affording a most interesting view of the plain and valley around, covered with lava vomited forth from the Tartaret. Some of the existing constructions of the castle are as late as the 18th centy., and none appear older than the 15th; the first mention of it occurs in 1223, when its seigneur was named Jean Chambre Chevarier.

The *Puy de Tartaret* deserves the attention of the geologist; it consists of loose scoriæ, lapilli, and fragments of granite, which have been forced up through the fundamental granite rock. "It has 2 deep and regular bowl-shaped craters, separated by a high ridge, and each broken down on one side:" the lava current which they have furnished first spreads over the plain, then, contracting, confines itself to the valley, whose sinuosities it follows as far as Neschers, a distance of 13 m., occupying the channel of the former river. Near Neschers and Champeix it assumes a regular columnar form. Neschers is a picturesque village, and the curé, the Abbé Croizet, has a collection of fossils.

Rather more than an hour's walk (4½ m.) from Murol, passing partly over the lava from the Puy de Tartaret, and near the waterfall Des Granges, one of the prettiest in Auvergne, lies *St. Nectaire* (*Inn:* H. Meudon, fair), a village possessing *hot Baths* and an *incrusting spring*, much more remarkable than that at Clermont, which issues from the granite and deposits large quantities of lime. The curious Romanesque *church* is a very ancient and unaltered specimen of the style, no part of it apparently older than the 12th centy.; lately repaired. It is surmounted at the cross by an octagonal tower, and terminates at the E. end in 3 apses. The capitals of the pillars in the choir, carved with bas-reliefs of Scriptural and legendary subjects, are curious. In this church are preserved a curious Byzantine crucifix of copper gilt, and a reliquiary, in the form of a bust, of embossed copper gilt, also Byzantine, and probably of the 11th centy. The *Castle of St. Nectaire*, the cradle of a noble family, whence sprang 2 marshals of France, has been destroyed. Here are a curious natural grotto and remains of Roman Baths. On the rt. of the road to Neschers, a little way out of St. Nectaire, is the arch of a Roman bridge, the piers of which stand on the lava of Tartaret.

On the heights above the Bains de Boite, not far from St. Nectaire, are some *Druidical remains*, consisting of a dolmen or altar formed of the unhewn blocks of the granite found in the country. On the summit of the hill of *Cornadore* are extensive excavations supposed to be of great antiquity, formed, perhaps, by the Gauls as store-houses, or places of refuge; they are now used as sheep-sheds.

Another interesting excursion, especially for the geologist, may be made to the rocks of La Thuillière and la Sanadoire, 1½ hour from Mont d'Or. The columnar feldspar or phonolite of the Roche Sanadoire is curious, and the view fine. 1½ hour more takes the traveller to the Lake of Servières, from which he may gain the great road to Clermont by descending the valley of the Sioule by Vernines (old castle) and St. Bonnet.

ROUTE 111.

MONT DORE LES BAINS TO LE PUY, BY ISSOIRE.

The traveller who wishes to go from Mont Dore les Bains to Issoire, and thence to Le Puy or elsewhere, need not go round by Clermont. He may ride across the hills on horseback, a journey of about 7 hours, or of 10 hours if the ascent of the Pic de Sancy be taken en route, which is quite practicable. There is also a very fair road direct to Issoire, and a voiture may be hired at Mont Dore for the journey, which will take about 8 hours, including stoppages. The road goes by the *Château of Murol* and the *baths of St. Nectaire* (Rte. 110), both of which may be visited, especially as the latter is the usual resting-place for the horses. After quitting St. Nectaire, the road passes through Sailhens, and leaves Verrières on the rt., at which latter place it enters a defile called the Valley of Montaigut, about 3 m. in length, the scenery of which is very striking, the carriage-way being cut along the side of a torrent, and hemmed in by precipitous rocks of great height, on one side mostly covered with wood, on the other bare and rugged. The scenery of this pass is well worth the attention of the traveller, and, though perhaps not equal to some similar defiles among the Alps, is certainly of a very high order. About two-thirds down the pass, upon the top of the rocks to the l., stand the ruins of the *Castle of Montaigut*, and at the end of the pass the village of the same name. At the small town of Champeix the road turns to the S., and, ascending a hill, passes by Pardines on the l., where are visible the remains of a very remarkable landslip, which took place June 25th, 1737, destroying almost the whole village and many of the inhabitants. The vast fragments extend nearly a mile from the crag whence they fell. It is well worth the traveller's while to mount to the top, and look down on the immense fragments and the fissures in the upper part of the rock, which did not actually give way. From this spot also a very beautiful panorama of all the Auvergne mountains, including the Puy de Dome and the range about Mont Dore, may be obtained. About 2 m. from Issoire the road passes the rough Perrier, where, in the rocks to the l., are a great number of caverns, many of which are inhabited. The ruins of the tower of Maurifolet are seen above the village.

Issoire. } Rte. 109.
Le Puy.

ROUTE 112.

CLERMONT TO LYONS, BY THIERS: — MONTBRISON.

177 kilom. = 109 Eng. m.
Diligence daily.—*Railway* 1855.

The road out of Clermont runs nealy due W., passing on the l. the *Puy de la Poix*, an eminence of basaltic tufa, having on the N. side a spring of bitumen, or mineral pitch, which issues out of the earth along with a source of water.

15 Pont du Château, a prettily situated town, named from a bridge over the Allier, by which our road crosses it. " About ½ m. above the bridge, on the rt. bank of the river, there is an interesting geological display of fossiliferous freshwater limestone strata, alternating with calcareous beds containing volcanic substances."—*T. J. T.*

The *Château of Beauregard*, a little on the l. of the road, was formerly the country seat of the bishops of Clermont, and the residence of Massillon as such.

13 Lezoux, a small town on the verge of the Limagne, has an ancient church.

The *Castle of Ravel* belonged to Philippe le Bel. Our road is hilly, threading a part of the chain of the mountains of Forez, which separate the Allier from the Loire.

12 *Thiers* (*Inns*: Poste; — H. de l'Europe; new and good), an industrious manufacturing town, built on the top and slope of a peaked granitic hill, at whose base the Durole flows in a deep rocky bed, turning many paper-mills and forges, where various articles of *cutlery* are wrought, the staple manufacture of the town, giving employment to a large portion of its 9830 Inhab. The town, so picturesque at a distance, with its houses rising one above another, on nearer approach is found to consist of dirty lanes; but from the upper part of it, especially from the high *terrace*, fine views are obtained over the Limagne and the distant chain of the Monts Dôme. Here also is situated the antique church of *St. Genes*, a Romanesque building, chiefly of the 12th centy., though the vaults of the roof are newer: the end of the S. transept is ornamented with coarse mosaics. More curious to the antiquary is the church *Du Moutier*, in the lower part of the town; the E. extremity of the choir has been referred to the 8th centy.

A portion of the old *castle* remains.

The road for about 4 m. is carried along the edge of a precipice, and is called Le Cordon. The views over the rich plain of the Limagne, to the range of the Monts Dôme in one direction, and of the chain of the Forez in the other, are very fine.

14 La Bergière.

13 Noiretable, a village at the foot of the high Montagne de l'Hermitage.

12 St. Thurin.

15 Boën (*Inn* : Poste; tolerable, clean beds), a dirty village. [It is about 11 m. distant from *Montbrison*, chef-lieu of the Dépt. of the Loire, though inferior in extent and population (7000) both to Roanne and St. Etienne. It stands at the base of a lofty and precipitous rock, from the top of which, or from the tower of the neighbouring church, as some say, the ferocious leader of the Calvinists, Le Baron des Adrets, compelled his Roman Catholic prisoners to leap, to their certain destruction. When one of the condemned, after twice approaching the brink, faltered in taking the leap, the tyrant exclaimed, "Two chances are too much." " I'll wager that *you* will not do it in ten," was the ready reply; and, it is said, saved the waverer's life. The *Cathedral* is a Gothic building (1205), and contains the tomb of its founder, Guy IV., Comte de Forez. The Salle de Diane, once the chapter-house, is decorated with curious armorial bearings.] (*Inns* : H. du Nord; du Centre.)

From Boën the road to Lyons crosses the flat and marshy plain of the Loire, and runs parallel with the Lignon, which is seen on the rt.; it is crossed, and at a short distance the river Loire also, before entering

18 Feurs, which occupies the site of one of the most important cities of the Gauls—*Forum Segusianorum*. In this name may be traced the modern one of Forez, given to the district of which it

was the capital, during the middle ages. Extensive fragments of Roman walls, aqueducts, inscribed stones, &c., attest its ancient consequence. Pop. 2250.

The *railroad* from Roanne to St. Etienne (Rte. 119) runs past the town on the E., directly across our line of route.

Soon after, the road ascends out of the fertile valley of the Loire.

10 St. Barthélemy l'Estrà.
13 Sainte Foy l'Argentière.
6 Duerne.

A high mountain ridge, a continuation of the hill of Tarare, described in Rte. 105, commanding an extensive view over the valley of the Rhône, and extending even, it is said, as far as Mont Blanc, is traversed in this stage.

11 La Braly.
14 Grand Buisson.
LYON. (Rte. 108.)

ROUTE 114.

CLERMONT TO TOULOUSE, BY THE CANTAL AND AURILLAC.

322 kilom. = 199½ Eng. m.

Those who wish to avail themselves of a public conveyance must take the Montpellier diligence as far as St. Flour, whence a private vehicle may be procured to Aurillac.

The most direct road from Clermont to Aurillac is by Rochefort (Rte. 110) and Mauriac, but it is not provided with post-horses, and it avoids the picturesque district of *Cantal*, so interesting to geologists, through the heart of which the following road through Murat is carried.

It is the same as Rte. 109 as far as

55 Lempde, where it turns to the l., ascending a long hill as it quits the town. By another hill, du Grenier, you descend in zigzags to

18 Massiac (Dépt. Cantal), where you turn to the left out of the St. Flour road, by a very pretty branch line carried up the vale of the Alagnon. This new road lies through scenery of uninterrupted beauty and interest, passing the picturesque castle of Merdogne, perched on a crag of basalt.

14 Ferrières (Cantal).
22 Murat.—*Inn:* Chez Dolly; tolerable, excepting the dirt. Fine trout here and elsewhere in the Cantal.

Murat is a dirty and antiquated town of 2655 Inhab., in the upland valley of the Alagnon, here bare of trees, but surrounded by hills of uncommon appearance, capped by basalt. One of these rises immediately behind Murat, in a tall cliff called *Roche Bonnevie*, composed of lofty and regular basaltic pillars, 30 to 50 ft. long. The castle on its summit was razed by Louis XI., after he had put to death its owner, Jacques d'Armagnac, 1477.

Opposite the town is another remarkable hill, also topped with basalt, on which stands the pilgrimage chapel of N. D. de Bredom.

Soon after quitting the town, the convent of St. Gal, now an hospital, is passed on the l., and the Castle of Anterroches on the rt. An excellent road is carried up the valley of the Alagnon, constantly ascending, amidst cliffs and precipices of granite. Near the Pont de Pierre Taillée, a bridge thrown over a stream which falls in a pretty cascade, a good geological section of the trachyte and tufa has been exposed. Above this, the fine fir forest of Lioran, which clothes the upper part of the valley, commences. The additional steepness of the valley near its head has hitherto been surmounted by a series of tourniquets or zigzags; but in order to avoid this, as well as the snow which blocks up the highest part of the road, frequently for weeks and months in winter and spring, a *Tunnel* is carried through a saddle-shaped ridge, which divides the waters of the Alagnon from those of the Cère, a little to the E. of the highest point of the old road, and about 400 or 500 ft. below it. This Tunnel is driven through the trachytic rock for a distance of about 4593 ft. (1400 mètres); it is nearly 18 ft. high, ascends slightly in the centre, and terminates a little below the village of les Chazes. On emerging from it, the *Puy de Griou*, a pointed, wedge-shaped peak of white rock, with a stream of débris descending from it, is seen on the rt.: and the *Plomb de Cantal,* a boss like a camel's hump surmounting a precipice, rises on the l. Those, however, who are content merely to pass through the tunnel will miss altogether the grand and striking scenery of the vast volcanic amphitheatre, through the midst of which the old road is carried, in proximity to the sources of the Alagnan and Cère.

The traveller, whether geologist or merely a lover of picturesque, will be well rewarded by making the ascent of the *Puy de Griou*, which may be effected in about an hour from the hamlet of les Chazes, even without a guide. It is fatiguing from the extreme steepness of the slope; but the only difficulty is in surmounting the bare crest of white clinkstone, covered with loose fallen masses, which rattle down under your feet into the depths below. But even here a sort of path has been formed, over the scanty grass tufts springing up between the stones. The summit itself is a mere crest only 3 or 4 ft. wide and 20 yds. long, plunging precipitously down on all sides. The Puy de Griou rises in the midst of an irregular circle of precipices, supposed by geologists to have been the fiery mouth or crater whence the volcanic rocks of the Cantal were erupted, and whence they spread for 15 or 20 m. around, from this centre as far as Aurillac, Murat, and St. Flour. It is also supposed that, at a later period, the volcanic forces acting from below, at the same point, burst through these deposits of trachyte, tufa, and basalt, fracturing the strata with radiating cracks like those in a starred pane of glass, and that these cracks, gradually widening, became the valleys of the Alagnon, Cère, Jourdanne, Dienne, &c. The circuit of precipices which composed the walls of this crater is broken by gaps formed by the openings of the different valleys radiating from this point like the spokes of a wheel. These walls are most perfect on the E. below the basaltic hump called Plomb de Cantal, the highest summit in the district, 6095 ft. above the sea-level; on the N. in the Puy Mary, 5459 ft.; and on the W. in the Puy Chavaroche. Through the gaps between them the eye ranges down the vistas of the valleys over an extensive horizon of plain and distant hills. The dimensions of this crater greatly exceed those of any in Auvergne, as it is more than 6 Eng. m. in diameter. Within and beneath its bounding walls are rounded slopes, wooded or covered with turf, forming the lining of the crater, and presenting a pleasing picture. Quite at the foot of the Puy de Griou is a remarkable kettle-shaped hollow, covered with the brightest verdure, and dotted over with 2 or 3 cabins, and with herds, for it is the best piece of pasturage in the district. From its shape it might be mistaken for a minor crater, hemmed in by wooded eminences. It is called *le Font du Vacher.*

Quitting the volcanic amphitheatre at les Chazes, we commence the descent of the valley of the Cère, which is far more picturesque in its scenery than that of the Alagnon, but is best seen in ascending, as the forms of the mountains at its head lend to the views their most striking features. The first village, St. Jacques des Blats, produces excellent cheeses of goat's milk, called *cabeçons*. The numerous projections on either side of the valley conceal the villages from view until you are close upon them. The river cuts through a rocky bed, and the road, skilfully engineered, is carried in terraces hewn out of the trachytic rock along the edge of deep precipices, the most remarkable of which, called Pas de Compain, terminates within a few hundred yards of the village of

26 Thiézac, where the Poste (Tête Noire), though most forbidding externally, by reason of its dirt, can afford 2 clean beds and a tolerable supper, with trout; for which and a breakfast only 5 fr. are charged. Below Thiézac calcined flints shattered by heat, like unannealed glass, may be seen embedded in the trachyte rock at the road side.

The most strikingly pictureque scene in the whole valley is at a spot called *Pas de la Cère*, a little way above the solitary projecting rock (Rocher de Murat), rendered conspicuous by the single round-headed lime-tree which crowns its summit. Here the valley at once expands considerably, and makes a deep descent or step, and the river has forced for itself a passage, at a great depth below the road, in a fissure lined by smooth walls of rock, and nearly shrouded by a luxuriant growth of trees. The rocks towering above the road imitate the forms of old castles. The little town of Vic (Vic-en-Carladés, or Vic-sur-Cère) is the chief place in the very picturesque valley. (*Inn:* Chez Vialette.) Close to it there are mineral *springs* of acidulous water, received into a *bathing establishment.* 1 m. out of the town, at the roadside, stands the Château de Comblat, belonging to an ancient and loyal family settled here for ages, the present owner being the Comte Charles de la Baume. At Polminhac is a far more picturesque *castle*, towering over the road, a fit subject for the artist's pencil. The valley of Vic, here widening out into a small plain, covered with meadows and corn-fields, is yet enlivened by a pretty distribution of wood and hedgerows, amidst which rise numerous châteaux and modern country houses, indicating that the proprietors reside on their estates. At this point our road quits the vale of the Cère, gradually ascending in a sloping terrace cut through the white tertiary limestone, containing flints, in appearance closely resembling the upper chalk of England, though of a very different age, which has been disturbed and baked by the trachytic rocks. Turning the shoulders of the hills, we enter the valley of the Jourdanne, a tributary of the Cère, at the mouth of which stands

27 *Aurillac* (*Inn:* Trois Frères; best and good), chef-lieu of the Dépt. du Cantal, and anciently one of the 6 good towns of la Haute Auvergne, a dull town of 9886 Inhab., without objects of interest, in a tame and bare valley watered by the Jourdanne. The churches, convents, and palace of the abbot were destroyed by the Huguenots, who took the town, 1569, by assault, and kept it for a year: the existing public buildings are modern and commonplace. The *Castle of St. Etienne*, rising on a rock above the town to the W., is said to have belonged to the ancestors of St. Géraud (d. 918), the patron of the town: it was held by the abbots, and now belongs to the bishop of Clermont, but is not worth visiting.

The chief manufactures carried on here are of copper kettles and coarse lace.

The infamous J. B. Carrier, the author and inventor of the Noyades at Nantes, was born, 1756, in the village of Yolet, close to Aurillac.

Diligences daily to Paris, to Rodez, 3 times a week to Toulouse, by Figeac. The road to Figeac, after crossing the level verdant valley of the Cère, and the river itself, mounts into a hilly district of gneiss and mica slate rocks, barely covered with heath. From the high ground fine views are obtained of the volcanic group of the Cantal.

27 Cayrols.

A very long and winding descent, doubling the shoulders of the hills, and diving deep into the recesses of the glens, leads down a wooded valley to

18 Maurs. Another hilly tract intervenes before we reach

24 Figeac (*Inn:* Poste), a town of 6400 Inhab., in the Dépt. of Lot, lying snugly at the bottom of a small valley, so shut in by steep hills that the high roads are obliged to make the most singular and circuitous contortions in order to reach it. The town, whose naturally obscure name has become familiar through its illustrious citizen Champollion, who was born here, and to whom a monumental *obelisk* has been erected at the water-side, contains a great number of antique houses and 2 curious churches. The abbey *Church of St. Sauveur*, in the lower part of the town, consists of a Romanesque basement, with a later pointed superstructure, of the 15th centy., and a modern front of the 19th. The choir, however, seems almost entirely of the 11th cent. Attached to the S. transept is a small chapter-house, resting on pointed arches.

On an eminence, above the town, stands *Notre Dame de Puy*, a church of the 11th centy., though much altered, in the form of a basilica, ending towards the E. in 3 apses. At the bottom of the choir is a very fine *altar screen* of wood richly carved and ornamented, a masterly work of the early part of the 17th centy., judging from its style.

The *Château de la Balcine*, now Palais de Justice, fortified and moated, also deserves attention.

A high table-land of limestone, bounded by very abrupt slopes, separates Figeac from the valley of the Lot. After reaching its summit by a steep ascent, the road to Villefranche passes near a singular stone *pillar*, or obelisk, rising on the brow of the hill above Figeac. Its use and age are equally unknown. Some consider it to have been a beacon: it was more probably a landmark to designate the boundary of some jurisdiction. There is a similar pillar on the other side of Figeac.

From the high ground a view is obtained, on the l. of the town, of Capdenac, on the rt. bank of the Lot, supposed by Champollion to be the ancient "*Uxellodunum*," besieged by Cæsar, and mentioned in his Commentaries.

The Lot is crossed by a wire suspension bridge: the hills bordering on the river sides are very steep.

18 La Remise.

17 Villefranche (*Inn*: Grand Soleil). This town of 9540 Inhab., on the Aveyron, was one of the Bastides, or Free Towns, built in the 14th centy., and retains its original plan (p. 228). Its principal building is the large *Collegiate Church*, in the pointed Gothic style of the 15th and 16th centuries, standing in a market-place surrounded by arcades. Its W. façade, though bare of ornament, is imposing from its proportions, and is surmounted by a lofty tower, supported by obliquely set buttresses, at the base of which a porch, furnished with triple arches, gives entrance to the interior.

There are many *ancient houses* of the 15th and 16th centuries, very picturesque in their architecture, in the principal street. "In the suburb beyond the river stands the *Hospital*, formerly a Carthusian convent, the buildings of which are preserved nearly entire, including a good flamboyant church and the refectory, with rich pulpit, and 2 cloisters—the smaller one very rich."—*J. H. P.*

Steep hills lead into and out of

29 Caylus (*Inn*: Poste), a town of most picturesque character, both in itself and in its situation, buried as it were in the deep recess of a valley. In the midst, its *castle*, rising on a rock, towers above the houses clustering round its base; and by its side rises the church spire. Opposite the W. door of the Ch. is a remarkable house of the 14th centy.; the front curious and well preserved.

The road emerges from this bowl-shaped hollow, by being carried in bends round its nearly vertical sides.

22 Caussade.

["On a cross-road from Caussade to Alby lies *St. Antonin* (*Inn*: H. de Commerce; homely, but clean), a small town with a pretty *H. de Ville*, chiefly of the 12th centy., well restored under M. Viollet-le-Duc. There are a number of old houses.

"*Cordes* (*Inn* on the top of the hill, good; not so the one below, H. de Commerce), a curious little town on the top of a steep sugar-loaf hill, which no antiquary should pass without ascending. The old fortification and gates remain, and within them a number of elaborate and well-preserved houses of the 13th and 14th centuries.]

23 Montauban } described in Rte.
51 Toulouse } 70.

ROUTE 116.

CLERMONT TO TOULOUSE, BY ST. FLOUR, THE BATHS OF CHAUDES AIGUES, RODEZ, AND ALBY.

385 kilom. = $238\frac{1}{2}$ Eng. m.

Malleposte as far as St. Flour, and thence to Montpellier, in 31 hrs.

The route is identical with Rte. 109 as far as

54 Lempde (*Inn*: la Poste). At

18 Massiac (Cantal) it turns to the l. away from the road to Aurillac, and reaches, by an ascent requiring $1\frac{1}{2}$ hr. to surmount, an elevated plain called la Fageole, formed by a great basaltic plateau.

10 La Barraque is a solitary post-

house, surrounded by a few farm-buildings, in a desolate spot.

About 5 m. short of St. Flour, a good view of it, and of the volcanic group of the Cantal beyond, is obtained.

19 St. Flour (*Inns:* Chez Aubertot, tolerable; supper, bed, and coffee cost 3 fr. 5 sous. H. de France).

St. Flour, the 2nd town in importance of the Cantal, is strikingly conspicuous at a distance, owing to its elevated position on the top of a table mount, whose platform is of basalt. The high road from Clermont to Montpellier passes through a suburb at its base; but the upper town is rendered accessible for carriages by a road carried in winding terraces cut into the basaltic rock, and laying bare a regular natural colonnade near the crest of the hill. Excepting its singular and picturesque situation, bounded on 3 sides by escarped precipices, the town, consisting of narrow streets and houses built of basalt, and containing 6464 Inhab., is deficient in attraction. Its *Cathedral*, the chief edifice, is a Gothic structure, not remarkable, dedicated 1496, but not finished till 1566; its towers, demolished in 1593, have been recently rebuilt. The roof is finely groined, and rests on piers without capitals.

From a little terrace behind the Cathedral, from another behind the Séminaire, and from the *Promenade*, or *Cours Chazeret*, occupying the neck of land by which the town is alone connected with the adjoining high ground of the Planèse, views may be obtained over the country and distant hills, but they are arid and bare, and over the contiguous valley watered by the Arder, on whose banks the suburb, the most busy part of the town, is planted. The basaltic rocks in the neighbouring mountains are covered with the lichen archil (orseille) used in dyeing, which is collected and largely exported hence.

St. Flour was anciently a very strong fortress, and withstood many sieges from the English in the 14th centy.

At this point the road to Chaudes Aigues and Rodez separates from that to Montpellier; a *malleposte* from Clermont follows the latter through St. Chely, Marvejols, and Milhau.

The road to Chaudes Aigues traverses for a considerable distance elevated basaltic plateau called la Planèse. The volcanic group of the Cantal mountains is visible for a long time on the W.

On the way to Chaudes Aigues, but considerably to the l. of the road, lies Alleuzes, mentioned by Froissart under the name Louise, a castle which belonged to the celebrated robber-chief of the 14th centy., Aymerigot Marcel, whence his band used to sally forth to pillage on the highways. A little further in the same direction is *Montbrun*, another castle, which was taken and held for the English, 1357, by John Chandos, constable of Guienne.

The approach to Chaudes Aigues is by the steep hill called Côte de Laneau, where the road has been terraced through rocks of gneiss and mica-schist, whose contortions are laid open in sections, at the edge of ravines and precipices. After passing the ravine called Saut du Loup, from a fanciful resemblance in the rock to a wolf's head, it descends into the valley or gorge of the Truyère, a tributary of the Lot. That river is passed on a handsome stone bridge.

33 *Chaudes Aigues* (*Inns:* the best is Chez Fabre, recently rebuilt. H. Felgère, furnished with baths).

This is an old but rustic-looking town of 2351 Inhab., planted in a narrow and picturesque gorge, which about 3 m. below opens into that of the Truyère. The *mineral waters*, from which it has obtained some resort as a watering-place, are almost pure warm water: they issue out of the slate-rock, and are 4 in number. That called *Source du Par* is the hottest spring in Europe, except the Geysers in Iceland, having a temperature of 177° Fahrenheit, and is one of the most copious sources in France; the others, *de Felgère*, *du Ban*, and *de la Grotte*, vary in heat between 135° and 162° Fahr. The waters are taken in baths, and are drunk, being considered efficacious in rheumatism, swellings of the joints, and some cutaneous disorders, though by no means richly impregnated with mineral particles. They are also turned to various domestic and economic purposes : they have the property of discharging most rapidly the grease from sheep's wool, and a vast number of fleeces are sent hither from the Dépt. Aveyron to be washed. From the month of Nov. to April the hot water is used for warming the town, being conducted in pipes into some of the houses, called in the patois of the country *Maison Caoudo;* and it thus saves the inhabitants the cost of many tons of coal or whole forests of firewood : the equal distribution of the waters is watched over by the police. The hot streams are also partly employed for cookery, for boiling eggs, prepared soups, and scalding pigs. They have also been turned to the artificial incubation of chickens with considerable success.

There is no object of interest in or near the town except the waters. A ruin at a short distance, near the chapel, is called *le Fort des Anglais;* indeed, the English are said to have captured the town in the 14th centy., in the 2 incursions which they made, in 1357, under the command of Robert Knollys, and in 1387. A large portion of the inhabitants of Chaudes Aigues migrate every winter to Paris, to obtain employment in various menial offices, as water-carriers, décrotteurs, &c.—a practice common among the lower orders throughout Auvergne. From Chaudes Aigues it is possible to ascend on foot the Plomb de Cantal and descend on Thiézac (p. 399), but this cannot be accomplished in a single day.

Scarcely a human habitation occurs on the long stage from Chaudes Aigues, except the poor hamlet of Lecalm, where the road enters the Dépt. Aveyron ; a hilly road.

32 Laguiole, built on the slope of a basaltic hill, trades in the excellent cheese made in this district.

The road skirts on the l. a valley, in whose recesses, once shrouded by forests, stood the venerable and wealthy Bernardine Monastery of Bonneval, now entirely swept away. The descent into the fertile and verdant valley of the Lot is very pleasing. Above the winding course of the river, which is bordered with wooded and vine-clad slopes, rise the escarped peaks crowned with the ruined *castles* of Caumont and of Roquelaure.

24 Espalion (*Inn:* Chez Aigalenz ; tolerable) is a prettily-situated small town, residence of a sous-préfet, on the Lot. There is nothing of interest in the town itself, but in its vicinity the 2 castles already mentioned, and a curious *chapel* in the cemetery of the village of Perse.

The road to Rodez ascends out of the valley of the Lot after crossing it, under the castle-crowned height of Caumont. From a distance of many miles the traveller discerns the picturesque towers of

31 *Rodez* (*Inns:* H. du Midi ; best. Ville de Paris ; good. H. des Voyageurs. Des Princes), chef-lieu of the Dépt. Aveyron, a town of 9685 Inhab., and occupying a commanding site on an escarped peninsula, surrounded on 3 sides by a curve of the Aveyron, which flows at a depth of 150 ft. below. The tongue of land, which alone connects it with the neighbouring plain, is traversed by the road from Paris and Espalion; from all other sides the town is accessible only by steep ascents.

The *Cathedral,* so imposing and conspicuous at a distance, will probably not altogether justify the impression it has produced on a near approach, though it is of large size, and possesses some elegant details. It was founded 1274, but carried on slowly through the 2 following centuries, and never finished. The W. end is destitute of entrance, because fitted up internally with a high altar as well as the E. end. The entrances are at the sides, and, though mutilated, display some rich ornaments; near the N. transept rises the *belfry,* the pride and boast of Rodez, 265 ft. high, consisting of a square base supporting an octagonal summit, richly ornamented in the upper part with florid tracery. It is surmounted by a statue of the Virgin, and was finished 1531.

The interior of the church, 110 ft. high, rests on piers without capitals, and the style of its decorations resembles the perpendicular of English Gothic. At the entrance of the choir is a fine *Jubé* (rood-loft), which, though mutilated, exhibits workmanship of surprising beauty, in the delicate sculpture of its curled foliage. A part of the *screen* intended to surround the choir is of like beauty. The woodwork of the *stalls* and bishop's throne in the choir are of good execution, and were well preserved until painted recently. One of the side-chapels contains a fine *altar-screen* of wood, elaborately carved with bas-reliefs, arabesques, and ornaments partly Gothic, partly classic, in the style of the 16th centy. The whole is painted and illuminated. The partition *screen* to this chapel is of rich open work in stone, flamboyant in its style. The woodwork of the organ-loft, a tomb in the form of a sarcophagus, adorned with bas-reliefs of the 9th centy.; another tomb of Bishop Guirbert, 14th centy.; an altar-table of white marble, 6 ft. long, with Byzantine ornaments, 10th centy., now used as an altar-screen, and painted with a figure of the Virgin, —also deserve attention.

The town abounds in antique houses of the 15th and 16th centuries, and contains some of perhaps a still older date. In the *Place d'Omet* there is a house charmingly decorated, in the style of the Renaissance, with arabesques, medallions rich framed, and in the upper story with a range of fantastic consoles. (See Merimée, 157-169.)

Terraces run round the town upon the line of the old fortifications, and afford agreeable views, though the country round Rodez is not particularly attractive, the valley of the Aveyron being bare, and not very fertile.

Rodez was the *Segodunum* of the Romans, and capital of the Gaulish tribe the Ruteni, whence comes its present name.

Fromage de Roquefort, the choicest cheese which France produces, which was sent to ancient Rome, and was enthusiastically praised by Pliny, is made with ewe milk, in the mountains of La Lozère, about 28 m. E. and S. of Rodez, in the district around St. Rome, St. Afrique, St. Georges, and Milhau. It is kept in cellars, belonging to the cheesemongers, to ripen. About 10,000 cheeses are made annually. The village of Roquefort, where are the principal cellars, is situated near St. Afrique, in the midst of the pastures of Larza, which support more than 100,000 sheep.

Diligences go to Toulouse and Montauban.

[The *Valley of Marcillac*, beginning at Salles Compteaux, about 5 m. N. of Rodez, forms an agreeable contrast to the barren district immediately around that town. This beautiful green dell, gushing with springs and waterfalls, covered with trees and orchards, is excavated out of a high plain destitute of vegetation, which must be crossed to reach it. At the head of the valley rises an old castle, near which a copious spring bursts forth. Following this valley past Marcillac (5 m.) along the banks of the Dourdou for about 12 m. below that town, you reach *Conques*, a small town half hidden in a rocky ravine, in the midst of the wildest mountains of the Rouergue, scarcely accessible at some seasons, owing to the badness of the roads. It owes its origin to an ancient abbey, whose site it occupies, but the buildings of which have all disappeared, except the *Church of St. Foy*, constructed to all appearance at the beginning of the 11th centy. by Abbot Odalric. It is entirely in the Romanesque style, with semicircular vaults and arches; it terminates at the E. in 3 apses, and is surmounted at the cross by an octagonal tower more modern than the rest (14th centy.). The W. end is flanked by 2 towers; the central portal is ornamented with a curious bas-relief in the tympanum, representing the Last Judgment, divided into 3 horizontal friezes; in the centre, Christ within the Vesica piscis; on his rt. the good, on his l. the wicked; above, angels; below, on one side, the gates of Paradise, with bolts and a huge lock, and the dead rising from beneath their grave-stones; in the centre, below Christ, an angel and devil weighing souls; on the other side, the gate of hell, an enormous open jaw, into which the devil is thrusting the condemned.

Each group and portion of the relief is designated by inscriptions in Leonine verses. The figures are coloured.

The *Trésor* of the ch. contains the following curious and valuable relics of ancient art, which at the Revolution were intrusted to the care of different inhabitants of the town, and were most carefully preserved, and religiously restored by them when the political storm had passed away. An ancient *reliquiary*, called Charlemagne's A, from its triangular form, and the tradition that it was given by that monarch to the abbey; it is of silver gilt and partly enamelled, and set with polished gems and some antiques; at the base are 2 little figures of gilt bronze, supposed to be less ancient than the upper portion. A statue of St. Foy, 18 inches high, of silver gilt, and studded with precious stones and antique gems, cameos, &c.; a Byzantine enamel of the figure of a saint, on a plate of copper; a silver crucifix of beautiful workmanship; a square slab of red porphyry in a frame of silver, covered with heads of Christ, the Virgin, and Saints in niello. There are also some tapestries of the 16th centy.

About 3 m. below Conques the Dourdou falls into the Lot.]

The high road from Rodez runs through

26 La Motte. *Inn:* Chez Nave.

30 Farguette.

At Carmeaux a coal-field is worked, which furnishes good fuel.

22 Alby (*Inns:* H. des Ambassadeurs; de l'Europe; du Nord, good) — an ancient city, chef-lieu of the Dépt. of the Tarn, in the midst of the flat but fertile plain of Languedoc, watered by the river Tarn—has 11,662 Inhab. Its buildings are of brick, as is the case throughout the plain of Languedoc; the ramparts are thrown down and planted, and, especially on the side next the new Quartier de Vigan, there are extensive *walks*, avenues, and gardens, partly on the site of the ancient lists (les Lices), where tournaments were held.

The *Cathedral of St. Cecile* is the chief building in the town; it is a noble Gothic edifice of brick, founded 1282, and not completed till 1512. The tower at the W. end, raised by Louis d'Amboise, 1475, is 290 ft. high and of curious construction. The nave, without transepts, and unsupported by pillars, is 88 ft. wide and 98 ft. high. The choir is separated from the nave by a *rood-loft* (*jubé*) of extreme beauty of design, and elaborate delicacy of execution in its Gothic tracery, foliage, &c.; the enclosure of the choir is of equally rich workmanship. But the most striking feature of interest is the profusion of *fresco paintings* on the roof and walls, which escaped destruction at the Revolution; portions in the vaults are untouched, and of the utmost freshness and beauty, on an azure ground, the work of Italian artists, 1505. In some of the side chapels, and near the entrance, are paintings of a still earlier date (14th centy.), and in a style resembling that of the German schools. The stone carvings of the choir, consisting of elaborate tabernacle work with a profusion of statues, were executed for Cardinal d'Amboise by a company of itinerant masons from Strasburg.

The *Préfecture*, formerly the Episcopal Palace, but at a still earlier period the residence of the counts of the Albigeois, is, in part, a heavy castellated edifice of brick, at the margin of the Tarn, on its l. bank. Its terraced garden, overlooking the river, is pleasing.

The *Ch. of St. Salvi* presents some architectural features of interest.

Some manufactures are carried on here of coarse linen cloths, candles, and tools, files, scythes; also of *woad* (pastel), which has been made here from a very early period. The chief commerce is in grain; the plain of Alby being one of the richest corn countries in France.

Alby has given its name to the sect of dissenters from the Ch. of Rome, the *Albigeois*, who abounded in the district during the 12th and beginning of the 13th centuries, and who were condemned as heretics by a council held here, 1254, and soon after nearly exterminated at the siege of Beziers. (Rte. 126.)

Alby is the birth-place of the unfortunate sea captain and circumnavigator of the globe, La Peyrouse.

The little *Ch.* of *Lescures*, on the opposite side of the river, is quite a model of the Byzantine style of the 11th centy. as it exists in this part of France.

At *Saut de Sabot*, about 3 m. off, the course of the Tarn is intercepted by rapids of considerable descent, by the side of which a furnace and forge for the manufacture of steel is established.

The *Castle* of Castenau de Levi, on the rt. bank of the Tarn, is a picturesque object. The Tarn is crossed at the village of Marsac.

21 Gaillac stands on the rt. bank of the Tarn, in a country producing abundance of wine. Its population exceeds 7000.

23 Pointe-Sainte-Sulpice.
16 Montbert.
15 TOULOUSE. Rte. 70.

ROUTE 117.

MONTAUBAN TO BEZIERS, BY CASTRES.

198 kilom. = 123 Eng. m.
12 La Bastide.

The road runs by the side of the Tarn as far as

32 Pointe St. Sulpice.

Hence it follows the Agout.
14 La Vaur.
15 St. Paul.

23 *Castres* (*Inn:* H. Sabatier, dirty), a picturesque but dirty town, situated on a gentle rise, with public walks, a Place, Halle au Blé, some manufactures and dye-works.

A pretty drive; pleasing valley enlivened with country houses.

27 St. Amans la Bastide (*Inns:* Lion d'Or;—St. Denis), a bustling little place; its streets lined with trees.

25 St. Pons.

The next stage is over a pretty country, and through a grand defile, having the Montagnes Noires on the S. and the Monts Espinouses on the N.E. The road is skilfully carried up the pass. The mountains are literally covered with wild lavender of exquisite fragrance. Every patch in the valley is cultivated; grapes, figs, almonds, walnuts, chestnuts, olives, wheat, and maize are among its varied produce, yet the people are most miserable.

23 St. Chinian (*Inn:* Grand Soleil), a wretched place, streets scarce wide enough for a carriage to pass.

27 *Beziers* (in Rte. 126).

ROUTE 118.

LYONS TO LE PUY, AUBENAS, AND MENDE, BY ST. ETIENNE.—RAILWAY TO ST. ETIENNE.—ARDÈCHE, AND CEVENNES.

220 kilom. = 134 Eng. m.

Railroad from Lyons to St. Etienne, $14\frac{1}{2}$ leagues = $35\frac{1}{3}$ Eng. m. Trains go 3 times a day in 4 hours, returning in $3\frac{1}{2}$; the line is not well made, the jolting is great, and the carriages, except the first-class (coupés), are large and dirty, and filled with workmen and market-people; stoppages are frequent at the numerous villages near the line. It was opened 1837. It is carried through more than a dozen tunnels. Private carriages cannot be taken. Its chief use is to supply Lyons with coal from St. Etienne. The *terminus*, or depôt, is situated outside the town of Lyons, in the *Faubourg de Perrache*, between the Saône and Rhône, but passengers are conveyed thither in huge omnibuses, which start from the Place Bellecour. The railway is carried over the Gare, or safety dock for barges, opening into the Saône, and crosses the Saône itself just above its junction with the Rhône, by the suspension *Pont de la Mulatière*, and thenceforth skirts the rt. bank of the Rhône as far as Givors, sometimes close to the river, sometimes separated from it by low meadows and rows of plantations of willows, which intercept much of the view.

The course of the Rhône is described in Rte. 125.

Oullins (Stat.) village is surrounded by country seats of Lyonese manufacturers; in its churchyard Jacquard, the inventor of the loom named after him, is buried. The line is carried through several small tunnels and cuttings past the villages Irigny, Vernaison (Stat.) and Grigny, before reaching Givors.

13 Brignais, the first post-station on the high road, is about 5 m. to the W. of the railway.

Givors (Stat.), a dirty and smoky town, abounding in manufactories, especially of glass bottles, on the rt. bank of the Rhône, at the point where it receives the stream of the Gier and the *Canal de Givors*, which transports much coal and ironstone. Pop. about 5000.

Omnibuses go hence to Vienne (Rte. 125), 5 m., in about an hour, corresponding with the railway trains.

The railroad here quits the side of the Rhône, and ascends the valley of the Gier, keeping that stream and the canal on the rt. hand. Industry prevails everywhere; manufactories occur at every step, and envelop the country with their dense smoke.

A tunnel about ¾ m. (1500 mètres) long is driven through a hill of the coal-measures, near

17 La Rousillière.

22 Rive de Gier (Stat.), a very flourishing and increasing manufacturing town of 12,000 Inhab., on the rt. bank of the Gier, at the commencement of the Canal de Givors, situated in a productive coal-field, which is the chief source of its prosperity. More than 40 coal-mines in the vicinity are provided with steam-engines. There are very large glass-works here, and a manufactory of steel carried on by Englishmen, Messrs. Jackson, which produces the best steel in France.

Here are also manufactories of steam-engines and other machinery, and some silk-mills. Lyons is chiefly supplied hence with fuel; but Marseilles, Mulhausen, Paris, and Nantes also receive fuel in large quantities from this coal-field, the most important in France, from its extent and position. Above this, owing to the steep inclination of the railway, horse power has hitherto been alone employed; but a new and more level line is being cut (1843) to admit of the use of locomotives. The railroad and post-road run side by side to

15 St. Chamond (Stat.), another manufacturing town, where ribbons and staylaces are made. More than 1200 frames (métiers à la poupée) are employed in weaving staylaces, which are largely exported. Here are besides numerous iron furnaces, foundries, and forges, and several silk-mills. Pop. 8246. This place has been much injured by the railway not passing through it. Between St. Chamond and St. Etienne runs the ridge separating the waters flowing into the Mediterranean through the Rhône, from those which go to the Atlantic through the Loire.

Another *tunnel*, about 1 m. long, traverses a hill under the considerable village of Terre Noire (Stat.), immediately before reaching St. Etienne. It is very narrow and low, affording space for only one line of rails. The latter part of the line is an inclined plane, which the train descends by its own impetus in going to Lyons.

12 ST. ETIENNE Station in Rte. 119.

The diligence takes 12 hours to make the journey from St. Etienne to Le Puy. The road is very hilly and varied: crossing a long ridge out of the valley of the Furens, it continues to traverse a district very populous, and abounding in manufactures as far as the coal-measures extend. At Le Chambon are manufactures of cutlery, nails, saws, &c. At

12 Firmigny there are many coal-mines, some of them, worked after the fashion of quarries, open to the sky, in a coal-bed more than 32 feet thick; also glass-works, ribbon and silk mills. The valley is bristling with chimneys, coal-heaps, manufactories; but they cease before you reach St. Ferreol, just within the borders of the Dépt. de la Haute Loire. The road is admirably engineered, and partly cut through the granite rock in a terrace winding round the shoulders of the hills.

17 Monistrol: the château, formerly a country seat of the Bishop of Le Puy, is now a ribbon manufactory. Some ribbons are woven here, but the manufacture extends no farther. 4 m. beyond Monistrol our road approaches

the Loire, and crosses, by a very long and steep descent and ascent, the deep and picturesque gorge of the Langon, which falls into the Loire about ½ m. below the bridge. The course of that river and its deep and wide valley may be traced for a considerable distance on the rt. from the heights beyond the Langon.

A road turns off rt. E. to Annonay and Valence on the Rhone, by St. Bonnet le Froid and the beautiful Val de Vocance. (See Rte. 119.)

20 Yssingeaux.—*Inn:* H. de l'Europe; not good. A town of no particular interest; Pop. 6700.

Near this we enter the volcanic district of the Velay: on either side of the road rise hills of basalt and trachyte, and from the summit of the trachytic ridge of the Montagne de Pertuis, which it traverses by a long ascent, an excellent panorama is presented of the country. A part of Le Puy itself is visible. The hills generally assume a conic form, and are frequently capped with basalt. The top of the Mt. Pertuis is of slaty clinkstone, which is used for roofing houses.

On the rt. of the road is passed the ruined *Castle Lardeyrolles*, perched on the top of such a volcanic eminence.

Within 3 m. of Le Puy the Loire is crossed, here an insignificant stream, descending from its source at Gerbier des Joncs, at the base of the Mont Mezène in the Dépt. de l'Ardèche. The pedestrian may proceed direct from Le Puy to Montpezat and Aubenas by the Source of the Loire.

A good view is obtained of the town of Le Puy in approaching it, though it is partly concealed by the Rocher de Corneille.

28 *Le Puy*, in Rte. 109.

The road to Mende is now furnished with post-horses; it is very hilly, being carried over part of the range of the Cevennes, in which some of the principal rivers of France take their rise. At first it ascends the valley of the Dolaison. From that stream as far as Pradelles the country is all volcanic.

19 Castaros.

About 3 m. W. of this is the Lac de Bouchet, a mountain tarn occupying the basin of an ancient crater, 91 ft. deep in the centre, without visible outlet.

[At the small and elevated town of Pradelles (no endurable *Inn*, but carriages at reasonable charge may be had chez Jouve), near which the granite rock shows itself, a cross road strikes off to Aubenas by Savilatte, over the mountains into the valley of the Ardèche, near its source, and follows its course downwards, by Mayras, to Thueyts. (*Inn:* H. de Voyageurs, good head-quarters for geological excursions.) Thueyts is built on a current of basaltic lava, which has flowed from a crater a little to the E. of it, and has occupied the bed of the Ardèche; but the river has cut for itself a passage on one side, laying bare a majestic colonnade of basalt 150 ft. high, stretching with a few interruptions 1½ m. down the valley. Its situation and environs are most picturesque and interesting (see Rte. 121). About 4 m. below Thueyts, the river Alignon enters the Ardèche from the S. The course of that stream for about 3 m. up, lies at the base of vertical cliffs, formed of columns of basalt 150 ft. high, the section of another lava current, made by the Alignon, which has gnawed for itself a channel between the granite and the basalt. This lava current is traced up to a large volcanic crater, called, from its regular cup-shape, *La Coupe de Jaujac*. It has been breached and broken down on one side. Its cone and slopes are covered with Spanish chestnut trees, which grow in the greatest luxuriance on volcanic soils, as is especially seen on the slopes of Mount Etna. This crater of Jaujac has burst forth through a coal formation, which lines the bottom of a triangular-shaped valley, bounded by mountains of granite and gneiss. The village of Jaujac stands in a very striking and singular position, on the edge of the basaltic precipice, on the rt. bank of the Alignon, near the base of the crater, whence a mineral spring and copious jets of carbonic acid gas issue. Another lava current enters the Alignon about 300 yards above its junction with the Ardèche: its origin is to be sought in another volcanic

CENTRAL FRANCE.   *Route* 118.—*Mende—Mont Lozère.*   409

cone, the *Gravenne de Souillols*. It has spread for a considerable distance down the valley of the Ardèche. Numerous picturesque ranges of columnar basalt are presented on the river banks from time to time. Some of the most striking occur near *Pont de la Beaume*, at the junction of the Fontaulier, which flows from Montpezat, with the Ardèche. The excursion to Montpezat, and the rest of the road to *Aubenas*, are described in Rte. 121.]

The road from Pradelles descends into the valley of the Allier, which it crosses before entering
21 Langogne, a town of 2720 Inhab., in the Dépt. de la Lozère. It has an ancient church, which belonged to a monastery founded in the 10th centy.
20 La Vitarelle. About 6 m. to the S. and E. of this the rivers Allier and Lot take their rise. A stone has been set up here to commemorate the death of the chivalrous Du Guesclin, who breathed his last while besieging a company of marauding mercenaries of the bands called "compagnies" in the petty fortress of Châteauneuf le Randon, a little on the rt. of the road, which still retains the ruins of its castle. The commander had promised to yield the place to Du Guesclin in a fortnight, provided no succour arrived; but the constable, who was adored by the compagnies as their father, who had spent his own fortune in ransoms for them when taken prisoners, died in the interval. The governor of the fortress nevertheless kept his word by placing the keys on the dead warrior's coffin on the appointed day.

The road is carried over a very high pass in the granitic range, a part of the Mont Margaride, often blocked up with snow, called in irony Le Palais du Roi.
29 Mende (*Inn*; H. de Commerce), chef-lieu of the Dépt. de la Lozère, anciently of the province of Gévaudun, is a feudal and monastic town of 5909 Inhab., in a hollow, surrounded by mountains, on the Lot. It has a fine *cathedral*, surmounted by 2 spires.

The ancient *Bishop's Palace* is now the *préfecture*. On the slope of the Mont Mimat, above the town, is perched the *Hermitage de St. Privast*, over the grotto of that saint, the apostle of the Gévaudun.

Some considerable manufactures of serges and other coarse cloths are carried on here.

The direct road from Paris to Montpellier runs through Marvijols, about 12 m. W. of Mende.

About 6 m. S.E. of Mende rises the *Mont Lozère*, whence the Département is named, whose summit, 1490 mètres above the sea-level, is covered with extensive pastures occupied in summer by large flocks of sheep, to the number, it is said, of 200,000, which migrate in the winter to the plains of Languedoc; and its base is girt round with large forests, which still abound in wolves.

At 3 m. from Mende our road quits the valley of the Lot, and, crossing a calcareous table-land, utterly bare and arid, destitute of habitation, cultivation, and almost of soil, called *Causse de Sauveterre*, descends into the valley of the Tarn, and the country of the Cevennes. (Introduction, Sect. V.)
26 Molines.

The principal source of the Tarn is in the Plateau de l'Hôpital: on its borders lies Grisac, birth-place of Pope Urban V., and about 6 m. from its source the Pont de Montvert, a small village, deep sunk between the Mont Lozère and Bougès, the scene of some remarkable events in the war of the Cevénnes. The insurrection in fact commenced here by the murder of the archdeacon Chayla, a cruel persecutor of the Calvinists, who had scoured the country backed by a troop of dragoons, seizing, imprisoning, and torturing women and men. On the night of July 24, 1702, the house, still standing at the N. end of the bridge, at that time occupied by Chayla and a party of priests and soldiers, was beset by a band of armed Camisards, headed by one of their prophets, Seguier, who, after breaking down the door with the trunk of a tree and releasing the prisoners, set fire to it, and slew those who attempted to escape.

A few of its inmates were allowed quarter, but Chayla, whose death was

France.   T

the motive for the assault, having broken his leg in letting himself down from a window, was discovered and killed without mercy. He fell, pierced with 52 wounds, 24 of which were mortal. The prophet and his companions, having perpetrated this act of vengeance, passed the night on their knees around the corpses, singing psalms, and did not withdraw before the morning. Seguier was captured shortly after, and expiated his crime by being *burned alive* on the 10th August, 1702. As Pont de Montvert was the cradle, so was it also the tomb of the insurrection: the last bold act of the Camisard chief Roland before his death was an assault upon the Miguelets or Spanish soldiers posted in the village, from which he was repulsed. Joani, one of the last of the Camisard leaders, having been made prisoner near this (1710), slipped off from behind the horse of the "archer" or policeman who was conveying him to a dungeon, as he was passing the bridge, like Rob Roy in Scott's novel, and leaped down into the Tarn, a height of 20 ft. He was shot, however, by the captain of the archers, and perished in the river. Our road quits the Tarn to follow its tributary, the Tarnon, shortly before reaching

11 Florac, a town of 2200 Inhab., situated under a hill, whose bare cleft ridge rises in the form of castellated towers on the Tarnon, close to the influx of the Mimente. The 3 valleys of the 3 head-waters of the Tarn lead into the inextricable labyrinth of defiles composing the mountainous district of the Hautes Cevennes. The Mimente rises in the mountain of Bougès, whose N. summit is crowned by the forest *Altefage*, in the depths of which the murderers of the archpriest Chayla had their rendezvous under 3 huge beech-trees, one of which was standing in 1837, reduced to a shattered trunk. At Cassagnas, a village near the source of the Mimente, 13 m. from Florac, many of the *caverns* which were converted into storehouses and arsenals by the Camisards still exist, and serve as habitations. They were filled with corn, wine, oil, chestnuts, and other provisions taken from convents and Romish villages, or contributed by the Protestants to their leaders. The provisions were conveyed thence to the spots where the insurgents met, either in conventicle for prayer, or in battle-array, and there distributed in rations. The corn was for the most part ground in hand-mills, the watermills having been destroyed by the military commander of Languedoc, who, at the same time, laid waste and burned all the villages in the Upper Cevennes, to the number of nearly 400, driving away their inhabitants. Other caves were filled with living flocks and herds or with meat salted, while others again were used as powder magazines and mills; for the Camisards made powder for themselves from the saltpetre collected in their caverns, and the ashes of the willows growing on all the streams. Their principal supply, however, was purchased at Papal Avignon; so that the Papists were shot chiefly by the Pope's own powder. The most airy and wholesome caverns were transformed into hospitals for the wounded, and stored with drugs from Montpellier— to such an extent was the commissariat organised by Roland and other leaders of that fearful civil strife. The mountains skirted by the road on the l., from Molines down to Ledignan, may be regarded as the citadel of the Camisard insurgents; but their ravages and incursions extended S. of the Gardon, and as far as the sea. Among these desolate solitudes they met, like the Cameronians of Scotland, with arms in their hands, in secret conventicles, where the harangues of their prophets and their hymns and prayers were often interrupted by an onset of the royal troops, and the congregation arose from their knees to do battle. After some miles we ascend out of the valley of the Tarnon, leaving it and the road to Montpellier on the rt., and, crossing the high land of Hospitalet, enter the valley of the Gardon, in which lies

23 Pompidou.

The road runs along a sort of hog's back or ridge, dividing the Dépt. de la Lozère from that of Gard, and traverses a sterile and dreary country.

30 St. Jean du Gard, on the l. bank of the Gardon, contains silk mills: 4128 Inhab.

Within this canton, 6 or 8 m. to the N.E., among the mountains, lies Mialet, a village of 1358 Inhab., the stronghold and head-quarters of Roland, chief of the Camisards, who was born at Massoubeyran, close to Mialet. It is also remarkable for the caves and grottoes around it, converted by him into arsenals and storehouses during the war of the Cevennes. Another position of strength held by him was Durfort, among the mountains on the rt. of the Gardon and considerably to the S. of Anduze.

To the S.W. of St. Jean rise the mountains of the Basses Cevennes, the chief of which is the Aigoal, at whose base the river Herault rises.

Anduze (no post) is a town of 5554 Inhab., on the rt. bank of the Gardon, and protected from its furious inundations by a strong dyke forming a terrace and promenade. It is overhung by escarped rocks of the Monts Peyremale and St. Julien. It was the centre of the religious wars which followed the death of Henri IV., and the head-quarters of the Calvinist leader Rohan. A large portion of its inhab. are still Calvinists. During the Camisard insurrection this town as well as Alais was constantly beset by the Camisards up to its very walls.

Florian, the author of 'Gonzalvo de Cordova,' was born in the castle of Florian, between Anduze and St. Hyppolite. The valley of the Gardon below Anduze, between Fornac and Ners, is called *Vallée de Beaurivage*, and is described in his pastoral romances Estelle and Némorin, but with so much exaggeration as scarcely to be distinguished.

Near Lezan our road quits the valley of the Gardon.

27 Ledignan.

Ribaute, a village situated among the hills to the N. of this, was the birth-place of Cavalier, who, having been bred a shepherd, and afterwards apprenticed to a baker at Anduze, was elected, at the age of 17, second in command of the Camisard insurgents, and proved himself a most able general, as well as powerful prophet or preacher. He died a pensioner in Chelsea Hospital.

13 Les Barragues de Fons.
18 Nismes, in Route 126.

ROUTE 119.

ROANNE TO VALENCE ON THE RHÔNE, BY ST. ETIENNE AND ANNONAY.—RAILWAY FROM ROANNE TO ST. ETIENNE.

179 kilom. = 110¾ Eng. m.
Diligences go daily.
Roanne is described in Rte. 105.

A *Railroad*, 42½ m. long, has been carried from Roanne to St. Etienne: the branch from Andresieux to St. Etienne was the first railway constructed in France: horses and not locomotives are used on it, and, though passenger trains traverse it in about 6 hours, it is chiefly used for the conveyance of coals and merchandise; its construction is very imperfect, and it is *not* recommended to English travellers. Carriages are not taken.

From Roanne it is carried up the valley of the Rhins, a small tributary of the Loire, parallel with the post-road to Lyons, as far as St. Symphorien de Lay, where it turns S. The post-road to St. Etienne turns off previously at L'Hôpital to

20 Neulise Stat., beyond which it meets the railway, and the two proceed side by side up the valley of the Loire along its rt. bank. Near the village Pouilly the Loire is confined between huge *dykes*, faced with stones cemented and clamped together, called *Mole de Pinè*, the original construction of which is attributed to the Romans. The rapids thus produced in the river prevent the ascent of boats.

20 Feurs Stat., in Rte. 112.

11 Montrond Stat., a village on the rt. bank of the Loire, 1½ m. W. of the railway. Above it rise the majestic ruins of its old *castle*, burned at the Revolution by order of an itinerant representative of the people.

Montbrison (Rte. 112) is 10 m. distant from Montrond.

14 La Gouyonnière.

The railway reaches the banks of the Loire at Andresieux, to which place large quantities of coal are conveyed from St. Etienne, to be embarked on the Loire for the supply of the centre and W. of France. Beyond Andresieux the line quits the side of the Loire, and ascends the industrious valley of its tributary the Furens, which, in the course of 9 m., sets in motion more than 100 forges and mills. The line from Roanne meets that from St. Etienne at a place called Quérillère, near La Fouillouse.

14 ST. ETIENNE.—*Inns :* H. du Nord, large ; and comfortable, in the Rue Royale ;—Poste, also good.

St. Etienne, the largest and most populous town in the Dépt. de la Loire, although not its chef-lieu, now numbering with its suburbs about 72,000 Inhab., is a remarkable example of a sudden rise, and of still increasing prosperity, owing to two very dissimilar but flourishing branches of manufacture—the making of fire-arms and the weaving of ribbons. To use the words of a French topographer, " ce sont les ateliers de Mars à côté de ceux de Vénus." The town is advantageously situated on the banks of the Furens, which furnishes water-power to move its machinery, in the midst of one of the most productive coal-fields of France. It may be called a French Birmingham, and, like that of England, it is the "child of coal," surrounded by mines, and even seated on coal-deposits, so that some galleries are driven beneath its very streets, though under strict superintendence of the authorities. It is by no means an inviting place to tarry in: little regularity is preserved in the building of streets so suddenly thrown up ; and the fine white sandstone of its houses, many of them 5 and 6 stories high, is soon tarnished and blackened by the coal-smoke which constantly hangs in clouds over it. It has one fine broad street, divided into 2 "Places," planted with trees, by the *Hôtel de Ville*, which stands in the centre of it and of the town. It is a building of no great merit, but of large size. It contains the *Bourse* and the commercial tribunal called *Conseil des Prudhommes*.

Within its walls is an incipient *Museum* (*Musée industriel*), containing specimens of the staple manufactures of the town, ribbons of all kinds, gun-barrels, locks, and stocks, engraved and carved by local workmen; also a collection of the minerals of the neighbourhood, and of the fossils of its coal-field, &c.

There are more than 200 master-manufacturers of *ribbons* here. The number of persons in the town and neighbouring communes employed in this branch of industry has been estimated at 40,000, and the number of looms at about 20,000. The weavers live chiefly on the outskirts of the town and in the adjoining villages, where they avoid the smoke, and live cheaper by escaping the octroi.

The beauty and varied invention shown in the patterns, and the delicate combinations of colours, are admirable. An English traveller should not omit to visit a ribbon-weaver's atelier. About 60 artists are employed in designing and drawing patterns. The total annual value of ribbons made here is estimated at 45 millions of francs.

The *gunsmiths' shops* may be better seen at Birmingham, or even at Liege, both which places produce a larger quantity of arms. About 30,000 or 40,000 stand of arms are made here annually in time of peace, besides 30,000 fowling-pieces, and 1500 pair of pistols; and during the sway of Napoleon not less than from 60,000 to 100,000 were turned out; but it is stated that at a push 300,000 muskets might be produced in 12 months. A musket may be bought for 12 or even 10 fr.; but the price paid by government is from 24 fr. to 35 fr. apiece. About 500 men are employed in the *Manufacture Royale des Armes*, which is carried on by contractors, under the superintendence of artillery officers; but many more out-labourers are employed. All the barrels made must pass through a trial at the proof-house (*Maison d'Epreuve*), open twice a-week. There are also considerable manufacturers of quincaillerie, hardware, and cutlery.

CENTRAL FRANCE. *Route* 119.—*La République—Annonay.* 413

The making of bayonets, gun-locks, gun-stocks of walnut-wood seasoned by steam, employs a great number of hands

St. Etienne is lighted with gas. Its *Cathedral* exhibits in its choir an ancient specimen of Romanesque architecture.

There is a *Theatre* here.

Chemins de Fer.—Two short railways branch off from St. Etienne— 1. to Lyons: the terminus is at the end of the Rue Royale, on the E. of the town, and there are 3 trains daily (see Rte. 118); 2. to Roanne. The station is also about ¼ hour's walk from the centre of the town. Trains go once a-day. (See p. 407.)

Diligences daily to Lyons (3 times); to Le Puy; to Annonay and Valence; to Clermont; to Roanne.

The road to Annonay, almost immediately on quitting the town, passes out of the coal-basin, and commences a long but gradual ascent through a rugged valley, over the high mountain-ridge separating the waters flowing into the Atlantic from those which run into the Mediterranean, and the valley of the Loire from that of the Rhône. These two rivers run parallel to each other, but in an opposite direction, for not less than 120 m. A short way below the summit stands

12 La République, the first relay, a solitary cabaret, which will furnish a tolerable meal and glass of wine. The ridge which our road crosses is a continuation of the granitic range of the Mont Pilas (pileatus), so conspicuous from the banks of the Rhône, near Vienne (Rte. 125), whose peak is visible on the l. near La République. The summit of the pass, and country around, is occupied by a vast forest of firs, le Grand Bois, on emerging from which, and beginning to descend, a fine view opens out, at the end of the valley, of the Alps of Dauphiné stretching along the horizon, of the minor chain running from them down the valley of the Isère, and more near, on the rt., of the mountains of the Ardèche.

The road is finely engineered, carried gradually down along the flanks of the mountains, following their sinuosities. It passes above the ruined *Castle d'Argental*, planted on a sort of promontory, where the rocks are naked and inaccessible. The Bourg, once attached to it, has prudently descended from this feudal platform,

(16 Bourg d'Argental), and now occupies a more genial and sunny site lower down, in a part of the valley where the vine grows and the white mulberry flourishes. The white silk produced here is the best in France for the manufacture of blonde lace, and bears a high price.

A little below this town the road passes out of the Dépt. of the Loire into that of the Ardèche.

The valley of the Dieune, in which lie both Bourg d'Argental and Annonay, has no very striking features of beauty; naked rocks intermixed with formal mulberry plantations, with green meadows, aspens, and willows, are the components of its scenery. Lower down, the river is bestridden by several large paper-mills, chiefly belonging to the respected family Montgolfier. The road, carried high up, looks over slopes occupied by vineyards, beyond which rises the Alpine chain, and between which, in a deep ravine, runs the river. Numerous country houses, or boxes, among the vines announce the approach to Annonay.

15 *Annonay. Inns:* H. du Midi; H. du Nord. This active and increasing manufacturing town, the largest in the Dépt. de l'Ardèche (Pop. 10,000), is situated in the rocky gorges of the Dieune and the Cance, which join their streams in the very centre of the town. The houses are either crammed in between the rocks, or carried up their sides in tiers, or in ranges along their tops, so that its ground plan is very irregular, and from no point can the whole town be seen at once. It has no public buildings of the least interest, merit, or good taste. The *Grande Place* includes in its centre the Bascule, and on one side an *Obelisk* to the memory of the ingenious brothers Joseph and Etienne Montgolfier, natives of Annonay, the inventors of the air-balloon, and founders of the cele-

brated paper-mills near this; it was erected "parleurs concitoyens." Their first ascent into the air was made from this spot, June 1783, in the presence of the Estates of the province. The descendants of the brothers still reside in the neighbourhood, where the family is distinguished by its well-earned opulence and intelligence. Boissy d'Anglas, the firm and unbending president of the Convention, was also born here.

The chief manufacture of Annonay is that of *paper*, celebrated all over France, produced in 8 paper-mills on the neighbouring streams. The preparation of kid and other *glove leather* occupies 65 master manufacturers and 600 men: 350,000 dozen of skins are prepared annually, of which half are sent to England. The cultivation of the silk-worm, and the production of silk, chiefly the white kind, prized for blondes, is rapidly advancing in the neighbourhood. Vast quantities of mulberries have been planted within a few years, and numerous silk-mills (filatures) established.

The name Annonay is said to come from the Latin *annona*, corn magazines, established by the Romans on this spot (?).

There is a good and interesting road from Annonay to Le Puy—penetrating the romantic *Val de Vocance*, and carried out of it by a series of zigzags, by which a great elevation is reached, upon which stands the miserable auberge and post-house St. Bonnet le Froid. It falls into the road to Le Puy (Rte. 118) near Yssingeaux.

Diligences daily; to St. Etienne; to Paris; to Lyons; to Grenoble; to Valence and Avignon.

A steep ascent leads out of Annonay: from the heights above it, and nearly all the way to the Rhône, the Alps form a fine feature in the view.

The borders of the Rhône are reached a little below la Tour des Martyrs, near Andance, picturesquely situated among granitic hills, on whose sides every inch of space opening to the sun is occupied by vines. A crag rising above the village is surmounted by a Calvary. Near this the sad effects of the inundations of the Rhône, in 1840-41-46, meet the traveller's sight, in fields and vineyards overwhelmed with sand, broken bridges, and ruined houses, until the Rhône is crossed, by a wire bridge, at

21 St. Vallier,
32 *Valence (Inn :* Poste), } described in Rte. 125.

ROUTE 120.

LE PUY TO ALAIS.

Diligence daily.

This Route is the same as No. 118 as far as

Langogne (p. 409), whence a new line has been carried over the chain of mountains of Lozère, passing through scenery of truly Alpine grandeur. The country is desperately barren and cheerless until you cross the summit level and begin to descend, when a gradual change comes over the scene; bold, shivered precipices rising on either side of the bed which a mountain torrent, flowing at an immense depth below, has hollowed out for itself. In the scanty clefts of the rock chesnuts have taken root and flourish amazingly. Perched on the edge of a precipice stands the ruined *Castle of Lagarde*, below which extends a savage-looking rocky den. It is a marvellous feat of engineering to have conducted through it an easy carriage-road. By a series of zigzags the region of chesnuts is reached, and, after traversing woods of some extent, the valley is crossed and re-crossed several times on bold and substantial bridges, one consisting of 2 tiers of arches, 9 above and 3 below. A long tunnel bored through the granite, and another bridge, conduct to the romantic village of *Villefort*, with a venerable bridge, and quaint, decaying, picturesque houses. Another summit, the Mont Lozère properly so called, is next surmounted by zigzags. On its S. slope chesnuts begin to be replaced by mulberries, growing on a white sandy soil. Through vines, olives, oleanders, fig-trees, we reach

ALAIS. Route 121.

ROUTE 121.

VALENCE TO NISMES, BY PRIVAS.—AUBENAS AND ALAIS.—VOLCANOES OF THE ARDÈCHE.

184 kilom.=115 Eng. m.
A post-road, but not good in places, and very hilly. A *diligence* goes daily to Aubenas, but it takes 12 hours, owing to the defects of the road, which, while it continues along the Rhône, is carried through several rivers by fords, and beyond is very hilly. Throughout it is interrupted by numerous villages, the passage of whose narrow and ill-paved streets is very difficult and tedious.

The Rhône is crossed by the wire bridge at Valence to the rt. bank: and the Eyrieu by another wire bridge to

19 Lavoulte; all which is described in Rte. 125.

The Valley of La Payre, up which the road turns on quiting the Rhône, is not remarkable for beauty; owing to the extreme aridity of the hills, which are of bare limestone, with a drapery of vines too scanty to cover their nakedness. There is some pasture in the low ground; but the district must properly be considered one vast grove of mulberries, for rearing the silkworm,—the source of wealth to the Ardèche. (See Rte. 125.)

The large white buildings which line the banks of the useful stream traversing the valley are, for the most part, silk-mills, for the moulinage (reeling) and filature (throwing) of the silk. They are very numerous near Chomerac, the most considerable place in this valley. A low ridge separates it from that in which is situated

20 *Privas.—Inns:* La Croix d'Or; tolerable, but dear;—H. du Commerce. Avoid stopping here for the night if possible, in autumn, on account of the mosquitoes.

Privas, chef-lieu of the Dépt. de l'Ardèche, 4619 Inhab., and one of the smallest chef-lieux in France, is situated on a steep ridge, a root of the range of the Coiron, projecting between the valley of the Ouvèze and that of a smaller stream falling into it, within an amphitheatre of rugged and arid hills. Its principal street running along this back-bone is prolonged, at either end, into terraces planted with trees, whence a good view is obtained of the valleys around, their slopes clad with vines and dotted with country houses; their depths, along the line of the streams, studded with silk-mills.

The town has an aspect of some pretension at a distance, with the Greek portico of its Palais de Justice, but contains nothing worth notice except its establishments for the reeling and throwing of silk. It was in the 16th and 17th centuries a fortress and stronghold of Protestantism, so that in 1612 a synod of all the Reformed Churches of France was held here; and in the reign of Henri IV. there was not a single Roman Catholic in the town or its territory. It has now quite a modern appearance, owing to its having been burned to the ground, and levelled with the dust, by Louis XIII., who assisted in person to besiege it, in the train of Card. Richelieu. The defence was conducted by the brave St. André de Montbrun, and a garrison of 1200 men, assisted by the inhabitants. At the end of 2 months a general assault was made by the royal forces, who were repulsed with a loss of 500 men; but the place being no longer tenable was abandoned by Montbrun, who retired to the Fort de Toulon, where the want of provisions compelled him soon after to surrender. The king caused him and all his companions to be hung; he confiscated the property of all the inhabitants of the town who were in it during the siege, and forbade, by an edict, any person living there without letters issued under the great seal. The site of this fort is marked by a conical hill, surmounted by 3 crosses, and a Protestant temple near the Esplanade marks the position of the old castle, which was razed to the ground. Privas had, in a previous war of religion, 1574, successfully resisted the royal forces, under the Duc de Montpensier, and had become a sort of metropolitan church to the

Protestants: hence the exasperation of the Roman Catholic party against it.

The road to Aubenas surmounts the chain of the Coiron mountains, which traverse the Dépt. Ardèche from N.W. to S.E., by a steep ascent, requiring 2 hours to climb to the summit of the pass. It passes through large plantations of sweet chestnuts. The famed "marrons de Lyon" come chiefly from the Ardèche. The country is not interesting, the extreme nakedness of the hills being a great drawback. The mountains on either side of the gap or col over which the road passes are capped by basalt. From the slope and top of the pass the mountains of the Dépt. of the Drome beyond the Rhône are well seen. On the opposite slope, a little way down, stands

16 Les Moulins, a single house. On the descent towards Aubenas, the hills are not less parched and naked, nor more picturesque, than on the side of Privas. The vine grows very high up, and it is curious to see it flourishing upon the dry disintegrated débris of rock fallen from the tops of the mountains, streaking their whitened flanks with the faintest tinge of verdure. The descent is very long, and the road towards the bottom of the valley as bad as possible; not properly made.

The river Ardèche is crossed immediately before reaching Aubenas, in a suburb of that town composed chiefly of silk-mills. A series of zigzags carried up the face of the hill are surmounted in order to enter

14 Aubenas.—*Inn:* H. de l'Union, kept by Barry; good, and tolerably comfortable, with capital cuisine, and not expensive. Truffles abound here; chestnuts, figs, ortolans are to be had in perfection. The house, being situated on the brow of the hill, commands a fine view from its terrace.

Aubenas (4685 Inhab.) is a town of very striking appearance at a distance, from the commanding height on which it stands, and the picturesque forms of its old Gothic castle, feudal walls, and other chief buildings. From this elevated platform, the foot of which is washed by the Ardèche, you command a view of some interest over its industrious and productive vale, clothed in its lower slopes with vines, fig-trees, and mulberry groves, surmounted in the distance by the usual bare arid mountains. You trace the river's course upwards to the point where it issues out of the more confined gorge of Vals, and, as it were rejoicing in riotous liberty, widens its bed, and overspreads the valley with gravel, bare at most seasons but winter and after autumnal storms, when the whole channel is covered by its muddy stream. It is nevertheless useful, serving to irrigate the fields, and turn the machinery of a long array of silk-mills which line its banks.

Aubenas is of importance as a place of trade, having become the staple for the silks of the Ardèche, Drome, Gard, and L'Hérault, which are deposited here in commission houses, sometimes to the value of 3 millions of francs, to be disposed of and distributed to the consumers in Lyons, St. Etienne, &c., who find here an assortment of all the different qualities of silk, suited to the exigence of the various manufactures. The canton of Aubenas furnishes about the 30th part of the silks sold in its market: in 1838 it possessed 60 mills for reeling and throwing the silk, which employed 1600 persons, chiefly females: the number has since greatly increased.

The *Collége Royal* was originally placed under the care of the Jesuits, established here in the 16th centy. for the conversion of the Protestants, who abounded in the Vivarais, as well as for the dissemination of learning. Neither the building nor its church merit notice.

The *castle*, an ancient and picturesque edifice, flanked by round and square towers, was occupied alternately by Romanists and Huguenots during the wars of religion: it is now converted into municipal and police offices; and the public *scales* for weighing all the silk brought to market are deposited in it.

Diligences daily to Privas and Valence; a courier to Bourg St. Andeol; and 3 times a week to Montélimart.

Although there is little worth seeing in Aubenas itself, it makes capital head-quarters (more especially considering the goodness of its Inn) for exploring the surrounding district of the Vivarais, so interesting in a geological point of view.

The course of the river Ardèche and its tributaries, above Aubenas, and within a range of 15 or 20 m., exhibits a series of interesting volcanic phenomena, which the geologist will not fail to explore, and which may be visited with interest even by the ordinary traveller, merely on account of the picturesqueness and singularity of the scenery.

Some of the valleys of the Bas Vivarais present an exquisite combination of beauty and magnificence. Their scenery has been compared by Mr. Scrope, in his excellent geological description of this district, to that of the Apennines, but with a more luxuriant vegetation. The rich glow of the chestnut forests, tinted by a soft and brilliant atmosphere, are admirably adapted to painting.

Excursions.—1. *Antraigues* and the *Coupe d'Ayzac* are distant about 8 m. above Aubenas. A good road leads thither, turning out of that to Le Puy at La Begude, and crossing the river Ardèche, by a wire bridge, to the village of Vals (H. de l'Europe; a good Inn, and convenient head-quarters for geological excursions), resorted to on account of its mineral baths, supplied by a spring of cold acidulo-ferruginous water. Vals lies on the l. bank of the Volane, a tributary of the Ardèche; and for nearly 6 m. above Vals the valley, which is very picturesque, and alternately well wooded or bounded by rocks of gneiss and granite, is studded at intervals by patches of basalt, forming platforms and regular colonnades, like those of the Giant's Causeway, but on a much smaller scale, although at times 100 or 150 ft. high. These fragments are all that remain of a lava current which once, undoubtedly, filled the bottom of the valley, but was cut away by the Volane, in forcing a passage for its waters. They appear to be composed of 3 beds, or stories, of which the lower one presents the most regular columns, and the upper is nearly amorphous. In places the current of the river, or of some minor rivulet, still saws through or undermines the basalt, and strews the bed of the Volane with detached pillars, mostly regular prisms of 5 or 6 sides. In some places you look down on the top of the lava stream, which presents the appearance of a gigantic tesselated pavement. The origin of this eruption is to be traced in a volcanic cone, called *La Coupe d'Ayzac*, rising on the l. bank of the Volane, opposite Antraigues, a picturesque village, which occupies a commanding platform on the top of a high rock of gneiss near the head of the valley. Around the base of this rock still cluster numerous groups of columns, corresponding with a much finer colonnade, on the opposite or rt. bank of the river, at the same level, which were doubtless originally united. Antraigues affords no accommodation but a miserable cabaret. To reach the Coupe d'Ayzac is a walk of ¾ hour from the bridge over the Volane, leaving on the rt. hand the road up to Antraigues. It is a very regular crater, but slightly broken down on the N.W. side, facing the Col d'Ayzac; and from this breach the stream of basaltic lava which has flowed down the course of the Volane may be seen to issue.

The stout pedestrian may find his way over the mountains from this to Burzet and Montpezat, but the aid of a guide may be desirable; otherwise he must retrace his steps down the Volane to Vals.

2. To *Montpezat, Thueyts, Jaujac.* It is a long day's excursion to Montpezat alone, which is probably 16 m. from Aubenas—a ride of nearly 4 hrs. by a bad road. The road to Le Puy, up the valley of the Ardèche, is followed; but, instead of crossing the bridge at La Begude, you continue along the rt. bank, leaving on one side the dirty village of Prades, where coal in small quantity is found, and, proceeding to La Baume (6½ m. from Aubenas), a village picturesquely situated, under a mass of basalt, exhibiting in the face of its cliffs a fine architectural façade of columns, and

T 3

occupying an angle in the valley, nearly opposite to the junction of the Fontaulier with the Ardèche. The top of this platform of basalt, called *Chaussée du Pont la Baume*, is covered with vines, and its mass is penetrated by a sort of grotto, lined and vaulted with natural pillars. This chaussée is probably the production of no less than 4 or 5 extinct volcanoes situated in the side valleys opening into the Ardèche, above this, whose lava streams united at this point, just as the waters flowing out of them now do. Between the two rivers, on the top of a domineering rock, its shattered towers and walls picturesquely draped with ivy, rises an old *Castle*, which once belonged to the Ducs de Ventadour: it is one of the finest feudal relics in the district.

The road to Montpezat (a bridle or cart road only) here quits that to Thueyts and Le Puy (see Rte. 118), crosses the Ardèche by the Pont de la Baume, and ascends the valley of the Fontaulier, having the castle on the l., and commanding a fine view of it and the 2 valleys. Ranges of basalt appear from time to time on either side of the valley.

On the rt., a little beyond the village of Meyras, the valley of Burzet opens out on the rt.; a bed of basalt occupies the bottom of it, and the river frequently flows over the tops of its columns, instead of cutting through them. About 6 m. up this valley is a village.

The vale of the Fontaulier expands as you ascend it; its lower slopes are covered with one vast forest of sweet *chestnut*, which flourishes in the congenial soil, composed of volcanic ashes, many of the trees being centuries old. The roads are strewn with their fruit in September, yet, productive as they are, and valuable to the peasant, who exports the best to Lyons or Paris, and feeds on the inferior fruit himself in winter, they are gradually giving place to the stll more profitable mulberry-trees and the culture of silk. The higher slopes, nearly to the tops of the hills, are terraced to plant vines. The red ashes, or scoriæ, which compose the soil of the valley, have issued from a volcanic crater near its head, easily distinguished for some distance below by its red hue, called *La Gravenne de Montpezat*. It is a regular bowl-shaped orifice, composed of porous scoriæ, roasted like the slag of a furnace, or of puzzolana (here called gravier). The crater is slightly inclined on one side; and from the lowest edge of its rim the lava current which occupies the valley below Montpezat has been discharged, filling the beds of the streams to a depth of 130 ft., and for the width of nearly ½ a m. The road to and from the bridge leading to Montpezat passes under cliffs cut through this eruption of lava, and showing on their face columns of considerable regularity. A branch of the lava current from the Gravenne has descended, on the opposite side of the crater, towards Thueyts, into the Ardèche. Volcanic tears, bombs, black and white cinders, are among the productions of its lava.

Montpezat (*Inn*: a dirty, miserable cabaret, de France) is a poor and dirty town, composed of singular gloomy houses, in a narrow street, at the foot of the granitic range of the Coiron mountains. A carriage-road has recently been made from the town up the valley, and over the bridge behind, as far as the village Pal (1¼ hr.'s walk), beyond which, on the opposite slope, is the very perfect volcano of Pal, in the midst of which rise 3 cones.

About 15 m. N. of Montpezat, near Gerbier des Joncs, at the base of the Mount Mezène, is the *source of the Loire*, 4711 ft. above the sea-level. There is a bridle-path by it to Le Puy (Rte. 109).

It is possible to cross the mountain from the Gravenne of Montpezat direct to Thueyts; the only other way is to return to Pont de la Baume.

A short way above La Baume the Ardèche is joined by the river Alignon, in whose valley are situated the singular *craters* of *Jaujac* and *Souillols*. (See Rte. 118.) There is a road from Jaujac down the valley of the Liane to L'Argentière.

Thueyts (*Inn*: Chez Burine; far better than that at Montpezat) lies on the l. bank of the Ardèche, surrounded by the most splendid volcanic scenery, about 4 m. above La Baume (see Rte. 118); it stands on a volcanic current, which has issued from the same ridge as the Gravenne de Montpezat, if not from that very crater. For nearly 1 m. below Thueyts the river is lined by the majestic colonnade of basalt proceeding from it. A stair, the steps of which are basaltic prisms, has been formed up the rock, and is called *Escalier du Roi*. A stream dashing down into a tremendous ravine called *La Gueule d'Enfer* forms a remarkable waterfall.

The road from Aubenas to Nismes is that by which the silk produced in the S. is transported to the market of Aubenas, and thence transferred to the manufactories of Lyons and St. Etienne. It leaves the town of L'Argentière a little on the rt. before reaching

23 Joyeuse, a small town on the Baume, at the foot of the Cevennes. An excursion might be made hence by Ruoms and Vallons (famed for the caves in its vicinity) to the *Pont de l'Arc*, a natural bridge of limestone spanning the river Ardèche, open to a height of 90 ft. above it, and 160 ft. wide. It was once the common line of passage from the Vivarais into the Cevennes, and was fortified in the religious wars.

29 St. Ambroix, in the Dépt. Gard, a town of 3000 Inhab., on the Cèze, surmounted by an old castle.

The coal-mines of Bessège, near which the road passes, are remarkable for the quantity and size of the fossil vegetables occurring in them.

The rivers Cèze and the 2 Gardons take their rise in the mountains of the *Hautes Cevennes*,—the wild theatre of the insurrection of the Protestant mountaineers, known as Camisards, or "Enfans de Dieu," as they called themselves; while they distinguished their native mountains, whose roots our road may be said to skirt on the rt. from St. Ambroix to Ners, by the name "le Désert." Their desolating irruptions and bloody contests with the forces of Louis XIV. spread far and wide over the country we are about to traverse, on both sides of our route, up to the very gates of Nismes and Alais; and almost every step will recall to those familiar with the history of that fearful contest some melancholy memorial of bloodshed and violence.

19 Alais (*Inns:* H. du Commerce;— Lion d'Or), an important manufacturing town, containing 17,831 Inhab., in the midst of a productive coal-field, which has only recently begun to be worked to any extent, and which furnishes iron as well as coal. The chief collieries are at Grande Combe on the railway. They supply the French steam-navy at Toulon. There are in the vicinity of Alais numerous iron-furnaces, silk-mills, glass-works, and many steam-engines hard at work.

The Place de la Maréchale is surrounded by low porticoes or arcades.

The town contains no fine buildings. It was taken by Louis XIII., as a stronghold of Protestantism, and its fortifications destroyed.

A *railroad* connects Alais with Nismes; trains go twice a day. Distance 49 kilom. = 30 Eng. m. A branch extends from Alais to Grande Combe, 10 m.

At la Tour de Bellot, a deserted sheep-farm and watch-tower to the W. of Alais, between it and Anduze, a band of 1500 Camisards, betrayed by a miller on the Gardon, who had supplied them with provisions, were surprised at night by the troops of Louis XIV., 1704. The Camisard outposts had barely time to sound an alarm, when they were cut to pieces, so that only the leader and a part of the band were able to issue forth from the tower before it was invested. The Camisard chief, Cavalier, made furious efforts to drive back the soldiery, and relieve his brethren in the tower, but in vain. Its garrison, however, blocked up every entry, pouring a deadly fire from every window and cranny, and were only subdued, after an obstinate resistance of 8 hours, by fire being set to the building, in which 298 of them perished, besides 100 left dead outside the walls. The loss of the king's troops was estimated at 1200 killed and wounded. Wild justice was soon after done by the Camisards on the traitorous miller; he was seized, condemned to death, and led out to execution in front of the insurgents, who, as was their custom, knelt around him the while, offering up prayers for his soul. His 2 sons, who served in their ranks, refused his parting embrace, and looked on unmoved during his punishment.

13 Vezenobre (Stat.), is frequently mentioned in the history of the Cevenol war; and the inhabitants of Euzet, a village a few miles to the E., were put to the sword, 1704, by a king's officer, Lalande. Entering the town suddenly, he found great store of provisions, heaps of bread, hams, sausages, and a bullock skinned, evidently destined for the Camisards, whom a brief search disclosed concealed in the neighbourhood. They were the remains of the force of Cavalier, defeated at Nages (Rte. 126), and were here again routed with a loss of 170 killed, including several prophetesses. Further evidence that the inhabitants of Euzet were aiding and abetting the rebels was furnished by the discovery in their vicinity of one of those caverns which the Camisards converted into hospitals and arsenals. It was filled with wounded, medicines, arms, and ammunition. This sealed their fate; they were all slaughtered, including the patients in the cavern, and Euzet was destroyed. Such was the system on which this exterminating war was carried on. The Camisard commissariat was supplied by requisitions upon towns and villages, both Catholic and Protestant: when not furnished with good will, a missive of this sort preceded their appearance, addressed to the chief men of the place:—"MM., vous ne manquerez point de nous préparer demain le dîner, sous peine d'être assiégé et mis à feu et à sang.—Cavalier."

15 Ners (Stat.) is a village on the l. bank of the Gardon, at the angle formed by the junction of its 2 branches, the Gardon d'Anduze and d'Alais. The river in winter rolls down a flood of water with the force of a torrent, but in summer is dried up to a few rills or threads. Owing to its impetuosity and sudden rising, no attempt to throw a bridge across it has succeeded.

Not far from Ners, on the W., is the Castle of *Castelnau* (8 m. S. of Uzès). It is remarkable as the spot where Roland, the chief and generalissimo of the Cevenol insurgents, ended his career, Aug. 13, 1704. His presence on the spot had probably been betrayed to Marshal Villars, for in the middle of the night, when Roland and his companions (including a female called Mademoiselle de Cornelli) were fast asleep, their sentinel on the tower heard the noise of horses' feet approaching at a gallop. He gave the alarm just as the cavalry were about to enter. The Camisards started up half-naked, rushed to the stable, and, mounting the bare backs of their horses, galloped off for their lives, but without saddles, belt, or spurs. They were soon overtaken, compelled to dismount, and, having been discovered trying to conceal themselves in a hollow way, were forced to face about. Roland, planting his back against the trunk of an old olive-tree, made a desperate resistance; answering to the summons, "Rendezvous! Bas les armes!" by killing 3 of the dragoons with 3 successive shots of his blunderbuss, and he was drawing his pistols, of which he carried a row at his girdle, when a musket-shot brought him down. The wound was mortal, and his companions, seeing his fall, at once threw themselves on his body, and allowed themselves to be seized and bound like lambs. The body of Roland was publicly burned at Nismes.

19 Boucoiron Stat. On a rock rises the tall tower of the modernized castle.

21 Nozières Stat.

25 St. Geniez Stat.

30 Fons Stat.

39 Mas. de Ponges.

The road passes near the limestone quarries, whence the Romans obtained the material for the amphitheatre of

49 Nismes Station. (Rte. 126.)

SECTION VI.

PROVENCE AND LANGUEDOC.

ROUTE	PAGE	ROUTE	PAGE
125 THE RHONE (B)—Lyons to Avignon and *Arles*, by *Vienne*, *Valence*, *Orange* (*Vaucluse*), *Tarascon*, *Beaucaire*, and *St. Remy*.—Rail	424	127 Avignon to Marseilles, Rail [and Aix], by Tarascon [Beaucaire], Arles, and St. Chamas:—The Rhone from Avignon to Arles	457
126 Avignon to *Narbonne*, by the *Pont du Gard*, *Nismes*, *Montpellier*, and *Beziers*.—*St. Gilles* and *Aigues Mortes* (*Rail*. Nismes to Cette.)	445	128 Marseilles to Toulon and Hyères	471
		129 Avignon to Marseilles and Nice, by *Aix*, *Fréjus*, and *Cannes*	475
		130 Nismes to Marseilles, by Beaucaire and Arles.—Rail . .	481

PRELIMINARY INFORMATION.

1. Features of Provence.—Climate, People.—2. Mistral.—3. Mosquitoes.—4. Fertility and Varied Productions.—5. The True Garden of Provence.—6. The Roman Antiquities.—7. Gothic Architecture.—8. The Rhône.

§ 1. THE Englishman who knows the S. of France only from books—who there finds Provence described as the cradle of Poetry and Romance, the paradise of the Troubadours, a land teeming with oil, wine, silk, and perfumes, has probably formed in his mind a picture of a region beautiful to behold, and charming to inhabit. Excepting, however, in a small and favoured district near Cannes, which is indeed a little paradise in climate and vegetation, these anticipations will not be realised on the spot, and at least it is not from this quarter that France deserves the epithet "La Belle." Nature has altogether an arid character;—in summer a sky of copper, an atmosphere loaded with dust, the earth scorched rather than parched by the unmitigated rays of the sun, which overspread everything with a lurid glare. The hills rise above the surface in masses of bare rock, without any covering of soil, like the dry bones of a wasted skeleton. Only on the low grounds, which can be reached by irrigation, does any verdure appear. There is a sombre, melancholy sternness in the landscape of the South. The aching eye in vain seeks to repose on a patch of green, and the inhabitant of the North would not readily purchase the clear cloudless sky of Provence with the verdure of misty England. Neither the bush-like vine nor the mop-headed mulberry, stripped of its leaves for a great part of the summer, nor the tawny green olive, whose foliage looks as though powdered with dust, will at all compensate in a picturesque point of view for forests of oak, ash, and beech.

"After Nice, the *austere* South of France, silent, burnt up, shadeless, and glaring, with houses all closed, showed the misery of a hot climate, while in Italy its *luxury* had struck us. The sun had bleached everything, and the atmosphere was thickened with the perpetual dust of habitual drought, for here it is said not to rain for seven months together in summer. The roads were of a dusky buffy white; the farm-houses, built of the materials nearest at hand, of the same colour; roads, soil, houses, men, trees, animals, all partaking of the same hue of universal dust, as the caterpillar does of the leaf on which it feeds. Now and then parched and scanty grass sprang up among the clodded earth, and long-legged sheep were feeding anxiously upon it, in the scorching sun, without a single tree of shelter. All the inns, however miserable, have large *remises*, to afford coolness and shade, during the middle of the day, for travellers and horses."—*P.*

The character of the people appears influenced by the fiery sun, and soil which looks as though it never cooled. Their fervid temperament knows no control or moderation; hasty and headstrong in disposition, they are led by very slight religious or political excitement, on sudden impulses, to the committal of acts of violence unknown in the North. They are rude in manner, coarse in aspect, and harsh in speech, their patois being unintelligible, even to the French themselves, not unlike the Spanish dialect of Catalonia. From the loudness of tone and energy of gesture, they appear always as though going to fight when merely carrying on an ordinary conversation. The traveller who happens to fall into the hands of the ruffianly porters at Avignon will be able to judge if this be an exaggerated picture.

Those who are prone to complain of the climate of England should be sent to try that of the South of France. If they expect an unvarying serene sky and warm temperature, they will be wofully disappointed. The variations between summer and winter are marked by the dead olive, and vine-trees killed by the frost; and the torrid influence of summer by the naked beds of torrents left without water. In many years not a drop of rain falls in June, July, and August, and the quantity is commonly very small: the great heats occur between the middle of July and the end of September, yet even in summer scorching heat alternates with the most piercing cold; and the vicissitudes are so sudden and severe, that strong persons, much more invalids, should beware how they yield to the temptation of wearing thin clothing, and of abandoning cloaks and great-coats.

§ 2. The cause of these sudden changes in temperature is the *Mistral* or N. W. wind, one of the scourges of Provence, from the occurrence of which no season is exempt. It is a most violent, bitterly cold, and drying wind, which fills the atmosphere with a yellow haze, and is very painful to the eyes and face. It prevails chiefly in spring all along the coast, and up the Rhône as far as Valence.

"Voilà le vent, le tourbillon, l'ouragan, les diables déchaînés qui veulent emporter votre château; quel ébranlement universel!" are the words in which *Madame de Sévigné* describes it: it overthrows at times the largest trees; their branches generally grow in a direction contrary to its cutting blasts, and while it rages, vessels are not unfrequently prevented putting out to sea in the teeth of it. It was well known to the ancients, and is supposed to be the Melamborias of Strabo, which he describes as sweeping stones and gravel from the ground. It is sufficient to blow a man from his horse. "In the winter months, December, January, February, the weather is truly charming, with the mistral very rarely."

§ 3. Another plague of the South of France is the *mosquitoes*, cousins, or moucherons, which, to an inhabitant of the North, unaccustomed to their venomous bite, will alone suffice to destroy all pleasure in travelling. They appear in May, and last sometimes to November; and the only good which the mistral effects is that it modifies the intensely hot air of summer, and represses, momentarily, these pestilential insects. They are not idle by day, but it is at night that the worn-out traveller needing repose is most exposed to the excruciating torments inflicted by this cruel insect. Woe to him who for the sake of coolness leaves his window open for a minute; attracted by the light, they will pour in by myriads. It is better to be stifled by the most oppressive heat than to go mad. Even closed shutters and a mosquito curtain (*cousinière*), with which all beds in good inns are provided, are ineffectual in protecting the sleeper. A scrutiny of the walls, and a butchery of all that appear, may lessen the number of enemies; but a single one effecting an entry, after closing the curtains and tucking up the bed-clothes with the utmost care, does all the mischief. The sufferer awakes in the middle of the night in a state of fever, and adieu to all further prospect of rest. The pain inflicted by the bites is bad enough, but it is the air of triumph with which the enemy blows his trumpet, the tingling, agonising buzzing which fills the air, gradually advancing nearer and nearer, announcing the certainty of a fresh attack, which carries the irritation to the highest pitch.

The pain and swellings usually last for several days, and there is no remedy but patience. The state of the blood at the time, however, considerably modifies or increases the amount and duration of suffering. It is said to be the female only which inflicts the sting. Mosquitoes, of course, are not peculiar to the S. of France, but there the traveller from the N. will probably first encounter them; and it is necessary that he should be prepared.

The *scorpion* is not uncommon in Languedoc and Provence, and even now and then makes his entrance into the houses, being brought in along with fire-wood; and it is even not uncommon to discover it in the folds of the bed-curtains or sheets. Instances, however, of persons being bitten by this foul insect are very rare indeed: from its nature it is fearful, and, when discovered, endeavours to run away and hide itself.

§ 4. The foregoing description of Provence and Bas Languedoc has been limited to the dark side of the picture: it remains to examine the resources, fertility, and curiosities of the country.

Its valleys, and lowlands accessible to irrigation, are most fertile; and the earth, where it can be sufficiently supplied with moisture, teems with varied productions all the year round. Before the spring is over, the mulberry-trees, which line the roads and cross the fields, in ugly cabbage-headed rows, are stripped of their juicy foliage to feed the silkworm—silk alone being a source of immense and increasing wealth in the S. provinces of France. Early in summer comes the corn-harvest, the crops having grown, for the most part, under the boughs of the mulberry, olive, or vine; sunshine and soil sufficing for both. Autumn is the season of the vintage; and the wines of Lunel and Frontignan have a widely-established reputation, though the bulk of the produce is used in the *manufacture* of wines and for mixing with other sorts. Chestnuts are another crop collected in the same season, and furnishing a store of wholesome food for the peasant during winter. The winter has set in before the olives are gathered and pressed. A visit to the market-place in every town will show with what abundance the earth brings forth fruits and vegetables of endless variety—grapes, figs, melons, almonds, citrons, mushrooms, tomatas, truffles, &c. The drying and preserving of fruits of various kinds is a great source of mercantile wealth to Provence.

§ 5. There is one little corner of Provence which combines remarkable picturesque beauty with a climate so serene and warm, and well protected from injurious blasts, that its productions are almost tropical in their nature. This is a narrow strip in the Department of the Var, bordering on the blue Mediterranean, extending from Toulon to Nice, stretching inland to Grasse and Draguignan. In this favoured region, the true garden of Provence, the real paradise of the Troubadours, in the valleys, and on the S. slopes of the small mountain-chains of Les Maures and Les Estrelles, sheltered from the injurious mistral, and open only to the S., the aloe, the cactus, the pine of Aleppo, the umbrella-pine, the pomegranate, the orange, and even the palm-tree, may be seen flourishing in the open air. This is especially the case at St. Maxime, Hyères, Antibes, and Cannes, whose gardens, luxuriant with aromatic herbs, heliotropes, orange-flowers,

424   § 6.—*Roman Antiquities.*   § 8.—*The Rhône.*   Sect. VI.

jasmines, &c., supply the perfume-distilleries of Grasse, where more scents, pomades, essences, &c., are made than in any town in Europe, save Paris.

§ 6. The chief attraction, however, of these southern provinces is their *Roman remains*, not surpassed in beauty and preservation by any in Italy. No traveller should miss seeing the *Pont du Gard*, between Avignon and Nismes, and the walls of the *Theatre at Orange*, stupendous and most impressive structures, perfectly characteristic of the great people that raised them; the *Amphitheatres of Nismes* and *Arles*, though far less enormous than the Colosseum, are more interesting on account of their better preservation. The *Maison Carrée* is a gem of architecture: the *monuments* at *St. Rémy*, and the *arch* at *Orange*, are also of great excellence, besides many other curious relics, which are described in their proper place. It may be interesting to compare the Roman aqueduct with that recently erected to convey water to Marseilles, at Roquefavour.

§ 7. The student of *Christian architecture* will find much to interest him in the churches of Arles and its vicinity, of St. Gilles, of Aix, of Avignon (the cathedral), where the stupendous Papal palace is also a very interesting historical monument, and many more.

In these and other mediæval monuments of S. E. France the traveller will not fail to observe the long-perpetuated influence of Roman architecture on the ecclesiastical edifices of the district, which still retains its Roman name of THE *Province*, par excellence. "A marked difference of character prevails between the church architecture of the S. of France and that of the N., in the smallness of the windows, designed no doubt to exclude the glare and heat. This gives the southern churches a much greater solemnity than those immense lantern-structures of the N.: unless where the windows are entirely filled with stained glass, it is difficult to produce the same effect. The influence of climate evidently gave rise to the distinctions in the two styles."—*E. o. S.*

§ 8. The *Rhône*, the great highway to Provence and to Italy, since the establishment of steamers, is not of commercial utility proportioned to its length and volume, owing to its turbulence and shifting sand-banks. Yet it is a noble river, and its scenery very striking, and some have preferred it to the Rhine; but, in truth, the two have a totally different character, and each its own excellences: the writer of this, however, cannot conceal his preference for the German stream. The traffic upon the Rhine is at least fourfold greater than that on the Rhône. The Rhine is navigated by 42 steamers, and, although there are 28 at present on the Rhône, they make on an average only 50 passages in the year, while a great part of the Rhenish steamers are, with the exception of a few weeks, in action all the year through.

The works which will best afford detailed information respecting Provence and the S. of France are—Millin, 'Voyage dans le Midi de la France;' Frossard, 'Tableau de Nîmes;' Merimée, 'Rapport sur les Monumens du Midi de la France' (for architecture); and Hughes' 'Itinerary of Provence and the Rhône.

ROUTE 125.

THE RHÔNE (B)—LYONS TO AVIGNON AND ARLES, BY VIENNE, VALENCE, ORANGE.

By land, 263 kilom.= 163 Eng. m.
By water to Arles, 285 kilom.

Steamers, belonging to several companies, but almost without exception managed by English engineers, start every morning from the Quai on the rt. bank of the Rhône, except when the river is too high to allow them to pass under the bridges, or too low, which sometimes happens. The hour of departure varies, according to the season, from 5 to 7 A.M. The time occupied in the voyage varies according to the efficiency of the steamers, and the state of the river and atmosphere. "The Ex-

PLANCHE (S) EN 2.
PRISES DE VUE

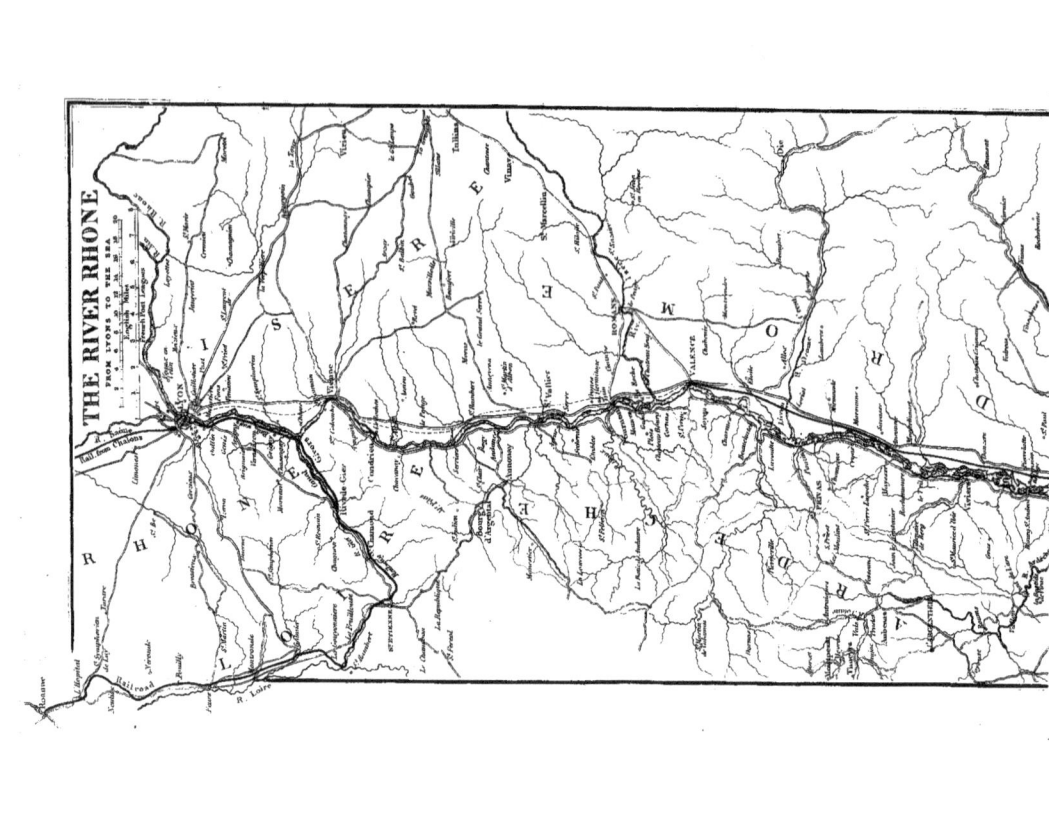

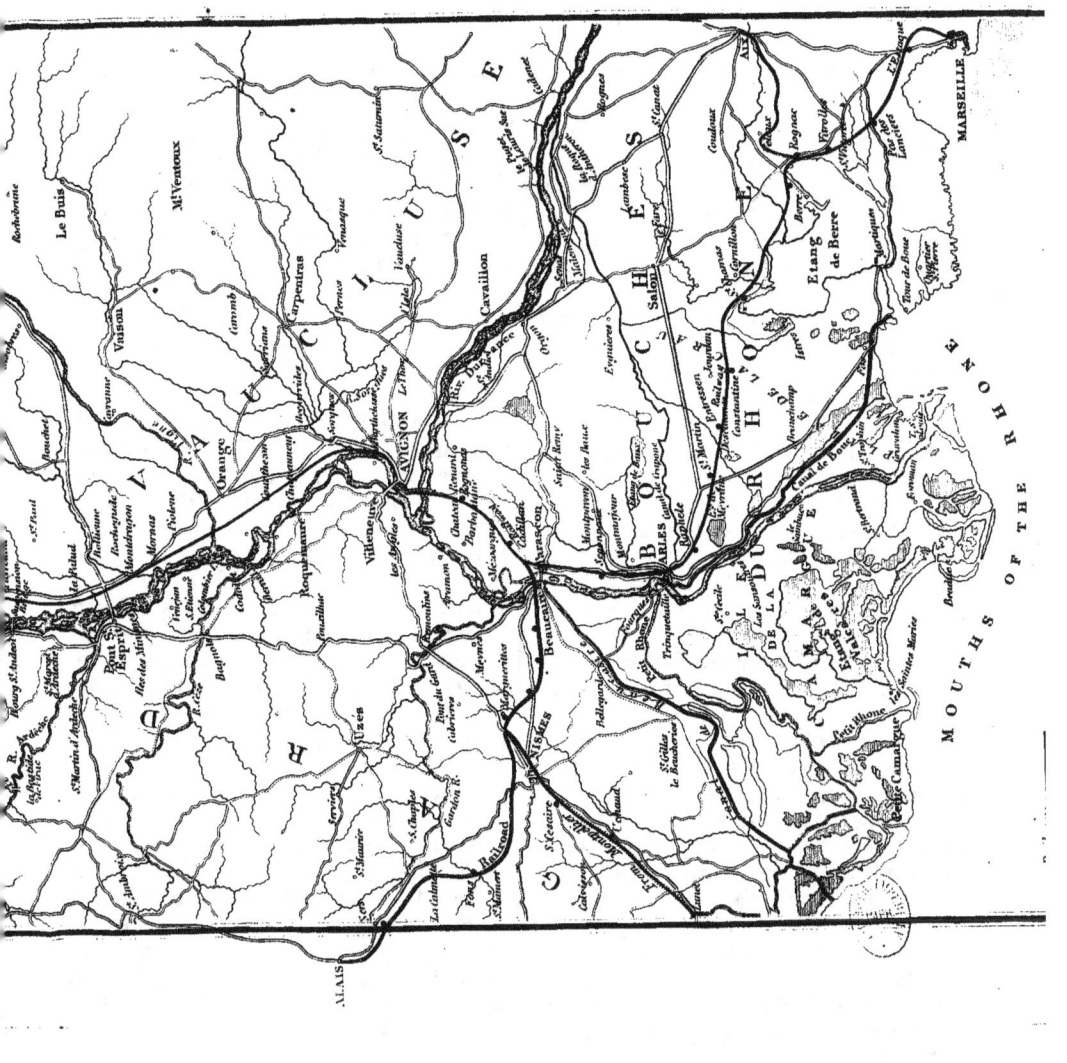

PROVENCE. *Route* 125.—*The Rhône* (B)—*Givors.*

press" steamboats profess to descend to Avignon in 7 hours, and return upwards to Lyons in 10. Other boats make the voyage to Avignon, a distance of at least 165 Eng. m., in 10 or 11 hrs.; while some, starting in the afternoon, stop at Valence for the night. They take carriages at a charge varying from 60 fr. for a light calèche to 160 for a Berline. The captain manages the embarkation and landing of carriages, transporting them to and from the hotel. The passenger's fare varies from 10 to 20 or 30 fr., so that it is cheaper than posting for a party in a light carriage (?). They are by no means clean, and are often crowded with merchandise. There is a Restaurant on board. They touch at Vienne, Tournon, Valence, Avignon, Beaucaire, Arles. It is very advisable to go either by railway when opened or by water *down* the Rhône, as the road is bad. It scarcely answers for passengers *to ascend* the river, as the vessels take as long as the diligences.

Diligences* run daily, along the l. bank, to Valence, and many more between the intermediate towns.

Railroad from Valence to Avignon was opened 1854. From Lyons to Valence will be finished 1855.

There is little interest at first in the banks of the Rhône, after getting clear of Lyons, its bustling quays and tall stately houses, and passing,

rt., the junction of the Saône with the Rhône,—

" Ubi Rhodanus ingens amne præräpido fluit,
Ararque dubitans quo suos cursus agat
Tacitus quietis alluit ripas vadis,"—*Seneca.*

under the wire suspension-bridge of La Mulatière, which carries the Rly. to St. Etienne over the Saône (Rte. 118). The junction of the Rhodanus and Arar originally took place nearly 2 m. higher up, until 1770, when the architect Perrache constructed dykes between the rivers, and gained from the water the

* By land, 263 kilom. = 163 Eng. m.
The *post-road* quits Lyons, after traversing the Rhone, by the Faubourg Guillotière, passes on the l. the detached *Fort de la Motte*, one of the modern defences of Lyons, named after an old castle occupied by Henri IV. at his marriage with Marie de Medicis, and, shortly before reaching

8 St. Fons, enters the Dépt. de l'Isère.

long tongue of land now partly occupied by an important suburb of Lyons. Cæsar appears to have visited the junction from his description of it: "Arar in Rhodanum influit incredibili lenitate, ita ut oculis in utram partem fluat, judicari non possit." (See p. 376.)

The united waters form a broad majestic flood; the banks are studded with small villages, scattered among willow and poplar avenues.

l. The high road along the l. bank of the Rhône is often out of order; a series of ups and downs, liable to constant injury from the torrents descending from the hills across it; but, above all, tremendously cut up by the immense number of broad-wheeled waggons which traverse it at all seasons. Even though the Rhône, the largest river in France, runs parallel with it, such is the rapidity of the current, and the perversity of the navigation, from shifting sand-banks, that the transport up its valley of most of the bulky articles the produce of Provence, soap, oils, silk, dried fruits, &c., and of the colonial imports of Marseilles, is made on the axle. Every mile or two the road is studded with enormous barn-like Remises, whose open portals yawn invitingly to receive in their shade the loaded waggon and its 6 or 8 horses. They have a cabaret or carter's hostel attached to them.

The traveller " journeys onwards in the dazzling dreariness of the sunshine, amidst clouds of intolerable dust, crossed ever and anon by long caravans of roulage, drawn by tall mules."

rt. The railway to St. Etienne (Rte. 118) continues near the water's edge as far as the dirty manufacturing town of

rt. Givors, distinguished at a distance by the smoke of its glass-houses. It is a place of some importance from its position on the railway, and at the mouth of the canal, which brings down coal, iron, &c., from Rive de Gier (see Rte. 118). Its population is 4900. Omnibuses run between Givors and Vienne, corresponding with the railway trains.

Along the banks of the Rhône, from Lyons to Valence, a "poste aux ânes," or relays of donkeys, for the convenience of bargemen and such persons, was at one time established. The cultivation of the vine is very general in the neighbourhood of Vienne: vineyards here cover all the slopes.

1.* *Vienne.* (*Inn:* Table Ronde, best, but charges high, and *not clean.*) Vienne, a town of 19,052 Inhab., stretches its buildings along the l. bank of the Rhône, faced by a tolerably handsome quay, at the foot of precipitous hills, and runs up a small valley between 2 heights: the one, *Mont Salomon*, crowned by a ruined castle of the middle ages; the other, *Mont Pipet*, originally a fortified camp of the Romans. The *Castle of Salomon* passes with the common people for the prison of Pilate, who was banished to Vienne in Gaul, according to Eusebius and others, after his return from Judæa to Rome.

From the valley behind Vienne, the Gère issues out into the Rhône, turning in its passage many mill-wheels, and giving activity to manufactures of coarse cloth, pasteboard, iron-forges, &c.

Vienne is one of the most ancient towns in France, having been already a flourishing place before Lyons is known to have existed. It is mentioned by Cæsar, by Ausonius, in the line,

"Accolit Alpinis opulenta Vienna calonis,"

and by Martial, who calls it "opulenta Vienna," and it is natural to expect to find some remains of its Roman possessors. Besides numerous water-conduits and substructions of masonry, the chief Roman building is a *Temple*, supposed to have been dedicated to Augustus, in form somewhat like the Maison Carrée at Nismes, but much injured during the middle ages by having the interstices of its columns built up with masonry, and the columns themselves rasped to bring them to a level with the walls, in order to convert it into a church. It is now a *museum*, and contains a number of sculptured and architectural fragments found in and about the town, a very rich frieze, capitals of columns, &c. A Greyhound, in marble, two Boys quarrelling about a Bird (a common subject of antique sculpture), and 2 copper Dolphins found in the Rhône, are worth notice.

Behind the Place du Pilori is a lofty double arch and vault, with pillars inside, called *Arche de Triomphe,* but in reality part of the portico of the ancient Forum. It now leads to the modern theatre, and is unimportant.

On the slopes of Mont Pipet the remains of the seats of a *Roman theatre* may, it is said, be traced among the vineyards, but they are very inconsiderable. Lastly, outside the town, below it, is the Roman obelisk, or *Aiguille*, described p. 427.

The *Cathedral of St. Maurice* is a stately and interesting edifice in the lower part of the town, raised upon an elevated basement or parvis, facing the river, on a line with the bridge, and approached by a broad flight of steps. Its W. front, flanked by 2 massive towers, is rich in flamboyant ornaments, but they are clumsy and without delicacy. It was much mutilated, like all the churches on the Rhône, by the fanatic Huguenot soldiery (1562), less than 30 years after its completion. The interior wants height. The pointed roof, painted blue, and sprinkled with stars, and the 4 compartments nearest to the W. end, seem of the same age, viz. 15th or 16th centy. The pillars of the choir, and the apses at the E. end, are said to be of the 12th centy. The delicate carving of the capitals and of other ornaments is very remarkable. There are no transepts. A marble monument of an Archbishop Montmorin, on the rt. of the altar, though much vaunted, seems a heavy piece of work; its artist was called Michel Angelo Slodtz. The N. porch retains some statues in a stiff style.

The Romanesque tower of *St. Andre le Bas* will be admired by the architect for its composition and proportions; but the cloister, so interesting for the varied sculpture of its capitals, is now included in a private garden, and its pillars built up in a wall.

In the suburb Pont l'Evêque, in a hill on the l. bank of the Gère, there is a lead-mine.

Many who have occupied themselves in tracing the route of *Hannibal* over the Alps suppose that he quitted the

---
* The *post-road* continues through 8 St. Symphorien, at a considerable distance from the river, but it approaches it at 13 Vienne.

1. bank of the Rhône at Vienne (which was one of the chief towns of the Allobroges), proceeding hence, by Bourgouin and Yenne, to the Little St. Bernard.

Vienne is interesting as the cradle of Christianity in the West: the Epistle of its early Martyrs to their brethren in the E. is a very instructive and perfectly authentic document.

Vienne was capital of the 1st kingdom of Burgundy in the 5th centy., and at a later period was the capital and residence of the Dauphins. A celebrated ecclesiastical *council* held here 1307, and presided over by Pope Clement V. and Philippe le Bel, condemned the Order of the Templars. The archbishops long enjoyed considerable temporal sway: they had the privilege of naming the governor of the forts Salomon and Pipet, who was always a canon of the cathedral, but had a military deputy under him.

A *suspension-bridge*, reconstructed since 1840, the previous one having been washed down by the inundation, connects Vienne with,

rt., its suburb, St. Colombe, where stands by the water side an old square *tower*, sometimes called "Tour de Mauconseil," from a tradition that Pilate threw himself off from the top of it. In reality it was built by Philippe de Valois as a tête-du-pont to the original stone bridge, destroyed by the Rhône, 1651, except the trunks of some of its piers, still visible when the water is low.

Diligences daily to Grenoble (Rte. 131) and Lyons, and omnibuses along the rt. bank of the Rhône to Givors, to meet the trains on the railway to St. Etienne and Lyons (Rte. 118).

l. Immediately below Vienne, in the midst of a field, on the rt. of the road to Avignon, stands a Roman obelisk, called *L'Aiguille*, 76 ft. high, rising from a square base, pierced by a double arch, and supported at the angles by pillars of clumsy proportions. The whole is of excellent masonry, the stones being fastened together, not by mortar, but by iron clamps. Its destination is unknown, and it bears no trace of an inscription, but was probably a sepulchral monument.

rt. The uniformity of the vine-clad slopes which border the river is relieved by the lofty irregular ridge and picturesque outline of *Mont Pilas*, 3516 ft. above the sea-level, a member of the chain of hills which divides the Rhône from the Loire.

rt. Ampuis.* At its base is a small village, from the flat behind which rise the sunny slopes of *Côte Rôtie*, called "the burnt side," from their happy exposure to the sun, which, striking full on them, as on a forcing wall, matures the excellent wine named after them. 3 m. below the hills of Côte Rôtie is

rt. Condrieux, a town of 4000 Inhab., famed for its wines; it has a suspension-bridge over the Rhône.

The soil of the valley of the Rhône abounds with rolled pebbles, which in places almost exclusively compose it; yet upon this grows the mulberry-tree in vast quantities, planted in rows across the fields, while beneath, and in spite of its shade, luxuriant crops of corn are produced.

rt. There is another suspension-bridge at Serrières, and hence a road strikes off to Annonay. (Rte. 119.)

rt. The church of Champagne is a Romanesque edifice of the 13th centy., well worth the attention of the antiquary, on account of the singular bas-reliefs with which its outer walls are incrusted, consisting of heads of animals, monsters, &c., and for the sculptured cornice running under the roof. Some of these carvings have been conjectured to belong to a more ancient structure. Two of them represent David and Goliah, and Judith and Holofernes. The interior ends in an apse at the E. The grand portal is decorated above with 6 bas-reliefs in medallions, representing, 1. a satyr; 2. a lion couchant; 3 and 4. 2 young fauns; 5. a tiger; 6. a group of 2 genii embracing. The meaning of these sculptures seems difficult to explain.

Before the Revolution the towns of Andance, Champagne, Annonay, though

---

* The *Post-road* continues near to the Rhône until almost opposite Ampuis, where it turns away to the station.
13 Auberive, situated outside the village, which it leaves on the rt.
6 Péage de Roussillon. A toll here.

on the rt. bank of the Rhône, belonged to Dauphiné, having been ancient possessions of the Dauphins of Vienne.

l.* St. Rambert. Just below this the Rhône passes from the Dépt. de l'Isère into that of La Drôme. A branch *Railway* is projected from St. Rambert to Grenoble.

rt. The road from St. Etienne to Marseilles, by Annonay, descends through a gap in the vine-clad granite hills near

rt. Andance (Rte. 119), and crosses the Rhône, a little lower down, by the *suspension-bridge* of

l. St. Vallier† (*Inn:* Poste or Grand Sauvage, fair), a town of 2455 Inhab., consisting of a long street, extending on a terrace above the Rhône. It has a large modern château. There are numerous silk-mills here.

Behind the town, in the gorge of the Galaure, rise the picturesque ruins of the *castle of Vals;* and near it is the *Roche Taillée,* a passage cut in the rock, through which a small road is carried.

l. The Château de Ponsas (derived, by the vulgar, from Pontius Pilate, who, according to the tradition, ended his days here by throwing himself from the rock) is a fine object, frowning with towers and battlements over river and village from the summit of a lofty precipice.

The valley of the Rhône is narrowed to a pass, by rocks projecting on either side, on approaching Tain. Nearly opposite the mouth of the considerable river Doux, which is crossed by a wire bridge,

l. A lofty round-topped hill, with a scanty scarf of black bushes round its shoulder, pushes forward its naked and almost precipitous sides into the river, which, along with the road, winds closely round its base. On doubling the sort of cape which it forms, its southern side will be found to consist of a more gradual slope, descending in a succession of steps, or terraces, formed by the natural divisions of the slaty beds of gneiss rock, all covered from top to bottom with vines. This is the celebrated vineyard of *L'Hermitage,* named from the ruin on its summit, once, perhaps, a hermit's cell. On its favoured slopes the sun plays all day long, maturing the juices of its grapes, which produce the Hermitage wine, one of the finest which grows on the Rhône. The white sort will keep for half a century; the red, of the best quality, is sent to Bordeaux, to be mixed with clarets of first growth, principally the kinds exported to England, which derive from it, and not from brandy, as is commonly supposed, that body which fits them for exportation, and adapts them to the English palate. The whole extent of the vineyard does not, perhaps, exceed 300 acres, and of this only a part near the centre, where a calcareous band traverses the gneiss rock, produces first-rate wines; the soil below is too rich, and above is too cold. The hill is divided among numerous proprietors; it is cultivated with vast labour, and at great expense; the vines are manured with sheep or horse dung. The grape grown for the red wine is called Ceras, and is said to have been brought from Shiraz, in Persia, by one of the hermits of the mountain.

l.* Tain (*Inns,* mere cabarets), a town of 2338 Inhab., connected by a wire suspension-bridge, the first, on a large scale, erected in France, with

rt. Tournon, one of the chief towns of the Dépt. de l'Ardèche (4522 Inhab.). Above the bridge the picturesque towers of the old *castle* of the Counts of Tournon and Ducs de Soubise rise on a precipitous rock, at the foot of the hills; it is now converted into the purposes of a mairie, tribunal, and a prison. Below the bridge, at the water side, stands the *Collège Royal,* originally founded by the Cardinal de Tournon, a favourite of Francis I. (1542), and a few years after, 1561, delivered over to the care of the Jesuits in order to extirpate the seeds of Protestantism, and they maintained their post here until the suppression of the Order in 1766. It next became an Ecole Militaire. *Inn:* H. de l'Europe, exorbitant charges.

Diligences run from Tain to Romans on the Isère, on the way to Grenoble. (Rte. 132.)

---

* *Post-road.*—9 St. Rambert.
† 12 St. Vallier.

* *Post-road.*—14 Tain.

PROVENCE. *Route* 125.—*The Rhône (B)—Valence.* 429

l. The *valley of the river Isère*, one of the chief tributaries of the Rhône, rising at the foot of the Little St. Bernard, now opens out into a wide and monotonous plain, after traversing which, and being crossed itself by the high road, on a handsome bridge of 7 arches, the river falls into the Rhône. Its waters have usually a black tint contrasting with the white muddy Rhône. Hannibal is supposed by some to have reached the foot of the Alps by ascending this valley, having passed the Rhône lower down, perhaps near Roquemaure.

l. The vista, opening out through the valley of the Isère, is terminated by the majestic snowy mass of *Mont Blanc*, clearly distinguished from among the Alps of Dauphiné; a magnificent object, although 70 or 80 m. distant as the crow flies. The deck of the *steamer* is too low to command it, but it is well seen from the road, or rt. bank.

rt. The picturesque white feudal castle, *Châteaubourg*, perched on a pedestal of rock, projecting into the Rhône, with a little hamlet at its foot, stands in the eye of Mont Blanc, and the everlasting snows of the monarch of mountains add magnificence to the distant horizon of a view, in which the exulting and swelling Rhone occupies the foreground. The Castle is besides of historic interest, since in it St. Lewis, on his way to the Crusade, spent the eve and festival of the Assumption, A.D. 1248. It had fallen to ruin and was condemned to destruction when rescued by its present owner, Mr. L. Giraud.

rt. Cornas, at the foot of limestone hills of considerable elevation, produces a tolerable red wine.

rt. On approaching Valence, the bare limestone precipices, rising behind the village of St. Peray, and crowned by the picturesque *castle* of *Crussol*, arrest the attention. (See p. 431.)

l. *Valence.** — *Inn:* Poste, outside the walls ; not at all bad, with some pretensions to English comforts ; not dear, and very civil people :— H. du Nord, close to the steamer, from which the others are remote, small and quiet.

• *Post-road.*—18 Valence.

Try here the sparkling St. Peray, an excellent wine, not inferior to Champagne. It costs here 2 fr. the bottle, and Châteauneuf des Papes 1½ fr.

The *steamer* passes the town and the Citadel, which is conspicuous from the Rhône, but is separated from it by a considerable space of garden-ground, and comes to her moorings below the *wire Suspension-Bridge*, one of the handsomest on the Rhône, supported in the centre by a fine lofty arch of classical architecture.

The high road from Lyons to Avignon skirts the outside of the town, which lies between it and the river, through a faubourg, in which the Poste and other inns are situated.

Valence is an ancient town of 13,829 Inhab., still surrounded by its feudal ramparts, battlemented, flanked by towers, and entered by arched gates. It is chef-lieu of the Dépt. de la Drôme, and was formerly capital of the Valentinois, created a dukedom for the infamous Cæsar Borgia, by Louis XII.

The *Cathedral*, a Romanesque building, small in size and very plain, is yet interesting to the architect for its age and constructive peculiarities. It is a cross with long transepts. Outside the nave, above the aisle roof, runs a small arcade of arches, alternately round and straight sided. The interior is simple ; the piers, surmounted by nearly pure Corinthian capitals, support round arches, from which rises the cylindrical roof, without triforium or clerestory. The E. end is an apse, roofed with a semi-dome. The Ch. contains a bust and bas-relief, by Canova, to the memory of Pope Pius VI., who, after having been carried off a prisoner from the Vatican and loaded with insults by the French, which he bore with resignation, died here, 1799.

On the N. side of the Ch. is a singular building, known as *Le Pendentif*, of classical architecture, erected 1548, as a monument to the family Mistral, whose arms are still visible on it. It is square in form, consisting of 4 piers, with pillars in the angles, and arches between them, supporting a vault, the first of its kind erected, and regarded as a type in architecture. In the rusticated space occupying the sides, carvings of monstrous birds may be discovered.

The ancient *Evêché*, now subdivided, and partly destroyed, was often visited by Madame de Sévigné.

The semicircular E. end of the cathedral adjoins the *Place aux Clercs*, an Esplanade between the Faubourg and the river, ornamented with a bronze *statue* of the Napoleonist General Championnet, a native of Valence.

In the "Grande Rue," leading out of this Place, will be found a very rich and interesting specimen of domestic architecture, in a *Mansion* of the 16th centy., now converted into a bookseller's shop. Its origin and destination are not clearly known. It has a Gothic front, covered with elegant Florid tracery, now sadly mutilated, combined with a certain mixture of classic ornament, such as rows of heads and statues, the upper heads representing the 4 Seasons. The doorway is an elegant flattened arch; the transoms of the windows have unfortunately been knocked out. The front of the house is not in one plane, but projects forward; only one part of it is ornamented, and that which is unadorned retreats backward at a slight angle, so as to be partly concealed from view as you approach it from the Place aux Clercs, probably with design on the part of the architect. The groined and vaulted passage, and the walls towards the inner court, also deserve notice. In the same street, at No. 4, on the 1st floor, *Napoleon* lodged, while yet a poor and obscure sous-lieutenant of artillery; and some of his first essays in the art of war were made in the Champs de Mars here. The *staircase* at the back of the house of Madame Dupré, Rue Perolierie, is a good specimen of the Renaissance in architecture, enriched with sculpture.

The *Citadelle*, begun by Francis I., and bastioned only on the side facing the town, but of no use now as a fortress, is converted into r Caserne du Génie. From the finished bastion there is a good view over the river, of St. Peray, and the Castle of Crussol on its arid rock beyond the Rhône.

Valence is the seat of an *Ecole d'Artillerie*, and the practice of gunnery is taught on the *polygone*, a large sandy area on the outskirts of the town, bordering on the Lyons road.

The reeling (filature) and throwing (moulinage) of silk affords employment to a large number of persons at Valence. (See p. 433.)

Steamers up and down the Rhône daily. The ascent to Lyons is made in one day.

Railway to Avignon and Marseilles.

Diligences daily (4) to Lyons; 2 to Grenoble (Rte. 132); 1 to Aubenas and Privas (Rte. 121); to St. Etienne and Annonay.

Rly. to Lyons in 1855.

[rt. *St. Peray*, famed for one of the best wines of the Rhône, is 2 Eng. m. from Valence, on the opposite side of the Rhône, within the Dépt. of the Ardèche: an omnibus goes thither several times a day.

The little village of St. Peray lies snugly in the quiet nook of a sheltered valley running down to the Rhône opposite Valence. Its most conspicuous buildings are the house of the proprietor of the *vineyards* around; and on the height, a little above it, the *Château de Beauregard*, a singular mansion on the plan of a mimic fortress, bastioned and curtained, with loopholed walls, portcullis, &c., built, it is said, by Marshal Vauban, as a freak, reminding one of Uncle Toby and Corporal Trim, now converted into a depôt for the wine of the district, for which it is better suited than for a dwelling, being constructed over cellars of vast extent.

The slopes of the hills around St. Peray are covered with one uninterrupted vineyard, and wherever they present an aspect to the S.E., so as to receive the sun's rays during nearly the whole day, the best wines grow: such are the Côte de Hongrie, Chapelle de Crussol, and the Prieuré vineyards. The soil is a decomposed granite, and the vine seems to flourish most on this mere dry gravel. Great pains are taken in digging about the roots, but the only manure employed is the leaves of the box, cut small. The grape, when ripe, assumes a beautiful golden hue; its taste is cloyingly sweet, and the saccharine matter exuding often covers the bunches with a brown stain.

The sparkling *St. Peray wine* is distinguished from Champagne in this respect, that its sweetness arises from the natural juice of the grape, and not from the addition of sugar to the grape-juice : and it is consequently a far more wholesome and not less palatable wine. The red St. Peray derives its colour, a delicate rose tint, from the hue of the skins of the grapes. The vintage takes place about the middle or end of September, and the juice is at once transferred to the cask before the fermentation has begun, and rests there for 6 or 7 months, during which time it is fined. In March or April it is bottled, and remains 2 or 3 years to mature, and allow the dregs to deposit. The bottles are piled up in stacks, each row separated by laths, to allow of the bottles which burst (and they form 14 or 15 per cent. of the whole) to be withdrawn. After this the wine is racked, i.e. every bottle is taken out, and is thrust, with its neck downwards, into a hole cut in a board. By this means the dregs sink down gradually into the neck, and, as they descend, day by day, the bottle is tilted more and more until its position becomes nearly vertical. To expedite the falling of the sediment the bottles are lifted and set down with a jerk once or twice a day; and after receiving 200 of these jerks, the bottle is taken up, and the sediment is discharged by cutting the string and letting the cork fly, and with it the lees at the neck of the bottle, but as little as possible of the wine. The vacancy thus caused is filled with clear wine; and this process of corking and uncorking is repeated 2 or 3 times, until no more sediment is deposited. The wine is then fit for use, and an excellent wine it is, the "St. Peray grand Mousseux" of M. Faure being equal to a first-class Champagne.]

The Lyons Rly. was finished 1854, between Valence and Avignon.

rt. A very conspicuous but unsightly line of cliffs of limestone, naked, arid, and partly stained black and yellow, bounds the W. side of the Rhône valley, opposite to and below Valence. Quarries of building-stone are worked in these rocks. The highest peak of all, a castled crag rising above the entrance of the valley in which lies St. Peray, is crowned by the ruins of the *Castle of Crussol*, called, from its 2 projecting and roofless gables, Les Cornes de Crussol, and conspicuous from a great distance. It belonged to the ancient family of the Crussols, Ducs d'Uzès, and once enclosed within its fortifications, which may be seen running down the rock, a small village long since deserted. Owing to the precipice, from whose very edges its walls start up, it must have been impregnable in the olden time.

rt. Lower down, on the top of the same escarpment of limestone, stands *Soyons Castle*, now an utter ruin, once a stronghold of the Calvinists, who by means of it held the key of the Rhône, intercepting the communication between Lyons and the S. in 1627, under their chief, Brisson: it was taken and demolished the same year by the Prince de Condé. A flight of steps cut in the rock leads to the summit.

l. Among the Dauphiné mountains the *Roche Courbe* becomes a conspicuous feature in the landscape, from its precipitous sides and horned brow. A little further down it changes its aspect, presenting a series of peaks as seen from the river.

l. L'Etoile, a pretty village.

rt. The river Eyrieu pours itself into the Rhône, a little below Charmes, at Beauchastel, where a new wire bridge shortens the way to Lavoulte by more than 2 m. Formerly it was necessary to ascend as high as St. Laurent du Pape to cross the Eyrieu.

rt. Lavoulte, a little town, piled up in a heap against a rock, is distinguished by the large *castle* on the summit of the height above it, and the clouds of smoke rising from the 4 large iron-furnaces at its base. The *Castle*, an ancient possession of the house of Ventadour, and residence of Louis XIII. in 1629, is now occupied by an iron-company, and partly serves as a fire-brick kiln: 1 or 2 picturesque towers remain of its older feudal part. The furnaces at its base are supplied with a very rich ore (red carbonate or hæmatite), from mines a short way up the valley. More than 300 persons are employed in them and in the ironworks; and the red tinge from the ore pervades the hideously filthy streets, and its dirty inhabitants, whose flesh, clothes, and even hair, acquire the same ruddy stain. The coal comes from St. Étienne, and the metal is sent hence in barges, for whose reception a little basin has been formed here at the water side.

A little below Lavoulte

rt. Pousin, a small town with a suspension bridge; activity is caused by the establishment of two large iron furnaces nearly opposite.

l. The river Drôme, which gives its name to a Dépt., pours itself into the Rhône.

l. On either side of the Drôme, about 2 m. above its confluence, stand the towns of Livrons (half of whose 3457 Inhab. are Protestants) and Loriol* (*Inn*: Chariot d'Or, 2nd rate). A fine bridge over the Drôme connects them, and the high road passes through both. On the l. in the valley is the Château of Crest, well placed. Loriol was the birth-place and residence of Faujas de St. Fond, who wrote a bulky tome on the extinct Volcanoes of Central France in his own neighbourhood which, as the author had never seen an *active* volcano, abounds in fallacies, and is now little valued.

The road to the volcanic district of the Ardèche by Privas and Aubenas (Rte. 121), turns away from the Rhône near Pouzin.

rt. Cruas, a curious fortified Abbey on a hill, in ruins, but retaining its antique ramparts, gates, and donjon, which stood sieges in 1584 and 1585, from the Calvinists, who were repulsed by the Monks. The Ch., below the road, and half buried under the deposits brought down by a neighbouring torrent, is a curious specimen of Romanesque architecture: beneath it are crypts. It contains the monument of Count Adhemar, founder of Montélimart and Rochemaure.

One of the most striking scenes on the banks of the Rhône is

rt. Rochemaure, a small village at the base of a hill from which project 3 peaked masses of black basalt, contrasting vividly with the light-coloured limestone around. The middle peak, rising precipitously 300 ft. above the river, is surmounted by the ruins of a feudal cas*t*le, which belonged to the families of Ventadour and Soubise. The donjon, crowning a now isolated peak, was formerly joined to the rest of the fortress by bridges thrown across the abyss. In these precipices of Rochemaure you behold the last root or limb of the Coiron chain of hills which, after traversing the whole of the Ardèche, terminates here, on the margin of the Rhône. The black rocks are 3 dykes of basalt, branches of the vast lava current which caps that mountain plateau. The basalt assumes in places a columnar form, and some of the houses and a part of the castle are built of regular prisms. From the top of the rock of Rochemaure there is a fine view over the course of the Rhône, the Alps of Dauphiné, &c.

About 3 m. lower down, but 1½ from the river-side, stands

l. *Montélimart** (*Inn:* Poste, outside the town on the S.), an ancient town of 8632 Inhab., entirely surrounded by Gothic ramparts flanked with watchtowers, and entered by 4 gates. On a rising ground within it stands the *castle* or *citadelle*. It obtained its name, Monteil d'Adhemar, from a powerful family of magnates, who held possession here from the days of Charlemagne, and from whom many of the old noblesse of the province traced their lineage. Some morocco leather is made here, and the manufacture is mentioned by Rabelais. The almond-cakes (nougat), in texture resembling a piece of soap, enjoy some celebrity. Near this the olive is first seen, though it cannot be said to flourish farther to the N. than Avignon: black truffles abound; and the mulberry-tree is cul-

* *Post-road.*—11 Pailasse. 11 Loriol.

* *Post-road.*—13 Derbières. 10 Montélimart.

tivated to a very great extent for the silkworm.

At a small village called Allan, about 9 m. S.E. of Montélimart, and the same from the Rhône, there existed, down to 1802, the first white mulberry planted in France. It was brought thither from Naples, by Guy Pope de St. Auban, seigneur of Allan, one of the soldiers who accompanied Charles VIII. on his Italian campaign, 1494. It spread hence all over the S. of France, where the culture of the silkworm is now one of the chief sources of industry and prosperity to the people. The silkworm is here called *magnan*, and the establishments in which it is reared *magnaneries*. A single tree will furnish 5 or 6 quintaux of leaves, and not unfrequently as much as 9 or 10 quintaux.

At the time when the eggs (la graine) are beginning to be hatched, sheets of paper pierced with holes are laid upon them, and through these the worms, extricating themselves from the shells, climb to reach the mulberry leaves hung over them, whence they are transferred to hurdles formed of reeds, arranged like shelves, for their future habitation. The worms live in that state (as larvæ) about 34 days, and in the course of that period change their skin 4 times. Before each of these sloughings, called "*ages*" by the peasant, they become torpid, and cease to eat, but, having changed their skin, their appetite increases enormously. The periods of appetite preceding the 4 first changes are called petites frèzes, and that before the 5th change grande frèze. The consumption of leaves increases with each age. The worms produced by an ounce of eggs devour 7 lbs. of leaves during the 1st age, and as much as 200 to 300 lbs. of leaves during the final period. At that time they make a noise in eating which resembles that of a heavy shower falling. On the 10th day of this 5th age they cease to eat, and try to climb up to the small twigs of heath or other plants purposely hung over the shelves, in order to spin their cocoon, which they complete in 3 or 4 days. Formerly it was usual to bake the cocoons in an oven, in order to kill the worm and

France.

prevent its biting through the silk; a more effectual method, unattended by risk of burning the silk, is to enclose the cocoon in a copper filled with steam, and hermetically sealed, and thus to stifle the worm. It is then fit for reeling (*filature*).

[17 m. S. E. of Montélimart is *Château Grignan*, celebrated in the letters of Madame de Sévigné, and the residence of her son-in-law. It was originally a stately pile, "un château vraiment royal," as Madame de S. calls it, seated on a commanding height above the town, fronted with a terrace raised partly on a rock, partly on masonry, 100 ft. high, commanding an extensive view, bounded by the Mont Ventoux. But it was burnt and gutted at the Revolution by a band of robbers composed of the scum of Orange and the neighbouring towns, and now stands a mere shell; yet the window of the bed-chamber and boudoir of the Sévigné is still pointed out. In the *church*, whose tower adjoins the castle terrace, and rises to a level with it, Madame de Sévigné (who died at Grignan) is buried. A black stone in the pavement marks the entrance of the family vault, which was saved from desecration at the hands of the Revolutionist pillagers of the church by the removal of this stone, so as to conceal the position of the vault.

The traveller may regain the banks of the Rhône from Grignan by a different road, leading direct to La Palud, near Pont St. Esprit. The cross-roads, however, to and from Grignan are very bad indeed.]

A considerable hill occurs on quitting Montélimart.

In this portion of the route the finest scenery occurs, and the superior transparency of a southern atmosphere becomes perceptible in the remarkable blueness of the distant hills, approximating in intensity to ultramarine. The inhabitant of a northern climate, who has, perhaps, regarded as exaggerations the azure mountains in the backgrounds of the paintings of Titian, will be surprised to find them here realised in nature.

U

The Rhône is confined between high but arid limestone cliffs abreast of

rt. Viviers, a town of only 2500 Inhab., yet a bishop's see, and anciently the capital of the province of Vivarais, which is named after it. The town, enclosed within its old walls, is a complicated labyrinth of narrow streets, partly crossed by arches, not unlike the interior of a hive. On an eminence, near the verge of the cliff, rising abruptly from the Rhône, stands the *Cathedral*, overtopping the other buildings: it is small, and not very remarkable; the nave modern, surmounted by a tower. Near it is the Evêché. At the upper end of the town stands the *Seminaire*, a huge modern edifice of 6 stories, for the education of priests. A private house in the principal Place presents in its richly ornamented front a good specimen of domestic architecture. Viviers suffered much during the wars of Religion, having been one of the first towns to declare against the king in favour of the Prince de Condé and the Protestant party, 1562. It was several times besieged and captured by both parties.

There is a road from Viviers to Aubenas, by Villeneuve de Berg, the birth-place of Olivier de Serres; near which is a curious volcanic mountain, known as les Rampes de Montbrul, pierced with grottoes.

l. The majestic summit of the *Mont Ventoux*, the extreme buttress or root pushed forth from the French Alps towards the Rhône, continues in view, a noble object and landmark from this as far as Avignon.

Below Viviers* the river expands, and its current is divided by numerous willowy islands. A fine suspension-bridge of 3 curves, rebuilt since 1840, when the inundation destroyed it, crosses the Rhône at

rt. Bourg St. Andeol, a town of 4300 Inhab., built on a slope. Close to it is a copious source rising from the base of a rock, on the face of which, about 20 ft. from the ground, is a rudely-sculptured group, representing the Sacrifice of a Bull to the god Mithras, to whom the source seems to have been dedicated. It is now nearly effaced.

Those who intend to visit the antiquities of Orange, on their way to Avignon, must quit the steamer at the bridge of Bourg St. Andeol.

l. Opposite to St. Andeol, but removed 1½ m. from the river, is Pierrelatte, so called from the broad isolated mass of rock rising out of the plain behind it, to a height of 300 or 400 ft. For many miles beyond this, nearly as far as Avignon, the road runs at such a distance from the Rhône that it is rarely seen at all.

l. La Palud,* the first place in the Dépt. Vaucluse, is about 2 m. distant from the Rhône, but the crocketed stone spire of its Gothic church may be distinguished. A few miles to the E. of the road is St. Paul Trois Châteaux, the Roman Augusta Tricastinorum.

rt. The river Ardèche pours its waters into the Rhône nearly opposite La Palud, and its deposits seem to have formed the numerous islands occurring near its mouth.

rt. About 2. m. lower down, at *Pont St. Esprit*, a town of 4500 Inhab., whose citadel was built by Louis XIII. to keep in awe the Protestants, the Rhône is crossed by a *bridge* of 19 arches, and 4 small land arches, the longest stone bridge in the world, and down to 1806 the only one over the Rhône. It was built 1310 by an associated brotherhood formed in the town, then called St. Saturnin, and 45 years were occupied in its construction, the first stone having been laid 1265 by the prior of the convent. The cost of this great public work was defrayed by subscriptions raised among the inhabitants of both banks of the Rhône, and by offerings made by the pious at a little chapel dedicated to the Holy Ghost at the end of the bridge, whence its actual name. The stones for it were brought by water from the quarries of St. Andeol, and a company of monks and nuns was established on the bank, the one to superintend the works, the other to attend the sick or

* *Post-road.*—14 Donzère.

* *Post-road.*—16 La Palud.

PROVENCE. *Route* 125.—*The Rhône (B)—Orange.*

wounded workmen. It is 2550 Fr. ft., or 2717 Eng. ft. long, more than three times as long as London Bridge, and 17 ft. wide: the arches are irregular in size; the widest have an opening of 108 ft.; the piers are pierced with small, round-headed, flood-water arches. It is not straight, but makes an angle against the stream. The passage under the Pont St. Esprit used to be thought an achievement like that of shooting old London Bridge, owing to the rapidity of the current; but the experience of the pilots is a guarantee from all danger, and the steamers pass in perfect safety, although the eddying river, rushing through the low arches, has an alarming look, increased by the sudden twist which the steersman is obliged to give to the vessel the moment it has passed through. The bridge is about 2 m. distant from the high road to Avignon. Roads branch off from it E. to Gap, and S.W. to Nismes, by the Pont du Gard. (Rte. 126.)

1. The Avignon road, having crossed that from Pont St. Esprit to Gap, skirts the towns of Montdragon and Mornas, both seated at the foot of precipitous cliffs crowned by ruined *castles*. From that of Mornas, as the story goes, the ferocious Huguenot leader, the Baron des Adrets, forced his prisoners to leap down on the pikes of his soldiers below.

1. After passing a small stream, the Aigues, a glimpse may be obtained from the river of a huge structure surmounting the town of Orange, 3 m. inland from the Rhône: it is the wall of its Roman theatre. (See below.) The post-road, just before it reaches Orange, flanked by poplars, is carried in a double sweep round the antique Roman Arch.

1. *Orange.**—*Inns:* H. des Princes; Griffin d'Or; both dear: mosquitoes are to be much dreaded here. (§ 3.) This town of 9254 Inhab., situated about 3 m. E. of the Rhône, was the ancient Arausio, and is remarkable for the interesting Roman remains which it possesses. Its name has been rendered familiar and illustrious by hav-

* *Post-road*—12 Mornas. 11 *Orange.*

ing been borne by the noble family of Nassau. It was the chief town of a small but independent principality which had existed from the 11th centy., and on the death of Philibert de Châlons, Prince of Orange, 1531, without children, became the inheritance of his sister, who was married to the Prince of Nassau Dillingen. The family of Nassau was confirmed in the possession by the Treaty of Ryswick; but upon the death of William III. of England the King of Prussia claimed it, as a descendant of the princes of Nassau-Orange, and in spite of other, rightful perhaps, but weaker claimants, he was allowed by the Treaty of Utrecht to make over the principality, in exchange for other possessions, to the King of France, from whose dominions it has never since been separated. The house of Nassau consequently retains at present no more than the title of Prince of Orange, which is borne by the heir to the throne of Holland.

The principal Roman remains are, 1. The *Triumphal Arch, situated about ¼ m. outside the town, on the road to Valence. It is a handsome structure, in a good, if not in the best style of Roman architecture: its preservation is remarkable, considering that it was incorporated in the palace of the Princes of Orange; and the deep yellow tints of the stone (a tertiary limestone abounding in fossils) of which it is composed have a rich effect. The bas-reliefs with which it is adorned represent chiefly naval trophies,—rostra, masts, yards, shrouds, anchors, and a number of barbaric shields skilfully disposed; others consist of groups of figures, but the subjects are not satisfactorily explained: one female holds her finger to her ear. The sunken panels (caissons) in the vault of the central archway are very elegant. The date and destination of this arch are unknown; no inscription is visible, excepting certain names inscribed on the shields, among which the most distinct is MARIO, and some have, in consequence, supposed that it was raised in commemoration of Marius' victory over the Cimbri near

U 2

Aix. But arches of triumph were not known, it appears, until the time of the emperors, and the generally-received opinion at present refers it to the reign of Marcus Aurelius, and to his successes on the Danube and in Germany.

The building has been very judiciously repaired.

Quite at the other end of the dirty little town stands, 2. The *Roman Theatre*, at the foot of a hill, whose side, with skilful economy, was excavated into semicircular ranges of seats for the spectators, and whose top was crowned by the citadel of the Romans first, and afterwards of the Princes of Orange, finally razed by Louis XIV. The colossal wall forming the scena, the chord of the semicircle, built over against the hill, overtops all the puny edifices of modern times, and is conspicuous for miles around. Few such walls, it may safely be asserted, exist in any part of the world: its dimensions are, 34 mèt. = 121 ft. high, 102 mèt. = 334½ ft. long, and 4 mèt. = 13 ft. thick. It is formed of huge blocks, fitted accurately together without cement. It had 3 doorways below, and near the top ran 2 rows of projecting corbel stones, those nearest the extremities being pierced with holes for the masts, by which an awning was stretched over the scene. Owing, however, to the projection of the crowning cornice, the masts must have inclined outwards. The inner face of the wall is denuded of ornament; in its centre is an arch, and on either side a curious and lofty recess. The interior has recently been cleared of the miserable hovels which filled it, and whose tenants, in some instances, burrowing like moles, had formed cellars in the thickness of the wall, regardless of the risk of undermining it, and of being buried in its ruins. The removal of 100 of these cabins now enables the spectator to judge, to a certain extent, of the arrangement of the scene on its inner face. It is still accessible by stone stairs nearly to the top. Some of the corridors are vaulted with long stone beams. Near the top the stone is calcined and reddened by the action of fire. The apartments at the side were destined for the actors, scenery, and other accessories of a theatre. A few seats remain on the slope, formed by excavating the limestone rock: on one may be seen the letters Eq. C. III. (Knights' 3rd row). —Round the semicircle run 3 passages, lined with masonry of small stones. A great many fragments of architecture and sculpture, slabs of marble, pillars of granite, &c., dug up within the enclosure, are preserved here.

Side by side with this theatre ran a *circus*, or hippodrome, the greater part of which has disappeared, quarried out to build the houses of the town, except a few arches of the portico, which joined it to the theatre.

The ancient *Arausio*, which could construct and maintain edifices of such splendour and magnitude as these, far exceeded in extent the present provincial town; and, judging from the range of the Roman walls, part of whose circuit still remains, they may have enclosed a population of 40,000. A good survey of it may be made from the heights above the theatre, where the citadel, now reduced to fragments of masonry, and the base of a round tower, once stood.

The people of Orange have a character for ferocity, of which they certainly displayed a sample during the Revolution; 378 persons perished here by the guillotine, in the space of 3 months, in compliance with the decree of the revolutionary tribunal.

[At Vaison, 15 m. N. E. of Orange, are some scanty ancient remains, 2 arches of a *theatre*, and a *Roman bridge*, of a single arch, over the torrent Lou Vèze, beyond which, in the modern town, are 2 old Romanesque churches, *St. Quinin*, partly of the 8th centy., and the *cathedral*, calculated to interest the antiquarian architect.

The most curious of the bas-reliefs and other antiquities, built into the walls of the house called Château Maraudy, have been removed to Avignon.]

The Rhône, below Orange, traverses

a wide plain, with little variety of surface.

rt. Roquemaure, distinguished by its tower, perched on the edge of a cliff, excavated below by stone-quarries, is fixed on by various authors as the spot where Hannibal passed the Rhône with his army and elephants, 4 days' march below the junction of the Isère, on his way to the Little St. Bernard, where he crossed the Alps.

l. Nearly opposite is Châteauneuf des Papes, where the Popes had a country residence.

l. The stony plain on the E. of the Rhône is nearly barren, but supports a few olives and willows. The road passes by Courthezon, near which is a salt lake, the only one in France; in its bed salt is collected when ·the waters dry up. There is greater fertility near Bédarrides (Biturritæ, from 2 towers which it possessed), and Sorgues, a village named from the clear stream flowing through it, which rises at Vaucluse. At its junction with the Rhône, that river divides into 2 branches, separated by broad islands.

The spires of Avignon, and the gigantic towers of the Papal palace, now rise conspicuously to view, whether we approach by land or water.

The steamers stop at the quay, outside the lofty battlemented city wall, just above the broken *stone bridge* of *St. Benezet*, and its little chapel, which is about a mile from the Inns. Passengers are left in the hands of the *porters* of Avignon, who are notoriously a brutal set, and whose exactions and insolence ought to be repressed by the police.

1. AVIGNON.*—*Inns:* Hôtel de l'Europe, excellent in all respects—a most attentive landlord; H. du Palais National, also very good and moderate. There are few better inns in France than these.

This ancient city of the Popes, now chef-lieu of the Dépt. Vaucluse. is seated on the l. bank of the Rhône, a little above the influx of the Durance into it, and is still enclosed by the

* *Post-road*.—18 Sorgues. 10 Avignon.

lofty *walls*, surmounted by a cornice of machicolated battlements, and flanked by watch-towers, which were constructed for its defence by Clement VI. in the middle of the 14th centy. They are very perfect and picturesque, interrupted only on the side towards the Rhône by the cliffs of the *Rocher des Dons*, which, starting up abruptly, nearly from the water's edge, abuts against the wall, serves as a rampart, and renders other defence needless. Within the circuit of these fortifications, however, will be found large spaces, now vacant, once covered with habitations; for Avignon, though now numbering only 31,812 Inhab., possessed down to the time of Louis XIV. a population of 80,000. It has indeed several thriving suburbs outside its walls. A suspension-bridge is thrown over the branches of the Rhône, from the Port d'Oulle to Villeneuve-les-Avignon, on the rt. bank of the river. In the Place d'Oulle, just within this gate, stand the two principal hotels, and a small *Theatre*, designed by the architect Mignard, now a warehouse. On this place Marshal Brune, in passing through Avignon, 1815, furnished with Lord Exmouth's passport, was murdered by an infuriated mob of Provençal royalists, who, upon the news of the battle of Waterloo, and instigated by hatred of Buonaparte, rose upon their adversaries, and committed all sorts of excesses and massacres. The Marshal was shot by the pistol of an assassin in his chamber at the Hôtel du Palais Royal, his body was thrown into the Rhône, and his murderers escaped justice.

To obtain an idea of the leading features of Avignon and its vicinity, the traveller must penetrate through its ill-paved and dirty streets, so narrow that an awning is often stretched across, from house to house, to keep off the sun, to the *height of the Dons*. On reaching its platform, now planted, converted into a public walk, and ornamented with a bronze statue of Alten, who introduced the culture of garance (madder) into France, in the Dépt. of Vaucluse, close to the telegraph, he will find himself on the brink of a precipice, looking over the Rhône, here divided by an island, towards the stately towers of Villeneuve, which was long a frontier fortress of France, on the opposite bank. In the S. appears the barren range bordering the valley of the Durance, and the Durance itself hurrying on to join the Rhône. On the N.E. rise the Mont Ventoux, and the blue hills at whose feet lies Vaucluse; and close at hand the buildings of the city are spread out, surmounted by the palace of the popes, and its ill-omened tower of the Glacière, and by the cathedral, planted side by side.

The *Cathedral, called Notre Dame des Dons (de Dominis), is founded on the rock, and approached by a long flight of steps. It is entered by a projecting porch, calculated to interest and puzzle the architect and antiquary, consisting of a circular arch, flanked by 2 Corinthian columns at the corners, so completely Roman in character that some have supposed it to have formed the porch of a Roman building, a temple of Hercules ; and, judging from a juncture perceptible in the masonry behind, it is probably of a different date from the body of the church. The pediment surmounting it is rather higher pitched than is usual in classic buildings; its tympanum is pierced with a circular opening, and over the doorway are the remains of frescoes of the 14th centy. Behind this rises a massy W. tower, and the cross is surmounted by an octagon, supported at the angles and flanked externally by fluted Corinthian columns. The roof is Pointed; the side chapels date from the 14th centy.; that of St. Joseph was once a passage leading into the papal palace. It contains the *tomb of Pope Jean XXII.*, a florid Gothic canopy, richly carved, but mutilated, and its niches emptied since the Revolution; beneath it reclines his broken effigy. Here is preserved a very ancient *altar*, a slab of marble supported on 5 pillars with classic capitals. Benedict XII. has a plainer monument in a N. chapel. In the choir is placed the *papal throne*, now the seat of the archbishop, of marble, carved with the Winged Bull of St. Luke, and the Lion of St. Mark. Near it is shown the monument of the brave Crillon. 4 or 5 popes were consecrated in this church.*

Besides what it suffered at the Revolution, this edifice was, in 1814, made the receptacle for some hundred Spanish prisoners. It has lately undergone repairs, and has been modernised with bad effect. One chapel is decorated with frescoes by *Deveria*; in one a statue of the Virgin, by *Pradier*, has been placed.

The ancient *Palace of the Popes*, now degraded into a barrack, is magnificent from its colossal vastness, and very impressive in spite of its present degradation and mutilations. Of late no part has been shown to strangers but the Chapelle du St. Office. It has been injuriously modernised. Those who heretofore explored its recesses were subjected to fatiguing ascents of lofty staircases, bad smells, and other annoyances inseparable from a barrack. It partakes of the mixed character of a feudal castle and convent. Its walls are 100 ft. high, and some of its towers 150 ft., with a proportionate thickness of masonry.

It is an edifice rich in associations!

* The Popes gained possession of Avignon on the strength of a grant made by Joanna of Naples, while yet a minor, 1348: she was to receive for it 80,000 gold crowns, which were never paid.

List of the Popes who reigned at Avignon—all Frenchmen.

1305. Clement V. Born near Bordeaux.
1316. John XXII. Born at Cahors.
1334. Benedict XII. Born at Verdun, Comté de Foix.
1342. Clement VI. Born near Limoges.
1352. Innocent VI. Born near Limoges.
1362. Urban V. Born in diocese of Mende.
1370. Gregory XI. Born in Limousin. Quitted Avignon for Rome, 1376. Thus ended the Babylonish Captivity of the Romish Church, as it is called, "L'Empia Babilonia" of *Petrarch's* Sonnet, 91.

Afterwards the following schismatic Popes set up their throne at Avignon, and resided there 40 years.

1378. Clement VII.
1394. Benedict XIII. (Pierre de Luna.)
1424. Clement VIII.

On the termination of the Schism, Avignon became the residence of the Papal Legate. Louis XIV., "the eldest son of the Church," seized Avignon to revenge a pretended affront on his ambassador at Rome. Louis XV. held possession of it for 10 years. It was not united with France until 1791.

It was founded by Clement V., 1319, and during the greater part of the 14th centy., the period of its construction by successive rulers, it was the seat of the Papal court, which had become a by-word for its luxury, profligacy, and venality. In those halls, now echoing to the blasphemous oaths of prisoners, or subdivided and filled with soldiers' cribs and accoutrements, the conclave of cardinals sate, by whom the pope was elected. Here *Petrarch* was a guest. Giotto and his scholars adorned its walls, and in its dungeons *Rienzi* was a prisoner. Here the once formidable Tribune of Rome, who had ruled from the Capitol with the sway of the Cæsars, now humble and despicable, owed his life to the intercession of his friend the poet. He was imprisoned in the tower *des Oubliettes*, and fettered with a single chain, fastened into the vault of the dungeon; in other respects kept in honourable custody, and had his meals from the remnants of the papal table, which were distributed to the poor. He could pursue his beloved studies: the Bible, and the history of the ancient Romans, particularly the books of Livy, were his companions in his prison, as formerly at the height of his prosperity. These battlemented walls and towers defied for several years a French army under Marshal Bouçicault, who in vain besieged within them the anti-pope Benedict XIII. (Pierre de Luna), who finally escaped by a postern.

Above the entrance, originally defended by drawbridges, portcullis, and iron gates, now removed, is the *balcony* whence the popes bestowed their benediction upon the people. The first court is disfigured by new buildings. A wide vaulted and finely groined stone staircase, under a depressed arch, on the rt. hand, leads up to what was once the great *hall* of the palace, called Salle Brûlée, ever since Pierre de Lude, papal legate in 1441, caused it to be blown up, with the guests assembled in it, consisting of the nobles of Avignon, in revenge for the murder of his nephew, a young libertine, who had outraged them by his excesses! Attached to it are side chapels, and the Salle du Consistoire, having traces of *frescoes* executed in the 14th centy.; but they are partly effaced or concealed from view by the modern division of this lofty range of halls, by floors, into 3 stories, to convert them into dormitories, except the compartment attributed to Giotto.

Another stair, on the opposite side of the building, leads to the chamber occupied by the *Inquisition*, which was established here in the 13th centy. The *Chapelle du Saint Office*, vaulted and groined, retains scarcely any traces of the frescoes with which it was decorated by Giotto, 1324-27. Christ's Baptism, and Interview with the Woman of Samaria; Theodosius repulsed by St. Ambrose; and St. Louis in Egypt, the Pyramids in the background, may still be distinguished. A large portion, including the Last Judgment, are effaced. Here the Jews inhabiting Avignon were assembled at stated times to hear a sermon, designed to promote their conversion to Christianity. The *chamber* of *torture* (salle de la question) adjoining, is built with funnel-shaped walls, contracting upwards, in the manner of a glass-house; a form devised, it is said, to stifle the cries of the miserable victims. In the thickness of the wall, in one corner, are the remains of a furnace for heating torturing irons, according to the tradition. Near it are the holes to which was attached the instrument called *La Veille*, a pointed stake upon which the condemned was seated, suspended by cords from above, so as only to prevent his falling, but allowing his whole weight to bear upon the point.

These are the associations of the dark ages, and they are dismal enough; but this building has beheld events in modern and enlightened times which far distance them in their horrors and atrocities. The crimes accumulated during a few hours of the French Revolution exceed those dispersed through previous ages. Who has not heard of the *Glacière* of Avignon? The tower so called, from an ice-house in a garden near it, stands close to the tower of the Inquisition. Until lately the stranger, through an aperture in its walls, might discern, near the bottom, long black stains; they are streaks of human blood; and into those dark depths below were hurled from above no less than 60 unfortunate and innocent persons, females as well as men, massacred by a band of democrats more savage than wild beasts, in Oct. 1791. The prisoners were dragged from their cells, and poignarded or struck down in the door; but in the blind haste of the ruffians, it is believed that some of their victims were precipitated from above before life was yet extinct; but to finish the deed of infamy, quicklime in large quantities was thrown down over them upon the mangled heap of dead and dying. The actual scene of these atrocities is no longer visible, the tower having been floored and fitted up.

In the narrow passage, shut up within lofty walls, by which you approach this part of the castle, some of the prisoners of the revolutionary executioner Jourdan, called Coupetête, from his butcheries, were thrust, and, cannon being brought to the gate, were despatched by grape-shot, the marks of which still indent the walls.

A later building facing the Papal palace, *Caserne de Gendarmerie*, but temporarily the Hôtel de Ville, fantastically ornamented in front with large garlands carved in stone, was the *papal mint*.

A lane S. of the Palace, passing into the Rue Peirollerie, under a huge flying buttress, which connects the castle wall with the ancient building, once residence of the Podestat or Governor of Avignon, leads to the *Ch. of St. Pierre*, having a richly florid front, built 1512, nearly in the Perpendicular style, but mutilated. It contains a stone pulpit, carved and surrounded by little statues, in canopied niches. Scarcely any other of the numerous churches here deserve notice; but to give an idea how completely ecclesiastical Avignon was before the Revolution, we may mention that it contained 8 chapters, 35 convents of both sexes, 10 hospitals, 7 fraternities of penitents, 3 séminaires, a university, and 60 churches, of which 18 now remain; ⅓ of its population were dedicated to the church, and it possessed between 200 and 300 towers and spires. Rabelais, in consequence of the number of bells, called it "La Ville sonnante."

The *Place de l'Horloge* is overlooked by the clock-tower, or belfry, called Jacquemart, from the figures in armour, who strike the hours, attached to the *Hôtel de Ville*, once a palace of the Colonna, now marred by a modern Grecian portico. Here are situated the principal cafés and the theatre.

In the Rue Calade is situated the *Musée*, founded by Calvet, a native of Avignon. Its collections are of considerable interest. The Roman antiquities found in the neighbourhood are numerous, though few are derived from Avignon itself, the ancient Avenio. Several large monuments, carved in high relief, have been brought from Vaison near Orange (p. 436), among them a chariot carrying 2 persons and a driver, drawn by horses harnessed with traces, and shod (this use of horseshoes has been attributed to later times); another represents the Sacrifice of a Bull (? Mithraic). They are overladen with ornament, and in the debased style of the Lower Empire. An amphora or wine-jar, 5 ft. high, and 8 or 10 in circumference, deserves notice for its size.

In the upper rooms are a large collection of antique bronzes, arms, utensils, &c., found in Provence and the Comtat Venaissin, in fine preservation: some of them have a Greek character. Among them is the Head of a Roman Standard (the Eagle of a Legion?), and a Head of Jupiter, cut in agate. The collection of Roman glass is large and perfect. Many of these objects were obtained from the Roman town Vaison by excavations in 1838–1840. There are 2 perfect Egyptian paintings on papyrus, and other Egyptian antiquities. The coins and medals amount to 14,000: among them is a suit of Papal medals struck at Avignon; also the seals of the Popes and their Legates, and the last seal used by the *Inquisition* here.

In the *Picture Gallery*, besides many early paintings of the 15th and 16th centuries, which seem to have been retouched, there are 2 portraits attri-

PROVENCE.   *Route* 125.—*Avignon—Picture Gallery.*   441

buted to *Holbein*; another head, like John Knox, 1535, in an oval; and a Holy Family of the Milanese school. A Crucifixion, by *Eckhout*, is not unworthy of Rembrandt, and is, perhaps, the best picture in the gallery. There are paintings by the 3 *Vernets*; by *Joseph*, who was a native of Avignon, one of his best landscapes; by *Carl*, several landscapes; and by *Horace* (whose bust, by Thorwaldsen, is placed in the room), Mazeppa on the Wild Horse. Many of old *Vernet's* sketches for the views of French seaports in the Louvre exist here.

The *library* amounts to 42,000 vols. derived from suppressed convents in the town; it includes 700 MSS. and many early printed editions of the 15th centy.

The large Benedictine convent adjoining it has been converted into a *Museum of Natural History*. In this collection may be seen specimens of the *flamingo* caught in the delta of the Rhône, where it frequents the ponds (étangs) of the Camargue. (See Index.) It is stated to be a permanent inhabitant of that part of France, forming a nest of mud, in the form of a truncated cone, on which it sits over its eggs, with its long legs dangling down on the outside. The bird does not assume its red plumage until it is 2 years old.

Here is the *beaver* of the Rhône, an animal now nearly exterminated, since the late inundations drove most of them from their retired haunts. Its colour is tawny, and its hair harsh compared with the American beaver. It does not build houses nor lay up stores in Europe, but burrows in the dykes or river bed, and feeds on willows or other brushwood, whole plantations of which are often laid prostrate by its sharp teeth. Here are collections of the minerals and fossils of the Dépt. de Vaucluse; also of fossil insects and fishes from Aix. The museum has been enriched by the splendid bequest of M. Riquet, and the whole appears well arranged. Behind is the *botanic garden*.

Continuing in the same direction, as far as Rue des Lices (No. 8), a street abounding with dyers and tanners, at the back of the Maison des Orphelins,

a charitable institution for the education of 50 poor children, we shall find the last relic of the *church of the Cordeliers*, in which Petrarch's Laura, a married lady of the family De Sade in Avignon, was buried. The church, destroyed at the Revolution, is now reduced to a fragment of the tower and side walls, sold probably for the value of the materials, but not worth pulling down.

Laura's tomb, described by Arthur Young as "nothing but a stone in the pavement, with a figure engraved on it, partly effaced, surrounded by an inscription in Gothic letters, and another on the wall adjoining, with the armorial bearings of the family De Sade," has entirely disappeared, having been broken open, and the contents of the tomb, as well as that of the brave Crillon, scattered by the Revolutionists. In a sort of tea-garden behind the fragment of the church, a vulgar, tasteless monument has been raised to Laura, bearing the pompous inscription, "Hunc cippum posuit Carolus Kelsall Anglicus." Petrarch has recorded that he first saw Laura in the church of St. Claire, 1327, in the time of his early youth.

In this church of the Cordeliers, June 1791, the mob of Avignon, irritated at the tyranny, spoliations, and sacrilegious acts of the democratic municipality, put to death its agent and secretary Lescuyère: the chief actors in this deed of blood were women, who actually tore out his eyes with their scissors.

Behind the church and convent of St. Martial is the *Hôtel des Invalides*, subordinate to, and dependent on, that of Paris, founded for old soldiers, after the expulsion of the French from Egypt. It occupies the buildings of 2 suppressed convents, between which a park extends. The upper part of a *chapel*, in the roof of which are traces of fresco, serves as the Lingerie. The establishment is furnished with a good library for the use of the inmates.

There is a *French Protestant Ch.* in the Rue Dorée, behind the Préfecture. Service at 11.

Steamers on the Rhône—to Lyons in

u 3

one long day, starting very early, during summer; at other seasons they stop for the night at Valence or Tournon, if possible: some vessels take more, and bring to at night without reference to any inn being near the spot. 2 to Arles in the afternoon.

Railway to Arles, Nismes, and Marseilles. (Rte. 129.) The Stat. is some distance out of the town.—*Railway* to Valence; to Lyons in progress.

Diligences, daily, to Nismes 3 (in 4 hrs.); to Lyons.

rt. Opposite to Avignon, but 1 m. higher, on the rt. bank of the Rhône, at the extremity of the wooden bridge, stands Villeneuve-lès-Avignon, an ancient town of 4000 Inhab., which was much encouraged by the kings of France, as a border-fortress, on the frontier of Languedoc, confronting the foreign territory of the Pope, on the opposite shore of Provence. It contains several objects of curiosity. In the chapel of the *Hôpital* is placed the very elegant Gothic *tomb of Pope Innocent VI.*, composed of tabernacle work, and niches beautifully carved. It was removed from the ruined convent of the Chartreuse, and has been carefully restored.

The ruins of the Gothic *Church* of the *Chartreuse*, and the tower which formed the Tête du Pont of the broken bridge of St. Benazet, faced with stones cut in diamond facettes, built by Philippe le Bel, also merit notice. The *Fort St. André*, on an elevated platform above the town, is a nearly unaltered citadel of feudal times, entered between grand drum towers. From the top is an extensive view.

The climate of Avignon is described in the proverbial line, "Avenio ventosa, sine vento venenosa, cum vento fastidiosa."

The following very interesting *Excursions* may be made from Avignon:— a. To Vaucluse; b. To the Pont du Gard, on the way to Nismes (Rte. 126); on no account to be omitted: either of these may be seen in one day from Avignon. The traveller should not return to Avignon from the P. du G., but by all means go on to Nismes. c. To Orange, on the way to Lyons (p. 435); d. To St. Remy (p. 459); e. To Carpentras. The Roman remains of Nismes (p. 446) and Arles (p. 460), more distant from Avignon, are scarcely inferior in interest to any in Italy.

a. To *Vaucluse*. 29 kilom. = 18 Eng. m. *Diligence* every morning at 6, to L'Isle for 30 sous, returning in the afternoon: it takes about an hour to walk from L'Isle to Vaucluse.

A carriage with 2 horses costs 18 or 20 frs., or with 1 horse 10 frs., to go and return; the excursion will take about 8 hrs.

It is incumbent upon all travellers to perform this "sentimental journey," not only on account of Petrarch and Laura, but because Vaucluse itself is a striking scene. You quit Avignon by the Porte St. Lazare, traverse long avenues of willows and poplars, leaving on either hand numerous country-houses, each fronted with an avenue of planes; and, after crossing the *Canal de Crillon*, which conducts the waters of the Durance to fertilise the fields of madder around Avignon (Rte. 128), reach the village of Le Thor, so named from a *bull*, which, by constantly falling on its knees, when brought to water on the margin of a pond, led to the discovery of a miraculous image of the Virgin, which was fished out of the mud, and deposited in the Church of *St. Marie du Lac!* This is an ancient and curious Romanesque building; its W. doorway resembles that of Notre Dame des Dons, and is probably of the 11th centy.; an ornamented portal at the E. end is rather later. The country is dreary as far as

22 L'Isle (*Inns:* H. du Petrarque et Laure; not very good, and dear;—Poste, better), a town of 5000 Inhab., 12 m. from Avignon, on an *island* surrounded by branches of the Sorgues, whose waters, employed in irrigation, spread fertility and verdure around. This is a green oasis in the desert, affording bubbling streams and grateful shade. There is a road from L'Isle to Carpentras. (See p. 444.)

The valley of the Sorgues, whose course we trace hence upwards, is excavated in a mountain-chain, branching from the lofty Mont Ventoux. Near its head lies the little village

7 *Vaucluse.—Inn:* H. de Laure; small, and not very clean. The landlord is a capital cook, and, judging from the Strangers' Book—a singular record of frivolous sentiment and selfish "gourmandise,"—his fried trout and eels, soupe à la bisque, and coquille d'écrevisse, have made a far deeper and more lasting impression on his visitors than the souvenir of Laura; and indeed they are not to be despised; even Petrarch himself has mentioned the fish of the Sorgues with praise. Close to the village stands a tasteless *monument* to Petrarch, which the Academy of Avignon planted at the mouth of the grotto itself, whence it was judiciously removed by order of the late Duchesse d'Angoulême, when she visited the spot. A path leads from the village to the fountain by the side of the Sorgues, whose exquisitely limpid waters are dried up near the head, in summer, and, instead of bursting out exuberantly from the cavern, filtrate underground, and issue out, some hundred yards lower down, in numerous streamlets, out of holes in the limestone rock.

The *valley of Vaucluse* (vallis clausa) is a complete cul de sac, a semicircular excavation in the side of a mountain, which seems to have been split from top to bottom, so as to disclose the secret storehouse of water within it, whence the sparkling Sorgues derives its supplies. All around rise walls of rock from 500 to 600 ft. high, intermixed with bristling pyramids, arid, destitute of verdure, and glaringly white. The sides and bottom are strewn with broken fragments of stone, which, where the Sorgues rolls over them, are covered with a luxuriant mantle of green moss. It is a desolate and arid scene. On a ledge half way up, to the rt., is perched a ruined *castle*, which belonged to the bishops of Cavaillon, one of whom, the Cardinal de Cabassole, was Petrarch's friend. Though popularly known as Petrarch's Castle, it never belonged either to him or to Laura; but the site of his house is pointed out between the castle and the village. Here, beside a natural grotto in the rock, mentioned in his letters, one of the gardens which he formed with so much care was probably situated.

At the extremity of this majestic recess, at the base of the precipice, yawns the cavern which contains the *fountain of Vaucluse*. According to the season, and the abundance of the water, it presents alternately a gushing cataract, tumbling over the moss-clad stones, from step to step, or a quiet, pellucid, dark-blue pool, sunken within its grotto, so that you may enter under the vault beside it, and, gazing into its funnel-shaped basin, watch the stones which are thrown in gradually descend into its fathomless depths. A wild fig-tree, springing from a crevice in the face of the rock, above the natural vault, marks, with its roots, the height which the waters attain when they fill the cave.

Around this spot must have been the other garden mentioned by Petrarch in his letters; that consecrated to Apollo, adapted to study, "where art surpasses nature."

It is more agreeable to contemplate Petrarch in these haunts, as the laborious student retired from the world, than as the mawkish lover, sighing for a married mistress, and converted, as in the sentimental verses of Delille, into a sort of Italian Werther. Listen to his own account of his occupations at Vaucluse.

"The Sorgues, transparent as crystal, rolls over its emerald bed; and by its bank I cultivate a little sterile and stony spot, which I have destined to the Muses; but the jealous Nymphs dispute the possession of it with me; they destroy, in the spring, the labours of my summer. I had conquered from them a little meadow, and had not enjoyed it long, when, upon my return from a journey into Italy, I found that they had robbed me of all my possession. But I was not to be discouraged; I collected the labourers, the fishermen, and the shepherds, and raised a rampart against the Nymphs; and there we raised an altar to the Muses; but, alas! experience has proved that it is in vain to battle with the elements. I no longer dispute with the

Sorgues a part of its bed; the Nymphs have gained the victory.

"Here I please myself with my little gardens and my narrow dwelling. I want nothing, and look for no favours from fortune. If you come to me, you will see a solitary, who wanders in the meadows, the fields, the forests, and the mountains, resting on the mossy grottoes, or beneath the shady trees. Your friend detests the intrigues of court, the tumult of cities, and flies from the abodes of pageantry and pride.—Equally removed from joy or sadness, he passes his days in the most profound calm, happy to have the Muses for his companions, and the song of birds and the murmur of the stream for his serenade. . . . . I have few servants, but many books. Sometimes you will find me seated upon the bank of the river, sometimes stretched upon the yielding grass: and, enviable power! I have all my hours at my own disposal, for it is rarely that I see any one. Above all things, I delight to taste the sweets of leisure."

e. *Carpentras.* 23 kilom. = 14 Eng. m. from Avignon, and the *Mont Ventoux.*

The road thither from Avignon lies through Entraigues and Monteux, crossing the Sorgues, here as limpid as at Vaucluse, between the two villages. The country around Carpentras is a fertile plain, which, by means of irrigation, and of a southern sun, produces crops of all kinds in abundance.

23 Carpentras is a flourishing town of 10,000 Inhab., still retaining, like most of those in the old Papal territory (the Comtat Venaissin), its feudal walls, towers, and gates; the *Porte d' Orange* being particularly perfect and stately. It was an important Roman station; but almost the only relic of that people remaining is an *Arch of Triumph*, formerly built up into the bishop's palace, and serving as his kitchen, but recently set free from that degradation, and detached from the buildings surrounding it. It is a ruin, reduced to the mere stone vault, without the attic, resting on the side piers. Upon these are curious sculptures in relief, representing Barbarian Captives, their hands bound behind their backs to trophies.

Nothing is known of the date or destination of this arch; but it is doubtless a work of the Lower Empire.

The *cathedral*, rebuilt 1405, has a tower attached to it of the 10th centy., and contains a nail of the Cross, made into a bit, and used for that purpose by Constantine, if we may believe the tradition.

There is a *musée* here containing antiquities, and a public library of 12,000 volumes and 700 MSS.

The *aqueduct* of Carpentras, a massive structure of 48 arches, was finished 1734.

The ascent of the *Mont Ventoux* may be made from Carpentras by way of Malaucène, whence it is 6 m. distant. Its top, reached by Petrarch in 1345, is 6427 ft. above the sea-level, and is covered for half the year with snow, which supplies the Dépt. with ice in summer. The view from it includes a portion of the chain of the Alps, the Cevennes, the Coiron, the course of the Rhône and Durance, and, it is said, extends to the Mediterranean. At the foot of the mountain stands *Bedouin*, a miserable village rising from amidst the blackened ruins of a former village destroyed at the Revolution. There is no darker spot in the black history of that period than the burning of Bedouin and the massacre of its inhabitants by the revolutionary committee. Their agent, the apostate priest Maignet, directed this atrocious crime, and Suchet, afterwards so eminent a general, with his soldiers, carried it into execution, setting fire to the houses, blowing up the public buildings, hurrying the peaceful inhabitants to the scaffold, and picking off with musketry those who tried to escape, until 180 had perished. And these horrors were enacted, not in a hostile country and in time of war, but upon fellow-countrymen, women, and children, Frenchmen being the executioners; and all because a tree of liberty planted within the parish had been sawn through in the night ! !

N.B. The railway from Avignon to Tarascon, Arles, and Marseilles is described Rte. 127.

ROUTE 126.

AVIGNON TO NARBONNE, BY THE PONT DU GARD, NISMES, MONTPELLIER, AND BÉZIERS.—EXCURSIONS TO ST. GILLES, CETTE, AND AIGUES MORTES.

200 kilom. = 124 Eng. m.

Malleposte from Montpellier to Narbonne daily.

Diligences from Avignon to Nismes, in 4 hrs. daily. The Pont du Gard may be seen on the way to Nismes. 9 kilom. extra are charged by the postmaster for making the détour by the Pont du Gard.

You quit Avignon by the Suspension bridge which crosses the Rhône, resting on the island. From the slope and summit of the long steep ascent which carries the road over the hills forming the rt. bank of the Rhône, you have a fine view of it and of Avignon, and then a dreary country succeeds; hills bare as dry bones; but in the low ground olives, mulberries, and vines.

12 Begude de Saze.

The point where our road approaches nearest to the Pont du Gard is at Remoulins (1¼ m. distant from it), a small town on the l. bank of the Gardon, now at length connected by a bridge of wire with

11 La Foux. (Fabre's restaurant. Beware the *Inn* here: it is extortionate and bad. Do not allow your coachman to drive into the remise, and force you to walk 2 m. of hot, dusty road to the Pont du Gard, unless you like it.) La Foux is a village and post stat. on the rt. bank. 9 kilom. extra are charged if the traveller posting chooses to be driven round by the *Pont du Gard (1¾ m. distant, turning to the rt. up the rt. bank of the river).

The sight of this noble edifice, one of the grandest monuments which the Romans have left, in France or any other country, would well repay for a very long détour. Like Stonehenge, it is the monument of a people's greatness, a standard by which to measure their power and intellect. It consists of 3 tiers of arches; the lowest of 6 arches supporting 11 of equal span in the central tier, surmounted by 35 of smaller size; the whole in a simple, if not stern style of architecture, destitute of ornament. It is by its magnitude, and the skilful fitting of its enormous blocks, that it makes an impression upon the mind. It is the more striking from the utter solitude in which it stands, a rocky valley, partly covered with brushwood and greensward, with scarcely a human habitation in sight, only a few goats browsing. After the lapse of 16 centuries this colossal monument still spans the valley, joining hill to hill, in a nearly perfect state, only the upper part, at the N. extremity, being broken away. The highest range of arches carries a covered canal about 5 ft. high, and 2 ft. wide, shaped like the letter U, just large enough for a man to walk through, still retaining a thick lining of Roman cement. It is covered with thick stone slabs, along which it is possible to walk from one end to the other, and to overlook the valley of the Gardon. The arches of the middle tier are formed of 3 distinct ribs or bands, apparently unconnected. The height of the Pont du Gard is 180 ft., and the length of the highest arcade 873 ft. Its use was to convey to the town of Nismes the water of 2 springs, 25 m. distant, the Airan rising near St. Quentin, and the Ure near Uzès. It forms only a small portion of the conduit constructed for this purpose, whose course, partly raised on low arches, some of which exist on the N. of the Pont du Gard, partly cut in the rock round the shoulders of the hills, may be traced at the village of St. Maximin, near Uzès, and above that of Vers, to the Pont du Gard; thence, by St. Bonnet and Sernhac, to the hill of the Tour Magne, and Bassin des Thermes at Nismes.

The sole object and use of this gigantic structure was for the conveyance of this small stream, an end which could be obtained in modern times by iron pipes laid under the Gardon, of sufficient strength to withstand the weight of the column of water from above. Its date and builder are alike lost in oblivion, but it is attributed to M. Agrippa, son-in-law of Augustus, B.C. 19. The quarry whence the stone was obtained is a little way down the Gardon, on its l. bank. The bridge by which the road crosses the Gardon, on a level with the lower tier of arches, and formed by merely widening them, is a modern addition to the ancient structure, having been erected in 1743 by the States of Languedoc.

Close to La Foux the road to Nismes turns rt. out of the valley of the Gardon, and traverses a more fertile and productive, but uninteresting country, by

10 St. Gervasy, to

10 *Nismes*. *Inns:* H. du Luxembourg, the best; H. du Midi, middling.

Nismes, chef-lieu of the Dépt. du Gard, a flourishing manufacturing town of 49,480 Inhab., consists of a central nucleus of narrow intricate streets and old houses, encircled by a girdle of open *boulevard*, which separates it from its modern fauxbourgs, composed of wide streets and new houses. The boulevard is itself a fine broad street, planted with trees, lined with handsome buildings; and there is little need for the passing traveller to penetrate into the old town, as the chief curiosities and objects of interest are situated on the edge of this boulevard, or at a short distance from it. They consist almost exclusively of Roman monuments, relics of the ancient city of *Nemausus*, which, though passed over in oblivion by classic authors, so that its origin is unknown, and merely mentioned in the geographical catalogues of Strabo and Ptolemy, yet affords more palpable testimony of its ancient extent and splendour than most cities celebrated in classic page. While the renowned cities of Marseilles and Narbonne have few relics and no existing edifices of the ancient masters of the world, the obscure Nismes is richer in well-preserved antiquities than any town in France or Northern Europe.

A walk along the boulevard, starting from the H. du Luxembourg, and keeping to the l., will bring you first to the *Esplanade*, a square terraced platform, planted with trees, furnishing a promenade of considerable extent. Facing it is the new *Palais de Justice*, fronted with an imposing portico, and a little further on stands

The *Amphitheatre, Les Arènes, now isolated by the removal of the buildings which obstructed it within and without, in the middle of a wide Place, allowing unimpeded view of its very perfect oval circuit. It consists of 2 stories, each of 60 arcades, 70 ft. high; the lower arches serving as so many doors: the arches of the upper arcade are double, but the inner arches are not concentric with the lower. It is far better preserved, externally, than the Coliseum at Rome, although like it converted into a fortress during the middle ages, and retains even its projecting stones, pierced with holes, for inserting the masts to which the awnings (velaria) were attached.

The interior, though less perfect, retains some of the original seats, especially of the lower and upper rows. The modern French architect employed on the building, not content with preserving and protecting the parts which remain, has committed the fault of restoring, or rather reconstructing, in a somewhat clumsy manner, part of them and some of the arcades. There were originally 32 rows of seats, and the number of spectators which it is supposed the building may have contained is estimated at from 17,000 to 23,000.

A long corridor, surrounding the building, runs within the arches on the ground story, and a smaller corridor encircles the upper story. It is worth while to make the circuit of these, and, indeed, to penetrate every part of this extraordinary structure. The vaults of the lower corridor or portico are like some vast natural cavern; the upper one is roofed with huge stone beams, 18 ft. long, reaching from side to side, many of them cracked, either by an earthquake, or by the conflagration which consumed the Arènes in the times of Charles Martel. It is interesting to penetrate the wedge-shaped passages, radiating from the centre, and widening outwards, so contrived as to facilitate the egress of the hastening crowds, and allow them to depart without any check; to ascend the stairs, by which ready access was given to every part of the huge structure; to clamber over the broken seats, some still marked with the line indicating the space allotted to each spectator, scaring the frightened lizard, which starts away from under your foot, out of the sunshine in which it has been basking, to the shelter of the tufts of grass or weeds springing up among the crevices of the masonry; and, finally, to stand on the topmost stone, the rim of this huge oval basin, surveying its whole interior, dismantled, and almost glutted. Here you may examine the round holes cut in the projecting stones, and corresponding with hollows in the exterior cornice below, into which the poles were put, in order to fasten the awnings stretched over the spectators. A very narrow stair in the thickness of the wall, near the N. side, was destined, it is supposed, for the men who had charge of the awning. The zones of seats, as is well known, were divided into 4 tiers (præcinctiones) by spaces wider than the seats themselves, and were destined for spectators of different rank; the patricians occupied the lower, equivalent to the dress circle, the plebeians the upper, corresponding with the gallery. These spaces, or landing-places, were each reached by 10 passages or vomitories. The 3 uppermost rows of seats rest upon a half arch, whose only support is the outer wall.

The *dimensions* are, length 437 ft., width 332 ft., height 70 ft.

The founder of this building and its date are unknown: it is attributed to Antoninus Pius, whose ancestors came from Nismes, but by others to Titus and Adrian.

The Visigoths converted it into a fortress, and it was known as the "Castrum Arenarum." The Saracens occupied it as such in the beginning of the 8th centy., until expelled by Charles Martel, who endeavoured to destroy the building altogether, by filling its vaults and passages with wood, and setting fire to it; finally, down to the middle of the 18th centy., it was occupied by mean hovels, all of which are now swept away. The people of Nismes use the Arènes for bull-fights and an entertainment called *Ferrade*, which consists in teasing a number of wild bulls from the Camargue (p. 463), previous to branding them with hot *iron*. The sport is but a poor imitation of a Spanish bull-fight; nearly as cruel, without being so exciting.

Continuing through the boulevard, from the Arènes, and passing on the l. the Great Hospital, you reach the modern *Theatre*, remarkable only for its tasteless portico, contrasting very unfavourably with a neighbouring building, which, though of an age deemed barbarous, shows yet a far greater refinement in taste,—

***The Maison Carrée*, the vulgar name given to a beautiful Corinthian temple, a gem of architecture, which has come down to the present time in a state of wonderful preservation, considering its various fortunes and the purposes to which it has been converted. Originally a temple, consecrated in the reign of Augustus, according to some; of Antoninus Pius, according to others: it became afterwards a Christian church, and, in the 11th centy., the Hôtel de Ville; still later it was converted into a stable, and its owner, to extend his space, built walls between the pillars of the portico, and pared away the flutings of the central columns to allow his carts to pass; it then became attached to the Augustine convent, and was used as a tomb-house for burial; its next changes were into a Revolutionary tribunal and corn warehouse; and, finally, at present it is converted into a *museum*.

It is surrounded by 30 elegant Corinthian columns, 10 of them detached, forming the portico, and 20 engaged: their height is equal to 10¼ diameters; and learned architects will tell you that these proportions are contrary to Vitruvian rules, and that the building is debased and defective in consequence. This, however, appears a case in which ignorance is bliss; the ordinary and unlearned spectator will scarcely fail to be impressed with the elegance of its general effect, as well as with the simplicity of its form, the beauty of its fluted Corinthian columns, and the richness of the capitals, frieze, and cornice which they support.

M. Séguier, an antiquary of Nismes, first hit upon the ingenious idea of restoring the inscription on the frieze above the portico from the holes left in it, by which the bronze letters composing it were attached, the letters themselves having long since disappeared. According to his reading, it ran thus:—C. CAESARI. AUGVSTI. F. COS. L. CAESARI. AUGUSTI. F. COS. DESIGNATO. PRINCIPIBUS. JUVENTUTIS.; thus attributing the dedication of this temple to "Marcus and Julius Cæsar, grandsons of Augustus, Consuls Elect, Princes of Youth." The style, however, of the building, and the profusion of ornament, indicate a period much later than Augustus; and another antiquary, on examining the original state of the holes in the frieze, discovers 3 holes preceding the 2 to which M. Séguier's first letter C was fastened, and thus converts the C into an M. This slight alteration shifts the date of the Maison Carrée from the era of Augustus to that of Antoninus, for it appears that the only 2 princes bearing such names who enjoyed together the title Principes Juventutis, after the sons of Agrippa, were Marcus Aurelius and Lucius Verus, adopted sons of Antoninus. It is evident, however, that the determination of the letters from such data must, in a great degree, be a mere piece of guess-work, owing to the confusion and number of the holes. Excavations have laid bare the foundations of walls, extending on either side of the temple, showing that it was only the centre of a larger edifice, from which two long colonnades extended, in the manner of wings, on either hand, and it is supposed that it occupied one end of the ancient *forum* of Nemausus.

The whole is now enclosed by an iron railing, within which are deposited numerous antique fragments found in and about the town.

The contents of the *Museum* (into which the temple is now turned) consist of other antiquities, including a bronze head (of Apollo?); a marble bust of Venus, and a quantity of *pictures*, very poor and commonplace for the most part, excepting *Paul Delaroche's* master-piece, Cromwell opening the Coffin of Charles I., and Nero trying upon a Slave the Poison destined for his Brother Britannicus, by *Sigalon.*

Opposite the entrance to the Maison Carrée is the small, though rich, *Museum of Antiquities,* formed by *M. Perrot.*

Returning to the boulevard, and continuing along it as far as the irregular Place de la Bouquerie, you come upon a handsome canal, supplied with water from the ancient *Fountain of the Nymphs*. It must not, however, be judged of at first sight, for at this point nothing can be more unclassical; its limpid rills are stained with soapsuds, and in the place of nymphs a swarm of blanchisseuses convert it into a public washing tub. Trace it upwards, however, and you will find its source within a fine *Public Garden,* planted with trees, in the midst of which it bursts forth in exuberant copiousness from the foot of a hill, and is received into a large reservoir, originally a *Roman bath for Women.* It is surrounded by a large colonnade below the level of the ground, and is conducted through a formal canal lined with masonry, like the ditch of a fortification, and bordered with a handsome stone balustrade. A part of this enclosure is of antique masonry, but the whole has been restored in modern times. It is a very handsome, but formal construction, and it and the fine *Garden* which it traverses form a principal ornament of the town. On one side of it is a *ruined Roman building*, supposed at one time to have been a *temple of Diana,* but now regarded as a *Nymphæum* (or fane dedicated to the Nymphs), and connected with the neighbouring baths. It appears to have had a semi-cylindrical roof rising from an entablature, supported by columns. It is proved by inscriptions to have been built, along with the baths, by Augustus. It was reduced to ruin 1577. The ancient aqueduct which the Pont du Gard carried across the valley of the Gardon (p. 445) terminated near the fountain at Nismes, in a basin or reservoir 16 ft. diameter, and about 5 ft. deep, recently discovered.

The hill rising behind the fountain, planted with trees, and rendered accessible by zigzag walks, is surmounted by another singular ancient monument, known as *La Tourmagne*, a dismantled tomb of rough ashlar, not unlike several still existing in the vicinity of Rome, but which has passed at different times with learned antiquaries for a lighthouse (50 m. inland, and remote from any river!), a Gallic temple, and a treasury. It is hollow within, having a rude conical shape, resembling that of a glass-house. The walls are very thick below, but taper upwards; externally it was an octagon, but the surface-stonework is for the most part removed. It is, perhaps, the oldest building in the town. Some have referred its origin to times preceding the Romans: in their time it was included in the defences of the town, and connected with the walls. It was originally filled with earth, and it seems not unlikely that it was built upon a nucleus of earth, for its cone is not properly vaulted, but consists of small stones, held together by the strength of the cement alone. It was cleared out by a gardener, who obtained leave from Henri IV. to search the building for treasure, a scheme which turned out eminently unprofitable.

A staircase is now erected to the top, whence the *view* is very fine. The situation of the Tourmagne is very commanding; at the foot of the heights, on which it stands, the whole city is displayed, and the distant horizon includes the bifurcation of the Rhône, and, perhaps, the site of Aigues Mortes on the Mediterranean.

Nismes retains two of its original Roman gates, the *Porte d' Auguste*, founded in the reign of that Emperor, B.C. 16, consisting of a double arch with two side doors for foot passengers, flanked by 2 towers, and the *Porte de France*.

In the heart of the old town stands the *Cathedral*, an ancient building, but so injured during the wars of religion of the 16th and 17th centuries, and now so much modernised, as to possess little interest. High up, on the W. front, above a circular window, a curious sculptured frieze, representing events from the book of Genesis, is introduced; it is very ancient.

The cabinet of *antiquities of M. Pelet*, and the cork models made by him of the ancient buildings in Nismes, are well worth seeing.

There are 12,000 Protestants at Nismes, who have 2 churches (*temples*) and a chapel: they have endured severe persecutions at different times. So little even now do the Protestants and Catholics coalesce, that each party frequents distinct cafés.

The *Maison centrale de Détention* was originally a citadel, erected by Louis XIV. to keep down the Protestants.

The *manufactures* of Nismes consist of various articles of silk and cotton, which change with the fashion and the demand; it has large printing and dyeing works; but cotton handkerchiefs seem the staple production. A considerable trade in the wines and spirits of Languedoc, in raw silks, and in oil, is carried on here. It is a very thriving town on the whole.

In the garden of the Convent of Recollets, now occupied by the Theatre, Marshal Villars had an interview in 1704 with the chief of the Camisards, Cavalier, who, originally a baker's boy, and at that time a mere youth, had raised himself by his talents for command and his fanatic eloquence to be the head of the formidable rebellion of the Cevennes. He appeared on that occasion magnificently mounted, and attired in laced coat, cocked hat, and plume of white feathers, escorted by a body-guard on horseback. The result of this memorable conference was to detach him from the insurgents by flattery and promises of rank and reward in the service of Louis XIV., as the price of his defection, coupled with assurances of justice and tolerance in religion to the persecuted Protestants of the Cevennes. Neither the one nor the other was destined to be kept or fulfilled. Villars, however, thus dealt a death-blow to the insurrection, by depriving it of one of its heads; and Cavalier, despised and hated for his desertion by his own party, and neglected by the court, was soon driven into exile, and died a pensioner at Chelsea.

On the Place de Boucairie in 1705 were erected the gibbet, the wheel, and the stake, at which a vast number of the Camisards concerned in the rebellion of the Cevennes perished miserably, after suffering horrid tortures in the prison of the fortress. The most memorable execution was that of the chiefs (April 22) Catenat and Ravenel, who were burnt alive, almost within sight of the battle-field where 2 years before they had defeated the royal forces under the Comte de Broglie; while their companions, Jonquet and Villas, were broken on the wheel and then burnt. On the 16th August, 1704, the body of Roland Laporte, general of the Camisards (see Rte. 121), was dragged into Nismes at the tail of a cart and burnt, while 5 of his companions were broken on the wheel around his funeral pyre.

Nismes is the birthplace of Nicot, a physician who first introduced from Portugal into France *tobacco* (called after him Nicotiana). Some one proposed to raise a monument to him in the form of a snuff-box, bearing the inscription, "Dieu vous bénisse." M. Guizot, ex-Minister of France, also comes from Nismes, where his father, an avocat, was guillotined during the Reign of Terror.

Railroads to Alais and its coal-field (R. 121), trains twice a day; to Beaucaire (R. 127); to Arles and Marseilles; to Montpellier and Cette.

Diligences daily to Avignon, to Mende, St. Flour, and Clermont; to St. Gilles and Aigues Mortes.

The *Pont du Gard* (p. 445), distant about 15 m. from Nismes, on the way to Avignon, ought to be visited expressly by those whose route does not lead them past it. It is about 2 hours' drive; a carriage may be hired for 12 fr. to go and return. Make the driver understand before setting out that he is not to leave you at La Foux, but to drive to the Pont.

About 13 m. nearly due S. of Nismes is *St. Gilles*, a town of great antiquity, originally *Rhoda Rhodiorum*, a colony founded by the Rhodians according to Pliny, situated on the Petit Rhône, chiefly remarkable at present for its magnificent *abbey church*, which will interest the antiquary. The upper church was begun 1116, on a scale of great magnificence, by Alphonso, son of Raymond IV., Count of St. Gilles, called Jourdain, because baptised in the Jordan, but was destroyed during the wars of religion, having been turned into a fortress by the Huguenots in 1562, and demolished, when no longer tenable as such, by the Duc de Rohan, 1622. It has been replaced by a temporary structure of late date and inferior architecture.

The *lower Church*, however, which is not subterranean, but on a level with the cloister, is, perhaps, of the 11th centy., having been dedicated, 1096, by Pope Urban II.; and the *West Front* is a masterpiece of the Romanesque style, upon which every species of ornamental decoration and rich sculpture seems to have been lavished. It has been described as one immense bas-relief, crowded with pillars, statues, panelling, foliage, &c., combined with a strange infusion of the elements of classical architecture, columns, capitals, entablatures, and friezes. Sculptured lions are frequently introduced as supports to the pillars, and in other parts; and as the abbots of St. Gilles, powerful seigneurs in ancient days, used to sit at the gate of the ch. to dispense justice, many of the old charters begin with the words "Domino NN. sedente inter leones." In the vestibule of this ch., Raymond VI., Comte de Toulouse, accused of favouring the persecuted Albigenses, underwent, in 1209, the ignominious penance of being scourged on his naked back, in the presence of the papal legate and of 12 French bishops. The lower church is supposed to be a little older than the porch.

A detached pile of ruin, behind the actual church, is the only relic of the old priory which escaped being destroyed in the 16th centy.; it contains a corkscrew *staircase*, called *Le Vis de St. Gilles*, and is celebrated for its masterly construction as a piece of masonry. It was again saved from destruction at the Revolution by the influence of M. Michel, a lawyer of St. Gilles. In a narrow street facing the ch. is a curious old house, deserving attention as a remarkable specimen of the civil architecture of the middle ages.]

A *Railway*, finished 1844, joins Nismes to Montpellier (52 kilom.), and is carried thence to the seaport of Cette, 27 kilom. = total 45 Eng. m. 4 trains daily, in 2 hours. Fare, 1st class, 2 frs. 10 sous, carriage 32 frs. Its chief work is a viaduct of 96 arches. It passes by Lunel.

The way from Nismes to Montpellier lies across an extensive plain, reaching from a range of low rocky limestone hills on the N., the extreme roots of the Cevennes, to the salt marshes bordering on the Mediterranean, S.

The fertile district to the W. of Nismes is called the *Vaunage* or Valley of Nages, from a small and reduced town of that name, a little to the N. of our road. It was the scene of one of the most remarkable engagements in the war of the Cevennes (April 6, 1704), in which Cavalier, at the head of 900 foot and 300 horse, well equipped, intending to waylay the Maréchal de Montreval on his way to Montpellier, was himself betrayed into a vast ambuscade, surrounded on all sides by the royal troops (among whom were 100 Irish from the Boyne), and caught as in a trap. Undismayed by numbers 6 times exceeding his own, the Camisard chief, perceiving the design of the enemy to outflank him, wheeled his column rapidly round under the hottest fire, and in the face of a charge of bayonets, and drew off his men, retreating en échelon —a masterly manœuvre of the baker's boy, which drew forth the admiration of Marshal Villars. Cavalier's retreat, however, was cut off; the royal army occupied every pass, every height; not an opening remained; and his only course was to cut his way through. Throwing aside his magnificent uniform and white plume, he put on a common dress, and, bidding his followers close their ranks, dashed forward directly against the enemy. With the fiercest struggle he broke through the first line, but was soon singled out and discovered: at one time a soldier caught his horse's bridle, but a Camisard behind cut off the hand; another dragoon who had seized him he shot with his pistol. But in front now appeared a second rank barring his way, and a squadron of dragoons occupying the Pont de Rosni, the only issue. The fugitive cavalry poured down upon it, forced their way through, forgetful of their leader, who was in the rear, and would probably have been cut off after all but for his brother, a boy 10 years old, who drew up his horse across the bridge, and, with a pistol presented to the fugitives, summoned them to defend their chief, and not abandon him. Cavalier, with the rest of his infantry, escaped into the wood of Cannes. This battle, or series of combats, extended from the mill of Langlade to the village of Nages; 1000 dead were left on the field, half of whom were Camisards.

At the commencement of the fight one of the Prophets of the Enfans de Dieu, named Daniel Gui, planted on the top of a rock, surrounded by 5 or 6 prophetesses, 3 of whom were afterwards found among the slain, called on the God of battles to favour their cause.

12 Uchau, anciently *Ad Octavum Lapidem* (the 8th milestone).

The turbulent torrent Vidourle, which separates the Dépt. du Gard from that of L'Hérault, is crossed shortly before reaching

14 Lunel *Stat.* (*Inn:* H. du Palais), a town of 6385 Inhab., owing its prosperity to the sweet wine and brandy which form its chief articles of commerce. The best Lunel wine is grown on the Côte de Mazet. The lower ground in which the town is situated is often inundated in winter and spring, is infested with mosquitoes in summer, and with fevers in autumn. Human bones, with pottery, have been found in caves in the tertiary limestone at Pondres, 6 m. N. of Lunel.

[22 kilom. = 13½ m. S. of Lunel is *Aigues Mortes*, singularly situated in the midst of salt marshes and lagoons, whose exhalations render it very unhealthy. It is approached by a causeway raised above the marsh and spanned midway by an ancient gate-tower, *La Carbonnière*. Aigues Mortes, itself a miserable and deserted town, is of interest only as a perfect example of a feudal fortress; its walls and gates, more entire and less altered than even those of Avignon, give a perfect idea of the art of fortification in the 13th centy. Its foss has been filled up, on account of the malaria produced by its stagnant water. In advance of the place, to the N., is a single round tower, which served as a citadel, 90 ft. high, 65 in diameter, surmounted by an old lighthouse turret of 34 ft. In the centre of each floor is a hole communicating with a reservoir for water below. Some of its chambers served as a prison, in which Protestants, chiefly females, who refused to abjure their faith, were confined after the Revocation of the Edict of Nantes. Some of them had been shut up here for 35 years, when they were released in 1769. From the upper story of this tower the Camisard chief Abraham, with 17 companions, made a wonderful escape, letting themselves down from a height of 80 ft. by their blankets tied together. This tower is called *Tour de Constance*, for what reason is unknown. It is proved to have been built by St. Louis, who embarked here on his unsuccessful Crusade in 1270, having assembled at this spot a fleet of 800 galleys and an army of 40,000 men. As Aigues Mortes lies nearly 3 m. inland, some have supposed from this that the sea must have retired since the 13th centy.; modern investigations have proved, however, the existence of a small port close to the town, in whose walls the ancient mooring rings still remain; and of a canal, now filled with sand, extending thence to the harbour of Grau du Roi, on the sea, doubtless the place of rendezvous for the royal fleet. The walls of the town were built after the death of St. Louis, in Africa, by his son Philippe le Hardi, on the plan, it is said, of those of Damietta. Salt is the chief article of commerce produced in the vicinity; and after the massacre by the royal forces, aided by the townsfolk, of the Burgundian troops, who had obtained possession of the town in 1421, the bodies of the slain were thrown into the tower still called *Tour des Bourguinons*, between layers of salt, it is said, in order to prevent their putrefying and breeding miasma in the town. In 1538 an interview took place here between the Emperor Charles V. and Francis I.; and in 1542 the Turkish corsair Barbarossa, the ally of the French king against the emperor, moored his fleet in the harbour.]

There is little to observe on the road between Lunel and Montpellier; the country rich and monotonously flat.

Lunel Viel, St. Brès, Les Mazes, Stations.

10 Columbier Stat., a land of oil and wine.

13 *Montpellier Stat.* — *Inns:* Hôtel Nevet, a splendid large edifice, 200 bed-rooms — one of the best hotels in France;—H. du Midi, good;—H. de Londres, good;—H. des Ambassadeurs. The name of Montpellier, familiar to every one who has been in an English watering-place, as the type of salubrity and mildness of climate, will not in reality answer the expectations of those who anticipate either a soft air or a beautiful position. Indeed it is difficult to understand how it came to be chosen by the physicians of the North as a retreat for consumptive patients; since nothing can be more trying to weak lungs than its variable climate, its blazing sunshine alternating with the piercingly cold blasts of the *mistral*. Though its sky be clear, its atmosphere is filled with dust, which must be hurtful to the lungs; and the glare from the chalky ground and white houses, unmodified by shade, is exceedingly painful to the eyes. The town is chef-lieu of the Dépt. de l'Hérault, and a place of importance, since it contains 40,746 Inhab.; in its streets and buildings it is not much distinguished.

The *Promenade du Peyrou* (a provincial form for pierreux, stony, the spot having been originally a bare rock), an elevated platform, reached by flights of stairs, and surrounded by balustrades in the style of the time of Louis XIV., whose equestrian statue is in the centre, was constructed 1766, and is referred to as the ne plus ultra of a public walk. It has, it is true, shady avenues and neat parterres. At the extremity of it rises the Château d'Eau, a sort of fountain-temple, which receives and distributes through the town the waters conveyed across the fertile valley from the opposite hill by the *Aqueduct*, a very noble construction, though modern, begun 1753, consisting of 53 large arches, surmounted by 183 smaller, measuring 2896 ft. The source whence the water is derived is about 2 m. distant. The beauty of the view from the Peyrou has been somewhat exaggerated ; the Pyrenees are too distant to give it interest, though the peak of the Canigou is said to be sometimes visible; the Mediterranean is ill represented in its border of marshes and lagoons; and the Alps (in spite of what the guide-books say) are out of the scope of vision. The chief feature is the bare Pic de St. Loup, a buttress of the Cevennes projecting from the N., visible from the road to Nismes. On the S. is seen the church-tower of Maguelonne.

The town *gate* on one side of the Peyrou was erected to commemorate the *glories* of the reign of Louis XIV. The bas-reliefs towards the town are meant to represent the union of the Mediterranean to the Atlantic by the Canal du Midi, and the Revocation of the Edict of Nantes; the one a benefit, the other a curse to France. There are, indeed, mournful recollections connected with the Peyrou : here were raised, during the reigns of Louis XIV. and XV., the scaffolds on which perished, by being burnt alive or broken alive on the wheel, not only many of the fanatic Camisards, among others their chief Castanet, but also many "Pastors of the Desert," Protestant ministers whose only crime was praying to God according to the impulse of their own conscience.

The *Jardin des Plantes* was the first established in France, in the reign of Henri IV., and it is well kept up, under the able direction of M. Martins. Here may be seen the Galactodendron, the cow or milk tree of S. America, mentioned by Humboldt. In one corner of the garden, shaded by cypress, is an arched recess, fenced with a trellis rail, within which a simple tablet bears these words: " *Placandis Narcissæ manibus.*" This is pointed out as the tomb of Mrs. Temple, the adopted daughter of Young, the poet, who died suddenly here, at a time when the atrocious laws which accompanied the revocation of the Edict of Nantes, backed by the superstition of a fanatic populace, denied Christian burial to Protestants. Such a refusal gave rise to the following passage in the ' Night Thoughts :'—

" Snatch'd ere thy prime! and in thy bridal hour !
And when kind fortune, with thy lover, smiled !
And when high-flavour'd thy fresh opening joys !
And when blind man pronounced thy bliss complete !
And on a foreign shore, where strangers wept !
Strangers to thee ; and, more surprising still, Strangers to kindness, wept: their eyes let fall Inhuman tears ! strange tears ! that trickled down
From marbled hearts ! obdurate tenderness !
A tenderness that call'd them more severe ;
In spite of nature's soft persuasion steel'd ;
While nature melted, superstition raved ;
That mourn'd the dead, and this denied a grave—
Denied the charity of dust to spread
O'er dust ! a charity their dogs enjoy.
What could I do ? What succour ? What resource ?
With pious sacrilege a grave I stole ;
With impious piety that grave I wrong'd ;
Short in my duty ; coward in my grief !
More like her murderer than friend, I crept,
With soft suspended step, and muffled deep,
In midnight darkness, whisper'd my last sigh.
I whisper'd what should echo through their realms ;
Nor writ her name whose tomb should pierce the skies."

Evidence has been brought forward to prove that Narcissa (Mrs. Temple) was, in reality, buried at Lyons.

The student of medicine should not fail to see the *Ecole de Médecine*, situated in the old building, formerly the bishop's palace. It contains valuable anatomical collections, and the doctor's *robe* with which Rabelais was here installed, and which is employed for the same purpose at present, but so much patched and mended that scarcely a thread of the original garment remains. The school of medicine here is of great antiquity, having been founded, it is said, by Arab physicians, driven out of Spain, and patronised by the Comtes de Montpellier. Adjoining this building is the *Cathedral*, modernised, and of no interest. It has a singular porch, projecting from the wall, and resting on 2 round piers or turrets. The building suffered much from the Huguenots. It contains an altarpiece by *Sebastian Bourdon*, a native of Montpellier, the Fall of Simon Magus.

The principal object of curiosity here, however, is the *Musée Fabre*, named from its founder, a native of Montpellier, an artist, and the friend of Alfieri and his mistress the Countess of Albany. It comprises a collection of paintings, of an excellence rarely found away from the capital; among them a portrait of Lorenzo de' Medicis, father of Catherine de' Medici (d. 1519), by *Raphael*, probably genuine, and good; and a head of a Young Man with a Beard, also attributed to *Raphael*, brought from a villa near Sienna; and at least a good copy by his scholars, if not original. The Infant Samuel in Prayer, *Sir Joshua Reynolds*. There are also many other pictures of the Italian schools, and a number by artists of the modern French school.

The *library of Alfieri*, 15,000 vols., including many works on art, is also deposited in this museum. The Marquis de Montcalm has a good collection of *Paintings* by the old masters, which is shown.

Cambacérès, Grand Chamberlain of Napoleon, Seb. Bourdon the painter, and Chaptal the chemist, were born here.

Montpellier has some considerable *manufactures* of cottons, dye-works, &c.; and some which are nearly peculiar to itself and its neighbourhood, such as the making of *verdigris*, which is obtained by laying plates of copper between layers of grape-husks, and allowing them to remain in cellars for 18 or 20 days, after which the coating of green rust (acetate of copper), produced by the oxidizing of the metal plates by the grape-juice, is scraped off. There are extensive *chemical works* here, founded by the Comte de Chaptal, consisting of alum, Prussian blue, sulphuric and nitric acids; also a considerable quantity of perfumes, essences, and liqueurs. The distilleries of brandy from the wines of the district are very numerous.

The excellent Roquefort cheese is made about 15 m. to the N. of this, in the Dépt. de la Lozère. (See Index.)

Diligences daily, to Toulouse in 27 hrs.; to Perpignan; to Narbonne in 10 hrs.

[The *Railway*, 17 m. long, from Montpellier to Cette, passes through Villeneuve, whose *Church* is in part as old, probably, as the 8th centy., and *Frontignan*, celebrated for its sweet wine, the best being of the kind called Muscat.

The flourishing town and seaport of Cette (*Inns :* Poste, very good;—H. du Grand Galion; dear; beware mosquitoes) contains a population of 13,413, and is situated on a tongue of land running between the sea and the salt lake called Etang de Thau: it stands at the foot of an eminence, surmounted by a fort. The town is entered by a causeway elevated above the lagoon, and by a bridge of 52 arches. The town was founded by Louis XIV.; and the works of the harbour, piers, &c., were executed by Riquet, the engineer of the *Canal du Midi*. There is an extensive *manufacture* here of the *wines of all countries*, port, sherry, claret, champagne, for the English and other markets, produced by the mixture of various kinds of French and Spanish wine and brandy; Benicarlo wine being imported from Spain to mix with inferior claret. The salt-works on the lagoon are numerous. In 1710 a descent was made here from the fleet of Commodore Norris by a small British force designed to cause a diversion on the side of Spain, and effect a junction with the insurgents of the Cevennes. They took possession of Cette, but after holding it for a few days were driven back to their ships with some loss.

Steamers to Marseilles, chiefly for merchandise, in 10 or 12 hours; to Onglous, near Agde, at the mouth of the Canal du Midi, crossing the Etang de Thau: 36 hours are required to reach Toulouse from Cette by the canal, owing to the number of locks; so that this mode of conveyance is not to be recommended.

A *canal* passes through the series of lagoons from Cette to Aigues Mortes, fenced in by dykes of stone or mud, and thence to Beaucaire. The Canal du Midi opens out also into the Etang de Thau, and thus Cette communicates both with the Rhône and Garonne.

The ruined church of *Maguelonne*, on an island between the sea and the lagoons, beyond the Canal du Grave, will interest the antiquary, but he will require a guide to it across the heath and marsh, though the distance is only 6 m. from Montpellier. It appears more like a castle than a church, little ornament being expended on its exterior. Its W. doorway is curious, consisting of a pointed arch of coloured marble, resting on a sculptured frieze, with a bas-relief of the Saviour in the tympanum, and a triangular bas-relief on either side of the door, representing St. Peter with the Keys, and St. Paul with the Sword. The body of the church, a nave ending in an apse, contains some ancient tombs of bishops, but is filled with hay. The building dates from 1110 to 1180. It is the sole relic of a populous town which existed on this spot down to the 16th centy.]

From Cette to Béziers the Canal du Midi is not a disagreeable mode of conveyance for those who have long been jolted along high roads in Diligences.

The road from Montpellier to Narbonne passes through a country abounding in vineyards, which cover all the low ground, while olives occupy the hills: it is very thickly inhabited.

11 Fabrègues.

8 Gigean; from this the town of Cette, rising on a promontory out of the sea, is well seen. Skirting the margin of the lagoon of Thau, we proceed to

12 Mèze (*Inn:* Couronne, tolerable), an increasing seaport and fishing station. Near this are the baths of Balarue, supplied by a hot salt spring: they are good for rheumatism, paralysis, &c. There is a very bad road (1846) from Mèze to Béziers by Agde (20 kilom.—*Inn:* Poste), a small seaport, Béziers (22 kilom.).

Beyond Mèze the road turns away from the sea; the country is very pretty, especially in the vicinity of

18 Pezenas, a town of 7800 Inhab., agreeably situated on the l. bank of the Hérault, at the confluence of the Peine. It was anciently called *Pissecanum*. Molière wrote here his comedy Les Précieuses Ridicules, while director of a troop of strolling players. The chair in which he used to sit to be shaved by the barber is still preserved in the town. Pezenas is one of the chief brandy markets in Europe.

10 La Begude de Jordy. A very steep ascent, for which an extra horse is required, leads into

12 Béziers. — *Inns:* H. du Nord; —Poste, filthy in the extreme and exorbitant;—Croix Blanche.

Béziers, an ancient town of 17,376 Inhab., has an imposing appearance at a distance, seated as it is upon a commanding eminence, its topmost building being its *Cathedral*. The interior, however, is confined, gloomy, and filthy; but some improvements have lately been made, including a new bridge to lead into the town. The view from the *Terrace*, in front of the cathedral and évêché, is fine, extending over the course of the Orbe, and of the Canal du Midi, both of which pass near the foot of the hill, and pursue their way to the sea in different directions. The Cathedral of *St. Nazaire* is a Gothic building, surmounted by battlements, so as somewhat to resemble a castle externally, and contains some old painted glass. It was the chief scene of the horrible slaughter of 1209, with which the name of Béziers is always associated, at that terrible siege by the crusading army raised at the call of the church of Rome to exterminate the unfortunate Albigenses, who were numerous in this devoted city. The inhabitants refusing to yield, the crusaders forced their way into the town, their leaders being its bishop and the abbé of Citeaux, who had prepared a list of the proscribed persons. In the confusion of the assault, however, the soldiers were perplexed to distinguish the heretics from the orthodox ; "Kill all," exclaimed the abbot ; "the Lord will recognise his own " (Cædite eos, novit enim Dominus qui sunt ejus). The result was the massacre of every living soul, to the number of 60,000 according to some historians, though the abbot of Citeaux himself, in his letter to Innocent III., humbly avows that he could only slay 20,000. A *Maison Centrale de Detention* has been built on the terrace in front of the Cathedral.

The chief trade here is in eau de vie, produced in the numerous distilleries. On the Promenade is a *Statue* in bronze of Paul Riquet, Baron de Bonrepos, a native of Béziers, the projector of the *Canal du Midi*, which is carried through 9 locks close to the town. (See Rte. 93.) It opens into the sea, 13 m. S. of this, at Agde, called "Ville Noire," from the black volcanic basalt of which it is built. Agde (*Inn*: Poste; 8230 Inhab.) has a curious *cathedral*, and a cloister, whose arcades are perfect, though walled up. The Hérault is here crossed by a suspension bridge.

Hence to Narbonne the country is very uninteresting.

10 Nissan. The Etang de Capestang is passed on the rt., and the river Aude (Atax), which gives its name to the Dépt, is crossed between this and

17 *Narbonne*. *Inns:* H. de la Daurade, good;—H. de France.

This very ancient town was the Narbo Martius of the Romans, one of the first colonies established by them beyond the Alps, and capital of the vast province of Gallia Narbonensis, which extended from the Alps to the Pyrenees. It was the spot where Julius Cæsar settled the remains of his 10th Legion, at the termination of the civil wars, and the "pulcherrima Narbo" of Martial; yet it retains surprisingly scanty vestiges of its ancient masters compared with the importance and celebrity which it maintains in history. Not one Roman building remains; and the chief traces of its former splendour are the numerous bas-reliefs, friezes, inscriptions, &c., built into the town walls, erected by Francis I., who fortified the place with the ruins of Roman buildings. The ramparts may consequently be looked upon as a museum of antiquities. A local antiquarian society, however, has collected together in a *Museum* within the ancient Archevêché a number of fragments, and several antique tombs of the 3rd and 4th centuries, a bas-relief of 2 Eagles supporting a Garland, &c. At present it is a very dirty town.

Attached to the *Archevêché*, a heavy castellated building, rises a square *tower*, the lower part of which, of large cubical stones, dates probably from the time of the Lower Empire, and the upper part from the 8th centy. This building retains one curious doorway. Within it Louis XIII. signed the order for the delivery of Cinq Mars and De Thou to a commission named by their enemy the Cardinal Richelieu for trial.

The *Cathedral of St. Just* is a fine Gothic edifice, of which the choir only is finished. It was founded in 1272; the height of the roof is 40 mètres (? 131 ft.). The side chapels were added during the 13th centy.; and some of the windows having flamboyant tracery are of the 15th. There is a good deal of painted glass in them. The high altar is rich in marble of the country. The magnificent white marble monument of Bishop de la Jugie (1272) is a model of Gothic art of the 13th centy., and well worth study. The statues of saints and bishops are admirably executed, but in the revolutionary frenzy the head of every statue was knocked off, and the Bishop's effigy removed. There are other tombs of the 16th centy., and a fine organ of the age of Louis XIII. Repairs and additions are being made to the building, and the completion of the nave is intended.

Behind the altar are some curious iron seats, in the form of an X, of considerable antiquity. Sebastian del Piombo's "Raising of Lazarus," now in the National Gallery, was painted for this church: there is a copy of it here. The *Ch. of St. Paul*, founded 1229, may interest the architect. The carved capitals of the columns on the outside represent monsters, devils, and other objects designed to disgust men with vice, and to remind them of the punishment of the wicked.

Narbonne is a city of 11,855 Inhab.,

but, though once so important, it is now not even chef-lieu of the department. It is about 8 m. from the sea; and a branch of the Canal du Midi, called *La Robine*, runs through it to the Mediterranean. The principal Promenade is an avenue of trees, which lines its side, called *Allée des Soupirs*. Narbonne is an intricate, curious, but lifeless town, though it possesses some manufactures. The *honey* of Narbonne is the best in France; it is very white, and has a highly aromatic flavour. A distant view of the Pyrenees is obtained from hence.

The two great roads, to Perpignan (Rte. 94) and to Toulouse (Rte. 93), branch off from this. *Diligences* traverse both daily.

The *Canal du Midi* is shortly described in Rte. 93.

ROUTE 127.

AVIGNON TO MARSEILLES (AND AIX), BY TARASCON [BEAUCAIRE], ARLES, AND ST. CHAMAS, RAILWAY:—THE RHONE, FROM AVIGNON TO ARLES.

120 kilom. = 74½ Eng. m.—4 trains daily in 4½ to 5 hrs.; 5 trains to Arles.

The first portion of this Rly. was opened 1847, and it was completed by aid of advances from Government, 1849. It cost £3,400,000 !!

As far as Arles its course is parallel with the Rhône, at a short distance from the l. bank of the river.

The Rhône opposite Avignon always belonged to the King of France, even when its l. bank formed the territory of the Pope, and, in consequence, during an inundation of the river, which had laid a quarter of the town under water, the royal bailiff entered the streets in a boat, and claimed all those parts which the river had occupied, for his master.

3 m. S. of Avignon the turbulent river Durance is crossed by a Viaduct 656 yds. long.

The course of the Rhône below this possesses very little interest. The high road to Arles is equally uninteresting, but more direct than the

river: traversing at first a country rendered fertile by irrigation, it crosses the Durance, at a distance of 1½ m. from Avignon, by a very long suspension bridge, rendered necessary by the broad bed of gravel, not half of which is occupied by the wild river, except in times of flood.

l. At Barbantane there are extensive quarries.

l. A low ridge of hills, called *Alpines*, remarkable for their utter nakedness, now approaches the Rhône, running from E. to W. In the distance, upon their flanks, the white houses of St. Remy, and its 2 Roman monuments, may be distinguished.

rt. Aramon is a town of 2800 Inhab.: and a little below it the river Gardon, which gives its name to the Dépt., flows into the Rhône.

8 kilom. Rognonas Stat.

12 Cadellan Stat.

A cast-iron *Viaduct* of 7 wide arches carries the Gard Rly. over the Rhône from Beaucaire to Tarascon. It is a construction of great merit.

A wire bridge, suspended from 4 piers, 1446 ft. long, over which the high road from Marseilles to Nismes and Narbonne passes (Rte. 126, 127), connects

l. Tarascon, whose massive square castle at the water-side is overtopped by the spire of its Gothic church behind, with

rt. Beaucaire, lying at the base of cliffs of bare rock, one of them surmounted by a Calvary, the other by a ruined castle. The bridge was erected in 6 months in 1829 by M. Seguin, of Lyons, at a cost of 600,000*l*.

21 TARASCON STAT.

rt. Here the Rly. is joined by the Gard line from Nismes and Montpellier (Rte. 126).

l.* *Tarascon* (*Inns:* H. des Empereurs, close to the bridge; not recommended) is a town of about 11,000 Inhab. Etymologists have been bold enough to derive its name from the Greek ταράσσω, disturb, connecting it with the tradition of a dragon called *Tarasque*, which, once upon a time, infested the borders of the

* *Post-road.*—23 Tarascon.

X

Rhône, preying upon human flesh, to the great terror and disturbance of the inhabitants. They were at length delivered from the pest by St. Martha, sister of Lazarus, since adopted as the patron saint of the town, who conquered the monster with no other weapon than the Cross, and made him a prisoner with her girdle. This deliverance was commemorated until within a few years by a procession of mummers, attended by the clergy, who paraded the town escorting the figure of a dragon, made of canvas, and wielding a huge beam of wood by way of a tail, to the imminent danger of the legs of all who approached. The ceremony was attended by numerous practical jokes, and led to acts of violence, in consequence of which it has been suppressed. The effigy of the dragon now slumbers in the lumber-room of the playhouse.

The *Ch. of St. Martha* is a pointed Gothic building of the 14th centy., with the exception of the S. portal, which is circular and recessed with deep mouldings; between these the dog-tooth ornament appears: it dates from 1187. In a crypt beneath the nave of the church is the shrine and tomb of St. Martha, ornamented with her reclining effigy of white marble, not badly executed, but modern. Against the walls the history of Martha is represented in a series of bas-reliefs. Here also is the tomb of a Neapolitan knight, a follower of Roi René, and a well in the floor, the water of which is said to rise and fall with the Rhône.

The picturesque *Castle*, remarkable for its massive construction and perfect preservation, was begun by Henri II. in 1400, and finished by King René of Anjou, who frequently resided here, spending his time in festivities and fêtes, during one of which he and his queen appeared in the attire of shepherd and shepherdess: it is now a prison, and contains nothing remarkable.

The road from Tarascon to Nismes is in Rte. 130.

rt. *Beaucaire* (*Inn:* H. du Luxembourg), though it contains only 9937 Inhab., is a town of more life than its opposite neighbour Tarascon. It stands at the mouth of the Canal de Beaucaire, which joins the Canal du Midi, and thus unites the Rhône and Garonne, and it is the terminus of the Rly. to Nismes and Alais (Rte. 127). It is, besides, the locality of the celebrated fair, held here every year between the 1st and 28th of July, on the wide space of ground, planted with rows of trees, extending between the Rhône and the castle rock. This space is then covered with booths and sheds, arranged in streets, forming a sort of supplemental town of wood and canvas, within which the various kinds of merchandise are deposited, each classed by itself. The shore is lined by a flotilla of barges, the roads are choked with waggons, and the inns are filled to overflowing. Though somewhat fallen off of late, this fair collects together about 100,000 persons, and is attended by merchants not only from all parts of France, Spain, Italy, Portugal, but by many Jews, Turks, Armenians, Greeks, and even Moors from Barbary, who sell dates, &c. It terminates July 28, at midnight. It is said to date as far back as 1168.

The *Castle*, standing on the top of an escarped rock, was an ancient possession of the Counts of Toulouse, and was recovered by Count Raymond VII., when only 19 years of age, from the usurping Simon de Montfort and his sons, after a long and memorable siege (1216), in which he, besieging the garrison, was himself surrounded by an army from without. It is now reduced to a complete ruin; one stately triangular tower, and a curious Romanesque *chapel* of great antiquity, in which St. Louis is said to have heard mass before he embarked for the Crusade, alone surmounting the crumbling walls. There is a good view, from the castle rock, of the Rhône, the bridge, the scene of the fair, the distant arid range of the Alpines on the opposite side of the river, and the equally naked hills of the Calvary and gallows (fourche patibulaire) on this side; but verdure is wanting. The rock, which serves as the pedestal to the castle, is being cut through, to allow the passage of a road to the Rhône.

Beaucaire is the scene of the old Provençal romance of Aucassin and Nicolette.

St. Gilles (Rte. 126) is about 15 m. distant.

[From Tarascon an excursion may be made to *St. Remy* (10 m.), a deserted town, remarkable only for two well-preserved Roman buildings, detached from all others, and about ¾ m. from the town: the one is a funereal *Monument*, of most elegant design, about 50 ft. high, ornamented on its square base with bas-reliefs. On the N. side is a Skirmish of Cavalry; on the W. a Combat of Infantry; on the S. the Sacrifices and Erection of Trophies after a Battle; on the E. a winged Victory supporting a wounded Soldier: above this rises a double arch with engaged columns in the angles, and the whole is surmounted by a circular temple enclosing 2 statues. It bears this inscription, which throws no light on its date:—

SEX.L.M.JVLIEI.C.F.PARENTIBVS. SVEIS.

The *Arch of Triumph*, standing within a few yards of it, is less perfect, having lost its upper story, but the stones of its vaults remain, beautifully carved in hexagonal compartments, or sunk panels. Much of the sculpture has perished; the bas-reliefs remaining represent captives, bound, with women beside them. The date of this monument is as little known as that of the former: it has been supposed to commemorate the victories of Marc Aurelius. St. Remy was the ancient *Glanum:* it stands on the slope of the naked Alpines, and one of the limestone crests near the town is pierced through and through by a natural orifice. The ancient quarries remain, from which stones were obtained for the Roman edifices in the neighbourhood, and there exist 2 wells. St. Remy was the birthplace of Nostradamus (1503), the astrologer and fortune-teller.]

[About 5 m. S. of St. Remy is *les Baux*, an exceedingly curious town of the middle ages, wonderfully little altered, except that it has fallen into utter decay, only 60 of its houses occupied, and only 200 Inhab. left. It is seated on an escarped platform of rock, surmounted by a *Castle*, begun about 485, including a *Church*, both in ruins. It belonged to the *Counts des Baux*, who during the middle ages were constantly engaged in feud with the Counts of Provence, who frequently laid siege to their stronghold. This place would well reward an antiquary to visit it.]

———

rt., close to the bridge of Beaucaire is the mouth of the canal joining the Rhône to the Canal du Midi. The plain around was overwhelmed by débris brought down by the Rhône, which broke its banks hereabouts during the inundation of 1840. This irruption, covering the low grounds, destroyed the crops, but has left behind a deep deposit of mud over much waste land, which it is hoped may produce permanent fertility.

l. The country between Tarascon and Arles is a flat and uninteresting alluvial marshy plain, intersected by ditches, and the olive here gives place to the willow.

27 Ségonnaux Stat.

l. A little on the l. of the road, about 2 m. from Arles, a singular rock rises, like an island, above a marshy pond, crowned with the ruins of the once celebrated *Abbey of Montmajour*, founded in the 10th centy., and continued down to the 18th. Of the latter period are the vast palatial constructions of Italian architecture, which formed the convent, now rapidly falling to pieces. The *Church* is partly Romanesque, partly Pointed; but beneath it is a vast *crypt*, of the 11th centy, running under nearly the whole upper church. Behind the altar of this crypt stretches a semicircular wall, pierced with windows so as to render the altar visible from the side-chapels. Attached to the church is a ruined *cloister*, in which 2 mutilated monumental effigies remain of princes of the house of Anjou.

At the foot of the rock, on the N.E., is the very curious *Chapel of Sainte*

x 2

Croix, consisting of a central square tower, from which project 4 equal semicircular apsides, that on the W. having a porch attached. It is in the Romanesque style, but destitute of all ornament. It is proved by records to have been dedicated by Pons de Marignan, Bishop of Arles, in 1019. An *inscription*, forged by the monks of Montmajeur at a comparatively late period, attributed its origin to Charlemagne, to commemorate a victory here gained over the Saracens. Down to 1789 this chapel was resorted to every year, on the festival of the Discovery of the True Cross, by infinite multitudes of pilgrims, anxious to reap the advantages promised by papal indulgence to all who then flocked hither. The rock on which the chapel is built is honeycombed with tombs of all sizes excavated in it: some are said to have been the last resting-place of early Christians.

1. The Rhône first forks off into 2 branches, forming the head of its delta, about a mile to the N. of Arles. The branch which it sends off to the W., called Petit Rhône, is crossed by a wire suspension bridge at the village Fourques.

34 *Arles Stat.* is situated on the ancient Roman Cemetery, still called Eliscamp.

L.* ARLES.—*Inns*: H. du Nord, in the Place du Forum; improved (*E. o. S.*) and tolerably comfortable; H. du Forum, good; Gauthier, who keeps it, was cook to Lord Salisbury; H. du Commerce, on the Quai, kept by the wife of one of the English engineers on the steamboats.

Arles, one of the most ancient, and once the most important city in France, the Rome of Gaul ("Gallula Roma Arelas," as Ausonius calls it), the residence of a Roman Prefect, and, after the fall of the Roman Empire (A.D. 876), the capital of the kingdom of Arles, or of Trans-Jurane Burgundy, is now shrunken up into a dull provincial town. It is, however, rich in ancient remains of the period of its greatness; and the stranger who succeeds in threading its labyrinth of dirty narrow streets, more intricate than any other perhaps in France, will be duly rewarded, if he takes an interest in antiquities. Arles is justly celebrated for the beauty of its women.

It is a seaport town of 22,788 Inhab. (but its population is on the decrease), standing on the l. bank of the Rhône, near the apex of its delta, about 28 m. from the sea. The river bank is lined by a quay, at which may be seen moored a number of heavy barges, with one mast and a very long yard, and a prow not unlike that of the antique galleys. A *bridge of boats* unites the town with its suburb rt. Trinquetaille, and supplies the place of an old bridge, over which passed the Aurelian Way, extending from Rome to Cadiz,

Per quem Romani commercia suscipis orbis,

to use the words of Ausonius, in his description of Arles.

The most interesting ancient monuments existing at Arles are,

1. *The Amphitheatre*, a magnificent and most interesting relic of former days, larger than that of Nismes (measuring 459 ft. by 338 ft., having 5 corridors and 43 rows of seats, and capable of holding 25,000 spectators), but by no means so well preserved, owing to the devastations of human hands, rather than those of time. It consists of 2 stories of 60 arches, the lower Doric, the upper Corinthian, both rude in style, and of most massive construction, formed of enormous blocks, very exactly fitted together. Owing to the unevenness of the ground, it is supported on one side by vast substructions. The outer wall is now nearly separated from the second by the removal of the vaults, and the interior is completely gutted. Yet the lower portion, including the podium, or parapet surrounding the arena, faced with marble slabs, is even more perfect than at Nismes, having been covered up with earth until 1830. It was also filled within and choked up without by an accumulation of mean hovels, occupied by the poorest and worst part of the population of the town, to the number of 2000. Some of them had even

* *Post-road*—15 Arles.

burrowed under the vaults, or nestled in its recesses. An excrescence, not forming part of the original structure, are the two *square towers* surmounting the entire edifice. But they are interesting historical relics, having been raised in the 8th centy., either by the Saracens, who, under Jussouf-Ben-Abdelrahman, Wali of Narbonne, then obtained possession of Arles, or by Charles Martel, who expelled them from the city 739. At all events the amphitheatre, like the Coliseum of Rome, was at that period converted into a fortress, and withstood sieges and assaults, while 4 towers of defence were erected at the 4 cardinal points. From the top of the loftiest remaining tower the best view is obtained of the amphitheatre, and of the city of Arles, of the course of the Rhône upwards to Beaucaire, of the distant outline of the Alpines and Mont Ventoux, and of the plain of the Crau: the sea is not visible.

The stranger will not fail to remark the beauty of the masonry of the amphitheatre, the arches sometimes turned flat, of small stones, sometimes replaced by huge single beams of stone. The vaulted chambers communicating with the arena are supposed to have been the dens for wild beasts. The very scanty traces of inscriptions remaining on this building throw no light on its date, but it is supposed to be older than the arènes of Nismes, and is attributed to the age of Titus.

The *Roman Theatre*, more recently disinterred from the earth than even the amphitheatre, has suffered equal if not greater dilapidations in the course of ages. It is said to have been demolished by order of the early Christian bishops, who regarded it as the focus of idolatry and vice. Although reduced to a mere fragment, the costly marbles, the columns, the sculptured friezes (some preserved in the museum), and the statues found in it, one of which, called the Vénus *d'Arles*, forms an ornament to the Louvre, attest its ancient magnificence. The portions remaining are two Corinthian columns, surmounted by part of their entablature, which stand isolated like those in the forum of Rome; they formed part of the Proscenium, the rest of which is reduced to the pedestals of other pillars on a line with these, to truncated walls pierced by openings for doors, by which the actors made their entrance and exit, and furnished with niches for statues. Opposite to this wall is the semicircular space destined for the audience, scooped out of the rock, and still retaining some of its stone seats, rising in steps one above the other. In the middle are some very curious substructions, attached apparently to the orchestra, consisting of 3 parallel walls, 6 or 8 ft. high, stretching quite across the building, leaving a space of about 1 ft. between them, which is set with grooved ridges projecting alternately from either wall at regular distances. Within these was probably placed the wooden support of the proscenium or pulpitum, the stage in fact. It is difficult to explain the uses of this very peculiar construction. Near the theatre there is a very beautiful *Doric gateway*, or arch, with both frieze and architrave richly sculptured.

In the midst of the *Place Royale*, or de l'Hôtel de Ville, in which are situated the church of St. Trophime, the Hôtel de Ville, and the museum, rises an *Obelisk* of a single shaft of grey granite, antique, but not Egyptian, since it is ascertained to have been brought from a quarry in the Estrelle mountains, near Fréjus: and it differs in shape from those of Egypt, tapering more rapidly from its base to its summit. After having been for centuries prostrate in the mud of the Rhône, it was elevated in its present position in 1676. It is supported on 4 lions, and surmounted by a very tasteless gilt sun, set off with eyes, cheeks, and mouth. It is supposed to have stood upon the spina in an ancient circus, all traces of which are gone; it is 47 ft. high (the Luxor obelisk is 72 ft.), and is destitute of inscription or hieroglyph.

The *Museum* occupies the suppressed church of St. Anne; it is filled with an interesting collection of ancient remains discovered in or near Arles, a large proportion in the theatre, including a very rich marble frieze, and numerous statues, whose merit as works of art is small, except a head of a female (? Diana, or the Empress Livia) without a nose, and a head of Augustus found in 1834, belonging to a torso previously sent to the Louvre, both very fine. An altar to Apollo bears representations of the Delphic Tripod and of Marsyas flayed alive. A leaden pipe, more than 40 ft. long, stamped with the name of the Roman plumber, was discovered in the bed of the Rhône, and is supposed to have conveyed fresh water to the opposite bank. The cemetery called Aliscamps (p. 463) has furnished a great number of sarcophagi, some pagan, but the majority Christian, ornamented with bas-reliefs of good design and execution, showing that Roman art survived long after the extinction of paganism, though the subjects on which it was exercised were taken from the Bible. Those most commonly represented are Adam and Eve, the Deluge, the Passage of the Red Sea, Moses striking the Rock, Jonah and the Whale, the Sacrifice of Isaac, &c. On one is seen the Oil Press and Olive Harvest. A mutilated statue of the God Mithras, wanting the feet and head, is very curious. It is a human body entwined by a serpent, between whose folds the signs of the zodiac are sculptured.

The *Cathedral of St. Trophimus, who is said to have been a disciple of St. Paul, and to have first planted the Cross here, is entered from the Place by a very curious projecting porch, constructed in the 12th or early in the 13th centy. It consists of a deeply recessed semicircular arch, with mouldings not unlike our late Norman, resting upon a horizontal sculptured frieze which forms the lintel of the door, and is continued from beneath the arch on the rt. and l. of the façade, supported on pillars. There are 6 of these pillars, round, square, and octagonal, on either side of the door, of stone, resembling metal in colour, and one in the middle of the door forms the support of the lintel. They are based upon carved lions, some of them devouring men. Between the pillars are statues of Apostles and Saints, those in the angles being St. Trophimus and St. Stephen. The tympanum over the door is occupied by the figure of the Saviour as Judge of the World, with the attributes of the 4 Evangelists; and the sculptured frieze below represents in the centre the 12 Apostles, and on the sides the Last Judgment; the Good being on the l. of the spectator, the Bad, bound by a rope and dragged by devils, on the rt. The archivolt is filled with the Heavenly Host in the shape of rows of cherubims.

The interior is modernized, and less interesting; it contains 3 antique sculptured sarcophagi, one of which serves as a font.

The *cloisters* on the S. side are very curious; two of the sides have round arches, and two pointed, resting on double shafts, or square piers, carved on the sides with figures of saints, and projecting towards the courtyard in the form of fluted Corinthian pilasters. The capitals of the pillars are very curiously but rudely sculptured, in part with Scripture groups.

The square tower is also ancient, and in its upper story Corinthian pilasters again appear.

The *Hôtel de Ville* was built 1673, from designs of *Mansard*, contiguous to the clock-tower, which is somewhat older. It contains a collection of natural history.

Besides the more important Roman remains already described, there are, within the town, in the Place du *Forum*, 2 granite pillars and part of a Corinthian pediment, let into the wall in front of the Hôtel du Nord; they are supposed to have been moved, from some building now destroyed, into their present position. Other constructions, which may have belonged to the *forum*, are known to exist beneath the houses. In a narrow street near the Rhône is a tower of brick, called *Tour de la Trouille*, supposed to have been built by Constantine the Great, who resided much at Arles, and whose eldest son was born here.

PROVENCE.   *Route* 127.—*Aliscamps—Camargue.*   463

Beyond the walls, to the E. of the town, near the Rly. Stat., is situated the ancient Cemetery of Arles, still called *Aliscamps*, a slight variation from the original name (*Elisii Campi*) by which it was known 18 centuries ago. It was of vast extent, a complete Necropolis, and the dead were brought hither from other cities, as far distant as Lyons, for interment. *Dante* mentions it in the *Inferno*, IX. 112:

"Si come ad Arli ove 'l Rodano stagna,
Fanno i sepolcri tutto 'l loco varo."

And Ariosto alludes to it in the *Orlando Furioso:*

" Piena di sepolture è la campagna."

One portion of the ground was used for burials in pagan times; another, marked off with crosses, was afterwards designated for the interment of Christians. The ground teems with gravestones, sepulchral memorials, and sarcophagi, but the most curious have been removed to the museums of Arles, Toulouse, Marseilles, &c. In the neighbouring farms the cattle drink out of stone troughs which are nothing but empty coffins, and with their lids the ditches are bridged. Several chapels were erected within the area of this vast churchyard : the most remarkable is that of *St. Honorat*, or of Notre Dame de Grace, now falling to ruin. It is surmounted by an elegant octagonal tower, of two stories, having 2 circular-headed windows in each face ; the interior, except the crypt, is not older than the 14th centy.

The ecclesiastical constructions of the middle ages on the *Montmajeur* are described at p. 459.

Although, in the days of the Romans, Arles was plentifully supplied with spring water, conveyed to it from the chain of the Alpines in aqueducts of masonry many miles long, the modern town is destitute of this important commodity, and the inhabitants suffer severely from the want of drinking water. Owing to the marshes and pools in the vicinity, the town and the district around Arles are unhealthy at certain seasons; and intermitting fevers are very prevalent, but less so now than formerly, in consequence of the extended drainage.

A *Canal* has been formed from Arles to Bouc, on the sea-coast, at the mouth of the salt lake called Etang de Berre, which opens a more direct communication to Marseilles than the course of the Rhône. This canal, begun 1802, with the double object of draining the marshes on the l. bank of the Rhône, and of facilitating traffic by avoiding the bars and sandbanks at the mouth of the river, was not completed until 1835. It is about 30 m. long. It was traversed regularly by barges until 1840, when the great inundation of the Rhône overwhelmed a part of it with sand.

The wide uninterrupted plain stretching from Arles to the sea, S. and E., nearly as far as Marseilles, including the *delta* of the Rhône, or the island of *Camargue* (derived from Καμαξ, marsh, and αγρος, field ?), presents some singular phenomena not unworthy of attention. Indeed, both its climate and its soil of mud banks, arid sand, or vast bare gravel beds, alternating with salt marshes and lagoons, raised from 2 to 7 feet above the sea, assimilate it rather to Africa and the borders of the Nile than to France. Even some of the animals which resort to it, the ibis, the pelican, and the flamingo, properly belong to the African continent. The ground is so impregnated with salt, that the water is brackish; the surface of the soil is, in summer, covered with a white saline efflorescence, like a coating of snow, and, when the pools are dried up, the salt forms in a cake 2 in. thick. Here, as in the deserts of Asia and Africa, the *mirage* constantly occurs during the heats, transforming the arid plain in appearance into a wide lake. Cultivation can only be pursued by excluding the sea by dykes, which entirely surround the Camargue, and the saline influence is counteracted by covering the surface with the muddy deposits brought down by the Rhône, In this manner the district produces extensive pastures, on which large flocks of sheep are fed, together with herds of swall cattle, and wild horses, or rather ponies, said to be of a stock originally brought from Africa by the Arabs, in their frequent invasions of this part of France. At stated times the young bulls are chased and separated from the herd by horsemen armed with tridents, in order to be branded, and receive the marks of their different proprietors; this is called *La Ferrade*. A considerable portion of the district is ploughed land, furnishing crops of corn, madder, &c., which are produced in abundance, and the culture of rice has lately been introduced; but this fertility, as well as the rich pasturages, arises entirely from irrigation, and the distribution in all directions of the waters of the Rhône, derived from the river in cuts and canals. The salt marshes and lagoons are unprofitable except in producing salt. There is only one village in the Camargue, that of Saintes Maries, but many isolated farms are scattered over it. At harvest time, in the month of July, the corn is threshed in the Oriental fashion, by driving 10 or 12 young horses, held with a long rein by a man in the centre of the threshing-floor, over the sheaves laid in heaps around, but this practice exists throughout Provence. The winnowing is performed by tossing the straw, chaff, and grain into the air, and allowing the wind to separate them.

It has been calculated that the Rhône discharges into the sea, in 24 hrs., more than 5 million cubic mètres of earthy matter, similar to the deposits composing the Camargue. Its banks are in consequence extending daily, and the *Tower of St. Louis*, built 1737, at a distance of 2600 mètres (1 m. 3 furl.) from the sea, is now 7200 mètres (4 m. 3 furl.) from it. In consequence the mouths of the Rhône are beset by sand-banks so as to be pronounced by Vauban "incorrigibles," and their navigation is dangerous.

At Arles are situated the workshop, engine-house, and carriage depôt of the Company. On quitting Arles Stat. the Rly. turns away from the Rhône and pursues a S.E. direction.

The railroad, issuing out of the antique Necropolis of Arles, the Aliscamps (p. 463), passes near an Aqueduct, comprising part of the line of a Roman one, which conveyed the waters of the Durance by St. Remy to Arles. A short distance from Arles the railway is carried over some low grounds by a viaduct of great length, which is a fine piece of work. From thence to Salon the railroad traverses the *Crau*, a singular stony plain extending S. to the Mediterranean, covered all over with rolled boulders and pebbles, deposited doubtless by the Rhône and its tributaries, especially the Durance, under circumstances differing from their present physical condition. This "campus lapideus" was well known to the ancients; not only is it described by Strabo, Pliny, and Mela, but Æschylus, in a fragment preserved by Pomponius Mela, lays on it the scene of the combat between Hercules and the Ligurians, when the son of Jove, having exhausted his arrows, was supplied with artillery from heaven by a discharge of stones from the sky, sent for his use by Jupiter.

Ἰδὼν δ' ἀμηχανοῦντα σ' ὁ Ζεὺς οἰκτερεῖ,
νεφέλην δ' ὑποσχὼν νιφάδι στρογγύλων
 πέτρων
ὑπόσκιον θήσει χθόνα, οἷς ἔπειτα συμ
-βαλὼν δηώσεις ῥᾳδίως λίγυν στρατόν.

One ancient writer remarks that the assistance of Jupiter would have been more effectual had he showered down the stones at once on the heads of the Ligurians. Such is the mythological history of the Crau. Its modern name is traced by some to the Celtic *craig*, a rock (?). "It is composed entirely of shingle, being so uniform a mass of round stones, some to the size of a man's head, but of all sizes less, that the newly thrown up shingle of a seashore is hardly less free from soil; beneath these surface-stones is not so much a sand as a cemented rubble, a small mixture of loam. Vegetation is rare and miserable; some of the absinthium and lavender so low and poor as scarcely to be recognised, and 2 or 3 miserable grasses, with Centaurea calycitropes and solstitialis, were the principal plants I could find."—*A. Young.*

Through the greater portion of its

Provence. *Route 127.—Salon—St. Chamas—Railway.*

extent its condition is that of a semi-desert; but under the stones which cover it grows a short sweet herbage, which the sheep accustomed to the locality obtain by turning over the stones. It is consequently covered over in the winter months with flocks driven hither from the French Alps, where they spend the summer, passing annually to and fro like the merino flocks of the Mesta in Spain. There the practice of migrating from the plains to the Pyrenees, and *vice versâ*, is as old as the 7th centy. Here, however, it must be traced to a far earlier period, since it is mentioned by Pliny, "e longinquis regionibus pecudum millibus convenientibus ut vescantur."

The small portion of the Crau which can be reached by irrigation is exceedingly fertile, producing vines, olives, mulberries, and corn. Arthur Young says, "The meadows I viewed are among the most extraordinary spectacles the world can afford, in respect to the amazing contrast between the soil in its natural and in its watered state, covered richly and luxuriantly with clover, chicory, rib-grass, and avena elatior." The chief means by which this useful purpose is effected is the *Canal de Craponne*, so called from its projector, who began it in 1554; it is cut from the Durance at a place called La Roque, and extends to the Rhône at Arles, a distance of 33 m., sending out branches to Salon and elsewhere. The whole agriculture of the district depends upon this canal, as Egypt does upon the Nile: it is besides of no small use in turning oil and corn mills. It is followed for a considerable distance, and crossed, by our road. Previous to its construction the stony desert reached up to the very outskirts of Arles and Salon. In the remoter and uncultivated parts of the Crau, the *Mirage*, which so often in the African deserts cheats the parched traveller with the appearance of inland lakes in spots most destitute of water, is of frequent occurrence. The irrigation and evaporation from a vast body of stagnant water renders this district very unhealthy, and the funereal cypresses, thickly planted around all the houses, are symbolic of the fate of their inhabitants, worn out with fever and ague.

43 Raphele Stat.
50 St. Martin Stat., a post-station on the high road.
63 Entressen Stat.
67 Constantine Stat.

[4 m. N. is
Salon.—*Inns:* Poste, improved; — Croix de Malte. This is a rather considerable town of 6000 Inhab., carrying on an important trade in olive-oil. The high road is carried through a sort of Boulevard, in the neat modern quarter enclosing the old town; and passes the *Castle*, said to be that of Nostradamus, now a barrack. That celebrated astrologer died here 1566, and is buried in the *parish church.*]

The railway is carried round the margin of the Etang de Berre, a sort of inland sea, navigable for small vessels, which is about to be connected with the sea by a new canal at Bouc.

72 *St. Chamas Stat.*, a town of 2443 Inhab., on the Etang de Berre. It is divided into 2 parts by a narrow marly ridge pierced with caverns, some of them inhabited. On the ridge stands the old *Church* of *St. Amand*.

Part of the ancient ramparts surround the town. There is a Government powder-mill here. 500 paces out of the town, in the midst of the plain, stands the *Pont Flavien*, a Roman bridge, built over the Touloubre, a single arch of large blocks, approached by arches of triumph of elegant Corinthian architecture at either end. On the frieze is this inscription:—

L. DONNIVS . C . FLAVOS . FLAMEN.
ROME ET. AVGVSTI. TESTAMENTO. FIERI
JVSSIT. ARBITRATV. C DONNII. VENÆ
ET. CATTEL. RVFI.

87 Berre Stat.
93 Rognac *Junction* Stat.; branch Railway to Aix, p. 477. 24 kilom. to be finished in 1855.
102 Pas des Lanciers Stat.
   m. is Martigues; an omnibus runs thither. Near St. Chamas and Vitrolles the railway encounters a triple range of mountains, which hem in Marseilles on this side. It clears a series of ridges and ravines by tunnels

x 3

and embankments. It traverses the Estaque by a tunnel 2¾ Eng. m. long, driven under the Montagne de la Nerthe, which cost 400,000l., and a second tunnel at St. Louis, 492 yards long, and emerges at the

120 *Marseilles Stat.*, at St. Charles, on a height 160 ft. above the Mediterranean; a handsome structure, commanding a strikingly grand view. A branch line 1¾ m. long is carried down to the port of La Joliette, or New Harbour.

15 MARSEILLES.—*Inns*, all inferior, dirty, and noisy: H. d'Orient;—H. des Empereurs, on the Cannebière;—H. de Noailles, select;—H. Beauveau;—H. de Paradis, Place Royale;—H. des Bains, on the Prado on the sea-shore, out of town; same proprietors as H. des Empereurs.

Marseilles, capital of the Dépt. des Bouches-du-Rhône, is a busy and flourishing city, and the most important seaport of France, having a population of about 193,000 souls; but it has few fine public buildings or sights for strangers. The entrance from the side of Aix is by an *Arch of Triumph*, not remarkable for elegance of design, originality of elevation, or elegance of decoration. It was intended to commemorate the campaign of the French in Spain in 1823, but its destination was changed to that of celebrating "all the glories of France;" and it is now inscribed to Louis Napoleon. From this arch a fine broad street, called the Cours and Rue de Rome, stretches entirely across the town to the Porte de Rome. Near the centre of it another wide street, called Rue de la Cannebière (Κάνναβις, *flax*), strikes off from it at right angles, down to the *Port* or *Harbour*, a natural oblong basin 1000 yards long by 330 broad, extending into the heart of the town, occupying an area of 45,000 mètres (nearly 70 acres), about equal to two of the docks at Liverpool. The depth of water varies from 18 ft. at its mouth to 24 ft., and it is capable of holding 1000 or 1200 merchant-vessels. This is the focus of that extensive commerce which renders Marseilles the first seaport of France and of the Mediterranean. The number of vessels entering and quitting in a year amounts to 18,000, and their tonnage exceeds 2,000,000 tons, about one-fourth of that of Liverpool: 633 vessels, of 53,973 tons, belong to the port. To this harbour Marseilles is indebted for her commercial consequence, which dates nearly 3000 years back, from the days when the Phocæans first set foot on her shore, inoculating the barbarous realms of W. Europe with the civilization of the East. The connexion of France with Algiers has given a great impetus to the prosperity of Marseilles, as it engrosses nearly the whole trade with the new colony in Africa. It has risen also to considerable importance since 1830 as a steam-packet station (see p. 470).

A *new Harbour* (le nouveau Port), called *La Joliette*, is being constructed a little to the N. of the old works, and it is a stupendous undertaking. It is formed by a breakwater, 1224 yards long, thrown into the sea parallel to the shore, and at a distance of 1312 ft. from it: 2 moles or piers stretch from the shore towards it, at a distance of 550 yards from each other, but leaving openings for the entrance of vessels. This will form an inner basin and 2 outer harbours, and they will be connected by a canal, running behind Fort St. Jean, with the old Port.

From the margin of the old harbour, lined with quays, the ground rises on all sides, covered with houses, forming a basin or amphitheatre, terminating only with the encircling chain of hills. From this disposition of the ground, the port becomes the sewer of the city, and is offensive from the filth which, flowing into it, is allowed to stagnate in its tideless sea. A plan is preparing to remedy this evil by carrying the town drainage in distinct culverts and sewers, out to sea, or to a distance from the town. Were it not for the bad smells, its *Quais* would be an agreeable walk, presenting as they do an amusing scene of bustle and variety, Greek, Turkish, and Neapolitan costumes. Among its shipping, the picturesque latteen sails of the Mediterranean are very common.

The direction of the old harbour is from E. to W. On its N. side, and within the angle formed by the Rue Cannebière and the Cours, lies the old town of narrow dirty streets, scarce worth entering. In the line of the quay, on this side, stands the *Hôtel de Ville*, a heavy building, and overloaded with tasteless ornaments, attributed to Puget, but not by him, his really beautiful design having been rejected. Farther on, near the harbour mouth, is the *Consigne*, or health office, where everything relating to quarantine is transacted, and whence the permission for vessels to enter the harbour is issued. To this office the captains of vessels come to give an account of themselves (raisonner), and to show their bill of health. The council-room contains a few paintings, chiefly having reference to the plague : by *Girard*, the Plague at Marseilles, in which Bishop Belzunce is introduced ; and another showing the self-devotion of the Chevalier Rose in burying the dead, when even the galley-slaves had refused ; by *David*, St. Roch healing the Sick ; a bas-relief, by *Puget*, of the Plague at Milan ; the Cholera at Marseilles by *Vernet*; the Yellow Fever at Barcelona, 1822. The subjects are all horrible, and the execution not good enough to compensate.

The mouth of the old port is narrow, and was once closed by a chain. It is defended by two forts : on the N. by the old castle and tower of St. Jean, built in the 15th centy., in which Philippe Egalité was imprisoned with his youngest son, and whence after a time they escaped ; on the S. the *Fort St. Nicolas*, recently repaired and extended, guards the entrance. It was founded by Louis XIV., who, after capturing the disobedient city, and entering it by a breach in the walls, observed that "he also would have a Bastide at Marseilles ;" and forthwith laid the foundation of this fort, of which the first stone bore the inscription—" Ne fidelis Massilia, aliquorum motibus concitata vel audaciorum petulantiâ, vel unicâ libertatis cupiditate tandem ruerit, Ludovic. XIV. optimatum populique securitate hâc arce prodivit." Close beside Fort St. Nicolas a new wet dock, Bassin de Carénage has been formed, by costly excavations out of the rock, on the site of an ancient cemetery.

Not far from this is *St. Victor*, the most ancient church of Marseilles, though its crypts and substructures alone are of the 11th centy. The upper part dates from 1200, except the two battlemented towers, which give it the air of a castle, erected 1350, by Pope Urban V., who had been abbot of St. Victor. The entrance under the tower is by a round arch : near it is a curious pointed arch, its mouldings relieved with the dog-tooth ornament. St. Victor was one of the most celebrated abbeys in Christendom, and possessed a host of other abbeys and religious houses dependent on it.

Above St. Victor, to the S. of the town and harbour, rises the bare rocky hill of *Notre Dame de la Garde*, so called from the curious *chapel*, situated within a small fort on its summit, a spot exposed to all the winds that blow. An image of the Virgin, carved in olive-wood, and of great antiquity, is enclosed within this humble shrine ; it is held in the highest veneration thoughout the Mediterranean by the sailors and fishermen and their wives, and its walls and roof are hung with ex-votos, chiefly paintings representing moving accidents by flood and field—all the veriest daubs, but very curious, as illustrating the religious feeling of the people. Besides a vast number of shipwrecks, storms, steamboat explosions, escapes from British vessels of war, there is a whole host of surgical operations, sick-beds, road-side accidents, &c. The cholera panic produced numerous offerings : among them a silver tunny-fish, presented by the Marseillaise fish-wives. Many ostrich-eggs and models of ships are suspended from the roof, and one corner is filled with cast-off crutches, the gifts of grateful cripples, now no longer lame, and with ropes' ends by which men have been saved from drowning ! The silver statue of the Virgin, 4 ft. high, over the altar, is modern.

The view from the top of the hill,

beside the chapel, is perhaps the best that can be had of Marseilles itself, spread over a gradually sloping basin, a city remarkably deficient in spires, towers, or domes. It is surrounded by hills which are covered with vineyards and olive-gardens, and speckled with white country-houses, called *Bastides*, to the number of 5000 or 6000, belonging to the citizens and shopkeepers. *Monte Christo*, well known from Dumas's novel, is conspicuous. It is an arid prospect of dazzling white, interspersed, but unrelieved, by dark streaks of dusky green. From this the eye is delighted to turn and repose upon the deep blue of the Mediterranean, the graceful curves of the coast of the Gulf of Lyons, and the little group of islands. *If* is crowned by a *castle*, once a state prison, in which Mirabeau was shut up, and Pomègue and Ratoneau, behind which a fleet of vessels in quarantine find shelter. The stripe of blue sea is prolonged into the heart of the city in the harbour, partly hidden from view by its forests of masts.

The Fort de la Garde was built by Francis I., and was never of great importance as a defence: hence the verses,

"Gouvernement commode et beau,
Où l'on ne voit, pour toute garde,
Qu'un Suisse, avec sa hallebarde,
Peint sur la porte du château."

Along the lower slope of the same hill, within the town, stretches a wide promenade planted with trees, called *Cours Bonaparte*, leading up to an eminence called Montagne Bonaparte. Those who have not time or patience for the long and somewhat fatiguing ascent of N. D. de la Garde, may content themselves with the *view* from this. Lower down, at the water-side, stands the *Customhouse*, with its piles of warehouses, isolated by a canal cut round it from the port.

The *Prado* is a handsome and very agreeable public walk and drive, a prolongation of the Rue de Rome by the sea-side, 3 Eng. m. It commands a fine sea-view. Here are *Sea Baths*.

The *Museum*, situated beyond the Marché aux Capucins, contains the few relics of antiquity which alone remain of the time-honoured city *Massilia*, founded (B.C. 578) by Phocæan exiles flying from Asia Minor. In spite of its wealth, power, and progress in civilization, the ancient city has left no remains of buildings, nor any traces of its existence beyond inscriptions (some in Greek), sarcophagi, mostly of the 5th, 6th, and 7th centuries, and a few fragments of sculpture. Among the antiques is a draped torso of a female with a child, wearing a peaked cap of Greek workmanship: a marble sarcophagus (No. 13) brought from Arles, sculptured with a combat between centaurs and lions: several Christian tombs, brought, for the most part, from the crypt of St. Victor; one (No. 27) of marble, designed for a child, contained the relics of St. Victor, and seems to be the most curious; another of Abbot Isarn (d. 1048), whose effigy is covered with his epitaph in Latin verse, allowing only his head, which exhibits the tonsure, and the feet to appear. None are so old as the capture of the city by Julius Cæsar.

The *Picture Gallery* in the same building contains about 150 very badly-lighted pictures, of which the following seem the best :—St. John carried up on the eagle, inspired to write the Revelations; a portion of the isle of Patmos appearing below: a copy after *Raphael*. The 3 Maries, as mothers, with St. Joseph, St. Cleophas, St. Simeon, &c., by *Perugino*; a very pleasing and genuine picture, though faded; very like Raphael's early manner. *Rubens* (perhaps by Jordaens): a boar-hunt; spirited, but the figures rather huddled together. A Prince of Orange with his family, attributed to Rubens. Lord Strafford, a copy from Vandyke. One or two small paintings by *Puget* merit notice, as he was a native of Marseilles, and architect and sculptor, as well as painter.

It is remarkable that so extensive and wealthy a mercantile community as that of Marseilles should not possess a permanent *Exchange*, yet the bourse is a mere temporary structure of wood and canvas, not much better than a show-booth in a fair. In front of it is a fountain of heavy design, basins resting on griffins. Some wag wrote upon them, when the fountain was first erected, "N'approchez pas:—ils sont mauvais."

Another fountain surmounted by a bust of Homer bears this inscription: "Les descendants des Phocéens à Homère, 1803." ! !

The *Lazaret*, to the N. of the port, is a well-regulated establishment; one of the first placed on a sound footing in Europe, and so large that it held the entire French army on its return from Egypt. It covers an area of 50 acres, is enclosed within a double wall, and is of course not accessible to any persons but such as enter it for quarantine. It is to be pulled down, and docks excavated on its site, 1852.

If a case of plague shows itself, the vessel is sunk and the goods burned. Merchandize is released from quarantine after exposure to the air, and especially to the dew. The Lazaret owes its foundation to the fearful ravages of the *plague at Marseilles* in 1720, which destroyed between 40,000 and 50,000 persons, *i.e.* half the population of the town. Amidst the general despair, selfishness, and depravity which accompanied this dire calamity, many individuals distinguished themselves by their noble self-devotion. One of them has been commemorated by Pope:—

"Why drew Marseilles' good bishop purer breath
When nature sicken'd and each gale was death?"

The name of the good bishop was *Belzunce*, who offered a rare example of courage and piety by his intrepid intercourse with the sick in the hospitals, where, aided by pious nuns, he constantly ministered to the support and consolation of the plague-stricken inmates. A *statue* of the good bishop has been set up on the Cours. The 2 échevins of the town, Estelle and Moustier, likewise exposed their lives. The streets soon became choked with dead, and of the galley-slaves, supplied at the rate of 80 a-week to conduct the dead-carts, none survived. The Chevalier Rose with his own hands then helped to bury the dead, when the very galley-slaves refused the dangerous duty. 3 physicians, also, from Montpellier, repaired to the city of death to aid the sick and dying, when all the native doctors were dead or had fled. The pestilence, which had broken out in the spring, continued with dreadful fury till September, but abated after a violent storm, and disappeared in November.

A Breakwater has been thrown between the islands of Pomègue and Ratonneau, connecting them together so as to form a quarantine roadstead, called *Port du Frioul* (fretum Julii). At this spot Cæsar's squadron, under the command of D. Brutus, was stationed during the siege of Marseilles.

One of the chief *manufactures* here is that of *soap*, which is said to employ 700 men. The process is worth seeing, and, as it is made exclusively of vegetable oil, it is not so unsavoury as in England. The manufacture of *Coral*, celebrated in the earliest times, has greatly fallen off, and has been transferred to Leghorn, Genoa, and Naples. Shipbuilding is a very important branch of trade. The manufactory of steam-engines, belonging to Mr. Philip Taylor and Sons, is one of the most considerable in France.

The *Fish-market* displays a number of the finny inhabitants of the Mediterranean unknown in the seas of the N.; among others, the tunny is abundant at certain seasons. The *Flower-market* also, at the N. end of Rue Cannebière, deserves a visit, and the *Jardin des Plantes*.

The *climate* of Marseilles for a portion of the year is delightful, but in summer and autumn the heat is at times intense—the streets like an oven, so that it is scarcely possible to move abroad during the daytime, and all rest during the night is liable to be destroyed by the *mosquitoes*. To this not unfrequently succeeds the *Mistral*, or cutting dry N.E. wind, whose effects are described p. 422. The N.W. wind, called *le Libech* (Ital. Libeccio), exercises a terrific force over the Mediterranean.

Consuls reside here from the principal states of Europe and America. Mr. Turnbull is the worthy representative of England.

The *English Church Service* is performed in an apartment in the Rue Sylvabelle, on Sundays, by a resident clergyman. The *French Protestant Ch.* adjoins the H. d'Orient.

"Dr. de Chargé is a very clever homœopathic physician."—*E. o. S.*

The *Cafés* are very splendid in their decorations; the Café Turc is frequented by Greek merchants.

Baths. *The Bains de la Méditerranée,* about 1½ m. out of the town, on the S. of the road to Aix, in an agreeable situation, commanding a view of the bay, and receiving the sea-breeze, is a well-conducted establishment. The *New Sea-Baths,* at the extremity of the Prado, are even superior.

With this exception the *Environs of Marseilles* possess but slight attractions—nothing but dust, scorched rocks, and bare high walls, amidst which the eye in vain seeks for some verdure to rest on. The *Bastides* already mentioned are little country boxes, which entirely dot the slopes around the town, prolonging it apparently to the tops of the surrounding hills. Some of them are handsome, and surrounded by gardens, but the greater part stand in mere bare enclosures, between 4 walls, destitute of shade and water, their only recommendation being that they are out of town. Every merchant, citizen, or shopkeeper must have one, and their number is said to exceed 6000. The stupendous *Canal* which supplies Marseilles with *water from the Durance* is gradually altering the aspect of the country around the town, by the irrigation which it furnishes. Travellers should visit the *aqueduct* of *Roquefavour* (see p. 476). It will take a day to go and return.

A common excursion is a "promenade sur eau," from the harbour's mouth to the islands of If, &c. (p. 468). Courty's Restaurant, "La Muette de Portici," at the *Prado,* on the beach, 2 m. out of Marseilles, affords a good specimen of la Cuisine Provençale. At *La Reserve,* at the entrance of the harbour, the cuisine is capital.

Some of the best shops are in the Rues St. Ferréol, Beauvau, and Paradis, and the *Post Office* is in a street running out of it, Rue Jeune Anacharsis. Letters reach this from England on the 4th day.

Railways to Avignon and Valence (Rte. 127)—Terminus at St. Charles, not far from the Arc de Triomphe;—to Arles, Nismes, and Montpellier (Rte. 126-130), in progress to Toulon.

Diligences daily to Aix; to Toulon; to Nice, by Antibes and Draguinan, in 24 hours (Rte. 129); to Grenoble in 38 hours.

Steamers.

To *Italy* 12 to 15 times a-month; Government mail, and several private Companies, touching at Genoa, Leghorn, Civita Vecchia, Naples, and Sicily.

To Genoa, Leghorn, Civita Vecchia, and Naples (Gov.), 3 times a-month.

To Malta, Syra, Smyrna, Constantinople (Gov.), 3 times a-month.

To Alexandria and Beyrout (Gov.) twice a-month.

To *Spain,* Barcelona, Valencia, Malaga, Gibraltar, 3 or 4 times a-month; to Cadiz 3 times a-month.

To *Algiers* (Gov.) 6 times a-month.

To *Corsica,* Ajaccio, and Bastia, once a-week.

To *Cette* twice a-week, chiefly for merchandise.

N.B. The *Peninsular and Oriental Company's* fast and clean vessels—A. the India Line—to *Malta* and *Alexandria* (with India mail and overland passengers) the 10th and 26th of every month. Takes the mail despatched from London on the 8th and 24th, and reaches Malta in about 50 hrs. Fare, 1st class 9*l.*, 2nd class 5*l.*

To Cannes and Nice twice a-week.

History. Classical tradition assigns the foundation of *Massilia* to a colony of Phocœans, who left their native country, Asia Minor, with their wives and children, rather than submit to Cyrus, and sought for liberty on the then barbarous shores of Gaul. Their emigration (B.C. 5) is described by Herodotus, and alluded to by Horace:—

"Phocæorum
Velut profugit execrata civitas,
Agros atque lares patrios, habitandaque rura
Apris reliquit et rapacibus lupis:
Ire pedes quocunque ferent, quocunque per undas
Notus vocabit, aut protervus Africus."

Favourably received by the inhabitants of the country, the settlement increased and prospered; became great in commerce and navigation, eminent in the arts and literature; was sought and esteemed by Rome as an ally, until, wishing to remain neutral in the wars between Cæsar and Pompey, and finally siding with the latter, she was besieged, taken, and reduced to great distress by his successful antagonist, who records that he preserved it "magis pro nomine et vetustate quam pro meritis in se."—*Cæsar.* Lucan has described the siege, but evidently without local knowledge. Cicero says, in his Oration for Flaccus, that Greece alone could compete with Marseilles as a seat of learning; Tacitus calls her " magistram studiorum." Her importance continued during the middle ages; she formed a sort of independent state, electing her own magistrates, and forming alliances with other states. She furnished alone all the galleys required by St. Louis to transport his army on the Crusade. The famous commercial code *Le Consulat de la Mer* is supposed to have been drawn up here. At length, conquered by Charles d'Anjou, Comte de Provence, she yielded to the rising superiority on the sea of Pisa, Genoa, and Venice.

Marseilles held out against Henri IV. long after Paris had submitted; when at length he was informed of its surrender, he exclaimed, "C'est maintenant que je suis Roi." Yet was its turbulent spirit of independence not subdued, since, in consequence of an outbreak against Louis XIV., that monarch entered the city by a breach in its wall (see above, p. 467).

At the Revolution, which inflamed to madness the fiery spirits of the people of the south, among whom moderation and restraint are unknown or little practised, Marseilles furnished, from the dregs of its own population, and the outcasts of other lands, the bands of assassins who perpetrated the greater portion of the September massacres in Paris. The Reign of Terror at Marseilles itself, under the rule of the infamous Fréron and Barras, produced more than its usual proportion of atrocities and follies. The usual wholesale murders were committed, amounting to 400 persons, attended by confiscation of their property.

But not satisfied with this, it was proposed by one of the Représentants du Peuple to fill up its harbour. The name of Marseilles was absolutely abolished by a decree, which enacted that it should pass under the denomination of "la Commune sans Nom!" Even the death of Robespierre, which, for the most part, put an end to the Reign of Terror in other places, was here and elsewhere in the south the signal for fresh assassinations. Vengeance against those who had been the instruments of the revolutionary massacres was now the cry; the Fort St. Jean, in which about 200 of them had been confined, was broken open, and they were all murdered by an irritated mob of insurgents, employing cannon loaded with grape to finish their victims in their cells.

Marseilles is the birthplace of Mascaron the preacher, of Bishop Belzunce, and of Puget, the architect who built the old British Museum.

ROUTE 128.

MARSEILLES TO TOULON AND HYÈRES.

59 kilom. = $36\frac{1}{2}$ Eng. m.

Diligences daily. Railway to open 1855.

It takes about 5 hrs. to post from Marseilles to Toulon. The first part of the road is dreary so long as it runs between white stone walls which enclose Bastides and intercept all view and fresh air. " The most dusty road I ever saw; the vines for 20 rods on each side like a dressed (powdered) head: the country all mountains of rock with poor pines."—*A. Young.*

17 Aubagne. Near this a little verdure is visible in the pretty vale of Gemenos. The Abbé Barthélemy, author of the 'Voyages du Jeune Anacharsis,' was born at Aubagne.

The caper, a pretty flowering plant, is cultivated near

12 Cujes, a miserable-looking town (like most of those on the road) of 3000 Inhab., but the country around most productive and well cultivated.

A hilly road leads to the poor town of

13 Beausset, in the Dépt. du Var. The sea is now and then seen through breaks on the rt.

About 3 m. farther the road penetrates the mountains, through a deep chasm or defile of wild and savage features, called the *Pass of Ollioules*. Bare, bleached, and nearly precipitous rocks of limestone, surmounted by a ruined *Castle*, which once guarded the passage, hem in on either side, for a distance of nearly 3 m., a scene of desolation, nakedness, and solitude. On emerging from it, the landscape is more cheerful; the orange-tree is first seen; the pomegranate grows in the hedges; the olive-trees, the cactus, and palm occur at intervals in the favoured region, sheltered from the N. by the Estrelle, extending hence to the Var.

17 *Toulon* (*Inns*: Croix de Malte; civil people, and good cuisine. Croix d'Or; very good; table-d'hôte 3 francs at 5. Hôtel de France.)

Toulon is the Plymouth of France, the seat of her naval power in the Mediterranean, the greatest naval arsenal in that sea, and second only to that of Brest on the Atlantic. It is a strongly fortified town, situated at the bottom of a deep double bay, which forms the roads. Behind it runs an amphitheatre of hills rising on the N. into the heights of Mount Pharon, too bare to be picturesque, which stretch their arms as it were round the bay, so as nearly to landlock it, rendering it a safe anchorage, except from the S. and E., where it is somewhat unprotected. 6 forts on the land side defend the town, while the mouth of the harbour and hills commanding it are studded with forts and redoubts.

The *Port* is divided into the old and new, separated from the roadstead by moles, hollow and bomb-proof, begun in the reign of Henri IV., formed externally into batteries on a level with the water's edge,—very formidable against ships. The Port du Commerce, or *Darse Vieille*, on the E., is appropriated to merchant-vessels, and is bordered by a quay. The *Darse Neuve*, on the W., is surrounded by the dockyard, slips, the arsenal, the storehouses for provisions, &c., equipments, cannon foundry, park of artillery, &c.

The town itself contains 45,510 Inhab., exclusive of the garrison; but, confined within ramparts, its streets are narrow, its shops inferior, and its buildings (exclusive of those of the dockyard) unimportant.

The *Hôtel de Ville*, facing the harbour, is ornamented in front with 2 colossal thermæ, serving as caryatides to support a balcony, executed by *Puget*, and of good design. Behind the Hôtel de Ville, at the corner of the Rue d'Orléans, is a house built by that variously accomplished artist.

The dockyard and fleet of Toulon were destroyed by a British force under Sir Sidney Smith, detached from the fleet of Lord Hood, in November, 1793, previously to the evacuation of the town by the British. It was a work of danger, as the republicans, having already gained possession of the surrounding forts and heights, poured in a merciless hail of shot and shells; and the work was but imperfectly performed, that is to say, the great magazine and several vessels on the stocks escaped. 27 vessels were destroyed, being ignited in the harbour by a fire-ship, 2 of them blowing up: 15 ships were brought away. It must be remembered that the English gained possession of Toulon not by force of arms, but by convention with the royalist portion of its inhabitants, on condition of their being protected from the cruel vengeance of the republicans. But the means at the disposal of Admiral Hood, a fleet of 21 ships, aided by a Spanish squadron of 17, were totally inadequate to effect this; 5000 British troops, the amount of his land force, were far too few to garrison so vast an extent of works, and little good was done by our 8000 Neapolitan and Spanish allies. Although the surrounding forts were manned and put into a state of defence as far as possible, the important pass of Ollioules, commanding the only approach to Toulon from the W., was left unguarded, and the republican forces, reeking from the massacres of Lyons and Marseilles, marched in, and speedily invested the town to the

PROVENCE. *Route 128.—Toulon—Dockyard—Roadstead.* 473

number of 50,000, breathing vengeance against the inhabitants of Toulon for the defection of a place so important. When at length, at the end of 3 months, the harbour became no longer tenable, and the British fleet was obliged to weigh anchor, nearly 15,000 of the inhabitants were embarked on board the British fleet, by the light of the burning ships and dockyards, amidst the cries and groans of the multitude that remained behind, praying for the means of escape from the hands of the merciless republicans. Nor were their worst anticipations unfounded; more than 6000 miserable victims were sacrificed to the vengeance of the agents of the Committee of Public Safety, in spite of the remonstrances of Dugommier, the French general, and his lieutenant Buonaparte. With such blind rage did the besieging soldiery rush into the town, that they murdered, without question, 200 Jacobins who had gone forth to meet them. The horrors of the fusillades and the butcheries of the guillotine were then exercised against the inhabitants with a blind rage, which did not wait to distinguish those who had opposed from those who had favoured the English. Fréron and the other members of the Committee of Public Safety, including the younger Robespierre, presided in person over the fusillades (thank God, the word has no equivalent in English). They sent orders for 1200 masons to raze the town of Toulon, but their commands were only partly carried into execution, and they decreed that its name should be abolished, and that it should in future be known only as Port de la Montagne.

The *Dockyard* (Port Militaire), entered from the town by a handsome and appropriate gateway, is not readily shown to foreigners: the introduction of the English consul will, generally, obtain admission for Englishmen. Excepting, however, the *Bagne*, or prison for the *forçats* (convicts), they will see nothing here that they may not see as well at home, at Portsmouth or Plymouth, &c. The description already given of Brest (Rte. 36) renders a further detailed account of a French dockyard unnecessary. This arsenal covers a space of 55 acres, of which 35 are occupied by the Basin, which has a depth of water throughout for the largest ships fully equipped. In 1841, 13 vessels were building here; only 2 of the slips (cales) are roofed; but there are nearly twice as many vessels laid up in ordinary here as in any other French port. The store of oak timber is very large. The ropehouse (corderie) is nearly 1200 ft. long, of 3 vaulted aisles of masonry, fire-proof, except the floor. In the centre of the surface of the yard is an opening out into the Petite Rade, and a line-of-battle ship, fully armed and stored, may sail at once from the basin or port right out to sea. Immediately after crossing this opening on the rt. is *Le Bagne*, a large airy building. The number of forçats here varies from 3000 to 3500; they are most rigidly superintended, chained each night to their beds, as at Brest, and there are loopholes for guns in the walls at the extremity of the dormitory, which would sweep it from end to end in the event of a mutiny. The number of free workmen, in 1841, was about 4500.

The *Musée de la Marine* contains a large collection of models of inventions, ship-building, &c.

" 2 first-rate Docks have been constructed at the S. angle of the Basin. They are not excavations from the land, but formed by quays carried into the port. A large frame of wood (caisse) was sunk with ballast at the spot, and of the size of the dock, and the masonry was built in around it." —*W.*

A new or supplemental dockyard has been formed at Mourillon, in the S. of the town, between it and Fort la Malgue; here are 5 large slips.

The *Roadstead* and *Harbour* is the most picturesque and interesting feature about Toulon, and the views of it from the neighbouring heights are very pleasing. A small *steamer* plies across to the village of La Seyne. The inner road is divided from the outer by 2 capes or headlands; that on the E. is defended at its point by an advanced fort, called Grosse Tour; and on its neck or root, between the little and great "Rade," stands the strong *Fort la Malgue*, surrounded by ramparts 30 ft. high, capable of holding 800 men, and defended by 200 pieces of cannon. Opposite to this, from the W. side of the bay, stretches forth a two-horned hilly promontory, the two points of which are occupied by the strong forts of *Eguillette* and *Ballaguier*, at the water's edge, while the commanding heights, de Caire, above them are crowned by the Fort Napoleon, which replaces the field-works of 1793, styled *le Petit Gibraltar*, and which is the key of the whole defences. Eguillette was regarded as the key of the British position in 1793, but was occupied by a garrison of which unfortunately only a small part were British, the rest Spaniards and Neapolitans. After keeping possession of it between 3 and 4 months, in spite of the besieging French force from without, on the 16th of December a range of batteries, which had been formed secretly by the French and concealed behind the olive-gardens, suddenly opened their fire upon le Petit Gibraltar and the Fort Eguillette from the heights behind, throwing, in the course of 36 hours, 8000 shot and shells. Early the next morning, the French, led by Dugommier, their commander-in-chief, advanced to the attack, but were so warmly received, that at first there seemed no hope of success, until the brave Muiron, followed by his men, entering by an embrasure on the side of the line intrusted to the Spaniards, overpowered them, and cut to pieces the British detachment of 300 men.

The planner of this attack, the constructor of the concealed batteries which now opened by hundreds of fiery mouths from the crests of all the hills upon the detachment of the allies below, was a young officer of artillery, aged 23, named Buonaparte, who for the first time received a command and enjoyed an opportunity of displaying his vast military genius on the heights above Toulon. On arriving 2 or 3 months previously to take the subordinate command, he found that the incapables who had preceded him had raised their batteries at a distance of 2 gun-shots from Toulon, and were directing vain efforts against the place itself. His quick eye at once perceived the defect, and singled out the points where an impression was to be made. In 5 or 6 weeks, under his directions, batteries were constructed, mounting 200 pieces of cannon, on the heights of Brégaillon, Evesca, and Lambert, commanding the forts held by the British. While awaiting the time when all should be ready to make his great effort, the Representatives of the People, discovering so many guns lying idle, would have caused an immediate cannonade, and would in their ignorance thus have spoiled all. Then it was that the young officer had the boldness to reply to one of them, Barras, "Tenez-vous à votre métier de Représentant, et laissez-moi faire le mien d'artilleur. Cette batterie restera là, et je réponds du succès sur ma tête." He promised that, in 2 days after gaining the fort, Toulon would fall, nor was he wrong: the morning after the capture of Petit Gibraltar, Eguillette, and Fort Pharon (an important work on the heights to the N. of the town), whose guns together swept the roadstead from end to end, the British and Spanish fleets had weighed anchor, and were standing out to sea.

A previous attempt was made upon Toulon, in 1707, by the Austrian and Sardinian army, under Prince Eugene and the Duke of Savoy, aided by an English and Dutch fleet, under Sir Cloudesley Shovel; but after an ineffectual bombardment of the town, they found it so stoutly defended that they were compelled to retire.

The *Outer Road* is formed by a hilly peninsula stretching from W. to E., terminating in Cap Sepet, corresponding with Cap Brun on the opposite side of the bay.

There is an extensive *Naval Hospital* at St. Mandrier, on the S. side of the roadstead, farthest from the town, a

PROVENCE. R. 128.—*Hyères*. R. 129.—*Avignon to Nice*. 475

splendid building with 2000 beds. Near it is the Lazaret.

Steamers twice every week to Corsica, touching at Ajaccio (22 hours' passage) and Bastia (24 hours) alternately.

The *view* from the hill to the S.E. of Toulon, on which stands Fort la Malgue, is one of the finest in the S. of France.

The *Botanic Garden*, outside the town, is worth a visit, on account of the number of plants of tropical or southern countries which here first begin to flourish in the open air; among others, the date-palm. Several palms may also be seen in the neighbourhood of.

18 *Hyères* (*Inns*: H. Les Iles d'Or, best, and very good;—H. des Ambassadeurs;—H. de l'Europe), a town of 4591 Inhab., on the slope of a hill, crowned by ruins, sheltered from the mistral by the chain of Les Maures, so that it enjoys a temperature nearly as mild as that of Nice. It faces the Mediterranean, but is separated from it by an intervening space, partly common, partly marsh, 3 m. broad: hence it enjoys little view of the sea. There is a want of good accommodation and pure water to drink.

The mildness of its climate causes Hyères to be chosen as a winter residence for invalids, and renders it perhaps one of the best resorts for invalids, during that season, in Europe, but it is not so satisfactory during the summer months. For the passing traveller there is little beauty in its situation. Here alone in France the orange bears fruit, but, though a novelty to strangers from the N., the *orange groves* are not an agreeable feature in the landscape, the trees being shut up in walled gardens. The palm-tree, of which there are 4 or 5 in the neighbourhood, produces no fruit in this latitude. The old or upper town, composed of narrow streets, steep and dirty, retains a fragment of its old *Castle*, and part of the line of the former fortifications still climbing up the steep. It is the birthplace of Massillon, the preacher, to whom a marble *pillar* and *bust* have been raised in the Place Royale.

The low ground is richly culti-

vated: olives, vines, figs, mulberries abound; the pomegranate, pistachio, caper, myrtle, jessamine flourish; but the hills are bare. On the shore, about 3 m. to the E., are large saltworks, and off the coast is the group of islands called

[*Diligence* daily in 7 hours to St. Tropez, (37 m). (*Inn*: H. du Commerce, supported by Commis Voyageurs, no good Inn.) In its first aspect St. Tropez is a little like Cadiz on a small scale, its white houses rising out of the blue sea. General Allard, long employed at Lahore by Runjeet Singh, was a native of St. Tropez.]

Diligences run daily between Toulon and Hyères.

The road hence to Nice passes through

23 Cuers.
15 Pignan.
15 Le Luc (*Inn*: Poste), where it falls into Rte. 129.

ROUTE 129.

AVIGNON TO NICE, BY AIX, FRÉJUS, AND CANNES.

274 kilom. = 170 Eng. m.

Diligences several times a-day. The railway from Avignon to Marseilles being completed by Arles (Rtes. 127 and 129), the first part of this road is deserted.

The road on quitting Avignon runs along the rt. bank of the Durance (Druentia), a turbulent and ill-conducted stream, whose wide and desolate bed of gravel, laid bare in summer, bears so large a proportion to the reduced stream flowing in threads towards the Rhône, that a passing traveller has no idea of the considerable volume of water poured down by it even at that season from the supplies furnished by the melting snows of the Alps. In winter, swollen in a few hours to a torrent, it not only fills its channel, but often inundates its banks. Its waters are employed in irrigating the neighbouring land. One considerable *Canal*, called *de Crillon*, from the grandson of le

Brave Crillon, who caused it to be made, is passed by our road near Bonpas. Here we cross the Durance by a long wooden bridge. A road runs hence to l'Isle, by which the traveller visiting *Vaucluse* (Rte. 126) may gain the route to Marseilles without returning from Avignon.

Near Bonpas is the village Noves, reputed the birthplace of Petrarch's Laura.

Higher up the Durance, on its rt. bank, is Cavaillon (7000 Inhab.), where are some mutilated Roman remains, an *Arch of Triumph*, half buried in the ground, attributed to the Empr. Constantine, and a curious Romanesque *Cathedral* (St. Véran) of the 13th centy., with an apse of the 12th; attached to it is a curious *Cloister*.

The Durance separates the Dépt. of Vaucluse from that of Bouches du Rhône.

18 St. Andéol. There is a cross-road from this to St. Remy, whose Roman monuments are described at p. 459. It lies at the foot of the low chain of bare limestone hills visible to the S., extending from Tarascon to Orgon, called *Les Alpines*.

10 Orgon (*Inn*: Poste; dear, and not to be recommended). This is a town of 2000 Inhab., near the l. bank of the Durance, at the foot of a hill crowned by a ruined castle.

The *Canal de Boisgelin*, a branch of the Canal de Craponne, which conveys the fresh water of the Durance to the Rhône at Arles, fertilising the land on its passage, is here carried through the rock in a *Tunnel*, known as the Pierre Percée, of no great length.

Napoleon, on his way from Fontainebleau to Elba, was nearly torn in pieces here by the infuriated populace, and became so much alarmed as to disguise himself as a courier, and ride on before his own carriage.

The Canal de Craponne is crossed at 18 Pont Royal: there is a pretty fountain near the post-house.

Canal to Marseilles from the Durance.

This highly important hydraulic work has been in progress since 1830, under the able direction of the engineer M. Montricher. The canal derives its waters from the river Durance at a point near to Pertuis, 28 m. in a *direct* line from Marseilles; but from the mountainous and difficult character of the country, its length extends to 60 m. before it reaches that city. The point of derivation, at Pertuis, is 614 ft. above the sea, between which place and Les Beaumes St. Antoine, near Marseilles, a length of 51 m., it falls to the level of 490 ft. (about 29 in. per m.) The section of this portion of the canal is calculated to pass the enormous quantity of $1\frac{1}{4}$ million tons of water per day, or 198,000 gallons per minute. In its course three chains of limestone mountains are pierced by 45 tunnels, forming an aggregate length of $8\frac{1}{2}$ m., and numerous intervening valleys are crossed by aqueducts. The *Aqueduct* of *Roquefavour*, over the ravine of the river Arc (about 5 m. from Aix), is a structure of gigantic dimensions, and well worthy the attention of the traveller. In admiring this work many will doubtless be surprised to find so large a volume of water, with such ample fall, still carried across on the same principles as those adopted by the Romans, instead of the modern substitution of iron pipes, which, owing to the facilities of the manufacture of iron, now so generally supersede the necessity of such constructions. As a work of art this aqueduct will not suffer in comparison with the famous Pont du Gard, which it surpasses in height; while it partakes much of the same character in design. The whole is carried out in excellent taste, but it is to be regretted that its principal arches are not of a more noble span. The entire elevation of the aqueduct is 262 ft. and its length 1287 ft. Its total cost has been 151,394*l.* sterling, and it contains 51,000 cubic yards of masonry. In the execution of the tunnels great difficulties were encountered owing to the hardness of the rock and the presence of large quantities of water, particularly in sinking the shafts of the tunnel of Taillades, which is above 2 m. in length, where the expense amounted to an average of 24*l.* each yard in depth. The

PROVENCE.   Route 129.—Canal to Marseilles—Aix.   477

total cost of these shafts, added to the expense of the tunnel, 22*l*. per yard, amounted to 57,200*l*. per mile. The whole work, from its origin to St. Antoine, have cost 666,546*l*., or 13,069*l*. per mile.

The object and use of this canal is to convey to the arid territory of Marseilles an almost unlimited supply of water for irrigation, and to the city a quantity sufficient for domestic and public distribution; and for giving activity to various branches of industry which may require water power.

Perhaps no work of this description has been undertaken in modern times with a greater amount of hardy conception, and determination to complete it to its fullest extent, almost regardless of expense. It has already succeeded in converting an arid soil, almost unproductive hitherto, under the effects of a southern sun, to that of a well-watered district. The waters of the Durance, it is true, are delivered at their destination in the same state in which they issue from the river, which at first sight is likely to give rise to much disappointment; but the useful effects of the undertaking are already perceptible in the district. The principal channel is continued from St. Antoine, but reduced in size one-third, and progressively diminishes, taking a circuit round Marseilles of 25 m., at an elevation of from 200 to 300 ft., commanding an area of many square miles. 5 other branch canals strike out of this, the aggregate lengths of which, including the main line and trunk canal to St. Antoine, amount to 97 m.

One of these branch canals is executed for the supply of the city of Marseilles, where it arrives at the level of 242 ft. above the sea.

Large filtering and service reservoirs are in the course of construction, and a considerable extent of iron pipeage for distributing the water is completed.

The entire cost of this important undertaking it is stated has already amounted to above 2,000,000*l*. sterling.

Lambesc is passed on the way to

14 St. Cannat, where our road is joined by that from Arles and Nismes. (Rte. 127.)

A hilly country succeeds, bare and bleak, but abounding in olives, and not interesting. A long and steep hill leads down to Aix; on its brow, close to the road, are subterranean *Quarries of Gypsum*, in connexion with which a great number of well-preserved fossil fish and insects are found. They occur in a fresh-water shale, whose laminations are so minute as to resemble the leaves of a book; on splitting them open the fossils are found between.

The Montagne de St. Victor, rising to the E. of Aix, is a conspicuous feature in the landscape (see p. 479).

16 *Aix*. (*Inns:* H. des Princes, the first house as you enter the Cours, good; Palais Royal, good.)

Aix is a flourishing town of 24,255 Inhab., agreeably situated in a basin surrounded by hills of abundant fertility, amidst almond-groves and plantations of olives, which furnish the much-esteemed *sweet oil of Aix*, the best produced in France.

The broad street called the *Cours*, by which you enter the town, is very striking; it is lined with handsome modern houses, including the chief hotels, closed at one end by an iron rail, and ornamented with 3 fountains, one of which bears a statue, by *David*, of *le Bon Roi René*, who is represented holding a bunch of Muscat grapes, which he introduced into France. During his reign Aix was the scene of gaiety and luxury, and the seat of art and literature. Within the modern and external quarters of the town, which assume somewhat the aspect of boulevards, is the *Old Town*, the ancient capital of Provence, the resort of the troubadours, the home of poetry, gallantry, and politeness; the theatre of the courts of love, and of gay fêtes and tournaments, during the reign of Raymond Berenger IV. as well as of René of Anjou. It still retains in part its feudal walls and gates, and its streets are narrow and foul. Here stands, surmounted by an octagon belfry, without a roof, the *Cathedral of St. Sauveur*, parts of which are very ancient, as the S. aisle of the nave, resting partly on a wall of Roman masonry, entered by a curious portal flanked by 2 Corinthian columns, probably antique, within which is a plain round arch. Attached to the aisle is a *Baptistery* recently restored, around which are arranged a number of antique pillars of polished granite, supporting round arches. These portions are all Romanesque, of the 12th centy., as well as the *Cloister*, remarkable for the variety of the columns supporting it. The central aisle is later, in the florid Gothic, and the N. aisle shows traces of the Italian style. The main W. *entrance* resembles in character somewhat the perpendicular English Gothic, overloaded with ornaments. The heads of the statues ornamenting it, destroyed at the Revolution, have been restored in the worst manner. The carved cedar-wood doors merit notice; they were executed 1503. The bas-reliefs upon them represent the 12 Theological Virtues (or the Sibyls), and the 4 Greater Prophets, below: the ornaments, a mixture of Gothic and Renaissance, are very delicately executed. These *doors* are covered with a sort of shutter to protect them, which the sacristan will remove for a small fee.

Within the ch. is a very good *old picture* of the Virgin and Child, on the top of a clump of trees, surrounded by a glory. Below, an angel appears to a shepherd, probably intended to represent Moses and the burning bush. On the outside of the two wings or shutters which cover the picture, painted in black and white, is the angel Gabriel appearing to the Virgin; and within are King René, and his second wife, Jeanne de Laval, both evidently portraits; he, attended by his patron saints, the Magdalen, St. Anthony, and St. Maurice; she, accompanied by St. John, St. Nicholas, and St. Catherine, the last a beauteous and most elevated countenance. This picture is attributed, like many others in different parts of France, to the pencil of King René; it is probably the work of a Flemish artist of the school of Van Eyck: its date must be posterior to 1455, as René did not marry Jeanne de Laval until that year.

There are some marble bas-reliefs, which probably belonged to an antique sarcophagus, representing Christ and the Apostles, in the chapel of *St. Mitre*, and others of the 15th centy. behind the altar of *St. Maurice*.

The *Ch. of St. John* includes some monuments to the Counts of Provence. The building is Gothic. The sacristy of the modern ch. of *La Madeleine* contains a curious painting of the Annunciation, attributed to *Alb. Dürer*.

The *Museum* contains numerous fragments of antiquity, inscriptions, mosaics, sculpture, bronzes, chiefly Roman, and found in the neighbourhood; including a torso of a youth, a tripod carved with a dancing female in relief, and a statue, said to be Hercules. The *Pictures*, as usual, are for the most part very mediocre; but among the modern works is a sample of *Granet*, a native of Aix.

The *Public Library* in the H. de Ville consists of 100,000 volumes, and possesses many letters of Mary Stuart.

In the Place de l'Hôtel de Ville is an old gateway with a clock bearing the date 1512. There are many pretty *bits* of carved stone, and other relics of ancient taste and splendour, in the filthy little closes of this most filthy town.

Aix, the *Aquæ Sextiæ* of the Romans, derives its origin from a Roman colony sent hither to defend the Phocæan colonists of Marseilles from the attacks of the Salyes, in the year 630 after the building of Rome. Its warm *mineral waters* served probably as an inducement for them to select this spot. The hot saline spring still exists, but it is neither very strong nor in high repute.

A *Bath-house* is erected over the source in the suburb, and there are remains of vaults near it, said to be Roman. The water is so weak that the baths may with safety be taken as ordinary warm baths. The chief spring, called Source de Sextius, from the founder of the Roman colony, Caius Sextius Calvinus, has a temperature of 78° Fahr. At the beginning of last century it diminished greatly in quantity, in consequence of wells being dug at a place called Barret, 2 m. off, which brought to light, at a short distance from the surface, very copious springs, similar in nature to those in the town, but cold. The magistrates, however, ordered these sources to be stopped up; and 22 days after, the warm spring of Sextius had regained ⅔ths of its original volume. It would appear, from this remarkable occurrence, that the source of heat must lie between the Source de Barret and that of Sextius.

Few provincial towns in France have produced a greater number of remarkable men than Aix: among them the learned Peiresc, the Marquis d'Argens, the naturalists Tournefort and Adanson, the painters J. B. Vanloo and Granet, and General Miollis.

The commerce in the *sweet oil of Aix* has greatly fallen off since 1830, when an unusually severe frost killed a large proportion of the olive-trees in this neighbourhood.

Diligences to Nice; to Gap; Digne; Toulon. *Omnibus* to Rognac Stat. on the Marseilles Railway.

Railway (branch in progress) to Rognac Stat. on Marseilles and Avignon line, described in Rte. 127.

The road to Nice passes under the precipitous heights of the *Mont St. Victoire*, and not far from the spot where Marius is supposed to have defeated the Cimbri, B. C. 125. 100,000 of the barbarians are stated to have been slain or taken prisoners, and the battle-field on the banks of the Arc was long known by the name "Campi Putridi," whence the modern village Pourrières.

12 Châteauneuf-le-Rouge.
11 Grande Pugère.

St. Maximin (H. du Var, indifferent) has a rather fine Gothic *Ch.*, very lofty within, but destitute of a W. front, without transepts, but ending in 3 apses. It was founded by Charles II., King of Naples and Count of Provence, 1279, but seems chiefly of the 15th centy. The woodwork of the pulpit and sacristy is well preserved. Here are treasured up the bones of the Magdalen, over the altar; her skull, with a bit of flesh adhering to the forehead, where our Saviour touched it! her arm gilt, and the coffins of several saints, her servants; also some curious old vestments.

22 Tourves, a wretched town of 2800 Inhab., in the Dépt. du Var. No Inn. There is a *direct road* from Tourves, by Roquevaire 30 kilom., Aubagne 8 kilom., to Marseilles 17 kilom.

12 Brignolles. (*Inn:* Poste.) In this town of 6000 Inhab. an extensive trade is carried on in dried fruits. The "prunes de Brignolles," though sold here, are in fact produced in the country around Digne (Basses Alpes.)

23 Le Luc. *Inn:* Poste, very dirty. Here the road from Toulon and Hyères falls in. (See Rte. 128.)

14 Vidauban. *Inns:* H. de Provence; Poste, good beds. Scenery interesting; myrtle, stone-pine, and cork trees. An abrupt turn of the road at *

13 Le Muy. H. Jourdan or La Poste.

15 *Fréjus*. *Inns:* H. du Midi, best; —Poste; not good, and bad smells: Buonaparte stayed 3 days at the Poste.

Outside the walls of this small and dirty town (not 3000 Inhab.), the once celebrated *Forum Julii* founded by Cæsar, on the W., are the remains of a small *Circus*, recently cleared out, far inferior in size and preservation to those of Nismes and Arles. The direction of the old Roman town walls may also be traced by existing fragments of them. The ancient harbour, in which Augustus posted the fleet of 300 galleys captured at Actium from Antony, is now sanded up by the deposits of the Argens (Argentius). The mole and tower (? lighthouse), which commanded the entrance to the old port, now rise out of the midst of a grass-grown plain. The town is now a mile from the sea.

Between the sea and the town is a *Roman arch*, formed of small stones alternating with layers of tiles, called *Porte Dorée*. The *Cathedral of St. Etienne* is neither large nor handsome, but may interest the antiquary as a Romanesque edifice of the 11th or 12th centy. Adjoining it is a *Baptistery*, resting on 8 antique columns of grey granite with marble capitals.

The most considerable and interesting Roman remains here are those of an *Aqueduct*, passed on the way to Cannes. It has been traced for more than 24 m. up the valley of the Ciagne, whose clear water it conveyed to the town. Many of the arches and piers remain perfect. It is a picturesque subject for the pencil.

Napoleon landed at the small port of St. Raphael near this, 1799, on his return from Egypt, and embarked hence, 1814, for Elba. This is the birthplace of the Abbé Sièyes, and is said to be that of Julius Agricola.

The French coast between Toulon and Nice is bordered by 2 small hilly chains called *les Maures* (because once occupied by Saracen brigands) and *l'Estrelle*. They are, as it were, the roots or footstool of the Alps, whose higher ridges protect them from the N. Consequently in their recesses and on their S. slopes they seem to enjoy a peculiar and privileged climate. Though their peaks are bare, near their bases the aloe, cactus, and palm flourish in the open air; and the umbrella pine, as in Italy, raises its graceful head close to the sea-shore. This is the true "garden of Provence." The Estrelle mountains are partly of porphyry, and are highly picturesque in their forms, as is invariably the case where that rock occurs. The red porphyry was worked by the Romans, and used by them for the buildings of Fréjus, and was even sent to Rome; the ancient quarry has been discovered about 1½ m. from the shore.

A new and improved line of road has been constructed over the Pass of

14 L'Estrelle. The scenery, varied by the fine foliage of the cork-tree, arbutus, and evergreen oak, is very pleasing, and is diversified by fine sea views.

20 Cannes. *Inns*: La Poste; H. du Nord ; Pinshinat's Hotel, outside the town, beautifully situated. The fish called St. Pierre is reputed the ortolan of the sea.

This is a neat and cheerful small town, finely situated in a mountainous country at the bottom of a beautiful bay. It is the port of Grasse.

About ½ a mile off is the villa Louise Eléonore, built by *Lord Brougham*, in one of the most charming situations in the S. of France, approached through iron gates by a long straight avenue. *Sir Herbert Taylor's* (now Mr. Woodfall's) *Villa* has even a finer site—between the road and the sea.

Napoleon landed 1½ m. E. of Cannes from Elba, in March, 1815, with an army composed of 500 grenadier guards, 200 dragoons, and 100 lancers without horses. He took the road to Grasse, and bivouacked the first night in an olive-garden there.

Opposite Cannes, about 2½ m. from the shore, lies the *Ile Ste. Marguerite*, covered with wood, one of the group of 2 isles called Lérins, in whose fort, once a state prison, the Man in the *Iron Mask* long lingered. The dungeon in which he was confined (1686 to 1698) is still pointed out ; its walls are 12 ft. thick, and its solitary window is guarded by treble iron bars. The only approach to it was through the governor's rooms. In the midst of a small garden is a curious square building, with a door in each face. On the *Ile St. Honorat* are remains of a fortified convent, a church, and a baptistery, recently reduced to ruin, and all deserving the attention of the antiquary. On the top of the hill washed by the sea above Cannes is the *Ch. of Notre Dame d'Espérance*, much revered by sailors. The road to Nice merely skirts, and does not enter, the town of

11 Antibes (*Inn*: Poste, not good), a flourishing little seaport (5976 Inhab.), finely situated on a promontory jutting out into the sea, and looking beautiful at a distance, and commanding views of the Maritime Alps. Here are portions of 2 square Roman towers. "Travellers should stop outside the gates, and send in for horses ; they will thus save time, and their carriage will escape the risk of accidents, in being twice dragged through the most odious streets."— *W. M.* A pier thrown out from the shore connects it with some islets in the bay : it was the work of Vauban.

It is a delightful ride hence to Nice. The torrent Var, crossed by a bridge of wood, divides France from the Sardinian states. It is an unmanageable stream, rolling enormous masses of shingle down into the sea, which the current of the Mediterranean pushes constantly to the W., grinding them smaller the further they are carried.

The French custom-house is strict (see INTRODUCTION). N. B. The Douanes on either side of the Var open about 8 A.M., and close at 5 in winter, 6 in summer. The gates on the Pont du Var are locked during the intermediate hours, and are not opened for travellers.

Trains daily in 2 hrs.

24 NICE (*Inns:* H. Victoria ; H. de France; H. des Etrangers) is described in HANDBOOK FOR NORTH ITALY.

ROUTE 130.

NISMES TO MARSEILLES BY BEAUCAIRE AND ARLES—RAILWAY.

Railway trains 4 times a-day, and 10 or 12 times during the fair of Beaucaire ; it takes carriages. The journey to Beaucaire is performed in 35 min. ; the distance 24 kilom. = 15 m. This railroad is carried through olive-grounds and vineyards, and, on approaching Beaucaire, is terraced along the shoulder of a hill overlooking the muddy Rhône, and the canal leading to Cette. It passes 1 or 2 small tunnels and cuttings.

[The *post-road*, direct from Nismes to Arles, crosses the Canal de Beaucaire and the Rhône, by

17 Bellegarde (about 7 m. S. of this lies St. Gilles, see p. 450),

15 ARLES, and avoiding Beaucaire altogether.]

24 Beaucaire Stat. (*Inn:* H. du Grand Jardin ; tolerable). Here are no post-horses ; and it is necessary to cross the Rhône to

15 Tarascon, described in Rte. 125.

A viaduct of 7 arches of cast iron carries the railroad over the Rhône to Tarascon Stat.

The railroad hence to Marseilles is described Rte. 127.

SECTION VII.

DAUPHINÉ.*

ROUTE	PAGE	ROUTE	PAGE
131 Lyons to *Grenoble* by *Vienne*, or by *Bourgoin.—Excursion to the Grande Chartreuse* . . 483		136 Lyons to Nice, by Grenoble, *Digne*, and *Grasse* . . . 495	
132 Valence on the Rhône to Grenoble and Chambéry, through the *Valley of Grésivaudan* . 490		137 Grenoble to *Briançon*, by *Bourg d'Oysans* and the *Col de Lauteret*, and by the *Mont Genèvre* to Susa . . . 496	
134 Grenoble to Marseilles, by *Gap* and *Sisteron*,—*Protestant Valleys of Dauphiné* . . 492		139 Gap to Briançon, by *Embrun*. —*Protestant Valleys* (continued); *Val Queyras, Val d'Arvieux*, and *Val Fressinière* . 499	
135 Grenoble to Marseilles, by the *Croix Haute* . . . 495			

INTRODUCTION.—SKETCH OF THE COUNTRY.

This province has been as much neglected by travellers as many other parts of France, yet its scenery is of first-rate beauty and grandeur. "I saw nothing among the Alps," says Arthur Young, "that offered such pleasing scenes as the N. parts of Dauphiné." The valley of the Isère is made up of a series of beautiful scenes, and the part of it about Grenoble, the deservedly vaunted Vallée de Grésivaudan, combines with the mountain forms of Switzerland the luxuriant vegetation and umbrageous foliage which usually characterise the S. slope of the Alps.

The *Grande Chartreuse* has been rarely visited by the English since Gray and Horace Walpole first drew their attention to it, yet the approach to it from St. Laurent is by a gorge as fine as any in the Alps. Grenoble itself is a striking city in a very romantic situation. The new carriage-road, begun by Napoleon, and at length nearly finished, from Grenoble to Briançon, by Bourg d'Oysans and the Col of the Lauteret, lays open a magnificent Alpine pass.

In addition to all this, however, Dauphiné includes, in the block of mountains which separate the basin of the Romanche from that of the Durance and the sources of the Drac, the *highest mountain in France, Mont Pelvoux*, whose culminating peak, the Pointe des Arcines or des Ecrins, attains an elevation of 13,468 ft. above the sea-level. Yet, though the loftiest summit in the Alpine chain between Mont Blanc and the Mediterranean, and considerably higher than Monte Viso, its name rarely appears on maps and in books of geography even published in France. Among the few persons who have visited it, besides engineers employed in the vicinity, are M. Elie de Beaumont, and our own countryman, Prof. Forbes, of Edinburgh, who have examined it geologically.† The scenery around Mont Pelvoux will well repay the trouble of a visit: it is of a sublime but desolate and savage character. It is best approached from Bourg d'Oysans, whence a path runs up Val Christophe to Berarde, a desolate

---

* The name *Dauphin* (Delphinus, whence Dauphiné), borne by the eldest son of the King of France down to 1830, is of unknown origin, but belonged to the Counts of Vienne, who also carried a dolphin as their coat of arms, from the 11th or 12th century down to 1349, when Count Humbert II., the last *native* Dauphin, made over his title and domains to the eldest son of Philip of Valois.

† See *Forbes*' 'Norway and its Glaciers, with Excursions in Dauphiné,' &c.—1853.

village at its base, buried by snow 7 months of the year, and hemmed in by precipices, with the scantiest vegetation around, and beyond it moraines and the glacier of la Condamine. It is destitute of any accommodation; indeed, the traveller who explores the Montagnes d'Oysans must be prepared to rough it; the mere tourist is an animal nearly unknown as yet among them. Mont Pelvoux is surrounded by other lofty peaks, all inclining their heads to him as in homage to the monarch of the French Alps, but presenting sides nearly precipitous, surrounding the desolate valley of Bérarde as it were with a colossal circus, 36 miles in circumference, forming an arrangement which has been compared to the petals of a flower.

The *Valleys of the Hautes Alpes*, including the Val Fressinière to the S. of Mont Pelvoux, and the Vals Queyras and Pragelas, running E. from Embrun and Mont Dauphin towards Monte Viso, although destitute of roads and accessible only by the pedestrian, will be explored with a double interest, not only for their noble scenery, but also as the refuge of persecuted Protestants, the kindred of the Albigenses and Vaudois, and also in recent times as the scene of the labours of the virtuous pastor Felix Neff.

Gen. *Bourcet's* 'Carte du Haut Dauphiné' is an indispensable travelling companion, and is not to be surpassed for accuracy.

Gilly's 'Life of Felix Neff,' of which there is a pocket edition, will be read with interest amidst the scenes of his ministry.

ROUTE 131.

LYONS TO GRENOBLE, BY VIENNE, OR BY BOURGOIN. — EXCURSION TO THE GRANDE CHARTREUSE.

A *Railway* is projected starting from St. Rambart Stat. on the Rhône between Lyons and Valence.

a. By Vienne 113 kilom. = 70 Eng. m. Diligences daily in 10 or 11 hrs. The road is the same as Rte. 125 as far as

27 Vienne.
15 La Detourbe.
14 Chatonay.
17 La Frette.
13 Rives.
13 Voreppe, p. 484.
14 *Grenoble*, p. 488.

b. The route by Bourgoin is shorter than the preceding by 7 kilom.; it is the road to Chambéry and Turin as far as Bourgoin.

4 *Diligences* go daily; and 2 or 3 to Chambéry and Turin follow the road by Bourgoin and Pont de Beauvoisin.

The road quits Lyons by the Pont Guillotière, and the long suburb of that name, emerging between 2 of the detached forts. It enters the Dépt. de l'Isère before reaching

10 Bron, a solitary post-house.

8 St. Laurent des Mûres (? so called from the mulberry-trees).

11 La Verpillière.

12 Bourgoin (Poste, good), a neat manufacturing town of about 3750 Inhab., whose industry is promoted by the Bourbre and 2 other small streams flowing through it. Here are manufactures of cotton, calico, cloth, and paper. A considerable trade is carried on in flour and wool; and the prosperity of the place is promoted by its position at the point where the roads from Lyons to Chambéry and Grenoble branch off.

The way to Chambéry and Turin runs through

15 La Tour du Pin (Poste; tolerable), a town of 2559 Inhab.

8 Gaz (no inn). A road runs hence by Voirons (*Inn:* Poste), a town of 6924 Inhab., where great quantities of sailcloth and other coarse cloths are made, to Voreppe and Grenoble.

10 Pont du Beauvoisin.(Poste; fallen off), a frontier town on the Guier, which here separates France from Sardinia. The respective custom-houses of the two countries are situated at the two extremities of the bridge over it.

The road runs along up the rt. bank of the Guier, but high above it, through

Y 2

a picturesque and fertile country at first, and afterwards through the grand gorge of La Chaille.

15 (2 posts) Les Echelles, a village situated at the junction of 2 streams, the Guiers Vif and Mort.

About 8 m. S. of this, up the Guiers Mort, is St. Laurent du Pont, the p int from which the Grande Chartreuse is visited (see below).

A good road leads from Les Echelles to Grenoble, through St. Laurent.

Chambéry is fully described, together with the road thither from Pont Beauvoisin, in the SWISS HANDBOOK.

Road to Grenoble.—The direct road from Lyons to Grenoble turns off from the preceding route at

40 Bourgoin.

11 Eclose.

15 La Frette. We here fall into the road *a* to Grenoble by Vienne.

The Château of La Frette was the birth-place of the terrible Baron des Adrets, a sort of French Alva, at whose name and war-cry "Beaumont," squadrons used to turn and fly. At the age of 60 he led on the Huguenots against the Romanists, and especially against the party of the Guises. He died here, after having become himself a Romanist, at the age of 80.

La Côte St. André, a little to the W., is famed for its distilleries of liqueurs.

13 Rives, on a stream called La Fure.

After surmounting a hill the road descends at Moirans into the beautiful valley of the Isère. The portion of it extending upwards from Voreppe to Chapareillan is called the *Valley of Grésivaudan*, and is deservedly celebrated as one of the most productive and beautiful in France. In its culture and its different kinds of produce, it is scarce surpassed by those luxuriant valleys stretching down into Italy on the S. side of the Alps. Up to the point where the mountains rise in bare precipitous rocks, or are girt with dark forests, every portion is constantly subject to tillage, and produces a vast variety of crops. Besides corn and clover, hemp, for which the valley is celebrated, grows often to the height of 15 feet. Orchards, chestnuts, and mulberry-trees rise above these; and the vine also, very abundant, instead of being allowed to crawl along the ground, or being clipped like a currant-bush, slings its graceful festoons from tree to tree, or is trained along wooden trellises. The roads are lined and shaded with trees, and it is difficult to see across the valley for the dense screen of foliage, but it hides the somewhat arid peaks and ridges from view, and thus modifies an unpleasing feature. Industry, abundant irrigation, and manure, have brought the whole to the condition of a luxuriant garden, and a great portion of the bottom is carpeted with meadows.

13 Voreppe, a flourishing village abounding in inns, chiefly resorted to by waggoners, of which the Petit Paris seems the best. A tolerably good cross-road, practicable for carriages, strikes off from Voreppe N. to the Grande Chartreuse and Les Echelles.

THE GRANDE CHARTREUSE.

"Per invias rupes, fera per juga,
Clivosque præruptos, sonantes
Inter aquas, nemorumque noctem."
GRAY.

"There are certain scenes that would awe an atheist into belief without the help of other argument. I am well persuaded St. Bruno was a man of no common genius to choose such a place for his retirement."—*Gray's Letters.*

N.B.—Those who cannot content themselves with Carthusian fare, viz. soupe maigre, herbs, and an omelet, had better take some cold meat and wine with them on this excursion.

The road from Voreppe to the Grande Chartreuse runs up a side valley shaded by walnut-trees, ascending steeply at first. At a distance of about 6 m., where the valley has widened out, the road from Voiron (*Inn :* Poste) and Le Gaz (p. 483) falls in, and 4 m. farther lies St. Laurent du Pont, a small village, with 2 poor and not very moderate inns. Here the traveller bound to the Chartreuse must turn out of the carriage-road, which continues on to Les Echelles, and the rest of the way must be performed on horseback or on foot. A mule or horse may be hired here for

Route 131.—La Grande Chartreuse.

4 or 5 frs.; a guide to show the way is unnecessary.

St. Laurent lies on the stream called Guiers Mort, up whose valley our way lies: it is at first bounded by gentle slopes covered with pasture below, and above with wood; but it soon contracts into a wooded gorge, not exceeded for picturesque grandeur among the Alps. At Fourvoirie, a little more than a mile from St. Laurent, near an iron-forge, now bankrupt and deserted, the mountains close together; the river, hemmed in by vertical precipices of vast height, is spanned by a single-arched bridge, and gushes forth from between the smoothed rocks with the swiftness of a cataract, in one deep sea-green flood. The jaws of the gorge seem barely rent asunder sufficiently to allow the stream to pass. The space cut out for the road between the torrent and the mountain precipice is occupied by a gateway, a pointed arch, faced by a modern and less picturesque one. It originally served for defence, and marked the limit of the domain of the monastery, or of the "Desert of St. Bruno" as it was styled. The bridge, the forge, the gateway, the river, and the precipices combine to form a most romantic natural picture, which will gratify the artist's eye, and has often employed the pencil. Within this grand portal the sides of the defile, up which the rough mule-path is carried, are rocks and precipices of limestone many hundred feet high; but their savageness is subdued by the dense foliage which lines them, so that it is a ride through a forest the whole way. The varied combinations of rock, tree, and river,—of rocks at a vast height overhead, inclining over the tree-tops and the wayfarer,—of the torrent foaming and rushing in the depths below, now spanned by a bridge, now studded by saw-mills,—its constant roar, as it frets and worms its way, indicating its presence, even when lost to view by the bends of the gorge or the intervention of rocks and trees,—and the varied forms and tints of the foliage, especially in autumn,—redeem the defile from all monotony. The road, though narrow, must have cost the monks much, and could only have been executed in a long time, and with great labour, being cut out of the rock great part of the way. Since the Revolution, however, which ruined the monks, it has gone to decay also, and in places is now barely passable, intersected by holes in which you might bury a mule, filled with mud, in which your animal plunges knee-deep. In places the torrents from the mountains have adopted it as their bed; in others it is no better than a steep staircase of bare rock. Owing to the badness of the road, no wheeled cart can pass, and the timber cut in the surrounding forests, and sawn into planks in the mills on the Guiers, is transported down the valley slung with ropes by the middle to the sides of mules. The deals thus nicely poised "traverse" like the needle of a compass, and at every movement of the animal perform segments of circles sweeping the road, and all that is upon it. It is by no means agreeable to meet a train of beasts so laden, with a precipice on one side of the narrow path, and a wall of rock on the other; nor are the huge sacks of charcoal more pleasant to encounter, as they at least leave their marks on the clothes, if they do not push you down the abyss, as the loaded animal brushes past. About half-way up, the path is carried by a narrow bridge, destitute of parapet, across the Guiers to its rt. bank, and after a very severe ascent it reaches a *second Gateway*, jammed in as it were between the precipice and a colossal Obelisk of limestone (pain de sucre), beyond which, in former times, no female could pass,—such was the rigid regulation of St. Bruno. A guard of soldiers was anciently posted here to keep the pass. The mountains here separate, and from the height you look down upon their sloping sides, covered with nearly unbroken forest, stretching over several minor valleys. The path, quitting the defile, turns to the l., still through woods, but slightly thinned, though the charcoal-burners are habitually settled in them. At the end of a ride of 1½ hr. the traveller reaches

La Grande Chartreuse, the Escurial

of Dauphiné, seated at a height of 1210 mèt. (4268 ft.) above the sea, shrouded in umbrageous woods, with only small patches of meadow and little or no level ground about it, being quite hemmed in by wooded heights. The position is not grand, but solitary, desolate, and monotonous, from the confined prospect. The *convent* is a huge unpicturesque pile, having neither age nor architecture to recommend it, since, owing to repeated conflagrations, which destroyed 6 or 8 previous buildings, very little of it is older than the 17th centy. Externally, its tent-like roofs of slate, higher than the body of the building which they cover, are its most conspicuous feature. Various straggling outhouses surround the main edifice: one is a cowhouse, another the infirmary, and one tenement is now set apart for females, who, though no longer restricted to the limits of the gateway, are not permitted to set foot in the convent itself. Male visitors are received by one of the fathers, called le Père Procureur, who is absolved from the obligation of silence, and conducted along its cold corridors, one of which is 660 ft. long, and includes part of a Gothic cloister, perhaps of the 15th centy., to the *burial-ground*, a simple enclosure without tombstones. The graves of the Generals of the order alone were formerly marked by stone crosses, but these were destroyed at the Revolution. When one of the monks dies, a cross of lath is set up over his head; but it soon disappears. Each father has a small habitation and garden to himself, in which a crucifix and a skull invite him to prayer and the contemplation of death. The cells are lined with plain deals, and furnished with bookshelves. No one is allowed to address a brother without special permission. The *chapel* is a lofty apartment, quite plain, in which service is performed by night and day. Strangers are not admitted between the evening and morning. The chapterhouse has been painted with portraits of the Generals of the order, of no great merit, and contains a marble statue of St. Bruno. The number of monks (pères) is now reduced to 33, who are dressed in white cloth, and 18 servitors (frères) clad in brown. By the rule of the order, the members were originally prohibited from speaking except on Sundays and fêtes; but this seems now not to be rigidly enforced. On certain days the monks walk abroad, and ascend in company to the chapel of St. Bruno; this they call "le Spaciment," and they afterwards dine together in the refectory; on other occasions they eat alone, excepting on fête-days. Previous to 1789 the monks were owners of St. Laurent du Pont and of many other villages: their tenants were well off, the ground well tilled, and they gave away much in charity. They were excellent landlords, managing their estates prudently, and were just to their tenants. The convent was stripped of its vast possessions at the Revolution, and escaped being sold only because no purchaser could be found for it; but the woods around, forfeited at that time, still belong to the government, and all that remains to the monks is a garden, with the right of cutting wood in the forest, and of pasturage for their cows, of which they have about 50. They depend much upon charity, and it is customary for strangers who visit the convent to make a small donation to the alms-box, and, if they remain for the night, they are charged for board and lodging. Male visitors are entertained with the humble fare of the convent, eggs, fish, and vegetables, and are lodged in a little cell provided with a small bed. Strangers are not allowed to remain beyond 2 days, and few would be tempted to prolong a sojourn in so melancholy a residence. The monks are famed for distilling *liqueurs*; the finest quality, *l' Elixir*,* is used as a medicine and cordial.

About 1½ m. higher up the mountain is the *Chapelle de St. Bruno*, where the founder of the order, descended from an opulent family at Cologne, established himself, 1084, having resolved to abandon the world. He retired to this spot, pointed out to him by Hugues Bishop of Grenoble, as a

* It may be had of Morel, in Piccadilly, of best quality.

desert quite beyond the haunts of man, and named, from a neighbouring hamlet, Cartuse, or Chartreuse, whence the order derives its name. Bruno lived in a cave or cleft of the rock, which is pointed out still higher up, and left no written rule for his order; that was compiled 44 years after his death by Dom Guignes.

At a less elevation than St. Bruno's is the chapel of the Virgin.

From *Le Grand Som* (sommet), the highest neighbouring cliff or peak, many hundred ft. above the convent, marked by a crucifix, an extensive view may be obtained, including part of the Lac de Bourget, on the side of Savoy.

There is only one other outlet from this upland valley, besides the road to St. Laurent du Pont. It is a path leading to the small hamlet of St. Pierre de Chartreuse, and Sapey, 3310 ft. above the sea-level. It is much shorter than the other, and Grenoble may be reached by it in 3 or 4 hrs. From the summit of the heights, as you descend towards that city, a beautiful view is obtained of the Vale of Grésivaudan.

The foundation of the Grande Chartreuse by St. Bruno is attributed, in the legendary histories of him, to the effect produced on him, by the apparition, after death, of a learned doctor of Paris, who, as the funeral procession was proceeding to the place of burial, burst from his coffin, exclaiming, "I am accused by the just judgment of God." This occurrence sank so deeply on St. Bruno's mind, that he, with 6 friends, determined to quit the world and retire into the wilderness. At first his only habitation was in the clefts of the rock, and the spot was inhabited at that time only by wild beasts. The first cells were higher up than the present convent, near the chapel of St. Bruno. These mere huts were swept away by an avalanche. The first convent, on the actual site of the present one, was built of wood by the 5th prior, Guignes, who died 1137. He first committed to writing the rules of the order, one of which runs thus:—
" Nous ne permettons jamais aux femmes d'entrer dans notre enceinte ; car nous savons que ni le sage, ni le prophète, ni le juge, ni l'hôte de Dieu, ni ses enfans, ni même le premier modèle sort de ses mains, n'ont pu échapper aux caresses ou aux tromperies des femmes. Qu'on se rappelle Salomon, David, Samson, Loth, et ceux qui ont pris les femmes qu'ils avoient choisies, et Adam lui-même; et qu'on sache bien que l'homme ne peut cacher du feu dans son sein sans que ses vêtemens soient embrasés, ni marcher sur des charbons ardents sans se brûler la plante des pieds."

Between Voreppe and Grenoble is, perhaps, the most picturesque portion of the *Vale of Grésivaudan*: the valley is here bounded by mountains precipitous as well as lofty. The road winds under such a one near the village of La Buisserade, which is particularly imposing. Under the dark woods and heights on the opposite bank lies Sassenage, and near this the river Drac pours itself into the Isère.

Little is seen of Grenoble, at a distance, in approaching from this side. A tall mountain buttress, nearly precipitous, projects forward to the Isère, leaving barely space for the road at its foot, and hides the town from view. This shoulder of rock has been recently studded with fortifications, rising one above another nearly to the clouds, 918 ft. above the river. They took more than 10 years to construct; the natural strength of the height having been increased by blasting and scarping the rock with gunpowder. The position of this fortress, the *Citadel of Grenoble, at an angle in the valley where the Isère makes a bend, and opposite the opening of the Vale of the Drac, gives it the command of these valleys, which would be swept by its guns. The chief work is the crowning battery, to defend the place in the rear, where it is surmounted by the superior heights of the Mont Rachet. It is called *La Bastille*, from an old feudal castle, a bit of which remains in the midst of modern works. It is worth while to ascend the hill of the Bastille, the Ehrenbreitstein of the

Isère, for the sake of the view. It embraces the town of Grenoble at your feet, laid open as on a plan, surrounded by its stellated ramparts, on a flat and fertile tongue of land watered by canals, bounded on one side by the Isère and by the Drac on the other. The courses of both rivers may be traced from their junction upwards; that of the Isère is very winding, and its valley is terminated by the snowy mass of Mont Blanc. In front stretches the straight road leading to Vizille, and pointing to the mouth of the valley of the Romanche, bounded by mountains of very picturesque outline.

Permission to enter the fortress must be obtained from the commandant at the little citadel in the town.

At the foot of the rock, crowned by the Bastille, stands the narrow suburb of St. Laurent, wedged in between precipices and the river. One side of its confined street has recently been pulled down and converted into a cheerful quay.

St. Laurent occupies the site of the original Gaulish town, called *Cularo*, mentioned in the letters of Plancus to Cicero: it changed its name, out of compliment to the Emperor Gratian, into that of *Gratianopolis*, whence Grenoble.

A handsome *stone bridge*, and a suspension wire bridge, replacing an old one of wood, connect this suburb with

14 GRENOBLE.—*Inns:* H. des Trois Dauphins, Rue Montorge; table-d'hôte 3 fr., breakfast à-la-fourchette 2 fr. In this house Napoleon lodged on his return from Elba: the room he occupied (No. 10) remains nearly in the same state.—H. de l'Europe, comfortable and reasonable, on the Grande Place.—H. des Ambassadeurs, very good.

Grenoble, formerly capital of Dauphiné, and now of the Dépt. de l'Isère, is a fortified city of 26,852 Inhab., pleasingly situated on the Isère, in a basin of great fertility and beauty, surrounded by high mountains, within which the Romanche and the Drac unite with the Isère, joining it a little below Grenoble. The full and rapid flood of the Isère, which is here confined within handsome *quays*, lined with fine houses, contributes much to the beauty of the town. Grenoble has been much improved and enlarged of late, and it is proposed to extend it considerably, and reconstruct the fortifications around it, so as to enclose a much larger space of ground. It has scarcely any fine public building: its churches are not remarkable: the *Cathedral* is a heavy mixture of ancient and modern masonry, having been ravaged and almost destroyed in the 16th centy. by the ferocious Baron des Adrets, who also destroyed, in the ch. of *St. André*, the monuments of the Dauphins. *St. Laurent* is the oldest church.

One of the most pleasing features of the town is its *Public Garden*, on the l. bank of the Isère, shaded with umbrageous trees, planted with flowers, and set out with orange-trees in pots. It was originally laid out by the Duc de Lesdiguières, and attached to his palace, now the *Préfecture*.

In the midst of the neighbouring Place St. André is a bronze colossal *Statue of Bayard*, the "chevalier sans peur et sans reproche," who was born in the valley of the Isère, and buried in the neighbouring church of the Minimes, (?) some say in the cathedral, where there is an inscription to his memory. It is meant to represent him in the moment of death, mortally wounded, kissing the cross formed by the hilt of his sword; but it is theatrical, and unworthy of the hero. It stands opposite the *Palais de Justice*, originally the palace of the Dauphin, the most interesting old building in the town, retaining a Gothic oriel, and other portions in the style of the Renaissance. The Place *Grenette* is the largest open space in the town : in it are the chief cafés and *diligence offices*. There are several handsome *Fountains*; observe one on the quai—a Lion crushing a Snake.

Attached to the *College* is a *Museum*, in which may be seen some of the old busts of the Dauphins, removed from their Palace. Here is a large collection of *paintings*, mostly mediocre: the best seem to be a portrait by *Philip de*

DAUPHINÉ.   *Route* 131.—*Grenoble—Environs.*   489

Champagne of Jean Duvergier de Hauranne, a member of Port-Royal; a Venetian in Velvet, by *Tintoret* (?); the Entry of the Emperor Sigismond into Mantua; a sketch by *J. Romano*; Pope Julius II., do. (?); St. Gregory, with Prudence and Force, by *Rubens* (or one of his school). Here are 2 bronze lions of Byzantine art, brought from an abbey at St. Marcellin.

The *library* contains some books brought from the Grande Chartreuse; also portraits of some of the celebrities of Grenoble—Vaucanson the mechanician, and Dolomieu, with busts of Mably and Condillac.

In the *cabinet of natural history* may be seen specimens of the minerals of Dauphiné,—its huge rock crystals, 2 feet long and 1 foot broad, its axinite, anatase, &c., with silver ore from Allemont, and gold from La Gardette, both mines near Bourg d'Oysans, no longer worked : but the collection is dirty and ill-arranged. Here are stuffed specimens of the wild animals from the neighbouring Alps, the bear and wolf.

A *Museum* of Natural History has been built on the S. side of the town, and merits notice.

Diligences daily (4 or 5), to Lyons, in 10 hours; to Vienne; to Valence; to Chambéry (2); to Marseilles, by Sisteron; to Gap; to St. Laurent; to Bourg d'Oysans.—*N.B.* The gates of Grenoble are closed at 11 P.M., and there is no means of gaining admittance except an order from the commandant. Those who are shut out must sleep where they are, and there is no inn, outside.

No one should omit to ascend the fortifications on the rt. bank of the Isère (p. 487): the *view* from them is one of the finest in Dauphiné.

Though Grenoble itself is deficient in objects of curiosity, the country around has great beauty, and many interesting excursions may be made from it: the chief of these are,

1. To the *Grande Chartreuse* (described at p. 484). There are two ways, either *a*, by Voreppe and St. Laurent du Pont, practicable as far as that place in carriages, and traversed by a daily diligence in summer, by which one can go in the morning and return in the evening; or *b*, by Sapey, a mule-path, the shorter of the two, by which the convent may be reached in 4 hrs. The most interesting part of the excursion, however, is the wooded gorge on the other road, between St. Laurent du Pont and the convent.

2. To Sassenage, a beautifully situated village on the opposite side of the Drac, in the midst of thick woods, and falling waters, and fine pasturages, producing an excellent *cheese*, resembling that of Roquefort. The distance is about 5 m.; a one-horse carriage may be hired in Grenoble to go and return for 5 francs. It is a pleasant drive. A turning to the rt. leads out of La Cours, the long avenue extending from Grenoble to Vizille, and conducts you to the iron suspension-bridge over the Drac. The river is here retained within stout dykes, originally the work of Lesdiguières; the plain is intersected with canals for the sake of irrigation. A small streamlet, a tributary of the Furon, which traverses the valley of Sassenage, bursts out of a hole in the limestone mountain above the village. The rock is pierced by several small caves, rather difficult of access.

3. *Château Bayard*, the birthplace of the model of French chivalry, is about 27 m. up the valley of the Isère, on the l. bank. (See Rte. 132.)

4. 7½ m. from Grenoble, at the mouth of the gorge of the Sonnant, is the fine feudal castle *Uriage;* and near it Mineral *Baths*, with a large hotel, affording very good accommodation. The waters are sulphureous, rising near a junction of the granite with the lias rock, at a temperature of 70° Fahrenheit.

5. *La Tour St. Venin*, on the hill of Parisot, on the l. bank of the Drac, classed among the wonders of Dauphiné, from a vulgar belief that no poisonous reptiles can live on it, is a fine point of view, 4 or 5 m. from Grenoble, commanding the junction of the valleys of the Isère and Drac. It appears to have been a chapel or hermitage, attached to a castle now swept away, dedicated to St. Verin; and that a misprint or mispronunciation gave

Y 3

rise to the present name and to the vulgar fable.

The staple manufacture of Grenoble is that of *leather gloves:* it is the most considerable in France. They are made of the skins of kid, the best sorts of which are obtained from Annonay, of chamois (beaver), and of lamb. Much leather also comes from Romans and Milhau. The gloves are chiefly sewed by the hand by women, between 4000 and 5000 being employed in and about the town in cutting out and sewing; machinery is also employed.

Grenoble was the first place which openly received Napoleon on his return from Elba. After having been joined at La Mûre by the troops sent out against him (see p. 492), and still nearer at hand by Labedoyère, he approached the walls, which were strongly guarded by troops and cannon. Although the garrison dared not disobey their commandant by opening the gates, yet not a shot was fired on him; he was permitted to come up to the gates and direct against them a howitzer to blow them open. Once within the walls he was received both by citizens and soldiers with the utmost enthusiasm, and borne in triumph, amidst shouts of " Vive l'Empereur !" to the Hôtel des Trois Dauphins. The Bourbonist governor was obliged to decamp, leaving him at the head of a force of 7000 men. Before the Emperor retired to rest the gates of the Porte de Bonne, which he had been obliged to burst open, were unhinged and brought before his windows by the young men of the town, instead of the keys, of which they could not obtain possession to present them to him.

ROUTE 132.

VALENCE ON THE RHÔNE TO GRENOBLE AND CHAMBÉRY, THROUGH THE VALLEY OF GRÉSIVAUDAN.

147 kilom. = 92 Eng. m.
Diligence daily in 11 hours.

The ascent of the valley of the Isère is a very agreeable journey, the country being alike remarkable for its beauty and fertility. The river is spanned by 12 or 15 iron-wire suspension-bridges, erected for the most part within a few years. Our road crosses it at Bourg du Péage, by a stone bridge, connecting that place with

18 Romans (*Inn:* Coupe d'Or ?), a thriving town of 9972 Inhab., in a picturesque situation, still partly surrounded by ramparts and flanking towers, one of which leans considerably out of the perpendicular. The ch. of *St. Antoine* is said to be a curious Gothic edifice.

At this place the last Dauphin, or native prince of Dauphiné, Humbert II., having lost his only son, who leaped from his nurse's arms out of a window of the castle of Mazard into the Isère, and was drowned, signed his abdication, 1349, by which he resigned his domains to Philippe de Valois, on condition that they should be an appanage of the heir to the French crown, and that he should bear the title of Dauphin.

18 Fauries, in the Dépt. de l'Isère.

At La Sône, where the Isère is crossed by a wire bridge, is an old *castle*, now turned into a silk-mill, part of the machinery for which was made by Vaucanson, who was a native of Dauphiné.

14 St. Marcellin. *Inn:* Petit Paris, not good. This little town, of 3344 Inhab., is situated near the Isère. On the height above it, called Mont Surjeu, is a fine terrace walk, commanding one of the best views of the valley.

11 L'Allegrerie.

From the top of the descent to Tullins, commencing at the inn of Morette, a beautiful view opens out over the valley of the Isère, and the serpentine windings of the river, backed by the chain of Alps, and by the Grand Som, which surmounts the Grande Chartreuse, in front. The charms of the landscape, the diversified nature of the ground, the variety of crops, the number and denseness of the trees, and the luxuriant productiveness of the valley, one of the very finest and richest in France, appear to be constantly increasing as far as

11 Tullins (*Inn:* La Poste), a town of 3500 Inhab., only remarkable for its situation in a spot teeming with fer-

tility. This is a great market for hemp grown in the vicinity.

The stream of the Fure, crossed a little beyond Tullins, is studded with iron-forges.

At Moirans, a town of 2500 Inhab., we enter the high road to Lyons (Rte. 131), and the valley of Grésivaudan at

13 Voreppe, which, with the excursion thence to the *Grande Chartreuse*, and the remainder of the route to

14 GRENOBLE, are described in Rte. 131.

There are two roads up the valley of the Isère above Grenoble.

a. On the rt. bank of the river is the post-road, and the shortest way to Chambéry. It is carried along a sort of terrace at the roots of the mountains which rise abruptly towards the Grande Chartreuse. The bridle-road thither turns off to the l. by Sapey at Montbonot. The lower slopes are sprinkled with the country seats of the Grenoblois.

21 Lumbin. It is asserted that goître and crétinism are unknown on this the sunny side of the valley, while they abound on the opposite bank of the Isère.

10 Le Touvet. *Inn*, clean ; vines and walnuts abound. Beautiful scenery.

On the opposite side of the Isère rise the ruins of Château Bayard.

A little farther on our road passes on the rt. *Fort Barraux,* commanding it and the passage up and down the valley ; it was built by Charles Emmanuel Duke of Savoy, in the presence of a French army, commanded by Lesdiguières. That general, on being reproved by Henri IV. for his inertness in allowing this to proceed, replied, " Your Majesty has need of a fortress on the side of Savoy, to hold in check that of Montmeillant ; and since the duke is willing to undertake the expense, we may as well permit it, and as soon as it is properly furnished with cannon and provision I undertake to capture it ;" and he kept his word, surprising the fort by moonlight, March 13, 1598. It was afterwards strengthened by Vauban. It commands a charming view from its elevated position. The road, as it rises over the base of the hill, overlooks the charming valley of the Isère, with the river itself, and in the N.E. the snowy top of Mont Blanc—a scene of grandeur and beauty scarcely to be surpassed.

10 Chapareillan. Here is the French custom-house. As there are 3 to pass on entering from Savoy, it is as well to have the baggage examined and plombé here ; the charge is small and it saves further delay. The Mont Grenier rises 3700 ft. high, close above this village.

16 *Chambéry*, described in the HANDBOOK FOR SWITZERLAND.

b. The road on the l. bank of the Isère is interesting and picturesque, but is not furnished with post-horses.

At St. Domène there is a wire suspension-bridge over the Isère: others have been erected at Brignon and La Gache.

At Tencin, which is about half-way, the traveller, while his horses rest, may explore a pretty shady glen, traversed by a gushing stream, leaping in a miniature fall down the rocks.

Goncelin.

[A road strikes off to the rt. from hence to the iron mines and works of *Allevard*, 6 m. distant. They are situated in a picturesque gorge or rent, stretching from the lias up to the granite mountains. Within a short distance of the junction of the lias with the primitive talc-slate rise sulphur springs, much used medicinally. Higher up, in the valley of the Breda, is La Ferrière, a poor hamlet, from which a walk of 5 hrs. leads to *Les Sept Laux* or Lacs, up a steep ascent. These 7 small and beautiful tarns lie at the bottom of a deep ravine, fed by springs. It is a wild and gloomy spot.]

About 27 m. from Grenoble stands *Château Bayard ;* a foot-path leads up to it from the ch. of Grignan. Its remains are situated on a height which commands the road, and a fine view of the beautiful valley from its terraces. In the mouldering turrets and shattered walls there is little beauty, but as the birth-place of the " Chevalier sans peur et sans reproche," they possess great interest. A gateway with the two flanking towers is the part best preserved. The walls of the castle are, in some places, 6 ft. thick. The situation of the room in which Bayard was born (1476) is pointed out by those who show the place, but without authority for what they state. Nearly opposite, beyond the Isère, is the modern fort Barraux. The conspicuous mountain of La Tuille, remarkable for the contortions of the strata in its limestone precipices, appears to close the valley at its upper end.

Pontecharra, the frontier town of France, is about a mile distant. (Inns very dirty and uncomfortable.)

Before a hired carriage can cross the frontier it is necessary that the driver procure from the douaniers a permit (termed in French *caution*, in Savoyard *bolletone*), containing a description of the horse and carriage, which enables them to pass without paying duty.

ROUTE 134.

GRENOBLE TO MARSEILLES, BY GAP AND SISTERON.—PROTESTANT VALLEYS OF DAUPHINÉ.

282 kilom. = 175 Eng. m.

A *courier* goes daily to Gap in 14 hours, taking passengers:—also a *diligence*.

This is a very hilly and a little more circuitous way to Marseilles than the new road by La Croix Haute. (Rte. 135.)

The road on quitting Grenoble is carried within an avenue of trees across the plain of the Drac, at a short distance from its rt. bank, in a straight line from the Porte de la Graille, as far as Claix, where there is a fine *bridge* of a single arch, built on dry land by Lesdiguières, who afterwards turned the course of the river below it. Here the new road by Croix Haute crosses the river, while ours, turning to the l. along high dykes, passes near the junction of the rivers, the Grèze on the l., and the Romanche on the rt., with the Drac. We here bid adieu for the present to the Drac, and follow up its tributary, the Romanche, as far as

18 Vizille (*Inns* wretched), an ancient town of 2750 Inhab., on the rt. bank of the Romanche, carrying on some manufactures of cotton-spinning, calico-weaving, &c., chiefly founded by the Périer family, one of whom was the French minister Casimir Périer.

The *Château*, partly destroyed by fire 1825, was built, between 1611 and 1620, by Lesdiguières, the Protestant commander, and governor of Dauphiné under Henri IV., "ce fin reynard," as the Duke of Savoy called him, who compelled the peasants on his estate to contribute their unpaid labour in constructing it, conformably with the old tax called Corvée. In 1788 the Estates of Dauphiné, assembled by Louis XVI. to appease the discontent and outcries of the people of the province, met in this building, and here prepared the bold remonstrance against aristocratic privileges, and in favour of popular representation by the assembly of the Tiers Etat, which served as a signal for the Revolution. This event occurred a year before the opening of the States General at Versailles; Barnave and Mounier were the leading orators. The actual building is now a calico and silk-printing work, and belongs to the family Périer. One apartment is preserved as it was in the time of Lesdiguières, and a bronze bas-relief of him, on horseback, still exists.

The route to Briançon and the Mont Genèvre, across the grand mountains of Bourg d'Oysans, here turns to the l. (Rte. 137.)

The road to Gap crosses the Romanche beyond Vizille, and proceeds by a very steep ascent, requiring 2 hours to surmount. The view from its slope over Vizille and the Romanche, and over an intervening hilly ridge to Grenoble and the valley of the Isère, is very fine.

7 Lafrey.

On the l. of the road 3 small lakes, la Motte, l'Aveillan, and Pierre Châtel, are passed in succession. Napoleon on his way from Elba, with little more than 200 men, was encountered, a little to the S. of Lafrey, by a battalion despatched by the governor of

Grenoble and drawn up across the road to intercept his march, between the hill on one side, and the stream which runs out of the lake on the other. Napoleon, on coming in sight of them, turned off into a meadow on the rt., and sent forward Bertrand to parley with the commanding officer and soldiers opposed to him. The two parties remained thus an hour in view of each other, when Napoleon, advancing to the battalion, opened his grey riding-coat, and baring his breast, so as to show the Star of the Legion of Honour, exclaimed, "Si quelqu'un de vous veut tuer son Empereur, qu'il tire." They were most of them soldiers of his own armies, and their commanding officer had served under him in Egypt. The command given by their officer to "fire" was unheeded by them; the ranks were broken, and the veterans crowded around him; some, embracing his knees, swore never to quit him; many burst into tears, while the air resounded with the cry of " Vive l'Empereur !" On his way hence to Grenoble, at the head of this reinforcement, he was met by the regiment of Labedoyère, which at once joined his ranks, their colonel at their head.

After leaving behind the 3 lakes some coal-mines are passed on the rt.; they are worked to a considerable extent, and produce anthracite coal (charbon-à-pierre).

14 La Mure (*Inn:* Poste, dear), an industrious town, on the top of a high hill, visible from afar; it abounds in mean cabarets and cafés; the chief occupation of the people is nail-making. Capital honey here. The mineral springs of *La Motte* occur near an outbreak of granite in a ravine extremely narrow, with a temperature of 45° Réaum. They are conveyed on mules' backs to the Baths.

A long-continued and very circuitous descent leads into the valley of the Drac; the road, however, does not approach it closely, but skirts the shattered and deep gorges of its tributaries until a favourable opportunity occurs for crossing them. It is a hilly stage to

11 Souchons. The mountains of the district are mostly of the Jura limestone formation, and are readily disintegrated by the washing of the rivers and by the weather. One very conspicuous conical summit rising on the W. is called the Mont Aiguille, or Mont Inaccessible, and was regarded as one of the wonders of Dauphiné. It is 6562 ft. above the sea-level. Another mountain, still higher, called L'Obieux, rises above

14 Corps; no good inns.

On the opposite (l.) bank of the Drac are the shapeless and uninteresting ruins of the *Château Lesdiguières,* built by the Constable as a resting-place after death, for he never inhabited it living. His body, transferred hither from Italy, was torn up at the Revolution, and his monument removed to Gap.

We enter the Dépt. des Hautes Alpes and cross the Drac, before reaching the relay of

14 Guinguette de Boyer.

St. Bonnet, on the rt. bank of the Drac, was the birthplace of Lesdiguières.

The upper part of the valley of the Drac, which we now leave on the l., is called *Champsaur* (campus aureus); it is fertile and picturesque, and a large portion of its inhabitants are Protestants. They formed part of the flock of Felix Neff, who often resided at St. Laurent. This valley communicates at its upper extremity, by the difficult pass of the *Col d'Orcières,* with the village of Dormilleuse, and the sterile and dreary Val Fressinière (Rte. 139).

10 Brutinel. In this stage the high chain which separates the vale of the Drac from that in which Gap is situated is crossed by a long and tedious ascent, requiring 2 hours to surmount.

13 *Gap.* Inns: H. du Nord;—de Provence; only tolerable. This little mountain capital, the chef-lieu of the Dépt. des Hautes Alpes, with 7726 Inhab., need scarcely detain the traveller, since it possesses no objects of curiosity, but is pleasingly situated, approached by avenues of walnuts, and surrounded by slopes on which

the vine still flourishes, although the height above the sea amounts to 2424 ft. In the *Préfecture*, a modern building, is deposited the monument of the Duc de Lesdiguières, François de Bonne, who, after having been the successful leader and defender of the Protestants in Dauphiné, abjured his faith for the rank of Constable of France, imitating, in his apostacy, the example of his master Henri IV. The monument was originally erected over his grave, in his own castle on the Drac, the spot chosen by himself, but was torn thence by revolutionary spoilers. It is of little merit as a work of sculpture, and consists of a white marble effigy, stiffly reclining on his side, in armour.

Gap was the ancient *Vapincum*: it was burnt 1692, by Victor Amedeus of Savoy. Here is an experimental Horticultural Garden.

William Farel, the Reformer, was born in the hamlet of Tareau, just outside of Gap: his first sermon was preached in the mill of Burée, but his followers soon drove out the Roman Catholics from Gap, and he took possession of the pulpit of St. Colomb.

The road from Gap to Briançon is given in Rte. 139. That to Marseilles descends a tributary valley of the Durance, and reaches the borders of that turbulent river at

17 La Saulce: passing previously, a little on the l., the ruined *castle* of *Tallard*, once the property of the family d'Auriac, now of that of Béranger: the ruins are extensive and picturesque.

16 Rourebeau.

The considerable river Buech is crossed before entering

14 Sisteron (*Inn:* H. Wagram, tolerable). This antiquated fortress, which once commanded the passage from Dauphiné into Provence, is composed of narrow dirty streets, cooped up within useless ramparts (4356 Inhab.). It is built at the foot of a perpendicular rock, which is surmounted by a *citadelle*, once the prison of Casimir, brother of Ladislaus VII. of Poland; but so many attempts were made by his friends for his rescue that he was removed to Vincennes. The works now in progress to strengthen it will, it is said, render it impregnable. There is a curious ancient *Cathedral* here; and fine remains of a monastery, now turned to lay purposes. Sisteron has a picturesque exterior, and its position in a sort of defile of the Durance, here hemmed in by cliffs, is well worthy of the pencil of the artist.

Here the roads to Grenoble by La Croix Haute (Rte. 135), and to Nice by Digne (Rte. 136), diverge from our route.

23 Peyruis.

12 Brillane. The Durance, throughout the greater part of its course, is nothing better than a large devastating torrent, at no time a picturesque object, and in summer so far diminished as to be incapable of covering its bed, so that, though its volume is always considerable, its shrunken rivulets of water seem nearly lost amidst beds of gravel and rolled stones, so broad as in places to appear like a dried lake bed.

15 Manosque (*Inns:* Poste; fair. Petit Versailles) is a flourishing little town, with double the population of Digne, the chef-lieu of the Dépt. des Basses Alpes. The olive is cultivated to a considerable extent in its vicinity.

20 Mirabeau. About $\frac{1}{4}$ m. from the post-house, on a height, is the ruined *Château* of the family of the celebrated leader and orator of the French Revolution. He frequently resided here in his early years, but was not born here. It is flanked by 4 round towers; and a group of poor houses form a hamlet about its base.

We are now within the limits of scorched and dreary Provence (Sect. VI.). About a mile from the post-house the Durance, hemmed in between high cliffs, is spanned by a suspension bridge, by which the road is transferred to its l. bank, and is carried along it partly on terraces.

11 Peyrolles.

The road begins to ascend near Meyrargues; and a little beyond the village, which is surmounted by a stately castle, the remains of an ancient aqueduct of brick, designed by the Romans, it is said, to convey the water of the Durance to Aix, are passed. From the top of the hill which succeeds, the eye wanders for many miles down the vale of the Durance, traversed by two more suspension bridges in this part of its course.

The new and wonderful *Canal* which is to supply Marseilles with water commences on the Durance, near the suspension bridge of Pertuis. (See Rte. 129.)

A considerable tract of well-cultivated table-land is traversed, commanding a view of Mont St. Victoire on the E. (see p. 479), before descending the long hill which leads into

21 Aix,   } in Rte. 128.
29 MARSEILLES,

ROUTE 135.

GRENOBLE TO MARSEILLES, BY THE CROIX HAUTE.

277 kilom. = 172 Eng. m.
This road was opened 1841, and is excellent. The *diligences* now follow it, having abandoned the old road. As there are many precipices, and few parapet-walls, the journey was at first attended with danger. No one should attempt this road without being prepared to rough it. It is well to engage post-horses to be in readiness at a fixed time beforehand.

There is *no inn* fit to sleep in before reaching Sisteron.

The relays, after crossing the plain of the Drac, below Vizille (Rte. 134), are
16 Vif.
18 Monestier de Clermont.

The country near Grenoble is very beautiful; woods of walnut and chestnut abound; in the distance snowy peaks appear.
17 Clelles.
14 Lalley. The mountains assume a very wild and desolate appearance, and there is scarcely any vegetation, on approaching
11 Lus la Croix Haute.
14 La Faurie.
8 Aspres les Veynes.
15 Serres.

16 Larogne. No inn, but a wretched cabaret.
17 Sisteron (*Inn*: see Rte. 134).
131 MARSEILLES. (Rte. 127 and 134.)

N. B. Additional information respecting this road and its inns is requested by the Editor.

ROUTE 136.

LYONS TO NICE, BY GRENOBLE, DIGNE, AND GRASSE.

This is the shortest route from Lyons to Nice; but a considerable portion of the road is very hilly; and it is by no means the most comfortable as regards accommodation. It is, however, a fine road, well engineered, and passes through magnificent mountain scenery on the grandest scale. The distance between Digne and Grasse is not furnished with post-horses, consequently the traveller must hire horses at Digne for the whole distance, which takes 2 days to perform. Diligence (very ill-managed) from Grenoble to Digne, stopping at Sisteron 5 hrs. and at Gap 3, in the middle of the night! From Lyons to Grenoble (see Rte. 131). Thence to Sisteron (see Rte. 134). The road is carried hence along the l. bank of the Durance, and then alongside one of its tributaries, the Bléone, which overspreads the valley with débris, to

20 Malijay.
20 Digne (*Inns*: Petit Paris; Bras d'Or), a town of 4119 Inhab., of narrow, steep, and dirty streets, and mean houses, stands in the midst of a cultivated oasis of this desert, through which the torrent passes, restrained within dykes. It is chef-lieu of the Dépt. des Basses Alpes, and its chief building is the Préfecture, once the Bishop's Palace, a very ordinary building.

The ancient *Cathedral* exists only in a scanty ruined fragment on the road to Barcelonnette, and is very curious.

Pliny mentions the town under the name Dina.

About 1½ m. off are *Warm Baths*, supplied by thermal springs, recommended in cases of rheumatism. The accommodation is very simple.

The philosopher Pierre Gassend, or *Gassendi*, was born at the neighbouring village, Champtercier, of poor parents, 1592.

29 Barrême (*Inn*: H. du Midi, tolerable). 1750 Inhab.

25 Castellane (*Inn*: Sauvère, tolerable), a small town of 2160 Inhab., at the foot of an escarped rock, on the Verdon, surrounded by precipices, and in the midst of scenes of the highest grandeur. The road hence commands magnificent views over the coast of the Mediterranean — Nice, Antibes, Ile Ste. Marguerite, and Sardinia.

24 Logis-du-Pin.
22 Nans.
18 *Grasse*. *Inn*: H. des Ministres, comfortable; best between Nice and Grenoble. Grasse (12,888 Inhab.) has, after Paris, the most extensive manufacture of perfumery in France, made from the flowers, roses, &c., which flourish in its neighbourhood, favoured by the mild climate. Some of the nursery-gardens near Cannes (10 m. S.) produce annually 200,000 frs.-worth of flowers of orange, lemon, heliotrope, hyacinth, which are sent to Grasse to supply its distilleries. The views of the Alps from its *Public Walks* are very striking; so is that from the high road. It is a drive of 6 hrs. by

23 k. Antibes to }
24 Nice.   } Rte. 129.

ROUTE 137.

GRENOBLE TO BRIANÇON, BY BOURG D'OYSANS AND THE COL DE LAUTERET, AND BY THE MONT GENÈVRE TO SUSA.—EXCURSION UP THE VAL ST. CHRISTOPHE.

To Briançon is about 50 Eng. m.

This magnificent carriage-road, begun by Napoleon in 1804, has been many years in progress, under the direction of the meritorious engineer of Mont Cenis, M. Dausse, but, owing to the extent and difficulty of the works to be executed, it was not completed until 1851. Between Briançon and Grenoble *diligences* run daily; and it is practicable for the whole distance, with a light carriage, when the ground is clear of snow. The accommodation on the way, as yet, is bad. "It abounds with some of the finest scenes in the Alps."

As far as Vizille the road is the same as Rte. 134, but, instead of crossing the Romanche, it adheres to its rt. bank, and enters a narrow and finely-wooded glen, threaded by the river for many miles, called Combe de Gavet.

In 1081, a landslip, or fall of a mountain, washed down by the fury of the torrents, formed such an accumulation of earth at the upper end of this defile as to dam up the river Romanche until it formed a lake, which covered the entire plain of Bourg d'Oysans, and rose to a height of 60 or 80 ft. It lasted for two centuries until 1229, when the dyke burst, and the emancipated flood swept all before it, cultivated lands and villages, as far as the city of Grenoble, part of which it also destroyed.

At the upper end of the combe, where the valley opens out, the river Olle flows into the Romanche from the N. [A few miles up it are the iron-foundries of Allemont and the lead and silver mine of Chalanche. At the head of the valley of Allemont a difficult and dangerous pass leads across to the *Sept Laux*, 7 small lakes, one of the "wonders" of Dauphiné, abounding in trout. From the Sept Laux you descend to the iron-mines and Baths of Allevard in the valley of the Isère (Rte. 13?).]

Bourg d'Oysans, 7½ leagues (*Inns*: very bad: Poste, civil;—Chez Manuel —? Etoile), a town of 3052 Inhab., possessing a manufacture of cotton. It lies in a swampy flat more than a mile broad, hemmed in by rocky precipices of great height, in the face of which is the gold-mine of *La Gardelle*. Bourg d'Oysans is about 42 Eng. m. distant from Briançon.

["An interesting excursion may be made from Bourg d'Oysans to La Bérarde, in the upper part of the valley of St. Christophe, 10 hours' walk from the Bourg. The only good Inn on the whole route is at the finely situated village of Venos, 3 hrs. from Bourg d'Oysans, where there are tolerable quarters, but the traveller must carry his own provisions thither. St. Christophe is 2 hrs. above Venos. Between the 2 hamlets a mountain has fallen in pieces, nearly filling the valley with huge fragments through which the path and the river wind. La Bérarde lies at the foot of Mont Pelvoux, the highest mountain in France, or in the S. Alps; its loftiest summit—the Point d'Arcines or des Ecrins—being 13,123 ft. above the sea-level. The scenery of the whole valley, and especially at and above La Bérarde, may vie in grandeur and savage sterility with any in the Alps. The valley is less known than Chamouni was before the time of Wyndham and Pocock; but a day devoted to visiting it from Bourg d'Oysans will always be remembered with gratification by the lover of sublime scenery."]

A char might be hired at Bourg d'Oysans to cross the Lauteret to Briançon for 18 or 20 fr., in 12 or 14 hrs. About 3 m. above Bourg d'Oysans the plain terminates, and the Veneon, coming from the l., pours itself into the Romanche. Between these 2 streams rises the snowy Mont de Lens. The road is carried along a tremendous gorge called *Les Infernets*, on the N. side of this mountain, through which the Romanche forces its way, by terraces and tunnels cut out of the solid rocks. Two very long tunnels have thus been formed for the passage of the road. The first of these, more than 234 yards long, and very wide and high, is one of the finest works of the kind in the Alps.

The gorge of Infernets is succeeded by a sterile upland valley, strewn with rocks. A little above this, on the l., is a fine waterfall, called *Le Saut de la Pucelle*. The road is completed, and fit for carriages, with the exception of some cuttings near the mouth of Les Infernets, as far as Le Dauphin (4 leagues), in a bare and dreary situation, with scarce a habitation around.

Between Le Dauphin and La Grave a stupendous narrow gorge is traversed by the Romanche, remarkable for the extraordinary grandeur and utter nakedness of the precipices of gneiss which form its sides. It is called *La Combe de Malval*. These precipices are the escarpments of vast mountains covered over with eternal snow and glaciers, which terminate at the edge of the cliff overhanging the combe; and numerous streams descend from them in falls across the road.

At the end of the gorge de Malval the road ceases, or was not made passable for carriages in 1849. The passengers by the diligence walk from the one to the other (1½ hour), where a fresh vehicle takes them on.

We pass from the Dépt. d'Isère into that of the Hautes Alpes, about a mile before reaching the miserable village of La Grave, grandly situated on a projecting rock, backed on the S. by vast snowy heights. There is a small and tolerably clean *cabaret* at La Grave. The church is worth looking at, and the view from it is splendid. [A long day's walk leads hence over the *Col des Infernets*, a wild and high but not difficult pass, to St. Jean Maurienne.]

There are copper-mines worked in the apparently inaccessible cliffs above La Grave; the ore is sent down through wooden tubes attached to the face of the rocks, and includes fine crystals of copper. A steep ascent succeeds over a crumbling, black, slaty limestone. The Glacier of La Grave is in full view, while the Romanche dashes down in a fine fall into the depths below.

Villars d'Arène (4 leagues), another wretched village, is situated at the foot of the pass of the Lauteret, which the route now ascends, leaving on the rt. the Romanche, whose source is in an upland valley to the S., at the foot of the snowy *Mont Pelvoux*.

The mountain opposite Villars d'Arène exhibits a section of granite or gneiss rock overlying limestone, of great interest to the geologist.

The *Col of the Lauteret*, which separates the waters of the Romanche from those of the Guisanne, is 6869 ft. above the sea-level, about 500 ft.

higher than the Mont Genèvre. Its summit is covered with some of the most beautiful pasturages in the Alps. Near the crest of the Col, which is not more than 50 yards broad, is an ancient

Hospice (2 leagues), founded by Humbert II., Count of Dauphiné. The view from the summit is fine: the Montagne d'Oursine (13,123 ft. high) is a grand object on the S.W.; from the glacier at its base rises the Guisanne, while in that of Tabouchet, to the S., is one of the sources of the Romanche. The Mont Pelvoux from this point appears lower, because more distant.

A steep descent leads down the valley of the Guisanne by Le Lauzet and Le Casset, near the glacier of Lusciale, to

Monestier (4 leagues), a town of 2500 Inhab., with several indifferent Inns, 12 m. from Briançon, having in its neighbourhood *hot sulphureous springs*, used for baths, and so abundant, that within a short distance of the source they serve to turn a mill. The valley around, and from hence to Briançon, is fertile, well cultivated, and studded with numerous villages; the upper slopes clothed with fir woods, while the view of the course of the Guisanne, backed in the distance by Briançon, and its extraordinary group of forts, piled one over the other, forms a magnificent scene.

From Monestier to Briançon (15 kilom.) the road is completed. This part of the valley is remarkable for its populousness, there being not less than 22 villages between the foot of the Lauteret and

15 *Briançon.* Inn: H. de la Paix, not clean; but great civility and tolerable cuisine.

Briançon, a first-class fortress of great strength, a sort of Alpine Gibraltar, commanding the passage from Italy into France by the Mont Genèvre, is a most picturesque and imposing object at a distance. It stands at the meeting of 3 valleys, at the foot of an isolated and escarped rock, whose summit is crowned by the *Fort du Château*, so named from an old castle, now demolished. Many of the streets of the town are so highly inclined that they are impassable for vehicles, and the carriage-road makes a circuit, and enters it by a series of zigzags. All the heights around are converted into points of defence; fort rises over fort up to the very clouds, which frequently shroud from view the upper works. Where the position is not inaccessible through natural precipices, it has been rendered so by artificial escarpments. The rivers Guisanne and Clairée, which unite beneath the walls of the town with the infant Durance, run in deep gullies, whose sides are precipices, forming as it were natural ditches to the fortress. The principal works are on the l., or E., bank of the Clairée, whose deep and savage gorge is crossed by a bridge of a single bold arch, 130 ft. span, and 168 ft. above the water, constructed 1734. An excellent road leads, in zigzags, up the abrupt heights from this bridge to the different forts, which communicate with each other by subterraneous ways. The largest fort is called *Les Trois Têtes*, because it occupies a triple-headed crag; on a level with it is *Fort Dauphin* ; 330 ft. higher, towards the Durance, is *Fort Randouillet*, whose batteries are partly excavated in the rock ; nearly 2000 ft. above this is the *Donjon* ; and finally the *Point du Jour*, commanding all the other defences. The different points, or mamelons of rock on which these forts are built, all belong to the *Mont Infernet*, whose summit still supports the ruins of a fort built in 1814, at a height of 9350 ft. above the sea-level. From its crest the Mont Pelvoux is a magnificent object, and the valley Des Prés or De Neuvache, down which pours the Clairée, and that leading up to the Mont Genèvre, are well seen. Permission to visit the forts may be obtained from the commandant in the town. If the weather be clear, it is worth while to ascend to Randouillet, on account of the view up the beautiful valley of Guisanne, studded with villages, and towards the Col de Lauteret (p. 497), otherwise the traveller may content himself with seeing the Fort du Château. The fortifications of Briançon have been greatly strengthened of late, and the improvements are not yet completed.

In the town itself there is nothing to see. The Port d'Embrun bore this inscription: "Aux braves Briançonnois, pour la conservation de cette ville, Louis-Philippe reconnaissant:" alluding to the refusal of the inhabitants, in spite of the orders of the préfet, to deliver up the town, though defended by a weak garrison, to the allies in 1815. The name of L. P. was erased in 1848.

Briançon has 3455 Inhab.; it stands at an elevation of 4285 ft. above the sea-level, and may be said to endure 7 months of winter. It was until 1848-51 cut off, in a manner, from the rest of the world, being accesible by only one carriage-road from the side of Gap. The Sardinian government has at length rendered the Mont Genèvre practicable for 4-wheeled carriages. The carriage-road, direct from Grenoble over the Lauteret, many years in progress, has been finished, and is practicable in a light char.

It takes 12 or 14 hours to reach Bourg d'Oysans by this route. A *diligence* goes daily to Embrun and Gap. (Rte. 139.)

The *Pass of the Mont Genèvre* leads from Briançon to Susa, a day's journey, 15 hours, traversed 3 times a week by a *diligence*. The road leaves the Val des Prés on the l., traversing thick forests of fir, and at the end of about 2 leagues of ascent, by zigzags, reaches the summit of the pass at Bourg Mont Genèvre, a hamlet on a plain, 6476 ft. above the sea-level, on which barley ripens. From this plain, at a short distance from each other, rise the Doira, which flows through the Po into the Adriatic, and the Durance; hence the verses

"Adieu ma sœur la Durance,
  Nous nous séparons sur ce mont;
Tu vas ravager la Provence,
  Moi féconder le Piedmont."

An obelisk erected on the summit commemorates the construction of this road, under Napoleon.

This pass was crossed in 1494 by Charles VIII. of France with the army with which he invaded Italy, dragging with him several hundred pieces of artillery.

The descent into Piedmont lies through

Cesanne   2 leagues.
Oulx   2   ,,
Salabertrand 2   ,,
Fort Exiles 1   ,,

Susa (22 m. from Cesanne) described in the HANDBOOKS for SWITZERLAND and N. ITALY. Rly. to Turin.

ROUTE 139.

GAP TO BRIANÇON, BY EMBRUN, AND EXCURSON INTO THE VAL DE QUEYRAS, VAL D'ARVIEUX, AND VAL FRESSINIÈRE.

91 kilom. = 56 Eng. m. to Briançon. A *diligence* (very slow) daily.

The valley above Gap is stony and dreary.

17 Chorges appears to have preserved traces of the name of the ancient inhabitants of this district, the "Caturigæ."

After crossing a high ridge the road descends in a gradual sweep into the valley of the Durance, which it reaches at the foot of a precipitous mountain. The valley hereabouts is a scene of unmitigated desolation: the turbulent river rolls along a furious flood of dirty water, undermining the loose shaly rocks (? Jura limestone) composing its sides, strewing the bottom with rubbish, and constantly forcing its banks. The road is frequently swept away by inundations, and for some distance is carried along temporary causeways. The Durance is crossed by a wooden bridge at

14 Savines, and again before reaching

10 Embrun. *Inn:* the best is indifferent. Embrun (anciently *Ebrodunum*), an old-fashioned fortress, surrounded by loopholed ramparts, overlooks the valley from the top of a singular platform or table of puddingstone rock, escarped on the side facing

the river, and separated by a ditch from the mountain behind it. The *Cathedral* has a fine lofty Romanesque tower ornamented with circular arches, and a N. portal, whose round mouldings rest on pillars of the red marble of the country, the two outer ones being supported on rudely-carved lions. The W. end is chequered with slabs of yellow limestone and black shale. It has a tolerable wheel window, filled with stained glass. The interior is not otherwise remarkable: the roof is Pointed. Against the N. door is nailed a horseshoe, said to have been thrown by the horse of Lesdiguières, the Protestant leader, which is reported to have stumbled and thrown its master in the porch as he was spurring on his steed to enter the church, and thus saved it from desecration. Such is the Romanist legend. The image of Notre Dame d'Embrun was held in great reverence by Louis XI., who, as dauphin, resided long in Dauphiné. (See 'Quentin Durward.')

Beside the cathedral stands the building formerly the archbishop's palace, now a barrack; and near it rises a curious tower of ancient masonry called *Tour Brunc*.

The first church at Embrun is said to have been built by Constantine the Great. The line of its archbishops is traced back, uninterruptedly, to his time: they were made princes, and endowed with the sovereignty of a large part of Dauphiné, by the Emperor Conrad II. A portion of their archives, captured with the town by Lesdiguières in 1585, are now in the public library of Cambridge.

Embrun is a poor town of narrow dirty streets; the view from its ramparts is striking, but the mountains around are bare in the extreme.

Little occurs worthy of remark in pursuing the course of the Durance upwards, until, after crossing the river to its l. bank, we approach the very picturesque and strong fortress of *Mont Dauphin*, the key of the pass into Italy, standing conspicuous on an elevated platform of rock, appearing to close the mouth of the lateral valley of the Guil, which here enters the Durance from the N.E. It was fortified by Vauban, who constructed its bastions of the rough pink marble of Eygliers, a neighbouring village, and completely commands the 2 valleys—presenting escarped precipices on either side, so as to be almost impregnable. Our road is carried under the base of the rock of pudding-stone, crowned by the fortress, 500 or 600 ft. above the river, and near it is the post-house,

16 Plan de Phazy.

[The *river Guil* rises at the base of the Monte Viso, on the Piedmontese frontier: its valley, called *Val de Queyras*, consists chiefly of a series of narrow defiles, through which the river seems to have forced its passage. About 1½ m. up, on its l. bank, is Guillestre, which was one of the stations for English prisoners during the war. Above this the valley is rent by an extraordinary fissure, called *Gorge de Chapelue*, bounded by precipices from 700 to 800 ft. high, described by Brockedon as "one of the *finest in the Alps*." Nearly 2 hours are required to traverse it. In places the rocks almost meet overhead, and the road crosses the depths, in which the Guil flows far below, from side to side, as the rocks present a shelf for its passage; but at times they are so completely precipitous that it is necessary to ascend the heights, and go over their summits. At the upper end of the defile, about 4 hours' walk from Mont Dauphin, is the *castle of Queyras*, an ancient feudal stronghold of the seigneurs of Château-Ville-Vieille, perched on the top of a monstrous rock, which seems to have been detached from the neighbouring peak in order to guard the passage. It is now converted into a military post, and is occupied by a company of infantry. A tolerable inn here, chez Bosi.

Two passes, the Col des Hayes and Col d'Isoard, lead N. over the mountains to Briançon.

In the remote valleys around Queyras the Protestants are very numerous, especially in the *Val d'Arvieux*, reached by a rough road branching off on the l. about 1½ m. below Château Queyras; as well as in the Commune of Molines, and its hamlets, St. Veran, Pierre Grosse, and Fousillarde. They have churches at Arvieux, St. Veran, and Fousillarde, in all of which service is performed once in 3 weeks by a minister who resides for a week in each parish alternately.

Felix Neff's residence was at La Chalp, in the Val d'Arvieux, above the village of that name; a foot path runs thence over the mountains to Briançon. *St. Veran*, where he had also a small Protestant flock, is situated in another valley, 8 or 10 m. to the S. of Château Queyras, on the very verge of vegetation: it is the loftiest human habitation in France, 6692 ft. above the sea-level, and the nearest towards the snowy summits of the Viso. Neff said of it that it was "the highest and consequently the most pious village in the Val Queyras."

About 2 m. above Queyras is Abries, where the Guil bends to the S.E. towards the Monte Viso, whose unscaled peak forms a striking object amidst the wild and savage scenery of this upland valley, here contracted and strewn with rocks. It is very grand, and well worth exploring, not only on its own account, but because through the two passes issuing out over the mountains at its head most interesting excursions may be made into Piedmont.

a. The *Col de la Croix* leads from the village Ristolas and Monta (French custom-house) to the Protestant valleys of the Vaudois, and their capital La Tour.

b. The *Col de Viso* conducts from La Chalp, a hamlet 1½ m. above Monta, along the rt. bank of the Guil, by a path only practicable on foot, in 5 hours, from Abries to the summit of the pass, 10,150 ft. above the sea-level, whence the view over the valley of the Po and plains of Piedmont, comprising an horizon of 100 m., "is one of the most magnificent in the world."
—*B*. The traveller may enter Italy by the Col de Viso, and return by La Tour and Col de la Croix. The routes are described in the HANDBOOK for SWITZERLAND.]

From Mont Dauphin to Briançon the road constantly follows the course of the Durance, sometimes on a level with it, at others at an elevation of many hundred feet above it. The river runs for a long distance at the bottom of a deep gash, whose sides, rarely susceptible of cultivation, slope at a very high angle.

[About 6 m. above Mont Dauphin, near the village of La Roche, prettily situated beside a small lake, a long timber bridge crosses the Durance, and an abrupt shepherd's path, scaling the mountain, leads up into the Val Fressinière, the poor Alpine valley once blessed by the ministering care of Felix Neff, and which now serves as his last resting-place. "The path creeps up the mountain in an oblique direction, and then over some rugged ground leads to a defile through which a torrent rushes, bordered on each side by groups of cottages, crossed by an Alpine bridge, below which is a cascade. This hamlet is Palons, and the torrent, called the Rimasse, is the guide which conducts to the Val Fressinière. There is no mistaking the way. The villages passed are Fressinière, whence the valley is named (1 league), in a lovely fertile vale, producing grain of several kinds and fruit-trees: Violins (1 league); here is a Protestant church, built by Neff, to which a tower has lately been added: Minsas (2 m.). Then comes the toilsome, rough, and clambering path, through a country perfectly savage and appalling, to Dormilleuse (3 m., or 5 leagues from La Roche), a miserable village at the very foot of the glaciers, constructed like an eagle's nest upon the side of a mountain, the most repulsive, perhaps, of all the habitable spots of Europe. Nature is here stern and terrible, offering nothing to repay the traveller but the satisfaction of planting his foot on the rock which has been hallowed as the asylum of Christians of whom the world was not worthy. It consists of a few poor detached huts, from which fresh air, comfort, and cleanliness are all banished; some without chimneys or glazed windows, others consisting of a mere miserable kitchen and stable, seldom cleaned out more than once a year, where the inhabitants spend the greater part of the winter along with their cattle, for the sake of the warmth. Their few sterile fields hang over precipices, and are partly covered with blocks of granite. In some seasons even rye will not ripen. Many of the pasturages are inaccessible to cattle, and scarcely safe for sheep. Yet in this gloomy spot did the virtuous Protestant pastor, Felix Neff, sit himself down, because his services seemed here to be most required, where he had everything to teach, even to the planting of a potato."—*Gilly's Memoir of Neff.*

A mountain pass leads over the *Col d' Orcière*, at the head of the Val Fressinière, into the valley of Champsaur, traversed by the Drac. (Rte. 134.)

Near Palons are several caves in the rocks, which served the inhabitants in time of persecution as places of refuge and of worship: one of them is called Glesia (L'Eglise).]

----

17 La Bessée. Near this a step or rise occurs in the valley of the Durance, which seems barred by a high bank or natural dam. Up this the road to Briançon toils in zigzags. A little above La Bessée the ruins of an embattled wall are visible, running across the valley from either bank of the Durance to the summit of the heights commanding it on the rt. and l., evidently designed to close the passage up, and check the incursions of a people from the S.

[Nearly opposite La Bessée to the N.W. opens out the Val Louise, which terminates in the *glaciers* and peaks of the *Mont Pelvoux*, whose top rises 13,468 ft. above the sea-level. "The poor village called *La Ville de Val Louise* is the chief place. Its environs are very picturesque. The valley branches into two: that on the rt. leads to Mt. Pelvoux; through it 2 French engineers most nearly attained the summit, but not quite. By the other branch there is a difficult pass into the Val Godemar, called Col de Celar."—*Pr. F.*

Within this valley is a cavern called Baume des Vaudois, from a number of those unfortunate professors of an ancient faith, who concealed themselves within it in 1488, carrying with them their children, and as much food as they could collect, relying on its inaccessible position, and the snows around, for their defence. When the officer despatched by Charles VIII. arrived with his soldiers in the valley, none of its inhabitants were found; but at length tracing out their hiding-place, he commanded a great quantity of wood to be set fire to at the mouth of the cave to burn or smoke them out. "Some were slain in attempting to escape, others threw themselves headlong on the rocks below, others were smothered; there were afterwards found within the caverns 400 infants stifled in the arms of their dead mothers. It is believed as a certain fact that 3000 persons perished on that occasion in this valley."—*Gilly's Mem. of Neff.*

Above this the valley is more wooded, while low down little patches are cleared of stones to allow the grass to grow.]

17 *Briançon*, in Rte. 137.

(503)

SECTION VIII.

BURGUNDY.—FRANCHE-COMTÉ.

ROUTE	PAGE
143 Montereau to *Troyes*, by *Nogent* (RAIL)	503
144 Paris to *Dijon*, by Troyes	505
148 Dijon to Geneva, by *Dôle*	507
150 Dôle to Lausanne, by *Pontarlier*	508
153 Châlons to Geneva by Lons-le-Saulnier	509
155 *Descent of the Haut Rhône.*—Aix in Savoy to Lyons	510
156 Lyons to Geneva, by *Nantua* and *Bellegarde*	511
159 Lyons to *Besançon*, by *Bourg* and *Lons-le-Saulnier*	512

ROUTE 143.

MONTEREAU TO TROYES, BY NOGENT—RAILWAY.

100 kilom. = 62 Eng. m. 5 trains daily, in 3 to 5 hrs.

Montereau (79 kilom. from Paris) is described in Rte. 106. A single line of railway was finished and opened to traffic 1848. It runs up the fertile valley of the Seine without tunnels or any extensive work.

13 Chatenay Stat.
8 Vimpelles Stat.
3 Les Ormes Stat. (Buffet, refreshment room.) Diligence to Provins. (See Rte. 144.)
10 Hermé Stat.
4 Melz Stat.
7 Nogent Stat. (*Inns:* Cygne d'Or;—Cygne de la Croix), a thriving town (3365 Inhab.) prettily situated on the l. bank of the Seine, at the point where it becomes navigable. It is intersected in the middle by the Ile des Ecluses, which is connected with either bank by stone bridges, one of which was blown up on February 11, 1814; when Nogent was bravely defended, step by step, and house by house, by a small body of French, under Bourmont, against the Allies, who finally carried the place by storm.

Here is a handsome *church*, in the late Gothic of the 15th centy., surmounted by a fine tower, constructed between 1521 and 1542; also *agreeable walks* round the town.

9 Pont-sur-Seine Stat.
9 Romilly Stat.
12 Mesgrigny Stat. Coach to Sézanne.
6 St. Mesmin Stat.
7 Payne Stat.
7 Barberey Stat.
5 *Troyes Station* is near the public walks.

This railway is intended to be prolonged to Chaumont. *Diligences* thither to Bar-sur-Aube, to Châtillon, Epernay, to Langres, to Nancy.

TROYES (*Inn:* Grand Mulet; good, clean, and cheap) is chef-lieu of the Dépt. de l'Aube (pop. 25,656), and is seated on the l. bank of the Seine, branches of which, conducted through the town in canals, contribute to its industry and cleanliness. In the reign of Henri IV. Troyes had 60,000 Inhab., so that it will be perceived its present state is one of decay, many of its most industrious citizens having been banished by the revocation of the Edict of Nantes. "This ancient capital of Champagne, in which the peculiar provincial character of the 'Francs Champenois' is thought to be exhibited in its most genuine aspect, still contains much that is interesting. The greater part is of timber and plaster, or pargeting, exactly in the old English style, though, as in England, the number of these venerable buildings diminishes day by day.

"The *Cathedral*, dedicated to St. Peter, is a splendid specimen of the *flamboyant* Gothic, full of bold inverted curves, open borders of festooned pendants, and all those luxuriances which preceded the abandonment of the style. The church is 374 ft. long, 96 ft. high to the point of the roof, and has 5 aisles, producing beautiful combinations of perspective. Those who are fond of painted glass will here have much enjoyment, for the windows are most brilliant and elegant. They exhibit the finest and most delicate mosaic patterns, which are more rare than other styles in this species of art. The clerestory is here really a *clear story* from the size of its windows, filled with as fine painted glass as the rest. In this church, and before the high altar, May 20, 1420, was our Henry V. affianced to the Princess Katherine; and on the following day was signed the memorable *Treaty of Troyes*,—that treaty so full of disaster, by which the victor of Azincour was declared to be the heir of Charles VI., and his successor in the kingdom. Charles VI. was present, together with very many magnates and nobles, English and French; but, above all, Philip Duke of Burgundy, by whose intervention the treaty was negotiated and concluded.

"The *Ch. of St. Urbain* is unfinished. It contains a great deal of open tracery, such as is found at Cologne, but of which there are very few examples on this side of the Rhine. Maréchal Vauban, who studied Gothic architecture attentively, used to say of this church that it was built of *coupons*."—*F. P.*

St. Urbain was founded by Pope Urban IV., son of a shoemaker of Troyes, 1262, on the site of his paternal abode, and is remarkable as an example of great richness of middle pointed Gothic, yet uninfluenced by the Flamboyant style.

The marriage of Henry V. took place June 2, 1420, in the *Church of St. Jean*, now much mutilated externally. It encloses a well which furnishes water to the neighbouring quarter of the town, and possesses an altar-piece, painted and given by *Mignard*, who was born in the parish.

The *Sainte Madeleine* possesses a stone *rood-loft* (jubé) of great beauty and richness of decoration, the work of John Gualdo, an Italian, 1518. Most of the statues have been destroyed, and some replaced by wood. Those which remain are good. In this church, at *St. Nicholas*, and at *St. Nazaire*, are painted glass windows.

St. Pantaleon is ornamented internally with statues, the best of which are attributed to an artist named François Gentil.

In *St. Remi* there is a bronze statue of Christ by *Girardon*.

The *H. de Ville* was built 1624-70 from a design of Mansard.

The *Public Library* is said to contain 50,000 vols. and 5000 MSS.: the hall in which they are deposited is decorated with painted windows representing events in the life of Henri IV.

"The ancient *Boucheries* consist of several long low ranges of timber buildings, evidently quite as old as the time of our Henry V. It used to be an article of popular belief that flies never entered this building, which some writers ascribed to a property of the wood, others to the construction of the edifice, and others to a spell or charm of St. Loup. The immunity, however, like all other privileges, has disappeared.

"Troyes would delight an architect. The houses are generally old and picturesque, and there are several churches besides those which we have noticed, Troyes having suffered less than many places during the Revolution."—*F. P.*

The *Hôtel Megrigny* is a good specimen of the architecture of the Renaissance, flanked by 2 turrets.

The name of Troyes will always be familiar to us from our *Troy-weight*, which obtains its name from the standard of this town.

The city has little commercial activity; it is evidently the centre of an agricultural community. A new *Canal*, however, is in progress to form a communication from Troyes to the navigable part of the Seine, and also to the

Canal of Burgundy; it will doubtless contribute to the prosperity of the town.

The chief manufacture carried on in and around Troyes is that of *nightcaps*.

Troyes is a very important place in a military point of view, being the centre where various roads meet on the l. of the Seine, in the midst of a plain cut up by streams and woody morasses. As a proof of this, in the course of the wonderful campaign of 1814, when Napoleon kept at bay so many enemies pressing on him from all sides, it was twice taken by the Allies and once by the French. In the month of February the portion of the Allied armies encamped round the walls amounted to 100,000 men, and they required 12 hrs. to march through it. Here the first steps for the Restoration of the Bourbons were taken, and the white cockade was publicly displayed in France for the first time after a lapse of more than 20 years.

ROUTE 144.

PARIS TO DIJON, BY TROYES.

310 kilom. = 192 Eng. m.

This road is little frequented since the completion of the railway by way of Melun. Montereau, Nogent, and Troyes. (Rte. 143.)

The road turns out of Rte. 106 beyond

7 Charenton.

14 Grosbois. The *Château* was the property of Monsieur, afterwards Louis XVIII., and now belongs to the Prince de Wagram.

8 Brie Comte Robert. The name of this little town comes from its situation in the district of Brie, an ancient dependence of the province of Champagne, and from Robert Comte de Dreux and Seigneur of Brie, its founder or benefactor. The parish *church* is Gothic of different periods from the 13th to the 16th centy. It contains some painted glass. The *old castle* is an utter ruin. The ruined chapel attached to the Hôtel Dieu merits notice.

16 Guignes.

Near this is the *château La Grange*, the residence of Lafayette, a moated

France.

mansion, whither he retired during the rule of Napoleon, occupying himself with agricultural pursuits; here he was visited by Fox, who planted the ivy which covers one of the towers.

8 Mormant.

11 Nangis.—*Inns:* Lion d'Or;—Sauvage. There is an ancient church and ruined castle here. (?)

11 Maison Rouge.

11 Provins.—*Inn:* H. de la Fontaine. The ancient *walls*, flanked by watch-towers, of this venerable but decayed town, enclose, besides the houses, a wide open space now occupied by gardens and vineyards. It lies between 2 hills, the old town on the highest ground, the new town on the lower slopes.

In the upper town, which abounds in ruins, rises, conspicuous far and wide, an ancient tower of great size and solid masonry, known as the *Grosse Tour de César*, though undoubtedly a work of the middle ages. It is square at the base; but in its upper story 4 turrets detach themselves from the centre, which becomes octagonal, and is connected by flying buttresses with the turrets. This building, containing 2 curious halls and dungeons, now serves as bell-tower to the neighbouring church of *St. Quiriace*, remarkable for its early date and plain massive architecture; it is surmounted in the centre by a cupola, and beneath is a curious *crypt*.

Under various buildings in the high town run extensive *vaults* and *caves*, arched over and partly sustained on pillars: they appear to have been formed out of ancient stone-quarries, and may have served as places of refuge, or for warehouses and cellars, in former times. The two old gates of St. Jean and Jouy still lead through the bastioned antique fortifications to the upper town.

In the *lower town*, which is also surrounded by ramparts and boulevards, stands the church of *Ste. Croix*, completed in 1538, but it includes a more ancient chapel of *St. Laurent*, of the 15th centy., containing delicate sculptures. This church is much modernised, but supported in the interior

z

by piers of primitive form, 2 of them twisted, and contains fine carved wood. The church of *St. Ayoul*, a simple nave without transepts or apse, in the Round style, may reward the notice of the antiquary.

The *chapel of the hospital* contains the monument in which was deposited the heart of Thibault VII., Comte de Champagne, who founded here, 1050, an hospital for pilgrims.

Provins has for centuries been celebrated for *Roses* (improperly called Provence roses); and though the cultivation of them for purposes of commerce has now nearly ceased, they are still partially grown to make "conserve," and to colour bonbons. The Provins rose has a rich crimson hue, and is said to have been brought by the Crusaders from the Holy Land.

The 2 small rivers, the Durtin and Vouzie, above whose confluence Provins is built, turn no less than 50 or 60 corn-mills; their waters are thought to be well fitted for dyeing, and there are consequently numerous dye-works on their banks. Pop. 6009.

The road affords little subject for remark until you reach

18 Nogent-sur-Seine.

Railway, Nogent to Troyes. Rte. 143.

At St. Aubin, about 4 m. beyond Nogent, the road passes within view of the chimneys and roofs of an iron-forge, now abandoned, which occupies the site of the famous monastery of the *Paraclète*, founded by Abélard, 1123. It afterwards became the retreat of Heloïse, and the final resting-place of both. In 1792, when the abbey was sold, the coffin containing their bodies was removed to Nogent, and afterwards transferred to Paris, where it is now deposited in Père la Chaise, under a Gothic monument, originally erected at the monastery of St. Marcel, near Châlons, over the remains of Abélard. The monument raised over the two lovers at the Paraclète, ornamented with a figure of the Trinity, was destroyed at the Revolution, 1794. A marble *pillar* was placed over the mouth of their burial vault, within the area once occupied by the church of the Paraclete, by the late Gen. Pajol, the owner of the ground, and within it still remains the stone sarcophagus which once enclosed their leaden coffin. The abbot's house is now inhabited by a peasant.

8 Pont le Roi, a town of 2000 Inhab., at the junction of the Aube with the Seine: the *Château* was built by Casimir Périer in 1830.

14 Granges. (Aube.)

15 Grês. The country possesses slight interest.

19 TROYES. Rte. 143.

Railway to Paris by Nogent and Montereau. Rte. 143.

At Troyes the high road from Paris to Basle (Rte. 162) branches off from that to Besançon and Dijon.

19 St. Parres-les-Vaudes.

14 Bar-sur-Seine. Pleasantly situated on the banks of the infant Seine, here a clear rivulet. A quiet country town. *The Church* has great elegance.

19 Mussy.—"The *wine* character of the country now becomes very apparent. The vineyards are, however, principally in strips, alternating with corn, potatoes, haricots, hemp, clover, altogether conveying a cheerful impression. This country begins again to vary from its hitherto swelling or undulating monotonous level. Towards the west, hills of a tabular shape appear, which continue increasing until they form almost a connected chain. This is the commencement of the well-known *Côte d' Or*, of which more hereafter."—*F. P.*

15 Châtillon-sur-Seine (*Inns: Poste* (?); —*H. de la Côte d' Or*; dirty, and barely tolerable), a neat small town. A congress of representatives of the allied sovereigns, at which Lord Castlereagh appeared on behalf of England, was held here, February 1814, to offer to Napoleon the throne of France, provided he would be content with its limits previous to the Revolution; he rejected these terms, and, emboldened by the successes he gained in the course of the campaign, broke off the negotiations, and the result was his dethronement.

Marshal Marmont was born here, and built on the spot a fine *château*.

"The road now becomes more hilly,

masses of grey rock, coloured and stained with iron hues, starting abruptly from the sides of the hills. The fields and soil generally stony, yet pleasantly watered by sparkling streams. On the hill sides many little ancient towns or *bourgades* are seen, even now strongly bearing the impress of feudality. Surrounded by walls and gates, it seems as if not a house could venture to stray out of the protecting circuit, indicating the ancient unsettled state of the country, or, at "least, of the habits which arose from its insecurity."—*F. P.*

14 Aisey-le-Duc.

15 Ampilly-le-Sec.

15 Chanceaux, celebrated for the manufacture of preserved barberries (*épinettes*). Here is a comfortable little inn, where a good stock of the preserve is kept.

The Seine takes its rise in the high land of the Côte d'Or, within about 1 m. of Chanceaux.

"The country now begins to assume a picturesque character; you begin, as it were, to cross the fibres of the roots of the Jura, and the beauty of the scene gains as you advance.

"12 St. Seyne, beautifully situated amongst a ridge of bold hills, almost of a mountainous character. The town, which contains about 1000 Inhab., is at the bottom of the valley. Above, on the brow of the hill, are the remains of a celebrated *Abbey* of Benedictines, founded by St. Seguanus before 580. The church, whose construction dates from the beginning of the 15th centy., is yet standing, and contains much that is remarkable; amongst other things, a series of ancient frescoes representing the life of the patron founder. This church has some peculiarities in its architecture, and the stalls of the monks continue undisturbed."—*F. P.*

10 Val de Suzon, so called from the torrent Suzon, which flows through the very pretty valley. The general aspect of the village, which you reach by a steep descent, continues to remind the traveller of his gradual approach to Switzerland; and indeed, throughout the whole of this district, he will observe how overcharged is the opinion of the monotony of French scenery, even in the provinces which are not professedly mountainous.

17 Dijon (in Rte. 104).

ROUTE 148.

DIJON TO GENEVA, BY DÔLE.

196 kilom. = 120 Eng. m.

Malleposte (2 places) daily in 15 hrs.

Diligences: 2 or 3 daily in about 16 hrs.

The journey may be divided into 2 days' posting: 1st day to Champagnole, 8 or 9 hrs.; 2nd day, Geneva, 10 hrs.

For some distance along the road there is little worth description or notice; the country fertile, but flat and monotonous. As you advance, the distant blue outline of the Jura mountains is discovered on the horizon.

17 Genlis—must not be confounded with the place of the same name in Picardy, whence Madame de Genlis derived her title.

A causeway 1½ m. long, pierced with 23 arches, to allow the escape of the water of the Saône during inundations, leads into

14 Auxonne (*Inn*: Grand Cerf), a second-class fortress of minor importance, owing to its distance from the frontier, in the rear of Besançon. It stands on the l. bank of the Saône, here crossed by a bridge. The fortifications were planned by Vauban. It was taken by the Austrians 1815. The pop. 5150.

From the heights above Dôle the snowy mass of the Mont Blanc, more than 100 m. distant as the crow flies, is apparent in clear weather.

16 Dôle (*Inns*: H. de France;—Ville de Lyon;—H. de Paris; said to be good) is a town of 9913 Inhab., in the Dépt. of the Jura, seated on the Doubs. It belonged for a long time to Spain, having been the capital of Franche-Comté, which was not united to France, until the reign of Louis XIV. The Emp. Charles V. fortified it; but the works were destroyed by Louis.

The *Parish Church* is Gothic, and the *Tour de Vergy*, which now serves as a prison, is one of the few ancient edifices.

The *Canal* which joins the Rhine to the Rhône passes near the town.

z 2

[The road to Besançon turns off here, passing through
14 Orchamps.
13 St. Wit.
18 *Besançon.* (Rte. 159.)]
18 Mont-sous-Vaudrey, a town of 1000 Inhab.
A road branches off here to Lausanne, by Salins and Pontarlier. (Rte. 150.)
19 *Poligny.* (Inns : Grand Cerf;—Grand Alexandre; tolerable, but arrange beforehand about charges.) This old town (5615 Inhab.) occupies a commanding site at the foot of the Jura, and enjoys a pure air and abundance of provisions, and stands in the midst of vine-culture. It was once walled, and a visit to the ruins of the old *Citadel* will repay for the climb by the extent and beauty of the view. The first ascent of the Jura commences on quitting Poligny. The road was made by Napoleon, and commands from the summits, after an hour's march, a good view into the valley called Culée de Vaux, and over the plains of Franche-Comté and Burgundy, as far as the Côte d'Or.
12 Mentrond. Picturesque Castle. The Mont Blanc appears over the top of a saddle-backed hill.
10 Champagnole. (Dupuis' *Inn;* clean and reasonable; mountain-trout, honey, cream, and butter, all good.) A town of 3150 Inhab., on the Ain, here crossed by a high bridge. Through a picturesque gorge to
12 Maisonneuve. A picturesque stage, passing from the first platform or step of the Jura to the second.
10 St. Laurent. (*Inn:* l'Ecu de France; very clean, and most civil people.) French custom-house on entering France. The staple productions of the Jura are cheese (resembling Gruyère) and timber; saw-mills stud all the streams.
Fine pastures. Soon after passing Morbier, the 2nd French custom-house, we reach the culminating point in the ascent of the Jura, and begin to descend by a fine road to Morez (*Inn*   ), an industrious and rapidly increasing bourg of 3600 Inhab., seated at the bottom of a defile, on the Bienne, which turns the machinery of numerous mills and works, where clockwork, jacks, nails, &c., are made. The 3rd and last step of the Jura is ascended on this stage, passing fine mountain farms.
20 Les Rousses (*Inn* small; Poste best), a hideous village on the Swiss frontier, in a cold, arid, upland country. The French Government is converting Les Rousses into a strong fortress for the defence of the frontier.
Here is the first French custom-house encountered by travellers coming from Switzerland. Geneva trinkets, boxes, &c., must be declared; watches are admitted on paying a duty of 5 fr. each.
Those who wish to ascend the *Dôle*, one of the highest summits of the Jura, on account of its surprising view, must turn out of the high road at Les Rousses, and proceed to St. Cergue (12 kilom.), whence the top may be attained in 3 hrs. See SWISS HANDBOOK.
The descent of the Jura to Gex is now made safe and easy by an excellent new road. About a mile beyond the douane you pass out of France.
A little beyond
19 La Faucille, a miserable solitary house, at the extremity of a narrow gorge, on a sudden turn in the road, opens out the celebrated and sublime view over the Lake of Geneva, the Mont Blanc, and the range of the Alps; a view not to be forgotten in a lifetime. Long and steep descent to
11 Gex (*Inn:* La Poste), through Ferney Voltaire, to
17 GENEVA (described in SWISS HANDBOOK).

ROUTE 150.

DÔLE TO LAUSANNE, BY PONTARLIER.

100 kilom. = 62 Eng. m. to Jougne, *i. e.* the French frontier.

A journey of 2 days, stopping the first night at Pontarlier, 8 hours; thence to Lausanne, 10 hours.

A very agreeable road, through a romantic and beautiful country, quitting that to Geneva by Morez at
18 Mont-sous-Vaudrey.
16 Mouchard.
9 Salins (*Inns :* Poste ;—Tête Noir;

tolerable), a town of 9000 Inhab., which had the misfortune to be almost entirely consumed by a fire, which lasted for 3 days, in 1825. It is romantically situated in a narrow rocky gorge, and owes its name to the salt-works, *Salines Royales*, a vast edifice, 918 ft. long, surrounded by walls, in the midst of the valley. The salt is obtained from brine-springs rising below vaults of ancient construction. The weaker springs are conducted in pipes to the forest of Chaux, 15 m. off, where, after being evaporated in "maisons de graduation," they are boiled.

The Church of *St. Anatole* is an interesting edifice, and contains some good woodwork in the stalls of the choir.

There are quarries of gypsum here.

The road ascends, on quitting Salins, through a country having much of the Swiss character, abounding in rocks and dark fir-woods.

21 Levier.

21 *Pontarlier*. *Inns*: Poste; very good;—Croix Blanche;—Lion d'Or. This is the frontier town of France, a place of considerable antiquity and interest, containing 4890 Inhab., seated at a height of 2716 ft. above the sea-level, at the foot of the second ridge of the Jura, and at the débouché of the principal routes leading through that chain. It is the loftiest town in France.

The road hence first ascends by the side of the river Doubs, and through the pass of La Cluse, which may be called a mountain gateway between France and Switzerland, to St. Pierre de Joux. The defile is commanded by the *Château de Joux*, situated on the summit of a precipitous and nearly inaccessible rock, at the foot of which the roads from Pontarlier, Neufchâtel, and Lausanne unite. This frontier-fort was the prison of the unfortunate Toussaint L'Ouverture, when treacherously carried off from St. Domingo by command of Napoleon. He ended his days here, some say by violent means; but the sudden transition from the climate of the tropics to a dark dungeon, so dank and cold that the water drops from the roof in summer, and icicles congeal on the walls in winter, in the elevated region and biting atmosphere of the Jura, sufficiently explains the cause of his death, without the need of violence. His miserable cell still exists, and has been described by Miss Martineau. He was buried in the prison church, with nothing to mark the grave, but it was bricked over, and is included in the new wall of the church. Here also was confined previously, "dans ce nid de hibous, égayé par une compagnie d'invalides," as he termed it, another remarkable prisoner, *Mirabeau*. He was sent hither (1776) by virtue of a lettre de cachet obtained by his father, "L'Ami des Hommes," as he called himself, and the tyrant of his own family, as he proved himself. Mirabeau, having by his insinuating manners obtained leave from the governor to visit the town of Pontarlier on parole, made love to Sophie Monnier, the wife of a magistrate there, and eloped with her to Holland. She was the Sophie to whom he addressed some of his obscene writings, the "Lettres datées du donjon de Vincennes."

A desolate country, chiefly of forest, inhabited by charcoal-burners, succeeds.

10 Jougne, in a narrow pass, between high mountains. Here is the French custom-house.

$2\frac{1}{2}$ Orbe.
$1\frac{3}{4}$ Cossonay. } Distances in posts.
2 LAUSANNE.

The routes from the Fort de Joux to Neufchâtel by Val Travers, and to Lausanne by Orbe, are described in the HANDBOOK for SWITZERLAND.

ROUTE 153.

CHÂLONS-SUR-SAÔNE TO GENEVA, BY LONS-LE-SAULNIER.

177 kilom.=$109\frac{3}{4}$ Eng. m. *Diligence* in 19 hrs.

Since the completion of the railway from Paris to Châlons, Geneva may be reached more quickly by this route than by the road from Dijon by Dôle. [202 kilom.=125 Eng. m.] Rte. 148.

20 St. Etienne en Bresse.
17 Louhans.
14 Beaurepaire.
13 *Lons-le-Saulnier*, in Rte. 159.

The ordinary post-road runs through
23 Clairvaux.
23 St. Laurent. *Inn* here.
20 Les Rousses. } Rte. 149.
30 Gex.
17 GENEVA. (2 posts of Geneva.)
There is a shorter road from Lons-le Saulnier by
Orgelet.
Ste. Claude. (*Inn*: Ecu de France; best, but wretched.) This is a romantically situated town, in the most beautiful part of the Jura. It has a fine *Cathedral*.

The scenery of the pass of the Jura traversed by this road is superior to any other leading to Geneva.

Gex.

GENEVA. (SWISS HANDBOOK.)

ROUTE 155.

DESCENT OF THE HAUT RHÔNE.—AIX IN SAVOY TO LYONS.

N. B.—A diligence runs several times a week from Geneva to Seyssel, to meet the steamer to Lyons.

The Upper Rhône is navigated, in summer, by *Steamers*, which perform the voyage, descending from Aix to Lyons, in 8 hours, but require 13 hours for the ascent. A vexatious delay takes place at the custom-houses of France and Savoy.

The voyage across the Lac de Bourget from Aix, passing the Abbey of Haute-Combe, at the foot of the Mont du Chat, is described in the SWISS HANDBOOK, and is very delightful. The outlet from the lake is a narrow winding channel, called Canal de Savières, traversing the flat meadows in a serpentine course, which some have supposed artificial, but which has, probably, only been enlarged by art. By this issue the Lac de Bourget disgorges its waters into the Rhône, near the Savoyard village of Chana. The course of the Rhône hereabouts is nearly due N. and S., and parallel with the lake, from which it is separated by the mass of the *Mont du Chat*, whose ridges are called Dents, and over whose shoulder Hannibal is supposed to have led his army to the foot of the high Alps. On entering the Rhône we have this mountain on the l.

The Rhône has been navigated by steam above this, as high as Seyssel, a small town on both banks of the river, one part belonging to France, the other to Savoy.

Except at one or two points, the scenery of the Upper Rhône is not very remarkable. It runs through a series of basins, terminated at either end by gorges (étranglemens, *i. e.* throttlings, as the French expressively term them), caused by the approximation of the hills on either side. Below Seyssel

l. the Fière, a turbid river, which drains the Lake of Annecy, enters the Rhône.

l. At Yenne, opposite Belley, is a suspension bridge, traversed by the high road from Chambéry to Châlons. A monotonous sandy plain extends thence to Chana, across which the navigation is difficult, on account of sand-banks in its bed.

The Rhône, however, narrowed within a reduced channel, traverses a contracted defile abreast of

rt. Pierre Châtel, a fort of imposing appearance, belonging to France, built on the summit of a rock 400 or 500 ft. high. The river rushes through the gorge at its base with a furious speed; but the steamer, steered by a skilful pilot, passes safely over the rapids, which, at the point of greatest fury, are crossed by a wire suspension bridge.

The river below alters its course; turning to the N.W., and emerging upon an open country, it is intersected by numerous low islands, the resort of smugglers. Between St. Genis and (l.) St. Didier, the river Guiers, which descends from the Grande Chartreuse (Rte. 131), joins the Rhône : it is the boundary of Savoy, separating it from the Dépt. de l'Isère; below this, therefore, both banks of the Rhône are French. Above the junction of the Guiers there is a suspension bridge, and a castle on the height near it.

rt. the ruined *Castle of Groslée*.

l. Castle of Quinsonas.

To this succeeds the defile of St. Albin, where the channel is contracted to a width of 60 ft.; it is walled in by bare rocks, destitute of verdure.

The Rhône is traversed from side to side by a reef of rocks a little above (rt.) the village of Le Sault, so called from the leap, or *rapid*, formed by the river over them. They are smooth, and not very dangerous, but the steamer in ascending has difficulty in stemming the torrent which sweeps over this inclined plane. Here the river is crossed by a handsome stone bridge, the central arch being 105 ft. span. On either side are extensive quarries of limestone, furnishing building materials for Lyons and other towns on the banks of the Rhône below.

rt. St. Sorlin, with the remains of ancient fortifications.

l. Vertrieux, a modern château in the foreground, near the river, and behind it, on an isolated rock, its ancient castle rises in picturesque ruins.

rt. At Lagnieux, where a suspension bridge of wire spans the Rhône, the hills subside into a monotonous plain, stretching away to Lyons.

l. The entry of the cave called Grotte de la Balme is about 10 minutes' walk from the river.

rt. We pass the embouchure of the Ain, which gives its name to the Département extending along the rt. bank of the Rhône from Fort l'Ecluse nearly to Lyons. The Rhône below this assumes a very tortuous course between islands and sand-banks, unrelieved by objects of interest. Nothing announces the approach to a vast city, the borders of the river are so desolate and lonely. The steamer at length brings to, under the fortress-crowned heights of La Croix Rousse, at the quai in the Faubourg of Bresse, on the outskirts of

rt. LYONS, described in Rte. 108.

ROUTE 156.

LYONS TO GENEVA, BY NANTUA AND BELLEGARDE.

151 kilom.=93½ Eng. m. *Diligences* in 12 hrs.; a beautiful and interesting drive.

A *Railroad* is in progress (1854), passing up the rt. bank of the Rhône, by Amberieux, St. Rambert, Culoz (near the frontier of Savoie, and 22 m. from Chambéry), touches Bellegarde, and crosses the Swiss frontier near Fort l'Ecluse.

The road, for some distance after quitting Lyons, runs parallel with the Rhône, up its rt. bank. The river, left to its own wayward impulse, straggles onward, overspreading the plain with wrecks of sterile sand and stones. The slope of La Pape, whence there is a good view of the river and the distant Alps of Dauphiné, is next ascended.

13 Miribel.

9 Montluel Stat. is a small town of about 3000 Inhab., on the Seraine, which is crossed on quitting the place.

13 Meximieux Stat. We reach the borders of the river Ain at Mollon.

11 Bublanne. A branch Rly. is designed to be carried from Amberieux by Pont d'Ain to Macon.

11 Pont d'Ain (*Inn:* H.   ), a town of 1266 Inhab., on the rt. bank of the Ain, at the foot of a height crowned by a *castle*, built by the dukes of Savoy. Here the road to Bourg strikes off (Rte. 159).

The Ain is crossed by a stone bridge at Neuville, and its valley is quitted by the road at Poncin, remarkable for the ruins of a feudal castle, in order to reach

13 Cerdon. After 3 or 4 m. over the plain the road begins to ascend the Jura along the flank of a mountain, forming one side of a gorge, varied by the pretty fall of St. Marcellin, and by the ruined castles of Labatie and St. Julien.

The approach to Nantua, along the borders of its lake, is very pleasing, surrounded by mountains. It is about 1½ m. long.

19 Nantua (*Inns:* H. du Nord;— l'Ecu de France) is a town of 3700 Inhab., finely situated in the midst of the Jura mountains, at the extremity of its lake, hemmed in by bare precipices and dark woods. It possesses some considerable manufactures.

The *Parish Church*, originally attached to an abbey, is a "venerable and picturesque edifice, in the Romanesque style." The entrance, a round-headed arch, is surmounted by a circular window, and nearly all the rest of the building is early Pointed. The centre is surmounted by an octagonal lantern. Charles le Chauve, who died at Briord, 877, was buried here.

The lake produces capital trout and crawfish.

The scenery of the Jura mountains, through which the road winds, continues very interesting for the rest of the way. A little beyond Neyrolles we attain the summit of the pass, and, descending, skirt the shore of the Lake Sylant, about 2 m. long.

13 St. Germain de Joux (*Inn*: H. de la Paix ; clean and good).

At Châtillon de Michaille we cross the Valserine, and leave on the rt. the road leading to Seyssel (Rte. 155). We reach the valley of the Rhône at

12 *Bellegarde* (*Inn*: Poste), the frontier town of France, placed at the junction of the Valserine with the Rhône. Passports are here called for, and baggage examined likewise, on entering France. Ten minutes' walk from the inn is the *Perte du Rhône*, a contracted portion of the channel, encumbered with rocks, where the river plunges into the earth, and continues its subterraneous course through caverns neither explored nor fathomed, which it has probably excavated by its own torrent in the limestone rocks, for about 120 yards. This phenomenon, however, is seen to perfection only when the river is low. At other times, when its volume exceeds that which the subterranean passage is able to contain, it flows along its upper bed, open to day, as well as below ground. At such times, says M. Simond, "la Perte du Rhône est perdue pour les voyageurs." The vault of rock which covers the subterranean canal has of late been partly removed by blasting, to facilitate the flotage of timber in detached trunks down the Rhône at high water ; this tends to diminish the wonder of the Perte.

The width of the Rhône, which, on quitting the Lake of Geneva, is about 115 ft., is contracted at the Pont de Grezin, in the neighbourhood of the Perte, to 15 or 16 ft.

The bed of the Valserine is more picturesque and scarcely less curious than the Perte. It is worth while to descend from the garden of the inn into the worn channel of this little river, which is almost dry in summer time, except when a rivulet of its water burrows into the clefts and fantastic bends of its calcareous rock.

The wild and narrowly contracted gorge through which the Rhône forces its way between Bellegarde and Collonges, formed by the Mont Vouache on the side of Savoy, and the Mont Credo, the extremity of the Jura, on that of France, is thus described by Cæsar :—" Angustum et difficile inter Montem Juram, et flumen Rhodanum, quâ vix singuli currus ducerentur ; mons autem altissimus impendebat, ut facile perpauci prohibere possent." Near the upper end of this defile, commanding the entrance into France, stands the very strong and picturesque fortress *Fort de l'Ecluse*, originally planned by Vauban, but ruined by the Austrians, and repaired since 1824 by the French government, who have used infinite labour and expense to strengthen this position. Additional batteries have been cut in the rock above the lower fortress, and these communicate with the barracks below by a broad staircase, 100 ft. high, hewn inside the solid mountain"— *H. R.* The high road is carried through the fortress. Permission to see it in detail may generally be obtained from the governor.

12 Collonges. Here the defile opens out. On quitting

16 St. Genix, you enter Switzerland.

12 GENEVA (2 postes extra charged), in HANDBOOK for SWITZERLAND.

ROUTE 159.

LYONS TO BESANÇON, BY BOURG AND LONS-LE-SAULNIER.

217 kilom. = 134½ Eng. m.
Malleposte daily in 14 hrs.
Diligences daily.

The road from Lyons is the same as Rte. 156, as far as

58 Pont d'Ain.

20 *Bourg (en Bresse).*—*Inns:* H. de l'Europe (?) ;—du Nord (?). This place was capital of the ancient division of La Bresse, and is now chef-lieu of the Dépt. de l'Ain ; its population is 8996. It belonged to the Dukes of Savoy from the 11th to the 17th centy., and was not finally gained by the French until 1600. It has neither trade nor manufactures, and the only object of

interest is the *Church of Notre Dame de Brou*, outside the walls, a very remarkable edifice in the latest style of Gothic, verging into the Renaissance, constructed between 1511 and 1536 by Margaret of Austria, who was created by her father, the Emperor Maximilian, and confirmed by her nephew, Charles V., governor of the Netherlands. Her motto,* *fortune—infortune —forte une*, is repeated in various parts of the building. The architect was "Maistre Loys Van Boglem," and the sculptor "Maistre Conrad." The W. front is surmounted by 3 gables, that in the centre being the most lofty; under it is a *portal*, consisting of a flattened arch, highly enriched with carvings, arabesques, and other ornaments. The decorations of the interior are concentrated upon the *choir*: rich and varied marbles, and peculiarly fine painted windows, contribute to the splendour of the shrine, which contains the superb monuments of Margaret, the founder of the church, of her mother-in-law, Margaret de Bourbon (wife of Philip II., prince of Savoy), who made the vow, which her daughter accomplished, of building this church; and in the centre that of her husband, Philibert le Beau, which is the finest of all. The prince is represented above as dead, and below as dying. These tombs, all of white marble, are the work of an artist of Dijon named *Colomban*. The carving and decoration of the *rood screen*, the wood-work of the choir, and the altar-piece delicately sculptured out of alabaster, all deserve minute attention. The sun-dial in front of the portal, originally made in the 16th centy., was reconstructed by the astronomer *Joseph de Lalande*, who was born at Bourg, 1732.

The district of La Bresse is famed for its poultry, honey, &c.

11 St. Etienne du Bois.

Coligny, a little beyond this relay, is the cradle of the illustrious family which sent forth the leader of the Protestants, the Admiral Coligny. He was born at Châtillon-sur-Loing.

18 St. Amours.

* " In fortune or misfortune, there is one (woman) strong of heart."

18 Beaufort.

15 *Lons-le-Saulnier* (*Inn*: Chapeau Rouge) is situated in a basin nearly, surrounded by the mountains of the Jura, whose lower slopes are covered with vines. It is chef-lieu of the Dépt. of the Jura, and a flourishing town of nearly 8000 Inhab.

At one end of the town is the *brine-spring*, or *well*, 60 ft. deep, supplying the salt-works, *Salines* (whence the town received its ancient name, Ledo Salinarius), situated about a mile from the town, including vast evaporating houses for sparing fuel, by strengthening the brine before it is boiled.

Above the salt-well rise the ruins of the *Castle Montmorot*.

This is the birthplace of the revolutionary general Lecourbe.

14 Mauffans.

15 Poligny, on the high road from Dijon to Geneva, Rte. 148.

11 Arbois. A good sparkling wine is grown here. It is the native place of General Pichegru.

9 Mouchard. Near this the stately ruins of the Castle of Vaudgrenan.

17 Quingey, in the Dépt. of the Doubs.—*Inn*: La Poste, comfortable; good fishing quarters for trout in the river Loue.

12 Larnod. The picturesque ruins of the Château de Montferrand are seen. A continuous descent of nearly 6 m. leads down the steep hills forming one side of the gorge of the Doubs, through grand scenery, to

10 Besançon (*Inns*: H. du Nord, best; H. National, pretty good; H. de l'Europe).

This ancient and interesting city and first-rate fortress, originally capital of Franche-Comté, and a free city of the empire, now chef-lieu of the Dépt. of the Doubs (Pop. 35,345), is seated on the Doubs, which divides it into 2 parts, and nearly surrounds the ville haute, the larger and older portion. It is defended by a *Citadel*, built by Vauban, on an inaccessible rock, occupying the isthmus of the peninsula on which the town stands, and by several detached forts. There is a fine *view* from the citadel.

Besançon was the ancient *Vesontio* mentioned by Cæsar, and his descrip-

z 3

tion of it is so exact, that no other will better portray its position. He tells us that it was the largest town of the Sequani, and so strong by nature, as to form an excellent basis for a campaign, because nearly surrounded by the river Dubis (Doubs), making a curve like a horseshoe about it, except for the space of about 600 ft., occupied by an eminence washed by the river on either side. A wall which surrounds this height converts it into a citadel, and unites it with the town. "Oppidum maximum Sequanorum; naturâ loci sic muniebatur ut magnam ad ducendum bellum daret facultatem: propterea quod flumen Dubis ut circino circumductum, pene totum oppidum cingit: reliquum spatium quod non est amplius pedum DC, quâ flumen intermittit, mons continet magnâ altitudine, ita ut radices montis ejus ex utrâque parte ripæ fluminis contingunt."—L. i. It is interesting to find the classical description backed as it were by still existing remains of the Roman city, which are both numerous and curious, consisting not only of inscriptions, mosaics, pillars, and other fragments, but of buildings, the chief and oldest of which is a *Triumphal Arch*, still tolerably perfect, ornamented with niches, statues, and reliefs, called *la Porte Noire*. It is of a low period of art, and much defaced by time and violence; it leads up to the Citadel.

The old and narrow bridge over the Doubs is said also to rest on Roman foundations.

The *Porte Taillée*, on the E. side, is an ancient gateway of solid masonry, built in a cleft of the rock, which was tunnelled through by the Romans for the passage of an *aqueduct*, constructed by them, to convey water to the city from the village Arcier, 7 m. distant, considerable fragments of which are still visible along the road leading to that village from the Porte Rivotte. Outside the walls are the remains of an *Amphitheatre*.

The extensive promenade of *Chamars*, traversed by 2 branches of the Doubs, is said to occupy the site, as well as retain in part the name, of the Roman "Campus Martius."

The *Cathedral* of *St. Jean* has a fine Gothic nave.

The other churches are comparatively modern. The *Palais de Justice* was built 1749 to receive the court of the parliament of the province, removed hither from Dôle by Louis XIV.

The Cardinal Granvelle, the able minister of the Emperor Charles V. and of Philip II. in the Low Countries, himself a native of Franche-Comté, born at Ornans, spent many years here, when disgraced through the intrigues of his enemies, occupying himself with literary pursuits. He contributed to the enlargement of the *College* founded by his father, and he built the *Palais Granvelle*, in the style of the Renaissance, uniting (like the schools at Oxford) the various orders of architecture, one above another. The library contains 60 folio vols. of his letters. The *Café Granville*, in this building, is the best in the town.

In the *Musée*, partly the bequest of a native named Paris, are assembled objects of art and antiquity of various degrees of interest. There are 400 paintings. On the W. of the town is an Arsenal; also a School of Artillery.

Trout are abundant in the Doubs; fly-fishing is little known or practised. 20 lbs. fish are caught here.

Watch-making, introduced from Switzerland about 40 years ago, is the most important manufacture here, employing 2000 persons, who work at home for large houses.

Besançon stands on the important line of inland navigation formed to connect the Rhine with the Rhône, partly by making the Doubs navigable: it was originally called *Canal du Monsieur*, now *Canal du Rhône au Rhin*.

History.—In the vicinity of this city Cæsar defeated Ariovistus. Besançon was taken by Louis XIV. in person 1660, and the possession of it was confirmed to France at the peace of Nimeguen. It was fruitlessly besieged by the Allies in 1814.

Conveyances. *Malleposte* daily to Dijon by Dôle.

Diligences daily to Dijon (whence railway to Paris); to Strasburg (Rte. 171)—the scenery of the valley of the Doubs is beautiful; to Lyons.

(515)

SECTION IX.

CHAMPAGNE.—LORRAINE.—ALSACE.—THE VOSGES MOUNTAINS.

ROUTE	PAGE
162 Troyes to Mühlhausen and Bâle, by *Bar-sur-Aube, Chaumont, Langres,* and *Vesoul*	515
164 Paris to Nancy, by *Sézanne* and *Bar-le-Duc*	518
165 Paris to *Strasburg* (Railway), by *Meaux, Château-Thierry, Épernay, Châlons-sur-Marne, Bar-le-Duc, Nancy, Lunéville*	519
166 Paris to *Bourbonne-les-Bains,* by *Neufchâteau, Domrémy,* and *Commercey*	531
167 Nancy to Besançon and Geneva, by *Épinal* and the Baths of *Plombières*	531
168 The *Vosges.*—Strasburg to Epinal, by *Mutzig* and *St. Diey.*—Excursion to the *Ban de la Roche*	533
170 Strasburg to Bâle.—RAILROAD, by *Schlestadt, Colmar,* and *Mühlhausen*	534
171 Strasburg to Besançon, by Colmar, *Thann, Belfort,* and *Montbelliard*	538
175 Châlons-sur-Marne to *Metz* and Forbach, by *Verdun*	539
178 Paris to *Mezières* and *Sédan,* by *Soissons* and *Reims*	542
180 Reims to Luxembourg, by Stenay and Longwy	548
181 Nancy to Trèves, by Metz and Thionville (*Rail.*).—Descent of the Moselle.—And Nancy to Forbach.	549
182 Metz to Luxembourg, or Arlon, by Longwy.	550

ROUTE 162.

TROYES TO MÜHLHAUSEN AND BÂLE, BY BAR-SUR-AUBE, CHAUMONT, LANGRES, AND VESOUL.

Troyes is described in Rte. 143. There is a Rly. thence to Paris by Montereau.

Diligences daily.

The road ascends the valley of the Barse, traversing the theatre of the memorable campaign of 1814. The bridge of La Guilottière over the Barse was stormed and carried by the Bavarians, March 4, after a stout resistance from the French. Lusigny, a little farther on, was the scene of a conference, followed by an armistice, Feb. 24.

19 Montiéramey.
13 Vendeuvre.

The Barse rises at the very foot of the old *castle*, built, it is supposed, in the 13th centy.

A ridge of high land is now surmounted, and the road descends into the valley of the Aube, whence the Dépt. gets its name.

That river is crossed, and the road carried up its rt. bank as far as

21 Bar-sur-Aube.—*Inn*: La Poste. Bar is a town of 4380 Inhab., at the foot of Mont St. Germaine, on the rt. bank of the Aube, here crossed by a stone bridge, upon which a chapel was erected to mark the spot where Charles VII. caused the Bastard de Bourbon, who had revolted against him, to be broken on the wheel, and his body, sewn up in a sack, to be cast into the river, 1440.

There are 2 churches here: *St. Pierre* is very ancient, and its pavement sunk considerably below the level of the ground; and *St. Maclou*, which has a curious altar-piece of wood, carved and gilt. There is good trout-fishing in the Aube.

An important and hard-contested action was fought here, Feb. 27, 1814, when the Allies, under Schwartzenberg, retreating before the French general Oudinot, turned round and made a stand, the result of which was that the French were obliged to retire across the river, having lost 3000 men, the Allies 2000. Schwartzenberg and Wittgenstein were both wounded here. On the preceding 25th of February a conference of the ministers of the allied sovereigns was held here, in which the firmness of Lord Castlereagh in refusing the English subsidies to Bernadotte, who was hanging on the French frontier unwilling to take a part in the invasion of France, unless he detached 2 corps of his army in support of Blücher, contributed in no slight degree to decide the wavering policy of the Allies, and to bring the war to an end. These reinforcements, thus extorted from the Swedish army, enabled the Allies to fight the battle of Laon, and put a stop to Napoleon's successful efforts to arrest the march of the Allies on Paris.

[At *Brienne le Château*, 19 m. lower down the Aube, Napoleon went to school—a poor friendless Corsican boy, not 10 years old, able to speak no language but Italian, 1779. The military college which he attended was suppressed 1790, and the building sold and pulled down. At this spot, 25 years after, he attempted the masterly manœuvre of cutting the army of Silesia in two, by marching suddenly from Châlons and interposing his forces between Blücher and Schwartzenberg, so as to prevent their junction.

The town is named after its handsome *Château*, built by Louis de Lomenie, last Comte de Brienne, with the fortune obtained by his marriage with the daughter of a fermier général. It was the head-quarters of Blücher during the memorable engagement of Jan. 29, 1814, alluded to above. After resisting the assaults and bombardments of the French during the whole day, by which the town had been set on fire, and nearly destroyed, the Prussian commander was very nearly surprised and made prisoner by a party of French grenadiers, who burst into the town at night through the park. He escaped, it is said, by leading his horse down a stair. Almost at the same spot, and at the same time, the career of Buonaparte, who was advancing to enter the town, was nearly cut short by a Cossack, one of a band who had dashed unawares upon the Emperor's staff, and, singling him out from the rest, charged him with his lance in rest, and was only arrested by a bullet from the pistol of Gourgaud, which brought the daring lancer to the ground, when so near to the Emperor that he fell at his feet. Napoleon took up his head-quarters in the Château, which he promised to make an imperial residence or military school, to compensate to the inhabitants for the losses his cannon had caused them. But his promises were not destined to be fulfilled. However, he left by his will a million of francs to the town, where he received the first rudiments of his military education.]

[About 10 m. from Bar-sur-Aube, in an opposite direction, up the valley, is (or rather was) the *Abbey of Clairvaux*, founded 1114, in a savage glen, previously known as the Vallée d'Absinthe, by St. Bernard, then only 24 years old. It is now converted into a very capacious prison, or Maison Centrale de Détention.

Its noble *church*, in which kings and princes were interred, not inferior to Notre Dame of Paris, no longer exists. After withstanding the storm of the Revolution, it was pulled down in the first year of the Restoration, without leaving one stone upon another, not even St. Bernard's monument, in order to make room for a prison-yard!]

———

We quit the valley of the Aube on leaving Bar, and soon after enter the Dépt. Haute Marne.

CHAMPAGNE. Route 162.—*Chaumont—Langres.* 517

15 Colombey les Deux Eglises. About 15 m. to the N. is the *Château de Cirey*, where Voltaire passed 5 years of his life in a degrading retirement, in the company of the Marquise de Châtelet. He composed in this retreat, 'Mahomet,' 'Merope,' 'L'Enfant Prodigue,' and the 'Discours Philosophique sur l'Homme.'

8 Juzennecourt.

In the midst of a country destitute of picturesqueness, but abounding in iron furnaces, works, forges, &c., stands

17 *Chaumont* (*Inn:* Ecu de France?), chef-lieu of the Dépt. de la Haute Marne, a dull town of 6318 Inhab., planted on a sort of elevated platform on the l. bank of the Marne, and retaining some fragments of old fortifications. A square tower alone remains of the *Castle* of *Haute Feuille*, which belonged to the Comtes de Champagne. Here is a sort of *Triumphal Arch*, begun by Napoleon, finished by Louis XVIII.

The *Treaty of Chaumont* signed here by the ministers of the allied sovereigns, March 1st, 1814, stipulated that, in case Napoleon should refuse to agree to the reduction of the territory of France to the limits existing previous to the Revolution, the four allied powers, Austria, Russia, Prussia and England, should each maintain an army of 150,000 men in the field, and that Great Britain should contribute a subsidy of 5 millions a year towards their support; it also provided for the reorganization of the other states of Europe.

There are some manufactures in the town, and it has a large trade in the *iron* made in the neighbouring iron-works: iron is the staple manufacture of the Dépt. Charcoal is chiefly employed in smelting the ore. From Chaumont a road strikes off to Bourbonne-les-Bains.

The country from Chaumont to Langres is such as one would wish to pass in the dark, so few attractions has it for the eye. The road runs up the valley of the Marne.

17 Vesaignes.

A steep ascent leads into

18 *Langres* (*Inns:* H. de l'Europe, exceedingly good;—Poste?), situated on the slope of a hill skirted by the Marne, at a considerable elevation: 8303 Inhab. It is of military importance, as commanding the passage from the basin of the Saône into that of the Seine, and it has consequently been converted into a strong fortress. It is mentioned by Cæsar as capital of the Lingones, and its antiquity is undoubted. The *Cathedral* (St. Mammée) is its finest edifice: it is built chiefly in the Romanesque style, with ornaments, such as rams' heads, borrowed apparently from classic architecture; some portion, however, is Gothic. The portal, a work of the last centy., is quite inappropriate, and the choir-screen, resembling an arch of triumph, built 1555, is not much better.

St. Didier, the oldest church, is turned into a *Museum*, in which not only various Roman remains dug up on the spot, but also some Egyptian antiquities, pictures, and a collection of birds from S. Africa, have been deposited.

The only vestige of a Roman building is an *arch* built into the town wall, raised in honour of the 2 Gordians A.D. 240.

Diderot was born at Langres: he was the son of a cutler.

Langres is a sort of French Sheffield, and produces the best fine *cutlery*.

13 Griffonotes.

11 Fayl-Billot (*Inn:* Lion d'Or?), 2411 Inhab.

From the heights surmounted by the road views are obtained of the Vosges mountains.

13 Cintrey (Dépt. Haute Saône).

12 Combeau Fontaine.

12 Port-sur-Saône, 2067 Inhab., is situated on the Saône, here crossed by a bridge, over which our road is carried. The Romans called it Portus Abucinus. The Saône becomes navigable at Gray, 30 m. lower down; but a canal has been undertaken to extend the water-way up to this point. It is a hilly country.

13 *Vesoul* (*Inns:* Cigogne ;— Madeleine). Although chef-lieu of the Dépt. Haute Saône, this is a dull but considerable town of 6061 Inhab., possessing absolutely no interest, but seated in a fertile country.

11 Calmoutier, a dirty village.

A tolerably level road through a country diversified with woodland of oak, birch, and hazels.

18 Lure (*Inn:* H. de France, clean), a town of 3346 Inhab., in the midst of a marshy plain.

The road reaches the hills at

18 Champagne, near which there are coal-mines employing many hands.

The Dept. of the Haut Rhin is entered at Essort, a little short of

14 *Belfort*, described in Rte. 171.

Here the road to Mühlhausen turns off on the l. (Rte. 171). The distance hence is 18 kilom. The road lies through a hilly country, passing the iron-mines of Perouse; and from the high hill, surmounted on quitting

15 Chavannes, commands a fine view of the Swiss mountains. Here the Canal du Rhône au Rhin is crossed (see p. 514).

19 Altkirch is a manufacturing town of 3028 Inhab., and a place of some antiquity. Its old *castle*, in ruins, was occupied by the archdukes of Austria when they visited Alsace. It is seated on the Ill.

15 Lochwürth.

13 St. Louis, the last French town.

A little to the l. of the road lies *Huningen*, once an important fortress, built by Vauban for Louis XIV., 1681, close to the l. bank of the Rhine and to the Swiss frontier, but now a heap of ruins, having been captured by the Austrians in 1815, and blown up pursuant to treaty.

4 BÂLE, in the SWISS HANDBOOK.

ROUTE 164.

PARIS TO NANCY, BY SÉZANNE AND BAR-LE-DUC.

455 kilom. = 282 Eng. m.

The *Railway* from Paris to Strasburg (Rte. 165) has drawn off the traffic from this road.

The inns on this road, generally speaking, are dirty and bad.

14 Champigny.

13 Ozouer la Ferrière.

17 Fontenay.

16 Vauday.

17 Courtacon.

20 Retourneloup.

13 *Sézanne* (*Inn:* H. de France) (Dépt. de la Marne), a town of 4016 Inhab. The *church* is curious; it is pewed and contains some painted glass. The Boulevards are good. Sézanne was taken and burnt by the Earl of Salisbury, 1423.

[About 15 m. N.W. of this is *Montmirail*, the scene of one of the most decisive of Napoleon's victories during his so-called "expedition of the Marne," when his arms were 3 times successful in the course of 5 days (February 9-14, 1814), beating Blücher, and taking 7000 Prussian prisoners, besides cannon and standards.

Montmirail was the birthplace of the Cardinal de Retz, 1614.]

"The solitariness of the road from Sézanne to Vitry is most striking and unusual to one fresh from well-peopled England. It crosses a vast, upland, arable plain, whose entire population must exist in towns and villages widely separated from one another, since there are no hamlets or single cottages : the consequence of which must be a loss of time and labour to every cultivator, who must go 3 or 4 miles, or perhaps more, to and from his labour-field every morning and evening."—*R. H. I.*

21 Fère Champenoise.

On the 24th of March, 1814, this town (of 2049 Inhab.) witnessed the decisive defeat of the French, under Marmont and Mortier, by the allied army, vastly superior to them in numbers, but consisting of 20,000 cavalry and artillery alone. Nearly at the same time, and only a short distance off, another French corps, conveying guns and bread, was surrounded by Russian and Prussian cavalry, and having, in spite of the superiority of numbers opposed to them, bravely refused to yield, was cut to pieces.

3000 French fell here, many of them National Guards. By this victory Paris was laid open to the Allies; 7000 prisoners, 80 guns, 200 baggage-waggons, fell into their hands. It is said not a musket was fired on their side, the day having been decided by charges, by the sabre, and by artillery.

16 Sommesous, a hamlet made apparently by the passage of the new road.

14 Coole. "A new hamlet, smaller than Sommesous. Between Coole and Vitry not one house occurs : it is one immense open plain, without a tree or a village in sight."—*R. I.*

15 Vitry-le-Français, a Stat. on the Strasburg Railway. Rte. 165.

16 Longchamp.

At the point where the Marne first becomes navigable stands

12 St. Dizier (*Inn*: Soleil; tolerable), a very long and very narrow town, with 6400 Inhab., of a modern aspect, having been almost entirely burnt down 1775 through the carelessness of a baker. The *Church*, at the N. end, has a pretty and singular variety of Gothic windows. A portion remains of the old *Castle*, which must have witnessed the siege of the place in 1544, by the Spanish army of Charles V., commanded by Ferdinand de Gonzaga, assisted by Maurice of Saxony, Albert of Brandenburg, and the Prince of Orange (killed at a spot marked by a cross), who served under him. The town, commanded by the Comte de Sancerre and the Seigneur de Lalande, resisted for a month ; and, by thus delaying the march of the Spaniards on Paris, enabled Francis I. to collect his forces to oppose them. St. Dizier is now no longer a fortress. The produce of the forges and forests of the Dépt. of the Haute Marne, which is more abundantly supplied with wood and iron than almost any other in France, is embarked here on the river.

[About 14 m. S.E. of St. Dizier is *Joinville* (*Inn*: Soleil d'Or), an interesting town, prettily situated on the Marne, surrounded by vineyards. The ancient and noble castle of the Prince de Joinville, the cradle of the Ducs de Guise, in which the famous "Ligue du Bien Public" was signed, 1585, was sold, in order to be pulled down, by Philippe Egalité, Duc d'Orléans, 1790, and no vestiges of it exist. The building called *Petit Château* was a country seat of the Duc de Guise, the owner of the town. The domain was created a principality by Henri II., in behalf of François Duc de Guise, who was assassinated by Poltrot. The Sire de Joinville, the faithful servant and biographer of St. Louis, was born here. There are many iron-works on the borders of the river, the supply of ore being very abundant.]

12 Sandrupt (Dépt. de la Meuse).

12 *Bar-le-Duc*, a Stat. on the Raily. See Rte. 165.

16 Ligny (*Inn:* Sauvage ?) is a town of 3012 Inhab. It has pretty walks, formed in what was the park of the old château.

9 St. Aubin.

14 Void.—*Inn:* Aigle Noir ; not recommended.

About 24 m. S. of Void, in the Dépt. des Vosges, is the village of Domrémy, the birthplace of Joan of Arc. (Rte. 166.)

About 16 m. N. of Void is St. Mihiel en Lorraine, where De Retz wrote his Memoirs.

In the stage beyond Void we cross the infant Meuse, and afterwards traverse the mountain ridge separating that river from the Moselle.

11 Lay St. Remy.

11 *Toul*, a Stat. on the Strasburg Railway. (See Rte. 165.)

11 Velaine.

11 NANCY, in Rte. 165.

ROUTE 165.

PARIS TO STRASBURG (RAILWAY), BY MEAUX, CHATEAU-THIERRY, EPERNAY, CHÂLONS-SUR-MARNE—BAR-LE-DUC, NANCY, LUNÉVILLE.

500 kilom.=about 300 Eng. m.

Fast trains run in 10 or 12 hours; stopping trains in 15 hours.

Terminus in Paris, Rue et Place de Strasbourg. It is a splendid edifice, with a rose window at one end. This Railway, the Great Eastern of France, communicates by branches with Reims, and with Metz and the Prussian frontier from Frouard.

It issues forth on the N. side of Paris, between the Fauxbourgs St. Denis and St. Martin; it is carried over the Canal St. Denis, the ditch of the Fortifications, and the Route de Flandres.

9 Noisy-le-Sec Stat.
11 Bondy Stat.
14 Villemomble Stat.
19 Chelles Stat.

The banks of the Marne are reached near

28 Lagny Stat., a town on the l. bank of the Marne.

37 Esbly Stat.

The winding Marne is twice crossed, at Chalifert (short tunnel, 1) and at Isle; and the Railway runs between it (rt.) and the Canal de l'Ourcq, to

45 *Meaux Stat.* (*Inns:* La Sirène;— Palais Royal), traversed by the Marne and the Canal de l'Ourcq, with a population of 8356. It is a bishop's see, and its *Cathedral* (*St. Etienne*) is a noble Gothic edifice, begun in the 12th and continued until the 16th century, but not finished; its vaulted roof is 109 feet high. It contains the tombs of several bishops, and the *Monument of Bossuet,* "the Eagle of Meaux," as he has been called, who long time filled the see. His marble statue, erected by the Dépt., 1820, is stiff, hard, and by no means successful as a work of art. His grave escaped, by a wonder, violation from the Vandals of the Revolution, and even the pulpit from which he preached remains. Some relics of him are preserved in the *Evêché*—the study in which he wrote, and the avenue of yews in the garden where he used to meditate. A house behind the cathedral is a good specimen of domestic architecture of the 15th century, of stone, flanked by turrets. There is an ancient *Hôtel Dieu* here, and an Hospice, founded by a citizen, Jean Rose, is now turned into a Séminaire. Three abbeys, numerous convents, and 4 out of its 7 churches, were destroyed at the Revolution, and scanty ruins alone exist. A magnificent *Hôpital Général* has been built here, and the *Ch. of St. Nicholas* has been restored. Meaux furnishes Paris with a large supply of corn and flour from the water-mills on the Marne. A sort of *cream cheese* (fromage de Brie), known as Fromage de la Poste aux Chevaux à Meaux, is peculiar to the place, and is considered very delicate.

The Marne is crossed by a wooden bridge: one of stone which preceded it having been blown up by the French in 1814.

Coaches to Dammartin—Villers Cotterets (Rte. 178)—Coulommiers—Nanteuil.

51 Trilport Stat. The Marne is crossed before and after traversing the tunnel (2) of Armentières, 672 yards.

58 Changis Stat.

66 La Ferté-sous-Jouarre Stat. (*Inns:* Epée; France; H. du Grand Condé); a town of 2907 Inhab. (Jovis Ara ?), on the Marne, here varied by islands, in one of which, united to the banks by a bridge of 5 arches, is an old mill. Here is a pretty *Pavillon,* of the time of Louis XIII., which, it is said, once belonged to the Duc de St. Simon. The Château de Laguy, in the Faubourg de Condets, and the Castle of La Barre, flanked by turrets, near the rt. bank of the Marne, deserve mention. La Ferté is famed for its *millstones,* the best in the world, quarried in the vicinity out of beds of a siliceous cellular rock, known as Burr stone, almost peculiar to the freshwater basin of Paris, in which it forms nearly the uppermost stratum. The stone is very full of cavities, formed chiefly by shells, which have been turned into flint. The blocks are extracted in cylinders, by driving in wedges of wood and iron. A good millstone, $6\frac{1}{2}$ ft. diameter, costs about 48*l.*; but many of those which are used are composed of small pieces (carreaux) bound together with iron-hoops. The number of millstones extracted amounts to 1200 pairs yearly, which are chiefly sent to England and America.

On an island in the Marne stands the ancient and half-ruined Castle of

La Barre; the height opposite La Ferté is crowned by the antiquated town of Jouarre. La Ferté, as before noticed, means la fortifiée. The Marne is crossed by a suspension bridge.

74 Nanteuil Stat. Tunnel (3), 937 yds.

84 Nogent Stat. Tunnel (4), Chézy-l'Abbaye, 440 yards.

The banks of the Marne are very prettily varied to

95 *Château-Thierry* Stat. (*Inn*: H. d'Angleterre, tolerable), a neat and pretty town of 4697 Inhab., agreeably situated on the Marne. On the summit of the gently sloping hill on which it is built are the fragments of a *Castle*, which has now nearly disappeared, constructed, it is said, by Charles Martel for the young King Thierry IV. The site, and the ground around these mouldering walls, are converted into a pleasant and well-kept *public walk*, and command a pleasing prospect of the town and river. The most perfect of the towers is turned into a powder magazine. The *Church of St. Crispin*, on the heights, of massive pointed architecture, resembling a fortress, surmounted by a huge tower and entered by high flights of steps, deserves the notice of the antiquary. In the *Rue des Cordeliers* (the name given in France to the Franciscan friars from the knotted *cord* which they wore round the waist) the house is preserved in which the charming poet *Jean de la Fontaine* was born, 1621. A *statue* of him has been erected at the end of the promenade called *La Levée*.

This town suffered much in the campaign of 1814, when the plain of Brie was covered over with uncouth hordes of Calmucks and Lesghian Cossacks, having been taken and retaken several times (Feb. 8-12).

The Rly. crosses the Marne for the 8th and last time.

The valley of the Marne, between Château-Thierry and Epernay, well deserves a visit; it is the prettiest part of the ancient province of Champagne, the country of the champagne wine.

Coaches to Soissons.

104 Mezy Stat.

106 Varennes Stat.

117 Dormans Stat. (*Inn*: Lion d'Or?), a town of 2000 Inhab., in the Dépt. Marne, has a port on the river. The ruins of the Château of Châtillon, on an elevated and apparently intrenched position, have a very picturesque aspect.

126 Port à Binson Stat.

Epernay Junction Stat. (*Inn*: H. de l'Europe), a town of 5318 Inhab., on the l. bank of the Marne. It is the head-quarters of *Vins de Champagne;* the kinds which are grown in the vicinity are distinguished from those produced near Rheims, as "Vins de la Rivière." Aï, which gives its name to one of the best sorts, is a hill a little higher up the Marne, on its rt. bank. Almost the only "lion" is the *Cellars* cut out in the chalk rock; they are of vast extent; a perfect labyrinth, and always contain several millions of bottles, a great part of which are sold on the spot, wholesale, at 2 or 3 frs. the bottle.

"Formerly wines from these particular spots were esteemed for their peculiar qualities; but now that the wine of Aï or any celebrated locality is no longer prepared without the admixture of the wine of other places, the general quality of champagne wines is greatly improved. These growths are now of value chiefly for admixture; and a skilful wine preparer gives to his wine a quality and character fitted for different markets and countries by his judicious proportions of the wine grown in different soils or aspects. Thus a light wine is preferred in Russia, and a full-flavoured wine in England; and these depend on the selection of the wine, and the degree of sweetness artificially imparted.

"It is a common mistake to suppose that champagne wine is obtained from unripe fruit. The grapes are small, but extremely sweet; and fine wine is never produced unless the season be most favourable to the ripening of the fruit. The summer of 1842 was one of the finest ever remembered for quality and quantity.

"When the fruit is gathered and pressed, the juice is exquisitely sweet, but in a few days this is destroyed by fermentation in the casks in which it is placed. When this subsides the wine is vapid and very disagreeable; it is then stopped, and fined to as great a degree of brightness as can be obtained before the bottling season, usually in March following the vintage. When it is bottled, a second fermentation is induced, by putting into each bottle a small glass of what is called *liqueur*—sugar-candy dissolved in wine, and fined to brightness. This fermentation produces a fresh deposit of sediment or lees, however bright the wine may be when bottled. In this process the greatest attention is necessary, and the bottles are closely watched, the temperature of the air carefully regulated, to promote or check the fermentation; yet thousands of bottles explode—so many, indeed, that 10 per cent. is always charged as a cost of manufacture: but in seasons of early and great and sudden heat 20 per cent. and even 25 per cent. are broken. It was reported that Madame Cliquot of Rheims, the largest grower in France, lost in the latter proportion 400,000 bottles in the great heat of April, 1843, before the fermentation could be checked by supplies of ice from Paris thrown into the caves.

"The destruction of so large a proportion as 10 per cent. is never considered a loss, for the wine-buyers, who go round to the growers and merchants to purchase stock, always inquire the amount of breakage. They despise the wine that has lost only 5 per cent., and expect to pay more for wine that has fermented destructively.

"When the wine, after clouding with fermentation in the bottles, begins to deposit a sediment, the bottles are placed, with the necks downward, in long beds or shelves, having holes obliquely cut in them, so that the bottoms are scarcely raised. Every day the man whose business it is to attend to this process lifts the end of each bottle, and after a slight vibration replaces it a little more upright in the hole, thus detaching the sediment from the side, and letting it pass towards the neck of the bottle. This is done for some time, until the bottle is placed quite upright, and the sediment is entirely deposited in the neck of the bottle; which is then ready for *disgorging*. In this process, a man holds the bottle steadily, with the mouth downwards, before a recess prepared for the operation, cuts the wire, when the internal force drives out the cork, and with it the foul sediment. The skill of the workman is shown in his preserving all the bright pure wine, and losing only the foul. There is an indescribable manipulation in this. An old cork is ready to replace that blown out, which in its turn serves again; the bottle is filled up from some previously purified wine, and again stacked. A second disgorgement is always necessary when the wine is prepared for sale; sometimes a third: when ready, it is sweetened for the particular market, or taste of customers: this preparation is in fact a second disgorgement. But the wine now gets another dose of *liqueur*, which is prepared with great care and purity, by candy dissolved in white wine for ordinary champagne, and in red wine for *pink*; and the colouring thus given is sufficient. The quantity put into each bottle depends upon the market to which it is to be sent,—generally a good wine-glassful: this gives it the requisite sweetness, and aids its sparkling condition when opened. The high price of genuine champagne may be accounted for by the loss from breakage and the cost of preparing. So large is the demand now for this class of wines, that many of the wine districts make mousseaux wines in imitation, under the names of sparkling Hock, Burgundy, and Moselle; and even in Hungary they make and send 8 millions of bottles annually to Russia, which country consumes more than 3 times that amount from France. A large quantity of wine is made and sold as champagne in France; and a company exists in Paris, Cette, and in many other towns for this manufacture. Light, poor wines, such as inferior Chablis, are sweetened with candy, and fined or strained bright: the liquor is then passed through an apparatus which charges it with carbonic acid gas: in this state it is bottled, and in 10 min. is ready for the market. There is another establishment of the same sort in London. The English imitation by gooseberries is well known; and lately a patent has been granted, which is worked profitably, for making champagne of the juice of the stalks of rhubarb: but all these imitations fall miserably short of the real article. The genuine productions of France in the champagne districts exceed 50 millions of bottles. Moet was a name long celebrated, but it is now more than rivalled in fame, and surpassed in extent, by several others."—*W. B.*

Large quantities of coarse *earthenware* are made at Epernay from clay called *Terre de Champagne*, obtained from the neighbouring hill of Montigny.

One of the principal buildings is the house of *M. Moet*, the eminent winemerchant, in which Napoleon slept at the time of the battle of Montmirail, 1814.

The town was taken by Henri IV., 1592, after an obstinate siege, in which Marshal Biron was killed. In the hideous modern *Church* remain a fragment of a portal in the style of the Renaissance, and 16 windows filled with curious *painted* glass of the 16th centy.

Coach to Ay.

[1. A *branch Railway* to Reims (Rte. 178) diverges at Epernay, crossing the Marne just above that town, and traversing the chalk range, dividing its valley from that of the Vesle by a tunnel 3450 mètres long.]

The journey continues up the l. bank of the Marne, through a region of vines; the vineyard of Aï being conspicuous on the opposite bank. The landscape somewhat monotonous, the river appearing only now and then.

159 Jalons Stat.

172 *Châlons-sur-Marne Stat.* (*Inns*: La Cloche d'Or et Palais Royal; not a good house, but the only tolerable one; —H. de Nancy;—H. de la Haute Mère Dieu, Place du Marché.) This is the chef-lieu of the Dépt. Marne; and has a pop. of 14,468. During the middle ages, and under its Count-Bishops, it enjoyed much greater prosperity as a commercial entrepôt, numbering 60,000 Inhab. Its privileges were withdrawn, and its celebrated fairs dwindled away, after the union of Champagne with France in 1284.

The town is old; principally of timber, lath, and plaster. The *Cathedral* was built in the 16th centy.; the front has been modernised, but in other parts it is in a rich and florid style: at the W. end is a bold and elaborate gallery, within which is a pretty chapel in the style of the Renaissance, and some good painted glass, including a rose window. It is 360 ft. long and 96 ft. high. The spires are of a beautiful open work, a style of which the finest example is found at Freyburg, in the Breisgau. The Marne runs through the city; and on the banks is another fine Church, *Notre Dame*, of early Romanesque architecture, and forming a striking object in many points of view. Outside the walls is the *promenade du Jard*, planted with 2000 ash-trees (ormes).

Close to the Rly. Stat. are the *Champagne cellars* of M. Jaqueson, of Châlons, perhaps the most extensive in France: they now hold, as an ordinary stock, 4 millions of bottles; and yet he is greatly extending them.* On approaching Châlons his buildings crown the hill and line the road; and their extent may be imagined, when one portion only—that which contains his stores in cask, and his sheds for packing, where he keeps his wood and straw—were let for 6 months to the French Government as barracks for 4000 men. The galleries excavated in the chalk rock are six miles long, through which loaded waggons are driven. Through part of them runs a tramway. They are perfectly lighted by metal reflectors placed at the bottom of the air-shafts. Every bottle passes through the workmen's hands nearly 200 times before the wine is cleared and fit for use. M. Jaqueson expends 6000*l.* a year in corks alone.

Diligences—to Troyes—to Metz (?)— St. Menehould.

An account of the *Battle of Attila*, fought near Châlons, is given in Rte. 187.

The church of *N. D. de l'Epine*, 6 m. E. of Châlons, is described in Rte. 175.

205 Vitry-le-Français Stat. (*Inn*: La Cloche; landlady English) is a town

* Cutler and Lee are his agents in London.

of modern origin, on the Marne (Matrona), which is here navigable, built 1545 by Francis I., and fortified, to supply the place of Vitry-le-Brûlé, 2 m. off, which had been taken and destroyed by Charles V.: 6976 Inhab.

Coaches to St. Dizier, Joinville, Chaumont, Langres. Railway in progress.

The Rly. penetrates into the vale of the Saulx, and thence into that of the Ornain, to reach

12 Bar-le-Duc Stat. (*Inn*: Le Cygne). This town, the chef-lieu of the Dépt. of La Meuse, has 14,303 Inhab., and stands on the Ornain. It was for several centuries the seat of the line of Dukes of Bar, whose castle is destroyed all but a small fragment. The view from the upper town is fine, and here are two trees of enormous size.

In the *Church of St. Pierre*, in the upper town, is the monument of René de Châlons, Prince of Orange, who was killed before the walls of St. Dizier. It bears an emaciated effigy or skeleton of white marble on a black altar tomb.

The lower town, close to which is the Rly Stat., has some handsome wide streets and buildings. Here is a Statue of Marshal Oudinot, a native of Bar, (as was also General Excelmans); and near it is the *Café des Oiseaux*, furnished with a collection of Natural History. There is some trade here in timber, iron, and vins de Bar, which resemble champagne.

Diligence to Verdun, Stenay, and Longwy.

265 Nançois le Petit Stat. Coach to Ligny. Deep cuttings over the hills near

276 Loxeville Stat.

Lerouville Stat. [Coach to St. Mihiel en Lorraine, a town of 6000 Inhab., on the Meuse, with a curious church, containing a small bas-relief of the Entombment, by Ligier-Richier. It was here that Cardinal de Retz wrote his Memoirs.]

294 Commercy Stat., a town of 4000 Inhab., on the Meuse. Here is a *Château* built by king Stanislas of Poland. Coaches to Vaucouleurs, Bourbonne les Bains. (Rte. 166).

The railway crosses the Meuse by a bridge nearly 100 yds. long. Through a tunnel (5) of 62 yds., near Pagny Stat., and another (6) at Foug Stat., of 1203 yds., it reaches

319 *Toul Stat.* (*Inn*: H. de l'Europe), a fourth-rate fortress, irregularly bastioned, seated on the Moselle, and containing 7314 Inhab. It was not definitively added to France until 1552, having previously maintained a sort of independence as a free city of the German empire, under the nominal control of a long line of bishops.

The chief edifice is the fine *Cathedral of St. Etienne*, a type of the Lorraine Gothic style of the 15th centy., surmounted by twin spires. Its portal and W. front, designed and raised by Jacquemin de Commercy (1447), are surpassed by few in France: the façade is 227 ft. high. The interior has some peculiarities of structure deserving notice; and there is a very remarkable *cloister*. The *Ch. of St. Gengoult* has some good painted glass, a tomb of 15th centy., and a ruined cloister. The H. de Ville, a modern building, was originally the Bishop's palace.

Toul is the birth-place of Marshal Gouvion St. Cyr. The valley and river Moselle are crossed by a bridge of 7 arches, each 52 ft. span, at Fontenoy. 2 other bridges occur before

344 Frouard Junction Stat.

1. Here the branch line to Metz (Rte. 175, about 30 Eng. m.) diverges.

NANCY STATION, between the Fauxbourgs Stanislas and St. Jean, occupies the site of the ponds where, according to tradition, Charles the Bold was slain. *Inns:* H. d'Angleterre (formerly de France); H. de Paris; H. de l'Europe.

Nancy, formerly capital of Lorraine, now chef-lieu of the Dépt. de la Meurthe, is a city of 40,289 Inhab., seated on a fertile plain, not far from the Meurthe. It has been styled the prettiest town in France; it is, at least, clean and orderly, and is distinguished for the regularity and uniformity of its buildings and breadth of its streets. The *Place Royale* is surrounded by 6 or 7 fine public buildings, including the H. de Ville and theatre, and ornamented with a *statue of Stanislas Lesczynski*, ex-king of Poland, to whom Nancy is indebted for its modern aspect and architectural embellishments. After abdicating the throne of Poland (1735), he resided here many years as Duke of Lorraine and Bar until his death (1766), when these domains fell to the crown of France. The Place Royale communicates by a triumphal arch, also erected by Stanislas, with the Place Carrière, which is prolonged into the Cours d'Orléans, terminating in the gateway called *Porte Neuve*, erected 1785 to celebrate the birth of the Dauphin, the victories of France, and her alliance with the United States.

In the old town, a network of lanes, except the Cours d'Orléans and Place de Grève, stands a portion of the old *Palace of the Dukes of Lorraine*, an elegant specimen of the Flamboyant Gothic of the 16th centy. Its portal and gatehouse deserve special notice. A part of the building is devoted to a museum of local antiquities.

In the *Ch. of the Cordeliers* are tombs of the Cardl. de Vaudémont, consisting of a kneeling statue, by *Drouin*; of Antoine de Vaudémont and his lady, 1447; of Philippa of Gueldres, much praised as a work of art, by the sculptor *Ligier-Richier*, and others. From the nave you enter the *Chapelle Ducale* or *Rotonde*, an octagonal structure, of singular grace and elegance, rich in marbles, prefaced by the arms of Lorraine and Austria, erected as a funeral chapel for the Dukes of Lorraine. The black marble contrasted with the white gives a solemn, funereal, but not too gloomy an air to the whole. The coffins were taken up at the Revolution, and thrown into a public cemetery; the ch. and chapel were converted into a warehouse.

The *Cathedral* is a modern Italian edifice in the new town. The *H. de l'Université* contains the Public Library. The *Musée de la Ville*, in the Palais de Justice, Place Stanislas, contains modern pictures, &c., by *Isabey* (a native of Nancy), a portrait of Gen. Druot, and some relics of Napoleon, left by Druot to the town.

The *Ch. of St. Evre* or *Epvre*. From its tower the Burgundian officers of Charles the Bold, to the number of nearly 100, were hanged in revenge for the death of Suffron du Bachier, chamberlain of René II., Duke of Lorraine, whom Charles had seized and put to death while besieging Nancy (1477). Behind the altar a bas-relief of the Last Supper, by *Drouin*, a sculptor of Nancy. In the Chapel of the Conception are ancient frescoes, much injured by repainting.

The *Gate* of St. Jean leads out of the town to the *Croix du Duc de Bourgogne*, raised to mark the spot where the lifeless body of Charles the Bold was discovered in a pond, near what was then the Marais de St. Jean, two days after the battle of 1477, when the might of Burgundy was laid prostrate by hireling Swiss and German landsknechts engaged to support Duke René of Lorraine, whose domains Charles had unjustly invaded. He rushed on certain destruction with a dispirited army, inferior to that of his opponents, and betrayed by his Neapolitan favourite, Campo Basso.

At the extremity of the Faubourg St. Pierre stands the *Ch. of N. D. de Bon Secours*, occupying the site of one raised by the Duc René to commemorate this victory. Having fallen to ruin, it was rebuilt 1738 by the ex-king of Poland, Stanislas, and contains the *Tombs*, in white marble, of himself and his queen. He was burned to death by his clothes accidentally catching fire as he sat at the fire-side. Here are or were preserved several standards taken from the Turks by various Princes of Lorraine in 1664, 1687, 1716.

The *Public Gardens* are spacious, and laid out with taste.

Callot, the artist and clever etcher, Marshal Bassompière, and Napoleon's General of Artillery, Druot, were natives of Nancy.

The *Cotton* manufacture is carried on to a considerable extent at Nancy, as well as that of Cloth; but *Embroidery*, of the kind called "plumetis," upon cambric, muslin, and jaconots, employs the greatest number of hands, amounting to 20,000 persons, in and about the town. The prices asked here are much below those of Paris.

Diligences to Epinal and Plombières. *Railway* to Metz (Rte. 181); to Thionville (in progress).

[From Nancy run Diligences also to Moyenvic and Château Salins.

Moyenvic, a town of 1295 Inhab., which formerly possessed salt-works, abandoned 1831, since the discovery of a mine of rock-salt at Dieuze (3892 Inhab.), about 9 m. off, where the most extensive *salt-works* in France have been established, producing annually 145,000 quintals, supplied chiefly from very copious brine springs, as well as rock-salt, and employing 400 men. There is also a considerable manufacture of soda and other chemical products.

6 m. N. of Moyenvic is the town of Château Salins.

"From Moyenvic, or even farther W., the country is a vast unenclosed arable plain, uninhabited, save in the towns or villages; scarcely one hamlet or farm-house, hardly a solitary cabaret at the road-side."—*R. I.*]

The Rly., quitting Nancy, runs by the side of the Canal de la Marne au Rhin as far as

365 Varengeville Stat. Canal and Rly. cross the Meurthe on one bridge at St. Phlin. It traverses the several branches of the Meurthe at

385 *Lunéville Stat.* (*Inn:* Sauvage; the only one, and very bad), a *decayed* town of 12,476 Inhab., near the junction of the Vezouse with the Meurthe, consisting chiefly of straight streets and regular buildings, but scarcely otherwise remarkable than for the *Treaty of Peace* signed here 1801 between France and Austria, by which the frontier of the Rhine was conceded to France, as a consequence of the campaign of Marengo. The *Palace* built by Leopold Duke of Lorraine at the beginning of the last centy., and sometime occupied by the ex-king of Poland, Stanislas, has long been turned into a Caserne de cavalerie. Its gardens are become a *public* walk. Here is a very large riding-school.

This is one of the chief stations for *cavalry* in France, and has a large riding-school.

393 Marainville Stat.

423 Heming Stat.

431 Sarrebourg Stat. (*Inns:* Le Sauvage;—Grand Hôtel), a town of 2494 Inhab., on the rt. bank of the Sarre, or Saar. Here are enormous *military* *storehouses* and bakeries, destined for a depôt of provisions in the event of a war on the Rhine. Here begins the portion of the *Railway* completed in 1851 hence to Strasburg. It descends the valley of the Zorn, and turns the hill of Saverne, an offshoot from the Vosges. The Rly. is carried in a tunnel under the Castle to

448 Lutzelbourg Stat. [7 m. N. is Phalsbourg (*Inn:* H. de la Ville de Metz), one of Louis XIV.'s fortresses, planned by Vauban in the place of older works: it is of importance from its position, under the crest of the Vosges, as commanding the defiles of those mountains, and is itself built on the living rock.]

The passage of the Vosges chain of hills is effected by a series of tunnels (7), near Hommarting, about 1¾ mile (2778 mètres) in length; (8) at Hoffmuhl; (9) at Lutzelbourg; (10), (11), and (12) in the Dépt. du Bas Rhin.

The Hommarting tunnel, the longest on the line, in its subterranean course dips under the Canal of the Marne and Rhine.

We now enter the Dépt. du Bas Rhin. The entrance into Alsace is very picturesque, presenting a pleasing picture of fertility. The people differ much in customs, dress, and language from the French. The *Castles* of Haut-Barr and Geroldseck are seen on the hills as you approach

458 *Saverne Stat.* (Germ. Zabern), (*Inn:* Poste), a town of 5733 Inhab., on the river Zorn., and on the E. slope of the Vosges, here surmounted by the great highway to Paris in zigzags. This was once the residence of the Bishops of Strasburg. It suffered severely in the 30 Years' War, but has ceased to be fortified since 1696. In the vicinity is the *Château*, converted by Louis Napoleon (1852) into an asylum for the widows of military and civil public servants. The Castle of Saverne, formerly the country residence of the Bishops of Strasburg, was rebuilt (the former one having been destroyed by fire in 1780) by the notorious Bishop-Prince de Rohan. It is an immense edifice. Since the first revolution it has been used as an extensive barrack for infantry and artillery. The ruined

LORRAINE.   Route 165.—*Paris to Strasburg—Strasburg.*   527

towers of Haut-Barr, Geroldseck, and of Greiffenstein, on the heights above the valley, are very picturesque objects. S.E. of Saverne is *Marmoutier*, the oldest Abbey in Alsace.

About 21 m. N. of Saverne is the fortress of Bitche, where many English were confined prisoners of war.

You now enter the level plain of Alsace, inhabited by people of the German race, one of the richest scenes, as far as regards soil and cultivation, to be met with in France.

At Marlenheim, near Wasselonne, are the quarries which furnished stone for Strasburg Minster.

462 Steinbourg Stat., down the valley of the Zorn.
488 Dettwiller Stat.
474 Hochfelden Stat.
484 Brumath Stat.
492 Vendenheim Stat.

The Rly. from Paris is joined by that from Basle on the Glacis of Strasburg, and they penetrate together to

501 *Strasburg Terminus*, in the heart of the city.—*Inns:* H. de Paris; the best, but dear; table-d-hôte at 1, 3 fr.; at 5, 4½ fr.; breakfast 1½ fr.; rooms from 2 to 4 fr.; omnibuses run from the inns to the Rhine steamers and to the railway;—H. de Metz, near the Rly. Stat.;—Maison Rouge (Rothes Haus);—La Fleur; in a centrical situation;—Rebstock (the Vine), a 2nd-class German inn, but good.

Strasburg, capital of the ancient province of Alsace (Elsass), is a very strong frontier fortress, with 64,242 Inhab., and a garrison of 6000 men, even in time of peace; situated at the distance of about 1½ m. from the Rhine, on the Ill, which, on its way to join that important river, intersects the town, divided into several channels and a canal. Strasburg is the *Argentoratum* of the Romans.

Though it has now for a long time been united to France, and forms at present the chief town of the Dépt. du Bas Rhin, yet it bears all the external aspect of a German town in the appearance of the streets and houses, and in the costume and language of its inhabitants. German is generally spoken by the lower orders, though French is taught in the schools.

Louis XIV. got possession of Strasburg, which was an imperial city of the German empire, in 1681, by an unwarrantable attack during the time of peace.

The principal and most interesting building in the town is the **Cathedral*, or *Münster*, one of the noblest Gothic edifices in Europe, remarkable for its spire, the highest in the world, rising 474 ft. above the pavement; 24 ft. higher than the great Pyramid of Egypt, and 140 ft. higher than St. Paul's. The artist who designed this admirable masterpiece of airy open-work was *Erwin of Steinbach:* his plans are still preserved in the town. He died in 1318, when the work was only half finished: it was continued by his son, and afterwards by his daughter Sabina. The remains of this family of architects are interred within the cathedral. The tower, begun 1277, was not completed till 1439, long after their deaths, and 424 years after the church was commenced, by John Hültz of Cologne, who was summoned to Strasburg for this end. Had the original design been carried into execution, both the towers would have been raised to the same height. A doorway, in the south side of the truncated tower, leads to the summit of the spire. On the platform, about ⅔ds of the way up, is a station for the watchmen, who are set to look out for fires; and on a turret a telegraph. One of them will accompany those who wish to mount the upper spire, and will unlock the iron gate which closes the passage. There is no difficulty or danger in the ascent to a person of ordinary nerve or steadiness of head; but the stonework of the steeple is so completely open, and the pillars which support it are so wide apart, and cut so thin, that they more nearly resemble a collection of bars of iron or wood; so that at such a height one might almost fancy one's self suspended in a cage over the city; and, if the foot were to slip, the body might possibly drop through the open fret-work. At the same time, the elaborateness of the tracery, and the sharpness of the angles and ornaments, are proofs of the skill of the architect, and the excellent materials he had chosen; and it is only by a close inspection that the delicacy of the workmanship can be truly appreciated. Within a few feet of the top, the winding stair terminates, under a species of carved rosette. Several instances are recorded of persons who have either fallen, or have thrown themselves, off the top. The upper part of the spire, within and without, is covered with neatly carved names of those who have visited it; among them may be read Stolberg, Göthe, Schlosser, Herder.

The view of the multitude of rusty-coloured tiled roofs of the town is not very pleasing; nor is it the bird's-eye panorama of the rich district around, of the Rhine and Black Forest in Germany, and of the Vosges Mountains on the side of France, that will reward the adventurous climber; but rather the exploit, the great elevation, and the near view which it affords of the steeple.

Now to descend to the body of the church. The exterior of the W. end deserves minute examination.

"The gigantic mass, over the solid part of which is thrown a netting of detached arcades and pillars, which, notwithstanding their delicacy, from the hardness and excellent preservation of the stone, are so true and sharp as to look like a veil of the finest cast-iron, contains a circular window 48 ft. in diameter, and rises to the height of 230 ft.: *i. e.* higher than the TOWERS of York Minster." — *Hope's Architecture.*

"The building," says Dr. Whewell, "looks as though it were placed behind a rich open screen, or in a case of woven stone. The effect of the combination is very gorgeous, but with a sacrifice of distinctness from the multiplicity and intersections of the lines." The *triple portal* in the W. front deserves to be studied, on account of its sculptures, statues, and bas-reliefs; as does also the porch on the S. side, executed by *Sabina*, the daughter of Erwin. Although the greater portion of these carvings are modern, the originals having been destroyed by the democrats of the Revolution, who melted down the great doors of brass into sous-pieces, yet they have been restored with a perfect exactness, with great truth of sentiment, and good taste, by MM. Kirstein et Haumack. The group of the Death of the Virgin is executed in a masterly manner.

The nave was begun in 1015, and finished in 1275. The choir, far inferior to it in size and proportion, is part of an older building, attributed to the time of Charlemagne. The most remarkable things in the interior are the rich painted *glass*, executed partly in 1348, partly in the 15th centy., the vast and beautiful marigold window, the pulpit of carved stone (date 1487), and the famous *clock* in the S. transept, made in 1571, which, after standing still for more than 50 years, has been repaired by a mechanician of Strasburg, named *Schwilge*, who was occupied 5 years upon the calculations alone for the remarkable work. At 12, all its clockwork, puppets, and images are set in motion. The part of the church where it is now placed is supported by a beautiful single pillar, ornamented with statues : above the Gothic border, which runs along the wall, appears a figure of the architect of the minster, Erwin of Steinbach, carved by himself : he is interred here; and in 1835 the tombstone was discovered in the little court behind the chapel of St. John. A statue of him has lately been erected in the porch on the S. side of the nave.

The *Guild of Freemasons* has existed at Strasburg since the foundation of the minster, and is the parent of the lodges throughout Germany.

Two ancient Gothic houses near the Palais deserve notice: they have been repaired.

The *Church of St. Thomas*, appropriated to the use of a Protestant congregation, contains the *Monument of Marshal Saxe*, erected to his memory by Louis XV., the masterpiece of the sculptor Pigalle, and the result of 25 years' labour. It represents the General descending with a calm mien to the grave, while France, personified in a beautiful female figure, endeavours to detain him, and at the same time to stay the threatening advance of Death. It is looked upon as a very successful effort of the chisel: though somewhat theatrical, there is a tenderness of expression about the female figure which is truly charming. This monument was saved from destruction at the Revolution by a citizen of Strasburg, named Mangelschott, who covered it up with bundles of hay and straw, the church having been turned into a straw warehouse. Schöpflin, and a brother of the pastor Oberlin, are buried in this church; and there are one or two other small monuments. Two bodies, said to be of a Count of Nassau Saarwerden and his daughter, are shown, on account of the wonderfully perfect state in which flesh and clothes have been preserved after the lapse of more than a century. This is truly a disgusting spectacle.

Some curious portions of a "Dance of Death" were discovered in 1823, painted on the walls of the *new Church*.

The *Mairie*, in the Brandgasse contains a museum of bad or second-rate *pictures*.

The *Académie Royale*, originally a Protestant school, founded 1538, raised to the dignity of an University in 1621, but suppressed at the Revolution, has produced several remarkable scholars, as Schöpflin, Oberlin, Schweighäuser, &c.: here also Göthe completed his studies, and took his degree of Doctor in Laws, 1772. His residence at Strasburg is admirably described in his autobiography. The Academy possesses a *Museum of Natural History*, which ranks far higher than the common average of provincial collections. It is very complete in the productions of Alsace, and especially in the fossils of the grès bigarré; and there is a large series of the fossil plants discovered at Sulz-les-Bains and Mühlhausen. The botanical collection contains the section of the trunk of a silver fir, from the Hochwald, near Barr; its diameter was 8 ft. close to the ground, its height 150 ft. There are many other specimens of woods, preserved in such a manner as not only to interest the botanist, but to be useful to the practical man, to the carpenter, and the like, by showing the texture and quality of the timber.

France.

The *Public Library*, near the new Church, boasts of many literary curiosities: the principal are, the 'Landsberg Missal,' or 'Hortus Deliciarum,' of Herrade, Abbess of Hohenberg, richly and copiously decorated with illuminations and miniatures in the early Byzantine style, executed in 1180; many early printed books; Cicero, printed by Faust, 1465; a Bible, printed at Strasburg, 1466, by Eggestein; Mentelin's Bible, printed here in the same year.

Here also is deposited a collection of antiquities, chiefly Roman, and found in Alsace; also some monuments of the middle ages; a statue of Rudolph of Habsburg; and the town standard (carroccio) of Strasburg, and some painted glass from Molsheim.

The earliest attempt at printing was made at Strasburg (about 1436) by John Guttemberg, who finally brought his invention to perfection at Mayence. Peter Schöffer, who assisted him, and made many improvements, particularly in the casting of metallic letters, was a citizen of Strasburg. The total number of volumes in the Strasburg library exceeds 100,000. The *statue of Guttemberg*, on the Marché aux Herbes, now called Place Guttemberg, was modelled by *David*, and it appears, on the whole, not inferior to the one at Mayence.

Strasburg is regarded as one of the strongest fortresses in France, or in Europe; its fortifications, including the *citadel* of 5 bastions, whose outer works extend to the arm of the Rhine, were laid out by Vauban, 1682-84. Persons interested in military matters will be disposed to visit the *arsenal* of a fortress so important as Strasburg: it contains fire-arms for 155,000 men, and 952 pieces of cannon, 412 of which are required for the defence of the town and the citadel. There is a *cannon foundry* here, and one of the largest depôts of artillery in France. By means of large sluices, constructed in the time of Louis XV., by Vauban, at the spot where the Ill enters the town, the country around Strasburg, between the Rhine and the Ill, can be laid under water, except on the side of the

2 A

Porte des Mines, and on that side the glacis is mined, and the city rendered unapproachable by an army, and almost impregnable. The attempt of Louis Napoleon to seize Strasburg was made Oct. 30, 1836.

The *Palais du Roi* is a handsome edifice, close to the cathedral : it was originally the Bishop's palace.

There is a good provincial *Theatre* here, near the square called Broglie, from a governor of Alsace of that name. A very splendid *Synagogue* was erected in 1834 by the Jews. It is curious to contrast the present with the former condition of that people in this city. Nowhere did they suffer more cruel or tyrannical persecutions. The street called Brand Gasse (Fire-street) was so named because on the spot where the Préfecture now stands a bonfire was made, in 1348, to burn the Hebrews ; and 2000 of that devoted race, accused of having poisoned the wells and fountains, and thus caused the plague which desolated the city about that time, were consumed in the flames. From thenceforth no Jew was allowed to live within the walls ; and the summons of a horn, blown every evening from the Minster tower, compelled them all to depart.

The body of General Kleber (a native of Strasburg), originally interred in the Minster, has been removed to a vault in the centre of the Place Kleber, and a monument has been erected over it.

Strasburg is famous for its *Pâtés de foie gras*, made of the livers of geese, which are enlarged to an unnatural size by the simple process of shutting the birds up singly in coops, too narrow to allow them to turn, and stuffing them twice a day with maize formed into a paste, and injected through a syringe. They are generally kept in a dark cellar, and the winter is the season for fattening them, coolness being essential. There is such a coop in almost every house in the town. Sulphur is steeped in the water given to the birds, to increase their appetite. Instances are known of a goose's liver having attained the weight of 2 or even 3 lbs. Henri, Rue de la Mesange, and Hummel, No. 9, Rue des Serruriers, are said to make good pâtés. A heavy duty is charged on them in England.

The gates of Strasburg are shut in winter at 8 and in summer at 10 o'clock, but ingress or egress is allowed after that time for diligences, and for travellers by post and by steamboat; and some of the gates remain longer open in summer.

The principal *Promenade* is the *Ruprechtsau*, an extensive space, laid out in walks and gardens, beyond the walls.

Railways—To Paris, 4 trains daily in 12 and 15 hrs.—to Bâle (Rte. 170), trains 4 times a day; starting from Bâle by the early train (7 A.M.), you may reach Mayence at 10 the same night—to Baden-Baden, Freyburg, Carlsruhe, Heidelberg, and Frankfurt.

Diligences—to Besançon and Lyons ; to Metz ; to Haguenau (several) ; to Epinal ; to Mutzig and Bischweiler.

Steamers descend the Rhine to Mannheim and Mayence daily, starting from the Canal of the Ill, in the middle of the city ; they reach Mayence in 11 hrs. : but take 2 long days to mount upwards from Mayence.

The distance from Strasburg to the boat bridge over the Rhine at Kehl is rather more than 1½ m. On the way thither you pass, on the rt., in the middle of an island formed by a branch of the Rhine, a monumental cenotaph, inscribed "Au Général Desaix—l'Armée du Rhin—1801," bearing a medallion portrait of him ; and bas-reliefs representing the passage of the Rhine, the Battle of the Pyramids, and the Death of Desaix at Marengo. His body lies on the summit of the Great St. Bernard.

Kehl and the Rhine are described in the HANDBOOK FOR NORTH GERMANY.

The *Ban de la Roche*, or Steinthal (Stone Valley), the scene of the Pastor Oberlin's beneficent life and labours, is about 30 m. S.W. of Strasburg. It is described in Rte. 168.

Strasburg communicates with Provence and the Mediterranean by the

Canal du Rhin au Rhône, and with the Loire and Atlantic by the Canals de Bourgogne and du Centre, which supply the manufacturers of Alsace with fuel from the coal-basin of the Loire, just at the time when their own coal-mines had been exhausted.

ROUTE 166.

PARIS TO BOURBONNE LES BAINS, BY VOID, VAUCOULEURS, DOMRÉMY, AND NEUFCHATEAU.

kilom.=246 Eng. m.

The Paris and Strasburg Rly. (Rte. 165) is followed as far as

294 *Commercy Stat.*, whence diligences run daily to

The Baths of Bourbonne, by *Void* (see Rte. 164).

Domrémy (la Pucelle.) This retired and insignificant village, on the Meuse, has been rendered celebrated as the birthplace (1410) of *Jeanne d'Arc*, the simple untaught peasant girl, who quitted her flocks to rescue her country from foreign invaders, and to place the crown of France on the rightful sovereign's head. Here, in the deep shade of the neighbouring haunted wood, Bois Chénus (Nemus Canutum), she heard the mysterious voices of her guardian saints, St. Margaret and St. Catherine, urging her to the enterprise, and counselling her how to act; and here in the village chapel dedicated to them, now in ruins, she would spend whole days in prayer, avoiding the pastimes of her companions. After the accomplishment of her mission, by the coronation at Rheims of Charles VII., Jeanne d'Arc entreated to be allowed to return hither to join her parents, and become a shepherd girl again, an intention she was persuaded to abandon to her own destruction. The only favour that she asked from the king, for whom she had effected so much, was that her native village should be exempt from every tax. This privilege was conceded, and remained in force down to the Revolution. In the registry-book of taxes, the space opposite the name Domrémy was filled up with the words, "Néant, à cause de la *Pucelle,*" instead of the amount of contribution. The humble *cottage* in which she was born, having always been treated with a sort of veneration, is still preserved. A *monument* and a girls' school have also been raised in her honour: and King Louis-Philippe has presented to the village a cast of the beautiful statue of the Pucelle by his own daughter, "another inspired Maid of Orleans."

Vaucouleurs. Here the Maid first disclosed her mission to the Sire de Baudricourt, and hence she set forth on a journey of nearly 300 miles, to declare to the king at Chinon, in Touraine, the assistance which Heaven destined in support of his cause.

11 Neufchâteau,—*Inns :* Couronne (?) ;—La Providence (?),—a town of 3650 Inhab., on a stream which runs into the Meuse, not far off.

Bourmont.

La Marche.

Bourbonne-les-Bains (Inns : H. du Commerce;—Vosges;—Tête du Bœuf). This watering-place lies about 30 m. N.E. of Langres; it is resorted to on account of its saline hot springs, which have a temperature of 131° Fahr., and are efficacious in rheumatism, scrofula, and paralysis. The bathing establishment contains about 50 baths, and there is accommodation for more than 1000 visitors. The number usually exceeds 800, exclusive of military, who are received in a Government hospital. The situation is elevated, the climate rainy, and the resources are said to be few.]

ROUTE 167.

NANCY TO BESANÇON AND GENEVA, BY EPINAL AND THE BATHS OF PLOMBIÈRES.

kilom = Eng. miles. Nancy is described in Rte. 165. *Diligences* daily thence to Plombières; excellent road leading through the heart of Franche Comté and Lorraine—an interesting country.

13 Flavigny. The road enters the lovely valley of the Moselle, and continues along it as far as Remiremont.
12 Neuvillers.
16 Charmes. On the rt. bank of the Moselle is seen the town of Châtel.
14 Igney.
9 *Epinal* (*Inn:* La Poste), chef-lieu of the Dépt. des Vosges, is a clean little town of 10,183 Inhab. It stands on the W. declivity of the Vosges mountains, on the infant Moselle, which makes several small falls in passing through it, and it is surmounted by the ruins of an old *Castle*, whose gardens are much admired. It has a large Gothic church.

Diligences to Nancy; to Thann and Mülhausen; to Strasburg.

The shortest road to Plombières is by Xertigny (16 and 11 kilom.), but the pleasantest is to follow the valley of the Moselle, which becomes narrower and prettier above Epinal.

13 Pouxeux. A rapid ascent leads to
13 *Remiremont* (*Inn* apparently good), an old and interesting town of 5091 Inhab. on the l. bank of the Moselle, commanding fine views of the thickly wooded hills of the Vosges. Vin du Pays here and at Epinal excellent.

11 *Plombières* (*Inns:* Ours; Tête d'Or; and several boarding-houses: *charges* vary according to season, from 5 to 13 frs. per diem, all things included, except wine and lights. There is no lack of lodgings in the town.

Plombières is a town of 1600 permanent Inhab., situated in a deep narrow valley running E. and W. on the Eaugronne, at a height of 1382 ft. above the sea-level. It possesses celebrated mineral springs, and may be regarded as one of the most fashionable watering places in France. The *waters* are chiefly saline and thermal; but there are some cold springs, one of them ferruginous, *La Bourdeille*. They are very numerous; the principal are the Sources du Romains, du Crucifix, de l'Enfer, du Grand Bain (147° Fahr.), des Capucins (127° Fahr.), du Bain des Dames. They are used chiefly for baths; but some, as the Crucifix, Bain des Dames, are taken internally.

The bath-houses belong to Government; the principal ones are *Bain Imperial*, containing two public baths (piscines), one for male, the other for female bathers, each capable of holding 25 persons, besides private baths. The building also contains a subscription reading-room, which serves for balls and concerts. The others are the Bains des Capucins, Bain Tempéré, Bain des Dames (so called from the Nuns of Remiremont, to whom it belonged), and Grand Bain, or Bain des Pauvres. In all there is a public as well as private bath, and in some are douche and vapour baths.

The waters are considered beneficial in chronic diseases of the digestive organs, dyspepsia, &c. The season lasts from May till October; in June and July is the greatest throng.

In the neighbourhood of Plombières are some agreeable *walks*, especially that along the banks of the stream which traverses the town, but there is little scenery calculated to satisfy the sketcher. Vast forests of oak, beech, and fir, cover the surrounding mountains. The *Fontaine Stanislas* is a well on the side of an eminence overhung by rocks, carved with inscriptions recording the benefactions of the Polish king, who also founded a hospital here. The eminence called *La Feuillée* commands a fine view over the fertile Val d'Ajol.

A rapid ascent leads out of Plombières; a lovely and extensive view over Franche-Comté before reaching
11 Fougerolles l'Eglise: well-wooded upland scenery.
9 *Luxeuil* (*Inn:* Lion d'Or), a quiet old town, far more pleasing in site and scenery than Plombières, and possessing hot *baths*, which, though less known, are probably as efficacious. Observe the picturesque tower of the H. de Ville. A fine trout stream passes a little to the S. of the town.
15 *Saulx*, a dirty village, country less pleasing.
13 *Vesoul*, in Rte. 164.
24 Ryoz. Peeps of the Jura are obtained this stage, and towards the end of it is a rapid descent, commanding fine views of

ALSACE.   Route 168.—*Strasburg to Epinal—Oberlin.*   533

13 *Besançon* (*Inn*: H. du Nord). See Rte. 159 for description of that city, as well as of the romantic road to *Poligny*. Rte. 148.

ROUTE 168.

THE VOSGES—STRASBURG TO EPINAL, BY MUTZIG AND ST. DIEY.—EXCURSION TO THE BAN DE LA ROCHE.

139 kilom. = 86 Eng. m. *Diligences* daily to Epinal and Mutzig.

This road, through the heart of the Vosges mountains, will possess an interest with many English travellers from its leading them close to the country of the estimable pastor Oberlin. The following account is derived from the journal of an English traveller:—" We left Strasburg by the Porte de Nancy, and, crossing the Ill, passed over a country whose chief productions seemed to be tobacco, flax, and potatoes.

11 " Entzheim. In several villages the houses were hung with double rows of tobacco-leaves drying in the sun. 3 m. on rt. is the château of M. Humann, late Minister of Finance. At Altorf, the near undulating hills are covered with vineyards; in the distance the mountains of the Vosges show themselves with great beauty. At Molzheim, a prettily situated village, is a large manufactory of saws, files, and other edge tools." Near this are the saline thermal springs of Sulz-les-Bains, little frequented at present.

" At Darlesheim we cross the river Bruche, and entering a defile of the mountains lose sight of Strasburg spire, hitherto visible far above the level plain."

14 Mutzig, a small walled town of 3551 Inhab., prettily situated on the Bruche. The *Château* of the bishops of Strasburg is turned into a manufactory of fire-arms. Behind the wooded hills to the W. rises the bald head of the Donon, 3314 ft.

" At Diersheim, 2 m. farther, a fine view of mountain scenery: the valley only ½ m. broad; on l. a level greensward, from which the hills rise precipitously about 500 ft., covered with young oak, beeches, fir, &c.; before us the mountain stream, the narrow but fresh-looking valley shut up by the mountains of the Vosges, of which we trace 7 ridges rising one above another in the distance.

22 " Schirmeck, a village prettily situated at the junction of another small stream with the Bruche, has 2 large ribbon manufactories. We are now in the Dépt. of the Vosges. 4 m. farther, at Rothau, a village situated at the N.E. extremity of the Ban de la Roche, we turn to the l. out of the road to St. Diey, and crossing the Bruche by a bridge which supplies the place of that originally constructed, as well as the road itself, in part by the labour of Oberlin's own hands, reach the quiet village of *Fouday*, within the Dépt. Bas Rhin, at the entrance of the valley of Waldersbach, which, though naturally sterile, enclosed by schistose hills, rising 1000 ft. above it, is much improved by cultivation and irrigation. A cotton-ribbon factory has been established here by M. Legrand, which, unlike most other establishments of the kind, has proved a blessing instead of a curse. The children, who are chiefly employed, work at home under their parents' eyes, and thus reap all the benefits of industry without the risk of health or morals attendant upon a crowded room."—*C. W.*

In the churchyard is the *grave of Oberlin*, a plain stone with his name engraved on it, and the words " Il fut 60 ans Père de ce Canton," and round the edge, " La mémoire du juste sera en bénédiction."—" *His* memory is indeed blessed: no cottager in this valley ever mentions his name without the affectionate addition of Father. Look around; every smiling field, every cultivated spot, every tree bearing fruit, reminds them of their lost benefactor: the education of their children, the comforts they enjoy in their cottages, the very roads by which they communicate, and, of infinitely more importance, the knowledge of the road that leads to heaven, which was constantly and faithfully taught them both by precept and example,—all forcibly recall the memory of their ' Father Oberlin.' "—*Capt. W.*

At Waldbach, a few miles farther, is Oberlin's parsonage, where his study, books, MSS., specimens of natural history, and drawings remain nearly as he left them; the walls and doors decorated by him with texts from Scripture.

In the plain village church is a *monument* to him, a medallion head by *Ohmacht*. The school established by him, which in one generation redeemed the inhabitants of this district nearly from barbarism, will not be looked on without interest.

There is no inn at Fouday or Waldbach. There is a road from Fouday by St. Blaise and Villy to Schlestadt (see p. 535).

The principal mass of the *Vosges* mountains lies between Giromagny and the valley of the Breusch; they are about 120 m. in extent, running parallel to the Rhine, and separating its basin from that of the Moselle. They consist chiefly of rounded dome-shaped hills abounding in forests and often turfed on the top. The name "ballon" applied to several of them is doubtless derived from this swelling rounded form. Les Chaumes (Calvi montes), so called from their bareness, form the highest ground in the Ban de la Roche. The bulk, or thickest mass of the Vosges, rises between the Ballon d'Alsace (4124 ft.), the Donon (3314), and the Ballon de Sultz, the highest of all (4693). The rivers Seine, Saône, Moselle, and Saar rise in the Vosges.

The road from Schirmeck to St. Diey runs by

20 Saules.

19 *St. Diey* or *Dié* (*Inn*: La Poste). The name of this town of 7707 Inhab. comes from St. Dieu Donné (Deodatus), to whom it and the valley were given by Childeric II. It stands on the Meurthe, here a mere torrent. Having been burnt down 1756, it was rebuilt, chiefly by the ex-king of Poland, Stanislas.

11 L'Hôte du Bois.
16 Rambervillars.
13 Girecourt.
15 *Epinal*, in Rte. 166.

The *Baths of Plombières* are about 18 m. to the S. of this: Rte. 167.

ROUTE 170.

STRASBURG TO BÂLE.—RAILROAD, BY SCHLESTADT, COLMAR, AND MÜHLHAUSEN.

140 kilom. $\rightleftharpoons$ 86 Eng. m.

Trains go 4 times a-day: the stoppages by the slow trains are very numerous, 28 in all, and the journey in consequence tedious, occupying 5 hours.

There is 1 fast train daily from Strasburg at (?) 5 P.M., and from Bâle at 1 A.M., which makes the journey in 4 hours. Passengers by this train pass the Douane without examination, if on their way to the Lower Rhine. Carriages and baggage may be plombé at either end of the line, in order that the search may be deferred till the end of the journey; or, if you are going out of France, the plombage will relieve you from all search.

"The transit by the railroad from Basle to the steam-packet at Strasburg is, *on the whole,* well managed, and yet rather puzzling to those who make it for the first time. At the office they give you three sets of tickets, for— 1. omnibus to railroad (yellow); 2. railroad (white); 3. omnibus from Strasburg terminus to water-side (green); 4. steam-boat (white): these tickets clear all your luggage. The railroad ticket which was given to you at Basle must be produced to the booking-clerk. All the luggage must be taken to the examination room; and upon your stating that it is for the *Cologne Company's* steamer, it is registered accordingly, and you receive a ticket in the usual manner. All the steamboat luggage is put into a separate van, and being plombé is driven to the water-side, in charge of a douanier; and the van being opened, you must select your luggage, and see it on board. The conductor of the om-

ALSACE.   Route 170.—*Strasburg to Bâle—Schlestadt.*   535

nibus takes your steamboat ticket from you, and you must go for it to the office at the river-side, where it is re-delivered to you, having been countersigned."—*F. P.*

The transport of a carriage costs 50 fr.

The construction of this railway is chiefly due to the enterprise of MM. Koechlin and Brothers, of Mühlhausen.

Omnibuses ply to and from almost all the stations on the line; the fare is 30 centimes.

The *terminus*, at present but a temporary one, is on the glacis, close to the Porte de Saverne.

There are no great works on this line, owing to its passing over a dead level country, up the valley of the Ill and parallel with the Canal du Rhône au Rhin, and with the Rhine, though at some distance from them.

It is carried over many hundred small bridges, which allow the streamlets descending from the Vosges to pass. It skirts, as it were, the roots of that mountain chain, and commands some pleasing views of them and of their old castles.

7 Geispolzheim Stat.
3 Fegersheim Stat.
3½ Limersheim Stat.
4½ Erstein Stat., a town of 3550 Inhab. The Strasburghers destroyed its walls and the neighbouring fort of Schwanau in the 14th centy. Hence an interesting excursion may be made to the *Odilienberg* (11 m.), commanding one of the finest views in the range of the Vosges; the Convent of St. Odilia, with a church built 1696, with 5 or 6 ancient chapels near it.

3 Matzenheim Stat.
3½ *Benfeld* Stat. (*Inn*: Poste). This small town was taken by the Swedes 1632, and fortified by Count Horn.

A little to the W. of Benfeld and Schlestadt lies *Barr*, a town of 4200 Inhab., remarkable for the beauties of the surrounding country.

Close to Barr are the 2 castles and Abbey of Andlau, and near Barr are the fine castles of Landsberg on a lofty height, Birkenfeld and Spesburg, also the Heidenmauer or Pagan's Wall. Hüttenheim, on the l. of the railway, is distinguished by one of the finest and loftiest church towers in Alsace.

5½ Kogenheim Stat.
4½ Ebersheim Stat.
6½ *Schlestadt* Stat. (Germ. *Schlettstadt*) (*Inn*: Le Bouc), seated on the l. bank of the Ill, anciently an Imperial Free City, has now 10,000 Inhab. and some manufactures, and is a fortress of fourth class, laid out by Vauban. It was besieged by the Allies in 1815.

The *Church* of *St. George* is rather an elegant Gothic building of the 14th centy., and that of *St. Foy* is remarkable for its antiquity, having been built 1094, on the model of the Holy Sepulchre church. Adjoining it is a large convent, called *Le Pavillon*, occupied in turn by Benedictines and Jesuits, but now a barrack.

The *Tour d'Horloge*, or *Fausse-porte*, is a fine Gothic gate-tower, pierced by a Pointed archway. *Martin Bucer*, the Reformer, was born here.

Diligences go hence to the industrious town of St. Marie aux Mines, which is entirely engaged in the cotton manufacture.

From the vicinity of Schlestadt, and from other points on the railway between Strasburg and Mühlhausen, good views are obtained of the *Vosges Mountains* (p. 533), stretching nearly parallel to the Rhine on the W., and gradually sinking into the plain traversed by the railway. They have mostly a tame, rounded outline; here and there an escarpment of red sandstone, of which they are chiefly composed, breaks through the green forest, and ever and anon upon some projecting cape stands forth a ruined castle. The beauties of the Val de Villée, near Schlestadt, are extolled. 2½ m. from Schlestadt is the old castle *Kientzheim*.

5½ St. Hyppolite (Germ. St. Pilt) Stat. The town (2¼ m. from Stat.—*Inn*: Couronne) is a good point from which to start on an excursion into the Vosges mountains. It lies at the foot of a hill crowned by the ruined castle of *Hoher Königsburg*, the most extensive in the Vosges range, and very picturesque. From the top (a walk of 1½ hr.) of its massive towers a fine view over Alsace and the Rhine valley is obtained. Its origin is unknown, but it is recorded that it was taken and dismantled (1462) by an army of Strasburghers and of Bâlois, who combined their forces, and placed themselves under the Bishop of Strasburg as general, in order to put down the robber knights, its owners, on account of the depredations they had committed. It was ruined and sacked by the Swedes in the 30 Years' War, 1633. Near this are coal-mines.

4½ Ribeauvillé Stat. The best wine produced in the Vosges is grown here.

The hill rising on the W. of this town of 6568 Inhab. is crowned by the castle of *Ribeaupierre*, which was besieged in turn by Rudolph of Habsburg and Adolphus of Nassau. Lower down, on neighbouring heights, are the castles of *Giersburg* and St. Ulrich. Along the crest of the advanced line of hills forming the Vosges range above Ribeauvillé runs the curious and mysterious bulwark, of unknown antiquity, called *Heidenmauer*, or Pagan Wall. It is composed of unhewn stones, heaped together without cement, from 8 to 10 ft. high.

3 Ostheim Stat.

3 Bennwihr Stat.

6 *Colmar* Stat. (*Inns:* Deux Clefs; good;—Ange). This is a flourishing town of 12,000 Inhab., and chef-lieu of the Dépt. Haut Rhin. It is situated near the foot of the Vosges, at the distance of 1½ m. from the Ill, on 2 of its tributaries, which do much service in turning millwheels in their passage through the town. Its chief manufactures are cotton and printed goods. There are many large factories on the outskirts. In the 13th centy. it was made a Free Imperial city, and was joined to France 1697. Louis XIV., who took it in 1673, razed the fortifications, and they are now replaced by agreeable *Boulevards*.

In the *Cathedral*, or Minster, built 1363, a respectable Gothic edifice, containing some monuments and painted glass in the choir, is a remarkable painting, of the old German school, by *Martin Schön*, or *Schöngauer*, a native of Colmar. It is placed behind the altar, and represents the Virgin Mary in a bower of Roses with the infant Jesus, attended by Angels. It is remarkable for its size and composition: the figures, rather larger than life, are on a gold ground. In the *public library* (containing 36,000 vols.) are several other paintings by M. Schön; 2 altarpieces of 6 compartments each, filled with events in the Life of Christ; 6 subjects from the Passion; an Annunciation and Adoration of the Magi, also by *M. Schön*, with other pictures attributed to *Alb. Dürer* and *Grunewald*.

The *Halle aux Blés* is a desecrated church; the nave is very elegant. In the *Musée* is preserved an *aërolite*, which fell from the sky here in 1492.

The fine choir of the *Protestant Church* is now a warehouse; and several other religious edifices are degraded to similar purposes.

General Rapp, celebrated for his defence of Danzig, was a native of Colmar.

The road to Besançon and Lyons (Rte. 171) here diverges from that to Bâle.

Diligences to Lyons; to New Breisach (an octagon fortress, built by Vauban, 1699); to Old Breisach and Fribourg, crossing the Rhine; also to *Munster* (15 m.), a manufacturing town, of 4340 Inhab., on the Fecht, in a pretty, narrow valley, shut in by hills, where factories and country seats alternate with vineyards and gardens. The principal factory is that of MM. Hartman, for cotton prints, one of the largest in France, employing about 1200 workpeople: there are also spinning and paper mills.

Sulzbad, in the valley of Munster, 9 m. from Colmar, has mineral springs of acidulous water, sometimes called "bain des fous," because considered to be efficacious in hypochondriac and hysterical complaints.

4 m. W. of Colmar is *Turckheim*, where Turenne gained a victory (1675) over the Imperialists.

4½ Eguisheim Stat. This was the birthplace of Leo IX. Above the town rises the castle, conspicuous for its 3 towers.

2½ Herrlisheim Stat.

6½ Rouffach (Stat.) is the birth-place of General Lefèbre, Duke of Danzig.

ALSACE.   Route 170.—Strasburg to Bâle—Mühlhausen.   537

5½ Merxheim Stat. Here stood the castle of Isemburg, inhabited by the Merovingian kings of France.

7 Bollwiller Stat. There is a large nursery garden here, where all the known species of vine are cultivated. Some of the best wines of Alsace are grown near this.

At Guebweiler, a few m. up the valley of the Lauch, is an extensive manufacture of spinning machinery.

The Ballon de Guebweiler, or de Sultz, the highest of the Vosges mountains, is 4693 ft. above the sea-level, and 10 m. distant from Bollwiller.

4½ Wittelsheim Stat.
7 Lutterbach Stat.
2¼ Dornach Stat.
3 *Mühlhausen* Stat. *Inns:* H. de Paris;—Couronne. This town, containing many large new buildings, but for the most part old and irregular, surrounded by the Ill, and situated close to the Canal du Rhin au Rhône, was formerly capital of a small democratic and independent state, and an ally of the Swiss Confederation from 1466 down to 1798, when it was united to France. Since the beginning of the present centy. it has rapidly risen to be one of the most important manufacturing towns in France. Its population amounts to 20,129 by the last census; and 7000 workmen repair daily to the town from the neighbouring communes. An entirely new quarter has lately sprung into existence. The branch of industry from which this sudden progress is derived is the *manufacture* of *cotton prints* and *muslins.* The quantity made here probably exceeds that of any other place in the world; they are particularly distinguished by the perfection and variety of their patterns, and the fineness of the colours. Another manufacture, the *spinning of cotton,* does not flourish to an equal extent, having difficulty in competing with Manchester and Glasgow. There are several extensive manufactories of machinery. Cotton printing was first introduced here, 1746, by Samuel Kœchlin (the Orrel, Marshal, or Cobden of France, whose descendants are still at the head of the manufacturers here), in conjunction with J. Schmalzer and H. Dollfus.

Many of the mills and factories of Mühlhausen are carried on, and set a-going, by the capital of the bankers of Bâle. The condition of the workpeople is not good; they are badly clothed, and lodged generally in cellars. (See Bowring's Report.)

Mühlhausen has to contend against the serious disadvantage of its long distance from the sea (raw cotton being transported hither all the way from Havre and Marseilles), and the want of coal in the neighbourhood. Its supply of fuel is obtained chiefly from St. Etienne and Rive de Gier, through the Canal du Rhin au Rhône.

The octagonal church of *Ottmarsheim*, m. from Mühlhausen, will interest the architect and antiquary by many peculiarities of construction.

Malleposte daily to Lyons in 24 hours. *Diligences* to Paris; to Lyons. There is a branch railroad from Mühlhausen to Thann (Rte. 171), by Dornach, Lutterbach, and Cernay. Lutterbach is on the line from Strasburg to Mühlhausen, and here the branch to Thann properly begins.

5¼ Rixheim Stat. Here are made the *stained papers* for rooms, including those very flashy pictures which commonly decorate the walls of salles-à-manger at inns; and one of the chief establishments employs 200 workmen.

1½ Habsheim Stat.
10 Sierentz Stat.
3¾ Bartenheim Stat.
7½ St. Louis Stat. Baggage searched in coming from Switzerland. (p. 534.)

3 BÂLE TERMINUS (see SWISS HANDBOOK). The Bâle omnibus meets every train, fare 50 cents.

N.B.—Travellers setting out from Bâle by the early train (7 A.M.) find, on their arrival at Strasburg, a steamer ready to start at 11 A.M., and by it they may reach Mayence at 10 P.M. the same night; or they may continue the journey from Strasburg by the Baden Railroad from Kêhl to Mannheim, or Frankfurt.

2 A 3

Bâle to Paris, by Strasburg Railway, in 28 hours.

ROUTE 171.

STRASBURG TO BESANÇON BY COLMAR, THANN, BELFORT, AND MONTBELLIARD.

228 kilom. = 142 Eng. m.

The railroad is the best mode of travelling as far as Colmar, or even Thann. (See Rte. 170.)

69 *Colmar* (Rte. 170). *Diligences* hence.

10 Hattstatt. The road continues along the level plain of the Rhine as far as

14 Isenheim, where the country becomes hilly.

The pretty little town of *Thann* (Pop. 3937) has a superb Gothic *Church* dedicated to *St. Thiebaut*, surmounted by a fine spire of delicate open work more than 300 ft. high. The *doorway* is highly enriched with sculpture, representing saints and Scriptural subjects, of very good execution; it is, in short, a miniature of Strasburg, and has lately been repaired.

On the hill above are the ruins of the Castle of Engelburg. There are manufactories of cotton prints here.

A branch *Railway* connects Thann with Mühlhausen, and with the railway from Strasburg to Bâle (Rte. 170)

19 Aspach. At

14 La Chapelle, the heights which connect the chain of the Vosges with the Jura mountains are crossed; and leaving the fertile and industrious province of Alsace, we enter that of Franche-Comté.

16 *Belfort*, or *Béfort* (*Inn*: L'Ancienne Poste), a fortress of first class in strength and importance, commanded by a *Citadel*, defending the entrance into France from the side of Switzerland, by the pass between the Jura and Vosges. It was laid out by Vauban; but, besides its own formidable fortifications, it is protected by an intrenched camp capable of holding 30,000 men. The town numbers about 6000 Inhab., and is seated on the Savoreuse.

The road from Paris to Bâle (Rte. 162) passes through Béfort.

Country barren and hilly to

11 Héricourt.

21 L'Ile sur le Doubs, a bourg of 1100 Inhab., on the l. bank of the winding Doubs, and on the Canal du Rhin au Rhône.

[A détour from Béfort of 5½ m. will carry the traveller through *Montbelliard* (Germ. Mümpelgard) (*Inns*: Lion Rouge; Balance), a small walled town of 5000 Inhab., the majority Protestants, and industrious; it is prettily situated in the valley of the Allan and Luzine. The most conspicuous building is the *Château*, on a commanding height; the greater part a modern construction of the last centy., flanked by ancient round towers. It is now converted into a prison. This town has to boast of being the birth-place of the distinguished naturalist *Geo. Cuvier* (b. 1769): a bronze statue of him by *David* D'Angers has been raised to his memory by his countrymen, opposite the house in which he was born.]

2 m. from Montbelliard the road reaches the Doubs, and continues down its rt. bank at the foot of well-wooded limestone hills to the Ile sur Doubs.

Here the river is crossed by a bridge; the road still following its beautiful clear stream between hills 200 or 300 ft. high, covered with every variety of wild flowers.

The Doubs, a *doubling* stream, rises in the Jura, at the foot of Mont Rixon, 3122 ft. above the sea-level, and flows for 60 m. to the N.E. as if to join the Rhine, but is turned to the S.W., on approaching Montbelliard, by the spur or ridge which connects the Vosges with the Jura, traversed by our road between Thann and Béfort. It descends past Besançon and joins the Saône below Dôle. It has been canalised and made navigable for barges of 20 tons, and forms a limb of the inland water communication connecting the Rhine with the Rhône. It is crossed by numerous wire suspension bridges. At

11 Clerval, a pretty village on its l. bank, at the foot of hills 1000 ft.

high, the Doubs is recrossed. 10 m. farther a mass of naked rock, 500 ft. high, of the most picturesque form overhangs the road, which has barely room to pass between it and the river.

A steep hill is now to be surmounted, whose top commands a very extensive view of the mountain scenery of the Jura, to the S.E. Immediately at the foot of this hill lies the retired town of

15 Beaume les Dames, pop. 2447. It is famous for its pâtés and for its fish.

The Doubs is again crossed, and another steep hill succeeds, from whose slope there is a fine prospect of the valley and of a ruined *castle* on the opposite side, which belonged to Charles the Bold, of Burgundy.

12 Roulans.

The scenery of the Doubs valley is not unlike that of the Meuse between Liege and Namur, but surpasses it in beauty. A sharp descent brings us to the fortified town of

19 Besançon (in Rte. 159).

ROUTE 175.

CHÂLONS SUR MARNE TO METZ, BY VERDUN.

Diligences daily to St. Menehould.

Châlons-sur-Marne is described in Rte. 165. The Railway from Nancy to Metz (Rte. 181) is generally preferred to this route.

6 m. from Châlons the road to Ste. Menehould passes the beautiful Gothic *Church of N. D. de l'Epine*, a perfect cathedral in size and beauty, surmounted by a most elegant spire of filagree open work, contrasting forcibly with the hovels of the poor hamlet around it. "The exterior is especially beautiful, full of bold and graceful devices, the whole more like some luxuriant tropical plant than a mass of stone."—*S. A*. It was constructed towards the end of the 16th centy., partly at the expense of Charles V.; and its present ruinous condition is much to be lamented. Its triple portal at the W. end richly adorned with sculptures of holy persons and sacred subjects, the fine rose windows surmounting them, the gargoyls round the eaves, quaintly carved, the elegance of the piers and arches, the choir screen, or jubé, delicately carved, a bas-relief of wood over the high altar, and some curious painted glass, all merit examination.

The truncated tower was deprived of its spire at the end of the 18th centy., in order to erect upon it the *Telegraph*, which still holds its place.

13 Somme Vesle.

16 Orbeval.

8 Sainte Menehould.—*Inn:* La Ville de Metz: "c'est une auberge excellente," and its kitchen is a "cuisine modèle," says *Victor Hugo*. This town of 3900 Inhab. has nothing worth notice, except its very pleasing aspect and position; it stands on the Aisne.

[6 m. off is *Valmy*, where the French under Kellerman defeated the Prussian army and compelled it to evacuate the territory of France, 1792. Louis-Philippe was present in this battle. The French commander, who became Duke of Valmy, desired at his death (aged 82, in 1820) that his heart should be transported to the battle-field, in order that it might rest among the remains of his brave companions in arms who fell there. This wish has been complied with, and a simple monument erected on the spot.]

The road to Metz passes through a nearly uninterrupted orchard, as far as the large village of

14 Clermont en Argonne, previously entering the Dépt. of the Meuse, across the very pretty wooded valley of the Brième, and the defile of les Islettes. 11 m. to the N. lies the small town of *Varennes*, where the unfortunate Louis XVI. and his family were arrested, June 21, 1791, while endeavouring to escape across the frontier, by Drouet, post-master of Ste. Menehould, as the king's carriage was crossing the little place or square.

The ridge of land called Monts de la Meuse, separating the basin of the Marne from that of the Meuse, is crossed between

10 Dombaslé and Verdun. The passes of these hills were the scene of the campaign of 1792, when Dumouriez was opposed to the Prussians; but they have lost their military importance, now that the country of l'Argonne is drained, and its forests cleared.

We now enter the valley of the Meuse and the territory formerly known as Les Trois Evêchés (Metz Toul, and Verdun).

15 *Verdun* (*Inns* : H. de l'Europe; Trois Maures, dear—*J. L.*) is an ancient and historical town, and a fortress of the fourth class, containing a population of 10,540: it is seated on the Meuse, which here first becomes navigable. It is well known to many Englishmen as the *prison* in which they spent 11 weary years from 1803, when so cruelly and unjustly seized by Napoleon on the sudden breaking out of the war, and kept until his fall in 1814.

The *citadel*, which is alone of importance as commanding the course of the Meuse, was planned by Vauban. The beautiful Gothic chapel of St. Vannes, in the midst of it, was pulled down in 1825 to give place to a barrack.

The great event which renders Verdun distinguished in history is the dismemberment of the vast empire of Charlemagne in 843, between the 3 brothers—Louis, who received all Germany as far as the Rhine; Charles, who took the Gallic provinces S. of a line formed by the Scheldt, Meuse, Saône, and Rhône ; and Lothaire, who kept Italy and the E. part of Gaul. This act is known as the "Treaty of Verdun."

Verdun was a free city of the Empire down to 1552, and was not finally united to France until the peace of Münster, 1648.

It was taken by the Prussians, 1792, after a bombardment of 15 hours, in spite of the opposition of Marceau, Lemoine, and other brave officers, who wished to hold out still longer. It was, however, soon evacuated by the Prussians in consequence of the victory of Valmy. When the French regained possession, the revolutionary tribunal sent to the guillotine 15 young women, all under 15 years of age, for the *crime* of having danced at a ball given by the Prussian officers.

Verdun is celebrated for its *manufacture of sugar-plums* (dragées) and liqueurs.

Beyond Verdun you pass through a beautifully wooded country.

18 Manheules.

10 Harville.

12 Mars la Tour (Dépt. Moselle).

11 Gravelotte.

Immediately beneath the steep hill and corkscrew road, leading down into the plain where lies Metz, and winds the Moselle, is the beautiful village Roseillyeuse: the banks of the Moselle are flat and uninteresting.

14 METZ. *Inns :* H. de l'Europe ; very dear;—du Nord;—de France.

Metz is considered the strongest fortress in France, and forms the centre of defence on the frontier of Germany between the Meuse and the Rhine. It is also chef-lieu of the Dépt. of the Moselle ; and an important city on the score of its population (44,131), of its trade, and of its manufactures. It is seated on the Moselle, at the junction of a small stream, la Seille. The streets in the centre of the town are narrow, and the houses lofty, but the river is lined with open *quays* and crossed by fine bridges. The situation of Metz, its public gardens and quays, will repay the traveller for a halt of some hours. It possesses a magnificent Gothic *Cathedral*, whose construction was continued from the 14th to the 16th centuries, with some incongruous additions (Portal, 1754) in the style of Louis XIV. It is surmounted at the cross by an elegant spire of open work 373 ft. high (built 1427), but is without towers at the extremities. It is 373 ft. long, and the elevation of the vaulted roof above the pavement is 141 ft. (?). The painted glass of the choir, executed 1526 by Anthon Busch of Strasburg, is remarkably fine, the design good, and the colours very brilliant. The font, called Cuve de César, is very ancient, probably Roman, and oblong in shape. Here are preserved the ancient stone *throne* of the early bishops; 2 processional crosses, 12th and 14th centuries; a cope of red silk, embroidered, said to be Charlemagne's; mass-books, &c.; and a *dragon* of pasteboard, or canvas, on a wooden frame, called le Gracelli, which was formerly carried through the streets in procession, with a man inside of it. It is worth while to ascend to the clerestory gallery, to view the stained glass close at hand, and to pass on to the roof, in order to examine the skilful arrangement of the flying buttresses, and the details of sculpture, as well as to enjoy the view over the city.

Another church, *Notre Dame de la Ronde*, has a *choir*, built 1130. Within the citadel is a *Round Church, Eglise du Temple*, which belonged to the Knights Templars, somewhat like the round churches of Cambridge and Northampton. It is wholly Romanesque in style; the nave is externally an octagon: it has a low apsidal E. end. Within it, and in a building near it, probably the Knights' Refectory, are traces of painting of the 13th centy.

The *Church* of St. Ségolène may interest the antiquary.

Some of the ancient city gates remain, and retain the machinery for raising the portcullis.

The *Esplanade*, its shady walks and gardens brilliant with flowers, planted with lofty acacias, and "confided to the care of each citizen," overlooking the river Moselle with its bridges and fine buildings, are much to be admired.

Metz has one of the largest *Arsenals* in France, with cannon foundry, &c., the machinery moved by water. It is shown only Monday and Thursday, by order. The immense *Military Hospital* is capable of holding 1500 patients. Metz is abundantly supplied with barracks. There is also a *School* for the application and practice of *Artillery and Engineering*.

The fortifications were planned by Vauban, and continued by Marshal Belleisle. The most important works are the forts of *Belle Croix*, a chef-d'œuvre of military construction, begun 1731; and *la Double Couronne*, surrounded by a triple ditch filled with water. In addition to these, there is a considerable redoubt called *le Paté*, so contrived that it may be converted into an island, by closing the sluices on the Seille, whose waters may be raised 24 feet, so as to form a lake more than 6 m. in extent.

Metz, for a long time capital of the kingdom of Austrasia, became, under the Emperor Otho II., a free imperial city, and residence of a prince-bishop. At length, in 1552, the Constable Montmorency gained possession of it by stratagem for Henri II. The Emperor Charles V., furious at the loss of so strong a fortress and important a city, containing at that time 60,000 Inhab., assembled an army of 100,000 men, determined at all risks to regain it. The defence, however, had been undertaken by the youthful and chivalrous François Duc de Guise, the same who afterwards wrested Calais from the English, who threw himself into the place with the *élite* of the French noblesse, among them the Prince de Condé. The Guise, by his address and activity, conciliated the citizens, inducing them to endure patiently the horrors of a siege, and strengthened the walls by new works thrown up in an incredibly short space of time. The details of this hard-contested siege are familiar to all who have read Robertson's *Charles V*. On Jan. 1, 1553, at the end of 10 months, the Emperor, experienced general as he was, was compelled to raise the siege, having lost 30,000 men before the place. "Fortune is a woman," he exclaimed bitterly, "and she favours only the young." The Duc de Guise was at that time only 30 years of age.

There are more *Jews* in Metz than in any other city of France, except Paris.

Metz is the native place of Generals Kellerman, the hero of Valmy, and Custine, who was guillotined.

Though Metz was an important city under the Romans, who called it *Divodurum* and *Metis*, yet there are few traces of their buildings in the town itself. Without the walls, however, at the village of *Jouy aux Arches*, 6 m. off, on the road to Nancy, are the very interesting remains of a *Roman Aque-*

duct, which conveyed the waters of a streamlet from Gorze to Metz, a distance of more than 15 m. Five arches are still standing on the l. bank of the Moselle, and 17 in the village of Jouy on the rt., out of 118 : that under which the road passes is 60 ft. high.

The *gates* of Metz are shut at 11; in winter even earlier.

Travellers entering France must here have their passports signed, which is attended with some difficulty for those who wish to continue on to Paris with the train without detention.

Railways—to Nancy (Rte. 181) ; to Thionville; to Forbach on the German frontier (Rte. 181).

Diligence daily to Trèves, by Luxembourg. (See N.-GERM. HANDBOOK.

ROUTE 178.

PARIS TO MÉZIÈRES AND SÉDAN, BY SOISSONS AND REIMS.

257 kilom. = 157 Eng. m.

The Strasburg Railway (Rte. 165) is the quickest way to reach the places on this route. There is a branch railway from Epernay to Reims.

The old post-road quits Paris by the Faubourg St. Martin, and traverses the village of la Villette, situated on the basin of the Canal de l'Ourcq. At this point the most desperate resistance was made by the French in defence of Paris, against the allied armies, in March 1814, and several bloody combats were fought here.

11 Le Bourget. Napoleon on his way from Waterloo stopped here some hours, in order not to enter Paris by daylight. At the radiation of roads called Patte d'Oie (goose's foot), you leave on the l. the route to Senlis, Lille, and Amiens. (Rte. 1 and 185.)

16 Mesnil Amelot (Seine et Marne.)

8 Dammartin. The Ch. of *Notre Dame* contains the monument of its founder, Antoine de Chabannes, leader of the ferocious brigands called "Ecorcheurs:" died 1488.

[A little on the l. of the road lies the village of *Ermenonville*. In the *Château* (which belonged to M. de Girardin) Jean Jacques Rousseau resided 3 or 4 months, and here terminated his miserable existence, it is supposed by poison, if not by the additional aid of a pistol, 1778, aged 66. (See Musset-Pathay, Vie de J. J. R., 1822.) His tomb is in the midst of the *Ile des Peupliers*, in the grounds of his host.]

14 Nanteuil-le-Haudouin (Oise).

A tower of the *Château* of the time of Francis I. alone exists.

10 Levignen.

15 Villers-Cotterets, a town of 2689 Inhab. Its magnificent manor-house, belonging to the Duc de Valois, of the age of Francis I., is now degraded into a poor-house (Dépôt de Mendicité). Its former parc was laid out by Le Nôtre. Coach to Meaux Stat.

[La Ferté Milon, a walled town on the Ourcq, with an old castle, about 9 m. S. of our road, on the way to Château-Thierry, deserves mention as the birthplace of *Racine*.]

11 Verte Feuille.

13 *Soissons*. (*Inns:* Croix d'Or ; Couronne ; Lion Rouge.) Pop. 7893.

This is a truly historical city, and one of the oldest in France as regards its foundation. Cæsar found the territory of the Suessones most extensive and fertile, and under the rule of a king not only the most powerful in the whole of Gaul, but who ruled over part of Britain. *Noviodunum*, at that time the name of this city, is mentioned thus in the Commentaries : " Cæsar in fines Suessionum qui proximi Rhemis erant, exercitum duxit, et ad oppidum Noviodunum contendit." Under its walls, Clovis, by defeating Syagrius, in 486, put an end to the Roman rule in France. He established here the throne of the Francs, and made Soissons his capital. Afterwards, and because some of his successors made it the seat of government, they were called Kings of Soissons. Charles the Simple was here defeated 924.

Its importance, in a military point of view, as commanding a passage over the Aisne, is shown by its fortunes in the campaign of 1814, when it was twice taken and retaken within 4 weeks —first, by the Russian general Chernicheff with his Cossacks, by a coup-de-main, February 13th, when its governor, the brave General Rusca, was killed by a cannon-shot on its walls. The French, however, regained it the same day, Chernicheff being compelled to withdraw. Napoleon laid the greatest stress upon the possession of it, enjoining the garrison to hold it to the last drop of their blood; and, if his injunction had been complied with, Blücher and the Silesian army, pursued by Napoleon across the Marne, and pent up between his army and Soissons, with the army of Marmont and Mortier behind it, would probably have been annihilated. Fortunately for the old Prussian Marshal, he obtained possession of the place by a disgraceful capitulation on the part of the French governor, which deranged all Napoleon's plans, March 3rd, and Blücher thus escaped out of the trap which Napoleon had laid for him.

Soissons in 1814 was defended only by antiquated ramparts; it has since been converted into a regular fortress. It is a city of 8149 Inhab., pleasantly situated on the banks of the Aisne.

Owing to what it has suffered from time and from the wars of 1567, when it was sacked by the Huguenots, and that of 1814, Soissons of the present day is a new town, and has a modern air, with few tangible relics to which one may attach the recollections of ancient times. The chief buildings remaining here consist of the *Castle*, occupying only the site of that inhabited by the Merovingian kings.

The *Cathedral*, surmounted by a solitary tower, is a very dilapidated edifice, founded in the 12th centy., whose venerable appearance is much injured by injudicious repair. The choir is of the 13th centy. (1212). The S. transept ends in a semicircle. Soissons is one of the oldest episcopal sees in France; indeed, traditions of the Church would refer its origin to the primitive Christians.

Of the once magnificent *Abbey of St. Jean des Vignes*, where Thomas Becket was received when in exile, which was castellated and moated, and formed a fortress by itself, detached from the town, only the W. end of the church, surmounted by 2 towers, crowned by spires, remains. These are a great ornament to the town, and were spared at the entreaty of the citizens, when the ruthless democrats destroyed the rest. The towers and the portal are probably of the 13th centy., the spires are more modern. The *Church of St. Leger* is interesting for its architecture, and tolerably perfect.

Some fragments of antiquities found in and near the town are stored away in a *Museum*. The famous tomb of St. Drausen, and the statues of several abbesses, have been saved from destruction.

A short walk across the fields, along the rt. bank of the Aisne, leads to an institute for *Deaf* and *Dumb*, occupying the site of the once celebrated *Abbey of St. Médard*, which has been razed to the ground, the only remnant being a subterranean *Crypt*, the date of which is referred by some to the 11th centy. (?) It is remarkable for the beauty of the construction, the sharpness of the stone, and the good preservation of the colours upon it. Here were buried the kings Clothaire and Sigebert; and in a dismal dungeon adjoining it, measuring 8 feet by 3 feet, which is still pointed out, Louis le Débonnaire is supposed to have been confined by his own son, Clothaire, 833. The verses on the wall, apparently referring to him, are not older than the 15th centy.

Among the natives of Soissons are kings Caribert, Chilperic, and Clothaire II., and the Duc de Mayenne, chief of the League, the opponent of Henri IV., who died here.

Diligences run to Laon (22 Eng. m.) (see Rte. 187); to Compiègne, Amiens, &c.; to Chateau-Thierry Stat.

[About 10 m. N. of Soissons is the very curious Gothic fortress of *Coucy le Château*, the beau ideal, in extent, arrangement, and picturesqueness, of a feudal castle, and perhaps the finest in France, though in ruins. It is attached to an old and picturesque walled town (*Inn:* Pomme d'Or), situated on the extremity of a high headland overlooking a deep valley. The castle consists of an outer bail or court, whose walls, garnished with circular towers at the angles about 100 ft. high, and with semicircular ones, or bastions, along the curtains, were partly blown up by Mazarin, 1652. Within this is the inner bail or ward, out of which rises the majestic circular *Donjon*, the prominent feature of the building—fit emblem of the proud barons that built and held it — whose boastful motto was,—

" Roi je ne suis,
Prince, ni Comte aussi,
Je suis le Sire de Coucy."

Time has made little impression on it, and even the earthquake's shock, though it has cleft its walls vertically from top to bottom in 1692, leaving the cracks still perceptible, has not altered its symmetry, nor caused it to swerve out of the perpendicular. It is 187 ft. high and 325 ft. in circumference; and its walls, massive in proportion, are 34 ft. thick. Except a row of windows surmounting its circlet of machicolations at the top, almost the only external openings are mere loopholes. It was entered by a narrow bridge now removed; over the door is the fragment of a bas-relief, sculptured with the device of the Coucy, a combat between a man and a lion. The interior, divided into 4 stories originally, is now entirely gutted, but around each stage runs an arcade of pointed recesses. On the ground floor, to the rt. as you enter, is a well 200 ft. deep, cut in the rock. Beside it was originally a flour-mill and oven. Excepting the topmost story, the halls of the donjon must have been inconveniently dark. Two of the external round towers are furnished with dungeons, whose only entrance was a hole in their roof, like the mouth of a well. Vast casemates ran under the outer walls.

The construction of Coucy Castle dates from the 13th centy.: its founder was Enguerrand III. de Coucy.

La Belle Gabrielle had a house here, which still exists, where she was visited by Henri IV. Her son, the Duc de Vendôme, was born here.]

The road to Reims follows the course of the Vesle, a small stream, upwards through

18 Brain-sur-Vesle.
13 Fismes.
10 Jonchery.
17 REIMS. (*Inn*: Lion d'Or; excellent; fronting the Cathedral.) "This city of 43,643 Inhab., the largest (though not chef-lieu) in the Dépt. Marne, so inseparably connected with the history of the Frankish monarchy, retains many vestiges of the Roman domination. The 4 gates of the city were called respectively the *Porta Martis, Porta Cereris, Porta Veneris,* and *Porta Bacchi:* the first 2 still preserve their appellations. The ancient *Porta Martis* (for there is a modern one beside it) is a splendid triumphal arch, recently restored. The fragments of the Corinthian columns are most delicately fluted, and acquire additional grace from the Gothic towers and rough walls around them. This noble relic has undergone strange vicissitudes. It was employed as the city gate until 1554, when earthworks were raised against it, and the adjoining gate opened. It was uncovered in 1595, but afterwards walled over again. In 1677 it was uncovered, but the apertures were walled. M. Guizot's commission brought it to its present state.

" **The Cathedral,* built 1241, is one of the most sumptuous Gothic edifices in France. It is, perhaps, the finest shrine of masonry N. of the Alps (for Milan must be reckoned as the finest in the world); and highly as the expectations of the stranger may have been raised, they will not be disappointed. The building, as it now stands, was the work of Robert de Coucy, begun 1212. The towers are unfinished; they were to have been crowned by open-work spires, such as did exist in the now demolished church of St. Nicaise; and by their absence the elevation loses much of its completeness. Extensive restorations in good taste have been for many years in progress. The great merit of Reims arises from the unity of the conception. Completely as the portal is covered and filled with ornaments, not one can be considered as an afterthought. Having massed the whole design, the architect then worked out the details, without interfering with the general effect. Many of the 600 statues on the portal are colossal, and generally elegant, both in design and workmanship; those in the transepts are not so good. The *rose windows* in the W. front, of which there are two, a large one above, more than 40 ft. in diameter, and one within the vast portal, are filled with the most brilliant painted glass. The gemmed windows of Aladdin's palace could hardly have been more splendid. Size of the building: its length is 466 ft., its height 121. The architecture of the interior bears a near resemblance, in the main outlines, to Westminster Abbey, excepting that it is bolder and simpler. It is much less florid and decorated than the exterior, and this has sometimes been considered as a defect; but it is evident that the architect calculated upon the gloom produced by the painted glass. The W. wall is ornamented with tiers of statues, placed, not in arches, but in deep cells, so that each figure is brought out by a background of shade. Almost all the monuments have been swept away; but the sarcophagus of Jovinus, prefect of Reims, is here, brought from the Abbey of *St. Nicaise* —a curious national monument. It is composed of a single block of pure white marble, about 9 ft. in length and 4 in height. Jovinus is represented in fine bas-relief, on horseback, having just broken his spear in the neck of a lion, which was leaping on a man. Many figures surround Jovinus; some, as well as himself, apparently portraits, beautiful in countenance, and perfectly made out in dress and accoutrements. A dead boar and other animals are in the foreground. The figures are about half the size of life; and on the sides of the tomb, shaped like an altar, the story is continued in very low relief. Much learned controversy has been excited on the subject of the bas-reliefs Some antiquarians are of opinion that they refer (though *how* it would be difficult to conjecture) to the defeat of the *Alemanni* (A.D. 367) by this consular general. Jovinus was a Christian; but there is no token of his faith upon this very curious monument. Amongst the curiosities of the Cathedral, the clock, standing in the N. transept, must not be omitted, inasmuch as it is probably the oldest moving piece of horology in existence. From the style of the Gothic tracery and carvings, it seems to belong to the 15th centy. When it strikes, a door opens, and the effigy of a man looks out; other smaller figures sally forth and make the round, as in the common Dutch clocks. This, without doubt, was considered in its time as a masterpiece. It is well worth while to ascend the tower, in order to inspect closely the details of the upper part of the building.

" The *Abbey Church of St. Remi is the burial-place of St. Remigius, the Apostle of the Franks (d. 545). Clovis and Clotilda founded the Church: the monastery owes its origin to Archbishop Turpin, who will be better recollected from the history which passes under his name, so often quoted in romance, than from any other of his deeds. Amongst its treasures was the *Sainte Ampoule*, employed in the coronation of the kings of France, and of which a fragment, said to have been preserved when the rest of the relics were dispersed, was produced at the consecration of Charles X. As it now stands, the principal portions were erected between 1048 and 1162: the choir is of the latter period, of a fully developed and beautiful Gothic. The S. transept, in the flamboyant style, was built in 1506. It is a most curious and harmonious mixture of inharmonious parts, of different periods and different styles. It is a large Ch. 350 ft. long.; it was extremely injured during the Revolution, but has undergone a thorough repair. The bodies of Carloman, Louis d'Outremer, Lothaire, and of 25 archbishops buried in its walls, were torn up, 1793. *The tomb of St. Remi*, erected by Cardinal Abbot Robert de Lenoncourt, about 1533, escaped the iconoclasts; and, though not in accordance with the Church, for it is in a Flemish-Italian style, is grand from its size and sumptuousness. It was reconstructed by a private individual in 1803. It is ornamented with 12 statues, as large as life, of the 12 peers of France, to whom Turpin gave so much chivalrous celebrity: 6 are the prelates of Rheims, Laon, Langres, Beauvais, Châlons, Noyon; 6 lay peers—the Dukes of Burgundy, Normandy, and Aquitaine, the Counts of Flanders, Champagne, and Toulouse: the figures are of white marble, finely sculptured, but in the rather theatrical and exaggerated taste of the time.

"Many of the streets of Reims will remind the traveller of an old English town. In these the houses are low, usually of one story. The smart new portions of the town, in which great improvements are making, are of the usual French character" (*F. P.*); yet, on the whole, the stranger who has heard Reims described as one of the oldest towns in France will be surprised to find that it has so very little appearance of antiquity. A few examples of picturesque street-architecture remain : in the *Rue du Tambour* is the hotel of the Comtes de Champagne—*la Maison des Musiciens* (13th cent.); in the *Marché au Blé*, a house decorated externally with rich and well-preserved oak carving. The inn called *Maison Rouje*, near the Cathedral, is interesting as being the same (or occupying the same site as that) in which Jeanne d'Arc was lodged at the coronation of Charles VII., though it then bore the sign of L'Ane Rayé (Zebra). In the Rue de Cérès is the house in which Colbert, the enlightened minister of Louis XIV., was born, 1619; his father is supposed to have been a draper, and he to have served as a shopman and traveller. The Abbé Pluche, author of the 'Spectacle de la Nature,' was also a native of Rheims. Mr. Pitt spent some months here in 1786 with his friend Wilberforce, in order to learn French. Drouet, Comte d'Erlon, is buried in the *Cemetery*; his sword is at the foot of the pedestal bearing his bust.

The ramparts and fosse have been planted and converted into agreeable *public walks* surrounding the town, and commanding fine views. The promenade is large and well laid out. The *Café Courtois* is handsomely fitted up.

Diligences to Mezières and Sédan, Railway to Paris by Epernay; and to Strasburg.

Reims is the metropolitan see of France, and one of the nuclei of the civilisation of that country; and was the place of *coronation* of the French kings from the time of Philippe Auguste to that of Charles X., with the two exceptions of Henri IV. and Louis XVIII. It was selected for that distinction, probably, as the place of deposit of the *Sainte Ampoule*, or holy flask of oil, brought by a dove from heaven to St. Remy as he was about to baptize Clovis (496). The persuasion of Clothilda, his queen, and a vow made before the decisive battle of Zulpich, had induced the Frankish conqueror to receive the Christian rite from the hands of the bishop; who, as the new convert kneeled before him, received him as a member of the church with these haughty words:—"Mitis depone colla Sicamber; incende quod adorâsti, et adora quod incendisti." The story of the Ampoule, however, is said to have been an invention of the Bishop Hinckmar, 360 years after Clovis; it is certain that no contemporary records make mention of it. After having been publicly smashed to pieces by a sansculotte named Ruhl, in 1793, it most unaccountably reappeared at the coronation of Charles X.

No celebration of the august ceremony of the "Sacre" in that imposing and well-proportioned pile, the Cathedral, can have exceeded in interest that of Charles VII., the result of the enthusiasm of the Maid of Orleans. "The people looked on with wonder and with awe. Thus had really come to pass the fantastic visions that floated before the eyes of the poor shepherd-girl of Domrémy! Thus did she perform her two-fold promise to the king within 3 months from the day when she first appeared in arms at Blois. During the coronation of her sovereign —so long the aim of her thoughts and prayers, and reserved to be at length achieved by her own prowess — the Maid stood before the high altar by the side of the king, with her banner unfurled in her hand. 'It had shared the danger,' she observed; 'it had a right to share the glory.'

"The holy rites having been performed, the Maid knelt down before the newly-crowned monarch, her eyes streaming with tears. 'Gentle King,' she said, 'now is fulfilled the pleasure of God, who willed that you should come to Reims and be anointed, showing that you are the true king, and he to whom the kingdom should belong.' She now regarded her mission as accomplished, and her inspiration as fled. 'I wish,' she said, 'that the gentle king should allow me to return towards my father and mother, keep my flocks and herds as before, and do all things as I was wont to do.'"—*Lord Mahon*.

In the campaign of 1814 Reims was surprised and taken by a Russian force under St. Priest, the French garrison being quite inadequate, from their small numbers, to defend the walls; but Napoleon did not allow the Russians to keep it many hours. Hurrying to the spot with an army broken by the defeat of Laon, he nevertheless completely took by surprise St. Priest, who was mortally wounded while endeavouring to stem the torrent and secure his retreat. This was almost the last military success which Buonaparte gained.

The situation of Reims is agreeable, on the rt. bank of the Vesle, surrounded by slopes covered with vineyards.

CHAMPAGNE WINES.—"This city is thriving: the chief article of commerce is the *wine*, which, in spite of all the powers of revolutionary geography, will perpetually keep the ancient name of the province of *Champagne* in remembrance. These *wines* are divided into 'Vins de la Rivière,' and the 'Vins de la Montagne;' the former being for the most part white, and the latter red. The best *river wines*, strictly so called, are obtained from the vineyards situate in the valleys and on the sides of the hills that border the Marne at Aï, Hautvilliers, Epernay, Dizy, Avernay, &c., and occupy a tract of country of about 5 leagues in extent; but the estate of Cumières, though in the midst of these vineyards, lying under the same line and with the same exposure, yields red wines only, and of a superior quality to the others that are grown in the same neighbourhood. In general, it may be observed that the vineyards on the banks of the Marne supply the choicest wines. (Rte. 165.)

The road to Mézières lies through an uninteresting portion of that part of Champagne called "La Pouilleuse," passing

17 Isle, beyond which it enters the Dépt. of the Ardennes, and reaches

20 *Rethel*, a town of 6800 Inhab., prettily seated on the Aisne, whose branches divide it into several parts.

A hilly country succeeds; once forest, now cleared for the most part, and bare and sad of aspect in consequence.

12 Saulces au Bois.

10 Launay.

19 *Mézières* (*Inn:* H. du Palais Royal; very good), one of Vauban's strong fortresses, and at the same time the cheflieu of the Dépt. des Ardennes, is seated on the rt. bank of the Meuse, on the isthmus of a promontory formed by the river, which washes its walls on two sides, and separates it from Charleville. It has 4083 Inhab.

The *parish Church* is a very fine flamboyant Gothic edifice of the 16th centy., in which the marriage of Charles IX. with Isabelle d'Autriche was solemnised 1570. Among the good points about it are its lateral portals, in the style of the latter part of the 15th centy., and 2 curious bas-reliefs in the choir. There are some bits of painted glass inserted in blank windows, and over the N. aisle is a bomb-shell, one of those thrown by the Allies when they invested the place after the battle of Waterloo, which has remained sticking in the roof ever since the town capitulated.

A more glorious event in the annals of Mézières was the resistance which it made to the Spanish army of Charles V., 40,000 strong, in 1521. The Chevalier Bayard gallantly took the command of the town at a time when Francis I. had proposed to blow it up and abandon it, as too weak to offer any resistance, and to lay waste the country around, as the only means of stopping the enemy. With a force of only 2000 men Bayard endured a siege of 6 weeks, in the course of which *bombs* were for the first time used, and were most plentifully showered upon the garrison, but with little effect. The *banner of Bayard* is said to be still preserved in the H de Ville.

Charleville, a town of 7773 Inhab., is only a mile distant from Mézières, and is connected with it by an avenue and suspension-bridge. It has become a thriving place since it ceased to be a fortress at the end of the 17th centy., and manufactures nails, hardware, fire-arms, &c.

The *Meuse* makes a wide sweep around, and then dives into a narrow trench or *defile* cut by it in the slate rocks, which stretch with the most contorted windings nearly as far as Givet. The depths into which the Meuse enters are a narrow and deep chasm in the chain of the Ardennes; the breach is in places no wider than the river itself, its sides often vertical, sometimes 130 ft. high. It expands suddenly at Fumay, a town most picturesquely planted on a holm on the banks of the river, overhung by precipitous rocks, called *Les Dames de la Meuse*, 130 ft. high, and overlooked by the picturesque *ruins* of the castle of Hierches. Slate is the chief product of this desolate district; it is sent down the Meuse to Holland from Fumay, where there are extensive quarries. In 1623 slates were sent from the Ardennes to roof the ch. of St. James of Compostella in Spain.

[20 m. N. of Mézières is *Rocroy,* a small fortress, in front of which *le Grand Condé* gained the greatest of his victories over the Spaniards, at the age of 22 years. The army opposed to him were veteran bands of Walloons, Spaniards, and Italians, commanded by a mature and experienced general; and it was only after thrice heading the charge against this serried infantry, that Condé at length broke their array. The Spanish general Fuentes, who conducted the battle from a litter, being wounded, was found among the dead. The battle-field is on a plain, at that time (May 19, 1643) surrounded by marshes and dense forests on all sides, but now much changed by clearing and drainage.]

The road to Sédan lies through a pretty country.

9 Flize. The Meuse is crossed on quitting Mézières, and again twice before entering

13 SÉDAN.—*Inns:* Croix d'Or; good; —H. de Turenne (?);—Croix d'Argent; nasty. Sédan, situated on the rt. bank of the Meuse, is both an important frontier fortress, commanding the entrance from Luxembourg into France, and a prosperous manufacturing town of 13,719 Inhab., but is a dirty, disagreeable place. It is celebrated for the *fine cloths*, especially the black, which are made here, and not less than 11,000 or 12,000 persons are employed in this branch of industry.

Down to the time of Louis XIII. it was capital of a principality belonging to the family of La Tour d'Auvergne, Ducs de Bouillon; but in 1642 the Duc de B., having engaged in the conspiracy of Cinq-Mars against Richelieu, was too happy to give it up to save his head. Marshal Turenne was born here 1611, in a small pavilion attached to the *château,* which was razed to the ground at the Revolution, and no souvenir of him remains, save a black stone to mark the spot where it stood. An ugly statue of him has been set up in the Place. The château itself is also demolished. In fact, Sédan has nothing of interest to detain the traveller.

At Bazeilles, a neighbouring village, is, or was, the château where Turenne was nursed, and an *avenue* planted by him. At this place the Comte de Soissons defeated the army of Richelieu 1641, but perished on the field of battle.

Malleposte to Rheims and Epernay Stat. on the Railway to Paris. (Rte. 165.)

ROUTE 180.

REIMS TO LUXEMBOURG, BY STENAY AND LONGWY.

REIMS, in Rte. 178.
17 Isle (Marne), in Rte. 178.

23 Pauvres.

16 Vouziers (Ardennes), a town of 2000 Inhab.; on the l. bank of the Aisne.

13 Boux aux Bois.

9 Buzaney, a bourg of less than 1000 Inhab., retaining portions of its old fortifications, and an entrance-gate called Porte St. Germaine. On the site of the Citadel is the *Château de la Cour*, anciently the habitation of St. Remy, Bishop of Reims. To the N. of the village, and in the upper part of it, stands the singular edifice called *Mahomet*, said to have been a mosque built by Pierre d'Angluré, who, having followed St. Louis to the Holy Wars, was taken prisoner by the Saracens, and released after a long captivity, on giving his word of honour that he would himself bring back his ransom. He accordingly sold part of his lands to raise the money, and returned, after many adventures, in the course of which he lost an eye, to the Sultan, who was so pleased with his honourable conduct that he restored the gold to the Christian knight, on the condition that he should build a mosque on his return home. The building is constructed of large stones, and the door on the E. was originally the only opening; the windows have been broken out.

The Dépt. of the Meuse is entered shortly before reaching

21 Stenay, an ancient town of 3140 Inhab., once an important frontier fortress, but after its capture by Louis XIV. its fortifications were razed, 1654. It belonged to the family of Condé down to 1791, and the Vicomte de Turenne, when in rebellion against the Court and Mazarin, threw himself into it, and was joined by the Duchesse de Longueville, so celebrated in the wars of the Fronde. They here signed a treaty of alliance with Spain.

The country around is flat, and subject to inundations from the Meuse.

15 Montmédy is a fourth-class fortress, consisting of an upper town surrounded by 8 bastions, and a lower one badly fortified. It stands on the Chiers, a tributary of the Meuse, and was taken from the Spaniards 1657. 3169 Inhab.

28 Longuyon.

18 Longwy (*Inn:* Croix d'Or; very good, and the only tolerable inn on the road). This is another fortress; the works of the upper town were laid out by Vauban, 1682, and Louis XIV. styled it the Iron Gate of France, from its important military position, at an angle of the French territory projecting into Luxembourg. It was taken by the Duke of Brunswick and the Prussians, 1792, and again 1815, when, after a severe bombardment, and a noble resistance on the part of the French General Ducos and a small garrison, it surrendered on honourable terms to the Allies commanded by the Prince of Hesse-Homburg.

Mercy, the Bavarian General, the antagonist of le Grand Condé at Fribourg and Nordlingen, where he fell nobly on the battle-field, 1645, was born here.

We cross the French frontier and enter the Duchy of Luxembourg before reaching

6 Auhange.

3½ posts, *Luxembourg.* See HANDBOOK FOR NORTH GERMANY.

ROUTE 181.

NANCY TO TRÈVES, BY METZ AND THIONVILLE (RAIL) — DESCENT OF THE MOSELLE — AND NANCY TO FORBACH.

Railway to Metz 35¼ kilom.—trains in 2 hours; and to Forbach 78¾ kilom.

The Moselle flows at a distance of about 7 m. from Nancy, and is crossed by the Railroad.

6½ Frouard Junction Stat. Here the Metz Rly. diverges from the Paris and Strasburg lines (Rte. 165).

9½ Marbache Stat.

13¾ Dieulouard Stat.

18¾ *Pont-à-Mousson* Stat. (*Inn:* H. d'Angleterre), a town of 7218 Inhab., on the Moselle, here crossed by a bridge. The fine Gothic *Ch. of St. Martin*, ending in 3 apses and ornamented with paintings of the Lorraine school, in the style of the latter part of the 13th centy., and in the square or Place, which is surrounded by arcades, an ancient mansion curiously decorated externally with sculptures, called *Maison des 7 Péchés Capitaux*, deserve notice. The buildings of the ancient Abbaye de St. Marie are converted into a Séminaire.

This is the birthplace of Marshal Duroc, the friend of Napoleon, in whose arms he died mortally wounded at the battle of Bautzen, 1813. The high road here crosses the Moselle to its rt. bank.

23¼ Pagny Stat.
27¾ Novéant Stat.

The ruined Roman aqueduct, described p. 445, is at *Jouy aux Arches*.

35¼ METZ *Station*, in Rte. 175.
[The Stations from Metz to Forbach are—
40 Peltre
44¼ Courcelles
49½ Remilly
53½ Herny
60½ Faulquemont
66¾ SAINT-AVOLD
71¼ Hombourg
75½ Cocheren
78¾ FORBACH TERMINUS. The frontier town of Germany: 4281 Inhab.

Malleposte hence to Mayence and Frankfurt (see NORTH GERMAN HANDBOOK) in 18 hrs.

Metz to Trèves—Railway to *Thionville*.
17 Mondelange. The correction of the course of the Moselle below Metz has been carried to such an extent, that it resembles a canal running between dykes. In Prussia little has been done: in many places the current is so strong that the steamer, in ascending, stems the rapids only by the aid of a towing-horse.

The small town of Richemont stands prettily on the l. bank of the Moselle, at the confluence of the Orne.

11 *Thionville* (Germ. Diedenhofen) (*Inns:* H. du Luxembourg;—du Commerce;—Lion d'Or), a town of 5800 Inhab., a fortress of third class, constructed by Vauban, consisting of 11 bastions covered by some external works, and by a fort on the rt. bank of the Moselle. It contains 5600 Inhab.; many of its houses bear the date of the 16th centy.

It was taken from the Spaniards, 1558, by the Duc de Guise, but was restored to Philip II. by the treaty of Cateau Cambresis. The Grand Condé, while yet Duc d'Enghien, captured it, 1643, after 3 months of siege and 40 days of open trenches. The Prussian custom-house on the river is near Serl, the French at . The *cuisines de Charlemagne* are not older than the 16th centy. The *Tour aux Puces* is now Magasin d'Artillerie.

17 Sierck, the last town in France, is agreeably situated on the rt. bank of the Moselle, between the Stromberg and the rocks of the valley of Montenach, surmounted at a considerable height by an old *Castle* in ruins, commanding the course of the Moselle: it is a fine point of view.

A little below Sierck is the camp of Kunsberg, thrown up by Vauban, a series of fortified lines, in which Marshal Villars arrested the march of Marlborough.

26 Sarrebourg (3 Pruss. posts).
TRÈVES. HANDBOOK FOR NORTH GERMANY.

ROUTE 182.

METZ TO LUXEMBOURG, OR ARLON, BY LONGWY.

The Inn at Longwy is the best and almost the only good one on these lines.

a. to Metz.
17 Mondelange.   } Rail.
11 Thionville (Rte. 181).
19 (or 2¼ posts) Frisange in Luxembourg.
1¾ posts, LUXEMBOURG. HANDBOOK FOR N. GERMANY.

b. to Arlon.
17 Mondelange.
20 Fontoy.
9 Aumetz.
20 Longwy (*Inn:* tolerable), a fortress: the upper town was fortified by Louis XIV., after the treaty of Nymegen.
Arlon. HANDBOOK FOR N. GERMANY.

SECTION X.

ILE DE FRANCE.—FLANDRES.—ARTOIS.

ROUTE	PAGE
183 Paris to Valenciennes, by Creil, Compiègne, Noyon, Chauny, St. Quentin (RAILWAY), and Cambrai	551
184 Chemin de Fer du Nord. Paris to Brussels, by Amiens, Arras, Douai, and Valenciennes	555
186 Lille to Brussels, by Roubaix, Mouscron, Tournay, and Mons.—Lille to Gand	556
187 Calais to Dijon, by Douai, Cambrai, St. Quentin, Laon, Rheims, Châlons-sur-Marne, and Troyes	557
188 Lille to Dunkerque, by Cassel	559
189 Calais to Dunkerque and Courtrai, by Gravelines and Bergues	560

ROUTE 183.

PARIS TO VALENCIENNES, BY CREIL, COMPIÈGNE, NOYON, CHAUNY, ST. QUENTIN (RAILWAY), AND CAMBRAI.

The *Chemin de Fer du Nord* has been described between Paris and

67 *Creil Stat.*, in Rte. 3. A branch Railway extends thence to St. Quentin, 167 kilom.=$103\frac{1}{2}$ Eng. m.

rt. extends the Forest of Chantilly.

78 Pont St. Maxence Stat. This town is prettily situated on the Oise, and its Bridge was built by the architect Peyronnet.

Coaches hence and also from Creil to Senlis (*Inn:* Grand Cerf), a town of 5000 Inhab., consisting of an old town still surrounded by ramparts and boulevards, among which are traces of Roman constructions, and of 3 modern suburbs, in which are cotton-mills and other manufactories. The *Porte de Meaux*, now in ruins, was a fort in itself, approached by a bridge; the Porte Bellon is also curious. In the interior of the Cité are remains of the *Castle*, dating from the time of St. Louis, in which may be distinguished the chapel, the hall bearing the initials of Henri II. and Diana of Poitiers, and the chamber of Louis XIII.

The *Cathedral* is a small and simple but stately building, chiefly of the 12th centy. The W. portal, with its statues, has been restored. The lateral portals, the façades of the transepts, which are very rich, are of the age of Francis I. and Louis XII. It is surmounted by a fine tower and twin spires 211 feet high.

Several other desecrated churches merit notice, as the *Abbey of St. Vincent*, well preserved; the *Church of St. Pierre*, now a hay-store, with a porch rich in sculpture; the Chapel of the *Hôtel Dieu*; and the nave of *St. Frambourg*.

The ruins of the *Abbey of Chaalis*, and the Chapelle du Roi, near Senlis, may deserve a visit from those who take an interest in Gothic remains.]

88 Villeneuve-sur-Verberie Stat. The river Oise runs parallel with our road at some distance on the l.

100 *Compiègne Stat.* (*Inns:* La Cloche (?);—le Lion), a mean town of 8986 Inhab., on the l. bank of the Oise, a little below its junction with the Aisne. The Romans gave it the name *Compendium*, because their military stores and ammunition of all sorts were kept here. It has been a favourite residence of the French monarchs, with few exceptions, from the time of

Clovis. They often repaired hither to enjoy the pleasures of the chace in its very extensive park and neighbouring forest.

The *Royal Palace*, as it at present stands, is a building of the time of Louis XV., erected from designs of Gabriel. Napoleon added a splendid hall or gallery : it was here that he received his bride Marie Louise. Charles X. spent much of his time here, in his favourite sport of shooting. The interior is elegantly furnished. The *Gardens* are prettily laid out, and a sort of arbour, or berceau walk, 4800 ft. long, leads from them to the forest. The façade towards the forest is very grand.

The *Hôtel de Ville* is a curious Gothic edifice, surmounted by a beffroi and turrets.

The *Church of St. André* is of the pure Gothic of the 13th centy., except the aisles and side chapels, which date from the end of the 15th. In the *Ch. of St. Anne* is a curious marble font.

The *Forest* occupies an area of nearly 30,000 acres, and contains some fine oak timber.

A camp for military manœuvres is sometimes formed here in the autumn.

Though the fortifications are now entirely razed, Compiègne was once a strong place ; and it was before its walls that the dauntless Maid of Orleans was made a prisoner and entered on a captivity which ended only in her miserable and cruel death, 1430. She had thrown herself into the town, then besieged by the Duke of Burgundy, and had courageously headed the garrison in a sally across the bridge, when, in retreating last of the rearguard, she found the town-gate partly closed, and choked by the throng eager to escape from the enemy, who closely pursued them. In consequence of this, while endeavouring to protect the fugitives, and before she could obtain an entrance, she was seized by an archer of Picardy, and transferred to John of Luxembourg, from whom she was purchased by the English. The spot of her capture, near the old gateway de Vieux Pont, is still pointed out, although the old bridge, close to which it occurred, has been removed, and replaced by another higher up the stream.

Diligence daily to Soissons. (Rte. 178.)

The Railroad ascends the valley of the Oise on its rt. bank, by

109 Thourotte Stat.,

117 Ourscamps Stat., to

124 *Noyon Stat.* (*Inn:* H. des Chevalets), a very ancient town, on a small stream, the Vorse, about a mile from the right side of the Oise, with 6250 Inhab., remarkable as the birthplace of the reformer, John Calvin,* son of a notary, grandson of a cooper, b. 1509. The house at the corner of the Rue Fromenteresse has been pulled down, it is said out of hatred to the heresiarch. Noyon was besieged by Julius Cæsar, who calls it *Noviodunum Belgarum*. Charlemagne resided here; and Hugues Capet was elected by his vassals King of France at this place in 987.

The *Cathedral* is of interest to the antiquary and architect. It is a fine Romanesque edifice, begun in the 12th centy., and completed on a uniform plan early in the 13th. The transepts and nave have semicircular terminations. The lower arches and the 9 side-chapels outside the choir are Round ; the triforium gallery running above them has Pointed arches. This church presents an interesting example of the transition from the Round to the Pointed style.

[A *Diligence* runs from Noyon by Guiscard to Ham, crossing the ridge which divides the basin of the Seine from that of the Somme, and enters the Dépt. of the Somme before reaching

Ham (*Inns:* H. de France;—Cornet d'Or), a small town on the Somme, surrounded by marshes, with 1663 Inhab. Its *Citadel* has been much strengthened by modern works, so as to be now a fortress of importance : it serves as a *state prison*, for which purpose it is well fitted. The central tower or *donjon* is 100 ft. high, 100 ft. wide, and the walls are of masonry 36 ft. thick. It was built 1470 by the Comte de St. Pol, afterwards be-

* See Dyer's ' Life of Calvin.'

headed by Louis XI., and bears over the gate his motto, "Mon Mieux." The Prince de Polignac, and 3 other ministers of Charles X., who signed the Ordonnances of July 25, 1830, were confined here; and Prince Louis Napoleon, after the failure of his rash attempt at Boulogne, 1840, remained here for 6 years, until, in 1846, he escaped in the disguise of a labourer, carrying a plank on his shoulder. Strangers are not admitted.

The *Church* is said to be an interesting building, and contains some curious bas-reliefs.

General Foy was born here.

Between Ham and a village called Nesle, Henry V. crossed the Somme, by a ford which the French had left unguarded, with his brave army, destined, 2 days after, to fight and gain the battle of Azincour, 1415.]

132 Appely Stat.

140 *Chauny Stat.*, an ancient town of 5154 Inhab., partly built on an island in the Oise, which is here connected with the Canal de St. Quentin.

169 ST. QUENTIN *Terminus* (*Inn*: H. du Cygne ; comfortable), a flourishing manufacturing town, whose population has more than doubled in 25 years, and now amounts to 25,000. It was the ancient capital of the Vermandois, the "Augusta Viromanduorum" of the Romans, and is situated on the Somme (Samarobriva of Cæsar).

The principal *Church*, once collegiate, is less known than it ought to be. It is one of the finest, boldest, and purest Gothic buildings in this part of Belgic Gaul. The vault of the roof is 127 ft. high. It has a double transept; the choir is braced with iron ; the E. apse has fine painted glass in 7 windows. The King of France was premier canon of this church, and the chapter possessed privileges over the municipal community which kept up constant feuds between *town* and *gown*, and this continued, more or less, until chapter and community sustained a simultaneous annihilation. The *Hôtel de Ville* is a very fine specimen of these structures in what may be termed the Flemish-Gothic style ; and this and many other portions of the town afford good subjects for the pencil. It probably dates from the 15th centy.

The wharfs on the banks of the Somme bear testimony to the increasing consumption of coal in this district. It is brought from the vicinity of Valenciennes, Condé, and Mons, by the Canal de St. Quentin, and is of an inferior quality, but it is extensively employed in the various manufactures which are springing up, and which may hereafter become formidable rivals to those of England.

St. Quentin is the centre of the manufacture of *Linen Cloths* (toile de fil), muslins and gauzes (battistes et gazes), which spread over the country for 30 m. around, as far as Cambrai, Bapeaume, and Peronne. Flanders and Picardy furnish the *flax:* the finest quality comes from Marchiennes; that of St. Quentin is coarse. The weavers are obliged to work below ground and in cellars, by the moist and even temperature of which they are alone enabled to prevent the fine thread breaking. It has been calculated that 100,000 persons are employed in weaving and spinning flax. *Cotton spinning* and weaving also employ a great many hands.

Under the walls of St. Quentin was fought (July 28, 1557) the great *battle* between the Spanish troops, commanded by Emanuel Philibert Duke of Savoy, and Ferdinand Gonzaga, and the French, headed by Coligny and the Connétable Anne de Montmorency, in which the latter were entirely routed. Queen Mary of England aided her husband Philip II. on this occasion with a considerable levy of English troops, under the command of the Earl of Pembroke, who contributed not a little to the victory. This defeat left Paris unprotected ; and, had the victors profited by their advantage, France and Spain might perhaps have been united into one vast monarchy. But Philip, who joined the army after the battle, hesitated, and occupied himself in the siege of the town, which, just capable of defence, might with safety have been left in the occupation of the French garrison. Commanded by Coligny and Jarnac, the town sustained eleven assaults before it was taken. The inhabitants were treated with great cruelty, the Spaniards revenging themselves upon the burgesses, who had defended the town-walls with great valour. Even the clergy were not spared, and they all quitted the town, and did not return until St. Quentin was restored to France by the treaty of Câteau Cambresis, 1559.

Diligences daily to Cambrai, to Câteau, to Laon and Rheims (Rte. 187), to Avesnes.

Railway in progress to the Belgian frontier, by Câteau and Maubeuge. It will be the direct road from Paris to Brussels, shorter by 100 kilom. than the present route.

The *Canal of St. Quentin* connects the basin of the Somme with that of the Scheldt, and is carried through the intervening hills by tunnels,—one at Tronquoi, ½ m. long; another at Riqueval, 3¾ m. long, cut through the solid rock : it is 20 ft. high, and 20 ft. broad ; it admits only 1 barge to pass at a time, towed by men. By means of this canal a communication is opened between the river Scheldt and the extreme eastern departments of France and the Atlantic, through the rivers Somme, Seine, and Loire ; it was completed by Napoleon in 1810 ; it enters the Oise at Chauny. It runs parallel with our road as far as Cambrai.

14 Bellicourt. The road is hilly to Cambrai. Near the little village of Castelet, traversed by the road, the Scheldt (l'Escaut) rises from behind the gardens of Mont St. Martin ; it issues from an arch in the side of a hill.

14 Bonavy.

11 *Cambrai* (*Inn*: H. de l'Europe, formerly au Grand Canard ; good) is an industrious and considerable town and fortress on the Scheldt, with 19,000 Inhab., principally remarkable for the fine muslin manufactured here, named by the English, after the place where it is made, *Cambric*. The Revolution stripped it of all its principal ornaments. It was the episcopal see of the venerable Fénélon, author of *Télémaque*, who was buried here. The sacrilegious hands of the Revolutionists, in 1793, tore his body from the peaceful grave, and melted the lead of his coffin into bullets. The beautiful *Cathedral* was utterly razed to the ground at the same time. By way of making some atonement for the outrage, a handsome *monument* was erected to his memory in 1825, in the present cathedral, a modern church of indifferent architecture. His statue, "half rising from an altar tomb, apparently ready to obey the sound of the last trumpet, is not ill conceived nor executed." The three bas-reliefs represent memorable events of his life —the education of the Duke of Burgundy, the Archbishop attending the wounded soldier after the battle of Malplaquet, and the cow restored to the peasant. His remains are deposited beneath the monument, which is the work of *David*, the sculptor. An ancient Greek painting of the Virgin, attributed, as is usual with pictures of this class, to St. Luke, is preserved in the cathedral, and is yet carried in procession.

Of the 12 churches which existed before the Revolution, 2 alone remain. That of St. Gery has a roodloft. The only other public building of consequence is the *Hôtel de Ville*, of modern construction. Cambrai is called Camaracum in the Itinerary of Antonine.

Cambrai is celebrated in the annals of diplomacy for the famous *League* against the republic of Venice concocted here in 1508 : a treaty of peace between Charles V. and Francis I. was also signed in 1529. The citadel was raised by Charles V. Cambrai was taken by a detachment of the British army under Sir Charles Colville, June 24, 1815. It is the native place of the historian Monstrelet, and of General Dumouriez (1739).

Diligences daily to Douai and Arras, on the Northern Railway.

The *Canal of St. Quentin* begins at Cambrai, where it issues out of the Scheldt (see above). It is of the highest utility in promoting the industry and prosperity of the district through which it passes.

[15 m. E. of Cambrai lies *Le Cateau Cambresis*, famous for the *treaty* signed there (1595) between Philip II. and Henri II. It was also the birthplace of Marshal Mortier, Duke of Trevise, who perished in Paris by Fieschi's assassination-machine. Cateau was the head-quarters of the Duke of Wellington when he entered France in 1815; hence he issued his order to his troops to abstain from pillage, and to maintain the strictest discipline.]

15 Bouchain, a small 2nd class fortress on the Scheldt.

On quitting Bouchain the road passes on the l. *Denain*, the battle-field where Marshal Villars defeated and made prisoner Lord Albemarle, commander of the allied forces, posted in a strong position, 1712. An Obelisk was erected on the field to commemorate the success, with these lines of Voltaire:—

"Regardez dans Denain l'audacieux Villars
Disputant le tonnerre à l'aigle des Césars."

The innermost douane to be passed on entering France is at Douchy. There is a railroad from Denain to Anzin by St. Waast, 16 kilom.

On approaching Valenciennes the road passes the great coal-field of the Dépt. du Nord, the most important in France, discovered about 1736, in a portion of Hainault which was not ceded to France until 1678. It is a prolongation of the Belgian coal-field. The chief collieries are at Anzin, Denain, Lourches, Fresnes, Vieux Condé, &c.; 40 mines are worked in this district; some of them are 1640 ft. deep. Paris is supplied with a large quantity of coal from hence by the canal of St. Quentin, and the fuel derived from hence imparts life to the numerous and varied manufactures scattered over the industrious Dépt. du Nord, including 3000 manufactories around the walls of

Valenciennes, within a circle of 10 or 15 m. (Rte. 184.)

ROUTE 184.

PARIS TO BRUSSELS.—CHEMIN DE FER DU NORD, BY AMIENS, ARRAS, DOUAI, AND VALENCIENNES.

370 kilom. = about 228 Eng. m.
5 trains daily to Douai in 8¼ h.
2 trains daily to Brussels in 12¼ h.
This railway is described in Rtes. 1 and 3 as far as

147 AMIENS Stat.
163 Carbie Stat.
179 Albert Stat. *Diligence* to *Péronne* (*Inns:* H. St. Martin; H. d'Angleterre), a fortress on the N. bank of the Somme. It bore the epithet "la Pucelle," because it never was captured by an enemy down to 1815, when the Duke of Wellington deprived it of its virgin reputation. He thus describes its capture in his Despatches:— "I attacked Péronne with the first division of British Guards, under Major-Gen. Maitland, on the 26th in the afternoon. The troops took the hornwork, which covers the suburb on the l. of the Somme, by storm, with but small loss, and the town immediately afterwards surrendered, on the condition that the garrison should lay down their arms and be allowed to return to their homes."—*June 26th*, 1815. The number of the inhabitants in the town exceeds 4000.

It was in the *Castle of Péronne* that Charles the Bold detained the crafty Louis XI, his prisoner, in the way so admirably described in *Quentin Durward*, on receiving intelligence of the revolt of the Liègeois, and restored him to liberty only after he had signed conditions most disadvantageous to himself, and known in history as the "treaty of Péronne." The castle is much dilapidated, and a large part is probably not older than the 16th centy., yet there remain many dismal dungeons on the ground-floor. The chamber occupied by Louis is still pointed out in the Tour Herbert, and beside it the miserable cell, on a level with the moat, where Charles the Simple ended his days, a wretched captive. He was buried in the church of St. Farcy, now destroyed. The *Church of St. John*, near the *Beffroi*, or bell-tower, date 1376, is a handsome Gothic edifice, apparently of the 16th centy.; its lithe piers without capitals spread out into multiplied groinings over the roof, and it has a little painted glass. The situation of Péronne is unwholesome, owing to the marshes which surround it.

197 Achiet Stat. *Coach* to Bapeaume, a dull and dirty fortress, where some linen and muslin are made.

206 Boileux Stat.

215 *Arras Stat.* in Rte. 1. *Diligence* to Cambrai, &c.

224 Roux Stat.

231 Vitry Stat.

241 DOUAI Stat. in Rte. 1.

249 Montigny Stat.

256 Somain Stat.

265 Wallers Stat.

274 Raismes Stat.

277 *Valenciennes Stat.*

VALENCIENNES (*Inns:* La Poste; H. des Princes, very good and comfortable; H. du Commerce, ditto; La Canard; La Biche), a fortress of the 2nd class, with a strong citadel constructed by the engineer Vauban, is a dark and ill-built town, lying on the Scheldt, and has a population of 20,625 souls. In 1793 it was taken by the Allies under the Duke of York and General Abercromby, after a siege of 84 days and a severe bombardment, which destroyed a part of the town: it was yielded back next year. In the grand square, or Place d'Armes, are situated the *Hôtel de Ville*, a fine building, half Gothic half Italian in style, built 1612, and containing 3 pictures by *Rubens* (?), brought from the abbey of St. Amand; the *Beffroi*, 170 ft. high, built 1237, fell 1843, and caused a serious loss of life; the *Theatre*. The *Church of St. Gery* is the principal one.

The celebrated Valenciennes *Lace* is manufactured here, and a considerable quantity of fine cambric. This is the birthplace of Watteau the painter, of Froissart the historian, and of the minister D'Argenson.

On entering France, passports must be delivered up here; and on quitting the country they are strictly examined by the police.

The country around Valenciennes offers no picturesque beauty; the rivers are sluggish, and have flat, uninteresting banks.

There is a triple row of French custom-houses on this frontier; and the repeated searches to which the traveller is subjected are often very annoying, and occasion considerable delay.

Diligences to Mézières, Sédan, and Strasburg; to Péronne; Landrecies; to Maubeuge and Avesnes.

The *Railway* from Valenciennes to the Belgian frontier (14 kilom.), and thence to BRUSSELS (11½ posts), is described in the HANDBOOK FOR NORTH GERMANY.

288 Blanc Misseron Stat.

289 Quiévrain Stat.

308 *Mons Stat.*

370 BRUSSELS *Terminus* (see HANDBOOK FOR BELGIUM AND NORTH GERMANY).

ROUTE 186.

LILLE TO BRUSSELS, BY ROUBAIX, MOUSCRON, AND MONS.—LILLE TO GAND.

3 trains daily, in about 5½ hrs.

11 *Roubaix Stat.* An industrious town of 24,000 Inhab.—a focus of the cotton manufacture.

Tourcoing Stat. A town of 20,000 Inhab. Celebrated manufactures of table-linen.

Mouscron Stat.

[Here the branch Railway to Gand diverges.]

The Brussels line proceeds by

Tournai Stat.
Mons Stat. } described in HAND-
Braine-le-Comte } BOOK FOR NORTH
  Stat. } GERMANY.
BRUSSELS STATION.

ROUTE 187.

CALAIS TO DIJON, BY DOUAI, CAMBRAI, ST. QUENTIN, LAON, REIMS, CHÂLONS-SUR-MARNE, AND TROYES.

559 kilom. = 346½ Eng. m.

This is the direct road for travellers to Switzerland or Italy, not wishing to pass through Paris. The saving in distance is not great, only 7 m. less than the route by Paris and Sens, and the road is very bad : the railway route by Paris is, of course, far preferable in point of speed ; but by this route they will pass through a series of places possessing great interest. The country is interesting, but the road as far as Châlons-sur-Marne is wretched ; rough paving worn into holes. Beyond C. s. M. the railway is open. Those who travel by *diligence* will not find a public conveyance direct to carry them from one end of the journey to the other without interruption, and may have to wait at various points; but they will invariably meet with diligences running from one great town to another.

Calais is described in Rte. 1.

16 Ardres, \
 8 La Recousse, } Railway. (Rte 1.) \
18 St. Omer, /

18 Aire.

13 Lillers, a town of 4620 Inhab. Here the first *Artesian well*, so called from the province Artois, was bored by the engineer Belidor, in the 18th century, and hence the practice has extended all over Europe ; it had been, however, previously tried in Italy.

13 *Béthune* (*Inn:* H. du Roi, comfortable). The post-house is outside the town, which was formerly considered third in importance in Artois. It has 6890 Inhab. In its large marketplace rises a singular old *Beffroi*, a heavy square truncated tower, on which a Gothic spire has been engrafted.

Water is scarce here, and wells few and very deep. *Coach* to Arras Stat.

There are 2 roads hence to Cambrai.

Branch a. by

18 Souchez, a shady and picturesque village.

"The country, which near Calais is very marshy and bleak, gradually improves. Very few hedges are seen. The crops divide the ownership, and some growths become apparent to which we are not accustomed at home : flax and hemp in great abundance, and large strips of the white poppy, cultivated for the purpose of extracting oil from the seed. The pale petals have a large lilac fleck at their base, and the crop is handsome when in flower. One unpleasing result of the want of hedges is the absence of their feathered tenants."—*F. P.*

12 Arras (Rte. 1). Railway to Paris.

24 Marquion.

11 Cambrai.

Branch b. from Béthune to

19 Lens.

15 Bac en Bencheul.

11 *Cambrai*, in Rte. 183.

---

11 Bonavy, \
14 Bellicourt, } in Rte. 183. \
13 ST. QUENTIN, /

10 Cerisy, a pretty village.

12 La Fère, a fortified town of 2085 Inhab., on the Oise, which we here cross. It has a school of artillery.

La Fère to Reims ; a railway projected 1852. 80 kilom. = 50 m.

The road is very bad, but the country improves in picturesqueness on approaching Laon, which is entered by a long and steep ascent.

23 Laon.—*Inn:* La Hure, *i. e.* the Boar's Head ; not a splendid house, but comfortable.

Laon, the chef-lieu of the Dépt. de l'Aisne (8043 Inhab.), " is situated upon a lofty and almost isolated hill, crowned by the noble *Cathedral of Notre Dame*. This edifice, which is in a very pure and simple Gothic style, much resembling the early English of Salisbury, was dedicated Sept. 6, 1114, having been built from the very ground in the space of the 2 years preceding ; so that it is a century older than any specimen of the same kind in England. It has 4 towers, which have very large, lofty, unglazed windows, through which the light shines, and the beginnings of 2 others. The façade, with its great receding cavern-like portals and arches, is singularly venerable; and the traveller will do well to mark its outline, for he will here see, in its simplest aspect, the type which at Rheims is expanded to the highest grade of decoration and exuberance. As a matter of taste, however, it may be doubtful whether the simplicity be not as satisfactory. It is 400 ft. long within, and has a double triforium, making 4 stories in all. The *choir*, like our English cathedrals, ends square. The circular window is remarkable for its size, and for its painted glass, of which there is more in the choir. The Cathedral is much neglected, and the *cloisters* have been demolished quite recently by the Vandalism of the municipality. The Bishop of Laon was one of the 12 ecclesiastical peers of France; but this dignity did not deter the citizens from violently contesting his authority. In this Cathedral is preserved an ancient painting of St. Veronica, brought from a suppressed monastery, with an inscription which greatly puzzled the savans of the age of Louis Quatorze. It is in the ancient Sclavonian dialect and character, merely indicating the object which it represents."—*F. P.*

The *Ch. of St. Martin*, on the side of the town opposite to the cathedral, is only remarkable for its 2 fine and lofty towers.

The *Préfecture* is established in the ancient abbey of St. Jean, which also contains the public *Library*, and the *Hôtel Dieu* is the former *Abbey of Martin.*

The grand massive tower of Louis d'Outremer, one of the oldest monuments in France, has been pulled down to make way for a *Citadelle*, which has been deemed necessary to defend this side of France from invasion. Its massive foundations, however, have hitherto resisted the attempt to remove them. Near the Porte St. Martin is a curious *Leaning Tower*, called Tour Penchée, or de la Dame Eve, inclining nearly 10 degrees out of the perpendicular. Queen Brunehault, who fixed her court at Laon, gives her name to another tower. "The fine masses of the ancient walls and towers which encircle the town, mixing with the rocks, add much to its picturesque aspect. These walls are said to have been built by Guillaume Harulin, the physician who attended Charles VI. during his insanity; so that, if this tradition be correct, they give a great idea of his fees. There are many fine points of view here, and perhaps none of them are more pleasing than those gained from the summit of the *ramparts*. The landscape is extensive and varied. Vineyards clothe the slopes of the hills, the plains are covered with cultivation, the earth seems literally teeming."—*F. P.*

One of the finest views of the town is from the road called "Chemin des Creuttes," near the Calvary, on the way to the *Abbey of St. Vincent*, of which no part escaped the fury of the democrats, except its outer walls (creuttes), moated and embattled like a fortress as it was; they now enclose a private garden.

In March (9 and 10), 1814, a *battle*, which lasted 2 days, was fought between the Allies, commanded by Blücher and Witzingerode, who occupied the town and neighbouring heights, and the French army, much inferior to them in numbers. Here the success of Napoleon was arrested for the first time in the campaign, and he was compelled to retire towards Soissons, with a loss of 6000 men and 46 cannon.

20 Corbény. "Crossing the Aisne, the road enters the ancient province of *Champagne*, which derives its name from the many plains which it contains, and which constitute its great natural features, as soon as you advance beyond the borders."—*F. P.*

9 Berry au Bac. "From Laon the country continues varied, though less hilly, as you approach Rheims. It is tolerably wooded, and the luxuriance of the wild flowers, French honeysuckle, and many which are cultivated in gardens with us, is very pleasing."—*F. P.*

19 RHEIMS, in Rte. 178.

"11 Sillery; not the locality which produces the celebrated Sillery Champagne. That wine derives its name from Sillery by a secondary process. Under its name is comprehended the produce of the vineyards of Verzenay, Mailly, Raunent, &c., situated at the N.E. termination of the chain of hills which separate the Maine from the Verle, and formerly belonging to the Marquis de Sillery, husband of Madame de Genlis. Having been originally brought into vogue by the greater care bestowed upon the manufacture of it by the Maréchale d'Estrées, it was long known by the name of *Vin de la Maréchale*.

"19 Les Grandes Loges.

"The road from Rheims to Châlons passes through plains extending far and wide, in which the course of the Marne may be traced by the long rows of poplars upon its bank, by the Campi Catalaunici, where the *great battle* took place between the combined armies of Rome and Theodoric, and the 'innumerable host' of Attila (A.D. 451). Here, as Gibbon observes, were assembled the natives of the various countries from the Volga to the Atlantic. The number of the slain amounted to 162,000, or, according to another account, 300,000. Attila, whose valour was always guided by his prudence, had waited for the enemy in these plains, as being best adapted to the operations of his Scythian cavalry. Great as was the slaughter, the conflict was undecided: Attila retreated into his camp, which he had fortified, according to the Scythian usage, by a vast circle of the waggons in which they dwelt. The allied armies separated at the moment when the magnanimous Barbarian had resolved, if his intrenchments should be forced, to rush headlong into the flames of the funeral pile formed of the saddles and rich furniture of the cavalry, and thus to deprive his enemies of the glory which they might have acquired by his captivity. Attila continued for several days within the circle of his waggons after this defeat, dreading some hostile stratagem; but his ultimate retreat beyond the Rhine 'confessed the last victory which was achieved in the name of the Western Empire.' Near the villages of Chape and Cuperly, about 5 m. from Châlons, there are vestiges of ancient earthworks, traditionally known as the Camps of Attila; and the expositors of the productions of the ancient German bards find the battle of Châlons recorded in the Niebelungen Lay."
—*F. P.*

13 Châlons-sur-Marne (Rte. 165), on the Railway to Strasburg.
18 Vatry.
10 Sommesous.

After leaving Châlons the country becomes less fertile, the crops generally thin and scanty. The vineyards of Champagne seem to be replaced by plantations of Scotch firs, which add nothing to the beauty and little to the shelter of the scenery. The road continues straight before and behind, marked in white chalk along the yellow and russet fields. At length it begins to undulate; till, after a long ascent and descent, you reach

20 Arcis-sur-Aube (*Inn:* Poste; small but decent), a town of 3000 Inhab., nearly all burnt down March 20, 1814, during a combat between Napoleon and the Allies. Much grain is shipped from its bridge. Danton the Terrorist was born here.

9 Voué.
19 *Troyes* (Rte. 143, p. 503).
19 St. Parre-les-Vaudes.
14 Bar-sur-Seine.
19 Musse-sur-Seine,
15 Châtillon-sur-Seine. } Rte. 144.
14 Aisey-le-Duc.
15 Ampilly-le-Sec.
15 Chanceaux.
39 DIJON (Rte. 104).

ROUTE 188.

LILLE TO DUNKERQUE, BY CASSEL.

51 kilom. = 32 Eng. m.

From Lille to Hazebrouck is described in Rte. 1.

Hazebrouck Stat.

20 *Cassel Stat.* H. du Sauvage, good. It is worth while in fine weather to stop here for a short time to enjoy the view.

Cassel is an ancient town of 4234 Inhab., agreeably situated on a hill commanding one of the most extensive views in Europe. Although it has no striking features, it exhibits, on a clear day, an unusually extensive tract of highly cultivated and productive country. Its most remarkable feature is, that the horizon is almost equally distant in every direction, as no rising ground interrupts the sight. It extends over the flat and fertile plains of Flanders, and as far as the white cliffs of England, into 3 different kingdoms; includes 32 towns and 100 villages. St. Omer, Dunkerque, Ypres, Ostend, and the beautiful steeple of Hazebrouck are the most prominent objects: no fresh water is visible in this vast expanse. Mont Cassel is only 800 Eng. ft. high: it was one of the principal signal stations of the great trigonometrical survey carried on during the reign of Napoleon. A small map of the country visible may be purchased on the spot for 20 sous.

General Vandamme was born here.

Flemish is the general language of the entire population in the northern parts of the Dépt. du Nord: it is spoken at Cassel, and as far as Watel.

Arnecke Stat.

Esquelbecq Stat.

Bergues Stat., in Rte. 189.

Dunkerque Stat., in Rte. 189.

ROUTE 189.

CALAIS TO DUNKERQUE AND COURTRAI, BY GRAVELINES AND BERGUES.

51 kilom. = 31½ Eng. m. to Bergues, and 8 posts thence to Courtrai.

Calais, in Rte. 1.

It is a good road to

20 *Gravelines*, a fortress, and desolate-looking small town, with grass growing in its streets; it has 3000 Inhab. "It is," to use the words of an old writer, "very strong, by reason that they can drown it round in 4 hrs., so as no land shall be within a mile of it." It is surrounded by a plain, once a vast marsh, below the level of the sea, nearly 20 m. long by 12 broad; almost all this can be laid under water in case of need, to ward off a hostile invasion on this side of France. At present this district supports a population of 60,000. It is protected from the sea by the dunes or sandhills, and is gradually being drained by its inhabitants. It would cost the arrondissement 10 millions of frs. to repair the damage caused by admitting the waters upon the land.

The Emperor Charles V. here paid a visit to Henry VIII. on his return from his interview with Francis I. at the Field of the Cloth of Gold, 1520.

Beyond Gravelines the road is paved.

21 Dunkerque (*Inns:* H. de Flandres; very good, and not dear; table d'hôte at 6, good, 2½ frs.; breakfast, with eggs, 1 fr. 75 c.; — Chaperon Rouge), a considerable fortified town and seaport, with 25,400 Inhab. Large sums have been expended in endeavouring to clear the mouth of the harbour from the bar of sand which obstructs it, by means of basins and sluices, which are filled by the flowing of the tide, and discharged at low water, so as to scour a channel through the mud. They are said to have failed in producing the results anticipated. Dunkerque nevertheless is the best harbour which France possesses in the N. Sea, and ranks fourth in the value of its exports and imports of all the seaports in the kingdom. It serves as the outlet for the manufacturing district of the Dépt. du Nord. "It is one of the cleanest towns in France, with wide streets, well paved, living cheap: baths, very good."—*D. C.*

The *Quai*, usually crowded with vessels, and *pier*, extending far into the sea, are worth seeing: so is the Corinthian portico of the *Church of St. Eloi*, a handsome but most incongruous frontispiece to a Gothic building; in front of it is a fine detached Gothic belfry, containing the chimes.

There is an *English Protestant Church*, Rue des Sœurs Blanches—a proof of the number of British residents.

A *Statue* of John Bart, a famous sea-captain, born here (temp. Louis XIV.), stands in the Great Market Place.

Dunkerque owes its origin to a chapel built by St. Eloi in the 7th century among the dunes or sandhills, and thence comes its name, "Church of the Dunes." Here was equipped the Flemish division of the *Spanish* Armada, designed to combine in the invasion of England, under the command of the Prince of Parma; but that skilful general, perhaps foreseeing the result, refrained from putting out to sea. Dunkerque, after having been hardly won by the English under Oliver Cromwell from the Spaniards, 1658, was basely sold by Charles II. to Louis XIV. for 6 millions of livres in 1662.

By the Treaty of Utrecht (1715) the French were compelled to demolish the town and fortifications, and an English commissioner was actually sent hither to ascertain that the stipulations of the treaty were complied with to the letter; a source of deep humiliation to French pride, but of more immediate misery to the poor inhabitants. The port and fortifications were not restored and rebuilt until 1740.

The country around is little better than a dreary waste of sandhills thrown up by the wind. It was in the neighbourhood of them that Turenne defeated, in 1658, the Spanish army under Don John of Austria and the Great Condé, who had sided at that time with the enemies of France, in the *Battle of the Dunes*. The siege of the town had been commenced by Mazarin, at the dictation of Cromwell, whose fleet blockaded it by sea. The Spaniards, unprovided with artillery, advanced to attack the French, by marching close to the sea. Condé remonstrated in vain with Don John against a measure so perilous: "Vous ne connaissez pas M. de Turenne," said he; "on ne fait pas impunément des fautes devant un si grand homme;" and just as the action began, he turned to the young Duke of Gloucester, and asked if he had ever been in a battle before. "No," answered the Duke. "Then you will see one lost in half an hour." The action was commenced by 6000 English soldiers of Cromwell, commanded by Lockhart, his ambassador, who formed the left wing of the French army, and distinguished themselves eminently: their charge carried everything before it, and contributed not a little to the result. The Duke of York (afterwards James II.) fought in the opposite ranks, at the head of a regiment of Cavaliers, and it was from them that their fellow-countrymen suffered most. The Spaniards lost 4000 men, and Dunkerque surrendered 10 days after, in consequence of this defeat.

A pleasant excursion may be made by rail to the hill of Cassel, about 18¾ m. off (Rte. 188).

Diligences daily to Calais; to Ostend. *Steamers* to London; to Rotterdam; to Hamburg; to Havre. *Railway* to Hazebrouck, where it joins the lines from Lille to Paris.

There is a *canal* from Dunkerque to Furnes, Ostend, and Bruges, traversed daily by a barge, and another canal to Bergues.

10 Bergues (*Inn*: Tête d'Or), a small and poor fortified town of 6000 Inhab., situated on an elevation, surrounded by marshes and salt lakes called Möere, formerly waste and insalubrious; but having been drained within a few years by the construction of hydraulic works, they are now becoming productive, and less unwholesome. Though only a fortress of the 3rd class, the possession of Bergues has been deemed of such consequence in every war, that it has been 8 times taken and retaken, and 9 times pillaged, in the course of 8 centuries. It has a picturesque *Beffroi*, 150 ft. high. A very important *corn-market* is held here every Monday. The gates are closed at 10, after which neither ingress nor egress is allowed.

The French frontier and customhouse is reached at Oest Kappel: here the "acquit à caution" must be delivered up. (See INTRODUCTION, § *e*.)

Belgian Posts:
1¾ Rousbrugge, a Belgian village.
2¾ YPRES.
2¼ Ménin, on the Lys.
1¼ COURTRAI.
} See HANDBOOK FOR NORTH GERMANY.

INDEX.

ABBEVILLE.

A.
Abbeville, 16
Abélard (at St. Gildas), 150; his birthplace, 204; his death at St. Marcel, 366
Ablon, 169
Accous, 282
Adour, passage of the, 270; cradle of, 304
Adrets, Baron des, 397, 435, 484, 488
Æschylus, 464
st. Afrique, 404
Agde, 455, 456
Agen, 252
Agincourt, 9
Agnes Sorel, 53, 56, 192, 194, 214
d'Aguesseau, 380
Aï, 521
Aidat, Lac d', 393
l'Aigle, 165
st. Aignan, 182
Aigrefeuille, 208
Aigueperse, 380
Aigues Mortes, 451
Aiguillon, 253
Ailly, 16
Ain, 511
—— river, 511
Airaines, 23
Aire, 9, 278
Aisey-le-Duc, 507
Aix, 477
—— in Savoy to Lyons, 510
—— Ile d', 210
Alagnon, 398
Alais, 419. To Nismes, railway, *ib.*
Albigeois, 324, 405, 455
st. Albin, 368
Albret, 267
Alby, 405
Alençon, 123
Alfieri's library, 454
Alfort, 344
Allan, 433
Alleaume, 81
Allemont, 496
Allevard, 491
Allier, 359, 379, 384, 389
Alpines, 457, 476
Alsace, 515
Altkirch, 518
Alzonne, 324
st. Amand, 238

ARMENTIÈRE.

st. Amand Montrond, 342
st. Amans la Bastide, 406
Ambleteuse, 22
Amboise, 182
st. Ambroix, 419
Amiens, 16. Cathedral, *ib.*
Amphitheatre at Nismes, 446
—— Arles, 460
Ampilly-le-Sec, 507
Ampoulle, sainte, 546
Ampuis, 427
Amyot, Jacques, 349
Ancenis, 203
Ancy-le-Franc, 352
Andance, 414, 428
Andaye, 274
Andelle, 51
les Andelys, 51
st. Andéol, 476
Andorre, 332
st. André le Bas, 426
Andresieux, 412
Andresis, 49
Anduze, 411
Anet, château d', 122
Angers, 154-159
Angerville, 168, 171
Angoulême, 219
Anjou, 155
Annonay, 413
Antibes, 480, 495
st. Antonin, 401
Antraigues, 417
Anzin, 555
Aragnouet, 307
Arago, M., 327
Aramon, 457
Aran, Val d', 314, 317, 320
Arbois, 513
l'Arboust, Val, 307, 315
Arc, Pont de l', 419
Arcis-sur-Aube, 559
Arcy, les Grottes d', 350
Ardèche, 335
—— river, 408, 434
Ardenne, 76
Ardevon, 93
Ardres, 9
Argelez, 292, 293
Argental, Bourg, 413
Argentan, 99
Argenton, 236
Ariége, 322, 329
ARLES, en Provence, 460
Arles-les-Bains, 333
Armentière, 6

AZUN.

Arpajon, 170
Arques, 28
Arras, 8
Arreau, 306
Arrhune, 273
Artenay, 168, 171
Artesian wells, 557
Artigues, 305
—— Tellina, 320
Artix, 277
Artois, 551
Arvieux, Val d', 500
Asnières, 31
Aspe, Val d', 282
Aspin, 306
Athis, Mont, 169
Attila, 559
Aubagne, 471
Aube, 515
Aubenas, 336, 416
st. Aubin du Cormier, 101
Auch, 321
Aude, 323
Auffay, 30
Aumetz, 550
Auray, 148
Aure, Val d', 306
Auriac, 278
Aurigny (Alderney), 87
Aurillac, 400
Ausonius, 260, 460
Auteuil, 120
Autrerive, 330
Autun, 366
AUVERGNE, 335, 379, 381
Auxerre, 349
Auxonne, 507
Avalon, 134
Avallon, 350
Avenières, 118
Avesnes, 554
AVIGNON, 437-442
—— to Marseilles, by Arles, St. Chamas, Etang de Berre (Railway), 457
—— to Narbonne, by Nismes and Montpellier, 445
—— to Nice, by Aix, 475
Avignonet, 323
Avranches, 91
Ax, 331
st. Ay, 177
Ayzac, Coupe d', 417
Azay-le-Rideau, 193
Azincour, 9
Azun, Val d', 292

BAGNÈRES.

B.

Bagnères de Bigorre, 230, 310
—— to Luchon, mountain road, 305
—— *de Luchon*, 230, 315
Bagnes, the, 129, 211, 473
Bailleul, 6
Balarue, 455
Ballons, 534
Ban de la Roche, 530, 533
Bapaume, 53
Bar-le-Duc, 519, 524
Bar-sur-Aube, 515
—— Seine, 506
la Baraque, 401
Barbaste, 277
st. Barbe, 151
Barbe Bleu, 202
—— Ile, 369, 378
Barbeira, 326
Barbezieu, 221
Barcelonnette, 495
Barèges, 230, 302. Crêpe de, 303, 312
Barentin, 60
Barfleur, 82
Barr, 535
Barraux, Fort, 491
Barre-y-va, 54
Barrême, 496
Barsac, 254, 267
Barse, 515
Basques, 227, 272
Bastan valley, 274, 302
Bastide, 239
Bastides at Marseilles, 228, 468, 470, 471
Batignolles, 31
Batz, 135
Baud, 148
Baudéan, 305
la Baume, 417
les Baux, 459
Bayard, 488, 547. Château, 489, 491
Bayeux, 78. Tapestry, 79
—— to St. Lo, 101
Bayle, 329
Bayonne, 268
—— to Irun in Spain, 272
—— to Pau, 276
Bayonnette, 271, 274
Bazas, 267, 277
Bazeilles, 548
Bazïege, 323
Bazoche, château de, 351
Bazouges la Perouse, 102
Béarn, 225, 278, 282
st. Béat, 314, 321
Beaucaire, 457, 458, 481
—— fair of, 458
la Beauce, 113, 175
Beaufort, 513
Beaugency, 178
Beaujeu, 369
Beaumanoir, 140
la Beaume, Pont de, 409, 418
Beaume les Dames, 539

BLOSSEVILLE.

Beaumont, 70
—— sur-Oise, 19, 25
Beaune, 365
Beauport Abbey, 133
Beaupreau, château, 161
Beauregard, 397, 430
Beausoleil, 238
Beausset, 472
Beauvais, 23
Beauvoir, 93
Beaver of the Rhône, 441
Bec Abbey, 69
—— d'Ambés, 264
Becket, Thomas, 73, 350, 351, 543
Bédarrides, 437
Bédeillac, 330
Bedouin, 444
Bédous, 282
Béfort, 538
Begude de Jordy, 455
—— Saze, 445
Behobia, 273
Behuard, Ile, 201
Bellegarde, 481
—— fort, 328
—— (Ain), 512
Belle Isle, 147
Belle-Ile-en-Terre, 125
Belley, 510
Belzunce, Bp., 469
Benfeld, 535
la Bérarde, 496
Bergons, Pic de, 296, 297
Bergues, 561
Bernadotte, 281, 516
Bernay, 22, 68
Berre, Etang de, 463, 465
Berri, 335
—— Duchesse de, 161, 264
st. Bertrand de Comminges, 314
Besançon, 513
Bétharram, 290
Béthune, 557
Beycheville, 265
Beza, 351
Béziers, 455
Bezons, 31
Biaritz, 272
Biaudos, 276
Bicêtre, 356
Bidart, 272
Bidassoa, 273
Bielle, 285
Bielsa, 307
Bienne, 508
Bignon, 356
Bilhère, 277
Binic, 132
Bischweiler, 530
Bitche, 527
Black Prince, 217, 228, 237, 260, 291, 309, 325
Blaisy, 353
Blanchelande, 88
Blanquefort, 260, 261
Blaye, 264
Bléré, 184
Blois, 178
Blosseville, 43

BOUT DE BOIS.

Blücher, 516
le Bocage, 99
Boën, 397
Bois Robert, 29
Bolbec, 61
Bolingbroke's château, 175
Bollwiller, 537
Bonaparte at Boulogne, 14
—— at Brienne, 516
—— at Cannes, 480
—— at Fontainebleau, 345
—— at Fréjus, 480
—— at Grenoble, 488, 490, 492
—— at Lyons, 379
—— at Malmaison, 44
—— at Montmirail, 518
—— at Orgon, 476
—— at Rochefort, 211
—— at Surville, 348
—— at Toulon, 473, 474
—— at Valence, 430
Bonavy, 554
Bondy, 520
st. Bonnet, 393, 493
Bonneval, 191, 403
Bonnières, 33
Bord'haut, 47
BORDEAUX, 255-261
—— to Auch, 277
—— to Bayonne, 266
—— —— by the Landes, 274
—— Bridge of, 222, 255
—— to Pau, 278
—— Richard of, 260
—— to la Tour de Cordouan, 261
—— wines, 258, 261
Bore in the Seine, 54
Boscherville, St. George de, 53, 56
Bosost, 321
Bossuet, 355, 520
Bouc, 463
Bouchain, 555
Boucoiron, 420
Boulogne-sur-Mer, 11-15
—— flotilla, 14
—— to Paris, 11
Boulou, 328
Bourbon l'Archambault, 360
—— Vendée, 208
Bourbonnais, 359
Bourbonne-les-Bains, 531
Bourdaloue, 342
Bourgachard, 69
Bourg, 264
—— (Ain), 512
—— St. Andéol, 434
—— d'Argental, 413
—— Dieu or Déols, 236
—— Dun, 65
—— d'Oysans, 496
—— la Reine, 168
Bourges, 339-342
le Bourget, 542
Bourget, lac de, 510
Bourgoin, 431
Bourgtheroude, 69
Bouscaut, 255, 267
Bout de Bois, 144

INDEX.

BRANILIS.

Branilis, 142
Brèche de Roland, 298, 300, 301
—— ascent to, 300
la Brède, château de la, 260, 267
Bréhal, 90
la Bresse, 369, 513
Bressuire, 207
Brest, 127-132. Roadstead of, 130
—— to Nantes, 144
Breteuil, 9
Bretigny, 115, 170
Bretteville, 78
Briançon, 498
—— to Susa, 499
Briare, 357
Bricquebec, 81, 88
Brie Comte Robert, 505
—— Cheese, 520
Brienne, 516
st. Brieuc, 125
—— to Brest, 132
Brignais, 407
Brignolles, 479
Brionne, 69
Brioude, 388
Brissac, château, 201
BRITTANY, 103-109
Brives, 239
Brix or Bruis, 82
Broglie, 68
Broons, 124
Brou (Ain), church of, 512
Brougham, Lord, 480
Brummel, Beau, 76
Brune, Marshal, 437
Brunel, Mark Isambart, birthplace of, 47
st. Bruno, 486
Buffon, 352
Buisson, Haut, 22
Burgundy, 503. Wines, 363
Burzet, 418
la Bussière, 357
Buzançais, 193
Buzaney, 549

C.

Cacolet, 272
Caen, 73-78. Stone-quarries, 77
—— to Cherbourg, 78
—— to Rennes, 99
—— to Tours, 98
Cæsar at Gergovia, 387
Cafés, xxxi
Cagots, 227, 297
Cahors, 240
Calais, 3
—— to Dijon, by Douai, Cambrai, St. Quentin, Laon, Rheims, Châlons-sur-Marne, and Troyes, 557
—— to Dunkerque and Courtrai, 560
—— to Paris by Amiens, 9
—— to Paris by Boulogne, 22
—— to Paris by Lille, 3
Calas, Jean, 246

CAUNES.

Calmoutier, 518
Calvados, Dept., 73
Calvin, 552
Calvinet, Mont, 248
Camargue, 447, 463
Cambacérès, 454
Cambiel, 307
Cambo, 271
Cambrai, 554
Camisards, 337, 409, 419, 450, 451
Campan, Val de, 305, 311
Campfranc, 283
Canal of Arles, 463
—— de Beaucaire, 458
—— de Boisgelin, 476
—— de Briare, 357
—— de Brienne, 248
—— du Centre, 365, 368, 531
—— du Cher, 343
—— de Crillon, 442, 475
—— de Givors, 407
—— d'Ille et Rance, 138
—— de Marseilles, 476
—— du Midi, 241, 248, 323, 455
—— d'Orléans, 177
—— de l'Ourcq, 520
—— de St. Quentin, 554
—— du Rhin au Rhône, 531, 538
Cancale, Rochers du, 95, 96
Candes, 196
Canigou, 327, 333
st. Cannat, 477
Cannes, 480
Cantal, 335, 398
Canteleu, 53
Cany, 65
Capbern, 314
Capdenac, 401
Captieux, 267
Carbonne, 322
Carcassonne, 324
Cardillac, 254
Carentan, 80
Carhaix, 142
Carla-le-Comte, 329
Carnac, 150
Carnot, 365
Carpentras, 444
Carriages, duty on, xxiii
Carrier, the infamous, 162, 400
Cassagnas, 410
Cassel, 559
st. Cast, 140
Castanet, 323
Castel Jaloux, 277, 285
Castellane, 496
Castelnau Castle, 420
Castelnaudary, 324
Castel Sarrazin, 252
Castels, 275
Castillon, 251
Castres, 255, 267, 406
Câteau Cambresis, 555
ste. Catherine de Fierbois, 214
Cauchoise, 60
Caudebec, 54, 57
Caumont, M. de, 76
Caunes, 325

CHÂTEAUBRIANT.

Caussade, 240, 401
Cauterets, 230, 293, 299
Caux, Pays de, 60
Cavaillon, 476
Cavalier, 411, 419, 420, 449, 451
Caylus, 401
Cazeau, 308
Cère valley, 399
Ceret, 333
Cerisy, 101, 557
Cérons, 255
Cesson, Tour de, 125
Cette, 454
Cevennes, 335, 336, 408, 410, 419
Cèze, 419
Châblis, 350
Chabrol Castle, 249
Chagny, 365
Chailly, 356
Chaise Dieu, 388
Chalais, 221
Chalabre, 329
Chalonnes, 202
Châlons to Lyons, 367
—— to Metz, 539
Châlons-sur-Marne, 523
Châlons-sur-Saône, 365
—— to Geneva, 509
la Chalp, 500
Chalus, 249
Chalusset, 238
st. Chamas, 465
Chambertin, 364
Chambord, château, 180
st. Chamond, 407
Champagne, 515, 518, 558
—— church of, 427
—— vins de, 521, 523, 547
Champagnole, 508
Champigny, 195, 518
Champollion's birthplace, 400
Champsaur, 493
Champtercier, 496
Champtocé, 202
Champtoceaux, 204
Chanceaux, 507
Chanteloup, 184
Chantilly, 9
Chaos, 299
Chapareillan, 491
la Chapelle, 538
Chaptal, 454
Chaptuzat, 380
Charente, 209
Charenton, 344, 505
la Charité, 357
Charleville, 548
Charmes, 431, 532
Charroux, 218
Chartres, 113; Cathedral, *ib.*
—— to Tours, 191
Chartreuse, la Grande, 482, 484
Chasselas grapes, 347
Château d'Adam, 82
Châteaubourg, 429
Châteaubriand, M. de, birthplace and tomb of, 97
Châteaubriant, 140

INDEX.

CHÂTEAU CHINON.

Château Chinon, 366
Châteaudun, 191
Château le Forêt, 127
— Gaillard, 33, 50
— Gonthier, 118
— Lafitte, 265
— Latour, 265
Châteaulin, 145
Château du Loir, 99
Château Margaux, 264
Châteauneuf, 137
— des Papes, 437
— St. Pierre, 82
— le Randon, 409
— le-Rouge, 479
Château Regnault, 191
Châteauroux, 236
Château Salins, 526
Château-Thierry, 521
Châtelaudren, 125
Châtellerault, 214
Châtenay, 168, 503
Châtillon-en-Bazois, 366
— sur-Indre, 193
— sur-Loing, 357
— de Michaille, 512
— sur-Seine, 506
— sur-Sèvre, 207
Châtonay, 483
Châtou, 45
Chaudes Aigues, 402
Chaumont, 182
— Haut Marne, 517
Chauny, 553
Chauvigny, 222
Chavagnac, 389
Chavannes, 518
Chayla, death of, 409
Chazes, 399
Chénonceaux, château of, 184
Cherbourg, 83; Digue, 84
— to St. Malo, 87
Chessy, 363
Chevilly, 168, 171
Chevreuse, 112
st. Chinian, 406
Chinon, 193
Choisy, 169
Chollet, 207
Chorges, 499
la Chouannerie, 108, 118
Chouzé, 196
Christian architecture, 424
st. Christophe, 496
Cierp, 314
Cinq Mars, la Pile de, 196
Cintegabelle, 329
Cirey, 517
Cirque, 226, 298
— de Gavarnie, 298, 300
Citeaux Abbey, 365
Civray, 218
Clain, 214
ste. Claire-sur-Epte, 246
Clairvaux, 516
Claix, 492
Clamart, 110
Clarbide, Port de, 307
Claret Wine, 258
ste. Claude, 510

CORMERY.

Clémence Isaure, 242
— de Maillé, 236, 239, 260, 342
Clermont en Argonne, 539
— *Ferrand*, 381
— to Mont Dore, 392
— to Lyons, by Thiers, 397
— sur-Oise, 19
— to Toulouse, by the Cantal, 398
— to Toulouse, by St. Flour, Alby, Rodez, 401
Clerval, 538
Cléry, N. Dame de, 177
Clichy, 31
Clisson, 164, 204
Clos-Vougeot, 364
st. Cloud, 111
Clovis, 542, 545
Cluny, 369
Cluse, 509
Coarrase, 290
Cocherel, 71
Cœur, Jacques, 341
Cognac, 213
Coiron, 416
Coligny, 10, 220, 352, 357, 513
Collioure, 328
Collonges, 512
Collot d'Herbois, 373, 376
Colmar, 536
Colombes, 31
Colombey, 517
Combat des Trente, 143
Combe de Malval, 497
Comblat, 400
Combourg, 102
st. Côme, 253
Comines, 16
la Commanderie, 72
Commentry, 343
Commercy, 524
Compiègne, 551
Concarneau, 146
Condé, le Grand, at Chantilly, 10; at Montrond, 342; at Fontainebleau, 346; at Montargis, 357; at Rocroy, 548; at the Dunes, 561
Condé, Huguenot leader, at Havre, 63; at Jarnac, 220
Condillac, 178
Condom, 278
Condorcet, 168
Condrieux, 427
Conflans, 49
Conqueror, Wm. the, his residence at Lillebonne, 59; his birth, 98; his death and funeral, 39, 74; his grave, 74
Conques, 404
Conquet, 131
Coole, 519
Corbeil, 169
Corbény, 558
Corday, Charlotte, 76
Cordes, 401
Cordouan, Tour de, 266
Cormery, 191

DIEPPEDALE.

Cornas, 429
Corneille, 41
Corps Nuds, 140
Corrèze, 239
Corseulles, 77
Cosne, 357
Côte des Deux Amans, 51
— d'Or, 352, 363, 506
— Rôtie, 427
Côtentin, 80
Coucy le Château, 543
Coudes, 387
Couësnon, river, 95
Courbassil, 332
Courbevoie, 44, 111
Cournouaille, 108, 142
Couronne, Grande, 69
la Couronne, abbey, 221
Courthezon, 437
Courville, 116
Coustouges, 333
Coutances, 88
Coutras, 221, 251
Couthon, 375
Crach, 150
Craon, 25
Craponne, Canal de, 465
Crau, 464
Crécy, 22
Creil, 19
Cressensac, 239
Cresset, 362
Crest, 432
Creuilly, 78
Creuzot, 367
Crillon, 475
Croix Court, 141
— Daurade, 241
— Haute, 495
— Rousse, 377, 511
Croquelardit, 252
Croutelle, 223
Cruas, 432
Crussol, 429, 431
Cubsac, Pont de, 221
Cujes, 471
Cussy la Colonne, 365
Cuvier, 65, 538
Cylindre, Mt., 300
st. Cyr, 121

D.

Dammartin, 542
Dampierre, 198
— château de, 112
Dante, allusion to Arles, 463
Daoulas, 145
Dauphiné, 482
Dax, 268
Delas, 264
Denain, 555
st. Denis, 20
Departments of France, xxxvi
Diderot, 517
Dieppe, 26-29
— to Paris, 26
— to Rouen, 30
Dieppedale, 53

INDEX.

DIEUZE.

Dieuze, 526
st. Diey, or Dié, 534
Digne, 495
Dijon, 353-355
—— to Châlons-sur-Saône, 363
—— to Geneva, by Dôle, 507
Diligences, xxv
Dinan, 137
st. Dizier, 519
Doira, 499
Dol, 95
Dôle, 507
—— to Pontarlier and Lausanne, 508
Dolmens, 105, 116, 135, 146, 149, 150, 200, 217
Dombasle, 540
Dombes, 369
Domrémy la Pucelle, 519, 531
Donzenac, 239
Dordogne, 221, 251, 394
Dore les Bains, Mont, 393
Dormans, 521
Dormilleuse, 493, 501
Douai, 8
Doubs, river, 514, 538; Dept., 514
Doullens, 9
Dozulle, 70
Drac, river, 488, 489, 492
Dragonnades, 241, 337
Dreux, 121; battle of, *ib.*
—— to Argentan, 165
Drevant, 343
Droiturier, 362
Drôme, 428, 432
Duclair, 53, 56
Duguesclin, 92, 124, 138, 148, 391; his death, 409
Dumouriez, 554
Dunes, battle of the, 561
Dunkerque, 560
Durance, 437, 457, 475, 499
Duretal, 154
Durfort, 411
Duroc, Marshal, 550

E.

Eaux-Bonnes, 230, 288
—— to Cauterets or Luz, 289
Eaux-Chaudes, 230, 286
Ebro, rise of, 314
les Echelles, 484
Ecluse, Fort, 512
Ecommoy, 99
Ecouen, 11
Ecouis, 48
Efflat, 361
Eguisheim, 536
Elbœuf, 52
st. Elne, 327
Elven, 153
Embrun, 499
st. Emilion, 251
Enghien-les-Bains, 19
English abroad, xxxvii
Entre Deux Mers, 222, 263

ST. FLORENT.

Entzheim, 533
Epernay, 521
Epernon, 112
Epinac, 367
Epinal, 532
Epinay, 170
Epone, 32
Epouville, 65
Epte, river, 49
Erdevan, 151
Ermenonville, 542
Ers, 248
Erstein, 535
Escaladieu, 313
Escot, 282
Espalion, 403
st. Esprit, 139, 434
Essonne, 356
Essort, 518
Estagel, 327
Estrelle, 461, 480
Etampes, 170
Etaples, 15
Etauliers, 213
st. *Etienne*, 412
—— to Lyons, 406
Etoile, 431
Etrécy, 168, 170
Etrétat, 65
Eu, 65
Eure, 51
Euzet, 420
Evreux, 71
Eyrieu, 431

F.

Falaise, 98
Faou, 144
Faouet, 142
Farel, 494
le Fay, 237
Fayl-Billot, 517
Fécamp, 65
la Fère, 557
—— Champenois, 518
st. Féréol, 323
la Ferrade, 447, 464
Ferrières, 398
la Ferté, meaning of, 236
Ferté-Bernard, 116
—— sous-Jouarre, 520
—— Milon, 542
Feurs, 397, 411
Field of the Cloth of Gold, 5
Figeac, 400
Finisterre, Dept., 125
Fire-arms, manufacture of, 412
Firmigny, 407
Fitou, 326
Flamboyant Gothic, 107, 159, 191, 504
Flamingo, 441
Flanders, 551
la Flèche, 154
Fleury-sur-Andelle, 48
Florac, 410
st. Florent, 203

GARONNE.

st. Florentin, 351
Florian, 176, 411
st. Flour, 397, 402
Foix, 329
Folgoat, church of, 132, 135
st. Fons, 425
Fontainebleau, 344
—— sandstone and grapes, 346, 347
Fontaine Henri, 77
Fontaines, 355
Fontanelle, 57
Fontaulier, 409, 418
Fontenay-le-Marmion, 98
—— abbey, 353
Fontevrault Abbey, 197
Forbach, 550
Forez, 379, 397
Forges les Eaux, 29
Formigny, 80
Fouday, 533
Fougères, 101
—— to Dinan, 102
Fourchamboult, 358
Fourvières, 370
la Foux, 445
FRANCE, introductory information respecting, ix-xxxix; modes of travelling in, xx; inns, &c., xxix; a traveller's view of, xxxii; Departments and Provinces, xxxvi
Franche-Comté, 503
Francs, table of, x
Fréjus, 479
Frèsne-Camilly, 78
Fresnes, 555
Fressinière, 493, 501
la Frette, 484
la Frey, 492
Frillière, 185
Froissart, 76, 228, 277, 291, 556
Fromenteau, 356
Frontignan, 454
Fruges, 9
Fumay, 548
Furens, 412

G.

Gabas, 287
Gaillac, 406
Gaillard, château, 33, 50
Gaillon, 33
Galgals, 106
Galignani, 25
Gan, 283
Gannat, 380
Gap, 493
—— to Briançon, 499
la Garaye, 140
Gard, St. Jean du, 411
—— Pont du (Aqueduct), 445
Gardon, 411, 419, 449
GARONNE, river, 252
—— below Bordeaux, 261
—— sources of, 314, 319, 320

GASCONY.

Gascony, 225
Gassendi, 496
Gatteville, 82
Gaube, lac de, 295
st. Gaudens, 322
—— to Foix and Carcassonne, 328
Gavarnie, 299
Gave de Gavarnie, 296-299
Gaves, 225
Gâvr Innis, 149
Gaz, 483
Gèdre, 298
Geloz, 285
Gemenos, 471
Gensdarmes, xviii
st. Genes, 397
Geneva, 508
st. Geneviève, 45
st. Genix, 512
Genlis (Burgundy), 507
Gennes, 200
st. George Boscherville, 53, 56
st. Gerard-le-Puy, 360
Gerbier des Joncs, 392, 408, 418
Gère, 426
Gergovia, 387
st. Germain-en-Laye, 45
—— to Rouen, 48
—— Railway, 44
—— de Joux, 512
Gervais, 39
Geuçay, 218
Gevray, 364
Gex, 508
Gibaud, Pont, 386
Gien, 176
—— to Orleans, 176
Gigean, 455
Gildas de Rhuys, 150
st. Gilles, 450
Giromagny, 534
Gironde, 221, 264
Girondins, 76, 261, 264
st. Girons, 328
Gisors, 29
Givors, 407, 425
Glacière at Avignon, 439
Gobelins tapestries, 346
Godemar, Val, 502
Goderville, 65
Goncelin, 491
Gournay, 29
Grande Chartreuse, 482, 484
—— Combe, 419
Grandvilliers, 23
la Grange, 505
Granges (Aube), 506
Granville, 90
Grasse, 496
la Grave, 497
Gravelines, 560
Graviers, 213
Graville, 61
Gray, 517
Grenelle, 110
Grenoble, 488
—— to Briançon, by Bourg d'Oysans, 496

HOUDAN.

Grenoble to Gap and Marseilles, 492
—— to Marseilles, by Croix Haute, 494
Grenoux, 118
Grésivaudan, Val de, 482, 484, 487
Greuze, 368
Grignan, château, 433
Grip, 305
Grisac, 409
Grolaud, 209
Grosbois, 505
Guebweiler, 537
Guerche, château de, 214
Guichen, 306
Guienne, 225
Guier, 133, 483
Guil river, 500
Guillestre, 500
Guillotière, 376, 515
Guingamp, 125
Guinguette de Boyer, 493
la Guiole, 403
Guisanne, Val de, 498
Guise, Duc de, 68
—— assassination of, 174
Guisnes, 5
Guizot, 450
Gypsum quarries, 477

H.

Hacqueville, Brunel's birthplace, 47
Hague, Cap la, 87
Ham, 552
Hambye, 90
Hannibal's route over the Alps, 426, 429, 437, 510
Harcourt, 72
Harfleur, 61
Hautes Pyrénées, 290
Hauteville, 102
le Havre, 62
—— to Caen, 70
—— to Dieppe, 64
la Haye, 214
—— du Puits, 88
Hazebrouck, 6
Héas, Val d', 299
Hectares and Acres, xvi
Hédé, 140
Heidenmauer, 535
Hennebon, 147
Henri Quatre, birth of, 279
Herblay, 29
st. Herbot, 142
Héricourt, 538
Hermitage, 428
st. Hilaire du Harcouet, 101
Honfleur, 70
Honorat, 463, 480
Hôpital, 409, 411
Hospitalet, 331
Hot springs of the Pyrenees, 230
Houdan, 121

JOUX.

la Hougue, Cape, battle of, 81
Hourat, 285
Hourquettes, 226
Hourquette d'Aspin, 306
Huelgoat, 141
Huguenot, derivation of, 190
Huningen, 518
Hyères, 475
st. Hyppolite, 535

I.

If, 468
Ile Belle, 49
—— sur Doubs, 538
—— des Faisans, 274
—— de France, 551
—— Jourdain, 321
Ille, 332
Indre, 193
Indret, 164
les Infernets, 497
Ingouville, 64
Ingrande, 203, 214
Inns, xxix
Inquisition in France, 246, 439
Iron Mask, the Man in the, 480
Isenheim, 537
Isère, river, 429, 491
Isigny, 80
l'Isle, 442
Isle, 547
Issoire, 388
Issy, 110
Ivry, battle, 71, 122
Izard, 227, 284

J.

Jacquerie, 25
James II. at St. Germain-en-Laye, 45
st. James, 243
Jargeau, 176
Jarnac, 220
Jaujac, 408, 417
st. Jean d'Angely, 208
—— du Doigt, 134
—— du Gard, 411
—— de Luz, 273
Jean-sans-peur, 348, 355
Jeanne d'Arc, at Rouen, 40; at Patay, 171; souvenirs at Orleans, 173; at Jargeau, 176; at Chinon, 194; at Domrémy, 531; at Reims, 546; at Compiègne, 552
Jeux Floraux, 242
Joigny, 349
Joinville, 519
Josephine, Empress, 44
Josselin, 143
Jouarre, 521
Jougne, 509
Joux, Fort de, 509

INDEX. 569

JOUY AUX ARCHES.

Jouy aux Arches, 541
Joyeuse, 419
st. Julien, 187, 265, 411
Jumièges Abbey, 56
st. Junien, 238
Jura, 513
Jurançon, 277, 283
st. Just, 9, 456
Juvisy, 169

K.

Kellerman, 539, 541
Kersanton stone, 107, 132, 135, 145
Kilogrammes reduced to English pounds, xv
Kilomètres reduced to English miles, xv, xx
Kistvaens, 106

L.

Labedoyère, 490
Labourd, Pays de, 271
Labrit, 267
Lac Bleu, 313
—— d'Espingo, 308
—— d'Oncet, 304
—— Vert, 313
Lace, manufacture of, 10, 76, 391, 556
Lafayette, 389, 505
Lafoux, 446
Lafrey, 492
Lagnieux, 511
Lagny, 520
Lailly, 178
Lalande, 513
Lamartine, M. Alphonse de, 368
Lamballe, 124
Lambert, 474
Lambesc, 477
La Mothe Fénélon, 239
Lanbader, 127
Landerneau, 127
Landes, 259, 262, 274
Landevan, 148
Landivisiau, 126
Landrecies, 556
Langeais, 196
Langogne, 409
Langoiron, 255
Langon, 254, 267, 408
Langres, 517
Languedoc, 225, 240, 421
Lanleff, 108, 132
Lanmeur, 134
Lannemezan, 314
Lannion, 133
Lanriouaré, 131
Laon, 557. Battle, 558
Laplace, 70
Larochejacquelin, 91, 117, 199, 204; his death, 207

LORRAINE.

Laruns, 285
La Tour d'Auvergne, 142
Laura's tomb, 441
st. Laurent, 508, 510
—— des Mûres, 483
—— du Pont, 484
Lauteret, Col de, 497
Laval, 118
Lavedan, Val, 292
Lavelanet, 329
Lavoulte, 431
Ledignan, 411
Légué, 125
Lehon, 139
Lemans, 116
Lempde, 388, 398, 401
Lens, 557
Lescar, 277
Lescure, 101, 207
Lescures, 406
Lesdiguières, 491, 492, 493
Lesneven, 135
Lesparre, 265
Lesponne, 305, 313
Lessay, 88
Lestelle, 290
st. Leu, 19
Leucate, 326
la Levée de la Loire, 182
Lezardrieux, 133
Lezoux, 397
Libech, 469
Libourne, 221, 251
Lieues de poste, xv
Lieuvin, 72
Liffré, 101
Ligny, 519
Lille, 6
—— to Brussels, 556
—— to Dunkerque, 559
Lillebonne, 54, 58
Lillers, 557
la Limagne, 344, 361, 379
Limetz, 49
Limoges, 237; Enamels, 238
—— to Bordeaux, 249
Limonest, 369
Limousin, 225
Limoux, 329
Lisieux, 72
Livres Tournois, 190
Livrons, 432
st. Lo, 101
Loches, castle of, 191
Locmariaker, 149
LOIRE river, 166, 191
—— A. Gien to Orleans, 176
—— B. Orleans to Tours, 177
—— C. Tours to Nantes, 195
—— below Nantes, 164
——, source of the, 418
Loiret, 177
Longéac, 391
Longjumeau, 168
Longueville, 30
Longwy, 549, 550
Lons-le-Saulnier, 513
Lorient, 146
Loriol, 432
Lorraine, 515

MAISON CARRÉE.

Lothiers, 236
st. Louis, 31, 212, 452, 518
Louis Napoleon, Prince, 553
Louis XI., 177, 188, 192
Louise Eléonore, Lord Brougham's villa, near Cannes, 480
Louise, Val, 502
Lourdes, 291
Louviers, 46
Louvigné, 101
Lowendahl, 236
la Lozère, 409
Luc, 77
le Luc, 475, 479
Luchon, 315
Luciennes, 44
Luçon, 209
Lucy-le-Bois, 350
Lunel, 451
Lunéville, 526
Lure, 518
Lusignan on the Vonne, 223
Lussac les Châteaux, 223
Luxeuil, 532
Luynes, 195
—— duc de, 195, 241
Luz, 297
—— to Gavarnie, 298
—— to Barèges, 302
Luzarches, 11
Luzerne, 91
Lyonnais, 335
LYONS, 370-379; Fourvières, 370; Cathedral, 371; Ainay, 372; Museum, 373; Pierre Scise, 374; P. Bellecour, 375; Siege of, 375; Inundation, 376; Fortifications, 377; Silk trade, 378.
—— to Avignon and Arles, 424
Lyons to Besançon, by Bourg, 512
—— to Geneva, by Nantua, 511
—— to Grenoble and Chambéry, 483
—— to Nice, by Grenoble, Digne, and Grasse, 495
—— to Le Puy, Aubenas, St. Etienne, 406
Lys, Val de, 316

M.

st. Macaire, 254
st. Maclou, Rouen, 36
Mâcon, 368
la Magdeleine, 240
Magistère, 252
Magny, 47, 359
Maguelonne, 455
Mailleraye-sur-Seine, 53
Mailly, 559
Maine, 208
Maintenon and its aqueduct, 112
Maison Carrée, 447

Maison Neuve, 508
—— Rouge, 237, 366, 505, 527
Maisons, 31
st. Maixent, 208, 223
Maladetta, 304, 306, 318, 319, 320
Malause, 252
Malijay, 495
Mallespostes, xxiv
Malmaison, 44
st. Malo, 96
——, to Nantes, 137
Mamet, 316
Manny, Sir Walter de, 148
Manosque, 494
le Mans, 116
—— to Nantes, 153
Mansle, 218
Mantes, 32
Marans, 209
Marboré, 298, 300
Marcadaou, 288, 295
st. Marcellin, 490
Marchiennes, 553
Marcillac, 404
Marennes, 212
Mareuil, 209
Margaux, 264
Marguerite, Ile Ste., 480
—— de Valois, 219, 253
st. Marie aux Mines, 535
stes. Maries, 464
Marigny, Enguerrand de, 39, 48
Marlborough at Brest, 131
Marly, 44
Marman, Puy de, 387
Marmande, 254, 342
Marmoutiers Abbey, 186, 527
Marot, 76, 240
Marquise, 22
Marrac, château de, 271
st. Mars-la-Bruyère, 116
MARSEILLES, 466-471
—— to Toulon and Hyères, 471
Marseille-sur-Oise, 23
Martinvaast, 87
st. Martory, 322
Martres, 245, 322
Marvejols, 402
Massiac, 398, 401
Massillon, 475
st. Mathurin, 201
st. Matthew, Abbey of, 131
Maubeuge, 556
Mauléon, 234
st. Maur, 200
les Maures, 475, 480
st. Maurice, 155, 426
Maurs, 400
Mauves, 204
Mauvezin, castle, 313
st. Maximin, 445, 479
Mayenne, 124
Mayet d'École, 380
Mazères, 329
Meaux, 520
st. Médard, 251
Médoc and its wines, 261-266
Médous, 305
Mehun, 178

Mehun sur-Yèvre, 339
Meillant, 343
la Meilleraye, 140
Melun, 344
Menars-le-Château, 178
Menat, 344
Mende, 409
ste. Menehould, 539
Menez Arrés hills, 103, 141
Menhirs, 96, 105, 131, 135, 149
st. Menoux, 360
ste. Mère l'Eglise, 80
Méreville, 168
st. Merxheim, 537
Mesnil-sous-Jumièges, 53
MÈTRE, the, xii ; Table of, reduced to feet, xiv
Mettray, 190
Metz, 540
—— to Luxembourg, 550
Meudon, 110
Meulan, 31
Meung, 178
Meuse river, 548
Meximieux, 511
Mèze, 455
Mezène, Mt., 392
Mézières, 547
Mialet, 411
st. Michel-aux-Lions, 237
Michel, Mont St., 93, 94
Midi, Canal du, 241, 248, 323, 455
Miélan, 322
Mihiel en Lorraine, 524
Milhau, 490
Mimat, 409
Mirabeau, 356, 468, 494, 509
Mirage, 463, 465
Mirande, 322
Mistral, 422, 452, 469
Moirans, 491
Moissac, 252
Moisselles, 25
Molesme, 365
Molière, 181, 455
Molzheim, 533
Monaldeschi, 346
Moncada, castle of, 276
Monestier, 498
—— de Clermont, 495
Money of France, x
Monistrol, 407
Montaigne, Michel de, 251
Montaigu, 208, 313, 344
Montaigut, 396
Montargis, 356
Montauban, 240
—— to Béziers, 406
Montbard, 352
Montbazon, 214
Montbelliard, 538
Montbert, 406
Mont Blanc, 429
Montbrison, 397, 411
Montbrun, 402, 415
Mont Cassel, 560
Mont du Chat, 510
Mont Dauphin, 500
Mont Dol, 96

Mont Dore les Bains, 393
—— to Le Puy, 396
Mont d'Ours, 390
Montdragon, 435
Montélimart, 432
Montereau, 347, 503
—— to Troyes, 503
Montesquieu's château, 267
Montferrand, 263, 381
Montfort castle, 70
Montfort, Jean de, 143, 204
—— Simon de, 322, 325, 458
Mont Genèvre, 499
Montgolfier, 413
Montigny, 556
Montivilliers, 64
Mont Jan, 202
Montlhéry, 170
Montlosier, 393
Mont Louis, 185, 334
—— Lozère, 409
Montluçon, 343
Montluel, 511
Montmajeur, 459
Mont de Marsan, 267
Montmédy, 549
Montmirail, 518
Mont Mirat, 99
Montmoreau, 221
Montmorency, 20
Montmorillon, 223
Montpellier, 452
Montpensier, Butte de, 380
Mont Perdu, 298, 301
—— Pertuis, 408
Montpeyroux, 387
Montpezat, 417, 418
Mont Pilas, 413, 427
—— Pipet, 426
Montpont, 251
Montrejeau, 314
Montrelais, 203
Montreuil, 111, 207
—— sur-Mer, 22
Montreval, 451
Montricher, 476
Montrodeix, 384
Montrognon, 386
Montrond, 342, 411, 508
Montrouge, 110
Mont Salomon, 426
—— St. Michel, 93, 94
—— Valérien, 44
Mont-sous-Vaudrey, 508
Mont St. Victoire, 479
Morbihan, 149
Moreilles, 209
Moret, 347
Morez, 508
Morlaas, 282
Morlaix, 125
—— to Nantes, 141
Mornas, 435
Mortagne, 123, 266
—— (Vendée), 207
Mortain, 100
Mortemer, Abbey of, 48
Mortier, Marshal, 555
Morvan, 351, 367
Mosac, or Mosat, 381

INDEX. 571

MOSELLE.

Moselle, 549
Mosquitoes, 422, 435, 469
la Mothe Fénélon, 239
la Motte, 405
Mouchard, 508, 513
Moulineaux, 53
Moulin Mauguin, 366
Moulins, 359
—— to Clermont and le Puy, 379
Moyenvic, 526
Mühlhausen, 537
Mulberry, 433
Munster, 536
Murat, 239, 398
la Mure, 493
Muret, 275, 322
Muriac, 393
Murol, 395
Mutzig, 533
le Muy, 479
Myriamètre, xii, xv

N.

Nages, 451
Nampont, 22
Nancy, 524
—— to Besançon and Geneva, 531
—— to Trèves, 549
Nangis, 505
Nanterre, 45
NANTES, 159-164
—— to Poitiers, 204
—— to Rochelle and Bordeaux, 208
Nanteuil, 521, 542
Nantua, 511
Narbonne, 456
—— to Perpignan, 326
Narcissa, 453
Navarre, 225
st. Nazaire, 325, 455
st. Nectaire, 395
Neff, Felix, 493, 501, 502
Nemours, 356
Nérac, 277
Néris-les-Bains, 343
Nerondes,
Ners, 420
Neschers, 395
Neuchâtel, 15
Neufbreisach, 536
Neufchâteau, 531
Neufchâtel, 29
Neuilly, 43
Neuvy, 357
Nevers, 358
—— to Châlons-sur-Saône, 366
Nice, 481
st. Nicolas, 38
Nicot, 450
Niort, 208, 223
NISMES, 446
—— to Alais and Aubenas, 419

OULLINS.

Nismes to Marseilles, 481
Nivelle, 273
st. Nizier, 373
Noailles, 239
Noë, 322
Nogent-sur-Seine, 503, 506
—— le Rotrou, 116
—— sur Vernisson, 357
Noiretable, 397
Noirlac, 342
Noirmoutiers, île, 165
Noisy-le-Sec, 520
Nonancourt, 123
Nord, Départ. du, 555
NORMANDY, 1-3. Routes, 3-102
Norrey, 78
Nort, 141
Nostradamus, 459, 465
Nouvion, 23
Noyades of the Loire, 162
Noyon, 552
Nuits, 352, 365

O.

Oberlin, 533
Octeville, 87
Odilienberg, 535
Oissel, 52
Oléron, Ile d', 210
Olette, 332, 334
Olivet, 235, 312
Ollioules, 472
Oloron, 282
st. Omer, 5, 557
Oo, Lac d', 307
Orange, 435
Orcières, Col d', 493, 502
Orgon, 476
Orival, 52
ORLEANS, 171
—— forest of, 168
—— siege of, 173
—— Maid of, 173, 174, 176, 214
—— railroad to Paris, 169
—— to Bourges and Clermont, 339
—— to Gien, 176
—— to Rouen, 175
—— to Toulouse, 235
—— to Tours, 177
d'Orléans, Duc, 43
les Ormes, 503
Ornain, 524
Orthez, 276
Ossau, Val d', 282, 284
Osse, 282
Ossouë, 296
Ossuary, 107
Ottmarsheim, 537
Oudon, 204
Ouessant, 22, 132
Oule, 226, 298
Oullins, 406

PAVILLY.

P.

la Pacaudière, 362
Pacy-sur-Eure, 71
Paillette, 283
Paillole, 306
Paimbœuf, 164
Paimpol, 133
Pain Bouchain, 362
Palais du Roi, 409
la Palisse, 362
le Pallet, 204
Palombière, the, 312
Palons, 501
la Palud, 434
Pamiers, 329
Panticosa, 287
Paper manufacture, 414
Paraclète, church of the, 506
st. Pardoux, 344
PARIS, 25
—— to Bourbonne les Bains, 531
—— to Brussels — Chemin de Fer du Nord, by Amiens, Arras, Douai, and Valenciennes, 555
—— to Caen and Cherbourg, 71
—— to Dijon, by Melun, 344
—— —— by Troyes, 505
—— to Lyons, Route du Bourbonnais, 356
—— to Mézières and Sédan, by Rheims, 542
—— to Nancy, 518
—— to Orleans, 168. Railway, 169
—— to Rennes, 109, 120
—— to Rouen (railway), 30
—— to Rouen (railway), lower road, 43
—— ——, upper road, 47
—— to Sceaux (railroad), 175
—— to Strasburg, by Nancy, 519
—— to Valenciennes, by St. Quentin and Cambrai, 551
—— to Versailles (railroad), 109
Parthenay, 207
PASSPORTS AND POLICE, xvi-xviii
Passy, 120
Patay, 171
st. Patrice, 196
Pau, 278
—— to Bagnères de Bigorre and de Luchon, 308
—— to Campfranc in Spain, by Oloron and Val d'Aspe, 282
—— to Cauterets and Barèges, 290
—— to Eaux-Bonnes and Eaux-Chaudes, 283
Pauillac, 265
st. Paul, 252, 305, 406
—— de Dax, 268
Pavilly, 60

ST. PÉ.

st. Pé, 290
Péage, 175
le Pecq, 44, 45
Pedauque, la Reine, 245
Pelacoy, 239
Pelvoux, Mont, 482, 502
Pendentif, 429
st. Peray, 430. Wine, 431
Perci, 90, 102
Perdu, Mont, 298, 301
st. Père, 351
Périers, 88
Perigueux, 250
Péronne, 555
Perpignan, 326
—— to Mont Louis and Puycerda, 332
Perrache, 376
Perte du Rhône, 512
Perthus, 328
Petit Rhône, 460
Petrarch, 439, 441, 443
Peulvens, 105
Peyrada, 299
Peyrehorade, 276
Peyresourde, 307
Peyrolles, 494
Peyruis, 494
Pezenas, 455
Phalsbourg, 526
Picade, port de, 317
Picardy, 1
Pic de Bergons, 296, 297
—— Génos, 307
—— Gers, 288
—— du Midi de Bigorre, 279, 304
—— du Midi d'Ossau, 277, 284, 286
Picquigny, 16
Pierre Châtel, 510
—— de Couars, 366
—— Scise, 374
st. Pierre le Moutier, 359
—— les Eglises, 72, 73
—— de Vauvray, 33
Pierrefitte, 292, 307
Pierrelatte, 434
Pignadas, 275
Pilas, Mont, 413, 427
Pimené, 299
Pique, valley of the, 314
Pithiviers, 171
Plantagenet, 103
Plessis les Tours, 188
Pleyben, 145
Ploërmel, 153
Plomb de Cantal, 398
Plombières, 353, 532
Plouarzel, 131
Plougastel, 132
Plouha, 132
Podensac, 255
Poissy, 31
Poitiers, 214. Battle of, 217
—— to Châteauroux, 222
—— to Rochefort by Niort, 223
Poix, 23
st. Pol, 9

PUGÈRE.

st. Pol de Léon, 134
Polignac, 389, 553
Poligny, 508
Polminhac, 400
Pomard, 365
Pommereau, port de, 320
Pommereval, 29
Pompadour, 239
Pompidou, 410
Pons, 213
Ponsas, 428
Pont-à-Mousson, 549
Pontarlier, 509
Pont Audemer, 69
Pontchâteau, 397
Pontecharra, 492
Pont d'Ain, 511, 512
Pont du Beauvoisin, 483
Ponts de Cé, 201
Pont Flavien, 465
Pont de l'Arc, 419
—— de l'Arche, 33
—— du Château, 397
—— d'Espagne, 295
—— DU GARD, 445
—— de Montvert, 409
Pontgibaud, 386
Pontigny, 351
Pontius Pilate, 428
Pontivy, 143
Pont l'Evêque, 70
—— le Roi, 506
Pontoise, 19
Pont Orson, 92
Pontouvre, 218
Pont St. Esprit, 434
—— St. Maxence, 551
—— Scorff, 147
Pont sans Pareil, 5
Pont-sur-Yonne, 348
Popes at Avignon, 438
st. Porchaire, 212
Pornic, 165
Port de Launay, 144
Port St. Hubert, 137
Port-Royal des Champs, 111
Port-sur-Saône, 517
—— Vendres, 328
Portets, 255, 322, 329
Portillons, 226
Ports, 226
Poste aux ânes, 425
Posting in France, xx
Pouges, 358
Pouilly, 357, 411
Poulahouan, 142
st. Pourçain, 379
Poussin, Nicolas, 51
Pouy, 268
Pradelles, 408
Prades, 332, 417
Pratz de Mollo, 333
Preignac, 254
Pretender (the) 135, 162
Privas, 415
st. Privast, 409
Privat d'Allier, 391
PROVENCE, 421
Provins, 505
Pugère, 479

RAMBOUILLET.

Puiseux, 25
le Puy, 389
—— to Alais, 414
Puy du Chopine, 386
—— de Cliersou, 385
—— Come, 386
—— de Dôme, 383
—— Girou, 386
—— du Grand Sarcouy, 386
—— Gravenoire, 386
—— Griou, 398, 399
—— Louchadière, 386
—— Marman, 387
—— Pariou, 384
—— la Poix, 386, 397
—— de Tartaret, 395
Puymaurins, 332
Puyoo, 276
PYRENEES, 225, 290, 305, 308.
Routes, 80, 82, 83, 84, 85, 86, 87, 91, 94, 97, 98
—— directions for travelling, 231-235
—— *the Eastern*, 329, 332
—— Marbles of the, 311

Q.

Quélern, 130, 144
st. Quentin, 553
—— in Normandy, 98
Querqueville, 87
Quevilly, 53
Queyras, Val, 500
Quiberon, 151
Quillebœuf, 54
Quimper, 145
Quimperlé, 146
Quinéville, 80
Quingey, 513
Quinipily, Venus of, 148

R.

Rabastens, 322
Rabelais, 110, 195, 453
Rachet, 487
Racine, 112, 542
Raillère, 294
RAILROADS, xxvii
—— Bordeaux to La Teste, 259
—— Boulogne to Paris, 15
—— Lille to Courtrai, 8
—— Lyons to St. Etienne, 406
—— Montpellier to Cette, 454
—— Nismes to Beaucaire, 481
—— Paris to Corbeil, 169
—— —— to St. Germain, 44
—— —— to Orleans, 169
—— —— to Rouen, 30
—— —— to Versailles, 109, 110
—— Roanne to St. Etienne, 362, 411
—— Strasburg to Bâle, 534
Raismes, 556
st. Rambert, 428
Rambouillet, 112

LA RANCE.

la Rance, river, 137
Rancié, mines de, 330
Rancogne, Grottes de, 219
Randan, 362
Randanne, 393
Raz, Pointe du, 146
Ré, Ile de, 210
Rébénac, 283
la Recousse, 9
Redon, 143
Reims, 544
—— to Luxembourg, 548
Remiremont, 532
Remoulins, 445
st. Remy, 459
Renaissance, style, 160, 173, 181, 187, 354, 430
René d'Anjou, 477
Rennes, 119
—— to Brest, 124
—— to Vannes, 153
la Réole, 254
la République, 413
Rethel, 547
de Retz, Card., 161, 518
—— Gilles, 202
Rhins, 411
RHÔNE, 424
—— the Haut, Aix to Lyons, 510
—— Junction with the Saône, 425
—— Lyons to Avignon and Arles, 424
—— Perte du, 512
Rhuys, 150
Ribbon manufacture, 412
Ribeauville, 536
Richard Cœur-de-Lion, 36, 52, 197; death of, 249
Richebourg, 364
Richelieu, 44, 210
Richemont, 550
Rienzi at Avignon, 439
Riom, 380
st. Riquier, 23
Rive de Gier, 407
Rivesaltes, 326
Rixheim, 537
Roanne, 362
—— to St. Etienne (Railway) and Valence, 411
Robert the Devil, 53
la Roche-sur-Yonne, 208
la Roche Bernard, 152
—— Guyon, 49
—— Maurice, 127
Roche Corbon, 185, 370
—— Cotte, 196
—— Courbe, 431
—— Taillée, 369, 428
Rochefort, 202, 211, 393
la Rochefoucauld, 219
la Rochelle, 209
la Roche Jagu, castle, 133
Rochemaure, 432
les Rochers, 119
Rocroy, 548
Rodez, 403
Rohan, 143, 411

SAÔNE.

Roland, Camisard chief, 337, 410, 411, 420, 450
—— the Girondist, 48
—— the Paladin, 298
Rolleboise, 49
Rollo the Pirate, 47
st. Romain, 41, 369
Roman remains, 424, 426, 435, 445, 447, 448, 449, 459, 460, 464, 465, 541
Romanche, Val, 496
Romanêche, 369
Romanée, 365
Romanesque style, 108, 160, 256, 427, 429, 450, 459
Romans, 490
Romilly copper-works, 51
Roncesvaux, 228
Roquefavour, aqueduct of, 476
Roquefort, 267, 278; cheese, 404
Roquemaure, 437
Roscoff, 135
les Rosiers, 200
Rosny, château, 32
Rosporden, 146
Roubaix, 556
ROUEN, 34-43
—— to Alençon, 68
—— to Caen, 69
—— to Havre, 52, 55; by Yvetot, 59
—— to Orleans, 175
—— to Paris (railroad), 30, 43
Rouffach, 536
Rousseau, 20, 185, 542
les Rousses, 508
Roussillon, 225, 326
Rouvray, St. Etienne de, 52
Royan, 212, 266
Royat, 385
Rue, 15
Ruel, 44
Ruelle, 219
Ruffec, 218
Rumengol, 144

S.

Sablé, 154
les Sables, 209
le Sage, birthplace of, 150; his death, 13
Saintes, 212
Salbris, 236
Salces, 326
Salients, 287
Salins, 508
Salles Compteaux, 404
Sallies, 276
Salon, 465
Samer, 22
Samadoire, 396
Sancerre, 357
Sancy, Pic de, 393, 395
Sandrupt, 519
SAÔNE, *river*, Châlons to Lyons, 367; junction of, with Rhône, 425

SOAP MANUFACTURE.

Sapey, 487
Sarrebourg, 526
Sarzeau, 152
Sassenage, 487, 489
le Saulce, 494
le Sault, 511
Saulx, 532
Saumur, 198
—— to Saintes and Bordeaux, 207
Saut de Sabot, 406
Sauterne, 267
Sauveterre, 276
st. Sauveur les Bains, 230, 297
—— le Vicomte, 81, 88
Savenay, 153
Savenières, 202
Saverdun, 329
Saverne, 526
Savigny, Abbey, 101; village, 170
st. Savin, 222
Scarron, 117, 154
Sceaux, 176
Scheldt, 554
Schirmeck, 533
Schlestadt, 535
Schön, Martin, 536
Schwartzenberg, 516
Scorpions, 423
St. Sebastian, 271
Seculéjo, 308
Sédan, 548
Séez, 69
Seguier, death of, 410
la Seilleraie, 204
SEINE RIVER, rise of, 507
—— Paris to Rouen, 43
—— st. Germain to Rouen, 48
—— Rouen to Havre, 52
Selles-sur-Cher, 181
Semur, 353
Senlis, 551
Sens, 348
Sept Laux, 491, 496
st. Sernin, 243
Serres, 495
Serrant, château de, 201
st. Servan, 97
Servières, 396
st. Sever, 34, 39
Sévignac, 283
Sévigné, Mad. de, 119, 153, 161, 204, 422, 433
Sèvre Nantaise, 159, 207
—— Niortaise, 209
Sèvres china, 120
st. Seyne, 507
Seyssel, 510
Sézanne, 518
Sierck, 550
Sièyes, 480
Sigean, 326
Silkworm, 433
Silk manufacture, 378, 415, 416
Sillery, 558
—— Champagne, 558
Sisteron, 494
Skeleton Tour of France, xxxix
Soap manufacture, 469

SOISSONS.

Soissons, 542
Solesmes, 154
Soligny, 123
la Sologne, 236
Sommesous, 519
la Sône, 490
Sorgues, 437, 443
Sotteville, 34
Souillac, 239
Souchez, 557
Soult, Marshal, 249, 270
la Source du Loiret, 175
Souvigny, 360
Souzé, 197
Soyons, 431
Steamboats, xxviii
Stenay, 549
STRASBURG, 527-531; pâtés, 530
—— to Bâle (railroad) 534
—— to Besançon, by Colmar, 538
—— to Epinal, 533
Succinio, 150
Suchet, Marshal, 444
Sully, 32, 176; his castle, 116; his grave, ib.
—— town and castle, 176
Sulz les Bains, 533
Sulzbad, 536
Suzon, Val de, 507
Symphorien-en-Lay, 362

T.

Tables d'hôte, xxix
Taillebourg, 212
Tain, 428
Talbot's death, 251
Tallard, 494
Talleyrand's residence at Valençay, 181; his tomb, 181
Tamarville, 81
Tancarville, 54
Tanlay, 352
Tarare, 362
Tarascon, 457
—— (Ariége), 330
Tarbes, 309
Tarn, 405, 409
Tartas, 268
Tech, valley of the, 333
Tencin, 491
Teste de Buch (railway), 259
Tet, 326, 332
Thau, Etang de, 455
Thann (Alsace), 538
—— near Caen, 77
Theatres, Roman, at Lillebonne, 58
—— at Arles, 461
—— at Orange, 436
Théogonec, 126
Thiers, 397
Thiézac, 399
Thionville, 550
le Thor, 442
Thouars, 207

TROYES.

Thourie, 140
Thueyts, 408, 417, 418
Tiffauges, 206
Tinchebray, 100
Tocqueville, 65, 82
Toissey, 369
Tombeleine, 92, 95
Tonnay Charente, 212
Tonneins, 254
Tonnerre, 352
Tonquedec, 134
Torfou, 206
Torigni, 102
Torte, 288, 289
Tôtes, 30
Toul, 519, 524
Toulon, 472; siege, *ib.*
Toulouse, 241-249; battle of, 248
—— to Auch and Pau, 321
—— to Bagnères, 322
—— to Bordeaux, 252
—— to Foix, 329
—— to Narbonne, 323
Touraine, 167
Tour de Bellot, 419
—— en Bessin, 80
—— du Carol, 332
—— de Cordouan, 266
—— du Pin, 483
Tourcoing, 556
Tourlaville castle, 82
la Tourmagne, 449
Tourmalet, 303, 304
Tournai, 556
Tournebride, 204
Tournoëlle, 381
Tournon, 428
Tournus, 368
Tours, 186-190
—— to Chinon and Saumur, 193
—— to Loches, 191
—— to Nantes, 195
—— to Poitiers and Bordeaux, 213
Tourves, 479
Tourville, 34
Toussaint l'Ouverture, 509
le Touvet, 491
Tramesaigues (Val d'Aure), 304, 306
la Trappe près Soligny, 123
Trappist Convents, 88, 123, 140
Tréguier, 133
Trépassés, Baie des, 146
Treport, 68
Trèves, 200
Trévoux, 369
Tricherie, 214
Triel, 31
Troarn, 70
st. Tropez, 475
Trou du Taureau, 319
Trouille, 462
Troumouse, 299
Trouville, 70
Troyes, 503; treaty of, 504; weight, 504
—— to Mülhausen, 515

VÉNASQUE.

Tulle, 239
Tullins, 490
Turckheim, 536
Turenne, 239
—— Marshal, 536, 548, 561
Turpin, Archbishop, 545

U.

Uchau, 451
Urdos, 283
Uriage, 489
Urtubi, 273
Urugne, 273
Ussat, 330
Utrecht, Treaty of, 561
Uzerche, 238
Uzès, 420
Uzeste, 267

V.

st. Vaast la Hougue, 81
Vaison, 436
Val d'Ante, 99
—— d'Aspe, 282
—— d'Enfer, 394
—— d'Ossau, 282, 284
Valençay, 181
Valence, 429
—— to Aubenas, Privas, and Nismes, 414
—— to Grenoble, 490
Valenciennes, 556
Valérien, Mt., 44
st. Valery-sur-Somme, 15
Vallery en Caux, 65
Vallery, 349
st. Vallier, 428
Vallière, Mad. de la, 45
Vallons, 419
Valmy, 539
Valognes, 81
Vals, 336, 417, 428
Vandamme, General, 560
Vannes, 152
Vanvres, 110
Var, 480
Varades, 203
Varennes, 360, 539
Vaubadon, 101
Vauban, Marshal, 6, 83, 127, 269, 351, 430, 529
Vaucanson, 490
Vaucelles, 75
Vaucluse, 443
Vaucouleurs, 531
Vaudémont, 525
Vaudreuil, 47
Vaugirard, 110
le Vaunage, 451
Vaux de Vire, 100
Vayre, 387
Velaine, 519
le Velay, 391, 408
Venasque, 319; port de, 315, 317, 318

INDEX.

VENDÉANS.

Vendéans at Chollet, 207
— at Granville, 91
— at Laval, 118
— at le Mans, 117
— at Nantes, 163
— at Saumur, 199
— at Savenay, 153
— at St. Florent, 203
la Vendée, 118, 167, 208
Vendôme, 191
Vendres, Port, 328
Vénérand, 118
Venin, la Tour st., 489
Venos, 497
Ventoux, Mont, 434, 444
st. Veran, 501
Verberie, 551
Verdigris, manufacture of, 454
Verdun, 540
Veretz, 195
Vergy, 507
Vermanton, 350
Vernet, 334
— Horace, 441
Verneuil, 123
Vernon, 33
la Verpillière, 483
Versailles, 111, 121
Vertrieux, 511
Vesaignes, 517
Vesoul, 518
Vexin, 47
Vézelay, 350
Vezenobre, 420
Vicdessos, 330
Vichy Baths, 360
Vic-sur-Cère, 400
st. Victor, 30
Vidauban, 479
Vieille-Brioude, 389
Viella, 320
Vielle, 306
Vienne, 426
— to Grenoble, 483
Vierzon, 236, 339
Vif, 495
Vigan, 405
Vignemale, 296

VOUGEOT.

Vigny, 47
Vilaine, river, 119
Villandraut, 254
Villars, 338, 359, 449, 550, 555
— d'Arène, 497
— Bocage, 99
Villebaudon, 102
Villebon, 116
Villedieu les Poêles, 102
— du Perron, 223
Villefranche, 323, 333
— sur-Saône, 369
— (Aveyron), 401
Villejuif, 356
Villeneuve lès Avignon, 442
— St. George, 344
— la Guiard, 348
— de Marsan, 278
— le Roi, 169, 349
Villers-Cotterets, 542
la Villette, 542
Villiquier, 54
Violins, 501
Vire, 99
Viry, 169
Viso, Monte, 500
la Vitarelle, 252, 409
Vitré, 119
Vitry le Français, 519, 523
Vivarais, 335, 416
Viviers, 329, 434
Vizille, 492
Vocance, Val de, 414
Void, 519
Voirons, 483
Volane, 417
Volcanoes, extinct, of Auvergne, 335
Volnay, 365
Voltaire, 31, 168, 175, 185, 247, 517
Volvic, 381
Voreppe, 484
Vosges mountains (Routes 168, 170), 515, 532, 533, 534, 535
Voué, 559
Vougeot, Clos de, 364

ZABERN.

la Voulte, 431
Vouziers, 549

W.

Waldbach, 534
Waldersbach, 533
st. Wandrille, 57
Wasselonne, 527
Weights and measures, xii-xvi
Wellington, Duke of, 155; in the Pyrenees, 229, 249, 273; at Bayonne, 269; at Cateau Cambresis, 555; at Péronne, 555
Wimille, 22
Witsand, 22

X.

Xantrailles, 277
Xertigny, 532

Y.

Yèvre, 339
Yonne, river, 348
Young, the poet, 453
st. Yrieix, 238
Yssingeaux, 407
Yvetot, 60; Roi d', *ib.*

Z.

Zabern, 526

THE END.

London: Printed by WILLIAM CLOWES and SONS, Stamford Street, and Charing Cross.

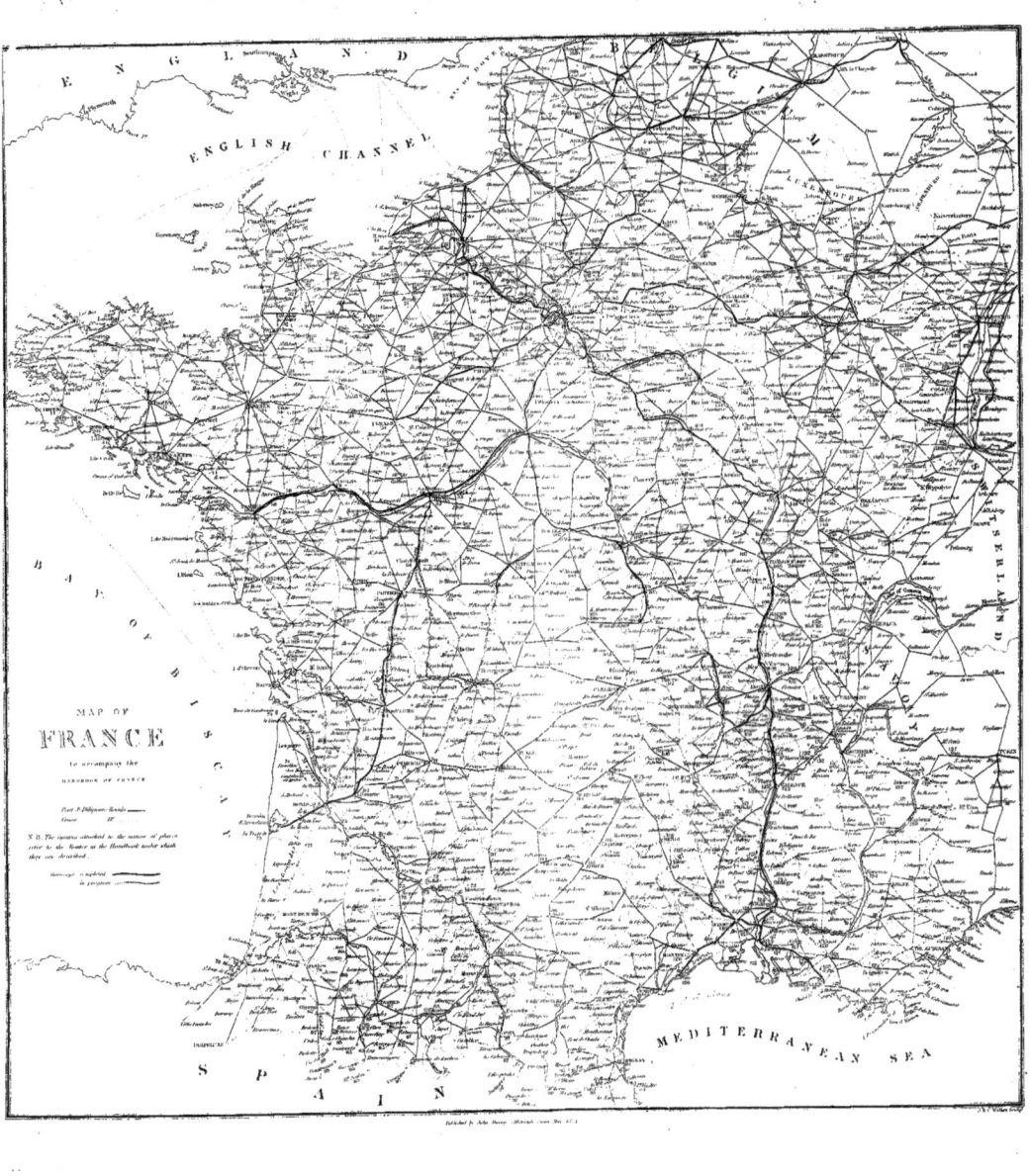

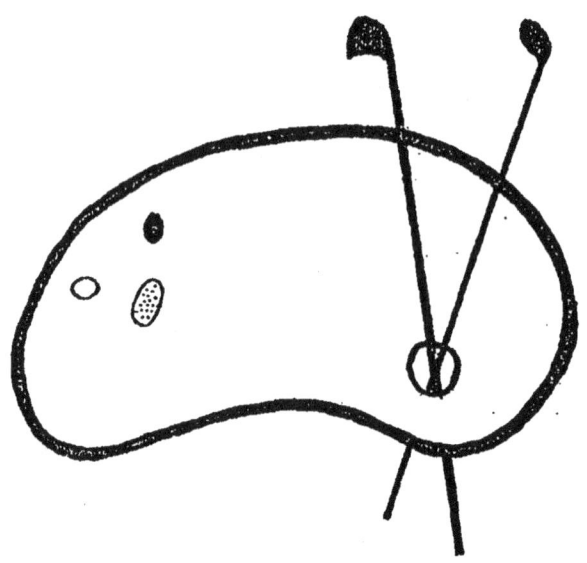

DEBUT D'UNE SERIE DE DOCUMENTS
EN COULEUR

MURRAY'S HANDBOOK ADVERTISER.

1854.

PRINTED FOR THE CONVENIENCE OF THOSE WHO ARE DESIROUS OF COMMUNICATING INFORMATION TO

TRAVELLERS ON THE CONTINENT.

PUBLISHED ANNUALLY.

The Editor is not responsible for any statements made in the Advertisements.

SCALE OF CHARGES:—

	£	s.	d.		£	s.	d.
For Eight Lines	0	8	6	Half a Column	1	2	0
Every Line additional	0	0	9	A Column, or Half-page	2	2	0
An entire Page				£4 0 0			

INDEX TO ADVERTISEMENTS.

GERMANY.

FRANKFORT.—Tacchi's Glass Warehouse . 10
    Bing's Manufactory . . 9
MUNICH.—Steigerwald's Glass Rooms . 6
    Wimmer's Magazine . . 8
COLOGNE.—Farina's Eau de Cologne . 11
    Martin's Eau de Cologne . 18
DRESDEN.—Magazine of Fine Arts . 12
PRAGUE.—Hofmann's Glass Manufactory 12
VIENNA.—Lobmeyr's Glass Manufactory 13
    Hofmann's Glass Manufactory 12
MARIENBURG.—Baskerville's School . 13
CARLSBAD.—Wolf's Glass Manufactory . 20

HOLLAND.

ROTTERDAM Steam Packets . . . 13

FRANCE.

BOULOGNE.—Hôtel Windsor . . . 19

ITALY.

FLORENCE.—Bianchini's Mosaic . . 7
    Roberts's Pharmacy . . 21
GENOA.—Loleo's Silver Filigree Work . 7
    Hôtel de Londres . . . 20

NICE.—How's English Warehouse . 8
    Lattes, General Agent . . 8
LEGHORN.—Micali's Marble Works . 12
ROME.—English Pharmacy . . . 7
    Shea, House Agent . . . 20

SWITZERLAND.

ZURICH.—Kerez, Chemist 20

ENGLAND.

Custom House Agents—McCracken . 4
Union Bank of London 14
London and Westminster Bank . . 16
Meohl's Dressing Cases 16
Black's Guide Books 17
Thimm's Foreign Book Depôt . . 21
Locock's Cough Wafers 16
Ocean-Parcels Company 19
Athenæum 18
Cary's Pocket Telescope . . . 19
Galignani's Guide to Paris . . 12
South-Eastern Railway 15
French Prompter 18
Assyrian Excavation Fund . . . 22
Hodgson's Parlour Library . . 24
Murray's Handbooks, &c. . . . 25
Lee's Guide-Book Depôt 32

B

LIST OF DUTIES

Now payable in London upon the Importation of Works of Art, Curiosities, &c., from the Continent.

The following Articles are ALL FREE OF DUTY.

ALABASTER and MARBLE.
AMBER, Manufactures of.
ANCHOVIES.
AGATES and CORNELIANS, set or unset.
BOOKS, of editions printed prior to 1801.
BRONZE Works of Art (antiques and original works only).
BULLION, Coins and Medals of all kinds, and battered Plate.
CAMBRICS, Lawns, Damask and Diapers of Linen, or Linen and Cotton.
CAMEOS, *not* set.
CARRIAGES of all sorts.
CATLINGS, and Harp Strings, silvered or not.
CASTS of Busts, Statues, or Figures.
CORAL, whole, polished, unpolished, and fragments.
COTTON, Manufactures of, *not* being articles wholly or in part made up.
DIAMONDS, Emeralds, Pearls, and other Precious Stones, *not* set.
FLOWER Roots.
FRAMES for Pictures, Prints, Drawings, and Mirrors.
FURS and SKINS, and Articles thereof.
GLASS, all Plate, Cast or Rolled Glass.
——— Paintings on Glass.
GLASS Beads and Bugles.
GLASS Bottles, Wine Glasses, and Tumblers, and all white flint and common green-glass goods, *not* being cut or ornamented.
LINEN Manufactures, *not* being *articles* wholly or in part made up.
LAY Figures, imported by British Artists for their own use.
MAGNA GRECIA Ware, and Antique Earthen Vases.
MANUSCRIPTS.
MAPS and CHARTS, and parts thereof.
MINERAL Waters.
MODELS of Cork and Wood.
OLIVES and Olive Oil.
PAINTERS' COLOURS, Brushes, Pencils, and Crayons.
PICTURES.
PLANTS and TREES, alive.
SEEDS.
SAUSAGES.
SPECIMENS of Natural History, Minerals, Fossils, and Ores.
STONE, all Sculpture and Articles of Stone, Alabaster, and Marble.
SULPHUR Impressions, or Casts.
TELESCOPES.
TILES.
VASES, Ancient, *not* of Stone or Marble.

On the following Articles the duty is 5 per cent. ad valorem.

CASHMERE SHAWLS, and all Articles of Goats' Hair or Wool.
COTTON Articles, wholly or in part made up.
LINEN Articles, wholly or in part made up.
WOOLLEN Articles, wholly or in part made up.

On the following Articles the Duty is 10 per cent. ad valorem.

BOXES of all sorts.
EGYPTIAN, and all other Antiquities.
EMBROIDERY and Needlework.
FURNITURE of all kinds.
JAPANNED and Lacquered Ware.
JEWELLERY, and all Jewels set.
LACE made by hand.
MOSAIC, small Ornaments for Jewellery.
MUSICAL Instruments, *excepting* Musical Boxes, Brass Instruments, Pianos, and Accordions.
SCAGLIOLA Tables.

LIST OF DUTIES—continued.

		£	s	d
ARQUEBUSADE WATER	the gallon	1	0	0
BEADS of CORAL	the lb.	0	1	6
———— Crystal, Jet, and Mock Pearl	ditto	0	0	2
BOOKS, of editions printed in and since 1801	the cwt.	1	10	0
———— imported under International Treaties of Copyright	ditto	0	15	0
(Pirated Editions of English Works, of which the Copyright exists in England, totally prohibited.)				
———— English, reimported (unless declared that no Drawback was claimed on Export)	the lb.	0	0	1½
BROCADE of GOLD and SILVER	ditto	0	5	0
BRONZE, BRASS, and COPPER, } all Manufactures of	the cwt.	0	10	0
CARPETS and RUGS (woollen)	the square yard	0	0	6
CORAL NEGLIGEES	the lb.	0	1	0
CHINA, PORCELAIN, and EARTHENWARE, all	the cwt.	0	10	0
CLOCKS, not exceeding the value of 5s. each	the dozen	0	4	0
———— exceeding 5s., and not exceeding the value of 12s. 6d. each	ditto	0	8	0
———— exceeding 12s. 6d., and not exceeding the value of 3l. each	each	0	2	0
———— exceeding 3l., and not exceeding the value of 10l.	ditto	0	4	0
———— exceeding 10l. value	ditto	0	10	0
CIGARS and TOBACCO, manufactured (3 lbs. only allowed in a passenger's baggage)	the lb.	0	9	0
TOBACCO, unmanufactured (with 5 per cent. additional on the Duty)	ditto	0	3	0
(N.B.—Unmanufactured Tobacco cannot be imported in less quantity than 300 lbs., or Cigars 100 lbs. in a Package; but small quantities are allowed for Private Use on declaration, and payment of a Fine of 1s. 6d. per lb. in addition to the Duty.)				
COFFEE	the lb.	0	0	4
CONFECTIONERY, Sweetmeats and Succades	ditto	0	0	2
CORDIALS and LIQUEURS	the gallon	1	0	0
CURTAINS, embroidered on Muslin or Net, called Swiss Curtains	the lb.	0	1	0
EAU DE COLOGNE, in long flasks	the flask	0	0	8
———— in any other description of bottles	the gallon	1	0	0
FLOWERS, Artificial, the cubic foot as packed		0	12	0
GLASS, Flint, Cut, Coloured, and Fancy Ornamental Glass, of whatever kind	the cwt.	0	10	0
GLOVES, of Leather (not less than 100 dozen pairs can be imported in one package)	the dozen pair	0	3	6
MACCARONI and VERMICELLI	the cwt.	0	1	0
NAPLES SOAP	ditto	1	0	0
PERFUMERY	the lb.	0	0	2
PERFUMED SPIRITS	the gallon	1	0	0
PAPER-HANGINGS, Flock Paper, and Paper printed, painted, or stained	the square yard	0	0	1
PIANOFORTES, horizontal grand	each	3	0	0
———————— upright and square	ditto	2	0	0
PLATE, of Gold	the oz. troy	1	1	0
———— of Silver, gilt or ungilt	ditto	0	1	8
PRINTS and DRAWINGS, single or bound, plain or coloured	the lb.	0	0	3
SILK, MILLINERY, Turbans or Caps	each	0	3	6
———————— Hats or Bonnets	ditto	0	7	0
———————— Dresses	ditto	1	10	0
———— HANGINGS, and other Manufactures of Silk	the 100l. value	15	0	0
———— VELVETS, plain or figured	the lb.	0	9	0
TEA, till 5th of April, 1854	the lb.	0	1	10
———— after 5th of April, 1854, to April, 1855	ditto	0	1	6
TOYS and TURNERY	the cubic foot	0	0	4
WINE in Casks or Bottles (in bottles 6 to the gallon)	the gallon	0	5	6
SPIRITS in Cask or Bottle	ditto	0	15	0
No Cask can be imported of less contents than 21 Gallons.				

MESSRS. J. & R. McCRACKEN,
7, OLD JEWRY, LONDON,
AGENTS BY APPOINTMENT TO THE ROYAL ACADEMY,

And Agents generally for the Reception and Shipment of Works of Art, Baggage, &c.,

FROM AND TO ALL PARTS OF THE WORLD,

RETURN their sincere acknowledgments to the Nobility and Gentry for the liberal patronage hitherto conferred on them. They hope, by the moderation of their charges, and their unremitting care in passing through the CUSTOM-HOUSE Property confided to them, to merit a continuance of the favours they have heretofore enjoyed. Their establishment comprises DRY AND SPACIOUS WAREHOUSES, where Works of Art and all descriptions of Property can be kept during the Owner's absence, at most moderate rates of rent.

J. & R. McC. undertake to execute Commissions for the purchase of Pictures, Statuary in Marble and Alabaster, Bronzes, &c., being in direct correspondence with Artists, Agents, and Bankers throughout the Continent.

British Artists resident abroad, having occasion to send home their works for Exhibition, or to be passed by the Academy, will find it advantageous to address them to the care of Messrs. J. & R. McCRACKEN, whose appointment enables them to offer every facility.

Parties favouring J. & R. McC. with Consignments, are requested to be particular in having the Bills of Lading sent to them DIRECT by post, and also to forward their Keys with the Packages, as all Goods MUST BE EXAMINED immediately on arrival.

J. & R. McC. keep Lachrymæ Christi and Marsala Wines of first quality, also Port and Sherry; and are general Importers of French and other Foreign Wines.

Packages sent, by Steamers or otherwise, to Southampton or Liverpool, also attended to; but all Letters of Advice and Bills of Lading to be addressed to 7, OLD JEWRY, LONDON.

THEIR PRINCIPAL CORRESPONDENTS ARE AT

CALAIS............	Messrs. CHARTIER, MORY, & VOGUE. Messrs. ISAAC VITAL & FILS.
BOULOGNE S. M...	Messrs. CHARTIER, MORY, & VOGUE. Mr. H. SIRE.
PARIS	Mr. M. CHENUE, Packer, Rue Croix Petits Champs, No. 24. Messrs. KLEINFELDER & HOFMANN, 15, Rue du Chabrol.
HAVRE............	Mr. A. CHAUMONT, Mr. THOMAS TAYLOR, Messrs. P. DEVOT & Co.
MARSEILLES......	Messrs. HORACE BOUCHET & Co. Messrs. CLAUDE CLERC & Co. Mr. PHILIGRET, 8, Rue Suffren.
BAGNERES DE BIGORRE, (Hautes Pyrénées..........	Mr. AIMÉ GÉRUZET, Marble Works,
BORDEAUX	Mr. AIMÉ GÉRUZET, 8, Place des Quinconces.
GIBRALTAR	Messrs. ARCHBOLD, JOHNSON, & POWERS. Messrs. TURNER & Co.
LISBON............	Mr. ARTHUR VAN ZELLER, Penin. & Orient. St. Nav. Co.'s Offices.
SEVILLE	Mr. JULIAN B. WILLIAMS, British Vice-Consul. Don JUAN ANTO. BAILLY.
NICE	Messrs. A. LACROIX & Co., British Consulate. Mr. T. W. HOW.
GENOA............	Messrs. GIBBS & Co. Sig. G. LOLEO, Croce di Malta. Mr. GOMERSALL, British Vice-Consul.
MILAN	Messrs. BUFFET & BERUTO, Piazzale di S. Sepolcro, No. 3176. Messrs. BRAMBILLA.
CARRARA.........	Sig. F. BIENAIMÉ. Mr. VINCENZO LIVY, Sculptor.
LEGHORN	Messrs. W. MACBEAN & Co. Messrs. HENDERSON BROTHERS. Messrs. THOMAS PATE & SONS. Messrs. MAQUAY, PAKENHAM, & SMYTH. Messrs. GIACO. MICALI & FIGO. Sculptors in Alabaster and Marble. Mr. M. RISTORI. Mr. JOSEPH GUANO. Messrs. DELLA VALLE BROTHERS, Artists in Scagliola. Messrs. G. GALLIANI & Co.
PISA..............	Messrs. HUGUET & VAN LINT, Sculptors in Alabaster and Marble.
FLORENCE	Messrs. EMMle. FENZI & Co. Messrs. PLOWDEN & FRENCH. Messrs. MAQUAY & PAKENHAM. Mr. GAETO. BIANCHINI, Mosaic Worker, opposite the Capella de' Medici. Mr. ANTONIO DI LUIGI PIACENTI. Mr. J. TOUGH. Mr. S. LOWE. Messrs. Flii. PACETTI, Picture-frame Makers, Via del Palagio. Messrs. NESTI CIARDI & Co. Mr. F. LEOPOLDO PISANI, Sculptor, No. 1, sul Prato. Sig. CARLO NOCCIOLI. Sig. LUIGI RAMACCI.
VOLTERRA	Sig. OTTO. CALLAJ. Sig. GIUSe. CHERICI.
BOLOGNA	Mr. FLAVIO PEROTTI, British Vice-Consul.
ANCONA	Messrs. MOORE, MERELLET, & Co.

MESSRS. J. & R. McCRACKEN'S CORRESPONDENTS—continued.

ROME	Messrs. FREEBORN & Co. Messrs. TORLONIA & Co. Messrs. MACBEAN & Co. Mr. EDWARD TREBBI. Messrs. PLOWDEN, CHOLMELEY, & Co. Messrs. PAKENHAM, HOOKER, & Co. Mr. LUIGI BRANCHINI, at the English College.
CIVITA VECCHIA	Messrs. LOWE BROTHERS, British Vice-Consulate. Mr. T. ARATA.
NAPLES	Messrs. IGGULDEN & Co. Messrs. W. J. TURNER & Co. Messrs. CUMMING, WOOD, & Co.
PALERMO	Messrs. PRIOR, TURNER, & THOMAS.
MESSINA	Messrs. CAILLER & Co.
MALTA	Mr. EMANUEL ZAMMIT. Mr. J. ASPINALL. Mr. P. P. DECESARE, 53, Strada Reale, Sculptor in Malta Stone. Mr. FORTUNATO TESTA, 92, Strada Sta. Lucia. Messrs. Josh. DARMANIN & SONS, 45, Strada Levante, Mosaic Workers.
CORFU	Mr. J. W. TAYLOR.
ALEXANDRIA.....	Messrs. BRIGGS & Co.
CONSTANTINOPLE	Messrs. C. HANSON & Co. Mr. BLACK.
SMYRNA	Messrs. HANSON & Co.
BEYROUT	Mr. HENRY HEALD.
ATHENS, PIRÆUS	Mr. J. J. BUCHERER.
VENICE	Messrs. FRERES SCHIELIN. Messrs. MUDIE & Co. Messrs. S. & A. BLUMENTHAL & Co. Mr. JOHN HARRIS.
TRIESTE	Messrs. GEORGE MOORE & Co.
OSTEND	Mr. F. A. BELLEROCHE. Messrs. BACH & Co. Mr. ST. AMOUR.
GHENT	Mr. J. DE BUYSER, Dealer in Antiquities, Marché au Beurre, 21.
BRUSSELS.........	
ANTWERP	Messrs. F. MACK & Co., Kipdorp, 1748. Mr. P. VAN ZEEBROECK, Picture Dealer, &c., Rue des Récollets, 2076.
ROTTERDAM......	Messrs. PRESTON & Co. Messrs. S. A. LEVINO & Co. Messrs. L. MAYER & Co. Messrs. C. HEMMANN & Co. Messrs. BOUTMY & Co.
COLOGNE..........	Mr. J. M. FARINA, vis-à-vis la Place Juliers. Messrs. Gme. TILMES & Co. Mr. ALBERT HEIMANN, 29, Bishofsgartenstrasse.
MAYENCE	Mr. G. L. KAYSER, Expéditeur.
FRANKFORT O. M.	Mr. JOSEPH THUQUET. Mr. KNUSSMAN, Cabinet Maker. Mr. P. A. TACCHI'S SUCCESSOR, Glass Manufacturer, Zeil D, 17. Madame Veuve J. H. STIEBEL, Zeil D, 30. Messrs. BING BROTHERS, Zeil D, 31. Mr. F. BÜHLER, Zeil. Mr. G. A. ZIPF, Ross Markt.
HEIDELBERG	Mr. PH. ZIMMERMANN.
MANNHEIM	Mr. DINKELSPEIL. Messrs. EYSSEN & CLAUS.
MUNICH...........	Mr. HY. WIMMER, Printseller, Promenade St. No. 12. Messrs. MAY & WIDMAYER, Printsellers. Mr. F. STEIGERWALD, Glass Manufacturer. Messrs. L. NEGRIOLI & Co.
KISSINGEN........	Mr. F. STEIGERWALD, Glass Manufacturer. Messrs. J. BERGMANN & Co.
RATISBON.........	Mr. AUGUSTE KOCH, Dealer in Antiquities.
NUREMBERG......	Mr. PAOLO GALIMBERTI, at the Red Horse, Dealer in Antiquities. Mr. JOHN CONRAD CNOPF, Banker and Forwarding Agent.
BASLE	Messrs. JEAN PREISWERK & FILS. Mr. BISCHOFF DE ST. ALBAN. Messrs. SCHNEWLIN & Co. Mr. BENOIT LA ROCHE.
BERNE	Mr. AUGUSTE BUECHE. Mr. ALBERT TRUMPY.
GENEVA	Mr. RITZCHEL, Fils, Grand Quai. Messrs. AUG. & VICTOR SNELL.
LAUSANNE	Mr. L. LONGCHAMPS.
INTERLACKEN....	Mr. J. WYDER. Mr. J. GROSSMANN.
GRINDELWALD...	Mr. S. ROTHACHER, Fils.
HAMBURG	Messrs. SCHAAR & CLAUSS. ZAHN & VIVIE. Mr. G. J. F. RODE.
PRAGUE...........	Mr. W. HOFMANN, Glass Manufacturer, Blauern Stern. Mr. A. V. LEBEDA, Gun Maker, &c.
CARLSBAD	Mr. THOMAS WOLF, Glass Manufacturer. Mr. CARL KNOLL, au Lion Blanc.
VIENNA...........	Mr. W. HOFMANN, Glass Manufacturer, am Lugeck, No. 768. Mr. JOS. LOBMEYR.
SALSBURG	Mr. ALOIS DUREGGER.
BERLIN	Messrs. GEBRUDER ROCCA, Printsellers, Unter den Linden. Messrs. PHALAND & DIETRICH, Carriers. Mr. LION M. COHN, Commre. Expéditeur.
DRESDEN	Messrs. H. W. BASSENGE & Co. Messrs. G. F. THODE Söhne. Madame HELENA WOLFSOHN, Schössergasse, No. 5.
NEW YORK	Messrs. WILBUR & SCOTT.

MUNICH.

FRANCIS STEIGERWALD,

MANUFACTURER OF ALL KINDS OF

FANCY ARTICLES,

AND

SERVICES IN WHITE & COLOURED CRYSTAL GLASS,

CUT, OR ORNAMENTED WITH GILDING, PAINTING, OR ENGRAVING,

Begs respectfully to inform the Public that his large Stock at MUNICH, the acknowledged seat of the Fine Arts in Germany, is, as it has been for many years, carefully supplied with the NEWEST and CHOICEST PRODUCE of his FACTORY.

Francis Steigerwald has also an Establishment at Kissingen during the Season.

Requesting his Customers and Correspondents in ENGLAND to continue to this Establishment the favour and confidence they have been pleased to bestow on his former one at FRANKFORT ON THE MAINE, he begs to state that Purchases or Orders will be transmitted on the shortest notice, and without any further trouble, through the medium of his Agents, Messrs. J. & R. M'Cracken, No. 7, Old Jewry, London.

ROME.

ENGLISH PHARMACY.
460, CORSO,
Near the Piazza St. Carlo and the Via de' Pontefici.

SINIMBERGHI AND WHITBURN,
DISPENSING CHEMISTS AND DRUGGISTS,

MEMBERS OF THE ROYAL PHARMACEUTICAL SOCIETY OF GREAT BRITAIN,

BEG to inform Visitors to Rome, that their Establishment is well provided with genuine English and French Patent Medicines.

Prescriptions prepared with the greatest care according to the formulary of the London, Edinburgh, Dublin, and United States Pharmacopeias, and the quality of the drugs may be confidently relied on, as they are chiefly supplied direct from Apothecaries' Hall.

GENOA.

SILVER FILIGREE WORK.
G. LOLEO,
(SUCCESSOR TO FELIX PERNETTI),

No. 81, in the Albergo della Croce di Malta,

KEEPS a Magazine which boasts the most elegant and complete assortment of every description of objects of this renowned and special production of Genoese industry. The exhibition of it in London, on the glorious occasion of the 1st May, 1851, obtained, for its variety, elegance, and solidity, the admiration of the visitors to the Crystal Palace, and was honoured with a Prize Medal. He invites Foreigners and Travellers to visit his Establishment (without being expected to purchase), where every article is sold at fixed prices.

His Agents in England are Messrs. J. & R. M'CRACKEN, 7, Old Jewry, London.

* In his Show-room may be seen a Monumental Column in filigree work in commemoration of the Great Exhibition.

FLORENCE.

G. BIANCHINI,
MANUFACTURER OF TABLES AND LADIES' ORNAMENTS OF FLORENTINE MOSAIC,

No. 4844, VIA DE' NELLI,

Opposite the Royal Chapel of the Medici,

INVITES the English Nobility and Gentry to visit his Establishment, where may always be seen numerous specimens of this celebrated and beautiful Manufacture, in every description of Rare and Precious Stones. Orders for Tables and other Ornaments executed to any Design.

G. BIANCHINI's Agents in England are Messrs. J. & R. M'CRACKEN, 7, Old Jewry, London.

NICE.

ENGLISH WAREHOUSE.

T. W. HOW,

WINE MERCHANT, GROCER, &c.,

Quai du Jardin des Plantes,

(Two doors from the Hôtel de France).

Wines and Teas of the choicest qualities. Bass's and Allsopp's Pale and Burton Ales, Stout, Porter, &c. Lemann's Biscuits, English Cheese, York Hams, Pickles, Sauces, and a variety of other condiments and articles too numerous to mention.

Correspondents in London, Messrs. J. and R. M'CRACKEN, 7, Old Jewry.

NICE.

F. LATTES,

Near the Pont Neuf,

GENERAL AGENT,

AND

AGENT FOR LETTING FURNISHED APARTMENTS.

Letters addressed as above from parties requiring any information respecting Apartments, &c., will meet with immediate attention.

MUNICH.

HENRY WIMMER,

SUCCESSOR TO

J. M. DE HERMANN,

PRINT AND PICTURE SELLER TO HIS MAJESTY THE KING OF BAVARIA,

ROYAL PROMENADE STRASSE, No. 12,

MAGAZINE OF OBJECTS OF FINE ARTS,

PICTURES, PRINTS, DRAWINGS, AND LITHOGRAPHS,

INVITES the Nobility and Gentry to visit his Establishment, where he has always on Sale an extensive collection of Pictures by Modern Artists, Paintings on Glass and Porcelain, Miniatures, Drawings, Engravings, and Lithographs, the latter comprising the Complete Collections of the various Galleries, of which Single Copies may be selected.

He has also on Sale all that relates to the Fine Arts.

H. WIMMER undertakes to forward to England all purchases made at his Establishment, through his Agents, Messrs. J. & R. M'CRACKEN, 7, Old Jewry, London.

FRANKFORT O. M.

BING BROTHERS,

ZEIL, No. 31,
(OPPOSITE THE HOTEL DE RUSSIE,)

MANUFACTORY OF ARTICLES IN STAG'S HORN,
DEPOT OF DRESDEN CHINA.
COPY OF THE STATUE OF ARIADNE.
₊ ALL KINDS OF PARISIAN FANCY ARTICLES.

MESSRS. BING BROTHERS beg respectfully to invite the Public to visit their Establishment, where they have always on show, and for sale, a most extensive Assortment of Articles in Stag's Horn, of their own manufacture; consisting of Brooches, Ear-rings, Bracelets, Pen and Pencil Holders, Seals, Inkstands, Watch-stands, Snuff-boxes, Cigar-boxes, Whips, Walking-sticks, Knives, Card-cases, and every description of article for the Writing and Work Table, besides Vases and other ornamental objects too various to be here enumerated.

Messrs. BING have also the finest Copies, both in Biscuit-China and Bronze, of the Statue of Ariadne, the chef-d'œuvre of the Sculptor DANNECKER, of which the original is in Bethman's Museum at Frankfort O. M.

Messrs. BING have likewise the *Sole Depôt* in FRANKFORT of the Porcelain of the Royal Manufactory of Dresden; and at their Establishment may be seen the most splendid assortment of Figures after the Ancient Models, ornamented with Lace-work of the most extraordinary fineness; likewise Dinner, Dessert, and Tea Services; Plates, Vases, Candelabras, Baskets, &c. &c., in the Antique Style, ornamented with flowers in relief, and the finest paintings.

Besides the above-named objects, they have a superb assortment of Clocks, Bronzes, Porcelain, and other Fancy Objects, the productions of Germany, France, and England.

DEPOT OF THE VERITABLE EAU DE COLOGNE OF JEAN MARIA FARINA, OF COLOGNE.

☞ Their Agents in London are J. and R. M'CRACKEN, 7, Old Jewry.

FRANKFORT O. M.

P. A. TACCHI'S SUCCESSOR,

(LATE FRANCIS STEIGERWALD,)

ZEIL D, No. 17,

BOHEMIAN FANCY GLASS AND CRYSTAL WAREHOUSE.

P. A. TACCHI'S SUCCESSOR begs to acquaint the Public that he has become the Purchaser of Mr. F. STEIGERWALD'S ESTABLISHMENT in this Town, for the Sale of Bohemian Fancy Cut Glass and Crystals.

He has always an extensive and choice Assortment of the Newest and most Elegant Patterns of

ORNAMENTAL CUT, ENGRAVED, GILT, & PAINTED GLASS,

BOTH WHITE AND COLOURED,

In Dessert Services, Chandeliers, Articles for the Table and Toilet, and every possible variety of objects in this beautiful branch of manufacture. He solicits, and will endeavour to merit, a continuance of the favours of the Public, which the late well-known House enjoyed in an eminent degree during a considerable number of years.

P. A. TACCHI'S SUCCESSOR has BRANCH ESTABLISHMENTS during the Season at

WIESBADEN AND EMS,

Where will always be found Selections of the newest Articles from his principal Establishment.

His Agents in England, to whom he undertakes to forward Purchases made of him, are Messrs. J. & R. M'CRACKEN, 7, Old Jewry, London.

COLOGNE O. RHINE.

JOHN MARIA FARINA

(OPPOSITE THE JULICH'S PLACE),

PURVEYOR TO H. M. QUEEN VICTORIA;
TO H. M. F. W. III., KING OF PRUSSIA; H. M. NICOLAS I., EMPEROR OF RUSSIA;
THE KING OF HANOVER, ETC. ETC.,

OF THE

ONLY GENUINE EAU DE COLOGNE.

THE frequency of mistakes, which are sometimes accidental, but for the most part the result of deception practised by interested individuals, induces me to request the attention of the English travellers to the following statement:—

Since the first establishment of my house in 1709, there has never been any partner in the business who did not bear the name of FARINA, nor has the manufacture of a second and cheaper quality of EAU DE COLOGNE ever been attempted. Since 1828, however, several inhabitants of Cologne have entered into engagements with Italians of the name of Farina, and, by employing that name, have succeeded to a very great extent in foisting an inferior and spurious article upon the Public.

But they have to this rivalry in trade not been satisfied with the mere usurpation of my name; the concluding phrase, "*opposite the Julich's Place,*" which had so long existed my special property, was not allowed to remain in its integrity. To deceive and lead astray again those of the public who are not fully conversant with the locality and circumstances, the competition seized hold of the word "*opposite,*" and more than once settled in my immediate neighbourhood, that they might avail themselves to the full extent of the phrase "*opposite the Julich's Place.*" When tried before the courts, the use only of the word "*opposite*" was forbidden, which, however, has been supplied by the word "*at*" or "*near,*" with the addition of the number of their houses. It is true, another less flagrant, but not less deceitful invention was, that several of my imitators established the sites of their manufactories in other public places of the town, to enable them to make use of the phrase "*opposite —— Place,* or *Market,*" on their address cards or labels, speculating, with respect to the proper name "*Julich,*" on the carelessness or forgetfulness of the consumer. I therefore beg to inform all strangers visiting Cologne that my establishment, which has existed since 1709, is exactly opposite the Julich's Place, forming the corner of the two streets, Unter Goldschmidt and Oben Marspforten, No. 23; and that it may be the more easily recognised, I have put up the arms of England, Russia, &c. &c., in the front of my house. By calling the attention of the public to this notice, I hope to check that system of imposition which has been so long practised towards foreigners by coachmen, valets-de-place, and others who receive bribes from the vendors of the many spurious compounds sold under my name.

A new proof of the excellence of MY manufacture has been put beyond all doubt by the fact of the Jury of the Great Exhibition in London having awarded ME the Prize Medal.—See the Official Statement in No. 20,934, page 6, of the '*Times*' of this month.

COLOGNE, *October*, 1851.

J. M. FARINA,
Opposite the Julich's Place.

** *My Agents in London are* MESSRS. J. & R. M'CRACKEN, 7, *Old Jewry, by whom orders are received for me.*

DRESDEN.

MAGAZINE OF ANTIQUITIES AND FINE ARTS.
HELENA WOLFSOHN, née MEYER,
(SUCCESSOR OF L. MEYER AND SONS,)
5, SCHLOSSERGASSE,

BEGS respectfully to solicit the inspection of her Establishment, where she has always on show and for sale a most extensive assortment of Old Saxon China, Old Sèvres and Japan, Antique Furniture, Bronzes, Old Lace, such as Points de Bruxelles and d'Alençon, Points de Venise, Guipure, &c. &c. Venetian, Ruby and Painted Glass, Rock Crystal, Ivory Work, Enamels, Mosaic Work, Armour, Gobelins Tapestry, Fans, and many other remarkable and curious articles.

HER AGENTS IN ENGLAND ARE

Messrs. J. & R. M'CRACKEN, 7, Old Jewry, London.

WILLIAM HOFMANN,
BOHEMIAN GLASS MANUFACTURER,
TO HIS MAJESTY THE EMPEROR OF AUSTRIA,

RECOMMENDS his great assortment of Glass Ware, from his own Manufactories in Bohemia. The choicest Articles in every Colour, Shape, and Description, are sold, at the same moderate prices, at both his Establishments—

At Prague, Hotel Blue Star; at Vienna, 768, Lugeck.

Agents in London, Messrs. J. and R. M'CRACKEN, 7, Old Jewry.

Goods forwarded direct to England, America, &c.

LEGHORN.

HIACINTH MICALI AND SON,
Via Ferdinanda, No. 1230.

Manufactory of Marble, Alabaster, and Scagliola Tables, and Depôt of objects of Fine Arts.

Their extensive Show-rooms are always open to Visitors.

THEIR AGENTS IN ENGLAND ARE

MESSRS. J. AND R. M'CRACKEN,
7, Old Jewry, London.

GUIDE TO PARIS.

Price 7s. 6d., or with Plates 10s. 6d.,

GALIGNANI'S GUIDE TO PARIS,

Compiled from the best authorities, revised and verified by personal inspection, and arranged on an entirely new plan, with Map.

"Galignani's Paris Guide appears so good as to relieve the Editor of this work from the necessity of entering into any description, at present, of the French capital."—*Murray's Handbook of France.*

London: SIMPKIN, MARSHALL, & Co.

VIENNA.

BOHEMIAN WHITE AND COLOURED CRYSTAL GLASS WAREHOUSE.

JOSEPH LOBMEYR,
GLASS MANUFACTURER,
No. 940, KARTHNERSTRASSE,

BEGS to inform Visitors to Vienna that he has considerably enlarged his Establishment. The most complete assortment of all kinds of Bohemian White and Coloured Crystal Glass, and of all articles in this branch of industry, in the newest and most elegant style, is always on hand. The rich collections of all Articles of Luxury, viz., Table, Dessert, and other Services, Vases, Candelabras, Lustres, Looking-glasses, &c. &c., will, he feels assured, satisfy every visitor.

The prices are fixed at very moderate and reasonable charges.—The English language is spoken.

His Agents in England, Messrs. J. and R. M'CRACKEN, No. 7, Old Jewry, London, will execute all orders with the greatest care and attention.

ROTTERDAM AND THE RHINE.

THE NETHERLANDS STEAM-BOAT COMPANY'S Steam Ship BATAVIER leaves LONDON every SUNDAY, and ROTTERDAM every TUESDAY; and the Screw Steamer FYENOVID from LONDON every THURSDAY MORNING, and from ROTTERDAM every SUNDAY.

Fast Steamers up and down the Rhine are in regular communication with the above, and belong to the same Company.

FARES TO ROTTERDAM.—First Class, £1. 10s.; Second Class, 17s. 6d. Return Tickets, £2. 5s., and £1. 6s. 3d.—Fares up the Rhine are very reasonable.

Agents in London, PHILLIPPS, GRAVES, & PHILLIPPS, 11, Rood Lane, City.

MARIENBURG, NEAR COLOGNE.

ESTABLISHMENT FOR THE
EDUCATION OF YOUNG GENTLEMEN,
CONDUCTED BY MR. ALFRED BASKERVILLE,
ASSISTED BY RESIDENT GERMAN AND FRENCH MASTERS.

THE object of this Establishment is to afford the Sons of Gentlemen a Superior Education, combined with a thorough knowledge of the Modern Languages.

Marienburg House is beautifully and healthily situated near the Rhine, at a short distance from Cologne. The Recreation and Pleasure Grounds are upwards of ten acres in extent.

TERMS per annum, without any extras, including Music, Drawing, and Dancing, if required, Books, Stationery, and Seat in the English Church:—

Under twelve . . 70 Guineas. | Above twelve . . . 80 Guineas

UNION BANK OF LONDON.

SIR PETER LAURIE, ALDERMAN, *Governor.*
WILLIAM MOUNTFORD NURSE, ESQ., *Deputy-Governor.*

J. BARNES, Esq.	J. CHAPMAN, Esq.	J. SCOTT, Esq.
J. FARQUHAR, Esq.	H. HULBERT, Esq.	LEO SCHUSTER, Esq.
P. NORTHALL LAURIE, Esq.	A. BOYD, Esq.	Sir JOHN MUSGROVE, Bart.
C. LYALL, Esq.	Lt.-Col. MATHESON, M.P.	WILLIAM S. BINNY, Esq.

WILLIAM WILSON SCRIMGEOUR, *General Manager.*   WALTER LAURIE, *Secretary.*

CIRCULAR NOTES.

CIRCULAR NOTES of the value of £10 and upwards, *free of expense*, and LETTERS OF CREDIT payable at the places indicated below, may be obtained at the HEAD OFFICE, 2, PRINCES STREET, MANSION HOUSE; ARGYLL PLACE; and 4, PALL MALL, EAST.

Abbeville	Cambrai	Gotha	Middlebourg	San Francisco
Aix-en-Provence	Canada	Gottenbourg	Milan	San Sebastian
Aix-la-Chapelle	Canton	Gottingen	Modena	Santa Cruz
Alexandria	Cape Town	Graefenburg	Montpellier	Schwalback
Aleppo	Carlsbad	Granville	Montreal	Seville
Algiers	Carlsruhe	Grasse	Moreton Bay	Shaffhausen
Alicante	Cassel	Gratz	Moscow	Siena
Almeria	Catania	Grenada	Moulins	Singapore
Amiens	Cephalonia	Grenoble	Moulmein	Smyrna
Amsterdam	Cette	Halifax	Munich	Spa
Ancona	Ceylon	Hamburg	Munster	Stettin
Angers	Chalon	Hanover	Murcia	St. Galle
Antwerp	Chambery	Havre	Nancy	St. Malo
Archangel	Chaux de fonds	Hague	Nantes	St. Omer
Athens	Cherbourg	Heidelburg	Naples	St. Petersburg
Augsbourg	Christiana	Hermanstadt	Neufchâtel	St. Quentin
Avignon	Christiansand	Homburg es monts	New Orleans	St. Thomas
Avranches	Cività Vecchia		New York	Stockholm
Baden-Baden	Clermont Ferrand	Hong Kong	Nice	Strasbourg
Bagdad		Innspruck	Nismes	Stuttgardt
Bagnères de Bigorre	Coblenz	Interlaken	Nurembourg	Sydney
	Cobourg	Jaffa	Odessa	Tarbes
Bahia	Coire	Jerusalem	Oleron	Teneriffe
Barcelona	Cologne	Kissengen	Oporto	Töplitz
Basle	Constance	Königsberg	Orleans	Toronto
Bayonne	Constantinople	Lausanne	Ostend	Toulon
Beirout	Copenhagen	Leghorn	Palermo	Toulouse
Bergen	Cordova	Leipsic	Paris	Tours
Berlin	Corfu	Liege	Parma	Treves
Berne	Corunna	Lille	Patras	Trieste
Besançon	Creuznach	Lisbon	Pau	Turin
Bilbao	Damascus	Locle	Perpignan	Utrecht
Blois	Dantzic	L'Orient	Pesth	Valenciennes
Bologna	Darmstadt	Lubeck	Pisa	Valencia
Bombay	Delhi	Lucca	Port St. Mary	Venice
Bonn	Dieppe	Lucerne	Prague	Verona
Bordeaux	Dijon	Lyons	Presbourg	Vevey
Botzen	Dresden	Madeira	Quebec	Vienna
Boulogne	Drontheim	Madras	Rastadt	Vigo
Bremen	Dunkirk	Madrid	Ratisbonne	Vitoria
Breslau	Dusseldorf	Magdebourg	Rennes	Warsaw
Bruges	Elberfeld	Malaga	Rheims	Weimar
Brünn	Elsinore	Malta	Riga	Wiesbaden
Brunswick	Emms	Mannheim	Rio de Janeiro	Wildbad
Brussels	Florence	Mantua	Rome	Worms
Burgos	Foix	Marlenbad	Rostock	Wurzbourg
Cadiz	Francfort	Marseilles	Rotterdam	Yverdon
Caen	Geneva	Mauritius	Rouen	Zante
Cairo	Genoa	Mayence	Salamanca	Zaragosa
Calais	Ghent	Melbourne	Salzburg	Zurich
Calcutta	Gibraltar	Messina		

SOUTH-EASTERN RAILWAY,

The Direct Mail Route to all Parts of the Continent, with the Shortest Sea Passage.

DAILY COMMUNICATION BETWEEN LONDON AND PARIS IN TWELVE HOURS.

London and Brussels in Fourteen Hours.
London and Cologne in Twenty-two Hours.
Sea Passage only Two Hours.

LONDON TO PARIS BY TIDAL TRAINS

Viâ Folkestone and Boulogne.

THIS is the quickest and most comfortable means of communication between London and Paris; it is performed every day, the time of departure varying in accordance with the tide. (Time Table published daily in front page of 'The Times.') The Passengers are conveyed by Express Train to Folkestone, where they find a powerful Steamer waiting in the harbour to receive them; they walk on board, and two hours afterwards are landed at Boulogne, where another Train is in readiness to convey them immediately to Paris. The whole journey is thus accomplished without interruption, in the shortest possible time, no small boats for embarking and disembarking being required.

By these Trains, luggage can be registered for Paris direct, relieving the Passenger from all trouble about it until the arrival in Paris, and avoiding the Customs examination at Boulogne.

The same correspondence of Trains and Steamers is arranged for the journey from Paris to London.

FIXED CONTINENTAL SERVICES VIÂ DOVER AND CALAIS.

FROM LONDON.

London	depart	8.10 a.m.	*11.30 a.m.	*8.30 p.m.
Dover	„	11. 0 „	2.30 p.m.	11.15 „
Calais	„	3. 0 p.m.	6.30 „	3. 0 a.m.
Paris	arrive	11. 5 „	5. 5 a.m.	10. 0 „
Brussels	„	10.10 „	5.45 „	10.50 „
Cologne	„	5. 0 a.m.	4.15 p.m.	6.20 p.m.

TO LONDON.

Cologne	depart	11.30 p.m.	—	*6.30 & 7.30 a.m.
Brussels	„	7. 0 a.m.	10.30 a.m.	2.45 & 4.45 p.m.
Paris	„	7. 0 „	11.45 „	7.30 p.m.
Calais	„	3. 0 p.m.	10. 0 p.m.	2.30 a.m.
Dover	„	7.30 „	2. 0 a.m.	5.20 „
London	arrive	10.15 „	4.50 „	7.45 „

* These Trains are not direct on Sundays.

Offices for Through Tickets, Time Bills, &c.:—

In **LONDON—40, Regent Circus, Piccadilly;**
In **PARIS—4, Boulevard des Italiens;**
In **BRUSSELS—74, Montagne de la Cour.**

G. S. HERBERT, *Secretary.*

London Bridge Terminus, May, 1854.

PERFECT FREEDOM FROM COUGHS IN 10 MINUTES,
AND INSTANT RELIEF AND A RAPID CURE OF
ASTHMA AND CONSUMPTION, COUGHS, COLDS,
AND ALL DISORDERS OF THE BREATH AND LUNGS, ARE INSURED BY

DR. LOCOCK'S PULMONIC WAFERS.

*** Small Books, containing many hundreds of properly authenticated Testimonials, may be had from every Agent.

From the Author of the 'Narrative of the Second Sikh War.'

Sir,—I had long suffered from a deep seated Cough, when Providence placed in my way a box of your Pulmonic Wafers. I experienced instantaneous relief, and have such a high estimate of their efficacy that I firmly believe they would effect the cure of the most consumptive person. You may make any use you please of this letter.
(Signed)   EDWARD JOSEPH THACKWELL,
Lieut. 3rd Light Dragoons, Union Club, London.

To **SINGERS** and **PUBLIC SPEAKERS** they are invaluable, as in a few hours they remove all hoarseness, and wonderfully increase the power and flexibility of the voice. They have a pleasant taste. Price 1s. 1½d., 2s. 9d., and 11s. per box. Also may be had,

DR. LOCOCK'S COSMETIC.

A DELIGHTFULLY FRAGRANT PREPARATION
FOR IMPROVING AND BEAUTIFYING THE COMPLEXION,
Rendering the Skin clear, soft, and transparent, removing all Eruptions, Freckles, Sunburn, Tan, Pimples, and Roughness; curing Gnat Bites, and the Stings of Insects generally.

In the process of Shaving, it allays all smarting, and renders the Skin soft and smooth. Sold in Bottles, at 1s. 1½d., 2s. 9d., and 4s. 6d. each. Beware of counterfeits. Observe the name on the Government Stamp outside the Wrapper.

SOLD BY ALL RESPECTABLE CHEMISTS.

WHOLESALE WAREHOUSE, 26, BRIDE LANE, LONDON.

To all Persons of Taste intending to Visit London.

MECHI,

OF No. 4, LEADENHALL STREET, NEAR GRACECHURCH STREET, LONDON,

HAS LONG BEEN RENOWNED THROUGHOUT THE CIVILISED WORLD FOR

RAZORS, STROPS, CUTLERY IN GENERAL,

NEEDLES, DRESSING-CASES, WORK-BOXES, TEA-TRAYS,

AND PAPIER MACHE IN ALL ITS VARIOUS APPLICATIONS,

AS WELL AS EVERY REQUISITE FOR THE TOILET AND WORK-TABLE.

His well-known Emporium has been re-decorated in a style suitable to the improved spirit of the age, and has received an accession of Stock calculated to meet the extraordinary demand which he anticipates. Among the sights of London, none are more interesting and extraordinary than its shops, and for a combination of taste and elegance, there is not one more conspicuous than MECHI's. Those who wish to see the Manufactures of England displayed in the most attractive manner must not omit to visit MECHI's, where they will find an abundance of objects adapted to the requirements of every class of purchasers. Catalogues will be furnished Gratis, or sent to any address in England, post free.

4, Leadenhall Street, near the India House.

THE LONDON AND WESTMINSTER BANK
Issues Circular Notes of £10 each,

FOR THE USE OF TRAVELLERS AND RESIDENTS ON THE CONTINENT.

They are payable at every important place in Europe, and enable a Traveller to vary his route without inconvenience. No expense is incurred, and when cashed, no charge is made for commission. They may be obtained at the head office of the London and Westminster Bank, in Lothbury; or of its Branches, viz.—1, St. James's Square; 214, High Holborn; 3, Wellington Street, Borough; 87, High Street, Whitechapel; and 4, Stratford Place, Oxford Street.
                        J. W. GILBART, *General Manager.*

To Tourists in Britain {BLACK'S GUIDE BOOKS & TRAVELLING MAPS.

In neat Portable Volumes, profusely illustrated by Maps, Charts, and Views of the Scenery, containing all the latest information regarding Hotels, Inns, Distances, and whatever is likely to prove useful or instructive to the Tourist.

"They should find a corner in the portmanteau of every person about to undertake a journey of pleasure or business either in England and Wales, or Scotland."—JOHN BULL.

"The most valuable series of Picturesque Guide Books issued by Messrs. Black of Edinburgh. We have looked carefully through the volumes; they are admirably 'got up;' the descriptions are accurate, and remarkably clear and comprehensive. Altogether the series of Works is of immense value to Tourists."—ART JOURNAL.

England, complete. 3rd Edition	10s. 6d.
Scotland, complete. 10th Edition	8s. 6d.
Ireland, complete. Just Published	5s.
Highlands, by Messrs. Anderson, Inverness	10s. 6d.
Trosachs, Illustrated by Foster	5s.
English Lake District, with Geology, by Phillips	5s.
Wales, North and South, and Monmouthshire	5s.

CHEAP GUIDES—ONE SHILLING EACH.
IN FANCY COVERS, WITH MAPS, CHARTS, AND ALL THE MOST RECENT INFORMATION.

Highlands of Perthshire.	**Aberdeen, Braemar, and Deeside.**
Trosachs, Lochlomond, &c.	
The Clyde and Argyleshire.	**Moffat and St. Mary's Loch.**
Staffa, Iona, Glencoe, &c.	**Edinburgh and Environs.**
Island of Skye.	**English Lakes.**

CHEAP IRISH GUIDES—EIGHTEEN PENCE EACH.
STRONGLY BOUND IN CLOTH LIMP.

Dublin & Wicklow Mountains.	**The Shannon and the West.**
Killarney and the South.	**Belfast and the North.**

ROAD AND RAILWAY TRAVELLING MAPS.

Carefully constructed from the Maps of the Ordnance Survey and other Authorities, and containing all the Roads, Railroads, Villages, Country Seats, Fishing Streams, Rivers, Lakes, and Mountains, and every Topographical Information required by the Tourist on pleasure or business. Well coloured, lined with cloth, and neatly bound in portable cases.

England and Wales. 32 Inches by 22¼		4s. 6d.
English Lake District. 19 Inches by 14		2s. 6d.
Wales, North and South. 14 Inches by 11¼	each	1s. 6d.
Scotland. 32 Inches by 22¼		4s. 6d.
Ireland. 20 Inches by 14¼		2s. 6d.
Continent of Europe. 17 Inches by 24		4s. 6d.

Cheaper Maps on Paper, Uncoloured, 1s. each.

EDINBURGH: A. & C. BLACK. AND SOLD BY ALL BOOKSELLERS.

Price **FOURPENCE** of any Bookseller.
Permanently Enlarged to Twenty-four Large Quarto Pages.

THE ATHENÆUM
JOURNAL OF LITERATURE, SCIENCE, AND ART.
(STAMPED TO GO FREE BY POST, 5*d*.) CONTAINS:

Reviews, with copious extracts, of every important New English Book, and of the more important Foreign Works.
Reports of the Proceedings of the Learned and Scientific Societies, with Abstracts of all Papers of Interest.
Authentic Accounts of all Scientific Voyages and Expeditions.
Foreign Correspondence on Literature, Science, and Art.
Criticisms on Art, with Critical Notices of Exhibitions, Picture Collections, New Prints, &c.
Music and Drama, including Reports on the Opera, Concerts, Theatres, New Music, &c.
Biographical Notices of Men distinguished in Literature, Science, and Art.
Original Papers and Poems.
Miscellanea, including all that is likely to interest the informed and intelligent.

THE ATHENÆUM
Is so conducted that the reader, however far distant, is, in respect to Literature, Science, and the Arts, on an equality in point of information with the best-informed circles of the Metropolis.

*** The ATHENÆUM is published every *Saturday*, but is re-issued each Month stitched in a Wrapper.

Wholesale Agents: for SCOTLAND, Messrs. BELL and BRADFUTE, Edinburgh; for IRELAND, JOHN ROBERTSON, Dublin; for FRANCE, M. BAUDRY, 3, Quai Malaquais, Paris.

EAU DE COLOGNE.
The most superior EAU DE COLOGNE in the Exhibition of London in 1851 was found to be that prepared by

MARY CLEMENTINE MARTIN, NUN,
DOMHOF, No. 17, AT COLOGNE.

See the following *Extract from the Official Report in the Exhibition of Industry of all Nations held in London in the year* 1851. Third Volume, 30th Number, 29th Class:—

"The sample of Eau de Cologne presented by the Nun Mary Clementine Martin, of Cologne, to the Exhibition, was unanimously regarded by the Jury as the best. This precious liquid seemed to embody simultaneously all perfumes, without at the evaporation any single one being distinguishable. In examining other perfumes of the kind, the Eau de Cologne of the Nun Martin, to which the Prize Medal was naturally adjudged, regularly served as a standard of comparison. Next to this sample of Eau de Cologne, that furnished by Mr. Jean Marie Farina, opposite the Julich's Place, Cologne, was judged to be the best, and was rewarded with the Medal also."

N.B.—This EAU DE COLOGNE can be purchased at the Manufactory, No. 17, Domhof (*opposite the Cathedral*), Cologne; or in London of Mr. C. DOLMAN, Bookseller, No. 61, New Bond Street.

FOR TRAVELLERS ON THE CONTINENT, FAMILIES, TEACHERS, AND STUDENTS.
Fifth Edition, with Additions, and a Key to French Pronunciation, in a pocket Volume, 5*s*. in limp cloth, or post free on receipt of 66 Queen's heads,

THE FRENCH PROMPTER:
A HANDBOOK of CONVERSATION in ENGLISH and FRENCH, Alphabetically Arranged, containing all the Words and Phrases in constant use. By MONS. LE PAGE, Author of 'L'Echo de Paris,' 'Petit Musée de Littérature Française,' &c.

"It supplies travellers, families, and students with a ready and complete translation of their thoughts on all common occurrences."—*Economist.*

"It will prove of service to the proficient, and will be altogether invaluable to that large class which modestly confesses that it only knows a little French."—*Athenæum.*

London: EFFINGHAM WILSON, 11, Royal Exchange; and Messrs. LONGMAN.

OCEAN PARCELS DELIVERY COMPANY

HAVE made arrangements with DIEZINGER and DIESCH'S CONTINENTAL EXPRESS for the conveyance of Goods and Parcels viâ ANTWERP or OSTEND to all parts of GERMANY, BELGIUM, &c. The rates of charges are much reduced, and the speed of transit is the same as the post.

Packages are received
At the COMPANY'S OFFICE, 4, AGAR STREET, STRAND,
opposite Charing Cross Hospital;
By HICKIE, BORMAN, & Co., 127, LEADENHALL STREET;
And by E. JONES, 68, SOUTH CASTLE STREET, LIVERPOOL.

OCEAN PARCELS DELIVERY COMPANY,

4, AGAR STREET, STRAND,
OPPOSITE CHARING-CROSS HOSPITAL.

DESPATCHES are regularly made up for

INDIA,	BELGIUM,
AUSTRALIA,	GERMANY,
THE UNITED STATES,	ITALY,
CANADA,	MALTA,
THE WEST INDIES,	THE BALTIC, and
FRANCE,	CONSTANTINOPLE.

RATES FOR SMALL PACKAGES.
5 lb. weight, 5s.; 10 lb., 7s. 6d.; 20 lb., 10s. 6d.

Merchandize forwarded on the lowest terms. Parcels are also received by

HICKIE, BORMAN, & Co.,
127, LEADENHALL STREET, and 4, ORIENTAL PLACE, SOUTHAMPTON;

AND BY

E. JONES,
68, SOUTH CASTLE STREET, LIVERPOOL.

CARY'S IMPROVED POCKET
TOURIST'S TELESCOPE.
(SEE MURRAY'S HANDBOOK.)

Just Published, 16th Edition of
GOULD'S
COMPANION to the MICROSCOPE,
Revised and Improved by H. GOULD.

CARY, Mathematical and Optical Instrument Maker to the Admiralty and Royal Military College, &c. &c., 181, STRAND.

BOULOGNE-SUR-MER.

HOTEL WINDSOR.

VISITORS to this delightful Watering Place will find every Accommodation at the above Hotel, which is most conveniently situate for those who may purpose sojourning, as well as for those en route for Paris.

PROPRIETOR—G. OZANNE.

ROME.

J. P. SHEA'S
ENGLISH HOUSE-AGENCY OFFICES,
14 & 15, PIAZZA DE SPAGNA.

THE only practical establishment of the kind ever known here, where the comforts and requirements of a family are thoroughly understood, and the interest of employers properly attended to.

The undeniable improvement which J. P. S. has in a short time effected in the system of House Letting, and the satisfaction expressed by those who have patronised him, will, he hopes, recommend him to Visitors requiring large or small Furnished Apartments.

Experience enables J. P. S. to hold himself responsible for the correct execution of any commission sent by letter, wherein requirements are properly specified.

GENOA.—HÔTEL DE LONDRES.

THE Proprietor of this old-established Hotel begs to inform Travellers that it has lately been greatly renovated and improved, nothing being neglected which can contribute to comfort and economy.

BEDROOMS from 1½ fr. upwards; TABLE D'HÔTE at 2½ fr.

ZURICH.

TO TOURISTS AND TRAVELLERS IN SWITZERLAND.

J. H. KEREZ,
Apothecaries' Hall, Zurich,

RESPECTFULLY informs Tourists and Travellers that he keeps a choice Stock of Drugs, Chemicals, and Toilette Articles.

J. H. KEREZ, having lived some time in England in a house of large business as Dispensing Assistant, is fully competent to prepare and dispense Prescriptions according to the English Pharmacopeia, and to which he pays the utmost care and personal attention.

J. H. K. has also on hand a Select Assortment of the most popular English Patent Medicines.

J. H. KEREZ,
DISPENSING CHEMIST,
Weinplatz, 141, *Zurich.*

CARLSBAD.

THOMAS WOLF,
MANUFACTURER OF

ORNAMENTAL GLASS WARES.

THOMAS WOLF begs to inform the Visitors to Carlsbad that at his Establishment will be found the finest and richest Assortment of the Crystal and Glass Wares of Bohemia—especially

Table and Dessert Services—all at reasonable and fixed prices.

AGENTS IN ENGLAND,
MESSRS. J. & R. M·CRACKEN,
7, *Old Jewry.*

FLORENCE.

PHARMACY OF THE BRITISH LEGATION,
No. 4190, VIA TORNABUONI,

Between the Piazza San Gaetano and the Palazzo Strozzi,

KEPT BY

H. ROBERTS,

MEMBER OF THE PHARMACEUTICAL SOCIETY OF GREAT BRITAIN.

Agent for

HENRY'S CALCINED MAGNESIA.	ROWLAND'S MACASSAR OIL.	CLEAVER'S SCENTED SOAPS.
,, AROMATIC VINEGAR.	,, KALYDOR.	METCALFE'S TOOTH BRUSHES.
DINNEFORD'S FLUID MAGNESIA.	,, ODONTO.	ROBINSON'S PATENT GROATS.

SAVORY'S SEIDLITZ POWDERS, ETC.

COD-LIVER OIL OF THE FINEST QUALITY, IMPORTED DIRECT FROM NEWFOUNDLAND.
GENUINE BERMUDA ARROWROOT; MANNA CROUP; ETC.
ELASTIC STOCKINGS, TRUSSES, ETC., FROM THE BEST LONDON MAKERS.
HEADLAND'S HOMŒOPATHIC COCOA AND CHOCOLATE. CHOCOLAT DE MENIER.
GERMAN SELTZER AND EMS WATER.

Prescriptions prepared by English Assistants with Drugs from London.

Mr. ROBERTS has lately added to his Establishment the improved and powerful Soda Water Machine which attracted so much attention at the Great Exhibition, by means of which he is enabled to prepare all kinds of Aërated Waters.

The water employed being from the celebrated Fountain at Santa Croce, these beverages are of unrivalled excellence.

Now ready, with a Clue Map, 18mo., 5s.,

HANDBOOK OF MODERN LONDON:

BEING A GUIDE TO ALL OBJECTS OF INTEREST IN THE METROPOLIS.

BY PETER CUNNINGHAM, F.S.A.

"Without a rival for intelligence and accuracy."—*Times.*

JOHN MURRAY, ALBEMARLE STREET.

THE BEST GRAMMARS
FOR A RAPID ACQUISITION OF FOREIGN LANGUAGES.

	s.	d.
AHN'S German Grammar and Key	4	2
MEISSNER'S German Idiomatic Dialogues	2	6
AHN'S French Grammar, cloth	3	6
,, Italian Grammar and Key	5	0
,, Spanish Grammar and Key	5	0
,, Dutch Grammar	4	0
RASK'S Danish Grammar	5	0
MAY'S Swedish Grammar	5	0
REIFF'S Russian Grammar	5	6

DIALOGUES, DICTIONARIES, and READERS, in all European Languages,

Published by FRANZ THIMM, 3, Brook Street, New Bond Street, London.

Now Ready, 2 vols. Post 8vo., 16s.,

SIX MONTHS IN ITALY.

BY GEORGE HILLARD.

Fcap. 8vo., 2s.,

A MONTH IN NORWAY.

BY J. G. HOLLWAY.

JOHN MURRAY, Albemarle Street.

ASSYRIAN EXCAVATION FUND.

SOCIETY FOR EXPLORING THE RUINS OF ASSYRIA AND BABYLONIA:

WITH

ESPECIAL REFERENCE TO BIBLICAL ILLUSTRATION.

PATRON,—HIS ROYAL HIGHNESS PRINCE ALBERT.

THE limited means hitherto at the command of the British Explorers in Assyria have prevented their carrying on their researches in a systematic manner and on an adequate scale. As yet, according to the accounts furnished by Mr. Layard, only the more recent ruins of Assyria—the surface of the mounds—have been examined, and even these only partially. It is all but certain that the rich discoveries already made by M. Botta and Mr. Layard bear no proportion to the treasures that still lie undetected in the earth. The results of limited exploration, however, have, in connection with biblical and profane history, been of so extraordinary a nature, that it would be matter of deep regret and of national reproach if further excavations on the part of England were now altogether abandoned.

It would appear from a statement by Mr. Layard, that, since the publication of his second work, remains have been found of a much earlier period than any previously taken from the Assyrian mounds. From one inscription it would even seem that temples existed of the 19th or 20th century before Christ, ascending almost to the earliest known Egyptian period. The annals of those Assyrian kings who are mentioned in Scripture, and who were closely connected with the Jewish people, have not yet been fully completed, and the chronicles of the wars with Samaria and of the destruction of that city are, as yet, unfortunately not entire, although reference to them has been met with on several fragments. It is believed that diligent research will speedily supply the missing information.

Besides the ruins of Assyria, enormous remains exist in Babylonia which have been scarcely visited by Europeans, and which there is every reason to conclude contain objects of the very highest interest. Owing to the overflowing of the banks of the Euphrates vast marshes are now forming in South Mesopotamia, which threaten ere long to destroy many of the remains entirely. Some indeed are already under water and inaccessible; but others are still free, and will, undoubtedly, upon examination, furnish relics of the first importance. Captain Jones, who, as commander of the steamer on the Euphrates and Tigris, has passed the last thirteen years in these regions, and who, within these few weeks, has returned to this country, distinctly states that funds only are wanting to obtain from South Babylonia or Lower Chaldea the most remarkable additions to the knowledge we now possess of the earliest recorded history of the world.

In order to extend still further the successful labours of Col. Rawlinson and Mr. Layard, the Assyrian Excavation Society has been formed, with the view of raising a fund for the immediate prosecution of the work indicated.

The staff for carrying forward excavations exists; and an expedition has already proceeded to Assyria to carry forward the necessary operations. A photographic artist accompanied the expedition, and will take copies of all objects of interest discovered.

In England facsimiles of the more interesting drawings and inscriptions will be issued from time to time, together with explanatory letterpress, the publication of which Mr. Layard has kindly undertaken to superintend. [*Continued.*

ASSYRIAN EXCAVATION FUND—continued.

It will be less the object of the Expedition to obtain bulky sculptures than to collect materials for completing the history of Assyria and Babylonia, especially as connected with Scripture. These materials consist chiefly of inscribed tablets in stone and in clay, bronzes, bricks and sculptured monuments of various kinds, all illustrating the remarkable advancement of that ancient civilisation. It is confidently believed that the whole history of Assyria may be restored to a very early period, and that discoveries of the most important character will be made in connection with the literature and science of the Assyrian people.

His Royal Highness Prince Albert has been pleased to honour the Society with his countenance and approval, and to head the List of Subscriptions with a Donation of One Hundred Guineas.

It is presumed that the sum of £10,000 will be required to commence operations at once in various parts of Mesopotamia, and to sustain necessary activity during a period of three years. But as it is of the utmost consequence to proceed with the greatest vigour during the first twelvemonth, it is calculated that up to August, 1854, £5000 of the sum named might be expended. In additions to the Donations, it is intended to raise Annual Subscriptions of a guinea each, the payment of which shall entitle the Subscriber to the Reports and Memoirs issued by the Society.

The present undertaking being regarded as a continuation of the researches already commenced by the British Museum, it is determined that the Monuments shall ultimately become the property of the nation.

Donations and Annual Subscriptions are solicited by the Society, and will be received by the London and Westminster Bank, Lothbury, and 4, Stratford Place, Oxford Street; Bosanquet and Co., 73, Lombard Street; by John Murray, Esq., Treasurer, 50, Albemarle Street; also by the Hon. Secretaries at the Royal Asiatic Society's House, 5, New Burlington Street.

COMMITTEE.

President—THE EARL SOMERS.

LORD ASHBURTON.	OWEN JONES, ESQ.
SAMUEL BIRCH, ESQ., F.R.S.	CAPTAIN FELIX JONES, I.N.
J. W. BOSANQUET, ESQ.	S. LAING, ESQ., M.P.
THE CHEVALIER BUNSEN.	THE MARQUESS OF LANSDOWNE.
LORD CARINGTON.	AUSTEN H. LAYARD, ESQ., M.P.
R. CLARKE, ESQ.	LORD MAHON.
LORD COWLEY.	SIR MOSES MONTEFIORE, BART.
HON. R. CURZON.	E. NORRIS, ESQ.
THE EARL OF ELLENBOROUGH.	COLONEL RAWLINSON.
THE EARL OF ELLESMERE.	LORD STRATFORD DE REDCLIFFE.
JAMES FERGUSSON, ESQ.	HENRY DANBY SEYMOUR, ESQ., M.P.
BARON DE GOLDSMID.	THE EARL OF SHAFTESBURY.
EARL GRANVILLE.	COLONEL SYKES.
HENRY HALLAM, ESQ.	W. S. W. VAUX, ESQ.
E. HAWKINS, ESQ., F.R.S.	SIR J. GARDNER WILKINSON.
REV. DR. E. HINCKS.	PROFESSOR H. H. WILSON.
SIR JAMES WEIR HOGG, BART., M.P.	

Bankers.

THE LONDON AND WESTMINSTER BANK, Lothbury; also, 4, Stratford Place, Oxford Street; and
BOSANQUET AND CO., 76, Lombard Street.

Honorary Secretaries.

VISCOUNT MANDEVILLE, M.P.; SAMUEL PHILLIPS, ESQ.

Treasurer.

JOHN MURRAY, ESQ.

AMUSING BOOKS FOR TRAVELLERS.

THE PARLOUR LIBRARY.

Price 1s. each Volume; or Double Volumes marked thus*, price 1s. 6d. in boards.

*Sir Theodore Broughton, by G. P. R. James.
*Forgery, by James.
*False Heir, by James.
*Arabella Stuart, by James.
*Henry of Guise, by James.
*Beauchamp, or the Error, by James.
*Attila, by James.
*Huguenot, by James.
*Jacquerie, by James.
*Whim and its Consequences, by James.
*Gentleman of the Old School, by James.
*Philip Augustus, by James.
*Agincourt, by James.
*Gowrie, by James.
*Henry Masterton, by James.
*John Marston Hall, by James.
*Smuggler, by James.
*Brigand, by James.
*Convict, by James.
*Gipsy, by James.
*King's Highway, by James.
*Forest Days, by James.
*Heidelberg, by James.
*Darnley, by James.
*Arrah Neil, by James.
*Morley Ernstein, by James.
Charles Tyrrell, by James.
Castelneau, by James.
One in a Thousand, by James.
Robber, by James.
Mary of Burgundy, by James.
Emilia Wyndham.
*Wilmingtons, by the Author of 'Emilia Wyndham.'
*Mordaunt Hall, by ditto.
*Time, the Avenger, by ditto.
Tales of Woods and Fields, by ditto.
Two Old Men's Tales, by ditto.
Previsions of Lady Evelyn, by ditto.
Bellah, by Feuillet, edited by ditto.
Geneviève, by A. Lamartine.
Pictures of First French Revolution, by Lamartine.
Wanderer and his Home, by Lamartine.
Parsonage, by Rodolph Toppfer.
Tales and Sketches, by Rodolph Toppfer.

*Tenant of Wildfel Hall, by Acton Bell.
Scottish Heiress, by R. M. Daniels.
*Cardinal's Daughter, by R. M. Daniels.
Dark Lady of Doona, by W. H. Maxwell.
*English Envoy at the Court of Nicholas I., by Miss Corner.
Magician, by Leitch Ritchie.
Crohoore of the Billhook, by Banim.
John Doe, by Banim.
The Nowlans, by Banim.
Emma, by Miss Austen.
Northanger Abbey, and Persuasion, by Miss Austen.
Mansfield Park, by Miss Austen.
Black Prophet, by William Carleton.
Collegians, by Gerald Griffin.
Rivals, by Griffin.
Lover upon Trial, by Lady Lyons.
Olivia, by Lady Lyons.
Sir Philip Hetherington, by Lady Lyons.
*Cagot's Hut, by T. C. Grattan.
*Agnes de Mansfelt, by T. C. Grattan.
Heir of Wast Wayland, by Mary Howitt.
Wood Leighton, by Mary Howitt.
Angela and other Tales, by A. Stifter.
*Memoirs of a Physician, by Dumas, 2 vols.
Rosa, or the Black Tulip, by Dumas.
Monte Christo, by Dumas, 3 vols.
George, the Planter of France, by Dumas.
*Stuart of Dunleath, by Hon. Mrs. Norton.
*Scalp Hunters, by Mayne Reid.
*Rifle Rangers, by Reid.
*Margaret Catchpole, by Rev. R. Cobbold.
Remembrances of a Monthy Nurse, by Mrs. H. Downing.
Miller of Angibault, by George Sand.
Khan's Tale, by J. B. Fraser.
Zenobia, by Rev. W. Ware.
Two Friends, by Marriott Oldfield.
Violet's Travels, by Capt. Marryat.
Country Stories, by Miss Mitford.
Family Pictures, by La Fontaine.
Marian, by Mrs. S. C. Hall.
Simple Story, by Mrs. Inchbald.
Sidonia, by W. Meinhold.
Andrew the Savoyard, by Paul de Kock.

THOMAS HODGSON, 13, PATERNOSTER ROW, LONDON.

Sold at every Railway Station, and by every Bookseller in Town and Country.

WORKS FOR OFFICERS.

1. A SELECTION FROM THE WELLINGTON DESPATCHES AND GENERAL ORDERS. By Col. Gurwood, C.B. *New Edition.* 8vo. 18s.

2. A MANUAL OF MILITARY OPERATIONS, for the USE OF OFFICERS. By Lieut. Jervis, R.A. Post 8vo. 9s. 6d.

3. THE PRINCIPLE OF MILITARY BRIDGES, AND THE PASSAGE OF RIVERS IN MILITARY OPERATIONS. By Gen^{L.} Sir Howard Douglas. *Third Edition.* Plates. 8vo. 21s.

4. A TREATISE ON IMPROVED GUNNERY. By Gen^{L.} Sir Howard Douglas. *Third Edition.* Plates. 8vo. 21s.

5. HISTORY OF THE SIEGE OF GIBRALTAR, 1779-83. With a Description of that Garrison. By Capt. Drinkwater. Post 8vo. 2s. 6d.

6. THE STORY OF THE BATTLE OF WATERLOO. From Public and Private Sources. By Rev. G. R. Gleig, Chaplain-General to the Forces. Post 8vo. 6s.

7. THE ADMIRALTY MANUAL OF SCIENTIFIC ENQUIRY; Prepared for the Use of Officers on Foreign Service. Edited by Sir John Herschel, Bart. *Second Edition.* Maps. Post 8vo. 10s. 6d.

8. DEEDS OF NAVAL DARING; or, ANECDOTES OF THE BRITISH NAVY. By Edward Giffard. 2 vols. post 8vo. 5s.

9. A NAVAL BIOGRAPHICAL DICTIONARY OF ALL LIVING OFFICERS, from the rank of Admiral of the Fleet to that of Lieutenant, inclusive; with Authentic Details of their Services. By W. R. O'Byrne. Royal 8vo. 42s.

10. A MILITARY AND NAVAL DICTIONARY OF TECHNICAL WORDS AND PHRASES. (English and French—French and English.) By Col. Burn, R.A. *Second Edition.* Crown 8vo. 15s.

11. THE LAW AND PRACTICE OF NAVAL COURTS MARTIAL. By William Hickman, R.N. 8vo. 10s. 6d.

12. PRACTICAL SURVEYING, PLAN DRAWING, AND SKETCHING GROUND, WITHOUT INSTRUMENTS. By G. D. Burr. *Second Edition.* Plates. Post 8vo. 7s. 6d.

JOHN MURRAY, ALBEMARLE STREET.

"Mr. Murray's meritorious Series."—*The Times*.

Now Ready, complete in 76 Parts, Post 8vo., 2s. 6d. each, or 37 Vols. cloth,

MURRAY'S
HOME AND COLONIAL LIBRARY.

Forming a compact and portable work, the bulk of which does not exceed the compass of a single shelf, or of one trunk, suited for all classes and all climates.

CONTENTS OF THE SERIES.

The Bible in Spain. By George Borrow.
Journals in India. By Bishop Heber.
Travels in Egypt and the Holy Land. By Irby and Mangles.
The Siege of Gibraltar. By John Drinkwater.
Morocco and the Moors. By Drummond Hay.
Letters from the Baltic. By a Lady.
The Amber Witch.
Cromwell and Bunyan. By Robert Southey.
New South Wales. By Mrs. Charles Meredith.
Life of Drake. By John Barrow.
The Court of Pekin. By Father Ripa.
The West Indies. By M. G. Lewis.
Sketches of Persia. By Sir John Malcolm.
The French in Algiers.
Fall of the Jesuits in the 19th Century.
Bracebridge Hall. By Washington Irving.
A Naturalist's Voyage round the World. By Charles Darwin.
Life of Condé. By Lord Mahon.
The Gypsies of Spain. By George Borrow.
Typee and Omoo. By Herman Melville.
Livonian Tales. By a Lady.
The Church Missionary in Canada. By Rev. J. Abbott.
Sale's Brigade in Affghanistan. By Rev. G. R. Gleig.
Letters from Madras. By a Lady.
Highland Sports. By Charles St. John.
Pampas Journeys. By Sir Francis Head.
The Sieges of Vienna. Translated by Lord Ellesmere.
Gatherings from Spain. By Richard Ford.
Sketches of German Life during the War of Liberation.
Story of the Battle of Waterloo. By Rev. G. R. Gleig.
A Voyage up the Amazon. By W. H. Edwards.
The Wayside Cross. By Captain Milman.
A Popular Account of India. By Rev. Charles Acland.
The British Army at Washington. By Rev. G. R. Gleig.
Adventures in Mexico. By George F. Ruxton.
Portugal and Galicia. By Lord Carnarvon.
Life of Lord Clive. By Rev. G. R. Gleig.
Bush Life in Australia. By H. W. Haygarth.
Autobiography of Henry Steffens.
Tales of a Traveller. By Washington Irving.
Lives of the British Poets. By Thomas Campbell.
Historical Essays. By Lord Mahon.
Stokers and Pokers. By Author of 'Bubbles.'
The Libyan Desert. By Bayle St. John.
Letters from Sierra Leone. By a Lady.
Life of Sir Thomas Munro. By Rev. G. R. Gleig.
Memoirs of Sir Fowell Buxton. By his Son.
Life of Goldsmith. By Washington Irving.

*** *Subscribers should complete their copies of the above Series, as the issue of the* SEPARATE PARTS *will be shortly discontinued.*

JOHN MURRAY, ALBEMARLE STREET.

RUSSIA, TURKEY, AND GREECE.

The following Works may now be had :—

THE RUSSIANS IN BULGARIA AND RUMELIA, 1828-9, during the Campaign of the Danube, the Sieges of Brailow, Varna, Silistria, Shumla, and the Passage of the Balkan. By BARON VON MOLTKE. With 13 Plans. 8vo.

II.

PROGRESS OF RUSSIA IN THE EAST: An Historical Summary, continued to the present time. With Map by ARROWSMITH of Russian Encroachments. 3rd *Edition.* 8vo. 6s. 6d.

III.

COMMENTARIES ON THE WAR IN RUSSIA AND GERMANY. 1812-13. By GENERAL SIR GEORGE CATHCART. With 28 Plans. 8vo. 14s.

IV.

THE CAMPAIGN IN RUSSIA OF 1812. By GENERAL CLAUSEWITZ. Translated from the German. With Map. 8vo. 10s. 6d.

V.

RUSSIA IN EUROPE AND THE URAL MOUNTAINS. Geologically Illustrated. By SIR RODERICK MURCHISON. With Coloured Maps, Plates, Sections, &c. 2 Vols. 4to.

VI.

LETTERS FROM THE SHORES OF THE BALTIC. Post 8vo. 2s. 6d.

VII.

DOMESTIC MANNERS OF THE RUSSIANS. Described from a Year's Residence in that Country. By Rev. R. VENABLES. Post 8vo. 9s. 6d.

VIII.

LETTERS ON TURKEY; descriptive of the Country and its Inhabitants— the Moslems, Greeks, Armenians, &c.; the Reformed Institutions, Army, &c. By M. A. UBICINI. 2 vols. post 8vo.

IX.

TURKEY AND ITS DESTINY; being an Account of Journeys made to examine into the true state of that Country. By C. MAC FARLANE. 2 vols. 8vo. 28s.

X.

ARMENIA. A YEAR at ERZEROOM, and on the Frontiers of RUSSIA, TURKEY, and PERSIA. By HON. ROBERT CURZON. *Third Edition.* Woodcuts. Post 8vo. 7s. 6d.

XI.

THE MONASTERIES OF THE LEVANT. By HON. ROBERT CURZON. *Fourth Edition.* Woodcuts. Post 8vo. 15s.

XII.

THE CONDITION AND PROSPECTS OF THE GREEK CHURCH. By DEAN WADDINGTON. *New Edition.* Fcap. 8vo.

XIII.

TRAVELS IN NORTHERN GREECE. By COLONEL W. M. LEAKE. Maps. 4 vols. 8vo. 60s.

XIV.

TRAVELS AND RESEARCHES IN ASIA MINOR, more particularly in the Province of LYCIA. By SIR CHARLES FELLOWS. Maps. Post 8vo. 9s.

XV.

RESEARCHES IN ASIA MINOR, THE SHORES OF THE BLACK SEA, AND ARMENIA; with some Account of the Antiquities and Geology of these Countries. By W. J. HAMILTON. Map and Plates. 2 vols. 8vo. 38s.

XVI.

SKETCHES OF PERSIA. By SIR JOHN MALCOLM. Post 8vo. 6s.

JOHN MURRAY, ALBEMARLE STREET.

MURRAY'S HANDBOOKS FOR TRAVELLERS.

HANDBOOK OF TRAVEL TALK.—ENGLISH, FRENCH, GERMAN. AND ITALIAN. 18mo., 3s. 6d.

HANDBOOK FOR TURKEY.—CONSTANTINOPLE, THE DANUBE, ASIA MINOR, ARMENIA, MESOPOTAMIA, &c. Maps. Post 8vo., 10s.

HANDBOOK FOR NORTH EUROPE.—RUSSIA, THE BALTIC, FINLAND, ICELAND, DENMARK, NORWAY, AND SWEDEN. Maps. 2 vols. Post 8vo., 24s.

HANDBOOK FOR GREECE.—THE IONIAN ISLANDS, ALBANIA, THESSALY, AND MACEDONIA. Maps. Post 8vo., 15s.

HANDBOOK FOR EGYPT.—MALTA, THE NILE, ALEXANDRIA, CAIRO, THEBES, AND THE OVERLAND ROUTE TO INDIA. Map. Post 8vo., 15s.

HANDBOOK FOR SOUTH GERMANY.—THE TYROL, BAVARIA, AUSTRIA, SALZBURG, STYRIA, HUNGARY, AND THE DANUBE FROM ULM TO THE BLACK SEA. Map. Post 8vo., 9s.

HANDBOOK FOR BELGIUM AND THE RHINE. Maps. Post 8vo., 5s.

HANDBOOK FOR NORTH GERMANY.—HOLLAND, BELGIUM, PRUSSIA, AND THE RHINE TO SWITZERLAND. Map. Post 8vo., 9s.

HANDBOOK FOR SWITZERLAND.—THE ALPS OF SAVOY AND PIEDMONT. Map. Post 8vo., 7s. 6d.

HANDBOOK FOR FRANCE.—NORMANDY, BRITTANY, THE FRENCH ALPS, DAUPHINE, PROVENCE, AND THE PYRENEES. Maps. Post 8vo., 9s.

HANDBOOK FOR SPAIN.—ANDALUSIA, RONDA, GRENADA, CATALONIA, GALLICIA, THE BASQUES, ARRAGON, &c. Maps. Post 8vo., 16s.

HANDBOOK OF PAINTING.—THE GERMAN, DUTCH, SPANISH, AND FRENCH SCHOOLS. Woodcuts. 2 vols. Post 8vo., 24s.

HANDBOOK FOR NORTH ITALY.—SARDINIA, LOMBARDY, VENICE, PARMA, PIACENZA, MODENA, LUCCA, FLORENCE, AND TUSCANY, as far as the VAL D'ARNO. Maps. Post 8vo., 9s.

HANDBOOK FOR CENTRAL ITALY.—SOUTHERN TUSCANY AND THE PAPAL STATES. Maps. Post 8vo., 7s.

HANDBOOK FOR ROME—AND ITS ENVIRONS. Maps. Post 8vo., 7s.

HANDBOOK FOR SOUTH ITALY.—THE TWO SICILIES, NAPLES, POMPEII, HERCULANEUM, VESUVIUS, &c. Maps. Post 8vo., 15s.

JOHN MURRAY, ALBEMARLE STREET.

MURRAY'S RAILWAY READING:

Containing Works of SOUND INFORMATION and INNOCENT AMUSEMENT, printed in large Readable Type, *varying in size and price,* and suited for ALL CLASSES OF READERS.

SELECTIONS FROM LORD BYRON'S WRITINGS. PROSE AND VERSE. 3s.

HISTORY OF THE GUILLOTINE. By MR. CROKER. 1s.

A POPULAR ACCOUNT OF THE ANCIENT EGYPTIANS. By SIR J. GARDNER WILKINSON. With 500 Woodcuts. 2 vols., 12s.

ANCIENT SPANISH BALLADS. By J. G. LOCKHART. 2s. 6d.

MUSIC AND DRESS. Two Essays. By A LADY. 1s.

THE "FORTY-FIVE;" or a History of the Rebellion in Scotland. By LORD MAHON. 3s.

WELLINGTON: His Character, his Actions, and his Writings. By JULES MAUREL. 1s. 6d.

A POPULAR ACCOUNT OF NINEVEH. By A. H. LAYARD. Woodcuts, 5s.

LITERARY ESSAYS AND CHARACTERS. By HENRY HALLAM. 2s.

THE FALL OF JERUSALEM. By DEAN MILMAN. 1s.

LIFE OF LORD CHANCELLOR BACON. By LORD CAMPBELL. 2s. 6d.

NIMROD ON THE CHACE, THE TURF, AND THE ROAD. 3s. 6d.

A MONTH IN NORWAY. By JOHN GEORGE HOLLWAY. 2s.

THE EMIGRANT. By SIR F. B. HEAD. 2s. 6d.

LIFE OF THEODORE HOOK. From the 'Quarterly Review.' 1s.

LITERARY ESSAYS FROM 'THE TIMES.' 2 Vols. 8s.

THE ART OF DINING; or Gastronomy and Gastronomers. 1s. 6d.

DEEDS OF NAVAL DARING. By EDWARD GIFFARD. 2 Vols. 5s.

THE CHARACTER OF WELLINGTON. By LORD ELLESMERE. 6d.

FABLES OF ÆSOP. By REV. THOMAS JAMES. 100 Woodcuts. 2s. 6d.

STORY OF JOAN OF ARC. By LORD MAHON. 1s.

A VISIT TO NEPAUL. By LAURENCE OLIPHANT. 2s. 6d.

BEES AND FLOWERS. Two Essays. By A CLERGYMAN. 2s.

JOHN MURRAY, ALBEMARLE STREET.

WORKS CONNECTED WITH

THE FINE ARTS.

I.
THE TREASURES OF ART IN GREAT BRITAIN. Being an Account of the chief Collections of Paintings, Drawings, Sculptures, MSS., &c., in this Country. By Dr. WAAGEN, Director of the Royal Gallery of Pictures at Berlin. 3 vols. 8vo. 36s.

II.
KUGLER'S HANDBOOK OF PAINTING. (The ITALIAN SCHOOLS.) Edited by SIR CHARLES EASTLAKE. With Illustrations. 2 vols. Post 8vo. 24s.

III.
KUGLER'S HANDBOOK OF PAINTING. (The GERMAN, DUTCH, SPANISH, and FRENCH SCHOOLS.) Edited by SIR EDMUND HEAD. With Illustrations. 2 vols. Post 8vo. 24s.

IV.
LIFE OF THOMAS STOTHARD, R.A. By MRS. BRAY. With Portrait and 70 illustrative Woodcuts. 4to. 21s.

V.
THE LIFE AND WORKS OF HORACE. Edited by DEAN MILMAN. With 300 Woodcuts of Coins and Gems, from the Antique. 2 vols. 8vo. 30s.

VI.
THE BOOK OF COMMON PRAYER. With 1000 Illustrations of Vignettes, Initials, and Historical Engravings from the Old Masters. 8vo. 21s.

VII.
CHILDE HAROLD'S PILGRIMAGE. By LORD BYRON. Illustrated with Portrait of Ada, and 30 Vignettes. Crown 8vo. 10s. 6d.

VIII.
THE ARABIAN NIGHTS. Translated, with Explanatory Notes, by E. W. LANE. Illustrated with 600 Woodcuts by HARVEY. Royal 8vo. 21s.

IX.
THE FABLES OF ÆSOP. A new Version. By REV. THOMAS JAMES. With 100 Original Designs by JOHN TENNIEL. Crown 8vo. 2s. 6d.

JOHN MURRAY, ALBEMARLE STREET.

MURRAY'S BRITISH CLASSICS.

PUBLISHING MONTHLY, IN DEMY OCTAVO VOLUMES.

EXAMINER.—"*Mr. Murray's British Classics, so edited and printed as to take the highest place in any library. Beyond all question the cheapest books of the day.*"

ATHENÆUM.—"*Those who love to collect our standard authors in handsome library editions may well congratulate themselves on the issue.*"

NOTES AND QUERIES.—"*Distinguished by skilful editorship, beautiful and legible type, fine paper, compactness of bulk, and economy of price.*"

With Portrait and Maps, Vols. 1, 2, & 3 (to be completed in 8 vols.), 8vo., 7s. 6d. each,

GIBBON'S DECLINE AND FALL
OF THE
ROMAN EMPIRE.

WITH NOTES AND PREFACE BY MILMAN AND GUIZOT.

EDITED BY WM. SMITH, LL.D.,

Editor of the 'Dictionary of Greek and Roman Antiquities,' &c.

This Edition includes the Autobiography of Gibbon, and is distinguished by careful revision of the text, verification of all the references to ancient writers, and notes incorporating the results of the researches of Modern Scholars and the discoveries of Recent Travellers.

Examiner.—"*An edition that must for very many years remain incomparably the best in every respect that has hitherto appeared. It is a first-rate library edition produced in the best style.*"

Athenæum.—"*If there be any man capable of bringing to bear upon the improvement of Gibbon's work the various additions which have been made to our knowledge since his time, it is Dr. Wm. Smith.*"

Now Ready, with Vignettes, 4 Vols. 8vo., 7s. 6d. each,

THE
WORKS OF OLIVER GOLDSMITH:
A New Edition.

EDITED BY PETER CUNNINGHAM, F.S.A.,

Author of the 'Handbook of London.'

This Edition is printed from the last revised by the Author, and not only contains more pieces than any other, but is also the first in which the works appear together exactly as their author left them.

The Times.—"*A library edition, well edited and beautifully printed.*"

Literary Gazette.—"*Much pains appears to have been bestowed in obtaining the text with the author's last revisions.*"

Guardian.—"*The best editions have been consulted, and the present volume gives evidence of careful and conscientious editing.*"

Spectator.—"*Laboured correctness of text, with sufficient annotation.*"

Examiner.—"*There will be no other edition to compare with this.*"

Press.—"*Mr. Cunningham is an editor, not a commentator, and he does not confound these functions. The volume is beautifully printed.*"

JOHN MURRAY, ALBEMARLE STREET.

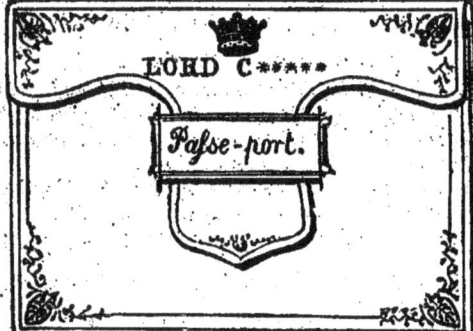

PASSPORTS

Carefully Mounted and inserted in morocco cases, with name lettered in gold.

Ambassadors' Signatures obtained to British Secretary of State's Passports, at one Shilling each.

The latest editions of all MURRAY's HAND-BOOKS; which can generally be supplied when out of print and not to be obtained elsewhere.

COURIERS, or TRAVELLING SERVANTS, can be obtained at

LEE'S Polyglot Washing Books,
(To save Travellers the trouble of translating their Washing Bills)
For Ladies.
DITTO
For Gentlemen.
English & French.
English & Italian.
English & German.
English & Spanish.
English & Portuguese.
1s. each.

Foreign Letter Paper,
Extra Large Size,
VERY THIN,
1s. per Quire.

BOOKS FOR JOURNALS, &c.

LUGGAGE LABELS.

DOOR FASTENERS.

BERRY'S PATENT INKSTANDS.

Leather Money-Bags.

JOHN LEE'S GUIDE DEPÔT,
440, WEST STRAND,
TWO DOORS WEST OF LOWTHER ARCADE,

Where an EXTENSIVE COLLECTION OF GUIDES, HAND-BOOKS, MAPS, DICTIONARIES, DIALOGUES, GRAMMARS, INTERPRETERS, &c., useful for Travellers upon the Continent and elsewhere, and much useful information concerning PASSPORTS, can be obtained.

MURRAY'S HAND-BOOKS, rendered convenient POCKET-BOOKS by J. LEE's limp leather binding, at 2s. additional charge.

MOROCCO and RUSSIA PORTABLE ROLL-UP CASES, containing every essential for Writing.

Moore's German Interpreter.
With the exact Pronunciation in English on a separate column, price 5s. cloth, 6s. in leather.

LONDON: W. CLOWES AND SONS, STAMFORD STREET, AND CHARING CROSS.

NOW COMPLETE.
MURRAY'S HOME AND COLONIAL LIBRARY.

In 76 Parts, or 37 Volumes, Post 8vo.

A compact and portable work, the bulk of which does not exceed the compass of a single shelf, or of one trunk, suited for all classes and all climates.

LIST OF WORKS INCLUDED IN THE SERIES.

- BORROW'S BIBLE IN SPAIN.
- HEBER'S JOURNALS IN INDIA.
- IRBY AND MANGLES' HOLY LAND.
- DRINKWATER'S SIEGE OF GIBRALTAR.
- HAY'S MOROCCO AND THE MOORS.
- LETTERS FROM THE BALTIC.
- THE AMBER WITCH.
- SOUTHEY'S CROMWELL AND BUNYAN.
- MEREDITH'S NEW SOUTH WALES.
- LIFE OF SIR FRANCIS DRAKE.
- FATHER RIPA'S COURT OF PEKING.
- LEWIS'S WEST INDIES.
- MALCOLM'S SKETCHES OF PERSIA.
- THE FRENCH IN ALGIERS.
- IRVING'S BRACEBRIDGE HALL.
- DARWIN'S NATURALIST'S VOYAGE.
- THE FALL OF THE JESUITS.
- MAHON'S LIFE OF CONDE.
- BORROW'S GYPSIES OF SPAIN.
- MELVILLE'S MARQUESAS ISLANDS.
- LIVONIAN TALES. BY A LADY.
- MISSIONARY LIFE IN CANADA.
- SALE'S BRIGADE IN AFFGHANISTAN.
- LETTERS FROM MADRAS.
- ST. JOHN'S HIGHLAND SPORTS.
- HEAD'S PAMPAS JOURNEYS.
- FORD'S SPANISH GATHERINGS.
- THE TWO SIEGES OF VIENNA.
- SKETCHES OF GERMAN LIFE.
- MELVILLE'S SOUTH SEAS.
- GLEIG'S BATTLE OF WATERLOO.
- EDWARD'S VOYAGE UP THE AMAZON.
- MILMAN'S WAYSIDE CROSS.
- ACLAND'S CUSTOMS OF INDIA.
- GLEIG'S CAMPAIGNS AT WASHINGTON.
- RUXTON'S MEXICAN TRAVELS.
- CARNARVON'S PORTUGAL AND GALICIA.
- GLEIG'S LIFE OF LORD CLIVE.
- HAYGARTH'S BUSH LIFE.
- STEFFENS' PERSONAL ADVENTURES.
- TALES OF A TRAVELLER.
- CAMPBELL'S ESSAY ON POETRY.
- MAHON'S HISTORICAL ESSAYS.
- STOKERS AND POKERS—HIGH-WAYS AND DRY-WAYS.
- ST. JOHN'S LIBYAN DESERT.
- SIERRA LEONE. BY A LADY.
- GLEIG'S LIFE OF SIR THOMAS MUNRO.
- SIR FOWELL BUXTON'S MEMOIRS.
- IRVING'S LIFE OF GOLDSMITH.

Books that you may carry to the fire and hold readily in your hand, are the most useful after all. A man will often look at them, and be tempted to go on, when he would have been frightened at books of a larger size and of a more erudite appearance.—DR. JOHNSON.

January, 1854.

BOOKS FOR TRAVELLERS.

ADMIRALTY MANUAL OF SCIENTIFIC ENQUIRY. Edited by SIR J. W. HERSCHEL. Maps. Post 8vo, 10s. 6d.

THE SANATIVE INFLUENCE OF CLIMATE. With an Account of the best Places of Resort for Invalids. By SIR JAMES CLARK. Post 8vo, 10s. 6d.

HUMBOLDT'S COSMOS. A PHYSICAL DESCRIPTION OF THE UNIVERSE. Translated by SABINE. 3 vols. Post 8vo, 10s. 6d.

HUMBOLDT'S ASPECTS OF NATURE in DIFFERENT LANDS and DIFFERENT CLIMATES. Translated by SABINE. 2 vols. Post 8vo, 5s.

PHYSICAL GEOGRAPHY. By MRS. SOMERVILLE. Portrait. 2 vols. 12mo, 12s.

CONNEXION OF THE PHYSICAL SCIENCES. By MRS. SOMERVILLE. Plates. Fcap. 8vo, 10s. 6d.

LYELL'S PRINCIPLES OF GEOLOGY, or the MODERN CHANGES of the EARTH, and its INHABITANTS. Woodcuts. 8vo, 18s.

LYELL'S MANUAL OF ELEMENTARY GEOLOGY, or the ANCIENT CHANGES of the EARTH, and its INHABITANTS. Woodcuts. 8vo, 12s.

LORD BYRON'S LIFE AND POETICAL WORKS. Portraits. 2 vols. Royal 8vo, 12s. each.

BOSWELL'S LIFE OF JOHNSON. Edited by MR. CROKER. Portraits. Royal 8vo, 15s.

CRABBE'S LIFE AND POETICAL WORKS. Portrait. Royal 8vo, 10s. 6d.

HORACE. A NEW EDITION OF THE TEXT. Illustrated by 300 Vignettes. 8vo, 21s.

CONSOLATIONS IN TRAVEL. By SIR HUMPHRY DAVY. Fcap. 8vo, 6s.

SALMONIA. By SIR HUMPHRY DAVY. Woodcuts. Fcap. 8vo, 6s.

SPECIMENS OF COLERIDGE'S TABLE TALK. Portrait. Fcap. 8vo, 6s.

ABERCROMBIE'S ENQUIRIES ON THE INTELLECTUAL POWERS. Fcap. 8vo, 6s. 6d.

ABERCROMBIE'S PHILOSOPHY OF THE MORAL FEELINGS. Fcap. 8vo, 4s.

HEAD'S TOUR THROUGH THE MANUFACTURING DISTRICTS OF ENGLAND. Post 8vo, 12s.

PEDESTRIAN WANDERINGS in the PYRENEES. By T. C. PARIS. Woodcuts. Post 8vo, 10s. 6d.

DALMATIA & MONTENEGRO. By SIR J. G. WILKINSON. 2 vols. 8vo, 42s.

ETRURIA; ITS CITIES AND CEMETERIES. By GEORGE DENNIS. Plates. 2 vols. 8vo, 42s.

BUBBLES from the BRUNNEN of NASSAU. By AN OLD MAN. 16mo, 5s

THE MONASTERIES OF THE LEVANT. By ROBERT CURZON. Woodcuts. Post 8vo, 15s.

HUNGARY & TRANSYLVANIA. By JOHN PAGET. 2 vols. 8vo, 24s.

TRAVELS IN ASIA MINOR AND LYCIA. By SIR CHARLES FELLOWS. Post 8vo, 9s.

January, 1854.

www.ingramcontent.com/pod-product-compliance
Lightning Source LLC
Chambersburg PA
CBHW050317240426
43673CB00042B/1439